ENCYCLOPEDIA OF AFRICAN-AMERICAN CULTURE AND HISTORY

EDITORIAL BOARD

ENCYCLOPEDIA OF AFRICAN-AMERICAN CULTURE AND HISTORY

Edited by

JACK SALZMAN
DAVID LIONEL SMITH
CORNEL WEST

Volume 4

MACMILLAN LIBRARY REFERENCE USA
SIMON & SCHUSTER MACMILLAN
NEW YORK

SIMON & SCHUSTER AND PRENTICE HALL INTERNATIONAL
LONDON   MEXICO CITY   NEW DELHI   SINGAPORE   SYDNEY   TORONTO

95-341

Simon & Schuster Macmillan
866 Third Avenue, New York, NY 10022

PRINTED IN THE UNITED STATES OF AMERICA

printing number

1 2 3 4 5 6 7 8 9 10

LIBRARY OF CONGRESS CATALOGING-IN-PUBLICATION DATA
Encyclopedia of African-American culture and history /
    edited by Jack Salzman, David Lionel Smith, Cornel West.
        p.   cm.
    Includes bibliographical references and index.
    ISBN 0-02-897345-3 (set)
    1. Afro-Americans—Encyclopedias. 2.
Afro-Americans—History—Encyclopedias. I. Salzman,
Jack. II. Smith, David L., 1954–   . III. West, Cornel.
E185E54 1995
973'.0496073'003—dc20   95-33607
                                                  CIP

This paper meets the requirements of ANSI/NISO Z39.48-1992
(Permanence of Paper)

M

(Continued)

Miami Riot of 1980. In May 1980, Liberty City, a black enclave in Miami, Florida, was the scene of a major riot. Unlike the "property riots" of the 1960s, where blacks vented their anger by looting shops and setting fire to buildings, black anger in Miami was expressed directly through violence against whites, with a fury that terrified the white community.

Racial tension was chronic in Miami, whose population was an uneasy mix of whites, blacks, and Latinos, the latter population containing a large number of Cubans. Major racial riots had occurred in 1968 and 1970, and minor racial incidents had taken place during the 1970s. African-American anger at the Miami Police Department (MPD) and Dade County Department of Public Safety (DPS) peaked in 1980, after a series of highly publicized cases of brutality and sexual assault by the police. The light punishments that the perpetrators received shook black Miamians' faith in the justice system. On December 16, 1979, Arthur McDuffie, a black motorist, ignored Miami police officers' orders to pull over and was caught after a high-speed chase. He swung at an officer, grazing the policeman's cheek, whereupon six officers beat him to death with their flashlights. A police cover-up of the fatal beating ensued. In early 1980, five officers went to trial at the Metro Justice Building for manslaughter. Defense attorneys used peremptory challenges to remove black potential jurors. On May 17, 1980, an all-white jury acquitted all the police defendants, after conferring for less than three hours.

That evening, as news of the verdict reached Liberty City, blacks began throwing rocks and bottles at cars on 62nd Street (Martin Luther King Boulevard) a wide street used by white suburbanites to get to the city's major highway. As wild rumors spread of white motorists shooting black children, the stoning grew so serious that police established a roadblock. However, the officer directing traffic was called away to protect a white derelict set upon by a black mob, and several cars went through the roadblock into the area before the roadblock was reestablished. One car, under the shower of bricks and concrete blocks, went out of control onto the sidewalk, wounding a black girl. One of the car's three white occupants fled, but the other two were set upon by the mob. They were so severely beaten that one died and one was maimed for life. Several other cars were stoned by the mobs, and motorists were beaten and murdered. Meanwhile, that same evening, outside the Metro Justice Building, the local NAACP sponsored a protest. Crowds became restless when no speaker system appeared, and blacks kicked in glass doors and windows and set fires. After an attempt to invade DPS headquarters and state office buildings was repulsed by heavily armed riot police, crowds moved to Liberty City, where they burned down white-owned businesses.

The next day, black leaders attempting to halt the violence met with police authorities and County Attorney General Janet Reno (later U.S. Attorney General in the Clinton administration), who refused their pleas to "save lives" and resign. That evening, as rioting continued, a squad made up of police from all of Dade County patrolled Miami's streets, arresting rioters. Armed white motorists shot blacks who approached their cars. By the following morning, May 19, when order had been restored, eighteen people had died (eight white motorists and ten black rioters), and $80 million of property had been destroyed. Although 855 people were arrested, only 135 were sentenced, and just three served prison terms.

See also URBAN RIOTS AND REBELLIONS.

REFERENCE

PORTER, BRUCE, and MARVIN DUNN. *The Miami Riot of 1980: Crossing the Boundaries.* Lexington, Mass., 1984.

GREG ROBINSON

Michaux, Elder Lightfoot Solomon (November 7, 1884–October 2, 1968), religious leader and radio evangelist. One of thirteen children, Michaux was born in Newport News, Va. During his youth he worked in the family seafood business, peddling fish to soldiers on the wharves. It was there he learned, as he would later state, "the power of persuasion."

As a young adult Michaux maintained a successful wholesale food business, and remained uninterested in a religious career until 1917, when his wife, a devout Baptist, convinced him to finance the building of a branch of the Church of Christ (Holiness) in Hopewell, Va. Soon Michaux was called to the pulpit by his wife and friends who were impressed with his rhetorical skills, and he became the permanent pastor of the church. When the end of World War I depopulated Hopewell, Michaux's fledgling church was forced to close, and in late 1919 he moved back to Newport News to organize a church under his own denomination, the Church of God.

Michaux's services were notable for their attendance by significant numbers of white people. In 1924 Michaux even traveled to Baltimore to preach to an all-white congregation dominated by members of the KU KLUX KLAN. He was arrested in 1926 after he held racially integrated services to challenge Virginia's laws banning interracial religious gatherings. Michaux appeared in court as his own counsel. Citing the Bible as his defense, he declared, "the sacred word of the Supreme Being makes no reference to class, division or race." He was fined, but continued to hold integrated services despite repeated harassment by the police and townspeople.

In 1928 Michaux moved to Washington, D.C., "to save souls on a larger scale." There he established a branch of the Church of God, and in 1929 began his first radio broadcasts from local station WJSV. By 1933 Michaux's broadcasts were broadcast nationally by CBS. Known as the "Happy Am I" evangelist,

Michaux used his radio pulpit to support numerous causes, among them President Franklin D. Roosevelt and the NEW DEAL. Along with his political pronouncements, Michaux developed a social dimension to his ministry and, through the Church of God, provided shelter and food to destitute persons in Washington during the GREAT DEPRESSION.

In the 1930s Michaux also gained fame by holding mass baptisms, first in the Potomac River and after 1938 at Griffith Stadium. In the ballpark, home to the Washington Senators baseball team, Michaux baptized hundreds at a time in a large tank filled with water allegedly drawn from the river Jordan. The mass baptisms were accompanied by fireworks and colorful pageantry, including floats, marching bands, and elaborate enactments of the second coming of Christ. Michaux's mass baptisms continued into the 1960s, when they were moved to other large, outdoor venues. A reporter for the *Washington Post* noted, "Michaux made headlines for many feats, but the 'Happy Am I' preacher probably will be remembered longest for his ball park meetings, religious extravaganzas that qualify him as a great showman."

In addition to his religious and political work, Michaux developed Mayfair Mansions, one of the largest privately owned housing projects for African Americans, which opened in Washington, D.C., in 1946. In the 1950s Michaux's popularity among African Americans waned when he broke with the Democratic party to endorse President Dwight D. Eisenhower. At the end of his career Michaux became embroiled in controversies over his and the church's finances, which were both heavily invested in real estate. Many in his congregation accused Michaux of hiding financial information on the church and of secretly transferring assets to his personal accounts. Despite the dark clouds over his final years, Michaux's Church of God has remained after his death as a monument to his successful and flamboyant career.

REFERENCES

LOGAN, RAYFORD W., and MICHAEL R. WINSTON, eds. *Dictionary of American Negro Biography.* New York, 1982.

WEBB, LILLIAN ASHCRAFT. *About My Father's Business: The Life of Elder Michaux.* Westport, Conn., 1981.

THADDEUS RUSSELL

Micheaux, Oscar (January 2, 1884–March 25, 1951), novelist and filmmaker. Oscar Micheaux was born in Metropolis, Ill., one of thirteen children of former slaves. The early events of his life are not clear and must be gleaned from several fictionalized versions he published. He evidently worked as a Pullman porter, acquiring enough capital to buy two 160-acre tracts of land in South Dakota, where he homesteaded. Micheaux's homesteading experiences were the basis of his first novel, *The Conquest: The Story of a Negro Pioneer* (1913). In order to publicize the book, Micheaux established the Western Book Supply Company and toured the Midwest. He sold most of the books and stock in his first company to white farmers, although his later ventures were financed by African-American entrepreneurs. From his bookselling experiences, he wrote a second novel, *The Forged Note: A Romance of the Darker Races* (1915). Micheaux's third novel, *The Homesteader* (1917), attracted the attention of George P. JOHNSON, who, with his Hollywood actor brother Noble, owned the Lincoln Film Company, with offices in Los Angeles and Omaha. The Johnson brothers were part of the first wave of African-American independent filmmakers to take up the challenge to D. W. Griffith's white supremacist version of American History, BIRTH OF A NATION (1915), and to produce their own stories of African-American life. Fascinated by the new medium, Micheaux offered to sell the Johnson Brothers film rights to his novel, on the condition that he direct the motion picture version. When they refused, Micheaux decided to produce and direct the film himself, financing it through what became the Micheaux Book and Film Company, with offices located in New York, Chicago, and Sioux City, Iowa.

The film version of Micheaux's third novel, *The Homesteader* (1918), was the first of about fifty films he directed. He distributed the films himself, carrying the prints from town to town, often for one-night stands. His films played mostly in white-owned (but often black-managed) black theaters in the North and in the South. He even had some luck convincing southern white cinema owners to let him show his films at all-black matinees and interracial midnight shows in white theaters. While the black press at the time sometimes criticized Micheaux for projecting a rich black fantasy world and ignoring ghetto problems, he dealt frankly with such social themes as interracial relationships, "passing," intraracial as well as interracial prejudice, and the intimidation of African Americans by the KU KLUX KLAN. Micheaux's second film, *Within Our Gates* (1919), contains a disturbing sequence representing a white lynch mob hanging an innocent black man and his wife. When Micheaux tried to exhibit the film in Chicago, less than a year after a major race riot in the city, both black and white groups urged city authorities to ban the film. Micheaux's response to such censorship was to cut and reedit his films from town

The pioneering African-American filmmaker Oscar Micheaux made over three dozen films between 1920 and 1950. (Moorland-Spingarn Research Center, Howard University)

to town. Showman and entrepreneur that he was, he would promote a film that had been banned in one town by indicating in the next town that it contained "censored" footage. Produced on a shoestring, his films earned him just enough money to continue his filmmaking.

Some twelve of Micheaux's films are extant, and they give an idea, though incomplete, of his style. His interior scenes are often dimly lit, but his location scenes of urban streets are usually crisp and clear, providing a documentary-like glimpse of the period. He seldom had money for more than one take, with the result that the actors' mistakes are sometimes left on screen. However, Micheaux had a genius for negotiating around tight budgets, improvising with limited resources, and synchronizing production with distribution. In the early 1920s, in order to purchase the rights to African-American author Charles Waddell CHESNUTT's *The House Behind the Cedars* (1900), he offered the author shares in his film company.

To create appeal for his films, Micheaux features some of the most talented African-American actors of his time: Andrew Bishop, Lawrence-Chenault, A. B. Comithiere, Lawrence Criner, Shingzie Howard, and Evelyn Preer, many of whom were associated with the Lafayette Players stock company. Actor and singer Paul ROBESON made his first motion picture appearance in Micheaux's *Body and Soul* (1924), in a dual role as both a venal preacher and his virtuous brother. Micheaux returned often to the theme of the hypocritical preacher, a portrait inspired by the betrayal of his father-in-law, a Chicago minister. Of the actors Micheaux made celebrities in the black community, the most notable was Lorenzo TUCKER, a handsome, light-skinned actor, dubbed "the colored Valentino." Micheaux's films also featured cabaret scenes and chorus line dancers, and, after the coming of sound, jazz musicians and comedians.

Although his company went bankrupt in 1928, Micheaux managed to survive the early depression, continuing to produce silent films. Although *Daughter of the Congo* (1930) featured some songs and a musical score, *The Exile* (1931) was thought to be the first African-American-produced all-talking picture. Micheaux went on to make a number of sound films, but many moments in these films are undercut because his technicians could not surmount the challenges produced by the new sound-recording technology. In the late 1930s, after the brief notoriety of *God's Stepchildren* (1937), Micheaux's film activities began to wind down and he returned to writing novels. He published *The Wind from Nowhere* (1941), a reworking of *The Homesteader,* and three other novels during the next five years. In 1948, he produced a large-budget version of *The Wind from Nowhere,* titled *The Betrayal* and billed as the first African-American motion picture to play in major white theaters. However, the film received unfavorable reviews in the press, including *The New York Times.* At a time of his decline in popularity as both novelist and filmmaker, Micheaux died during a promotional tour in 1951 in Charlotte, N.C.

Micheaux's work was first rediscovered by film scholars in the early 1970s. However, these critics still disdained the wooden acting and unmatched shots in his films and decried what they thought to be the escapist nature of his stories. More recent critics, however, have hailed Micheaux as a maverick stylist who understood but was not bound by classical Hollywood cutting style, who used precious footage economically, who was adept in his use of the flashback device, and whose "rough draft" films were vaguely avant-garde. Similarly, Micheaux is not recognized for his "protest" films and his use of social types to oppose caricature rather than to reinforce stereotype.

Largely ignored during his lifetime, Micheaux has received recognition in recent years. The Black Filmmakers Hall of Fame inaugurated an annual Oscar Micheaux Award in 1974. In 1985, the Directors' Guild presented Micheaux with a special Golden Jubilee Award, and in 1987, he received a star on the Hollywood Walk of Fame. The recent discovery of prints of two silent films, *Within Our Gates* (1919) and *Symbol of the Unconquered* (1920) in archives in Spain and Belgium, respectively, has increased the interest in his work.

REFERENCES

CRIPPS, THOMAS. *Slow Fade to Black: The Negro in American Film, 1900–1942.* 2nd ed. New York, 1989.

GAINES, JANE M. "Fire and Desire: Race, Melodrama, and Oscar Micheaux." In Manthia Diawara, ed. *Black American Cinema: History, Theory, Criticism.* New York, 1993.

GREEN, RON. "Oscar Micheaux's Production Values." In Manthia Diawara, ed. *Black American Cinema: History, Theory, Criticism.* New York, 1993.

PETERSON, BERNARD L., JR. "A Filmography of Oscar Micheaux: America's Legendary Black Filmmaker." In David Platt, ed. *Celluloid Power.* Metuchen, N.J., 1992.

REGESTER, CHARLENE. "Lynched, Assaulted, and Intimidated: Oscar Micheaux's Most Controversial Films." *Popular Culture Review* 5, no. 1 (February 1994): 47–55.

JANE GAINES
CHARLENE REGESTER

Michigan. The history of Michigan's African-American population is a study of contrasting experiences. African Americans lived as FUGITIVE SLAVES and as freepeople, in urban areas as laborers and merchants, and in rural areas as prosperous farmers, at opposite ends of the political spectrum. Economic choices and opportunities, limited by institutional racism and the resulting political and social structures, shaped these contrasting experiences.

Black men explored the Great Lakes region in what would become Michigan as early as 1679 when they accompanied French explorers Father Louis Hennepin and Sieur de LaSalle on the good ship *Griffon,* twenty-one years before Count Cadillac established his base at Detroit. Records found in the parish register of the Church of Ste. Anne at Michilimackinac on the Upper Peninsula, where black slaves were brought in to build church buildings and raise food, indicate that between 1731 and 1750, sixteen slaves received rites from parish priests. In 1774, Ann

Wiley, a slave woman, was caught after stealing money and setting fire to a trading post; she was later hanged. Slaves generally worked as lumberjacks, dockworkers, carriage drivers, or farmhands. A few ran away and formed maroon colonies (*see* MAROON-AGE). Around 1780, the trader Jean Baptiste Du Sable, founder of Chicago, moved to the Michigan area and allegedly married a Potawatomi women. Near the end of the American Revolution, he was imprisoned by the English at Fort Michilimackinac for favoring American forces.

After American independence, slavery was preserved in the Old Northwest, despite the passage of control of the land from the French to the English in 1763 and then in 1796, following Jay's Treaty, to the Americans. Although slavery was technically prohibited in Michigan by the Northwest Ordinance of 1787, slaves previously owned by the British continued in bondage. Slavery persisted into the 1830s, leaving its mark on the laws of territory and state. In 1807, many Detroit residents freed their slaves to form militia and repel Indian attacks, but when the danger passed, the African Americans were reenslaved. When Peter and Elizabeth Denison applied for freedom, Judge Augustus Woodward ruled that while slavery was forbidden in Michigan, prior treaties with Great Britain protected all property, including slaves, and he ordered the Denisons returned to their master.

When the Michigan Territory was established in 1805, there were relatively few African-American residents. The first territorial census, taken in 1810, counted only twenty-four slaves and 120 free blacks. The free population slowly increased, though in 1829, the legislature enacted a law that forbade free blacks to settle unless they could prove they were self-supporting. In 1837, the year Michigan became a state, the legislature formally abolished slavery. However, in 1850, African Americans were barred from militia service, public schools were formally segregated, and African Americans were denied suffrage.

In the latter part of the eighteenth century, slaves began escaping through Michigan into Canada. Detroit became a major transfer point on the UNDERGROUND RAILROAD to Canada. Such leaders among the city's black settlers as Jean and George DeBaptiste, Joseph Ferguson, John G. Reynolds, William Webb, William C. Moore, and William Lambert were all stationmasters in Detroit. In 1843, Detroit was the site of the First "State Convention of the Colored Men of Michigan," organized to lobby for suffrage. A second Convention of Colored Men was held at Battle Creek in 1860. The distinguished abolitionist Sojourner TRUTH moved to Battle Creek in the mid-1850s. She lived there until her death in 1883,

and a memorial marks her grave there. The rural black settlements that were established near the villages of Ann Arbor and Marshall also played a part in antislavery activities. In 1836, the Michigan Anti-Slavery Society was created in Ann Arbor, and the Abolitionist newspaper *Signal of Liberty* was printed there. In 1848, when a posse of slavecatchers arrived in Marshall seeking the Crosswaite family, local residents jailed them long enough to allow the fugitives to flee across the border to Canada. Meanwhile, in 1848, three brothers—Joseph, Levi, and Prior Foster—founded the Woodstock Manual Labor Institute in the town of Woodstock, one of the first interracial training schools.

The oldest and largest of the rural black communities in Michigan is in Cass County, located in the southwest part of the state. Originally settled in 1832 by antislavery Quakers and free black Southerners who migrated from Virginia and North Carolina, it became the meeting point of three Underground Railroad paths that followed the route of the Michigan Central Railroad, completed in 1852. Land became available for free black farmers. Escaping slaves were harbored by free black settlers, Quakers, and the Pokagon band of the Potawatomi. The Quakers also provided jobs clearing land, tools, housing, and wages for fugitives who preferred to settle in the area. By 1850, African Americans represented 25 percent of the county's population. After the Fugitive Slave Law of 1850 was passed (*see* FUGITIVE SLAVE LAWS) to aid southern masters in recovering their slaves, black settlers poured into the safe confines of Cass County, and Calvin Township had a majority black population by 1860.

The CIVIL WAR galvanized Michigan's black community, and the state's black residents vigorously endorsed the Union cause. Beginning in 1863, when the armed forces began to accept African-American recruits, nearly 1,400 infantry men were mustered into the U.S. Army. They served in the Michigan First Colored Infantry, later recommissioned as the 102nd Regiment.

After 1865, African Americans lobbied intensely for suffrage, which was granted in 1870. In 1868, the first blacks were admitted to the University of Michigan, and in 1869, the state supreme court desegregated the state's public schools. By the end of the Civil War, Michigan's black population of nearly 3,000 had spread between Detroit and the central and southwest area counties. Migration from the upper South swelled the African-American population between 1870 and 1880, and again between 1890 and 1900, in response to the demand for labor in Detroit industries. Nevertheless, African Americans represented less than 1 percent of the state's population throughout the period.

Among the migrants were a large number of highly educated and successful African Americans, who built a strong black community in Detroit. As a result of their lobbying efforts, in 1883 the legislature repealed its twelve-year-old law forbidding intermarriage. In 1885, it passed the first of a series of laws banning discrimination in public accommodations. In spite of these achievements, prejudice remained widespread in the state, and the laws were largely unenforced. In 1893, William Ferguson became the first African-American state representative. Elsewhere in the state lived such notable figures as Frederick Pelham, an engineer whose bridges near Pelham still stand; inventor/state legislator Joseph Dickinson of Detroit; Katherine Crawford, a graduate of the University of Michigan Medical School and one of the first African-American women doctors; and Elijah MCCOY, developer of the "oil cup" for railroad engines and other inventions.

Compared with the surrounding area, Cass County retained a greater measure of equality. Black farmers continued to live on relatively equal terms with their white counterparts, attending integrated schools and voting. In 1903, Booker T. WASHINGTON visited the black farming community in Cass County. He was impressed with the unusual prosperity, political power, and educational attainment of its residents. The 1910 federal census listed the value of African-American agricultural holdings at more than $650,000—the price of 13,515 acres of land—located on 171 farm units. These farms, the majority of which ranged in size from 90 to 800 acres, were located in Calvin Township and in a portion of Porter Township, approximately eight miles from the county seat and principal marketplace of Cassopolis. Beginning in 1880, with votes from the black majority, African Americans were elected to offices such as justice of the peace, supervisor, clerk, treasurer, school inspector, highway commissioner, and constable. In 1899, the first black was elected to the county board of supervisors from Calvin Township.

The Great Migration of the 1910s and early 1920s brought an enormous number of southern black people to Michigan. Some went to small towns such as Ann Arbor, whose black population had doubled to 1,200 by 1930. However, most settled in the Detroit area, which has since remained the home of the vast majority of Michigan's African Americans. African-American workers migrated in response to the unusual opportunities offered by the Detroit auto industry and the demand for labor in related industries. Detroit's black population jumped from 5,741 in 1910 to 40,838 ten years later. The Ford Motor Company was one of the first large manufacturers in the nation to hire black workers. General Motors plants in the cities of Pontiac, Saginaw, and Flint, in the Detroit

metropolitan area, also attracted workers. The proportion of black workers in the industry nationwide stabilized at about 4 percent by 1920, with very few outside Michigan.

The auto industry was largely nonunionized, and employers were willing to hire cheaper black labor. The Detroit Urban League, founded in 1918, together with the local branch of the NATIONAL ASSOCIATION FOR THE ADVANCEMENT OF COLORED PEOPLE, were promanagement (reflecting the views of Detroit's black elite on labor and union questions in general) and strong supporters of the Ford Motor Company. The Detroit Urban League was an important supplier of workers for white employers. During the 1920s, half of the city's black wage earners reported that they had obtained work through the Urban League at the Chrysler, Dodge, Studebaker, and Cadillac plants.

The GREAT DEPRESSION hit Michigan blacks very hard. In Detroit, large numbers of African-American laborers were laid off. In the farming counties of the central and southwest areas, the continuing agricultural depression impoverished black landowners. Many of their children were forced to migrate to towns to seek work. In Cass County, where black farmers still owned nearly 10,000 acres in 1930, black landholdings declined. The depression aggravated the strong prejudices of many Michigan whites. White supremacist groups such as the KU KLUX KLAN, a strong force in Michigan, grew in numbers. In 1930, a white terror group called the Black Legion allegedly murdered minister Earl Little (father of future Black Nationalist MALCOLM X) and burned down the family home in Lansing.

During the 1930s, African Americans played a prominent role in the unionization of Detroit industries. Many black leaders, future Detroit mayor Coleman YOUNG being the most notable, started their careers as labor organizers. In the mid- to late 1930s, blacks had allied with white unionists from the United Auto Workers and had participated in strikes at General Motors' Flint plant and at Ford's River Rouge factory.

The coming of WORLD WAR II brought war contracts and prosperity to Detroit's industries and sparked renewed black population growth. The population surge overburdened the city and race relations worsened. In 1943, Detroit exploded into violence. Conflict between black and white residents resulted in an enormous race riot. The rioting lasted two days, and by the time it was over, thirty-four people were dead, including twenty-five African Americans. There were also more than 600 people injured.

In the years after World War II, Michigan's blacks became a powerful political force. Detroit and the other black communities in Michigan contrasted strongly in political allegiance. The black population in Detroit, influenced by labor organizers and New Deal social policies, was largely DEMOCRATIC, while the farmers in the central and southwest areas were REPUBLICAN (and have remained so despite the changes brought on by the CIVIL RIGHTS MOVEMENT). African Americans were named to state commissions and assisted in the offices of such officials as the secretary of state. A few blacks gained seats on city councils in Ann Arbor and elsewhere. In 1954, Charles C. DIGGS of Detroit became Michigan's first African American in Congress. In 1961, largely through the efforts of delegate Daisy Elliott, Michigan approved a new constitution with a strong antidiscrimination clause.

During the early 1960s, the civil rights movement became a powerful force in Michigan black life. In 1961, the Ann Arbor Fair Housing Association spent eight months picketing Pittsfield Village, a housing development, after it refused to sell to an interracial couple. With help from the local NAACP, a city housing ordinance was passed in March 1962. In 1963, activists from the CONGRESS OF RACIAL EQUALITY (CORE) began protests in Grand Rapids to open up rental housing to blacks. The same year, in Detroit, a Walk for Freedom led by the Rev. Dr. Martin Luther King, Jr., attracted 125,000 participants.

Attempts at reform in the early 1960s were insufficient to correct the imbalance within the state's racist class structure. In 1966, Floyd McCree, an African American, was elected mayor of Flint by a largely black vote. The same year, African Americans in Lansing and Benton Harbor expressed their disgust and anger in a riot. In July 1967, Detroit was torn for three days by a major race rebellion, which left forty-three people dead and large sections of the city damaged. Additional riots broke out the following month in Kalamazoo, Saginaw, and other places in Michigan instigated by racist oppression.

Since the 1960s, Michigan's African-American community has made noteworthy political gains. Coleman Young, elected mayor of Detroit in 1973, became one of the most powerful leaders in the state, and Rep. John CONYERS of Detroit, elected in 1964, later became the dean of African Americans in Congress. In 1987, William Lucas ran a strong but unsuccessful campaign as Republican candidate for governor of Michigan.

Michigan's African-American population, both rural and urban, has suffered from chronic unemployment since 1950, and the jobless rate rose sharply after 1970. Black workers have been adversely affected by the decline of the auto industry in Detroit, and, to a lesser extent, by layoffs in the industrial areas of Grand Rapids and Lansing.

Institutionalized racism has nearly devastated Detroit's black community and continues to make land ownership very tenuous for black farmers in the central and southwestern counties. In Cass County, which remained strongly committed to agriculture, black land ownership was reduced to 8,000 acres by 1968. That year, Elijah MUHAMMAD, Sr. and Sons, together with a firm named the Progressive Land Corporation, began making land purchases in Cass County on behalf of the NATION OF ISLAM. Cass County was selected as the site for these purchases because of the historical presence of African-American farmers, high soil productivity, and proximity to markets in Detroit and Chicago. The Progressive Land Corporation acquired at least 550 acres, or nearly a square mile, for $155,000. Nevertheless, black landholdings in Cass County continued to decline in the following decades.

In recent years, Michigan has been the home of prominent African-American artists and entertainers. Some of the more significant figures are basketball star Earvin "Magic" JOHNSON, born in Lansing; singers Diana ROSS and Della Reese, born in Detroit; Betty CARTER, born in Flint; and Stevie WONDER, born in Saginaw; composer Willis Charles Patterson, born in Ann Arbor; actor James Earl JONES, who grew up near Jackson; jazz musicians Melvin "Sy" Oliver, born in Battle Creek, Milt JACKSON and Herb Jeffries, born in Detroit; and the brothers Hank, Thad, and Elvin JONES, natives of Pontiac.

The African-American legacy in Michigan is one of pride and determined effort. Although Michigan's African Americans continue to face severe obstacles to political and economic progress, the legacy of struggle and resistance exemplified by the actions of the operators of the Underground Railroad throughout the state is vital as an example of hope and determination necessary for advancement in the twenty-first century.

REFERENCES

BANNER, MELVIN E. *The Black Pioneer in Michigan.* Midland, Mich., 1973.

CLASPY, EVERETT. *The Negro in Southwestern Michigan: Negroes in the North in a Rural Environment.* Dowagiac, Mich., 1967.

DEVRIES, JAMES E. *Race and Kinship in a Midwestern Town: The Black Experience in Monroe, Michigan, 1900–1915.* Urbana, Ill., 1984.

GRAFF, GEORGE P. *The People of Michigan.* Lansing, Mich., 1974.

HESSLINK, GEORGE K. *Black Neighbors: Negroes in a Northern Rural Community.* New York, 1974.

LARRIE, REGINALD R. *Makin' Free: African Americans in the Northwest Territory.* Detroit, 1981.

Michigan Historical Commission. *Negroes in Michigan History.* Lansing, Mich., 1970.

WILSON, BENJAMIN C. *The Rural Black Heritage Between Chicago and Detroit: 1850–1929.* Kalamazoo, Mich., 1985.

MARCIA R. SAWYER

Middle Passage.   *See* Slave Trade.

Midwifery.   The evocation of the word *midwifery* calls up two images. The first is a medically trained nurse who specializes in obstetrics and gynecology and is licensed to attend childbirths in the hospital and, less frequently, in freestanding birthing centers or the homes of clients. The second and older image is the tradition of social childbirth in which women gave birth at home in the presence of other women and with the guidance of a skilled folk practitioner. Due to a number of economic, cultural, and political factors, social childbirth declined in significance for native-born northern white women relatively early. By the late 1760s, they had already begun to rely on male physicians to deliver their children. Traditional midwifery, however, continued to flourish among European immigrants who settled in the cities along the northeastern seaboard from the late nineteenth through the early twentieth century.

In the South, the midwifery tradition has been for the most part an African-American one, with the midwife mediating the reproductive experiences of both black and white women, especially in the region's rural communities from the early seventeenth to the closing decades of the twentieth century. By the 1940s, social childbirth had been largely replaced by scientific childbirth in the hospital, but a few surviving traditional African-American midwives continued to offer their services in the late 1980s as reported by Debra Susie (1988) in Florida and by Linda Holmes (1986) and Annie Logan (1989) in Alabama.

Throughout the slaveholding South, African-American midwives had the responsibility for managing pregnancy and childbirth. Often these women were slaves practicing not only on the plantations where they resided, but also attending births on neighboring plantations, for which their owners collected a fee. In the rural areas of the South, slave midwives also delivered the children of white women. Powerful in their knowledge of the physiological, medicinal, and spiritual aspects of childbirth, slave midwives inhabited an intensely ambiguous role. They wielded an expertise that allowed them to compete successfully with "scientifically" trained

Savannah Brown's midwife application, October 27, 1941. (Florida State Archives)

white male physicians of the period while they remained classified as property, rarely receiving renumeration, and subject to sanctions should the infant or mother die. Given the close association of childbirth with other aspects of bodily functioning, slave midwives were also generally recognized as healers and attended the sick as part of their practice. Todd Savitt notes that free black women also marketed their skills as birth attendants to a white clientele, while at the same time offering their services to neighbors and kin in their own communities (Savitt 1978, 182).

In the African-American community, across historical periods, women who became midwives did so either through apprenticeship to another midwife, often a family member, or through the experience of having given birth themselves. Whatever the practical route of transmission, however, the emphasis in the articulation of an identity as a midwife was on the spiritual nature of the practice. Women were said to be called to become midwives in the same manner that a person is called to religious ministry; the decision was not under the control of the individual practitioner. So too were prayer and divine guidance crucial to the midwife's success in delivering babies and nurturing the mother back to health.

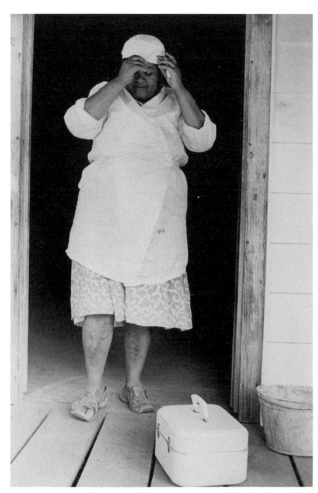

Frances Mae Carson, thirty-seven, midwife in Dallas County, Ala., getting dressed to leave on her patient rounds in the district, May 4, 1966. (© Charmian Reading)

Childbirth, in this framework, did not end with the physical emergence of the infant. The midwife was responsible for postpartum care, ensuring that both mother and child—spiritually as well as physically vulnerable—were protected from harm. Though the length of time varied, new mothers were expected to refrain from normal activities, avoid eating certain foods, and keep close to home for up to a month after birth, under the guidance of their midwives.

The dual nature of midwifery as skilled craft and as spiritual service to others was intrinsic to its emergence during the slave period, and continued as an essential feature through the end of the twentieth century. It is important to recognize, then, that African-American midwives historically viewed themselves as socially embedded in the cultural and religious belief systems of their own communities, but also as having control of a set of skills that allowed them a measure of independence and authority in the broader society.

REFERENCES

HOLMES, LINDA J. "African-American Midwives in the South." In Pamela S. Eakins, ed. *The American Way of Birth*. Philadelphia, 1986, pp. 273–291.

LOGAN, ANNIE LEE, as told to Katherine Clark. *Motherwit: An Alabama Midwife's Story*. New York, 1989.

SAVITT, TODD. *Medicine and Slavery: The Diseases and Health Care of Blacks in Antebellum Virginia*. Urbana, Ill., 1978.

SUSIE, DEBRA A. *In the Way of Our Grandmothers: A Cultural View of Twentieth-Century Midwifery in Florida*. Athens, Ga., 1988.

GERTRUDE J. FRASER

Migration/Population.   Migration has been a persistent theme throughout African-American history. Africans entered the New World as slaves, unlike European immigrants and their Asian counterparts. With the advent of the CIVIL WAR and EMANCIPATION, black population movement took on a voluntary character and slowly converged with that of other groups. Nonetheless, only with the coming of WORLD WAR I and its aftermath did blacks make a fundamental break with the land and move into cities in growing numbers. The Great Migration of the early twentieth century foreshadowed the long-run transformation of African Americans from a predominantly rural to a predominantly urban population. It reflected their quest for freedom, jobs, and social justice; the rise of new classes and social relations within the African-American community; and the emergence of new patterns of race, class, and ethnic relations in American society as a whole.

From the colonial period through the antebellum era, Africans and their American descendants experienced forced migration from one agricultural region to another. One and a half million blacks reached the United States via the international SLAVE TRADE, primarily from the west coast of Africa. Through natural increase, their numbers rose to an estimated four million by 1860. By 1750, there were more than 144,000 blacks in the tobacco-growing states of Maryland and Virginia, representing the highest concentration of slaves in the country. In the wake of the American Revolution, however, slaves experienced a dramatic relocation from the tobacco region of the upper South to the emerging cotton-growing areas of the deep South. The tobacco country slowly declined in fertility during the late eighteenth century, and planters first transported or sold their slaves to the neighboring states of Kentucky and Tennessee. After the close of the international slave trade to the United States in 1808, this movement accelerated. Between 1810 and 1820, an estimated 137,000 slaves left the Chesapeake Bay region and North Carolina for the cotton-growing states of the deep South, particularly Alabama and Mississippi.

Some slaves entered the deep South with their masters, but growing numbers came via the domestic slave trade. Whether they traveled by water or by land, they moved to their new homes in handcuffs and chains. As one ex-slave recalled, "We were hand-cuffed in pairs, with iron staples and bolts, with a short chain about a foot long uniting the handcuffs and their wearers." Contemporary travelers frequently commented on the sight of migrating slaves. In 1834, for example, an English traveler reported on his trip from Virginia to Alabama: "In the early grey of the morning, we came up with a singular spectacle, the most striking one of the kind I have ever witnessed. It was a camp of negro slave-drivers, just

packing up to start; they had about three hundred slaves with them, who had bivouacked the preceding night in chains in the woods; these they were conducting to Natchez, upon the Mississippi River."

Although Africans, and increasingly African Americans, were the victims of coerced migrations during this period, they were by no means passive. Slaves acted in their own behalf by running away, planning rebellions, and deepening their efforts to build a viable slave community. One historian concludes, for example, that the transition from an African to a predominantly American-born slave-labor force facilitated the emergence of new forms of rebellion and demands for liberation in the new republic. As slaves learned the language, gained familiarity with the terrain, and built linkages to slaves on other plantations, they increased their efforts to resist bondage. Newspaper advertisements for runaways increased as planters and slave traders mediated the transfer of slaves from the tobacco-growing regions to the "cotton kingdom." Advertisements for runaways not only reflected the slaves' resistance, but

Like millions of other blacks between 1915 and 1940, this Florida family left the states of the old Confederacy for a new home in the North. (Prints and Photographs Division, Library of Congress)

also the harsh conditions they faced: "Bill is a large fellow, very black, shows the whites of his eyes more than usual, has a scar on his right cheek bone, several on his breast, one on his arm, occasioned by the bite of a dog, his back very badly scarred with the whip."

The Civil War and RECONSTRUCTION radically transformed the context of black migration. Black population movement accelerated, spurred by the presence of federal troops, the ending of chattel slavery, the enactment of full citizenship legislation, and rising white hostility. In the first years following Emancipation, one Florida planter informed his cousin in North Carolina, "The negroes don't seem to feel free unless they leave their old homes . . . just to make it sure they can go when and where they choose." A South Carolina family offered to pay its cook double the amount that she would receive in another village, but the woman insisted, "No, Miss, I must go. . . . If I stay here I'll never know I am free."

When the promise of freedom faded during the late 1870s, the Exodus of 1879 (see EXODUSTERS) symbolized the new mobility of the black population. Within a few months, some six thousand blacks left their homes in Louisiana, Mississippi, and Texas for a new life in Kansas. As one black contemporary stated, "There are no words which can fully express or explain the real condition of my people throughout the south, nor how deeply and keenly they feel the necessity of fleeing from the wrath and long pent-up hatred of their old masters which they feel assured will ere long burst loose like the pent-up-fires of a volcano and crush them if they remain here many years longer." Still, the Exodus was a rural-to-rural migration, with blacks moving to Kansas when an earlier Tennessee option proved fruitless. African Americans expected to resettle on available farmland and continue their familiar, but hopefully freer, rural way of life.

Despite the predominance of rural-to-rural migration, the migration of blacks to American cities had deep antebellum roots. Boston launched its career as a slaveholding city as early as 1638, when the Salem ship *Desire* returned from the West Indies with a cargo of "salt, cotton, tobacco, and Negroes." Slavery in New York City, beginning under Dutch control in 1626, entered an era of unprecedented growth under the British in 1664. In Philadelphia in 1684, within three years after the first Quakers settled in Pennsylvania, the first fifty Africans arrived. The number of slaves in the seaports of the Northeast rose from negligible numbers during the seventeenth century to sizable proportions by the mid-eighteenth century: to over 1,500 in Boston, 1,400 in Philadelphia, and over 2,000 in New York. Southern cities such as New Orleans, Mobile, Charleston, Balti-more, Louisville, Savannah, and Richmond also had sizable antebellum black populations.

Black migration to American cities escalated during the late eighteenth and early nineteenth centuries. Moreover, in the aftermath of the Civil War and Reconstruction, blacks increasingly moved into rural industrial settings such as the coalfields of Alabama, Tennessee, Kentucky, and West Virginia. Others gained increasing access to nonagricultural jobs as lumber and railroad hands in the expanding industrial order. Still, as late as 1910, nearly 90 percent of the nation's black population lived in the South, and fewer than 22 percent of southern blacks lived in cities.

Under the impact of World War I, blacks made a fundamental break with their southern rural heritage and moved into cities in growing numbers. An estimated 700,000 to one million blacks left the South between 1917 and 1920. Another 800,000 to one million left during the 1920s. Whereas the prewar migrants moved to southern cities such as Norfolk, Louisville, Birmingham, and Atlanta and to a few northern cities such as Chicago, Philadelphia, and New York, blacks now moved throughout the urban North and West. Beginning with relatively small numbers on the eve of World War I, the black urban population in the Midwest and Great Lakes region increased even more dramatically than that of the old Northeast. Detroit's black population increased by 611 percent during the war years and by nearly 200 percent during the 1920s, rising from fewer than 6,000 to over 120,000. Cleveland's black population rose from fewer than 8,500 to nearly 72,000. In St. Louis, the increase was from under 45,000 in 1910 to nearly 94,000 in 1930. In the urban West, the black population increased most dramatically in Los Angeles, growing from 7,600 in 1910 to nearly 40,000 in 1930. Nonetheless, as in the prewar era, New York City, Chicago, and Philadelphia continued to absorb disproportionately large numbers of black newcomers. Between 1910 and 1930, Chicago's black population increased more than fivefold, from 44,000 to 234,000; New York's more than tripled, from about 100,000 to 328,000; and Philadelphia's grew from 84,500 to an estimated 220,600.

Upper South and border states remained important sources of black migrants during World War I and the 1920s, but deep South states increased their importance. Blacks born in Mississippi, Alabama, Georgia, South Carolina, and Louisiana now dominated the migration stream to Illinois and Chicago, for example, making up over 60 percent of the black population increase in that area between 1910 and 1920. African Americans from the upper South predominated in New York City more so than in Chicago, but blacks from South Carolina, Georgia, and

Florida came in growing numbers. In the rapidly industrializing cities of Cleveland and Detroit, the percentage of black men to women escalated from just a few more men than women in 1910 to between 120 and 140 men to every 100 women during the war years. In Milwaukee, where the ratio of men to women was 95 to 100 in 1910, the ratio reversed itself, and the number of men versus women increased between 1910 and 1920. Finally, in the northeastern cities of New York and Philadelphia, where women significantly outnumbered men before the war, the ratio evened out.

A variety of factors underlay black population movement. African Americans sought an alternative to sharecropping, disfranchisement, and racial injustice in the South. In 1917, the *AME Review* articulated the forces that propelled blacks outward from the South: "Neither character, the accumulation of property, the fostering of the Church, the schools and a better and higher standard of the home" had made a difference in the status of black Southerners. "Confidence in the sense of justice, humanity and fair play of the white South is gone," the paper concluded. One migrant articulated the same mood in verse: "An' let one race have all de South—Where color lines are drawn—For 'Hagar's child' done [stem] de tide—Farewell—we're good and gone."

African Americans were also attracted by the lure of opportunities in the North. The labor demands of northern industries, immigration-restriction legislation, and greater access to the rights of citizens (including the franchise) all encouraged the movement of blacks into northern cities. Wages in northern industries usually ranged from $3 to $5 per eight-hour day, compared with as little as 75 cents to $1 per day in southern agriculture and with no more than $2.50 for a nine-hour day in southern industries. Moreover, between 1915 and 1925, the average wages of domestics in some northern cities doubled. Northern cities also promised access to better health care. The nonwhite infant-mortality rate dropped in New York City from 176 in 1917 to 105 in 1930; in Boston, from 167 to 90; and in Philadelphia, from 193 to 100. Between 1911 and 1926, according to the Metropolitan Life Insurance Company, the incidence of tuberculosis among the nation's blacks declined by 44 percent for black males and 43 percent for black females. New York, Philadelphia, and Chicago showed similar patterns of decline.

Better social conditions, higher wages, and the franchise—it is no wonder that African Americans viewed the Great Migration to northern cities in glowing terms with references to "the Promised Land," the "flight out of Egypt," and "going into Canaan." One black man wrote back to his southern home, "The (Col.) men are making good. [The job]

never pays less than $3.00 per day for (10) hours." In her letter home, a black woman related, "I am well and thankful to say I am doing well . . . I work in Swifts Packing Company." "Up here," another migrant said, "our people are in a different light." Over and over again, African Americans confirmed that: "Up here, a man can be a man." As one southern black man wrote home from the North, "I should have been here twenty years ago . . . I just begin to feel like a man . . . My children are going to the same school with the whites and I don't have to humble to no one. I have registered. Will vote in the next election and there isn't any yes Sir or no Sir. It's all yes and no, Sam and Bill."

The Great Migration was by no means a simple move from southern agriculture to northern cities. It had specific regional and subregional components. More blacks migrated to southern cities between 1900 and 1920 than to northern ones. Moreover, African Americans frequently made up from 25 percent to 50 percent of the total population in southern cities, compared with little more than 10 percent in northern cities. Before moving to Philadelphia, Boston, or New York, for example, rural migrants first moved to cities such as New Orleans, Jacksonville, Savannah, Memphis, Charleston, and Birmingham. The Jefferson County cities of Birmingham and Bessemer, with extensive rail connections, served as the major distribution points for blacks going north from Alabama. The Southern, the Louisville and Nashville, the Chicago, St. Louis, and San Francisco, and the Illinois Central railroads all traveled northward from Birmingham and Bessemer. In Georgia, cities such as Columbus, Americus, and Albany served as distribution points for blacks leaving from western Georgia and eastern Alabama, while Valdosta, Waycross, Brunswick, and Savannah were distribution centers for those leaving the depressed agricultural counties of southern and southeastern Georgia. To blacks moving north from Mississippi, Arkansas, Alabama, Louisiana, and Texas, Chicago was the logical destination, whereas cities in Pennsylvania, New Jersey, New York, and New England attracted blacks from Florida, South Carolina, Virginia, and Georgia.

Upon the arrival of blacks in northern cities, their population movement usually developed secondary streams. As one contemporary observer noted, "All of the arrivals here [Chicago] did not stay. . . . They were only temporary guests awaiting the opportunity to proceed further and settle in surrounding cities and towns." "With Chicago as a center there are within a radius of from one hundred to one hundred and fifty miles a number of smaller industrial centers. . . . A great many of the migrants who came to Chicago found employment in these satellite places." In Philadelphia, black migration also "broke bulk" and radiated outward to Lancaster, York, Altoona, and Harrisburg in central Pennsylvania, as well as to Wilmington in Delaware.

Southern blacks helped to organize their own movement into the urban North. They developed an extensive communications network, which included railroad employees, who traveled back and forth between northern and southern cities; northern black weeklies such as the *Chicago Defender* and the *Pittsburgh Courier;* and an expanding chain of kin and friends. Using their networks of families and friends, African Americans learned about transportation, jobs, and housing beforehand. As one contemporary observer noted, "The chief stimuli was discussion . . . . The talk in the barber shops and grocery stores . . . soon began to take the form of reasons for leaving." Also fueling the migration process were the letters, money, and testimonies of migrants who returned to visit. One South Carolina migrant to Pittsburgh recalled, "I was plowing in the field and it was real hot. And I stayed with some of the boys who would leave home and [come] back . . . and would have money, and they had clothes. I didn't have that. We all grew up together. And I said, 'Well, as long as I stay here I'm going to get nowhere.' And I tied that mule to a tree and caught a train."

Other migrants formed migration clubs, pooled their resources, and moved in groups. Black women, deeply enmeshed in black kin and friendship networks, played a conspicuous role in helping to organize the black migration. As recent scholarship suggests, women were the "primary kinkeepers." Moreover, they often had their own gender-specific reasons for leaving the rural South. African-American women resented stereotyped images of the black mammy, who presumably placed loyalty to white families above attachment to her own. Black women's migration reinforced the notion that lifting the race and improving the image of black women were compatible goals.

As blacks moved into northern cities in growing numbers, a black industrial working class emerged. Black migration was fundamentally a movement of workers. Southern black sharecroppers, farm laborers, sawmill hands, dock workers, and railroad hands all moved into new positions in the urban economy. Labor agents helped to recruit black workers for jobs in meat-packing, auto, steel, and other mass-production industries. As suggested above, however, these labor agents were soon supplanted by the expansion of black familial and communal networks. Employers attested: " 'After the initial group movement by agents, Negroes kept going by twos and threes. These were drawn by letters, and by actual advances of money, from Negroes who had already settled in the North.' . . . 'Every Negro that makes good in the North and writes back to his friends starts off a new group.' "

Wartime labor demands undermined the color barrier in basic industries. In Cleveland, Pittsburgh, Detroit, and Milwaukee, the percentage of black men employed in industrial jobs increased from an estimated 10 to 20 percent of the black labor force in 1910 to about 60 percent or 70 percent in 1920 and 1930. An official of Cleveland's National Malleable Casting company exclaimed: "We have [black] molders, core makers, chippers, fitters, locomotive crane operators, melting furnace operators, general foremen, foremen, assistant foremen, clerks, timekeepers[;] in fact, there is no work in our shop that they cannot do and do well, if properly supervised." In the Pittsburgh district, the number of black steelworkers rose to nearly 17,000 by 1923, from less than 800 on the eve of World War I. In Detroit, the Ford Motor Company outdistanced other automakers in the employment of African Americans, the number of black employees rising from fewer than 100 in 1916 to nearly 10,000 ten years later. Black women also entered industrial jobs, although their gains were far less than those of black men. In Chicago, the number of black women in manufacturing trades increased from fewer than 1,000 in 1910 to over 3,000 in 1920. Industrial jobs now employed 15 percent of the black female labor force, compared with less than 7 percent in 1910. Buffalo and Pittsburgh offered neither black nor white women substantial industrial opportunities, but the war nonetheless increased their numbers in manufacturing. In Harlem, black women gained increasing employment in the garment industry and in commercial laundries. Still, few black women entered the major factories of the industrial North. Moreover, despite black men's increasing participation in the new industrial sectors, most moved into jobs at the bottom rung of the industrial ladder.

If African Americans helped to shape their own movement into cities, they also played a role in shaping their experiences within the labor force. In order to change the terms on which they labored, they frequently moved from job to job seeking higher wages and better working conditions. In Milwaukee, at one very disagreeable tannery plant, a black worker related, "I worked there one night and I quit." During the war years, the steel mills of western Pennsylvania frequently experienced a 300 percent turnover rate among black workers. In 1923, for instance, the A. M. Byers iron mill in Pittsburgh employed 1,408 African Americans in order to maintain a work force of 228. At the same time, some African Americans served as strikebreakers; they expressed bitter resentment over the discriminatory practices of white workers, who frequently referred to blacks as a "scab race" and justified their exclusionary policies. Black workers also organized independent all-black unions such as the BROTHERHOOD OF SLEEPING CAR PORTERS. When whites occasionally lowered racial barriers, others joined white unions such as the Amalgamated Meat Cutters and Butcher Workmen. During the 1930s, the Congress of Industrial Organizations built upon these traditions of collective action among black workers.

Closely intertwined with the increasing urbanization of the black population was the rise of the GHETTO. As the black urban population increased, residential segregation increased in all major cities. The index of dissimilarity (a statistical device for measuring the extent of residential segregation) rose from 66.8 to 85.2 percent in Chicago; 60.6 to 85.0 percent in Cleveland; 64.1 to 77.9 percent in Boston; and 46.0 to 63.0 percent in Philadelphia. The increasing segregation of blacks in the city not only reflected their precarious position in the urban economy but the intensification of racial restrictions in the urban housing market as well. In cities with large black populations like New York and Chicago, the World War I migration intensified a process that was already well under way. HARLEM, planned as an exclusive, stable, upper- and upper-middle-class white community, represented a desirable location to the city's expanding black population.

Although an economic depression undercut the flow of whites into Harlem, white residents resisted black occupancy. Between 1910 and 1915, the Harlem Property Owners' Improvement Corporation waged a vigorous fight to keep blacks out. It launched a restrictive covenant campaign and informed black realtors that houses in the area were not available to black buyers. Although the movement failed to keep Harlem white, discriminatory prices, along with the dearth of necessary repairs, undermined housing quality during the 1920s.

In Chicago and elsewhere, North and South, blacks faced similar restrictions in the housing market. When legal tactics failed, whites resorted to violence. Race violence erupted in Chicago, East St. Louis, Pittsburgh, and Philadelphia during the era of the Great Migration. Race riots not only helped to reinforce residential segregation in northern cities, they highlighted the growing nationalization of the "race question" in American society.

African Americans developed cross-class alliances and fought racial discrimination in the housing, institutional, and political life of the cities. The black migration reinforced a long tradition of black urban institution-building activities. As early as the 1790s, blacks launched the AFRICAN METHODIST EPISCOPAL CHURCH in Philadelphia, followed closely by the AFRICAN METHODIST EPISCOPAL ZION church in New York, and the Baptist church (see BAPTISTS) in both cities. In 1886, African Americans formed the NATIONAL BAPTIST CONVENTION and spearheaded the formation of new churches.

Along with churches, blacks soon formed a variety of mutual-aid societies and FRATERNAL ORDERS, including the Masons, Odd Fellows, and Independent Order of St. Luke. The NATIONAL ASSOCIATION OF COLORED WOMEN, formed in 1895, emphasized service to the community. Mobilizing under its credo "Lifting as We Climb," the association organized, administered, and supported a variety of social-welfare activities: homes for the aged, young women, and children; relief funds for the unemployed; and legal aid to combat injustice before the law. Under the impact of World War I and its aftermath, new expressions of black consciousness (as reflected in the emergence of the HARLEM RENAISSANCE) and the growing participation of blacks in northern politics both demonstrated solidarity across class and status lines.

The alliance between black workers and black elites was by no means unproblematic. As the new black middle class expanded during the 1920s, for example, it slowly moved into better housing vacated by whites, leaving the black poor concentrated in certain sections. In his studies of Chicago and New York, sociologist E. Franklin FRAZIER demonstrated the increasing division of the black urban community along socioeconomic lines. While each city contained significant areas of interclass mixing, poverty increasingly characterized specific sections of the ghetto.

Moreover, the rise of working-class-oriented organizations such as the UNIVERSAL NEGRO IMPROVEMENT ASSOCIATION created substantial conflicts between black workers and established middle-class leadership. Emphasizing "race first," black pride, and solidarity with Africa, the Garvey movement struck a responsive chord among large numbers of black workers. Its Jamaican-born leader, Marcus GARVEY, frequently exclaimed, "The Universal Negro Improvement Association . . . believes that the Negro race is as good as any other race, and therefore should be as proud of itself as others are. . . . It believes in the spiritual Fatherhood of God and the Brotherhood of Man." As one migrant stated, "We will make a great mistake if we step out of the path of the Universal Negro Improvement Association." While race-conscious black business and professional people endorsed aspects of Garvey's ideas, they feared his growing appeal and often complained that his message appealed primarily to the "ignorant class" of newcomers from the South.

Despite conflicts between black workers and middle-class black leaders, African Americans continued to forge cross-class alliances. As early as 1914,

Oscar DEPRIEST defeated his white opponents and became Chicago's first black alderman. In 1928, DePriest also symbolized the growing shift of black electoral power from the South to northern urban centers when he gained the party's endorsements and won a seat in the U.S. Congress, serving the First Congressional District of Illinois. When blacks sought a similar goal in New York, they failed because skillful gerrymandering had split the black vote between the Nineteenth and Twenty-First Assembly districts. In 1944, when boundaries were redrawn, blacks elected the black minister Adam Clayton POWELL, Jr., to the House of Representatives; Harlem thus became the second northern congressional district to send a black to Congress. By then, African Americans had realigned their party affiliation from Republican to Democrat and had become an indispensable element in the New Deal coalition.

Although black electoral politics reflected the growing segregation of the urban environment, black elites retained a core of white allies. African Americans had cultivated a small number of white friends and launched the interracial NATIONAL URBAN LEAGUE in 1911 and the NATIONAL ASSOCIATION FOR THE ADVANCEMENT OF COLORED PEOPLE (NAACP) in 1909. During the 1930s and 1940s, this inter- and intraracial unity gained even greater expression with the rise of the Congress of Industrial Organizations, New Deal social-welfare programs, and the March on Washington movement. When President Franklin D. Roosevelt issued Executive Order 8802 in 1941, calling for an end to racial barriers in defense industries, African Americans achieved a major victory against racial exploitation.

As the nation entered the years after World War II, a variety of forces again transformed the context of black migration. The technological revolution in southern agriculture, the emergence of the welfare state, and the militant civil rights and Black Power movements all helped to complete the long-run transformation of blacks from a predominantly rural to a predominantly urban people. The African-American population increased from thirteen million in 1940 to over twenty-two million in 1970. The proportion of blacks living in cities rose to over 80 percent, 10 percent higher than the population at large. Beginning as the most rural of Americans, blacks had become the most urbanized.

The Great Migration helped to transform both black and white America. It elevated the issues of race and southern black culture from regional to national phenomena. It was often a volatile process, involving both intra- and interracial conflicts. Distributed almost equally among regions, by the late 1970s the black urban migration had run its familiar twentieth-century course. Increases in black urban population were now primarily the product of births over deaths rather than interregional movements. Moreover, southern-born blacks from the North and West returned home in rising numbers. During the 1980s, the proportion of African Americans living in the South increased, after declining for more than a century. At the same time, black migration to American suburbs escalated. While the outcome of this new migration is yet to be determined, the suburban migrants are faring better than their inner-city counterparts. The returning migrants are also much better off than those who left, and they envision a "New South," one that is much different from the one their forebears abandoned.

REFERENCES

BERLIN, IRA, and RONALD HOFFMAN, eds. *Slavery and Freedom in the Age of the American Revolution.* Urbana, Ill., 1983.

GROSSMAN, JAMES R. *Land of Hope: Chicago, Black Southerners, and the Great Migration.* Chicago, 1989.

HARRIS, ROBERT L., JR. "Coming of Age: The Transformation of Afro-American Historiography." *Journal of Negro History* 57, no. 2 (1982): 107–121.

HARRISON, ALFERDTEEN. *Black Exodus: The Great Migration from the American South.* Jackson, Miss., 1991.

HINE, DARLENE CLARK, ed. *The State of Afro-American History: Past, Present and Future.* Baton Rouge, La., 1986.

LEMANN, NICHOLAS. *The Promised Land: The Great Black Migration and How It Changed America.* New York, 1991.

LEWIS, EARL. *In Their Own Interests: Race, Class, and Power in Twentieth-Century Norfolk, Virginia.* Berkeley, Calif., 1991.

MARKS, CAROLE. *Farewell—We're Good and Gone: The Great Migration.* Bloomington, Ind., 1989.

MEIER, AUGUST, and ELLIOT RUDWICK. *Black History and the Historical Profession, 1915–1980.* Urbana, Ill., 1986.

NASH, GARY. *Forging Freedom: The Formation of Philadelphia's Black Community, 1720–1840.* Cambridge, Mass., 1988.

PAINTER, NELL IRVIN. *Exodusters: Black Migration to Kansas after Reconstruction.* 1976. Reprint. Lawrence, Kans., 1986.

TROTTER, JOE W., JR. "Afro-American Urban History: A Critique of the Literature." In *Black Milwaukee: The Making of an Industrial Proletariat, 1915–45.* Urbana, Ill., 1985.

———, ed. *The Great Migration in Historical Perspective: New Dimensions of Race, Class, and Gender.* Bloomington, Ind., 1991.

WILSON, WILLIAM J. *The Truly Disadvantaged: The Inner City, the Underclass, and Public Policy.* Chicago, 1987.

JOE W. TROTTER, JR.

Miles, William (April 18, 1931–), filmmaker. Born in Harlem, William Miles is known for his documentaries on the history of African Americans. As a boy growing up on 126th Street behind the Apollo Theatre, Miles was fascinated by the movies and black history. While still a teenager, he persuaded the projectionist at the Apollo to show him how to splice film, and this provided him with his entry into Sterling Films. For approximately the next twenty-five years, Miles reedited films for television and restored old film stock. He eventually became involved in the production of films, although he did not receive credit.

His first film, *Men of Bronze* (1977), launched Miles's career as a filmmaker and exemplified his passion for uncovering the history of forgotten black Americans through archival film footage, oral histories, and historic photographs. It premiered at the New York Film Festival and won the American Film Festival Award and the CINE Golden Eagle Award. More films followed, including *I Remember Harlem* (1981), *The Different Drummer: Blacks in the Military* (1983), *Black Champions* (1986), *Black Stars in Orbit* (1990), and *Liberators: Fighting on Two Fronts in World War II* (1992), which was nominated for an Academy Award. Miles has received numerous awards, including a Guggenheim Award, an Alfred I. DuPont Columbia University Citation, and CEBA Awards.

REFERENCE

WILLIS-THOMAS, DEBORAH. "Documentary Artist: William Miles: Award-Winning Filmmaker." *Schomburg Center Journal* 2, no. 4 (Fall 1983): 2–3.

SARAH M. KEISLING

Miley, James Wesley "Bubber" (April 3, 1903–May 20, 1932), jazz trumpeter and composer. Bubber Miley was born in Aiken, S.C. His parents moved to New York City in 1909, where he was introduced to the trombone, then the cornet, in school. He joined the U.S. Navy in 1918 for eighteen months of service in World War I. On his discharge, Miley began working as a professional trumpeter and by 1921 had become a member of the Jazz Hounds, the group that accompanied blues singer Mamie SMITH. Miley had by that time become an accomplished player in the wa-wa or "plunger" style pioneered by trumpeter Joseph "King" OLIVER. (The style involved the careful manipulation of the rubber end of a plumber's plunger as a mute to produce plaintive, highly vocalized sounds.) In 1923, Miley joined the band known as the Washingtonians, at first led by Elmer Snowden but thereafter by Duke ELLINGTON; Miley's contributions soon became central to the development of Ellington's style and sound and to his early development as a composer. Miley's themes, particularly "Black and Tan Fantasy" (1927), "East St. Louis Toodle-Oo" (1928), and "The Mooche" (1928) account for the earliest Ellington masterpieces. With some brief absences, Miley remained with Ellington until 1929. On his departure he worked with several other leaders, including Noble SISSLE on a trip to Paris later in 1929, and as a special guest with the society dance orchestra of Leo Reisman. Miley formed his own orchestra in 1932, but he succumbed to tuberculosis that same year in New York.

REFERENCES

DODGE, ROGER PRYOR. "Bubber Miley." *Jazz Monthly* 4 (May 1958): 2–4.
TUCKER, MARK. *Ellington: The Early Years.* Urbana, Ill., and Chicago, 1991.

MARTIN WILLIAMS

Military. Military service has traditionally afforded African Americans a means of economic, social, and political advancement. In time of emergency, the British North American colonies found room in the ranks for free blacks and slaves. The United States has turned to blacks during military crises throughout its history, and today African Americans continue to help themselves by helping defend their country.

Colonial Wars and the American Revolution

In colonial times, black slaves accompanied their white masters to war, sometimes as cooks, occasionally as soldiers or sailors. South Carolina, where able-bodied male slaves outnumbered free whites of military age, enrolled trusted slaves in the militia, promising them freedom for exceptional service. Despite the shortage of white manpower, South Carolina remained wary of the slave militia, concerned that it might join in a slave rebellion. Actually, organized mutinies proved rare in colonial North America, although some individual slaves did seek vengeance by attacking the person, family, or property of the master. A planned uprising jolted the city of New York in April 1712, when some twenty slaves set fire to a building and killed nine of the whites who tried to put out the flames; the incident triggered arrests, trials, executions, and repression. South Carolina experienced a similar revolt, the Stono War of 1739, when a group of slaves from Angola rallied behind one of their number, killed several whites, and set out for the safety of Spanish Florida. White militiamen and their Native

American allies tracked down and killed the fugitives. Significantly, the colony did not on this occasion call on its armed slaves, who had fought under white leaders against the Yamasee Indians in 1715.

Like the slave who might earn freedom, the free black could benefit personally from helping defend his colony. George Gire of Massachusetts earned a pension for service during the French and Indian War (1754–1763) and also enhanced his standing in the community. Moreover, the free black who shipped out in a privateer shared with other crewmen in the proceeds from the sale of captured merchantmen, money that could establish him in a craft or trade.

When the American colonies rebelled against Great Britain in 1775, blacks fought in the Massachusetts militia at Lexington and Concord in April and in Gen. George Washington's Continental Army at Bunker Hill in June. The rebellious southern colonies, however, refused to employ blacks except as military labor. Even South Carolina, which had admitted slaves into the militia as recently as 1760, now refused them weapons for fear of a slave insurrection. Southern resistance to the arming of blacks proved so stubborn that Washington considered purging them from his army. Circumstances, however, persuaded him not only to allow black veterans to reenlist but also to admit other African Americans to the ranks.

John Murray, Lord Dunmore, the last royal governor of Virginia, inadvertently helped determine the racial policy of the Continental Army when, in November 1775, he offered slaves their freedom in return for military service on the loyalist side. The enthusiastic response enabled him to organize a regiment of escaped slaves. Lord Dunmore demonstrated that slaves would fight for their freedom, and some of the mutinous colonies followed his example.

In 1777, Connecticut adopted a policy of buying slaves, using them to fill quotas for the Continental Army, and declaring them forever free. Rhode Island followed Connecticut's lead, raising a battalion of slaves during 1778 who earned their freedom on battlegrounds in Rhode Island, New Jersey, and New York.

The plantation South came under pressure to emulate Connecticut and Rhode Island, and legislatures from Maryland southward debated the policy but failed to follow through. As late as 1779, with British forces on the offensive in the region, South Carolina refused to arm blacks, an attitude that Henry Laurens, a member of the Continental Congress, later blamed on the "triple-headed monster, in which prejudice, avarice, and pusillanimity were united." James Madison, a future president of the United States, tried unsuccessfully to persuade Virginia to recruit its most trusted slaves, assuring the planters that those who earned freedom through military service, far from leading a slave rebellion, would have only contempt for those remaining in bondage.

Although the southern governments forbade blacks to bear arms, policy and practice did not always coincide. The Continental Congress kept calling for troops as the war dragged on, but white volunteers became increasingly scarce. Prominent citizens, though they supported the Revolution, tended to prefer service in the local militia to that in the Continental Army, which might fight anywhere. Consequently, someone could stay close to home by arranging freedom for a slave to help fill the Continental quota.

The New Nation's Armed Forces

Although some 5,000 blacks served the American cause during the Revolutionary War, the United States—its independence confirmed when the Treaty of Paris took effect in 1783—soon excluded them from its armed forces. The new nation tried to make the militia its first line of defense, requiring in 1792 that all white males between the ages of eighteen and forty-five arm themselves and report for periodic training. Those states already admitting free blacks into the militia interpreted the federal law as a ban on African Americans and expelled them. Louisiana, after becoming American territory in 1803, disbanded a battalion of free blacks at New Orleans, a unit dating from the period of Spanish rule. During the American Revolution, when Spain aided the rebellious colonies against Great Britain, black soldiers from New Orleans had helped defeat the British on the Gulf coast.

In 1794, the War Department built a few frigates to protect American commerce against the Barbary pirates, but not until the very eve of the undeclared naval war with France (1798–1800) did the nation establish the departments of the Navy, Marine Corps, and Army. The Navy became the first of the armed forces to accept blacks, for it discovered while fighting France that white Americans flinched from the discomfort and harsh discipline of a dangerous cruise. In 1818, after black soldiers had fought first against the French and, with specific congressional approval, against the British in the WAR OF 1812, navy regulations at last approved the recruiting of free black Americans, thus confirming existing practices. The U.S. Navy continued, however, to bar slaves from enlisting or serving as workmen at navy yards. By 1839, the response of African Americans had proved so overwhelming that Secretary of the Navy Isaac B. Chauncey, who had commanded black sailors on the Great Lakes in the War of 1812, imposed a ceiling of 5 percent on black enlistments; so many reenlisted, however, that the proportion on active duty remained much higher.

Though a few African Americans had served in the Continental Marines during the American Revolution, the U.S. Marine Corps shunned them from its inception in 1798 until 1942. The Marine Corps needed fewer men than the Navy, and those it accepted did not require the special skills of a sailor. As a result, the number of white applicants proved adequate.

Like the militia, the new national Army accepted no blacks until the War of 1812 compelled it to do so. When Maj. Gen. Andrew Jackson arrived at New Orleans to organize the city's defenses, he called on free blacks to volunteer. The black militia unit, revived to meet the emergency, stepped forward, as did another 500 volunteers organized into two battalions under black officers. These African Americans helped win a series of clashes fought after the Treaty of Ghent, signed on Christmas Eve 1814, had officially ended the war. The climax came on January 8, 1815, when the final British assault broke under the massed fire of blacks and whites manning makeshift breastworks.

The African-American volunteers received the same pay and bonuses as whites, but such equality did not last. In 1834, Louisiana again disbanded the black militia, and all state militias, like the Army, became exclusively white. A window of opportunity, briefly opened, thus slammed shut.

Although the free black could no longer improve his lot in the Army or the militia, the slave of an army officer might become free if he accompanied his master to a post on free soil. In 1834, a household slave of Lt. J. W. B. Stockton successfully sued for her freedom on the grounds of residence at Fort Snelling in Wisconsin, a free territory. Dred Scott, a slave whom an army surgeon brought to the same post, invoked the earlier decision, but in 1857 a majority of the Supreme Court rejected the argument and ruled that no slave or descendant of a slave could aspire to American citizenship (*see* DRED SCOTT V. SANFORD).

The Civil War and Citizenship

Although the U.S. Navy continued to recruit blacks, none entered the Army or the state militias between the disbandment of the black militia at New Orleans and the outbreak of the CIVIL WAR. In the spring of 1861, when the South seceded and hostilities erupted, Louisiana again raised a militia unit among the free black residents of New Orleans. The Confederate States of America, however, used Louisiana's black troops only for guard duty.

Outside Louisiana, the Confederacy resisted making military use of African Americans, except to build fortifications. In 1864, as Confederate fortunes declined, Maj. Gen. Pat Cleburne recommended freeing slaves in return for military service, but he was

John Lawson was awarded the Medal of Honor for his valor during the August 1864 Battle of Mobile Bay, upon the recommendation of Adm. David Farragut. (Photographs and Prints Division, Schomburg Center for Research in Black Culture, The New York Public Library, Astor, Lenox and Tilden Foundations)

killed in battle; the idea languished until January 1865, when a desperate Robert E. Lee endorsed it. An ambitious scheme to recruit slaves took shape late in March of that year but never went into effect: time had run out on the Confederacy, and Lee surrendered the Army of Northern Virginia on April 9.

Fear of a slave rebellion, along with the need for agricultural labor, deterred the Confederacy from recruiting slaves as soldiers. The Union also moved slowly, even though Frederick DOUGLASS, the escaped slave and abolitionist, predicted that the first side to mobilize black manpower would win the war. President Abraham Lincoln hoped to avoid alienating the slaveholding Unionists in the border states. He postponed arming free blacks or abolishing slavery and insisted that the war was being fought solely to preserve the Union. During 1862, however, thousands of slaves, liberated from bondage by the advance of northern armies, created a human reservoir that the North could not ignore. At first, Union officers employed the freedmen as paid workers and servants. But in the spring of that year, commanders such as James H. Lane, Benjamin F. Butler, and Thomas Wentworth Higginson began training the former slaves to fight.

In July 1862, radical Republicans in Congress authorized the reluctant president to recruit black soldiers, and freeing the slaves became a war aim after Lincoln's Emancipation Proclamation went into effect January 1, 1863. The northern states thereupon began recruiting black regiments, administered after May 1863 by the Bureau of U.S. Colored Troops. The Union Army's black soldiers fought a succession of major battles. Higginson's FIRST SOUTH CAROLINA VOLUNTEER REGIMENT probed the St. Mary's River, the boundary between Georgia and Florida, capturing bricks, iron, and lumber needed by the Confederacy. Lane's Kansas regiment fought at Island Mound, Mo., and the FIFTY–FOURTH REGIMENT OF MASSACHUSETTS VOLUNTEER INFANTRY led the assault on FORT WAGNER, one of the fortifications guarding Charleston harbor, in South Carolina. Brig. Gen. Edward Ferrero's black Fourth Division of the Ninth Corps surged into the crater gouged in the earth after sappers tunneled beneath the Confederate defenses, planted explosives, and tried unsuccessfully to blast a path to Petersburg, Va. At FORT PILLOW, TENNESSEE, attacking Confederates under Nathan Bedford Forrest, a former slave trader who would later help organize the postwar Ku Klux Klan, killed black artillerymen trying to surrender. When the last Confederate forces lay down their weapons in May 1865, 186,000 African Americans had enlisted in the U.S. Colored Troops, and perhaps 30,000 had entered the U.S. Navy during wartime, joining black soldiers already on duty when the fighting began.

Of all the Army's Colored Troops fewer than a hundred became officers, and not one black received a navy commission. Although free blacks and liberated slaves provided a welcome source of enlisted men, the Navy refused to appoint black officers, a policy that survived until World War II. In May 1862, when Robert SMALLS, an experienced coastal pilot, fled slavery with his family and friends in the steamship *Planter,* he accepted a commission in the U.S. Colored Troops, rather than the Navy, though he commanded a number of steamers. Moreover, the Navy paid its wartime black recruits less than their white counterparts, as did the U.S. Colored Troops, although the War Department was correcting the inequity when the conflict ended.

Despite bitterness about the discriminatory pay scale—which triggered protests in the Army that led to the execution of a black sergeant for mutiny— African Americans benefited from service in the Civil War. Black soldiers and sailors contributed to the defeat of the Confederacy, and the fruits of victory included the Thirteenth, Fourteenth, and Fifteenth amendments to the Constitution, which abolished slavery and, backed by civil rights legislation, extended citizenship to blacks.

Reconstruction and Reaction

After the Civil War, Congress in 1866 created six regular-army black regiments, but this was reduced three years later to just four. This action was less an acknowledgment of the obligations of newly won citizenship than a repayment to African Americans for service against the Confederacy. With a handful of exceptions, white officers led the black troops. Between the organization of the black regiments and the SPANISH-AMERICAN WAR, only three African-American officers graduated from the U.S. Military Academy and reported to these units. One was dismissed from the Army; another died; and the third, Charles O. Young, remained the only black officer (except for chaplains) until he was joined in 1902 by Benjamin O. DAVIS and two other second lieutenants commissioned from the ranks. In 1936 Davis's son, Benjamin DAVIS, Jr., would become the first African American to graduate from the U.S. Military Academy since Young in 1889.

The radical Republicans, advocates of arming blacks during the war and of afterward incorporating them into the regular Army, embarked upon a program of RECONSTRUCTION. To effect a social and political revolution in the defeated South, the radicals sought to install government by freedmen in place of the traditional leadership. Once the last federal occupation forces withdrew in 1877, the defense of the Reconstruction governments rested exclusively on black militia units.

The reforms of Reconstruction proved short-lived, as did most of the black militia companies in the former Confederacy. During the decade immediately after the war, the radicals lost control of the Republican party; the new leadership emphasized economic development rather than the rights of black Americans, making common cause with white southern politicians who hoped to industrialize the region with northern capital. Throughout the old Confederacy a white coalition, representing every economic class, crushed the black militia—using such force as necessary—and ousted the Reconstruction governments. Only a handful of black militia units survived in the South into the twentieth century, though these organizations were more common in northern cities.

Racial segregation spread from the South throughout the nation, affecting opportunities for African Americans in the military services and the treatment they received there. As the U.S. Navy converted from sail to steam power, it sought a large number of men, at ease with machinery, who could learn to be sailors, instead of a lesser number of experienced seamen, many of them blacks. Whites tended to have the mechanical background that qualified them for the new Navy, and, in a time of pervasive racism, they would no longer willingly serve alongside African Americans. The Navy, therefore, accepted fewer blacks, diverting the trickle of recruits into specialties where they could be isolated from white crewmen.

In 1896, the Supreme Court in PLESSY V. FERGUSON endorsed the principle of separate but equal, enshrining racial segregation as the law of the land and, in effect, reversing the results of the Civil War. Social acceptance and economic opportunity diminished, and the basic rights of citizenship followed them into oblivion; only the pretense of separate but equal remained. Racial segregation, personified as JIM CROW, fastened its grip on every aspect of society.

The Armed Forces in the Era of Jim Crow

Since the rights of citizenship had been won on the battlefields of the Civil War, some influential blacks believed that in a future war African Americans could demonstrate heroism that would shame the federal government into restoring constitutional guarantees. When the United States went to war with Spain in 1898, E. E. Cooper, editor of the Washington *Colored American*, predicted that the fighting would "cement the races in a more compact brotherhood." Despite the courage of black soldiers and sailors, this age of racial harmony never dawned.

In August 1906, nighttime marauders shot up Brownsville, Tex., killing one civilian, and wounding two others. Suspicion fell on a recently arrived battalion of black infantrymen, and President Theodore Roosevelt, although lacking the evidence for a court-marital, approved dishonorable discharges for every soldier who might possibly have fired the shots. A few gained reinstatement, but despite persuasive evidence that townspeople had done the shooting, the injustice persisted until 1972, when the dishonorable discharges were changed to honorable ones. By that time, only one of the soldiers still lived.

When the United States entered WORLD WAR I in April 1917, W. E. B. DU BOIS saw another opportunity to regain the rights of citizenship and urged his fellow African Americans to forget their "special grievances" and fight "shoulder to shoulder with . . . white fellow citizens." Once again, military service failed to recapture the civil, social, and political rights that Jim Crow had confiscated. Du Bois acknowledged as much in 1919, when he reported the cruel treatment of black soldiers during the war not against Germany but against the white oppressor.

Shortly after the United States declared war on Germany, the War Department authorized sixteen new regiments of black infantrymen to fight in France, but the plan never reached fruition. In August 1917 black soldiers, recently transferred to Houston, rebelled against the city's Jim Crow laws. The riot claimed the lives of sixteen whites, including an army officer apparently mistaken for a policeman. Four of the rioters died, one by his own hand, and nineteen were hanged after courts-martial convicted them of desertion and murder. Shaken by the violence, the Army formed only two divisions of African Americans, with half the number of regiments originally planned.

In the Ninety-second Division, one of the two, veteran sergeants received commissions as wartime junior officers, the senior officers were white, and the bulk of the soldiers were draftees. The nation's few black National Guard units—their white senior officers supplemented by other white officers of the regular army—manned the other unit, the Ninety-third Division (Provisional), which also included African-American draftees and a number of recently commissioned blacks. Of the 380,000 African Americans in the wartime Army, only 11 percent fought in the two combat divisions, where they might display the kind of heroism that some black leaders believed could restore constitutional rights. The remaining 89 percent built roads, camps, and railroads and loaded or unloaded ships.

Although the Ninety-third Division (Provisional) distinguished itself fighting alongside French troops, the postwar American Army wrote off the black soldier. The War Department concluded that any future conflict would, like World War I, require only a token force of black combat soldiers, including members of the Organized Reserve and National Guard. The vast majority would wield the pick and shovel. From the armistice of November 1918 until the eve of WORLD WAR II, the Army reduced the regular black regiment to skeleton strength and barred black Americans from aviation and other new specialties.

The racial polices of the Army and Navy reduced opportunities for blacks to serve. The Great Depression, generating unemployment rates of 25 percent in the United States, bore down hard on the black civilian work force, but federal programs for relief and recovery, administered by white politicians and their black lieutenants, held out the promise of survival in the great northern cities. Consequently, urban blacks tended to sever their ties to the Republicans, the party of Lincoln, and become valuable cogs in local Democratic machines. President Franklin D. Roosevelt and his New Deal came to symbolize the opportunity that military service no longer provided.

Broader Opportunity in the Segregated Services

In 1940, the political leverage of the black community indirectly forced the armed services to modify

(Left) New York State 369th National Guard leaving for Fort Smith, Ark., to train for antiaircraft duty. They were the first black National Guardsmen to receive such training. (Right) Sgt. Peter Biggins, Sr., of the 369th, bids farewell to his family before leaving for Fort Smith. (Photographs and Prints Division, Schomburg Center for Research in Black Culture, The New York Public Library, Astor, Lenox and Tilden Foundations)

their restrictive racial policies. As the United States rearmed to meet the threat of Nazi Germany and militaristic Japan, Roosevelt sought an unprecedented third term. The danger of involvement in a foreign war aroused the opposition of America's isolationists, and the decision to defy political tradition alienated many of the president's supporters. He needed the help of the nation's black voter, and leaders such as A. Philip RANDOLPH could offer African-American support for Roosevelt and rearmament in exchange for greater opportunity and better treatment in the armed forces and in defense industries. On the other hand, Roosevelt's foreign policy depended on the support of the senators and representatives from the South, many of them unbending segregationists. He therefore sought to effect a tacit compromise that would satisfy blacks without alienating the white segregationists.

On the surface, the chief executive seemed to be offering African Americans symbols rather than substance. On October 25, 1940, with the election fast approaching, he announced two appointments: Col. Benjamin O. Davis, Sr., would become the nation's first black general officer; and William H. HASTIE, a black civil rights attorney and former dean of the Howard University school of law, who served as a

judge in the Virgin Islands, would become a special assistant to the secretary of war dealing with racial matters. Neither Davis nor Hastie proved content to be a mere symbol. Although subject to military discipline, the general struggled to improve the treatment of black soldiers; Hastie, an avowed integrationist, resigned early in 1943, disgusted by the Army's reluctance to lower racial barriers.

In another dramatic gesture that formed part of his reelection campaign, Roosevelt prodded the Army Air Corps into admitting blacks to pilot training. The candidates included Capt. Benjamin O. DAVIS, Jr., the son of the recently promoted general. Since the president sought to improve opportunities for black servicemen without undermining racial segregation, the younger Davis and his fellow airmen trained and served separately from whites.

After Japan attacked Pearl Harbor on December 7, 1941, the armed forces gradually discovered they would have to do more than Roosevelt anticipated. The Army found it could not afford the cost, in money and morale, of racially exclusive clubs and exchanges in the United States, and permitted a degree of integration. Overseas, black and white units, though theoretically separate, shared a common danger. Moreover, in the final months of the war in

Gen. Benjamin O. Davis, Sr., with troops. (Prints and Photographs Division, Library of Congress)

Europe, the Army ran short of white infantrymen and called for volunteers from among the black service units in that theater. Some 4,500 African Americans stepped forward, underwent a brief period of infantry training, and formed platoons assigned to formerly all-white rifle companies. The arrival of a black platoon meant that one soldier in five was an African American in a rifle company where teamwork was essential and close contact unavoidable. Racial integration inevitably resulted. The Navy and Coast Guard (a part of the wartime Navy) discovered that keeping African Americans out of combat undermined black morale as well as that of whites, who would have to endure additional sea duty because blacks could not replace them. The Coast Guard pioneered the racial integration of ships' crews, and the Navy, after experimenting with all-black crews, in-

tegrated the races on board a number of fleet auxiliaries. Only the Marine Corps, after accepting its first black recruits since the American Revolution, succeeded in maintaining racial segregation.

After the fighting ended in August 1945, the armed forces abandoned their wartime efforts at racial integration. Although a panel of senior officers predicted in 1946 that a racially integrated army would fight the next war, the military leadership feared that immediate integration would alienate white public opinion. Despite the occasional anomaly—the first black officer in the Marine Corps Reserve, or the first African-American graduate of the U.S. Naval Academy—the armed forces embraced segregation, imposing quotas on black enlistments, discharging those already in uniform who had scored poorly on the aptitude tests, and assigning the rest to menial

Sailors of the destroyer escort USS *Mason,* the first U.S. naval vessel with a predominantly black crew. (Photographs and Prints Division, Schomburg Center for Research in Black Culture, The New York Public Library, Astor, Lenox and Tilden Foundations)

duties. In the immediate postwar years, even the Army Air Force, in spite of its investment in black pilots, devoted more energy to isolating African Americans than to utilizing their skills.

The Decision to Integrate

Except for providing access to the benefits of the GI Bill, military service failed to help the average black advance himself, but some progress did occur. A succession of decisions by federal courts, beginning in 1938 and continuing after the war, eroded the legal foundation of racial segregation, but local authorities often ignored what the judges decreed. In the 1940 presidential election, black voters in the northern cities, rather than lawyers or the military, had triggered a change in race relations within the armed forces; a similar situation occurred in 1948. Harry S. Truman, who had become president in April 1945 after Roosevelt died early in his fourth term, faced a mutinous Democratic party. To win a close contest, Truman needed the votes of African Americans. Since a hostile Congress would not cooperate by passing civil rights legislation, Truman had no choice but to use his power as commander in chief to end segregation in the military services, providing a model for society and gaining the support of blacks. On July 26, 1948, he issued Executive Order 9981, directing the armed forces to provide equal treatment and opportunity regardless of race. His stand against racism contributed to his victory at the polls.

The Air Force, independent of the Army since September 1947, laid the foundations for integration even before the president's directive. The newest of the services, burdened with volatile concentrations of black airmen doing meaningless work, saw an opportunity to dissolve these units and force all enlisted personnel, regardless of race, to compete for technical training and useful duties. Moreover, the Air Force demanded the largest share of the defense budget to buy and operate weapons intended to deter nuclear war. So heavy an investment could scarcely be justified if the Air Force discriminated against African Americans, roughly 11 percent of the populace.

The other services lagged behind the Air Force in integrating the races. In June 1950, when North Korea invaded South Korea, the Army still maintained exclusively black combat and support units, while the Navy and Marine Corps tended to train their African-American servicemen as messmen, stewards, or members of security detachments. The demands of the KOREAN WAR changed all this. Combat ships and frontline units could not wait for the sluggish functioning of a personnel system that made race, rather than the needs of the service, the principal criterion for training and assignment. Recruits had to learn useful skills and serve wherever needed, an impossibility unless the races were truly integrated.

The need to use manpower efficiently forced the services to provide equal treatment and opportunity regardless of race, a process under way when the Korean fighting ended in July 1953. African Americans were now eligible for most specialties, though not yet all, and could expect a meaningful assignment when they completed training. Skills took time to

acquire, however, and promotions did not come easily, so that blacks were underrepresented in the more demanding technical fields and among noncommissioned officers. Black commissioned officers were especially rare. As late as 1962, African Americans made up 3.2 percent of the Army's officer corps, roughly 1 percent in the Marine Corps and Navy, and 1.2 percent in the Air Force. But, despite vestiges of racial segregation that survived in the late 1950s and early 1960s, blacks as a rule enjoyed greater opportunity and better treatment in uniform than in civilian jobs.

Even as the armed forces advanced—albeit imperfectly—toward Truman's goal of racial integration, the CIVIL RIGHTS MOVEMENT, a loose coalition of black activists and their white allies, launched a struggle to regain the rights guaranteed to all citizens by the Constitution. The racial integration of the military slipped from the national consciousness as leaders such as the Rev. Dr. Martin Luther KING, Jr., challenged the federal government to protect black

Cadets reporting to their officer-instructor on October 3, 1942, for basic (or second phase) training at Tuskegee Army Flying School. The instructor is 1st Lt. Gabe C. Hawkins. Cadets are (left to right) H. B. Perry, Thomasville, Ga.; R. C. Ceasar, Lake Village, Ark.; and J. A. Henson, Salisbury, Md. (Photographs and Prints Division, Schomburg Center for Research in Black Culture, The New York Public Library, Astor, Lenox and Tilden Foundations)

Americans in the exercise of their legal rights. The response of presidents John F. Kennedy and Lyndon B. Johnson culminated between 1964 and 1968 in legislation to ensure that African Americans had equal access to jobs, public accommodations, and decent housing and that they could exercise the right to vote.

A Breakdown in Racial Understanding

During 1963 and 1964, a committee headed by Gerhard A. Gesell, a Washington attorney, evaluated the progress of the armed forces toward racial integration and warned of danger. Some forms of segregation persisted, and a breakdown in communication between the races prevented the predominantly white officer corps from understanding how deeply black servicemen resented the remaining manifestations of racism. In response to the Gesell Committee's warning, Secretary of Defense Robert S. McNamara enforced equal treatment and opportunity at military and naval bases, and used moral pressure and economic leverage to integrate housing and public accommodations in nearby communities. For a brief time in the mid-1960s, the military establishment more closely approached the ideal of racial integration than any other American institution.

Scarcely had the reaction to the Gesell Committee begun when, in the spring of 1965, the United States intensified the VIETNAM WAR. As the years passed and casualties mounted, the Army and the Marine Corps relied on the Selective Service System to maintain combat strength, and the possibility of being drafted motivated young men to enlist for less dangerous duty in the Air Force or Navy. Both the volunteers and the draftees included many resentful urban blacks, bypassed by the gains of the civil rights movement, and whites from a comparable social class who feared that anything they had or hoped for would be handed over to African Americans as compensation for past discrimination. Frustrated blacks rioted in Detroit, in the Watts district of Los Angeles, and, after a white gunman murdered the Rev. Dr. Martin Luther King in April 1968, in major cities throughout the nation. Since the armed forces reflected the mood of the society they defended, the mutual hatred found its way into the services and ignited worldwide race riots beginning in 1968.

Amity Restored

A riot in May 1971 at Travis Air Force Base, in California, lent urgency to a plan, drawn up under the guidance of a black Air Force officer, Col. Lucius Theus, to teach racial understanding and cooperation throughout the armed forces. The Defense Race Relations Institute (in 1979 redesignated the Defense Equal Opportunity Management Institute) began al-

2nd Lt. Mildred L. Osby of the Women's Army Auxiliary Corps (WAAC), later known as the Women's Army Corps (WAC). Black women served in segregated units in the WAC, both stateside and in Europe. (Prints and Photographs Division, Library of Congress)

most immediately to train instructors, who returned to their units and conducted classes to heighten racial sensitivity. In conjunction with interracial councils and fostered by the exercise of common sense on the part of commanders, the program flourished and received much of the credit for a revival of racial amity.

Success, however, stemmed in part from the suspension of the draft, reserved in 1973 for possible use in some future emergency, and the truce that ended the Vietnam fighting in January of that year. The decision to rely on volunteers instead of draftees attracted recruits who wanted to serve and would do what was expected of them—even cooperating harmoniously with members of other races. Nevertheless, the all-volunteer force included a disproportionate number of African Americans, especially when the economy faltered and jobs became scarce. In 1983, a decade after Selective Service went on the shelf, blacks in the enlisted force approached 20 percent, almost twice their proportion in society as a whole. The Army led with 33 percent; the Marine Corps followed with 22 percent; and the Air Force and Navy had 14 and 12 percent, respectively. The

Army also had the greatest proportion of African Americans in the officer corps, almost 10 percent; the Air Force had 5 percent, the Marine Corps 4, and the Navy 3. The Army also had the largest proportion of African Americans among women in uniform, some 17 percent of its officers and 20 percent of enlisted women. For the Air Force, the percentages were 11 and 20; for the Marine Corps, 5 and 23; and for the Navy, 5 and 18.

As happened during the Vietnam conflict, blacks serving in the 1980s tended to gravitate toward combat units, attracted perhaps by the challenge, the status, or the premium pay. What would happen if large numbers of black Americans were killed and wounded in a future war fought mainly by the Army and Marine Corps? Just such a conflict loomed early in 1991, when a coalition led by the United States sought to expel the army of Iraq from Kuwait. Roughly 30 percent of the American force deployed to the Middle East consisted of African Americans. Fortunately, American casualties were few, since Iraqi resistance collapsed rapidly, and the war had scant effect on race relations in the United States. Military service continued to present black Americans with an opportunity to assume responsibility, learn skills, and earn respect, and compared to whites a vastly greater proportion of young blacks took advantage of the offer.

REFERENCES

BARBEAU, ARTHUR E., and FLORETTE, HENRI. *The Unknown Soldiers: Black American Troops in World War I*. Philadelphia, 1974.

BERLIN, IRA, ed., with Joseph P. Reidy and Leslie S. Rowlands. *Freedom: A Documentary History of Emancipation, 1861–1865*. Series II, *The Black Military Experience*. Cambridge, Mass., 1982.

CORNISH, DUDLEY TAYLOR. *The Sable Arm: Negro Troops in the Union Army, 1861–1865*. 1956. Reprint. Lawrence, Kans., 1987.

DALFIUME, RICHARD M. *Desegregation of the U.S. Armed Forces: Fighting on Two Fronts, 1939–1953*. Columbia, Mo., 1969.

FLETCHER, MARVIN E. *America's First Black General: Benjamin O. Davis, Sr., 1880–1970*. Lawrence, Kans., 1989.

FOWLER, ARLEN. *The Black Infantry in the West, 1869–1891*. Westport, Conn., 1971.

GROPMAN, ALAN L. *The Air Force Integrates, 1945–1964*. 1977. Reprint. Washington, D.C., 1986.

HAYNES, ROBERT V. *A Night of Violence: The Houston Riot of 1917*. Baton Rouge, La., 1976.

LECKIE, WILLIAM H. *The Buffalo Soldiers: A Narrative of the Negro Cavalry in the West*. 1967. Reprint. Norman, Okla., 1975.

LEE, ULYSSES. *The United States Army in World War II; Special Studies: The Employment of Negro Troops*. Washington, D.C., 1966.

MACGREGOR, MORRIS J. *Defense Studies: Integration of the Armed Forces, 1940–1965*. Washington, D.C., 1981.

MACGREGOR, MORRIS J., and BERNARD C. NALTY, eds. *Blacks in the United States Armed Forces: Basic Documents*. 13 vols. Wilmington, Del., 1977.

MCGUIRE, PHILLIP. *He, Too, Spoke for Democracy: Judge Hastie, World War II, and the Black Soldier*. Westport, Conn., 1988.

NALTY, BERNARD C. *Strength for the Fight: A History of Black Americans in the Military*. 1986. Reprint. New York, 1989.

OSUR, ALAN M. *Blacks in the Army Air Forces during World War II*. Washington, D.C., 1977.

QUARLES, BENJAMIN. *The Negro in the American Revolution*. Chapel Hill, N.C., 1961.

———. *The Negro in the Civil War*. 1953. Reprint. Boston, 1989.

SHAW, HENRY I., JR., and RALPH N. DONNELLY. *Blacks in the Marine Corps*. Washington, D.C., 1975.

SINGLETARY, OTIS A. *The Negro Militia and Reconstruction*. Austin, Tex., 1971.

WEAVER, JOHN D. *The Brownsville Raid*. New York, 1970.

BERNARD C. NALTY

Miller, Bebe (September 20, 1950–), modern dancer. Born in Brooklyn, N.Y., where she was raised by her mother, Bebe Miller began childhood dance study with Murray Louis at the Henry Street Settlement on Manhattan's Lower East Side. In 1971 she graduated from Earlham College in Richmond, Ind., with a degree in art, and four years later earned her master's degree in dance from Ohio State University. From 1976 to 1982 Miller danced with Nina Weiner and Dancers, where she developed a quietly intense, passionate style. In 1984 she formed the Bebe Miller Company with an "interest in finding a physical language for the human condition." Miller's choreography has been noted for its mix of virtuosic, athletic speed and the fragile human impulse behind it. Miller has choreographed works for the Boston Ballet, Oregon Ballet Theatre, Dayton Contemporary Dance Company, the Alvin Ailey Repertory Ensemble, and the PACT Dance Company of Johannesburg, South Africa. Among her awards and fellowships are two Bessie awards for performance (1986 and 1987), a Guggenheim Fellowship (1988), and an American Choreographer Award (1988).

REFERENCES

HIGHWATER, JAMAKE. "Bebe Miller, Picky Postmodernist." *Christian Science Monitor*, July 11, 1990.

ZIMMER, ELIZABETH. "Bebe Miller Comes Home." *Dance Magazine* (December 1989): 34–38.

THOMAS F. DEFRANTZ

PORTER, DAVID L., ed. *Biographical Dictionary of American Sports: Basketball and Other Indoor Sports.* New York, 1989.

LYDIA MCNEILL

Miller, Cheryl DeAnne (January 3, 1964–), basketball player. Born in Riverside, Calif., the third of five children (a younger brother, Reggie Miller, would go on to become a star player in the National Basketball Association), Cheryl Miller gained recognition for her superb play on her hometown Polytechnic High School women's BASKETBALL team. While at Polytechnic, she scored a record 105 points in one game, and was named to the *Parade* All-American Team four years in a row, the only person ever recognized in this way.

A 6'3" forward, Miller is considered by many to be the most dominant female basketball player of all time. She played college basketball for the University of Southern California (USC; 1982–1986), leading her team to two National Collegiate Athletic Association (NCAA) championships. She was named an All-American four times, NCAA Player of the Year three times, and Most Valuable Player of the NCAA playoffs twice. She graduated in 1986 with a degree in communications.

Miller was the highest scorer on the U.S. Women's gold-medal-winning basketball team at the 1984 Summer Olympics held in Los Angeles. In the summer of 1986 she played for the gold medal U.S. team in the World Championships, as well as for the U.S. team in the Goodwill Games in Moscow. That year she was drafted in the first round by the California Stars of the National Women's Basketball Association (NWBA), but the league dissolved later in the year. Miller joined ABC Sports as a television broadcaster in January 1988, and reported on the Winter Olympic Games held in Calgary, Alberta. However, a knee injury kept her from the 1988 Summer Olympic team.

On September 3, 1993, Miller became the coach of the USC women's basketball team. During her rookie coaching season, her team won the Pac 10 Conference championship, and reached the NCAA tournament quarterfinals. In acknowledgment of this feat, the Black Coaches Association named Miller one of the Coaches of the Year in 1994.

REFERENCES

ASHE, ARTHUR R., JR. *A Hard Road to Glory: A History of the African-American Athlete Since 1946.* New York, 1988.

McCALLUM, JACK. "It's Not Miller Time—!" *Sports Illustrated* (April 11, 1994): 17.

Miller, Dorie (October 12, 1919–November 24, 1943), war hero. Born near Waco, Tex., Dorie Miller was the son of poor sharecroppers. He spent his youth working on his parents' farm, and attended only a few years of elementary school. In 1940, after seeing a navy recruiting officer in Waco, Miller enlisted in the navy. At the time, the navy did not accept African Americans except as cooks and menial laborers on ships. Miller was given limited military training before being assigned as a messman on the battleship *Arizona*. After a tour of duty, the U.S.S. *Arizona* docked in Pearl Harbor, Hawaii.

On December 7, 1941, the Japanese launched a surprise attack on Pearl Harbor. The *Arizona*, which was being refitted and was unable to leave its moorings, was heavily hit. Miller ran to the ship's deck. Though briefly knocked down by the force of an explosion, he pulled the *Arizona*'s mortally wounded captain from the line of fire, and took up a position at an antiaircraft gun. He had never been taught how to fire a gun, but he quickly figured out how it worked, and began firing. Miller shot down four Japanese planes before being ordered to leave the badly damaged ship.

While the mainstream press largely ignored Miller's exploits, the African-American press publicized his heroism. In Spring, 1942, under pressure from black leaders, Miller was awarded the Navy Cross, promoted to mess attendant first class, and invited to speak before a graduating training class at the Great Lakes Training Center in Illinois. However, navy policy remained intact. Miller was denied military training and was assigned for training as a cook. In 1943 he was assigned to the aircraft carrier U.S.S. *Liscome Bay*, which sailed to the South Pacific. Miller died after the carrier was sunk by a Japanese submarine.

An authentic American war hero, the first of World War II, Miller has been remembered in many ways since his death. In 1943 the Dorie Miller commemoration and the Dorie Miller Trophy in race relations was instituted. Shortly thereafter, a recreation center in Newport, Va., and a housing project in Corona, New York City were named after him. Miller was honored by the navy with a Dorie Miller recruiting poster, and by the christening of the Dorie Miller Barracks at the Great Lakes training camp in 1971. In 1973 a destroyer-escort ship, the U.S.S.

Miller, was commissioned in his memory, and in 1985 a memorial monument was erected at the Veterans Administration hospital in Waco. Still, Miller has been denied complete official recognition for his heroism. In 1988 a bill was introduced in the U.S. House of Representatives to award Miller a posthumous Congressional Medal of Honor. This would have made him the first African-American recipient for service in World War II, but it failed to pass.

REFERENCE

NELSON, DENNIS D. *The Integration of the Negro into the U.S. Navy.* New York, 1951.

GREG ROBINSON

Miller, George Frazier (November 28, 1864–May 9, 1943), minister and socialist. George Frazier Miller was born in Aiken, S.C., the only son of Alfred Abram and Ellen Collins DeReef Miller. Through his white grandmother Isabella Fowler, daughter of Jonathan Fowler, Miller was linked to South Carolina's plantocracy. After attending public schools in Charleston, he earned an A.B. degree at Howard University in 1888 and advanced degrees at General Theological Seminary in New York and Howard and New York universities. In 1891, he was ordained a deacon in the Episcopal Diocese of South Carolina and assigned to Charleston's Calvary Church, a former slave chapel. In 1892, he was ordained a priest. He married Ellen M. Bulkley in 1893 and they had four children; Ellen died in 1923, and Miller never remarried.

In 1896, he was called to Saint Augustine's Episcopal Church in Brooklyn, N.Y., as rector, where he remained until his death. In New York, Miller came into his own as a fiery social critic and a popular radio preacher, one of the first African Americans to achieve such a status. In 1906, like many black intellectuals, he joined the Socialist party, which—together with his religious beliefs—shaped many of his unpopular political positions during the unbridled patriotism of World War I, when most blacks supported the war effort. He preached and wrote against the war, even refusing to fly the American flag either inside or outside his parish; he called himself "cosmopolitan" rather than patriotic, which he thought was provincial. FBI agents infiltrated Sunday services to take notes on his sermons. He was also one of the "Original 29" of the NIAGARA MOVEMENT, the forerunner of the NAACP. In 1919, he ran as a Socialist candidate from Harlem for Congress.

"Rector" Miller, as he was called by his members, early on grasped the role of the media for commu-

nicating his vision and his sermons. He wrote a column in the MESSENGER, the socialist journal founded in 1917 by A. Philip Randolph and Chandler Owen. In May 1936, Miller gave his first public address on radio, entitled "To What Extent Censorship?" in which he identified as "inalienable rights" the right to strike, the right to collective bargaining, and the right to support different ideologies.

On May 9, 1943, Miller died, and his funeral attracted people from across New York City. W. E. B. DU BOIS called Miller one of the "strongest fighting radicals" he knew, "but a clean, frank fighter." Among his extant publications are *Adventism Answered: The Sabbath Question* (Brooklyn, 1905); a pamphlet, "The Colored Ministry in New York" (New York, 1915); several sermons: "A Reply to the 'Political Plea' . . ." (Brooklyn, 1913), "The Sacredness of Humanity: Annual Sermon of the Conference of Church Workers among Colored People at St. Philip's Church, New York" (Brooklyn, 1914), and "The Resurrection of a Witnessed Fact" (n.d.); two published addresses: "To What Extent Censorship—A Radio Address" (New York, 1936) and "Socialism and Its Ethical Basis" (n.d.); and his contribution to a discussion entitled "Is Religion Reasonable?" (Brooklyn, n.d.).

ROBERT E. HOOD

Miller, Joan (1936–), dancer, choreographer, instructor. Born and raised in Harlem, Joan Miller began dance training in a local troop of the Girl Scouts, performing folk and ballet work. While a Brooklyn College physical education major, she continued to study dance at the José Limon studio with Ruth Currier and Betty Jones. In the late 1950s, Miller continued to study with Limon, and went on to study choreography and work with Doris Humphrey, Louis Horst, and Pauline Koner.

Miller completed a master's degree at Teachers College, Columbia University (1960), and earned a professional diploma in dance from Juilliard (1962). From 1960 to 1967 Miller performed with Ruth Currier and was featured in Currier's *The Antagonists.* Miller also began teaching at the Hunter College Bronx campus (later Lehman College) in 1963. Also in 1963 and in 1964 Miller danced with the Merry-Go-Rounders, a group that performed for children. From 1965 to 1968 she worked with James Waring, Remy Charlip, and Yvonne Rainer, members of the experimental Judson Church group. Between 1968 and 1970 she performed with both Rod Rodgers in African traditional dance and Rudy Perez, an exponent of avant-garde dancing.

In 1970, Miller founded her own troupe, the Dance Players, which became a forum for her socio-political ideas and satires. Her company enjoyed resident status at Lehman College from 1970 until 1980, from which time they stayed on unofficially and also performed in New York, New Jersey, and Connecticut. The Dance Players' repertory consists primarily of Miller's creations, such as the 1970 solo, *Pass Fe White*, and the group work, *Manhattan Thoroughfare 1980*. Her company also performs works by Rael Lamb, Eleo POMARE, and her former student Abdel Salaam, director of the Forces of Nature Dance Company.

REFERENCES

BANES, SALLY. *Terpsichore in Sneakers: Post-Modern Dance*. Boston, 1980.
MCDONAGH, DON. *Complete Guide to Modern Dance*. New York, 1977.

JULINDA LEWIS-FERGUSON

Miller, Kelly (July 23, 1863–December 27, 1939), historian and educator. Born in Winnsboro, S.C., to a Confederate military father and an enslaved mother, Miller believed the surest road to freedom from bondage was through education. He worked his way through school, graduating from HOWARD UNIVERSITY in 1886, and continued studying mathematics and physics at Johns Hopkins University, earning an A.M. in 1901 and an LL.D. in 1903 from Howard. Miller taught at Howard from 1890 to 1934, and became the dean of the College of Arts and Sciences in 1936. Under his leadership the school expanded dramatically, with the development of a sociology department, a steady recruitment of students, and modernization of the curriculum.

As a journalist, Miller wrote essays and a weekly column for the black press, in which he discussed the promise and progress of African Americans since Emancipation, and proposed solutions for global racial equality. In addition, he wrote several books, including *Race Adjustment* (1903); *Out of the House of Bondage* (1917); *History of the World War and the Important Part Taken by the Negroes* (1919); and *The Everlasting Stain* (1924). Considered a voice of reason and a person of enormous intellectual range, Miller was a believer in the philosophy that different races would eventually assimilate and color would become an irrelevant issue in the United States.

REFERENCES

LOGAN, RAYFORD, ed. *Dictionary of American Negro Biography*. New York, 1982.

A mathematician and sociologist at Howard University for more than four decades, Kelly Miller was one of the leading black intellectuals in the early decades of the twentieth century. In the political battles of the era, Miller usually managed to stay in the middle between the warring camps around Booker T. Washington and W. E. B. Du Bois. (Moorland-Spingarn Research Center, Howard University)

PLOSKI, HARRY A., ed. *The Negro Almanac*. New York, 1982.

NEIL GOLDSTEIN

Miller, Norma (1919–), dancer and choreographer. Norma Miller was born in Harlem one month after the death of her father and was raised by her mother, an immigrant from Barbados. Miller honed her skills as a dancer by absorbing the vital dance scene in Harlem and soon became a regular at the SAVOY and other Harlem ballrooms. At age twelve, she danced with one of the regulars on a Savoy Sunday afternoon exhibition, where she impressed the audience. Two years later she became a member of one of the Savoy's dance groups, Whitey's Lindy Hoppers, and won the 1935 *New York Daily News* Harvest Moon Ball Lindy Hop competition.

As a member of Herbert White's Savoy dance teams, she traveled internationally and appeared with such great bands as those of Duke ELLINGTON, Chick

WEBB, Count BASIE, and Cab CALLOWAY. Miller appeared in several Broadway shows including *Knickerbocker Holiday* (1938), *Hellzapoppin'* (1938), the *Hot Mikado* (1939) with Bill Robinson, and *Swingin' the Dream* (1939). Miller's film credits include *A Day at the Races* (1937) and *Hellzapoppin'* (1941).

When Whitey's Lindy Hoppers disbanded in the early forties, Miller left for the West Coast where she danced and staged shows. She formed the Norma Miller Jazz Dancers in 1952. Two years later Miller reorganized the group with male dancers using the name Norma Miller & Her Jazz Men. Miller and her four dancers toured Europe successfully in the early sixties and then traveled extensively with the Count Basie band.

In the late sixties, Miller began a career in comedy appearing at the Redd FOXX Club in California. Miller's association with Foxx led to the co-authorship of the *Encyclopedia of Black Humor* published in 1977. She revived her dance career in the early eighties when she returned to the East Coast and helped introduce authentic jazz dance to a new generation through the formation of a company based in New York City. She served as a dance consultant for Spike Lee's film *Malcolm X* (1992). Since the early 1990s she has been living in Las Vegas and directing a company of Lindy-Hoppers.

REFERENCES

Black Arts New York Staff. "Norma Miller: Harlem Treasure." *Black Arts New York* (March 1992): 7, 8.
CREASE, ROBERT. "Last of the Lindy Hoppers." *Village Voice* (August 25, 1987): 27–32.

JACKIE MALONE

Miller, Thomas Ezekial (June 17, 1849–April 8, 1938), politician. Thomas E. Miller was born in Ferrebeeville, S.C., in 1849. His ancestry was ambiguous: although his birth records indicated that he was the son of free black parents, Richard Miller and Mary Ferrebee, his descendants later believed that the light-skinned Thomas was actually the son of white parents who gave the infant Thomas away to the Millers. Whatever his true ancestry, Thomas Miller identified himself as an African American. He first attended school in Charleston, S.C., then worked as a newsboy while attending school in Hudson, N.Y. Receiving a scholarship to Lincoln University in Chester County, Pa., he graduated in 1872. After studying law privately under the tutelage of individual lawyers and judges, he gained admittance to the bar in 1874 and established a private practice in Beaufort, S.C.

Shortly after beginning his practice, Miller was elected county school commissioner of Beaufort. He subsequently won the 1874 election to the state House of Representatives. He served three terms in the statehouse before being elected to the state Senate and obtaining membership in the Republican state executive committee. By 1884, he was state party chairman, and over the next four years he raised revenue for Republican campaigns at both the state and local levels. In 1888, he won election to Congress from the seventh congressional district, after convincing famed black Rep. Robert Smalls (who had once held that seat himself) not to run.

To circumvent the heavily African-American population of the seventh district and the overwhelming preference of that population for the Republican party, the Democrats in the district used fraudulent techniques to win the election for Miller's white Democratic Party opponent, William Elliott. Miller contested the election before the U.S. House of Representatives, which considered Miller's claim in 1890. After Elliott had already been in office ten months—and with only a week remaining in the congressional session—the House voted, 157–1, to concede the seat to Miller. Immediately after Miller secured his post and a seat on the Library of Congress Committee, he began to campaign for reelection. Although he won more votes than Elliott in the second election, Elliott appealed the count on the grounds that Miller's ballots were not of the legal size and color. The South Carolina Supreme Court accepted Elliott's argument and decided the election in the Democrat's favor.

Before leaving his congressional seat in 1891, Miller forcefully refuted the allegations of Georgia Sen. Alfred H. Colquitt that blacks were uncultured and primitive—and that these qualities made African Americans responsible for the economic deprivation of the South. Miller eloquently retorted in the House chamber that it was systematized racism on the part of white elites that had retarded the South's progress toward economic prosperity.

Miller returned to his private law practice in 1891 and shortly afterward was reelected to the South Carolina House of Representatives. During the 1895 state constitutional convention, he and Robert Smalls struggled unsuccessfully against proposed literacy amendments to the state voting law. In 1896, Miller helped found State Negro College (later known as South Carolina State College) in Orangeburg. As its first president, he encouraged the hiring of black teachers for Charleston's black schools. After opposing a new state governor, whom he believed to be an opponent of civil rights, Miller was asked to resign from the presidency of the college in 1911. After his retirement from State Negro College, Miller moved to Philadelphia. In 1930, at the age of eighty, he addressed the Association for the Study of Negro Life and History on the subject of opportunities for blacks in elected office. In the following eight years, he attempted unsuccessfully to finish his autobiography. He left instructions for the book's completion and publication in his will. After his death on April 8, 1938, the manuscript was distributed amongst various scholarly collections, but never published.

REFERENCES

CHRISTOPHER, MAURINE. *Black Americans in Congress.* New York, 1976.

CLAY, WILLIAM L. *Just Permanent Interests: Black Americans in Congress, 1870–1991.* New York, 1992.

DURAHN TAYLOR

Mills, Florence (1896–1927), singer and dancer. Florence Mills was born January 25, 1896, in Washington, D.C., the daughter of John and Nellie (Simons) Winfrey, immigrants from Virginia's depressed tobacco industry. A talented singer and dancer, she appeared at age six in the Washington production of Bert WILLIAMS and George WALKER's *Sons of Ham* singing "Miss Hannah from Savannah." She traveled with the white vaudeville team of Bonita and Hearn, and then at age fourteen organized a vaudeville act with her sisters. Around 1915 she worked at Chicago's notorious Panama Cafe with Cora GREENE and Ada "Bricktop" SMITH as the Panama Trio, with Tony Jackson on piano. When the police closed the Panama, she joined the Tennessee Ten on the Keith vaudeville circuit, where she met and married the acrobatic dancer Ulysses "Slow Kid" Thompson.

Mills came to national attention when she replaced Gertrude Saunders as the ingenue in Noble SISSLE and Eubie BLAKE's trend-setting all-black 1921 musical *Shuffle Along.* Taken up by producer Lew Leslie, she starred in his *Plantation Revue* (1922), then went to London in Charles B. Cochran's *Dover Street to Dixie* (1923), where she made a profound impression. Offered a major role by Florenz Ziegfeld in the *Follies,* she turned him down to create more all-black revues. In 1924, *From Dixie to Broadway* opened in the heart of Broadway with Mills singing "I'm a Little Blackbird," and later that year she headlined at the Palace. *Blackbirds of 1926* captivated London, but Mills died unexpectedly in New York on November 1, 1927, before the show could return to the United States. She was beloved in Harlem; over 150,000 people lined the streets for her funeral.

Florence Mills, the "Black Beauty" of Duke Ellington's composition, was one of the most charismatic performers in black musicals in the 1920s. Her early death in 1927 was the occasion for a huge, spontaneous, and long-remembered Harlem funeral. (Photographs and Prints Division, Schomburg Center for Research in Black Culture, The New York Public Library, Astor, Lenox and Tilden Foundations)

REFERENCES

NEWMAN, RICHARD. "Florence Mills." In *Notable Black American Women.* Detroit, 1992, pp. 752–756.

JAMES E. MUMFORD

Mills Brothers, pop vocal group. The principal members of the group were three brothers, Herbert (1912–), Harry (1912–1982), and Donald Mills (1915–), all born in Piqua, Ohio; another brother, John, played guitar and sang bass until his death in 1935, when he was replaced by his father, John, Sr. (1882–1967), who performed with the group until his retirement in 1957. (Billy Mills, the father of John, Sr., had been a singer in the popular nineteenth-century jubilee group the Stinson Singers.) The Mills Brothers were one of a small number of black male vocal groups that popularized the songs of Tin Pan Alley before and during World War II; their fairly conventional pop manner pleased both black and white audiences, and served as a model for aspiring black vocalists. They were among the earliest African-American vocal groups to achieve a national following.

The brothers began their career singing in small-town vaudeville and tent shows. A ten-month stint during the late 1920s on radio station WLW in Cincinnati provided them with their first big break; in 1929 they became the first black group to be given sponsorship on a national network (CBS). By 1930 the brothers were in New York appearing in theaters, clubs, and on radio as well as recording for Brunswick and appearing in films. Early in their career, the brothers sang to the accompaniment of a guitar; after becoming well known, they fronted orchestras and big bands and recorded with Louis ARMSTRONG and other jazz artists, but their signature style remained a smooth three- of four-part barbershop-style harmony. Among their many hit songs in the 1930s and 1940s were "Tiger Rag" (1930), which sold one million copies; their biggest success, "Paper Doll" (1943), which sold six million copies; and "You Always Hurt the One You Love" (1944), another million-seller. The group, which made its first recording in 1925, continued to perform as a threesome until 1982; altogether, the Mills Brothers are credited with making more than 1,200 recordings.

REFERENCES

"1920s–1970s: 50 Years in Show Business Celebrated by Mills Brothers." *Jet* (March 13, 1975): 62.
"Twenty-five Years with the Mills Brothers." *Hue* (February 1954): 46–49.

ROBERT W. STEPHENS

Milner, Ronald (May 29, 1938–) playwright. Born in Detroit, Mich., Ronald Milner grew up in a poor but vibrant part of the city and decided while he was in high school that the characters among whom he lived were as worthy of being written about as those in the novels he read in class. In 1965, in pursuit of his writing vocation, he attended Harvey Swados's writing workshop at Columbia University in New York.

Milner's first play, *Who's Got His Own*, was produced off-Broadway in 1966. When his one-act play "The Warning—A Theme for Linda" was performed in 1969 with three other one-act plays written by African Americans under the collective title "A Black Quartet," Milner established himself as one of the leading proponents of the Black Theater Movement. An outgrowth of the Black Power movement, the Black Theater movement aimed at fostering rebellion

Starting in 1930, the close harmonies and smooth, easygoing vocal style of the Mills Brothers made them popular favorites for more than half a century. In this 1977 picture from Reno, Nev., are (from left to right) Herbert, Don, and Harry Mills. (AP/Wide World Photos)

among African Americans and creating a positive image of black life to counteract the negative image often present when white authors portrayed black characters.

Milner himself eschewed calls to violence in his writing, preferring to create realistic portrayals of black characters who triumph over hardship. His plays have received a warm response in the black community, especially *What the Wine-Sellers Buy,* which opened in New York in 1973 and traveled around the country, breaking house records in Chicago and elsewhere. He has had many other plays produced, including *Jazz Set* (1980), *Checkmates* (1987), and *Don't Get God Started* (1987).

In 1962, along with Woodie KING, Jr., a black producer and director, Milner founded Concept-East, a theater company in Detroit. In the early 1970s he founded the Spirit of Shango Theater Company, which eventually merged with Concept-East. In 1971, he and King coedited *Black Drama Anthology.* Milner was writer in residence at Lincoln University from 1966 to 1967, and taught at Michigan State University from 1971 to 1972. He has been a recipient of a Rockefeller grant and a John Hay Whitney fellowship.

REFERENCES

METZGER, LINDA, ed. *Black Writers.* Detroit, Mich. 1989.

WILLIAMS, MANCE. *Black Theatre in the 1960s and 1970s.* Westport, Conn., 1985.

LYDIA McNEILL

Mingus, Charles, Jr. (April 22, 1922–January 5, 1979), jazz musician. Born in Nogales, Ariz., Charles Mingus straddled the bebop and free jazz eras. Although he became a virtuoso bassist early in his career, his main contribution to jazz was as a composer and bandleader. For over thirty years Mingus created a body of compositions matched in quality and variety only by Duke ELLINGTON and Thelonious MONK, and ranging from somber but gritty tributes to Lester YOUNG, Charlie PARKER, and Eric DOLPHY to roaring evocations of African-American gospel prayer meetings. Taking a cue from Ellington, Mingus generally wrote music for particular individuals in his superb ensembles, and such compositions were developed or "workshopped" through in-concert rehearsals rather than from fixed and polished scores prior to performance and recording. Mingus's mercurial personality thrived in these improvisational settings, but this process often made for chaos and disaster as well. He was notorious for berating audiences and musicians from the bandstand, even firing and rehiring band members during the course of performances. However, the workshops also achieved a spontaneity and musical passion unmatched in the history of jazz, as Mingus conducted and shouted instructions and comments from the piano or bass, at times in a wheelchair at the end of his life, even improvising speeches on civil rights.

Mingus grew up in the Watts section of Los Angeles, and in his youth studied trombone and cello before switching at age sixteen to the bass. He studied with Britt Woodman, Red Callender, Lloyd Reese, and Herman Rheinschagen, and began performing professionally while still a teenager. He played in the rhythm sections of the bands of Lee Young (1940), Louis ARMSTRONG (1941–1943), Barney Bigard (1942), and Lionel HAMPTON (1947–1948). He made his first recordings with Hampton in 1947, a session that included Mingus's first recorded composition, "Mingus Fingers." Mingus played in Red Norvo's trio from 1950 to 1951, quitting in anger after Mingus, who was not a member of the local musicians' union, was replaced by a white bassist for a television performance. Mingus settled in New York in 1951, and played stints with Duke Ellington, Billy TAYLOR, Stan Getz, and Art TATUM. His most important work in his early period was a single concert he organized and recorded for his own record label, Debut Records, at Toronto's Massey Hall in May 1953, featuring pianist Bud POWELL, drummer Max ROACH, and the reunited team of Charlie Parker and Dizzy GILLESPIE—the definitive bebop quintet.

Mingus formed his own music workshop in 1955 in order to develop compositions for a core of performers, and it is from this point that his mature style dates. He had played in the cooperative Jazz Composers' Workshop from 1953 to 1955, but it was as the tempestuous leader of his own group that he created his most famous works, which in concerts often became long, brooding performances, building to aggressive, even savage climaxes. His compositions used folk elements such as blues shouts, field hollers, call and response, and gospel-style improvised accompanying riffs. In this middle period, which lasted from 1955 to 1966, Mingus employed a number of notable musicians, including saxophonists Eric Dolphy, Rahsaan Roland Kirk, Jackie MCLEAN, Booker Ervin, John Handy, Clifford JORDAN, and Charles McPherson; drummer Dannie Richmond; pianists Mal Waldron and Jaki Byard; trombonist Jimmy Knepper; and trumpeter Ted Curson. He produced numerous albums that are considered classics, including *Tijuana Moods* (1957), *Mingus Ah-Um* (1959), the orchestral *Pre-Bird* (1960), *Mingus Oh Yeah* (1961),

Bassist Charles Mingus, one of the major figures of postbebop jazz, emulated his idol, Duke Ellington, in his creation of jazz compositions and suites of surpassing virtuosity, acidic forcefulness, and lyrical elegance. (© Atlantic Records)

Town Hall Concerts (1962, 1964), and *Mingus Mingus Mingus* (1963), and notable compositions such as "Love Chant" (1955), "Foggy Day" (1955), "Percussion Discussion" (1955), "Pithecanthropus Erectus" (1956), "Reincarnation of a Lovebird" (1957), "Haitian Fight Song" (1957), and "The Black Saint and the Sinner Lady" (1963).

Politics also began to enter Mingus's music in the 1950s, and the two eventually became inseparable, with Mingus issuing explicit musical attacks against segregation and racism. "Meditations on Integration" (1964) was written in response to the segregation and mistreatment of black prisoners in the American South and recorded live at the Monterey Jazz Festival, while "Fables of Faubus" (1959) protested Orval Faubus, the segregationist governor of Arkansas. Mingus's activism also extended to attempts at having jazz musicians wrest control of their careers out of the hands of club owners and recording executives. He twice organized his own record companies, Debut Records in 1952 and Charles Mingus Records in 1963. In 1960 he helped lead a musical revolt against the staid Newport Jazz Festival, and along with Ornette COLEMAN, Coleman HAWKINS, and Max Roach, he formed a group known as the Newport Rebels, which held a counter-festival.

In his peak years Mingus often performed in settings outside the workshops. In 1958 he led a quintet accompanying Langston HUGHES reciting his poetry on *The Weary Blues of Langston Hughes.* Further,

though he gained fame early as a bassist in the tradition of Jimmy BLANTON and Oscar PETTIFORD, he also on occasion hired a bassist and performed at the piano, and he released *Mingus Plays Piano* in 1963. In 1962 he recorded *Money Jungle,* a trio album with Duke Ellington and Max Roach.

In 1966 Mingus stopped performing, largely as a result of the psychological problems that had always plagued him. In 1969 financial problems forced him out of retirement, and despite his deteriorating physical condition due to amyotrophic lateral sclerosis, a progressive degenerative disease of the nervous system (also known as Lou Gehrig's disease), he experienced a new burst of creativity in the 1970s. He published his picaresque, fictionalized autobiography, *Beneath the Underdog,* and was awarded a Guggenheim fellowship in 1971. He thereafter worked regularly, recording *Mingus Moves* (1973), until 1977, when he fell ill after recording *Three or Four Shades of Blue.* He released his last albums, *Me, Myself an Eye* and *Something like a Bird,* in 1978. His last appearance on record was on *Mingus,* an album by the singer Joni Mitchell, in 1978. He died in Cuernavaca, Mexico.

REFERENCES

BERENDT, JOACHIM. "Mingus and the Shadow of Duke Ellington." *Jazz* 4, no. 4 (1965): 17–25.

COLEMAN, JANET. *Mingus/Mingus: Two Memoirs.* New York, 1991.

JOST, E. "Charles Mingus." In *Free Jazz*. Graz, Austria, 1974, pp. 35–44..

MINGUS, CHARLES. *Beneath the Underdog*. New York, 1971.

PRIESTLEY, BRIAN. *Mingus: A Critical Biography*. New York, 1983.

EDDIE S. MEADOWS

Minnesota. Located on the upper reaches of the Mississippi River, Minnesota has historically been a center for agriculture, banking/finance, and light manufacturing for the upper Midwest. This economic mix, along with the opportunity for employment, has attracted African Americans to the area, notably to the port and transportation hubs of St. Paul/Minneapolis, although in smaller numbers than usually associated with industrialized northern metropolitan areas.

African Americans in Minnesota predate the state's territorial status. They often accompanied French fur trappers and acted as interpreters between Europeans and Native Americans. The earliest record of blacks in Minnesota dates from the end of the eighteenth century and centers on George Bonga. Born to Pierre Bonga, a free black employed by the Northwest (Trade) Company, and an Ojibwa woman near the site of Duluth, Minnesota, in 1802, Bonga was raised in the Northwest Territory and educated in Montreal. He went on to become one of Minnesota's territorial fathers. Initially employed by the American Fur Company, he later established his own trading post. Eventually he was called upon to negotiate treaties between the United States government and the Ojibwa people because of his language skills. He died in 1872, leaving behind children who would produce hundreds of descendants.

Although Minnesota, as part of the Wisconsin Territory, forbade slavery under the Northwest Ordinance of 1787, African-American slaves came to the area as early as 1825. They worked as servants to officers stationed at Fort Snelling and as domestics to the wealthy southern slave owners who frequently vacationed in Minnesota during the summer. The best-known of these was Dred Scott, who was brought to Minnesota in 1836 by his owner, Dr. John Emerson, an army surgeon, and remained there two years. In 1848, he sued for his freedom in a Missouri district court, claiming that he had been freed as a result of his residence in a free territory. The case eventually led to the U.S. Supreme Court's notorious 1857 decision, *Dred Scott* v. *Sanford*, which defined blacks as without constitutional rights and therefore lacking the right to petition the federal courts for relief from their condition as slaves (*see* DRED SCOTT DECISION).

By the time Minnesota achieved territorial status in 1849, approximately forty free persons of African descent were recorded as territorial residents, of whom thirty lived in St. Paul. At least one attended public school in St. Peter's (now Mendota). During the 1850s, more free blacks entered the territory, many as laborers and cooks on Mississippi River steamboats. Minnesota faced the same struggle over slavery that the rest of the nation did, and the area was torn by conflict between antislavery sentiment and economic interest in Southern slave owner sojourners. In 1854, a restrictive BLACK CODE was narrowly defeated in the territorial legislature. Antislavery activists worked against enforcement of the 1850 FUGITIVE SLAVE LAW. In 1857, the first black school opened in St. Paul. By 1860, two years after Minnesota became the thirty-second state, some 259 blacks resided in twenty-two of the state's eighty-seven counties, with seventy in St. Paul (Ramsey County). In 1860, abolitionists helped Eliza Winston, slave of a visiting southerner, to win her freedom in court by arguing that the state banned slavery. When prosouthern residents threatened violent protest, Winston was spirited to safety in Canada.

In 1863, during the CIVIL WAR, a group of blacks from Missouri migrated to Minnesota. In the face of white hostility, mainly from Irish-American laborers, the migrants were dispersed in small groups to Fort Snelling and other places. A group in St. Paul founded the Pilgrim Baptist Church, the state's oldest black church. The same year, the elite St. James African Methodist Episcopal Church was founded in Minneapolis (then called St. Anthony). Subsequent migrants were not permitted to land at St. Paul, so they continued to more sparsely settled towns. Although black men were not initially allowed to become members of the state's militia, 104 black men from Minnesota ultimately served in the Union army during the Civil War.

The black population in Minnesota grew after the Civil War. Most settled in St. Paul, in what is now the city's business section, and in Minneapolis, first in the Seven Corners district and then in North Minneapolis. African Americans migrated to Minnesota for the same reasons as other immigrants: to homestead land, to improve their economic circumstances, and to acquire education. Most blacks were unable to secure land and worked in service jobs such as barbers and clerks, or as waiters or porters. One of the 1863 migrants, John W. Cheatham, was hired by the St. Paul Fire Department, and in 1899 became the city's fire captain. The Twin Cities community grew fast. In 1867, with the aid of wealthy barber/beauticians Thomas and Amanda Lyles, the St. Mark's

Frederick L. McGhee, a criminal lawyer in St. Paul, Minn., was a cofounder of the Niagara Movement in 1905. (Minnesota Historical Society)

Episcopal Church was formed. By 1870, there was a black newspaper. Lyles also formed Robert Bank's Literary Society, an elite "lyceum" and literary group.

In 1868, whites voted to grant African Americans the franchise. The following year, the first black state convention for the Sons of Freedom was held in St. Paul. The Sons of Freedom, led by teacher Moses DIXON, businessmen J. K. Hilyard and Jacob Pritchard, and a few others, was created to promote black self-help and to lobby for civil rights. By 1898, three state laws had been passed prohibiting racial discrimination in public accommodations. Nevertheless, occasional discrimination remained.

Unsatisfied with their protection under Minnesota statutes, blacks in St. Paul organized civil rights efforts. In 1887, they formed the Minnesota Protective and Industrial League, which grew into the local chapters of such late nineteenth-century national civil rights organizations as the Afro-American League and the Afro-American Council. Nationally recognized leaders such as Booker T. WASHINGTON, William Monroe TROTTER and W. E. B. DU BOIS often traveled to Minnesota to consult with local black leaders. In 1902, St. Paul was the site of the national meeting of the Afro-American Council. In 1905, St. Paul attorney Frederick McGhee helped Du Bois and Trotter in the founding of the NIAGARA

MOVEMENT. In 1913, the Twin Cities branch of the NATIONAL ASSOCIATION FOR THE ADVANCEMENT OF COLORED PEOPLE (NAACP) was formed.

The leading civil rights activist in Minnesota was editor John Quincy Adams, a graduate of Oberlin College and recent migrant from Kentucky who took over the two-year-old Western Appeal newspaper in 1887. He ran the paper until his death in 1922. Under Adams, the St. Paul Appeal became a leading militant voice. In the 1890s, Adams became one of the founders of the National Negro Press Association. After 1900, Adams sponsored a local branch of the National Equal Rights League and worked with the St. Paul NAACP.

By 1900, Minnesota's black population had reached about 5,000. Immigration then slowed, though the population doubled in the following forty years. The population remained centered in the Twin Cities and in the growing industrial center of Duluth. Roy Wilkins, later the head of the NAACP, grew up in Duluth during these years, and eventually attended the University of Minnesota. The Twin Cities community was educated and largely successful. St. Paul had the highest percentage of black homeowners of any city in the United States and included many black professionals. Attorney William Morris was one of the first black lawyers to practice before the U.S. Supreme Court. In 1898, John Francis Wheaton, an African American, was elected to a term in the state legislature from a nearly all-white district in Minneapolis (no other African Americans would be elected to public office until the 1960s, though many were appointed to important posts). Clubs were formed, such as the Afro-American Social Club, founded in 1894, and the Self Culture Club, begun in 1907. The black community also supported the St. Paul Colored Gophers, a powerful baseball team of the 1910s.

However, despite civil rights laws, housing and employment discrimination remained widespread. The Twin Cities black population was largely restricted to the areas of North Minneapolis and St. Paul's Rondo district, a formerly Jewish neighborhood. In 1913, the state's African-American community lobbied strongly in the legislature to defeat a law forbidding intermarriage.

After the United States entered World War I in 1917, African Americans in Minnesota struggled to be permitted to participate. Eventually over 500 black Minnesotans were drafted. However, their actions did not bring about improved conditions. In June of 1920, following the end of the war, three black men working with a traveling circus in Duluth were accused of raping a white girl and were lynched. Nellie Francis (the wife of William T. Francis, a prominent St. Paul attorney and later U.S. Ambassador to Liberia) successfully lobbied the state legislature for

John Quincy Adams was a leader of the African-American community in Minneapolis–St.Paul in the early twentieth century and the longtime editor of *The Appeal,* a combative local newspaper. (Minnesota Historical Society)

passage of the first antilynching law in the United States. A. Phillip RANDOLPH successfully organized a chapter of the BROTHERHOOD OF SLEEPING CAR PORTERS in St. Paul in 1920, and even Marcus GARVEY's UNIVERSAL NEGRO IMPROVEMENT ASSOCIATION had a small following in the Twin Cities. The Twin Cities branch of the NATIONAL URBAN LEAGUE, organized in 1923, attempted to persuade local businesses to hire blacks. The league helped build the Phillis WHEATLEY House in Minneapolis and the Hallie Q. BROWN Community House in St. Paul as educational and recreational centers. In 1926, the Minneapolis Urban League's secretary, economist Abram Harris, wrote a report, *The Negro Population in Minneapolis,* which sparked reform efforts in that city. In 1934, the *Minneapolis Spokesman/St. Paul Recorder* newspaper was founded. It has remained the civil rights voice of the local black community.

By the late 1920s, due to limited job prospects, many blacks were unemployed, and educated African Americans such as Roy WILKINS were forced to leave the state in search of work. The depression further eroded the state's African-American economy, as many blacks occupied domestic or personal service

positions, which evaporated in the crisis. African Americans in the Civilian Conservation Corps were sent to segregated bases in the South, while whites worked within the state. Housing remained scarce and often substandard, despite the opening of a black housing project, Sumner Field Houses, in St. Paul in 1935. By 1936, an estimated sixty-two percent of the Twin Cities' black population was on relief or dependent on charity. Federal aid was distributed in a discriminatory fashion. In 1938, Clarence Mitchell, an expert on labor problems, became secretary of the St. Paul Urban League. He managed to place many blacks in federal jobs programs. The Associated Negro Credit Union and the Joint Negro Labor Council also aided workers.

The coming of World War II brought widespread prosperity, as well as thousands of black immigrants, to Minnesota. By the war's end, 702 black Minnesotans had served in the U.S. armed forces. While the army remained segregated, many war industries integrated after pressure from the federal FAIR EMPLOYMENT PRACTICES COMMISSION (FEPC) and the Congress of Industrial Organizations. The giant Twin Cities Ordnance plant employed up to one-fifth of the state's adult black population by itself. Governor Edward Thye's Interracial Commission (after 1955

William T. Francis, of Minneapolis–St. Paul, was appointed minister to Liberia in 1927. (Minnesota Historical Society)

called the Human Rights Commission), organized in the wake of the Detroit Riot of 1943, produced important studies of employment and housing discrimination in the state. In 1944, the state's Democratic party officially allied with the populist Farmer-Labor party, and reformers such as Hubert H. Humphrey, mayor of Minneapolis and later U.S. senator, made civil rights a major concern.

In the years following World War II, the African-American population of Minnesota continued its expansion. Jobs opened up in formerly all-white industries, in part through the efforts of civil rights leader Whitney M. YOUNG, Jr., industrial relations secretary of the St. Paul Urban League in the late 1940s. St. Paul and Minneapolis created municipal FEPCs in 1949, and in 1955, after years of lobbying by black leaders, the Minnesota legislature created a statewide FEPC. Still, housing discrimination remained a chronic problem. Despite a 1953 law banning racially restrictive covenants and a 1961 open housing law, de facto segregation increased. Ghetto conditions were aggravated by "slum clearance" and highway construction which broke up black neighborhoods. African Americans who tried to move into white suburban areas were harassed or threatened. In 1961, a cross was burned on the lawn of an African American in St. Paul.

The CIVIL RIGHTS MOVEMENT began full-scale efforts in Minnesota in 1960, when members of the Youth Council of the Minneapolis NAACP began picketing lunch counters which refused to serve African Americans and stores which would not hire black workers. However, progress was not sufficient to avert rising tensions. In the summers of 1966 and 1967, there were racial disturbances in North Minneapolis. In 1968, following the assassination of the Rev. Dr. Martin Luther KING, Jr., several hundred demonstrators participated in an interracial march through the Selby-Dale area of St. Paul.

Minnesota is the home of a black population which is unique in many ways. The 1990 federal census records 94,944 blacks living in Minnesota, an increase of 78 percent from 1980. This unprecedented growth over a decade has been attributed to the migration of black individuals seeking employment opportunities. Ninety-four percent of the state's black residents live in the seven-county Twin Cities metropolitan area: approximately 21 percent in St. Paul, 51 percent in Minneapolis, and 22 percent in scattered suburban communities. The remainder can be found in such secondary population centers as Duluth, Rochester, and Moorehead. Males comprise 51.7 percent of the population. Literacy is very high. Eighty-five percent of African-American adults twenty-five years of age or older possess a high school diploma, and 26 percent of these adults have educational degrees

higher than the degree of associate of arts. Thirty percent of black householders own their own homes. Black men and women can be found employed in all sectors of the economy, including corporate management, medicine, education, and business. African Americans—such as Sharon Sayles Belton, the first African-American and first woman mayor of Minneapolis—have been active in state and local government, and in the state judiciary (notably former Minnesota Vikings star Alan PAGE, elected to the Minnesota Supreme Court in 1992). Unfortunately, prejudice has not evaporated. The important 1992 U.S. Supreme Court "hate crime" decision *R.A.V. v. St. Paul* stemmed from the actions of a group of "skinheads" in St. Paul who burned a cross in a black family's yard.

The Twin Cities black community has a very rich and vibrant tradition in the black cultural arts. St. Paul is the home of the Penumbra Theater, one of five professional black repertory theaters in the United States. It is also the former home of August WILSON, Pulitzer Prize–winning playwright and author. The state is the home of rock music superstar PRINCE, creator of the "Minneapolis Sound," the Grammy Award–winning "Sounds of Blackness," and of Minneapolis Gospel Sound, as well as musicians Jimmy Jam, Terry Lewis, and others. In 1981, the Minnesota Black Music Awards ceremony began, and in 1989 the Minnesota Black Music Expo, an annual music business conference, was inaugurated.

Other Minnesotans who have achieved prominence in the last one hundred years include Anna Arnold HEDGEMAN, educator, author, and literata of the HARLEM RENAISSANCE Movement; Dr. Catherine Lealtad, physician and humanitarian; Frederick McKinley, inventor of the semaphore stoplight and other inventions; Carl T. Rowan, columnist, ambassador to Finland and United States Information Agency director; Richard K. Fox, former U.S. Ambassador to Spain and Jamaica; and baseball star Dave Winfield.

REFERENCES

HARRIS, ABRAM L., JR. *The Negro Population in Minneapolis.* Minneapolis, Minn., 1930.
HOLMQUIST, JUNE DRENNING, ed. *They Chose Minnesota: A Survey of the State's Ethnic Groups.* St. Paul, Minn., 1981.
Minnesota Interracial Commission. *Race Relations in Minnesota: Reports of the Commission.* St. Paul, Minn., 1948.
SPANGLER, EARL. *The Negro in Minnesota.* Minneapolis, Minn., 1961.
TAYLOR, DAVID. "Black Minnesotans: Roots for Discovering Minnesota's History." *Roots Magazine* 17, no. 1 (Fall 1988).

———. Pilgrim's Progress: Black St. Paul and the Making of an Urban Ghetto, 1870–1930. Ph.D. diss., University of Minnesota, 1977.

DAVID V. TAYLOR

Minns, Albert David. *See* James, Leon Edgehill, and Minns, Albert David.

Minority Business Development Agency. Citing a need to "remove commercial obstacles which have too often stood in the way of minority-group members," President Richard Nixon signed Executive Order 11458 in March 1971, creating the Office of Minority Business Enterprise (OMBE). The obstacles were identified as the unavailability of credit, insurance, and technical assistance for aspiring minority entrepreneurs. Only African Americans and those officially classified as minorities qualified for assistance. During the administration of President Jimmy Carter, the OMBE became the Minority Business Development Agency (MBDA) and received a larger staff and increased responsibilities.

Since its inception, the MBDA has primarily disseminated advice through over one hundred Minority Business Development Centers (MBDC), run by independent business consultants. (There were 107 such centers in 1993.) Consultants charge business clients a nominal fee for services, which include advice on management, finance, and marketing; the agency supplies the rest of the costs. From 1987 through 1992, the organization advised on average between 10,000 and 12,000 clients a year. A 1989 General Accounting Office (GAO) report stated that only 17 percent of the MBDA's clients were dissatisfied with the services they received from MBDA. In the early 1990s, the MBDA created two Minority Enterprise Growth Assistance (MEGA) centers, one in Chicago, Ill., and another in Los Angeles, Calif., which was awarded funding in early 1994. The MEGA centers provide more comprehensive assistance and are better funded than the MBDCs; they cater primarily to clients with technology-based firms or firms with specialized needs.

The MBDA's status, especially during the 1980s, was increasingly precarious as Reagan administration officials urged the consolidation of the MBDA with the Small Business Administration. While critics of the plan aided the MBDA in maintaining its independence, funding for the agency has decreased markedly. During the 1980s, funding fell from approximately $56 million in 1982 to $39 million in 1990.

However, funding increased slightly during the first years of the Clinton administration.

REFERENCES

"Banking on the Man from Hope." *Black Enterprise* 24, no. 3 (November 1993): 53–57.

DINGLE, DEREK T. "Whatever Happened to Black Capitalism?" *Black Enterprise* 21, no. 1 (August 1990): 161–168.

SULSKI, JIM. "Obstacle Course: Minority Firms Say Bias Persists Despite Many Gains." *Chicago Tribune*, October 27, 1993, p. C8.

TREADWELL, DAVID. "Hard Road for Black Businesses." *Los Angeles Times*, September 20, 1991, p. A1.

JOHN C. STONER

Minority Business Set-Asides. Minority set-aside policies require that a certain proportion of government contract work be performed by minority-owned businesses. Eligible firms are those for which at least 51 percent is owned by a socially or economically disadvantaged individual. Designated eligible races and ethnicities normally include African Americans, Hispanics, Asian Americans, and Native Americans. Individuals not belonging to a designated group may be declared eligible on a case-by-case basis after proving disadvantage through racial or ethnic bias. These policies are found at all levels of government, largely for public works and construction projects, but also in government procurement. In 1989, the last year statistics were collected, there were 234 programs in effect at the state, county, city, and district levels, usually styled after federal programs.

Set-asides are most often presented as remedies for current or past discrimination against particular racial or ethnic groups, while opponents have argued that they perpetuate the discrimination they were designed to remedy, and should be used only to remedy proved discrimination against individuals. The programs serve many purposes other than strictly remedying job discrimination. They have often been aimed at building or supporting a middle-class base in poor communities, which would function as example and local employer. The programs' multiple purposes make their success difficult to evaluate.

Federal set-aside programs are an offshoot of affirmative action policies that began in the late 1960s with executive orders by the Johnson and Nixon Administrations. They grew quickly during the 1970s, and became regular features of congressional appropriations. Despite opposition from whites, the programs were preserved after political action by representatives of beneficiary groups. The first important legal challenge to the principle of set-asides came in 1979–1980, when the Supreme Court heard the case of *Fullilove* v. *Klutznick*. In the Public Works Employment Act of 1977, Congress had provided a 10 percent set-aside for minority business enterprises. The Court ruled 6 to 3 that such a law was constitutional, although the majority disagreed on whether or not authority to order set-asides rested only with Congress. In 1989, in *Richmond* v. *J. A. Croson Co.*, the Court ruled that states and localities did not have the same power as Congress. Their plans would be judged by "strict scrutiny," which meant lawmakers would be held to a "higher standard" of evidence in determining constitutionality.

REFERENCE

ORLANS, HAROLD, and JUNE O'NEILL, eds. *Affirmative Action Revisited*. Annals of the American Academy for Political and Social Science, vol. 523. Newbery Park, Calif., 1992.

ELAINE REARDON

Minstrels/Minstrelsy. The minstrel show was the first uniquely American form of stage entertainment. Begun by white performers using black makeup and dialect to portray African Americans, the minstrel show was a popular sensation in the 1840s, dominated American show business until the 1890s, and had profound and enduring impacts on show business, racial STEREOTYPES, and African Americans in the performing arts.

White men in blackface had portrayed black people almost since the first contact of the races. But in the 1820s—when American show business was in its infancy, and audiences demanded stage shows about American, not European, characters and themes—some white performers began to specialize in blackfaced acts they called "Ethiopian Delineation." In 1828 in Louisville, Ky., one of these "Delineators," Thomas D. Rice, saw a crippled African-American stablehand named Jim Crow doing an unusual song and dance. Rice bought the man's clothes, learned the routine, and became a stage star with his "Jump Jim Crow" act (*see also* JIM CROW). After that, blackfaced whites became more and more popular on America's stages.

In 1843 in New York City, four of these blackfaced entertainers, calling themselves the Virginia Minstrels, staged the first full evening of what they billed as "the oddities, peculiarities, eccentricities, and comicalities of that Sable Genus of Humanity." The Virginia Minstrels were a great hit. Within a

year, the minstrel show became a separate entertainment form that audiences loved. Although it was centered in the big cities of the North, it was performed almost everywhere, from frontier camps to the White House. In fact, when Commodore Perry's fleet entered Japan in 1853–1854, the sailors put on a blackfaced minstrel show for the Japanese.

Minstrel shows had three distinct parts. The first opened with a rousing group song and dance. Then the minstrels sat in a semicircle facing the audience. The dignified man in the middle, the interlocutor, used a commanding voice and precise, pompous language as the master of ceremonies. Flanking him, holding instruments such as banjos and fiddles, were

A number of minstrel songs by James A. Bland, including "Carry Me Back to Ole Virginny" and "Oh, Dem Golden Slippers," remain part of America's collective musical memory more than a century after they were composed. (Photographs and Prints Division, Schomburg Center for Research in Black Culture, The New York Public Library, Astor, Lenox and Tilden Foundations)

entertainers who performed the musical numbers, most notably the songs of Stephen Foster. In his string of minstrel hits, including "Old Folks at Home," "Oh Susanna," "My Old Kentucky Home," and "Old Black Joe," Foster was a pioneer of a new eclectic American popular music, blending European parlor music he heard at home, frontier music he heard in Cincinnati theaters, and African-American music he heard in a servant's church. On the ends of the semicircle sat the most popular minstrels, the comedians, "Mr. Tambo" and "Mr. Bones," who were named after their instruments, the tambourine and the rhythm clacker bones. (Various performers assumed these two roles.) Wearing flashy clothes and exaggerated black makeup and speaking in heavy dialects laden with humorous malapropisms, the endmen traded puns, riddles, and jokes with the interlocutor (the man in the middle between them). This new fast-paced verbal humor later matured in vaudeville and radio. The first part ended with an upbeat song and dance.

The second part, the olio, was essentially a variety show with performers coming on stage one at a time to do their specialties, everything from acrobatics to animal acts. This was again a forerunner of vaudeville and of radio and television variety shows.

The third part, a one-act production with costumes, props, and a set, was at times a parody of a popular play or a current event. But in the early years, it was usually a happy plantation scene with dances, banjo playing, sentimentalism, slapstick, and songs such as "Dixie," a minstrel hit first introduced in New York City. These productions mixing music, comedy, and dance provided the seeds for the later development of the musical comedy.

Minstrelsy was not just precedent-setting entertainment. It was entertainment in blackface. It was about race and slavery, and it was born when those issues threatened to plunge America into civil war. During that period of rising tensions northern whites, with little knowledge of African Americans, packed into theaters to watch white men in blackface act out images of slavery and black people that the white public wanted to see. From its inception, in every part of the show, minstrelsy used makeup, props, gestures, and descriptions to create grotesque physical caricatures of African Americans—big mouths and lips, pop eyes, huge feet, woolly hair, and literally black skin. Minstrels also evolved sharp contrasts between African Americans in the North and in the South. In the show's first part, some of the olio, and the nonplantation farces, northern minstrel blacks were either lazy, ignorant good-for-nothings or flashy, preening dandies. Southern minstrel blacks, in first-part songs and plantation finales, were happy, frolicking "darkies" or nostalgic "old uncles" and

loving "mammies" devoted to their kind, doting masters and mistresses. In the 1850s, as political conflicts grew, minstrelsy often portrayed unhappy plantation runaways who longed to be back in the land of cotton. It even converted the powerful antislavery messages of UNCLE TOM'S CABIN into closing plantation farces of "Happy Uncle Tom."

Minstrelsy never pretended to be anything but escapist entertainment, but its racial caricatures and stereotypes allowed its huge northern white audiences to believe that African Americans were inferior people who did not belong in the North and were happy and secure only on southern plantations. So there was no need for a civil war over slavery or for acceptance of African Americans as equals. Even after the Civil War and the abolition of slavery, minstrelsy continued these stereotypes, as if to support the racial caste system that replaced slavery and kept African Americans "in their place" in the South.

After the Civil War, for the first time a large number of African Americans themselves became minstrels. Realizing that the popularity of blackfaced whites gave them a unique wedge into show business, early African-American minstrels emphasized their race. They billed themselves as "genuine," "bona fide" "colored" people who were untrained ex-slaves re-creating their lives on the plantation. Except for the endmen, they rarely wore blackface. Northern white audiences were astonished by the variety of African Americans' skin colors and delighted by their shows. Although African-American minstrels did modify and diversify their material in subtle ways, the bulk of their shows reproduced and in effect added credibility to ingrained minstrel stereotypes. African-American minstrel troupes were so popular that they performed all over the United States, in Europe, and in the South Pacific, and forced white minstrels to cut back their plantation material to avoid the new competition. One "Minstrel Wanted" ad in 1883 even warned, "Non-colored performers need not apply."

By the 1880s, as a result of minstrelsy, African Americans were established in all phases of show business as performers, composers, managers, and owners, though the most successful troupes were owned by whites. But the successes of African-American minstrels came at great expense. Personally, they faced discrimination daily. Professionally, they did not get the credit they deserved as performing artists because of their image as untrained, natural entertainers. Creatively, they had to stay within restrictive roles. Racially, they appeared to confirm negative stereotypes of African Americans. But for decades, there were no other real choices for blacks in show business. For instance, Sam Lucas, a top minstrel composer and star by 1873, repeatedly tried to break free of minstrelsy. In 1875, he costarred in *Out of Bondage,* a serious musical drama about blacks' progress from slavery to the "attainment of education and refinement," and in 1878, he was the first of his race to star in a serious production of *Uncle Tom's Cabin,* a role long considered too difficult for an African American. But each time, he had to return to minstrelsy to make a living. Still, he and the other pioneers laid the foundation for future generations.

Although minstrelsy as an entertainment institution was originally created and shaped by white performers playing to white audiences, African-American culture was part of its appeal from the beginning. Some blackfaced stars, like Thomas D. Rice, admitted copying their acts directly from individual African Americans. More often, touring white minstrels bragged in general of learning new material and performance styles from black people, and there is considerable evidence in early minstrelsy that they did. Hans Nathan has identified African-derived syncopated rhythms in early banjo tunes that were the forerunners of RAGTIME and JAZZ. Robert C. Toll has found characteristically African-American folklore and humor in the early shows. And minstrelsy's biggest debts to African-American culture were in dance. In fact, the only African-American star in early minstrelsy was the dancer William Henry "Juba" LANE. Before emigrating to England in 1848, he repeatedly outdanced whites with "the manner in which he beats time with his feet." Virtually the father of American tap dance, Lane was, according to dance historian Marian Hannah Winter, the "most influential single performer of nineteenth century American dance." Most African-American influence on minstrel dance was less direct but no less real, as Marshall Stearns and Jean Stearns have demonstrated, with everything from the "buck and wing" to the "soft shoe."

When a number of black people became minstrels, they brought a new infusion of African-American culture. For the first time, spirituals were part of minstrelsy. Black composers drew on traditional culture, as black dancers did with African-American steps and styles. Comedians, such as Billy Kersands, used the double-edged wit and guile of the black folk to get the African Americans seated in segregated sections laughing *with* them at the same time that whites laughed *at* them.

Since these examples have to be gleaned from the few studies of the sparse nineteenth-century sources, they are probably the tip of the iceberg. Still, they do indicate that minstrelsy was the first example of the enormous influence that African-American culture would have on the performing arts in America. It was also the first example of white Americans exploiting and profiting from the creativity of African Americans.

By the 1890s, as public interest shifted from plantations and ex-slaves to big cities and new European immigrants, minstrelsy's national popularity faded, though it survived in some areas for a long time. For white minstrels, the blackface that was once such an asset became a handicap, limiting their ability to compete with vaudeville—which could make race just one part of its shows—and with nonracial musicals. Ultimately, the blackfaced dialect act moved into vaudeville, musicals, movies, and radio. For African Americans, though minstrelsy remained a limited possibility, more promising opportunities opened up in musicals, popular music, and vaudeville. But the struggles against bias, restrictions, and discrimination had only begun. Long after minstrelsy was gone, its negative stereotypes and caricatures of African Americans remained deeply embedded in American show business and popular culture.

REFERENCES

FLETCHER, TOM. *One Hundred Years of the Negro in Show Business.* New York, 1954.

NATHAN, HANS. *Dan Emmett and the Rise of Early Negro Minstrelsy.* Norman, Okla., 1962.

SIMOND, IKE. *Old Slack's Reminiscences and Pocket History of the Colored Profession from 1865 to 1891.* Edited by Robert C. Toll and Francis Lee Utley. Bowling Green, Ohio, 1974.

STEARNS, MARSHALL, and JEAN STEARNS. *Jazz Dance.* New York, 1968.

TOLL, ROBERT C. *Blacking Up: The Minstrel Show in Nineteenth Century America.* New York, 1974.

———. "From Folktype to Stereotype: Images of Slaves in Antebellum Minstrelsy." *Journal of the Folklore Institute* 8 (June 1971): 38–47.

———. "Showbiz in Blackface: The Evolution of the Minstrel Show as a Theatrical Form." In Myron Matlaw, ed. *American Popular Entertainment: Papers and Proceedings of the Conference on the History of American Popular Entertainment.* Westport, Conn., 1979, pp. 21–32.

WINTER, MARIAN HANNAH. "Juba and American Minstrelsy." *Dance Index* 6 (February 1947): 28–47.

WITTKE, CARL. *Tambo and Bones.* Durham, N.C., 1930.

ROBERT C. TOLL

Minton, Henry McKee (December 20, 1870–December 1946), physician and pharmacist. Henry McKee Minton was born in Columbia, S.C., to a prominent Philadelphia family who had moved temporarily to the South. After graduating from Phillips Exeter Academy in 1891, he earned a degree from the Philadelphia College of Pharmacy in 1895. Two years later, he established what is believed to be Pennsylvania's first black-owned drugstore. In 1903, Minton closed his pharmacy and chose to study medicine. In 1904, he and five associates founded Sigma Pi Phi, the first African-American Greek-letter fraternity. After graduating from the Jefferson Medical College in Philadelphia in 1906, Minton began a long, prominent career as a public health physician and civic activist.

Dr. Minton's medical career centered on tuberculosis treatment and control, teaching, and hospital administration. In 1915, Minton was hired by the Henry Phipps Institute for the Study, Prevention and Treatment of Tuberculosis to head its work in black sections of Philadelphia. He retained this position until his death in 1946. The Phipps Institute was a private philanthropic facility founded in 1903. The institute gained national recognition for its contribution to tuberculosis research, including its work with urban black and immigrant populations. Dr. Minton became the central figure behind the institute's successful opening of tuberculosis-control clinics throughout black sections of Philadelphia. In 1923, he was named supervisor of the Negro Tuberculosis Bureau in Philadelphia. He also was head of the Philadelphia-area black advisory committee of the Pennsylvania Society for the Prevention of Tuberculosis—the nation's first such organization.

Dr. Minton also was a seminal figure in the black-controlled hospitals that opened throughout the United States before World War II (*see* HOSPITALS, BLACK). From 1920 until 1944, he was the superintendent of Mercy Hospital in Philadelphia. He had been one of the key figures involved in the founding of the hospital in 1907. Under Minton's leadership, this institution offered valuable medical services to the black community. Furthermore, because Mercy was one of the nation's few black hospitals that was fully accredited, it provided some of the few internships available in the country for black medical school graduates, as well as an excellent nursing school.

In addition to his medical activities, Minton became heavily involved in social welfare work in Philadelphia and throughout Pennsylvania. He served on the board of the Whittier Center, a large Philadelphia charitable agency, and as a treasurer of the mainly black Downington Industrial School. He wrote articles for *New York Medical Journal* and the *Journal of the National Medical Association,* among others, and he published two pamphlets, *Early Negroes in Business in Philadelphia* (1913) and *Causes and Prevention of Tuberculosis* (1915). Minton died of a heart attack in Philadelphia in 1946.

REFERENCES

BATES, BARBARA. *Bargaining for Life: A Social History of Tuberculosis, 1876–1938.* Philadelphia, 1992.

COBB, W. MONTAGUE. "Henry McKee Minton, 1870–1946." *Journal of the National Medical Association* 47 (July 1955): 285–286.

DAVID MCBRIDE
LYDIA MCNEILL

Mirror of the Times, abolitionist newspaper. A relatively small number of prosperous African Americans living and working in California began to organize themselves into an abolitionist movement during the 1850s. Mifflin W. GIBBS and James Townsend, two wealthy businessmen, put up the money for publication of a newspaper addressed to African Americans in the state. William H. NEWBY, a self-educated writer, became the paper's founding editor. The *Mirror of the Times* was first published in 1855 in San Francisco. It became a broadsheet of news for African Americans and information about the antislavery movement.

In 1857, the CALIFORNIA COLORED CONVENTION was held in San Francisco, widely attended because of publicity it received in the *Mirror.* After the end of the Civil War and the abolition of slavery, the *Mirror* ceased printing, ceding its task of informing and addressing the African-American community in California to the new *Pacific Appeal.*

REFERENCE

DANIELS, HENRY DOUGLAS. *Pioneer Urbanites: A Social and Cultural History of Black San Francisco.* Philadelphia, 1980.

NANCY YOUSEF

Miscegenation and Intermarriage. The word *miscegenation* was coined during the presidential campaign of 1864 (from the Latin *miscere,* "to mix," and *genus,* "race") when the Democratic party asserted that Lincoln's Republican party advocated sex and marriage across the color line. Like *mulatto,* probably derived from the concept of mules and hybridity, the word was pejorative in its historical context.

People of European ancestry and people of African ancestry began reproducing together in America from their earliest contacts in the seventeenth-century South, when white servants and black slaves lived and labored together. Census counts of "mulattoes" (a category used in some, but not all, nineteenth-century U.S. census schedules) were subjectively based upon appearance, and while documentation of frequency can also be gathered from court records, slave narratives, and personal writings, such statistics are ultimately based on conjecture and are always cast in terms of proportions of European ancestry in the African-American population. With that said, perhaps 15 to 25 percent of African Americans in 1860 had some European ancestry; and perhaps 75 percent of modern-day African Americans do.

Colonial authorities wrote statutes against liaisons between Europeans and Africans from the 1660s forward, punishing liaisons between white women and black men most harshly. Under slavery, these laws largely reflected white fears of free African Americans. Because a child's legal status as slave or free followed the mother, when white women and black men reproduced together, their children would be free, but of partial African ancestry, thereby eroding racial slavery. On the contrary, children of slave women and white men were legally slaves, and usually remained enslaved throughout their lives.

Under the antebellum southern slave system, the sexual exploitation of black women by white masters and overseers, or the explicit or implicit threat of it, was a constant burden for slave families. Most liaisons between black women and white men were exploitive; resistance, on the part of black women and men alike, was ever present though often ineffective, and southern courts very rarely concerned themselves with the assault or rape of black women. These broad patterns differed markedly only in New Orleans, in which a system called *placage*, essentially concubinage, coupled free women of color with white men through formal dances.

Beyond testimony of cruelty, and the constant factor of unequal power between black women and white men, it is difficult to discern any uniformity of treatment; beyond entitlement on the part of masters, and anger and humiliation on the part of female slaves, it is difficult to discern the emotions that accompanied such relations in the context of a slave regime.

Under slavery, white southern communities displayed a degree of toleration for sexual liaisons between white women and black men, though this toleration was never as great as that displayed for the much more frequent master–female slave pairing. Sexual encounters with planter-class women presented the gravest dangers for black men, while dominant ideology was likely to cast lower-class white women as depraved agents of such illicit actions.

In the antebellum North, some states (though not all) had laws against intermarriage, and regardless of the law, liaisons between African Americans and whites remained socially taboo at least through the Civil War.

After Emancipation, the topic of liaisons between white women and black men entered Congressional debates about the Fourteenth and Fifteenth Amendments, with Democrats linking black male suffrage with fears of marriage to white women. Determined to retain a racial hierarchy, white Southerners then conflated the new political power of black men with sexual transgressions against white women. The Reconstruction years thus saw the development of full-scale white hysteria about black male sexuality, thereby commencing an era of terrorism and lynching that rapidly spread north and west.

In the decades following Emancipation, the sexual coercion and assault of black women by white men continued in the South, especially as Reconstruction drew to a close. Marriages across the color line were illegal in the post-Reconstruction South, while some Northern states had repealed those laws. Other laws, in both the North and West, ranged from declaring such marriages null and void, to imposing fines, to imprisonment; they were largely enforced against white women and black men only.

People of mixed European and African ancestry have never been considered a separate "race" in this country, although both the African American and white communities of antebellum New Orleans, Charleston, S.C., Mobile, Ala., and Savannah, Ga., recognized a "mulatto" or "brown" class. By the late nineteenth century, the "one-drop rule," which proclaimed that anyone with any known African ancestry would be classified as black, prevailed nationally.

While the numbers of mixed couples have increased in the second half of the twentieth century, percentages are still small; the majority of mixed couples since the end of World War II have been white women and black men, a phenomenon that caused considerable racial tension in the Civil Rights Movement of the 1960s. According to the U.S. Census Bureau, in 1970 there were 146 black-white married couples for every 100,000 married couples. In 1980 that number increased to 335 and in 1990, to 396. There are no reliable statistics on nonmarried couples. While recognizing legal sanctions as racist and a violation of rights, many African Americans have looked down on those who consorted with whites. As for dominant white attitudes, it was not until 1967, after nine years of trials and appeals in the case of *Loving* v. *Virginia,* that the United States Supreme Court ruled laws prohibiting marriages between blacks and whites unconstitutional; at that time, sixteen southern states had such laws.

The ongoing legacies of the legal and social history of this subject are apparent in issues ranging from the choice of racial categories on United States census forms, to the influence of racist ideology in sex crimes or alleged sex crimes, to antagonism from both white and black communities toward marriages and relationships across the color line.

REFERENCES

HIGGINBOTHAM, A. LEON, JR. *In the Matter of Color: Race and the American Legal Process: The Colonial Period.* New York, 1978.

HODES, MARTHA. "The Sexualization of Reconstruction Politics: White Women and Black Men in the South after the Civil War." *Journal of the History of Sexuality* 3 (1993): 402–417.

SPICKARD, PAUL R. *Mixed Blood: Intermarriage and Ethnic Identity in Twentieth-Century America.* Madison, Wis., 1989.

WILLIAMSON, JOEL. *New People: Miscegenation and Mulattoes in the United States.* New York, 1980.

MARTHA E. HODES

Missionary Movements. Missionary movements among African-American Christians in the United States can be characterized in a number of ways. First, the distinction should be made between domestic or home missions and overseas or foreign missions. Second, we may categorize the missionary efforts of African Americans based upon the activities of historically black denominations and agencies, or those of predominantly white groups, or some means of cooperation or joint endeavors between the two.

Third, mission movements are characterized by two dimensions, spiritual and temporal. The spiritual dimension refers to the efforts of Christians to convert others to the faith: preaching, religious instruction, and the construction of houses of worship. The temporal includes the educational, medical, and other humanitarian interests that cover the concerns of the body and not simply the soul. On a practical level it is often impossible to distinguish neatly between the domestic and the overseas, the various means of evangelizing, and the spiritual and the temporal. They are all often intimately related and interwoven, both organizationally and theologically.

The black missionary tradition derives from eighteenth-century evangelicalism. It was the evangelical type of Christianity that appealed to most blacks, whites, and Native Americans in the United States in that period. At the core of this religious approach was the conviction that God deals directly with the individual and that it was the sacred duty of every faithful Christian to share the faith with others. For black Christians and those whites committed to black and African evangelization, a scripture verse, Psalm 68:31, applied specifically to racial evangelization and uplift. According to the King James translation, princes were to come from Egypt, and Ethiopia was to extend hands to God. Egypt and Ethiopia together represented the totality of the African race, and this verse was understood to predict that the black race should and must be evangelized, as a result of which temporal progress would occur.

As the United States moved further from its Revolutionary era, the early antislavery ardor of many evangelical churches among Methodists, Baptists, Presbyterians, and others declined. This reduction of active religious opposition to slavery was also occasioned in part by the fact that white evangelicals in the South increasingly became slaveholders and slave traders. In addition, the 1780s and '90s witnessed a greater willingness on the part of white Christians to apply even stricter discriminatory measures against their black counterparts within the churches.

On the one hand, these antiblack developments led to the rise of independent black congregations and denominations. On the other hand, the rise in proslavery and discriminatory attitudes led some whites and blacks to conclude that African-American Christians would fare better on the mother continent, where they could, more successfully than whites, effect spiritual and temporal progress among their African kinfolk.

When black Christians began to secede from white-controlled congregations and denominations in the latter part of the 1700s, they sought greater freedom in worship and church leadership. They wanted to influence in a more organized manner the lives of fellow blacks, whom they considered to have been overlooked by white-controlled Christian bodies. Richard ALLEN, one of the founders of the African Methodist Episcopal (AME) denomination, cited the need at an early point in his ministry for more evangelical attention to African Americans.

During the Second Great Awakening (1790–1825), many black congregations saw the same need. Thus, one of the first steps taken by these new congregations and denominations was the organization of outreach agencies for domestic and foreign missions. Through their church disciplines, religious publications, active involvement in antislavery activities, and establishment of schools and institutes, these black Christians often made it clear that they associated spiritual salvation with temporal betterment and physical freedom.

It would be a mistake, however, to view black evangelistic enterprises as confined solely to ministry within the race. It is true that Christianity in the United States spread more intraracially than interracially, but the latter was quite substantial and commonplace. Henry Evans, an eighteenth-century black Methodist minister, established the Methodist Episcopal Church in the Fayetteville, N.C., area with his influential preaching and pastoral efforts. At one point his church's black members were crowded out by whites, who, after initial opposition, responded in great numbers to his ministry. "Black Harry" HOSIER, esteemed for his powerful preaching, was a frequent evangelistic companion of the famous white Methodist preacher and bishop Francis Asbury. He was highly regarded by Asbury, Freeborn Garrettson, Thomas Coke, and other eminent American Methodists.

The missionary labors of John STEWART indicate the profound impact that individual black Christians had upon white-controlled denominational and missionary endeavors. Stewart's missionary activities to the Wyandotte Indians in Ohio demonstrated not only the biracial but the multiracial character of American religious history. In addition, the racially mixed, but white-controlled, Methodist Episcopal General Conference of 1820, inspired by the work of Stewart, for the first time set up a separate denominational agency for missions. Blacks of other denominations also participated in ministry on an interracial or multiracial basis, including the Baptists William Lemon, Josiah Bishop, and "Uncle Jack."

In addition to denominational and local outreach efforts, Christianity spread during the eighteenth and nineteenth centuries through "camp meeting" revivalistic gatherings, to which people came from miles around to hear the preaching and exhortations of ministers of various denominations and races and both genders. The autobiographical accounts of nineteenth-century black female ministers such as Zilpha ELAW and Jarena LEE demonstrate the interracial character of many of these camp meetings, the powerful roles often played by women and blacks in them, and the crucial significance of itinerant preaching by black men and women.

By and large, the independent black denominations and associations were confined to northern, free states and territories prior to the 1860s, because of the antipathy of the southern slave system to independent black enterprises. With the advent of the CIVIL WAR, this situation changed profoundly. Many northern missionaries went south to do missionary work among the freedpeople. These missionaries included both clergy and laypeople, blacks and whites, males and females, and individuals and agencies representing practically all of the major denominations, black and white.

Included among these northern missionaries and church organizers were black Christians such as the Rev. James Walker HOOD of the African Methodist Episcopal Zion Church (AMEZ), who organized and built a host of churches in Virginia, North Carolina, and South Carolina during and following the Civil War. Charlotte L. Forten (see Charlotte Forten GRIMKÉ), a prominent laywoman in the African Methodist Episcopal church, left a moving and insightful account of her life, *The Journal of Charlotte L. Forten,* which includes descriptions of her years of missionary service and teaching during the Civil War among freedpeople of the Port Royal, S.C., area.

It would be misleading, however, to leave the impression that all missionary work among freedpeople was conducted by northern Christians. Though pre–Civil War enslaved black Christians did not enjoy the advantages of independent organized groups, they nevertheless played the greatest roles in spreading the faith within their own communities. By and large, blacks who were enslaved received religious teaching from other blacks, clergy and laity—not from white plantation preachers, as is often assumed. Similarly, southern black Christians, such as Rev. Joseph C. PRICE, who founded Livingstone College in Salisbury, N.C., continued to play a major role in missionary outreach after the Civil War. These activities during the nineteenth and twentieth centuries established or helped establish a host of churches, schools and colleges, hospitals and medical clinics, banks and insurance companies, farm cooperatives, newspapers, and social agencies dedicated to the uplift of the disadvantaged.

In foreign missions, the greatest expenditures of time, resources, and personnel of the black churches have been in Canada, the Caribbean, and Africa. During the eighteenth and nineteenth centuries, a number of blacks fleeing southern slavery and northern discrimination migrated to Canada. They sometimes took their churches with them, and sometimes were followed by churches of various denominations, especially Baptists and Methodists. There was also a conscious expansion of Christianity by black North Americans into the Caribbean and South America during the nineteenth century, especially prior to the Civil War. Sometimes this extension was carried on by black denominations and associations. At other times, black missionaries representing predominantly white denominations, such as the Episcopalian James Theodore HOLLY, ventured to countries such as Haiti to establish Protestantism there.

The loyalties of some black Christians and/or their slaveholders to the British during the Revolutionary War had forced some of them to retire or be transported to either the British-controlled Caribbean or portions of Canada. George LIELE, a Georgia Baptist, ventured to Jamaica and there established the first Baptist church on the island. David GEORGE, another Georgia Baptist, traveled to Nova Scotia, ministered there for a number of years, and then journeyed with a group of Afro-Canadians to the British colony for repatriated enslaved persons in West Africa, Sierra

Leone. There he helped found the first Baptist church on the continent. Black Baptist denominational historians have traditionally accorded these persons the distinction of being the first two black American missionaries.

In many ways, the African missions movement represents the most dramatic and sustained efforts of black Americans to evangelize other lands. All major denominations of black Christians—Baptists, Methodists, and Pentecostalists—have participated in missionizing the continent, especially in its western and southern regions. The Presbyterian William Henry Sheppard, a missionary to the Congo in the late nineteenth and early twentieth centuries, however, represents two other types of black missionaries: those who ventured to other portions of Africa and those supported by predominantly white denominations. African missions among black Christians may be divided into three major periods: the colonization phase, from the latter part of the eighteenth century to the American Civil War; the independent organizational phase, from the Civil War to World War I; and the phase since World War I.

Prior to the Civil War, a great deal of African missionary outreach by black Christians was carried out in conjunction with movements to establish free blacks on the continent of Africa; thus, most of the evangelization efforts were concentrated in Liberia or nearby regions. Shortly after the formation of the predominantly white General Missionary Convention of the Baptist Denomination of the United States for Foreign Missions (or Triennial Convention), in 1814, a white Baptist deacon in Richmond, Va., William Crane, along with two black ministers, Lott CAREY and Collin Teague, established the Richmond African Baptist Missionary Society for the express purpose of sending the Gospel to Africa. The efforts of the society coincided with the foreign-missions interest of the Triennial Convention and the rising colonization movement to repatriate free blacks to Africa. This was symbolized and represented by the founding of the AMERICAN COLONIZATION SOCIETY in 1816–1817. William W. Colley, Teague, and their families relocated in Liberia, as a result of their own fundraising activities and in cooperation with the Triennial Convention and the American Colonization Society. A similar scenario occurred with Rev. Daniel COKER of the AME Church. He ventured to Sierra Leone in 1820 as a colonist supported by the American Colonization Society. But while there he also received support from the AME Church in the United States and established mission stations on behalf of the denomination.

With the conclusion of the Civil War, black Christians were free (and usually encouraged by many of their white counterparts) to pursue independent ec-

clesiastical arrangements. Interwoven with this ecclesiastical independence was the continuing conviction that American black Christians had a providential role to lift Africa from religious "paganism" and cultural "barbarism." Thus, state, regional, and national black Baptist groups and the two major black Methodist groups began to establish institutional apparatuses that would be devoted wholly to, or focused heavily upon, African missions (e.g., Virginia Baptist State Convention, Baptist Foreign Mission Convention, Women's Home and Foreign Mission Society of the AMEZ Church). This second phase of African missions was sometimes related to, but usually not as directly dependent upon, the principle of black migration or colonization as the first period. William W. Colley, John and Lucy Coles, Emma B. DeLaney, and most other missionaries did not venture to Africa with the intention of renouncing American citizenship or encouraging others to do so. They were more strictly missionaries, not colonists.

In addition, African missions geographically broadened during this period. The first phase tended to focus upon West Africa, especially Liberia. The independent organizational phase continued that focus but also expanded to central and southern Africa. Though Henry McNeal TURNER, an AME bishop, at the turn of the century renounced his American citizenship and called for some form of limited emigration to Africa, his focus on missionary work in southern Africa transcended his politics and helped to commit the denomination to intense involvement in that region. Emma B. DeLaney, a Florida Baptist, was a missionary in both southern and western Africa during the first two decades of the twentieth century. Her missionary activities indicate the presence of women on the mission fields, sometimes as partners with their husbands and sometimes, as with Delaney, as unmarried missionaries and evangelistic pioneers.

The Azusa Street Revival (1906–1909), which originated among black worshipers in Los Angeles, Calif., was the major impetus for the rise of most modern denominations of Pentecostalism. Blacks, whites, and others came from throughout the United States, around the world, and all walks of life to receive Pentecostal blessings in a crusade led by the black preacher William J. SEYMOUR. Both in the domestic sphere and overseas, the Pentecostal movement gave rise to a host of missionary endeavors. The revival, therefore, played a great role in extending Christianity to Africa as well as other lands. It was the activities of this second period that most clearly established the foundation of African missions for black Christians.

The third phase, from the time of World War I, has been characterized by an expansion upon the earlier foundation, continued interaction between many black and continental African Christians, and a slow but steady recognition of greater participation of Africans in the denominational apparatuses of the American-based churches. The urgency for evangelism and sense of racial solidarity and commitment that characterized the former periods have significantly subsided from the African-American churches' missions programs, especially since World War II. To the extent that this is the case, it is partly related to the greater role continental Africans have played in both politics and religion, and increased opportunities for black American involvement in domestic matters.

REFERENCES

COKER, DANIEL. *Journal of Daniel Coker*. Baltimore, 1820.

DRAKE, ST. CLAIR. *The Redemption of Africa and Black Religion*. Chicago, 1977.

JACOBS, SYLVIA M., ed. *Black Americans and the Missionary Movement in Africa*. Westport, Conn., 1982.

MARTIN, SANDY D. *Black Baptists and African Missions: The Origins of a Movement, 1880–1915*. Macon, Ga., 1989.

SERNETT, MILTON C. *Black Religion and American Evangelicalism: White Protestants, Plantation Missions, and the Flowering of Negro Christianity, 1787–1865*. Metuchen, N.J., 1975.

WALKER, JAMES W. ST. G. *The Black Loyalists: The Search for a Promised Land in Nova Scotia and Sierra Leone, 1783–1870*. New York, 1976.

WILLIAMS, WALTER L. *Black Americans and the Evangelization of Africa, 1877–1900*. Madison, Wis., 1982.

WILLS, DAVID W., and RICHARD NEWMAN, eds. *Black Apostles at Home and Abroad: Afro-Americans and the Christian Mission from the Revolution to Reconstruction*. Boston, 1982.

SANDY DWAYNE MARTIN

Mississippi. "Mississippi to my mind," a black schoolmaster asserted in 1915, "was the darkest section of the South for a colored man." The thought echoes through the annals of the African–American experience. In the antebellum period, hard-to-manage slaves in Tennessee or North Carolina were threatened with the ultimate punishment: sale "down the river" to the plantations of Mississippi. Late in the twentieth century, some 130 years after the EMANCIPATION, the state was still the object of invidious comparison. As one expatriate put it, "Mississippi was everybody's choice as the state that was the South at its worst."

In fact, since the post–World War II freedom struggle, much has changed and Mississippians of both races often deplore persisting negative images of their state. Yet, at least through the 1960s, Mississippi deserved its benighted reputation. By whatever measure—whether by its record of unpunished white racial violence, its discriminatory social policy, or its inflammatory political discourse—Mississippi seemed to be the American state most determined to deny full citizenship to blacks.

Explanations abound, but the most plausible include a population mix that throughout much of the state's history made whites a minority race fearful of "inundation" by a sea of blackness. Upon statehood in 1817, more than four in ten residents were black. Thereafter, as it entered the boom years of the cotton economy and slave imports from the upper South rose to meet mounting demands for labor, Mississippi's black population soared: By 1840 slaves outnumbered whites statewide, and by 1860 the ratio of slaves to whites in the state's richest cotton counties was greater than nine to one.

Decade by decade, the state's black population grew until 1900, when nearly six in every ten Mississippians were African Americans and nearly one in every ten American blacks was a Mississippian. Not until 1940, under the pressure of massive black migration to northern cities, did the population balance tip in favor of whites (51 percent white); and even then, through the end of the twentieth century, the black share of Mississippi's population was greater than that of any other state (36 percent in 1990).

During the antebellum years, all but a tiny fraction (0.2 percent in 1860) of black Mississippians were slaves, the great majority of whom were employed in the production of cotton. Slave circumstances improved somewhat toward the end of the period, as pioneering conditions faded in this relatively late-developing state and as horse-drawn mechanization gradually replaced the more primitive forms of hand labor. Black life and labor on Mississippi river plantations, however, were never anything but hard. Until the 1840s, all but the most privileged bondsmen (i.e., drivers, house servants, or skilled craftsmen) typically lived in communal housing rather than as families in cabins of their own. Their diet was usually ample, but often deficient in important nutrients. The gang system was the rule, and field hands were generally worked like teams of oxen until the gradual introduction of a modified task system (emphasizing incentives rather than punishment) was effected following advances in agricultural technology in the 1840s and '50s.

Late in the period, slaves also frequently enjoyed the meager returns from production and sale of garden produce. A fortunate few slave carpenters or mechanics sometimes managed to hire their own time, paying their masters a monthly fee but otherwise

Selling cotton in Clarksdale, Miss., 1939. Law and custom often severely circumscribed the economic rights of southern black farmers, but they were not entirely without bargaining power. (Prints and Photographs Division, Library of Congress)

conducting their own affairs from homes and shops in urban areas. By 1860, roughly one third of the population of such cities as Natchez, Vicksburg, Jackson, and Columbus were slaves, the great majority of them employed as domestic or manual laborers.

The state's slave code, to which all Mississippi slaves were subject, was perhaps the region's harshest. Although punishment for minor infractions was left to the discretion of masters and overseers, slaves accused of more serious crimes were subject to special courts and brutal punishment.

Under Mississippi law, any black was assumed "*prima facie* to be a slave." In fact, however, some black Mississippians were not slaves, though free blacks were never numerous and never truly free. In 1840, the peak year, free blacks totaled 1,366 (compared to 195,211 slaves); by 1860 the number had fallen to 773. Had laws governing this anomalous (and largely mulatto) population been strictly enforced there would have been fewer still. Seeking first to contain and then to eradicate entirely the free

black element, state legislators in 1823 severely circumscribed grounds for MANUMISSION and in 1857 outlawed emancipation entirely.

In 1831 all free blacks from sixteen to fifty years of age and not certified by county courts to be of "good character" were expelled from the state. Denied virtually every right of free citizenship, free blacks often fared little better than slaves. Some few voluntarily petitioned the state legislature for enslavement. Yet, for all this, some free blacks prospered as small farmers, skilled tradesmen, and even as businessmen. William Tiller Johnson, celebrated in history as the "barber of Natchez," and Scott Keyes, an Aberdeen shopkeeper, numbered among the most notable men of their class. In 1830, seventeen free black Mississippians (Johnson among them) were themselves slaveowners.

During the CIVIL WAR, black Mississippians voted with their feet, absconding from the plantations to Union lines at the first opportunity. Following the war, despite early white efforts to institute new forms of black servitude under one of the most restrictive BLACK CODES anywhere in the former Confederacy, Mississippi's freedmen briefly entered the body politic as full citizens. They controlled neither the state REPUBLICAN PARTY nor state government. While they helped send two members of their race to the U.S. Senate (Blanche K. BRUCE and Hiram REVELS) and one to the House (John R. LYNCH), most of the public offices to which they were elected were relatively minor. Yet during congressional RECONSTRUCTION they developed sufficient political leadership and group solidarity to translate their commanding share of the electorate into more public services and civil amenities than they would know for a hundred years. During the period, three black colleges were set up in the state: Rust College and Tougaloo University (later Tougaloo College) by the AMERICAN MISSIONARY ASSOCIATION, and Jackson State University, a state-funded institution. Even after Reconstruction, these institutions trained the black teaching and professional class, and were oases of culture for black Mississippians denied education elsewhere.

All too soon, following the reassertion of white rule under the First Mississippi Plan of 1875 (electoral fraud, violence, and intimidation), the moment passed. Subsequent decades brought virtually complete segregation, exclusion, discrimination, and dependency. Under the blatantly white supremacist state constitution of 1890 (the "Second Mississippi Plan"), a relative handful of middle-class blacks continued to vote and participate in an ineffectual, faction-ridden "Black and Tan Republican Party"; in 1903, even these were excluded by law from the all-important Democratic primary elections. (The most prominent black Republican from Mississippi in the late nineteenth century, Isaiah MONTGOMERY, who was the sole black delegate to the 1890 convention, voted for the franchise restriction that was adopted there. He was also a supporter of black enterprise and founded the independent black town of MOUND BAYOU.) Under the influence of the extreme racist James K. Vardaman, elected governor in 1904, segregation and black disempowerment in Mississippi became nearly absolute.

In the years after the Civil War, a distinctive regional culture arose in the Mississippi Delta, which surrounds the junction of the Mississippi and Yazoo rivers in the northwest of the state. Despite its fertile alluvial soil, the area was subject to floods, and was not much inhabited before the war—only 10 percent of its land was cleared by 1860. After 1865, the promise of rich, plentiful land brought large numbers of blacks to the Delta. However, they were rarely able to secure title to lands in the face of white terrorism, and then they were unable to surmount supply and transportation difficulties. In the 1880s, the new railroad lines and levees on the Mississippi River made large-scale agriculture possible. Businessmen-planters took over large tracts in the region from both black and white subsistence farmers, and planted cotton. By 1890, when blacks were disfranchised, 25 percent of the state's African Americans lived in the Delta region, where most of the counties were 80 to 90 percent black. Whites exploited this large landless labor force as tenants or sharecroppers.

By 1910, the Delta region featured the nation's widest gap between rural rich and poor. The whites' desire to maintain and control the black workforce led to the creation of a closed, Old South–style plantation system with a rigid class hierarchy, brutally enforced. The caste deference imposed upon blacks effectively stifled pressure for change. Unlike other agricultural regions, the Delta retained its semi-feudal agricultural system throughout the first half of the twentieth century, and during the New Deal, planters were enriched by the government at the expense of the black workforce. Since the 1950s, however, under the impact of mechanization and political changes, the system has in many ways broken down.

Though Mississippi produced many fine African-American folk artists, its most famous artistic legacy is undoubtedly BLUES music, created in the Delta around the turn of the century. The blues offered a mode of expression for feelings of joy and anger, and the songs told of the financial, social, and sexual difficulties of Mississippi life. The blues were spread and popularized by black migrants to Chicago and other places in the North. Delta blues musicians such as Charley PATTON and Robert JOHNSON created one of American's most important musical genres.

Under JIM CROW, as under slavery, black Mississippians resisted oppression but generally avoided suicidal confrontations with white power. The threat of white violence in a state that led all others in unpunished LYNCHINGS could not silence black dissatisfactions, but it kept black protest either underground or safely nonconfrontational. Black grievances were typically expressed not through the NAACP, but through women's clubs or conservative black leadership councils. For instance, the Mississippi State Federation of Colored Women's Clubs, founded in 1903, was able to exert a modest measure of political influence on the state government to expand funding for black health care institutions. However, for most black Mississippians, the only available way of protesting the oppressive political conditions and lack of economic opportunity was by migrating, and between 1910 and 1960, over one million blacks left the state. Black Mississippians who found fame elsewhere include Richard WRIGHT, Leontyne PRICE, and a large number of blues musicians, such as MUDDY WATERS and HOWLIN' WOLF, who created an electrified version of the Delta blues in Chicago.

Meanwhile, Mississippi remained firmly controlled by segregationists. Race-baiting politicians such as Theodore Bilbo, James Eastland, Ross Barnett, and John Stennis dominated the state's politics for decades. Despite the huge migration out of the state, its black population continued to grow. The relatively good wages available in the Delta attracted blacks from elsewhere in the South.

In the wake of the BROWN V. BOARD OF EDUCATION OF TOPEKA, KANSAS decision in 1954, blacks in Mississippi began to challenge the system openly. Mississippi was the arena for some of the bloodiest racial conflicts of the 1950s and '60s, as it became the symbol of intransigent white resistance to changing federal social policy. In 1955, a fourteen-year-old African American from Chicago, Emmet TILL, who was visiting relatives in Mississippi, was lynched for whistling at a white woman. This act of savagery sparked national outrage. The state's NAACP branch, led by Medgar EVERS, began intense civil rights and voter registration efforts. The agents of change, it must be emphasized, were largely homegrown; in Mississippi, as elsewhere in the South, black protest originated at the community level. National civil rights organizations, including the region-wide VOTER EDUCATION PROJECT, and the Council of Federated Organizations (a coalition of the CONGRESS OF RACIAL EQUALITY, the SOUTHERN CHRISTIAN LEADERSHIP CONFERENCE, the STUDENT NONVIOLENT COORDINATING COMMITTEE, and the NAACP) contributed invaluably. The federal government contributed indispensable (if belated) support. The real heroes of the freedom struggle included not only such justly celebrated indigenous leaders as Aaron Henry, James MEREDITH, Medgar Evers, and Fannie Lou HAMER, but the black masses who marched in such communities as McComb and Greenwood and carried on voter registration efforts.

In 1940, 0.4 percent of all eligible black Mississippians were registered to vote, but despite intense black efforts, by 1964 the figure had risen to only 6.7 percent. The state was home to a region-wide, militant White Citizens' Council movement, organized to resist federally mandated school desegregation. State legislators also formed a State Sovereignty Commission (Mississippi's "KGB of race") and enacted more anti–civil rights measures than any other southern state. This campaign of massive resistance blocked the advancement of civil rights for a decade following *Brown* v. *Board of Education.*

Conflict in Mississippi came to a head during FREEDOM SUMMER in 1964. Civil rights organizations recruited black and white college students to travel to Mississippi in order to lead civil rights and voter registration efforts, and to fight illiteracy and teach about black history and culture by starting "Freedom Schools." Despite the disappearance at the beginning of the summer of three civil rights workers—James Chaney, an African American, and Michael Schwerner and Andrew Goodman, two whites—who were later found dead, the project continued, in the face of large-scale southern white harassment and violence. With the help of civil rights workers, the MISSISSIPPI FREEDOM DEMOCRATIC PARTY, an indigenous non-racial alternative political organization, was founded and its leaders traveled that summer to the Democratic convention in Atlantic City in an unsuccessful attempt to replace the regular white Democratic organization. Change came rapidly after the enactment of the Civil Rights Act of 1964 and the VOTING RIGHTS ACT in 1965, which brought token desegregation of schools and public accommodations and massive black enfranchisement.

Inevitably, in the new Mississippi born of such turmoil, tradition persisted within change. After 1965, despite continuing official efforts to vitiate the Voting Rights Act, the state emerged as a center of black political influence. In the early 1970s, for the first time in this century, blacks were appointed to state agencies and even to the state highway patrol. By 1980, Mississippi led the South in black voter registration (measured absolutely and as a percentage of those eligible); and by 1985, it had more black elected officials (613) than any other state. Although blacks did not win elections in proportion to their population—and such offices as they won were likely to be lesser posts in municipal and county government—some held major offices.

By 1985, there were twenty black state legislators and a black state supreme court justice. State Rep. Robert G. Clark, the first black to serve in the legislature since the 1890s and the first black congressional candidate ever nominated by the state Democratic Party, lost racially charged congressional races in 1982 and 1984. But in 1986, Democrat Michael Espy defeated a conservative white Republican incumbent to become the state's first black congressman since John R. Lynch. In 1993 he was appointed secretary of agriculture by President Bill Clinton.

By the early 1990s, 21 percent of the state's legislators were African American, the highest percentage in the nation. Notwithstanding these promising developments, racial division continued to trouble Mississippi's political life. Through the end of the 1980s, only the repeated intervention of federal authority denied official efforts to dilute the black vote in municipal, county, and statewide elections. Racial appeals, although usually fairly subtle, still sullied the political process and, in election after election, voting patterns were characterized by extreme racial polarization. In the 1970s, separate white and black factions merged to form a unified Democratic party, yet black candidates remained almost wholly dependent on black votes.

Although a few prominent black Mississippians, including Fayette mayor Charles EVERS, joined an increasingly viable state Republican party, the Mississippi GOP remained essentially white in membership and in appeal. National Republican "southern strategists," eager to capitalize on Democratic identification with civil rights, found a warm reception in Mississippi. Between 1956 and 1992, only one Democratic presidential candidate, southern-born Jimmy Carter (1976), carried Mississippi.

Still generally described as the most "southern" of the southern states—the poorest, the most rural, the "blackest," the most tradition-bound—Mississippi at the end of the twentieth century defies easy characterization. The state could no longer be called a "white man's country," but isolated anachronisms of the color line could be found in nearly any community. Though diminishing in number, "segregation academies" continued to provide white refuge from social change in counties with large black populations. Blacks and whites mingled on Mississippi's predominantly white college campuses about as easily as anywhere in the nation, yet in 1992 the U.S. Supreme Court found that its predominantly black institutions of higher learning remained largely separate and unequal.

These were vexing problems, but they were widely shared in a nation that was itself still plagued by racial divisions. Still haunted by their past, confronted at every hand by evidence that so much and so little has changed, Mississippians, perhaps for the first time since statehood, could claim that now at least their racial problems approximated those of the rest of the United States.

REFERENCES

CAGIN, SETH, and PHILIP DRAY. *We Are Not Afraid: The Story of Goodman, Schwerner, and Chaney and the Civil Rights Campaign for Mississippi.* New York, 1988.
COBB, JAMES A. *The Most Southern Place on Earth: The Mississippi Delta and the Roots of Southern Identity.* New York, 1992.
FERRIS, WILLIAM A. *Blues from the Delta.* New York, 1984.
MCADAM, DOUG. *Freedom Summer.* New York, 1988.
MCMILLEN, NEIL R. "Black Enfranchisement in Mississippi: Federal Enforcement and Black Protest in the 1960s." *Journal of Southern History* 43 (1977).
———. *Dark Journey: Black Mississippians in the Age of Jim Crow.* Urbana, Ill., 1989.
MOODY, ANNE. *Coming of Age in Mississippi.* New York, 1968.
PARKER, FRANK R. *Black Votes Count: Political Empowerment in Mississippi After 1965.* Chapel Hill, N.C. 1990.
SYDNOR, CHARLES S. "The Free Negro in Mississippi Before the Civil War." *American Historical Review* 32 (1927).
———. *Slavery in Mississippi.* New York, 1933.
WHARTON, VERNON LANE. *The Negro in Mississippi, 1865–1890.* New York, 1947.

NEIL R. MCMILLEN

Mississippi Freedom Democratic Party.

The Mississippi Freedom Democratic Party (MFDP), a predominantly African-American party that existed from 1964 to the early 1970s, was one of America's most significant third political parties. SNCC, the STUDENT NONVIOLENT COORDINATING COMMITTEE, did not establish MFDP to permanently replace the regular Mississippi Democratic party. On the contrary, SNCC intended MFDP to be an alternative that would allow black and white Mississippians to be in a party that shared the same views as the national organization.

MFDP contested the right of the regular Mississippi Democratic party to represent the state's black voting-age population at the Democratic National Committee's (DNC) 1964 and 1968 conventions. The state Democratic party and state election officials had deprived most blacks of the opportunity to take part in state politics (*see* MISSISSIPPI). In addition, the regular Mississippi Democratic party opposed the civil rights positions of the national party (*see* DEMOCRATIC PARTY). At the state Democratic convention of July 1964, delegates passed a resolution calling for the immediate repeal of the recently passed Civil Rights Act of 1964. Furthermore, in that same year the regular Mississippi party repudiated the Democratic presidential and vice presidential candidates, Lyndon Johnson and Hubert Humphrey, urging white citizens of the state to vote for Republican Barry Goldwater. On the other hand, MFDP supported the national party's positions and nominee. Initially, black Mississippians organized MFDP in part to take the place of the regular state party at the 1964 DNC's convention if the regular party walked out over the issue of civil rights. But in addition to being a party waiting in the wings, MFDP registered black voters by the tens of thousands. Thus, it succeeded in empowering blacks in Mississippi politics for the first time since the end of the nineteenth century, despite white harassment. It emphasized political education to help black Mississippians learn about the political process, so as to make informed choices once they exercised their right of franchise in earnest.

The idea for the formation of MFDP developed shortly after the end of SNCC's "Freedom Vote" campaign to protest the 1963 Mississippi gubernatorial election. Responding to the success of that campaign, Robert MOSES of SNCC proposed that blacks participate in mock state elections to vote for "Freedom candidates." To create national attention, the FREEDOM SUMMER campaign used white northern college students to help SNCC conduct a mock protest vote by registering thousands of blacks to express their outrage with the wholesale disfranchisement of blacks in Mississippi. Realizing the futility of registering thousands of blacks without challenging the discriminatory practices of the state Democratic party, SNCC in April 1964 founded MFDP to run candidates in Mississippi and to contest the loyalty of the Mississippi Democrats to the national party. SNCC took these measures to expose the fact that few blacks could take part in precinct meetings of the regular state party. In the few cases where party officials permitted blacks access to meetings, they denied blacks the right to speak or vote. After experi-

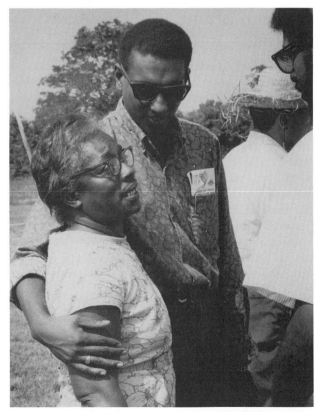

Annie Devine, founder with Victoria Gray and Fannie Lou Hamer of the Mississippi Freedom Democratic Party, with Stokely Carmichael at the James Meredith March in Mississippi, June 12, 1966. (© Charmian Reading)

encing similar treatment at county conventions and the state convention, members of MFDP conducted their own precinct meetings and held their own state convention in June 1964 to select delegates to the DNC in Atlantic City who would support the national ticket.

Members of MFDP went to Atlantic City believing that their planned contest of the seats assigned to the state party had a reasonable chance of success. In reality, the MFDP leadership received an education on how politics at the national level operated. While a number of MFDP delegates sincerely believed that moral persuasion would lead the DNC to refuse the regular state party the state's allotment of seats, President Johnson had his own agenda. Johnson, running without opposition for the nomination for president, wanted a smooth convention. He feared a southern walkout if the DNC seated MFDP. Johnson ordered the FBI to wiretap MFDP's office, as well as the hotel rooms of the Rev. Dr. Martin Luther KING, Jr., and Bayard RUSTIN. Johnson knew the positions of civil rights groups and key leaders throughout the convention. He also threatened the patronage of those who might have been inclined to support the MFDP. In addition, he coerced Walter Reuther, head of the United Auto Workers union, to threaten to cut off financial support to SNCC and MFDP in Mississippi if the challenge was not withdrawn.

This threat did not alter the determination of the protestors. Before a televised hearing of the Credentials Committee, the deeply affecting testimony of Fannie Lou HAMER led Johnson to stage a news conference in an effort to stop public opinion from mounting to the point that he had to give seats to MFDP. Johnson forced Hubert Humphrey to try to convince the challengers not to go forward. This was a test of Humphrey's personal loyalty. Johnson told him the vice presidential position on the ticket depended on how he handled the controversy. Humphrey offered MFDP two seats representing the state of Mississippi, and the rest of the MFDP delegation were to be "honored guests" at the convention. MFDP refused this offer, demanding at least the seats proportionate to the state's blacks of voting age. Unwilling to compromise, the challengers got no seats, but they did manage to obtain the credentials of sympathetic delegates from states that disapproved of the regular Mississippi delegation. Several members of MFDP staged a sit-in demonstration on the convention floor, but security guards quickly removed the protestors.

MFDP members left the convention embittered by their experience. Feeling betrayed by the actions of northern liberals and civil rights moderates such as King and Rustin who had supported the compromise option proposed by Humphrey, MFDP and SNCC became more militant after the convention. The DNC did unseat the regular Mississippi Democrats in 1968 (as promised at the 1964 convention) when the state party persisted in denying access to blacks. As a consequence of this action, the Mississippi Democratic party ended the discriminatory practices and customs it had used to exclude blacks from meaningful participation in party affairs.

REFERENCE

MCLEMORE, LESLIE B. The Mississippi Freedom Democratic Party: A Case Study of Grass Roots Politics. Ph.D. diss., University of Massachusetts, 1971.

MICHAEL A. COOKE

Missouri. The land that comprises present-day Missouri was colonized in the early part of the eighteenth century by France, as part of the Louisiana Territory. Around 1717 slaveowning Jesuit missionaries came to the area. In 1719 French explorer Marc Antoine de la Loëre Des Ursins, seeking silver mines in Upper Louisiana, brought five enslaved blacks from Saint Domingue (later Haiti) as workers. The following year, Philip Renault brought five hundred blacks into the region to work in lead mines. Slavery flourished, and Africans soon replaced enslaved Native American inhabitants as the colony's chief labor force. A rich planter named Valet worked one hundred slaves in lumbering and growing corn. Most worked in lead and salt mines, or as servants in the settlements of St. Louis, St. Charles, and Ste. Geneviève. The French *code noir* provided for slaves to be given instruction in the Roman Catholic faith, and by mid-century Ste. Geneviève had a thriving black Catholic community. After 1763, when Spain acquired Louisiana, cultivation of flax and hemp replaced mining as the main occupation of blacks. By 1803, when the United States acquired the territory of Missouri following the Louisiana Purchase, there were 10,340 people in the area, 1,320 of them black slaves. There were also seventy-seven free blacks, most in St. Louis. One notable free black Missourian of the period was Jean Baptiste DU SABLE, founder of Chicago, who settled in St. Charles around 1805 and died there in 1818.

Missouri was not as conducive to cotton growing in the nineteenth century as the Deep South, but possibilities existed for slave labor in tobacco and hemp production. The territory's good river outlets and mid-state band of fertile alluvial soil caused an influx of slaveowners and their chattels in the years after 1803, and again from 1812 to 1825. The Missouri Territory's BLACK CODE, passed in 1804, was relatively lenient, though those with one quarter or more African-American ancestry were denied suffrage and were forbidden to testify against whites in court.

In 1819 Missouri applied to join the Union as a slave state. Its admission was opposed by antislavery Northerners, but after the 1820 MISSOURI COMPROMISE, which provided that new slave states must be admitted paired with free states, it became a state in 1821. The state's first constitution mandated jury trials with court-appointed counsel for blacks accused of capital crimes, and equal punishment with whites for equal offenses.

Once admitted to the Union, Missouri's slave population grew steadily. Most slaveowners held only one or two slaves, who grew grains, tobacco, hemp, and flax, or were craftworkers. Others were hired out as railway or riverboat and dock workers, or toiled in iron factories and brickyards. While the percentage of slaves in the population declined after 1830, this was due to large-scale Irish and German immigration and not to the decline of the slave system. As a rule, masters allowed slaves to have Sunday afternoons to themselves, during which time they often manufactured small articles for sale or tended small plots of land adjoining slave quarters. Many slaves applied the proceeds of these ventures to the purchase of their freedom.

Not all blacks in antebellum Missouri were enslaved. Most free blacks lived in the cities because of greater opportunities there. By 1860 almost half of Missouri's 3,752 free African Americans were located in St. Louis. They served as farmers, cooks, painters, carpenters, blacksmiths, ministers, tinners, and shopkeepers. Despite numerous obstacles, some free blacks achieved success. The Rev. John Berry Meachum was the owner of a barrel factory and two steamboats, and he used his wealth to shield and help emancipate slaves. William Wells BROWN, a Missouri slave, became a famous author and abolitionist after escaping in 1834. In 1846, the Rev. Moses DICKSON of St. Louis met with eleven other black men and founded the TWELVE KNIGHTS OF TABOR, which Dickson later claimed led a secret revolutionary group, the Knights of Liberty, and aided hundreds of slaves to escape to freedom. The antebellum African-American Missourian who achieved the greatest fame in his time was Dred Scott, a St. Louis slave who in 1846 instituted a suit for his freedom that resulted in the epochal 1857 U.S. Supreme Court decision, *Dred Scott* v. *Sanford* (see DRED SCOTT DECISION). Although Scott lost the case, he was freed shortly thereafter.

Although surrounded by free states, most Missouri whites were belligerently proslavery. Treatment of African Americans, whether slave or free, remained harsh. In 1835 Missouri passed an act "to prevent free Negroes and mulattoes from coming to, and settling in, this state." According to the law, free blacks from the ages of seven to twenty-one were to be taken away from their parents and bound as "apprentices," a thinly disguised form of slavery. Free African Americans, to reside in a Missouri county, had to obtain county court licenses, and either arrange white guarantors or post a bond of $500 or more to ensure good behavior. For the next twenty years, there was little or no free black immigration to Missouri. As early as 1817, fearing insurrection, the territorial government passed an act that restricted black travel and made assembling, even for the purpose of education, illegal for African Americans. The law was strengthened in 1847, following the growth of abolitionist literature, specifically to forbid African Americans from learning to read and write.

Despite the laws, various schools were set up to teach blacks. St. Louis blacks ran church schools in the 1820s and '30s, and whites such as Timothy Flint, a northern minister who opened a school in St. Charles, also taught school. Both of the African Americans who were later to serve in the U.S. Senate during RECONSTRUCTION taught in antebellum Missouri. During the CIVIL WAR, Hiram REVELS operated a school in St. Louis, while Blanche K. BRUCE took over duties at the Rev. Tom Henderson's school in Hannibal. Catholic schools for blacks were founded near St. Louis in 1845 and in 1855, but both were forced to close shortly after opening.

As a border state, Missouri was torn by strife from within and without during the Civil War, as the state was riven by battles between pro-slavery and pro-Union factions. Despite the efforts of pro-Confederate Gov. Claiborne Jackson, Missouri remained pro-Union and did not secede. Shortly after the war began, Missouri was occupied by Union troops commanded by John C. Frémont, who issued an order emancipating all slaves within his jurisdiction. President Abraham Lincoln, fearing the order's effect on border state sentiment, almost immediately countermanded it. Slave contrabands were, however, employed by the Union Army as teamsters, cooks, and construction workers. Missouri was not covered by the 1863 Emancipation Proclamation (see EMANCIPATION), but many slaveowners rightly understood that slavery's existence was threatened by the conflict. In 1862 Missouri John W. Noell proposed in Congress that the state's masters be given $10 million in compensation for their property. Although black Kansas regiments served at the Battle of Mound Island, Mo., in 1862, Missouri African Americans were not recruited for service until July 1863. Slaves were drafted or volunteered to fill quotas. Bounties and compensation were given to slaveowners, but many

nevertheless opposed what they saw as legalized emancipation. Soon, despite terror campaigns against black recruits by pro-Southern bushwhackers, five black regiments were created, and Missouri ultimately sent 8,400 African Americans to fight in the Union Army. Many African-American women volunteered as nurses. Slaves also took advantage of the wartime confusion to escape from farms to cities or out of state. By 1864 only one fifth of the prewar slave population was still in bondage. That year, a Radical Unionist party gained power, and called a state constitutional convention. On January 11, 1865, eleven months before ratification of the THIRTEENTH AMENDMENT, slavery was formally banned in Missouri.

When the Civil War ended, Missouri freedmen found themselves in an extremely precarious position. In Boone County, a group of white terrorists, led by Jim Jackson, attacked and murdered blacks and destroyed schools. Many freedmen left the state in search of greater opportunity in states such as Illinois. Many sought work and education in towns and cities such as St. Louis, Jefferson City, Columbia, and Kansas City. Hannibal's booming lumber industry attracted an influx of black workers, which pushed the town's black population to 40 percent of the total before declining after the industry waned. Although the ban on black literacy was not officially overturned until 1870, blacks worked to educate themselves. In 1865 the Western Sanitary Commission, a white charitable organization, started four schools and a high school in St. Louis. Soon after, a colored school board was established. After 1865 the AMERICAN MISSIONARY ASSOCIATION established schools throughout the state. In 1866 the Missouri Legislature passed a school law which stated that separate schools should be provided for African-American children where they numbered more than twenty in a district. School segregation would be legally reinforced four times in the next dozen years. Also in 1866, Lincoln Institute (later LINCOLN UNIVERSITY) was founded at Jefferson City. Funded out of the contributions of soldiers of Missouri's 62nd and 65th U.S. Colored Infantry regiments who wished to educate their children, it stands as a tribute to them and to educators such as Inman PAGE, Nathan Young, and Wendell Rayburn.

Politically, Missouri freedmen remained largely powerless. Unlike in Deep South states that underwent federal Reconstruction, there were no black political office-holders during the postwar period. In 1865 the Missouri Equal Rights League, made up largely of St. Louis ministers, was created to press for voting rights. A seven-man steering committee, led by Moses DICKSON, drafted an *Address to the Friends of Equal Rights*, which called for suffrage as indispens-

Allegorical print commemorating the ordinance providing for the emancipation of slaves in Missouri. The ordinance was passed on January 11, 1865, three weeks before the Thirteenth Amendment was proposed in Congress. Originally published in *The Westliche Post* in St. Louis, Mo., 1865. (Prints and Photographs Division, Library of Congress)

able to progress and hired lawyer John Mercer LANG-STON as a speaker and lobbyist. No action, however, was taken until the passage of the FIFTEENTH AMENDMENT in 1870, when blacks were enfranchised. That year, James Milton Turner, a black writer and orator and Kansas City public school teacher who was later named U.S. Minister to Liberia, organized a convention in Jefferson City to push for civil rights legislation in exchange for political support. State politicians refused, but they did appropriate $5000 for Lincoln Institute toward the training of teachers, a gift that assured the Institute's survival. Although blacks retained the vote in the post-Reconstruction period, prejudice and lack of education kept African Americans from holding office or serving on juries. In 1879 the arrival of thousands of Southern black EXODUSTERS trying to make their way to Kansas inflamed racial tension in Missouri. By the 1880s, the REPUBLICAN PARTY had largely

abandoned its support of blacks. After repeated delegations to state and national officials failed to bring about aid, the Missouri Republican Union, the main black political group, planned a statewide convention in 1882, and announced that blacks would throw their support to the party that offered the best deal. Except in the cities, though, neither party generally campaigned for the African-American vote.

Although public transportation remained integrated, by the beginning of the twentieth century segregation was informal but almost universal. Beginning in 1903, rural Democrats attempted repeatedly to impose legal color bars, but such attempts were defeated by a coalition of Republicans and urban Democrats dependent on black support. Nevertheless, black Missourians were largely reduced to menial and domestic labor, or to tenant farming. Racial violence was a chronic threat. In 1906 three blacks were lynched in Springfield.

Excluded from white institutions, blacks formed their own churches, financial institutions, social clubs, and FRATERNITIES, such as the large Masonic Temple and Masonic Home in Hannibal. Throughout the period, a few Missouri African Americans made names for themselves. Pianist Scott JOPLIN, who lived and worked in Sedalia and St. Louis, popularized RAGTIME with his bestselling *Maple Leaf Rag* (1899), named for a Sedalia club. Joplin and other musicians such as Tom Turpin turned St. Louis into the center of the ragtime craze. Publisher John W. Wheeler made the *St. Louis Palladium* (1884–1911) into a source of news and advice. Missouri ex-slave Tom Bass was a famous show horse trainer. Kansas City also became a musical center during the 1920s and 1930s, and was home to such figures as Count BASIE, Mary Lou WILLIAMS, and the young Charlie PARKER. In 1910 physician and activist Dr. J. Edward PERRY organized the Perry Sanitarium and Nurse Training School (later Wheatly-Provident Hospital), the first black private hospital in Kansas City. During the first half of the century, several native-born African-American Missourians, including scientist George Washington CARVER (born a slave in Diamond Grove), entertainer Josephine BAKER, writer Langston HUGHES, and jazz artist Coleman HAWKINS (born in St. Joseph) achieved fame in other places.

In 1898 Missouri blacks from the 70th Regiment fought in the SPANISH–AMERICAN WAR. In 1916 a contingent was sent to Mexico to capture Pancho Villa. The coming of WORLD WAR I in 1917 prompted massive black enlistment, in the hope that Allied victory would gain them full citizenship. Eventually almost 10,000 of the state's blacks served in the armed forces during the period. Wartime labor shortages and the cutoff of European immigration brought thousands of blacks from rural Missouri and the Deep South to the towns and cities to fill the gaps in the factories and railroads. Widespread racial tension resulted from competition for jobs and scarce housing resources.

The postwar years brought little substantive improvement in the status of Missouri's black population. The Missouri State Negro Industrial Commission, founded in 1918, and the local branch of the NATIONAL URBAN LEAGUE, founded in the 1920s, tried to aid black business and train workers. White unions organized opposition to the introduction of African-American workers, whom they feared would lower wage scales. Labor leader A. Philip RANDOLPH made a special effort to organize Missouri's railway porters, but was able to organize only a handful out of the state's large force into a union. Segregation remained entrenched, and many blacks, particularly returning soldiers, were attacked and lynched. During the 1920s, Missouri became a center

of the KU KLUX KLAN, and in 1924, a particularly brutal lynching occurred in Charleston. In the meantime, blacks did organize politically. In 1920 the Colored Liberty League and the Missouri Negro Republican League joined forces to elect the state's first black legislator, Walthall Moore of St. Louis.

The GREAT DEPRESSION in Missouri hurt African Americans hardest of all. Many blacks were laid off from jobs once considered "black"—waiters, porters, and menial laborers—which were now being filled by whites. Lynchings occurred in St. Joseph in 1933 and Sikeston in 1941, and there were race riots in Holland and elsewhere during the 1934 election campaign, and in Oran in 1939.

President Franklin Roosevelt's New Deal brought hope for African Americans, and the president made key appointments of Missouri blacks. In 1935 Dr. William J. Thompkins, a Kansas City physician and politician, was named Recorder of Deeds for the District of Columbia, while St. Louis newspaperman Lester A. Walton was selected as Minister to Liberia. New Deal agencies helped African-American laborers. However, government officials were reluctant to challenge the racial status quo. In Kansas City, blacks were for several years excluded from work on Public Works Administration projects, though they had the city's highest unemployment rate. In 1937 St. Louis blacks secured Homer Phillips Hospital, a $3 million federally sponsored black medical facility, named for a local attorney who had been prominent in lobbying for it. White unions refused to allow black construction workers on the project. The sharecroppers of the southeastern Missouri "boot-heel" were also hit hard by the economic crisis. Both blacks and whites were reduced to living in crude, dilapidated shacks. Their average annual income was pitifully small, reaching only $251 in 1936. In search of better conditions, they formed the Southern Tenant Farmer's Union and asked employers to abolish tenant farming and the sharecropping system and institute a ten-hour day. In January 1939, more than 1,000 sharecroppers were evicted from their houses. Black and whites, led by black Baptist minister Owen W. Whitfield, together organized a roadside march along Highways 60 and 61 to publicize their situation. Without any source of income, they lived in misery for several months. Eventually, Lincoln University students raised money for their support, and helped buy land near Poplar Bluff to form a colony, "Cropperville." After the Farm Security Association provided home construction loans at low interest, and black leaders raised funds to set up a loan guarantee corporation and cooperative grocery store, the interracial settlement prospered.

The struggle for equality in Missouri was a long one. The NATIONAL ASSOCIATION FOR THE AD-

New Deal agencies set an important precedent by directly assisting local communities of southern blacks. Farming families in southeastern Missouri in 1938 listen to a Farm Security Agency project manager. (Prints and Photographs Division, Library of Congress)

VANCEMENT OF COLORED PEOPLE (NAACP) was growing and becoming more powerful through the mid-1930s, because of the efforts of Kansas City chair Roy WILKINS and others. In 1936 Lloyd Gaines, a Lincoln University student, was denied admission to the University of Missouri Law School. NAACP lawyers Charles R. Houston and Sidney Redmond of St. Louis took his case before the U.S. Supreme Court, which ruled in 1938 that the University of Missouri had to admit him or establish an equal facility. Although Gaines mysteriously vanished before the mandate was issued, the ruling was the prelude to all later assaults on the "separate but equal" doctrine. In any case, rather than admit Gaines, Missouri established a short-lived, inadequate law school at Lincoln University, which opened in the Poro building in St. Louis in 1940. Two years later, Missouri opened the Lincoln University School of Journalism rather than integrate state facilities.

WORLD WAR II brought many changes in the lives of African Americans, not the least of which was the promise of increased economic security. The wartime labor shortage led to large numbers of new jobs for blacks. Urbanization increased, and in its wake came problems with housing, recreation, employment, education, and other matters. This led African Americans to redouble their efforts to gain recognition of their rights. In 1947 Archbishop Joseph Ritter integrated St. Louis-area Catholic schools. The following year, the U.S. Supreme Court ruled in *Shelley* v. *Kramer*, a case originating in St. Louis, that restrictive housing covenants were unenforceable. In 1949 the University of Missouri opened its doors to black students. Most attempts to secure equal access through lawsuits, however, were unsuccessful, and school desegregation in Missouri was postponed until after the 1954 BROWN V. BOARD OF EDUCATION OF TOPEKA, KANSAS decision. (Lincoln University, integrated in 1954, became a white majority institution in the 1980s). Token desegregation was achieved in Missouri, mostly in the large cities, during the 1950s. In 1953 the legislature secured African-

American access to roadside restaurants for bus passengers. In 1957, with the support of liberal Gov. James T. Blair, the Missouri Human Rights Commission was created to investigate civil rights abuses.

The 1960s saw the most dramatic change in Missouri's pattern of race relations. In 1960, sit-ins forced stores and restaurants in St. Louis, Kansas City, and Jefferson City to serve blacks, and in 1963 further sit-ins forced city authorities to pass equal rights ordinances. Federal civil rights legislation led to increased economic and educational opportunity for black Missourians, but continued discrimination led to frustration and anger. In 1968, after the assassination of the Rev. Dr. Martin Luther KING, Jr., Kansas City erupted, and authorities were compelled to call out the entire 900-man police force, as well as 1,700 National Guardsmen and 168 state troopers to quell the violence. Jefferson City and other areas had smaller racial outbreaks.

Since the 1960s, the economic status of black Missourians has remained bleak, as unemployment and poverty have increased, and the social and educational picture is far from encouraging. During the 1980s alone, Missouri lost 35,000 African Americans to migration. Discrimination in housing and income have kept cities largely segregated. School desegregation has been a slow and painful process. Despite court orders in St. Louis and Kansas City, implementation is far from absolute. Yet the availability and nature of college education for African Americans has changed drastically. The black college population rose dramatically, and black educators such as Marguerite Ross Barnett, chancellor of the University of Missouri-St. Louis (later the first black female head of a major university) gained prominence. Many black Missourians of the period became prominent in other fields as well, some notable examples being scholar Oliver Cromwell COX, writer Chester HIMES, labor leader Andrew McKenzie, and Miss America Debbye Turner.

Black Missourians have made great strides in the political arena. In 1969 William Clay of St. Louis became the state's first black U.S. Congressman. Kansas City's Alan Wheat was elected to Congress in 1982. By 1993 St. Louis and Kansas City, neither of which was a black majority city, each had elected black mayors. There were also fourteen black state representatives, including three black state senators. However, a redistricting plan which threatened to reduce the number of African Americans in office, and which was challenged by African-American leaders, was upheld in 1993 by the U.S. Supreme Court. It remains to be seen how the decision will affect the political gains made by African Americans in Missouri.

REFERENCES

CANTOR, LOUIS. *A Prologue to the Protest Movement: The Missouri Sharecropper Roadside Demonstration of 1939*. Durham, N.C., 1969.

CURTIS, WILLIAM J. *A Rich Heritage: A Black History of Independence, Missouri*. Atlanta, 1985.

ELWONG, WILLIAM WILSON. *The Negroes of Columbia, Missouri: A Concrete Study of the Race Problem*. 1904. Reprint. Northbrook, Ill., 1972.

FOLEY, WILLIAM E. *The Genesis of Missouri: From Frontier Outpost to Statehood*. Columbia, Mo., 1989.

GREENE, LORENZO J., GARY R. KREMER, and ANTONIO F. HOLLAND, *Missouri's Black Heritage*. Rev. ed. Columbia, Mo., 1993.

HUGHES, JOHN STARRETT. *Lafayette County and the Aftermath of Slavery*. Columbia, Mo., 1980.

KREMER, GARY R. *James Milton Turner and the Promise of America: The Public Life of a Post-Civil War Black Leader*. Columbia, Mo., 1991.

MORRIS, ANN. *North Webster: A Photographic History of a Black Community*. Bloomington, Ind., 1993.

TREXLER, HARRISON. *Slavery in Missouri, 1804–1865*. 1914. Reprint. New York, 1986.

U.S. Commission on Civil Rights. *Race Relations in the "Kingdom" of Callaway*. Washington, D.C., 1979.

ANTONIO F. HOLLAND

Missouri Compromise. The Missouri Compromise of 1820 directly affected African Americans by prohibiting SLAVERY in the land acquired in the Louisiana Purchase north of the 36° 30' line, but allowing slavery in Missouri itself. At the time the American Southwest belonged to Mexico. Thus the Missouri Compromise implied that the nation would eventually have more free states than slave states. Congressional debates over it signaled the beginning of public discourse over the place of slavery and the rights of free blacks (*see* FREE BLACKS IN THE NORTH; FREE BLACKS, 1619-1860) in the United States.

The Missouri Compromise also allowed Maine, previously part of Massachusetts, to enter the Union as a free state. The new state of Maine had few blacks, but those who did live there had almost total equality. The state allowed blacks to vote on the same basis as whites and did not segregate its schools or any other institutions.

At the same time, Missouri would come into the Union as a slave state. When it entered the Union, Missouri adopted a constitution that prohibited the state legislature from ending slavery without the consent of slaveholders and required the legislature to prohibit the migration of free blacks into the state. Northern congressmen opposed these constitutional provisions—especially the one requiring a prohibition on the migration of free blacks. In the resolution admitting Missouri, Congress declared that the state constitution "shall never be construed to authorize the passage of any law" denying a citizen of "the privileges and immunities" of an American citizen. Despite this provision, in 1848 Missouri prohibited free blacks from entering the state.

The provisions of the Missouri Compromise were not to last. The Kansas–Nebraska Act of 1854 effectively superceded the Missouri Compromise by allowing popular sovereignty to determine the fate of slavery in the Nebraska territories. In the DRED SCOTT DECISION (1857), Chief Justice Taney declared that the entire provision violated the Constitution.

REFERENCES

FREEHLING, WILLIAM W. *The Road to Disunion: Secessionists at Bay, 1776–1854.* New York, 1990.
MOORE, GLOVER. *The Missouri Controversy, 1819–1821.* Lexington, Ky., 1953.

PAUL FINKELMAN

Mitchell, Abbie (1884–1960), singer and actress. Abbie Mitchell was born in New York City and grew up in Baltimore. In 1898, at the age of fourteen, she auditioned for Paul Laurence DUNBAR and Will Marion COOK's musical *Clorindy; or, The Origin of the Cakewalk.* She was cast in the show and in that year married Cook. Her first voice lessons were with Harry T. BURLEIGH and Mme. Emilia Serrano. Mitchell played many lead roles in musicals composed and/or conducted by Cook, and in other important shows of the time, including Bert WILLIAMS and George Walker's *In Dahomey* and Bob COLE and J. Rosamond JOHNSON's *Red Moon.* She toured from 1906 to 1908 in the United States and Europe with the Memphis Students, but interrupted her career to prepare for the concert stage.

Mitchell studied voice in Paris with Jean de Reszke. She specialized in German lieder, although her concert offerings from opera (e.g., "Rittonna Vincintor" from *Aida*), won uniformly high praise. Mitchell worked as an actress at New York's Lafayette Theatre from 1912 to 1924. In 1924 she collaborated with Flournoy Miller, Aubrey Lyles, and Cook to create *Negro Nuances,* a musical history of African Americans. In 1926 she played the mother in Paul Green's Pulitzer Prize–winning play *In Abraham's Bosom.* She also performed in *Damaged Goods, Madame X, Help Wanted,* and *Faust.*

After another period of voice study in Paris, Mitchell continued her concert and operatic career,

often on radio. Her roles included Santuzza in the Aeolian Opera Association's production of *Cavalleria rusticana,* with Todd DUNCAN and Ruby Elzy. In 1935 she created the role of Clara in the original cast of *Porgy and Bess,* and in 1939 she played Addie in the film *The Little Foxes.* Mitchell taught at Tuskegee Institute in Alabama, where she was head of the voice department. She died in Harlem Hospital March 16, 1960, survived by her son Mercer COOK.

REFERENCES

CUNEY-HARE, MAUDE. *Negro Musicians and Their Music.* Washington, D.C., 1936.
ISAACS, EDITH J. R. *The Negro in the American Theatre.* College Park, Md., 1947.

JAMES STANDIFER

Mitchell, Arthur Adams, Jr. (March 27, 1934–), dancer and choreographer. Born in New York City, the oldest son of five children, Mitchell began tap-dance lessons at the age of ten, sang in the Police Athletic League Glee Club and attended the High School of Performing Arts, where he progressed quickly through a modern dance major. He began his professional career while still a senior in high school when he appeared in the 1952 Paris revival of Virgil Thomson and Gertrude Stein's opera *Four Saints in Three Acts.* Upon graduation from high school he was the first male to receive the school's prestigious Dance Award.

Mitchell was accepted as a scholarship student at the School of American Ballet in 1952. Determined to overcome a late start in classical ballet technique, he also studied with ballet master Karel Shook at the Studio of Dance Arts in New York. His vibrant, agile performance style made him highly sought by contemporary modern dance choreographers; and during this period he performed with the Donald MCKAYLE Company, Sophie Maslow and the New Dance Group, Louis JOHNSON, and Anna Sokolow. In 1955, after only three years of concentrated ballet study, Mitchell joined the John Butler Company for a brief European tour. He returned to New York to join the New York City Ballet (NYCB) in November 1955.

Within his first week with NYCB, Mitchell danced a featured role in George Balanchine's *Western Symphony.* He became the first African-American principal dancer permanently associated with that company, but asked that there be no publicity about breaking a color barrier. In 1957 Balanchine created the centerpiece pas de deux of *Agon* for Mitchell and ballerina Diana Adams. Performances of this techni-

Arthur Mitchell, founder of the Dance Theater of Harlem. (Reprinted from *In the Shadow of the Great White Way: Images from the Black Theatre,* Thunder's Mouth Press, © 1957–1989 by Bert Andrews. Reprinted by permission of the Estate of Bert Andrews)

cally demanding, modernist work gained Mitchell international recognition as a principal dancer imbued with supple control and precise partnering skills. Mitchell stayed with the NYCB for fifteen years, dancing a range of leading roles that included spare, sensual works (Jerome Robbins's *Afternoon of a Faun*) neoclassic works (Balanchine's *Four Temperaments*), and pure classical ballets (Balanchine's *Allegro Brillante*). In 1962 Mitchell created the role of Puck in Balanchine's version of *A Midsummer Night's Dream,* winning critical and audience praise for his dramatic abilities and charismatic warmth.

Mitchell also performed in the Broadway productions of *House of Flowers* (1954), *Shinbone Alley* (1957), and *Noel Coward's Sweet Potato* (1968). He choreographed for Eartha KITT at the Newport Jazz Festival in 1957, and appeared at the 1960 and 1961 Festival of Two Worlds in Spoleto, Italy. He danced as a guest artist with the Metropolitan Opera (1962), the Munich Ballet Festival (1963), the Stuttgart Opera Ballet (1963), and the National Ballet of Canada (1964). In 1967, at the invitation of the United States government, he helped organize the National Ballet Company of Brazil.

Well aware of his role as a trailblazer, Mitchell encouraged others to follow his example of excellence in classical ballet. He taught at the Katherine Dunham School, the Karel Shook Studio, and the Harlem School of the Arts, as well as the Jones-Hayward School in Washington, D.C. In 1968

Mitchell and Shook reacted to the assassination of the Rev. Dr. Martin Luther KING, Jr., by forming the school that became the DANCE THEATRE OF HARLEM (DTH), although Mitchell "never actually started out to have a company. I wanted to start a school to get kids off the streets. But I couldn't tell the young people in the school to be the best they could when they had no place to go." DTH was cofounded in February 1969 by Mitchell and Shook to "prove that there is no difference, except color, between a black ballet dancer and a white ballet dancer."

Mitchell has received numerous honors and awards, including the 1975 Capezio Dance Award, the New York Public Library "Lion of the Performing Arts" Award for outstanding contributions to the performing arts, the NAACP's Image Award of Fame, and numerous honorary doctorates including ones from Harvard, Princeton, and Williams College. In 1993 Mitchell was honored by David DINKINS, mayor of New York City, with a Handel Medallion Award, and by President Bill Clinton at the Kennedy Center Honors for lifetime contribution to American culture. In June 1994 he was awarded a MacArthur Fellowship.

REFERENCES

"Arthur Mitchell." In *Current Biography Yearbook.* New York, 1966, pp. 278–280.

GOODMAN, SAUL. "Brief Biographies: Arthur Mitchell." *Dance Magazine* (December 1957): 47.

GRUEN, JOHN. *People Who Dance: Twenty-two Dancers Tell Their Own Stories.* Princeton, N.J., 1988.

LATHAM, JACQUELINE QUINN. A Biographical Study of the Lives and Contributions of Two Selected Contemporary Black Male Dance Artists—Arthur Mitchell and Alvin Ailey. Ph.D. diss., 1973.

MAYNARD, OLGA. "Arthur Mitchell and the Dance Theater of Harlem." *Dance Magazine* (March 1970): 52–62.

THOMAS F. DEFRANTZ

Mitchell, Arthur Wergs (December 22, 1883–May 9, 1968), politician. Born in Chambers County, Ala., in 1883, Arthur Mitchell left home at age fourteen and walked to Tuskegee Institute, where he obtained work as an office assistant for Booker T. WASHINGTON. He eventually entered Tuskegee as a student.

Mitchell taught in rural schools in Georgia and Alabama, and founded the Armstrong Agricultural School in West Butler, Ala., where he served as president for ten years. Mitchell continued his education at Columbia University and Harvard University School of Law, but never completed the requirements for a law degree. However, he was able to earn admission to the Washington, D.C., bar in 1927 and subsequently began to purchase tracts of real estate in the nation's capital. In 1928, Mitchell moved to Chicago, opened a law practice, and became involved with local Republican party politics.

Mitchell changed his political affiliation to the DEMOCRATIC PARTY when, in the wake of the Great Depression, the Democrats adopted a more activist position toward aiding the unemployed than did the Republicans. In 1934, Mitchell ran for the Democratic nomination for Congress from the first district of Chicago. He lost the nomination contest to Harry Baker, but Baker died before the general election. The Democratic committee selected Mitchell to run for the seat in his stead. Identifying his candidacy with the New Deal, Mitchell defeated black Republican Oscar DEPRIEST in the 1934 general election and, in doing so, became the first black Democrat elected to the House of Representatives. Mitchell began the first of his four terms in the House of Representatives in January 1935.

As a congressman, Mitchell supported President Franklin Roosevelt's New Deal and sided with the president during such controversial administration battles as the 1937 "court-packing plan" debate. Mitchell, by inclination something of a temporizer, was perhaps ill suited for his role as the sole African-American congressman and was often criticized for being insufficiently stalwart in his commitment to civil rights. Mitchell introduced an antilynching bill in Congress in 1935 that was attacked by Walter WHITE of the NATIONAL ASSOCIATION FOR THE ADVANCEMENT OF COLORED PEOPLE (NAACP) for being toothless. Mitchell garnered similar criticism when he was slow to condemn Italy's invasion of Ethiopia and for his support for the U.S. Supreme Court nomination of Alabama Sen. Hugo L. Black, a former member of the KU KLUX KLAN. (Despite the misgivings of many African-American leaders, Black was confirmed and proved to be a strong supporter of civil rights decisions during more than thirty years on the Court.)

Perhaps Mitchell's most significant civil rights battle occurred outside of the halls of Congress. In 1937, while riding on the Chicago and Rock Island Railroad in a first-class carriage, Mitchell was obliged to leave the first-class car when the train reached Arkansas. Mitchell brought suit against the railroad to the Interstate Commerce Commission, which dismissed the complaint. Mitchell then brought a civil suit against the railroad, which eventually reached the U.S. Supreme Court—with Mitchell himself arguing his case before the high court. In 1941, the U.S. Supreme Court ruled in *Mitchell* v. *United States*

that segregated coach laws for interstate travel were illegal. The decision, however, was largely ignored.

After leaving Congress after his fourth term, Mitchell moved to Pittsburgh, Va. For the next twenty-five years, he lived as a farmer and real-estate investor. He occasionally served as an unofficial adviser to the War and Defense departments and became involved in local political campaigns. Mitchell was also active in the Southern Regional Council, a moderate interracial organization that was dedicated to reform of discriminatory racial legislation. Mitchell died in his Pittsburgh, Va., home on May 9, 1968.

REFERENCES

CHRISTOPHER, MAURINE. *Black Americans in Congress.* New York, 1976.

CLAY, WILLIAM L. *Just Permanent Interests: Black Americans in Congress, 1870–1992.* New York, 1992.

KAREN E. REARDON
DURAHN TAYLOR

Mitchell, Clarence Maurice, Jr. (March 8, 1911–March 18, 1984), lawyer and lobbyist. Born in Baltimore, Md., Clarence Mitchell was the son of Clarence Maurice Mitchell, Sr., a chef in a fancy Annapolis restaurant, and Elsie Davis Mitchell. He attended Lincoln University in Pennsylvania, where he received an A.B. degree in 1932. The following year, he joined the *Baltimore Afro-American* as a reporter/columnist, covered the trials of the Scottsboro Boys, and reported on racial violence in Princess Anne County, Md. In 1934, he ran unsuccessfully for the Maryland House of Delegates on the socialist party ticket. In 1937, Mitchell spent a year doing graduate work at the Atlanta School of Social Work. That year, he briefly became Maryland State Director of the Negro National Youth Administration, during which time he married activist Juanita Jackson. The couple had four children, two of whom were later elected to local office in Baltimore.

In 1938, Mitchell was named executive secretary of the National Urban League branch in St. Paul, Minn., where he established his expertise in labor questions. In 1942, Mitchell became assistant director of Negro Manpower Service in the War Manpower Commission, and at the same time served on the FAIR EMPLOYMENT PRACTICES COMMITTEE (FEPC). The next year, he joined the FEPC full time, and became associate director of its Division of Field Operation. He supervised antidiscrimination efforts until it was disbanded in 1946.

In 1946, Mitchell joined the NAACP as labor secretary in the organization's Washington bureau,

Clarence Mitchell testifying before a Senate subcommittee in 1969. Mitchell, the chief lobbyist for the NAACP and the president of the Leadership Conference on Civil Rights, played a crucial role in the passage of civil rights legislation from the 1950s through the '70s. (AP/Wide World Photos)

where he cemented ties with organized labor and lobbied for civil rights legislation. Mitchell organized the National Council for a Permanent FEPC, and pushed for enforcement of executive orders banning discrimination. In 1949, he blocked the United Nations Food and Agricultural Organization from locating at the University of Maryland because of discriminatory University practices. The following year, Mitchell became head of the bureau.

In November 1949, Mitchell called a National Emergency Civil Rights Mobilization conference, in order to form a broad-based, interracial pressure group for equality which would be built on the nucleus of the National Council for a permanent FEPC. In January 1950, delegates from sixty organizations met and formed a steering committee, the Leadership Conference on Civil Rights. Mitchell was appointed legislative chairman, and served in that role for the next twenty-eight years. As the chief civil rights lobbyist on Capitol Hill, Mitchell was such a ubiquitous figure in Congress that he was often known as "the 101st senator." A courteous, gentle man, Mitchell

formed alliances with both Democrats (notably Senator and later President Lyndon B. Johnson) and Republicans (such as Sen. Everett Dirksen). In 1957, Mitchell marshaled support for a Civil Rights Bill, the first since Reconstruction. He aided the passage of the Civil Rights Acts in 1960, 1964, and 1968, as well as the 1965 VOTING RIGHTS ACT and its extension in 1975.

Mitchell was known for his devotion to legal processes. He once explained that "when you have a law, you have an instrument that will work for you permanently," whereas private agreements were more ephemeral. He was also willing to protest personally against discrimination. In 1956, he became nationally known when he was arrested in Florence, Ala., for using a whites-only door to the railroad station, an incident that became a cause célèbre. In 1958, he entered the University of Maryland's evening law school, where he obtained his law degree in 1962. In 1968, Mitchell opposed the efforts of civil rights supporters to procure an executive order banning housing discrimination, and pushed President Lyndon

Johnson to recommend congressional legislation. For his success in bringing about the Civil Rights Act of 1968, which provided legal protection against discrimination in rental housing, the NAACP awarded him the SPINGARN MEDAL in 1969.

In 1975, Mitchell was named a member of the United States delegation at the United Nations by President Gerald Ford. After his retirement in 1978, Mitchell served as a consultant and operated a law practice. In 1980, President Jimmy Carter awarded him the Presidential Medal of Freedom. He died in Washington, D.C., in 1984. The following year, the Baltimore city courthouse was named in his honor.

REFERENCES

WATSON, DENTON L. *Lion in the Lobby: Clarence Mitchell, Jr.'s Struggle for the Passage of Civil Rights Laws.* New York, 1990.

WHALEN, CHARLES, and BARBARA WHALEN. *The Longest Debate: A Legislative History of the 1964 Civil Rights Act.* Washington, D.C., 1985.

GREG ROBINSON

Mitchell, John R., Jr. (1863–December 3, 1929), journalist, banker, and politician. Born on the outskirts of Richmond, Va., John Mitchell worked as a carriage boy for his former master after Emancipation while attending Richmond's black schools. In 1881, he graduated from Richmond Normal High School and accepted a teaching position. During this time, Mitchell also worked as a correspondent for the *New York Globe.* This journalistic experience provided Mitchell with the necessary background to assume control in 1884 of the *Richmond Planet,* a weekly newspaper founded the previous year by E. A. Randolph.

As the *Planet's* editor, Mitchell established a reputation as a vocal opponent of racial discrimination. He gained initial recognition for his crusade against lynching and his counsel to blacks to arm themselves in self-defense. Mitchell's efforts to cultivate racial pride and his condemnation of racial injustice earned the *Planet* wide acclaim. Mitchell's aggressive stance, however, was increasingly tempered by his belief in the necessity of forging alliances with the white establishment in the South.

In recognition of his achievements, the Afro-American Press Association elected him president in 1890; he served in this position until 1894. Mitchell's renown as a journalist earned him a position in Richmond's political life as well. He served on Richmond's city council from 1888 to 1896, but he was defeated in the openly fradulent elections of 1896 and 1900. Mitchell had fallen into disfavor among the state's white Republicans because of his willingness to speak out against racial injustice.

Before and during the state constitutional convention called to resolve the question of black voting rights in 1901, Mitchell waged a bitter editorial campaign against the state's attempts to disfranchise African Americans. In seeming contradiction to his courageous attack, Mitchell endorsed voting restrictions based on property holdings and literacy tests.

Following the disfranchisement of Virginia's African-American population, Mitchell turned his attention from politics to business. In 1902, he founded the Mechanics Savings Bank of Richmond, and in 1910, he erected a four-story brick building in downtown Richmond to house the institution. Mitchell invested heavily in real estate during this time, using funds available to him as the grand chancellor of the Virginia Knights of Pythias. He purchased a movie theater, a cemetery, and other commercial property.

Mitchell's association with Richmond's leading white bankers was crucial to his success. With the help of the white banking establishment, Mitchell was admitted as the first black member of the American Bankers Association in 1904. While one can discern a growing, and somewhat uneasy acquiescence in some aspects of racial discrimination in his editorial policy during these years, he continued to write articles condemning disfranchisement. In 1904, Mitchell led a boycott of Richmond's segregated streetcars.

The lack of support Mitchell received from the city's white businessmen, especially in his attempt to block the passage of a citywide residential segregation ordinance in 1911, caused him to question the possibility of interracial cooperation. Mitchell again became more openly hostile to racial discrimination, and his series of articles about the mistreatment of African-American soldiers during World War I led to the confiscation of issues of the *Planet* by United States postal authorities.

In 1921, in a show of opposition to the racist policies of the state's white Republicans, Mitchell ran for governor of Virginia on an all-black ticket. In the year following his defeat, the Mechanics Savings Bank went into receivership, and Mitchell was indicted for mismanagement of the bank's funds. Mitchell was never convicted, but the scandal destroyed his standing within the city's black community. In 1929, before he could recover his losses and reestablish his bank, Mitchell died at his home in Richmond.

REFERENCES

BREWER, JAMES H. "Editorials from the Damned." *Journal of Southern History* 28 (1962): 225–233.

SIMMONS, WILLIAM J. *Men of Mark: Eminent, Progressive, and Rising.* 1888. Reprint. New York, 1968.

LOUISE P. MAXWELL

WATSON, DENTON L. *Lion in the Lobby: Clarence Mitchell Jr.'s Struggle for the Passage of Civil Rights.* New York, 1990.

NEIL GOLDSTEIN

Mitchell, Juanita Jackson (January 2, 1913–July 7, 1992), civil rights lawyer and activist. Born in Hot Springs, Ark., and raised in Baltimore, Md., Juanita Mitchell was from her youth committed to civil rights activity. She attended Morgan State College and the University of Pennsylvania (1927–1931). During the depression she returned home to found the City-Wide Young People's Forum of Baltimore, a vehicle for education and political activity. The Forum, led by Mitchell until 1934, sponsored antilynching petitions, employment campaigns, and numerous demonstrations. Walter WHITE, the executive secretary of the NATIONAL ASSOCIATION FOR THE ADVANCEMENT OF COLORED PEOPLE, noticed Mitchell's skills and invited her to New York City to lead the NAACP's first nationwide youth program, where she worked from 1935 to 1938. Organizing youth councils across the country, Mitchell concentrated on jobs, education, civil rights, and antilynching as critical issues for African-American youth.

Mitchell's political activism did not wane, despite her marriage in 1938 to the prominent civil rights leader Clarence M. MITCHELL, Jr., In the early 1940s she directed the first NAACP voter registration campaign in Baltimore, and in 1950 she received a law degree from the University of Maryland. Mitchell's legal accomplishments were significant. Besides being the first African-American women to practice law in Maryland, she won cases against segregation at Baltimore beaches and pools in 1950, and in 1953 she argued the case that led to desegregation of Baltimore's public schools.

During the 1960s, Mitchell was counsel for students who practiced civil disobedience by sitting-in at Baltimore restaurants that refused to serve black customers. She represented the students before the Supreme Court in the 1964 case *Robert Mack Bell v. Maryland* and won. Mitchell continued her various activities through the 1970s and 1980s with voter registration drives, while fulfilling her duties as the president of the Baltimore NAACP. In 1985 Mitchell was inducted into the Maryland Women's Hall of Fame. Upon her death on July 7, 1992, Benjamin HOOKS, then executive director of the NAACP, called Mitchell "one of the greatest freedom fighters in the history of Maryland and the nation."

REFERENCES

HINE, DARLENE CLARK, ed., *Black Women in America,* Vol. II. New York, 1993.

Mitchell, Loften (April 15, 1919–), playwright. Born near Columbia, N.C., Loften Mitchell was taken by his father, Ulysses Sanford Mitchell, and his mother, Willia Spaulding Mitchell, to Harlem before he was a month old. Reared with three brothers (Louis, Melvin, Clayton) and one sister (Gladys), Mitchell graduated in 1937 with honors from DeWitt Clinton High School in the Bronx. He then began to pursue his interest in theater by simultaneously working with the Rose McClendon Players in Harlem and attending City College of New York to study playwriting. He then enrolled at Talladega College, Alabama, where he received an A.B. in 1943. After serving in the navy as a seaman second class for one year, he enrolled at Columbia University to study playwriting with John Gassner from 1947 to 1951. In 1943 he married Helen Marsh, who bore him two sons, Thomas and Melvin. They were divorced in 1956. His second marriage was to Gloria Anderson in 1991.

Following his first successful play, *A Land Beyond the River* (1957), a drama built around the court case that ended school segregation, Mitchell received a Guggenheim Fellowship. A series of plays followed: *The Photographer* (1962); *Ballad of Bimshire* (1963); *Ballad for The Winter Soldiers* (1964); *Tell Pharaoh* (1967). His commercially successful musical, *Bubbling Brown Sugar*, written with Rosetta LeNoire, opened on Broadway in 1976 and traveled to the London stage. He was a professor of theater at the State University of New York at Binghamton from 1971 to 1985. Mitchell published one novel, *A Stubborn Old Lady* (1972), and two African-American theater histories: *Black Drama: The Story of the American Negro in the Theatre* (1967) and *Voices of the Black Theatre* (1975).

REFERENCE

PETERSON, BERNARD L., JR. *Contemporary Black American Playwrights and Their Plays.* Westport, Conn., 1988.

JAMES V. HATCH

Modern Dance. *See* Ballet.

Modern Jazz Quartet. Comprising vibraharpist Milt JACKSON, pianist-composer John LEWIS, bassist Percy Heath, and drummer Connie Kay, the Modern Jazz Quartet (MJQ) epitomizes the style that came to be known as "cool jazz." Although grounded in the fiery bebop style of the late 1940s, its repertory is characterized by elegant ensemble precision, a restrained emotional atmosphere (aided by the relatively cool timbres of the vibraharp and piano), and a self-conscious attempt to bring compositional technique derived from European art music into a working relationship with jazz improvisation.

Jackson and Lewis were originally members of Dizzy GILLESPIE's big band, and occasionally performed as a quartet in the late 1940s with Kenny CLARKE on drums and Ray Brown on bass. The Modern Jazz Quartet proper made its recording debut in 1952 for the Prestige label. Wearing tuxedos on stage, members of the MJQ brought jazz to audiences accustomed to European chamber music. Such early Lewis compositions as "Vendome" (1952) and "Concorde" (1955) attracted attention for their use of fugal textures, while later projects such as *The Comedy* (1962) made more ambitious use of a modern compositional idiom derived in part from contemporary European "classical" music and were associated with the Third Stream movement.

The music of the MJQ has nevertheless remained firmly rooted in African-American culture, through the soulful improvising of Jackson and a continuous exploration of the blues (e.g., the album *Blues at Carnegie Hall,* 1966). In 1974 the group disbanded, only to re-form for tours and recordings in 1981.

REFERENCE

WILLIAMS, MARTIN. "John Lewis and the Modern Jazz Quartet: Modern Conservative." In *The Jazz Tradition.* Rev. ed. New York and Oxford, 1983, pp. 172–182.

SCOTT DEVEAUX

Molineaux, Tom (c. 1784–August 4, 1818), boxer. As the first American to fight for the heavyweight championship, Tom Molineaux—his name was sometimes spelled Molyneux—garnered acclaim in early nineteenth-century Britain through his success as a bare-knuckle boxer. Little is certain about Molineaux's early life. He was born in either Virginia or Maryland in 1784. Some accounts place his birthdate as March 27, 1784, and maintain that both his father, Zachary, and his grandfather had been formidable plantation-slave fighters. It is likely that he won his freedom and $100 by defeating the slave of a neighboring plantation owner, Randolph Peyton, in a bout staged by his master, Algeron Molineaux.

However it happened, Molineaux was free by about the age of twenty, and he came to New York City in the early nineteenth century. First as a porter, and later as a stevedore, Molineaux earned a living on the New York City docks, probably engaging in informal fights. Developing a local reputation, by 1809 Molineaux had earned his way to London, where he hoped to participate in England's most popular sport, boxing. There he sought out fellow African-American boxer Bill RICHMOND, who agreed to become his patron, trainer, and second.

Molineaux's success was immediate: He quickly defeated eight British fighters, including "the Bristol Unknown" (Jack Burrows) on July 14, 1810, and Tom Blake on August 21, 1810. His successful record made him the first American contender, either black or white, to vie for the heavyweight championship. Molineaux's ability stirred considerable excitement among English boxing enthusiasts.

Molineaux and Tom Crib (or Cribb), the English titleholder, first met on December 18, 1810, at Copthall Common, where the 5'8", 198-pound Molineaux was finally defeated in the thirty-ninth round, but not before having demonstrated both endurance and considerable pugilistic skill.

Crib and Molineaux met again on September 28, 1811, in Thistleton Gap near London before a crowd of 20,000. But this time Molineaux, who was not in top fighting condition, crumbled beneath Crib's powerful blows. He endured a broken jaw in the ninth round and was knocked out in the eleventh.

Molineaux's ring career declined thereafter, along with his health and fortune. He drank excessively, engaged in street brawls, and failed to keep himself physically conditioned—all of which precipitated his break with Richmond. In an effort to regain his financial status Molineaux spent the last four years of his life touring unsuccessfully throughout Scotland and Ireland, both sparring and teaching self-defense. Unfortunately, Molineaux's meager earnings slipped away as rapidly as his health, attributable in part to his gullibility as well as to his drinking habits. He was sustained during his last ten months by friends in the 77th Regiment who were stationed in Galway, Ireland. Molineaux died August 4, 1818, in the Regiment's bandroom, penniless, homeless, and wasted by tuberculosis. He was nonetheless the first American professional boxer to garner international acclaim, and was inducted into *The Ring*'s Boxing Hall of Fame in 1958.

REFERENCES

EGAN, PIERCE. *Boxiana.* 1812. Reprint. London, 1976.
FLEISCHER, NAT. *Black Dynamite.* Vol. 1. New York, 1938.

GORN, ELLIOTT J. *The Manly Art: Bare-Knuckle Prize Fighting in America.* Ithaca, N.Y. 1986.

LISA MARIE MOORE

Monk, Thelonious Sphere (October 10, 1917–February 17, 1982), jazz pianist and composer. Thelonious Monk was born in Rocky Mount, N.C., but moved with his family to New York at age four and grew up in the San Juan Hill district of Manhattan. He began a career as a professional pianist in the mid-1930s, playing at house rent parties and touring for two years as the accompanist to a female evangelist. By 1940, he was a member of the house rhythm section at Minton's Playhouse, a nightclub in Harlem well known among musicians for its nightly jam sessions. Surviving live recordings from this period document a piano style firmly rooted in the stride-piano tradition, as well as a penchant for unusual reharmonizations of standard songs.

Monk had already written several of his best-known compositions by this period: "Epistrophy" and " 'Round Midnight" were performed and recorded by the Cootie WILLIAMS big band as early as 1944, while "Hackensack" (under the name "Rifftide") was recorded in Monk's professional recording debut with the Coleman HAWKINS Quartet in the same year. With their astringent and highly original approach to harmony, these compositions attracted the attention of the most adventurous jazz musicians, and placed Monk at the center of the emergent BEBOP movement during World War II.

Although well known within the inner circle of bebop musicians, Monk did not come to more general attention until later in the 1940s. Beginning in 1947, he made a series of recordings for the Blue Note label, documenting a wide range of his compositions. These recordings, which include "Criss Cross," "Ruby, My Dear," and "Straight, No Chaser," feature him as both improviser and composer.

While Monk was admired as a composer, his unusual approach to the piano keyboard, lacking the overt virtuosity of such bebop pianists as Bud POWELL and bristling with dissonant combinations that could easily be misinterpreted as "wrong notes," led many to dismiss him initially as a pianist. An incident in 1951 in which he was accused of drug possession led to the loss of his cabaret card, precluding further performances in New York City until 1957. But he continued to record for the Prestige label, including the famous "Bags Groove" session with Miles DAVIS in 1954, and he began making a series of recordings for Riverside, including *Brilliant Corners* (1956).

Thelonious Monk. (Photographs and Prints Division, Schomburg Center for Research in Black Culture, The New York Public Library, Astor, Lenox and Tilden Foundations)

An extended residency at the Five Spot, a New York night club, in the summer of 1957 with John COLTRANE finally drew attention to Monk as one of the most important figures in modern jazz. From the late 1950s through the 1960s, Monk worked primarily with his quartet, featuring tenor saxophonist Charlie Rouse, touring both in this country and abroad and recording prolifically for Columbia. Increasingly, he turned to the solo piano, recording idiosyncratic performances not only of his own compositions but also of such decades-old popular songs as "Just a Gigolo." The feature-length film *Straight, No Chaser* (1988; directed by Charlotte Zwerin) documents Monk's music and life in the late 1960s. After 1971, he virtually retired from public life. But his reputation continued to grow, as a younger generation of musicians discovered his compositions and responded to the challenge of improvising within their distinctive melodic and harmonic framework.

REFERENCES

BLAKE, RAN. "Round About Monk: The Music." Wire 10 (1984): 23–33.

WILLIAMS, MARTIN. "Thelonious Monk: Modern Jazz in Search of Maturity." In *The Jazz Tradition*. New York, 1983, pp. 154–171.

SCOTT DEVEAUX

Monroe, George A. "Alfred" (c. 1834–1886), stagecoach driver. There are conflicting stories concerning George Monroe's origins. Some versions of his biography claim that Monroe was born in Georgia in 1843; others indicate that he was born in California in 1834. All accounts agree, however, that when Monroe was a child, he moved with his parents—his father, a barber, ranch owner, and an early gold miner and his mother, a seamstress—to Mariposa, Calif.

Monroe was one of two black men to carry mail for the Pony Express during its years of operation from 1860 to 1861. In 1868, he started to work for the Yosemite Stage and Turnpike Company, driving a stagecoach for eighteen years until his death in 1886. His boss, Henry Washburn, called Monroe the "best all-round reinsman" he'd ever seen and relied on him to chauffeur important visitors to Yosemite Valley along the Wawona Road, which opened in 1876.

Monroe drove a number of well-known historical figures, including important statesmen, governors, artists, and journalists. In addition to driving Presidents Rutherford B. Hayes and James A. Garfield, he took former President Ulysses S. Grant on a twisting twenty-six-mile stagecoach tour of the mountainous S-curves of the Wawona Trail in 1879. In 1886 Monroe was thrown by a mule and fatally injured when the animal rolled on top of him. In recognition of Monroe's service to travelers along the frontier, Monroe Meadows in Yosemite National Park was named in his honor.

REFERENCES

KATZ, WILLIAM L. *The Black West*. Seattle, Wash., 1987.

REASONS, GEORGE, and SAM PATRICK. *They Had a Dream*. Vol. 2. Los Angeles, 1970.

LOUISE P. MAXWELL
LYDIA MCNEILL

Montana.　In a stark reversal of the general pattern of African-American population growth and community development, Montana's black population in the nineteenth century was larger and more influential than it was in the twentieth. Indeed, the state's black population of 1,800 in 1910 declined after that date and was not surpassed again until 1970. Limited employment opportunities and growing racial restrictions at the beginning of the twentieth century combined to discourage large-scale black migration to the state.

The first blacks to enter Montana were explorers and fur trappers. York, a servant of Lt. William Clark, crossed the region with the Lewis and Clark expedition of 1804–1806. Two black trappers, Edward Rose and James BECKWOURTH, lived in the region: Rose resided in Montana from 1806 to the 1830s; Beckwourth, who first visited Montana in 1829, returned regularly and died there in 1866.

Montana's first permanent black settlers were gold miners who arrived following discoveries there in the early 1860s. These men and women staked claims or worked in the hotels and stores of Virginia City and Helena, the territory's first towns. The 1870 census reported seventy-one blacks in Helena, with smaller concentrations of African-American miners in six other counties.

Some African Americans found gold. James Pratt, a former Union soldier, staked a successful mining claim at Marysville in 1869 that he worked until 1886,

William C. Irvin was a policeman in Helena, Mont., photographed in 1888 by J. P. Ball. (Montana Historical Society, Helena)

before selling the mine and moving to Helena to operate a saloon. Charles Porter Grove, a former slave, discovered gold in Broadwater County in 1885. After working the claim, he returned south to encourage blacks to migrate to Montana. Millie Ringgold, an ex-slave from Maryland, invested her mine earnings of $1,800 in a hotel and restaurant.

Montana had few African-American homesteaders, because of the expense of high-plains agriculture. Nevertheless, some blacks staked land claims. William Bairpaugh of Cascade County homesteaded farmland when he became twenty-one and eventually operated one of the largest wheat ranches in the state. Before his death in 1928, Bairpaugh donated much of his wealth to indigent blacks in Great Falls. Mattie Bell, a former North Carolina slave, migrated to Fort Benton in 1876, where she opened a laundry. After she married John Castner, a white settler, they filed claims on two thousand acres of farmland in eastern Montana Territory.

Nineteenth-century black Montanans included retired soldiers from the Twenty-fourth Infantry (who constituted much of the black community in Missoula) and cowboys such as Newt Glendennon and Bob Leavitt, who worked the cattle ranches in the eastern section of the territory, but black servants made up the largest occupational group. These men and women worked for wealthy families or in hotels, restaurants, and private clubs, such as the Montana Club in Helena and the Silver Bow Club in Butte, where they served the economic and political elite of the state. A. S. Webb and Charles Dorsey were valets of the two most important financiers and politicians in Montana, Sen. William A. Clark and F. Augustus Heinze, respectively; they used their positions to lobby for the abolition of discriminatory legislation.

Black Montana entrepreneurs operated restaurants and barbershops, particularly in Helena and Butte, but the largest enterprise was the Virginia City Waterworks, owned by Sarah Bickford. Born Sarah Gammon in 1855 in North Carolina, in 1888 she married Stephen Bickford, one of the early white pioneers of the area. The Bickfords bought two-thirds of the utility that supplied water to Virginia City. After Stephen Bickford's death in 1900, Sarah Bickford purchased the other third, acquired two fresh-water springs, and constructed a reservoir. She purchased many of Virginia City's older buildings for historic preservation, while managing the city's water company until her death in 1931.

Helena was home to the first, and for many years the largest, black community in Montana. The city began as a gold-mining camp in 1864, and three years later there were enough blacks to support the establishment of the Pioneer Social Club. In 1879 a black fraternal order, the Lodge of the Good Templars, was organized, and in 1888 Rev. James Hubbard established Saint James AME Church. By the 1890s, the community had a grocery store, barbershops, and a saloon that served both black and white customers. In 1900, Helena's black community could list two additional fraternal orders, a literary society, a women's benevolent association, a theatrical troupe, a nine-piece band, and a local baseball team. The city was also home of the *Helena Colored Citizen* and *Montana Plaindealer,* two of the state's three black newspapers.

Twentieth-century black Montana experienced economic decline. Although the African-American population rose steadily from 346 in 1880 to 1,834 in 1910, it decreased over the next three decades, as many blacks left because of declining employment opportunities and growing racial restrictions. Indeed, by 1910 Montana had enacted a number of racially restrictive laws, including measures that allowed segregated schools and outlawed interracial marriages. The economic decline was predictable; the fortunes of most of the state's blacks rested on the wealth that mining had generated for the local elite. That success was reflected in the patronage of the private clubs and elegant hotels and restaurants. When mining no longer produced such profits, the local elite and concomitant businesses declined, prompting many African Americans to migrate to other states.

Most of the state's African Americans who remained resided in four cities: Billings, Butte, Great Falls, and Helena. But, as if to indicate the deteriorating fortunes of blacks throughout the state, none of the populations in 1940—which averaged 150—rivaled the 420 blacks living in Helena in 1910. The shrinking populations took their toll on community institutions, such as the churches in various cities and the Great Falls NAACP, established in 1922 but defunct by 1930.

Nevertheless, Montana's small black population crusaded for civil rights legislation in the late 1940s and early 1950s. Arcella Hayes of Missoula initiated a successful campaign to repeal discriminatory statutes and enact the Fair Employment Practices Law. Hayes and her supporters received the backing of State Sen. Donald Nutter, a future governor of Montana, who introduced the legislation in 1949. Four years later, Hayes began a successful campaign to repeal the state's forty-four-year ban on interracial marriages.

The post–WORLD WAR II black population grew slowly, surpassing two thousand only in the 1980s. Most Montana blacks now resided in Great Falls or Billings, the state's largest cities. In 1974 Montana elected its first black state legislator, Geraldine Travis, a Great Falls librarian, who was chosen to represent a predominantly white district. Although her election was a milestone, the state's contemporary African-American community has yet to approach the levels of political, economic, and social activity that characterized black Montana at the end of the nineteenth century.

REFERENCES

LANG, WILLIAM L. "The Nearly Forgotten Negroes on the Last Chance Gulch." *Pacific Northwest Quarterly* 70 (1979): 50–57.

MILLS, ANGIE ARNOLD. *Montana Federation of Colored Women's Clubs.* Butte, Mont., 1921.

TAYLOR, QUINTARD. A History of Blacks in the Pacific Northwest: 1788–1970. Ph.D. diss., University of Minnesota, 1977.

———. "The Emergence of Afro-American Communities in the Pacific Northwest, 1865–1910." *Journal of Negro History* 64 (1979): 342–351.

QUINTARD TAYLOR

Montgomery, Isaiah Thornton (May 21, 1841–March 7, 1924), entrepreneur and politician. Isaiah Montgomery was born into slavery at the Hurricane Plantation at Davis Bend, Miss. His father, Benjamin, was the overseer/business manager for Joseph E. Davis and his brother Jefferson Davis (the future president of the Confederacy), who resided on the adjoining Brierfield plantation. Reluctantly, Benjamin secured for his son the position of hand servant to the Davises, which afforded the young boy an opportunity to study in the family's extensive library. His comprehensive education was overseen by Joseph Davis, regarded by many as a relatively progressive slave owner.

During the Civil War, Montgomery served the Union Army as a cabin boy under commander David D. Porter, but he was discharged in 1863 due to illness. Following the war, the Montgomery family, in exile in Cincinnati, Ohio, returned to Mississippi, where they eventually purchased the Davis plantations from the exiled first family for the sum of $300,000. They later purchased the adjoining Ursino plantation and enjoyed an unusual amount of social and economic freedom in an area rife with racial tension. Isaiah Montgomery became the bookkeeper and a partner in his family's business, Montgomery and Sons, one of the state's most successful cotton businesses. By 1876, however, declining cotton prices, infestation, and mounting interest payments pushed the Montgomery's to the brink of bankruptcy. By 1879, Montgomery and Sons was insolvent, and in 1881 the plantations were returned to the Davis heirs after a series of court hearings.

Shortly thereafter, Montgomery led an unsuccessful venture to found a colony of freedmen and women in Wabaunsee County, Kans. Then, in 1885, Montgomery and his cousins Benjamin T. Green and Joshua P.T. Montgomery struck a deal with the Louisville, New Orleans, and Texas (L.N.O.T.) Railroad and persuaded a small but industrious band of pioneers to turn a portion of thick Mississippi swampland into a colony exclusively for African Americans. This site, an 840-square-mile area of Bolivar County, Miss., was called MOUND BAYOU, so named for the two natural bayous that converged at a Chickasaw burial mound. By the time Mound Bayou was recognized by the state, it had become the largest black-governed town in the United States.

In 1890, Montgomery served as the only African-American delegate to the Mississippi State Constitutional Convention, where he declared his support for an amendment that resulted in the disfranchisement of over 124,000 black Mississippians, giving whites a majority of over 48,000 in the state. He justified his support of the measure (which included a substantial poll tax and subjective literacy requirements for voters) by contending that disfranchisement would lead to better race relations and force the race to focus on such practical self-help issues as education and property accumulation, though it has long been rumored that his actions resulted from a deal struck with the white hierarchy to leave his fledgling town out of the impending racial tensions. Montgomery was bitterly criticized for his decision by black leaders and later confessed to Booker T. WASHINGTON in a 1904 correspondence that his support of the amendment was a terrible blunder.

After a brief and scandal-ridden tenure with President Theodore Roosevelt's administration as collector of government monies in Jackson, Miss., Montgomery returned to Mound Bayou and served as its first mayor. In 1900, Montgomery helped found the NATIONAL NEGRO BUSINESS LEAGUE with Booker T. Washington. He remained a prominent businessman in Mound Bayou, promoting, among other endeavors, the Mound Bayou Cottonseed Oil Mill and Manufacturing Company. After its failure in 1915, he pursued assorted business ventures and generally lived a comfortable existence until his death in Mound Bayou.

REFERENCES

HAMILTON, KENNETH MARVIN. *Black Towns and Profit: Promotion and Development in the Trans-Appalachian West, 1877–1915.* Urbana, Ill., 1991.

HARLAN, LOUIS R., ed. *The Papers of Booker T. Washington.* 8 vols. Urbana, Ill., 1972–1979.

HERMANN, JANET SHARP. *The Pursuit of a Dream.* New York, 1981.

JOEL N. ROSEN

Montgomery, John Leslie "Wes" (March 6, 1923–June 15, 1968), jazz guitarist. John Leslie was born in Indianapolis, Ind., on March 6, 1923. He began playing the guitar at age nineteen. After playing in a variety of local bands, he toured with Lionel Hampton from 1948 to 1950. He quit music professionally for a time until he joined the Montgomery-Johnson Quintet (with brothers Monk and Buddy Montgomery) in 1955, when he recorded his first extended solos. He formed the Wes Montgomery Trio (with organ and drums) in 1959 and began recording for the Riverside label. It was these recordings that brought Montgomery recognition as a guitarist, winning multiple *Down Beat* and *Playboy* jazz polls for best guitarist. He moved to the San Francisco Bay Area in 1960, again appearing with his brothers before returning to Indianapolis in 1962. He began touring with his trio in 1963. In 1964 he initiated a series of recordings for the Verve label with large band or orchestral backing arrangements that brought him great commercial success, including a Grammy award for 1965's *Going Out of My Head*. His live performances continued to be in small ensembles, however.

Generally considered to be the most important jazz guitarist since Charlie Christian, Montgomery developed a solo style based on remarkable dexterity and rhythmic invention, building extended lines from simple melodies. His sound was distinctive, as he employed his right-hand thumb instead of a pick, creating a soft, warm tone. The trademarks of his style, however, became his extensive use of parallel octaves, sometimes used to play entire phrases.

REFERENCES

INGRAM, ADRIAN. *Wes Montgomery*. Gateshead, England, 1985.

———. "Wes Montgomery." *Jazz Journal International* 39, no. 7 (July 1986): 10.

DANIEL THOM

Montgomery, Ala., Bus Boycott. The Montgomery, Ala., Bus Boycott began on December 5, 1955, as an effort by black residents to protest the trial that day in the Montgomery Recorder's Court of Rosa McCauley PARKS. She had been arrested on December 1 for violating the city's ordinance requiring racial segregation of seating on buses. The boycott had initially been intended to last only for the single day of the trial, but local black support of the strike proved so great that, at a meeting that afternoon, black community leaders decided to continue the boycott until city and bus company authorities met black demands: the adoption by the bus company in Montgomery of the pattern of seating segregation used by the same company in Mobile; the hiring of black bus drivers on predominantly black routes, and greater courtesy by drivers toward passengers. The leaders formed the MONTGOMERY IMPROVEMENT ASSOCIATION (MIA) to run the extended boycott. At a mass meeting that evening, several thousand blacks ratified these decisions.

The Mobile plan sought by the boycott differed from the Montgomery pattern in that passengers, once seated, could not be unseated by drivers. In Mobile, blacks seated from the back and whites from the front, but after the bus was full, the racial division could be adjusted only when riders disembarked. On Montgomery's buses, the front ten seats were irrevocably reserved for whites, whether or not there were any whites aboard, and the rear ten seats were in theory similarly reserved for blacks. The racial designation of the middle sixteen seats, however, was adjusted by the drivers to accord with the changing racial composition of the ridership as the bus proceeded along its route. In Rosa Parks's case, when she had taken her seat, it had been in the black section of the bus. Two blocks farther on, all white seats and standing room were taken, but some standing room remained in the rear. Bus driver J. Fred Blake then ordered the row of seats in which Parks was sitting cleared to make room for boarding whites. Three blacks complied, but Mrs. Parks refused and was arrested. She was fined fourteen dollars.

Black Montgomerians had long been dissatisfied with the form of bus segregation used in their city. It had originally been adopted, for streetcars, in August 1900, and had provoked a boycott that had lasted for almost two years. In October 1952 a delegation from the black Women's Political Council had urged the city commission to permit the use of the Mobile seating plan. In a special election in the fall of 1953, a racial liberal with strong black support, Dave Birmingham, was elected to the three-member city commission. Following his inauguration, blacks again pressed the seating proposal at meetings in December 1953 and March 1954. In May 1954, the president of the Women's Political Council, JoAnn G. ROBINSON, a professor of English at Alabama State College for Negroes, wrote to the mayor to warn that blacks might launch a boycott if white authorities continued adamant. During the municipal election in the spring of 1955, black leaders held a candidates' forum at which they posed questions about issues of interest to the black community. At the head of the list was the adoption of the Mobile seating pattern.

On March 2, only weeks before the election, a black teenager, Claudette Colvin, was arrested for violation of the bus segregation ordinance. Following this incident, representatives of the city and the bus company promised black negotiators that a seating policy more favorable to African Americans would be adopted. However, Birmingham, the racially liberal city commissioner elected in 1953, had integrated the city police force in 1954. As a result of hostility to this action and other similar ones, he was defeated for reelection in 1955 by an outspoken segregationist, Clyde Sellers. The other commissioners at once became less accommodating. By the time that Rosa Parks was arrested in December, the discussions had come to a standstill. Mrs. Parks, the secretary of the Montgomery branch of the NATIONAL ASSOCIATION FOR THE ADVANCEMENT OF COLORED PEOPLE (NAACP), shared with other black leaders the frustration that grew out of the negotiations with municipal authorities. This frustration produced her refusal to vacate her seat.

From the city jail, Parks telephoned Edgar D. Nixon, a Pullman porter who was a former president of the Montgomery NAACP branch. After Nixon had posted bail for Parks, he called other prominent blacks to propose the one-day boycott. The response was generally positive. At JoAnn Robinson's suggestion, the Women's Political Council immediately began distributing leaflets urging the action. It was then endorsed by the city's black ministers and other leaders at a meeting at the Dexter Avenue Baptist Church. The result was almost universal black participation.

At the December 5 meeting, when it was decided to continue the boycott and to form the Montgomery Improvement Association (MIA), the Rev. Dr. Martin Luther KING, Jr., was chosen as the MIA's president, principally because, as a young man who had lived in the city only fifteen months, he was not as yet involved in the bitter rivalry for leadership of the black community between Nixon and funeral director Rufus A. Lewis. Nixon was elected the MIA's treasurer, and Lewis was appointed to organize car pools to transport blacks to their jobs without having to use buses. The Rev. Ralph D. ABERNATHY was named to head the committee designated to reopen negotiations with the city and the bus company.

Initially, the renewed negotiations seemed promising. Mayor William A. Gayle asked a committee of white community leaders to meet with the MIA's delegates. But by January 1956, these discussions had reached a stalemate. The MIA's attorney, Fred D. Gray, urged that the MIA abandon its request for the Mobile plan in favor of filing a federal court lawsuit seeking to declare unconstitutional all forms of seating segregation. The MIA's executive board resisted this proposal until January 30, when Martin Luther King's home was bombed. One day thereafter, the

executive board voted to authorize the suit, which was filed as *Browder* v. *Gayle* on February 1.

Meanwhile, similar strains were at work in the white community. A group of moderate businessmen, the Men of Montgomery, was attempting to mediate between the MIA and the city commission. But segregationists were pressing authorities to seek the indictment of the boycott's leaders in state court for violating the Alabama Anti-Boycott Act of 1921, which made it a misdemeanor to conspire to hinder any person from carrying on a lawful business. On February 20, an MIA mass meeting rejected the compromise proposals of the Men of Montgomery, and on February 21, the county grand jury returned indictments of eighty-nine blacks, twenty-four of whom were ministers, under the Anti-Boycott Act.

Martin Luther King, the first to be brought to trial, was convicted by Judge Eugene Carter at the end of March and was fined $500. King appealed, and the remainder of the prosecutions were suspended while the appellate courts considered his case. On May 11, a three-judge federal court heard *Browder* v. *Gayle* and on June 5, it ruled 2–1, in an opinion by Circuit Judge Richard Rives, that any law requiring racially segregated seating on buses violated the equal protection clause of the Constitution's Fourteenth Amendment. The city appealed to the U.S. Supreme Court. Both segregation and the boycott continued while the appeal was pending.

Throughout the thirteen months of negotiations and legal maneuvers, the boycott was sustained by mass meetings and its car-pool operation. The weekly mass meetings, rotated among the city's black churches, continually reinforced the high level of emotional commitment to the movement among the black population. Initially the car pool, modeled on one used during a brief bus boycott in Baton Rouge in 1953, consisted of private cars whose owners volunteered to participate. But as contributions flowed in from sympathetic Northerners, the MIA eventually purchased a fleet of station wagons, assigned ownership of them to the various black churches, hired drivers and established regular routes. Rufus Lewis administered the car pool until May 1956, when he was succeeded by the Rev. B. J. Simms.

White authorities eventually realized that the MIA's ability to perpetuate the boycott depended on its successful organization of the car pool. In November the city sued in state court for an injunction to forbid the car-pool operation on the ground that it was infringing on the bus company's exclusive franchise. On November 13, Judge Eugene Carter granted the injunction, and the car pool ceased operation the next day. But on that same day, the U.S. Supreme Court summarily affirmed the previous ruling of the lower federal court that bus segregation was unconstitutional. The city petitioned the Supreme Court for rehearing, and a final order was delayed until December 20. On December 21, 1956, the buses were integrated and the boycott ended.

The city was at once plunged into violence. Snipers fired into the buses; one of the shots shattered the leg of a pregnant black passenger, Rosa Jordan. The city commission ordered the suspension of night bus service. On January 10, 1957, four black churches and the homes of the Rev. Ralph Abernathy and of the MIA's only white board member, the Rev. Robert Graetz, were bombed and heavily damaged. All bus service was then suspended. On January 27, a home near that of Martin Luther King, was bombed and destroyed, and a bomb at King's own home was defused. On January 30, Montgomery police arrested seven bombers, all of whom were members of the KU KLUX KLAN.

The arrests ended the violence, and in March full bus service resumed. However, the first two of the bombers to come to trial were acquitted in May 1957, despite their confessions and the irrefutable evidence against them. Meanwhile, in April, the Alabama Court of Appeals had affirmed on technical grounds King's conviction under the Anti-Boycott Act. Because it was now clear that the other bombing prosecutions would be unsuccessful and because the boycott had ended in any case, prosecutors in November agreed to dismiss all the remaining bombing and antiboycott-law indictments in return for King's payment of his $500 fine.

The Montgomery Bus Boycott marked the beginning of the CIVIL RIGHTS MOVEMENT's direct action phase, and it made the Rev. Dr. Martin Luther King, Jr., a national figure. Although the integration of the buses was actually produced by the federal court injunction rather than by the boycott, it was the boycott that began the process of moving the civil rights movement out of the courtroom by demonstrating that ordinary African Americans possessed the power to control their own destiny.

REFERENCES

GARROW, DAVID J., ed. *The Walking City: The Montgomery Bus Boycott, 1955–1956.* In David J. Garrow, ed. *Martin Luther King, Jr., and the Civil Rights Movement,* vol. 7. Brooklyn N.Y., 1989.
GRAETZ, ROBERT S. *Montgomery: A White Preacher's Memoir.* Minneapolis, 1991.
KING, MARTIN LUTHER, JR. *Stride Toward Freedom: The Montgomery Story.* New York, 1958.
ROBINSON, JOANN GIBSON. *The Montgomery Bus Boycott and the Women Who Started It: The Memoir of JoAnn Gibson Robinson.* Knoxville, Tenn., 1987.
THORNTON, J. MILLS, III. "Challenge and Response in the Montgomery Bus Boycott of 1955–1956." *Alabama Review* 33 (1980): 163–235.
YEAKEY, LAMONT H. *The Montgomery, Alabama, Bus Boycott, 1955–1956.* Ph.D. diss., 1979.

J. MILLS THORNTON III

Montgomery Improvement Association. Montgomery Improvement Association (MIA) is the name of the organization formed in Montgomery, Ala., on December 5, 1955, to direct the black boycott of the city's bus system (*see* MONTGOMERY, ALA., BUS BOYCOTT). Black leaders had called a one-day boycott for December 5, to protest the trial of Mrs. Rosa L. PARKS, who had been arrested for violating the city ordinance requiring buses to maintain racially segregated seating. This boycott had proven so successful that on the afternoon of December 5, at a meeting of the community's black leaders at the Mount Zion African Methodist Episcopal Zion Church, those present decided to extend the boycott until the city and the bus company agreed to adopt the bus segregation pattern used in Mobile, Ala., which did not require the unseating of passengers who were already seated. The leaders decided to create a new organization to run the boycott, and at the suggestion of the Rev. Ralph D. ABERNATHY, they named it the Montgomery Improvement Association. Funeral director Rufus A. Lewis then nominated the Rev. Dr. Martin Luther KING, Jr., Lewis's pastor, as the association's president. The twenty-six-year-old King was taken by surprise at this unexpected designation, but he accepted it. That night, at a mass meeting at the Holt Street Baptist Church attended by some five thousand people, black Montgomerians ratified these actions.

During the course of the boycott, perhaps the MIA's most important achievement was the organization of an efficient carpool operation to replace the buses. Without this operation to get the mass of black participants to and from work, the boycott would soon have begun to weaken, and it was the ability of blacks to create and administer such an operation that most confounded the expectations of their white segregationist opponents. Rufus Lewis ran the carpool during the first six months of the boycott, and he was succeeded in May 1956 by the Rev. B. J. Simms. Almost equally as important as the carpool were the MIA's weekly mass meetings. These meetings, held in rotation at each of the city's principal black churches, were an effective means of maintaining the enthusiasm and commitment of the boycott's participants.

The MIA was governed by a self-constituted board of directors, consisting primarily of the leaders who had attended the December 5 organizational meeting. When a vacancy occurred, the remaining members themselves selected a person to fill it. The only white member was the Rev. Robert Graetz, a Lutheran pastor of an all-black congregation. The board proved extremely reluctant to move beyond the initial black demand for a more acceptable pattern of seating segregation. Throughout the boycott's first two months, board members refused to permit the association's attorney, Fred D. Gray, to file suit in federal court seeking a declaration that seating segregation ordinances were unconstitutional. Only when the Rev. Dr. Martin Luther King, Jr.'s home was bombed on January 30, 1956, was the board pushed into authorizing the suit. The resultant case, *Browder* v. *Gayle,* produced the U.S. Supreme Court's holding that bus segregation laws violated the Constitution's Fourteenth Amendment and thus led to a successful conclusion of the boycott on December 21, 1956.

The association continued to exist after the boycott. It became one of the founding organizations of the SOUTHERN CHRISTIAN LEADERSHIP CONFERENCE in 1957, conducted a largely ineffective voter registration drive in Montgomery, sought unsuccessfully to create a credit union for blacks, and in 1958 sponsored the filing of a suit to integrate the city's parks and playgrounds, a suit that only resulted in the city's closure of all of them. The MIA threatened a suit to integrate Montgomery's schools, but the suit was never filed. After King moved to Atlanta in 1960 and Abernathy followed him there in 1961, the association became less and less active. Its last important achievement came in the spring of 1962, when, under the leadership of the Rev. Solomon S. Seay, Sr., it managed to persuade the bus company to hire blacks as bus drivers, an action that had been one of the original demands of the boycott. Seay was succeeded by the Rev. Jesse Douglas, and Douglas by Mrs. Johnnie Carr. By the last decades of the twentieth century, however, the MIA had ceased to play any active role in the life of the community.

REFERENCES

GARROW, DAVID J. *Bearing the Cross: Martin Luther King, Jr., and the Southern Christian Leadership Conference.* New York, 1986.
KING, MARTIN LUTHER, JR. *Stride Toward Freedom: The Montgomery Story.* New York, 1958.
THORNTON, J. MILLS, III. "Challenge and Response in the Montgomery Bus Boycott of 1955–1956." *Alabama Review* 33 (1989): 163–235.

J. MILLS THORNTON III

Moody, Anne (September 15, 1940–), civil rights activist and writer. Born near Centreville, Miss., to poor sharecroppers, Anne Moody attended segregated schools in the area and worked as a domestic and at other jobs. She went to Natchez Junior College on a basketball scholarship in 1959 and to Tougaloo College in Jackson, receiving her B.S. in 1964.

While in college, Moody became involved in the CIVIL RIGHTS MOVEMENT and was jailed several times. In 1963 she and two other blacks were among the first sit-in demonstrators at a Woolworth's lunch counter in Jackson, Miss. Moody was a CONGRESS OF RACIAL EQUALITY (CORE) organizer in 1961–1963 and a fund-raiser in 1964. During 1964–1965, she served as the civil rights project coordinator for Cornell University. Complaining that the civil rights campaign had become "narrowly nationalistic," she shortly thereafter left the campaign, moved to New York, and began to pursue a writing career.

Moody's best known work is her autobiography *Coming of Age in Mississippi* (1968). It chronicles her growing up in poverty, her struggles to get an education, southern white racism, and the early battles of the civil rights movement. This compelling and moving book is among the best accounts of the southern black experience; it received many prizes, including the Best Book of the Year Award (1969) from the National Library Association.

In 1975, Moody published *Mr. Death,* which had been completed in 1972, four somber short stories for children. She has continued to write, but has published little since.

REFERENCES

MOODY, ANNE. *Coming of Age in Mississippi.* New York, 1968.
SEWELL, GEORGE, and MARGERET DWIGHT, eds. *Mississippi Black History Makers.* Jackson, Miss., 1984.
STONE, ALBERT E. "After *Black Boy* and *Dusk of Dawn:* Patterns in Recent Black Autobiography." *Phylon* 9, no. 1 (1978): 18–34.

QADRI ISMAIL

Moon, Henry Lee (1901–June 7, 1985), journalist. Henry Lee Moon was born and raised in Cleveland. He received a B.A. degree from Howard University and then attended Ohio State University, where he earned a degree in journalism in 1924. That year Moon became a press agent for the Tuskegee Institute in Alabama. In the late 1920s, Moon was hired as a reporter by the AMSTERDAM NEWS in New York City. In 1938, he was fired from the newspaper for attempting to form a union and was hired as a "race relations" adviser by the Federal Public Housing Authority (FPHA). Moon worked with the FPHA until 1944.

After World War II, he devoted himself to historical scholarship and in 1948 published *Balance of Power: The Negro Vote,* a study of black voting patterns after Reconstruction, which was part of a broader effort by civil rights leaders to argue that the black voting bloc was crucial in presidential elections.

In 1948, Moon took the post of public relations director with the NAACP, responsible for informing the press of the organization's activities as well as advancing the civil rights agenda through articles in magazines and newspapers. In 1965, he assumed the editorship of the CRISIS, the monthly magazine of the NATIONAL ASSOCIATION FOR THE ADVANCEMENT OF COLORED PEOPLE (NAACP). While heading *The Crisis,* Moon edited a collection of W. E. B. DU BOIS's essays entitled *The Emerging Thought of W. E. B. DuBois,* which was published in 1972. He retired from the NAACP staff in 1974. Moon died in Queens, New York, in 1985.

REFERENCES

BERGER, JOSEPH. "Henry Lee Moon Dead at 84; Ex-N.A.A.C.P. Spokesman." *New York Times,* June 8, 1985, p. 45.
MOON, HENRY LEE. *Balance of Power: The Negro Vote.* Garden City, N.Y., 1948.

THADDEUS RUSSELL

Moore, Archibald Lee "Archie" (c. December 13, 1913/1916–), boxer. Born in Benoit, Miss., in either 1913 or 1916, "Old Mongoose," as he liked to call himself, had more fights than any light heavyweight champion in BOXING history and was still knocking out people when he was forty-eight years old. He spent twenty-two months in reform school as a teenager for stealing coins from a train station in order to buy food. He learned to box there. Starting in 1935, the Mississippi-born Moore had 234 fights, with 199 wins, 145 by knockout. The phenomenal success of Joe LOUIS in the heavyweight division did not sit well with white boxing promoters, who were always convinced that a white champion could outdraw a black one. They continually denied the hard-punching Moore a title shot throughout the 1940s and early '50s. He was thirty-nine years old when he finally took the title, beating Joey Maxim, the tough veteran champ, in 1952. Moore held on to that title for a decade. Eager for the top rung on the ladder, he fought twice for the heavyweight title, but was knocked out by Rocky Marciano and Floyd PATTERSON. His eleventh-round knockout of Yvonne Durelle in 1958, after being floored five times, is considered one of the great comebacks in ring history.

Light-heavyweight champion Archie Moore stands over his kneeling opponent, Bert Whitehurst, in 1954. In his long career, Moore engaged in 220 recorded professional bouts, a record. (AP/Wide World Photos)

REFERENCES

ANDERSON, DAVE. "A Mongoose in a Beret and Goatee." *New York Times,* January 17, 1990.
MOORE, ARCHIE, with Leonard Pearl. *Any Boy Can.* New York, 1971.

BENJAMIN K. SCOTT

Moore, Audley "Queen Mother" (July 27, 1898–), activist. Queen Mother Moore's long career in service to African Americans provides an example of a consummate community organizer. Born and raised in Louisiana, Moore became a member of the UNIVERSAL NEGRO IMPROVEMENT ASSOCIATION and a follower of Marcus GARVEY in 1919. Through Garvey, she was first exposed to African history. Moore and her family moved to Harlem along with the flood of southern migrants during the 1920s. Here she founded the Harriet Tubman Association to assist black women workers. Moore also used the Communist party as a vehicle for achieving her aims. Impressed with its work on the Scottsboro case, she used the information and skills she acquired through the party to address the needs of the Harlem com-

Audley "Queen Mother" Moore of Harlem at the Women's Encampment, Seneca Falls, N.Y., September 4, 1983. (© Collette Fournier)

REFERENCES

HILL, RUTH EDMONDS, ed. *The Black Women Oral History Project.* Westport, Conn., 1991.
"Interview: Queen Mother Moore." *Black Scholar* 4 (March–April 1973): 47–55.
LANKER, BRIAN. *I Dream a World: Portraits of Black Women Who Changed the World.* New York, 1989.

JUDITH WEISENFELD

munity by organizing rent strikes, fighting evictions, and taking other actions. Eventually, the racism she encountered in the party moved Moore to resign.

The major theme of Moore's career has been a developing Pan-African consciousness. From Garvey through involvement with the NATIONAL COUNCIL OF NEGRO WOMEN to MALCOLM X's Organization of Afro-American Unity, Moore emphasized a knowledge of and pride in African history and its African-American connections. She brought this to the fore in her campaign for REPARATIONS, begun in 1955, as she did in founding other institutions in the black community. Among these are the World Federation of African People and a tribute to her sister in the Eloise Moore College of African Studies in Mount Addis Ababa, New York. She was also one of the founders of the Ethiopian Orthodox Church of North and South America, of which she is an archabbess. Moore received the title Queen Mother of the Ashanti people when in Ghana on one of her many trips to Africa.

Moore, Charles (May 22, 1928–January 23, 1986), dancer, choreographer, teacher. Born in Cleveland, Ohio, Charles Moore had early training in both music and dance. He arrived in New York City in 1948 with a Weidman scholarship. There he began studying ballet, modern and African dance from Asadata DAFORA, Pearl PRIMUS, and Katherine DUNHAM. From 1952 to 1960, Moore was a member of Dunham's company.

Tall, with a commanding presence, Moore had a lithe, muscular body and moved with clarity. Popular as a performer during the 1950s and 1960s, he danced with the companies of Geoffrey Holder, Donald MCKAYLE, Alvin AILEY, and in four Broadway shows and two opera productions.

In 1959 Moore began teaching Dunham's technique at the Clark Center in New York City, then continued at the New Dance Group, Harlem Youth Activities, and Hunter and Brooklyn colleges of the City College of New York; he also taught in Jamaica and Europe. An influential instructor, Moore fused Dunham's technique with his vocabulary of movement developed from his interest in African dance.

In 1972–1973 he founded the Charles Moore Center for Ethnic Studies in New York City, and a company, Dances and Drums of Africa. His choreography evolved from meticulous research in African dance, authenticated with actual costumes and African drummers. He also revived early pieces of Asadata Dafora (notably the *Ostrich Dance*) and brought distinguished African musicians to perform and teach in the United States. From 1973 to 1985, Dances and Drums of Africa toured nationally on the university circuit, also performing in Puerto Rico, the Bahamas, Nassau, and Haiti; in 1980 the company went to South and Central America.

Though Moore never went to Africa, reconstructions of his dances such as *Bundao, Maiden's Stick Dance, Spear Dance,* and *African Congo* were highly respected, and they inspired similar dances in most repertories of African dance companies in America. Moore died in New York City in 1986, survived by his wife, the dancer Ella Thompson, whom he had married in 1960.

REFERENCES

EMERY, LYNNE FAULEY. *Black Dance from 1619 to Today*. Princeton, N.J., 1988, p. 306.

"Reviews." *Dance Magazine* (August 1972).

DERRY SWAN

Moore, Ella Thompson

Moore, Ella Thompson (c. 1938–), dancer, teacher, choreographer. Although Ella Thompson Moore is most closely associated with her husband Charles MOORE, she is a dancer who has claimed high praise throughout her diverse career. She studied dance with Syvilla Fort, Walter Nicks, then at the Dunham School in New York City, where she met and married Charles Moore in 1960.

She worked in commercial theater in revivals of *Showboat, The King and I, Finian's Rainbow*, and in productions of *House of Flowers* (1955) and *Jamaica* (1957) with Lena Horne. In 1960 she was in the national touring company of *West Side Story* and she also danced for and with Alvin AILEY, Carmen DELAVALLADE, Thelma HILL, and later performed with Dances and Drums of Africa, her husband's company, in addition to assuming teaching and management duties and holding company rehearsals.

Thompson finished choreography for and opened Moore's evening-length work, *Traces*, after his death in 1986. The piece followed black dance styles from African roots through 1930s African-American social dances. It was acclaimed by *Dance Magazine* for "showing promise of developing into an important historical document of black styles." *Traces* stands as a fitting monument to the collaboration of Ella Thompson and Charles Moore. Dances and Drums of Africa continues to perform.

REFERENCES

STEVENS, LARRY. *Attitude* 2, no. 1 (June 1983).

TODD, ARTHUR. "Two Way Passage for Dance." *Dance Magazine* (July 1962): 39–41.

DERRY SWAN

Moore, Harry R. "Tim"

Moore, Harry R. "Tim" (1888–1958), actor. Born in Rock Island, Ill., Tim Moore left home at age twelve to join a vaudeville troupe, appearing in an act called Cora Misket and Her Gold Dust Twins. At age fifteen be became a jockey, and at seventeen a prizefighter. But he returned to show business while he was in his twenties and was successful enough in the Midwest to have his own show, *Tim Moore's Chicago Follies,* which ran from 1921 until 1925. Working in vaudeville theaters, Moore developed a broad comic style and a great rapport with audiences. In 1926 he played on Broadway in *Lucky Sam,* a comedy about a con man who discovers an oil well. The play was not a success, but Moore's performance as the con man included many of the features he would later employ as Kingfish on the television version of AMOS 'N' ANDY. Moore continued to enjoy moderate success, appearing notably in Lew Leslie's *Blackbirds of 1928* and *Harlem Scandals of 1932*. He also appeared in the film *Boy, What a Girl!* in 1946.

By the late 1940s, Moore, who was nearly sixty, decided to retire from show business. But in 1951 he was asked to play the role of Kingfish in the television version of *Amos 'n' Andy*. For the first time in his career, he received national recognition for his work, a performance in which a lifetime as a journeyman entertainer came to fruition. When *Amos 'n' Andy* ceased production in 1953, Moore remained in Los Angeles, working irregularly. He died there of pulmonary tuberculosis in 1958.

REFERENCES

BOGLE, DONALD. *Blacks in American Films and Television*. New York, 1988.

WOLL, ALLEN. *Black Musical Theatre: From Coontown to Dreamgirls*. Baton Rouge, La., 1989.

ANDREW BIENEN

Moore, Harry Tyson

Moore, Harry Tyson (November 17, 1905–December 25, 1951), teacher and civil rights activist. Harry T. Moore was born in Houston, Fla., the son of Rosalea Alberta Tyson and F. Johnny Moore, who deserted the family when his son was young. Harry attended school and grew up in the Houston area and around Lake Butler, a nearby small town where his uncle had a farm. He also lived for a while with his aunts in Jacksonville, where he may have attended a private high school. Moore began teaching fourth grade in the Brevard County, Fla., school system in 1925. From the mid-1920s until the mid-1930s, he taught at the Titusville Junior High School and was made principal of the Mims, Fla., school in 1936. In the same year he received a teaching diploma from BETHUNE-COOKMAN COLLEGE. He regularly attended summer classes until his death. Moore remained active as a teacher until 1946.

Moore was an activist in state and local branches of the NAACP during voter registration drives in the late 1940s and early '50s. His work is credited with being the primary reason that over 50 percent of Brevard County's African-American population was registered to vote (an unusually high percentage for a southern state at that time). He was also active on other fronts. After he and his wife Harriet led a campaign demanding equalization of pay for black and white teachers, both were fired from their teaching positions in 1946.

On the night of December 25, 1951, the Moores' twenty-fifth wedding anniversary, their home was rocked by a bomb that had been planted under the bedroom. Harry was fatally wounded; Harriett survived him by only a few days. The bombing provoked understandable outrage about the level of racial discrimination and racial violence both in Florida and in the country. Moore was posthumously awarded the NAACP's SPINGARN MEDAL, its highest award, in 1952.

Speculation over the identity of the culprits led to theories about the involvement of the KU KLUX KLAN or racist law enforcement agents. Moore had antagonized some elements of the white community by calling for the indictment of a sheriff involved in the much-publicized 1949 Groveland rape case. After their convictions were overturned by the U.S. Supreme Court in 1951 on account of obvious racial bias, the two black defendants were being transported to a new trial. Allegedly, they tried to escape, and as they did, the sheriff shot both of them. Political activists such as Moore claimed that the shooting was unprovoked.

After an FBI investigation into the Moore bombing, no indictments were handed down and no one was prosecuted. In 1991 pressure from civil rights organizations and relatives, such as Moore's daughter, Juanita Evangeline Moore, prodded Governor Lawton Chiles of Florida to reopen the Moore investigation and several others. The investigation, hampered by lack of physical evidence and the death of many potential witnesses, concluded that no new evidence existed to shed any light upon the culprits.

REFERENCES

KENNEDY, STETSON. "Florida's Christmas Murders." *New York Times*, December 23, 1991, p. A21.
———. "Murder by Bombing." *Nation* 174, no. 1 (1952): 4.
"No Day of Triumph." *Nation* 174, no. 1 (1952): 3.
PRICE, HUGH DOUGLAS. *The Negro and Southern Politics: A Chapter of Florida History.* New York, 1957.

JOHN C. STONER

Moore, Richard Benjamin (August 9, 1893–August 18, 1978), civil rights activist. Born in Hastings, Christ Church, Barbados, Richard B. Moore

left school at the age of eleven to work as a clerk in a department store. He emigrated to New York on July 4, 1909, and worked as an office boy and elevator operator and then at a silk manufacturing firm, where he received regular promotions until he became head of the stock department. The racism he encountered in the United States prompted Moore to a life of activism. In 1911 he served as president of the Ideal Tennis Club, which built Harlem's first tennis courts. In 1915, Moore founded and was treasurer of the Pioneer Cooperative Society, a grocery store featuring southern and West Indian products. A self-educated bibliophile, he began to amass an impressive book collection and formed the People's Educational Forum (later the Harlem Educational Forum), organizing debates and lectures.

In 1918, Moore became a member of 21st Assembly District Branch of the Socialist party (*see* SOCIALISM). Around this time he also joined the American Blood Brotherhood (ABB), a secret organization formed in response to race riots for purpose of the "liberation of people of African descent all over the world. . . ." In 1920, Moore was cofounder and contributing editor of *The Emancipator,* of which ten issues were produced.

In 1921 he left the Socialist party, disenchanted with its lack of concern for African Americans, and subsequently joined the COMMUNIST PARTY (the actual date of membership is uncertain). Moore was elected to the general executive board and council of directors of the American Negro Labor Congress (ANLC) at its founding meeting on October 25–31, 1925 and was a contributing editor to the ANLC's *The Negro Champion*. When Moore was fired from the silk manufacturing firm in 1926, he was put on the ANLC payroll as a paid organizer. In 1927, representing the ANLC at the International Congress Against Colonial Oppression and Imperialism and for National Independence in Brussels, Belgium, he drafted the Common Resolution on the Negro Question which was unanimously adopted. In August of that year he attended the Fourth Pan-African Congress held in New York (*see* PAN-AFRICANISM). In January 1928, as an employee of the ANLC, he organized and was president of The Harlem Tenants League. By 1931, Moore was vice president of the International Labor Defense (ILD), where he struggled during the 1930s on behalf of the Scottsboro boys (*see* SCOTTSBORO CASE), organizing mass demonstrations, preparing press releases, and making use of his brilliant gift for oratory in speeches delivered across the nation.

In February 1940, Moore founded the Pathway Press and the Frederick Douglass Historical and Cultural League and published the *Life and Times of Frederick Douglass* (1892), which had been out of print for

Richard B. Moore. (Photographs and Prints Division, Schomburg Center for Research in Black Culture, The New York Public Library, Astor, Lenox and Tilden Foundations)

forty years (*see* Frederick DOUGLASS). Moore had been motivated by his reading of this work during his early years in New York. In 1942 he opened the Frederick Douglass Book Center at 141 West 125th Street, a bookshop and meeting place specializing in African, Afro-American, and Caribbean history and literature, a Harlem landmark until it was razed in 1968.

After his expulsion from the Communist party in 1942, Moore shifted his attention to agitating for Caribbean independence. June 1940 marked the foundation of the West Indies National Emergency Committee (later the West Indies National Council [WINC]) of which he was vice president. He drafted "The Declaration of the Rights of the Caribbean Peoples to Self-Determination and Self-Government," which he submitted to the Pan-American Foreign Ministers' Conference held at Havana, Cuba, in July 1940. In 1945 Moore was a delegate of the West Indies National Council to the United Nations conference in San Francisco. He was secretary of the United Caribbean American Council founded in 1949.

In the 1960's Moore founded the Committee to Present the Truth About the Name Negro. In 1960 he published *The Name "Negro"—Its Origin and Evil Use* as a part of his campaign to promote the adoption of "Afro-American" as the preferred designation of black people. He was instrumental in convincing the Association for the Study of Negro Life and History to change its name to the ASSOCIATION FOR THE STUDY OF AFRO-AMERICAN LIFE AND HISTORY in 1972.

In 1966, Moore was invited by the government of Barbados to witness the Barbadian independence celebration. Although he continued to have his primary residence in the New York City area, he spent increasing amounts of time in the land of his birth. Moore died in Barbados in 1978; his extensive book collection is housed there at the University of the West Indies.

REFERENCES

ROSE, PETER I., ed. *Americans from Africa: Old Memories, New Moods*. Vol. 2. New York, 1970.
TURNER, W. BURGHARDT, and JOYCE MOORE TURNER. *Richard B. Moore, Caribbean Militant in Harlem: Collected Writings, 1920–1972*. Bloomington, Ind., 1988.

LYDIA MCNEILL

Moore, Samuel.   *See* Sam and Dave.

Moore, Undine Smith (August 23, 1904–February 6, 1989), composer. Born and reared in Jarratt, Va., Undine Moore was drawn into the musical traditions of the region by the singing of African-American spirituals in her home and church. She shared her mother's love for books and responded with equal ease to classical European music and to the folk expressions she heard in African-American music. Later, while studying performance at Fisk University, in Tennessee, she focused her attention on Western music theory and began to compose accordingly, choosing, primarily, nineteenth-century poets and composers as models of text and style.

In 1927, Moore began to teach at Virginia State College in Petersburg, where she continued writing music. She completed a master's degree at Columbia University in 1931 and did further study at the Juilliard School of Music, Manhattan School of Music, and Eastman School of Music. She heard spirituals again during visits home, wrote down the melodies with a heightened sense of their cultural significance, and began to set them in her own arrangements. Two of these became her first publications, in 1951.

Throughout a forty-five-year (1927–1972) professorship at Virginia State, Moore's prolific output included anthems, secular works, and chamber music, while she performed as choral conductor, organist, and pianist, becoming a master teacher of theory and, in 1977, music laureate of the Commonwealth of Virginia. Her cantata, *Scenes from the Life of a Martyr,* which epitomized her dedication to African-American art forms, philosophies, and social activism, received a Pulitzer Prize nomination in 1981. Her choral compositions "The Lamb," "Lord, We Give Thanks to Thee," and "Daniel, Daniel, Servant of the Lord," and her *Afro-American Suite* for flute, cello, and piano are among her most often performed works.

REFERENCES

BAKER, DAVID N., LIDA M. BELT, and HERMAN C. HUDSON, eds. "Undine Smith Moore." In *The Black Composer Speaks.* Metuchen, N.J., 1978, pp. 173–202.

HARRIS, CARL G. "Conversation with Undine Smith Moore: Composer and Master Teacher." *Black Perspective in Music* 13 (1985): 79–90.

GEORGIA A. RYDER

Moorhead, Scipio (fl. 1773), artist. Scipio Moorhead was enslaved in Massachusetts in the late eighteenth century and owned by the Rev. John Moorhead of Boston's Presbyterian Church on Long Lane. Scipio learned his craft from Moorhead's wife, Sarah, who was a drawing instructor and painter. He is best known for one painting, which scholars attribute to him despite little direct documentary proof. That painting is the portrait of Phillis WHEATLEY, which was the basis for the anonymous engraved frontispiece made in London for the 1773 first edition of her *Poems on Various Subjects, Religious and Moral.* Wheatley's *Poems* was the first published volume by an American woman to include the author's portrait as a frontispiece.

Moorhead and Wheatley knew each other, and the poet had ample opportunity to view Moorhead's work. Their families lived in the same community and socialized through local church networks. In 1773, Wheatley wrote a poem, "To S.M. a Young African Painter, on Seeing His Works," which scholars believe was inspired by Moorhead. The poem describes two of his paintings, "Aurora" and "Damon and Pythias." An advertisement in the January

7, 1773 edition of the *Boston News Letter* stated that a black artist, presumably Moorhead, "takes faces at the lowest Rates," working near the Town Hall down the street from where Wheatley lived.

Moorhead's alleged image of Wheatley depicts the poet at her desk, pen poised, eyes raised in contemplation. It features contemporary dress, furniture, and writing implements used by a woman of Wheatley's position in Boston society of the 1770s. The fragmentary evidence that exists suggests that Moorhead was an artist of considerable talent and enterprise.

REFERENCE

DRISKELL, DAVID. *Two Centuries of Black American Art.* New York, 1976.

RENEE NEWMAN
NANCY YOUSEF

Moorland, Jesse Edward (September 10, 1863–March 20, 1939), minister, YMCA executive, and civic leader. Jesse Moorland was born the only child of a farming family in Coldwater, Ohio. When he was an infant his mother died and his father left his son to be raised by his maternal grandparents. Moorland attended Northwestern Normal University in Ada, Ohio. After graduation he taught briefly in public schools in Urbana, Ohio, before moving to Washington, D.C. to enroll in the Department of Theology at HOWARD UNIVERSITY.

In 1891 Moorland received a master's degree from Howard and was ordained a Congregational minister. That same year he was appointed secretary of the colored branch of the Young Men's Christian Association in Washington, D.C. He held that position for two years and then in 1893 moved to Nashville, where he had been appointed pastor at Howard Chapel. In 1896 Moorland left Nashville to become pastor of the Mount Zion Congregational Church in Cleveland.

Moorland was a participant in the movement of the 1890s to make Protestantism "relevant" to existing social conditions. As part of the American moral reform tradition, he sought to develop a "practical, muscular Christianity" that would address worldly, human needs.

In 1898 Moorland accepted a position as an administrator and fund-raiser in the Colored Men's Department of the YMCA, located in Washington, D.C. Through the YMCA Moorland set out to create a refuge for young black men from the social disorganization among the growing numbers of migrants to American cities. He developed numerous programs for cultural self-improvement, including lectures, debates, Bible classes, workshops on job skills, literacy classes, and sports. With the help of the Rosenwald Fund, Moorland raised more than two million dollars for twenty-nine new YMCA buildings for blacks, which were erected in nineteen cities in the 1910s.

In 1914 Moorland succeeded William A. Hunton as senior secretary of the Colored Men's Department of the YMCA. By then Moorland had helped to build the department into a significant national institution. In 1917 it included 107 college student chapters, thirty-nine city associations, fourteen industrial associations, and two railroad associations. Moorland left the YMCA in 1923, having reached the mandatory retirement age of sixty.

After his retirement from the YMCA, Moorland devoted himself to black social organizations, including the National Health Circle for Colored People, the Association for the Study of Negro Life and History (which he helped found with Carter G. WOODSON in 1915), and Howard University, on whose Board of Trustees he had served since 1907. In the 1930s he held the chairmanship of the Executive Committee of the Board of Trustees. Moorland had long encouraged the university to establish a research library devoted to African-American studies, and in 1915 he donated his personal library on black history to Howard University. This collection later formed the basis of the Moorland-Spingarn Research Center, one of the leading research centers of its kind. Moorland died in New York in 1939.

REFERENCES

"JESSE E. MOORLAND." *Journal of Negro History* 25 (July 1940): 401–403.

LOGAN, RAYMOND W., and MICHAEL R. WINSTON. *Dictionary of American Negro Biography.* New York, 1982.

MOORLAND, JESSE. "The Young Men's Christian Association Among Negroes." *Journal of Negro History* 9 (April 1924): 127–138.

THADDEUS RUSSELL

Morehouse College.   In 1867 the Augusta Baptist Seminary was established in Augusta, Ga., with the aid of the Washington, D.C.–based National Theological Institute. The seminary soon became affiliated with the American Baptist Home Mission Society, which provided financial and moral support to

the fledgling venture. The first class of thirty-seven men and women took courses in the Springfield Baptist Church; the class had three female missionary teachers.

In 1871, Joseph T. Robert became the first president of the institution. After seven years of pressure to move the seminary to Atlanta, the ABHMS purchased land, and the seminary moved in 1879. It was rechristened the Atlanta Baptist Seminary. Accompanying the move was an increased determination to improve the quality of education at the seminary. Within three years, the all-male institution opened a collegiate department; students could enroll in either a four-year scientific course or a six-year classical course.

By the end of the nineteenth century, school officials sought to amend the charter, changing the name of the school to Atlanta Baptist College in 1897. Nine years later, John HOPE became the first African-American president; he would lead the college until 1931. Hope oversaw the rapid expansion of the institution and was largely responsible for its excellent reputation both in the region and the country. In 1913, the name of the college was again changed to honor longtime ABHMS stalwart Henry Lyman Morehouse. The newly renamed Morehouse College had about sixty students in the collegiate program in 1915.

Morehouse offered an education weighted heavily toward both spiritual and academic advancement. Teachers such as Morehouse alumnus Benjamin BRAWLEY, who taught there in 1902–1910 and 1912–1920, provided intellectual stimulation and served as role models for the student body. During John Hope's tenure, the "Morehouse man" began to symbolize an honest, intelligent African-American male who could succeed at anything. Partially as a result of the spread of this image, the school was criticized for catering primarily to the black elite and restricting its educational efforts to the Talented Tenth.

Morehouse College, Spelman College, and Atlanta University merged some of their operations together in 1929 to streamline administrative functions and pacify philanthropists who believed the merger would simplify donations to any of the participants. Academic resources were pooled. Atlanta became solely a university for graduate study; Spelman catered to undergraduate women, and Morehouse to undergraduate men. Students could take courses at the affiliated schools. Classroom space and some faculty responsibilities were also shared.

While the affiliation maintained each school's financial and administrative autonomy, the GREAT DEPRESSION caused Morehouse significant difficulty. John Hope's successor, Samuel Archer, turned over much of Morehouse's financial and budgetary control to Atlanta University, leaving Morehouse with almost no decision-making power.

Students and faculty at Morehouse chafed under the new arrangements. When Benjamin Elijah MAYS became president of Morehouse in 1940, he made the reempowerment of Morehouse a priority. Mays was responsible for drastically increasing the college's endowment, wresting financial control from Atlanta University, and instituting an aggressive program of construction and expansion. He was also leading Morehouse when the 1957 creation of Atlanta University Center further consolidated operations between the original three participants and the new additions of Morris Brown College, Gammon Theological Seminary, and Clark University.

Morehouse was ahead of some of its contemporaries by instituting a non-Western studies program in the early 1960s. Students at Morehouse were also active participants in the CIVIL RIGHTS MOVEMENT. The most notable Morehouse alumnus undoubtedly was the Rev. Dr. Martin Luther KING, Jr., a 1948 graduate. Julian BOND, a student at Morehouse in the early 1960s, left school to be a full-time activist with the STUDENT NONVIOLENT COORDINATING COMMITTEE (SNCC).

Mays retired in 1967, passing the torch to Hugh Gloster, who led Morehouse for the next twenty years. Gloster attempted to expand the endowment, which was always a critical issue at Morehouse. The late 1970s saw the establishment of the Morehouse School of Medicine (1978), originally a two-year institution providing a grounding in primary-care and preventive medicine to students who would then continue at four-year institutions. In 1981, the medical school, which remained autonomous from the college, switched to a four-year curriculum; its finances were bolstered by millions of dollars in donations from governmental and private donations.

Leroy Keith, Jr., became president of Morehouse in 1987. He faced many of the same problems as his predecessors had. Budget difficulties, the endowment, and other issues remained pressing crises. Other events, like fatalities caused by fraternity hazing, brought unwanted attention to the college and threatened to tarnish the image of the three thousand "Morehouse men" enrolled at the college. In September 1994, Keith resigned under pressure after a financial audit revealed that he might have received more than $200,000 in unapproved benefits. Despite these setbacks, Morehouse remained one of the most prestigious of historically black colleges, committed to academic excellence and the distinctive educational needs of African Americans.

REFERENCES

BRAWLEY, BENJAMIN G. *History of Morehouse College.* 1917. Reprint. College Park, Md., 1970.

BUTLER, ADDIE LOUIS JOYNER. *The Distinctive Black College: Talladega, Tuskegee, and Morehouse.* Metuchen, N.J., 1977.

JONES, EDWARD ALLEN. *A Candle in the Dark: A History of Morehouse College.* Valley Forge, Pa., 1967.

JOHN C. STONER

In 1906 John Hope was named president of Atlanta Baptist College, which became Morehouse College in 1913. He led the institution until 1931. (Photographs and Prints Division, Schomburg Center for Research in Black Culture, The New York Public Library, Astor, Lenox and Tilden Foundations)

Morgan, Garrett Augustus (March 4, 1875–July 27, 1963), inventor. Garrett Morgan was born in Paris, Ky. In 1889, he traveled to Cincinnati, where he found work as a handyman. Six years later, he moved to Cleveland and briefly worked fixing sewing machines for a clothing manufacturer. Morgan then began several successful enterprises on his own: a sewing machine repair service (1907), a tailor shop (1909), and a hair-straightening company (1913). He also tried his hand at a number of inventions, the most important being a "breathing device" which he patented in 1914. Morgan's device, as he noted in his patent application, enabled firefighters to breathe in smoke-filled buildings and protected engineers, chemists, and workers who labored near noxious fumes and dust. The apparatus consisted of a hood that fit over the head with two tubes leading from the face mask around the left and right sides of the body to a bag of fresh air.

In 1912, Morgan, along with several Cleveland business executives, formed the National Safety Device Company to manufacture and advertise the Morgan Safety Hood. Two years later, Morgan was awarded First Grand Prize by the National Safety Device Company at the Second International Exposition of Safety and Sanitation held in New York City. In 1916, Morgan's hoods were worn when he and others entered a smoke-filled tunnel, 250 feet below Lake Erie, to rescue workers trapped after an explosion in the Cleveland waterworks system—an incident known as the Lake Erie Crib Disaster. The following year, Morgan received a contract from the U.S. Navy to produce his gas mask for combat use.

In 1922, Morgan patented another important invention, the three-way automatic traffic signal. The "go-stop" signals used before Morgan's invention had no intermediate or neutral signal position; there was no "yellow light" as it was later known. Without a traffic officer present, the "go" and "stop" signals could change too abruptly, leading to accidents. Morgan's signal caused the "go" and "stop" armatures to pause briefly in a half-mast position to caution drivers to slow down. Morgan sold the rights to his signal to the General Electric Company for $40,000 in 1923. G.E. then converted the signal into the now commonly used three-way light.

Aside from his inventions, Morgan took an interest in civic affairs. From 1920 to 1923 he published the African-American newspaper *Cleveland Call*. He was a longtime member of the Cleveland NAACP and in 1931 ran unsuccessfully for city council. In 1943, Morgan contracted glaucoma, from which he gradually lost most of his sight. He died in Cleveland in 1963. Shortly after his death he was recognized at the Emancipation Centennial Celebration in Chicago. In 1976, a public school in Harlem was named in his honor.

REFERENCES

BAKER, HENRY E. *The Colored Inventor*. Washington, D.C., 1913.

HAYDEN, ROBERT C. *Nine African American Inventors*. Frederick, Md., 1992.

KING, WILLIAM M. "Guardian of the Public Safety: Garrett A. Morgan and the Lake Erie Crib Disaster." *Journal of Negro History* 70, nos. 1, 2 (Winter-Spring 1985): 1–13.

ROBERT C. HAYDEN

Morgan, Sister Gertrude (April 7, 1900–1980), painter and prophet. Gertrude Morgan was born in Lafayette, Ala., on April 7, 1900. Following her relocation to New Orleans during the 1950s and her belief she was mystically married to Jesus Christ in 1965, Morgan wore only white apparel and painted primarily biblical themes to illustrate her gospel teachings. She adopted the title "Sister" during the early 1950s when she was associated with two other street missionaries who built a chapel and child-care center in New Orleans. Morgan's paintings frequently depict herself and Jesus as bride and groom. She painted on any available materials: cardboard, windowshades, styrofoam supermarket trays, plastic utensils, jelly jars, lampshades, fire screens, picture frames, and her guitar case. She worked in a variety of mediums, including watercolors, acrylics, wax crayons, and ball point pens. The calligraphy which appears in most of her works to convey an important message or denote the specific verses of scripture illustrated is an integral and vital part of the compo-

The talents of folksinger, folk artist, and street preacher Sister Gertrude Morgan first came to recognition in New Orleans in the late 1950s. Morgan always wore white, the color of the bride of Christ. (Photographs and Prints Division, Schomburg Center for Research in Black Culture, The New York Public Library, Astor, Lenox and Tilden Foundations)

sitions. The majority of Morgan's paintings depict religious subjects and self-portraits showing the artist wearing black before and white after her mystical marriage. She painted a group of large narrative compositions which she called "charters" and illustrated with chapters from the Book of Revelation, and a number of handmade fans which she passed out during her prayer sessions. Some of her poems were set to music, and in 1971 an album of her original song-prayers, *Let's Make a Record*, was recorded by True Believer Records in the Prayer Room of her residence in New Orleans. The painted expressions of Morgan's religious beliefs were entirely original and unique among contemporary American folk artists. Her vivid imagination, innate gift of color, compositional arrangement, and intense religiosity resulted in a body of literal yet creative interpretations of the Bible.

REFERENCES

"Black Folk Art in America, 1930–1980." Corcoran Gallery of Art Washington, D.C., 1982, pp. 97–103.
"What It Is: Black American Folk Art from the Collection of Regenia Perry." Anderson Gallery, Virginia Commonwealth University, Richmond, Va., 1982.

REGENIA A. PERRY

Mormons. Within the Church of Jesus Christ of Latter-day Saints, popularly known as the Mormon church, the number of African Americans has always been relatively small. This has been the case from the 1830s, the period when the denomination was first organized. African Americans, however, have exerted an influence on Mormonism far beyond their small numbers.

A handful of free northern blacks, probably no more than one or two dozen, associated themselves with Mormonism in the 1830s and 1840s, during the church's formative years in upstate New York under the leadership of Joseph Smith. The small number was largely due to limited black-white contact involving members of the still-fledgling denomination. Also limiting African-American interest were Mormon scriptural writings, as articulated by Smith, asserting that various dark-skinned peoples, including blacks, were divinely less favored or inferior to whites. These writings, which included the *Book of Mormon* and the "Book of Moses" and the "Book of Abraham," which constituted the *Pearl of Great Price*, were considered holy scripture on a level with the Old and New Testaments. In time, they helped justify denying African-American ordination to the Mormon priesthood, a lay organization open to virtually all other adult male members of the church.

In addition, Joseph Smith committed his Latter-day Saint followers to an official anti-abolitionist position during the 1830s. The reason was that the Mormons sought to adjust to local conditions following the movement of the church's headquarters, first to Kirtland, Ohio (located near the Western Reserve—a hotbed of abolitionist conflict), and then to Missouri (a slave state). Blacks thus had little incentive to join the Mormon movement.

The few blacks who did join the Mormon church, however, left their mark. Among these was Elijah Abel, who joined in Kirtland and was apparently "intimately acquainted" with and "lived in the home" of Smith. In fact, Abel, despite his African-American lineage, was ordained to the Mormon priesthood, and served as a missionary for the church on three different occasions. He was ordained during the 1830s, prior to the imposition of Mormonism's ban on black ordination. The ban itself was affirmed by Brigham Young in 1847, after he became the principal Mormon leader following Smith's death three years earlier.

Young's immediate decision to ban blacks from the priesthood was encouraged, in large part, by the disruptive behavior of William McCary, an African-Indian who was associated briefly with the church at Winter Quarters, Nebr., during the time of the Mormon migration to the western Great Basin. Young, anxious to put an end to McCary's rival prophetic claims and his practice of polygamy (a still-secret practice to those outside the church's leadership), asserted that all blacks, including McCary, were ineligible for ordination.

By the time Young and his followers settled in the Great Basin, the number of African Americans who came in contact with the Mormon church had slightly increased. In contrast to the twenty or so free blacks associated with the Mormons in Nauvoo, Ill., during the 1840s, there were over one hundred blacks living in UTAH by the early 1850s—the majority being slaves belonging to Latter-day Saints who migrated west from the slaveholding South. In response to this situation, Brigham Young, in his capacity as Utah territorial governor, approved "An Act in Relation to Service," which legalized black slavery. This made Utah the only American territory west of the Mississippi River where slavery was legal prior to the Civil War. As a result, the number of blacks migrating to Utah and/or joining the Mormon church remained small in the years before and during the Civil War.

This situation continued as the number of blacks living in Utah associated with the Mormon church remained low during the next fifty to seventy-five years. Despite Emancipation, the Mormon ban on black ordination remained intact. In addition, Utah's small black population was subjected to civil restrictions upholding both de facto and de jure segregation and other forms of discrimination.

Although the number of blacks living in Utah increased from 118 to 1,235 between 1870 and 1940, their tiny percentage of the state's total population remained virtually unchanged—a mere 0.1 percent to 0.3 percent. The corresponding number of blacks within the Mormon church itself was even more negligible. Thus, both outsiders and those within the church had little need to pay attention to Utah's discriminatory civil statutes, or to Mormon ecclesiastical restrictions on black ordination during this period.

Starting in the 1950s, however, in the wake of the doubling of Utah's black population within just one decade, the state's small but active chapter of the NAACP worked for the elimination of all forms of civil discrimination. This occurred against the backdrop of a burgeoning nationwide civil rights movement. Under pressure from the NAACP and other civil rights groups, the Mormon church issued a statement of support for civil rights in 1963. Two years later, as a result of further NAACP pressure, the Mormon-dominated Utah legislature enacted both a Public Accommodations Act and a Fair Employment Act.

By the late 1960s, black activists and others exerted direct pressure on the Mormon church to lift its ban on black ordination to the priesthood. Protest was promoted mainly by black-rights activists rather than by the handful of blacks within the church. Such pressure coming from "outsiders" made Mormon officials even more resistant to change, particularly during the turbulent era of the late 1960s and early '70s.

In 1971, however, Mormon leaders did formulate a special organization for its black members known as the "Genesis group," designed to serve the needs of the estimated two hundred black Mormons living in and around Salt Lake City. In addition, room was made in the famed Mormon Tabernacle Choir for three blacks, and the church-owned Brigham Young University recruited blacks for its athletic teams. Finally, in June 1978, the church leadership lifted its black priesthood ban, allowing blacks full participation in the church. This change came less in response to Mormon–African American relations than to the emergence of the Mormon church as an international organization active in nonwhite areas outside the United States.

Indeed, during the years since the lifting of the ban, the church has enjoyed its greatest success among people of African descent Brazil, the Caribbean, and various parts of sub-Saharan Africa. By contrast, Mormonism continues to have much more limited appeal among blacks within the United States itself.

REFERENCES

BRINGHURST, NEWELL G. *Saints, Slaves, and Blacks: The Changing Place of Black People Within Mormonism.* Westport, Conn., 1981.
BUSH, LESTER E., and ARMAND L. MAUSS, eds. *Neither White nor Black: Mormon Scholars Confront the Race Issue in a Universal Church.* Midvale, Utah, 1984.
LAUNIUS, ROGER D. *Invisible Saints: A History of Black Americans in the Reorganized Church.* Independence, Mo., 1988.

NEWELL G. BRINGHURST

Morris, Elias Camp (May 7, 1855–September 5, 1922), minister and educator. Born a slave in Murray County, Ga., Elias C. Morris was trained in his early years as a shoemaker. After the Civil War, Morris went to Tennessee with his parents and then to Alabama, where he received a primary education and opened a successful shoemaker's shop. In 1874, Morris was baptized and received his BAPTIST preaching license. He traveled to Helena, Ark., where there was a missionary station of the Women's American Baptist Home Mission Society, and soon became pastor of the Centennial Baptist Church, where he remained for a number of years. His preaching and pastoral work for blacks gained him a popular following. In 1882, the same year Morris began a four-year stint as editor of a Baptist newspaper, the *Arkansas Times,* he briefly served as an official missionary for the white-dominated American Baptist Home Mission Society (ABHMS). In 1884, with funding from the ABHMS, Morris founded Arkansas Baptist College. He served as its president for two years.

In 1895, Morris, who had been president for several years of the Negro Baptist Convention of Arkansas, helped found the National Baptist Convention (NBC), still the largest African-American religious group. He was named president of the convention, a post he held until his death 27 years later.

As the official head of black Baptists throughout the world, Morris maintained the basic theological unity of black and white Baptists, but insisted that only African-American ministers were suited for black congregations. Morris represented black Baptists at ecumenical gatherings and helped start the Baptist World Alliance in 1905. Four years earlier, he had published a collection of his *Sermons, Addresses, and Reminiscences and Important Correspondence* (1901).

The National Baptist Convention controlled missionary work and publishing, which individual churches could not support by themselves. Morris's attempt to control the publishing arm of black Baptistry, as well as fears on the part of some ministers that Morris was strengthening the NBC at the expense of the traditionally loose congregational structure of the Baptist movement, prompted a major schism. As early as 1905, Morris tried to take control of R. H. Boyd's nominally independent National Baptist Publishing House, on the grounds that it was a part of the convention. At the 1915 convention, Boyd left with his followers to form the National Baptist Convention of America. The Morris group incorporated as the NATIONAL BAPTIST CONVENTION, U.S.A. Morris died in Little Rock in 1922.

REFERENCES

BLACKNEY, WILLIAM H. *The Baptists.* Westport, Conn., 1988.

LINCOLN, C. ERIC, and LAWRENCE H. MAMIYA. *The Black Church in the African American Experience.* Durham, N.C., 1980.

GREG ROBINSON

Morrison, Toni (February 18, 1931–), writer. By the 1980s, Toni Morrison was considered by the literary world to be one of the major American novelists. In 1992—five years after she received the Pulitzer Prize for *Beloved* and the year of publication both for her sixth novel, *Jazz,* and for a series of lectures on American literature, *Playing in the Dark*—Morrison was being referred to internationally as one of the greatest American writers of all time. In 1993 she became the first black woman in history to be awarded the Nobel Prize for literature.

The road to prominence began with Morrison's birth into a family she describes as a group of storytellers. Born Chloe Anthony Wofford in Lorain, Ohio, she was the second of four children of George Wofford (a steel-mill welder, car washer, and construction and shipyard worker) and Ramah Willis Wofford (who worked at home and sang in church).

Her grandparents came to the North from Alabama to escape poverty and racism. Her father's and mother's experiences with and responses to racial violence and economic inequality, as well as what Morrison learned about living in an economically cooperative neighborhood, have influenced the political edge of her art. Her early understanding of the "recognized and verifiable principles of Black art," principles she heard demonstrated in her family's stories

and saw demonstrated in the art and play of black people around her, has also had its effect. Morrison's ability to manipulate the linguistic qualities of both black art and conventional literary form manifests itself in a prose that some critics have described as lyrical and vernacular at the same time.

After earning a B.A. from Howard University in 1953, Morrison moved to Cornell University for graduate work in English and received an M.A. in 1955. She taught at Texas Southern University from 1955 to 1957 and then at Howard University (until 1964), where she met and married Harold Morrison, a Jamaican architect, and gave birth to two sons. Those were years that Morrison has described as a period of almost complete powerlessness, when she wrote quietly and participated in a writers' workshop, creating the story that would become *The Bluest Eye.*

In 1964, Morrison divorced her husband and moved to Syracuse, N.Y., where she began work for Random House. She later moved to a senior editor's position at the Random House headquarters in New York City—continuing to teach, along the way, at various universities. Since 1988, she has been Robert F. Goheen Professor of the Humanities at Princeton University.

Morrison's first novel, *The Bluest Eye* (1970), is a text that combines formal "play" between literary

Novelist Toni Morrison, photographed in New York City shortly after winning the 1993 Nobel Prize for Literature. Author of *The Song of Solomon* and *Beloved,* Morrison is the first American-born black to win the award. (AP/Wide World Photos)

aesthetics and pastoral imagery with criticism of the effects of racialized personal aesthetics. *Sula* (1973) takes the pattern of the heroic quest and the artist-outsider theme and disrupts both in a novel that juxtaposes those figurations with societal gender restrictions amid the historical constraint of racism. *Song of Solomon* (1977), *Tar Baby* (1981), and *Beloved* (1987) are engagements with the relation to history of culturally specific political dynamics, aesthetics, and ritualized cultural practices.

Song of Solomon sets group history within the parameters of a family romance; *Tar Baby* interweaves the effects of colonialism and multiple family interrelationships that are stand-ins for history with surreal descriptions of landscape; and *Beloved* negotiates narrative battles over story and history produced as a result of the imagination's inability to make sense of slavery. In *Jazz,* Morrison continues her engagement with the problems and productiveness of individual storytelling's relation to larger, public history.

The lectures published as *Playing in the Dark* continue Morrison's interest in history and narrative. The collection abstracts her ongoing dialogue with literary criticism and history around manifestations of race and racism as narrative forms themselves produced by (and producers of) the social effects of racism in the larger public imagination.

Morrison's work sets its own unique imprimatur on that public imagination as much as it does on the literary world. A consensus has emerged that articulates the importance of Morrison to the world of letters and demonstrates the permeability of the boundary between specific cultural production—the cultural production that comes out of living as part of the African-American group—and the realm of cultural production that critics perceive as having crossed boundaries between groups and nation-states.

Morrison's ability to cross the boundaries as cultural commentator is reflected in *Race-ing Justice and Engendering Power: Essays on Anita Hill, Clarence Thomas, and the Construction of Social Reality,* a collection of essays about the nomination of Supreme Court Justice Clarence THOMAS and the accusations of sexual harassment brought against him by law professor Anita Hill (*see also* HILL-THOMAS HEARINGS). The essays in the collection were written by scholars from various fields, then edited and introduced by Morrison.

REFERENCES

LUBIANO, WAHNEEMA. "Toni Morrison." In Lea Baechler and A. Walton Litz, eds. *African American Writers*. New York, 1991, pp. 321–334.

MIDDLETON, DAVID L. *Toni Morrison: An Annotated Bibliography*. New York, 1987.

MORRISON, TONI. "Memory, Creation, and Writing." *Thought* 59 (December 1984): 385–390.

WAHNEEMA LUBIANO

Morrow, Everett Frederick (April 20, 1909–), government official. Born in Hackensack, N.J., the son and grandson of ministers, E. Frederick Morrow graduated from Bowdoin College in 1930, then took a position as a field secretary for the NATIONAL ASSOCIATION FOR THE ADVANCEMENT OF COLORED PEOPLE (NAACP) during the 1930s and 1940s. He served in the Army from 1942 through 1946, reaching the rank of major. After his discharge, he attended the Rutgers University School of Law, and passed the bar exam in 1948. In 1951, Morrow left the NAACP and joined CBS News. The following year he worked as adviser and consultant for Dwight D. Eisenhower's presidential campaign. After the election, Morrow was promised a position on Eisenhower's White House staff. However, the position did not materialize; instead, Morrow was given a job as adviser on business affairs in the Department of Commerce.

On July 9, 1955, Morrow finally was offered a White House position, and was named administrative officer for the Special Projects group. He was the first African-American White House staff member, but he was not given much responsibility. He had difficulty obtaining a personal secretary and was not permitted to be alone in a room with women staff members. Contrary to normal practice, he was not even officially sworn in until 1957, after Eisenhower's second election, and the swearing-in took place in a closed, unannounced ceremony that Eisenhower did not attend.

Morrow spent a frustrating five and a half years in the White House, sending memos and trying to press Eisenhower out of his inertia in dealing with civil rights. Acting as a liaison between the black community and the administration, Morrow played a crucial role in arranging the 1958 meeting between President Eisenhower and the Rev. Dr. Martin Luther KING, Jr., and other black leaders. However, Morrow also was criticized by some staff members for pushing too hard on civil rights.

In 1960, Morrow was invited to address the Republican National Convention in Chicago. However, before he began his speech praising the REPUBLICAN PARTY, network telecasters, wary of white reaction to a black speaker, cut away from the convention. Morrow campaigned for Richard Nixon, but was unable to persuade the Republicans to take strong action on civil rights. After the election, Morrow became vice president of the African-American Institute in New York, and in 1964 was hired as vice president of the Bank of America International, where he spent the rest of his career. He has written three books, *Black Man in the White House: A Diary of the Eisenhower Years* (1963); *Way Down South Up North* (1975); and *Forty Years a Guinea Pig* (1980).

REFERENCE

MORROW, E. FREDERICK. *Forty Years a Guinea Pig.* New York, 1980.

BILL OLSEN

Mortality and Morbidity. In the United States, African Americans, in comparison with whites, suffer enormous disadvantages in health status. In general, African Americans are at greater health risks throughout their life span. Because of this inequality, they do not live as long as whites.

Infant Mortality

Over the past decades, infant mortality declined rapidly in the United States. Despite these declines, however, the United States still ranks twenty-second worldwide in infant mortality. The rate varies considerably by race in the United States. For example, despite the improvements that have been made, an African-American child is about twice as likely as a white child to die within the first year of life. Between 1960 and 1988, the infant-mortality rate for whites declined from 22.9 per 1,000 live births to 8.9 per 1,000 live births, whereas the African-American infant-mortality rate dropped from 44.3 per 1,000 to 18 per 1,000 live births. In some cities with large African-American populations, such as Washington, D.C., and Detroit, the infant-mortality rate of African-American babies exceeds those found in some developing countries of Central America. Some experts estimate that if African-American and white infant-mortality rates were equal, approximately 6,000 additional African-American babies would survive annually.

In the United States, the two leading causes of infant mortality are birth defects (21 percent) and low birth weight/prematurity/respiratory stress syndrome (17.7 percent). While birth defects are the leading cause, it is developmental disabilities such as low birth weights that appear to differentiate more greatly along racial lines. For example, African-American infants are twice as likely as white infants to be low-weight (5.5 pounds or less). To a large extent these racial disparities may be explained by the vestiges of poverty, including poor or no prenatal care, poor nutrition, and lack of information about health care during pregnancy.

Typically, maternal mortality is defined as the number of deaths to women per 100,000 live births due to complications of pregnancy or childbirth or within ninety days postpartum. The disparities between African-American and white maternal-mortality rates actually exceed the infant-mortality rate differences. Despite overall reductions in maternal-mortality rates for both races, African-American mothers continue to experience a mortality rate that is about three times that of whites. In 1984, for example, the maternal-mortality rate for African Americans was 19.7, compared with only 5.4 for whites. There is considerable evidence that many of these deaths could have been prevented through early and adequate prenatal care.

Life Expectancy

In 1960, white Americans could expect to live about 69.1 years, while African Americans and other races could expect to live roughly 8.3 years less. Ten years later, the life expectancy of white and African Americans had climbed to 71.1 and 64.1 years, respectively, a difference of 7.0 years. By 1984, the racial gap fell to 5.6 years. Since that time, however, the gap has risen again to 6.2 years (through 1987). The net effect was that life expectancy for whites continued to rise and reached 75.6 years, while African Americans could expect to live only 69.4 years. Health officials view this as a disturbing trend. Much of this recent differential is due to the alarmingly high death rates of young African-American males. In 1988, the life expectancy of African-American males was 8 years less than that of African-American females. In fact, one study revealed that African-American males living in New York City's Harlem had less chance of surviving to age 65 than a male in Bangladesh, one of the poorest nations in the world. However, the officials at the national Centers for Disease Control concluded that about one-third of the difference in African-American/white death rates was due to preventable risk factors.

LEADING CAUSES OF DEATH

Heart disease and stroke account for approximately 40 percent of all excess deaths for African Americans under age seventy. (*Excess deaths* refers to the differential between the actual deaths and the number that would have occurred had African Americans and whites had the same death rates for each cohort and both sexes.) In 1990, there was a higher prevalence among African Americans than whites for cancer of the esophagus, larynx, lung, stomach, cervix, and pancreas. Generally, African-American women are somewhat less likely than white women, and

African-American men are more likely than white men, to have cancer.

African-American female cancer patients are about 20 percent less likely than white females to survive cancer. Similarly, African-American males are about 30 percent less likely than white males to survive cancer. Despite an 11 percent decline in the cervical cancer rate between 1980 and 1987, African-American women are twice as likely as white women to die of the disease. Although African-American women are more likely than their white counterparts to obtain a Pap test, they fail to obtain the same kind of follow-up treatment or care as their white counterparts.

OTHER DISEASES

The rate of blindness and visual impairment among African Americans is nearly twice that of whites. Among white and African Americans between the ages of forty and seventy-nine, African Americans have a higher rate of visual impairment. Thereafter, blindness is only slightly higher for African Americans than whites (8 percent versus 7 percent).

Approximately 16 percent of all children in the United States suffer from lead poisoning. In sharp contrast, however, 55 percent of all African-American children have been contaminated by lead that causes neurological damage. The effects of lead poisoning have been associated with a number of social problems, including higher dropout rates, higher incidence of reading disabilities, and lower performance and achievement in school.

Among African-American men between the ages of twenty-five and forty-four who suffer from hypertension, the rate of kidney failure is about 20 times that of their white counterparts. Approximately 33 percent of the kidney failure incidence among African Americans can be attributed to hypertension. Of the 100,000 Americans in dialysis, about one-third are African-American. However, white males are about twice as likely as African-American males to receive a kidney transplant. These disparities could be greatly reduced by eliminating existing cultural barriers in organ donations and by aggressive action to find suitable matches between donors and recipients.

In 1981, Acquired Immune Deficiency Syndrome (AIDS) first received national media attention. The disease was widely regarded to be a gay disease, mostly affecting white males. During much of the 1980s, the African-American community was reluctant to acknowledge the problem among its citizens. Some scholars attributed this denial to the strong cultural taboo against homosexuality. As the disease spread to other segments of the population, African Americans could no longer deny the problem. Ac-

cording to reports published in 1989 by the federal Centers for Disease Control, African Americans are twice as likely as whites to contract AIDS. The reports conclude that more than one-half of all women afflicted with the disease in this country are African Americans; about 70 percent of babies born with the AIDS virus are African Americans, as are nearly one-fourth of all males with the disease. The incidence of AIDS in the African-American community is attributable, in large measure, to the higher rate of intravenous drug use, in which dirty needles are frequently exchanged by users. This practice of sharing needles is further complicated when the intravenous drug users engage in sexual practices that put themselves, their partners, and unborn children at risk.

REFERENCES

BLACKWELL, JAMES E. The Black Community: Diversity and Unity. 3rd ed. New York, 1991.

JAYNES, GERALD D., and ROBIN M. WILLIAMS, JR., eds. A Common Destiny: Blacks and American Society. Washington, D.C., 1989.

McCORD, C. and H. P. FREEMAN. "Excess Mortality in Harlem." New England Journal of Medicine 322 (1990):173–177.

WILLIE J. PEARSON, JR.

Morticians. See Undertakers, Embalmers, Morticians.

Morton, Ferdinand Joseph "Jelly Roll" (October 20, 1890–July 10, 1941), jazz pianist and composer. Although the facts concerning his early life remain in dispute, along with his claim to have singlehandedly invented jazz in the early years of the twentieth century, Jelly Roll Morton nonetheless remains the crucial figure in bridging nineteenth-century blues, vaudeville songs, and ragtime with the small jazz ensembles of the 1920s. He was born Ferdinand Joseph LaMothe in Gulfport, Miss. His father, a Creole carpenter and trombonist schooled in classical music, whose name has also been spelled "LeMenthe" and "Lemott," left the family when Ferdinand was a child. Ferdinand was raised in New Orleans, and took the last name of Ed Morton, his stepfather, who was a porter and trombonist. Jelly Roll played guitar and trombone before taking up piano as a teenager, performing at "sporting houses," which were bordellos in the red-light district of New

Orleans known as Storyville. He also learned from pianists during his travels along the Gulf Coast as far as Florida. Morton studied with a professor of music from St. Joseph's Seminary College in Saint Benedict, La., but it was his 1902 meeting in New Orleans with the elegant ragtime pianist Tony Jackson, the composer of "Pretty Baby" and "The Naked Dance," that determined the direction of his career.

Morton left New Orleans around 1906, working in Louisiana and Mississippi as a pianist and as a small-time pool hustler, card shark, gambler, and pimp. In 1908 he moved to Memphis to work in a vaudeville show, and the next year he went on the road again, playing with vaudeville shows throughout the South, and possibly in New York, Chicago, and California. In 1911, he was performing as a pianist and comedian with McCabe's Minstrel Troubadours in St. Louis and Kansas City, and he eventually went to Chicago, where he settled for three years, leading his own band and managing a cabaret. He also published his first composition, "Jelly Roll Blues" (1915), the title referring to Morton's self-bestowed nickname, a slang term for the female genitals and sex in general. In 1915 he traveled to San Francisco, Chicago, and Detroit, and the next year he

Jelly Roll Morton, c. 1926. (Photographs and Prints Division, Schomburg Center for Research in Black Culture, The New York Public Library, Astor, Lenox and Tilden Foundations)

performed and ran a hotel and nightclub in Los Angeles. Between 1917 and 1923 Morton traveled and worked up and down the West Coast, from Tijuana, Mexico, to Vancouver and Alaska, as well as to Colorado and Wyoming, and finally back to Los Angeles, where he worked for a time as a boxing promoter.

In 1923, Morton returned to Chicago for five years, working as a staff arranger for the Melrose Publishing House. But much more important, it was during this time that he took advantage of the growing market for "hot" records and made the recordings upon which his reputation rests. He recorded as a solo pianist in Richmond, Ind., in 1923 and 1924 ("London Blues," "Grandpa's Spell," "Milenburg Joys," "Wolverine Blues," "The Pearls"), and also with a white group called the New Orleans Rhythm Kings. Even better known are recordings he made from 1926 to 1930 in Chicago and New York ("Kansas City Stomps," "Sidewalk Blues," "Smokehouse Blues," "The Chant," "Mournful Serenade," "Shreveport Stomp," "Ponchartrain Blues") with his Red Hot Peppers, an ensemble which included trombonist Kid ORY, clarinetists Johnny DODDS and Omer Simeon, and drummer Baby DODDS. During this time Morton continued to perform, touring the Midwest with W. C. HANDY, playing second piano in Fate Marable's riverboat band, and fronting pianist Henry Crowder's band.

Morton was the first great JAZZ composer. In addition to those works already mentioned, notable compositions include "New Orleans Blues," "King Porter Stomp," "Frog-i-more Rag," "Mamanita," and "Black Bottom Stomp." Morton was also the most important pianist to emerge from early New Orleans jazz, playing in an artful blend of ornamental nineteenth-century salon music and stomping blues. His arranging provided a model for small jazz ensembles, allowing raw improvisational passages to animate sophisticated composed sections, always within the conventions of New Orleans instrumental ragtime. As an arranger and composer, Morton paid careful attention to instrumentation and ensemble effects. In this he was the prime forerunner of subsequent jazz composers.

In 1928 Morton moved to New York, where in addition to continuing recording with the Red Hot Peppers, he played for two months at Harlem's Rose Danceland, and in 1929 he led an all-girl revue in Chicago. In 1931 he again led his own ensemble in Harlem, and in 1932 he served as the accompanist for Harlem musical shows. In 1934 he worked as the house pianist at the Red Apple Club in Harlem, and recorded with the white trumpeter Wingy Manone. Despite his busy schedule, Morton found both his health and his career beginning to decline by the early

1930s. Interest in New Orleans jazz had ebbed in general, the Great Depression had caused a collapse of the record industry, and Morton was virtually financially ruined by investments in a cosmetics company.

In 1935 Morton moved to Washington, D.C., and played a two-year engagement at the Jungle Club. He worked as a nightclub manager in 1937. In 1938 he recorded eight hours of music and anecdotal reminiscences for John Lomax at the Library of Congress. While they are pioneering and indispensable as oral history, because of Morton's boastful obfuscations they raise as many historical questions as they answer. In addition to the dubious claim that he invented jazz in New Orleans in 1902 by playing four beats to the bar instead of ragtime's two, Morton, whose arrogant personality had earned him many enemies, bitterly complained that numerous famous jazz tunes had been stolen from him. Nevertheless, the interviews provide an unequaled glimpse into the creation of New Orleans jazz, along with Morton's often quite perceptive insights into the workings of his music. Alan Lomax's *Mister Jelly Roll* (1950) is a condensed version of the Library of Congress interviews.

In 1938 Morton also moved back to New York, organized a music publishing company, and began performing and recording again, just in time for a revival of interest in New Orleans jazz. In 1939 he performed solo, but a heart attack forced him into the hospital. The following year, with his health still in decline, Morton moved to Los Angeles, hoping to claim an inheritance from his godmother. There he formed a new music company and led a new group of musicians, but he was too sick to work, and died of heart disease in 1941. In 1992 Morton was the subject of a loosely biographical Broadway musical by George C. Wolfe, *Jelly's Last Jam,* which attracted national attention.

REFERENCES

DAPOGNY, JAMES. *Ferdinand "Jelly Roll" Morton: The Collected Piano Music.* New York, 1982.

GUSHEE, LAWRENCE. "A Preliminary Chronology of the Early Career of Ferd 'Jelly Roll' Morton." *American Music* 3 (1985): 389–412.

LOMAX, ALAN. *Mister Jelly Roll.* New York, 1950.

MORTON, JELLY ROLL. "I Created Jazz." *Downbeat* 8 (1938).

WILLIAMS, MARTIN. *Jazz Masters of New Orleans.* New York, 1979.

LAWRENCE GUSHEE

Moseka, Aminaka.   *See* Lincoln, Abbey.

Moseley-Braun, Carol (August 16, 1947–), politician. Carol Moseley was born and raised in Chicago, the daughter of a Chicago police officer. She was educated at public schools in Chicago and the University of Illinois at Chicago, and received a law degree from the University of Chicago in 1972. Although now divorced, she has used her married name throughout her public career but hyphenated it after joining the Senate.

Moseley-Braun worked for three years as a prosecutor in the U.S. Attorney's office in Chicago. For her work there she won the U.S. Attorney General's Special Achievement Award. She began her career in politics in 1978, when she successfully campaigned for a seat in the Illinois House of Representatives. While in the Illinois House she was an advocate for public education funding, particularly for schools in Chicago. She also sponsored a number of bills banning discrimination in housing and private clubs. After two terms Moseley-Braun became the first woman and first African American elected assistant majority leader in the Illinois legislature.

In 1987 Moseley-Braun again set a precedent by becoming the first woman and first African American to hold executive office in Cook County government when she was elected to the office of Cook County Recorder of Deeds. She held the office through 1992, when she waged a campaign for the U.S. Senate. When she defeated two-term incumbent Alan Dixon and wealthy Chicago attorney Al Hofeld in the Democratic primary, Moseley-Braun became the first black woman nominated for the Senate by a major party in American history. Moseley-Braun then went on to defeat Republican nominee Rich Williamson in a close general election, becoming the first black woman to hold a seat in the U.S. Senate.

During her first year in the Senate Moseley-Braun sponsored several pieces of civil rights legislation, including the Gender Equity in Education Act and the 1993 Violence Against Women Act, and reintroduced the Equal Rights Amendment.

REFERENCES

HINE, DARLENE CLARK, ed. *Black Women in America: An Historical Encyclopedia.* New York, 1993.

SHALIT, RUTH. "A Star Is Born." *New Republic* 209 (November 15, 1993): 18–25.

THADDEUS RUSSELL

Moses, Edwin Corley (August 31, 1955–), track and field athlete. Born and raised in Dayton, Ohio, Edwin Moses began running hurdles at Dayton Fairview High School. An excellent student, Moses accepted an academic scholarship at Morehouse College in Atlanta after he failed to secure a college athletic scholarship. In his junior year at Morehouse, he began to compete in the 400-meter hurdles and qualified for the United States Olympic Team. Moses was the first hurdler to perfect a thirteen-step approach between each hurdle (most runners required fourteen or fifteen steps). At the 1976 Montreal Summer Olympics, he won the 400-meter hurdles in the world-record time of 47.64 seconds. Following the Olympics, Moses returned to Morehouse to finish his degree in aerospace engineering. He graduated in 1978.

Beginning in 1977, Moses won 122 consecutive races, establishing a record for the most consecutive victories in TRACK AND FIELD competition. In 1983, he set a new world record in the 400-meter hurdles (47.02 second) and won the Sullivan award, given to the top amateur athlete in the United States. The following year, he won his second Olympic gold medal at the Los Angeles Games and was named Sportsman of the Year by both the U.S. Olympic Committee and *Sports Illustrated*. In 1985, Moses was elected to the U.S. Olympic Hall of Fame. He retired from competition in 1988 and subsequently served as chairman of substance abuse committees for the Athletic Congress and the United States Olympic Committee. Moses was one of several track and football stars who joined the United States Olympic bobsled program in the early 1990s. A brakeman for the top

Olympic champion Edwin Moses in the 400-meter hurdles in Helsinki, Finland, 1978. (AP/Wide World Photos)

two-man sled for the United States, he won a bronze medal at a 1990 World Cup event in Winterberg, Germany. Moses attempted to return to track and field competition for the 1992 Summer Games in Barcelona, but was hampered by injuries and did not qualify. He maintained his ties to the United States Olympic movement, however, through his involvement with the U.S. Olympic Committee's Athletes' Advisory Council.

REFERENCES

Ebony (May 1984): 95–102.
SWIFT, E. M. "Ice Follies." *Sports Illustrated* (February 4, 1991): 52–57.

BENJAMIN K. SCOTT

Moses, Robert Parris (January 23, 1935–), civil rights activist, educator. Bob Moses was born in New York City and raised in Harlem. He graduated from Hamilton College in 1956 and began graduate work in philosophy at Harvard University, receiving his M.A. one year later. Forced to leave school due to his mother's death, Moses taught mathematics at a private school in New York City. He first became active in the CIVIL RIGHTS MOVEMENT in 1959, when he worked with Bayard RUSTIN, a prominent SOUTHERN CHRISTIAN LEADERSHIP CONFERENCE (SCLC) activist, on organizing a youth march for integrated schools. A meeting with civil rights activist Ella BAKER inspired Moses to immerse himself in the civil rights movement that was sweeping the South. In 1960 Moses joined the STUDENT NONVIOLENT COORDINATING COMMITTEE (SNCC) and became the fledgling organization's first full-time voter registration worker in the deep south.

Moses, who often worked alone facing many dangerous situations, was arrested and jailed numerous times. In McComb, Miss., he spearheaded black voter registration drives and organized Freedom Schools. He grew to play a more central role in SNCC, and in 1962 he became the strategical coordinator and project director of the Congress of Federated Organizations (COFO)—a statewide coalition of the CONGRESS OF RACIAL EQUALITY (CORE), SNCC, and the NATIONAL ASSOCIATION FOR THE ADVANCEMENT OF COLORED PEOPLE (NAACP). In 1963, COFO, with Moses as the guiding force, launched a successful mock gubernatorial election campaign—"the Freedom Ballot"—in which black voters were allowed to vote for candidates of their choosing for the first time. Its success led Moses to champion an entire summer of voter registration and educational activities to challenge racism and segregation in 1964, the FREEDOM SUMMER, with the purpose of capturing national attention forcing federal intervention in Mississippi.

During the Freedom Summer, Moses played an integral role in organizing and advising the MISSISSIPPI FREEDOM DEMOCRATIC PARTY (MFDP)—an alternative third party which challenged the legitimacy of the all-white Democratic party delegation at the Democratic national convention in Atlantic City. After the 1964 summer project came to an end, SNCC erupted in factionalism. Moses's staunch belief in the Christian idea of a beloved community, nonhierarchical leadership, grassroots struggle, local initiative, and pacifism made him the leading ideologue in the early years of SNCC. Finding himself unwillingly drawn into the factional struggle, Moses left the organization and ended all involvement in civil rights activities. Later that year, he adopted Parris—his middle name—as his new last name, to elude his growing celebrity.

A conscientious objector to the Vietnam War, Moses fled to Canada to avoid the draft in 1966. Two years later he traveled with his family to Tanzania, where he taught mathematics. In 1976 Moses returned to the United States and resumed his graduate studies at Harvard University. Supplementing his children's math education at home, however, led him away from the pursuit of his doctorate and back into the classroom. In 1980 he founded the Algebra Project, with grants received from a MacArthur Fellowship, to help underprivileged children get an early grounding in mathematics to better their job opportunities in the future.

Moses viewed the Algebra Project—whose classes were directly modeled on Freedom Schools and Citizenship Schools from the early 1960s—as an integral continuation of his civil rights work. He personally oversaw all teacher training to insure that the emphasis was placed on student empowerment, rather than dependence on the teachers. Creating a five-step learning method to help children translate their concrete experiences into complex mathematical concepts, Moses pioneered innovative methods designed to help children become independent thinkers. After proven success in raising students' standardized test scores in Massachusetts public schools, the project branched out to schools in Chicago, Milwaukee, Oakland, and Los Angeles, and Moses was once again propelled into the public eye. In 1992, in what he saw as a spiritual homecoming, Moses returned to the same areas of Mississippi where he had registered African-American voters three decades earlier, and launched the Delta Algebra project to help ensure a brighter future for children of that impoverished region.

REFERENCES

CARSON, CLAYBORNE. *In Struggle: SNCC and the Black Awakening of the 1960s.* Cambridge, Mass., 1981.
JETTER, ALEXIS. "Mississippi Learning." *New York Times Magazine* (February 21, 1993): 28.
McADAM, DOUG. *Freedom Summer.* 1988.

MARSHALL HYATT

Mosley, Walter (January 12, 1952–), novelist. The son of an African-American janitor and a Jewish clerk, Walter Mosley was born in Los Angeles, Calif., and raised in the South Central section of that city. After graduating from high school on the west coast, he attended Goddard College and later Johnson State University, both in Vermont. Upon receiving his B.A. in 1975 from Johnson State, Mosley worked at various jobs, including that of potter and caterer. Mosley moved to New York City in 1981 and enrolled in a graduate writing program at City College, while supporting himself as a computer programmer. It was during this time that he wrote his first novel, *Gone Fishing,* for which he was unable to find a publisher. Shortly thereafter, he completed *Devil in a Blue Dress,* the first of his "Easy Rawlins" detective novels. Mosley waited for six months to show the book to his mentor, novelist Frederic Tuten. Within a week of submitting the manuscript, Mosley signed a publishing contract with the publishing company Norton, quit his job, and began writing full time.

Mosley's hero, Ezekiel "Easy" Rawlins, is an African-American detective working the South Central section of Los Angeles with his sidekick "Mouse." *Devil in a Blue Dress* (1990) finds him in his late thirties, struggling to make his way in the often violent and racist, yet colorful and endearing, working-class world of South Central just after World War II. Mosley's subsequent novels—*A Red Death* (1991), *A White Butterfly* (1992), and *Black Betty* (1994)—see Rawlins through the McCarthy era and into the early 1960s. From the outset, the series was praised by critics and sold relatively well, but it became exceptionally popular after President Bill Clinton mentioned Mosley as one of his favorite authors during his 1992 campaign. Three of the books were nominated for Gold Dagger Awards by the British Crime Writers Association; *A White Butterfly* was nominated for the Edgar Award by the Mystery Writers of America. In 1994, a film version of *Devil in a Blue Dress*—directed by Jonathan Demme and featuring Denzel WASHINGTON, Eddie MURPHY, and Wesley Snipes—was in production, and two books—Mosley's fifth Rawlins novel, *The Little Yellow Dog,* and *R.L.'s Dream,* a novel about the blues—were due for publication.

REFERENCES

LYALL, SARAH. "Heroes in Black, Not White." *New York Times,* June 15, 1994, p. C1, 8.
MCCULLOUGH, BOB. "Walter Mosley: Interview." *Publisher's Weekly* (May 23, 1994): 67–68.

PAMELA WILKINSON

Mossell, Nathan Francis (July 27, 1856–October 27, 1946), physician. Nathan F. Mossell was born in Hamilton, Canada West (now Ontario), to FUGITIVE SLAVES from Baltimore. In 1865 his family moved to Lockport, N.Y., where Mossell attended an integrated school. Mossell moved to Philadelphia in 1873 and graduated from Lincoln University near Philadelphia in 1879. He was then accepted by the School of Medicine at the University of Pennsylvania, receiving his M.D. in 1882.

Initially denied membership in the Philadelphia County Medical Society, Mossell and his professors won a three-year struggle to secure his admittance in 1885. To further his medical education, Mossell undertook postgraduate studies at Guy's and St. Thomas Hospitals in London. Returning to Philadelphia, Mossell found that local hospitals still denied training to black interns and nurses. Refusing the offers of local medical colleges to start a segregated hospital under their financing, Mossell set out to establish a hospital run by African Americans and open to patients on a nonsegregated basis.

At first the Pennsylvania state legislature refused appropriations for such a project, so Mossell raised funds through public appeals, church donations, and his private resources. He leased a three-story building and opened the doors of the Frederick Douglass Memorial Hospital in Philadelphia on October 31, 1895. Receiving 86 percent of its funding from black citizens and businesses (and later an annual $6,000 appropriation from the state legislature), the medical center was dedicated to providing proper health care for African Americans and adequate training opportunities for African-American doctors and nurses.

In 1908 a modern building was constructed to house the hospital on another property Mossell had bought. The new building helped expand the hospital to 100 beds by the end of 1908; by 1912 there were 3,500 inpatients and 40,000 outpatients. Mossell served as both superintendent and medical director of the hospital from 1895 until 1931, and continued as medical director until 1933. In 1948, following a forty-one year rivalry with Mercy Hospital in Philadelphia (founded in 1907 by Henry McKee MINTON and other black physicians), the Frederick Douglass Hospital merged with Mercy to become the Mercy-Douglass Hospital.

From 1907 to 1908, Mossell served as the eighth president of the National Medical Association. He was also active in issues of civil rights and social justice. An original member of the NIAGARA MOVEMENT, he attended its founding convention at Niagara Falls, Canada, in 1905. In 1915 he organized protests in Philadelphia against the showing of the film *The Birth of a Nation.* He fought to have his alma mater, Lincoln University, hire African-American professors, an effort that culminated in the desegregation of Lincoln's faculty in 1931. Mossell also worked to integrate the student body of Philadelphia's Girard College, a goal that was not accomplished until after his death. Mossell retired from medicine in 1944 and died two years later in Philadelphia at the age of ninety.

See HEALTH AND HEALTH CARE PROVIDERS for an overview of African Americans in medicine.

REFERENCES

BOND, HORACE MANN. *Education for Freedom.* Philadelphia, 1976.
COBB, W. MONTAGUE. "Nathan Francis Mossell, M.D., 1856–1946." *Journal of the National Medical Association* (March 1954): 118–130.
MORIAS, HERBERT M. *The History of the Negro in Medicine.* New York, 1967.

SIRAJ AHMED

Moten, Benjamin "Bennie" (November 13, 1894–April 2, 1935), jazz bandleader. Moten, born in Kansas City, Mo., was exposed to music as a child by his mother, who played piano. His first instrument was baritone saxophone, which he played in Lacy Blackburn's Juvenile Brass Band. He studied piano in Kansas City with two pupils of RAGTIME composer Scott JOPLIN, and in 1918 he led a ragtime-style trio. By 1923 he had added five members, recording "Elephant's Wobble" and "Crawdad Blues," which were among the earliest recordings by a regional, or "territory," band. As it grew, the ensemble pioneered the Kansas City style of big band swing, with soloists "riffing" over a background of short, close harmony passages.

Moten's group played throughout the Midwest in the early and mid-1920s, gaining fame as the greatest of territory bands for their driving dance rhythms and compelling soloists. In the late 1920s, Moten brought the band to New York, playing at several of the most popular ballrooms. By 1932 Moten's ensemble had absorbed most of the personnel of bassist Walter Page's Blue Devils, including pianist Count BASIE, vocalist Jimmy Rushing, trumpeter Oran "Hot Lips" Page, and tenor saxophonist Ben Webster. Many of Moten's later recordings—"Moten Stomp" (1927), "Kansas City Breakdown" (1928), "Lafayette" (1932), "Prince of Wails" (1932), "Moten Swing" (1932), and "Toby" (1932)—proved enormously influential among jazz musicians. After Moten died unexpectedly during an operation for a tonsillectomy in Kansas City in 1935, Basie assumed leadership of the ensemble, which eventually evolved into the Count Basie Orchestra.

REFERENCES

DRIGGS, FRANK. "Kansas City and the South West." In Nat Hentoff and A. J. McCarthy, eds. *Jazz: New Perspectives in the History of Jazz.* New York, 1959, pp. 189–230.

RUSSELL, ROSS. *Jazz Style in Kansas City and the Southwest.* Berkeley, Calif., 1971.

THEODORE R. HUDSON

Motion Pictures.   *See* Film.

Motley, Archibald John, Jr. (1891–1981), painter. Archibald John Motley, Jr., was born in New Orleans. In 1894, he and his family, who were Roman Catholic and of Creole ancestry, settled on Chicago's South Side. Motley graduated from Englewood High School in 1914, receiving his initial art training there, and then began four years of study at the School of the Art Institute of Chicago, from which he graduated in 1918.

During his study at the School of the Art Institute, Motley executed highly accomplished figure studies. In their subdued coloring, careful attention to modeling, and slightly broken brushwork, these works reflect the academic nature of the training he received at that institution. In the late 1910s and 1920s, as racial barriers thwarted his ambition to be a professional portraitist, Motley hired models and asked family members to pose for him. His sensitive, highly naturalistic portraits show his strong feeling for composition and color.

The young painter was honored in a commercially successful one-man exhibition of his work at New York City's New Gallery in 1928, and he spent the following year in Paris on a Guggenheim Fellowship. For this show Motley painted several imaginative depictions of African ethnic myths. Following the exhibition, he visited family members in rural Arkansas, where he created portraits and genre scenes, as well as landscapes of the region.

During his stay in Paris in 1929–1930, Motley portrayed the streets and cabarets of the French capital. In *Blues,* perhaps his best-known painting, he captured the vibrant and energetic mood of nightlife among Paris's African community.

After finding little outlet for his ambitions as a portraitist, Motley at an early point in his career turned his talents to the subject of everyday life in Chicago's Black Belt. Deeply influenced by the syncopated rhythms, vibrant colors, and dissonant and melodic harmonies of jazz, his paintings evoke the streets, bars, dance halls, and outdoor gathering spots of Chicago's Bronzeville during its heyday of the 1920s and 1930s. He treated these subjects in a broad, simplified abstract style distinct from that of his portraits. Motley's Bronzeville views are informed by a modernist aesthetic.

A figure in Chicago's creative Renaissance known as the NEW NEGRO movement and a participant in such mainstream artistic endeavors as the WPA FEDERAL ARTS PROJECT, Motley applied a modernist sense of color and composition to images whose subjects and spirit drew on his ethnic roots. Between 1938 and 1941, he joined numerous other Illinois artists as an employee of the federally sponsored arts projects of the depression era. For institutions in Chicago and other parts of the state he painted easel pictures and murals, the latter often on historical or allegorical themes.

Motley visited Mexico several times in the 1950s, where he joined his nephew Willard MOTLEY, the writer, and a host of expatriate artists. His Mexican work ranges from brightly colored, small-scale landscapes to large, mural-like works that were influenced in style and subject by the social realism of modern Mexican art.

At the end of his career, Motley experimented in several new directions. In his long lifetime he produced a relatively small number of works, of which the most important, *The First One Hundred Years,* is his only painting with an overt political message. Today Motley is recognized as one of the founding figures of twentieth-century African-American art.

REFERENCES

ROBINSON, JONTYLE THERESA. "Archibald John Motley, Jr.: Pioneer Artist of the Urban Scene." In Carroll Greene, Jr., ed. *American Visions: Afro-American Art–1986.* Washington, D.C., 1987.

Getting Religion by Archibald Motley. (National Archives)

———. "The Art of Archibald John Motley, Jr.: A Notable Anniversary for a Pioneer." In *Three Masters: Eldzier Cortor, Hughie Lee-Smith, Archibald John Motley, Jr.* Exhibition catalogue. New York, 1988.

ROBINSON, JONTYLE THERESA, and WENDY GREENHOUSE. *The Art of Archibald J. Motley, Jr.* Chicago, 1991.

JONTYLE THERESA ROBINSON

Motley, Constance Baker (September 14, 1921–), lawyer and judge. Constance Baker Motley was the first African-American woman to be elected to the New York State Senate, the first woman to be elected Manhattan borough president, and the first black woman to be appointed a federal judge. She was born in New Haven, Conn., to immigrants from the Caribbean island of Nevis. She graduated from high school with honors in 1939, but could not afford college. Impressed by her participation in a public discussion and by her high school record, Clarence Blakeslee, a local white businessman, offered to pay her college expenses.

Motley enrolled at Fisk University in February 1941, transferred to New York University, and received a bachelor's degree in economics in October 1943. She enrolled at Columbia Law School in February 1944 and graduated in 1946. In 1945, during her final year at Columbia, she began to work part-time as a law clerk for Thurgood MARSHALL at the NAACP Legal Defense and Educational Fund, and continued full-time after graduation, eventually becoming one of its associate counsels. Because Marshall's staff was small and there was little work being

Constance Baker Motley (center) helped Ruth Smith (left) and other parents win a case in favor of Atlanta school integration, June 6, 1959. A. T. Walden (right) is one of the attorneys representing the parents. (AP/Wide World Photos)

done in civil rights, Motley had the unusual opportunity to try major cases before circuit courts of appeal and the United States Supreme Court. From 1949 to 1964, she tried cases, primarily involving desegregation, in eleven southern states and the District of Columbia, including cases that desegregated the University of Mississippi (*Meredith* v. *Fair*, 1962) and the University of Georgia (*Homes* v. *Danner*, 1961). She helped write the briefs for the landmark desegregation case BROWN V. BOARD OF EDUCATION (1954), and won nine of the ten cases she argued before the Supreme Court.

She left the NAACP in 1964 to run for the New York State Senate, to which she was elected in February 1964, becoming only the second woman elected to that body. She left the Senate in February 1965, when she was elected Manhattan borough president, becoming only the third black to hold this office. On January 25, 1966, President Lyndon B. Johnson appointed her to the bench of the United States District Court for the Southern District of New York. She was confirmed in August 1966, becoming both the first black and the first woman to be a federal judge in that district. On June 1, 1982, she became the chief judge of her court, serving in this position until October 1, 1986, when she became a senior judge.

REFERENCES

LANKER, BRIAN. *I Dream a World*. New York, 1989.
MOTLEY, CONSTANCE BAKER. "Some Reflections on My Career." *Law and Inequality* 6 (May 1988): 35–40.

SIRAJ AHMED

Motley, Marion "Tank" (June 5, 1920–), professional football player. Marion Motley was born in Leesburg, Ga., but moved to Canton, Ohio, where he played high school football before entering the University of Nevada in 1941. He was drafted into the Navy during World War II, and played football under Paul Brown at the Great Lakes Naval Training Station. He left the Navy in 1945, and returned to Canton.

Although blacks had begun to play in the National Football League (NFL) in 1920, they were barred from it in 1934. In 1946, when the Los Angeles Rams reintegrated the NFL, the All-American Football Conference (AAFC) was formed, and Brown, now coach and general manager of the Cleveland Browns, made them the only integrated team in the league, signing Bill Willis on August 6, and Motley on August 9.

Motley was a fullback, linebacker, and placekicker for the Browns from 1946 to 1953. One of the greatest football dynasties, the Browns of this period played in eight consecutive championship games, winning six titles. During this period, Motley carried the ball 826 times for 4,712 yards and 39 touchdowns. He was all-league in his rookie season, and became the first black to lead the AAFC in rushing, with 946 yards, in 1948. Motley was the career rushing leader of the AAFC, and after the league folded in 1949, and the Browns were incorporated into the NFL in 1950, Motley became the first black to lead the NFL in rushing, with 810 yards. Having sustained a knee injury that greatly reduced his ability, he was traded to the Pittsburgh Steelers in 1954, but retired during the 1955 season. He ended his career with a 5.7 yard per carry average, highest in professional football history. In 1992, *Sports Illustrated* placed him in its "dream team" backfield, alongside Johnny Unitas and Jim BROWN. Some people consider Motley the greatest fullback ever, even better than Brown, because of his blocking ability. In 1968, he became the second black inducted into the Professional Football Hall of Fame, after Emlen Tunnell.

Upon his retirement, Motley sought a position with the Browns, but none was forthcoming. He subsequently worked in a post office, a parking lot, as a liquor salesman, and as a supervisor in the Ohio lottery system. Although Motley expressed interest in working as an assistant coach or as a full-time scout, no NFL team offered him a position (other than a temporary scouting assignment with the Washington Redskins). On April 16, 1993, Motley was inducted into the NFL Alumni Order of the Leather Helmet for his service to professional football.

REFERENCES

VECSEY, GEORGE. "Marion Motley's Dream." *New York Times,* February 26, 1982, p. 8B.
YOUNG, A. S. "The Black Athlete Makes His Mark." *Ebony* (May 1969): 110–20.

SIRAJ AHMED

Motley, Willard Francis (July 14, 1909–March 4, 1965), novelist. Born and raised in a middle-class Chicago neighborhood, Willard Motley decided to become a writer after traveling around the United States for many years, working at odd jobs, and observing at first hand the life of the working class during the GREAT DEPRESSION. He worked variously as a ranch hand, cook, migrant laborer, shipping clerk, photographer, interviewer for the Chicago Housing Authority, and writer for the Office of Civil Defense. In the 1940s Motley lived in Chicago's slums, an experience that provided him with material for his first novel, *Knock on Any Door* (1947), which treated predominantly white characters involved in criminal activity, and drug use in an impoverished urban environment. This novel, hailed by contemporary reviewers as a significant contribution to American literature in the naturalist tradition, became commercially successful and was made into a Hollywood film starring Humphrey Bogart in 1949.

In 1951 Motley published *We Fished All Night,* a novel that examines the experiences of three World War II veterans as they struggle to cope with postwar life. *Let No Man Write My Epitaph,* the sequel to *Knock on Any Door,* followed in 1958 and was made into a film in 1960. Motley's last novel, *Let Noon Be Fair,* appeared posthumously in 1966; it examines the gradual corruption and cultural demise of a Mexican fishing village that becomes popular with North American tourists. *The Diaries of Willard Motley* (1979) also was published posthumously. Motley lived in Mexico for the last twelve years of his life and died of gangrene in Mexico City on March 4, 1965.

REFERENCES

KLINKOWITZ, JEROME, ed. *The Diaries of Willard Motley.* Ames, Iowa, 1979.
METZGER, LINDA, ed. "Willard (Francis) Motley." In *Black Writers: A Selection of Sketches from Contemporary Authors,* Detroit, 1989, pp. 417–418.

CAMERON BARDRICK

Moton, Robert Russa (August 26, 1867–May 31, 1940), educator. Born in Amelia County, Va., and raised in Prince Edward County, Va., Robert Russa Moton was educated by the daughter of his parents' plantation master. He entered Hampton Institute in Hampton, Va., in 1885, but three years later interrupted his work to study law and teach. Moton received a license to practice law in 1888, then returned to Hampton. He studied and drilled in the student cadet corps, reaching the rank of assistant commandant. After graduation in 1890, he was named commandant of the corps and given the rank of "Major," the title he would use for the rest of his life. He was the school disciplinarian, assigned to check on students' rooms and work. He had faculty and administrative responsibilities, and was a liaison between the white faculty and the black student body.

During his later years at Hampton, Moton also became a protégé and lieutenant of Booker T. WASHINGTON, president of Tuskegee Institute in Tuskegee, Ala. He became active in Washington's National Negro Business League, and accompanied Washington on speaking and fundraising tours. Moton echoed Washington's views, emphasizing the need for self-improvement, thrift, and industrial education. In 1909, he helped the Tuskegee leader preview and comment on a draft of President Taft's Inaugural Address. In the early 1910s, after the creation of the NAACP, Moton tried to restrain its members from attacking accommodationist ideas. In 1915, Moton founded the Virginia Cooperative Association, a farmer's aid organization, which he hoped would be the basis of a nationwide movement.

In 1915, following the death of Booker T. Washington, Moton was chosen to succeed him as principal of Tuskegee Institute. Moton was never the charismatic figure Washington was, and he let Washington's political machine dissolve, but he continued Washington's work and racial leadership role. He lectured and wrote pieces extolling the Tuskegee philosophy, and became chair of the National Negro Business League in 1919. Moton also became active in forming government commissions, which he thought a better avenue than civil rights legislation for resolving racial conflict. During World War I, Moton spoke

Robert Russa Moton, Booker T. Washington's successor at Tuskegee Institute, was a leading voice of southern black conservatism from 1915 through the early 1930s. (Photographs and Prints Division, Schomburg Center for Research in Black Culture, The New York Public Library, Astor, Lenox and Tilden Foundations)

at Liberty Bond rallies and tried to drum up support for the war effort. In 1918, after a spate of LYNCHINGS in the South, he helped form the Commission on Interracial Cooperation, which thereafter annually published lynching statistics. Moton retained a measure of Washington's control over federal political patronage to African Americans, and advised government on racial policies. In 1918, after he privately warned President Woodrow Wilson of the growth of black unrest in America, Wilson sent him to France in order to speak to black soldiers and make a report on their treatment. Moton reported on his experiences in his autobiography, *Finding a Way Out* (1920).

During the 1920s, Moton restructured Tuskegee, adding an accredited junior college program and planning a four-year curriculum. The school offered its first B.S. degree program in 1926. A skilled fundraiser, Moton tripled Tuskegee's endowment. His concern for white donors' sensibilities caused him to crack down on black self-assertion and dissent at Tuskegee. However, Moton was willing to defend what he considered African Americans' best inter-

ests. He lobbied successfully for the creation of a black Veterans Administration hospital at Tuskegee Institute, to be staffed by African-American doctors and nurses. The KU KLUX KLAN threatened violence unless he installed white medical staff, and 100 Klansmen marched on Tuskegee. Moton barricaded the campus and called on alumni to help defend the Institute. His actions won him widespread applause among blacks, including W. E. B. DU BOIS, a frequent ideological adversary. Moton's general philosophy was expressed in his book *What the Negro Thinks* (1929). Moton forthrightly demanded an end to legislated racial inequality. However, he accepted segregation, and called for compromise and black patience and work rather than activism to achieve civil rights aims.

Throughout the 1920s and '30s, Moton undertook public duties. He devised and lobbied for government assistance with National Negro Health Week. He succeeded Booker T. Washington on the Board of Trustees for Fisk University. In 1924, Moton founded and became president of the National Negro Finance Corporation in Durham, N.C. In 1927, he headed a committee of African Americans involved with the Hoover presidential commission on the Mississippi Flood Disaster. He served on President Herbert Hoover's National Advisory Committee on Education, and recommended federal funding to reduce racial inequality in education. He also served on a commission on education in Liberia, and wrote a strong report on educational inequities in Haiti. For his work, Moton received the Harmon Award in Race Relations in 1930 and the NAACP's SPINGARN MEDAL in 1932. Moton retired from Tuskegee in 1935, and died five years later at his home in Capahosic, Va., where the Robert R. Moton foundation was later established in his memory to aid black scholars.

REFERENCES

ANDERSON, JAMES D. *The Education of Blacks in the South, 1860–1935*. Chapel Hill, N.C., 1988.
BUTLER, ADDIE LOUISE JOYNER. *The Distinctive Black College: Talladega, Tuskegee, and Morehouse*. Metuchen, N.J., 1977.
HARLAN, LOUIS, and RAYMOND W. SMOCK, eds. *The Booker T. Washington Papers* (Vols. 3, 10–13). Urbana, Ill., 1972–1989.

GREG ROBINSON

Motor Racing.   Popular mostly in the South and parts of the Midwest, motor racing has traditionally been one of the most segregated sports in the United

States. Most major automobile races, including the Indianapolis 500, were open only to whites until after World War II. In 1910 the American Automobile Association enforced this policy when it suspended Berna Eli "Barney" Oldfield, the most famous American race car driver of his time, for holding an unauthorized race with Jack JOHNSON, the black heavyweight boxing champion.

In the 1920s, several groups of black automobile enthusiasts established their own racing organizations, including the Western Race Drivers Association, which held a rally in Los Angeles in 1925, and the Negro Men's Automobile Racing Association in Georgia.

Through the 1920s and 1930s, a driver named Rojo Jack became the first black automobile racer to gain fame. He appeared in several major races around the country and gained a significant following, mostly among black fans of the sport.

The most important milestone in African-American auto racing occurred in 1924, when an all-black, 100-mile derby was held in Indianapolis. Malcolm Hannon won the race, in which only three of twenty-two drivers finished.

Black drivers did not begin to participate significantly in professional races until after World War II and the advent of stock car racing, which used ordinary cars that were specially adapted for high-speed racing. The first successful black stock car drivers were Wilbur Gaines, who claimed to be the inventor of the roll bar, and Mel Leighton, who won prize money in twenty-seven of forty races in 1947. Neither was as successful in National Association of Stock Car Automobile Racing (NASCAR) as Wendell SCOTT, who gained a national following and substantial prize money during his career, which spanned from the 1950s to the early 1970s on the Indy Car and related circuits. Willie T. RIBBS, the first African American to compete in the Indianapolis 500, was the most successful black driver in the late 1970s and 1980s, winning the 1978 Dunlop Championship in Europe and recording Trans-Am victories at Daytona Beach, Fla., and Brainerd, Minn., in 1984.

REFERENCE

ASHE, ARTHUR R., JR. *A Hard Road to Glory: A History of the African American Athlete.* 3 vols. New York, 1988.

THADDEUS RUSSELL
BENJAMIN K. SCOTT

Motown. Motown, which was founded in 1959 in the basement of Berry GORDY, Jr.'s Detroit home and grew to become the largest black-owned company in the United States, virtually defines the style of African-American popular music known as soul. Integrating the unrestrained vocals, hand claps, and tambourine accents of black gospel music, the strong backbeat of rhythm and blues, the heavily produced sound of white popular music, and the detailed, narrative-style love lyrics of doo-wop and vocal group songs, Motown has always signified a range of African-American pop music styles. Drawing on untrained recruits from the churches and projects of Detroit, Motown nurtured many prominent figures of postwar American popular music, including Smokey ROBINSON, Marvin GAYE, the TEMPTATIONS, the FOUR TOPS, Diana ROSS, Stevie WONDER, the Jackson 5, and the Commodores.

Gordy, a former boxer and record store owner who had worked on the assembly line at Ford and had written several of Jackie WILSON's hits, started his musical empire with two small record labels, Tamla Records and Gordy Records. At first, Gordy worked with his brothers, sisters, and friends to produce Motown's records. By 1962 Gordy was comparing Motown with the Detroit auto industry that gave the label its name, a contraction of "Motor Town." At the height of Motown's fame starting in

The Temptations, one of Motown's most successful singing groups, at the height of their popularity in 1966. Pictured are Eddie Kendricks (center) and, clockwise from top right, Paul Williams, Otis Williams, David Ruffin, and Melvin Franklin. (AP/Wide World Photos)

1963, the production schedules at "Detroit's other assembly line," were indeed arduous, but consistently successful.

Gordy and his producers created dozens of classic soul records in Motown's cramped basement studio. Even after 1963, when the Motown sound became more elaborate, recordings were largely improvised on the spot. Motown's house band of Joe Hunter or Earl Van Dyke on piano, drummer Benny Benjamin, and electric bassist James Jamerson (1938–1983) was provided with sketchy lead sheets of chords. They responded with the inventive figures behind hits like the Temptations' "My Girl" and Martha and the Vandellas' "Nowhere to Run," on which Jamerson is virtually the lead player.

Gordy also prepared his acts for performances on traveling tours known as the Motown Revue. In 1964 Gordy hired a consultant, Maxine Powell, to teach Motown's artists everything from makeup to deportment, readying them for audiences as racially diverse as those at Harlem's APOLLO THEATER, Las Vegas, and prime time television. In 1965 Motown hired the tap dancer Cholly ATKINS to choreograph its acts. Atkins perfected the "Temptations' Walk" and taught the SUPREMES their demure half-turns and dance steps.

Smokey Robinson was the first of Motown's songwriter-producers, writing and producing six of Motown's first ten Top Ten hits. He specialized in wistful tunes and surprising lyrics, such as "I don't like you/But I love you," from the Miracles' "You Really Got a Hold on Me" (1963), and "I've got sunshine on a cloudy day," from the Temptations' "My Girl" (1965). His other songs included "The One Who Really Loves You," "You Beat Me to the Punch," "Two Lovers," and "My Guy." Starting in 1964 Robinson took over the direction of the Temptations. He gave them a song he had written for himself, "The Way You Do the Things You Do," and picked Eddie Kendricks (1939–1992), whose falsetto resembled Robinson's, to sing lead. A year later he wrote "My Girl," but instead of Kendricks he chose David Ruffin (1941–1992), a gruff, raspy gospel-styled baritone, to sing lead. Robinson also had hits with Marvin Gaye and with the Marvelettes.

The most famous version of the "Motown Sound" was largely the creation of two brothers, Eddie and Brian Holland, and Lamont Dozier, usually known as Holland-Dozier-Holland, or H-D-H. Starting in 1963, while writing for and producing Martha and the Vandellas, the Four Tops, and the Supremes, they created an instantly recognizable style: drums and tambourines on all the beats, vibraphone in tandem with piano, a throaty baritone saxophone, Jamerson's pulsating bass lines, and melodic riffs that counterpointed the melody of the lyrics instead of merely

Longtime Motown producer and recording artist Smokey Robinson (left) greets Berry Gordy during a Los Angeles performance in 1981. (AP/Wide World Photos)

marking time. H-D-H cut thirty Top Ten pop hits, among them five straight number ones for the Supremes in 1964 and 1965: "Where Did Our Love Go?" "Baby Love," "Come See About Me," "Stop! In the Name of Love," and "Back in My Arms Again."

Although black-owned, many top financial positions at the cluster of companies that made up Motown—including Tamla Records, Gordy Records, Motown Records, Jobete Music Publishing, Hitsville USA, and International Talent Management—were eventually filled by whites. Gordy was often accused of mistreating his performers financially. Motown lawyers wrote contracts that performers often never saw and paid them royalties that were well below industry standards. Motown also used the money performers made from live shows and songwriting to subsidize production costs for their next recordings, a practice known as cross-collateralization. By the end of the decade, Mary WELLS, H-D-H, David Ruffin of the Temptations, and others had sued the company for keeping them in what Ruffin's lawyers called "economic peonage." Still, Motown grew steadily, and by 1965 the company was grossing $8 million a year, and had 100 employees in Detroit, New York, and Los Angeles.

By 1967, Motown was undergoing personnel and musical changes. Norman Whitfield (1943–) took charge of the Motown production line. Writing with his partner Barrett Strong (1941–) and producing by himself, he took over the Temptations in 1966 with "Ain't Too Proud to Beg." Whitfield highlighted the raspy gospel sound of David Ruffin's voice and the increasing influence of funk. New sounds like stutter-step polyrhythms, one-chord vamps, and fuzztone lead guitars all challenged the old Motown Sound, and resulted in the Temptations' "Cloud Nine" (1968), "Psychedelic Shack" (1969), and the eleven-minute "Papa Was a Rolling Stone" (1972).

The early 1970s saw important career changes for several musicians who had been with Motown almost from the start. Marvin Gaye's conceptual album, *What's Going On* (1971), originally rejected by Gordy, spawned three top-ten hits: "What's Going On," "Mercy, Mercy, Me," and "Inner City Blues." In the same year, 1971, Stevie Wonder turned twenty-one, and altered his contract with Motown in order to begin a series of albums which included *Where I'm Coming From* (1971), *Music of My Mind* (1972), *Talking Book* (1972) and *Innervisions* (1973). Wonder wrote and produced these records and played virtually every instrument himself. Motown's last discovery of the 1960s was the Jackson 5. Cut with musicians from Los Angeles, the Jackson's first four singles went to number one. Sizzling, danceable pop, the first two releases, "I Want You Back" (1969) and "ABC" (1970), featured vocals by Motown's new boy star, Michael Jackson.

As early as 1963, Gordy involved Motown in the CIVIL RIGHTS MOVEMENT, releasing *The Great March to Freedom* containing the Rev. Dr. Martin Luther KING, Jr.'s "I Have a Dream" speech. In the early 1970s Motown started a new spoken word label, Black Forum, which produced King's Grammy Award–winning *Why I Oppose the War in Vietnam* (1970), as well as *Guess Who's Coming Home: Black Fighting Men Recorded Live in Vietnam* (1970), and albums by Langston HUGHES and Margaret DANNER (1970), Stokely CARMICHAEL (1970), Amiri BARAKA (1972), Ossie DAVIS and Bill COSBY (1972), and Elaine Brown (1973).

In the early 1970s Gordy moved Motown to Los Angeles, where he became increasingly involved in television specials, which were quite successful, and films, which were not. In 1973 Motown was the biggest black-owned company in the United States, and Gordy helped finance and produce *Lady Sings the Blues* (1972), *Mahogany* (1975), and *The Wiz* (1978), all of which starred Diana Ross. Despite the departure of many of Motown's key musical and financial figures, the company remained strong. Diana Ross, Stevie Wonder, the Commodores, and Rick JAMES,

continued to put Motown's records on the charts.

By the 1970s, Motown had become a financial giant as well as a dominant musical influence. In 1973 the company had grossed $40 million. Five years later, that figure was up to $60 million. In 1981 Gordy made Suzanne De Passe president of Motown Productions. She concentrated on television specials, with great success, and in 1983 the company grossed $104 million. The next year, Gordy signed a distribution agreement with MCA, an ironic return to the corporate involvement that had inspired him to start his own record company. Further ventures in television and film, including *The Last Dragon* (1985), proved largely unsuccessful. Consequently, Gordy was soon entertaining offers for Motown, and in 1988 he sold the company—then the fifth largest black-owned business in the country, with $100 million in sales and 257 employees—to MCA for $61 million. Gordy remained in control of Motown's music publishing and television and film subsidiaries. However, in 1993, MCA in turn sold the company to Polygram for $325 million. Polygram revitalized Motown, developing several major pop acts, including the singer Johnny Gill, and the vocal group Boyz II Men. Since 1985 Motown's original headquarters, the house at 2468 West Grand Boulevard in Detroit, has been a museum dedicated to the history of the company.

REFERENCES

BIANCO, DAVID. *Heat Wave: The Motown Fact Book.* Ann Arbor, Mich., 1988.

GEORGE, NELSON. *Where Did Our Love Go? The Rise and Fall of the Motown Sound.* New York, 1985.

GUARALNICK, PETER. *Sweet Soul Music.* New York, 1986.

HIRSHEY, GERRI. *Nowhere to Run.* New York, 1984.

MORSE, DAVID. *Motown.* New York, 1971.

WALLER, DON. *The Motown Story.* New York, 1985.

HARRIS FRIEDBERG

Mound Bayou, Mississippi. Considered by many to be the first all African-American town in the South, Mound Bayou, Miss., was founded in 1888 by Isaiah T. MONTGOMERY and Benjamin Green. The two cousins created what they believed to be a haven for African Americans who sought self-determination; the community also served as a capital venture intended to improve the fortunes of the Montgomery family.

The idea for Mound Bayou was conceived in the 1880s after the Louisville, New Orleans, and Texas Railroad (L.N.O. & T.) began developing a railroad line stretching from Memphis, Tenn., to Vicksburg,

Miss. Railroad officials believed that few whites would settle along the swampy land where the potential for disease was high; they thought, however, that African Americans were racially suited to the climate and could flourish under such conditions. As a result, the company set aside tracts of wilderness along the route for sale. Mound Bayou was forged from an 840-acre section of wetland, including two merging bayous and a number of Native American burial mounds which lay on both sides of the tracks that ran through Bolivar County, Miss.

The first settlers cleared land, planted crops, and opened their own businesses. Through mass advertising campaigns, which encouraged black settlers to form an all-black community, and with the support of national figures such as Booker T. WASHINGTON, Mound Bayou thrived and grew to become one of the Mississippi Delta's most successful towns. It also had the distinction of being the largest African-American city in the nation. At its peak in 1907, Mound Bayou was home to more than 800 families, with a total of approximately 4,000 residents.

In an era of sharecropping and peonage for much of Mississippi's black population, inhabitants of Mound Bayou—mostly doctors, lawyers, and small farmers—had a standard of living that exceeded most black, and some white, communities. It was a close-knit town that brought local issues before town meetings and sought the approval of its citizens before embarking upon new projects. Residents, citing a negligible crime rate, boasted of having torn down the local jail. They attributed this fortune to community spirit.

Community spirit aside, much of Mound Bayou's good fortune came from outside sources. Booker T. Washington was a vocal supporter of Mound Bayou in the early twentieth century; through Washington's intercession with financiers around the country, Charles Banks (1873–1923), a leading developer in Mound Bayou at the time, was able to float several ambitious projects, including a cottonseed oil mill and the Bank of Mound Bayou. The oil mill, whose stock was bolstered by contributions from outside investors like white philanthropist Julius Rosenwald, was initially capitalized at $100,000; it promised to be the industrial centerpiece of the small town.

By 1914, however, economic problems plagued Mound Bayou. The falling price of cotton and a lack of capital forced many residents to depend upon credit extended by white merchants from other communities. As economic conditions worsened, it became more and more difficult for local farmers to get the credit they needed for planting. The much heralded oil mill, opened in dramatic fashion by Booker T. Washington in November 1912, never actually went into production under the supervision of African Americans; its owners and shareholders were forced to cede control of the mill to B. B. Harvey of Memphis, an unscrupulous white businessman, while the bank failed in the fall of 1914 amid allegations of mismanagement. As the price of cotton rose during WORLD WAR I, the corresponding drop in prices after the war brought little relief to the residents. Hundreds fled north as part of the first great migration during the war in search of better economic opportunities (*see* MIGRATION/POPULATION). Fewer than 900 residents remained by 1930.

Mound Bayou remained troubled during the 1930s and 1940s. A fire decimated most of the business district in 1941. In the same year, one observer noted that Mound Bayou was "mostly a town of old folks an' folks getting old." By WORLD WAR II, prosperity and pride had been replaced by poverty and disillusionment.

Mound Bayou, Miss., the most celebrated of the black towns in the South after the Civil War, was founded by Isaiah T. Montgomery (right, center) in 1887. In its heyday in the early twentieth century, Mound Bayou had more than four thousand residents, a cottonseed oil mill, and a bank. (Prints and Photographs Division, Library of Congress)

After World War II, general prosperity nationwide brought a limited degree of revitalization to Mound Bayou. In the 1960s, some black nationalists brought Mound Bayou back to the spotlight by endorsing the desirability of all-black towns. In 1966, the Tufts University Department of Community Medicine, funded by a grant from the federal Office of Economic Opportunity, established an outpatient health center in Mound Bayou. Although there was some population increase, the number of inhabitants never again reached its 1907 peak. The 1970 census showed a population of slightly more than two thousand.

The 1970s witnessed an economic upsurge. Under the administration of Mayor Earl Lucas, who was elected in 1969, Mound Bayou attracted outside support for various projects. Tufts University continued to channel funds from the federal government into the local clinic and hospital. Although the funds were now granted by the Department of Health and Human Services (HHS), Tufts was charged with the administration of the clinic, which served the four surrounding counties. The clinic merged with the Mound Bayou Community Hospital in 1978. The two facilities were responsible for 450 jobs and served as the bulwark of the local economy. In 1977, Mound Bayou also received $4.9 million in public works funds from the U.S. Economic Development Agency; the grant was almost half of the $10 million appropriation for the entire state. In the same year, civil rights activist Fannie Lou HAMER, who spent her last years in Mound Bayou, died at the local hospital.

Unfortunately, by the beginning of the 1980s, the town had once again fallen on hard times. Economic cutbacks under the Reagan administration eliminated the jobs of some townspeople; at one point, more than half of the residents of the town relied on either federal or state assistance for support. In 1982, a Memphis radio station raised $120,000 from the black community in one week to help diminish Mound Bayou's $209,000 debt. While this measure showed the overall support for the town, the 1990 census only registered 2200 residents; more than one quarter of the town's population left Mound Bayou during the 1980s.

In the 1990s, various other crises affected Mound Bayou. While Mayor Earl Lucas had been partly responsible for attracting funding for the hospital and federal grants, his administration left office after twenty-four years in 1993, with a municipal debt of more than $500,000, although Lucas had been defeated in a 1989 election. Due to a lawsuit alleging election improprieties in 1989, no new mayor was allowed to take office in Mound Bayou until Nerissa Norman became its first female mayor in a court-ordered special election in June 1993. Norman pledged to try and curtail municipal spending and attempted to reduce some of the small town's debt. *See also* BLACK TOWNS.

REFERENCES

CROCKETT, NORMAN L. *The Black Towns.* Lawrence, Kans., 1979.

HERMANN, JANET SHARP. *The Pursuit of a Dream.* New York, 1981.

Mound Bayou, Mississippi Centennial Celebration: July 6–12, 1987. Mound Bayou, Miss., 1987.

JOEL N. ROSEN

MOVE. A countercultural organization based in Philadelphia, MOVE, or the Movement, was started by John Africa (b. Vincent Leophart) sometime in the early 1970s. Africa dictated to Donald Glassey, a graduate student at the University of Pennsylvania, an 800-page manuscript known as *The Guideline.* It became the cornerstone of MOVE philosophy. MOVE members rejected anything considered "man-made" or "unnatural." They opposed using modern technology and machinery, even to cook food or heat their homes. They also refused to subscribe to "man's" laws, seeing them as the root of all racial hatred and violence against man and animals. MOVE children, therefore, did not attend public schools and often went unclothed, and all MOVE members accepted Africa as their family name. This radicalism led to confrontations with public health inspectors and social workers concerned over the care of children, and with neighbors, who complained of garbage and fecal odor, rat infestation, and large numbers of stray animals. MOVE, in turn, protested industrial and noise pollution, and the caging of animals at the Philadelphia zoo. In March 1978, the Philadelphia police attempted to force them out of their collective house in Powelton Village. Under Mayor Frank Rizzo, the police sealed off a four-block area preventing food, water, and other provisions from reaching MOVE members. The confrontation escalated into a shoot-out in which one police officer was killed. Nine MOVE members were convicted of third-degree manslaughter.

A final, climactic showdown occurred in 1985, under Mayor Wilson Goode. MOVE, with a membership of approximately fifty-five, had obtained a house on Osage Avenue in West Philadelphia. MOVE began to protest what they considered police harassment. They boarded up their house and began broadcasting their grievances night and day. On May 12, police ordered their eviction. Shots were fired from the MOVE house; police responded with over 10,000 rounds of ammunition. Tear gas was also used, but the group was not dislodged until an incendiary device was dropped from a helicopter. The ensuing blaze brought down two square residential blocks. Eleven MOVE members were killed; only two survived. Birdie Africa (Michael Moses Ward), a child survivor of the blaze, was awarded up to $9 million in damages by the City of Philadelphia in 1991. Ramona Africa, the other survivor, was imprisoned on riot and conspiracy charges. MOVE continued to have a small presence in Philadelphia afterward.

REFERENCE

ASSEFA, HIZKIAS, and PAUL WAHRHAFTIG. *Extremist Groups and Conflict Resolution: The MOVE Crisis in Philadelphia.* New York, 1988.

WALTER FRIEDMAN

Moynihan Report.   In early 1965, as the focus of government action toward African Americans turned from fighting legal segregation to the War on Poverty, Daniel Patrick Moynihan, a young sociologist from Harvard working as assistant secretary of labor, wrote a report entitled *The Negro Family: The Case for National Action.* Moynihan argued that aid for blacks must take account of the state of the black family. Relying on the African-American sociologist E. Franklin FRAZIER and other influential authorities, Moynihan argued that poor African-American families were caught in a "tangle of pathology." He noted that one-quarter of all black marriages ended in divorce, one-quarter of all black children were born out of wedlock, and one-quarter of all black households were female-headed. From the time blacks had been enslaved, Moynihan argued, their family structure had been warped, and after Emancipation it had been weakened by segregation and poverty. Black women's greater educational and employment opportunities had led to a "matriarchal" family pattern that eliminated proper role models and undermined black male self-esteem, leading to juvenile delinquency and crime. High fertility rates led to increased poverty and to welfare dependency. While blacks were not to blame for their original oppression, their pathological condition was now self-perpetuating. The report noted that instead of paralleling the unemployment rate, the number of welfare cases was now growing. Moynihan did not propose any solutions to the problems he delineated, but the report clearly looked to federal actions such as large-scale employment of black males to break the "matriarchal" mold of the black family and to curb welfare dependency. Moynihan suggested the armed forces were one arena in which black men could find masculine employment and role models.

At first, the report was circulated within the government, and portions of it were discussed by the media. President Lyndon B. Johnson covered Moynihan's main points at a commencement address at Howard University. The government officially released it in August 1965. Coming shortly after the Watts uprising in Los Angeles (*see* LOS ANGELES WATTS RIOT OF 1965; URBAN RIOTS AND REBELLIONS), the report seemed timely. Johnson called for a national conference on the black family.

The report was soon met, however, by a wave of opposition, both from social scientists debating Moynihan's conclusions and use of data and by African Americans and other civil rights activists who found it insulting. Activists felt that the emphasis on out-of-wedlock births and the "pathology" of black family relations seemed biased and demeaning. Since Moynihan had not proposed any solutions to his findings, he seemed, in the words of the white psychologist William Ryan, to be "blaming the victims" of oppression for their condition. Rather than urging federal programs for blacks, the report was interpreted as justifying inaction, since it argued that blacks were trapped in a "culture of poverty" and did not have the psychological resources to benefit from educational or employment opportunities. John Lewis of the STUDENT NONVIOLENT COORDINATING COMMITTEE criticized the report for assuming that white discrimination was no longer a factor in black life, and the nascent Black Power movement decried Moynihan's advocacy of socialization by the armed forces.

The report was also criticized by black women activists and white feminists. Dorothy HEIGHT of the National Council of Negro Women claimed the report criticized black women for holding their families together and assumed that women-headed families were inherently pathological. Social scientists have since amassed considerable statistical and demographic evidence refuting Moynihan's contention that black women enjoyed privileged employment and educational status in relation to black men, and have suggested that the problem of female-headed households arose from the fact that women were paid less than men, and could not support their families without assistance. Pauli MURRAY questioned why black women should be censured for working.

Rather than engendering a flood of federal action to support black families, as Moynihan had hoped, the report ended by dividing opinion. Ironically, instead of focusing attention on the black family, the report itself has continued to be the focus of huge efforts at rebuttal. Its historical premise, sociological theory, and conclusions have been repeatedly attacked. Historians such as Herbert Gutman have examined the history of the black family to demonstrate the strength of family ties despite slavery and later oppression.

The report dramatically shifted the debate among social scientists on how to fight poverty. The effect of Moynihan's conclusions has been to challenge the thesis that income redistribution alone could "solve" the problem of poverty, and to focus attention on the particular problems of inner-city blacks. Some contemporary thinkers, notably the African-American sociologist William Julius Wilson in *The Truly Disadvantaged* (1987), have devoted special attention to the problem of high unemployment among young black males and its effect on the black economy and family structure, as Moynihan discussed. The issues raised by the Moynihan report on whether black poverty is a function of inadequate "values" or socialization has echoed, in both simplistic and sophisticated fashion, in policy debates ever since.

REFERENCES

GUTMAN, HERBERT. *The Black Family in Slavery and Freedom, 1750–1925.* New York, 1976.

JONES, JACQUELINE. *Labor of Love, Labor of Sorrow: Black Women, Work, and the Family, from Slavery to the Present.* New York, 1985.

LEMANN, NICHOLAS. *The Promised Land.* New York, 1991.

RAINWATER, LEE, and WILLIAM YANCEY. *The Moynihan Report and the Politics of Controversy.* Cambridge, Mass., 1967.

MARGARET D. JACOBS

Muddy Waters (Morganfield, McKinley)

(April 4, 1915–April 30, 1983), blues singer and guitarist. Muddy Waters grew up in Clarksdale, Miss., and took up the harmonica at age seven. He switched to the guitar at seventeen and soon began playing at local gatherings. He recorded both as a soloist and with a string band in 1941–1942 for a Library of Congress field-recording project. Moving to Chicago in 1943, he began playing the electric guitar, recording for the Aristocrat label (later Chess Records) by 1947 under the name Muddy Waters. He began performing with a band that featured harmonica player Little Walter; their recording "Louisiana Blues," made late in 1950, became a nationwide hit, entering the rhythm and blues Top Ten. The band, which also included Otis Spencer (pianist) and Jimmy Rogers (guitar), had many Top Ten hits in the 1950s, including "I'm Your Hoochie Coochie Man" (1953) and "I'm Ready" (1954). Muddy Waters continued to tour throughout the United States and Europe in the

1960s and received much acclaim as a primary influence on many "British Invasion" musicians. He remained active as a performer for the rest of his life, winning Grammy awards for several later recordings. He was inducted into the Rock and Roll Hall of Fame in 1987.

Muddy Waters retained a style that evoked the sound of the Delta blues in a band contest. His Library of Congress recordings illustrate the influence of Son HOUSE through their searing slide guitar playing, which he maintained throughout his band recordings in the 1950s. In contrast to the smoother Chicago blues of Big Bill BROONZY, Muddy Waters brought a tough, aggressive edge to the urban blues, making him a seminal figure in the development of the style and establishing him among the most important post–World War II blues singers.

REFERENCES

OBRECHT, JAS. "Biography of a Bluesman." *Guitar Player* 17, no. 8 (August 1983): 48–57.

OLIVER, PAUL. *Muddy Waters.* Bexhill-on-Sea, England, 1964.

DANIEL THOM

Muhammad, Elijah

(October 10, 1897–February 25, 1975), religious leader. Born Robert Poole in Sandersville, Ga., Muhammad was one of thirteen children of an itinerant Baptist preacher and sharecropper. In 1919 he married Clara Evans and they joined the black migration to Detroit, where he worked in the auto plants. In 1931 he met Master Wallace FARD (or Wali Farad), founder of the NATION OF ISLAM, who eventually chose this devoted disciple as his chief aide. Fard named him "Minister of Islam," dropped his slave name, Poole, and restored his true Muslim name, Muhammad. As the movement grew, a Temple of Islam was established in a Detroit storefront. It is estimated that Fard had close to 8,000 members in the Nation of Islam, consisting of poor black migrants and some former members from Marcus GARVEY's UNITED NEGRO IMPROVEMENT ASSOCIATION and NOBLE DREW ALI's Moorish Science Temple.

After Fard mysteriously disappeared in 1934, the Nation of Islam was divided by internal schisms and Elijah Muhammad led a major faction to Chicago, where he established Temple of Islam No. 2 as the main headquarters for the Nation. He also instituted the worship of Master Fard as Allah and himself as the Messenger of Allah and head of the Nation of Islam, always addressed with the title "the Honourable." Muhammad built on the teachings of Fard and

Elijah Muhammad led the Nation of Islam for more than thirty years. He is photographed here in his Chicago home in 1969. (Shawn Walker)

combined aspects of Islam and Christianity with the black nationalism of Marcus Garvey into a "proto-Islam," an unorthodox Islam with a strong racial slant. The Honorable Elijah Muhammad's message of racial separation focused on the recognition of true black identity and stressed economic independence. "Knowledge of self" and "do for self" were the rallying cries. The economic ethic of the Black Muslims has been described as a kind of black puritanism—hard work, frugality, the avoidance of debt, self-improvement, and a conservative lifestyle. Muhammad's followers sold the Nation's newspaper, *Muhammad Speaks,* and established their own educational system of Clara Muhammad schools and small businesses such as bakeries, grocery stores, and outlets selling fish and bean pies. More than 100 temples were founded. The disciples also· followed strict dietary rules outlined in Muhammad's book *How to Eat to Live,* which enjoined one meal per day and complete abstention from pork, drugs, tobacco, and alcohol. The Nation itself owned farms in several states, a bank, trailer trucks for its fish and grocery businesses, an ultramodern printing press, and other assets.

Muhammad's ministers of Islam found the prisons and streets of the ghetto a fertile recruiting ground.

His message of self-reclamation and black manifest destiny struck a responsive chord in the thousands of black men and women whose hope and self-respect had been all but defeated by racial abuse and denigration. As a consequence of where they recruited and the militancy of their beliefs, the Black Muslims have attracted many more young black males than any other black movement.

Muhammad had an uncanny sense of the vulnerabilities of the black psyche during the social transitions brought on by two world wars; his *Message to the Black Man in America* diagnosed the problem as a confusion of identity and self-hatred caused by white racism. The cure he prescribed was radical surgery through the formation of a separate black nation. Muhammad's 120 "degrees," or lessons, and the major doctrines and beliefs of the Nation of Islam all elaborated on aspects of this central message. The white man is a "devil by nature," absolutely unredeemable and incapable of caring about or respecting anyone who is not white. He is the historic, persistent source of harm and injury to black people. The Nation of Islam's central theological myth tells of Yakub, a black mad scientist who rebelled against Allah by creating the white race, a weak, hybrid people who were permitted temporary dominance of the world. Whites achieved their power and position through devious means and "tricknology." But, according to the Black Muslim apocalyptic view, there will come a time in the not-too-distant future when the forces of good and the forces of evil—that is to say, blacks versus whites—will clash in a "Battle of Armageddon," and the blacks will emerge victorious to recreate their original hegemony under Allah throughout the world.

After spending four years in a federal prison for encouraging draft refusal during World War II, Elijah Muhammad was assisted by his chief protégé, Minister MALCOLM X, in building the movement and encouraging its rapid spread in the 1950s and 1960s. During its peak years, the Nation of Islam had more than half a million devoted followers, influencing millions more, and accumulated an economic empire worth an estimated $80 million. Besides his residence in Chicago, Muhammad also lived in a mansion outside of Phoenix, Arizona, since the climate helped to reduce his respiratory problems. He had eight children with his wife, Sister Clara Muhammad, but also fathered a number of illegitimate children with his secretaries, a circumstance that was one of the reasons for Malcolm X's final break with the Nation of Islam in 1964.

With only a third-grade education, Elijah Muhammad was the leader of the most enduring black militant movement in the United States. He died in Chicago and was succeeded by one of his six sons,

Wallace Deen Muhammad. After his death, Muhammad's estate and the property of the Nation were involved in several lawsuits over the question of support for his illegitimate children.

REFERENCES

LINCOLN, C. ERIC. *The Black Muslims in America.* Boston, 1961; rev. ed., 1973.

MUHAMMAD, ELIJAH. *How to Eat to Live.* Chicago, 1972.

————. *Message to the Black Man in America.* Chicago, 1965.

LAWRENCE H. MAMIYA

Muralists. A culturally hybrid art form, the African-American mural is deeply rooted in ancient and modern African cultures; it also draws from both traditional and modernist Euro-American aesthetic and sociopolitical values. Inspired as much by social and economic conditions as by artistic vision, the African-American mural has reflected historical developments in American life and also helped effect social change. In black communities and historically black college campuses across the United States, the African-American mural is an ongoing source of cultural pride. Because murals have been among the works most often selected by textbook editors to illustrate African-American achievement in the visual arts, murals by artists like Aaron DOUGLAS, Hale WOODRUFF, and Charles WHITE are among the most widely reproduced and readily recognized examples of African-American art.

While confronting the artist with numerous technical challenges, the mural form nonetheless enables him or her to reach countless individuals who may not visit museums or galleries. As a large-scale work of public art, the mural addresses great numbers of viewers from all walks of life. Its large size and usual placement in public spaces make it an especially forceful and effective communication medium. This essential democratic nature makes the mural ideal for celebrating the historical, mythic, and symbolic aspects of African-American life and culture.

Broadly speaking, a mural is a large-scale work of art specifically designed to fill and complement an interior or exterior architectural space—a wall, ceiling, or floor. Not all murals are painted; *bas* (low) *relief* murals may be carved from a flat wood or stone surface, creating a design which is raised in low relief from the background. Other materials may also be used. Glazed tiles, enameled steel panels, terrazzo, and other durable materials can make even exterior murals relatively permanent.

The mural's flat surface and spatial amplitude are especially well suited to telling a story, recounting a historic event, or celebrating the heroism and achievements of historical figures. Because its story or message is expressed through visual images rather than words, the mural enables an artist to communicate with viewers regardless of their language or literacy. A relatively permanent, site-specific work, a mural seldom changes owners and frequently remains in perpetuity under the custodianship of a public institution where it is preserved and presented as a cultural treasure.

The African-American Muralist

African-American muralists are neither an identifiable group nor a school of artists; their common features include only their ethnicity and their occasional production of murals. All have worked primarily in other media. Because they have pursued different visions and styles in different eras and at different stages of their careers, they cannot easily be categorized or characterized. While many have worked primarily with black subjects and themes and addressed their work primarily to minority audiences, others have chosen to work with cross-cultural subjects and themes, creating works for broader audiences. Some identify themselves as "*black* artists," others as "*artists who happen also to be black.*" Recognizing this multiplicity of aims, audiences, and self-identifications is central to understanding and appreciating African-American artists, for no single characterization adequately encompasses the rich diversity of subjects, themes, and styles with which they have worked.

Because the mural gives powerful voice to an artist's narrative, historical, and sometimes propagandistic or didactic impulses, artists sometimes choose this form when they wish to make an especially important and lasting statement. Socially conscious artists sometimes employ the mural to offer both aesthetic and intellectual nourishment to ordinary citizens who often assume that art is inaccessible or irrelevant to their lives.

From Africa to the Americas

Since the dawn of civilization in the great river valleys of AFRICA, visual artists have recorded, recounted, celebrated, and preserved human history, achievements, and cultural values by decorating their homes, tombs, and public buildings with figurative and symbolic representations of heroic events and everyday life. Throughout Africa, ancient and modern peoples have created murals using whatever materials were available to them. Ancient Egyptian artisans painted elaborate scenes on plastered or stuccoed interior walls and carved detailed bas relief scenes on stone panels to decorate exterior walls. Today, women of the Bantu-speaking peoples of southern Africa continue ancient traditions, covering the mud plaster exterior walls of their homes with painted, incised, and inlaid designs combining centuries-old patterns and symbols with images drawn from modern life. Whether the sophisticated products of highly skilled artists or the humble, individual expressions of housewives preserving the vernacular ancestral arts, African murals demonstrate a timeless impulse to decorate architectural surfaces with scenes, images, and symbols depicting a people's history, values, and aesthetic visions.

In Europe, the mural experienced its apex with the fresco painting of the Italian Renaissance. Although mural painting never died out completely in the West, it fell generally out of favor until Diego Rivera (1886–1957), Jose Clemente Orozco (1883–1949), and David Alfaro Siqueiros (1896–1974) revived the mural form in Mexico during the late 1920s and '30s. A flurry of mural painting in the United States soon followed. The Mexican muralists' methods and motives proved a pivotal influence on African-American artists during the 1930s. Observing how these masters of politically and socially charged public art effectively employed the mural form to educate and raise the nationalistic consciousness of a largely illiterate and disunited people in Mexico, leading black American artists recognized the mural's great potential for raising racial consciousness and validating racial identity among black Americans. The influence of the Mexican muralists is readily evident in the murals of Charles ALSTON, Aaron Douglas, Vertis HAYES, Charles White, Hale Woodruff, and many others.

Materials and Methods

African-American muralists work with both traditional and new materials and methods. Murals painted on plaster are called *frescoes*. To paint a fresco, artists first render the design in a small-scale drawing called a *cartoon*. Then they enlarge the design and transfers its basic outlines to the prepared surface. The painting may be done with the help of one or more skilled assistants. In the case of a *buon* (true) *fresco*, a smooth final layer of lime plaster (the *intonaco*) must be applied to the surface a small section at a time to ensure that it is still wet when painted. The artist must work quickly and cannot go back and make revisions. *Fresco secco* is more commonly used today. Less difficult but also less permanent, it is made by applying water-based paint to dry plaster.

Many murals today are painted in an artist's studio on large canvas panels, tailored to the exact dimensions and shapes of the architectural spaces they are to occupy. When completed, the canvas panels are assembled and installed under the artist's supervision in the spaces for which they were created, perhaps under the arc formed by a vaulted ceiling or on the wall of a multiple-storied atrium or stairwell.

History of the African-American Mural

The history of the African-American mural reflects the rough outlines of the development of African-American art. Its story is largely confined to the twentieth century and rooted in the institutions of the black community. The wide diversity among the murals black American artists have created over more than a century's time reflects broad developments in African-American art as well as the individual visions of the artists.

THE TRADITIONALISTS

Because opportunities for training and patronage were limited for African-American artists prior to the 1930s, few are known to have created murals before the revival brought on by the Mexican muralists. The finest example from the nineteenth century is Robert Scott DUNCANSON. Duncanson was a traditionalist painter best known for his classical-romantic landscape studies. Between 1848 and 1850, he painted a series of eight landscape frescoes for the foyer of a former Cincinnati mansion, now the Taft Museum.

Although William Édouard SCOTT's career bridged the romantic and modern eras, he remained a traditionalist painter long after his younger colleagues had embraced African art, European modernism, and NEW NEGRO themes. In 1913, Scott painted two murals for public schools in Indianapolis, each depicting childhood themes and featuring black subjects. In 1933, he completed two murals for the Harlem YMCA in New York City.

THE NEW NEGRO RENAISSANCE

The New Negro Renaissance of the late 1920s and 1930s was a watershed for African-American visual arts. Modernist aesthetic theories and styles joined forces with the ideas of the New Negro Movement, creating a fresh and vital artistic vision. By nurturing a community of race-conscious black artists and intellectuals, by providing new sources of training and patronage, and by establishing alternative means for validating the achievements of black artists within the institutions of the African-American community, the HARLEM RENAISSANCE set the intellectual and aesthetic stage for the flurry of mural painting activity in the 1930s.

Pioneering black modernist and New Negro artist Aaron Douglas was the first African-American artist successfully to combine African imagery and sensibilities with European modernist styles, creating a culturally hybrid African-American art. He was also the most prolific African-American muralist. Early in his career, Douglas painted murals for Harlem cabarets. Club Ebony (1927) and Club Harlem (1928) are long gone; with them disappeared Douglas's exotic Africanesque scenes fusing jungle drums, rhythms, and dances with the music and dance of the Jazz Age Harlem.

As the cultural Renaissance of the 1920s flowed seamlessly into the 1930s, Douglas undertook a number of important mural projects, perfecting his original and distinctive style. In these monumental works, he documented with heroic grandeur and mystical wonder his people's journey from ancient Africa to modern urban America, celebrating their aspirations and achievements. Douglas's mural style is distinguished by hard-edge, larger-than-life figures dominating flat, geometrically segmented grounds. His most significant murals include an extensive series of frescoes for Fisk University's Cravath Library (1930), nightclub murals for Chicago's Sherman Hotel (1930), a panel commemorating Harriet TUBMAN for Bennett College in Greensboro, N.C. (1931), a fresco for Harlem's 135th Street YMCA (1933), a series of four canvas panels for the 135th Street Branch of the New York Public Library (1934), and a series of four murals for the Texas Centennial Exposition (1936).

Although they did not turn to mural painting until well into the 1930s, several other important artists are also identified with this earliest generation of race-conscious black American artists. Although only a few years older than their students, this so-called "Harlem Renaissance generation" mentored younger artists whose careers began in the 1930s. Both generations were prolific producers of murals during the latter part of that decade.

Hale Woodruff's powerful 1939 series of three mural panels commemorating the centennial of the AMISTAD slave mutiny and trial stands among the finest examples of the African-American mural. It is owned by Talladega College in Talladega, Ala. Charles Alston's interest in the healing arts of ancient magic and modern medicine resulted in an important and compelling pair of canvas panels for Harlem Hospital (1936–1937). In 1938, sculptor Richmond BARTHE created a monumental pair of *bas relief* marble panels for the exterior facade of the Harlem River Housing Project in New York City. Archibald MOTLEY was the premiere black Chicago painter of his era. He created a number of murals for schools and public buildings, including "United States Mail" (1937), a vivid stagecoach scene for the Wood River, Ill. Post Office. On the West Coast, sculptor Sargent JOHNSON also produced several murals during the 1930s.

THE 1930S

New Negro artists' thinking about art and society was further refined by the new ideas of a new decade.

Strong leftist sympathies which swept through American artistic and intellectual circles in the 1930s joined forces with the "cultural democracy" aims of New Deal art programs, creating a compelling ideological base for a socially conscious, nonelitist "people's art." Many black muralists joined the radical left. For radicalized New Negro artists, cultural democracy meant employing their art to engender racial unity and pride. By using public art to teach the black masses about their rich history and cultural heritage, artists helped to raise black consciousness, setting the stage for the civil rights movement a generation later.

Increased patronage in the late 1930s further stimulated mural production among African-American artists. New Deal art programs provided unprecedented government patronage. The U.S. Treasury Department's Public Works of Art Project (PWAP) (1933–1934), Section of Painting and Sculpture (1934–1942), and Treasury Relief Art Project (TRAP) (1935–1936); the Federal Emergency Relief Act (FERA) programs administered through the states (1933–1935); and the Federal Arts Project (FAP) of the Works Progress Administration (WPA) (*see* WORKS PROJECT ADMINISTRATION) (1935–1942) hired artists to decorate public buildings across America. Although these programs professed a commitment to nondiscrimination, they hired few black artists until after the Harlem Artists Guild began lobbying federal agency officials for more jobs. Guild members included Charles Alston, Selma Day (active 1933–1951), Aaron Douglas, Vertis Hayes (1911–), Elba Lightfoot (1910–), Sara Murrell (active 1936–1939), and Georgette Seabrooke POWELL, all of whom secured employment on federal mural projects. The Guild's efforts significantly increased the number of black artists hired by New Deal agencies nationwide and helped to place a few black artists in supervisory positions. More than a hundred African-American artists were employed on New York City's WPA/FAP. Although black women artists benefitted in significant numbers, sexism usually relegated them to jobs teaching art rather than producing it. This may in part explain the relative dearth of black women muralists, for many of their male counterparts were initiated into the mural medium through their work on New Deal mural projects.

THE INTERIM YEARS

While the period spanning the first great black cultural awakening of the 1920s and '30s and the BLACK ARTS MOVEMENT of the late 1960s and '70s saw significantly less activity in African-American mural production, it nonetheless yielded some outstanding murals by well-established black artists. The loss of federal patronage was a significant factor in the decline in the number of mural commissions.

During these relatively lean years for black artists, much of their patronage came from within the black community. Blacks commissioned murals for their homes, businesses, and community gathering places. Aaron Douglas painted murals for two private residences in Wilmington, Del. Charles Alston and Hale Woodruff were commissioned in 1948 by the Golden State Mutual Life Insurance Company to paint a pair of mural panels documenting the contributions of black people in settling and building the state of California. In 1953, a Houston minister commissioned John T. BIGGERS to paint *The Contribution of Negro Women to American Life and Education* for the Blue Triangle Branch of the Houston YWCA.

America's historically black colleges and universities played a central and ongoing patronage role during these years. In 1943, Charles White completed Hampton University's "The Contribution of the Negro to American Democracy," a kaleidoscopic "visual textbook" surveying the faces and figures of more than twenty great African-American men and women. His mentorship had a lasting effect on Hampton undergraduates who watched him as he painted; Persis Jennings (active ca. 1942–1944) subsequently painted murals at Fort Eustis, Va. (1942) and the East End Baptist Church in Suffolk, Va. (ca. 1942–1944). Hale Woodruff's *Art of the Negro*, a series of six panels completed in 1950 for the Arnett Library at Atlanta University, is an outstanding example from this period.

For decades, white philanthropies—whose patronage and interest had been carefully cultivated in the 1920s and '30s by intermediary patrons like W. E. B. DU BOIS and Charles S. JOHNSON—continued to award fellowships to black artists. Yet their support dwindled after the 1930s. The Julius Rosenwald Fund of Chicago and the Carnegie Foundation of New York provided a good deal of support for black artists, but funded very few mural projects after their interests shifted to the education and training of artists.

THE BLACK ARTS MOVEMENT

The BLACK ARTS MOVEMENT of the late 1960s and '70s marks the second major cultural awakening in black America. Led by young artists radicalized by the Black Power movement, the Black Arts movement earned the support of some elder black artists but created sharp tensions among others. It helped to revitalize a languishing African-American art and stimulated a resurgent interest in mural painting.

The African-American mural moved out of doors and into the streets of America's urban ghettoes in the late 1960s, when radicalized artists recognized and seized upon the public mural's communication potential. In cities across the country, militant black artists organized massive-scale, collaborative mural projects in an effort to create a "people's art." Submerging the artists' individual identities and voices in a collective, revolutionary chorus, they brought art into neighborhoods where social and economic conditions attested to the oppression and exploitation these artists reviled. Covering entire exterior walls of inner city buildings with boldly colorful, naive images of black pride, black power, African heritage, and African-American heroes and heroines, they raised race consciousness and fostered pride and dignity among America's dispossessed minorities.

Best known of these outdoor murals is Chicago's "Wall of Respect" (1967). Created by AfriCobra (African Commune of Bad Relevant Artists) leader and Howard University art professor Jeff Donaldson (1932–) and other members of the Organization of Black American Culture (OBAC), this work spawned hundreds of similar outdoor murals in cities all across the United States. Conceived and executed as vehicles for community involvement, these projects brought skilled, socially committed artists together with young people who learned to reclaim their cultural heritage as they painted its imagery on neighborhood walls.

THE RECENT PAST

The mural is not a static art form; its evolution in black America reflects a changing American society over time, as well as the artists' changing relationship with that society. In recent decades, established and respected African-American artists have won prestigious mural commissions both in and outside the black community. Two of the most prominent artists are Romare BEARDEN and Jacob LAWRENCE. Both only undertook mural commissions in their mature years, after establishing their reputations in other media.

The pioneering and best-known collagist of his time, Bearden was nearly sixty when he created *The Block* (1971), a six-panel collage depicting life in the buildings of a block-long stretch of a busy Harlem street. A tape recording of street sounds is part of the mural's installation. His 1983 mosaic, *Baltimore Uproar*, marks the subway station near Billie HOLIDAY's birthplace in Baltimore. In 1984, Bearden completed *Pittsburgh Recollections*, a ceramic tile mosaic mural depicting that city's black history and installed in an underground subway station.

Jacob Lawrence, who for decades had expressed his narrative impulses through extensive series of small images collectively recounting long, heroic stories drawn from dramatic episodes in African-American history, was in his sixties before he began combining multiple images into murals. In 1979, he completed *Games*, a ten-panel sports mural for Seattle's Kingdome Stadium. In 1985, Lawrence completed *Theater* for the University of Washington.

Contemporary ideas, materials and styles have continued to keep African-American murals vital, fresh, and dynamic. Lawrence's *Exploration* (1980) is a thematically and visually connected series of twelve enamels on steel panels. A fresh and vital exploration of the interrelationships among the academic disciplines, the mural was installed in Howard University's Blackburn University Center in 1980. In *Origins*, Lawrence used the same materials for a visual exploration of Harlem history and life. This work was installed near *Exploration* in 1984.

One of the most unusual and moving murals of recent years is Houston CONWILL's 1990 floor mural, *Rivers*, inspired by Langston HUGHES's poem "The Negro Speaks of Rivers." Installed in the lobby outside the Langston Hughes Auditorium at the Schomburg Center for Research in Black History of the New York Public Library, Conwill's terrazzo "cosmogram" celebrates the spread of African culture throughout the world. The mural also covers the tomb in which the poet's ashes were interred in 1990.

One of the students who had watched Charles White paint his fresco at Hampton in 1942 and 1943 was John T. Biggers. Nearly four decades later, Biggers returned to his alma mater to paint two panels flanking the five-story atrium of the university's new Harvey Library. *House of the Turtle* and *Tree House* were completed in 1992. Their mystical, mythic figures, symbolic images, and repetitive geometric patterns express a cosmology that spiritually and functionally interconnects their human figures, the natural world, and the built environment.

REFERENCES

CAMPBELL, MARY SCHMIDT, et al. *Harlem Renaissance: Art of Black America*. New York, 1987.
CHANGUION, PAUL. *The African Mural*. London, 1989.
COCKCROFT, EVA, ET AL. *Toward a People's Art: The Contemporary Mural Movement*. New York, 1977.
DOVER, CEDRIC. *American Negro Art*. Greenwich, Conn., 1960.
DRISKELL, DAVID C. *Two Centuries of Black American Art*. New York, 1976.
FINE, ELSA HONIG. *The Afro-American Artist: A Search for Identity*. New York, 1973.
MCKINZIE, RICHARD D. *The New Deal for Artists*. Princeton, N.J., 1975.
MECKLENBURG, VIRGINIA. *The Public as Patron: A History of the Treasury Department Mural Program*. College Park, Md., 1979.
O'CONNOR, FRANCIS V., ed. *Art for the Millions: Essays from the 1930s by Artists and Administrators of the WPA Federal Art Project*. Boston, 1973.
PORTER, JAMES A. *Modern Negro Art*. New York, 1943.

LINDA NIEMAN

Murphy, Carl (January 17, 1889–February 26, 1967), publisher. Carl Murphy was born in Baltimore in 1889. Only three years later, his father, John Henry Murphy, edited and published the first issue of the *Baltimore Afro-American*. After attending high school in Baltimore, Carl Murphy graduated from HOWARD UNIVERSITY, receiving a B.A. in 1911. He continued on to Harvard, receiving an M.A. in German in 1913. Murphy studied in Germany for several months after his graduation, and then returned to the United States to become an instructor, later an assistant professor, in the German department at Howard.

Because of the poor health of his father, Murphy started to work at the *Baltimore Afro-American*, becoming editor in 1918. After his father's death in 1922, Murphy was suddenly thrust into the leadership of one of the most influential African-American newspapers in the country. By the end of Murphy's tenure in 1961, the Afro-American chain had grown to include newspapers in Newark, Philadelphia, Washington, D.C., and Richmond. At its peak, the *Baltimore Afro-American* alone had a circulation of over 200,000.

Murphy was active in both national and local debates, especially those over civil rights activities. As a member of the Board of Directors of the NATIONAL ASSOCIATION FOR THE ADVANCEMENT OF COLORED PEOPLE (he was appointed in 1931), he vigorously supported the NAACP's legal challenges to legal discrimination. He also participated in trade associations, serving as the president of the National Newspaper Publishers' Association in 1954 and 1955. Dedicated to improving education for African Americans, Murphy served as a member of the board of trustees at Morgan State College from 1953 to 1967 and as a member of numerous state committees dedicated to investigating education. His commitment to education and civil rights issues earned him the NAACP's SPINGARN MEDAL in 1955. Murphy died in Baltimore in 1967.

REFERENCES

Good News for You! The Afro-American Newspapers. Baltimore, 1969.

WOLSELEY, ROLAND E. *The Black Press, U.S.A.* 2nd ed. Ames, Iowa, 1990.

JOHN C. STONER

Murphy, Eddie (April 3, 1961–), actor and comedian. Eddie Murphy was born in Brooklyn, N.Y. His father was a New York policeman and amateur comedian, and his mother a phone operator. Murphy's father was killed on duty when his son was three years old; his mother remarried, and the family moved from Brooklyn, when Murphy was nine, to the Long Island, N.Y., town of Roosevelt.

Murphy's talent at "ranking," a version of the "dozens" (a traditional street pastime of trading witty insults), earned him a position as a host of an after-school talent show at a local hangout, the Roosevelt Youth Center. After the favorable response he received from his Al Green impression, Murphy became a stand-up comedian, and soon was making $25 and $50 a week performing at Long Island nightclubs. In 1979, when he was just out of high school, he appeared at the Comic Strip, in Manhattan, which led to a successful audition for the television show *Saturday Night Live.*

Murphy emerged as a success on *Saturday Night Live* through his satirical impressions of such well-known African Americans as Bill COSBY, Stevie WONDER, and Muhammad ALI. Among his most famous characters were "Mister Robinson," a mean-spirited inner-city version of the children's television host Mister Rogers; a grown-up "Buckwheat" from "The Little Rascals"; "Velvet Jones," a book-writing, irreverent pimp; and "Tyrone Green," an illiterate convict poet.

In 1982 Murphy recorded an album of live stand-up material, earning him a gold record and a Grammy nomination. In the same year he costarred in his first motion picture, the highly successful *48 Hours*, playing a fast-talking convict who is released for two days to help track down a criminal. Murphy reached the height of his popularity in the 1980s with the films *Trading Places* (1983), *Beverly Hills Cop* (1985), *The Golden Child* (1986), *Beverly Hills Cop II* (1987), and *Raw* (1987), a highly successful though controversial, full-length concert film. In 1989 Murphy wrote, directed, and starred in *Harlem Nights*; he also made his recording debut with the album *So Happy*. In 1992 Murphy starred in two more films, *Boomerang* and *The Distinguished Gentleman*, though their box office success was only moderate.

Murphy started his own company, Eddie Murphy Enterprises, Ltd., in 1986, which, in a special agreement with CBS, produced series, pilots, and specials for network television.

REFERENCES

"*Ebony* Interview with Eddie Murphy." *Ebony* (July 1985): 40–48.

"Eddie Murphy." In Barbara Carlisle Bigelow, ed. *Contemporary Black Biography*, vol. 4. Detroit, 1993, pp. 170–175.

ROOTH, MARIANNE. *Eddie: Eddie Murphy from A to Z.* Los Angeles, Calif., 1985.

SUSAN MCINTOSH

Murphy, Isaac (April 16, 1861–February 12, 1896), jockey. Isaac Murphy was born a slave in Fayette County, Ky. After emancipation, his family moved to Lexington, where Murphy apprenticed as a jockey. In 1878, he rode in his first horse race, and in 1879 he attracted national attention by riding to first place in the Phoenix Hotel Stakes and Clark Handicap and placed second in the Kentucky Derby. Over the next four years, Murphy emerged as a leading jockey on the national circuit and in 1883 won a remarkable 51 out of 133 races.

Murphy's greatest successes came in the 1884 and 1885 seasons, when he rode with the Corrigan Stable of New York City. In 1884, he took first place in the American Derby at Chicago and then rode Buchanon to the first of Murphy's three victories in the Kentucky Derby. Murphy's most famous race came in 1890, in a match with Snapper Garrison, the top white jockey of the time. A great deal of excitement surrounded the race, as horseracing enthusiasts had debated for a decade over who was the better jockey. Murphy rode Salvator to a tight, half-head decision over Garrison's mount, Tenny. In the same year, Murphy again took the Kentucky Derby crown aboard Riley, and in 1891 he won his third crown aboard Kingman.

Although they are virtually nonexistent today, black jockeys were prominent in horseracing until the end of the nineteenth century, when the emergence of JIM CROW laws forced virtually every African American from the sport. Creeping segregation, combined with Murphy's weight problems and alcoholism, essentially ended his career after 1891. He died of pneumonia in 1896.

Murphy's record is one of the greatest in the history of horseracing. He won a remarkable 44 percent of his races, was the first jockey to win three Kentucky Derbys, and in 1955 was the first jockey elected to the National Museum of Racing Hall of Fame.

REFERENCES

LOGAN, RAYFORD, W., and MICHAEL R. WINSTON, eds. *Dictionary of American Negro Biography*. New York, 1982.

PORTER, DAVID L., ed. *Biographical Dictionary of American Sports: Outdoor Sports*. Westport, Conn., 1988.

THADDEUS RUSSELL

LINDA SALZMAN

of the protagonist of *Train Whistle Guitar* at an Alabama college in the 1930s.

REFERENCES

BERRY, JASON. "Musical Literature." *Nation* 224 (1977): 55–57.

WIDEMAN, JOHN. "*Stomping the Blues*: Ritual in Black Music and Speech." *American Poetry Review* 7, no. 4 (1978): 42–45.

CAMERON BARDRICK

Murray, Albert L. (June 12, 1916–   ), critic and novelist. Born and raised in Nokomis, Ala., Albert Murray received his bachelor's degree in education from Tuskegee Institute in 1939 and his master's in English from New York University in 1948. He joined the U.S. Air Force in 1943, served as training officer during World War II, and retired from the military with the rank of major in 1962. During his career as educator, Murray taught at Tuskegee Institute (1940–1943, 1946–1951), Columbia University (1968), Colgate University (1970, 1973, 1982), the University of Massachusetts at Boston (1971), the University of Missouri (1972), and Barnard College (1981–1983).

Criticized by some for antipolitical conservative views, Murray's writings focus on the positive aspects of African-American culture rather than on the negative effects of SLAVERY. In essays and novels, he displays a particular interest in the BLUES tradition, emphasizes the rich complexity of a culture that defined itself not only against systematic oppression but within the traditional American hegemony, and argues that race should not be seen as the prime determinant of individual identity. *The Omni-Americans: New Perspectives on Black Experience and American Culture* (1970) is a collection of essays on the diversity of African-American cultural expression. *South to a Very Old Place* (1971) is a semiautobiographical account that contrasts a trip Murray took through the South in 1970 with his childhood memories of the region. *The Hero and the Blues* (1973), a collection of essays on the social function of the blues, relates the improvisational art form to the concept of personal heroism. Murray's first novel, *Train Whistle Guitar* (1974; it received the Lillian Smith Award for Southern Fiction), tells the story of a black youth coming of age in 1920s Alabama. *Stomping the Blues* (1976, recipient of the ASCAP Deems Taylor Award) is a history of the blues and jazz and their significance in contemporary American society. *Good Morning Blues: The Autobiography of Count Basie*, cowritten with Basie, was published in 1985. Murray's second novel, *The Spyglass Tree* (1991), relates the further experiences

Murray, George Washington (September 22, 1853–April 26, 1926), politician. George Washington Murray was born a slave in Sumpter County, S.C. He was apparently orphaned at an early age, and at Emancipation he was left to earn his own living. Relying on his own resources and what schooling was available, he successfully competed for a scholarship in 1874 to attend the University of South Carolina. Returning to Sumpter County in 1876, he taught in public schools there until appointed inspector of customs at the port of Charleston in February 1890.

Almost immediately after his appointment, Murray began campaigning for a congressional seat. An effort launched in 1890 failed, but he was elected to Congress in 1892, serving from 1893 to 1895. He was then elected to serve an additional term, but, due to accusations of irregularity within the electoral process, he was not allowed to assume office until June 1896.

Murray received many leaves of absence during his terms in Congress, providing ammunition for critics' charges that he was inattentive during his tenure. However, he often absented himself from his formal congressional duties in order to organize his black constituents against efforts to disfranchise them. He gave many memorable addresses before Congress, including a speech defending free silver during his first session, and an address during his second session in which he read the names of over ninety African-American inventors into the *Congressional Record,* his own among them. He received twelve patents for his own inventions of improved farm implements.

Murray was a working farmer and was also involved in real estate. After his last congressional term, he devised a scheme to purchase and resell thousands of acres of land to blacks in South Carolina. He sold land to nearly two hundred black families in an effort to undercut the property restrictions against voting. After legal difficulties stemming from his real-estate ventures, Murray and his wife, Cornelia, moved their family to Chicago in 1905. There he published two "race improvement" books, *Race*

Ideals in 1914 and *Light in Dark Places* in 1925. He remained active in Republican party politics and continued lecturing until his death on April 26, 1926.

REFERENCES

GABOURY, WILLIAM, J. "George Washington Murray and the Fight for Political Democracy in South Carolina." *Journal of Negro History* 62 (July 1977): 158–269.

TINDALL, GEORGE B. *South Carolina Negroes, 1877–1900.* Columbia, S.C., 1952.

PORTIA P. JAMES

Murray, Pauli (November 20, 1910–July 1, 1985), lawyer, poet, and minister. During the course of a remarkably diverse life, Pauli Murray was a pioneer among African Americans and women in a number of fields. She was born in Baltimore. Her postsecondary education spanned six decades, beginning at Hunter College (B.A., 1933); continuing at Howard University Law School (LL.B., 1944); the University of California, Berkeley (LL.M., 1945), and Yale Law School, where in 1965 she became the first African American to receive the degree of doctor of juridical science; and culminating in 1976 at General Theological Seminary in New York, where, as the only African-American female enrolled, she received the master of divinity degree. When not pursuing her studies, Murray maintained several distinct careers. She served as deputy attorney general of California, becoming, in January 1946, the first African American to hold that position. During the 1967–1968 school year, she was vice president of Benedict College. From 1968 to 1973, she was professor of American studies at Brandeis University; in 1972 she was named Louis Stulberg Professor of Law and Politics at Brandeis. From 1977 until her retirement from public life in 1984, she was an Episcopal priest in Washington and Baltimore.

Murray's published writings include *States' Laws on Race and Color* (1951), which Thurgood MARSHALL referred to as the bible for lawyers fighting segregation laws; *Dark Testament and Other Poems* (1970), a collection of poetry; her autobiography, *Song in a Weary Throat: An American Pilgrimage* (published posthumously in 1987, it received both the Robert F. Kennedy Book Award and the Christopher Award). Murray's achievements and honors also included being named Woman of the Year in 1946 by the National Council of Negro Women and in 1947 by *Mademoiselle* magazine; serving as one of the thirty-two founders of the National Organization for Women in 1966; receiving the Eleanor Roosevelt Award from the Profes-

The Rev. Pauli Murray, the first black woman Episcopal priest, at her 1977 ordination in Washington National Cathedral. (AP/Wide World Photos)

sional Women's Caucus in 1971; and, on January 8, 1977, becoming the first African-American woman ordained a priest in the Episcopal church. On July 1, 1985, Pauli Murray died of cancer in Pittsburgh.

REFERENCES

MURRAY, PAULI. *Song in a Weary Throat: An American Pilgrimage.* New York, 1987.

SMITH, JESSIE CARNEY, ed. *Notable Black American Women.* Detroit, 1992.

SIRAJ AHMED

Murray, Peter Marshall (June 9, 1888–December 19, 1969), surgeon, hospital administrator, and civil rights activist. Peter Marshall Murray was born in Houma, La. He received a bachelor's degree from New Orleans University (now Dillard University) in 1910, and graduated in 1914 with honors from the

HOWARD UNIVERSITY College of Medicine, with a specialization in surgery and obstetrics. The following year Murray established a private practice in Washington, D.C., and served as a medical inspector for the District of Columbia Public Schools from 1917 to 1918. That year, he became assistant surgeon-in-chief of FREEDMEN'S HOSPITAL (now Howard University Hospital).

In 1921 Murray moved to New York City, where he started his medical practice and was an active participant in the cultural and professional life of HARLEM. In 1928 he started at the Harlem Hospital clinic and rose to become director of the gynecology unit. In 1953 Murray retired after twenty-five years of service.

In 1954 Thomas Dewey, the governor of New York, appointed him to the board of trustees of the State University of New York, where he served as chairman of its Committee on Medical Education. Murray's appointment to the New York City Board of Hospitals, in 1958, made him its first African-American member. He was also a member of the President's National Medical Advisory Committee on Health Resources.

Murray was active in both the National Medical Association (NMA), the black physician organization, and the American Medical Association (AMA). He served as president of the NMA in 1932, was chairman of its Publications Committee from 1942 to 1957, and was awarded the NMA's Distinguished Service Medal in 1954.

In 1926, twelve years after his graduation, Howard University elected Murray to its board of trustees where he served until he retired as an emeritus trustee in 1961. In 1951 Murray became the first African-American member of the AMA's House of Delegates, where for twelve years he worked diligently for the elimination of restrictive racial provisions in all of its component societies. Murray died in New York City in 1969.

REFERENCES

COBB, W. MONTAGUE. "Peter Marshall Murray." *Journal of the National Medical Association* 61 (January 1970): 70.

MORAIS, HERBERT M. *The History of the Negro in Medicine.* New York, 1967.

KEVIN PARKER

Museums.   The spirit of innovation, survival, and black creative expression has been preserved for more than a century through a range of research libraries, archives, and museums. Devoted to the black experience in the Americas and throughout the globe, they document the history of struggle and achievement that are the hallmarks of African-American life and culture. Since the founding of the College Museum at HAMPTON INSTITUTE in Hampton, Va., in 1868, material culture—household artifacts, photographs, diaries and letters, and other memorabilia, as well as sculpture, paintings, and more contemporary media such as films and videos—has been vigorously collected and interpreted to enhance public awareness and appreciation. Today, this tradition of cultural presentation is maintained by nearly 120 institutions and galleries throughout the United States.

Hampton's College Museum was truly a pioneer in this effort. Established to enrich vocational and academic instruction and to provide the broader community with otherwise unavailable cultural experiences, the museum was the brainchild of Col. Samuel Chapman Armstrong. Today, the College Museum is noted for its important collection of African artworks, acquired by a black nineteenth-century missionary to Africa. Its holdings also include significant works of African-American and Native American artists (the latter group a reflection of the student body at the time of the museum's establishment) and a major bequest from the Harmon Foundation, which sponsored a prestigious national competition for African-American artists from 1926 until the early 1940s.

Black cultural preservation was also advanced through the formation of literary societies and church archives. Beginning with the Bethel Literary and Historical Association (founded c. 1880) and the Negro Historical Society (1887), and, following the turn of the century, the Negro Society for Historical Research, these organizations were, in many ways, precursors to African-American museums.

Early research collections were often formed from materials lovingly accumulated by race-conscious bibliographies and lay historians. Such was the case for Howard University's Library of Negro Life in Washington, D.C., which received a sixteen-hundred-volume library from Jesse Moorland in 1873. The collection was augmented in 1946 by a donation of the considerable library of fame civil rights attorney Arthur A. Spingarn, becoming in the process the Moorland-Spingarn Library. In New York, Arthur Alfonso SCHOMBURG, a black Puerto Rican immigrant, responded to a teacher's comment that "the Negro has no history" by exhaustively seeking information on Africans and their descendants throughout the world. He began seriously collecting in 1910 and rapidly developed diverse holdings of manuscripts, rare books, pamphlets, sheet music, and artworks. By 1926, the magnitude of the Schomburg Collection led to its purchase by the Carnegie Foundation for the Harlem branch of the New York Public Library. Today, the Schomburg Center for Research in Black Culture is considered the foremost research facility of its kind in the world, with holdings in excess of five million items detailing the histories of blacks in Africa, the Americas, and elsewhere.

With the racial pride and interest in Africa that emerged in the 1920s, the campuses of historically black galleries and museums intended to enhance teaching generally for the black academic community and to make works of art available to the general public. Howard University began the trend in 1928, soon followed by Fisk (Tennessee), Lincoln (Pennsylvania), Tuskegee (Alabama), Morgan State (Baltimore), and Talladega (Florida) universities, among others. The galleries at these schools provided one of the few sources for exhibition and criticism for a generation of black artists and performed a major service to contemporary African-American art history by preserving a body of artwork and related historical documents that might otherwise have been dispersed, lost, or destroyed. The significant outpouring of black creative expression that resulted from the HARLEM RENAISSANCE, and, later, the large number of works commissioned through the FEDERAL ARTS PROJECT of the WORKS PROJECT ADMINISTRATION (WPA) during the depression era, make up the primary holdings of many of these institutions.

Assisted by the WPA in the 1940s, organizations such as the Uptown Art Center in New York (founded in sculptor Augusta SAVAGE's garage studio), Cleveland's KARAMU HOUSE, and Chicago's South Side Community Art Center provided free art instruction for local residents and aspiring artists and in many ways performed museum-like functions. Major artists, including Charles WHITE, Archibald MOTLEY, Romare BEARDEN, and Jacob LAWRENCE, received early training through these centers. In a similar fashion, the Barnett-Aden Gallery in Washington, D.C., which opened in 1940, provided a focal point for artistic activity in that city by mounting numerous exhibitions of black artists of the late nineteenth and early twentieth centuries, in addition to hosting public lectures and gallery talks.

The civil rights movement of the 1950s and '60s created a new black cultural Renaissance. The museums created during this period moved awareness of African-American history to a new plateau. In their expression of a black perspective and through their efforts to preserve black history, these institutions sought to use their collections to motivate African Americans to "define themselves, their future and their understanding of their past" (Harding 1967, p. 40). This came at a time when information about black achievements was generally excluded from common history texts and from other museums. Black history was seen, says Vincent Harding, "as a weapon for the Civil Rights Movement." Responding to the void of available information, the San Francisco African American Historical and Cultural Society was founded in 1955, soon followed by the Du Sable Museum of African American History (originally the Ebony Museum) in 1961 and the Afro-American Museum of Detroit in 1965.

In this period, a unique effort involving students, scouts, local scholars, and government agencies in an urban-archaeology project in Brooklyn, N.Y., uncovered a black settlement dating back to the nineteenth century, and led to the formation of the Society for the Preservation of Historic Weeksville. Today it continues its archaeological research on a forgotten early black community. The efforts of the Museum of Afro-American History in Boston during this period were instrumental in the preservation of the oldest existing black church building, the African Meeting House. The restored building serves as the centerpiece of the fourteen-site Black Heritage Trail, which explores Boston's rich nineteenth-century African-American community. Also in Boston, the Museum of the National Center for African American Artists was created to provide a leading showcase for artists of the African diaspora.

The Smithsonian Institution created the ANACOSTIA NEIGHBORHOOD MUSEUM in 1967 as a "storefront" model for museum outreach. Its goal was to "enliven the community and enlighten the people it serves" (American Association of Museums 1972, p. 6). Such an outreach was invaluable in the wake of the civil unrest that followed the Rev. Dr. Martin Luther King, Jr.'s April 1968 assassination. Although the Smithsonian Institution provided funding support and technical expertise, exhibition planning, public programs, and overall administration were determined by the surrounding community. As a result, exhibition themes address community issues and urban problems as much as historical events. Other mainstream museums, often in response to confrontations with angry artists, were forced to reevaluate their relationships with urban communities and initiated outreach programs. Thus, the Junior Council of the Museum of Modern Art in New York played an important role in the creation of the Studio Museum of Harlem (1967), now the nation's foremost showcase for African-American artists; the Brooklyn Museum replicated the Smithsonian's effort by establishing an outreach center known as the New Muse.

With the Black Power movement of the 1960s and '70s, African-American museums were founded with increasing frequency with the view that such institutions fostered "a way of empowerment" and a method of moving black history to a new plateau of public awareness. To provide space for these expressions and to serve greatly heightened interest, museums were formed throughout the country. The Afro-American Historical Society in New Haven, Conn. was founded as a research library with an estimated 250,000 volumes; and in Providence, the Rhode Island Black Heritage Society instituted pioneering techniques to involve black audiences in the actual collection and cataloging of artifacts. The Black Archives of Mid-America, based in both Kansas and Missouri, collects black cultural information from the midwestern region. To preserve the experience of blacks in the West, the Great Plains Museum in Nebraska and the Black America West Museum were established. The United States's bicentennial led to the creation of Philadelphia's Afro-American Historical and Cultural Museum and led the way for tapping municipal, state, and federal support for African-American museums. Between 1975 and 1990, black museums were formed in California, Texas, South Carolina, Oklahoma, Colorado, Florida, Tennessee, Georgia, and Virginia, including new institutions devoted to the civil rights movement (Memphis) and, finally, a planned National African-American Museum, part of the Smithsonian Institution.

Struggling with limited economic and human resources, these institutions nonetheless serve the broadest possible mandate—cultural, educative, political, social, and civic. Their tradition of service forges a vital historical link between past and future.

REFERENCES

AMERICAN ASSOCIATION OF MUSEUMS. *Museums, Their New Audience.* Washington, D.C., 1972.

AUSTIN, JOY FORD. "Their Face to the Rising Sun: Trends in the Development of African American Museums." *Museum News* 6 (1986): 30–32.

COLLIER-THOMAS, BETTYE. "An Historical Overview of Black Museums and Institutions with Museums' Functions: 1800–1980." *Negro History Bulletin* 44, no. 3 (1981): 56–58.

DICKERSON, AMINA. "Afro-American Museums: A Future Full of Promise." *Roundtable Reports* 9, nos. 2 and 3 (1984): 14–18.

HARDING, VINCENT. "Power from Our People: The Source of the Modern Revival of Black History." *Black Scholar* 18 (1967): 40.

TRESCOTT, JACQUELINE. "Museums on the Move." *American Visions* 1, no. 2 (1986): 24–34.

AMINA DICKERSON

Music. The African-American music tradition comprises many different genres, including SPIRITU-ALS, work songs, BLUES, GOSPEL MUSIC, JAZZ, and popular music. Each genre includes a complex of subdivisions and is associated with a specific cultural function, social context, and historical period. Despite these distinguishing factors, the various genres exist as part of a musical continuum of African origin. The secular and sacred forms share musical features, demonstrating that the two spheres are complementary rather than oppositional.

The web of African-American musical genres is a product of interactions between people of African descent and various environmental forces in North America. The African-American music tradition documents the ways African Americans reconciled their dual national identity and forged a meaningful life in a foreign environment, first as slaves and later as second-class citizens.

African Culture in America

When Africans arrived as slaves in America, they brought a culture endowed with many traditions foreign to their European captors. Their rituals for worshiping African gods and celebrating ancestors, death, and holidays, for example, displayed features uncommon to Western Culture. Most noticeable among African practices was the prominent tie of music and movement. The description of a ritual for a dying woman, recorded by the daughter of a Virginia planter in her *Plantation Reminiscences* (n.d.), illustrates the centrality of these cultural expressions and the preservation of African traditions in slave culture:

> Several days before her death . . . [h]er room was crowded with Negroes who had come to perform their religious rites around the death bed. Joining hands they performed a savage dance, shouting wildly around her bed. Although [Aunt Fanny was] an intelligent woman, she seemed to cling to the superstitions of her race.
>
> After the savage dance and rites were over . . . I went, and said to her: ". . . we are afraid the noise [singing] and dancing have made you worse."
>
> Speaking feebly, she replied: "Honey, that kind of religion suits us black folks better than your kind. What suits Mars Charles' mind, don't suit mine." (Epstein 1977, p. 130)

Slaveholders and missionaries assumed that exposure to Euro-American cultural traditions would encourage slaves to abandon their African way of life. For some slaves, particularly those who were in constant contact with whites through work and leisure activities, such was the case. The majority of slaves, however, systematically resisted cultural imprisonment by reinterpreting European traditions through an African lens. A description of the slaves' celebration of Pinkster Day, a holiday of Dutch origin, illustrates how the event was transformed into an African-style festival characterized by dancing, drumming, and singing. Dr. James Eights, an observer of this celebration in the late 1700s, noted that the principal instrument accompanying the dancing was an eel-pot drum. This kettle-shaped drum consisted of a wide, single head covered with sheepskin. Over the rhythms the drummer repeated *"hi-a-bomba, bomba, bomba."*

> These vocal sounds were readily taken up and as oft repeated by the female portion of the spectators not otherwise engaged in the exercises of scene, accompanied by the beating of time with their ungloved hands, in strict accordance with the eel-pot melody.
>
> Merrily now the dance moved on, and briskly twirled the lads and lasses over the well trampled green sward; loud and more quickly swelled the sounds of music to the ear, as the excited movements increased in energy and action. (Eights [1867], reprinted in Southern, 1983b, pp. 45–46)

The physical detachment of African Americans from Africa and the widespread disappearance of many original African musical artifacts did not prevent Africans and their descendants from creating, interpreting, and experiencing music from an African perspective. Relegated to the status of slaves in America, Africans continued to perform songs of the past. They also created new musical forms and reinterpreted those of European cultures using the vocabulary, idiom, and aesthetic principles of African traditions. The earliest indigenous musical form created within the American context was known as the Negro spiritual.

The Evolution of Negro Spirituals

The original form of the Negro spiritual emerged at the turn of the nineteenth century. Later known as the folk spiritual, it was a form of expression that arose within a religious context and through black people's resistance to the cultural subjugation imposed by the larger resistance to the cultural subjugation imposed by the larger society. When missionaries introduced blacks to Christianity in systematic fashion (c. 1740s), slaves brought relevance to the instruction by reinterpreting Protestant ideals through an African prism. Negro spirituals, therefore, symbolized a unique religious expression, a black cultural identity and worldview that was illustrated in the religious and secular meanings that spirituals often held—a feature often referred to as double-entendre.

Many texts found in Negro spirituals compare the slave's worldly oppression to the persecution and suffering of Jesus Christ. Others protest their bondage, as in the familiar lines "Befor' I'd be a slave, I'd be buried in my grave, and go home to my Lord and be free." A large body of spiritual texts are laced with coded language that can be interpreted accurately only through an evaluation of the performance context. For example, a spiritual such as the one cited below could have been sung by slaves to organize clandestine meetings and plan escapes:

> If you want to find Jesus, go in the wilderness, Mournin' brudder,
> You want to find Jesus, go into the wilderness,
> I wait upon de Lord, I wait upon de Lord,
> I wait upon de Lord, my God, Who take away de sin of de world.

The text of this song provided instructions for slaves to escape from bondage: "Jesus" was the word for "freedom"; "wilderness" identified the meeting place; "de Lord" referred to the person who would lead slaves through the UNDERGROUND RAILROAD or secret route into the North (the land of freedom). This and other coded texts were incomprehensible to missionaries, planters, and other whites, who interpreted them as "meaningless and disjointed affirmations."

The folk spiritual tradition draws from two basic sources: African-derived songs and the Protestant repertory of psalms, hymns, and spirituals songs. Missionaries introduced blacks to Protestant traditions through Christian instruction, anticipating that these songs would replace those of African origin, which they referred to as "extravagant and nonsensical chants, and catches" (Epstein 1977, pp. 61–98). When slaves and free blacks worshiped with whites, they were expected to adhere to prescribed Euro-American norms. Therefore, blacks did not develop a distinct body of religious music until they gained religious autonomy.

When blacks were permitted to lead their own religious services, many transformed the worship into an African-inspired ritual of which singing was an integral part. The Reverend Robert Mallard described the character of this ritual, which he observed in Chattanooga in 1859:

> I stood at the door and looked in—and such confusion of sights and sounds! . . . Some were standing, others sitting, others moving from one seat to another, several exhorting along the aisles. The whole congregation kept up one monotonous strain, interrupted by various sounds: groans and screams and clapping of hands. One woman especially under the influence of the excitement went across the church in a quick succession of leaps: now [on] her knees . . . then up again; now with her arms about some brother or sister, and again tossing them wildly in the air and clapping her hands together and accompa-

nying the whole by a series of short, sharp shrieks. . . . (Myers 1972, pp. 482–483)

During these rituals slaves not only sang their own African-derived songs but reinterpreted European psalms and hymns as well.

An English musician, whose tour of the United States from 1833 to 1841 included a visit to a black church in Vicksburg, Va., described how slaves altered the original character of a psalm:

> When the minister gave out his own version of the Psalm, the choir commenced singing so rapidly that the original tune absolutely ceased to exist—in fact, the fine old psalm tune became thoroughly transformed into a kind of negro melody; and so sudden was the transformation, by accelerating the time. . . . (Russell 1895, pp. 84–85)

In 1853 Frederick Law Olmsted encountered a similar situation, witnessing a hymn change into a "confused wild kind of chant" (Olmsted 1904). The original tunes became unrecognizable because blacks altered the structure, melody, rhythm, and tempo in accordance with African aesthetic principles.

The clergy objected not only to such altered renditions of Protestant songs but also to songs created independently. John Watson, a white Methodist minister, referred to the latter as "short scraps of disjointed affirmations, pledges or prayers, lengthened out with long repetitive choruses." The rhythmic bodily movements that accompanied the singing caused even more concern among the clergy:

> With every word so sung, they have a sinking of one or other leg of the body alternately, producing an audible sound of the feet at every step. . . . If some in the meantime sit, they strike the sounds alternately on each thigh. What in the name of religion, can countenance or tolerate such gross perversions of true religion! (Watson [1819] in Southern 1983b, p. 63)

As they had long done in African traditions, audible physical gestures provided the rhythmic foundation for singing.

The slaves' interpretation of standard Christian doctrine and musical practice demonstrated their refusal to abandon their cultural values for those of their masters and the missionaries. Undergirding the slaves' independent worship services were African values that emphasized group participation and free expression. These principles govern the features of the folk spiritual tradition: (1) communal composition; (2) call-response; (3) repetitive choruses; (4) improvised melodies and texts; (5) extensive melodic ornamentation (slurs, bends, shouts, moans, groans, cries); (6) heterophonic (individually varied) group singing; (7) complex rhythmic structures; and (8) the integration of song and bodily movement.

The call-response structure promotes both individual expression and group participation. The soloist, who presents the call, is free to improvise on the melody and text; the congregation provides a fixed response. Repetitive chorus lines also encourage group participation. Melodic ornamentation enables singers to embellish and thus intensify performances. Clapped and stamped rhythmic patterns create layered metrical structures as a foundation for gestures and dance movements.

Folk spirituals were also commonplace among many free blacks who attended independent African-American churches in the eighteenth and nineteenth centuries. These blacks expressed their racial pride by consciously rejecting control and cultural domination by the affiliated white church. Richard ALLEN, founder of Bethel AME Church in Philadelphia in 1794, was the first African-American minister of an independent black church to alter the cultural style of Protestant worship so that it would have greater appeal for his black congregation (see AFRICAN METHODIST EPISCOPAL CHURCH).

Recognizing the importance of music, Allen chose to compile his own hymnal (which contained no music) rather than use the standard one for Methodist worship. The second edition of this hymnal, *A Collection of Spiritual Songs and Hymns Selected from Various Authors, by Richard Allen, Minister of the African Methodist Episcopal Church* (1801), contains some of Allen's original song texts as well as other hymns favored by his congregation. To some of these hymns Allen added refrain lines and choruses to the typical stanza or verse form to ensure full congregational participation in the singing. Allen's congregation performed these songs in the style of folk spirituals, which generated much criticism from white Methodist ministers. Despite such objections, other AME churches adopted the musical practices established at Bethel.

In the 1840s Daniel A. PAYNE, an AME minister who later became a bishop, campaigned to change the church's folk-style character. A former Presbyterian pastor educated in a white Lutheran seminary, Payne subscribed to the Euro-American view of the "right, fit, and proper way of serving God" (Payne [1888] in Southern 1983b, p. 69). Therefore he restructured the AME service to conform to the doctrines, literature, and musical practices of white elite churches. Payne introduced Western choral literature performed by a trained choir and instrumental music played by an organist. These forms replaced the congregational singing of folk spirituals, which Payne labeled "cornfield ditties." While some independent urban black churches adopted Payne's initiatives, discontented members left to join other churches or establish their own. However, the majority of the AME churches, especially those in the South, denounced Payne's "improvements" and continued their folk-style worship.

Payne and his black counterparts affiliated with other AME and with Episcopalian, Lutheran, and Presbyterian churches, represented an emerging black educated elite that demonstrated little if any tolerance for religious practices contrary to Euro-American Christian ideals of "reverence" and "refinement." Their training in white seminaries shaped their perspective on an "appropriate" style of worship. In the Protestant Episcopal Church, for example, a southern white member noted that these black leaders

> were accustomed to use *no other worship* than the regular course prescribed in the Book of Common Prayer, for the day. Hymns, or Psalms out of the same book were sung, and printed sermon read. . . . No extemporary address, exhortation, or prayer, was permitted, or used. . . . (Epstein 1977, p. 196)

Seminary-trained black ministers rejected traditional practices of black folk churches because they did not conform to aesthetic principles associated with written traditions. Sermons read from the written script, musical performances that strictly adhered to the printed score, and the notion of reserved behavior marked those religious practices considered most characteristic and appropriate within Euro-American liturgical worship.

In contrast, practices associated with the black folk church epitomize an oral tradition. Improvised sermons, prayers, testimonies, and singing, together with demonstrative behavior, preserve the African values of spontaneity and communal interaction.

Secular Music in the Slave Community

The core secular genres among African-American slaves were work songs, field calls and street cries, social and game songs, and dance music. Work songs accompanied all forms of labor, providing encouragement and strength and relieving boredom. The texts, improvised by field workers, stevedores, dockworkers, weavers, boat rowers, and others, frequently reflected the type of work performed. In sociopolitical terms, work songs provided an outlet for protest and criticism while the song rhythms coordinated the efforts of workers and regulated the rate of labor. Performances of work songs exhibit call-response and repetitive chorus structures; melodic, textual, and timbral variation; heterophonic vocal textures; and percussive delivery.

Field calls (rural) and street cries (urban) were used by workers for personal communication. Field calls enabled workers to maintain contact with one another from a distance, make their presence known (e.g., the water boy), attract attention, or communicate a mood. Street vendors used special cries to advertise their products. Both field calls and street cries consisted of short, improvised phrases performed in a free and highly individual style. These features contrast with the call-response and the repetitive choruses that characterize work songs.

Game songs accompanied children's activities, facilitating play and the development of motor and social skills. Song texts provided instructions for playing games as well as a vehicle for the expression of children's fantasies and worldview. Game songs embody all of the aesthetic features associated with folk spirituals, including group interaction, clapping, and stamping.

Slaves spent much of their leisure time singing and dancing. Accounts of these activities and holiday celebrations from the seventeenth and eighteenth centuries indicate that a variety of African instruments—drums, xylophones, calabashes, horns, banjos, musical bows, tambourines, triangles, and jawbones—were played in a distinctly African style and accompanied dancing.

Beginning in the 1740s, however, as a consequence of slave revolts, many colonies passed legislation that prohibited the playing of African drums and horns. Such legislation did not restrict the musical and dance activities of slaves. Over time, as traditional African instruments disappeared, blacks found functional substitutes for some of these instruments and constructed modified versions of others. Wooden boxes, stamping, and clapping replaced drums; spoons, washboards, and washtubs substituted for rattles, scrapers, and other percussion instruments; panpipes, fifes, and jugs substituted for flutes and other wind instruments; and the diddly bow and washtub bass were adapted versions of the musical bow. Using these instruments, slaves created new forms of dance accompaniment that later became a part of the blues tradition.

Slaves also adopted European instruments, which they learned to play as early as the 1690s. The fiddle and fife were popular among slaves, and they played them in conjunction with African instruments. By the nineteenth century the fiddle and banjo (a derivation from the African lute) had become the most common instruments to accompany dancing. Combining African-derived with European instruments, African Americans created an original form of improvised and rhythmically complex dance music that would give birth to RAGTIME and jazz in the late nineteenth and twentieth centuries, respectively.

The Reconstruction Era

The end of the CIVIL WAR in 1865 symbolically marked the freedom of slaves. The social upheaval and political maneuvering that followed the war, however, restricted the freedmen's integration into mainstream society. While some ex-slaves had access to the new educational institutions established for blacks, the vast majority had few if any options for social advancement and economic stability.

In the RECONSTRUCTION South many African-Americans remained effectively enslaved because of an emergent system called sharecropping. This system, defined by an inequitable economic arrangement between landlords (former slaveholders) and sharecroppers (freed blacks), kept blacks in debt and subjugated to southern whites. Most sharecroppers lived in the same shacks on the same farms and plantations that they had as slaves. For nearly a century this arrangement isolated most African Americans from mainstream society, restricted their mobility, and limited their economic empowerment. African Americans survived this oppressive environment by preserving fundamental values of the past, as they had done as slaves. These values manifested themselves in new forms of musical expression.

Arranged Spirituals

The evolution of new and diverse musical forms during the post–Civil War years paralleled the divergent life styles among African Americans. While the social and economic conditions of many ex-slaves remained virtually unchanged, the establishment of black colleges that had begun in 1856 (Wilberforce University in Wilberforce, Ohio) provided some with opportunities for social and economic advancement. Within this context, black students adopted various Euro-American cultural models dictated by the established Eurocentric college curriculam.

At FISK UNIVERSITY, founded in 1866 in Nashville, Tenn., the white treasurer, George White, organized the FISK JUBILEE SINGERS to raise money for the school. The Jubilee Singers initially performed both the standard European repertory and arranged Negro spirituals. Responding to the preferences of white audiences, White centered the group's performances around spirituals. The Fisk Jubilee Singers were the first to popularize the choral arrangement of spirituals. Their successful concerts, presented throughout the nation and world beginning in 1871, inspired the subsequent formation of similar groups at HAMPTON INSTITUTE in Virginia and other black colleges.

George White, influenced by his musical background, arranged the folk spiritual in a European concert form and insisted on a performance style that appealed to the aesthetic and preferences of white audiences. In doing so, according to John WORK, he "eliminated every element that detracted from the pure emotion of the song. . . . Finish, precision and sincerity were demanded by this leader. Mr. White strove for an art presentation" (Work 1940, p. 15).

White's "art presentation" of spirituals required strict conformity to the written tradition. In his arrangements four-part harmony replaced heterophonic singing, and strict adherence to the printed score eliminated melodic and textual improvisation and the clapping and stamping accompaniment. Despite the removal of elements associated with the oral tradition, evidence of the folk spiritual tradition remained in call-response, syncopation, polyrhythms, melodic and textual repetition, and linguistic dialect.

The legacy of the Fisk Jubilee Singers continued in the 1920s when Hall JOHNSON and Eva JESSYE formed professional choirs specializing in this idiom. Both choirs gave concerts in major halls, on radio, and appeared in theatrical and film productions.

During the second decade of the twentieth century, another concert version of the folk spiritual appeared. This form transformed the folk spiritual into an art song for solo voice. Conservatory-trained singer-composer Harry T. BURLEIGH provided the model, arranging "Deep River" (1916) for voice and piano. Burleigh's arrangement brought publication to this musical form, which eventually became a standard part of the repertory of African-American concert singers. Influenced by Burleigh, performers such as Roland HAYES, Marian ANDERSON, Paul ROBESON, and Dorothy MAYNOR concluded their solo concerts with arranged solo spirituals, as black college choirs continue to do even today. William Warfield, McHenry Boatwright, Willis Patterson, Rawn Spearman, Jessye NORMAN, Leontyne PRICE, Grace BUMBRY, Shirley VERRETT, George SHIRLEY, Simon ESTES, Martina ARROYO, and Kathleen BATTLE are among those who followed this tradition in the post–WORLD WAR II years.

The Use of Folk Idioms in Concert Music of African-American Composers

During the first decade of the twentieth century, a core group of black composers sought to create a school of composition using African and African-derived vernacular forms. Harry T. Burleigh, Samuel Coleridge-Taylor, Will Marion COOK, R. Nathaniel DETT, Clarence Cameron WHITE, and the brothers John Rosamond JOHNSON and James Weldon JOHNSON were among the first composers to arrange and/or write choral and small instrumental works inspired by folk spirituals, blues, ragtime, and other vernacular forms for the concert stage. They pioneered a nationalist school of composition that preserved the spirit and musical features of black folk idioms.

In *Six Plantation Melodies for Violin and Piano* (1901) and *Jubilee Songs of the United States of America* (1916) (a collection of spirituals arranged for solo voice and piano accompaniment), for example, Burleigh sought to maintain the racial flavor of the original folk melody. To achieve this, Eileen Southern noted, Burleigh's piano accompaniments "rarely overpower the simple melodies but rather set and sustain a dominant emotional mood throughout the song" (Southern 1983a, p. 268).

Samuel Coleridge-Taylor (born in England of African and British ancestry) also made every effort to preserve the integrity of original folk melodies in his compositions. Inspired by the appearance of the Fisk Jubilee Singers in London, Coleridge-Taylor arranged traditional African and African-American folk melodies in a piece for piano, *Twenty-four Negro Melodies,* Op. 59 (1904). Coleridge-Taylor's notes on this work emphasized that he employed original melodies without the "idea of 'improving' the original material any more than Brahms' Variations on the Haydn Theme 'improved' that" (reprint of liner notes to *Twenty-four Negro Melodies,* recorded by Francis Walker).

Sharing Coleridge-Taylor's perspective, other nationalist composers used vernacular materials with the intent of maintaining their original character. Dett's *In the Bottoms* (1913), a suite for piano, employs various dance rhythms associated with African-American folk culture. Its opening "Prelude" mimics the texture and rhythms of a syncopated banjo, and the last piece, "Dance (Juba)," captures the complex rhythms of "pattin' juba." "Pattin' juba" was a popular self-accompanying dance common among slaves that involved singing and stamping while alternately clapping the hands and striking each shoulder and thigh.

Dett's use of black folk rhythms, melodies, textures, and timbres demonstrates one way in which nationalist composers preserved the integrity of the folk idiom. Their efforts to create a distinct racial artistic identity using European models were advanced by African-American creative artists and intellectuals of the 1920s and 1930s in what became known as the HARLEM RENAISSANCE.

Throughout the Harlem Renaissance, African-American intellectuals and university-trained writers, musicians, and visual artists discussed ways to liberate themselves from the restrictions of European cultural expression. As a group they pioneered the concept of the NEW NEGRO—one who claimed an identity founded on self-respect, self-dependence, racial pride, and racial solidarity. The New Negro's ultimate concern, according to William Grant STILL, was "the development of our racial culture and . . . its *integration* (italics added) into American culture

(Still [n.d.], in Haas, 1972, p. 129). Both intellectuals and creative artists agreed that this goal could be achieved by incorporating African-American folk materials into European concert and literary forms. They disagreed, however, on the appropriate presentation of these materials.

Whereas the pioneer nationalists shared the belief that the original character of folk idioms should be preserved, the Harlem renaissance group expressed the need to adapt or "elevate" these idioms to the level of "high art" (Locke 1925, p. 28; Locke 1936, pp. 21–23; Still [n.d.], in Haas 1972, p. 134). The issues appear to have concerned the degree to which the folk idiom could be altered through thematic development without losing its authentic character, the use of arrangements that supported rather than diluted the spirit of the folk form, and the preservation of the folk quality without restricting the creative impulses of composers (Burleigh [1924], quoted in Southern 1983a, p. 268; Locke 1925, pp. 207–208). Composers of the Harlem Renaissance, including William Grant Still, William DAWSON, and Howard SWANSON, employed various approaches in establishing racial identity in their music. Some utilized authentic folk melodies; others composed thematic material in the spirit and with the flavor of vernacular idioms; and still others worked to capture the ambience of the folk environment.

Still, known as the dean of African-American composers, wrote many works using a broad range of African, American-African, and Caribbean folk material. In the first movement of his well-known *Afro-American Symphony* (1930), for example, Still juxtaposes original blues and spiritual melodies; in the third movement he introduces the banjo, the most familiar of all African instruments in the New World. In *Levee Land* (1925), a work for orchestra and soloist, he experiments with jazz elements. *Sahdji* (1930), a ballet for orchestra and chorus, and *Mota* (1951), an opera, dramatize African life. The opera *Troubled Island* (1941) captures the spirit of Haitian culture.

William Dawson, using a slightly different approach, juxtaposed existing folk and folk-inspired themes in his *Negro Folk Symphony* (1934). The Harlem Renaissance composers also established racial identities in their vocal and choral works by employing texts by such African-American writers as Langston HUGHES, Countee CULLEN, Paul Laurence DUNBAR, and Arna BONTEMPS. Langston Hughes, for example, wrote the poems for Howard Swanson's "The Negro Speaks of Rivers" (1942) and "Lady's Boogie" (1947) and the libretto for Still's opera *Troubled Island*.

Despite the efforts of these conservatory-trained musicians to preserve the integrity of folk expressions, their music had limited appeal outside middle-class audiences. Even within this group, some expressed concern about overelaboration and the tendency to place too much emphasis on formal European conventions. Anthropologist-folklorist Zora Neale HURSTON vehemently objected to concert presentations of Negro spirituals. She argued that the aesthetic ideas of oral traditions that allow for spontaneous, improvisatory, and interactive expression could not be captured in the written score or reproduced by trained musicians (Hurston 1976, pp. 344–345).

The wider African-American folk community shared Hurston's views, objecting that the new modes of presentation were too "pretty" (Work 1949, pp. 136–137). The community simply did not share the aesthetic ideals of the black elite. Even though many composers attempted to preserve vocabulary, form, structure, rhythms, textures, tonal qualities, and aesthetic devices of folk forms, the printed score changed the character of the original style. Because of this, most of the African-American folk community was unable to relate to the aesthetic qualities associated with concert presentations of folk idioms.

Ragtime

Ragtime refers to both a style of performance and a musical genre characterized by a syncopated, or "ragged," melody played over a quarter- or eighth-note bass pattern. The ragtime style evolved out of syncopated banjo melodies in the 1880s. It was popularized in African-American communities by itinerant pianists and brass bands. The pianists, who played in honky-tonks, saloons, and brothels, improvised on folk and popular tunes, transforming them into contemporary African-American dance music. In a similar fashion, black brass bands "ragged" the melodies of traditional marches, hymns, spirituals, and folk and popular songs during funeral processions, parades, and other celebrations, changing the character of these melodies.

By the late 1890s ragtime had come to identify a body of composed syncopated piano and vocal music published for mass consumption. As such, its improvisatory character and syncopated embellishments became formalized and simplified in written form. The availability of ragtime as sheet music resulted in the ragtime explosion of the first two decades of the twentieth century. Ragtime's syncopated rhythms quickly became popular among amateur and professional pianists. Responding to the demand for this music, publishers flooded the market with ragtime arrangements of popular and folk tunes, marches, and European classical songs for dance orchestras and marching and concert bands and vocal versions for singers. African-American ragtime composers include Thomas Turpin, Scott JOPLIN, Jelly Roll MORTON, Eubie BLAKE, and Artie Matthews.

The vocal counterparts of instrumental ragtime were labeled "coon songs." Popularized by minstrel performers in the late 1800s, coon songs became mainstays in vaudeville and Broadway productions in the 1900s. Coon songs are distinguished from other vocal genres of twentieth-century popular music by the use of black dialect and often denigrating lyrics. Between 1900 and 1920 vocal and instrumental ragtime dominated musical performances in theaters, saloons, ballrooms, and the homes of the white middle class, giving a degree of respectability to a form once associated with brothels and minstrel shows.

Blues

The blues evolved from work songs and field calls during the 1880s in response to the inhumane treatment and second-class citizenship that had defined black life in America for seven decades. The blues share the aesthetic qualities of folk spirituals, and like spirituals, they attempt to make sense of and give meaning to life. Two historic rulings by the U.S. Supreme Court, in 1883 and 1896, created the social and political environment from which the blues sprang. The first declared the 1875 Civil Rights Act unconstitutional, and the second upheld the "separate but equal" policy related to the PLESSY V. FERGUSON court case, which sanctioned segregation or JIM CROW as the law of the land. These decisions resulted in discriminatory state laws, violent activities of the KU KLUX KLAN, unfair treatment by landlords and employers, and political powerlessness. In effect, the Supreme Court rulings eliminated any hope for social equality and community empowerment and forced African Americans to struggle just to survive. Music, especially the blues, proved to be an important tool for enduring an oppressive existence.

Blues performers, like black preachers, served as spokespersons and community counselors; their messages addressed the social realities of daily life. As entertainers blues musicians provided a temporary escape from daily oppression by performing for barbecues, house parties, social clubs, and informal gatherings in juke joints and bars.

The blues became a way of life, as illustrated by the various blues styles—rural (folk), vaudeville (classic), urban, and boogie-woogie (instrumental form). The earliest blues form, known as rural or folk blues, is the product of the segregated rural South. Performed primarily by men, the texts address economic hardships, sharecropping experiences, unjust imprisonment, broken relationships, travels, and opposition to the Jim Crow system. Folk blues is performed as vocal and instrumental music and consists of a series of verses that vary in structure (largely eight to sixteen bars and two to five lines of text) and length. Chord structures often center around the tonic and sometimes the subdominant or dominant chords. Acoustic instruments, including the guitar, harmonica, banjo, mandolin, fiddle, diddly-bow, kazoo, jug, fife and drum, washboard, and washtub bass provide the accompaniment. The instruments, functioning as accompaniment and as substitute for singers, often double and respond to the vocal melody. Prominent rural blues musicians include Robert JOHNSON, Charley PATTON, Son HOUSE, Blind Lemon JEFFERSON, Blind Boy Fuller, Sonny TERRY, Brownie MCGHEE, Blind Blake, and Gus Cannon.

Boogie-Woogie

Boogie-woogie is a piano form of the blues that evolved between the late 1890s and the early 1900s in barrelhouses (also known as juke joints) in logging, sawmill, turpentine, levee, and railroad camps throughout the South. Barrelhouses, which served as social centers for migrant workers living in these camps, consisted of a room with a piano, dance area, and bar. Itinerant boogie-woogie pianists traveled the barrelhouse circuit providing the entertainment—music for dancing.

Early boogie-woogie styles incorporated the chord structures, bass patterns, form, and tonality of the folk blues and the melodic and rhythmic properties of ragtime. Boogie-woogie pianists adapted these elements to reflect the dance function of the music as well as their own percussive and regional improvisatory style. The various regional styles emphasized a heavy and rhythmic eight-note triadic bass line (1-3-5-6-1 or flatted 7) over which flowed syncopated melodic phrases.

Boogie-woogie pianists were among the southern migrants who moved to Chicago after WORLD WAR I. High rents and low wages forced Chicago's South Side residents to raise money to pay rent. To do so, they hosted rent parties that featured boogie-woogie pianists. This music was so popular among Chicago's southern migrants that it also provided the entertainment on excursion trains that transported blacks to the South on holidays. The trains, called honky-tonks, were converted baggage cars that contained a bar and a dance floor. Boogie-woogie remained the music associated with the lower social strata of black society until the 1930s, when the style entered the repertory of jazz bands and was featured in a concert at Carnegie Hall. By the 1940s boogie-woogie had become the new craze in American jazz and popular music, which brought respectability to the form. Pioneering boogie-woogie pianists include Charles "Cow Cow" Davenport, Clarence "Pine Top" SMITH, Little Brother Montgomery, Clarence Lofton, Roosevelt Sykes, Jimmy Blythe, Jimmy YANCEY, Meade Lux LEWIS, and Albert AMMONS.

Vaudeville Blues

At the turn of the century, a new blues style, which provided the transition from a folk to a commercial style, evolved within the context of traveling minstrel, carnival, and vaudeville shows. Known as vaudeville or classic blues, it showcased black female singers. Most of these women had grown up in the South, and they escaped their impoverished environments by becoming professional entertainers. Relocating in cities, they created widespread awareness of the blues tradition, appearing in cabarets, dance halls, off-Broadway productions, and on records.

Vaudeville blues was the first black music style recorded by a black performer and accompanied by black musicians. The popularity of the song "Crazy Blues," composed by the professional songwriter Perry Bradford and sung by Mamie SMITH in 1920, resulted in the recording of many types of black music written and performed by black musicians.

The vaudeville blues tradition is distinguished from rural blues by instrumentation, musical form, harmonic structure, and performance style. Vaudeville singers were accompanied by blues-ragtime-jazz pianists or a New Orleans–style jazz band. As a commercial form the blues structure became standardized through use of a twelve-bar, three-line (AAB) verse or stanza structure, the tonic-subdominant-dominant harmonic progression, and the blues tonality of the flatted third and seventh degrees.

As in rural blues, textual themes varied and included economic hardship, relationships, imprisonment, travels, urban experiences, and southern nostalgia. Many singers, including Ma RAINEY, Ida COX, Victoria SPIVEY, Alberta HUNTER, and Bessie SMITH, wrote their own blues songs, bringing a feminist perspective to many topics common to the blues tradition. Other songs were drawn from the folk blues and composed by professional black male songwriters.

The GREAT DEPRESSION led to a decline in the recording of black music during the 1930s. The demand for the blues, nevertheless, continued to grow. The World War II migration of rural southern blacks to urban centers engendered a consumer market for black music that surpassed the previous decades. Urban blues was one of the most popular black music forms to emerge during the 1940s.

Urban Blues

Urban blues shares the musical features (form, structure, tonality, and textual themes) of vaudeville blues. Musically it is more akin to the rural tradition, from which it is distinguished by a more developed instrumental style and influences from jazz and popular music.

Urban blues evolved in cities where southern black migrants struggled to cope with daily life. City life proved harsher than anticipated; the expectation of social and racial equality quickly abated in the face of covert discriminatory practices. Yet blacks adjusted by adapting southern traditions to the demands of city living. The blues played a pivotal role in this process.

In bars, lounges, and clubs where African Americans gathered to socialize, rural blues performers MUDDY WATERS, HOWLIN' WOLF, Sonny Boy WILLIAMSON, and Sam "Lightnin' " HOPKINS, among others, provided the entertainment. The noise level of these venues, combined with surrounding street and factory sounds, forced these musicians to amplify their voices and instruments. The density and intensity of these gatherings soon demanded that blues musicians expand their instrumentation to include a drummer and electric bass guitar and, in some cases, horns. Over these amplified instruments blues singers shouted and moaned about city life—the good times, the bad times, and the lonely times. Performers who brought inspiration to the inner-city dwellers included T-Bone WALKER, B. B. KING, Bobby "Blue" Bland, Elmore JAMES, Homesick James, Junior Wells, Buddy Guy, Otis Span, Willie DIXON, and Ko Ko Taylor.

Jazz

Jazz is a twentieth-century form, an ensemble-based instrumental music. Like the blues, it comprises many styles, each one associated with a specific historical period, social context, and cultural function. While the various styles may be distinguished by certain musical features and instrumentation, they share certain African-American aesthetic properties, which link them as a whole and to the larger body of African-American music.

Early jazz styles evolved around the turn of the century out of the syncopated brass band tradition. Brass bands borrowed ragtime's syncopated rhythmic style to create an ensemble-based dance music employing conventions of the oral tradition. The bands led by Joe "King" OLIVER, Louis ARMSTRONG, Kid ORY, and Bunk Johnson popularized this tradition, providing collectively improvised versions of marches, hymns, folk tunes, popular melodies, and original compositions. They performed in black entertainment venues throughout the urban South, at funerals, and at community social gatherings. Later known as New Orleans jazz, this style featured a small ensemble consisting of cornet, trombone, clarinet, banjo, tuba, and drums.

Many New Orleans musicians and those from other areas migrated to Chicago, Kansas City, or New York during the World War I era. In these cities social dancing had become popular, and the number of nightclubs, cabarets, and ballrooms increased dramatically. In this context and by the 1930s, a distinctive style of instrumental dance music labeled jazz had emerged out of the New Orleans tradition. This new jazz style, in which improvisation remained a salient feature, differed from the New Orleans tradition in composition, instrumentation, repertory, and musical structure. The number of musicians increased from six or seven to twelve to sixteen; the instrumentation consisted of trumpets, trombones, saxophones, piano, string bass, and drums; the repertory included complex rhythmic arrangements of popular songs, blues, and original compositions; and the musical structure which featured soloists, took on a more formal yet flexible quality. Prominent bands of this era (labeled big bands in the late 1920s and swing bands in the mid-1930s) included those of Bennie MOTEN, Count BASIE, Fletcher HENDERSON, Jimmie LUNCEFORD, Duke ELLINGTON, Andy Kirk, Chick WEBB, Cab CALLOWAY, Coleman HAWKINS, Earl "Fatha" HINES, and Lionel HAMPTON.

The World War II era engendered yet another change in the jazz tradition. During the war years the musical taste and social patterns of many Americans began to change. After the war small clubs replaced ballrooms as the center for musical activity, and experimental jazz combos (rhythm section, trumpet, saxophone, and trombone) came into vogue. Over the next six decades these combos created new and diverse styles of improvised music that were known as bebop, hard bop, cool jazz, soul jazz, jazz fusion, modern jazz, and new jazz swing. Each of these styles introduced new musical concepts to the jazz tradition.

Bebop (1940s), hard bop (1950s), cool jazz (1950s), and modern jazz (1960s) musicians experimented with timbre and texture and expanded harmonic language, melodic and rhythmic structures, and tempos beyond the parameters associated with big bands. Musicians of these styles altered and extended traditional chord structures, introduced unconventional chord sequences, and employed abstract, nonvocal melodies, and unpredictable rhythmic patterns. In the process, they transformed jazz from dance music to music for listening. Bebop's major innovators were Charlie PARKER, Dizzy GILLESPIE, Thelonius MONK, Kenny CLARKE, and Max ROACH. Hard bop's pioneers included Clifford BROWN, Lee Morgan, Sonny ROLLINS, John COLTRANE, J. J. JOHNSON, Horace SILVER, Cannonball ADDERLEY, Wes MONTGOMERY, and Kenny Burrell. Cool jazz is associated with Miles DAVIS and the

(Upper left) Art Tatum. (Upper right) Ella Fitzgerald. (Photographs and Prints Division, Schomburg Center for Research in Black Culture, The New York Public Library, Astor, Lenox and Tilden Foundations). (Lower left) Dizzy Gillespie. (Prints and Photographs Division, Library of Congress). (Lower right) Quincy Jones. (AP/Wide World Photos)

MODERN JAZZ QUARTET, among others. Modern jazz (also known as avant-garde or free jazz) innovators include Ornette COLEMAN, Cecil TAYLOR, Archie SHEPP, SUN RA, and the ART ENSEMBLE OF CHICAGO.

Some musicians rooted in the bebop or hard bop style experimented with various non-Western musical traditions. John Coltrane, Alice Coltrane, McCoy Tyner, and Ralph MacDonald, for example, drew inspiration from the music of India, Japan, Africa, the Caribbean, and Latin America. Some performers even employed instruments from these countries. While many musicians expanded on bebop's musical foundation during the 1950s and 1960s, others evolved jazz styles that differed conceptually from this tradition.

Retaining the sensibilities and improvisatory style of the jazz tradition, soul jazz (1960s), jazz fusion (1970s), and new jazz swing (1990s) musicians turned to popular idioms (soul music, funk, and RAP) for creative inspiration. Fusing the musical language, stylings, rhythms, and synthesized instruments of various popular forms with the harmonic vocabulary of jazz, they not only brought a new sound to the jazz tradition but recaptured jazz's original dance function as well.

Ramsey Lewis, Les McCann, Cannonball Adderley, Jimmy SMITH, and Richard "Groove" Holmes are among musicians who popularized the soul jazz style; Herbie HANCOCK (who introduced the synthesizer to jazz), George Duke, George BENSON, Noel Pointer, and Hurbert Laws forged the jazz fusion concept.

In the 1990s such jazz musicians as Greg Osby, Miles Davis, Roy Ayers, Donald Byrd, Lonnie Liston Smith, Courtney Pine, and Branford Marsalis teamed up with rap (also known as hip-hop) artists to produce a new sound called new jazz swing. This style fuses rap's lyrics, hip-hop rhythms, scratching (sounds produced with the needle by rotating a record backward and forward), RHYTHM AND BLUES and funk samples (phrases extracted from prerecorded songs), and multilayered textures with the improvisational character and vocabulary of jazz. The musical borrowings across genres gave birth not only to new jazz forms but also to a new body of religious music labeled gospel.

Gospel

Gospel is a twentieth-century form of sacred music developed by African-Americans within an urban context. As described by ethnomusicologist Mellonee Burnim, gospel functions multidimensionally holding historical, religious, cultural, and social significance among African Americans (Burnim 1988, pp. 112–120). As an urban response to the sociocultural climate that supported racial oppression, gospel provides a spiritual perspective on the secular events that negatively impacted the lives of African Americans. As such, it expresses the changing ideas and ideals held by blacks in their attempt to establish a meaningful life in an urban environment.

The gospel tradition relies on three primary sources for its repertory: (1) spontaneous creations by church congregations in the oral tradition; (2) original composition by individuals; and (3) rearrangements of hymns, spirituals, blues, and popular idioms. Given these distinct musical sources, gospel music utilizes many structural forms, including call-response, verse-chorus, blues, and theme and variation. Gospel performances, which are highly improvisatory, are accompanied by a variety of instruments, particular piano, Hammond organ, bass, tambourine, and drums.

GOSPEL AS ORAL COMPOSITION

Gospel music, as an oral form of religious expression, has its roots in PENTECOSTALISM, established at the turn of the century. The Pentecostal church, a by-product of the post–Civil War HOLINESS MOVEMENT, became a refuge for many African Americans from lower socioeconomic strata who sought spiritual uplift and deliverance from hardship and struggle. The worship style of the Pentecostal church appealed to these and other African Americans because it retained the improvisatory preaching style, spontaneous testimonies, prayer, and music traditions of the past. Pentecostal congregations brought an urban flavor to these expressions, especially the folk spiritual tradition, which they transformed into an urban folk gospel style.

The feature that distinguishes folk gospel from folk spirituals is the addition of accompanying instruments, including tambourines, washboards, triangles, guitars, pianos, horns, and drums. Pentecostal ministers sanctioned the use of these instruments, citing Psalm 150, which encouraged the use of trumpets, harps, lyres, tambourines, strings, flutes, and cymbals to praise the Lord. Blues, ragtime, and jazz performers were among those who responded to this invitation, bringing their instruments and secular style of performance into the Pentecostal church.

Congregational singing accompanied by instruments increased the intensity and spontaneity of urban black folk services. The bluesy guitar lines, ragtime and boogie-woogie rhythms, horn riffs, and polyrhythmic drum patterns brought a contemporary sound to old traditions.

GOSPEL AS WRITTEN COMPOSITION

Gospel music as written composition emerged as a distinct genre in independent black churches in the 1930s. The prototype, known as a gospel hymn, was developed during the first two decades of the twentieth century by the Philadelphia Methodist minister Charles A. TINDLEY. Tindley grew up in rural Maryland, where he attended a folk-style rural church. Influenced by this experience, his ministry catered to the spiritual, cultural, and social needs of black people. Tindley gave special attention to the poor, who flocked to his church in large numbers, as did people of all classes and races. His socioeconomically and culturally diverse congregation responded positively to his style of worship, which intertwined the liturgical and cultural practices of the Pentecostal, Baptist, and Methodist churches. These services

> embraced both the order and selections of well-loved "high" church literature and the practice, richness, intensity, and spontaneity found in the most traditionally based Black form of worship. These were hymns, anthems, prayers, and creeds. There were "amens" and hand-claps and shouts of "Thank you Jesus" and a spirit that ran throughout the service. (Reagon 1992, p. 39)

The music, woven into every component of worship, was as diverse as the liturgy. The choir performed Handel's *Messiah* at Christmas and the music of other Western classical composers and the African-American tradition during Sunday morning service. At evening testimonials the congregation sang spirituals, lined hymns, and other songs from the oral tradition.

The church's musical repertory also included Tindley's original compositions, which he wrote specifically for his congregation and as an extension of his sermons. His song texts related the Scriptures to everyday life experiences. A recurring theme in Tindley's songs and sermons, according to cultural historian Bernice Johnson Reagon, "is the belief that true change or release from worldly bondage can be attained only through struggle" (Reagon 1992, p. 45).

The theme of deliverance through struggle is one feature that distinguishes Tindley's gospel hymns from the hymns of white songwriters, whose texts focus on conversion, salvation, and heaven. Other distinguishing elements are the construction of melodies in a fashion that allows for improvisation and interpolation and the use of melodic, harmonic, and rhythmic components of the black folk tradition. Among Tindley's well-known songs are "Some Day," published in 1901, and "Stand By Me," "The Storm Is Passing Over, Hallelujah," and "By and By," all published in 1905. These and other compositions, which are included in hymnbooks of all denominations, have become part of the black oral tradition. They are sung in a variety of styles by congregations, gospel soloists, duos, quartets, and numerous traditional and contemporary ensembles and choirs.

Tindley's compositions had a profound impact on Thomas A. DORSEY, a Baptist, who evolved Tindley's gospel hymn model into an original gospel song. Dorsey, a former blues and ragtime performer, brought a different kind of song structure, melody, harmony, rhythm, and energy to the black sacred tradition. Dorsey was known as the Father of Gospel, and his compositions fuse blues-style melodies with blues and ragtime rhythms. His texts are testimonies about the power of Jesus Christ, which provides spiritually inspired yet earthly solutions to daily struggles. Among Dorsey's well-known compositions are "Take My Hand, Precious Lord" (1932), "There'll Be Peace in the Valley for Me" (1938), "Hide Me in Thy Bosom" (1939), "God Is Good to Me" (1943), and "Old Ship of Zion" (1950).

Despite the "good news" about Jesus Christ of which the gospels speak, most ministers of independent black churches rejected Dorsey's songs because of their "secular" beat and musical style and because they did not conform to the established religious musical conventions. He therefore used unorthodox strategies to introduce them to church congregations. Throughout the 1930s Dorsey along with Sallie MARTIN, Mahalia JACKSON, and Willie Mae Ford SMITH, sang his songs on the sidewalks outside churches, at church conventions, and at the gospel music convention, The National Convention of Choirs and Choruses, that Dorsey founded with Sallie Martin, Willie Mae Ford Smith, Theodore Fry, and Magnolia Lewis Butts in 1932.

Also during the 1930s, many established jubilee quartets added Dorsey's songs and those of such composers as Lucie Campbell, William Herbert Brewster, Roberta MARTIN, and Kenneth Morris, among others to their traditional repertory of Negro spirituals. By the 1940s several newly formed semiprofessional and professional gospel quartets, female and mixed groups, and local choirs specialized in gospel music. In the 1950s, as a result of the proliferation of gospel church choirs, gospel music became standard repertory in many independent black church choirs.

Groups that brought widespread public notice to the gospel music tradition of Dorsey and his contemporaries include the gospel quartets Fairfield Four, Famous Blue Jay Singers, Golden Gate Quartet, Soul Stirrers, Highway Q.C.'s, Dixie Hummingbirds, Swan Silvertones, and the Blind Boys; the gospel groups of Roberta Martin, Sally Ward, Clara Ward, and the Barrett Sisters; the soloists Mahalia Jackson, Sallie Martin, Willie Mae Ford Smith, Marion WILLIAMS, Bessie Griffin, Albertina Walker, Alex Bradford, James CLEVELAND, and Shirley CAESAR. Gospel quartets performed a cappella or with guitar accompaniment, and gospel groups and soloists performed with piano and Hammond organ.

The gospel songs of Dorsey and other songwriters were disseminated in printed form. The musical score, however, provides only the text and a skeletal outline of the basic melody and harmonies. Vocalists and instrumentalists bring their own interpretations to these songs, employing the aesthetic conventions of the oral tradition. Thus, gospel music represents both a style of performance and a body of original composition. This style of performance is manifested in the gospel arrangement of the white hymn "Oh, Happy Day," which transformed the traditional style of Thomas Dorsey into a contemporary sound.

CONTEMPORARY GOSPEL

When Edwin HAWKINS, a Pentecostal, recorded his version of the hymn "Oh, Happy Day" in 1969, he ushered in a new era of gospel music—an era that coincided with the changed social climate engendered by the CIVIL RIGHTS MOVEMENT. Hawkins and his contemporaries evolved the gospel sound by blending traditional elements with those of contemporary popular, jazz, blues, folk, and classical music. "Oh, Happy Day," for example, is laced with elements of soul music, particularly its danceable beat. This song attracted the attention of top forty and soul music programmers, who added it to their play list. The popularity of "Oh, Happy Day" within and outside the religious community inspired other gospel performers to exploit Hawkins's model.

In the 1970s Andrae CROUCH experimented with every black secular form, employing melodies, harmonies, rhythms, and instrumentation from ragtime, jazz, blues, and funk; Rance Allen borrowed rhythms and instrumentation from the rhythm and blues and soul music traditions; and Vernard Johnson elevated the saxophone to the status of a solo gospel instrument. Contemporary gospel songwriters-performers also introduced new textual themes to the tradition. While retaining the established theme of salvation in some compositions, they do not mention God or Jesus directly in others. Instead, themes of peace, compassion, and universal love inspired by the civil rights movement and the spiritually based teachings of Martin Luther KING, Jr., prevail. These themes and the musical innovations, which demonstrate the affinity between gospel and popular forms, led to debates regarding appropriate sacred musical expression.

Perhaps the most controversial practice of the 1970s and 1980s was the recording of popular songs as gospel. James Cleveland, for example, recorded a gospel version of George BENSON's "Everything Must Change"; the 21st Century Singers presented a rendition of Melba Moore's "Lean on Me" as "Lean on Him"; and Shirley Caesar and the Thompson Community Singers recorded Curtis MAYFIELD's

"People Get Ready," a song inspired by Mayfield's religious beliefs. The only significant change made to the original songs was the substitution of "Jesus" for "baby," "my woman," and "my man."

In the 1980s gospel and classical performers joined forces to record a historic album, *Edwin Hawkins Live* (1981), with the Oakland Symphony Orchestra. The fusion of classical elements with gospel has its origins in the style of the Roberta Martin Singers. During the 1940s Roberta Martin, a songwriter and classically trained pianist, incorporated scales and arpeggios in the piano accompaniment and operatic vocal stylings from the classical tradition in the group's performances. During the 1970s and 1980s Pearl Williams-Jones and Richard Smallwood, who also were trained classical pianists, continued Martin's tradition of fusing classical with gospel piano techniques in gospel music.

Throughout the 1980s and into the 1990s, gospel performers continued to borrow the language, instrumentation, and technology (synthesizers, drum machines, and sound effects) of popular idioms. At the same time, performers of popular music turned to the gospel tradition for inspiration, as they had done for the previous four decades, employing gospel vocal stylings, harmonies, and rhythms and recording gospel songs under the label of soul. The Clark Sisters, Vanessa Bell Armstrong, Tramaine Hawkins, Walter HAWKINS, Commissioned, Bebe and CeCe Winans, Take 6, Nu Colors, Sounds of Blackness, Daryl Coley, Keith Pringle, John P. Kee, Little Saints in Praise, and Kinnection (gospel rap) are among those performers who created new gospel styles by stretching traditional musical parameters.

Civil Rights Freedom Songs

Civil rights freedom songs are the products of the 1950s and 1960s civil rights and Black Power movements, respectively. In the mid-1950s African Americans from the South mounted a series of grassroots activities to protest their social status as second-class citizens. These activities, which gained widespread momentum and attracted national attention in the 1960s, evolved into the civil rights and Black Power movements. Music was integral to both and served a multitude of functions. It galvanized African Americans into political action; provided them with strength and courage; united protesters as a cohesive group; and supplied a creative medium for mass communication.

Freedom songs draw from many sources and traditions, including folk and arranged spirituals; unaccompanied congreagtional hymn singing; folk ballads; gospel quartets, groups, and choirs; rhythm and blues and soul music; and original creations. Protesters reinterpreted the musical repertory of African-Americans, communicating their determination to effect social and political change. The singing captured the energy and spirit of the movement. The power of the songs, according to Bernice Johnson Reagon, "came from the linking of traditional oral expression to the everyday experiences of the movement" (Reagon 1987, p. 106). Well-known freedom songs include "We Shall Overcome," "Come Bah Yah," "Ain't Gonna Let Nobody Turn Me Around," "99½ Won't Do," and "Get Your Rights, Jack."

Rhythm and Blues

During the World War II era a distinct body of African-American popular music emerged in urban areas throughout the country. Labeled rhythm and blues, this tradition consisted of many regional styles, reflecting the migration patterns of African Americans and the musical background of performers. In Los Angeles, for example, former swing band and blues musicians formed five- to eight-member combos (bass and rhythm guitar, drums, piano, saxophone, trumpet, and trombone) and created a distinctive rhythm and blues style. It was a hybrid dance form that fused the twelve-bar blues and boogie-woogie bass line with the repetitive melodic riffs and drum patterns of the southwestern and Kansas City swing bands. This tradition also featured instrumental solos by a saxophonist and vocals by a blues singer. Pioneers of this style included Louis JORDAN, Joe Liggins, Roy Milton, Johnny Otis, Big Jay McNeely, Harold Singer, Paul WILLIAMS, and Wild Bill Moore.

Another artifact of the rhythm and blues style, introduced in Los Angeles in the 1940s, was the ballad. First associated with the King Cole Trio, it was performed primarily in lounges and small, intimate clubs as background or listening music. It featured a self-accompanying jazz or blues-style pianist-vocalist augmented by guitar and bass performing in a subdued or tempered style, in contrast to the high-energy sounds of the dance combos. Popularizers of this form include Cecil Gant, Charles Brown and the Three Blazers, Roy Brown, Amos Milburn, and Ray CHARLES.

In New Orleans a younger generation of performers such as Fats DOMINO, LITTLE RICHARD, Lloyd Price, and Shirley & Lee pioneered a youthful-sounding rhythm and blues style. This tradition featured gospel-derived vocal stylings; the repeated triplet and rolling octave piano figures from the blues; and the Cuban-derived rhumba bass pattern and an underlying fast sixteenth-note cymbal pattern accented on beats two and four on the snare drum. These innovations transformed the Los Angeles rhythm and blues combo style into a contemporary sound marketed by the music industry under the label ROCK 'N' ROLL.

By the mid-1950s New Orleans rhythm and blues had inspired other combo styles, such as the Atlantic Sound (Atlantic Records), popularized by Ruth BROWN and La Vern Baker, and those of guitarist Chuck BERRY and Bo DIDDLEY and the up-tempo vocal group styles of the Cadillacs, El Dorados, Flamingos, and COASTERS. These and other artists (with their producers) borrowed elements from the New Orleans tradition and fashioned them into a personalized style.

The vocal group tradition emerged as the most popular rhythm and blues form among teenagers, especially those living on the East Coast, in Chicago, and in Detroit. In these densely populated cities teenagers formed a cappella groups that performed for school dances and other social activities. Rehearsing on street corners and in schoolyards and parks, they eventually arrived at a type of group harmony inspired by their musical training in church choirs and in gospel groups. The pioneering vocal groups of the early 1950s, the Orioles, Spaniels, and the Five Keys specialized in singing ballads that appealed to the romantic fantasies of teenagers.

By the mid-1950s vocal groups had transformed the ballad into the doo-wop style. This style highlighted the phrase "doo-doo-doo-wop" or "doo-doo-doo-doo," sung as a rhythmic accompaniment by the bass singer. The doo-wop concept, introduced by the Spaniels in the early 1950s, eventually replaced the sustained "oohs and ahs" background of the early groups, adding a rhythmic foundation to the a cappella vocal group tradition. Popularizers of the doo-wop style include the Moonglows, Monotones, Frankie Lymon and the Teenagers, Five Satins, Channels, Charts, Heartbeats, Chantels, and Crests.

Coexisting with the doo-wop style was a pop-oriented vocal group sound that featured orchestral arrangements, gospel-pop-oriented vocal stylings, sing-along (as opposed to call-response) phrases (known as "hook lines"), and Latin-derived rhythms. This style, popularized by the PLATTERS and the post-1956 Drifters, provided some of the elements (musical arrangements and hook lines) that undergirded the 1960s vocal group sound of Smokey Robinson and the Miracles, the SUPREMES, FOUR TOPS, TEMPTATIONS, Dells, and Impressions.

In the mid-1960s the rhythm and blues tradition began to exhibit new sounds that reflected the discontentment of many African-Americans engaged in the struggle for social and racial equality. The pop-oriented vocal stylings of the Drifters, the cha-cha beat of some rhythm and blues singers, and the youthful sound and teen lyrics of the MOTOWN groups gave way to a more spirited type of music labeled soul.

Soul Music

Soul music, distinguished by gospel music stylings and socially conscious messages, was a product of the 1960s Black Power movement, a movement led by college-age students who rejected the integrationist philosophy of the 1950s civil rights leaders. The ideology associated with this movement promoted nationalist concepts of racial pride, racial unity, self-empowerment, self-control, and self-identification. As a concept soul became associated with an attitude, a behavior, symbols, institutions, and cultural products that were distinctively black and reflected the values and worldview of people of African descent.

Many black musicians supported the Black Power movement, promoting the nationalist ideology and galvanizing African Americans into social and political action. They identified with their African heritage, wearing African-derived fashions and hairstyles; their song lyrics advocated national black unity, activism, and self-pride; and their musical styles, which captured the energy, convictions, and optimism of African-Americans, reinforced an African cultural identity.

Soul music embodies the vocal and piano stylings, call-response, polyrhythmic structures, and aesthetic conventions of gospel music. This style is represented in the recordings "Soul Finger" (1967) by the Bar-Kays; "Soul Man" (1967) by SAM AND DAVE; "Respect" (1967) by Aretha FRANKLIN; "We're a Winner" (1968) and "This Is My Country" (1968) by the Impressions; "Say It Loud, I'm Black and Proud" (1968) and "I Don't Want Nobody to Give Me Nothing" (1969) by James BROWN; "Freedom" (1970) by the Isley Brothers; "Respect Yourself" (1971) by the Staple Singers; "Give More Power to the People" (1971) by the Chi-Lites; and "Back Stabbers" (1972) by the O'Jays, among others.

During the early 1970s the optimism that had prevailed during the 1960s began to fade among a large segment of the African-American community. New opportunities for social and economic advancement engendered by pressures of the civil rights and Black Power movements resulted in opposition from mainstream society. Resistance to affirmative action programs, school desegregation, busing, open housing, and other federal policies designed to integrate African Americans fully into the mainstream hindered them in their progress toward social, economic, and racial equality. The musical style and lyrics of Marvin GAYE's "What's Going On" (1971) and "Inner City Blues" (1971); James Brown's "Down and Out in New York City" (1973) and "Funky President"

(1974); and the O'Jays' "Survival" (1975) express mixed feelings about social change. Reflecting the disappointments and the continued struggle toward racial equality, new forms of popular expressions labeled funk, disco, and rap emerged out of the soul style during the 1970s.

Funk Music

Funk describes a form of dance music rooted in the traditions of James Brown and Sly STONE. It is characterized by group singing, complex polyrhythmic structures, percussive instrumental and vocal timbres, a horn section, and lyrics that urge "partying" or "having a good time." The primary function of funk was to provide temporary escape from the unpleasant realities of daily life. Therefore, funk performers created an ambience that encouraged black people to express themselves freely and without the restrictions or cultural compromises often experienced in integrated settings.

The therapeutic potential of funk is reflected in key recurring phrases: "have a good time," "let yourself go," "give up the funk," and "it ain't nothing but a party." Among the pioneering funk performers were Sly and the Family Stone, Kool and the Gang, Ohio Players, Graham Central Station, Bar-Kays, and Parliament.

By the mid-1970s George CLINTON, the founder of Parliament and other funk groups had broadened the definition of funk to embrace a philosophy. Known as P-funk (pure funk), this philosophy emerges from the creation of an imaginary planet—the planet of funk. On this planet blacks acquire new values, a worldview, and a life style free of earthly social and cultural restrictions. Clinton's P-funk songs combined the party theme with social commentary in a comic style. This theme and the philosophy of P-funk prevail in Parliament's "Chocolate City" (1975); "P. Funk (Wants to Get Funked Up)" (1975); "Prelude" (1976); "Dr. Funkenstein" (1976); "Bop Gun (Endangered Species)" (1977); and "Funkentelechy" (1977). Musically, the P-funk style advances the concepts of Sly Stone, who achieved mood and textural variety through the use of electronic distorting devices and synthesizers.

Only a few 1970s and 1980s funk groups (including Zapp and Roger) incorporated synthesized technology into their performances. Most, such as Con Funk Shun, Rich JAMES and the Stone City Band, Bohannon, Lakeside, Gap Band, Cameo, and Instant Funk, remained faithful to the traditional funk style of the early pioneers.

Nevertheless, George Clinton's technological concepts inspired the new breed of 1980s composers who were technician-arrangers influenced by the innovations of European avant-garde composers. Using synthesizers, drum machines, computers, and other electronic equipment, they created the techno-funk style, which employs various sound effects. Techno-funk provided the sound tracks and sound effects for many rap music records. Rap music deejays Afrika Bambaataa and the Soul Sonic Force ("Planet Rock," 1982), Planet Patrol ("Play at Your Own Risk," 1982), and the Jonzun Crew ("Space Is the Place," 1982) are pioneers of this style.

Go-Go

Another derivative funk style is go-go music, which evolved in Washington, D.C.'s inner-city neighborhoods during the mid-1970s. It is distinguished from traditional funk by its continuous audience participation and by the use of percussion instruments to extend and connect different songs into a twenty- to ninety-minute performance. Live audience participation is an essential component of the go-go tradition. The audience and performers spontaneously create and exchange phrases in an antiphonal style. Musical variety results from the percussively played horn lines and extended percussion sections. Go-go pioneer Chuck Brown popularized this style with his first hit, "Bustin' Loose" (1978), and a later hit, "We Need Some Money" (1985). Spike LEE brought national notoriety to the idiom when he featured E. U. (Experience Unlimited) performing "Da' Butt" (1988) in his film *School Daze*. Other go-go groups include Trouble Funk, Rare Essence, Little Benny and the Masters, Slim, and Redds and the Boys.

Disco

Disco is a term first used to identify dance music played in discotheques during the 1970s. The "Top 50 Disco Hits" chart that appeared in *Billboard* (a music industry publication) for the first time in 1974 indicated that the majority of these songs were soul, Latin soul, funk, and the new sounds from Philadelphia International Records (known as the Philly Sound and created by the songwriters Kenny Gamble and Leon Huff).

By the late 1970s disco referred to a new body of extended play (i.e., exceeding the standard three-minute recording) dance music distinguished by instrumental arrangements that incorporated synthesized sound effects and a distinctive drum pattern known as the disco beat. Disco, as a distinct musical style, had its origins in the orchestral arrangements and drumbeat of the Philly Sound, which combines melodic strings with percussively played horn lines over a four-to-the-bar bass drum pattern subdivided by beats of the high-hat cymbal (and variations of this pattern). The Philly groups MFSB ("TSOP," 1973, "Love Is the Message," 1974) and Harold Melvin and the Blue Notes ("Bad Luck," 1975) and

Thelma Houston ("Don't Leave Me This Way," 1976) popularized this sound, which became known as disco and which became a worldwide musical phenomenon.

Both American and European disco producers and performers appropriated the Philly Sound, especially the drum pattern, to create various disco styles. They include the orchestral-style arrangements of Gloria Gaynor ("Never Can Say Good-bye," 1974, and "I Will Survive," 1978) and Salsoul Orchestra ("Tangerine," 1975); the Euro-disco styles of the Ritchie Family ("Brazil," 1975, and "The Best Disco in Town," 1976), Donna Summer ("Love to Love You, Baby," 1975), the Trammps ("That's Where the Happy People Go," 1976), and the Village People ("San Francisco, 1977, and "Macho Man," 1978); the Latin styles of Carl Douglas ("Doctor's Orders," 1974), and Van McCoy ("The Hustle," 1974, and "The Disco Kid," 1975); and the funk-based disco of Silver Convention ("Fly, Robin, Fly," 1975), B. T. Express ("B. T. Express," 1974), Taste of Honey ("Boogie Oogie Oogie," 1978), and Chic ("Good Times," 1979).

With the release of the disco film *Saturday Night Fever* (1978), disco crossed over from a primarily black and gay audience into the mainstream. The popularity of the film's sound track resulted in the disco craze. In response, record companies flooded the market with recordings that quickly reduced disco to a formula made up of the disco beat, synthesized sound effects, and repetitious vocal phrases. By the early 1980s disco had lost its originality and soon faded from the musical landscape.

The deejays in black gay basement clubs in Chicago and New York created a neodisco style known as house music in the mid-1980s. Their creations added gospel-style vocals over repetitive bass lines and drum patterns programmed on synthesizers and drum machines. Like those of disco and funk, house music lyrics encouraged dancers to have a good time. The pioneer of house music was deejay Frankie Knuckles, and its performers included Marshall Jefferson ("Move Your Body [The House Music Anthem]," 1986), Exit ("Let's Work It Out," 1987), Fast Eddie ("Yo Yo Get Funky," 1988), Inner City ("Big Fun," 1988), and Technotronic ("Pump Up the Jam," 1989, and "Move This," 1989).

Rap Music

Rap music is the product of inner-city black communities, where the proliferation of drugs and gangs, the rise in unemployment, and the lack of educational opportunities and traditional support institutions contributed to increased poverty and community decay during the years following the civil rights and Black Power movements. Between the late 1960s and the early 1970s gang violence escalated to new levels in New York City, a situation that inspired some ex-gang members to consider ways to reduce violent exchanges. They turned to rap music, which evolved in conjunction with BREAKDANCING and graffiti art as an urban street youth culture called hip-hop. In about 1975 these artistic forms came to provide an alternative to competitive gang warfare. In turn, rap music became the vehicle through which many young people elevated their social status and developed a sense of pride, displaying their technological and verbal skills. By 1977 this music and the broader hip-hop culture dominated the expressions of inner-city youth.

Rap is defined as rhymed poetry recited in rhythm over prerecorded instrumental music. Rapping is rooted in the black oral traditions of storytelling, toasting, boasting, signifying, and "the dozens." The performance style of rappers employs the rhyming couplets, rhythmic speech patterns, and rhetorical style of black personality deejays who talked, or "rapped," over music. Rap music consists of several song types: party rap (known in the 1990s as hip-hop), novelty or humorous rap, rap ballad, Afrocentric or nationalist rap, and hard-core, or "gangsta," rap.

The first commercial rap recording—"Rapper's Delight" by the Sugarhill Gang, released in 1979—established party rap as the model for other early rap recordings. This rap style exploited the art of boasting. Rappers, while bragging about their verbal facility and the technological skills of the deejay to "rock the house," emphasized their physical attributes, material possessions, and other personal characteristics. Rappers within the same group (known as a posse or crew) verbally competed with each other as well as members of other rap groups. The groups that popularized party raps include Sequence ("Funk You Up," 1979); Curtis Blow ("The Breaks," 1980); Grandmaster Flash and the Furious Five ("Freedom," 1980, and "Birthday Party," 1981); Funky Four Plus One ("Rapping and Rocking the House," 1980); Lady B. ("To the Beat [Y'all]," 1980); Grandmaster Flash and the Furious Five and Furious Five Meets the Sugarhill Gang ("Showdown," 1981).

The early rap groups used studio bands rather than street mixes of rap deejays in their live recordings. The success of Grandmaster Flash's recording "Adventures of Grandmaster Flash on the Wheels of Steel" (1981) brought the street technology and techniques of mobile rap deejays into the studio. In this recording Flash created musical collages (combined and remixed extracts from existing records) and employed the scratching and backspinning (repetition of key musical phrases and rhythms by manipulating the record) techniques and various other sound effects. The innovations of rap deejay Afrika Bambaataa and the introduction of drum machines, synthesizers, computers, analog and digital machines, and other systems advanced the techniques and technology for rap music production. The new technology eventually replaced live musicians and arrangers on rap recordings.

During the mid-1980s a new generation of rappers from both inner cities and suburbs broadened the scope of rap. While "rockin' the house," boasting about their emcee skills, and exchanging insults, these rappers introduced new lyric themes and musical styles to the tradition. Some told humorous stories and tall tales; many recounted adolescent pranks, fantasies, and romantic encounters; and others painted graphic images of suburban and inner-city life. Rappers from inner-city communities aggressively expounded on the social ills and political issues that adversely affected the lives of African Americans, while those from the suburbs often presented parodies of the middle class.

In 1984 UTFO ("Roxanne Roxanne"), Roxanne Shante ("Roxanne's Revenge"), and the Real Roxanne ("The Real Roxanne") popularized verbal dueling, or "signifyin'," between genders. Run-D.M.C. fused rock with rap in "Rock Box" (1984) and "Walk This Way" (1986) to create the first rap crossover hit ("Walk This Way"). In "La Di Da Di" (1985), Doug E. Fresh incorporated rhythmic vocal effects in a concept known as the "human beat box," which became the trademark of the comic group the Fat Boys ("Jail House Rap," 1984, and "The Fat Boys Are Back," 1985). L. L. Cool J introduced the rap ballad in "I Need Love" (1987), which brought to rap a softer edge and a romantic dimension. Jazzy Jeff and the Fresh Prince added a humorous suburban perspective in "Girls Ain't Nothing but Trouble" (1986) and "Parents Just Don't Understand" (1988), as did De La Soul in "Potholes in My Lawn" (1989), "Plug Tunin' " (1989), and "Me Myself and I" (1989). Queen Latifah, the Real Roxanne, and Positive K introduced a feminist perspective in "Ladies First" (1989), "Respect" (1988), and "I Got a Man" (1992), respectively.

In the late 1980s rap became a public forum for social and political commentary as well as the expression of inner-city rage and X-rated behavior. Inner-city communities deteriorated throughout the 1980s due to the dismantling of government programs, the continuing rise in unemployment, the proliferation of drugs, and the relocation of the black middle class to the suburbs. As an invisible group with limited resources, inner-city residents struggled to survive.

This situation, which led to chaos in inner-city communities, inspired a new aggressive tone and graphic descriptions of the harshness and diversity of inner-city life.

The first recordings that addressed the economic woes, social ills, and deteriorating conditions of inner cities were Curtis Blow's "Hard Times" (1980), Grandmaster Flash and the Furious Five's "The Message" (1982) and "New York, New York" (1983), and Grandmaster Flash and Melle Mel's "White Lines (Don't Do It)" (1983). In the late 1980s and 1990s a group of rappers expounded on these themes and promoted the 1960s black nationalism agenda associated with the NATION OF ISLAM and soul music. These rappers condemned social injustices, drugs, police brutality, violence, and black-on-black crime. Innovators of nationalist rap include Public Enemy ("It Takes a Nation of Millions to Hold Us Back," 1988, and "Fear of a Black Planet," 1989–1990); Jungle Brothers ("Straight Out of the Jungle," 1988, and "Done by the Forces of Nature," 1989); Boogie Down Productions ("By All Means Necessary," 1988, and "Ghetto Music: The Blueprint of Hip Hop," 1989); Paris ("The Devil Made Me Do It," 1989–1990); X-Clan ("To the East, Blackwards," 1990); Brand Nubian ("One for All," 1990, and "In God We Trust," 1992), and Sister Souljah ("360 Degrees of Power," 1992).

The political voices of nationalist rappers coexisted with the harsh messages of hard-core rappers who described the chaos, the rough and seedy side of inner-city life, using graphic language laced with expletices. Their raps, while portraying components of everyday life in inner-city communities, often exploited and dramatized these experiences to the point of glorifying drugs, violence, criminal acts, and misogynistic and X-rated behavior. Such rappers include Slick Rick ("Children's Story," 1988); N.W.A. ("Straight Outta Compton," 1988, and "Niggaz4life," 1991); Eazy-E ("Eazy-Duz-It," 1988); 2 Live Crew ("As Nasty As They Wanna Be," 1989); Geto Boys ("The Geto Boys," 1989, and "Uncut Dope," 1992); Ice Cube ("Amerikkka's Most Wanted," 1990); Dr. Dre ("The Chronic," 1992); and Snoop Doggy Dogg ("Doggystyle," 1993).

Hard-core and nationalist rappers occasionally have been accused of supporting racist and homophobic sentiments. Although these themes are not prominent in rap music, they are found in the lyrics of some artists, including Public Enemy ("Welcome to the Terrordome, 1989); Big Daddy Kane ("Pimpin' Ain't Easy," 1989); and Brand Nubian ("Punks Jump Up to Get Beat Down," 1992).

The musical style of nationalist and hard-core rap is aggressive, polytextured, polyrhythmic, and polysonic. Sampling, the repetitive remixing of chord sequences and rhythms from prerecorded music (especially the music of James Brown, George Clinton, and other soul and funk groups), combined with synthesized sound effects, is the primary technique used to create the distinctive sounds associated with these rap styles. The samples and the sounds of sirens, gunshots, babies crying, screams, and street noises reflect the ethos, chaos, tensions, anger, despair, and the sometimes violent nature of inner-city life. Many rappers express their commitment to improving conditions in inner-city communities. Despite the inclination of some to devalue human life, most rappers (including nationalist and some hard-core rappers) denounce behavior that negatively impacts African Americans. Dr. Jeckyll and Mr. Hyde ("Fast Life," 1984), Ice T ("I'm Your Pusher," and "High Rollers," 1988), for example, condemn drugs and criminal activity; N.W.A. "——— Tha Police," 1988) and Ice T ("Cop Killer," 1992) speak out against police brutality. Other rappers address a broader range of social issues, ranging from the plight of unwed mothers to that of the homeless and those on welfare. They include Snoop Doggy Dogg ("Keep Ya Head Up," 1993), Arrested Development ("Mama's Always on Stage," and "Mr. Wendall," 1992), and Queen Latifah "The Evil That Men Do," 1989).

New Jack Swing

By the late 1980s new black popular styles were being created by independent producers, including Teddy Riley, Dallas Austin, and the teams of James "Jimmy Jam" Harris and Terry Lewis and Antonio "L. A." Reid and Kenneth "Babyface" Edmonds. One style that evolved from the innovations of these producers and was imitated by others was termed new jack swing. The style, pioneered by Teddy Riley, represents postmodern soul; it is defined by its sparse instrumentation and a marked underlying drum pattern blended with or sometimes above the tempered vocals. Variations of this pattern incorporate a snare drum emphasis on the second and fourth beats, giving the sound a 1970s syncopated swing associated with James Brown and Earth, Wind, and Fire. The rhythms and production techniques of new jack swing became the beat and mix of the late 1980s and 1990s. It can be heard in Guy's "Groove Me" (1988), "You Can Call Me Crazy" (1988), and "Don't Clap . . . Just Dance" (1988); Heavy D. and The Boyz' "We Got Our Own Thang" (1989); Keith Sweat's "Make You Sweat" (1990); Hi Five's "I Just Can't Handle It" (1990); the gospel group Winans' "A Friend" (1990); and Michael Jackson's "Remember the Time" (1992), among others.

New Jack Swing Rhythmic Patterns
"Groove Me" (1988) by Guy

"Don't Clap...Just Dance" (1988) by Guy

Future trends in black popular music will be pioneered by individuals and groups who continue to cross traditional genres and borrow from existing styles to create music that expresses the changing ideas and ideals of the African-American community.

REFERENCES

BARLOW, WILLIAM. *Looking Up at Down: The Emergence of Blues Culture.* Philadelphia, 1989.

BEBEY, FRANCIS. *African Music: A People's Art.* Translated by Josephine Bennett. New York, 1974.

BERLIN, EDWARD A. *Ragtime: A Musical and Cultural History.* Berkeley, Calif., 1980.

BURNIM, MELLONEE. "Functional Dimensions of Gospel Music Performance." *Western Journal of Black Studies* 12 (1988): 112–120.

CHARTERS, SAMUEL B., and LEONARD KUNSTADT. *Jazz: A History of the New York Scene.* 1962. Reprint. New York, 1981.

CONE, JAMES. *The Spirituals and the Blues.* New York, 1972.

COURLANDER, HAROLD. *Negro Folk Music, U.S.A.* New York, 1963.

DE LERMA, DOMINIQUE. *Black Music in Our Culture.* Kent, Ohio, 1970.

DU BOIS, W. E. B. *The Souls of Black Folk.* 1903. Reprint. Greenwich, Conn., 1961.

EPSTEIN, DENA. *Sinful Tunes and Spirituals.* Urbana, Ill., 1977.

FLETCHER, TOM. *One Hundred Years of the Negro in Show Business.* 1954. Reprint. New York, 1984.

FLOYD, SAMUEL, JR. *Black Music in the Harlem Renaissance.* New York, 1990.

GARLAND, PHYL. *The Sound of Soul.* Chicago, 1969.

GEORGE, NELSON. *The Death of Rhythm & Blues.* New York, 1988.

GILLETT, CHARLIE. *The Sound of the City.* Rev. ed. New York, 1983.

HAAS, ROBERT BARTLETT, ed. *William Grant Still and the Fusion of Cultures in American Music.* Los Angeles, 1972.

HARRIS, MICHAEL. *The Rise of Gospel Blues: The Music of Thomas Andrew Dorsey.* New York, 1992.

HARRISON, DAPHNE DUVAL. *Black Pearls: Blues Queens of the 1920s.* New Brunswick, N.J., 1988.

HURSTON, ZORA NEALE. "Spirituals and Neo-Spirituals." In Nathan Huggins, ed. *Voices from the Harlem Renaissance.* New York, 1976, pp. 344–347.

KEIL, CHARLES. *Urban Blues.* 1961. Reprint. Chicago, 1991.

KILHAM, ELIZABETH. "Sketches in Color: IV." In Bruce Jackson, ed. *The Negro and His Folklore.* Austin, Tex., 1967, pp. 120–133.

LEIGH, JAMES WENTWORTH. *Other Days.* New York, 1921.

LEVINE, LAWRENCE. *Black Culture and Black Consciousness.* New York, 1977.

LOCKE, ALAIN. *The Negro and His Music.* 1936. Reprint. Port Washington, N.Y., 1968.

———. "The Negro Spirituals." In Alain Locke, ed. *The New Negro.* 1925. Reprint. New York, 1969, pp. 199–213.

MAULTSBY, PORTIA K. "Africanisms in African-American Music." In *Africanisms in American Culture*. Bloomington, Ind., 1990.

MYERS, ROBERT MANSON, ed. *The Children of Pride*. New Haven, Conn., 1972.

NKETIA, KWABENA J. H. "African Roots of Music in the Americas: An African View." In American Musicological Society, *Report of the 12th Congress*. London, 1981, pp. 82–88.

———. *The Music of Africa*. New York, 1974.

OLMSTED, FREDERICK LAW. *A Journey in the Seaboard Slave States in the Years 1853–1854, with Remarks on Their Economy*. 1856. Reprint. New York, 1904.

PEARSON, NATHAN W., JR. *Goin' to Kansas City*. Urbana, Ill., 1987.

PERETTI, BURTON W. *The Creation of Jazz*. Urbana, Ill., 1992.

REAGON, BERNICE JOHNSON. "Let the Church Sing 'Freedom' " *Black Music Research Journal* 7 (1987): 105–118.

———. *We'll Understand It Better By and By*. Washington, D.C., 1992.

ROSE, TRISA. *Black Noise*. Hanover, N.H., 1994.

RUSSELL, HENRY. *Cheer! Boys, Cheer! Memories of Men and Music*. London, 1895.

SCHAFER, WILLIAM J. *Brass Bands and New Orleans Jazz*. Baton Rouge, La., 1977.

SILVESTER, PETER J. *A Left Hand like God: A History of Boogie-Woogie Piano*. New York, 1989.

SOUTHERN, EILEEN. *The Music of Black Americans*. 2nd ed. New York, 1983a.

———, ed. *Readings in Black American Music*. 2nd ed. New York, 1983b.

STILL, WILLIAM GRANT. "A Composer's Viewpoint." In Dominique de Lerma, ed. *Black Music in Our Culture*. Kent, Ohio, 1970, pp. 93–108.

TOLL, ROBERT C. *Blacking Up: The Minstrel Show in Nineteenth-Century America*. New York, 1977.

TOOP, DAVID. "Changing Patterns in Negro Folk Songs." *Journal of American Folklore* 62 (1949): 136–144.

———. *The Rap Attack 2: African Rap to Global Hip, Hop*. Boston, 1992.

WORK, JOHN. *American Negro Songs and Spirituals*. New York, 1940.

PORTIA K. MAULTSBY

Music Collections, Black. Black music—that is, music composed or performed by people of African descent—is basic to the study of African-American history and culture, and to an understanding of American culture in general. Libraries collect it in all formats and genres, from scores and sheet music of classical compositions for study and performance to recordings of the latest popular music. Black music collections are found in institutions of all sorts, including major research collections, nationally recognized collections devoted to black culture, special-collections departments of college and university libraries, historical societies and museums, music libraries, and public-library collections. All have a role in the documentation and study of black music.

Specialized collections exist to preserve the various black music styles, including popular music, blues, and jazz, and to collect the works of black composers. Library collections also document the contributions of African-American performers in broader genres, such as opera and musical theater, and the work of African-American music educators and organizations. Black music collections can be used by researchers not only to study and perform the music itself, but to gain insight into historical and social processes, and to document the broader cultural contributions of African Americans.

Serious documentation of blacks in musical culture began early in the twentieth century with the establishment of library collections devoted to black history. Important special collections have been maintained by the historically black educational institutions, with the holdings of the Moorland-Spingarn Research Center at Howard University, in Washington, D.C., found in 1914, particularly outstanding. The Schomburg Center for Black History and Culture of the New York Public Library, containing one of the largest black collections, was established in 1926. Another respected research collection, the Amistad Research Center, established at Fisk University in Nashville in 1966, is now located at Tulane University in New Orleans. These three repositories, which cover the broad spectrum of black history and culture, have devoted serious efforts to collecting music materials.

The first publicly accessible collection devoted exclusively to black music and blacks in the performing arts was the E. Azalia Hackley Collection of the Detroit Public Library, founded in 1943. Collections focusing on jazz include the Institute of Jazz Studies at Rutgers University in New Brunswick, N.J., founded in 1952, and the William Ransom Hogan Jazz Archive at Tulane University, founded in 1958. A serious effort to collect and preserve scores by black composers began at the Music Library of Indiana University at Bloomington in 1970. The newest comprehensive black music collection can be found at the Center for Black Music Research at Columbia College, in Chicago, which opened formally in September 1992.

National agencies, such as the Library of Congress and the Smithsonian Institution, in Washington, D.C., are also important resources, as are general performing-arts collections, such as the New York Public Library for the Performing Arts at Lincoln Center. Popular-music collections such as those at the University of California at Los Angeles (UCLA), Bowling Green State University in Ohio, and Middle Tennessee State University in Murfreesboro are general in scope, but do justice to the importance of black popular styles. Specialist repositories, such as the University of Mississippi Blues Archive and various ethnomusicology archives, devote themselves to preserving oral and recorded traditions. The collections of these repositories will be discussed in greater detail.

Any attempt to describe black music collections in the United States is obsolete almost before it is completed, because collections are constantly growing and backlogs being cataloged, bringing newly processed materials to the attention of scholars. Many libraries now catalog their holdings on national library databases: the Online Computer Library Center (OCLC) and the Research Libraries Information Network (RLIN), making information available to any researcher who has access to these networks.

Archives often supplement their standard cataloging with in-house databases. An example is the CBMR Database at the Center for Black Music Research in Chicago, which indexes music and vertical file materials in the CBMR Library and Archives. [A bibliographic database with over thirty thousand entries is maintained at the Black Arts Research Center in Nyack, N.Y., which specializes in popular-music styles worldwide, classical music, and modern jazz.]

The catalogs of some of the major libraries, including the Schomburg and Moorland-Spingarn collections, were published in book form before the library community came to rely on the national on-line networks. A catalog of the Hackley Collection was published in 1979, and guides to other individual collections have also been published.

Black music is a broad field encompassing many material types, genres, and possible research approaches. In addition to art music in many compositional styles, there are the various genres in the oral tradition, including spirituals, jazz, blues, rhythm and blues, gospel, and a number of current popular styles. Music collections tend to concentrate on sheet music and scores, and on recordings in numerous formats, but they also collect ephemera, photographs, periodicals, and other unique documents, including letters, diaries, and music manuscripts, when they exist. Such written documents may be scarce, partly because musicians are often too busy to keep them, and sometimes because the musicians find written means of expression uncongenial. In some cases, especially when the music is itself orally transmitted (blues) or dependent on improvisation for

musical effect (jazz, some forms of gospel), libraries may turn to oral history, which ensures the survival of important information while freeing informants from the necessity of creating a written document.

Knowledge of black music is absolutely essential to the study of American popular music. Many general popular-music collections therefore collect black music as part of their larger holdings. Sheet music was the only format for music, popular or otherwise, before the advent of recording technology in the late nineteenth century, and collections of early sheet music tend to make few distinctions between popular and art genres. Such collections include the J. Francis Driscoll Collection at the Newberry Library in Chicago, the Corning Sheet Music Collection of the William L. Clements Library at the University of Michigan in Ann Arbor, and the sheet-music collection at the John Hay Library, Brown University, in Providence, R.I. All have substantial holdings of minstrel songs, and of nineteenth-century music by black composers or on black topics.

The Sam De Vincent Collection of Illustrated Sheet Music at the Archives Center of the Smithsonian Institution has a large component of black music. There are also sizable collections of popular sheet music at the Archive of Popular American Music at UCLA, and the Center for Popular Music at Middle Tennessee State University. Sheet music of minstrel songs, ragtime, and similar music, including songs by black composers, is highly collectible, and in recent years collectors have donated or sold their holdings to libraries in increasing numbers. Libraries now possessing such collections include the Special Collections Division of the Michigan State University Libraries in East Lansing and the music libraries of the University of Michigan and the University of Illinois at Urbana-Champaign. The American Music Collection of the New York Public Library for the Performing Arts has an extensive collection of piano ragtime compositions, and the Buffalo and Erie County Public Library has a collection of minstrel songs and songsters (collections of song lyrics). The Music Division of the Library of Congress retains sheet music deposited for copyright registration.

In addition to the collections named above, two major research repositories, the Schomburg Center for Research in Black Culture and the Moorland-Spingarn Research Center, have comprehensive collections of sheet music, popular and otherwise, by black composers. Many items in their collections are extremely rare. The Gershwin Memorial Collection at Fisk University contains photographs and other materials about black composers, as well as music. The Hackley Collection at the Detroit Public Library has an impressive sheet-music component. The NCNB Black Musical Heritage Collection in the

Special Collections Department of the University of South Florida Library in Tampa contains five thousand pieces of sheet music, much of it popular.

Recordings

Recordings are the primary source for the study of popular music during the twentieth century. One of the premier collections of popular-music recordings in the United States is in the Music Library and Sound Archives at Bowling Green State University, Bowling Green, Ohio. A collection of sound recordings numbering nearly six hundred thousand is supported by a research collection of printed materials, periodicals, and ephemera. The Center for Popular Music at Middle Tennessee State and the Archive of Popular American Music at UCLA both have extensive collections of sound recordings. Finally, the Library of Congress has a department devoted to recordings as part of its Motion Picture, Broadcasting and Recorded Sound Division. Again, these collections are general in scope but contain numerous recordings of black music and black performers.

Popular Music

Libraries have only begun to collect documentary materials relating to contemporary popular musicians. The Amistad Research Center has a small collection relating to James BROWN, and the Western Historical Manuscript Collection at the University of Missouri–St. Louis has a similar one devoted to Chuck BERRY. The Sue Cassidy Clark Collection at the Center for Black Music Research contains photographs and interviews with musicians from the 1970s. The music library at Bowling Green State University collects popular fan magazines and ephemeral publications. The Chicago Public Library's Music Information Center and the Center for Black Music Research keep vertical files on contemporary performers.

Folk Music

Ethnomusicology collections can be useful to researchers in African-American music, because these sources include noncommercial field recordings of traditional music from America and other parts of the world. Study of recordings of African, Afro-Caribbean, and South American musics can provide insights into the development of African-American musical forms. African-American folk music, encourage work songs, ballads, dance music, games, and sermons, along with well-known forms such as spirituals and folk blues, must be studied to obtain insights into both popular and classical compositions.

An extensive collection of field recordings of traditional African-American performers can be found at the Archive of Folk Culture at the American Folk-

life Center of the Library of Congress. Since its founding in 1928, a succession of folklorists—including Robert Winslow Gordon, John and Alan Lomax, Herbert Halpert, Zora Neale HURSTON, and Laura Bolton, working directly for the archive or for other government agencies—have recorded and documented American folk music and culture. Numerous other scholars have contributed additional collections. Among the many African-American musicians who are represented in the collections are Jelly Roll MORTON, James P. JOHNSON, Albert AMMONS, Meade "Lux" LEWIS and Pete Johnson, Leadbelly (Huddie LEDBETTER), and bluesmen Son HOUSE, John Hurt, and MUDDY WATERS. In addition to field recordings, the Archive of Folk Culture collects books, published sound recordings, manuscripts, photographs, and moving-image materials. It publishes an excellent series of commercial recordings based on its holdings, as well as a useful series of bibliographies and finding aids.

The Archives of Traditional Music at Indiana University in Bloomington has field collections of traditional music, spirituals, blues, gospel music, and sermons and tales collected by Natalie Curtis Burlin, Harold Courlander, Richard Dorson, John Hasse, Guy B. Johnson, and John, Alan, and Elizabeth Lomax, among others. It also holds numerous African collections and about forty thousand commercial recordings of blues, jazz, and other musical styles. Two other archives with holdings of commercial as well as field recordings are the Ethnomusicology Archive at UCLA and the Ethnomusicology Archives at the University of Washington, in Seattle, which has few American collections but over fifty collections of field recordings from sub-Saharan Africa. The archive of Folkways Records, a company that specialized in commercially issued field recordings, many of them African-American, is at the Smithsonian Institution.

Ethnographic films are another important source of information on traditional music. The Motion Picture Division of the Library of Congress and the Human Studies Film Archives at the Smithsonian Institution have African-American materials, both commercial films and field recordings. The Center for Southern Folklore in Memphis distributes several films on southern folk music and blues, and also holds the Rev. W. O. Taylor collection of photographs and film footage of religious events, including one hundred 78-rpm acetate recordings of religious music.

Repositories that specialize in traditional music away concentrate on a region. The Avery Research Center for African American History and Culture in Charleston, S.C., focuses on the Gullah culture of the Sea Islands. In its holdings are field recordings made in the Sea Islands by Lorenzo Dow Turner and recordings of the Moving Star Hall Singers. The

Southern Folklife Collection at the University of North Carolina at Chapel Hill holds both commercial and field recordings of black music in a general collection devoted to southern traditional music. The collection is particularly strong in early blues and gospel and in string-band music, a still-neglected area of study. An interesting component is a group of forty-six wax cylinders recorded on South Carolina's St. Helena Island in 1928 by folklorist Guy B. Johnson.

Blues Collections

Blues is the popular-music form closest to traditional music. The University of Mississippi Blues Archive has not only over twenty thousand sound recordings of blues and related genres, but also the files of *Living Blues* magazine, the business papers of Trumpet Records, and jazz and gospel session books of Savoy Records, plus collections relating to performers as diverse as B. B. KING and Gertrude "Ma" RAINEY. Oral-history holdings include interviews made for *Living Blues,* collections contributed by several blues journalists, and the archive's own oral-history project, carried out with north Mississippi musicians. The Chicago Blues Archives at the Music Information Center of the Chicago Public Library has recordings and files on blues musicians, and a collection of recordings and papers devoted to the annual Chicago Blues Festival, at which many contemporary musicians have performed.

Blues oral-history projects of note include the Bull City Blues oral histories and performances at the North Carolina Division of Archives and History in Raleigh, and the Robert Neff and Anthony Connor Blues Collection of interviews with blues musicians, housed at the Yale University School of Music's Oral History, American Music Project. An ongoing project entitled History of the Oakland Blues, initiated at the Regional Oral History Office of the Bancroft Library at the University of California, Berkeley, aims at documenting the blues in Oakland, Calif.

Gospel Music Collections

There are no repositories devoted exclusively to traditional black religious music, or to gospel music. The archives of the black colleges that first brought spirituals to a broader public after the Civil War have documented their performing groups: Fisk University has collections relating to the FISK JUBILEE SINGERS, and the Hampton University Archives has papers of the Hampton Singers, plus field recordings and papers of folklorist Natalie Curtis Burlin. A collection devoted to WINGS OVER JORDAN, including the personal papers of the choir's founder, Rev. Glynn T. Settle, can be found at the National Afro-

American Museum and Cultural Center in Wilberforce, Ohio. The Southern Folklife Collection at the University of North Carolina, Chapel Hill, has papers, recordings, and sheet music from the Gospel Light Music Store of Philadelphia. Included are original acetate recordings of local gospel groups from the 1950s.

Gospel sheet music can be found in the holdings of the Schomburg Center and the Library of Congress. Over fifteen hundred pieces of gospel music published by the Martin and Morris Publishing Company of Chicago are in the Chicago Public Library's Music Information Center. The Center for Popular Music at Middle Tennessee State University collects gospel songbooks and commercial and field recordings, with a specialty in black shape-note singing and gospel quartets, notably the Fairfield Four and the Four Eagles. The Chicago Public Library has videotapes of one hundred programs of the television series *Jubilee Showcase* (1963–1984), on which most major gospel artists performed. Despite efforts in the last few years, gospel music remains the most underdocumented genre of black music. Major collections are held by private collectors, or by the musicians themselves and their families, very few are accessible in libraries.

Jazz

The situation is much different with jazz. Not only do several specialist repositories and collections exist, but major figures have archives devoted solely to them. For example, papers, business records, photographs, manuscripts, and recordings of Duke ELLINGTON are in the Duke Ellington Collection, housed in the Archives Center of the Smithsonian Institution, and Queens College, New York, holds the Louis ARMSTRONG Archive. Such collections give important figures the emphasis they deserve.

The Institute of Jazz Studies at Rutgers collects jazz materials in all formats comprehensively, and publishes the *IJS Jazz Register and Indexes,* a catalog of recordings in microfiche form. In addition, the institute holds the world's most extensive collection of jazz periodicals, 122 interviews comprising the Jazz Oral History Project, and one hundred transcriptions of big-band arrangements.

The William Ransom Hogan Jazz Archive at Tulane University focuses on New Orleans jazz, with fifty thousand recordings, sheet music, vertical files, and manuscripts. Other New Orleans collections include the New Orleans Jazz Club Collection at the Louisiana State Museum, comprising recordings, sheet music, photographs, and ephemera, and the New Orleans Jazz and Heritage Foundation Oral History Project, interviews with forty-nine New Orleans musicians, which is housed at the Amistad Research Center. The Amistad Research Center also has papers of jazz arranger Fletcher HENDERSON, whose arrangements for Benny Goodman can be found in the American Music Collection of the New York Public Library for the Performing Arts.

Other cities important in the development of jazz have collections devoted to them. The Jazzmen Project at the Western Historical Manuscript Collection consists of recorded interviews and performances of St. Louis musicians. Microfilmed scrapbooks of riverboat musicians Eddie Johnson and Elijah Shaw are also available. The Jazz Institute of Chicago has placed its collection at the Chicago Jazz Archive at the University of Chicago. It contains recordings, oral histories, and collections devoted to Chicago musicians. Jazz in New York City is documented in the Otto Hess collection of photographs of jazz events from the 1940s and 1950s, held by the American Music Collection of the New York Public Library for the Performing Arts, and by the papers of the New York Jazz Museum at the Schomburg Center. On the West Coast, the Central Avenue Sounds Oral History Project of the UCLA Oral History Program documents Los Angeles's Central Avenue from the 1920s through the 1950s. Notable informants include Art Farmer, Frank Morgan, Buddy Collette, and Melba LISTON.

Jazz recordings can be found in the Maxwell O. Reade Collection in the African-American Music Collection at the University of Michigan, and at the Center for Black Music Research. The Valburn Ellington Collection at the Library of Congress contains 10,000 Duke ELLINGTON recordings, including nearly every commercial recording and hundreds of noncommercial recordings. Another major collection of the recordings of Duke Ellington, numbering over 800 commercial recordings and 88 tape recordings (some of them unique), is held by the University of North Texas Music Library.

The Boston University's Mugar Memorial Library specializes in collecting the papers of popular performers. Its jazz-related holdings include collections devoted to Cab CALLOWAY and Ella FITZGERALD. The papers of W. C. HANDY, Don Redman, Ronald L. CARTER, and Mabel Mercer are at the Schomburg Center. The W. C. Handy Museum in Handy's hometown of Florence, Ala., also has archival materials.

Oral-History Interviews

A relatively new development is the videotaped oral-history interview. The Standifer Video Archive in the African-American Music Collection at the University of Michigan has over one hundred interviews with major figures, including a number of jazz musicians as well as classical performers and composers.

The Schomburg Center also has a videotaping program aimed at recording musical events and interviews with individuals.

Musical Theater

Library collections pertaining to classically trained African-American composers and performers are diverse and sometimes scattered. Before the mid-twentieth century, racial discrimination shunted aspiring black performers and composers into vaudeville and musical theater. As in the case of popular music, materials from the early years of black theater can be found in general theater collections, including the Harvard Theatre Collection, the Theatre Arts Library at the University of Texas at Austin, and the New York Public Library for the Performing Arts at Lincoln Center. The Channing Pollock Theater Collection at Howard University and the Countee Cullen Memorial Collection at Atlanta University's Robert W. Woodruff Library specialize in African-American contributions in theater and the performing arts.

Other theater-oriented collections include the *Porgy and Bess* collection at the African-American Music Collection, University of Michigan, which includes files on the original production. Materials on other productions of *Porgy and Bess* are in the Robert E. Lee Theatre Research Institute at Ohio State University in Columbus. The Schomburg Center has the papers of theatrical composer Luther Henderson and actor/songwriter Emmet "Babe" Wallace. The George Peabody Collection at Hampton University consists of four scrapbooks on black music and musicians dating from 1824 to 1921. Scrapbooks of vocalist Sissieretta JONES are at the Moorland-Spingarn Research Center. The Maryland Historical Society in Baltimore has an archive devoted to composer and performer Eubie BLAKE.

Educators and Organizations

The papers of educators and organizations are of great importance, especially for the time when discrimination prohibited black performers and composers from full participation in mainstream organizations. The papers of George Washington Glover at the Schomburg Center contain extensive information on the National Association of Negro Musicians (NANM). Amistad Research Center has the records of two branches of NANM, the Chicago Music Association and the B-Sharp Music Club of New Orleans. The Schomburg Center has papers of educator and composer Blanche K. Thomas and educator Isabelle Taliaferro Spiller. Additional Spiller materials are at the Moorland-Spingarn Research Center, which also has papers of Gregoria Fraser Goins, prominent in several musical organizations in Washington, D.C., and records of the Washington Conservatory of Music. The papers of the National Opera Association are at the Library of Congress.

Classical Music

When it comes to archival collections of classical composers and performers, the major research collections have extensive holdings. The Music Division of the Library of Congress has correspondence and manuscripts of several black composers and performers. Outstanding examples include two manuscripts of William Grant STILL's *Afro-American Symphony* and manuscripts of several early works by Ulysses KAY. An in-house card file compiled by Walter E. Whittlesey, a library staff member, covers from c. 1900 through the 1930s and serves as an adjunct to the library's catalogs and copyright records. Researchers have found it extremely useful as a guide to information about otherwise obscure individuals.

The Schomburg Center has the records of the Symphony of the New World, and of Mary Caldwell DAWSON, founder of the National Negro Opera Company, plus the papers of composers Edward Boatner and Clarence Cameron WHITE. Classical performers documented at the Schomburg Center include Marion Cumbo, Julius BLEDSOE, Lawrence Brown, Melville Charlton, and Philippa Duke SCHUYLER.

The Amistad Research Center has also documented African-American performers and composers. The papers of composer Howard SWANSON are primarily music manuscripts; there are also collections relating to Roger Dickerson and Hale SMITH. Collections pertaining to performers include papers of Carol Brice, Camilla Williams, Mattiwilda DOBBS, William Warfield, and Jessie Covington Dent.

Collections dealing with individual performers are also scattered in other repositories. At least three have collections on Paul ROBESON: The Moorland-Spingarn Research Center has the bulk of Robeson's papers, but there are also collections of Robeson materials at the Schomburg Center and at the Charles L. Blockson Collection at Temple University in Philadelphia. The Hackley Collection received the papers of Roland HAYES in 1989. The Marian ANDERSON papers are in the Rare Book Collection of the Van Felt Library at the University of Pennsylvania in Philadelphia. The Center for Black Music Research has a collection on operatic baritone Ben Holt, and the Hampton University Archives has a collection relating to Dorothy MAYNOR. The papers of pianist and author Maude Cuney Hare are at Atlanta University. They also contain biographical information on other African-American composers and musicians.

Documenting the early years of African-American composition can be problematic, because so few materials have survived the passage of time. Fortunately, some manuscript materials from the nineteenth century have survived. These include a manuscript music book and sheet music of black bandleader and composer Francis JOHNSON, at the Library Company of Philadelphia, and a Johnson holograph manuscript at the Library of Congress.

Ragtime collections appear to consist mainly of sheet music and recordings, including piano rolls made by the composers. James Scott, Scott JOPLIN, and Blind BOONE are documented in the ragtime collection at State Fair Community College in Sedalia, Mo. The State Historical Society of Missouri also has collections relating to Boone and Joplin. A Joplin collection at Fisk University contains correspondence about the composer by his wife and others. The recently organized Scott Joplin House State Historic Site in St. Louis has piano rolls that were recorded by Joplin.

Papers and manuscripts of individual composers are to be found in numerous repositories. Papers of H. T. BURLEIGH can be found at the Erie County Historical Society in Erie, Pa., and at the Pennsylvania Historical and Museum Commission in Harrisburg. Three repositories have papers of R. Nathaniel DETT, including the Archives at Hampton University, with which he was associated for many years; the University Archives and Historical Collections at Michigan State University; and the Local History Department of the Niagara Falls Public Library, in Niagara Falls, N.Y. Papers and manuscripts of John Wesley WORK III are at Fisk University, which also has papers of contemporary composer Arthur Cunningham. The papers of J. Rosamond JOHNSON are in the Music Library at Yale University in New Haven, Conn. Manuscripts and published arrangements by N. Clark Smith are in the Conservatory Library of the University of Missouri in Kansas City. The music manuscripts of Edmund Thornton JENKINS, unlocated for years, are now at the Center for Black Music Research.

The Special Collections Department of the University of Arkansas Libraries has the papers of two major twentieth-century composers, Florence PRICE and William Grant Still. Still manuscripts can also be found in the Henry T. Sampson Library of Jackson State University in Jackson, Miss. The Center for Black Music Research has papers of James Furman, music manuscripts of Richard C. Moffatt, the papers of William Banfield, and collections of scores by Banfield, Leslie Adams, Ed Bland, and Michael Woods. The Eva JESSYE Collection is a major component of the African-American Music Collection at the University of Michigan, and Jessye materials can also be found at the Amistad Research Center of Tulane University; the Special Collections Department at Pittsburgh State University in Pittsburg, Kans., has a sizable amount of Jessye's correspondence and manuscripts, as well as photographs, interviews, and recordings of her folk oratorio *Paradise Lost and Regained*. The American Music Center in New York has a collection of scores by numerous contemporary black composers.

Mention should also be made of other personal collections of great research value. The James Weldon JOHNSON collection in the Beinecke Rare Book and Manuscript Library at Yale covers black music extensively, and contains holograph scores by several African-American composers. The American Music Research Center at the University of Colorado, Boulder, has music by black women composers collected and donated by Helen Walker-Hill, a prominent scholar and bibliographer in the field. The Dominique-René de Lerma Collection at the Center for Black Music Research in Chicago contains manuscripts and published scores, ephemera, recordings, and this pioneering scholar's correspondence with composers and musicians.

Archival collections documenting composers perform two functions: They provide materials for the study of an individual's life and times and also for the study of his or her music, including analysis of the compositional process. They point to obstacles and triumphs, and to the uniqueness of the African-American contribution to American music. The names of many libraries and of many individuals have been mentioned above, attesting to the preservation of African-American music materials in publicly accessible repositories. The tragedy, for the study of black music and American music and for recognition of the importance of the African-American heritage, is in the names that are missing; names of important composers whose works are scattered or destroyed, or are still inaccessible in private hands; names of performers who never made recordings, whose scrapbooks and letters are missing or destroyed, and whose contributions therefore will never be completely recognized.

REFERENCES

ASH, LEE, and WILLIAM G. MILLER. *Subject Collections*. 6th ed. New York, 1985

FLOYD, JR., SAMUEL A., and MARSHA J. REISSER. *Black Music in the United States: An Annotated Bibliography of Selected Reference and Research Materials*. Millwood, N.Y., 1983.

GEIST, CHRISTOPHER D, RAY B. BROWNE, MICHAEL T. MARSDEN, and CAROL E. PALMER. *Directory of Popular Culture Collections*. Phoenix, 1989.

KRUMMEL, D. W., JEAN GEIL, DORIS J. DYEN, and DEAN L. ROOT. *Resources of American Music History:*

A Directory of Source Materials from Colonial Times to World War II. Urbana, Ill., 1981.

SUZANNE FLANDREAU

Musical Instruments.   Many of the most popular musical instruments in American music derive from African Americans, who used traditional African instruments and developed new ones according not only to musical needs, but the natural and manufactured materials at hand, and the legal restrictions placed by slave owners regarding the making of music. The prominence of stringed instruments in early African-American music was no doubt due to plantation prohibitions on drum and wind instruments, which slave masters believed would be used for long-distance and mass communication among slaves.

Although the banjo, the earliest and most important African-American instrument, is today used almost exclusively in white music, the instrument derives from the West African "banja" or "banza" brought to the New World by slaves. References to a gourd covered with sheepskin and strung with four strings along an attached stick occur in accounts of the Americas as early as 1678. Both fretless and fretted banjos were used by African-American musicians, and open tunings were common. Slaves also pioneered most of the techniques that became standard on the modern instrument, including the various kinds of strumming and plucking heard in twentieth-century bluegrass and country music. Although informal banjo playing was a central feature of African-American domestic life in the eighteenth century, it was through nineteenth-century minstrel shows that the instrument was first widely noticed among whites. The banjo was used by white musicians before the Civil War, and was being commercially produced using a wood frame (contrary to some accounts, the now-standard fifth string was a feature of the banjo before the white minstrel musician Joel Walker Sweeney [1810—1860] helped popularize the instrument). Soon, the banjo was considered as much a parlor instrument among white families as a staple of rural black music. Among the best early recordings of black banjo music are "Long Gone Lost John" (1928) by Papa Charlie Jackson (1890–1950), and "Money Never Runs Out" (1930) by Gus Cannon (1883–1979), who recorded under the name Banjo Joe. Early jazz bands also used the banjo extensively, most notably Johnny St. Cyr (1890–1966), a sideman with Louis ARMSTRONG and Jelly Roll MORTON in the 1920s. After the late 1920s, however, the guitar supplanted the banjo as a rhythm instrument. After that time the banjo became the almost exclusive province of white country, bluegrass, and folk music, although some black folk musicians, including Elizabeth COTTEN, continued to play the banjo.

African Americans also developed many types of single-string instruments. The diddley bow was a type of simple guitar popular among black musicians in the South well into the twentieth century. As a child, Elias McDaniel's prowess on the instrument was so great that he was known by the name Bo DIDDLEY well before he gained fame as a blues musician in the 1950s. The blues guitarist and singer Elmore JAMES learned music on a jitterbug, a variant of the diddley bow that is strung along a wall. The washtub bass or gutbucket played a central role in folk blues and jug bands (the word "gutbucket" has also come to mean a crude, raucous, earthy style of jazz or blues). This instrument was created by stringing a rope from the bottom of an inverted metal washtub to the end of a stick, the other end of which stands on the tub. Plucked much in the manner of the modern jazz bass, the washtub bass is still in use today in informal street ensembles. It probably originated from an African instrument called the earthbow or mosquito drum, in which resonating material was stretched over a hole in the ground. The practice of using a hard object to create glissandos on the guitar is of unclear origin—certainly the "Hawaiian" style of picking with the right hand while using a slide with the left, introduced in the late nineteenth century was influential—but African-American musicians were the first to master the use of broken-off bottlenecks, knives, and medicine bottles for this purpose, now typical of blues guitar playing.

Numerous types of flutes, pipes, and fifes were brought by African slaves to the New World, and despite being outlawed in slave states, these wind instruments played a central part in the development of African-American music. Wooden or metal fifes, similar to European transverse flutes, were used in ubiquitous fife and drum bands as early as the eighteenth century. The kazoo, a small cylinder with a resonating membrane set into motion by humming or singing, was also probably of African-American origin—although it bears similarities to European musical devices—and became a popular folk instrument among whites and blacks after being manufactured commercially starting around 1850.

Perhaps the most distinctive African-American wind instrument is the quills. These pan pipes were traditionally made from cane, reed, or willow stalks cut from riverbanks, but their name suggests that at one time they may have been made with feathers. After being cut down to a length of approximately one foot, a hole was bored through the center, and finger and mouth holes were also created. Among the earliest and most representative of the quill recordings are "Arkansas" (1927) by Henry Thomas (1874–1930), and "Quill Blues" (1927) by Big Boy Clarence.

The domestic earthen jug, which produces a sound when blown across its mouth, was another wind instrument popular among African Americans, and gave its name to an independent genre of music in the late nineteenth century. Throughout the South, and well into the twentieth century, jug bands consisting of a jug, fiddle and bass, kazoo or harmonica, and often a washboard scraped and played as a percussion instrument, performed folk-blues music often suited for dancing. Early examples of jug bands include the Memphis Jug Band, the Dixieland Jug Blowers, who recorded "Skip Skat Doodle Do" in 1926, and Gus Cannon's Jug Stompers, which recorded "K.C. Moan" in 1929.

Many African-American percussion instruments were developed from common household or agricultural materials that lent themselves to use as knockers, rattles, and scrapers. Clapping together small sections of dried bone or wood was a long-standing feature of European folk music by the time the SLAVE TRADE began, but playing "the bones" was elevated to a virtuosic state by black minstrels in nineteenth-century America (see MINSTRELS/MINSTRELSY). In fact, the player of the bones was such an important part of African-American culture that the role was immortalized alongside the tambourine player in minstrel shows as the characters of Tambo and Bones. The practice of striking and shaking the weathered jawbone of a donkey or horse probably derives from African slaves—although visual images and literary references to jawbone percussion are also found in medieval and renaissance Europe—and was a conspicuous aspect of both white and black minstrel shows early in the nineteenth century.

Although the playing of drums was proscribed on most plantations, the striking of skin stretched on a sturdy frame remained a part of black musical life. The marching bands that were so popular in the nineteenth century, at both parades and military functions, were driven by drummers using a variety of instruments, from huge bass drums to smaller snare drums. Although the origin of the snare drum is not clear, the use of bamboo or feathers stretched across a drumhead to give an impure, buzzing tone is a characteristic of many African instruments. The tuned or talking drums of Africa also had their counterparts in America, as African-American musicians played peg drums, which used posts on the side of the frames to tighten or loosen the skin head, and therefore raise or lower the pitch of the drum.

The decline of marching music in favor of the dance music played at nightclubs where musicians remained stationary made possible the trap drum set, whose combination of bass drum, snare, tom-tom, and cymbals was developed by popular dance drummers, and early jazz musicians such as Baby DODDS and Zutty SINGLETON (1898–1975). In the 1940s Cuban musicians such as Chano POZO brought Latin-style drums and drumming to jazz. The Afro-Cuban tradition, which used congas and bongos played with the hands, as opposed to drumsticks, was directly linked to West African religious practices that had been carried over and sustained in Cuba.

The marimba is sometimes called an Amerindian creation, but some scholars believe that this melodic percussion instrument, with its parallel wooden blocks gathered together and struck with a mallet, was brought to the Americas by African slaves, and documented in Virginia as early as 1775.

In addition to using instruments of African origin, or creating ones, African Americans have also approached traditional European instruments from such a new perspective that instruments such as saxophone, violin, harmonica and piano were transformed into virtually new instruments. Perhaps the best such example is the double bass, which in the European tradition was almost always bowed, forming the harmonic underpinning of the orchestra. In the 1920s African Americans began to use the bass as a timekeeper, and made the pizzicato, or plucked technique, its main feature in jazz and jug bands. Among the finest early recorded example of jazz bass playing is that of the John Lindsay (1894–1950) performance on Jelly Roll Morton's "Black Bottom Stomp" (1926). A slightly different example of the metamorphosis of a purely European instrument is the plunger-muted trumpet. In the European tradition, trumpeters used mutes to muffle their sounds. In the 1920s, African-American jazz trumpeters such as Joe "King" OLIVER, Bubber MILEY, and, later, Cootie WILLIAMS, adapted rubber toilet plungers as mutes that, when manipulated in front of the bell of the horn, could create a whole new range of growls and speech-like sounds, a practice that was also extended to the trombone in the playing of Joe "Tricky Sam" NANTON.

The development of African-American instruments has continued in the twentieth century. The Chicago musicians' collective known as the ASSOCIATION FOR THE ADVANCEMENT OF CREATIVE MUSICIANS (AACM) integrated the use of unusual tools and household items into its percussion array. One AACM member, Henry THREADGILL, invented a percussion instrument made of automobile hubcaps. In more recent years, African-American disc jockeys have developed the technique of "scratching"—manually moving records backwards and forwards on turntables to create melodic rhythms. Digital electronics have allowed African-American musicians to develop "sampling," in which fragments of older recordings by musicians are integrated into new musical works. The fact that these techniques use modern technique demonstrates how the response by African Americans to both musical and material imperatives continues to inspire the development of new African-American musical instruments.

REFERENCES

EVANS, DAVID. "Afro-American One-Stringed Instruments." In William Ferris, ed. *Afro-American Folk Art and Crafts.* Boston, 1983, pp. 181–198.

———. "Black Fife and Drum Music in Mississippi." In William Ferris, ed. *Afro-American Folk Art and Crafts.* Boston, 1983, pp. 163–172.

MACLEOD, BRUCE. "The Musical Instruments of North American Slaves." *Mississippi Folklore Register* 11 (1977): 34–49.

———. "Quills, Fifes, and Flutes Before the Civil War." *Southern Folklore Quarterly* 42 (1978): 201–208.

WEBB, ROBERT LLOYD. *Ring the Banjar! The Banjo from Folklore to Factory.* Cambridge, Mass., 1984.

JONATHAN GILL

Musical Theater. Musical theater—formal, staged entertainments combining songs, skits, instrumental interludes, and dances—was relatively uncommon in America before the middle of the eighteenth century. It is very likely that slave musicians occasionally took part in the earliest colonial period musical theatricals, called ballad operas, at least in the orchestra pit, since many slaves were known to be musically accomplished. Less than fully developed theatrical shows that involved satirical skits by slaves about white masters are recorded in the late eighteenth century. These skits, related to African storytelling traditions, were the seeds from which black American theatricality sprang. "Negro songs" or "Negro jigs" are also recorded in the shows of this period, suggesting the impact of an unnotated tradition of black music making on the musical theater song repertory (Southern 1983, p. 89).

Up to the Civil War

The opening of the African Grove theater in 1821 near lower Broadway in New York inaugurated the staging of plays with music "agreeable to Ladies and Gentlemen of Colour" (Southern 1983, 119). Led by playwright Henry BROWN, the African Grove players produced Shakespeare's *Hamlet, Othello,* and

Richard III (including inserted songs), popular pot-pourris such as *Tom and Jerry; or Life in London,* and the pantomime *Obi; or, Three Finger'd Jack.* James Hewlett was the company's principal singer and actor. Ira ALDRIDGE, who later made his career in Europe, sang songs at the Grove. Despite the theater's popularity, it was plagued by hooligans and closed in 1829.

Various musical shows were produced with black performers periodically in Philadelphia and New Orleans, though very little information survives about these shows. New Orleans could command orchestral forces (as opposed to the modest pit band of violin, clarinet, and double bass at the African Grove) for theatricals, and it engaged black players in the 1840s. In the 1850s and '60s African-American actors became traveling entertainers or joined minstrel shows (*see* MINSTRELS/MINSTRELSY).

The Late Nineteenth Century

The HYERS Sisters touring company, founded in 1876, became the first established African-American musical comedy troupe. Managed by Sam Hyers, the company featured his two daughters, Emma Louise and Anna Madah, and a string of male comedy singer /actors: Fred Lyon, Sam Lucas, Billy Kersands, Wallace King, and John and Alexander Luca. The Hyers began as a concert-giving group but moved on to fully staged musical plays that often dealt with racial themes: *Out of Bondage* (1876); *Urlina, or The African Princess* (1879); *Peculiar Sam; or, The Underground Railroad* (1879); and *Plum Pudding* (1887). The music they presented included jubilee songs, spirituals, operatic excerpts, and new popular songs and dances (*see* SPIRITUALS).

By the 1890s a few specific plays regularly toured and featured parts for black singers, usually in the guise of "plantation slaves." Bucolic scenes or other scenarios in the cotton field, on the levee, or in a camp meeting were meant to evoke an idyllic antebellum South. Turner Dazey's *In Old Kentucky* (1892) and *The South before the War* (1893) included black singers and dancers, as did the most famous of all shows of this type, *Uncle Tom's Cabin* (based on Harriet Beecher Stowe's novel of 1852). The huge number and variety of staged versions of this powerful work made it a unique dramatic vehicle in American culture. Many African-American "jubilee" singing groups, typically male quartets, took part in the play, although early performances rarely used black actors. It served the careers of solo banjo virtuoso Horace Weston in 1877 and vaudevillian Sam Lucas, who played the role of Uncle Tom in the 1880s (*see* OPERA).

At least a half-dozen all-black companies, as well as some integrated ones, appeared before the end of the century. Black choral singers and supernumeraries, including children, brought literally hundreds of people to the stage in productions in the 1880s and 1890s. Other festivals featuring black vaudeville acts, musical specialties, and historical tableaux, with titles like *Black America* (1895) and *Darkest America* (1897), were well-attended showcases but did not present complete plays.

The most widely acclaimed operatic singer of the period to become involved with traveling musical theatrical companies was Sissieretta JONES, known as the Black Patti (after the renowned soprano Adelina Patti). In 1896 she formed the Black Patti Troubadours and remained an important presence on the road for two decades, eventually mounting full-fledged musical comedies.

White burlesque entrepreneur Sam T. Jack formed the Creole Company in 1890 to do the skit *The Beauty of the Nile; or, Doomed by Fire,* using the novelty of black women in a minstrel line that emphasized glittery, revealing costumes and diverse musical acts. John Isham, Jack's advance man, developed his own potpourri shows presented by mixed male and female companies known as the Octoroons (1895), one of which toured in Europe. All of Isham's shows exploited the popularity of exotic costumes, operatic excerpts, musical specialties, spectacular scenery, and attractive women, while avoiding farcical minstrel show caricatures.

The First Black Musicals and the Growth of Black Vaudeville, 1897–1920

Within this world of extravagant eclecticism, full-length musical comedies—plays in which songs were frequent and newly composed if not integral—became more and more common. The first musical written by and for African Americans, "Bob" COLE and Billy Johnson's *A Trip to Coontown* (1897), was built up from Cole's songs and vaudeville turns with the Black Patti Troubadours (Cole had also managed her show in its first season) and other elements: a trio from Verdi's opera *Attila,* Sousa's new march "The Stars and Stripes Forever," a tune by Cole that was later stolen to become Yale University's fight song "Boola Boola," energetic dancing, topical humor, and social commentary. The show eschewed the Old South nostalgia typical of the earlier touring shows. Minstrel tunes were replaced by snappy up-tempo, occasionally syncopated songs written by different composers.

At the same time, cakewalk dancers/comedians Bert Williams and George Walker, in the course of several productions from 1898 to 1908, expanded their routines to even more ambitious dimensions, with elaborate plots and often African settings: *The Policy Players* (1899); *The Sons of Ham* (1900); *In*

Dahomey (1902); *Abyssinia* (1905); and *Bandanna Land* (1907). Will Marion COOK, classical violinist and European-trained composer, wrote most of the music for these landmark shows in a unique syncopated style. Cook's sensational Broadway debut—his musical skit *Clorindy* was produced at the Casino Theatre Roof Garden in 1898—established him as a leading figure, along with its dancing star, Ernest Hogan.

In 1899 Bob Cole formed a partnership with the brothers J. Rosamond JOHNSON and James Weldon JOHNSON. This young trio wrote songs for many shows and performers, black and white, to great success, and later composed comic operettas for all-black casts entitled *The Shoo-Fly Regiment* (1906) and *The Red Moon* (1908); they also starred in the shows themselves. Black, white, and mixed audiences found these many early twentieth-century efforts attractive, but any hope for sustained development was dashed by the premature deaths of the leaders, Ernest Hogan, George Walker, and Bob Cole, around 1910 and the unremitting financial burden of mounting and tour-

J. Rosamond Johnson. (Photographs and Prints Division, Schomburg Center for Research in Black Culture, The New York Public Library, Astor, Lenox and Tilden Foundations)

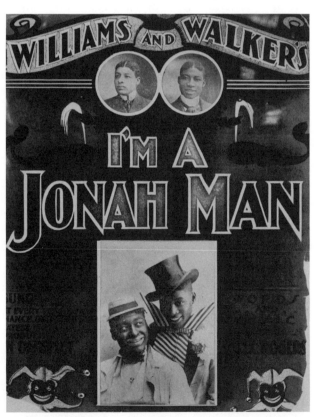

"I'm a Jonah Man," sheet music cover for Bert Williams's theme song in the Williams and Walker musical *In Dahomey*, which had a command performance at Buckingham Palace after a successful turn-of-the-century run in New York. (Photographs and Prints Division, Schomburg Center for Research in Black Culture, The New York Public Library, Astor, Lenox and Tilden Foundations)

ing with a large cast. Racism and professional jealousies among competing companies also limited the success of these shows.

Black-owned theaters rapidly increased in number in the early twentieth century, providing sites for a wide variety of musical-theater activities. Following the opening of the Pekin Theatre in Chicago in 1905, many black-owned or black-managed houses were built. By 1920 some 300 theaters around the country were serving black patrons (approximately one-third of these theaters were black-run). This in turn led to the formation of resident stock companies that provided a regular menu of musical plays and developed loyal audiences. Many short-lived shows of the 1920s and '30s filled the Lafayette, Lincoln, and Alhambra theaters in Harlem, the Howard in Washington, D.C., the Regal in Baltimore, Md., the Monogram in Chicago, the 81 in Atlanta, Ga., and the Booker T. Washington in St. Louis, Mo., among others (*see* LINCOLN THEATRE).

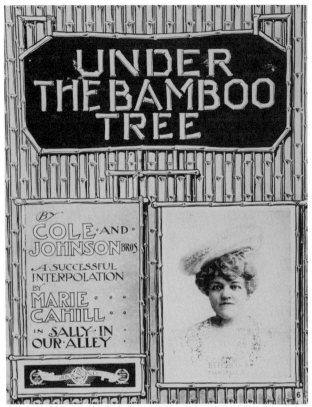

One of the hit songs of the 1902 Broadway season was "Under the Bamboo Tree" from the show *Sally in Our Alley,* composed by James Weldon Johnson, James Rosamond Johnson, and Bob Cole. The song's melody is related to the spiritual "Nobody Knows the Trouble I've Seen." (Photographs and Prints Division, Schomburg Center for Research in Black Culture, The New York Public Library, Astor, Lenox and Tilden Foundations)

A few large companies continued to tour—J. Leubrie Hill's Darktown Follies (from 1911 to 1916) and the various Smart Set shows run by S. H. Dudley, H. Tutt, and S. T. Whitney—but many acts appeared in vaudeville as well. By 1920 the THEATRE OWNERS' BOOKING ASSOCIATION (TOBA) was formed to facilitate the booking of black acts into theaters that served black audiences exclusively. The TOBA circuit of theaters eventually embraced houses all over the South and survived until the Great Depression.

Vaudeville acts and musicals of the first decades of the twentieth century served as apprenticeships for many young ragtime pianists and composers who wanted to break into the business (*see* RAGTIME). J. Tim Brymn, James Vaughan, Charles "Luckey" ROBERTS, James Price JOHNSON, and "Will" VODERY played, wrote songs for, and directed forgotten shows with titles like *George Washington Bullion Abroad* (1915) and *Baby Blues* (1919) before going on to arrange, perform, and write for military bands, Broadway shows, and films.

"Shuffle Along" and Its Successors, 1921–1939.

Eubie BLAKE and Noble SISSLE's *Shuffle Along* kicked off a major revival of black musical comedies in New York in 1921. Light, fast-moving, and filled with catchy melodies, it captured crowds for over 500 Broadway performances and spent two years on the road. Its lead comedians, still in blackface, were Aubrey Lyles and Flournoy Miller, who wrote the book, developing material that they had been using for years. Many members of the cast later found individual stardom: Florence MILLS, Josephine BAKER, Caterina Yarboro, Ethel WATERS, Adelaide Hall, Paul ROBESON, William Grant STILL, and Hall JOHNSON.

The upsurge in black shows in the wake of *Shuffle Along* has not been equaled since. Their number paralleled the high-water mark of new productions of all kinds on Broadway in the late 1920s. Many were close imitations of *Shuffle Along,* but a few broke new ground, with respect to both characters and music: *Put and Take* (1921); *Liza* (1922); *Strut Miss Lizzie* (1922); *Plantation Days* (1923); *Runnin' Wild* (1923); *Bottomland* (1927); *Africana* (1927); *Rang Tang* (1927); and five shows produced by Lew Leslie called *Blackbirds* (of 1926, 1928, 1930, 1933, and 1939).

Hot Chocolates (1929), by Andy Razaf and Fats WALLER, epitomized the successful post-*Shuffle Along*

Florence Mills and the Florence Mills Trio. (Photographs and Prints Division, Schomburg Center for Research in Black Culture, The New York Public Library, Astor, Lenox and Tilden Foundations)

show of the late 1920s: a revue (i.e., a string of topical acts and songs rather than a plotted story show) filled with new dance steps—the Black Bottom, the Lindy, the Shimmy, and the Charleston all appeared in these shows—with an attractive chorus line, blues songs, and repartee closer to the real speech of Harlem than either the pseudo-dialect of minstrelsy or the clean, cute shows of white Broadway. James P. Johnson, Tom Lemonier, Donald Heyward, Maceo Pinkard, Joe Jordan, Henry Creamer, Ford Dabney, and Perry Bradford emerged as songwriters with these shows.

The spirituals arranged by Hall Johnson and sung by his choir helped to make *The Green Pastures* the hit play of 1930. Weaving humor and gentleness together to create a naive picture of a black heaven, the superb cast was well received. Ironically, its very success led to bookings in exclusionary theaters where no blacks were admitted to the auditorium. Both this show and its successor, *Run Little Chillun* (1933), helped to ensure the continued employment of black players and singers during the general decline of the 1930s.

The Works Progress Administration (WPA) Negro Theatre Project (1935–1939) brought African Americans into all aspects of theater production, and a few musicals were performed: *Did Adam Sin?* (1936), using African-American folklore themes and music; Theodore Brown's *Natural Man* (1937), a retelling of the John Henry legend; *Swing It* (1937), by Cecil Mack (a.k.a. R. Cecil McPherson); and *Swing Mikado* (1939), a jazz transformation of Gilbert and Sullivan.

Developments since World War II.

The only major shows featuring black stars in the 1940s were *Cabin in the Sky* (1940) with Ethel Waters and *St. Louis Woman* (1946) with Pearl BAILEY and the NICOLAS BROTHERS. Otherwise, opportunities for blacks in the New York musical theater scene through the 1940s, 1950s, and 1960s were few. A desire to eliminate stereotyped roles for black actors and the problem of dealing with serious race-related social issues in the normally lighthearted style of musicals resulted in the temporary elimination of nearly all black participation. No all-black-cast shows were staged in the early 1950s, nor were more than a handful of African Americans employed on- or offstage during this period. A small group of shows with integrated casts or a single black star did well at the box office, notably *Jamaica* (1957) with Lena HORNE and *Golden Boy* (1964) with Sammy DAVIS, Jr.

In the wake of the CIVIL RIGHTS MOVEMENT, via the revival of older black musical styles and the folk songs that had always found an audience, African Americans returned to Broadway and touring companies. The plays of Langston HUGHES with various

musical collaborators, *Simply Heavenly* (1957), *Black Nativity* (1961), *Tambourines to Glory* (1963), and *The Prodigal Son* (1965), embraced black culture and ignored the politics of integration. Vinnette CARROLL adapted James Weldon Johnson's verse sermons for *Trumpets of the Lord* (1963). Gospel songs, spirituals, and folk songs also infused *A Hand Is at the Gate* (1966), *Don't Bother Me, I Can't Cope* (1972), and *Your Arms Too Short to Box with God* (1976).

More direct social criticism was offered in the calypso musical *Ballad for Bimshire* (1963) and in Melvin VAN PEEBLES's angry and challenging plays *Ain't Supposed to Die a Natural Death* (1971) and *Don't Play Us Cheap* (1972). Blues, jazz, and the special styles of famous artists in earlier eras of black music added a nostalgic aura to the shows of the rest of the 1970s and 1980s: *Me and Bessie* (1975), *One Mo' Time* (1979), *Eubie* (1979), *Sophisticated Ladies* (1981), *Blues in the Night* (1982), *Dreamgirls* (1982), *Williams and Walker* (1986), and *Black and Blue* (1989).

The same decades saw the successful conversion of straight plays by black playwrights (Ossie DAVIS, Lorraine HANSBERRY, and James BALDWIN) into musicals: *Purlie* (1970), *Raisin* (1973), *The Amen Corner* (1983), as well as the improbable remake of Sophocles into the fervid gospel music show *The Gospel at Colonus* (1988). A uniquely whimsical and tuneful adaptation of L. Frank Baum's *Wizard of Oz*, with music by Charles Smalls, became *The Wiz* (1975, revived in 1984), and black-cast versions of white shows *Hello Dolly* (1963 and 1975) and *Guys and Dolls* (1976) and self-conscious historical song summaries like *Bubbling Brown Sugar* (1976) and *Black Broadway* (1980) also appeared. As in the 1930s, the revue format succeeded best with audiences and critics. *Ain't Misbehavin'*, using the tunes of "Fats" Waller, won the Tony Award for Best Musical in 1978.

One of the most interesting and impassioned imports at the end of the 1980s was the anti-apartheid South African show *Sarafina!* (1987), featuring native song styles and enjoying a long run. This show was striking for its dramatic content, but in the main the homegrown shows of the most recent decades have not been such. Shows high on energy, retrospection, and dance numbers but less apt to be driven by a powerful book have been the norm. *Jelly's Last Jam* (1992) attempted to address some serious issues surrounding the life of the famous Creole jazzman "Jelly Roll" MORTON on his deathbed and portrayed the protagonist as a dancer to his own music; Gregory Hines starred. Part biography, part historical recreation, and part satire (complete with a blackface chorus of Pullman porters) this ambitious and brilliantly produced show—*Variety* called it "original, outrageous, and exuberant"—received eleven Tony Award nominations.

REFERENCES

CHARTERS, ANN. *Nobody: The Story of Bert Williams.* London, 1970.

COOK, WILL MARION. "Clorindy; or, The Origin of the Cakewalk." In Eileen Southern, ed. *Readings in Black American Music.* New York, 1983.

FLANAGAN, HALLIE. *Arena: The History of the Federal Theatre.* New York, 1940.

FLETCHER, TOM. *The Tom Fletcher Story: 100 Years of the Negro in Show Business.* 1954. Reprint. New York, 1984.

GRAZIANO, JOHN. "Black Musical Theatre and the Harlem Renaissance Movement." In Samuel A. Floyd, Jr., ed. *Black Music in the Harlem Renaissance.* Westport, Conn., 1990.

HATCH, JAMES V. *Black Image on the American Stage: A Bibliography of Plays and Musicals, 1770–1970.* New York, 1970.

HUGHES, LANGSTON, and MILTON MELTZER. *Black Magic: A Pictorial History of the Negro in American Entertainment.* Englewood Cliffs, N.J., 1967.

JOHNSON, JAMES WELDON. *Black Manhattan.* New York, 1930.

KIMBALL, ROBERT, and WILLIAM BOLCOM. *Reminiscing with Sissle and Blake.* New York, 1973.

RIIS, THOMAS L. *Just Before Jazz: Black Musical Theater in New York, 1890 to 1915.* Washington, D.C., 1989.

SAMPSON, HENRY. *Blacks in Blackface: A Sourcebook on Early Black Musical Shows.* New York, 1980.

SOUTHERN, EILEEN. *The Music of Black Americans: A History.* New York, 1983.

STEARNS, MARSHALL, and JEAN STEARNS. *Jazz Dance.* New York, 1968.

WOLL, ALLEN. *Black Musical Theatre: From Coontown to Dreamgirls.* Baton Rouge, 1989.

THOMAS L. RIIS

Music Museums and Historical Sites. In the 1960s, museums began paying serious attention to African-American music. New Orleans and New York both supported jazz museums for a period; the New Orleans collections were later absorbed by the Louisiana State Museum, which maintains a permanent exhibit. In 1971, the Smithsonian Institution began a jazz program that included record reissues such as *The Smithsonian Collection of Classic Jazz,* performances, and symposia. Beginning in the 1980s, the Smithsonian's National Museum of American History acquired artifacts such as Dizzy GILLESPIE's trumpet, and jazz photographs of Herman Leonard, and in 1988, with funds designated by the U.S. Congress, the 200,000-page Duke ELLINGTON archives; and it stepped up its activities in collecting, preserving, and disseminating jazz and African-American music. In 1991, the U.S. Congress established the eighteen-member Smithsonian Jazz Masterworks Orchestra, whose first musical directors were David Baker and Gunther Schuller. In 1992, a record-breaking $7 million grant from the Lila Wallace–Reader's Digest Fund to the Smithsonian established a ten-year program, "America's Jazz Heritage," offering major traveling exhibitions, educational programs, and radio broadcasts.

Berry GORDY and his family founded the Motown Historical Museum in Detroit, which displays memorabilia associated with the record label, and includes Studio A, where MOTOWN artists recorded from 1959 to 1972. Detroit's Graystone International Jazz Museum, named after the famous ballroom, preserves various artifacts, including some associated with the demolished Graystone. Clarksdale, Miss., has the Delta Blues Museum, housed within the city's Carnegie Public Library. The Alabama Jazz Hall of Fame, in Birmingham, focuses on musicians from that city, while the Alabama Music Hall of Fame, in Muscle Shoals, covers the entire state. The W. C. HANDY Birthplace, Florence, Ala., displays his piano, trumpet, music, and other artifacts. The Chattanooga, Tenn., Afro-American Museum and Research Center includes an exhibit on Bessie SMITH. The Songwriters' Hall of Fame in New York City has, among other items, Fats WALLER's piano. In Baltimore, the Eubie BLAKE Cultural Center displays artifacts of the songwriter-pianist; Coppin State College maintains an exhibit on Cab CALLOWAY; and the Great Blacks in Wax Museum has wax figures of Eubie Blake, Billie HOLIDAY, and others. Cleveland's Rock and Roll Hall of Fame completed construction of its own building in 1994. Cleveland is also the site of an African-American Museum whose coverage includes music; and the exhibits of the National Afro-American Museum and Cultural Center, in Wilberforce, Ohio, include a film on black music. The huge collections of the Country Music Hall of Fame and Museum in Nashville include coverage of blacks in country music such as Deford BAILEY and Charley PRIDE. The Museum of the City of New York's music and theater collections include material on black musicians and musicals. Among the many museums that collect and exhibit musical instruments, the Percussive Arts Society's museum in Lawton, Okla., which opened in 1992 and includes many types of drums, should be mentioned.

Meanwhile, the U.S. National Park Service designated as National Historic Landmarks the homes of Louis ARMSTRONG (Queens, N.Y.), Will Marion COOK, Duke Ellington, James Weldon JOHNSON, Florence MILLS, and Paul ROBESON (all Manhattan), as well as New York's Carnegie Hall, site of many important concerts, and St. George's Episcopal Church in New York, where for forty years Harry

Thacker BURLEIGH served as soloist. Also named National Historic Landmarks were the Beale Street Historic District in Memphis, including W. C. Handy's home; the Charleston, S.C., home of the white writer Dubose Hayward, author of *Porgy*; and Scott JOPLIN's home in St. Louis, which the state of Missouri has refurbished and opened to the public as the Scott Joplin Historic Site.

A lesser designation of the National Park Service, the National Register of Historic Places, includes many theaters, concert halls, and ballrooms which played a role in twentieth-century African-American music, including New York's APOLLO THEATER, Minton's Playhouse, and Town Hall; Washington's Howard Theater; Louisville's Madrid Ballroom; Chicago's Balaban and Katz Chicago Theater; Columbus, Ohio's Valley Dale Ballroom; San Antonio's Majestic Theatre; Indianapolis' Madame C. J. Walker Building; and St. Louis's Goldenrod showboat.

REFERENCES

American Association of Museums. *The Official Museum Directory, 1993*. New Providence, N.J., 1992.

BIRD, CHRISTIANE. *The Jazz and Blues Lover's Guide to the U.S.* Reading, Mass., 1991.

CANTOR, GEORGE. *Historic Black Landmarks*. Detroit, 1991.

HASSE, JOHN EDWARD. *Music Museums and Historical Sites of the United States*. Washington, D.C., 1993.

THUM, MARCELLA. *Hippocrene U.S.A. Guide to Black America*. New York, 1991.

JOHN EDWARD HASSE

Mutual Aid Associations.   *See* Fraternal Orders and Mutual Aid Associations.

Mutual Relief Societies.   *See* Fraternal Orders and Mutual Aid Associations.

Myers, Isaac (January 13, 1835–January 26, 1891), labor leader. Born free in Baltimore, Isaac Myers was the son of poor workers. He attended the Rev. John Fortie's day school, and at sixteen was apprenticed to James Jackson, a well-known African-American caulker in Baltimore's shipyards. By the time the CIVIL WAR broke out, Myers had become an independent caulker.

In October 1865, white caulkers angered by black competition went on strike, demanding that black workers be excluded from waterfront work. Police joined in, and African Americans were driven from the shipyards. The unemployed black caulkers and waterfront men held a meeting. Myers suggested they form their own union, buy up a shipyard and railway line, and run their own business cooperatively. Baltimore blacks responded to Myers' pleas for help by investing $10,000. Myers borrowed an additional $30,000 from a ship captain and set up a shipyard and railway. The cooperative, called the Chesapeake Marine Railway and Dry Dock, opened in February 1866, and paid its three hundred workers an average of three dollars per day. Myers also organized the Colored Caulkers' Trades Union, and was named its first president. He expanded his union role to political activism, calling for civil rights and black suffrage.

The shipyard was successful almost immediately, and Myers and his partners were able to pay off their original debts within five years. The cooperative's influence and example assured that white Baltimore workers did not exclude blacks from other fields. Soon it began hiring white workers, and Myers worked closely with the white caulkers' union. From his collaboration, he dreamed of interracial activism on a large scale. In 1868, he was one of nine blacks invited to attend the convention of the National Labor Union (NLU), the largest white labor organization, in Philadelphia. Myers underlined the importance of interracial collaboration, and asserted that blacks would be happy to work with whites for common goals. His efforts met with white indifference, but he invited white delegates to a National Labor Convention that December in Washington, D.C. At the convention, the (black) National Labor Union was born. Myers helped write the union's constitution and served as its president. He spent the next several months on a speaking tour, attempting unsuccessfully to draw support for the union. Myers reminded his audiences that labor could succeed only if both races united. That August, he attended another NLU convention, but white and black delegates divided over blacks' support of the REPUBLICAN PARTY. The black NLU remained small and financially strapped. It dissolved before the end of 1871, and Myers left the labor movement.

In later life, Myers became a detective in the Post Office Department, opened an unsuccessful coalyard, and became a United States tax collector. He headed several black business organizations in Baltimore, and was active in the African Methodist Episcopal (AME) Church, spending fifteen years as superintendent of Baltimore's Bethel A.M.E. School and writing an unpublished sacred drama. A grand master of Maryland's black Masons, he edited a *Mason's Digest*. He died in Baltimore in 1891, after a paralytic stroke.

REFERENCE

FONER, PHILIP S. *History of the Labor Movement in the United States.* Vol. 1. New York, 1947.

GREG ROBINSON

Myers, Milton (March 24, 1951–), modern dancer and choreographer. Born in Kansas City, Mo., Milton Myers became interested in dance while he was a math major at the University of Missouri and organized Black Exodus, an all-black company of modern dancers. In 1973 he moved to New York and auditioned for Alvin AILEY. Although he did not join Alvin Ailey, he met Ailey's assistant, Joyce Trisler. Myers was in New London, Conn., studying choreography with the American Dance Festival when Trisler formed her own dance troupe in 1974 and invited Myers to be a member. Myers joined the troupe as a dancer, and also served as Trisler's assistant choreographer from 1975 through 1980. In 1977 Myers joined the Alvin Ailey American Dance Theater as a dancer while still assisting Trisler. During that time he began making dances for both compa-nies, creating *Echoes in Blue* (1975) for Ailey and assisting Trisler in developing a new choreography for Igor Stravinsky's *Rite of Spring* (1974) and Paul Hindemith's *Four Temperaments* (1976). When Trisler died in 1980, Myers left Ailey to take over the helm of the Trisler Danscompany. He choreographed such dances as *Timesteps* (1981), a four-part work to the music of Stravinsky and Duke Ellington, and *Movin'* (1983), a dance set to the music of the alternative rock group Talking Heads. In 1991 Myers left the Trisler Danscompany to become the resident choreographer of Philadanco, a Philadelphia-based dance group. He has developed numerous pieces for the company, including *Ebony Concerto* (1991), a ballet to a Stravinsky jazz score of the same name, and *Love 'n' Pain* (1992), a dance for six women set to the songs of Aretha FRANKLIN.

REFERENCES

CARUSO, JOYCE. "Myers in First Position." *Other Stages* (September 25, 1980): 6.
HARDY, CAMILLE. "Joyce Trisler Dance Company." *Dance Magazine* (September 1986): 98.

CONSTANCE VALIS HILL

N

NAACP. *See* National Association for the Advancement of Colored People.

NAACP Legal Defense and Educational Fund. Created by the NATIONAL ASSOCIATION FOR THE ADVANCEMENT OF COLORED PEOPLE in 1940 as a tax-exempt fund for litigation and education, the NAACP Legal Defense and Educational Fund, (LDF), based in New York, has been the central organization for African-American civil rights advances through the legal system. While the LDF, popularly known as the "Inc. Fund," had from the beginning a board of directors and a separate fundraising apparatus from those of the NAACP, it was planned as an integrated component of the larger organization, designed to carry out Charles H. HOUSTON's plan for a legal assault on segregation in public education. The LDF's leadership was represented on the NAACP board, and helped design organizational strategy. The LDF was set up with a loose administrative structure, with a director-counsel as the chief officer. The first LDF director-counsel, former NAACP Counsel Thurgood MARSHALL, hired a staff of five lawyers.

During the 1940s and 1950s, such lawyers as Robert Carter, Franklin WILLIAMS, and Constance Baker MOTLEY joined the staff. Marshall made the LDF the main locus of civil rights law, and the LDF litigated a variety of landmark civil rights cases before the Supreme Court. In 1944, the LDF successfully argued in *Smith* v. *Allwright* that primaries which legally excluded blacks were unconstitutional. In 1946, *Morgan* v. *the Commonwealth of Virginia* outlawed segregation on interstate bus lines. In 1948 the LDF brought *Shelley* v. *Kramer* to the U.S. Supreme Court. The Court ruled that racially restrictive housing covenants that prohibited sales of homes to blacks were unenforceable.

However, much of the LDF's work was done not at the Supreme Court, but in small southern towns, fighting lawsuits or defending arrested blacks under adverse and dangerous conditions. LDF lawyers, forced to work on a shoestring budget, received death threats and ran from lynch mobs. While they frequently lost cases, their presence helped assure fair trials. In 1950, the Supreme Court ruling in *Shepard and Irvin* v. *Florida* helped establish the now-familiar doctrine that defendants must be tried in a venue free of prejudice against them.

Education cases were the centerpiece of LDF legal efforts. Following the NAACP's successful strategy in *Mississippi ex rel Gaines* v. *Canada* (1938), the LDF attacked discrimination in graduate education. Beginning in 1946, the LDF brought a series of cases before the Supreme Court, culminating in *Sipuel* v. *Board of Regents of the University of Oklahoma* (1948); *McLaurin* v. *Oklahoma State Regents* (1950); and SWEATT V. PAINTER (1950). In the latter, the Court ruled that segregated facilities led to discrimination, though the case did not directly challenge the principle of "separate but equal" in primary education.

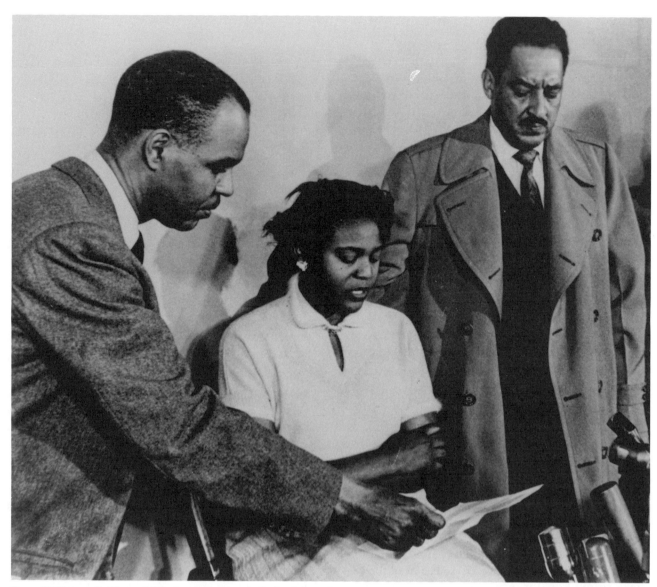

Roy Wilkins (left) and Thurgood Marshall flank Autherine Lucy, who in 1956, after months of litigation, became the first black admitted to the University of Alabama. However, she was soon suspended from classes when officials claimed they could not ensure her safety. A second black was not admitted to the university for another seven years. (Prints and Photographs Division, Library of Congress)

LDF lawyers also brought suit to eliminate pay differentials between white and black teachers, in part to demonstrate the enormous expense of a dual school system. By 1951, the LDF, preparing for a direct challenge to segregation, was working on twenty elementary and high school cases·and a dozen higher-education cases. The LDF's efforts were crowned·with success in 1954 with the decision in BROWN V. BOARD OF EDUCATION OF TOPEKA, KANSAS, argued by Thurgood Marshall.

By 1954, however, personal differences among staff members and disagreements over organizational mission led to a total split with the NAACP. The NAACP considered the LDF a vehicle for arguing

civil rights cases. LDF leaders considered achieving educational equality their prime responsibility. The LDF and the NAACP formally parted in 1956, establishing separate boards of directors.

After the implementation ruling in *Brown* v. *Board of Education*, which ordered desegregation "with all deliberate speed," was announced in 1955, the LDF began designing desegregation plans and fighting court cases to force compliance, notably *Cooper* v. *Aaron* (1958), in which the Court mandated the integration of Arkansas's Little Rock Central High School. LDF lawyers continued to work to combat segregation in other fields. In 1956, the LDF began a central involvement in the CIVIL RIGHTS MOVEMENT when it won *Gayle* v. *Browder*, the case of the MONT-GOMERY BUS BOYCOTT led by the Rev. Dr. Martin Luther KING, Jr.

At the same time, Southerners determined to keep the LDF from operating. Legislatures charged the LDF created cases in which it had no legitimate interest or standing. The Supreme Court finally ruled in 1963 that LDF litigation was constitutionally protected. By 1965, LDF lawyers had taken school cases as they had arisen in every southern state. Eventually, in *Griffin* v. *County School Board of Prince Edward County* (1964), the Court renounced "all deliberate speed," and in *Green* v. *County School Board of New Kent County* (1968) ordered immediate and total desegregation.

In 1961, Thurgood Marshall was appointed a federal judge by President John F. Kennedy, and left the LDF. Jack Greenberg, his white assistant, who had come to the LDF in 1949, succeeded him as the new director–counsel, a position he would hold for the next twenty-three years. During the 1960s, the LDF continued as an active force in the civil rights movement, defending sit-in protesters in cases such as *Boynton* v. *Virginia* (1961) and *Shuttlesworth* v. *Alabama* (1964), as well as defending Freedom Riders and providing bail funds for the many activists who were arrested during the struggle.

The Black Power movement of the late 1960s and early '70s brought about tensions within the LDF, over its white leadership and its refusal to defend black radicals except in those few cases where civil rights issues were involved, such as exorbitant bail fees for incarcerated BLACK PANTHER PARTY members. In 1970, several LDF lawyers pressed the organization to take up the defense of black radical Angela DAVIS after she was implicated in a courthouse shoot-out, but the LDF Board of Directors and Director-Counsel Greenberg vetoed the idea. The same year, when Julian BOND was refused his seat in the Georgia Legislature because he opposed the VIETNAM WAR, the LDF refused his case on the grounds that a white antiwar legislator would have suffered the same fate.

In recent decades, the LDF has concentrated on other pressing civil rights areas. In *Griggs* v. *Duke Power* (1971), the LDF persuaded the Supreme Court to strike down discriminatory educational or testing requirements irrelevant to job performance. The LDF then argued numerous affirmative action cases based on *Griggs* in the following years. The most important of these was *Regents of the University of California* v. *Bakke* (1979), in which the LDF worked largely successfully in contributing to opposing Allan Bakke's "reverse discrimination" suit.

Capital punishment was a particular focus of LDF's efforts. In preparation for the Supreme Court case *Maxwell* v. *Bishop* (1970), which involved an Arkansas African American convicted of the rape of a white woman, the LDF organized a study which showed that 89 percent of defendants around the country given the death penalty for rape between 1930 and 1962 were black, and demonstrated patterns of racial discrimination in death sentences given for rape in Arkansas between 1945 and 1965. While the Court declined to rule on the LDF's statistics, Jack Greenberg continued to lead the campaign against the death penalty, which achieved temporary victory in *Furman* v. *Georgia* (1972). Capital punishment was reinstated in 1976, but the death penalty in cases of rape, a special concern of blacks, was declared unconstitutional in *Coker* v. *Georgia* (1977). The LDF continued to appeal death penalty sentences for African Americans. In the early 1980s it commissioned the so-called "Baldus Study," a mammoth study of the influence of race on death penalty sentencing, following which lawyers argued *McCleskey* v. *Kemp* (1987). However, the Supreme Court refused to rule solely on the basis of this statistical evidence that the death penalty was arbitrary or racially discriminatory.

In 1984, Julius LeVonne Chambers took over as director–counsel and continued to concentrate on litigation in the areas of poverty law, education, fair housing, capital punishment, fair employment, environmental justice, and voting rights. A housing discrimination suit the LDF brought in the San Fernando Valley in 1992 was settled for $300,000, one of the largest awards ever granted victims of racial bias in housing.

In 1992, Chambers resigned and was replaced by Elaine Ruth Jones. Jones had previously been head of the LDF's regional office in Washington, D.C., where she had helped draft and implement civil rights legislation, notably the Civil Rights Restoration Act (1988), the 1988 Fair Housing Act, and the Civil Rights Act of 1991. Jones redirected LDF's focus toward cases of environmental and health care discrimination. Environmental activism covers suits to ensure equal treatment of blacks victimized by toxic wastes, and cases enforcing federal laws mandating free lead-poisoning exams for poor children. Examples of health care cases include a suit filed in Contra Costa, Calif., charging with violation of civil rights statutes officials who built a county hospital largely inaccessible to the district's African-American population. The LDF continues involvement in poverty law, such as its suit to block New Jersey from stopping welfare payments to women who have additional children while on welfare; education, through its attempts to preserve the University of Maryland's special scholarship program for African Americans, among other matters; criminal justice, through the

Capital Punishment Project; and voting rights, by its efforts to enforce the Voting Rights Act in judicial elections and to support black majority districts. The LDF also offers four scholarship programs to aid African-American law students. In the early 1990s, the LDF had twenty-eight staff lawyers in its New York, Washington, and Los Angeles offices, and a total annual budget of almost $8 million.

REFERENCES

BALDUS, DAVID, GEORGE WOODWORTH, and CHARLES A. PULASKI, JR. *Equal Justice and the Death Penalty: Legal and Empirical Analysis.* New York, 1990.

HALL, KERMIT, ed. *The Oxford Companion to the Supreme Court.* New York, 1992.

KLUGER, RICHARD. *Simple Justice.* New York, 1975.

ROWAN, CARL. *Dream Makers, Dream Breakers: The World of Justice Thurgood Marshall.* Boston, 1992.

TUSHNET, MARK. *The NAACP's Legal Strategy Against Segregation, 1925–1950.* New York, 1987.

GREG ROBINSON

Nabrit, James Madison (September 4, 1900–), lawyer, educator. Born in Atlanta, Ga., James Nabrit was the son of the Rev. J. M. and Gertrude Nabrit. In 1919, he received his high school diploma from Morehouse College, and four years later graduated from Morehouse with a B.A. degree. Although he left school in 1925 to teach political science and coach football at Leland College, Nabrit received a J.D. degree from Northwestern University Law School in 1927. While at Northwestern, he was an honor student and was elected to the Order of the Coif, the highest legal scholarship fraternity. After law school, he served as a dean at Arkansas State College for two years.

In 1930, Nabrit moved to Houston, Tex., where he practiced law. In his six years in Houston, Nabrit became involved in civil rights law (CIVIL RIGHTS AND THE LAW; CIVIL RIGHTS MOVEMENT). He participated in over 25 cases, most of which were concerned with voting rights. In 1936 Nabrit began his twenty-four-year career at HOWARD UNIVERSITY as an associate professor of law. While at Howard, he developed a syllabus that collected more than two thousand civil rights cases. He organized the first course in civil rights taught at a law school in the United States. In 1954, Nabrit served as the legal adviser to the governor of the Virgin Islands. He was an active member of various organizations, including the Texas Bar Association, the National Lawyers' Guild, the NATIONAL ASSOCIATION FOR THE ADVANCEMENT OF COLORED PEOPLE (NAACP), and

the New Negro Alliance. In 1981, Nabrit received an honorary degree from Howard University.

REFERENCES

"James Madison Nabrit." *Negro History Bulletin* 24, no. 4 (January 1961): 75–76.

LOGAN, RAYFORD. *Howard University: The First Hundred Years.* New York, 1969.

SASHA THOMAS

Names and Naming, African. Africans arriving in America continued to give their children African names well into the nineteenth century. In the seventeenth and eighteenth centuries African-American slaves had retained AFRICANISMS in their naming practices. The highest percentage of African names was found among male slaves in the eighteenth century, when the majority of the black population was still unacculturated. During the colonial period the practice of naming children after the days of the week, the months, and the seasons was retained. Such names as January, April, May, June, September, November, March, August, Christmas, and Midday were popular. There are numerous examples of Akan day names (sometimes modified or anglicized): Cudjoe (Monday), Cubbenah (Tuesday), Quao (Wednesday), Quaco (Thursday), Cuffe (Friday), Quamin (Saturday), and Quashee (Sunday). Many exist in numerous forms. Quao became Quaro and later Jacco, Jack, and Jackson. Other African names common in the eighteenth century were Sambo, Mongo, and Juba.

In western and central Africa names are given at stages in an individual's life, and—as among all people for whom magic is important—the identification of a name with the personality of its bearer is held to be so complete that the person's real name (usually the one given at birth) must be kept secret lest it be used by someone working evil magic against the person. That is why, among Africans, a person's name may in many instances change with time, a new designation being assumed on the occasion of some striking occurrence in life. When one of the rites marking a new stage in the person's development occurs, a name change also occurs to note the event.

African Americans also changed their names to correspond to major changes in the life of the individual. Take the case of Frederick DOUGLASS, for example. His original last name, Bailey, had an African origin. He was descended from Belali Mohomet, a Mande-speaking slave from Timbo, Futa Jallon. (Bailey is a common African-American surname along the Atlantic coast. In Talbot County, Md., the records list no white Baileys from whom the slave name Bailey could have been taken.) Belali was owned by Richard Skinner, a wealthy tobacco planter near the Miles River. Belali's granddaughter Betsy belonged to Skinner's granddaughter Ann Catherine. Frederick Bailey was born in 1817.

Soon after escaping slavery, Bailey changed his name to Douglass. In similar fashion, Sojourner TRUTH was known was Isabella Baumfree until she had a dream that told her about her new name and mission. Malcolm Little, at different stages of his life, was variously known as MALCOLM X, Homeboy, Detroit Red, Big Red, Satan, and el-Hajj Malik el-Shabazz.

Almost every black person is known by two names: a given name and a name used only within the family circle. Lorenzo Dow TURNER (1895–1972), a leading scholar of African retentions in American English, found a dual naming system among the GULLAHS in the Sea Islands of South Carolina. This system (which still exists) involves an English (American) name given at birth and a more intimate name—sometimes called a basket name or a day name—used exclusively by the family and community. Slave holders recognized this dual naming practice among enslaved Africans in the eighteenth century. In advertisements of runaways, owners always included "proper" (given) names and "country" names, which are the African names.

Among enslaved Africans the use of nicknames was also widespread. Pie Ya, Puddin'-tame, Frog, Tennie C., Monkey, Mush, Cooter, John de Baptist, Fat-Man, Preacher, Jack Rabbit, Sixty, Pop Corn, Old Gold, Dootes, Angle-Eye, Bad Luck, Sky-up-de-Greek, Cracker, Jabbo, Cat-Fish, Bear, Tip, Odessa, Pig Lasses, Rattler, Pearly, Luck, Buffalo, Old Blue, Red Fox, and Coon are some of the most common nicknames.

A few examples of Gullah basket names that are unchanged from their African roots are Ndomba, Mviluki, Sungila, Kamba, Anyika, and Sebe. Ndomba is the name given to a breech-delivered Gullah child whose hand protrudes first at birth. It means "I am begging (with outstretched hand)." Mviluki has a Gullah meaning of "a penitent." Its Luba source word is *mvuluki,* "one who doesn't forget his sins." The basket name Sungila means "to save, help, deliver," while Kamba, a very common Luba name, comes from *munkamba,* meaning "ancestor." Anyika, a Gullah name meaning "she is beautiful," is related to a Luba word meaning "to praise the beauty of." Sebe, a Gullah name meaning "a leather ornament," comes from the Luba word for hide or leather, *tshisebe.* Others—Tulu (sleep), Tuma (send), Pita (pass by), Mesu (eyes), Kudima (to work or hoe), and Kudiya (to eat)—are all Gullah day names, exactly the same in Gullah and Luba.

In the Sea Islands children sometimes have not only their given names and basket names but also community names. The community gives the child a name that characterizes or is characteristic of the individual, such as Smart Child or Shanty (showoff). This practice parallels Bantu naming practices in Zaire. The name of Georgetown University's former basketball center Dikambe Mutombo (he is from Zaire) illustrates this point. His full name is Dikamba Mutombo Mpolondo Munkamba Diken Jean-Jean Jacque wa Mutombo. In order, these names are his uncle's name, his family surname, his grandfather's name, his village nickname, his name given at birth, and his hometown village, wa Mutombo (which means "from the village of Mutombo").

Other creolized Gullah nicknames typical of Bantu naming practices are names of animals or fish: De Dog, Doggie, Kitty, Fish, Yellowtail Croker, Frog, Spider, Boy, Gal, Jumper, Tooti, Crocki, Don, Cuffy, Akebee, Dr. Buzzer, and Dr. Eagle.

In Gullah naming practices, as in African naming practices, children are named after parents because it is believed that the parent spirit resides in the children. The same name might appear in several generations of a family. In the Sea Islands the name Litia appeared in four generations of female children.

By the time of the Civil War and the emancipation of four million African-American slaves, African personal names had almost completely disappeared. It was not until the 1920s, when the early black Islamic revivalist NOBLE DREW ALI began to use Arabic and Islamic names, that the practice revived. These practices were followed by Elijah MUHAMMAD and the NATION OF ISLAM. They used African and Arabic words and names to instill in their followers a sense of racial pride.

By the 1960s and '70s African names had gained respectability in the wake of the civil rights, African independence, and Black Power movements. Movements such as KAWAIDA of Maulana KARENGA stressed the use of Swahili and Yoruba names. African names such as Dashanaba, Tameka, Kwame, and Maat again became common.

African names have come full circle. Their use reflects many changes in attitudes, from strong African identification to nationalism, from integration and assimilation back to cultural identification.

REFERENCES

DILLARD, J. L. *All American English.* New York, 1975.
———. *Black English: Its History and Usage in the United States.* New York, 1972.
———. *Black Names.* The Hague, 1976.
———. *Lexicon of Black English.* New York, 1977.
HALEY, ALEX. *The Autobiography of Malcolm X.* New York, 1965.

HOLLOWAY, JOSEPH E. *The African Heritage of American English*. Bloomington, Ind., 1993.

———. *Africanisms in American English*. Bloomington, Ind., 1990.

MCFEELEY, WILLIAM S. *Frederick Douglass*. New York, 1991.

MENCKEN, H. L. *The American Language: An Inquiry into the Development of English in the United States*. New York, 1936.

JOSEPH E. HOLLOWAY

Names Controversy. Naming has played an important role in developing a sense of group identity among African Americans. Black leaders have frequently argued that the names borne by African Americans influence their self-esteem and help determine their place in American life. Black journalist T. Thomas FORTUNE counseled in 1906 that "until we get this racial designation properly fixed in the language and literature of the country we shall be kicked and cuffed and sneered at." But what African Americans should collectively be called has often engendered controversy among the race's foremost voices.

Africans brought to the North American continent as slaves during the seventeenth and eighteenth centuries belonged to particular nations or ethnic groups (e.g., Ibo, Yoruba, Mandingo, Bakongo). But such diverse allegiances were difficult to maintain in the complex world of plantation slavery, and a new "African" identity emerged. Blacks consistently referred to themselves as Africans throughout the colonial period, and, as communities of free blacks emerged in the decades following the American Revolution, they placed the prefix "African" before the names of nearly all of their churches, schools, lodges, and social organizations.

Only in a few cities such as CHARLESTON, S.C., and NEW ORLEANS did free men and women of mixed African and European (and sometimes Native American) ancestry reject identification with their darker brothers and sisters and encourage the development of a tripartite racial system. They often preferred to be called "brown" or "creole."

The rise after 1816 of a white-led colonization movement bent on carrying African Americans back to the African continent caused a major shift in how free blacks referred to the race. Fearful that continuing to call themselves "African" would merely encourage the colonizationists, growing numbers of blacks avoided the term. Most opted for the safer appellation "colored." A few ultraintegrationists such as Philadelphian William Whipper urged that all racial designations be abandoned. He convinced the 1835 black national convention to pass a resolution exhorting African Americans to abandon the word "colored" and to remove "African" from the names of their institutions. Yet by the 1830s, "colored" was widely used throughout the North, a fact symbolized by the title of the leading black journal of the era, the *Colored American*. Between 1827 and 1899, 34 percent of all black newspapers and magazines containing a racial designation in their title bore the name "colored."

"Negro," a term derived from the Portuguese word for black, vied for primacy with "colored" after the CIVIL WAR. Blacks increasingly viewed the latter name as offensive, even though many whites continued to use it as a racial designation. After 1900 "Negro" gained broad acceptance among both races. As more and more blacks adopted the term, black leaders began to attack whites for spelling the word with a diminutive "n." Contending that whites spelled all other proper nouns with capital letters, they charged that their failure to capitalize "Negro" was a deliberate effort to label blacks as inferior. With the support of Booker T. WASHINGTON, W. E. B. DU BOIS, and a majority of black leaders, the capital "N" campaign convinced the federal government and most editors, even in the southern press, to adhere to the rule by 1950.

"Negro" was never a term of universal approbation. The Rev. J. C. Embry of Philadelphia argued in 1892 that slaveholders had invented the word to stigmatize blacks. Observing that "Negro" lacked a geographic locus and failed to recognize blacks' African past, Embry and Fortune led a campaign to adopt the name "Afro-American." From the late 1880s through the first decade of the twentieth century, "Afro-American" competed with "Negro" as a popular racial designation.

Some ordinary blacks simply opposed the term "Negro" because it was easily corrupted into derisive expressions such as "nigger" and "nigra." There was a steady increase in opposition to the name after 1920. One of the most intense and influential attacks came from the pen of Richard B. MOORE, an African-American activist of West Indian descent. His pamphlet "The Name 'Negro': Its Origin and Evil Use" (1960) summarized objections to the term and contended that the term itself—"because of its slave origin, its consequent degradation, and its still prevalent connection in the minds of people generally with prejudice, vileness, inferiority, and hostility"—was a major factor in keeping the race in a subordinate state.

In the midst of the turbulent battles of the CIVIL RIGHTS MOVEMENT of the 1960s, many African Americans abandoned the term "Negro"—what Moore called "the oppressors' vicious smear name." The Nation of ISLAM (especially MALCOLM X), "Black Power" advocates, and other black cultural nationalists renewed the assault on the term, linking it almost irrevocably in the minds of many young blacks with slavery and Uncle Tomism. "Black" quickly became the most popular racial identifier, in large part because it stood in symbolic opposition to white dominance—the enemy of Black Power. African Americans spoke proudly of being "black" and infused the term into their rhetoric, writing, and organizational names. Convinced anew of the value of recognizing their African heritage, black cultural nationalists also revived use of the term "Afro-American" (*see* BLACK NATIONALISM; BLACK PANTHER CONFERENCE OF NEWARK).

In 1988 civil rights leader Jesse JACKSON reopened the debate over racial nomenclature when he announced that blacks should begin to refer to themselves as "African Americans." Criticizing the term "black" for its singular reference to skin color, he maintained that the name offered African Americans no connection to their land of origin or their cultural heritage. "To be called black is baseless," he proclaimed, "to be called African American has cultural integrity." The new terminology has gained acceptance among activists and academics by the early 1990s. But it made only grudging inroads within the larger African-American population. A 1991 poll by the JOINT CENTER FOR POLITICAL AND ECONOMIC STUDIES found that 72 percent of Americans of African descent preferred the racial designation "black," while only 15 percent selected "African American."

The names controversy has been a source of continuing conflict among black leaders since the early nineteenth century. Yet in each era, a few have questioned the value of this debate to the advancement of the race. Some have labeled it a distraction and a waste of time, energy, and resources. Others have viewed it as a reflection of African-American powerlessness. Writing in *The Content of Our Character* (1990), Shelby Steele observed that "this self-conscious reaching for pride through nomenclature suggests nothing so much as a despair over the possibility of gaining the less conspicuous pride that follows real advancement."

REFERENCES

BERRY, MARY FRANCES, and JOHN W. BLASSINGAME. "Black Nationalism." In *Long Memory: The Black Experience in America.* New York, 1982, pp. 388–428.

SMITH, TOM W. "Changing Racial Labels: From 'Colored' to 'Negro' to 'Black' to 'African American'." *Public Opinion Quarterly* 56 (1992): 496–514.

STUCKEY, STERLING. "Identity and Ideology: The Names Controversy." In *Slave Culture: Nationalist Theory and the Foundations of Black America,* pp. 193–244. New York, 1987.

WILLIAMS, WALTER E., JOHN SIBLEY BUTLER, and DORIS WILKINSON. "Commentaries: Politics of Nomenclature." *Society* 27 (1990): 4–18.

ROY E. FINKENBINE

Nance, Ray Willis (December 10, 1913–January 28, 1976), trumpeter and violinist. Born in Chicago, Ray Nance held the trumpet chair in Duke ELLINGTON's orchestra for two decades and gained renown as one of the few prominent violinists in jazz. He studied piano and violin formally as a child, playing violin in his school orchestra and taking up trumpet in high school. In 1932, playing trumpet as well as violin, he formed his own sextet in Chicago and quickly gained a reputation as a sideman for Earl "Fatha" HINES in 1937–1938 and Horace Henderson in 1939–1940.

In 1940 Nance joined the Ellington orchestra, taking over the coveted "growl" trumpet chair from the departing Cootie WILLIAMS. In recordings and concerts all over the world, Nance carried on the tradition of the group's distinctive trumpet sound, playing not only "straight" but also with open and muted horns to suggest human voices, animal sounds, and the noises of machinery. His first recorded solo with the Ellington band, "Take the A Train" (1941), rapidly became a classic, as did the first recording of "Perdido" (1942). Ellington featured Nance's crisp violin playing on "Moon Mist" and " 'C' Jam Blues" (1942). Nance also lent a comic presence to the orchestra, earning the nickname Floorshow because of his singing, dancing, and trumpet twirling. Nance, who briefly left Ellington from 1944 to 1945 to pursue a solo career, switched to cornet in 1961 and again left Ellington two years later, leading his own small groups in 1964 and 1965. From 1966 to 1967 he toured Europe as a soloist, occasionally returning to the Ellington band in the late 1960s. He made a well-received album as a violinist, *Body and Soul,* in 1970, and continued recording and performing under his own name until shortly before his death in New York City six years later.

JOHN EDWARD HASSE

Nanton, Joseph "Tricky Sam" (February 1, 1904–July 20, 1946), jazz trombonist. Nanton, called "Tricky Sam" because of his ability to generate "jungle" sounds on the trombone, achieved his greatest fame during his years in the Duke ELLINGTON Orchestra.

Nanton was born to West Indian parents and raised in the San Juan Hill area of New York City. During the early 1920s, he worked in bands with Cliff Jackson and Elmer Snowden. His early style was based on study with Jake "Gutbucket" Green and Charlie Irvis, whom he replaced in the Ellington band in 1926. After joining Ellington, he was heavily influenced by trumpeter Bubber MILEY, with whom he perfected "jungle" sounds, created by "growling" and using plunger and wah-wah mutes. These sounds were "the first really distinguishable trademark of the Ellington band" (Schuller 1968, p. 332).

Although his range and technical proficiency were limited, Nanton crafted several original "talking" solos during his career with Ellington such as in "The Blues I Love to Sing" (1927), "Yellow Dog Blues" (1928), "Ko-Ko"(1940), and the "Work Song" portion of *Black, Brown, and Beige* (1943). In addition, Ellington used Nanton's tone to great effect in many compositions, such as the immortal "Mood Indigo" (1930).

Although he was not vocal about his political feelings, Nanton was a devoted follower of Marcus GARVEY. He was also considered to be a scholar by the other members of the Ellington band. After he died in San Francisco in 1946, no other player was ever able to duplicate his trombone style in the Ellington band.

REFERENCES

SCHULLER, GUNTHER. *Early Jazz: Its Roots and Musical Development*. New York, 1968.
STEWART, REX. "Tribute to Tricky Sam (Joe Nanton)." In *Jazz Masters of the Thirties*. New York, 1980, pp. 103–113.

TRAVIS JACKSON

Narratives, Slave.   *See* Slave Narratives.

Nash, Diane Bevel (May 15, 1938–), civil rights activist. Diane Nash was born in Chicago. She was raised in a middle-class Roman Catholic household and attended Howard University in Washington, D.C. In 1959 she transferred to Fisk University in Nashville, Tenn., majoring in English. In Nashville she was confronted by rigid racial segregation for the first time in her life, and later that year, she joined with other students from local colleges to organize protests against racism and segregation. She also began to attend nonviolence workshops led by James LAWSON, a student of Mahatma Gandhi's theories of nonviolent resistance. Skeptical at first, Nash found

the concept of moral resistance highly compatible with her strong religious beliefs and came to embrace nonviolence as a way of life.

Nash was elected chairperson of the Student Central Committee and was one of the key participants in SIT-INS in local department stores in Nashville which began in February, 1960. Nash's picture was printed in the local newspaper and she was often quoted as the spokesperson for the emerging student movement. She gained more celebrity when she confronted Nashville's mayor Ben West during a protest demonstration and forced him to admit that he felt local lunch counters should be desegregated.

In April 1960, Nash was one of the founding members of the STUDENT NONVIOLENT COORDINATING COMMITTEE (SNCC) in Raleigh, N.C. In February 1961, she and a group of ten other students were arrested in Rock Hill, S.C., for civil rights activities and refused the opportunity for bail. Their actions dramatized racial injustice, popularized the plight of African Americans in the South, and set a precedent of "jail, no bail" that was followed by many other activists during the civil rights movement.

In May 1961, SNCC activists recommended Freedom Rides, after the violent southern white response to the initial Freedom Rides led the CONGRESS OF RACIAL EQUALITY (CORE) to discontinue them. Leaving Fisk to devote herself full time to the movement, Nash played a pivotal role as coordinator of the SNCC Freedom Rides, serving as liaison with governmental officials and the press. Later that year she was appointed head of direct action in SNCC, married James BEVEL, a fellow civil rights activist, and moved to Jackson, Miss., where she continued her commitment to social activism. (She adopted her husband's last name as her middle name.) In August 1962, Nash and Bevel moved to Georgia and both became involved in the SOUTHERN CHRISTIAN LEADERSHIP CONFERENCE (SCLC).

The couple proved to be a highly effective organizing team and played an integral role in organizing many SCLC campaigns including the 1964–65 Selma voting rights campaign. In 1965 they were awarded the Rosa Parks Award from SCLC for their commitment to achieving social justice through nonviolent direct action.

Diane Nash's prominent role in the student sit-in movement made her one of the few well-known female activists of the civil rights movement. She has maintained an unwavering commitment to black empowerment and over the years has broadened the scope of her activism to include antiwar protest, and issues of economic injustice. Now divorced, Nash has remained politically active in the 1980s and '90s, living and teaching in Chicago, doing tenant organizing and advocating housing reform.

REFERENCES

BRANCH, TAYLOR. *Parting the Waters: America in the King Years, 1954–63.* New York, 1988.

CLAYBORNE, CARSON. *In Struggle: SNCC and the Black Awakening of the 1960s.* Cambridge, Mass., 1981.

POWLEDGE, FRED. *Free At Last?: The Civil Rights Movement and the People Who Made It.* Boston, 1991.

LYDIA MCNEILL
ROBYN SPENCER

Nash, William Beverly (c. 1822–January 19, 1888), southern politician. The Virginia-born slave William Nash, commonly known as Beverly, was brought at age thirteen to Columbia, S.C. Little is known of his early life except that before the Civil War he worked at Hunt's Hotel in Columbia and apparently held many jobs there, including work as a bootblack, porter, and waiter. At the hotel he learned to read; through his master, local politician W. C. Preston, and the clientele of the hotel, he was exposed to politics. In addition, it is possible that Nash may have been able to earn enough to buy his freedom from tips or from doing extra work for money. In his hotel work Nash acquired a veneer of gentility and social grace that would be advantageous in his political career.

During RECONSTRUCTION, Nash was a grocer and became active in the REPUBLICAN PARTY. In 1865 he represented Columbia in the South Carolina all-black convention convened to overturn the repressive BLACK CODES. He gained statewide prominence in 1866 when he criticized the Freedmen's Bureau's policy toward inland South Carolina and its alleged favoritism of the coastal regions (*see* BUREAU OF FREEDMEN, REFUGEES, AND ABANDONED LANDS). In 1867 he gained his first official political appointment, when he was named a magistrate for Columbia. Nash was also a delegate to the National Freedmen's Convention in 1867 in Washington, D.C., where he campaigned for a universal male suffrage plan without property or literacy qualifications. In 1868 he was elected to the state senate. To achieve a more equitable land distribution, he proposed that large plantations be taxed heavily, which would force landowners to sell property in parcels, thereby creating small farms that blacks and poor whites could afford. He also favored a law mandating schooling for all children. Essentially moderate in his policies, Nash opposed confiscation of the land of former Confederates, arguing that that power did not belong to the state.

Even though he was a Republican, Nash socialized and conducted business deals with prominent South Carolinians, many of them white Democrats. He made wide use of his contacts both in honorable and questionable transactions. In 1869 he and an associate bribed the land commissioner to resign so that an African American could take his post. Three years later, when railroad barons proposed that the state purchase a half-completed railroad, Nash accepted a $5,000 bribe in return for an affirmative vote in the South Carolina senate. The following year, Nash and two friends bought a brickyard and Nash persuaded the state senate to buy bricks from the yard for a new penitentiary. In 1877, as Reconstruction was ending, and as southern blacks were forced from positions of power, insurgent white Democrats threatened to expose his role in government graft. Nash resigned his position, paying back the money he had misappropriated. He continued his business, particularly real estate, but never again held public office. He died in Columbia in 1888.

REFERENCES

FONER, ERIC. *Freedom's Lawmakers: A Directory of Black Officeholders During Reconstruction.* New York, 1993.

WILLIAMSON, JOEL. *After Slavery: The Negro in South Carolina During Reconstruction, 1861–1877.* New York, 1965.

ALANA J. ERICKSON

National Afro-American League/Afro-American Council. In 1887, *New York Age* editor T. Thomas FORTUNE wrote editorials calling for the formation of a National Afro-American League. He planned for the League to seek the elimination of disfranchisement, LYNCHING, segregation on railroads and in public accommodations, and abuse of black prisoners. Although Fortune aimed most of his attacks at the segregated South, he also addressed discrimination in the North. He helped establish local league branches in New England, New York, Pennsylvania, and California.

The first convention of the league as a national organization, consisting of local branches from the South as well as the North, took place in Chicago in 1890. The convention, which consisted entirely of African-American delegates, adopted a constitution pledging to fight racial injustice by influencing popular opinion through the press, and by obtaining favorable decisions from the courts. Although Fortune was temporary chairman of the convention, the delegates did not elect him president, in part because

Fortune's distrust of political activity angered some delegates to the convention. Instead, the delegates chose North Carolina educator and clergyman Joseph C. PRICE as president, and made Fortune the league's secretary.

The league was short-lived, however, due to the inability of local branches to support themselves financially. The second convention in Knoxville in 1891 attracted far fewer delegates than the first. Although this convention elevated Fortune to the presidency, he did not have the funds to pursue a test case against railroad segregation, as he had planned. By 1893 Fortune was forced to admit the bankruptcy and imminent dissolution of the League.

Yet the persistence of lynching and disenfranchisement throughout the late 1890s gave impetus to a drive to restore the League. Fortune and Bishop Alexander WALTERS of the African Methodist Episcopal Zion Church, revived the organization as the Afro-American Council on September 15, 1898, in Rochester, N.Y. At the time of its founding the council was the largest organization of national African-American leaders in the nation. At the council's second meeting in December 1898, Bishop Walters became the council's first president, and Fortune the first chairman. Walters attacked Booker T. WASHINGTON's accommodationist approach to race relations, while Fortune attacked President William McKinley for failing to publicly oppose racial violence. Despite Walters's attacks, Washington, who was extremely influential in the council, was able to have most of the important positions filled with his loyal followers. Fortune depended upon Washington for political favors and the financing of the *New York Age*.

Washington did not openly oppose the council when it condemned segregation and lynching, and he joined the council in supporting President Theodore Roosevelt for being receptive to African-American concerns. Yet Washington did oppose other council proposals made under Walters's leadership; among these was an 1898 council motion that called for states that disfranchised blacks to have their congressional representation curtailed. Washington made efforts to have Walters replaced by Fortune as council president, and achieved this in 1902.

Fortune resigned from the council in 1904, in order to give more time and financial support to the *New York Age*. The council declined briefly as a result of Fortune's departure, but the next year Bishop Walters, with some support from Washington, revitalized the council as its new president. However, by 1907 Walters began to associate with members of W. E. B. Du Bois's NIAGARA MOVEMENT, and Washington withdrew his influence and support from the council. In 1908 Walters officially joined the Niagara

Movement, and in 1909 he joined the fledgling NATIONAL ASSOCIATION FOR THE ADVANCEMENT OF COLORED PEOPLE (NAACP). With Washington's abandonment of the council, the nervous collapse of Fortune in 1907, and the emerging alliance of Walters with Du Bois, the council became moribund by 1908.

REFERENCES

HARLAN, LOUIS R. *Booker T. Washington: The Wizard of Tuskegee, 1901–1915.* New York, 1983.
THORNBROUGH, EMMA LOU. "The National Afro-American League, 1887–1908." *Journal of Southern History* 37 (November 1961): 494–512.
THORNBROUGH, EMMA LOU. *T. Thomas Fortune, Militant Journalist.* Chicago, 1972.

DURAHN TAYLOR

National Association for the Advancement of Colored People (NAACP).

Since its organization in 1909, the National Association for the Advancement of Colored People (NAACP) has been the premier civil rights organization in the United States. It has been in the forefront of numerous successful campaigns on behalf of African-American rights, from the effort to suppress lynching to the long struggle to overturn legal segregation and the still-ongoing effort to secure the implementation of racial justice. The growth and evolution of the NAACP mirrors the growth of African-American political power and the vigorous debates this process engendered.

Founding and Early Days

The NAACP owes it origins to the coalescence of two political movements of the early twentieth century. The early years of the century saw the emergence of a group of black intellectuals opposed to the ACCOMODATIONISM of Booker T. WASHINGTON. While William Monroe TROTTER was the first important figure to break with Washington, he was temperamentally unsuited to the uniting of political forces, and it was W. E. B. DU BOIS who soon came to be the most prominent black figure among the anti-Bookerites, as Washington's opponents were called. At the same time there was a revival of political agitation by a small group of white "neo-abolitionists," many of them descended from those who had led the antebellum fight against slavery and who were increasingly distressed by the deterioration in the legal rights and social status of African Americans.

The NIAGARA MOVEMENT, formed by Du Bois, Trotter, and twenty-eight other African-American men at a conference on the Canadian side of Niagara Falls in August 1905, was the organized expression of anti-Bookerite sentiment. The movement was forthright in its opposition to Washingtonian accommodationism and in its commitment to civil equality. At a 1906 meeting of the organization at Harpers Ferry, West Va., the site of JOHN BROWN'S RAID, the organization declared:

> We shall not be satisfied with less than full manhood rights . . . We claim for ourselves every right that belongs to a free-born American—political, civil, and social—and until we get these rights, we shall never cease to protest and assail the ears of America with the story of its shameful deeds toward us.

Despite its oratory, the Niagara Movement was loosely organized and poorly funded and was largely ineffective as a national civil rights organization during its brief history. Bruised by internal controversy and hounded by members of Washington's extensive and effective network in the black community (the "Tuskegee Machine"), the Niagara Movement's existence was tentative and brief. After its dissolution, many of its active members joined the NAACP.

The catalyst for the founding of the NAACP was a violent race riot in 1908 in Springfield, Ill., Abraham Lincoln's home town (*see* SPRINGFIELD, ILLINOIS, RIOT OF 1908). William English Walling (1877–1936), a white socialist (*see* SOCIALISM) and labor activist, graphically described the violence he had witnessed in an article in *The Independent*. Walling invoked the spirit of Lincoln and the abolitionist Elijah Lovejoy in a call for citizens to come to the assistance of blacks and to fight for racial equality.

Walling's article was read by Mary White Ovington (1865–1951), a white journalist and social worker from a well-to-do abolitionist family who worked and lived in a black tenement in New York, doing research for her landmark sociological work *Half a Man: The Status of the Negro in New York* (1911). She responded to his plea and invited Dr. Henry Moskowitz (1879–1936), a labor reformer and social worker among New York immigrants, to join her in meeting with Walling in his New York apartment to discuss "the Negro Question." The three were the principal founders of the NAACP. Two other members of the core group were Charles Edward Russell (1860–1941), another socialist whose father had been the abolitionist editor of a small newspaper in Iowa, and Oswald Garrison Villard (1872–1949), grandson of the abolitionist William Lloyd Garrison and publisher of the liberal *New York Evening Post* journal and later the *Nation*.

Ovington also invited two prominent black New York clergymen, Bishop Alexander WALTERS of the

Roy Wilkins (left), Walter White (center), and Thurgood Marshall (right) directed the fortunes of the NAACP and the NAACP Legal Defense and Educational Fund for more than forty years. (Prints and Photographs Division, Library of Congress)

AFRICAN METHODIST EPISCOPAL ZION CHURCH, a former president of the National Afro-American Council, and the Rev. William Henry Brooks, minister of Mark's Methodist Episcopal Church, to join the continuing discussions. The expanded group agreed to issue a call on February 12, 1909, Lincoln's birthday, for a conference in New York.

Written by Villard, the call reflected the Niagara Movement's platform and emphasized protection of the civil and political rights of African Americans guaranteed under the Fourteenth and Fifteenth Amendments. Of the sixty people signing the call, seven were black: Professor William L. Bulkley, a New York school principal; Du Bois; the Rev. Francis J. GRIMKÉ of Washington; Mary Church TERRELL of Washington; Dr. J. Milton WALDRON of Washington; Bishop Walters; and Ida B. Wells (*see* Ida B. WELLS-BARNETT).

The founders' overriding concern was guaranteeing to all citizens the reality of equality. They demanded all rights "which underlie our American institutions and are guaranteed by our Constitution"—legal, educational, and political—as well as an end to all forms of segregation and intimidation. The organization was founded as a small elite organization which would rely primarily on agitation and legal battles rather than mass action against racial discrimination.

As a result of the call, the National Negro Conference met at the Charity Organization Hall in New York City on May 31 and June 1, 1909. The conference created the National Negro Committee (also known as the Committee of Forty on Permanent Organization and initially known as the National Committee for the Advancement of the Negro) to develop plans for an effective organization. The committee's plans were implemented a year later at a second meeting in New York, when the organization's permanent name was adopted. The organization chose to include the phrase "colored people" in its title to emphasize the broad and anti-imperialist concerns of its founders, and not to limit the scope of the organization to the United States. The NAACP's structure and mission inspired the formation of several other civil rights groups, such as South Africa's African National Congress, formed in 1912.

The NAACP's organizers created a formal institutional structure headed by an executive committee composed largely of members of the Committee of Forty. While Du Bois and a handful of other black men, largely moderates, were included, black women—notably Ida B. Wells—were excluded from the committee. Kathryn Johnson served as field secretary from 1910 through 1916 (on a volunteer basis for the first four years), becoming the first of many black women to serve as in that position; but black women were not offered leadership roles in the NAACP for several decades. Moorfield Storey (1845–1929), a former secretary to antislavery Sen. Charles Sumner, and one of the country's foremost constitutional lawyers, was named the organization's president. In addition to Storey and Du Bois, the only black and only salaried staffer, its first officers were Walling, chairman; John E. Milholland, treasurer; Villard, assistant treasurer; and Ovington, secretary. In addition to their official positions, Villard and Ovington were the principal organizers, providing direction and ideas. Francis Blascoer served as national secretary (becoming the second salaried staffer) from February 1910 to March 1911, when Ovington resumed the position pro bono for a year. May Childs Nerney took over the position in 1912.

Soon after the 1910 conference, the NAACP established an office at 20 Vesey St. in New York City (it moved to its longtime home of 70 Fifth Ave. a few years later). In its first year, it launched programs to increase job opportunities for blacks, and to obtain greater protection for them in the South by crusading against lynching and other forms of violence.

The organization's most important act by far that year was the hiring of Du Bois as director of publications and research. Du Bois's visionary ideas and militant program were his primary contributions to the NAACP. His hiring signaled the final demise of the Niagara Movement; while Du Bois brought its central vision to the new organization, the NAACP had better funding and a much more well-defined structure and program than the Niagara Movement.

In November 1910, Du Bois launched the CRISIS as the NAACP's house journal. *The Crisis* soon became the principal philosophical instrument of the black freedom struggle. From an initial publication of 1,000 copies in November 1910 the magazine's circulation increased to 100,000 a month in 1918. In its pages, Du Bois exposed and protested the scourge of racial oppression in order to educate both his black and white audiences on the nature of the struggle and to instill pride in his people. *The Crisis* was not only known for political articles; in its pages Du Bois introduced works by African-American writers, poets, and artists.

Following the report of a Committee on Program headed by Villard, the NAACP was incorporated in New York on June 20, 1911. The organizers invested overall control in a board of directors, which replaced the executive committee. Moorfield Storey remained as president, while Villard succeeded Walling as chairman of the board of directors. The chairman of the board, rather than the president, was designated the most powerful officer in the organization, because Storey had a highly successful practice in Boston and was unable to devote much attention to the NAACP.

The executive committee centralized control of the organization in a national body, to which memberships belonged; it decentralized other significant aspects of the organization's work through local groups called vigilance committees, which became its branches. To ensure that the movement spread as quickly as possible, the committee authorized mass meetings in Chicago, Cleveland, and Buffalo.

The first local NAACP branch was organized in New York in January 1911. Joel E. Spingarn (1874–1939), former chairman of the department of comparative literature at Columbia University, became the branch's first president. His brother Arthur, a lawyer, also became active in the branch. The following year, branches were created in Boston, Baltimore, Detroit, Indianapolis, St. Louis, and Quincy, Ill. In 1913, other branch offices were created in Chicago, Kansas City, Tacoma, Wash., and Washington, D.C. Membership in the organization was contingent upon acceptance of NAACP philosophy and programs.

While the local branches were largely staffed by African Americans, the national NAACP was a largely white group during its early days. Whites had the financial resources to devote themselves to NAACP work; throughout the NAACP's early days, all of the board members contributed a considerable amount of time to the organization. Arthur Spingarn, for example, estimated that he devoted "half and probably more" of his time to the NAACP. Also, whites had the education, the administrative experience, and the access to money that were required to build the organization. For example, Villard initially provided office space for the NAACP in his *New York Post* building. He also gave his personal funds to save the infant organization from imminent collapse. Joel Spingarn paid for his own travel from city to city, soliciting memberships and funds during what were called the New Abolition tours. While he did not make sizable personal contributions to the organization until 1919, Spingarn's knowledge of the management of stocks and bonds also enabled him to direct the organization's financial policies. Furthermore, he donated funds to establish the annual SPINGARN MEDAL, first awarded in 1915, which rapidly became the most prestigious African-American award.

Despite essential contributions of white activists, blacks were increasingly uneasy about white control of an organization that was meant for African Americans. Those differences had surfaced at the founding conference, when Ida B. Wells openly expressed concern over the leading roles that whites were playing in the movement. She and William Monroe Trotter shied away from involvement in the new organization because of its domination by whites. Black resentment about white control was manifested in the frequent clashes between Du Bois and Villard, two prickly and irreconcilable personalities.

Du Bois especially resented the intrusion of whites into the editorial affairs of *The Crisis,* which he maintained as an independent, self-supporting magazine. While it remained part of the NAACP, it had its own staff of eight to ten people (led by business manager Augustus DILL, one of the NAACP's few black staff members). Many whites, including Villard, felt that *The Crisis* did not report NAACP news sufficiently. They maintained that Du Bois's often acerbic denunciations of whites were inflammatory and said his editorial style was propagandistic and unbalanced, since he refused to cover negative topics, such as black crime.

In 1914, following clashes with Du Bois, Villard resigned as chairman of the board, and Joel Spingarn succeeded him. Even after Villard's departure, the issue of white control continued, and it caused considerable conflict between Du Bois and Spingarn, his long-time friend. Though, as Du Bois admitted, his haughty personality contributed to the problem, he also interpreted his role within a racial context and

felt that he could not accept even the appearance of inferiority or subservience to whites without betraying the race ideals for which he stood. Spingarn felt strongly that Du Bois devoted too much time to lecturing and writing at the expense of association work, but he and Ovington sided with Du Bois in board matters. After Ovington, a long-time ally and supporter, became NAACP chair in 1919, she too became a severe critic of Du Bois's refusal to follow board policy, though she accepted his independence in management of *The Crisis.*

The problem of white domination led to frank discussion about whether whites should continue in top-level positions in the NAACP. While Du Bois challenged any sign of black subordination, he feared that whites would refuse to aid a black-dominated organization and that it would compromise the NAACP's integrationist program. Spingarn and Ovington both acknowledged the difficulties inherent in white leadership, but felt it was a necessary evil until blacks had sufficient resources to run organizations without assistance.

In 1916 Mae Nerney resigned her post as secretary. She recommended that the board choose a black person to succeed her, but the board chose a white man, Roy Nash. It could not, however, escape the pressure to hire another black executive, so it chose James Weldon JOHNSON, a writer for the *New York Age* and a highly respected man of letters, as field secretary later that year.

Several events in the NAACP's first years combined to define and unite the fledgling organization. The first was the NAACP's ten-year protest campaign for the withdrawal of the film BIRTH OF A NATION, beginning in 1915. The film, directed by D. W. Griffith, featured racist portrayals of blacks. The NAACP charged that the film "assassinated" the character of black Americans and undermined the very basis of the struggle for racial equality. The organization arranged pickets of movie theaters and lobbied local governments to ban showings of the film. The NAACP branches succeeded in leading thousands of blacks in protests and forced the withdrawal of the film from several cities and states. The struggle provided important evidence that African Americans would display opposition to racist images and actions.

The following year, upon the death of Booker T. Washington in 1915, the NAACP reached another turning point. With the end of effective opposition by those who preferred accommodation with the South's Jim Crow policies, *The Crisis,* under Du Bois's leadership, became the leading principal instrument of black opinion. As leadership passed from Washington to the militant "race men" of the North, the NAACP fully established itself as the primary

Charles Houston became the NAACP's chief counsel in 1935 and organized its carefully crafted legal strategy for challenging segregation. Depicted here (from left to right) are Walter White, executive secretary of the NAACP; Houston; James G. Tyson; Leon Ransom; and Edward Lovett. Ransom was a professor of law at Harvard University's School of Law; Tyson and Lovett were former students there. All three worked with Houston in the preparation and arguing of important desegregation cases. (Moorland-Spingarn Research Center, Howard University)

black organization. Consolidating the NAACP's power, in 1916 Du Bois initiated a conference of black leaders, including Washington's men, and their friends. This was the first Amenia conference, which was held at Joel Spingarn's Troutbeck estate at Amenia, north of New York City (*see* AMENIA CONFERENCE OF 1916). The fifty or so participants adopted resolutions that were aimed at breaching the division between the Washington group and the NAACP. The conference participants endorsed all forms of education for African Americans—not just the type of industrial schooling that Washington had advocated; recognized complete political freedom as essential for the development of blacks; agreed that organization and a practical working understanding among race leaders was necessary for development; urged that old controversies, suspicions and factional alignments be eliminated; and suggested that there was a special need for understanding between leaders in the South

and in the North. Du Bois reiterated the African-American demand for full equality and political power.

World War I and related events combined to set the NAACP on its primary mission, a two-pronged legal and political course against racial violence. During the war, Du Bois instituted a controversial policy of black support for American military efforts, with the goal of greater recognition for civil rights afterward. However, the migration of southern blacks to northern urban areas during and after the war led to racial tension, and the clash between increasingly assertive blacks, and whites who refused to countenance changes in the racial status quo, led to violent riots, particularly during the postwar RED SUMMER of 1919.

Security of person was the most pressing problem that the blacks faced, since the taking of a person's life by mob action violated the most basic constitutional right. At first, the NAACP's primary strategy against lynching involved a publicity campaign backed by pamphlets, in-depth studies, and other educational activities to mobilize public support for ending the crime. From its earliest years, the NAACP devoted most of its resources to seeking an end to lynchings and other forms of mob violence; the organization's protest campaign after a lynching in Coatesville, Pa., in 1911 resulted in its first substantial publicity. In 1917 it led the celebrated silent protest parade of 15,000 people through Harlem with muffled drums to protest the violent riots that year against blacks in EAST ST. LOUIS, ILL., and discrimination in general.

The strengthening of the branch structure heightened NAACP influence. As field secretary, James Weldon Johnson was charged with organizing branches, which carried out most of the organization's protest activity. Johnson's most immediate challenge was to increase significantly the number of NAACP branches in the South, a mission that exposed him to the dangers of JIM CROW in the region. Johnson began by organizing a branch in Richmond, Va., in 1917. Initially, his progress was slow, but by the end of 1919, the NAACP had 310 branches, including 31 in the South. The Atlanta branch, founded in late 1916, had become one of the organization's strongest, with a membership of more than 1,000. The NAACP's total membership jumped from 9,282 in 1917 to 91,203 in 1919.

In 1921, Johnson became NAACP secretary, establishing the permanent line of blacks to hold the position. Johnson's assumption of this power reflected the clearer administrative lines that were developing within the NAACP, and signalled the rising influence of paid African-American staff members within the organization. Johnson's predecessor, John Shillady, hired in 1918, had served as the first professional secretary. Shillady assumed responsibility for fund raising, coordinating the branches, and developing the strategy for implementing the organization's programs. Johnson worked even harder to further the organization's goals. The NAACP strengthened its executive staff in 1922 when it hired Herbert J. Seligman as its first full-time director of publicity. Johnson was succeeded as field secretary by Dr. William A. Pickens, who later served as director of branches until 1942.

The NAACP During the "New Negro" Era

Despite its promising beginnings, by 1919 it was clear that the NAACP's reliance on agitation and education had proved largely ineffective against racial violence. The most promising avenue of redress was by political challenge. Walter WHITE, a young insurance salesman from Atlanta whom Johnson met dur-

ing an organizing trip, and who joined the national staff in 1918, was named assistant secretary with responsibility for investigating lynchings. White's effectiveness with this mission—in part because as a very light-skinned African American he could blend into white mobs—won him national respect.

In 1919, the NAACP published its report *Thirty Years of Lynching in the United States, 1889–1918*. The book provided documentation for the campaign against the crime that White was leading. A resurgence of violence helped the NAACP to get the Republican party during the 1920 campaign to urge Congress "to consider the most effective means to end lynching." Two years later, through Johnson's extraordinary effort, the House passed an antilynching bill introduced by Congressman L. C. Dyer of Missouri, but Southerners in the Senate killed the DYER BILL with a filibuster.

Even though Congress failed to pass antilynching legislation during the Coolidge and Hoover administrations, the Republican party's repeated pledge in 1924 to seek such a law was a strong indication that the NAACP's political emphasis held considerable promise. During the administration of Franklin D. Roosevelt the NAACP continued pressing for the passage of antilynching laws in Congress. Two more bills were introduced in this period, but one died in the House and the other in the Senate. Congress never passed an antilynching law, but the NAACP eventually helped end the crime through publicity.

Led by Du Bois, the NAACP continued to extend its influence abroad. In 1919, with NAACP support, Du Bois organized the first of a series of Pan African Congresses in Paris, as the most effective means for demeaning the removal of colonial shackles in Africa, India, the West Indies, and all other such territories. The following year, the NAACP expanded its international program by sending Johnson to Haiti to investigate the U.S. occupation of the country. After spending six weeks there, Johnson conducted an extensive campaign in the United States to get both the president and the Congress to take action to protect the sovereignty of Haiti and the rights of its citizens. Although his effort was not immediately fruitful, Johnson brought to national attention the occupation and the discriminatory treatment of persons of African descent by American troops in Haiti.

Despite its preeminent position in the black community, the NAACP was not without its critics during the 1920s. Proponents of radical protest, such as A. Philip RANDOLPH and Chandler OWEN of the journal the MESSENGER criticized the NAACP for excessive legalism, claiming the organization should support self-defense efforts against racial violence. Furthermore, the NAACP engaged in a strong rivalry with Marcus GARVEY and his UNIVERSAL NE-

GRO IMPROVEMENT ASSOCIATION. Garvey scorned the NAACP's interracial, integrationist philosophy and its predominantly light-skinned, middle-class black leadership. The NAACP, meanwhile, feared Garvey's Back-to-Africa movement as chauvinist and overly visionary. Du Bois called Garvey "the most dangerous man in America," while Robert BAGNALL, the NAACP's director of branches, said that Garvey was "insane" and collaborated with United States government officials in their successful attempt to deport Garvey.

Under James Weldon Johnson's leadership, the NAACP became a recognized power in the United States during the 1920s. In 1930, Johnson, who had taken a year's leave of absence to devote his time to creative writing, retired from the NAACP, and Walter White was appointed secretary. White, in turn, hired Roy WILKINS, a former managing editor of the *Kansas City Call,* as his assistant.

The NAACP began the 1930s with 325 branches, which were located in every state of the Union except Maine, New Hampshire, Vermont, Idaho, and North Dakota. The association's branch work was now directed by two field secretaries, Dr. William Pickens and Daisy E. LAMPKIN. The branches served as information bureaus for the national office and stimulated the cultural life of African Americans. In addition to the field staff, the national officers visited them regularly, led conferences, did intense organizational work, and solicited financial support as well as regular and life memberships. The broad organizational independence of the branches enabled them to put together actions, such as mass demonstrations, that differed strongly from national office policy.

The NAACP's influence was demonstrated by Walter White's successful campaign in 1930 to defeat President Herbert Hoover's nomination of Judge John J. Parker to the U.S. Supreme Court. Parker was from North Carolina and had previously, as a gubernatorial candidate, spoken against black suffrage. While he had opposition from labor unions and other groups, the NAACP was largely influential in forming coalitions and lobbying senators against Parker's confirmation. Parker's defeat, after a close vote, was a dramatic accomplishment for the NAACP, and widespread denunciation of the organization by white Southerners after the battle reinforced its stature as a formidable political force.

The NAACP Legal Campaign

Well before it had launched its political efforts, the NAACP had begun using the courts to improve the status of blacks (see also CIVIL RIGHTS AND THE LAW). The scarcity of good black lawyers during the organization's early years made it crucial for whites to dedicate their services to the organization. The NAACP engaged lawyers to conduct its legal work as the need arose and when funds permitted. Because of this inability to fund a legal program, Arthur Spingarn and his law partner Charles H. Studin, along with Moorfield Storey, volunteered their legal services. Arthur Spingarn assumed leadership of this program in 1929.

The NAACP's first significant court action was the legal struggle to save the life of Pink Franklin, an illiterate farmhand in South Carolina, which led the NAACP to establish a legal redress department in 1910. Franklin had been sentenced to death for killing a law officer attempting to arrest him for leaving his employer after he had received advances on his wages. This case was noteworthy because it forced the U.S. Supreme Court, which for some time had been evading all questions relating to the citizenship rights of African Americans, to rule on whether serfdom could be legally established in the country. While the Court affirmed the decision of the lower courts, the NAACP got the South Carolina governor to commute Franklin's sentence to life imprisonment.

An important victory came in 1915, when Storey wrote an *amicus curiae* brief of the NAACP in *Guinn* v. *United States,* challenging the constitutionality of the Oklahoma "grandfather clause." The U.S. Supreme Court ruled that the clause violated the Fifteenth Amendment, giving the NAACP its first legal victory and incentive to seek further redress of civil rights cases.

Through the early part of the century, the NAACP won other significant cases. In 1917 the NAACP struck a strong, though not final, blow against residential segregation when the U.S. Supreme Court ruled in *Buchanan* v. *Warley* that the Louisville, Ky., residential segregation ordinance was unconstitutional. The case resulted in the striking down of mandatory housing segregation in Norfolk, Baltimore, St. Louis, and other cities. In 1919, the NAACP conducted an investigation of the convictions of twelve black Elaine, Ark., farmers arrested during a riot in 1919 and sentenced to death, and took their case to the U.S. Supreme Court. The Court threw out the convictions in *Moore* v. *Dempsey* (1923), ruling that the trial had been dominated by a mob atmosphere. In 1935, in the Court's ruling in *Hollins* v. *Oklahoma,* the NAACP won the reversal of two death penalty convictions due to racial discrimination in jury selection.

Aside from opposition to lynching, the NAACP's primary fight in the 1920s continued to be against racial injustices in the courts, and it handled hundreds of civil rights cases. It considered its task of educating the public, both white and black, about racial wrongs to be an even greater challenge than resolving specific problems. Thus, it had two criteria for accepting a case: first, whether it involved discrimination and injustice based on race or color; second, whether it would establish a precedent for protecting the rights of African Americans as a group. The case of Dr. Ossian Sweet of Detroit met those criteria. In 1925, Sweet moved his family into a house he had purchased in a middle-class white neighborhood. The house was surrounded by a white mob. Sweet shot at the mob in self-defense, and killed one of its members. The NAACP hired Clarence Darrow, the greatest trial lawyer of the day, and he successfully defended Sweet.

One notable area of NAACP interest was the "White Primary," which effectively disfranchised southern blacks. In 1927, the Supreme Court declared in a unanimous decision in Nixon v. Herndon that a Texas state primary law that excluded blacks from voting was unconstitutional. Soon afterward, a special session of the Texas legislature passed a new statute authorizing the Democratic state committee to make its own decisions on the eligibility of voters in party primaries. The NAACP appealed, and in 1932 the Supreme Court ruled in Nixon v. Condon that the Fourteenth Amendment forbade such distinctions. (Despite NAACP efforts, however, in 1935, the U.S. Supreme Court ruled in Grovey v. Townshend that a party was a private body and could exclude blacks from primary elections; the white primary was finally struck down in 1944.)

Such victories led the NAACP to declare after 1932 that "for the present, the avenue of affirmation and defense of the Negro's fundamental rights in America lies through the courts." Those, of course, were the Supreme Court and the lower federal courts, which the NAACP regarded as bulwarks in this struggle, because at that level "the atmosphere of sectional prejudice is notably absent." Its legal victories, it concluded, were "clear-cut" and "matters of prominent record."

In 1929, Arthur Spingarn organized the NAACP legal committee, and served as its chair until 1939, when he succeeded his deceased brother Joel as president of the NAACP. The first members of the legal committee included the distinguished labor lawyer Clarence Darrow, Harvard law professor and future U.S. Supreme Court justice Felix Frankfurter; liberal Michigan governor and future U.S. Supreme Court justice Frank Murphy; and American Civil Liberties Union lawyer Arthur Garfield Hays.

Darrow and Hays represented the NAACP in the Sweet case, as well as the SCOTTSBORO CASE, which involved nine young black men who were convicted of raping two white women on a train passing through Scottsboro, Ala., in 1931. Eight of the Scottsboro defendants were sentenced to death. The NAACP, which lacked a regular legal department,

was unable to move quickly into action, and the International Labor Defense, closely allied with the COMMUNIST PARTY, took control of the case. In 1933, the NAACP, spurred by black community criticism of its inaction on the famous case, formed the Scottsboro Defense Committee in an uneasy alliance with the International Labor Defense. After a series of protracted legal battles, the defendants' lives were saved. (The ILD abandoned the case after it lost publicity value. On November 29, 1976, the NAACP finally won freedom for Clarence Norris, the last of the Scottsboro nine, when the Alabama Board for Pardons and Paroles pardoned him.)

The NAACP in the Depression

The frustrations of the Scottsboro case were the beginning of a contentious and difficult period for the NAACP. The collapse of the national economy in 1929 brought disproportionate hardship to the masses of African Americans. Many blacks hailed the New Deal's programs for economic recovery in the hope that minimum wage, maximum working hours, and other such reforms would benefit blacks (see also GREAT DEPRESSION AND THE NEW DEAL). However, early New Deal programs were unable to alter the low social and economic status of the African-American masses; in some cases these worsened their situation. Bitterly disappointed, many intellectuals were attracted by Marxism and other radical philosophies. The COMMUNIST PARTY and allied groups such as the League of Struggle for Negro Rights presented themselves in black areas as rivals to the NAACP, whose reformist stance they sought to discredit as inadequate for addressing the economic injustice African Americans were suffering.

Similarly, the Great Depression brought sharp criticisms of the NAACP by a generation of younger intellectuals, and pressure on the organization to make radical shifts in its strategies and programs to meet the needs of impoverished blacks. One of the severest critics was Ralph BUNCHE, a political scientist at Howard University. Bunche maintained that the NAACP's program of political and civil liberties was doomed to failure unless there was an improvement in the economic condition of the black masses. Bunche was also uncomfortable with having whites in policy-making positions in the NAACP, maintaining that its interracial structure was "an undoubted source of organizational weakness." He felt that the "white sympathizers were in the main either cautious liberals or mawkish, missionary-minded sentimentalists on the race question."

Another important critic was Dr. Abram L. HARRIS, a Howard University economics professor and member of the NAACP board of directors. Harris insisted that the NAACP launch a more vigorous attack on fundamental economic problems and that the masses of African Americans organized in the local branches play a more significant role in the organization's work. He and Bunche advocated efforts by the NAACP to reach out to white labor unions and secure greater union affiliation for black workers.

The organization did respond to economic discrimination during the early 1930s. For example, in 1931, Helen Boardman, a white NAACP investigator, reported that the 30,000 blacks on the War Department's Mississippi Flood Control project were receiving 10 cents an hour for an 84-hour week. In 1933, Roy Wilkins and George S. SCHUYLER, a former Socialist and writer for the *Messenger,* disguised themselves as laborers in order to investigate the deplorable, peonage-like conditions under which blacks on the project were working. White officials discovered their identities, and both men barely escaped with their lives. The Wilkins and Schuyler investigations enabled the NAACP to get the Secretary of War to quadruple the hourly pay for unskilled laborers and shorten their work week to thirty hours.

Nevertheless, while the NAACP leaders did not share Bunche's view of the futility of legal efforts, some staffers, notably Du Bois, felt that the NAACP lacked a clear sense of direction. The criticisms convinced younger staffers such as Wilkins that "among the liberals and radicals, both Negro and white, the impression prevails that the Association is weak because it has no economic program and no economic philosophy."

In the face of the criticisms, in August 1933 the NAACP held a second AMENIA CONFERENCE (*see* AMENIA CONFERENCE OF 1933). This time whites were barred from the assemblage on Joel Spingarn's estate. Among the delegates were several young leaders who would later achieve distinction. Notable were Bunche and Harris; sociologists E. Franklin FRAZIER and Ira De A. Reid; attorney Louis Redding; Sterling A. BROWN, a literary critic and poet; and Juanita Jackson, who with her mother Lillie Mae JACKSON in 1935 would begin leading the NAACP struggle to desegregate their home state of Maryland. The major emphasis at the conference was on economics and the need for power among blacks that could make the government more responsive to the demands of their community. The participants were upset by the national NAACP's reluctance to launch a mass movement, in contrast to the efforts of branches such as Baltimore.

There was general agreement on the need for the NAACP to develop the type of comprehensive economic program that the Amenia Conference delegates demanded. Not everyone within the organization, however, subscribed to the young activists' focus on race pride; neither did they initially support

their call for greater solidarity between the black and white working class. Walter White, for one, had grave reservations about moving toward a more "mass-oriented" program and felt that many of his colleagues were being "stampeded by temporary or emotional situations and conditions." Nevertheless, in the aftermath of the conference and significant prodding by Joel Spingarn, the NAACP created a Committee on Future Plan and Program in 1935 to consider the concerns raised by the Amenia Conference. The members of the committee were Harris, chairman; Rachel Davis Du Bois; Dr. Louis T. WRIGHT; James Weldon Johnson; Sterling Brown; and Mary White Ovington, who had resigned from the board in 1931 following disagreements with White. The committee reinforced the priority of economic concerns and urged solidarity between black and white workers. It forced the organization to declare that its interests were "inextricably intertwined with those of white workers." The importance of this emphasis was realized with the subsequent creation of the Congress of Industrial Organizations (CIO) which, unlike the American Federation of Labor (AFL), opened its ranks to black workers, and which was closely allied with the NAACP (*see also* LABOR AND LABOR UNIONS).

White made some modifications in the NAACP's programs to accommodate the economic concerns and activism of the young militants in the late 1930s. For example, the NAACP was one of the twenty-four civil rights and religious organizations supporting the Joint Committee on National Recovery, a Washington-based economic lobbying and information group founded by Robert C. WEAVER and John P. DAVIS in 1935. Also, the NAACP negotiated with leaders of the CIO on behalf of black automobile workers in Detroit. However, White redoubled the organization's efforts in its traditional areas of education, agitation, and court litigation. More than ever, court action defined the NAACP's identity, while direct action was left to small groups such as the NATIONAL NEGRO CONGRESS and the CONGRESS OF RACIAL EQUALITY (CORE), founded in 1942.

As discomforting as most of the criticisms from young radicals were for White, none created anything as near a schism as those offered by Du Bois. He too had grown impatient with the pace of the NAACP's achievements. Openly challenging White and the NAACP, he shifted from his long-held position of urging integration, because that was not achieving racial equality fast enough, and promoted independent black economic development. (One possible factor in Du Bois's 180-degree shift in position from emphasis on integration to tactical segregation was his deep, personal differences with White). Du Bois's stand made his departure from

The Crisis and the NAACP board inevitable, and he resigned in 1934. Wilkins, in addition to being in charge of the organization's administration, succeeded him as editor of *The Crisis*.

Another significant development was the revamping of the NAACP hierarchy. More and more, the paid staff exercised control of the organization. In effect, White made the executive secretary the association's chief executive officer as well as its chief spokesman. White was able to effect such changes because the bulk of the organization's strength and finances now came from its vastly expanded branch structure. Despite the severe hardships of the depression, the branches in 1936 contributed $26,288 toward the total income of $47,724. Most of the remaining income came from contributions, as well as a life membership program that was created in 1927. This pattern of support had been established from around 1920. Between that year and 1931, the NAACP raised $545,407 in general funds, of which $374,896 came from the branches.

The board, as a result, underwent a shift in direction. In 1934, Dr. Louis T. WRIGHT, a physician and Fellow in the American College of Surgeons, was elected as the first in the permanent line of blacks to be chairman of the NAACP board. As Charles Hamilton HOUSTON, who was chairman of the board revision committee explained, among other things, the changes made the board more representative of the organization's membership. Previously, he said, board meetings were "in substance executive committee meetings." He added, "I favor calling a spade by its name. The board meetings would deal with policies rather than details." While whites remained on the board in diminishing numbers, by mid-1936 the NAACP's organizational revolution was so stark that the NAACP no longer depended on whites for administrative expertise or for the bulk of its fiscal support. Mary White Ovington complained that the board of directors had adopted "the rubber stamp attitude" in sanctioning the staff's actions. She was especially unhappy with Walter White, whom she lamented was virtually "the dictator" of the organization. She complained that the board's discussions had little effect on its actual programs and policies.

Throughout the late 1930s, much of the NAACP's activism was organized by individual branches. For example, in Baltimore, Boston, and elsewhere, NAACP Youth Council leaders formed "don't-buy-where-you-can't-work" boycotts and pickets to protest job discrimination in stores located in black communities. In New Orleans, the NAACP paid residents' poll taxes to fight voting restrictions. In Kansas City, an NAACP-led protest campaign desegregated municipal golf courses. In New York, NAACP officials joined a committee to improve conditions in Harlem after a riot broke out in 1935.

The national NAACP also engaged in several campaigns during the 1930s, lobbying Congress for antilynching legislation and struggling against discrimination in New Deal programs. One important NAACP action was its protest against the Italian invasion of Ethiopia. The organization collected donations for war relief, sent official protests to the League of Nations and U.S. State Department, and lobbied against pro-Italian amendments in the 1935 Neutrality Act. Another important struggle dealt with media stereotypes. NAACP representatives met with newspaper editors to persuade them to offer positive coverage of African Americans and to cease the practice of discussing the race of alleged criminals. The NAACP also launched a campaign to end stereotypes in Hollywood films and radio programs, notably the popular radio series AMOS 'N' ANDY, which the organization claimed presented demeaning stereotypes of blacks. NAACP lobbying helped secure the signing of black performers such as Lena HORNE to film studio contracts.

The Legal Assault on Segregation

To end its dependence on volunteer lawyers, which had proved a large handicap in the Scottsboro case, as well as to wage an all-out fight against segregation, the NAACP in 1935 created its legal department. The creation of the NAACP legal department resulted from a comprehensive study of the association's legal program that Nathan Ross Margold, a white public service lawyer in New York, conducted in 1930 under a grant from the American Fund for Public Service (later the Garland Fund). Margold suggested that the NAACP "strike directly at the most prolific sources of discrimination" by boldly challenging "the constitutional validity of segregation if and when accompanied irremediably by discrimination." He recommended, furthermore, that the NAACP focus on the glaring disparities between white and black schools.

The NAACP hired Charles H. Houston, the highly respected dean of Howard University School of Law, as its first special counsel. Walter White was responsible for bringing Houston into the NAACP. White had become very impressed with Houston's brilliant defense in 1932 of George Crawford, an African American who was accused of murdering two white women in Virginia. Although a jury convicted Crawford and he was sentenced to life in prison, Houston saved him from the death penalty.

Houston diverged from the Margold report by attacking the unequal financial support of black schools in the South. His strategy was to force the states either to strengthen black institutions or to abandon them because it was too expensive to maintain the avowed "separate but equal" practice. In order to accumulate evidence of unequal funding, Houston and his protegé, Thurgood MARSHALL, toured the South, investigating conditions. Houston also laid the foundations of the NAACP's successful strategy of sociological jurisprudence in the subsequent direct attack on segregation.

Houston's first line of attack was graduate and professional schools. He successfully tested this strategy in the Maryland Supreme Court case *Murray* v. *Maryland* in 1935, the first of a series of challenges that would lead to the U.S. Supreme Court's landmark BROWN V. BOARD OF EDUCATION decision in 1954. Houston left the NAACP in 1938 to return to private law practice in Washington, and was succeeded by Marshall, a graduate of Howard University Law School who had been working with the Baltimore NAACP branch.

Continuing to attack racial inequalities in education, the NAACP filed its first teacher's discrimination pay case in behalf of William Gibbs against the Montgomery County Board of Education in Maryland. The county was paying Gibbs $612 a year, whereas a white school principal with comparable qualifications was receiving $1,475. In 1938 the court ordered the county to equalize teachers' salaries, setting a precedent for similar NAACP challenges in other parts of the country. The same year, the NAACP won in *Missouri* ex rel. *Gaines* v. *Canada.* Chief Justice Charles Evans Hughes said in the Supreme Court's majority opinion that Missouri's offer of tuition aid to Lloyd Gaines to attend an out-of-state university law school did not constitute equal treatment under the Constitution. In 1939, William H. HASTIE, a black scholar and federal judge, succeeded Arthur Spingarn as chairman of the NAACP Legal Committee. Soon after, the NAACP LEGAL DEFENSE AND EDUCATIONAL FUND was incorporated to receive tax deductible contributions for those areas of the NAACP's work that met the Internal Revenue Service's guidelines. The LDF, dubbed the "Inc. Fund" and headed by Thurgood MARSHALL, was tied to the parent NAACP by interlocking boards.

As in the earlier years, the NAACP's cases covered four major areas: disfranchisement, segregation ordinances, restrictive covenants and due process, and equal protection for blacks accused of crimes. Among the fundamental victories won before the Supreme Court were *Smith* v. *Allwright* (1944), in which the all-white Texas Democratic primary was declared unconstitutional; *Morgan* v. *Virginia* (1946), in which it was declared that state laws requiring segregated travel could not be enforced in interstate travel; and *Shelley* v. *Kraemer* and *McGhee* v. *Sipes* (1948), in which it was declared that restrictive housing cove-

nants could not be legally enforced. (Two other cases, *Hurd* v. *Hodge* and *Urciolo* v. *Hodge,* were argued with the *Kraemer* and *McGhee* cases.)

World War II and Postwar Periods

The NAACP's legal campaign during the 1940s was reinforced by its efforts at education and lobbying. During WORLD WAR II, the NAACP made an enormous effort to secure equal treatment for blacks in the military and in war industries. For example, NAACP officials lobbied successfully for a Navy officer training program for African Americans, and investigated reports of discrimination against black GIs; Walter White personally conducted investigations of discrimination complaints in the European and Pacific theaters. White also championed A. Philip Randolph's 1941 March on Washington Movement and was an adviser in the creation of the FAIR EMPLOYMENT PRACTICE COMMITTEE (FEPC). In 1942, NAACP investigators reported on living and working conditions in overcrowded cities, although they were largely ignored. After rioting broke out in Detroit and New York's Harlem in 1943 (*see* DETROIT RIOT OF 1943 and HARLEM RIOT OF 1943), the NAACP backed interracial committee efforts. In 1944, the NAACP organized a Wartime Conference, in which it recorded its "special stake in the abolition of imperialism," due to the preponderance of people of color in colonized nations. With the aid of such staffers as Ella BAKER, director of branches from 1943 through 1946, the NAACP grew from 355 branches and 50,556 members in 1940 to 1,073 branches and some 450,000 members by 1946.

After the end of the war, the NAACP redoubled its efforts to pass antilynching legislation. In the face of rising racial violence, such as an antiblack riot in Columbia, Tenn., the NAACP called for federal civil rights protection. In 1946, Walter White organized a National Emergency Committee against Mob Violence, and met with President Harry Truman to demand action. In 1947, the NAACP provided financial and logistical support for CORE's Journey of Reconciliation, a series of interracial bus rides to challenge discrimination in interstate travel. Clarence MITCHELL, Jr., director of the NAACP's Washington Bureau, led the fight for a permanent FEPC, which was realized in the Equal Employment Opportunity Commission, created by the 1964 Civil Rights Act.

An important factor in NAACP progress was the unprecedented support for civil rights shown by President Harry Truman. In fall 1946, in response to demands from the NAACP for presidential leadership on the civil rights, Truman appointed the President's Committee on Civil Rights and made Walter White a key adviser to it. The committee's 1947 report *To Secure These Rights* further sharpened the focus of the struggle to destroy segregation and grant full equality to African Americans. It closely followed NAACP recommendations for government action against segregation. In 1947 Truman became the first president to attend an NAACP convention when he addressed the organization's thirty-eighth annual convention in Washington.

In 1948, following NAACP pressure, President Truman issued an executive order barring segregation in the armed forces. The NAACP fought over the next years to implement the mandate. This fight was led by Thurgood Marshall, who conducted studies on the progress of military integration during the Korean War; and by Clarence Mitchell, who led the struggle in Washington to get President Eisenhower and the Defense Department to end all forms of segregation at military establishments in the United States and elsewhere.

During the late 1940s, the NAACP considerably strengthened its antidiscrimination programs and strategies. But with the rise of the Cold War and concerns over communism, the NAACP feared that it, too, would become a target for red baiting. To preserve its integrity, the NAACP adopted a strict anticommunist membership policy and avoided any association with the Communist party. The NAACP, furthermore, strongly opposed loyalty probes among government workers, fully realized that such investigations would make African Americans scapegoats purely on the basis of race. The organization scored a significant victory in this struggle when Frank Barnes, president of the NAACP's Santa Monica branch, was reinstated in his post office job as a result of the NAACP's intensive campaign to clear his name of charges of disloyalty to the United States.

At the same time, the NAACP directed worldwide attention to the problem of colonialism by sending Walter White and Du Bois as its representatives in 1945 to the founding United Nations Conference on International Organization in San Francisco. In 1947 Du Bois dramatically reinforced the NAACP's anticolonial program by presenting to the UN "An Appeal to the World," a 155-page petition composed of five chapters that linked the plight of Africans and other subjects of colonial imperialism with that of African Americans in the United States. The drafting committee of the UN Human Rights Commission debated the petition for two days at a meeting in Geneva.

In 1948 the NAACP continued to express its views on human rights, genocide, and colonialism at the Paris session of the UN General Assembly. That year, the NAACP welcomed the General Assembly's adoption of a Declaration of Human Rights and a Genocide Convention, and regretted that the colonial issue was not promptly settled. The NAACP won considerable support from other nongovernmental agencies for its demand that all colonial territories be placed under UN trusteeship and administered in a manner that would encourage development of indigenous populations. It strongly opposed attempts to return Somaliland and Eritrea, former colonies in Africa, to Italy or to turn them over to any other nation for administration.

Despite Du Bois's continuing contributions to the NAACP in raising world concern over the plight of the darker races in Africa, Asia, and the Caribbean, strong differences in 1948, caused by his inability to work with Walter White and resulting refusal to follow the organization's administrative procedures, led the NAACP board of directors to refuse to renew his contract. Thus, even though upon Du Bois's return in 1944 as director of special research he remained the symbol of NAACP history, he again left the organization in 1948.

In 1949, Roy Wilkins wrote an editorial in *The Crisis* strongly attacking black activist Paul ROBESON, who was accused of pro-Soviet sentiments. In 1950, the NAACP organized a National Emergency Civil Rights Mobilization in Washington to demand passage of civil rights laws. Led by Roy Wilkins, a group of 4,000 delegates representing 100 organizations met with Truman to enlist his support for the struggle in Congress. The mobilization, culminating a decade of NAACP efforts to get Congress to pass fair employment practice and other civil rights laws, signaled the birth of the LEADERSHIP COUNCIL ON CIVIL RIGHTS (LCCR).

The core of the NAACP's struggle for the passage of antiviolence and other civil rights laws was waged through its Washington bureau, which was created in 1942, as well as its branches. In addition to being executive secretary, Walter White served as the bureau's first director from its creation until 1950, when he relinquished the position to Clarence Mitchell, who also served as legislative chairman of the LCCR. Mitchell's function in developing the organization's political strategy and legislative program was similar to Thurgood Marshall's in the legal area. Both men served in positions that were a notch under the executive secretary.

The most important element in the civil rights struggle, nevertheless, was the NAACP's branches, which provided essential grassroots support and lobbying clout. In 1951, the association had 1,253 branches, youth councils, and college chapters, and a membership of 210,000 which for the first time since 1947 represented an encouraging increase. An indication of the NAACP's strength was that in 1950, for the first time in its history, it held its annual conference in the deep South in Atlanta. There, 7,500

In Baltimore, Paul Robeson joins the NAACP picket line in front of Ford's Theatre protesting its policy of racial segregation. (Left to right) Ada Jenkins; Paul Robeson; Earl Robinson, Hollywood composer of "Ballad for Americans" and accompanist for Robeson; Dr. J. E. T. Camper; Paul Kaufman; Rhoda Peasom; Dan Atwood. (Photographs and Prints Division, Schomburg Center for Research in Black Culture, The New York Public Library, Astor, Lenox and Tilden Foundations)

blacks and whites packed the municipal auditorium to hear Nobel Peace Prize laureate Ralph Bunche, the NAACP's onetime critic. Bunche, by then an NAACP board member, assailed the "tyranny of the segregation laws of the South" and the failure of Congress to pass civil rights legislation.

Since Southerners in Congress continued to block passage of civil rights laws, the best promise of success lay with the courts, as the NAACP had determined earlier. In 1950, the Supreme Court took decisive steps in two cases brought by the NAACP toward ending the "separate but equal" doctrine. In the first case, Sweatt v. Painter, the Court ruled that the separate black law school the state of Texas had established to accommodate Heman Sweatt was not and could not be equal to that provided for white students at the University of Texas. In the second case, McLaurin v. Oklahoma, the Supreme Court

ruled unanimously that the University of Oklahoma could not segregate G. W. McLaurin within its graduate school once he had been admitted.

Encouraged by the decisions in Sweatt v. Painter and McLaurin v. Oklahoma, the NAACP in 1951 launched a well-planned "Equality Under Law" campaign to overturn racial separation at its roots—in elementary and secondary schools. This drive was launched with the filing of lawsuits against school districts in Atlanta; Clarendon County, S.C.; Topeka, Kans.; and Wilmington, Del.

In 1953, Dr. Channing H. TOBIAS, the newly elected chairman of the NAACP board of directors, launched a "Fight for Freedom Fund" campaign and a goal of "Free by '63." This slogan was designed to mobilize all of the organization's resources for what the NAACP saw as the final phase of the struggle to eliminate all state-imposed discrimination in celebration of the centennial of Lincoln's Emancipation Proclamation. Reinforcing the climate of great anticipation within the civil rights community, President Eisenhower on May 10 addressed the NAACP's "Freedom Fulfillment" conference in Washington. He pledged that wherever the federal authority extended he would do his utmost to bring about racial equality. With help from the fund-raising campaign, the NAACP's membership grew to 240,000 by 1954.

On May 17, 1954, the Supreme Court handed down its landmark ruling in the four school desegregation cases that the NAACP had initiated, plus another case challenging segregation in the District of Columbia. Reasserting the full meaning of the Fourteenth Amendment, the court declared in *Brown* v. *Board of Education* that "in the field of public education the doctrine of 'separate but equal' has no place. Separate educational facilities are inherently unequal." Shortly thereafter, the NAACP won another historic victory, when the Department of Defense reported that as of August 31, 1954, there were "no longer any all-Negro units in the services."

Implementing Brown

Less than a year after he had led the celebrations of the school desegregation case victory, Walter White died. He had developed the organization that James Weldon Johnson had passed on to him into the most powerful vehicle of its kind for achieving racial equality. *Brown* v. *Board of Education* was his crowning achievement as much as it was Thurgood Marshall's. However, in his last years, White was an increasingly embattled figure. His flamboyant style and overinvolvement in outside activities had made him many enemies on the NAACP board, and many African Americans angrily criticized his marriage to a white woman in 1949. That year White took a leave of absence and, upon his return 1950, the board sharply restricted his policy-making power.

White left a staff of experienced professionals in their prime of productivity; in addition to Wilkins, White had hired Clarence Mitchell as labor secretary, Gloster B. Current as director of branches in 1946, and Henry Lee Moon, a former newspaper reporter, as director of public relations in 1948.

Roy Wilkins, who was elected in April 1955 to succeed White as NAACP executive director, faced enormous challenges. Wilkins's first problem was pressing for the enforcement of the *Brown* decision and for passage of FEPC and other civil rights laws. NAACP lawyers participated in the formation of desegregation plans and monitored compliance with *Brown*. In 1956, under NAACP sponsorship, Autherine Lucy, an African American, won a court ruling admitting her to the University of Alabama. However, university officials expelled her on the pretext

of preventing violence. The NAACP also made its struggle for passage of civil rights laws in Congress a top priority.

At the same time, the organization was forced to expend effort combatting the onslaught that the South had unleashed on the organization. The NAACP's trail-blazing victories in the courts, especially the *Brown* decision, made it a main target of the South's campaign of "massive resistance."

The resurgent KU KLUX KLAN figured strongly in the backlash of white violence, but it was not the only threat that NAACP faced from the South. Less than two months after the *Brown* decision was handed down, political leaders, businessmen and the professional elite organized the White Citizens' Council in Mississippi. Overnight, councils sprang up in other states. Regarded as "manicured kluxism," the White Citizens' Councils used economic and political pressure to prevent implementation of the *Brown* decision. In March 1956, nearly all of the southerners in Congress showed their defiance of *Brown* by signing the "Southern Manifesto," which called the Supreme Court decision "illegal."

Prior to this period, Southerners had targeted individual blacks through lynchings and other forms of violence in their campaign of terror. Now the NAACP was attacked by these groups. On Christmas night of 1951, the home of Harry T. MOORE, the NAACP's field secretary in Mims, Fla., was bombed. Moore died in the blast and his wife died a few days later from injuries she received that night. In 1955, NAACP officials the Rev. George W. Lee and Lamar Smith of Belzoni, Miss. were shot to death, and Gus Courts, president of the Belzoni NAACP branch, was shot, wounded, and later forced to abandon his store and flee to Chicago.

The NAACP charged that racial violence was a manifestation of the broader pattern of opposition to civil rights and demanded that the Justice Department protect blacks in the state and elsewhere in the South. The Justice Department, however, responded that it lacked authority to prosecute suspected murderers and civil rights violaters in what it claimed were state jurisdictions.

Despite the violence, the NAACP continued to grow. The number of branches in Mississippi increased from ten to twenty-one during 1955, while membership jumped 100 percent. The NAACP took several steps to aid local blacks. In December, the NAACP board of directors voted to deposit $20,000 in the Tri-State Bank in Memphis in order to increase the bank's reserves and enable it to make more loans to embattled blacks. The board called for an investigation of the operation in Mississippi of the federal "surplus commodities" program, which provided food to the destitute, to see if it discriminated against blacks. National NAACP officials also pushed for a meeting with the Mississippi Power and Light Company to inquire about cutoffs of power to businessmen active with the NAACP and overcharges for restoration.

In 1956, Louisiana led the South in a more deliberate assault on the NAACP when its attorney general demanded that the association's branches file their membership lists with the state. Because the NAACP refused to do so, the attorney general obtained an injunction barring the organization from operating in Louisiana. Alabama, Texas, and Georgia followed with similar punitive actions. In 1958, the Supreme Court (in *National Association for the Advancement of Colored People* v. *Alabama* ex rel. *Patterson*) overturned Alabama's fine of $100,000 against the NAACP because it refused to disclose the names and addresses of its members. But the Court then did not lift the injunction that barred the NAACP from operating in Alabama. Furthermore, the supreme courts in Arkansas and Florida held that the High Court's ruling did not affect those states. Not until June 1, 1964, after four appeals, would the U.S. Supreme Court rule unanimously that the NAACP had a right to register in Alabama as a foreign corporation. The ruling, in effect, overturned similar bans against the NAACP in other southern states and paved the way for it to resume operations in Alabama on October 29.

On January 14, 1963, for the Supreme Court in another significant case (*National Association for the Advancement of Colored People* v. *Button*) also overturned Virginia's antibarratry law, which was enacted in 1956, prohibiting the NAACP from sponsoring, financing, or providing legal counsel in suits challenging the validity of the state's segregation and other anti-civil rights laws.

One consequence of the southern crusade against the NAACP following the *Brown* decision was the splitting off of the NAACP LEGAL DEFENSE AND EDUCATIONAL FUND, a process that began in 1956 and ended in 1961. The split was caused by threats from the Southerners to rescind the LDF's tax-exempt status, and by personal differences within the NAACP. The LDF made the battle in the courts for school desegregation its main project, while the parent NAACP continued its strategy of legal and political action in numerous forms. Robert Carter, who was on the LDF's staff, was chosen as the NAACP's general counsel and he began setting up a new legal department. Carter led the NAACP's battle against the state injunctions.

The South's response to desegregation made the NAACP intensify its call for President Eisenhower to enforce *Brown,* and to provide the leadership which it regarded as essential for defeating the South's steadfast resistance to the passage of civil rights laws in Congress. NAACP leaders argued that the President's prestige could overwhelm the Southerners' use of committee chairmanships and the filibuster rule in the Senate to bottle up civil rights legislation. Eisenhower, a state's rights advocate, nevertheless supported the NAACP's demand that there should be no discrimination in federally funded programs and in the armed forces; but he was opposed to federal action to enforce *Brown*.

In 1956, responding to the NAACP's demands, election-year domestic considerations, and international pressure, Eisenhower called for civil rights legislation in his State of the Union address. The administration's package became the basis of debate in the bill H.R. 627. Senate Majority Leader Lyndon Baines Johnson of Texas, who believed that passage of some civil rights legislation was inevitable, began maneuvering to shape a compromise on the bill that would blunt its strongest provisions and break the southern filibuster. The civil rights forces were therefore left with what was essentially a weak voting rights law. Still, the 1957 Civil Rights Act created a division of civil rights in the Justice Department and a bipartisan Civil Rights Commission. Furthermore, the Civil Rights Act of 1957, the first such bill passed by Congress in eighty-two years, broke the psychological barrier to civil rights measures, making it easier for future efforts to succeed.

The encouraging breakthrough of the passage of the Civil Rights Act was somewhat overshadowed that September by the Little Rock crisis, in which Governor Orval Faubus used the Arkansas National Guard to block implementation of a federal court desegregation order at Central High School. To uphold the Constitution and end rioting, President Eisenhower federalized the Arkansas National Guard and ordered 1,000 members of the 101st Airborne Division into Little Rock. His action enabled nine black children (the "Little Rock Nine") to attend the school.

The Civil Rights Movement

The NAACP launched its "Golden Anniversary" celebrations on February 12, 1959, with services at the Community Church of New York City. One of the most promising indications of the organization's future strength was the presence of 624 youths among the 2,000 delegates who packed the New York Coliseum during the annual convention, which concluded with a rally at the Polo Grounds. In December, the NAACP held its third annual Freedom Fund dinner in New York, where it honored Marian ANDERSON, the celebrated concert singer, and Gardner Cowles, publisher of *Look* magazine. The celebrations revealed the broad acceptance of the

NAACP as an institution. However, its mastery was to be challenged in the 1960s by a new generation of more militant activists.

The first sign of the tensions the NAACP would face came in 1955 and 1956, when blacks in Alabama, led by the Rev. Dr. Martin Luther King, Jr., organized the MONTGOMERY IMPROVEMENT ASSOCIATION to lead the boycott against segregated city buses (*see also* MONTGOMERY BUS BOYCOTT). Although the movement was sparked by NAACP legal victories against segregation and the principal leaders of the boycott were also local NAACP leaders, the strategy of nonviolent demonstrations that they adopted was a substantial departure from the association's well-defined legal and political program. Similarly, while NAACP lawyers successfully argued the U.S. Supreme Court case *Gayle* v. *Browder* (1956), which handed victory to the boycotters, the MIA displayed impatience with the NAACP's carefully structured programs and centralized direction.

Inspired by the tactics of nonviolent protest, NAACP Youth Council chapters in Wichita, Kans., and Oklahoma City further successfully tested a new confrontation strategy in 1958 by staging "sit-downs" at lunch counters to protest segregation. The protests led to the desegregation of 60 or more lunch counters. In 1959, the NAACP chapter at Washington University in St. Louis conducted SIT-INS to end segregation at local lunch counters. The same year, the NAACP hired former CORE activist James FARMER as program director, but he was unable to move the association toward support for mass demonstrations, and he returned to CORE as executive director after less than two years.

As important as the Youth Council demonstrations were, however, they did not capture national media attention because they were not conducted in the deep South. On February 1, 1960, four students from North Carolina Agricultural and Technical College sat at a segregated store lunch counter in Greensboro and refused to leave until they were served. Two of the students, Ezell Blair and Joseph McNeil, were former officers of the NAACP's college chapter. The NAACP was heavily involved—the sit-in was conducted in consultation with Dr. George Simpkins, president of the Greensboro NAACP branch, and Ralph Jones, president of the branch's executive committee. The Greensboro actions set the stage for the sit-in movement, which spread like brush fire through the south.

The NAACP declared that it was proud that many of its youth members, from Virginia to Texas, were participating in the sit-ins. NAACP branch officials, notably Mississippi field secretary Medgar EVERS, coordinated protest campaigns. Nevertheless, the students' confrontations with Jim Crow was an expres-

sion of impatience with the NAACP's carefully executed legal and political programs. There was a dramatic clash of strategies, with the NAACP adhering firmly to its philosophy of change through court action and legislation, while King and the students marched under the banner of nonviolent direct action and local change. (The problems of strategy and organizational discipline merged as early as 1959, when Roy Wilkins suspended Robert WILLIAMS, president of the NAACP's Monroe, N.C., branch, for advocating that the NAACP meet "violence with violence.") Despite the ideological clash and the intense competition for financial contributions, media attention, and historical recognition, the young activists' strategy complemented the NAACP's. The NAACP provided large sums for bail money and legal support for the demonstrators and joined more militant movement groups in local alliances, such as the COUNCIL OF FEDERATED ORGANIZATIONS (COFO), which sponsored voter registration and other activities in Mississippi.

Despite the media attention that the demonstrations in the South drew, by 1962 the NAACP's 388,347 members in 46 states and the District of Columbia helped it to remain the leader in civil rights. That growth was especially significant, given that repeated court injunctions, state administrative regulations, punitive legislation, and other intimidating actions prevented many people from working with the NAACP in the South. The restrictions on the NAACP opened a window of opportunity for action by groups such as the SOUTHERN CHRISTIAN LEADERSHIP CONFERENCE (SCLC) and the Student Nonviolent Coordinating Committee (SNCC; organized with the aid of NAACP veteran Ella BAKER), as well as NAACP spinoffs such as the ALABAMA CHRISTIAN MOVEMENT FOR HUMAN RIGHTS.

Meanwhile, the NAACP's board was undergoing a change. Robert C. WEAVER, an economist and national housing expert, was elected chairman in 1960. Weaver resigned in 1961 when President John F. Kennedy appointed him administrator of the Federal Housing and Home Financing Administration. He was succeeded by Bishop Stephen Gil Spottswood of the African Methodist Episcopal Zion church.

The NAACP's most outstanding contribution to the civil rights movement continued to be its legal and lobbying efforts. In 1958, the NAACP forced the University of Florida to desegregate. A similar lawsuit was pending against the University of Georgia when it desegregated in 1961. In 1962, the NAACP led the battle to desegregate the University of Mississippi. The effort was directed by Constance Baker MOTLEY, of the LDF staff. Nevertheless, the fact that the parent NAACP featured the struggle in its 1962 annual report showed the extent to which the battle to enroll James H. MEREDITH in the university was also its own. After Mississippi governor Ross Barnett defied a federal court order, President Kennedy was forced to send in federal troops to quell a riot and assure Meredith's admittance.

The NAACP used the President's pleas for compliance, as well as the South's brutal opposition to the nonviolent demonstrations, to reinforce its struggle in Washington for passage of a meaningful civil rights law. Following the breakthrough in 1957, the NAACP had gotten Congress to pass the 1960 Civil Rights Act. That, however, was only a weak voting rights amendment to the 1957 act. Kennedy, insisting that comprehensive civil rights legislation would not pass, refused to send any to Congress. In February 1963, Kennedy submitted a weak civil rights bill. Mobilizing a historic coalition through the LCCR, the NAACP began an all-out struggle for passage of the bill as well as the strengthening of its provisions. NAACP pickets in Lawrence, Kans., New York City, Newark, and Philadelphia helped highlight the struggle for such provisions as a national fair employment practice law.

Events in 1963 reshaped the civil rights bill and the struggle. The demonstrations in Birmingham that King led during the spring provoked national outrage. On June 11th, in response to the demonstrations, President Kennedy delivered a televised civil rights address. The following night, Medgar Evers was assassinated in Jackson, Miss. On June 19, the day Evers was buried at Arlington Cemetery, Kennedy sent Congress a revised civil rights bill that was much stronger than the one he had submitted in February.

The climactic event of 1963 was the March On Washington for Jobs and Freedom (MOW). A. Philip Randolph had initiated the call for a march in January. The NAACP, nevertheless, led in organizing it and saw to it that the march, held on August 28 at the Lincoln Memorial, broadened its focus to include the legislative struggle. From a strategic point of view, Clarence Mitchell and the NAACP Washington bureau regarded the legislative conference it held with NAACP branch leaders earlier in August as more meaningful to the struggle in Congress than the MOW had been. Both, nevertheless, served the intended purpose.

Following the assassination of President Kennedy in November 1963, Lyndon Johnson vowed to ensure passage of his predecessor's civil rights bill and provided the leadership that the NAACP had demanded from the executive branch. In the final, crucial phase of the struggle in the Senate, Johnson orchestrated the coordinated leadership of Majority Leader Sen. Mike Mansfield (D-Mont.) and Minority Leader Sen. Everett Dirksen (R-Ill.) Debate on

the 1964 civil rights bill, H.R. 7152, began in earnest on March 10 and lasted until June 10, when the civil rights forces were finally able to break the filibuster.

The Civil Rights Act of 1964 was an immense victory for the NAACP. Following its passage, the NAACP began work on legislation to protect the right to vote. Following the Selma-to-Montgomery march, led by King, to protest the continuing disfranchisement of blacks in the South, the national climate was favorable to such a bill, and the NAACP was again left to direct the struggle in Congress for passage of the VOTING RIGHTS ACT OF 1965. This struggle was much less dramatic than that of 1964, perhaps because many expected its passage. Even so, as in 1957, the NAACP was hard-pressed to ward off attempts to weaken the bill. Its success in this battle was evident by the strong law that Congress passed.

Following passage of the civil rights laws, the NAACP switched its attention to enforcement, particularly in the areas of public school desegregation, employment, and housing. It also sought and won passage of strengthening provisions, such as amendments to the equal employment opportunity title of the 1964 Civil Rights Act. It won the first extension of the 1965 Voting Rights Act in 1970 with a provision extending protection for the right to vote, as well as subsequent ones. The programs remained centered in large part on the activities of the branches and its labor, education, and housing departments.

Despite the NAACP's crucial contribution to legislation which ended state-sponsored racial discrimination, the organization, with its interracial structure and integrationist philosophy, was scorned by increasing numbers of young blacks during the late 1960s as old-fashioned and overly cautious. The cycle of urban racial violence during the 1960s displayed the limits of the NAACP's program in appealing to frustrated urban blacks. President Johnson appointed Roy Wilkins a member of the National Advisory Commission on Civil Disorders, and the commission's well-known 1968 report reflected fully the NAACP's concerns.

Despite the radical criticism of the NAACP's program, the vitality of the organization's legal strategy was manifest by its success in passing legislation despite the embittered climate for black rights. While the NAACP shared credit with the other civil rights organizations for passage of the 1964 Civil Rights Act and the Voting Rights Act, there can be no doubt about its central role in 1968, when the Fair Housing Act was passed. Fearing the failure of a legislative struggle for fair housing legislation, many black leaders asked President Johnson to issue instead a comprehensive executive order barring discrimination in government-sponsored housing programs and federally insured mortgages. Johnson, however, did not want to deal with the problem piecemeal, and the NAACP supported him. The wisdom of that decision was evident on April 11, when President Johnson signed the 1968 Fair Housing Act, although its final version was somewhat weaker than the NAACP had originally intended. The final days of this struggle were overshadowed by the assassination of Dr. King in Memphis on April 4. The following day, at a meeting of civil rights leaders at the White House, the NAACP agreed to a suggestion that Congress be urged to pass the fair housing bill as a tribute to the slain leader.

During the late 1960s and early '70s, the NAACP faced new and sometimes more difficult challenges than in the past. These problems now resulted from systemic or endemic discrimination, which were more difficult to identify than state-imposed segregation and required the development of new strategies to correct. One of the organization's most important functions became the designing and implementing of affirmative action and minority hiring programs with government and private business. This struggle was led by Nathaniel R. Jones, who replaced Robert Carter as the NAACP's general counsel in 1969 (Jones served in this position for ten years, before leaving to become a judge on the United States Court of Appeals, Second Circuit, in Cincinnati. The NAACP brought suits or sent *amicus curiae* briefs in many notable affirmative action cases during the 1960s and '70s. For example, in 1969 the NAACP brought *Head* v. *Timken Roller Bearing Co., of Columbus, Ohio,* a landmark antidiscrimination lawsuit. In 1976, it won a consent decree, with a settlement by which twenty-five black workers were awarded back pay and won expanded promotional opportunities into previously all-white craft jobs. As a result of another lawsuit, filed against the Indiana State Police Department, twenty black troopers were hired, bringing the number on the thousand-man force to twenty-three.

Another aspect of the NAACP's legal struggle was the campaign against the death penalty. This struggle was led primarily by the NAACP Legal Defense and Educational Fund, which monitored death penalty cases and compiled statistics demonstrating racial disproportions in death penalty sentencing outcomes. As a result, in *Furman* v. *Georgi* (1972), the U.S. Supreme Court temporarily struck down the death penalty.

Among the NAACP's other achievements was a continuation of the thirty-eight-year-old struggle to defeat unfavorable nominees to the Supreme Court. The NAACP scored a double victory against the nomination in 1969 of Judge Clement F. Haynsworth of South Carolina and in 1970 of Judge G. Harrold Carswell of Florida as Supreme Court justices. The

NAACP opposed them because of their records on racial issues. The NAACP would continue to be influential in the confirmation process—for example, in 1987 the organization led the successful opposition to the Supreme Court appointment of Robert Bork and in 1990 helped defeat the confirmation of William Lucas, an African-American conservative, as assistant attorney for civil rights.

Still another focus of NAACP efforts was its ongoing campaign against media stereotypes. NAACP pressure had succeeded in removing AMOS 'N' ANDY from network first-run television in the early 1950s; in the 1960s, NAACP pressure was partly responsible for the creation of the TV series *Julia,* the first series with a positive African-American leading character. In the 1980s, the NAACP organized protests of Steven Spielberg's film *The Color Purple* owing to its white director and negative portrayal of black men.

The Search for New Direction

By the mid-1970s, the NAACP once again was forced into a period of transition. Henry Lee MOON retired in 1974. In 1976 Roy Wilkins retired as NAACP executive director. He had devoted forty-five years to the struggle and fulfilled most of his goals. In 1978 Clarence Mitchell also retired. Meanwhile, as a sign of the growing influence of women in the organization and the civil rights movement, in 1975 Margaret Bush Wilson, a St. Louis lawyer, was elected to chair the NAACP board of directors. Twenty years later, Myrlie Evers, the widow of Medgar Evers, was elected as its chair, and Hazel Dukes was named president of the powerful New York state chapter.

Along with the problems connected with the change in administration, the NAACP faced grave financial problems and some opposition to its program among blacks, who continued to criticize the NAACP as irrelevant to black needs. This opposition was an important challenge facing Benjamin L. HOOKS, a minister, lawyer, and member of the Federal Communications Commission, when he became executive director of the association in January 1977. Hooks assumed command of the NAACP at a time when it was not only struggling to devise an effective strategy for new civil rights challenges but battling for its very existence.

In 1976, two adverse judgments in lawsuits against the NAACP in Mississippi had presented it with the worst crisis in its lifetime: A court awarded Robert Moody, a state highway patrolman, $250,000 as a result of a lawsuit charging libel and slander that he had filed against the NAACP. Local NAACP officials and its state field director had charged Moody with police brutality because he had allegedly beaten a black man while arresting him on a reckless driving charge. To protect its assets, the NAACP had to borrow money to post the required $262,000 bond, though it eventually won reversal of the judgment in appeals.

Then, the Hinds County chancery court in Jackson, Miss., handed down a $1.25 million judgment against the NAACP as a result of a lawsuit that local businessmen had filed against the organization following a boycott of their stores. Under Mississippi law, in order to forestall the seizure of its assets pending an appeal, the NAACP had to post a cash bond amounting to 125 percent of the judgment, which was $1,563,374. The U.S. Supreme Court reversed the judgment in 1982. However, the experience was sobering.

The NAACP was disconcerted by the Supreme Court ruling in *Regents of the University of California v. Bakke* in 1978. The Court ruled five to four that Title VI of the 1964 Civil Rights Act barred a university medical school's special admissions program for blacks and ordered a white applicant's admission. Although another bare majority ruled that race was a constitutionally valid criterion for admission programs, the Court had increased the difficulty of developing specific programs to meet constitutional tests.

The election of Ronald Reagan as president in 1980, at a time when the NAACP was still groping for effective programs to meet new challenges, was an even more ominous development. The Reagan administration all but destroyed the effectiveness of the U.S. Civil Rights Commission, the Civil Rights Division of the Justice Department, and the Equal Employment Commission. In 1984, Benjamin Hooks led a 125,000-person March on Washington to protest the "legal lynching" of civil rights by the Reagan administration.

Questions concerning Hooks's leadership gained national attention in 1983 when Board Chair Margaret Wilson unilaterally suspended him. Outraged that Wilson had reprimanded Hooks without its approval, the board replaced her with Kelly Alexander, Sr., a North Carolina mortician. Following Alexander's death in 1986, the board elected Dr. William F. Gibson, a South Carolina dentist, as chairman. In order to oust Gibson, who was bitterly criticized for his leadership of the NAACP, Myrlie Evers led one of the fiercest internal battles in the organization's history.

Despite those setbacks, Hooks led the NAACP in winning several promising agreements from corporations, such as $1 billion from the American Gas Association, to provide jobs and other economic opportunities for blacks under a fair share program he inaugurated. In 1986, Hooks relocated the NAACP's national headquarters to Baltimore. Among his other accomplishments was the ACT-SO (Afro-Academic Cultural Technological Scientific Olympics) program he created to promote academic experience among minority youth through local, regional, and national competition. His goal was to seek proficiency in all academic areas, but with a special emphasis in the arts and humanities and the applied, technical, and social sciences. Hooks also continued the NAACP's political action programs with a special emphasis on voter registration.

In April 1993, Hooks retired as NAACP executive director. The board of directors had considerable difficulty deciding on a successor. Candidates included the Rev. Jesse Jackson. The board finally selected the Reverend Benjamin F. CHAVIS, Jr., an official of the United Church of Christ in Cleveland, who had once served more than four years in prison after being wrongly convicted on charges of conspiracy and arson for setting fire to a grocery store in Wilmington, N.C., in 1972. Chavis, much younger than his predecessor, was chosen in an attempt to revitalize the NAACP by attracting new sources of funding and reaching out to young African Americans. Chavis also called for the NAACP to expand its efforts to serve other minority interests.

Chavis's short tenure proved extremely controversial. In accord with his policy of attracting young African Americans, he shifted NAACP policy in a nationalistic direction and embraced black separatists, whom the NAACP had previously denounced. Chavis succeeded in increasing youth interest in the NAACP and was praised for his meetings with gang leaders, but he was widely criticized for inviting black radicals such as NATION OF ISLAM chair Louis FARRAKHAN to a black leadership conference, and for refusing to disassociate himself from the Nation's anti-Semitic policies. The NAACP's membership dropped significantly as a result.

Chavis also met with opposition to his administrative policies. NAACP board members were angered by his unauthorized policy statements, such as his approval of the North American Free Trade Agreement. Furthermore, Chavis was blamed for running up the organization's deficit, already swelled by declining memberships, to $1.2 million through staff salary increases. When in the summer of 1994 it was disclosed that Chavis had used organization money in an out-of-court settlement of a sexual harassment suit filed by a female staffer, there began to be calls for his resignation. On August 20, 1994, in a meeting of the board of directors, Chavis was removed as executive director.

The schism over Chavis's policies provided a forum for fundamental disagreements between blacks over the role of civil rights organizations. With full legal equality substantially achieved, the NAACP continued to face questions regarding the best use of its leadership and the appropriate strategy to employ in attacking the problems of African Americans.

REFERENCES

ARCHER, LEONARD COURTNEY. *Black Images in the American Theatre: NAACP Protest Campaigns—Stage, Screen, Radio & Television.* Brooklyn, N.Y., 1973.

CORTNER, RICHARD C. *A Mob Intent on Death: The NAACP and the Arkansas Riot Cases.* Middletown, Conn., 1988.

DALFIUME, RICHARD M. "The Forgotten Years of the Negro Revolution," *Journal of American History* 55 (June 1968): 105–106.

DOWNEY, DENNIS, and RAYMOND M. HYSTER. *No Crooked Death: Coatesville, Pennsylvania, and the Lynching of Zachariah Walker.* Urbana, Ill., 1991.

FINCH, MINNIE. *The NAACP, Its Fight for Justice.* Metuchen, N.J., 1981.

FOX, STEPHEN R. *The Guardian of Boston: William Monroe Trotter.* New York, 1970.

GOINGS, KENNETH W. *The NAACP Comes of Age: The Defeat of Judge John J. Parker.* Bloomington, Ind., 1990.

GREENBERG, JACK. *Crusaders in the Courts: How a Dedicated Bunch of Lawyers Fought For the Civil Rights Revolution.* New York, 1994.

HARLAN, LOUIS R. *Booker T. Washington: The Wizard of Tuskegee, 1901–1915.* New York, 1983.

HORNE, GERALD. *Black and Red: W. E. B. Du Bois and the Afro-American Response to the Cold War.* Albany, N.Y., 1986.

HUGHES, LANGSTON. *Fight for Freedom: The Story of the NAACP.* New York, 1962.

KELLOGG, CHARLES FLINT. *NAACP: A History of the National Association for the Advancement of Colored People,* vol. 1: *1909–1920.* Baltimore, 1967.

KELLOGG, PETER J. "Civil Rights Consciousness in the 1940s." *The Historian* 42, no. 1 (November 1979): 18–41.

KLUGER, RICHARD. *Simple Justice.* New York, 1976.

LAWRENCE, CHARLES RADFORD. *Negro Organizations in Crisis: Depression, New Deal, World War II.* Ph.D. diss. Columbia University, 1953.

LEWIS, DAVID LEVERING. *W. E. B. Du Bois: Biography of a Race, 1868–1919.* New York, 1993.

MCNEIL, GENNA RAE. *Groundwork, Charles Hamilton Houston and the Struggle for Civil Rights.* Philadelphia, 1983.

MCPHERSON, JAMES. *The Abolitionist Legacy.* Princeton, N.J., 1975.

MUSE, EDWARD B. *Paying For Freedom: History of the NAACP and the Life Membership Program, 1909–1987.* Baltimore, 1987.

NATIONAL NEGRO CONFERENCE. *Proceedings of the National Negro Conference.* New York, 1909.

OVINGTON, MARY WHITE. "How the National Association for the Advancement of Colored People Began." *The Crisis* 8 (August 1914): 184–188.

———. *The Walls Came Tumbling Down. 1947.* Reprint. New York, 1970.

RECORD, WILSON. *Race and Radicalism: The NAACP and the Communist Party in Conflict.* Ithaca, N.Y., 1964.

ROSS, D. JOYCE. *J. E. Spingarn and the Rise of the NAACP.* New York, 1972.

ROWAN, CARL. *Dream Makers, Dream Breakers: The World of Justice Thurgood Marshall.* Boston, 1992.

RUDWICK, ELLIOTT, and AUGUST MEIER. "The Rise of the Black Secretariat in the NAACP, 1909–1935." In *Along the Colored Line: Explorations in the Black Experience.* Urbana, Ill., 1976.

SITKOFF, HARVARD. *A New Deal for Blacks, The Emergence of Civil Rights as a National Issue: The Depression Decade.* New York, 1978.

ST. JAMES, WARREN D. *NAACP: Triumphs of a Pressure Group, 1909–1980.* Smithtown, N.Y., 1980.

TILLMAN, JR., NATHANIEL PATRICK. *Walter Francis White: A Study in Interest Group Leadership.* Ph.D. diss. University of Wisconsin, 1961.

TUSHNET, MARK. *The NAACP's Legal Strategy Against Segregation, 1925–1950.* New York, 1987.

VOSE, CLEMENT E. *Caucasians Only: The Supreme Court, the NAACP, and the Restrictive Covenant Cases.* Berkeley, Calif., 1959.

WATSON, DENTON L. *Lion in the Lobby, Clarence Mitchell, Jr.'s Struggle for the Passage of Civil Rights Laws.* New York, 1990.

WHITE, WALTER. *A Man Called White.* Bloomington, Ind., 1948.

WILKINS, ROY. "The Negro Wants Full Equality." In Rayford W. Logan, ed. *What the Negro Wants.* Chapel Hill, N.C., 1944.

WILKINS, ROY, with Tom Matthews. *Standing Fast, the Autobiography of Roy Wilkins.* New York, 1982.

WOLTERS, RAYMOND. *Negroes in the Great Depression.* Westport, Conn., 1970.

ZANGRANDO, ROBERT L. *The NAACP Crusade Against Lynching, 1909–1950.* Philadelphia, 1960.

DENTON L. WATSON

National Association of Colored Women.

Predating the NATIONAL ASSOCIATION FOR THE ADVANCEMENT OF COLORED PEOPLE and the NATIONAL URBAN LEAGUE, the National Association of Colored Women (NACW) was the first national black organization in the United States and has proved to be one of the longest lasting. Founded in 1896, NACW had roots that lay in decades of local political activity by African-American women. This often took the form of women's clubs, and was the result of heightened racism, a need for social services within the black community, and the exclusionary policies of many white-run organizations.

The local clubs and reform efforts of black women in churches, mutual aid societies, and literary clubs were part of a larger reform effort during the late nineteenth century. Little state assistance was available for the needy. Clubwomen provided aid to the aged, young, and other dependents, strengthened racial solidarity, and developed leadership. These local efforts, which were usually short-lived and unconnected, became the basis of a national coalition.

A series of events facilitated the emergence of the National Association of Colored Women. In 1895, a national convention of black women was called to respond to a racist letter sent by James Jacks, a southern journalist, to a British reformer. Jacks wrote that blacks lacked morality and that black women were prostitutes, natural liars, and thieves. Because of the local clubs and women's magazines that were in existence, in particular *The Woman's Era,* a national black women's journal, African-American women were able to respond quickly and effectively to the slanderous letter.

The 1895 convention led to the formation of the National Federation of Afro-American Women. Shortly thereafter, the National League of Colored Women broke from the Federation because of differences about how to deal with segregation at the Atlanta Exposition. But because of concerns about the lack of unity, the two organizations merged in 1896 to form the National Association of Colored Women. Committed to social reform and racial betterment, the NACW achieved its greatest growth from the 1890s to the 1920s. Shortly after it was founded, the NACW had 5,000 members. Twenty years later, it had 50,000 members in 28 federations and over 1,000 clubs. By 1924, it had reached 100,000 members.

The NACW was involved in a variety of projects to address problems of health, housing, education, and working conditions, and to create a social space for black women. It was the primary organization through which African-American women channeled their reform efforts. Embodied in their slogan "Lifting as we Climb" was a commitment not only to improve their own situation, but to aid the less fortunate. They built schools, ran orphanages, founded homes for the aged, set up kindergarten programs, and formed agencies in New York and Philadelphia to help female migrants from the South find jobs and affordable housing. Black women who formed the backbone of the NACW were primarily middle-class and often professional women involved in teaching or other social service occupations. Their local activities were the seeds for multiservice centers that combined the many goals of the NACW reform efforts. They provided material assistance through day care and health services and job training to help women secure jobs.

While the movement comprised many local groups with differing philosophies, the national agenda was dominated by women less interested in confrontation than in accommodation. In the early years, the NACW journal, *National Notes,* was printed at Tuskegee Institute under the direction of Margaret Murray WASHINGTON. The first president of the NACW, Mary Church TERRELL, was also a supporter of Booker T. Washington and accommodationist policies. At the request of organizers in Chicago, Terrell chose not to invite outspoken anti-accommodationist Ida B. WELLS-BARNETT to the first NACW meeting.

The political orientation of women in the NACW was also evident in the programs and policies of the organization. Black clubwomen adhered to middle-class values of self-improvement and moral purity. As Terrell expressed in 1902, "Self-preservation demands that [black women] go among the lowly, illiterate, and even vicious, to whom they are bound by ties of race and sex . . . to reclaim them." They taught thrift through penny-saving societies and supported the temperance movement. Some of their old-age homes accepted only the respectable poor and elderly, not those who were indigent because of what the NACW considered laziness or immorality. They conducted classes in domestic service and child rearing to teach the poor proper health and hygiene, how to maintain a household, and techniques to raise their children. They maintained that women could play an important role in reforming society by using their virtuous qualities and superior moral sensibilities to create a safe and comfortable home. Women in the NACW wanted to instill racial pride in African Americans and counter negative images of black women. They believed their commitment to racial solidarity and helping the poorest African Americans would improve the position of the entire race.

Although immersed in social reform and racial uplift efforts, the NACW also took strong stands against the roots of racial injustice. In the early years, black clubwomen opposed segregation and the brutal convict-lease system. The organization's publication, *National Notes,* became a tool to discuss ideas and disseminate information. By 1910, they had expanded their goals to include the women's suffrage amendment and the federal antilynching bill and had also come to believe that more than simply exposure of the brutalities that African Americans faced was necessary to effect change. After the RED SUMMER of 1919, the NACW, under the leadership of Mary TALBERT, joined the crusade against lynching and mobilized black women, raised money, and educated the public. While never a militant organization, the NACW made verbal protests against racial injustice and advocated boycotts of segregated facilities. It was successful in creating a national political voice for African-American women. As the organization expanded its agenda, its overwhelming influence by northeastern urban women was tempered by greater involvement of women from the South.

During the GREAT DEPRESSION, the stature and importance of the NACW began to decline, and for a time, the organization met only periodically. Many of the welfare and social services NACW provided were available through better-funded local, state, and private agencies created expressly for this purpose. In addition, obvious dire need for direct material assistance during the 1930s made the self-help and moral uplift ideology of the NACW somewhat anachronistic. These issues, coupled with a declining membership and financial insecurity, made the NACW a less effective organization.

In 1935, Mary McLeod BETHUNE, who served as president of NACW from 1924 to 1928, formed the NATIONAL COUNCIL OF NEGRO WOMEN, which acted as an umbrella for black women's organizations. This led to a redefinition of NACW, which was no longer the only national black women's organization. In 1957, NACW changed its name to the National Association of Colored Women's Clubs (NACWC). In the early 1990s the NACWC had close to 40,000 members in 1,500 local clubs. Today it is primarily involved in educational, social service, and fundraising activities. The NACWC sponsors forums on HIV infection, provides college scholarships for young black women, and raises money for children's hospitals. Despite the ebbs and flows in its work, the NACWC has admirably endured a century of service and commitment to African-American women.

REFERENCES

GIDDINGS, PAULA. *When and Where I Enter: The Impact of Black Women on Race and Sex in America.* New York, 1984.

SALEM, DOROTHY. *To Better Our World: Black Women in Organized Reform, 1890–1920.* New York, 1990.

WESLEY, CHARLES H. *The History of the National Association of Colored Women's Clubs: A Legacy of Service.* Washington, D.C., 1984.

PAM NADASEN

National Association of Negro Musicians.

The National Association of Negro Musicians (NANM) was established in 1919 at Chicago. Various nationally recognized musicians were associated with its founding, including composers Clarence Cameron WHITE and R. Nathaniel DETT, music critic

Nora D. Holt, and public-school music teacher Henry L. Grant. A committee was formed by Harriet G. MARSHALL of Washington, D.C., as early as 1906 for the purpose of establishing such a national organization. Later, White and Dett both made efforts to initiate a national meeting in 1916 and 1918, respectively, and finally in 1919 Holt called a meeting at her home at which plans were solidified for the NANM. Grant called together a preliminary meeting designated as the Initial Conference of Negro Musicians and Artists, held in May 1919 in Washington, D.C. In July of the same year, the first NANM meeting was held in Chicago and the first officers installed: Henry L. Grant (Washington, D.C.), president; Nora D. Holt (Chicago), vice president; Alice Carter Simmons (Tuskegee, Ala.), secretary; Fred ("Deacon") Johnson (New York), treasurer.

The purpose as stated in general terms by Nora D. Holt (1974, pp. 234–235) was that of "furthering and coordinating the musical forces of the Negro race for the promotion of economic, educational, and fraternal betterment." In specific terms the association sponsored young music students in recital, gave scholarships, attempted to gather information regarding the employment status of the black music teacher, encouraged performance of works by black composers, promoted concerts by its members, and provided opportunity for musicians to meet and discuss issues of interest. The membership was composed mainly of public-school music teachers and supervisors, private studio teachers, representatives from conservatories, concert artists, and students. Activities of the branches were covered by the black press and, in the first year, were reported on a monthly basis in Nora Holt's journal *Music and Poetry*.

At the second annual convention in 1920, held in New York and attended by 200 delegates, one of the features was a conference on Negro folk music, a theme that was continued as an emphasis of the organization. Conventions generally provided concerts, student recitals, lectures, workshops, and clinics. Musical events of unusual interest sometimes took place, such as the presentation of *Aida* by the National Negro Opera Company in 1941 at Pittsburgh in a fully staged production prior to the official opening of the company, and the presentation of Scott JOPLIN's opera *Treemonisha* in 1979 at St. Louis under the direction of Kenneth Billups, choral director and college and public-school music teacher.

The scholarship program was directed not only toward young musicians of promise, such as Marian ANDERSON, who was the first scholarship recipient (1921), but also, in later years, toward outstanding established musicians, such as Harriet Gibbs Marshall (founder of the Washington Conservatory of Music), R. Augustus Lawson (pianist), and Lulu V. Childers (founder of the School of Music at Howard University), all of whom were honored in 1939.

REFERENCES

ALLEN, CLARENCE G. "Negro Musicians Urge Against Perversion of Their Songs, at Second Convention." *Musical America* (August 7, 1920): 4.

HOLT, NORA. "The Chronological History of the NANM," *Music and Poetry* (July 1921); reprint ed. in *Black Perspective in Music* 2, no. 1 (Fall 1974): 234–235.

DORIS EVANS MCGINTY

National Bankers Association.

The National Bankers Association (NBA) was created in 1927 in response to discriminatory practices of the American Bankers Association (ABA), which would not accept African Americans into membership. In 1926, R. R. Wright of Citizens Bank and Trust Company of Philadelphia and C. C. Spaulding of Mechanics and Farmers Bank of Durham, N.C., met with representatives of nineteen black-owned and -operated banks and savings-and-loan institutions. The group met at Pythias Hall in Philadelphia and discussed the need to form an organization to serve the common needs of black bankers.

In 1927 the group met in Durham to form the National Negro Bankers Association. The principal purposes of the NBA were to develop programs designed to strengthen the existing member banks, increase their number, and increase their economic impact on their communities. Over the years, the NBA has become more aligned with the "mainstream" banking system. Beginning in the 1960s, NBA member banks were encouraged to become ABA members as well.

During this period, the NBA also began to consult with various local, state, and federal officials. They sought financial assistance because of their relatively weak position in the banking world, and in 1968, the NBA was awarded a grant from the Economic Development Administration. Despite its financial difficulties, the NBA has continued to survive and to maintain its commitment to aid in the expansion of capital and management resources in the African-American community.

See also BANKS AND BANKING.

REFERENCE

"The National Bankers Association: What's It All About?" *Black Business Digest* 2, no. 2 (December 1971): 31–32.

SASHA THOMAS

National Baptist Convention, U.S.A.

The National Baptist Convention, U.S.A., Inc., founded on September 24, 1895, constitutes the largest body of organized African-American Christians in the world. With over 7.5 million members, this influential body's roots go deep into the early religious and cooperative efforts of free blacks and slaves in antebellum America.

As early as 1834, African Americans in Ohio organized the Providence Baptist Association to strengthen the work of local Baptist churches (*see* BAPTISTS). The formation of this association established a trend for other local churches, resulting in the organization of other associations, state conventions, regional conventions, and national bodies. The first significant trend toward a national body was the organization in 1894 of the Tripartite Union, consisting of the New England Baptist Foreign Missionary Convention, the African Foreign Mission Convention, and the Foreign Mission Convention of America. Although this Tripartite Union attempt failed by 1895, the spirit of national cooperation eventually prevailed.

In 1895, Revs. S. E. GRIGGS, L. M. Luke, and A. W. Pegues, former leaders of the Tripartite Union movement, led another attempt at national unity among African-American Baptists. They successfully encouraged the Foreign Mission Convention, the National Baptist Educational Convention, and the American National Baptist Convention to merge into the National Baptist Convention, U.S.A.

The purpose of the newly formed national convention was multipartite. The former work of the National Baptist Educational Convention was increased through the new convention's aggressive involvement in the education of the race. Local churches were encouraged to increase their support of secondary schools and colleges throughout the southern region of the United States. Internationally, the National Baptist Convention, U.S.A., advanced foreign missionary projects in Africa, Central America, and the West Indies. Schools, churches, and medical institutions were expanded in various mission stations on these foreign fields. A large number of the leaders among Africans on the developing continent as well as Africans of the diaspora were trained by these institutions.

In order to facilitate practical operations in the National Baptist Convention, U.S.A., the leadership was careful to develop comprehensive plans for a viable structure. The basic strategy was to organize the work of the convention through specialized boards. The leadership organized a Foreign Mission Board, Home Mission Board, Educational Board, Baptist Young People's Union, and Publishing Board. These were designed to carry out the mandates of the convention as articulated by Rev. Elias Camp Morris, the organization's first president. The pattern of specialized boards was continued by the subsequent leadership of the convention, but proved problematic in practice.

Problem areas developed within two of the strongest boards, Foreign Mission and Publishing. By 1897 there was enough internal disturbance in the convention to threaten the unity of the denomination. When the annual session was convened at Ebenezer Baptist Church in Boston, a group of ministers of national prominence led a debate over several key emotion-laden issues: (1) the advisability of moving the Foreign Mission Board from Richmond to Louisville; (2) the use of American Baptist literature and cooperation with white Baptists in general; and (3) a greater emphasis on foreign missions as a primary policy of the convention. The leadership was not able to resolve the conflicts, especially the last. Consequently, several clergymen from Virginia and North Carolina who were in favor of stronger foreign missions issued a call to like-minded ministers to meet at Shiloh Baptist Church in Washington, D.C., on December 11, 1897, for the purpose of developing a new convention strategy. Out of this movement emerged the Lott Carey Baptist Home and Foreign Mission Convention, specializing in foreign missions.

The second problem area was the Publishing Board. The National Baptist Publishing Board, under the leadership of Revs. Henry Allen BOYD and C. H. Clark, was given the exclusive right to publish all church and Sunday-school literature for local Baptist churches. With a significant increase in its financial holdings, the National Baptist Publishing Board tended to act independently of the general leadership of the convention. This resulted in a split within the leadership and the formation of the National Baptist Convention of America in 1915.

The National Baptist Convention, U.S.A., Inc., emerged from these splits, however, as the majority convention among African-American Baptists. Its scheme of organizational structure through major boards remained intact. Morris, the national president, was careful to require responsibility and accountability from the specialized boards' leadership. This policy facilitated unity within the convention until the middle of the twentieth century.

In 1956, a serious debate erupted over the question of tenure. Rev. Joseph H. Jackson, president of the convention, had risen to a position of such power and prestige that a majority of the convention's leaders and delegates desired the continuation of his leadership beyond the tenure limits of the constitution. Tensions increased, resulting in a strong challenge to Jackson's leadership by a group favoring the election of Rev. Gardner C. Taylor of Brooklyn to the presidency. The 1961 presidential election became a crisis that resulted in a civil court battle between Jackson and "the Taylor team." Jackson's position was confirmed by the court.

The Jackson victory did not calm the troubled waters, however. On September 11, 1961, a national call was issued for the organization of the PROGRESSIVE NATIONAL BAPTIST CONVENTION. The rationale for creating a new convention was a protest against Jackson's policy of "gradualism" in civil rights issues, as well as a demonstration of support for Taylor's election bid for the presidency. Moreover, the new convention rallied to give stronger support to the civil rights movement under the leadership of the Rev. Dr. Martin Luther KING, Jr.

The National Baptist Convention remained the largest convention of African-American Baptists. But the advance of the civil rights revolution and the growth in power and influence of Martin Luther King, Jr., seriously challenged the moral and racial leadership of the majority convention. This trend continued until King's assassination and the rise of Rev. T. J. Jemison to the presidency of the convention. The new president, a veteran civil rights leader, made efforts to restore the convention to its previous leadership role.

REFERENCES

FITTS, LEROY. *A History of Black Baptists*. Nashville, Tenn., 1985.

WASHINGTON, JAMES M. *Frustrated Fellowship: The Black Baptist Quest for Social Power*. Macon, Ga., 1986.

LEROY FITTS

National Black Evangelical Association.

Founded in 1963 as the National Negro Evangelical Association, the National Black Evangelical Association (NBEA) functions as an umbrella association of individuals, organizations, and churches. A theologically conservative organization, the NBEA is one of the same theological genus as the larger, modern, white American fundamentalist movement. This modern American fundamentalist movement had its beginning in the late nineteenth and early twentieth century with the fundamentalist-versus-modernist religious controversy. The National Association of Evangelicals (NAE), founded in 1942 as an outgrowth of this controversy, brought together evangelicals from a variety of theological positions, including fundamentalist, dispensational, Calvinist,

Reformed, covenantal, pentecostal, and charismatic. These all hold in common the belief in the historic "fundamentals" of the Protestant tradition: the Reformation and Arminian doctrine of complete reliability and final authority of the Bible in matters of faith and practice; the real, historical character of God's saving work recorded in Scripture; personal eternal salvation only through belief in Jesus Christ; evidence of a spiritually transformed life; and the importance of sharing this belief and experience with others through evangelism and mission works.

In the early twentieth century, a distinct group of Christians within the African-American community aligned themselves with the fundamentalist movement and developed separately from traditional African-American churches. Traditional African-American churches, some of whose history dated back to the seventeenth century, emphasized moral and social reform in the areas of personal piety, slavery, and discrimination. They generally saw themselves as "Bible believers." Black fundamentalists, on the other hand, placed more emphasis on conservative, propositional, and doctrinal aspects of faith. The black fundamentalist charged that African-American churches were one of two types: poor congregations, who were "otherworldly" and emotionally focused in worship; or middle-class congregations, who were theological liberals and embraced modern science. This history caused some strains between these two movements. Some black evangelicals characterized the historic black church as "apostate and un-Biblical," and some in mainline black churches labeled black evangelicals as doctrinaire and schismatic "fanatics." This history led to the presence of African Americans in white fundamentalist and evangelical Bible schools and seminaries in the late 1940s and 1950s. Black alumni from these institutions helped to develop the NBEA.

At the time of its founding, the NBEA did not view itself as racially separatist but as an association focused on developing African-American leadership to minister with clear evangelical emphasis to the black community. During this early stage, many black evangelicals were also frustrated with the white evangelical movement. This tension focused on what blacks perceived as white evangelicals' indifference to and lack of sympathy for the evangelistic needs of the African-American community. This frustration eventually led some black evangelicals to charge their white counterparts with a spiritual "benign neglect." Eventually the charge of neglect evolved into a stronger allegation of racism. From the beginning its social-action commission raised social issues within the NBEA, yet major social concerns were not in the forefront of its work. Instead the NBEA concentrated on strategies for effectively communicating its particular brand of evangelicalism within the African-American community.

Like all social movements, black evangelicalism has not always been unified in its efforts. The movement could not avoid confronting the CIVIL RIGHTS and Black Power movements and their attendant black theology movements of the late 1960s and early '70s (see THEOLOGY, BLACK). The challenges of these new movements, with their emphasis on social justice and self-determination, created anxiety, ambivalence, and dissension within the black evangelical movement. These rifts became evident in several of the annual NBEA conventions.

The CIVIL RIGHTS MOVEMENT forced black evangelicals, in several NBEA conferences between 1968 and 1970, to look at the issues of social justice and racial discrimination and their relationship to presenting the gospel. The conservatives in the movement felt that their first priority was the promulgation of personal salvation rather than attacking social injustice. If society was to be changed, it would be through the changing of human hearts rather than through altering the individual person's social condition. The activists within the black evangelical movement argued that social action and the verbal proclamation of the gospel were equal tasks in evangelical missions. The whole truth of the gospel could be received only when the social concerns of the individual were met.

The Black Power movement challenged the black evangelical movement with issues of self-determination. This was reflected in several NBEA conferences from 1970 through 1975. Activist black evangelicals, drawing from Black Power advocates, believed that white evangelicals were too paternalistic in their support and that blacks were too dependent upon whites. The activists argued that African Americans should develop institutions and support within their own communities. They were not completely opposed to white support, however. Whites could contribute to the cause, but without any conditions attached. The conservative wing countered that this stance smacked of divisiveness within the body of Christ. They argued for a more conciliatory role with their white evangelical counterparts, emphasizing Christian reconciliation. This debate forced the movement to look anew at its historical links to the black church as a source of strength and self-determination. These discussions led to another major debate within the black evangelical movement revolving around the role of black theology and African-American culture in the movement as interpretative tools.

Black theology as a movement and the challenge of African-American history and culture were the catalysts of a major debate within the movement. This rift surfaced in several of the NBEA conferences in the late 1970s. Some within the black evangelical movement, such as William Bentley and Columbus Salley, closely followed the writings of black theologians. They disagreed with some black theologians' liberal assumptions regarding biblical authority. Yet these activist black evangelicals agreed with black theologians' interpretative critique of both the liberal and conservative European and white American theologians' claim of universality and, therefore, repudiated the appropriateness and normativeness of white theology in all situations. To these black critics, all theology was culturally bound and, therefore, culturally specific. Theology, then, had to be culturally relevant, and this was especially so for the African-American community. The conservatives countered that what was at stake in the activists' critique of conservative white theology was the very essence of the theological foundation of this movement. They felt that the use of black theology, with its liberal theological foundation, compromised too much. It contradicted the very basis of their faith. The conservatives also feared that the activists placed too much emphasis on the importance of black culture at the expense of the gospel message.

These issues drove the NBEA to examine the historic role of the black church as an institution and its relationship to social issues. This was evidence in the 1990 convention in which the delegates discussed the viability of dropping the term *evangelical* because it conjured images of political conservatism, which, some felt, further alienated the movement from the historic African-American church.

The NBEA's numerical strength is unknown, but its leadership estimates its mailing list at 5,000, with a larger black-evangelical constituency of between 30,000 and 40,000. Its annual convention draws several hundred participants, and smaller numbers participate in the meetings sponsored by local chapters. The NBEA has been an arena in which the differing factions of the black evangelical movement have been able to dialog, to discuss disagreements, and to reach compromise. It has been a delicate balancing act over the years. It remains to be seen whether the movement, and especially the NBEA as an organization, can continue to hold its various camps under its umbrella and simultaneously continue to stretch the canvas to include and win favor with the historic black church community as well.

REFERENCES

BENTLEY WILLIAM H. "Bible Believers in the Black Community." In David F. Wells and John D. Woodbridge, eds., *The Evangelicals: What They Believe, Who They Are, Where They Are Changing*, New York, 1975, pp. 108–121.

————. *The National Black Evangelical Association: Bellwether of a Movement*. Chicago, 1988.

————. *The National Black Evangelical Association: Evolution of a Concept of Ministry*. Chicago, 1979.

MARSDEN, GEORGE, ed. *Evangelicalism and Modern America*. Grand Rapids, Mich., 1984.

PANNELL, WILLIAM. *My Friend the Enemy*. Waco, Tex., 1968.

————. "The Religious Heritage of Blacks." In David F. Wells and John D. Woodbridge, eds. *The Evangelicals: What They Believe, Who They Are, Where They Are Changing*. New York, 1975, pp. 96–107.

QUEBEDEAUX, RICHARD. *The Young Evangelicals: Revolution in Orthodoxy*. New York, 1974.

SALLEY, COLUMBUS and RONALD BEHM. *What Color Is Your God? Black Consciousness and the Christian Faith*. Rev. ed. Foreword by Rep. Walter Fauntroy. Downers Grove, Ill., 1981.

ALBERT G. MILLER

National Black Political Convention of 1972. *See* Gary Convention.

National Council of Negro Women.

The National Council of Negro Women (NCNW) has been among the most influential African-American women's organizations of the twentieth century, particularly under the guidance of its founder, Mary McLeod BETHUNE, and its later president Dorothy HEIGHT. Bethune seized on the idea of an umbrella organization to bring together the skills and experience of black women in a variety of organizations. This national council would provide leadership and guidance in order to make African-American women's voices heard in every arena of social and political life. When Bethune began to pursue this goal in 1929, she met with some resistance from the leadership of other national organizations, particularly the NATIONAL ASSOCIATION OF COLORED WOMEN. But she was successful in convincing the skeptics that a National Council of Negro Women would respect the achievements and strengths of other groups and streamline the cooperative operations of black women's organizations, rather than supersede existing groups.

The NCNW was founded in New York City on December 5, 1935, after five years of planning. The true signs of Bethune's diplomatic ability were the presence at the founding meeting of representatives of twenty-nine organizations and the election of such important figures as Mary Church TERRELL and Charlotte Hawkins BROWN to leadership positions. Bethune was elected president by a unanimous vote. The effectiveness of the council and its leadership was immediately apparent. One of its areas of greatest success was labor issues. With Bethune's influence in the federal government, the NCNW, in conjunction with other organizations, pressed for federal jobs for African Americans, and was one of the forces behind the founding of the FAIR EMPLOYMENT PRACTICES COMMITTEE. Under Bethune's leadership the NCNW also established an important journal, the *Aframerican Woman's Journal,* which in 1949 became *Women United.* The council expressed an interest in international affairs, supporting the founding of the United Nations. From its founding, the United Nations has had an NCNW official observer at its proceedings.

Bethune retired from the presidency of the NCNW in 1949 and was succeeded by Dorothy Boulding Ferebee, the grandniece of Josephine St. Pierre RUFFIN and former NCNW treasurer. During Ferebee's tenure, the council continued to press the issues with which it had always been concerned—civil rights, education, jobs, and health care, among others. However, the organization experienced a crisis as it moved beyond merely defining goals and issues toward providing more tangible services to its constituency. This issue carried over to the term of its third president, Vivian Carter Mason, elected in 1953. During her four years in office, Mason employed administrative skills to improve the operation of the national headquarters and to forge closer ties between the local and national councils. Under Mason, the NCNW continued to develop as a force in the struggle for civil rights. Just as Bethune led the organization to fight for the integration of the military, Mason fought for swift implementation of school desegregation.

In 1957, the NCNW elected Dorothy I. Height to be the organization's fourth president. Height came to her work at the council with experience on the national board of the YOUNG WOMEN'S CHRISTIAN ASSOCIATION, eight years as president of Delta Sigma Theta, and involvement in a host of organizations and institutions. Height set out to place the NCNW on firm financial ground through gaining tax-exempt status (accomplished in 1966) and through grants from foundations. She was successful in garnering support from the Ford Foundation and the U.S. Department of Health, Education, and Welfare to expand the scope of the NCNW's work.

Among Height's other major accomplishments as president was the construction of the Bethune Memorial Statue, unveiled in Lincoln Park, Washington, D.C., in 1974. The memorial pays tribute to the contributions of an extraordinary woman. The

NCNW continued its commitment to preserve the history of black women through the founding of the National Archives for Black Women's History. Although the council desired such an institution from its founding, the archives did not become a reality until 1979. This collection preserves the papers of the NCNW, the National Committee on Household Employment, and the National Association of Fashion and Accessory Designers. The personal papers of a number of women are also housed there. Through this collection and through conferences sponsored by the archives, the NCNW has become an important force in preserving the records and achievements of black women in the twentieth century.

The list of organizations affiliated with the National Council of Negro Women is long and varied, reflecting the council's commitment to building bridges to create a united voice for black women. Affiliated groups include ten national sororities, the National Association of Negro Business and Professional Women's Clubs, Inc., the Auxiliary of the National Medical Association, women's missionary societies of the National Baptist Convention and the African Methodist Episcopal Church, and Trade Union Women of African Heritage. The NCNW has also developed an international component to its work. In addition to maintaining a presence at the United Nations, it has worked with women in Africa (in Togo and Senegal, for example) and other areas of the diaspora, such as Cuba.

The NCNW has been successful in creating a national organization through which African-American women can address the issues facing them and their families. It has enabled black women from a variety of backgrounds to design and implement programs and develop themselves as community leaders. The longevity and effectiveness of the council are due to the willingness of its leadership to change and to shape programs and methods to the emerging needs of African-American communities.

See also FRATERNITIES AND SORORITIES.

REFERENCES

COLLIER-THOMAS, BETTYE. *N.C.N.W., 1935–1980.* Washington, D.C., 1981.
GIDDINGS, PAULA. *When and Where I Enter: The Impact of Black Women on Race and Sex in America.* New York, 1984.

JUDITH WEISENFELD

National Federation of Afro-American Women.

Established in 1895 in Boston, the National Federation of Afro-American Women (NFAAW), was one of the first organizations created to represent

African-American women on a national scale. Founded during the First National Conference of Colored Women of America, its mandate was to improve the image of black women by uplifting the race through middle-class domestic values. During its one year of existence, the federation included 104 delegates representing 54 women's clubs from 14 states.

Several events crystallized the need for black women's groups to join together as a national entity in the early 1890s. The Women's Pavilion at the Columbian Exposition (1893) denied the participation of black women's organizations. The incident galvanized black women's groups in Washington, New York, Boston, and Chicago, and showed them they could no longer afford to limit their activism to the local arena.

The final catalyst toward unification was a letter written by James Jacks, President of the Missouri Press Association, to Florence Balgarnie, secretary of England's Anti-Lynching Society, in which Jacks attacked black women, claiming they were immoral, sexually promiscuous, and likely to be liars and thieves. Balgarnie sent the letter to Joseph Ruffin, founder of Boston's Women's Era Club, and Ruffin had it published in their journal the WOMEN'S ERA. Women from all over the country met at the First National Conference of Colored Women of America in Boston (1895) to discuss the letter and other issues facing women, such as education, employment, and child rearing. While they stressed that white women could join their organization, they were less eager to admit lower-class blacks and centered their agenda around middle-class concerns.

At the close of the conference, the women voted to create a new, permanent national organization called the National Federation of Afro-American Women which would try to change the image of the black woman, raise the moral standard of the lower class, and cultivate black middle-class women's domestic skills.

The National Federation of Afro-American Women coexisted with another organization, the National League of Colored Women, but both groups became convinced that to be effective they needed to come together in one organization. In 1896, the National Association of Colored Women was organized in an attempt to overcome the factionalism which had limited black women's political effectiveness throughout the 1890s. The merger spelled the dissolution of the National Federation of Afro-American Women after one year of existence.

REFERENCES

HARLY, SHARON, and ROSALYN TERBORG-PENN, eds. *The Afro-American Woman: Struggles and Images.* Port Washington, N.Y., 1978.

SALEM, DOROTHY. "Foundations for Organized Reform." In *To Better Our World: Black Women in Organized Reform, 1890–1920*, Vol. 14 of *Black Women in U.S. History*, ed. Darlene Clark Hine. New York, 1990.

MARIAN AGUIAR

National Hospital Association. The National Hospital Association (NHA) was established in August 1923 by the National Medical Association at its annual meeting in St. Louis. The parent body founded this new auxiliary organization to coordinate and guide its efforts in African-American hospital reform. The NHA's specific goals included the standardization of black hospitals and of the curricula at black nurse-training schools, the establishment of additional black hospitals, and the provision of more internships for black physicians.

African-American medical leaders' concerns that the growing importance of hospital standardization and accreditation would lead to the elimination of black hospitals prompted their establishment of the NHA. They recognized that many black hospitals were inferior institutions that were ineligible for approval by certifying agencies. But these facilities were critical to the careers of African-American physicians and, in many locations, to the lives of black patients. The NHA sought to improve black hospitals by attempting to ensure proper standards of education and efficiency in them. Therefore, one of its first actions was to issue in 1925 a set of minimum standards for its member hospitals. These standards included criteria on hospital supervision, record keeping, and the operation of nurse-training schools. Compared to the guidelines of the larger and more influential American College of Surgeons, these were rudimentary. Nonetheless, the NHA hoped that its efforts would forestall the closure of African-American hospitals and demonstrate to white physicians that their black colleagues could keep abreast of changes in medical and hospital practice.

Other activities of the NHA included the provision of technical assistance to hospitals, the sponsorship of professional conferences, and the publication of literature promoting proper hospital administration. The association also lobbied major health-care organizations such as the American Medical Association, the American College of Surgeons, and the American Hospital Association, urging them to take on a role in the improvement of black hospitals.

The NHA was a short-lived organization with limited effectiveness. It never had a full-time administrator or a permanent office. During its first ten years Knoxville physician H. M. Green served as its president while maintaining a busy medical practice. The NHA ran entirely on modest membership fees and often operated at a deficit. It never received financial or programmatic support from foundations or other health-care organizations. It lacked the financial and political muscle to implement and enforce its policies and failed to convince many black physicians of the importance of its goals. By the early 1940s the NHA had disbanded.

Despite these limitations the NHA played a significant role in African-American medical history. It provided black physicians and nurses with opportunities to learn about and discuss trends in hospital care. And it helped the National Medical Association to publicize and articulate the plight of black physicians, their patients, and their hospitals at a time when few outlets for voicing such concerns existed.

REFERENCES

GAMBLE, VANESSA NORTHINGTON. "The Negro Hospital Renaissance: The Black Hospital Movement." In Diana E. Long and Janet Golden, eds. *The American General Hospital*. Ithaca, N.Y., 1989, pp. 182–205.
GREEN, H. M. "Some Observations on and Lessons from the Experience of the Past Ten Years." *Journal of the National Medical Association* 26 (1934): 21–24.

VANESSA NORTHINGTON GAMBLE

National League for the Protection of Colored Women.

Founded by Frances Kellor and S. W. Layten in 1906, the National League for the Protection of Colored Women concerned itself with the predicament of women in domestic labor in northern cities. Job opportunities for African-American women in the cities were severely restricted; nearly 90 percent were in household employ as domestic servants. Wages were low and unregulated, and the hours were extremely long for women who worked as live-in domestics. Layten, a black Baptist activist, and Kellor, a white reformer, joined black and white women in New York to study these conditions and to try to change them. In addition to its base in New York, chapters of the league were active in Philadelphia, Baltimore, Washington, D.C., and Chicago.

A major focus of the league's work was the migration of southern African Americans to northern cities in search of a better life. While the numbers migrating at the turn of the century were fewer than would come later, the predicament of young women was a matter of great concern for workers in the league. Many women arrived knowing no one, with little money, and with no arrangements for lodging. The league feared that these women might fall into dangerous situations, especially associations with houses of prostitution. Additional difficulties were presented by labor agents working in the South to encourage migration. Often, anxious migrants were tricked into signing contracts that left them little of their wages at the end of the month.

In order to deal with these issues, the league distributed information among southern black women about the realities of life in the North and warning of unscrupulous labor agents. In addition, it sent out its own people to meet new arrivals at train stations and ports to guide them to safe places to lodge. The league worked in conjunction with existing black women's shelters and created an effective network to deal with these problems. In 1911, the league became one of the founding organizations under the umbrella of the NATIONAL URBAN LEAGUE.

REFERENCES

KELLOR, FRANCES A. *Out of Work: A Study in Unemployment*. 1915. Reprint. New York, 1974.
LAYTEN, S. W. "The Servant Problem." *Colored American* 12 (January 1907): 13–17.
WEISS, NANCY J. *The National Urban League, 1910–1940*. Oxford, 1974.

JUDITH WEISENFELD

National Medical Association. *See* Medical Associations.

National Negro Congress.

The National Negro Congress (NNC) was an organization that emerged from the May 1935 Washington, D.C., Howard University Conference on the status of the Negro. Formally getting under way in 1936, it held meetings at irregular intervals and was composed predominantly of organizations and individuals active in the African-American community. For Ralph BUNCHE and others, the National Negro Congress held the promise of an interclass alliance which included labor, clerics, entrepreneurs, and elected officials, among others. The mission of the NNC included protest against JIM CROW and organizing for the social, political, and economic advancement of African Americans.

Sponsors of the NNC included Charles H. HOUSTON of the NAACP, Alain LOCKE and Ralph Bunche of Howard University, Lester Granger of the NATIONAL URBAN LEAGUE, John P. Davis of the Joint

Committee on National Recovery, A. Philip RANDOLPH of the BROTHERHOOD OF SLEEPING CAR PORTERS, who served as the organization's first president, and James Ford of the COMMUNIST PARTY OF THE U.S.A.

The participation of the Communist party within the NNC caused controversy. From the beginning, the party played a prominent role within the NNC and grew after the 1937 convention. Their point of view was that the NNC was an expression of a "united front" of African Americans (i.e., despite class and ideological differences, blacks should unite for common goals). However, by 1938, some noncommunists, such as Bunche, troubled by the influence of the Communist party, left the NNC.

Critics of the NNC, a list that ultimately included Randolph, were of the opinion that the organization was a front for the party and that it refused to take positions at variance with those of the communists. These criticisms of the NNC became sharper after the concluding of the Nazi–Soviet pact in August 1939, which led to the German invasion of Poland and the onset of World War II.

While many communists were hesitant to criticize the pact, NNC critics (e.g., Randolph) began to drift away from the organization. Those who refused to leave the NNC felt that disputes over the pact were examples of the kind of ideological differences that should be submerged in the interest of a "united front" for the betterment of African Americans.

Despite these internecine conflicts, the NNC during its brief history rivaled the NAACP as a tribune for African Americans. It had fifty branch councils in nineteen states, published a number of communications organs, and sponsored numerous conferences.

In Harlem, where the NNC was particularly strong, it enjoyed the participation of the Rev. Adam Clayton POWELL, JR., and the Harvard-educated communist lawyer Benjamin J. DAVIS, and spearheaded campaigns to secure jobs for blacks in mass transit. Across the nation, the NNC could be found boycotting department stores that engaged in racial discrimination, protesting police brutality, and demanding federal antilynching legislation and investigation of the Ku Klux Klan and Black Legion. The NNC protested vigorously the Italian invasion of Ethiopia and the perceived laggard policies of the U.S. State Department in opposing this action.

In a number of communities, the NNC worked quite closely with NAACP branches, affiliates of the Congress of Industrial Organizations (CIO), the Southern Conference for Human Welfare, and the American Committee for the Protection of the Foreign Born. After the entry of the United States into World War II in 1941, this kind of collaboration increased. Since the United States was in an alliance with the Soviet Union from 1941 to 1945, the role of communists within the NNC was not seen by many noncommunists as a bar to cooperation. As such, the NNC experienced some growth during this period after the difficulties of 1939.

The NNC played a leading role during this period in the formation of the Negro Labor Victory Committee (NLVC; 1942–1945), which in Harlem and elsewhere mobilized African Americans against fascism abroad and Jim Crow at home.

Nevertheless, neither the NNC nor the NLVC was able to survive the end of the war and the onset of the Cold War and Red Scare. By 1946, it was quite common for the NNC to be referred to as a "communist front" and "tool of Moscow." The transformation of the Soviet Union from an ally to an enemy of the United States was a leading factor in this changed perception of the NNC and its eventual demise. During the period 1946–1947 the NNC was subsumed by the Civil Rights Congress, another organization closely related to the Communist party, but one that had a broader mission, less exclusively focused on African-American affairs, of fighting political and racist repression.

REFERENCES

HORNE, GERALD. *Communist Front? The Civil Rights Congress, 1946–56.* London, 1988.

HUGHES, CICERO ALVIN. "Toward a Black United Front: the National Negro Congress Movement." Ph.D. diss., Ohio University, 1982.

STREATER, JOHN BAXTER. The National Negro Congress, 1936–47. Ph.D. diss., University of Cincinnati, 1981.

GERALD HORNE

National Negro Labor Council.

The National Negro Labor Council (NNLC) was established in 1951 to promote the cause of African-American workers. Although beleaguered and ultimately extinguished by the repressive political environment of the 1950s, the organization contested economic discrimination in a variety of settings and thus helped to keep alive the battle for civil rights in the realm of labor.

During the New Deal and World War II, the CONGRESS OF INDUSTRIAL ORGANIZATIONS (CIO), along with such allies as the NATIONAL NEGRO CONGRESS, the MARCH ON WASHINGTON MOVEMENT, and at times, the NATIONAL ASSOCIATION FOR THE ADVANCEMENT OF COLORED PEOPLE, had done much to transform organized labor from a bastion of Jim Crow into a leading agent of civil rights struggle.

Mass campaigns for racial equality at work and in unions, together with the wartime mobilization, advanced the position of African Americans in the workplace and spawned a new generation of black union leadership. After the war, however, the outlook for black workers turned increasingly dismal. Peacetime reconversion, spreading mechanization, and a hardening of workplace discrimination conspired to squeeze large numbers of African Americans out of industry, even as thousands of displaced black farmers were moving from the rural South into the industrial North. Meanwhile, the conservative climate of the emerging Cold War era dampened the CIO's commitment to civil rights organizing; indeed, the expulsion from its ranks of communist-oriented unions in the late 1940s banished significant strongholds of black membership, along with many of the CIO's most energetic exponents of racial justice.

In June 1950, over 900 labor activists, predominantly black, gathered in Chicago at a National Labor Conference for Negro Rights. During the following year twenty-three Negro Labor Councils (NLCs) were established in key industrial centers around the country. In October 1951, representatives from these councils met in Cincinnati to form the National Negro Labor Council. In a founding Statement of Principles, the NNLC pledged to "work unitedly with the trade unions to bring about greater cooperation between all sections of the Negro people and the trade union movement." While it focused on equal economic opportunity, the NNLC advocated all measures essential to "full citizenship," including an end to police brutality and mob violence, the right to vote and hold public office, and the abolition of segregation in housing and in other public facilities.

The NNLC drew much of its leadership and active followers either from the unions recently expelled from the CIO—including the United Electrical, Radio, and Machine Workers; the International Mine, Mill, and Smelter Workers; the Food, Tobacco, Agricultural and Allied Workers; the National Union of Marine Cooks and Stewards; the International Fur and Leather Workers; and the International Longshoremen's and Warehousemen's Union—or from the left-wing bastions of mainstream unions, such as the United Packinghouse Workers, the Amalgamated Clothing Workers, and the United Auto Workers. (Detroit's vast UAW Local 600, a center of militant black leadership, made up a particularly vital base of the support). In cities such as San Francisco, Detroit, Washington, Chicago, Cleveland, New York, and Louisville, NLCs cultivated allies within the African-American community, as well as among sympathetic whites. William R. Hood, recording secretary of UAW Local 600, served as president of the national organization. Coleman A. YOUNG, then organizer for the Amalgamated Clothing Workers in Detroit, served as executive secretary. World-renowned singer, actor, and civil rights leader Paul ROBESON was an active supporter.

Over the first half of the 1950s, the NNLC initiated or rallied behind a series of public campaigns around the country. Local NLCs confronted racial barriers to hiring or advancement at a number of enterprises, including the Ford Motor Company, the Statler and Sherry Netherland hotels (New York), Sears-Roebuck (Cleveland, San Francisco), General Electric (Louisville), the U.S. Bureau of Engraving (Washington), the Detroit Tigers, Drexel National Bank (Chicago), and American Airlines. Through petitions and write-in drives, picket lines and local publications, visiting committees and job-training programs, the NNLC helped to open up employment for African-American men and women as streetcar motormen and conductors, hotel workers, truck drivers, clerks and salespeople, and bank officials, and in previously unobtainable levels of skilled industrial work. The NNLC called on unions to demand the inclusion of a model "Fair Employment Practices" clause in labor contracts (see FAIR EMPLOYMENT PRACTICES COMMITTEE), and to bring African Americans into leadership positions. The NNLC also mobilized support for strikes in which black workers figured prominently, including those at International Harvester in Chicago (1952) and among sugar cane workers in Louisiana (1953).

The NNLC encountered a formidable array of obstacles. Employers remained widely resistant to the call for nonracial hiring; the airline industry, for example, continued to deny blacks access to skilled jobs, as did virtually all employers around the South targeted by the NNLC. Most of the labor establishment, for its part, turned a cold shoulder to the NNLC. CIO leaders such as Walter Reuther and James B. Carey regularly condemned it as an agent of communism, while many AFL unions remained openly opposed to organizing black workers on an equal basis, if at all. Much of the African-American community remained aloof from the NNLC, or openly condemned it, because of its "communist" associations. The NAACP and the NATIONAL URBAN LEAGUE were particularly vocal in their denunciations. Finally, government repression took its toll. The NNLC was called before the House Committee on Un-American Activities and Subversive Activities Control Board to answer charges that it was a "Communist-Front organization." In 1956, faced with insurmountable legal expenses, the NNLC leadership voted to disband the organization.

Historical assessments of the NNLC have diverged sharply, reflecting, often extending, the heated debates of contemporaries. Anticommunist scholars have tended flatly to characterize it as a "front" organization, a creation of the COMMUNIST PARTY lacking authentic roots in the black community (Record 1964). Historians sympathetic to the Communist party, on the other hand, have stressed the self-directed enterprise of black labor activists as the driving force behind the NNLC, and deemphasized the role of the party (Foner 1974). In the 1980s and early 1990s, historians began to paint a more nuanced and varied picture of the relationship between African-American workers and the Communist party (Korstad and Lichtenstein 1988; Kelley 1990). But many of the campaigns in which the NNLC played a role still await in-depth scholarly attention. Such research is likely to bring to light an organization closely linked but not reducible to the Communist party—an expression at once of the party's rhetorical and tactical approach, and of the genuine initiative of black workers, both in and out of the party.

However portrayed, the NNLC left a mixed legacy. Its influence and impact, although at instances dramatic, were ultimately limited, and racial discrimination at the workplace and in unions remained pervasive at the time of its demise. A new civil rights movement was then in the making, but its center of gravity would materialize in the black church and independent protest organizations.

REFERENCES

FONER, PHILIP S. "The National Negro Labor Council, 1951–1955." In Philip Foner, *Organized Labor and the Black Worker, 1619–1973*. New York, 1974, pp. 293–311.

KELLEY, ROBIN D. G. *Hammer and Hoe: Alabama Communists During the Great Depression*. Chapel Hill, N.C., 1990.

KORSTAD, ROBERT, and NELSON LICHTENSTEIN. "Opportunities Found and Lost: Labor, Radicals, and the Early Civil Rights Movement." *Journal of American History* 75 (1988): 786–811.

RECORD, WILSON. "Since 1950." In *Race and Radicalism: The NAACP and the Communist Party in Conflict*. Ithaca, N.Y., 1964, pp. 169–221.

THOMAS, RICHARD. "Blacks and the CIO." In Paul Buhle and Alan Dawley, eds. *Working for Democracy: American Workers from the Revolution to the Present*. Urbana, Ill., 1985, pp. 93–100.

DANIEL LETWIN

National Urban League. Founded in New York City in 1911 through the consolidation of the Committee for Improving the Industrial Condition of Negroes in New York (1906), the NATIONAL LEAGUE FOR THE PROTECTION OF COLORED WOMEN (1906), and the Committee on Urban Conditions Among Negroes (1910), the National Urban League quickly established itself as the principal organization then dealing with the economic and social problems of blacks in American cities.

The league divided with its contemporary, the National Association for the Advancement of Colored People, the work of the emerging struggle for racial advancement. Securing the legal rights of black Americans was the principal business of the NAACP; promoting economic opportunity and social welfare was the responsibility of the Urban League.

Committed to improving employment opportunities for blacks, the Urban League placed workers in the private sector, attacked the color line in organized labor, and sponsored programs of vocational guidance and job training. While it first concentrated on changing discriminatory employment practices in the private sector, it became involved increasingly over time in trying to influence the development of public policy. During the GREAT DEPRESSION, it lobbied for the inclusion of blacks in federal relief and recovery programs; in the 1940s, it pressed for an end to discrimination in defense industries and for the desegregation of the armed forces.

In the 1950s the league still measured its accomplishments in terms of pilot placements of blacks in jobs previously closed to them because of race. In the 1960s, with the passage of civil rights legislation and the pressures of urban violence, the climate changed. Now the league reported tens of thousands of placements annually in new or upgraded jobs. It sponsored an array of new projects to improve employment opportunities: a national skills bank, for example, which matched blacks who had marketable skills with positions that utilized their talents, and an on-the-job-training program that placed unskilled workers in training slots in private industry. In the 1970s and 1980s, the league pioneered a range of other employment programs providing skills training, apprenticeships, and job placements.

The league grounded its work in social welfare in scientific investigations of conditions among urban blacks which provided the basis for practical reform. Its studies—some published independently, some reported in the league's magazine, OPPORTUNITY: JOURNAL OF NEGRO LIFE (1923–1949)—contributed importantly to the development of a body of reliable literature on aspects of black urban life and helped to shape public and private policy with respect to race.

The Urban League pioneered professional social service training for blacks. The agency encouraged black colleges to incorporate instruction in economics, sociology, and urban problems in their curricula, and it cooperated in establishing the first training center for black social workers. An Urban League fellowship program enabled promising blacks to pursue advanced studies at designated schools of social work while gaining some practical experience at the Urban League or similar agencies. The result was a corps of professional black social workers, whom the League placed in a wide range of social service agencies.

The Urban League adapted for blacks the welfare services already offered to whites by settlement houses, charitable agencies, and immigrant aid societies. Working principally through a network of local affiliates, the league counseled blacks new to the cities on behavior, dress, sanitation, health, and homemaking, and sponsored community centers, clinics, kindergartens and day nurseries, and summer camps. League staff members engaged in casework to deal with individual problems including juvenile delinquency, truancy, and marital adjustment.

In the 1960s the Urban League supplemented its traditional social service approach with a more activist commitment to civil rights. It embraced direct action and community organization, sponsored leadership development and voter education and registration projects, helped organize the March on Washington of 1963 and the POOR PEOPLE'S WASHINGTON CAMPAIGN of 1968, called for a domestic Marshall Plan, and began to concentrate on building economic and political power in inner cities. The agency's services reflected a combination of new activism and the traditional Urban League concerns: assistance to black veterans, campaigns for open housing, consumer protection, efforts to find adoptive families for hard-to-place black children, as well as tutoring programs for ghetto youngsters and street academies to prepare high school dropouts to go to college.

In the 1970s the league became a major subcontractor for government employment and social welfare programs and worked increasingly closely with Congress, the executive departments, and the regulatory agencies as an advocate of the interests of black Americans. It significantly expanded its research capacity, with a range of new monographs and special studies, a policy research journal, *The Urban League Review* (1975–), and a widely publicized annual report, *The State of Black America* (1976–). In the 1980s, as federal social programs were cut back, the organization looked increasingly to black self-help, seeking to mobilize the institutions of the black community to address some of the most persistent problems of the ghetto—the crisis in the public schools, and the high incidence of teenage pregnancy, single female-headed households, and crime.

Guided in its earliest years by George Edmund HAYNES, a sociologist who was the first black to earn

A gathering of the leadership of the National Urban League in about 1920. (Photographs and Prints Division, Schomburg Center for Research in Black Culture, The New York Public Library, Astor, Lenox and Tilden Foundations)

a Ph.D. from Columbia University, in 1917 the National Urban League came under the direction of his assistant, Eugene Kinckle Jones, a former high school teacher who also held an advanced degree in sociology. Jones was succeeded as executive secretary in 1941 by Lester B. Granger, a social worker who had been secretary of the league's Workers' Bureau. Granger stepped down in 1961, turning the League's leadership over the Whitney M. YOUNG, Jr., dean of the Atlanta School of Social Work, who served until his death in 1971. Vernon E. JORDAN, a lawyer then serving as executive director of the United Negro College Fund, was named president of the National Urban League in 1972. Jordan was succeeded in 1982 by John E. Jacob, also a social worker, who had spent his professional career in a number of Urban League posts, including that of executive vice president of the national organization.

REFERENCES

MOORE, JESSE THOMAS, JR. *A Search for Equality: The National Urban League, 1910–1961.* University Park, Pa., 1981.

NATIONAL URBAN LEAGUE. *Eightieth Anniversary, 1910–1990.* New York, 1990.

PARRIS, GUICHARD, and LESTER BROOKS. *Blacks in the City: A History of the National Urban League.* Boston, 1971.

WEISS, NANCY J. *The National Urban League, 1910–1940.* New York, 1974.

———. *Whitney M. Young, Jr., and the Struggle for Civil Rights.* Princeton, N.J., 1989.

NANCY J. WEISS

National Welfare Rights Organization.

The National Welfare Rights Organization (NWRO) was a militant organization of poor women on welfare that mobilized in the 1960s and early 1970s to lobby for changes in welfare policy, press for increased aid to recipients, and demand more humane treatment by government caseworkers. It was founded in spring 1966 by middle-class activists and women on welfare who had been organizing since the early 1960s. The organization was overwhelmingly African American and membership was limited to welfare recipients, most of whom received Aid to Families with Dependent Children (AFDC). The NWRO grew rapidly, more than doubling from 10,000 in 1968 to 22,000 in 1969. Actual participation in the movement was much higher, perhaps reaching 100,000 at its peak in 1969. The NWRO supported, coordinated, and directed efforts of local groups in places such as Los Angeles, Newark, Boston, Philadelphia, Baltimore, and Des Moines, with the largest chapter in New York City.

The welfare rights movement was an important example of the changing nature of political struggle in the 1960s. After years of intense protest around desegregation and voting rights, many civil rights leaders became disillusioned with a strategy that did not address the immediate needs of most members of the African-American community. They increasingly came to the conclusion that civil rights without economic justice was a hollow victory. In its early years, the NWRO got widespread support from liberal churches, civil rights organizations, and government antipoverty programs that were part of President Lyndon Johnson's Great Society program.

Welfare leaders of the NWRO sought to address problems of urban poverty by targeting the welfare system. They fought to get an adequate monthly grant, decent day care, and practical job training programs. They believed the state had a responsibility to provide for all of its citizens in need. One of their central demands was a guaranteed annual income, which they believed the federal government should provide for every American. They opposed "morality" investigations by government caseworkers, which they found degrading, and affirmed the legitimacy of female-headed households. The NWRO believed that AFDC recipients should have access to decent paying jobs, but also supported the right of these mothers to stay home and care for their children.

The primary strategy for the welfare rights movement was to apply for "special grants" for clothing and household items to which welfare recipients were entitled. Anywhere from thirty to 300 women would go to a welfare office together and demand money immediately for such things as school clothing and new furniture. If welfare officials refused their request, they would hold a sit-in or another form of protest until their demands were met. By inundating welfare offices with such requests, activists hoped to put pressure on the system and effect more fundamental changes to improve the lives of recipients. In the early years, this strategy was very successful and was the key way in which leaders built up the membership of their organization. The NWRO also developed alliances with other political groups, publicized their grievances, and held mass rallies and marches.

For the women on welfare, their goals became twofold: to pose direct and militant challenges to the state and to create an organization of poor women that was truly led by poor women. Women organizers on welfare, such as Johnnie Tillmon in Watts, Los Angeles, and Beulah Sanders in New York City, made up the National Coordinating Committee and were invested with formal decision-making authority. However, much of the day-to-day running of the organization was in the hands of the executive director and the mostly white, male, middle-class staff. George Wiley, an African-American chemistry professor and former associate director of the CONGRESS OF RACIAL EQUALITY (CORE), was elected executive director of NWRO in 1966 and remained in that position until 1973. Wiley and his staff raised money, planned conferences and meetings, and set short-term goals. However, tension developed within the NWRO as the women struggled to define their goals, outline their strategy, and assert their autonomy.

By the early 1970s the NWRO was in trouble. As the demands for special grants led to fewer material gains because of changes in state and city policy, membership began to decline. In addition, mainstream and liberal support waned as an antiwelfare backlash swept the nation and popular support for sweeping reforms diminished. This contributed to the decline of the NWRO. In 1972, the NWRO was $150,000 in debt. The following year, George Wiley, the primary fundraiser, resigned, which did little to resolve the financial difficulties of the organization. In 1975, NWRO was forced to file for bankruptcy, and it ceased operations shortly thereafter.

Although often defined as a movement of poor people, the welfare rights movement was also a movement of black women. They saw their struggle as one in which race, class, and gender were inextricably tied together. They fought for the right of economic security, challenged the popular assumption that families headed by black women were dysfunctional, and identified their movement as part of the larger struggle for black liberation. In so doing, they laid the groundwork for future grass-roots struggles by poor black women.

REFERENCES

PIVEN, FRANCES FOX, and RICHARD SLOWARD. *Poor People's Movements: How They Succeed, Why They Fail.* 1978.

POPE, JACQUELINE. *Biting the Hand That Feeds Them.* 1981.

WEST, GUIDA. *The National Welfare Rights Organization: The Social Protest of Poor Women.* 1981.

PAM NADASEN

Nation of Islam. In the midsummer of 1930, a friendly but mysterious peddler appeared among rural southern immigrants in a black ghetto of Detroit called "Paradise Valley," selling raincoats, silks, and other sundries but also giving advice to the poor residents about their health and spiritual development. He told them about their "true religion," not Christianity but the "religion of the Black Men" of Asia and Africa. Using both the Bible and the Qur'an in his messages, he taught at first in the private homes of his followers, then rented a hall that was called the Temple of Islam. This mysterious stranger often referred to himself as Mr. Farrad Mohammed, or sometimes as Mr. Wali Farrad, W. D. Fard, or Professor Ford.

Master FARD, as he came to be called, taught his followers about a period of temporary domination and persecution by white "blue-eyed devils," who had achieved their power by brutality, murder, and trickery. But as a prerequisite for black liberation, he stressed the importance of attaining "knowledge of self." He told his followers that they were not Americans and therefore owed no allegiance to the American flag. He wrote two manuals for the movement—*The Secret Ritual of the Nation of Islam,* which is transmitted orally to members, and *Teaching for the Lost-Found Nation of Islam in a Mathematical Way,* which is written in symbolic language and requires special interpretation. Fard established several organizations: the University of Islam, to propagate his teachings; the Muslim Girls Training, to teach female members home economics and how to be a proper Muslim woman; and the Fruit of Islam, consisting of

selected male members, to provide security for Muslim leaders and to enforce the disciplinary rules.

One of the earliest officers of the movement and Fard's most trusted lieutenant was Robert Poole, alias Elijah Poole, who was given the Muslim name Elijah MUHAMMAD (Perry 1991, p. 143). The son of a rural Baptist minister and sharecropper from Sandersville, Ga., Poole had immigrated with his family to Detroit in 1923; he and several of his brothers joined the Nation of Islam in 1931. Although he had only a third-grade education, Elijah Muhammad's shrewd native intelligence and hard work enabled him to rise through the ranks rapidly, and he was chosen by Fard as the chief minister of Islam to preside over the daily affairs of the organization.

Fard's mysterious disappearance in 1934 led to an internal struggle for the leadership of the Nation of Islam. As a result of this strife, Muhammad eventually moved his family and close followers, settling on the south side of Chicago in 1936. There they established Temple of Islam No. 2, which eventually became the national headquarters of the movement. Throughout the 1940s, Muhammad reshaped the Nation and gave it his own imprimatur. He firmly established the doctrine that Master Fard was "Allah," and that God is a black man, proclaiming that he, the "Honorable" Elijah Muhammad, knew Allah personally and was anointed his "Messenger." Prior to 1961, members of the Nation of Islam were called "Voodoo People" or "People of the Temple"; Professor C. Eric Lincoln's study *The Black Muslims in America* (1961) established the usage of the phrase "Black Muslims" in referring to the Nation of Islam.

Under Muhammad's guidance, the Nation developed a two-pronged attack on the problems of the black masses: the development of economic independence and the recovery of an acceptable identity. "Do for Self" became the rallying cry of the movement, which encouraged economic self-reliance for individuals and the black community. The economic ethic of the Black Muslims was a kind of black puritanism—hard work, frugality and the avoidance of debt, self-improvement, and a conservative lifestyle. During the forty-one-year period of his leadership, Muhammad and his followers established more than one hundred temples nationwide and innumerable grocery stores, restaurants, bakeries, and other small businesses. The Nation of Islam also became famous for the foods—bean pies and whiting—it peddled in black communities to improve the nutrition and physical health of African Americans. It strictly forbade alcohol, drugs, pork, and an unhealthy diet. Elijah Muhammad was prescient in his advice on nutrition: "You are what you eat," he often said.

In his *Message to the Black Man in America* (1965), Muhammad diagnosed the vulnerabilities of the black psyche as stemming from a confusion of identity and self-hatred caused by white racism; the cure he prescribed was radical surgery, the formation of a separate black nation. Muhammad's 120 "degrees," or lessons, and the major doctrines and beliefs of the Nation of Islam elaborated on aspects of this central message. The white man is a "devil by nature," unable to respect anyone who is not white and the historical and persistent source of harm and injury to black people. The central theological myth of the Nation tells of Yakub, a black mad scientist who rebelled against Allah by creating the white race, a weak hybrid people who were permitted temporary dominance of the world. But according to the apocalyptic beliefs of the Black Muslims, there will be a clash between the forces of good (blacks) and the forces of evil (whites) in the not-too-distant future, an Armageddon from which black people will emerge victorious and re-create their original hegemony under Allah throughout the world.

All these myths and doctrines have functioned as a theodicy for the Black Muslims, as an explanation and rationalization for the pain and suffering inflicted on black people in America. For example, Malcolm Little described the powerful, jarring impact that the revelation of religious truth had on him in the Norfolk State Prison in Massachusetts after his brother Reginald told him, "The white man is the Devil." The doctrines of the Nation transformed the chaos of the world behind prison bars into a cosmos, an ordered reality. Malcolm finally had an explanation for the extreme poverty and tragedies his family suffered, and for all the years he had spent hustling and pimping on the streets of Roxbury and Harlem as "Detroit Red." The conversion and total transformation of Malcolm Little into MALCOLM X in prison in 1947 is a story of the effectiveness of Elijah Muhammad's message, one that was repeated thousands of times during the period of Muhammad's leadership. Dropping one's surname and taking on an X, standard practice in the movement, was an outward symbol of inward changes: it meant ex-Christian, ex-Negro, ex-slave.

The years between Malcolm's release from prison and his assassination, 1952 to 1965, mark the period of the greatest growth and influence of the Nation of Islam. After meeting Elijah Muhammad in 1952, Malcolm began organizing Muslim temples in New York, Philadelphia, and Boston, and in the South and on the West Coast as well. He founded the Nation's newspaper, *Muhammad Speaks,* in the basement of his home and initiated the practice of requiring every male Muslim to sell an assigned quota of newspapers on the street as a recruiting and fund-raising device. He rose rapidly through the ranks to become minister of Boston Temple No. 11 and was later re-

warded with the post of minister of Temple No. 7 in Harlem, the largest and most prestigious of the temples after the Chicago headquarters. The Honorable Elijah Muhammad recognized his organizational talents, enormous charismatic appeal, and forensic abilities by naming Malcolm national representative of the Nation of Islam, second in rank to the Messenger himself. Under his lieutenancy, the Nation achieved a membership estimated at 500,000. But as in other movements of this kind, the numbers involved were quite fluid and the Nation's influence, refracted through the public charisma of Malcolm X, greatly exceeded its actual numbers.

Malcolm's keen intellect, incisive wit, and ardent radicalism made him a formidable critic of American society, including the civil rights movement. As a favorite media personality, he challenged the Rev. Dr. Martin Luther KING, Jr.'s central notions of "integration" and "nonviolence." Malcolm felt that what was at stake, at a deeper level than the civil right to sit in a restaurant or even to vote, was the integrity of black selfhood and its independence. His biting critique of the "so-called Negro" and his emphasis on the recovery of black self-identity and independence provided the intellectual foundations for the American BLACK POWER MOVEMENT and black-consciousness movement of the late 1960s and 1970s. In contrast to King's nonviolence, Malcolm urged his followers to defend themselves "by any means possible." He articulated the pent-up frustration, bitterness, and rage felt by the dispossessed black masses, the "grass roots."

As the result of a dispute on political philosophy and morality with Elijah Muhammad, Malcolm left the Nation of Islam in March 1964 in order to form his own organizations, the Muslim Mosque Inc. and the Organization for Afro-American Unity. He took the Muslim name el-Hajj Malik el-Shabazz after converting to orthodox Sunni ISLAM and participating in the hajj, the annual pilgrimage to Mecca. Malcolm was assassinated on February 21, 1965, while he was delivering a lecture at the Audubon Ballroom in Harlem.

From 1965 until Elijah Muhammad's death in February 1975, the Nation of Islam prospered economically, but its membership never surged again. Minister Louis X of Boston, also called Louis Abdul FARRAKHAN, replaced Malcolm as the national representative and the head minister of Temple No. 7 in New York. During this period, the Nation acquired an ultramodern printing press, cattle farms in Georgia and Alabama, and a bank in Chicago.

After a bout of illness, Muhammad died in Chicago and one of his six sons, Wallace Deen Muhammad (later Imam Warith Deen Muhammad), was named supreme minister of the Nation of Islam.

(Top) Muslim women prepare to leave the auditorium of Jones Armory in Chicago after listening to a speech given by Hon. Elijah Muhammad on Savior's Day, February 26, 1974; (bottom) the Fruit of Islam (F.O.I.), a security team, listens attentively as Nation of Islam leader Louis Farrakhan (not shown) speaks to an audience in Chicago, 1983. (© Ted Gray)

However, two months later Wallace shocked his followers and the world by declaring that whites were no longer viewed as devils and they could join the movement. He began to make radical changes in the doctrines and the structure of the Nation, moving it in the direction of orthodox Sunni Islam.

The changes introduced by Imam Warith Deen Muhammad led to a splintering of the movement, especially among the hard-core black-nationalist followers. In 1978, Louis Farrakhan led a schismatic group that succeeded in resurrecting the old Nation of Islam. Farrakhan's Nation, which is also based in Chicago, retains the black-nationalist and separatist beliefs and doctrines that were central to the teachings of Elijah Muhammad. Farrakhan displays much of the charisma and forensic candor of Malcolm X, and his message of black nationalism is again directed to those mired in the underclass, as well as to disillusioned intellectuals, via the Nation's *Final Call* newspaper and popular rap-music groups such as Public Enemy.

Through more than sixty years, the Nation of Islam in its various forms has become the longest-lasting and most enduring of the black militant and separatist movements that have appeared in the history of black people in the United States. Besides its crucial role in the development of the black-consciousness movement, the Nation is important for having introduced Islam as a fourth major religious tradition in American society, alongside Protestantism, Catholicism, and Judaism.

REFERENCES

BREITMAN, GEORGE, ed. *Malcolm X Speaks.* New York, 1965.
ESSIEN-UDOM, E. U. *Black Nationalism: A Search for Identity in America.* Chicago, 1962.
FARRAKHAN, LOUIS. *Seven Speeches.* Chicago, 1974.
LINCOLN, C. ERIC. *The Black Muslims in America.* Boston, 1961.
MALCOLM X and ALEX HALEY. *The Autobiography of Malcolm X.* New York, 1965.
MAMIYA, LAWRENCE H. "From Black Muslim to Bilalian: The Evolution of a Movement." *Journal for the Scientific Study of Religion* 21, no. 2 (June 1982): 138–152.
MUHAMMAD, ELIJAH. *Message to the Black Man in America.* Chicago, 1965.
MUHAMMAD, WARITH DEEN. *As the Light Shineth from the East.* Chicago, 1980.
PERRY, BRUCE. *Malcolm: The Life of a Man Who Changed Black America.* Barrytown, N.Y., 1991.
WAUGH, EARLE H., BAHA ABU-LABAN, and REGULA B. QURESHI, eds. *The Muslim Community in North America.* Edmonton, Alberta, 1983.

LAWRENCE H. MAMIYA
C. ERIC LINCOLN

Native Americans. *See* American Indians.

Nat Turner Controversy. William Styron's novel *The Confessions of Nat Turner* (1967) is a fictionalized version of Nat Turner's 1831 Virginia slave revolt (*see* NAT TURNER'S REBELLION) in the form of an expanded version of Turner's original narrative, transcribed by a white lawyer prior to Turner's execution, and published under the same title. Styron's book was awarded a Pulitzer Prize in 1968, and was widely acclaimed by many critics. However, it soon became the subject of a major controversy. Many African-American authors took issue with Styron's motives, abilities, and techniques, calling into question whether a white author could write honestly and convincingly about a black man. Their arguments culminated in the collection *William Styron's Nat Turner: Ten Black Writers Respond* (1968). Critics such as John Henrick Clarke and Vincent Harding accused Styron of committing a deliberately racist act and showing "moral cowardice" for having attempted the narrative depiction of Turner, claiming he distorted history and denied Turner's true character and motives.

The criticism took many different forms. Mike Thelwell claimed the author was ignorant of black speech patterns and metaphorical imagery and had distorted Turner's voice. Another significant criticism launched against Styron concerned his depiction of Turner as deriving his impetus for revolt from a religious "calling" rather than from the general condition of SLAVERY, thus reducing the Nat Turner rebellion to an episode of religious fanaticism. Many of the critics maintained that since the novel depicted incidences of warm, friendly relations between slaves and masters, it showed a sympathy for the slaveholding tradition and portrayed Turner's masters as "benevolent" victims of a crime. Critics such as Lerone BENNETT were also offended by the sexuality and lack of "virility" of Styron's character. In the novel, Nat Turner's only sexual relation is homosexual, while his sex-fantasies focus largely on "a nameless white girl . . . with golden curls." Bennett associated Turner's sexuality with his "weakness." When the rebellion breaks out in the novel, Turner is able to kill only one of the whites he attacks.

Styron countered his detractors by noting his lifelong interest in Nat Turner, whose actual rebellion took place only a few miles from the author's childhood home, and his painstaking research. He also emphasized that the work was a novel and that he relied on the liberated imagination over strict fidelity to fact where the historical record was unclear or incomplete. Meanwhile, several African-American writers, notably James BALDWIN, defended Styron and his work. The long-term effect of Styron's novel and the attacks it prompted were to increase popular interest in the historical Nat Turner and his actions. However, the violent dissonance between various white and black views on how Turner should be portrayed served as one of the first indicators of the divergence in racial attitudes that has characterized the last decades of the twentieth century.

REFERENCES

CLARKE, JOHN HENRIK, ed. *William Styron's Nat Turner: Ten Black Writers Respond.* New York, 1968.

GENOVESE, EUGENE. "William Styron Before the People's Court." In *In Red and Black: Marxian Explorations in Southern and Afro-American History.* 1969. Reprint. New York, 1971.

WEST, JAMES L. W., III, ed. *Conversations With William Styron.* Oxford, Miss., 1985.

GREG ROBINSON

Nat Turner's Rebellion.   Nat Turner (October 2, 1800–November 11, 1831) led the most significant slave revolt in U.S. history. Undertaken in 1831 in Virginia, Turner's Rebellion claimed more lives than any similar uprising. It had repercussions throughout the South, redrawing the lines of the American debate over slavery in ways that led toward all-out civil war within a generation. Indeed, some suggest that it represented the first major battle of the long war to end slavery.

In 1831 Virginia's Southampton County, bordering on North Carolina, contained roughly 6,500 whites and 9,500 blacks. Almost all of the latter, whether young or old, lived in perpetual bondage, including Nat Turner, a slave of Joseph Travis. Turner had been born in Southampton on October 2, 1800, only five days before the execution of black revolutionary Gabriel Prosser in Richmond (*see* GABRIEL PROSSER CONSPIRACY), and as a boy he must have heard stories of Prosser's intended insurrection. Tradition suggests his mother was born and raised in Africa. She told her son at an early age that, on the basis of his quick intelligence and the distinctive lumps on his head, he seemed "intended for some great purpose."

Turner learned to read as a small boy, and he built a strong and composite faith from listening to the African beliefs retained within his family and the Christian values of his first master, Benjamin Turner. Confident from childhood that he had a special role to play, Nat Turner found outward confirmations

for his messianic thoughts and eventually determined that his personal calling coincided with the most pressing public issue of the day—the termination of racial enslavement.

Most of what we know about the man must be drawn from his *Confessions*, a remarkable autobiographical statement taken down by a young lawyer named Thomas Ruffin Gray during the rebel's final days in jail. While one can question the validity of Turner's recollections and the motivations of the disillusioned and desperate Gray (who rapidly published his lurid transcript at a profit), the confession has an underlying ring of truth and represents one of the most extraordinary firsthand texts in American history.

According to this account, Turner experienced a powerful vision in 1825 in which he "saw white spirits and black spirits engaged in battle, and the sun was darkened—the thunder rolled in the Heavens, and blood flowed in streams. . . ." Three years later, another vision told him to prepare to slay his "ene-

For most blacks and abolitionists, Nat Turner, the leader of the slave revolt in Southampton County, Va., in 1831, immediately became a heroic and legendary figure. The most common reaction to Turner's insurrection, however, was one of revulsion and horror. (Prints and Photographs Division, Library of Congress)

mies with their own weapons." But it was not until February 1831 that a solar eclipse signaled to Turner that he must begin. He laid plans with others to act on the holiday of July 4, but when he fell ill, the date was allowed to pass. Then, on August 13, he awoke to find the sun a dim reflection of itself, changing from one hazy color to another. Taking this as another sign, he brought together a handful of collaborators on Sunday, August 21, and told them of his plan for a terrorist attack.

His intention, Turner explained, was to move through the countryside from household to household, killing whites regardless of age or sex. He hoped that this brutal show of force would be so swift as to prevent any warning and so compelling as to convince others to join in the cause. Having rallied supporters and gathered up more horses and weapons, they could march on Jerusalem, the county seat, and take the arsenal, which would give them a substantial beachhead of resistance. From there the rebellion could spread, aided by a network of enslaved black Christians, and perhaps by divine intervention as well. Turner made clear, according to the *Richmond Enquirer*, that "indiscriminate slaughter was not their intention after they obtained a foothold, and was resorted to in the first instance to strike terror and alarm. Women and children would afterwards have been spared, and men too who ceased to resist."

Shortly after midnight, Turner and five others launched their violent offensive, attacking the home of Turner's master and killing the Travis household, then proceeding on to other farmsteads to wreak similar vengeance. As their ranks grew, the band became more disorderly and the element of surprise was lost, but the first militiamen who offered resistance on Monday afternoon beat a hasty retreat. By Monday night, as many as sixty or seventy African Americans had joined the cause, and on Tuesday morning Turner's army set out for Jerusalem. Behind them at least fifty-seven whites of all ages had been killed in a stretch of twenty miles.

When some rebels stopped at James Parker's farm, within three miles of Jerusalem, to win recruits and refresh themselves, the pause proved fatal, for the local militia had regrouped. They managed to attack and disperse the insurgents, who were off guard and poorly armed. Although Turner attempted to rally his followers, he never regained the initiative, and on Tuesday, white reinforcements launched a harsh and indiscriminate counteroffensive that took well over a hundred lives. One cavalry company slaughtered forty blacks in two days, mounting more than a dozen severed heads atop poles as public warnings. Turner, his force destroyed, eluded authorities for six weeks—during which time another black preacher known as David attempted to ignite an uprising in North Carolina, fueling white fears of widespread rebellion. After an enormous manhunt, authorities captured Turner in a swamp on October 30 and hanged him publicly twelve days later.

Turner's unprecedented insurgency had a complex impact. It forced Virginia's legislature to consider openly, if briefly, the prospect of gradual emancipation. It also attracted proslavery whites to the colonization movement, since many saw African resettlement as a way to remove dangerous bondsmen and reduce the free black community. For black and white abolitionists in the North, Turner's Rebellion reinforced the idea, later espoused by John Brown (*see* JOHN BROWN'S RAID), that enslaved Southerners were willing and able to engage in armed revolt if only weapons and outside support could be arranged. Among churchgoing slaveholders, the uprising prompted tighter restrictions on black preaching and greater caution regarding slave access to the Gospel. Among African Americans, Turner became and has remained both a martyr and a folk hero never to be forgotten. As recently as 1969, one black Southampton resident could recall what his mother had learned in her childhood: that Nat Turner "was a man of war, and for legal rights, and for freedom."

REFERENCES

APTHEKER, HERBERT. *Nat Turner's Slave Rebellion.* New York, 1966.

MORRIS, CHARLES EDWARD. "Panic and Reprisal: Reaction in North Carolina to the Nat Turner Insurrection, 1831." *North Carolina Historical Review* 62 (1985): 29–52.

OATES, STEPHEN B. *The Fires of Jubilee: Nat Turner's Fierce Rebellion.* New York, 1975.

TRAGLE, HENRY IRVING. *The Southampton Slave Revolt of 1831: A Compilation of Source Material, Including the Full Text of 'The Confessions of Nat Turner.'* Amherst, Mass., 1971.

WOOD, PETER H. "Nat Turner: The Unknown Slave as Visionary Leader." In Leon Litwack and August Meier, eds. *Black Leaders of the Nineteenth Century.* Urbana, Ill., 1988, pp. 20–40.

PETER H. WOOD

Navarro, Theodore "Fats" (September 24, 1923–July 7, 1950), jazz trumpeter. Born in Key West, Fla., in 1923, Navarro was known affectionately to his peers as Fat Girl because of his weight. Navarro, along with Dizzy GILLESPIE, was considered one of the foremost trumpeters in the bebop idiom. His life was cut short due to an addiction to heroin, which was a factor in his contracting tuberculosis.

Navarro began his music studies as a pianist but soon switched to the tenor saxophone, and then at age thirteen to the trumpet. He was equally adept at both the sax and trumpet, but, sensing that his career chances were better on trumpet, he began touring on that instrument when he was seventeen. After working with Snookum Russell in the early 1940s, Navarro's first big break came as a member of the Andy Kirk band, with which he toured from 1943 to 1944. In this band he worked with another trumpeter, Howard McGhee, through whom he became known to other players in the East. In 1945 Navarro was recommended to Billy ECKSTINE by Dizzy Gillespie as Gillespie's replacement in that band. Navarro was such a fine player that he soon was nearly Gillespie's equal. He held his chair for eighteen months and then played with Illinois Jacquet, Tommy Reynolds, Lionel HAMPTON, and Coleman HAWKINS. Navarro worked with the pianist, arranger, and composer Tadd DAMERON during 1948 and 1949, and he continued to record until shortly before his death in 1950.

Navarro had an exceptionally clean sound, and his technique was flawless. He was also an innovative soloist. Both his ideas and his approach to the instrument were demonstrated in his recordings with Tadd Dameron and Bud POWELL, which contain the best illustrations of Navarro's improvisations.

Navarro was a big man, weighing at one point over three hundred pounds, but tuberculosis and heroin addiction wasted him away to little more than one hundred pounds when he died. In the last stage of his life Navarro was abandoned by other players because they feared contracting his disease. One exception, Miles DAVIS, befriended him and helped him to the end.

REFERENCES

BALLIETT, WHITNEY. "Jazz: Fat Girl." *New Yorker,* (June 12, 1978): 116.
COLLIER, JAMES LINCOLN. *The Making of Jazz,* pp. 399–400. New York, 1979.

WILLIAM S. COLE

Naylor, Gloria (January 25, 1950–), writer. Gloria Naylor was born in New York City to Roosevelt and Alberta Naylor. After traveling through New York, Florida, and North Carolina as a missionary for the Jehovah's Witnesses (1968–1975) she returned to New York, where she worked as a telephone operator at various hotels while she attended Brooklyn College (B.A., 1981). She received an M.A. in Afro-American Studies from Yale University in 1983.

Naylor's first published work, *The Women of Brewster Place* (1982), won the American Book Award for best first novel in 1983. Dealing with the lives of seven black women who live on one ghetto street, the novel conveys the oppression and spiritual strength that African-American women share. At the same time, by exploring the characters' differences, it emphasizes the variety of their experience. Naylor wrote a television screenplay adaptation of the novel which starred Oprah Winfrey and appeared on *American Playhouse* in 1984. Her next novel, *Linden Hills* (1985), is concerned with the spiritual decay of a group of black Americans who live in an affluent community, having forsaken their heritage in favor of material gain. *Mama Day,* published in 1988, tells of an elderly lady with magical powers. The best-selling *Bailey's Cafe* (1992) takes place in a 1940s American diner where neighborhood prostitutes congregate. Naylor wrote a play based on the novel which was produced and performed by the Hartford Stage Company in 1994. She also wrote the screenplay for the PBS presentation *In Our Own Words* (1985).

Naylor has said that she writes because her perspective, that of the black American woman, has been "underrepresented in American literature." Her goal is to present the diversity of the black experience. Although she reworks traditional Western sources in her novels, borrowing the structure of Dante's *Inferno* for *Linden Hills,* and elements of Shakespeare's *The Tempest* for *Mama Day,* Naylor utilizes black vernacular and other aspects of her own heritage in her writing.

Naylor has taught at George Washington University, New York University, Princeton, Cornell, and Boston University. She has received a National Endowment for the Arts Fellowship (1985), the Distinguished Writer Award from the Mid-Atlantic Writers Association (1983), the Candace Award from the National Coalition of 100 Black Women (1986), and a Guggenheim Fellowship (1988).

REFERENCES

HINE, DARLENE CLARK, ed. *Black Women in America.* Brooklyn, N.Y., 1993.
METZGER, LINDA, ed. *Black Writers: A Selection of Sketches from Contemporary Authors.* Detroit, 1989.

LILY PHILLIPS
LYDIA MCNEILL

Neal, Larry (September 5, 1937–January 6, 1981), writer. Larry Neal, one of the most prominent figures of the BLACK ARTS MOVEMENT of the 1960s and

1970s, was born in Atlanta and graduated from Lincoln University in Pennsylvania in 1961, receiving an M.A. from the University of Pennsylvania in 1963. Neal soon became one of the most prominent of the African-American writers that emerged in the early 1960s championing the search for a distinctive African-American aesthetic. His early articles, including "The Negro in the Theatre" (1964) and "Cultural Front" (1965), were among the earliest to assert the need for separate cultural forms as necessary to the development of black artists in a racist society.

Neal developed his perspective on black art in the influential anthology *Black Fire* (1968), coedited with Amiri BARAKA, and the essay "The Black Arts Movement" (1968), which helped give a name and direction to the nascent artistic trend. Neal argued that the purpose of black arts was to effect a "radical reordering of the Western cultural aesthetic" in part through a purging of the external European and white American cultural influences from black artistic expression. His critical thinking was further developed in a series of books: *Black Boogaloo: Notes on Black Liberation* (1969); *Trippin' a Need for Change* (1969), coauthored with Amiri Baraka and journalist A. B. Spellman; and *Hoodoo Hollerin Bebop Ghosts* (1971). Neal also authored plays (*The Glorious Monster in the Bell of the Horn,* 1976), screenplays (*Holler S.O.S.,* [1971]; *Moving on Up,* [1973]), and television scripts (*Lenox Avenue Sunday,* [1966]; *Deep River* [1967]).

Neal was an instructor at the City College of New York from 1968 to 1969, and subsequently taught at Wesleyan University (1969–1970) and Yale University (1970–1975). By the mid-1970s Neal was reconsidering his view of black culture. In "The Black Contribution to American Letters" (1976), he argued that while all African-American writers and literature must be in some sense political, it was important to separate the public persona of black writers from their specific private experiences, which are often wider and more inclusive than the polemical rejection of nonblack influences that characterized the Black Arts Movement. Other late works of Neal include a play, *In an Upstate Motel,* which premiered in New York in 1981. Neal died of a heart attack in Hamilton, N.Y., in 1981.

REFERENCES

MARTIN, REGINALD. "Total Life Is What We Want: The Progressive Stages of the New Black Aesthetic in Literature." *South Atlantic Review* (November 1986): 46–67.
NEAL, LARRY. "The Black Arts Movement," *Drama Review* 12 (Summer 1968).
———. "The Black Contribution to American Letters: Part II, The Writer as Activist—1960 and After." In Mabel M. Smythe, ed. *The Black American Reference Book.* Engelwood Cliffs, N.J., 1976.
———. "The Negro in the Theatre." *Drama Critique* 7 (Spring 1964).
VAN DEBURG, WILLIAM L. *New Day in Babylon: The Black Power Movement and American Culture, 1965–1975.* Chicago, 1992.

REGINALD MARTIN

Larry Neal giving a lecture. (Photographs and Prints Division, Schomburg Center for Research in Black Culture, The New York Public Library, Astor, Lenox and Tilden Foundations)

Nebraska. The Kansas-Nebraska Act of 1854 opened the territory to settlement. Nebraska escaped the violence that plagued the early settlement of Kansas, as very few slave holders migrated to the area. The census of 1860 listed only eighty-two blacks in the territory, of whom fifteen were slaves. Then, in 1861 the territorial legislature abolished SLAVERY.

Between the CIVIL WAR and WORLD WAR I, Nebraska, which had become a state in 1867, developed rapidly, but in staccato fashion due to the boom-bust economic cycles of the late nineteenth century. The transcontinental railroad traversed the state, the cattle kingdom moved north, and farmers occupied the plains. The state's population climbed to over one million and Omaha became the twentieth most populous city in the United States.

African Americans constituted a small but significant portion of the pre–World War I migration. Some blacks took up homesteads, but migrants attempted few short-lived EXODUSTER-style colonies. Most African Americans settled in towns. Usually they were accepted, or at least tolerated, although several violent incidents occurred. In 1879, for example, residents of Lincoln, the state capital, drove a group of 150 migrating black Mississippians out of town. Nonetheless, by the early twentieth century small numbers of African Americans resided in most of the sizable towns scattered throughout the state. Yet, because of available economic opportunities, the vast majority of blacks lived in Omaha. According to the 1910 census, of 1,192,214 people who lived in Nebraska, 7,689 (0.6 percent) were blacks, and of 124,096 people who resided in Omaha, 4,426 (3 percent) were blacks.

In race relations Nebraska did not follow the pre–World War I southern model. Except for an 1887 anti-miscegenation law, the legislature did not enact other JIM CROW provisions. In fact, in 1885 it passed a state civil rights law modeled on the national statute of 1875, although the courts adjudicated it erratically. However, discrimination remained personal and limited; income largely determined residence, social interaction was common, and employment opportunity existed in the white- and blue-collar sectors.

World War I dramatically altered race relations in Lincoln and Omaha. Nebraska's share of the Great Migration was small, but it did double the black population in both cities, to approximately 1,000 and 10,000 respectively. Competition for jobs and housing intensified, and rumors about black crime spread fear and anger. Thus, during the "Red Summer" of 1919, Omaha experienced a race riot. Subsequently, de facto segregation rapidly became pervasive.

Restrictive banking and realty practices quickly created residential ghettos. In Lincoln, "T" Town, named for a primary street in the neighborhood east of the University of Nebraska campus, emerged as an area of residential confinement for newly arrived African Americans. Actually, the small number of black migrants and the high rate of home ownership by the older African-American residents kept "T" Town integrated and overall black residence somewhat dispersed.

In Omaha two more densely settled ghettos emerged. The smaller was located in South Omaha, a suburb annexed in 1915, adjacent to the meat-packing plants, the major industrial employer of black labor. The larger neighborhood, the Near Northside, astride the downtown area, developed as African Americans replaced Scandinavians, Jews, and Italians in 1870s- and '80s-era rental units and modest single-family homes.

Economic opportunity also dwindled and a race-based job-classification system grew as blacks were limited to menial, nonindustrial, service-type employment. In education in Omaha, where the only sizeable African-American settlement existed, segre-gation evolved because of residential patterns, student-transfer policy, and the choice of where to build new schools. Moreover, black teachers could not obtain employment in the school systems statewide. Also, the University of Nebraska adopted a whites-only policy for student housing, the athletic teams, and the health-profession schools.

Finally, public access became racially selective. Restaurants, hotels, hospitals, cemeteries, and recreational establishments segregated or refused service to blacks. In Omaha, with its larger African-American population, some institutions separated the races by establishing an all-black satellite in one of the ghettos. In smaller communities, organizations that felt the need to serve blacks sometimes designated separate black-use time periods.

The patterns of segregation intensified from 1920 to 1940 despite the curtailing of the Great Migration. The African-American population in Nebraska increased only a few thousand during the interwar era. Small Urban League and NAACP affiliates in Lincoln and Omaha negotiated in nonpublic forums to improve conditions, but with extremely limited results. Their most significant success came in obtaining relatively equal access to NEW DEAL programs.

Then, war dramatically intervened again. Large-scale black migration resumed during WORLD WAR II, with Omaha absorbing the vast majority of it. By 1990, the city's African-American population quadrupled, as did Lincoln's, perpetuating the geographic concentration of blacks in Nebraska. Actually, 97 percent of the 57,404 blacks resided in three contiguous eastern counties—Douglas (Omaha), Sarpy (headquarters for the Strategic Air Command), and Lancaster (Lincoln). The population increase coincided with a war-induced civil rights militancy symbolized by the national African-American "Double V" slogan.

In Lincoln and Omaha, direct-action groups emerged to promote equal opportunity. In 1946 the Lincoln Urban League helped create the Central Social Action Committee, chaired by the Rev. Gordon Lippitt. During the late 1940s and early '50s, it and successor groups integrated restaurants, the municipal swimming pool, and some sports and women's housing at the University of Nebraska.

Simultaneously the Omaha Urban League led efforts that ended segregation of the public-housing projects and persuaded the Omaha Public School System to hire black teachers. In 1948, it cooperated with Fr. John Markoe and Denny Holland, founders of the integrated De Porres Club, which conducted successful boycotts that gained employment for blacks. However, into the 1960s all attempts by it and successor groups, such as the Citizens Coordinating Committee for Civil Liberties (4CL), failed to secure city or state open-housing or fair-employment laws. Only national legislation established those rights, and in 1976 the federal courts mandated the Omaha Public School District to integrate system-wide with busing. Furthermore, Omaha did not escape the violence of the 1960s, experiencing significant riots in 1966 and 1968.

In the 1990s, race relations and the status of blacks in Nebraska continued to evolve in the context of the state's distinct history and demography and in that of the CIVIL RIGHTS MOVEMENT. Monumental changes in legal rights occurred, but the full litany of urban racial problems persisted, especially in Omaha.

REFERENCES

ANTHONY-WELCH, LILIAN. "Black People: The Nation-Building Vision." In *Broken Hoops and Plains People.* Lincoln, Nebr., 1976, pp. 99–151.
FEDERAL WRITERS PROJECT. *The Negroes of Nebraska.* Lincoln, Nebr., 1940.
MIHELICH, DENNIS. "The Formation of the Lincoln Urban League." *Nebraska History* 68 (1987): 63–73.
———. "The Lincoln Urban League: The Travail of Depression and War." *Nebraska History* 70 (1989): 303–316.
———. "Omaha, Nebraska: Positive Planning for Peaceful Integration." In *Community Politics and Educational Change.* New York, 1980, pp. 260–297.
———. "World War II and the Transformation of the Omaha Urban League." *Nebraska History* 60 (1979): 401–423.

DENNIS MIHELICH

Négritude. It was in Aimé Césaire's revolutionary surrealist poem *Cahier d'un retour au pays natal* (*Return to My Native Land*), published in 1939, that the term *négritude* first appeared in print. It had been invented by Césaire, Senegalese poet Léopold Sédar Senghor tells us, perhaps as early as 1932. The term did not come into literary and cultural history until the publication in 1948 of Senghor's *Anthologie de la nouvelle poésie nègre et malgache* (Anthology of New Black and Malagasy Poetry), whose preface, "Orphée noir" (Black Orpheus), had been written by Jean-Paul Sartre. In addition to Senghor (future president of Senegal) and Césaire (future representative of Martinique to the French Assembly), the poets of négritude represented in the anthology included Léon Damas of Guyana; Gilbert Gratiant and Étienne Léro of Martinique; Guy Tirolien and Paul Niger of Guadeloupe; Léon Laleau, Jacques Roumain, Jean-François Brière, and René Belance of Haiti; Birago Diop and David Diop of Senegal; Jean-Joseph Rabéarivelo, Jacques Rabémananjara, and Flavien Rana-

ivo of Madagascar. Each of these poets had, in his particular fashion, "returned to the source," composed poems out of the matrix of African culture and experience. Négritude was a diverse phenomenon, but it has been associated chiefly with Senghor, its principal promoter, who defined it as the "totality of values of black African culture." It was at once a racial essence, common to all Africans and their descendants, and a conscious choice to embrace the "condition" of being black. In classic Senghorian négritude, the affirmation of African values is complemented by faith in the virtue of cultural mixing (*métissage*) and an aspiration toward a universal civilization or humanism:

Let us answer "present" at the rebirth of the World
As white flour cannot rise without the leaven.
Who else will teach *rhythm* to the world
Deadened by machines and cannons?
Who will sound the *shout of joy* at daybreak to wake orphans and the dead?
Tell me, who will give back the *memory of life* to the man of gutted hopes?
They call us men of cotton, coffee, oil.
They call us men of death.
But we are men of *dance,* whose feet get stronger
As we pound upon firm ground.

(From "Prayer to the Masks." In *Léopold Sédar Senghor: The Collected Poetry,* trans. Melvin Dixon. Charlottesville, Va., 1991, p. 13.)

It was in Paris in the 1930s, in the climate of modernism, jazz, African primitivism, and surrealism, that the idea of négritude arose. West Indian and African students had come to the capital to complete their education. They had attended French colonial schools whose objective, in keeping with the values of the Enlightenment and the French Revolution, was to make of them "black Frenchmen." The effect of this assimilation policy was that these subjects or citizens of France had learned to reject their African cultures of origin and to emulate the culture of the French. Yet these students now felt the pull of both cultures—or, as W. E. B. Du Bois had written three decades earlier, a double consciousness—and they sought the intellectual means to rehabilitate African civilization(s).

Paulette Nardal and her sisters were the midwives of this cultural reawakening. Their home was a meeting place for young black intellectuals and writers from Africa and the diaspora. Among the American visitors to the Nardal home and to that of their cousin, Louis Achille, Jr., were Alain LOCKE, the editor of *The New Negro* (1925), and Mercer COOK, a professor of French at HOWARD UNIVERSITY. In

1930–1931, the Nardal sisters published a bilingual journal, the *Revue du monde noir* (*Black World Review*), in which they and others set forth forceful arguments and appeals for racial pride and solidarity, across national and continental boundaries. In its brief existence the journal exposed the Parisian students to facets of black American life and to the poetry of Langston HUGHES and Claude MCKAY. Soon thereafter, Césaire and Senghor were reciting poems by these and other black American writers, among them Jean TOOMER, Sterling BROWN, and Countee CULLEN. Senghor read articles by W. E. B. DU BOIS and Carter G. WOODSON in the *Crisis* and *Opportunity,* respectively. The example of these black American brothers, these "new Negroes," was crucial in spurring on Senghor and Césaire, as had been the intellectual courage of René Maran (*Batouala,* 1921) and Jean Price-Mars (*Ainsi parla l'oncle* [Thus Spoke the Uncle], 1928), and the work of European anthropologists and ethnographers Maurice Delafosse, Leo Frobenius, and Robert Delavignette, who demonstrated that precolonial African civilizations were not devoid of culture.

The Nardal sisters, and Césaire and Senghor in a later and short-lived publication *L'Etudiant noir* (1935), privileged the cultural dimension of black life. Thus the publication in 1932 of the more political and militant manifesto *Légitime Défense,* by Étienne Léro, René Ménil, and Jules Monnerot, was but the first of many critiques to come. It was after the publication of the *Anthologie* that the flurry of attacks began. They were directed especially against Senghor and the proposition that "emotion is Negro as reason is Greek."

Above all, the idea of a "Negro soul"—collectivist, rhythmic, spiritual, and so on—was seen as a mystification that ignored the significance of national identity, historical circumstances, and modes of economic life, as well as the necessity of political action. Moreover, since négritude was a response to the psychological turmoil of a French-educated elite, it was deemed irrelevant to the unassimilated peasant masses of French Africa and to Africans governed under British indirect rule. One French critic observed that négritude merely corresponded to one strain of Western humanism that privileged the intuitive and the irrational. (See chapters 22 and 23 of Hymans 1971 for a discussion of négritude's early detractors.) More sustained critiques have been made by Stanislas Adotevi in *Négritude et négrologues* (1972) and Marcien Towa in *Léopold Sédar Senghor: Négritude ou servitude?* (1971). In fiction, Yambo Ouologuem's *Devoir de violence* (*Bound to Violence*; 1968) denounced romanticized notions of precolonial Africa, and Mariama Bâ's *Un chant écarlate* (*Scarlet Song*; 1981) revealed the masculinist bias of négritude.

Yet African writers and intellectuals acknowledge the stunning impact of négritude as a cultural and aesthetic philosophy that sought to affirm the humanity of those whose humanity had been denied by Europe on the basis of race. On American shores, Samuel W. Allen published "Black Orpheus," a translation of Sartre's preface, and an anthology of African writers, illustrated by Romare BEARDEN. Mercer Cook also taught, published, and lectured on African and West Indian writers. Langston Hughes, too, published several anthologies of African writing. That new renaissance of cultural nationalism, the Black Arts Movement of the 1960s, was an American version of négritude: The same themes resonated in the works of writers such as Don Lee, Larry NEAL, Sonia SANCHEZ, and Paul Carter HARRISON (*The Drama of Nommo,* 1972). Moreover, the recent elaboration of indigenous theoretical models for African-American literature by Houston Baker (*Blues, Ideology, and Afro-American Literature: A Vernacular Theory,* 1984) and Henry Louis Gates, Jr. (*The Signifying Monkey,* 1988) can be seen as the latest avatar of the aesthetic ideology at the heart of négritude.

REFERENCES

ARNOLD, JAMES. *Modernism and Negritude.* Cambridge, Mass., 1981.

COOK, MERCER, and STEPHEN HENDERSON. *The Militant Black Writer in Africa and the United States.* Madison, Wis., 1969.

FABRE, MICHEL. *From Harlem to Paris: Black American Writers in France 1840–1980.* Champaign, Ill., 1991.

HYMANS, JACQUES LOUIS. *Léopold Sédar Senghor: An Intellectual Biography.* Edinburgh, 1971.

KESTELOOT, LILYAN. *Black Writers in French.* Washington, D.C., 1990.

VAILLANT, JANET. *Black, French, and African: A Life of Léopold Sédar Senghor.* Cambridge, Mass., 1990.

EILEEN JULIEN

Negro American Labor Council. Shortly after the American Federation of Labor and Congress of Industrial Organizations (AFL-CIO) refused to adopt internal desegregation measures at its 1959 convention, seventy-five black trade union officials, led by A. Philip RANDOLPH, president of the BROTHERHOOD OF SLEEPING CAR PORTERS, AFL-CIO, formed the Negro American Labor Council (NALC) as a vehicle through which to pressure the labor federation to act against segregated and discriminatory unions. At its founding convention in 1960, the all-black NALC called for the elimination of JIM CROW union locals, racist bars to union leadership, and discriminatory job training programs. Randolph, who was elected president by the delegates, dominated the council for most of its brief life. By the end of its first year the NALC had enlisted 10,000 members nationally, with its largest chapter in Detroit.

In 1961 the NALC presented to the AFL-CIO Executive Council specific charges of discriminatory practices in affiliated unions along with the recommendation that such practices be rooted out and, as a final resort, unions refusing to comply be expelled from the federation. The Executive Council rejected the proposals, labeled the NALC "separatist," and officially censured Randolph, charging the longtime labor and civil rights leader as the cause of the black rank and file's discontent with AFL-CIO leadership.

The second NALC convention, held in Chicago in the fall of 1961, featured lengthy and vigorous denunciations of the AFL-CIO Executive Council for its response to the NALC's proposal in particular, and for the failure of organized labor historically to combat racist practices and extend class solidarity to black workers.

By the time of the second convention, the NALC's membership had fallen to a little more than 4,000, largely as a result of a lack of funds to wage a sustained organizing campaign. Moreover, a number of members notified the NALC that they were not allowed to organize on behalf of the council while holding official union positions. However, as a result of the pressure brought to bear by the NALC, the 1961 AFL-CIO convention adopted an unprecedented civil rights program which Randolph called the best anti-discrimination measure ever taken up by organized labor. The AFL-CIO's civil rights resolution instituted grievance procedures and called for affiliated unions to voluntarily eliminate segregated locals and discriminatory practices. The NALC criticized the resolution for its reliance on voluntary compliance, yet considered the AFL-CIO's measure an important, if insufficient, victory. One of the greater tangible achievements of the NALC was the election of an African American, Nelson Edwards, to the executive board of the United Auto Workers, for which the Detroit chapter had lobbied since its founding.

Shortly after the 1961 NALC convention, Randolph renewed his call from 1941 for a massive march on Washington to demand jobs and civil rights, partly as a way to satisfy militant black nationalists in the council. The NALC became one of the primary mobilizing organizations for the 1963 March on Washington for Jobs and Freedom. Although it was unable to win the official endorsement of the AFL-CIO, it was instrumental in gaining the support of various major unions for the demonstration. The NALC continued through the early 1960s as the leading liaison between the CIVIL RIGHTS MOVEMENT and organized labor.

At its fourth annual convention in 1964 the NALC adopted a resolution calling for a national one-day general strike on August 28, the anniversary of the March on Washington, if the pending civil rights bill were not passed by that time. The resolution became moot when the Civil Rights Act of 1964 was signed into law shortly after the NALC convention.

In 1966 Randolph resigned as president of the council and Cleveland Robinson, vice president of the Distributive, Processing, and Office Workers Union (District 65) and a longtime ally of Randolph, was elected to succeed him. The name of the organization was soon thereafter changed to the National Afro-American Labor Council, which was supplanted as the leading advocate of equality within the labor movement by the more moderate A. Philip Randolph Institute, founded by Randolph in 1964. Through the 1960s the institute also recruited black workers into the civil rights movement, assisted voter-registration drives in the South, and successfully lobbied the AFL-CIO leadership to support African-American political causes.

See also LABOR AND LABOR UNIONS.

REFERENCES

FONER, PHILIP S. *Organized Labor and the Black Worker, 1619–1973.* New York, 1974.

HILL, HERBERT. "Racial Practices of Organized Labor." In Julius Jacobson, ed. *The Negro and the American Labor Movement.* Garden City, N.Y., 1968.

PFEFFER, PAULA F. *A. Philip Randolph, Pioneer of the Civil Rights Movement.* Baton Rouge, La., 1990.

THADDEUS RUSSELL

Negro Digest. *See* Black World/Negro Digest.

Negro Elections Day. Negro Elections Day, a ceremony among African-American slaves in New England, is of disputed origin. Known also as Negro Governor's Day and by several other names, Negro Elections Day is a celebration that entailed costumes, feasting, and the election of a "governor" among certain slave populations. More of a symbolic position than anything else, an elected "governor" had no real legislative or political power.

In some cases, contests of cleverness and strength were designed as a means of picking a winner, who would then become governor; in other cases, personal character, morality, intelligence, and wisdom were prerequisites upon which a governor was appointed. In a few cases, the appointed governor was a descendent of African royalty or had actually been a prince or king prior to capture by slave traders.

Negro Elections Day generally fell on one of the days granted to slaves for rest and recreation. On this day, slave men and women dressed in fancy garb or costume, played music, and paraded through the streets on foot or on horseback, accompanying their elected governor. The governor usually wore military dress or emblems (such as a crown) of royalty. The parade was usually followed by a dinner and dance.

Some eighteenth-century writers speculate that the election of governors was a vestige of the ceremonies accompanying the election of a king or chief which had taken place in Africa. Other writers suggest that enslaved Africans, now politically powerless, were imitating the election process that they had witnessed in the company of their white masters. However, the fact that Negro Elections Day is documented as having grown less political and more ceremonial over the years (when fewer Africans with a knowledge of original customs were being imported), combined with the fact that similar celebrations took place among slave populations in the Caribbean and Latin America, seems to buttress the belief that the practice originated in Africa.

REFERENCES

AIMES, HUBERT H. S. "African Institutions in America." *Journal of American Folk-Lore* 18 (1905): 15–32.

SHELTON, JANE deFOREST. "The New England Negro—A Remnant." *Harper's New Monthly Magazine* 88 (1894): 533–538.

PETRA E. LEWIS

Negro Ensemble Company, The. The Negro Ensemble Company (NEC), the longest-lived black theater in the United States, was founded in 1967 by actor Robert Hooks, actor-director-playwright Douglas Turner WARD, and manager Gerald Krone. Supported with an initial Ford Foundation grant of $434,000, the NEC was founded as a not-for-profit institution to provide a place where black theatrical talent could be trained and presented on a continual basis, away from the pressures of commercial theater. In addition to producing plays, therefore, it offered a tuition-free training program for actors and a playwrights' unit where writers could develop their work. Founded during the height of the BLACK ARTS MOVEMENT (of which it was conspicuously not a part), the NEC was often criticized in its

early days for its integrated administrative staff (Krone, for example, was white), its ties to white-led institutions such as the Ford Foundation, and its selection of plays. The latter tended toward naturalistic representations of black family life, not the heavily polemical, revolutionary plays favored by the Black Arts movement.

Through the mid-1980s, the NEC nurtured a generation of important African-American playwrights. Productions included Lonne ELDER III's *Ceremonies in Dark Old Men* (1969), Philip Hayes Dean's *The Sty of the Blind Pig* (1971), Joseph WALKER's *The River Niger* (1972), Leslie Lee's *The First Breeze of Summer* (1975), Charles FULLER's *The Brownsville Raid* (1976) and *A Soldier's Play* (1982; winner of the Pulitzer Prize) and Samm-Art WILLIAMS's *Home* (1979). On occasion, the NEC ventured into styles other than realism, including the experimental *A Ballet Behind the Bridge* (1971) by Lennox Brown, and Paul Carter HARRISON's ritualistic *The Great McDaddy* (1973).

In the mid-1980s, severe financial crises forced the NEC to curtail its number of productions, disband its resident acting company, and discontinue most of its workshops. It produced plays only sporadically, and these, including Charles Fuller's cycle of one-act plays about African-American life since the Civil War, were less well received than many of its earlier productions. Between 1991 and 1993, the NEC suspended production altogether, although it continued to hold readings and occasional workshops. In 1993 the NEC produced Kenneth Hoke Witherspoon's *Last Night at Ace High* and hoped to return to a more active production schedule.

REFERENCES

DURHAM, WELDON, ed. *American Theatre Companies, 1931–1986.* New York, 1989.

WILLIAMS, MANCE. *Black Theatre in the 1960s and 1970s: A Historical-Critical Analysis of the Movement.* Westport, Conn., 1985.

MICHAEL PALLER

Negro History Week. *See* Black History Month/Negro History Week.

Negro National Anthem. "Lift Ev'ry Voice and Sing," with words by James Weldon JOHNSON and music by J. Rosamond JOHNSON, became known as the "Negro National Anthem" or "Negro National Hymn." James Weldon Johnson wrote this three-stanza hymn for a celebration of Lincoln's birthday at the Colored High School in Jacksonville, Fla. The school choir first performed the song on February 12, 1900. During the next twenty-five years, African Americans began to perform the hymn at churches, schools, and other large gatherings.

James Weldon Johnson did not write the song as an expression of African-American solidarity, but in 1926 he acknowledged that "the song not only epitomizes the history of the race, and its present condition, but voices their hope for the future." Some writers have objected to calling "Lift Ev'ry Voice" a "national" hymn; however, the song is still performed as the unofficial anthem of African Americans.

REFERENCES

JOHNSON, JAMES WELDON. *Along This Way*. New York, 1938.
"Lift Ev'ry Voice and Sing." *Crisis* 32 (September 1926): 234–236.

WILLIE STRONG

Negro Sanhedrin.

Negro Sanhedrin.   The Negro Sanhedrin was a short-lived organization established in 1924 with the purpose, according to its founder, Kelly MILLER, of fostering cooperation and coordination between black organizations and forming one unified voice for black America. Miller perceived that black organizations often duplicated each others' efforts or worked at cross-purposes, offering the nation neither a clear picture of the problems of African Americans nor a single agenda for action.

Actually, Miller envisioned several organizations formed along the lines of the ancient Hebrew Sanhedrins: a greater Sanhedrin, which would function nationally to coordinate black political and social policy and be composed of representatives from the leading national black organizations, and lesser Sanhedrins, operating on local levels. Miller took care to distinguish the Sanhedrin, which would concern itself with "the immediate problems of the Negro in the United States," from W. E. B. DU BOIS's Pan-African Conferences (*see* PAN-AFRICANISM), which explored the conditions of blacks worldwide, and UNIVERSAL NEGRO IMPROVEMENT ASSOCIATION of Marcus GARVEY, which sought the emigration of American blacks to Africa.

Miller, a leading essayist, sociologist, and dean of the College of Arts and Sciences at Howard University, used his influence among black moderates to attract representatives from sixty-three national black organizations, including the NATIONAL ASSOCIATION FOR THE ADVANCEMENT OF COLORED PEOPLE, the

Equal Rights League, the Race Congress, the International Uplift League, and the Friends of Negro Freedom, to an initial meeting in Chicago the week of February 11, 1924. Miller also invited several leading citizens unaffiliated with black organizations. In all, 300 delegates attended. The main address was delivered by the mayor of Chicago, William E. Dever.

In the course of their week-long meeting, the delegates identified seven problems of black American life which required interracial cooperation to resolve: the need to improve public health among black Americans; the necessity for equal schools; the end of the exploitation of black labor; the protection of the black franchise; equal rights for women; strengthening the right of protest and public utterance; and the improvement of interracial relations.

The delegates also recommended seven points of internal policy aimed at the internal improvement of the black community: the need to build a strong, independent business community; the creation of black fraternal and charitable organizations; the maintenance of a "less partisan" and "more dignified" black press; the establishment of relationships with blacks around the world; the encouragement and support of black youth; and the study and promotion of African and black American culture.

Miller, who referred to the Negro Sanhedrin as "an influence rather than an organization," envisioned biennial meetings on the national level, but the Negro Sanhedrin never met again.

REFERENCES

BRACEY, JOHN H., JR., AUGUST MEIER and ELLIOT RUDWICK, eds. *Black Nationalism in America*. New York, 1970.
MILLER, KELLY. *The Negro Sanhedrin: A Call to Conference*. Washington, D.C., 1923.

MICHAEL PALLER

Negro String Quartet.

Negro String Quartet.   Founded by Felix Weir and active from 1920 to 1933, the Negro String Quartet performed on musical programs of many churches and community organizations in Harlem and at Columbia University. Its members were Weir and Arthur Boyd, first and second violins respectively, Hall JOHNSON, viola; and Marion Cumbo, cello. They performed both European chamber music repertory and music of African-American composers, including Samuel COLERIDGE-TAYLOR and Clarence Cameron WHITE. Johnson, who later formed his own choir and arranged many African-American spirituals, also composed and arranged music for the quartet. The Negro String Quartet was the musical descendant of the American String Quartet, also founded by Weir. That group included Joseph Lymos, Hall Johnson, and Leonard Jeter. Despite a brief tenure (1914–1919), its members bequeathed a distinguished reputation to the Negro String Quartet: Johnson and Jeter were members of the original pit orchestra of the Broadway musical *Shuffle Along* (together with Eubie BLAKE and William Grant STILL). Jeter performed the Schumann *Cello Concerto* with the Boston Symphony Orchestra in 1914 and was one of the cello teachers of Marion Cumbo.

The most significant performance of the Negro String Quartet was on November 28, 1925, at Carnegie Hall, when it accompanied Roland HAYES singing spirituals arranged by Hall Johnson for tenor, piano, and string quartet. Of that performance *New York Times* music critic Olin Downes wrote: "The performance had the profound and mystical feeling that the slave songs possess—a spirituality and pathos given them in fact as well as in name. Thus the final group was not merely an expected item of an entertainment, but rather the contribution of musicians and artists together in the presence of a common ideal of beauty."

REFERENCES

DOWNES, OLIN. "Roland Hayes Sings." *New York Times,* November 28, 1925.

HARE, MAUDE CUNEY. *Negro Musicians and Their Music.* Washington, D.C., 1936.

WATERS, ETHEL, with Charles Samuels. *His Eye Is on the Sparrow.* New York, 1951.

TIMOTHY W. HOLLEY

Nell, William Cooper (December 20, 1816–May 25, 1874), historian and abolitionist. Born in Boston, William Cooper Nell graduated from the city's African school with honors, but despite his achievements was excluded because of color from citywide ceremonies honoring outstanding scholars. That incident inspired him to lead a campaign to integrate Boston schools during the 1840s and early '50s. He also championed equal access to railroads, theaters, and militia service. Nell joined the rising antislavery movement in 1831 and became one of the closest and most loyal African-American associates of abolitionist William Lloyd Garrison. In later years, Nell supported himself through work as a legal copyist.

In the early 1840s, Nell began a lengthy affiliation with Garrison's LIBERATOR, writing articles, supervising the paper's Negro Employment Office, corresponding with other abolitionists, and representing Garrison at various antislavery functions. Nell

moved to Rochester at the end of the 1840s, where he became the publisher of Frederick DOUGLASS's newspaper *The North Star* (1847). By 1850, he had returned to Boston, where he ran unsuccessfully for the Massachusetts Legislature on the Free Soil party ticket, and worked on the UNDERGROUND RAILROAD. When conflict arose between Douglass and Garrison after 1851, Nell eventually sided with Garrison, although his own political posture was probably somewhere in the middle.

Nell believed that African-American history could be a useful tool in stimulating racial pride and advancing the struggle against slavery and racial prejudice. He wrote two pioneering historical works, the pamphlet *The Services of Colored Americans in the Wars of 1776 and 1812* (1851), and the book *Colored Patriots of the American Revolution* (1855). His careful scholarship and innovative use of oral sources contributed in important ways to the developments of African-American historiography. Beginning in 1858, to protest the 1857 DRED SCOTT DECISION, Nell began organizing annual Crispus Attucks Day celebrations in Boston to commemorate African-American contributions to the American Revolution and to justify black claims to full citizenship. In 1861, he was appointed a postal clerk in Boston, becoming probably the first African American named to a position in a federal agency. He held this post until his death, from "paralysis of the brain," in 1874.

REFERENCES

SMITH, ROBERT P. "William Cooper Nell: Crusading Black Abolitionist." *Journal of Negro History* 55 (1970): 182–199.

WESLEY, DOROTHY PORTER. "Integration Versus Separatism: William Cooper Nell's Role in the Struggle for Equality." In Donald M. Jacobs, ed. *Courage and Conscience: Black and White Abolitionists in Boston.* Bloomington, Ind., 1993, pp. 207–224.

ROY E. FINKENBINE

Nelson, Prince Rogers. *See* Prince.

Nevada. Although African Americans arrived in large numbers only during WORLD WAR II, they have been present at every stage of Nevada's development. In the nineteenth century mountain man James P. BECKWOURTH went through the area; there is a pass named after him just north of Reno. African-American men accompanied Jedediah Smith, John C. Frémont and other fur traders or explorers. Rancher Ben Palmer, who arrived in Carson Valley in the early 1850s, was one of the wealthiest men in Douglas County for several decades during the nineteenth century. One of his sister's children was the first non–Native American child born in the territory.

Most nineteenth-century African Americans lived on the Comstock, the chief silver-producing area in nineteenth-century Nevada, and in Carson City. Almost entirely barred from mining, black men and women alike did menial labor. However, they also operated businesses from barbershops to cafés and hotels. W. H. C. Stephenson practiced medicine in Virginia City in the 1860s and '70s. The small black population supported two lodges of Prince Hall Masons, churches in Virginia City and Carson City, and other organizations. William M. Bird, a barber, ran for mayor of Virginia City in 1870. Another barber, Thomas Detter, who came to San Francisco from Washington, D.C., in the 1850s and lived in several places in the West, published a book, *Nellie Brown,* in 1871 while he lived in Elko. Poet James WHITFIELD was also a 19th century resident of Elko.

Nevada law was openly racist at its beginning; nonwhites could not vote, hold office, serve on juries, marry whites, testify against whites, or send their children to public schools, unless separate schools were established. Protests from the African-American community plus national developments eliminated much governmental discrimination by the mid 1870s. For example, parents in Carson City raised money, built a schoolhouse, and then sued when the school board refused to hire a teacher. In 1872 the state Supreme Court invalidated the discriminatory school law. Although complete data are lacking, it is probable that private discrimination lessened into the 1870s and then increased at the end of the century.

The African-American population declined even more rapidly than the overall population in the 1880s, when the Comstock mines ceased producing heavily, and did not recover until the 1940s. From 1900 to about 1940, the largest community was in Reno, where Bethel African Methodist Episcopal Church is the oldest African-American church in the state.

Substantial numbers of African-American workers were hired during World War II at a war plant, Basic Magnesium, in Henderson, in southern Nevada's Clark County. Before this, the small African-American population of Las Vegas (the principal city in Clark County) mostly lived downtown, where some operated businesses. The new workers from the South (principally Arkansas and Louisiana) found themselves largely confined to the Westside, across the railroad tracks from downtown Las Vegas.

The Westside continues to be the core of the black community in southern Nevada, but it has spilled over into North Las Vegas and other surrounding areas. The Westside for several decades was almost entirely black, with few African Americans living elsewhere, but higher proportions have moved out to live elsewhere in the southern metropolitan area in the last two decades.

For the last forty years the largest African-American population in the state has lived in Clark County, with smaller concentrations in Reno-Sparks and Mineral County. African Americans are scarce in almost all the small counties (which together comprise only about 15 percent of the state's population).

Rising private discrimination in the late 1930s earned Nevada the reputation of "the Mississippi of the West." Branches of the NATIONAL ASSOCIATION FOR THE ADVANCEMENT OF COLORED PEOPLE were organized in Las Vegas in the late 1920s and in Reno-Sparks in 1945. The Las Vegas branch began efforts to secure civil rights laws in 1939, but significant advances did not occur until 1959–1960, when a state district court judge invalidated the antimiscegenation law and the legislature, at the urging of Gov. Grant Sawyer, repealed various discriminatory laws left over from the nineteenth century and prohibited discrimination in apprenticeship programs. A threatened public march organized by the NAACP against discrimination by southern Nevada casinos, the largest employers in the state, ended public accommodations discrimination in southern but not northern Nevada.

Not until 1965 was a law passed forbidding discrimination in public accommodations and employment; only then did northern Nevada casinos admit black customers. Not until 1971 was a fair housing act passed, and the Equal Rights Commission has been weakened since it was created in 1961; Nevada retains some of its reluctance to abandon racial discrimination.

Court action—initiated largely by Nevada's first African-American attorney, Charles Kellar—brought about some desegregation of schools in Clark County in the 1970s, ended some discriminatory practices at the state prison, and opened up employment in southern Nevada's casino industry. Litigation in Reno led in the 1980s to the hiring of the first African-American firefighters in that area.

Nevada's first black state legislator was Woodrow Wilson, elected in 1966. The Rev. Willie Wynn became the first African-American cabinet officer in Nevada history under Gov. Paul Laxalt in the late 1960s. In 1992 there were several prominent black public officials, including the Sparks postmaster, local elected officials in both southern and northern Nevada, and a member of the board of regents of the university system. In 1993 State Sen. Joe Neal and Assemblymen Morse Arberry and Wendell Williams represented southern Nevada districts.

Dr. Charles I. West was the first African-American physician since Dr. Stephenson in the nineteenth century. Dr. James McMillan was the state's first black dentist; both arrived in the 1950s. Today there are many black health professionals in the state at all levels. The first laparoscopic operation in southern Nevada was performed by Dr. Harriston Lee Bass, Jr.

Attorney Kellar had to sue to get the right to practice law in Nevada, but there are now prominent African-American attorneys in both Las Vegas and Reno. Several have been elected to judgeships; in 1992 Addeliar Guy and Lee A. Gates were district court judges in Clark County.

There are many black educators in the state. Dr. Paul Meacham has been president of Southern Nevada Community College since 1983, and Claude G. Perkins was superintendent of Clark County schools from 1978 to 1981.

Churches, among which the BAPTIST and CHURCH OF GOD IN CHRIST congregations are numerous, are strong in Nevada's African-American community. Civil rights organizations other than the NAACP are scarce. The Northern Nevada Black Cultural Awareness Society developed vigorous programs in the 1990s. In Clark County, the Fordyce Club maintains social ties with Fordyce, Ark., one of the major sources of wartime immigration to Clark County.

Economic development has been slow, but by the early 1990s there were substantial numbers of successful black business people. In northern Nevada, Luther Mack owned several fast-food stores. In southern Nevada William "Bob" Bailey was continuing a long career helping black businesses, John J. Edmond owned a shopping center, and Donald Givens was hotel manager of the Excalibur casino, one of the largest in the state.

In the arts, Laverne Ligon's Simba dance group has been critically acclaimed. Young artists Wayne Horne, Jr., and Tony Trigg and poets Nancy Ellen-Webb Williams and Jimi S. Bufkin have received recognition.

The rise of a successful middle class should not obscure the fact that poverty rates are high in African-American communities. The ratio of African-American to white household incomes in Nevada in 1992 was 70.8 percent, higher than the national average of 62.9 percent, but close to the average for Western states.

Dr. Charles West founded the *Las Vegas Voice,* the state's first African-American newspaper, in the 1950s; it survives as the *Las Vegas Sentinel-Voice.* The Rev. Vincent L. Thompson published the *Reno Observer* in Reno during the 1970s. African-American-owned radio or TV stations have yet to appear, but there are prominent black media employees in southern Nevada.

Black Nevadans have made significant contributions to the state in spite of pervasive discrimination. Today there are prominent and successful black men and women in all occupational fields although a legacy of past discrimination survives.

REFERENCES

CORAY, MICHAEL S. "Blacks in Nevada." In *Nevada Comprehensive Preservation Plan.* Carson City, Nev., 1991, pp. 31-2 to 32-23.

EARL, PHILLIP I. "Blood Will Tell: A Short History of Nevada's Miscegenation Laws." *Nevada Public Affairs Review* (1987, no. 2): 82–86.

FITZGERALD, ROOSEVELT. "The Demographic Impact of Basic Magnesium Corporation on Southern Nevada." *Nevada Public Affairs Review* (1987, no. 2): 29–35.

———. "The Evolution of a Black Community in Las Vegas: 1905–1940." *Nevada Public Affairs Review* (1987, no. 2): 23–28.

NEVADA BLACK HISTORY PROJECT. *Nevada Black History: Yesterday and Today.* Reno, Nev., 1992.

RUSCO, ELMER R. "The Civil Rights Movement in Nevada." *Nevada Public Affairs Review* (1987, no. 2): 75–81.

———. *Good Time Coming? Black Nevadans in the 19th Century.* Westport, Conn., 1975.

ELMER R. RUSCO

New Africa, Republic of. *See* Republic of New Africa.

Newark, New Jersey. Situated on the Passaic River in northern New Jersey, Newark was founded in 1666. It remained largely agricultural for the next 150 years, and slavery was practiced on a small scale in the area through the beginning of the nineteenth century. Starting in the 1830s, industrialization caused a spurt in local economic and population growth. In 1832 the town of Newark received its charter, and four years later was incorporated as a city. As German and Irish immigrants came to Newark, the population increased almost tenfold in forty years. Slavery in Newark and New Jersey finally ended in the 1840s, though the city remained sympathetic to Southern interests and largely free of abolitionist activity.

The city's modest free black community of poor laborers and servants, which never exceeded 2,000, was molded during this period. The Baxter School, a private black school, was founded in 1828. In 1832 the city's first black church, the Thirteenth Street Presbyterian Church, was founded. St. James African Methodist Episcopal Church was founded in 1842, and St. Phillip's Episcopal Church followed not long after.

In the decades following the CIVIL WAR, small numbers of African Americans migrated to Newark, and the town's black population grew to 10,000 by WORLD WAR I, an overflow from the larger migration to nearby New York City. The thousands of immigrants from southern and eastern Europe who poured into Newark provided competition for labor and for scarce housing resources (one-fifth of the city's area was marshlands, and there was a chronic land and housing shortage). Meanwhile, the city's increasingly powerful industrial unions excluded black workers: In 1903, only six of the city's twenty-two major unions accepted black laborers.

During these decades, the city's black population remained almost exclusively trapped at the bottom of the economic ladder. In 1890 almost two-thirds of all male African Americans were engaged in unskilled labor or as servants, and 88 percent of women were maids or laundresses. Twenty years later, the picture was substantially the same. A few African Americans were able to found successful businesses. C. M. "Chicken" Brown operated a poultry stand, and Mary and Frank Anderson were the proprietors of a hotel with mostly white patrons. John S. Pinkman, who ran a furniture moving concern, became relatively wealthy.

At the same time, Newark was mostly free of overt racial tension, and the city's blacks were relatively integrated into community affairs. Housing stock, while poor, was open to blacks, and African Americans lived in integrated working-class areas throughout the city. The only all-black enclave was a district on the northern side of the downtown area. Public accommodations remained largely segregated, but schools integrated peacefully after the New Jersey Supreme Court's 1884 decision in *Pierce* v. *School Board of Burlington County,* which declared school segregation unconstitutional. In 1909, city authorities closed the all-black Baxter school, claiming separate schools were unnecessary.

The black community fostered several lasting institutions during this period. In 1871 the Bethany Baptist Church (later the city's largest black church) was founded. Bethany Church members also founded the Bethany Lodge, a masonic fraternity; the Sunday Afternoon Lyceum, a literary circle; and the Coloured Home for Aged and Orphans in nearby Montclair. In 1902, the *Appeal,* the city's first black newspaper, was founded. It was published through 1910. During the early 1900s, the Frederick Douglass Republican Club was organized to promote voting.

The Great Migration altered the face of black Newark. As the coming of World War I opened up jobs for African Americans in the city's steel mills and in war industries such as munitions plants, brickyards, and wire factories, southeastern blacks, the largest number from Georgia, poured into the city. The Negro Welfare League, an interracial group of black ministers and professionals and white businessmen founded in 1910 (transformed into the Newark branch of the NATIONAL URBAN LEAGUE in 1919) and led by African-American Thomas Puryear, attempted to find jobs and housing for the migrants, some of whom were forced into shantytowns and tent cities. The league obtained employment for black workers, who were largely excluded from white unions, often through the use of no-strike pledges. The only large protest by black workers during the period was that of the dockworkers, led by Prosper Brewer (later a political leader and the black ward's Republican ward committeeman), who struck successfully for higher wages in 1916.

By the end of the 1920s, Newark's economy was already depressed, and its white population began to decline. Many large industrial firms left the crowded city for larger sites. Business flight cost the city well-paid jobs and tax revenue for city services, and the city's commission system of government led to unresponsive and notoriously corrupt rule. Within such an environment, racial tension grew. Downtown stores, swimming pools, and theaters continued to exclude black patrons, who were forced into segregated neighborhoods in the old downtown areas. The Third Ward, better known as the "Hill District" and considered by many commentators "the worst slum in America," was the center of Newark's black community. By 1930, 30 percent of the city's 38,880 African-American residents lived there. Antiquated zoning laws, which prevented construction of new housing, meant that few blacks owned their homes, and most were forced to settle in overcrowded dilapidated, expensive, old, white-owned housing. Sanitation was primitive, and black residents were plagued by tuberculosis and venereal disease. In 1923, the city's Board of Health tried to use the tuberculosis epidemic as a pretext for deporting black migrants. In 1927, Dr. John Kenney founded Kenney Memorial Hospital to care for poor citizens. Police harassment was a chronic problem. In 1928, police Captain George Fohs prohibited interracial contact after midnight in the district. In 1930 white city residents vetoed a proposal by the Prudential Insurance Corporation to build a black housing development in the Hill district.

Despite the depressing living conditions, a thriving black culture grew up within the "Roaring Third" Ward during the 1920s and 1930s. Religious institutions flourished, including heterodox denominations such as FATHER DIVINE's movement and NO-

BLE DREW ALI's Moorish Science Temple, founded in 1915, a black nationalist religious group that prefigured the NATION OF ISLAM. An active JAZZ scene, loosely connected with New York City's, arose in the ward. It was centered on the core intersection of Spruce Street (the "Colored Broadway") and Broome Street. There, theaters such as the Orpheum and Paramount, and such nightclubs as the Kinney Club and the Skateland Club, featured New York performers and hopefuls such as Jimmy LUNCEFORD and Ella FITZGERALD. Newark also has been the home of many important musicians in various genres, such as Willie "The Lion" SMITH, Sarah VAUGHAN, Wayne SHORTER, Babs Gonzales, Larry Young, Woody Shaw, James Moody, Hank Mobley, and Dave Thomas. Another focus of black community interest during the period was Ruppert Stadium, home of the Newark Eagles of the Negro National League, who featured such players as Larry DOBY and future Hall-of-Famers Monte IRVIN, Ray Dandridge, and (briefly) Satchel PAIGE.

The GREAT DEPRESSION devastated Newark. In the face of white competition, many blacks were unable to find work. By 1931 there were 20,000 African Americans on relief, one-third of the city's total. Although almost all welfare recipients were longtime Newark residents, in 1932 city officials organized a movement to send back all newly arrived southern blacks in order to reduce welfare rolls. Black ministers and leaders campaigned successfully against the project, and Newark Urban League president Thomas Puryear, who collaborated on it, was forced to resign.

The depression and the struggle to remain in the city radicalized many young black Newark residents. In 1934, activist Harold Lett became director of the Newark Urban League and led protests over black job exclusion. The same year, Guy Moorehead organized the Essex County Worker's League, and in 1936 became New Jersey's first black Democratic state representative. In 1938 black community forces led by the Newark branch of the NATIONAL NEGRO CONGRESS successfully picketed chain stores to obtain jobs for African Americans. In 1939 Fred and Richard Martin bought the Newark Herald newspaper, renamed it the Newark Herald-News, and made it a powerful voice for civil rights during the 1940s.

The economic boom that followed the outbreak of World War II brought renewed black mass migration to Newark. African Americans, who had represented just 10 percent of the city's 1940 population, tripled over the next twenty years, growing to one-third of the city's total. Although black protesters won token access to public places, the rise in population was not accompanied by a rise in status. Indeed, whites ac-

tively opposed black equality. In 1949 the city Board of Education approved a policy of free transfers for white students from black majority schools, and by 1951, some 3,200 white students were attending schools outside their districts. In 1953 a reform city government was elected and replaced the corrupt city commission regime, which had systematically discriminated against blacks, with a mayor and city council.

The next year, Newark African Americans finally got their first voice in government, when former NAACP president Harry Hazelwood was named city magistrate, and newspaperman Irvine Turner was elected to the new city council, where he remained until 1970. Even so, the reform movement proved ephemeral, and Newark's Democratic machine soon regained control. Poor city services and police brutality remained chronic problems. Meanwhile, Turner became a corrupt and powerful "boss" in the black community. Famous for his fiery rhetorical denunciations of "slumlords" and racist practices, he tried to curtail efforts at reform by other blacks. The Newark NAACP, whose leaders were dependent on the machine, failed to press strongly for city action in support of black equality.

During the 1950s, even as the white population was reduced, the black population began to decline, as middle-class blacks moved to nearby suburbs. By the beginning of the 1960s, Newark was, in an often-used phrase, a "terminal case"—a city with little industry, high unemployment, corrupt government, and racial unrest. Its high crime rate and poor city services foreshadowed the problems of many urban areas in the United States at the end of the twentieth century.

Within the city, black residents unwilling to put up with discrimination began organizing civil rights efforts. In 1961 a chapter of the CONGRESS OF RACIAL EQUALITY (CORE) was formed, and members protested police brutality, housing discrimination, and began negotiations with employers for jobs. In 1963 CORE joined with other groups to form the Newark Coordination Council (NCC). When the NCC protested discrimination in hiring for city school construction projects, Mayor Hugh Addonizio, supported by Turner and NAACP leader Carlton Norris, refused to act or meet with "irresponsible" protesters. Police harassment of NCC members weakened the group.

Despite official opposition, the African-American community was growing more powerful in Newark. White flight led to an African-American majority population by mid-decade, and federal antipoverty projects designed to bypass the city machine and encourage community participation fostered such black organizations as the Newark Community Union Project. Post and community organizer Imamu Amiri BARAKA (formerly LeRoi Jones) returned to his native Newark, founded the community arts center Spirit House, and established the Temple of Kawaida as a center of African-American religion and culture. In 1966 Kenneth A. Gibson ran for Mayor. Though he was defeated, his strong showing clearly demonstrated the rise of African American political power in Newark. Meanwhile, radical protest groups were created. In 1967 Abdul-Jerud Hassan formed the Blackman's Liberation Army, and Baraka formed the Committee for a Unified Newark. The following year, Newark was the location of the first BLACK POWER CONFERENCE. Black community groups organized successfully to oppose the granting of land in a black neighborhood to a state medical college, and blocked the appointment of an unqualified white city councilman, James Callaghan, to the school board, though they were unable to secure the appointment of City Budget Director Wilbur Parker, an African American.

On July 12, 1967, John Smith, a black cabdriver, attempted to speed past a police car and was arrested, beaten, and taken to a police station. Rumors of his death spread through the black community. The next night, after a "Police Brutality Protest Rally" downtown, rioting broke out, and crowds began looting and setting fires throughout the city. National Guard troops arrived to arrest rioters and looters, but the violence continued for three nights. Twenty-one African Americans died, 1,600 were arrested, and over $10,000,000 in property was destroyed. In 1968, following the assassination of the Rev. Dr. Martin Luther KING, Jr., rioting broke out again.

The riots scarred Newark both physically and emotionally. During the following years, as whites continued to move out of the city, blacks concentrated on political organizing. In 1968 Mayor Addonizio was forced out of office after being convicted on criminal corruption charges. In 1970 Kenneth A. Gibson again ran for mayor. He received almost no white votes, but was elected by a coalition of black and Hispanic voters. Gibson was elected as a reformer, but was largely unable to dismantle existing police and educational structures. In 1971 Gibson appointed several new members to the city Board of Education in order to assure a nonwhite majority. The white-led city teacher's union went on strike for eleven weeks to protest the appointments, the longest teacher's strike ever in a large city in the United States.

Gibson remained in office for four terms. He attracted large amounts of federal money for improvements at Newark airport and the Port of Newark. He also was successful in persuading businesses such as Prudential Insurance to remain in Newark and secured funds to revive the downtown area. With the aid of federal grants, the city soon had the nation's largest percentage of families in public housing projects, including the Kawaida Towers development. Still, Newark remained a poor city, with high unemployment, crime, and homicide rates, dilapidated schools and housing, and poor city services. Gibson was increasingly criticized as ineffective in improving conditions, and in 1986 he was challenged and defeated in the Democratic mayoral primary by City Councilman Sharpe James. James was elected mayor and was reelected in 1990. By the early 1990s, blacks dominated the city's political scene. In 1988 Newark's Donald Payne became New Jersey's first black congressperson.

African-American life in Newark remained difficult in the early 1990s. The frustrations of the period were symbolized by an epidemic of car theft. Many young black men without jobs turned to stealing cars for joyrides as a form of excitement. Still, Newark's African-American residents have continued to struggle to improve conditions and enrich their lives. Institutions such as the Newark Museum and the Institute of Jazz Studies at Rutgers University–Newark (one of the city's two colleges) were particularly notable for their efforts to promote black culture. Newark also has been the home base of a large number of successful black business and professional people, as well as such entertainers as Dionne WARWICK, Melba MOORE, and Cissy and Whitney HOUSTON.

REFERENCES

CURVIN, ROBERT. The Persistent Minority: The Black Political Experience in Newark. Ph.D. diss. Newark, N.J., 1975.

HAYDEN, TOM. Rebellion in Newark: Official Violence and Ghetto Response. New York, 1967.

JACKSON, KENNETH T. and BARBARA B. JACKSON. "The Black Experience in Newark: The Growth of the Ghetto, 1870–1970." In William C. Wright, ed. New Jersey Since 1860: New Findings and Interpretations. Trenton, N.J., 1972.

KUKLA, BARBARA J. Swing City: Newark Nightlife, 1925–1950. Philadelphia, 1991.

PORAMBO, RON. No Cause for Indictment: An Autopsy of Newark. New York, 1971.

PRICE, CLEMLENT. "The Beleaguered City as Promised Land: Newark, New Jersey, 1917–1947." In William C. Wright, ed. Urban New Jersey Since 1870. Trenton, N.J., 1974.

WRIGHT, GILES R. Afro-Americans in New Jersey: A Short History. Trenton, N.J., 1988.

WRIGHT, NATHAN. Ready to Riot. New York, 1968.

GREG ROBINSON

Newby, William H. (1828–1859), journalist. William Newby was born in Virginia in 1828 to a slave father and free black mother. His father died soon after his birth and the family moved to Philadelphia, where Newby studied in segregated schools and eventually achieved some success as a daguerreotypist. He settled in San Francisco in 1851 and greatly influenced the political and cultural life of the city's emerging African-American community. In 1863 he joined with other local leaders to organize the San Francisco Athenaeum, the first black literary association in the state and a forum for the discussion of racial concerns.

Three years later, Newby and fellow activist Jonas H. Townsend founded and edited *The Mirror of the Times,* the first black journal in the state. He regularly reported on the San Francisco African-American community in letters written to *Frederick Douglass' Paper* under the pseudonym "Nubia." A strident voice at the 1855 and 1856 conventions of California blacks, Newby urged united action to overturn the state's laws prohibiting black testimony in the courts, and helped coordinate statewide petition campaigns for black rights. But the effects of tuberculosis and the intractability of American racism eventually prompted him to consider leaving the United States.

In late 1857, Newby accepted a position as private secretary to the French consul in Haiti. Upon his arrival there, he found that the consul had died and left him without employment. He returned to San Francisco in a weakened condition and spent his final months trying to resuscitate the Athenaeum, which had grown moribund in his absence.

REFERENCE

LAPP, RUDOLPH M. *Blacks in Gold Rush California.* New Haven, 1977.

ROY E. FINKENBINE

New Deal. *See* Great Depression and the New Deal.

New Era Club. The New Era Club was founded in 1893 in Boston by Josephine St. Pierre RUFFIN, a well-known social reformer, her daughter, Florida Ruffin Ridley, and Maria Louise BALDWIN, the first African-American female principal in a Massachusetts public school. Josephine Ruffin served as the club's president during its existence.

The New Era Club was founded primarily to meet the needs of the impoverished African-American community. Its middle-class members sought to nurture communal dignity and pride and to teach the less fortunate the importance of hard work and education. They believed that African Americans could overcome the debilitating racism of the period by forming their own organizations and networks and demonstrating their competence.

In essence, their program was a combination of removing racial barriers, expanding opportunities, and encouraging self-help. They organized kindergartens in Boston and supported children in educational institutions in Georgia. In 1894 they started the first magazine published by black women, the *Women's Era* (1894–1897), which covered topics such as legislation, health, family life, and fashion as well as the activities of the New Era Club. The magazine also served as a forum for black clubwomen from all over the country.

The New Era Club also played a critical role in the formation of the first national African-American women's organization. In 1895 Ruffin convened a conference in Boston to respond to charges by a Missouri newspaper editor that African-American women were immoral. She proposed "to teach an ignorant and suspicious world that our aims and interests are identical with those of all good aspiring women." Over one hundred delegates from thirty-six African-American women's organizations in twelve states attended the conference. They formed the National Federation of Afro-American Women, which in 1896 merged with the National League of Colored Women to become the National Association of Colored Women (NACW).

The New Era Club played a prominent role in the national organization and national club movement. Ruffin served as the first vice president of the NACW and the New Era Club was a charter member. In 1896 the *Women's Era* became the official organ of the NACW. The New Era Club also tried to join the all-white General Federation of Women's Clubs in 1900 when Ruffin attended their meeting in Milwaukee. The executive board of the General Federation would not ratify the membership of the Boston Club and refused to seat Ruffin as a representative of a black women's organization. The Massachusetts delegation protested the blatant racism of the white women's club movement. By 1904 as the NACW came to dominate the black women's club movement, the New Era Club had disbanded, but its former members continued to play an important role in the national club movement.

REFERENCES

GIDDINGS, PAULA. *When and Where I Enter: The Impact of Black Women on Race and Sex in America.* New York, 1984.

SALEM, DOROTHY. *To Better Our World: Black Women in Organized Reform, 1890–1920.* Brooklyn, N.Y., 1990.

PAM NADASEN

New Hampshire. Black people have been in New Hampshire since the first known African slave arrived in Portsmouth from Guinea in 1645. According to provincial census records, the number of slaves in the colony was seventy in 1707 and peaked at 656 in 1775. The majority of blacks, both enslaved and free, were located in the Portsmouth area and represented about 4 percent of the town's total population. The percentage of black people in the total state population has remained at less than 1 percent over time. Portsmouth still claims the largest percentage of African Americans (1,200 out of a total population of 26,000 in 1990); its numbers, though, fall short of those of the larger industrial city of Nashua (1,300 African Americans out of a total of 75,800) but exceed those of Manchester (970 African Americans out of a total of 96,550).

Slaves were brought to New Hampshire by prosperous residents whose wealth came in part from direct and indirect participation in the international slave trade. Typically, one to three slaves lived with a family. They shared chores, providing skilled and unskilled labor at home and in the workplace. Men worked in the shipyards, aboard ships at sea, in shops, and in the fields. Women performed the many tasks required to maintain a healthy household and a gracious home. The versatility required for survival in colonial New Hampshire is implied in newspaper advertisements for the sale of "negro" men and women who were described as suited for work in both town and country.

Children of slave fathers were born free under the prevailing English common law in the new colonies, but custom and tradition later followed Virginia's law of 1662, which assigned the mother's status as slave or free to the child. Laws restricting activities of "Negroes" and "mulattoes" applied equally to slaves and freedpeople. The laws limited rights of travel and assembly, imposed night curfew, forbade accommodations in public places, and prevented African Americans from being guests in a private home after nine o'clock at night.

Surveys of wills and inventories of the estates of prominent early families show that slaves were frequently passed on to family members upon the death of a master. Some slaves, such as Prince Whipple (1750?–1796), an aide to Gen. William Whipple during the Revolutionary War, earned freedom by serving in the colonial wars. Others purchased freedom. An example is Amos Fortune (1701?–1801), a tanner who had been a slave in MASSACHUSETTS until age sixty, when he bought freedom for himself and others, including Violate, the woman he married. The couple moved to Jaffrey, N.H., where Amos's tanning business flourished, and they became town philanthropists. The Amos Fortune Forum continues as a memorial and is funded by his estate. A few free blacks also gained renown. The most prominent was Wentworth CHESWILL of Newmarket, a Revolutionary War veteran who was elected several times to office in the town in the 1770s and '80s.

Portsmouth blacks were part of the abolitionist movement that was developing during the late eighteenth century. Leaders of the Negro Court, also known as the Slave Court, were elected annually from among their peers to conduct the business of the black community. Officials of the court were among the nineteen Portsmouth slaves who submitted a petition in 1779 to the state legislature urging the end of slavery in the state; no action was taken on the petition. Although the legislature did not address the issue of slavery in the state constitution drafted in 1783, its removal of slaves from the category of taxable property was indicative of the prevailing opposition to human bondage. As slaves were freed for military service or manumitted by masters, slavery disappeared in the state. There were only eight slaves in the state in 1800 and none soon after, although slavery was not officially abolished in the state until 1861. However, African Americans remained excluded from militia service and other citizenship rights.

During the early nineteenth century several New Hampshire towns had abolition societies. Frederick DOUGLASS was among the many abolitionists on the speaking circuit, appearing in Pittsfield, Dover, Portsmouth, Concord, Cornish, and Claremont between 1842 and 1845. UNDERGROUND RAILROAD stations were located in several towns from the Massachusetts border northward to VERMONT and CANADA. Antiabolition sentiment was also strong, with Senator Franklin Pierce (who later became president) the most famous New Hampshire antiabolitionist. One house in Canaan was a vital transfer station for escaping slaves, yet the town's notoriety came from the forced closing of a biracial school, Noyes Academy, in 1835. Angry residents yoked the school building to a team of oxen and dragged it into a swamp. Two men who had been among the academy's fourteen black students were Henry Highland GARNET, the future antislavery activist, and future EPISCOPALIAN priest Alexander CRUMMELL. After decades of effort by abolitionists, antislavery forces won a final victory in 1861, when the state supreme court affirmed that a person's color should not deny that person from full rights of citizenship, including the right to vote. Slavery was abolished, and slaves brought into the state were considered freed.

A few notable African Americans emerged from New Hampshire during the volatile decades of the nineteenth century. The PAUL brothers, Thomas (1773–1831) and Nathaniel (1793–1839), born free in Exeter, became active abolitionists. Thomas founded and served as the first pastor at the African Meeting House in Boston. Nathaniel founded a church in Albany, NEW YORK. In Portsmouth Prince Whipple's widow, Dinah, established a school for black children as part of the Ladies Charitable African Society. The poet James M. WHITFIELD (1822–1871) was born in Exeter. Harriet E. WILSON (fl. 1830–1870) of Milford wrote the novel *Our Nig; or, Sketches from the Life of a Free Black . . .* (1859), believed to be the first novel published by an African American in this country. Concert singer Nellie E. Brown of Dover won widespread acclaim for her voice during the 1860s.

Black communities became more clearly defined in the twentieth century. The first black church in the state was founded in Portsmouth in 1896; People's BAPTIST Church remained the only New Hampshire black church for the next half century. By the 1920s, as closings of shoe and textile mills throughout New Hampshire depressed the state's economy, tourism provided an alternative to industry. Black chauffeurs, maids, and cooks arrived with the influx of wealthy white families who summered on the coast of New Hampshire and southern MAINE. Some of the servants remained or returned to become permanent residents. During the same period a black community was forming in Nashua. Black laborers came to Nashua from the South in the 1920s to work in wood-treating plants that manufactured railway ties. Following the outbreak of WORLD WAR II, black soldiers and sailors were stationed at various military installations in southern New Hampshire. As civilian jobs at the Portsmouth Naval Shipyard became plentiful and accessible to African Americans, black men and women gave up employment in factories and private homes for the higher-paying, more challenging positions of "the yard."

A new wave of black migrant workers, including professionals, arrived in the 1950s with the growth of the electronics industry. Also, the opening of Pease Air Force Base near Portsmouth in 1954 significantly increased the local black population. Instances of racial discrimination, particularly in housing and public accommodations, became more frequent and blatant. A branch of the NAACP was chartered in 1958 in Portsmouth to address the problems of de facto segregation both in neighboring communities and on the air base itself. In 1961 the NAACP persuaded the legislature to pass a law banning discrimination in private housing.

In 1963 hearings were held in Portsmouth, Concord, and Nashua by the New Hampshire Advisory Commission to the U.S. Commission for Civil Rights to determine the extent of discriminatory practices in the state. The New Hampshire Human Rights Commission was created as a result of the findings, and the first Equal Employment Opportunities Commission was established at the shipyard. However, support for equal rights was far from universal. The *Manchester Union Leader,* New Hampshire's only statewide newspaper, remained opposed to integration and to those organizations that advocated legislative enforcement of equal rights and opportunities for minorities.

A few New Hampshire African Americans aroused attention. Albert Johnson, a black doctor living in a small town in the state and passing as white during the 1930s, faced an ugly pattern of prejudice when his racial identity was discovered. His story was later dramatized in the film *Lost Boundaries* (1949). The most bizarre episode in New Hampshire African-American history involved Barney Hill, an activist in the state civil rights commission and the NAACP, who claimed in 1966 that he and his wife, Betty, had been abducted and examined by extraterrestrials. The Hills' story brought them extensive media coverage, some of which focused on their status as an interracial couple.

New Hampshire remains the only state which does not officially celebrate the Martin Luther KING, Jr., holiday, although most school districts and many town offices are closed on that day. The Martin Luther King Holiday Coalition, comprising the Portsmouth and Manchester NAACP branches, the American Friends Service Committee, and dozens of other civic, educational, labor, and religious organizations, lobbied for more than fifteen years to establish a state holiday. Opposition was led by the *Union Leader.* In 1992 the threat of economic boycotts of the state caused the newspaper's editor to declare that it was time to adopt the holiday. Soon after, the state's legislature accepted a "civil rights day," celebrated on the third Monday in January, in exchange for eliminating the state's unique "fast day."

REFERENCES

CUNNINGHAM, VALERIE. "The First Blacks of Portsmouth." *Historical New Hampshire* (Winter 1989): 180–201.

U.S. COMMISSION ON CIVIL RIGHTS. *A Report of the New Hampshire Advisory Committee on Civil Rights.* Washington, D.C., 1964.

VALERIE CUNNINGHAM

New Jersey. It is not clear when persons of African descent first arrived on New Jersey soil. Certainly the Dutch from nearby New Amsterdam took the lead in introducing African slaves there in 1664. The Dutch were encouraged by the colony's allocation of additional land for every slave imported between 1664 and 1666. These inducements helped spawn a rapid increase in the slave-labor force by 1680, the date of the earliest documented black New Jersey presence. Most slaves were brought in from the West Indies, especially Barbados, until the mid-eighteenth century, when they began to be imported directly from Africa (*see* SLAVE TRADE).

Throughout the eighteenth century, New Jersey slaves—who numbered about 2,600 in 1726, 4,700 in 1745, and 12,000 in 1790—constituted roughly 8 percent of the overall population, although in several northern counties their proportion was much higher. Only New York in the colonial North exceeded New Jersey in the number and proportion of slaves.

Most New Jersey slaves worked on small farms that averaged about three slaves and produced grains and raised livestock. While their work conditions were generally less harsh than those on the large plantations of the South, many ran away and some considered insurrection, as exemplified in a plot discovered in 1734 near Somerville that led to the arrest of several hundred bondsmen.

The state's slave population peaked in 1800, when about 13,000 bondsmen were recorded. By this year, however, the egalitarian ideals of the AMERICAN REVOLUTION and the abolitionist efforts of the Quakers had weakened involuntary servitude, especially in Quaker-dominated South Jersey, where in 1800 free blacks outnumbered slaves by almost five to one. The struggle against SLAVERY in New Jersey achieved a milestone in 1786, when the slave trade was abolished.

The weakening of slavery enabled blacks to begin fashioning organizations that met a host of needs and helped them forge an identity as a people—a community. Around 1800 they founded their first institution, the Mt. Pisgah African Methodist Episcopal Church, in Salem.

In 1804 New Jersey became the last northern state to manumit its slaves, a fact that helped foster a view of the state as very South-like in its treatment of blacks. Under the gradual provisions of the 1804 abolition law, all children born of slaves after July 4 of that year were to be emancipated after serving apprenticeships to their mother's master—females after twenty-one years and males after twenty-five. The abolition act of 1846 freed all black children born after its passage. The state's few remaining slaves, however, became "apprentices for life," another form of bondage. Their numbers had dwindled to eighteen in 1860, as recorded in the U.S. census, making New Jersey the last state in the North to have slaves. The ratification of the THIRTEENTH AMENDMENT to the U.S. Constitution in 1865 ended the "peculiar institution" in New Jersey.

Both free southern blacks and FUGITIVE SLAVE participants in the UNDERGROUND RAILROAD settled in New Jersey during the antebellum period, establishing an immigration pattern that down to 1970 was the primary source of black population increase there. They helped create or expand all-black settlements such as Lawnside, which was incorporated in 1926 as a municipality, the state's first and only all-black community to achieve such a status.

By the CIVIL WAR, black New Jerseyans numbered nearly 26,000 and had structured a vibrant institutional life that included churches, schools, literary societies, fraternal lodges, and benevolent associations. They had also organized to protest racial injustice, in 1849 holding a statewide convention for restoring the franchise lost in 1807 through legislation. A similar meeting in 1865 proved equally unsuccessful; it was the Fifteenth Amendment in 1870 that returned black voting rights.

After the Civil War, a color line that kept New Jersey African Americans subservient became more heavily drawn, reinforcing the state's image of racial conservatism. The system of JIM CROW public schools, which existed primarily in southern New Jersey and lasted until the early 1950s, was strengthened in 1886 with the founding of the "Tuskegee of the North," the New Jersey Manual Training and Industrial School for Colored Youth, eventually located in Bordentown. Increased discrimination and insensitivity from the white community in other social realms stirred African Americans to reach inward for resources to build additional alternative institutions. These offered services ignored by the larger

Civil rights float for New Jersey in the Gay Pride parade, New York City. (© Martha Cooper)

society and provided much needed opportunities for blacks to be treated with dignity and respect. By 1915 the black associational network included newspapers, homes for the elderly and orphans, political clubs, women's social clubs, and such businesses as hotels, barbershops, and funeral homes.

Many of the southern blacks who trekked northward during the Great Migration triggered by World War I came to New Jersey. Some were attracted by the relatively small size of its industrial cities, with their slower pace. Arriving (like prior and later migrants) mainly from the states along the Atlantic coastline, they enlarged the state's African-American population on an unprecedented scale. Between 1910 and 1930 the black population more than doubled, from roughly 90,000 to 209,000; between 1920 and 1930 alone it grew by 78 percent, its highest decennial increase ever.

With the massive influx of southern newcomers, the state's black ghettos also began to take shape, giving rise to profound social, economic, and political changes in black community life. One immediate benefit of increased residential segregation was the enhancement of black political power, as reflected in the first election of an African American, Walter G. Alexander, to the General Assembly, the state legislature's lower house, in 1921. Still, migrants found much in New Jersey reminiscent of the South, such as considerable KU KLUX KLAN activity in the early 1920s. Blacks began calling the state the "Georgia of the North."

While the GREAT DEPRESSION slowed migration during the 1930s, WORLD WAR II renewed movement to the state. Because the war involved a struggle against racist and antidemocratic forces abroad, it also created a climate that strengthened the resolve of New Jersey African Americans to struggle against racial intolerance at home. Their deeds helped shape the state's third constitution. Adopted in 1947, it outlawed racial segregation in public schools and the state militia, making New Jersey the first state to make such provisions constitutional.

After the war and until the end of the 1960s, African Americans continued to arrive in New Jersey from the South on an even larger scale. A more than twofold increase in the black population, from 318,565 in 1950 to 770,292 in 1970, coincided with abandonment by whites of the state's cities and led to the enlargement of black ghettos. Their myriad social and economic ills caused many to erupt in violence during the 1960s. The violence that occurred in black NEWARK in 1967, involving twenty-six fatalities, was by far the most serious.

Black protest in the 1960s was also directed toward discriminatory treatment in housing and employment and, especially in South Jersey, public accommodations (hotels, restaurants, theaters, parks, and beaches). Perhaps the most important symbol of the success of political protest was the election of Newark's first African-American mayor, in 1970.

By 1980 virtually all black life in New Jersey, the nation's most urbanized state, had an urban texture and spirit; over 95 percent of the state's African Americans were urban dwellers. In 1990, when blacks numbered 1,036,825 and constituted 13.4 percent of the population—the highest percentage ever—they made up majorities in nine major New Jersey communities (Newark, East Orange, Camden, Irvington, Plainfield, Orange, Willingboro, Atlantic City, and Asbury Park).

New Jersey in 1990 had the fourth-highest black median household income among the fifty states, and its African-American community could count other gains in politics, housing, social status, and wage equality. Still, using various indices of poverty, some of the state's predominantly black municipalities were among the nation's most impoverished, serving as metaphors for urban squalor and decay.

REFERENCES

PRICE, CLEMENT ALEXANDER. *Freedom Not Far Distant: A Documentary History of Afro-Americans in New Jersey*. Newark, N.J., 1980.
WRIGHT, GILES R. *Afro-Americans in New Jersey: A Short History*. Trenton, N.J., 1988.

GILES R. WRIGHT

New Mexico. Although New Mexico has long been recognized as a state with a diverse cultural heritage, the state's African-American population has often received less attention than the interaction of the area's Anglos, Latinos, and Native Americans. Yet blacks have a history as old as the Latinos in the state. The black population has remained relatively small in numbers and percentage, but blacks have played an important role in New Mexico's culture, economy, and society.

The first important person of African descent in what is now New Mexico was Stephen Dorantes (also known as Estevanico, Black Steven, Little Steven, and Estevan), the slave of the Spanish explorer Andres Dorantes. Having crossed the Southwest as one of the survivors of the Cabeza de Vaca expedition in 1528, Estevanico was well acquainted with the area. He entered the territory of New Mexico as a guide for Fray Marcos de Niza in 1539 in search of the Seven Cities of Cibola (Seven Cities of Gold).

At the end of the sixteenth century, Spanish Gen. Juan de Oñate colonized New Mexico and brought some Africans along with him. Blacks remained a presence in the colony and in the more substantial capital of Santa Fe, founded in 1610. The contemporary Franciscan historian Fray Angélico Chávez has speculated that Domenico Naranjo, a mulatto, was one of the leaders of the Taos Pueblo revolt in 1680, which succeeded in expelling the Spaniards.

When Don Diego de Vargas resettled New Mexico in the 1690s, he brought with him several families of black ancestry. Sebastian Rodrigues Brito, the drummer for de Vargas, was a full-blooded African. During the following years, black men and women were brought to the colony as forced laborers in mining and agriculture. The attitude of the Spanish toward the black slaves who accompanied various expeditions to New Mexico is in direct contrast to the later American position. The Spanish were known for their lack of racial prejudice; they saw blacks as human beings who had merely lost their portion of external freedom. While Santa Fe was a highly stratified society, with six main "castas," or racial groups, cross-cultural marriages contributed to assimilation, and there was limited social mobility for mixed-race people. By 1792, there were forty-two mulatto men and forty-three mulatto women among Santa Fe's 2,540 residents. In 1821, when New Mexico passed from Spain to Mexico, slavery continued on a tiny scale.

The mid-nineteenth century brought fur traders, trappers, and mountain men into New Mexico. One of the best known was the African-American James BECKWOURTH. By his own account, Beckwourth settled long enough in New Mexico to marry a local girl in 1846 and open a hotel in Santa Fe. Later the same year he served as a dispatch rider for Gen. Stephen W. Kearney between Santa Fe and Ft. Leavenworth, Kan. He sold the hotel in 1848 and traveled to California. The Mexican War (1846–1848) brought other blacks into New Mexico with the military forces, notably with the Missouri Rifles, under Gen. Alexander Domiphan. One black teamster with the Missouri Rifles, Henry Boyer, recalled serving in the area at the Battle of Brazito in 1846.

The American victory brought the land occupied by New Mexico into the United States, and in 1850 the territory of New Mexico (including Arizona and part of Colorado) was organized. New Mexico sided with the South on the issue of slavery, which was not explicitly forbidden in the territory's constitution, but the climate made bondage unprofitable. In 1850 there were twenty-two blacks in the New Mexico Territory. Most of these were domestic servants who worked for military or government officials. There were only twenty-two slaves in New Mexico in 1861.

During the Civil War, Confederate troops invaded New Mexico, hoping to conquer the territory, but were repulsed. The territory remained in Union hands. In 1866, the laws preventing intermarriage were repealed, and blacks were enfranchised in 1870.

Between 1866 and 1900, from 3,000 to 3,800 black infantrymen and cavalrymen in the U.S. Army served at one time or another at eleven of the sixteen forts in New Mexico. They were called "Buffalo Soldiers," a term originated by the Native Americans, who thought the hair of black soldiers resembled the fur of the buffalo. The name was accepted with honor. The black troops protected the growing Anglo population from Native Americans and enforced the laws. Seven black soldiers were ultimately awarded the Congressional Medal of Honor for their efforts, including Sergeant Thomas Boyne and Sergeant John Denny, cited for their conduct under fire during a Mescalero Apache raid in 1879. In 1898, the troops participated in the SPANISH-AMERICAN WAR under the command of John Pershing, then a young lieutenant. In 1916, after New Mexico was invaded by the forces of the Mexican bandit Pancho Villa, Pershing, the commanding general of the forces sent to capture Villa, personally requested that the black soldiers of the Tenth Cavalry join his command.

The enlisted men of the Ninth and Tenth Cavalry regiments were major contributors in the final outcome of one of the most famous episodes in the history of the American West, namely the Lincoln County War (1878–1881), a large-scale civil conflict pitting together opposing factions of cattlemen and merchants. Blacks actively fought on both sides of the feud. The black troops were used to protect the trial judge, protect the life of citizens, and preserve the peace. The climax of the war came in April 1879, when a grand jury at Lincoln, N. Mex., handed down 100 indictments. A large-scale gun battle ensued, which the black troops managed to subdue after three days. A detachment of the Ninth Cavalry, Company H, traveled to the Chisum Ranch. They attempted to serve one of the leaders, Alexander McSween, with a warranty for his arrest, but he escaped.

The civilian black population remained under 200 until the 1870s, when many Civil War veterans and Southerners migrated to the West to work in the cattle industry. Although there were more than 5,000 blacks riding the cattle trails that penetrated new Mexico, the percentage of blacks in the permanent population was minuscule. Blacks never were regarded as a political threat to the status quo, and a man was judged by his capacity for work more than by his skin color. One black cowboy, George McJunkin, came to New Mexico in 1876, and went to work at the Pitchforks Ranch. In 1889, he became a local hero for protecting the lives of several white cowboys and saving a herd of cows during a ferocious blizzard.

Many blacks migrated to New Mexico. Under the Homestead Act of 1862, each adult person was entitled to 160 acres of land on payment of ten dollars and the filing of a claim on certified public domain. After residing on or cultivating the land for five years, the settler could receive a patent on payment of additional fees. In 1896, Frances Boyer, son of soldier Henry Boyer, walked from Georgia to New Mexico "to find a place for colored people to live and to be their own free agents." He organized an all-black town named Blackdom, and sent leaflets back to Georgia. Blackdom at its peak had about 300 residents. The decline of this town began in 1918 when a lack of water forced the settlers to move to other areas in New Mexico, mostly to the community of Vado.

Blacks migrating in the area brought with them many elements of southern black culture. One contribution was culinary. Blacks brought typical southern foods such as collard greens, cornbread, okra, sweet potatoes, red beans, pork dishes, black-eyed peas, and biscuits, and readily adopted the Mexican foods of the area: pinto beans, squash, green and red chili, enchiladas, and tortillas. Meals many times were a combination of foods from both cultures.

Once settled, blacks built community institutions. Underlying the strength of the blacks in New Mexico has been religion. Under Mexican rule, many blacks joined the Roman Catholic church. One early black served as sacristan for Saint Albino Church in Mesilla, N. Mex., during colonial times. As more blacks arrived, Protestant churches were organized, mainly Baptist and African Methodist. Such churches as Albuquerque's Cavalry Chapel have remained centers of black life throughout the twentieth century. Many of the clergy were educators, as example, the Rev. C. T. Hughes, who in the 1920s, organized Hughes Academy, an all-black high school, to serve the community of Vado. Blacks built social institutions, such as Albuquerque's Home Circle Club, founded in 1914 by teacher Lula Black.

By 1912, when New Mexico achieved statehood, prejudice against blacks was growing, although Nobel Prize-winning statesman Ralph BUNCHE, who spent part of his childhood in Albuquerque during this period, later recalled that there were too few blacks in the town for antiblack prejudice to be a major problem (anti-Mexican sentiments, however, were common). Discrimination became more blatant following the influx of southern whites to the state in the mid-1920s. Public schools, formerly open to blacks, were segregated in certain areas of the state during these years. For example, a separate school was established at Clayton in northeast Union County in 1926. Public schools in Santa Fe and Albuquerque were never segregated, but blacks in Albuquerque (who were offered and refused a separate school in the 1930s) were sometimes forced to sit in the rear of classrooms. During the 1940s, district boundaries were gerrymandered to assure that affluent whites attended a separate high school from blacks and Latinos. The schools remained segregated until the fall of 1954, shortly after the Supreme Court decision in BROWN V. BOARD OF EDUCATION, OF TOPEKA, KANSAS, banned segregation.

Except for a temporary influx of African Americans after World War I—mostly men working on the Santa Fe railroad who left after the assignment ended—blacks remained less than 1 percent of New Mexico's population through 1940. Most worked in the coal mines around Raton or in the cotton fields and farms of the southwestern Mesilla Valley. The black population of Albuquerque, forced into the dilapidated tenements in the city's "South Broadway" section, remained tiny. Two future celebrities, light-heavyweight boxing champion Bob Foster (born in the city in 1938) and jazz musician John LEWIS (born in 1920), grew up in Albuquerque.

World War II led a great number of blacks to move into the state. Some were in the military service and some employed in civil service positions allied to the defense industry. The federal government would remain the state's largest source of African American employment for the rest of the century. Many of these individuals, settling near military installations or in Albuquerque, played a significant role in New Mexico's labor force, economy, society, and culture. In the late 1940s, the newcomers helped found the state's first NAACP chapter. In 1952, Albuquerque passed an antidiscrimination ordinance. Despite its small membership, the NATIONAL ASSOCIATION FOR THE ADVANCEMENT OF COLORED PEOPLE (NAACP) gained influence through coalitions with Latino civil rights groups such as the GI Forum. However, the state did not pass civil rights legislation until 1964, and due to opposition by conservative white legislators from southeastern "Little Texas," the bill lacked enforcement power. In the late 1960s, the black Latino coalition began to fall apart, although radical groups such as the Alianza Federal de Mercedes—a Hispanic civil rights organization whose leaders called for restitution of community land rights—affirmed the importance of the African-American protest movement and ties with southern civil rights leaders such as the Rev. Dr. Martin Luther KING, Jr.

In the years since the 1960s, blacks in New Mexico have made enormous gains in education and status.

An elaborate public school system, compulsory attendance, and a quest for education has paid off for New Mexico's black population, although the black dropout rate remains above the state's average. Higher education has been readily available through the extensive two-year and four-year system of colleges and universities. Clara Belle Williams, the first black student in the state university system, graduated from New Mexico State University in 1937. Nevertheless, many obstacles remain to black equality. Discrimination has remained a problem. Black poverty and unemployment rates also have remained significantly higher than that of Anglos: in 1987, 29 percent of the state's African Americans lived in poverty.

In 1990, although there were only about 30,000 blacks in New Mexico (some 2 percent of the total population), they were participating actively in politics. Blacks have served on local school boards and have been elected to such positions as city and county commissioners, mayors, and state legislators. In 1984, Tommy Jewell of Albuquerque Metropolitan Court became the state's first black judge. In December 1985, James B. Lewis, a former Bernalillo Country Treasurer, attained the highest statewide office occupied by an African American when Governor Toney Anaya appointed him to the position of State Treasurer, left vacant by the previous treasurer's resignation. Lewis was elected to the position for a full term in 1986.

REFERENCES

BANKS, ROGER W. "Between the Tracks and the Freeway: The Negro in Albuquerque." In Henry Jack Tobias and Charles E. Woodhouse, eds. *Minorities and Politics*. Albuquerque, N.Mex., 1969, pp. 155–180.

BILLINGTON, MONROE LEE. *New Mexico's Buffalo Soldiers, 1866–1900*. Niwot, Colo., 1991.

CHÁVEZ FRAY ANGÉLICO. "Pohe-yemo's Representative and the Pueblo Revolt of 1680." *New Mexico Historical Review* 42 (1962): 85–126.

DROTNING, PHILLIP T. *Heroes in Our Nation's History*, New York, 1970.

JENSEN, JOAN, and DARLIS A. MILLER. *New Mexico Women: Intercultural Perspectives*. Albuquerque, N.Mex., 1980.

MILLER, DARLIS A. "Cross-Cultural Marriages in the Southwest: The New Mexico Experience, 1846–1900." *New Mexico Historical Review* (October 1982): 335–360.

MOCK, CHARLOTTE K. *Bridges: New Mexican Black Women, 1900–1950*. Albuquerque, N.Mex., 1985.

RICHARDSON, BARBARA J. *Black Directory of New Mexico*. Rio Rancho, N.Mex., 1976.

CLARENCE H. FIELDER

New Negro. The term *New Negro* was often used by whites in the colonial period to designate newly enslaved Africans. Ironically that same term began to be used at the end of the nineteenth century to measure and represent the distance that African Americans had come from the institution of slavery. Throughout the first three decades of this century, articles and books discussing the New Negro were commonplace. African-American leaders, journalists, artists, and some white Americans used the phrase to refer to a general sense of racial renewal among blacks that was characterized by a spirit of racial pride, cultural and economic self-assertion, and political militancy. William Pickens, for example, proclaimed the transformation of the "patient, unquestioning devoted semi-slave" into "the self-conscious, aspiring, proud young man" (Pickens, p. 236). While the notion of a New Negro was variously defined, it typically referred to the passing of an "old Negro," the "Uncle Tom" of racial STEREOTYPES, and the emergence of an educated, politically and culturally aware generation of blacks.

A New Negro for a New Century (1900), a volume of historical and social essays, with chapters by Booker T. WASHINGTON and other prominent blacks, was one of earliest of several books that sought to define the new racial personality. In subsequent decades, many African Americans referred to Washington's political leadership and educational philosophy as symbolic of an accommodation that marked the "old Negro" (*see* ACCOMMODATIONISM); yet Washington's chapter, "Afro-American Education," stressed the role of EDUCATION, "the grand army of school children" (p. 84), in remaking African-American consciousness. Fannie B. WILLIAMS's "Club Movement Among Colored Women in America" drew attention to the role of African-American women in the development of the "womanhood of a great nation and a great civilization," and she praised their organizations as the "beginning of self-respect and the respect" for the race (Washington, p. 404).

During the 1920s, the idea of the New Negro became an important symbol of racial progress, and different political groups vied with each other over who more properly represented the new racial consciousness. Most agreed that impact of black military service during WORLD WAR I, the MIGRATION of blacks to the North, and the example of blacks fighting against racial violence during the race riots of 1919 provided clear evidence of a reinvigorated African-American sense of self. Political organizations like the NATIONAL ASSOCIATION FOR THE ADVANCEMENT OF COLORED PEOPLE, the NATIONAL URBAN LEAGUE, and the UNIVERSAL NEGRO IMPROVEMENT ASSOCIATION of Marcus GARVEY each felt that they represented an unquenchable political and racial militancy. The group of socialist and political radicals like A. Philip RANDOLPH and Chandler OWEN who were identified with the monthly journal MESSENGER and the BROTHERHOOD OF SLEEPING CAR PORTERS consistently argued that they represented the political ideas as the ideal of the New Negro.

In 1925, Alain L. LOCKE, a philosophy professor at Howard University and a leading promoter of black writers and artists, published an anthology *The New Negro, An Interpretation*. That volume proposed African-American creative artists as contenders with political spokesmen for the title of New Negro. The anthology contained contributions from leading political leaders like W. E. B. DU BOIS, Jessie FAUSET, James Weldon JOHNSON, and Walter WHITE of the NAACP, and Charles H. JOHNSON of the National Urban League, yet Locke's essays, "Enter the New Negro" and "Negro Youth Speaks," focused exclusively on a group of young writers and artists: "Youth speaks and the voice of the New Negro is heard" (Locke, p. 47). Locke offered the drawings, poetry, and prose of Aaron DOUGLAS, Countee CULLEN, Langston HUGHES, Zora Neale HURSTON, Claude MCKAY, and Jean TOOMER, artists who drew inspiration from the vernacular—blues, jazz, spirituals, and the folktale—as the voice of a vibrant "new psychology" (Locke, p. 3). Locke's anthology, and the subsequent work of the young artists included in it, tied the notion of the New Negro to the work of African-American artists and firmly bound the image of the New Negro to the artistic products of the HARLEM RENAISSANCE.

After the 1920s, the expression *New Negro* passed out of fashion, largely because the spirit that it referred to was taken for granted. Subsequent generations of scholars, however, still debate about which of the various political and artistic philosophies best represented the ideal of the New Negro.

REFERENCES

LOCKE, ALAIN L., ed. *The New Negro, An Interpretation*. New York, 1925.

PICKENS, WILLIAM. *The New Negro: His Political, Civil, and Mental Status, and Related Essays*. New York, 1916.

WASHINGTON, BOOKER T., et al. *A New Negro for a New Century*. Chicago, 1900.

GEORGE P. CUNNINGHAM

New Orleans, Louisiana. New Orleans was founded in 1718 by Jean Baptiste, Sieur de Bienville, governor of the French Colony of Louisiana, and was made the capital of the colony in 1722. By 1721 the town contained 145 white men, 65 white women, 38 children, 29 white servants, 172 black slaves, and 21 Indian slaves. The first imported slaves, five hundred Africans bought on credit from the St. Domingue colony (now Haiti), came in 1719. In the following twelve years, twenty-three slave ships arrived in Louisiana.

While only a few slaves were imported in the following forty years, the black inhabitants, mainly Senegalese (brought directly from Africa, unlike most blacks in British North America) helped build a distinct Afro-French culture in New Orleans. The enslaved black community soon included most of the town's skilled laborers, and the "donated" labor of blacks built much of the city. Black CREOLES—the term usually refers to native Louisianian francophones—borrowed heavily in their cuisine and art from African models, and passed them along to whites. Africans contributed words to the creole dialect. The first *code noir* (BLACK CODE), passed in 1724, prohibited mixed-race marriage, provided for Roman Catholic religious training, outlawed Sunday labor, and allowed slaves to own property and marry. Many slave owners ignored the code.

New Orleans grew slowly into a major port. In 1763, along with the rest of the Louisiana Territory, it was ceded to Spain in the Treaty of Paris. In 1791, slave revolts in St. Domingue, plus smaller ones in rural Louisiana, brought large numbers of whites, free mulattos, and enslaved blacks, to New Orleans. Further immigrants from St. Domingue entered in 1809, when they were expelled from Spanish Cuba. In 1795, Spain granted the United States free navigation of the Mississippi River, and use of the large depot at New Orleans. Americans began to settle in the city. In 1800 France regained Louisiana in a secret treaty, though three years later, New Orleans and the Louisiana Territory were sold by Napoleon to the United States.

Throughout the years of Spanish rule, New Orleans remained largely French in culture. However, while slavery continued, the nature of the town's African-American population began to change, as a new, free colored community, mostly composed of mulattos, came into being. In 1769, the town contained 1,225 slaves, but only 100 free persons of color. The latter number would grow to 1,200 by the end of the Spanish era, against a slave population of 3,000, as a result of natural increase plus a huge Caribbean influx. The Spanish encouraged the growth of a free colored community as a buffer between blacks and whites. Spanish law made manumission easy and slaves worked to purchase their own freedom. Some earned their freedom by serving in militia units. Though most free blacks had enslaved relatives, authorities made use of them as city guards, in slave patrols, and as informers.

Under American rule, New Orleans became the most important city in the South, and a major port and banking center for the Mississippi River region. The city's French character, and its large black and immigrant population, highlighted its distinctiveness. Gen. Andrew Jackson recruited black troops from the city for the Battle of New Orleans in 1815, and in the mid-1840s black contingents fought in the *Mexican War.* Antebellum African-American culture in New Orleans took diverse forms. Congo Square in the center of the city, which took its name from the slaves who established a market there for their own produce, was the scene of funerals and public dances, with dances such as the *carabiné* and music provided by African instruments. The VOODOO religion, a syncretic combination of African snake worship, Haitian rituals, and Christian elements, attracted followers of all races and religions. Dr. John was dubbed the "king" of his voodoo, while his rival, Madame Marie LAVEAU, was acclaimed the "queen." Even the dominant Catholic religion was affected by African traditions. The famous Mardi Gras, the carnival preceding Lent, is adapted in part from African festivals. Blacks offered for sale at the slave auctions under the giant rotunda of the St. Louis Hotel often were presented in Mardi Gras–style costumes.

Although the Louisiana Civil Code of 1808 forbade mulattos from marrying either whites or black slaves, New Orleans became famous for its quadroon balls where white men trysted with mixed-race women. Mulatto women were kept under the arrangement known as *plaçage.* Under this system, white men took mulatto mistresses as "second wives," buying houses for the women and any children that resulted from their union. Mulatto children often legally inherited their parents' money and property, including slaves, and frequently traveled to France to vacation or be educated. Prominent mulatto citizens included Bastile Croquière, who instructed elite whites in fencing; Norbert RILLIEUX, inventor of the vacuum pump for sugar refining; Aristide Mary, philanthropist and real estate tycoon; Victor Sejour, a playwright; the doctors Louis Charles Roundanez, James Derham, and Alexandre Chaumette; the composer/conductor Edmond Dédé, who later led the Alcazar Orchestra in France; and the sculptor Eugene Warbourg. In 1845, a circle of writers, led by Armand LANUSSE, published a volume of verse, entitled LES CENELLES.

The free black community prospered and continued to grow. Job opportunities for skilled black laborers were reasonably plentiful, since few white immigrants were trained artisans. Legal manumission remained simple. Free Anglo-American blacks continued to migrate to the city, although they remained

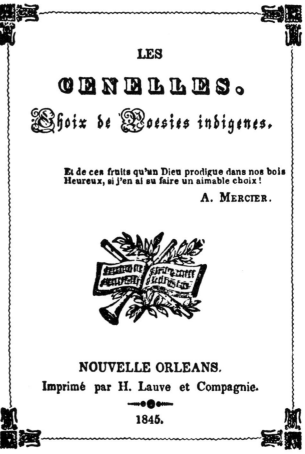

Les Cenelles (The Hawthorns), the first anthology of African-American poetry, was the product of the highly cultured francophone free black community in antebellum New Orleans. In translation, the quotation on the title page reads: "And these fruits that a generous God provides in our woods/Happy am I to be able to offer the finest." (Photographs and Prints Division, Schomburg Center for Research in Black Culture, The New York Public Library, Astor, Lenox and Tilden Foundations)

largely separate from the creole community. They formed BAPTIST and Methodist churches, and joined several Masonic groups.

Despite New Orleans's reputation for tolerance, segregation and discrimination hindered the lives of free people of color. Blacks were officially excluded when the New Orleans public school system was established in 1841, although some white fathers enrolled their mulatto children. Roman Catholic schools were established for blacks, such as the COUVENT INSTITUTE. The Institute, funded by a legacy from an ex-slave, was established in 1847. As the city's Anglo-American population became dominant, and whites aligned themselves with the other southern states, prejudice against free people of color increased. By the 1850s black organizations such as churches and fraternal societies were forced to lead increasingly clandestine existences. The French *code noir* was officially abrogated in the mid-1850s. Laws against free black migration were enforced, and manumission became difficult.

The coming of the CIVIL WAR in 1861 dramatically changed the situation of African Americans in the city. When the war began, some 1,400 free people of color (eventually 3,000), acting variously out of southern patriotism, slaveholder interest, and/or fear of white wrath, entered the Confederate Army as an unarmed unit, the New Orleans Home Guards. The Union takeover of New Orleans in 1862 galvanized the city's black population and that of the surrounding area. SLAVERY became almost extinct in the area, as slaves left their masters and poured into the city. Union Army Gen. Benjamin Butler, commanding the city, originally opposed efforts by blacks to enlist in the Union Army. By September 1862 this policy was reversed, and eventually three black New Orleans units, including the Corps D'Afrique, were established.

Despite the military ability of African Americans, and the creoles' evident dignity and social standing, civil rights efforts lagged. The Union occupation forces retained the harsh Black Codes of the 1850s. Since President Abraham Lincoln had exempted Louisiana from the Emancipation Proclamation (see EMANCIPATION), free people of color began to lobby to formally end slavery throughout the United States, and in March, 1864, two creole delegates, E. Arnold Bertonneau and Jean-Baptiste Roudanez, went to Washington to press Congress and President Lincoln to extend suffrage rights to Louisiana's blacks. Their efforts were unsuccessful. Black creole opinion had as its major forum *L'Union*, a French (later bilingual) biweekly journal that became the major black newspaper. It folded in mid-1864, but Paul Trévigne, its editor, quickly began the bilingual *Tribune*, which in fall 1864 became the first African-American daily newspaper. The creole elite and black Americans joined together at that time to form the National Equal Rights League of Louisiana. In 1864, league members lobbied in Congress against the bill readmitting Louisiana to the Union, since the government denied blacks suffrage. The end of the war brought fresh conflict to New Orleans.

In July 1866, a Radical Republican convention, organized to consider changing the 1864 state constitution to grant black suffrage, was held at the mechanics' Institute, Louisiana's capitol building. A group of freed blacks, led by a marching band, attempted to cross Canal Street, the city's wide main artery, to protest outside the convention. They were jeered by a white mob, organized by conservatives trying to break up the convention. A white protester shot at the blacks, who fired back. Police opened fire into the crowd of black marchers. Antiblack violence spread across the city. Neither the Union Army nor the Freedmen's Bureau intervened. By the time order was restored, 37 people were dead, 34 of them black; 136 people were wounded, 119 of them black; and police had made 293 arrests. Outrage over the violence in Congress led in part to the Civil Rights Act of 1866.

The following year, 1867, after African American William Nichols was thrown off a streetcar, New Orleans black leaders organized a successful sit-in campaign, and a mob of 500 blacks stoned segregated "star cars." Gen. Philip Sheridan, commanding the region, refused to support segregated facilities, and desegregation was achieved. The same year, Congress passed the Reconstruction Act (see RECONSTRUCTION), which dissolved the Louisiana government. The interim government enfranchised blacks. The next year, 1868, Sheridan organized a "Black and Tan" Radical Republican constitutional convention, of which two-thirds of the delegates were African-American. The new constitution provided for racial equality and integrated public schools, which opened in 1869. That same year, the Republican legislature passed a public accommodations law, which creoles and others enforced through large damage suits against violators.

In 1868, however, the race for the Republican nomination for governor, then tantamount to election, destroyed the fragile creole-American black alliance. That year, the black creole Francis Dumas, a Union army veteran and former slaveholder, ran for the gubernatorial nomination with the support of the *Tribune*, which refused to back a white candidate, Henry Warmoth. Warmoth, with the support of P.B.S. PINCHBACK, a powerful army veteran and political broker who had recently come to New Orleans, won a very close race. Warmoth named the black Oscar Dunn his lieutenant governor, but broke with the creoles, ending the public subsidies that kept the *Tribune* afloat. His ally, Pinchback, named lieutenant governor in 1871, briefly became the first African-American state governor after Warmoth's impeachment in 1872. Pinchback was later elected to the U.S. Senate.

New black and creole institutions were set up in the post-bellum era. Blacks formed their own churches and Scots rite Masonic lodges and benevolent societies, although creoles generally stayed in interracial Catholic churches and French rite Masonic lodges. Three colleges opened in New Orleans: Straight University (1869), founded under the aegis of the AMERICAN MISSIONARY ASSOCIATION; Leland University (1869), a private college; and New Orleans University (1873), a state-funded institution.

Originally integrated, eight of the ten graduates of its first Law School class in 1878 were white. Another college, Southern University, opened in 1879 (after it moved in 1914, its buildings housed Xavier University). The colleges remained intellectual centers through the JIM CROW era, and helped take the place of city high schools, which excluded blacks from 1879 to 1917 and segregated them afterwards.

Reconstruction also brought a cultural flowering in African-American New Orleans. Theaters opened, and public lectures—especially those of the African-American female suffragist and poet, Frances E. W. HARPER—were popular among creoles. Dance halls such as the Brown, the Natural, the Economy, and the Union were popular among blacks. There were even large dances held at the state capitol. Many people enjoyed horse races and regattas, often organized through the city's many social clubs. BASEBALL had a wide following in the city. There were interracial games in the 1870s.

Perhaps most importantly, music was played throughout the city: A New Orleans University group gave concerts of spirituals; minstrel shows and vaudeville were popular, as were many brass bands, the most famous of them Sylvester Decker's Excelsior Brass Band; and Professor Louis Martin's Negro Symphony Orchestra and black concert performers, such as Victor Eugene Macarthy, played classical music. When a French opera company was stranded in the city in 1875, the black creole community sponsored a season of performances.

In 1874, white rioters rose up against Louisiana's biracial government in the so-called Battle of Liberty Place. In 1876 white Democrats won a disputed election and immediately started "redeeming" the state. City schools and public accommodations were resegregated almost immediately, although public transportation remained integrated. Most blacks were now restricted to older, squalid and segregated residential areas. During the 1880s, the creole élite, led by real estate tycoon and philanthropist Aristide Mary and lawyer/journalist Rodolphe DESDUNES, began new efforts against discriminatory legislation. In 1887, Desdunes formed *L'Union Louisianaise,* which with creole financial support, grew into a newspaper, the New Orleans *Crusader,* for a time the nation's only African-American daily. In 1890, after the passage of a law segregating railroad transportation, the creoles formed a *Comité des Citoyens* to challenge the law in court, and raised money to defer legal expenses. A member of the *Comité,* Homer Plessy, agreed to serve as defendant. In 1896, however, the U.S. Supreme Court ruled in the PLESSY V. FERGUSON decision that "separate but equal" facilities were constitutional. The turn of the century brought the final decline of the creole community. The strict color bar eliminated the vestiges of their privileges, and promoted assimilation with blacks.

Despite official segregation and continuing racial tension, which broke into a major riot in 1900, New Orleans remained a culturally interracial city. One locus of interracial contact in these years, though clandestine and exploitative, was Storyville, the legal red-light district. Despite the romantic aura of Storyville, it played only a small part in African-American life in the city. The prostitutes, the majority African Americans, ranged in their pigmentation. The most expensive houses, which attracted an exclusively white clientele, usually featured light-skinned women. The owners of the larger brothels, except for "Miss Lulu" White, were all white.

The lively entertainment scene in New Orleans—of which Storyville was only one aspect—nurtured the growth of distinctive African-American musical forms, especially JAZZ. Early jazz, as played in the first years of the twentieth century by pioneers such as Buddy BOLDEN, Jelly Roll MORTON, and King OLIVER, developed from a melange of ragtime, marching bands, and the music of popular entertainment halls. New Orleans' unusual multiracial culture promoted its development. Early jazz was primarily collectively improvised polyphonic versions of rags and of blues melodies. After 1915, with the emergence of the white Original Dixieland Jazz Band (who made the first jazz recordings in 1917), and after 1920, with King Oliver and Louis Armstrong, jazz soon became successively a national and international craze. However, the lure of larger entertainment markets elsewhere, such as Chicago and New York City, led to an exodus of jazz musicians to the North. By 1925, New Orleans was largely depleted of its first-rank jazz musicians, and the dominance of "New Orleans Jazz" was essentially over.

The depression of 1893 brought conflict and rioting by whites over apportionment of labor on the docks, and destroyed the uneasy decade-long alliance between black and white unionized labor. The two sides recognized their interest in alliance, though, and by 1901 made fresh agreements, which held through a general strike in 1907, and lasted until the decline of the unions in 1923. During the following years, a few blacks were promoted to supervisory positions, but eventually the absence of union work rules and wage scales led to a steep decline in wages and working conditions. Beginning in 1929, the GREAT DEPRESSION further eroded black labor influence in the port.

Meanwhile, the city continued as a musical center. Traditional jazz remained a mainstay of New Orleans culture. In places such as Preservation Hall, early New Orleans jazz was lovingly preserved, primarily for the benefit of tourists. In 1969, the popular New

Orleans Jazz and Heritage Festival was inaugurated. New Orleans also helped spawn other popular African-American musical forms. The great gospel singer Mahalia JACKSON came from New Orleans, though the bulk of her career was spent in Chicago. In the 1930s and '40s local musicians, influenced by Latin and Caribbean rhythms, developed an infectious, fast-paced, piano-centered blues style generally known as New Orleans rhythm and blues. The pioneers include PROFESSOR LONGHAIR, Lloyd Price, and Dave Bartholomew, though the best-known exponent in the style was Fats DOMINO, one of the leading rock-and-roll performers of the 1950s. The Neville Brothers had a successful rhythm and blues career stretching from the 1950s through the 1990s. New Orleans is the hometown of a number of contemporary black musicians; avant-garde drummer Ed BLACKWELL hailed from New Orleans, and in the 1980s, natives Branford and Wynton MARSALIS came to national prominence as jazz artists. In tribute to its musical heritage, in the 1990s the city was selected as the home of the Black Music Hall of Fame and Museum.

The movement for black equality never completely died in New Orleans. During the 1920s the black Federation of Civic Leagues, an organization of social clubs led by creole activist A. P. Tureaud, sponsored a New Orleans branch of the NAACP. The NAACP successfully challenged a 1924 residential segregation ordinance in the U.S. Supreme Court, won salary equalization for African-American teachers in the early 1940s, and paid residents' poll taxes to further an unsuccessful electoral challenge to voter registration laws. In 1946, Tureaud sponsored a lawsuit, *Hall* v. *Nagel,* which eased white interference with black voter registration. In 1953, after another lawsuit, *Tureaud* v. *Board of Supervisors,* Tureaud opened the doors of Louisiana State University to blacks.

During the 1950s, a moderate mayor, Chep Morrison, eased police harassment of blacks. However, only a few small gains were made in desegregation. Blacks remained largely excluded from downtown areas. The NAACP, led by Ernest "Dutch" Morial, faced constant white opposition, although white harassment increased the NAACP's prestige in the black community. In 1958, following a suit in court, Judge Skelly Wright voided streetcar/bus segregation, and in 1960, despite Morrison's strong opposition, the first schools were desegregated. The same year, activists from the CONGRESS OF RACIAL EQUALITY (CORE) sponsored sit-ins and direct action on Canal St. White storeowners challenged the legality of the sit-ins, but the U.S. Supreme Court ruled in *Garner* v. *Louisiana* (1960) that they were constitutionally protected. The sit-ins eventually brought about the desegregation of city lunch counters in 1962. The NAACP joined CORE and other black groups in a short-lived Citizen's Committee, which sponsored a march on City Hall in September 1963. Nevertheless, the process of desegregation was slow. In 1965, African-American players staged a walkout at an American Football League All-Star game in New Orleans to protest racial discrimination in the city.

The U.S. VOTING RIGHTS ACT OF 1965 altered the city's political landscape. In 1967, Dutch Morial won a seat in the Louisiana legislature, and two years later, almost won a seat as councilman-at-large. The same year, with his support and that of two important black political clubs, Community Organization for Urban Politics (COUP) and Southern Organization for Unified Leadership (SOUL), the moderate liberal Moon Landrieu was elected mayor. Landrieu ended discrimination in public accommodations and awarded city patronage to black allies in COUP and SOUL, particularly jobs connected with the Superdome, the city's giant new sports arena. During the early 1970s, a combination of white flight and new economic opportunity, transformed New Orleans into an African-American majority city.

In 1978, Dutch Morial ran for mayor and won by a narrow margin, mostly on the strength of the black vote. Ironically, due to past personal and political disagreements, Morial was opposed or only half-heartedly supported by COUP and SOUL, whose leaders he proceeded to prosecute for corruption once in office. Morial served two terms, retaining popularity among his black constituency despite opposition from both whites and black leaders over his independent policy-making, including color-blind merit hiring. In 1985, Sidney Barthelemy of COUP, running as a moderate against another black candidate, became New Orleans' second African-American mayor. Ironically, he received barely 25 percent of the black vote, but won 85 percent of the white vote.

While racial divisions continue to plague New Orleans, there has been progress in certain areas. In 1989, city officials voted to store the Liberty Monument, an obelisk commemorating the Battle of Liberty Place, on the grounds that it commemorated prejudice and served as a rallying point for the Ku Klux Klan. White supremacists led by gubernatorial candidate David Duke challenged the removal. In 1993, after a court ordered the monument restored, the city's Human Rights Commission voted unanimously that it be removed. The same year, under pressure from the city council, the Rex organization, one of the four prestigious secret societies that plan the city's annual Mardi Gras festival, invited its first three blacks to become members.

REFERENCES

ARNESEN, ERIC. *Waterfront Workers of New Orleans: Race, Class, and Politics, 1863–1923.* New York, 1991.

BLASSINGAME, JOHN W. *Black New Orleans, 1860–1880.* Chicago, 1973.

DESDUNES, RODOLPHE. *Nos Hommes et Notre Histoire.* Translated as *Our People and Our History* by Sister Dorothea Olga McCants. 1911. Reprint. New Orleans, 1973.

HAIR, WILLIAM IVY. *Carnival of Fury: The New Orleans Riot of 1900.* Baton Rouge, La., 1976.

HALL, GWENDOLYN. *Africans in Colonial Louisiana: The Formation of an Afro-creole Culture in the Eighteenth Century.* Baton Rouge, La., 1992.

HIRSCH, ARNOLD R. and JOSEPH LOGSDON, eds. *creole New Orleans: Race and Americanization.* Baton Rouge, La., 1992.

JACKSON, JOY. *New Orleans in the Gilded Age.* Baton Rouge, La., 1969.

LEAVITT, MEL. *A Short History of New Orleans.* San Francisco, 1982.

MARCUS, FRANCES FRANK. "A Symbol of Racial Conflict Moves Nearer Removal Again." *New York Times,* July 6, 1993.

ROGERS, KIM LACY. *Righteous Lives: Narratives of the New Orleans Civil Rights Movement.* New York, 1993.

CHARLES VINCENT

New Orleans Riot of 1900.

New Orleans in the nineteenth century was notable for its relatively easy race relations and its wealthy, influential African-American community. However, after the PLESSY V. FERGUSON decision by the U.S. Supreme Court in 1896, race relations in New Orleans worsened as segregation was imposed on blacks and creoles. Control over African Americans was enforced by a policy of police harassment.

On the evening of July 23, 1900, Robert Charles, an unemployed migrant to the city who was a disciple of the black nationalist Bishop Henry McNeal TURNER, was waiting for his girlfriend when a group of police began to interrogate him. Charles resisted, and when one of the police officers grabbed his billy club, Charles ran. The police fired their guns. Charles pulled out his own gun and fired, wounding two police officers, before going into hiding. Police organized a dragnet and began conducting a house-to-house search.

Meanwhile the city's whites, aroused by Charles' actions, went on an antiblack rampage. African Americans on streetcars and the streets were attacked. By morning, 50 blacks had been beaten; three blacks were dead, six seriously injured. Black-owned houses and stores were looted and damaged. Over the following two days, as the hunt for Charles continued, two more blacks were killed and more were beaten by white rioters.

On July 27 Charles was cornered by police in a house. The police attempted to shoot their way in, but Charles defended himself. In all, he shot twenty-seven people, killing four police officers and seriously wounding three more, before he was himself shot. White rioters, in retaliation, shot two more blacks that night and set fire to the city's best black school building. As white firefighters looked on, the school burned to the ground. Ten blacks were arrested for complicity in Charles's concealment, but all were released. Six whites were arrested for murder on the testimony of white witnesses. Although their guilt was generally admitted the assailants were eventually released.

See also URBAN RIOTS AND REBELLIONS.

REFERENCE

HAIR, WILLIAM IVY. *Carnival of Fury: The New Orleans Riot of 1900.* Baton Rouge, La., 1976.

GREG ROBINSON

Newton, Huey P.

Newton, Huey P. (February 17, 1942–August 22, 1989), political activist. Huey Newton was born in Monroe, La. His family moved to Oakland, Calif., when he was young. Newton was the youngest of seven siblings. He attended Merritt College in Oakland and participated in the groundswell of political activities that were erupting on college campuses nationwide. He joined the increasing number of blacks who questioned the ability of the CIVIL RIGHTS MOVEMENT to deal with the problems of housing, unemployment, poverty, and police brutality that plagued urban African Americans.

In college, Newton and his friend Bobby SEALE were active in the effort to diversify the curriculum at Merritt, as well as lobbying for more black instructors. Newton joined the Afro-American Association but soon became a vocal critic of the organization's advocacy of capitalism. Instead, he sought inspiration from Robert Williams, a former head of the Monroe, N.C., NAACP, who advocated guerilla warfare, and from Third World revolutionaries such as Cuba's Fidel Castro, China's Mao Ze Dong, and Algeria's Franz Fanon. Newton believed that blacks were an oppressed colony being exploited economically and disfranchised politically within U.S. borders and argued that blacks should launch a liberation movement for self-empowerment.

In 1966, Newton and Seale founded the BLACK PANTHER PARTY FOR SELF-DEFENSE. Newton took on the title of minister of defense and acted as leader of the organization. Among the points raised in their initial program was the right to bear arms to defend their community from police repression.

In November, Newton and Seale, armed with shotguns—which was legal at the time as long as they were not concealed—instituted "justice patrols" to monitor the actions of the police and inform blacks of their rights when stopped by the police. The police responded with resentment and harassment. On October 28, 1967, in culmination of a year of hostile and antagonistic relations between the Panthers and the police, Newton was arrested and charged in the shooting of one police officer and the murder of another. Events of this incident are unclear and conflicting. Newton claimed to be unconscious after being shot by one of the policemen.

Newton's arrest heightened the awareness of police brutality in the black community. While in prison Newton was considered a political prisoner; rallies and speeches focused attention on his plight. His trial became a cause célèbre, and "Free Huey" became a slogan that galvanized thousands of people on the New Left. Massive rallies and demonstrations at the courthouse demanding his release were organized by BPP members.

Newton remained active in prison, issuing speeches and directives. He was convicted in September 1968 of voluntary manslaughter, and was sentenced to two to fifteen years in prison. His conviction was overturned by the Court of Appeals, because of procedural errors during his first trial. Newton, after being released from prison, tried to revive the organization. However, during the early 1970s, the BPP had declined due to legal problems, internal tensions, and a factional split among BPP members on the East and West Coast. This division was fostered by the disinformation campaign launched by the FBI, which created a climate of distrust and suspicion within the BPP. Many on the East Coast believed the ideology of Eldridge CLEAVER—who had become the public spokesperson for the BPP during Newton's incarceration and who advocated politically motivated armed actions. Newton articulated the feelings of many on the West Coast by arguing that the BPP, by becoming too militant, had moved onto a plane with which average blacks could no longer identify. He wanted to focus more on community programs and political education. Newton ordered a series of purges, which debilitated the party further.

Although Newton remained publicly identified with the party, many people no longer looked to him as leader. Increasingly isolated, Newton cultivated a small band of supporters. In 1974 Newton was ac-

The embodiment of revolutionary militancy, Huey Newton was one of the best-known leaders of the Black Panther party in the 1960s and early '70s. Newton had a troubled life after the heyday of the Panthers and was murdered in Oakland, Calif., in 1989. (AP/Wide World Photos)

cused of murder in the killing of a woman. The circumstances of this incident are unclear. Newton fled to Cuba, feeling that he would not get a fair trial here. In 1977 he returned to the United States to resume leadership of the weakened and splintering party. In his absence, Elaine Brown had assumed leadership of the organization and taken it in new directions. Newton's role in the organization continued to diminish. He was retried in the 1967 killing of the policeman and convicted, but that conviction was later overturned. He also faced trial for the murder of the woman, but the charge was dropped after two hung juries.

In 1980 Newton received a Ph.D. from the University of California. His thesis was "War Against the Panthers—A Study of Repression in America." While Newton remained politically active, his visibility as a public figure was waning. He was arrested in 1985 for embezzling funds from a nutritional program he headed. Three years later, he was convicted of possessing firearms. Increasingly addicted to drugs and involved in the drug trade, he was killed in a drug-related incident on the streets of Oakland in 1989.

REFERENCES

NEWTON, HUEY P. *Revolutionary Suicide.* New York, 1973.

———. *To Die for the People: The Writings of Huey P. Newton.* New York, 1972.

PEARSON, HUGH. *The Shadow of the Panther.* New York, 1994.

SEALE, BOBBY. *Seize the Time: The Story of the Black Panther Party and Huey Newton.* New York, 1970.

ROBYN SPENCER

Newton, James, Jr. (May 1, 1953–), flutist, composer, bandleader. Born in Los Angeles, Newton began his musical career in high school as an electric bass guitarist performing RHYTHM AND BLUES. In 1971 he switched to saxophones and flute and began to explore JAZZ with Arthur Blythe, David Murray, John Carter, and Bobby Bradford. He studied flute with Buddy Collette and earned a B.A. in music from California State University, Los Angeles, before moving to New York in early 1978. Focusing exclusively on the flute, he performed and recorded with Murray and Blythe and coled a group with Anthony DAVIS. By 1979 Newton had achieved international critical acclaim for his performances and recordings, which featured his distinctive full-bodied tone and exploitation of timbral shadings in the flute's higher registers. Developing flute vocalization techniques pioneered by Yusef LATEEF and Rahsaan Roland Kirk and incorporating Japanese *shakuhachi* techniques into his otherwise classical vocabulary, Newton has expanded the technical and timbral possibilities of the Western orchestral flute and is recognized as one of the leading innovators on the instrument. He has also broken new ground as a composer, again drawing on a range of influences that includes the black Baptist church, Duke ELLINGTON, Charles MINGUS, traditional and contemporary Asian repertory, and twentieth-century French and Viennese composers. In addition to his works for large and small jazz ensembles, other compositions include *Ninety-first Psalm* (1985) and soprano, piano, and chamber orchestra, *The King's Way* (1988) for chamber orchestra, and *The Line of Immortality* (1992) for chamber ensemble and jazz quartet. Newton's achievements as flutist, composer, and arranger in the jazz idiom are heard to best advantage on the recordings *Axum*

(1982), *Luella* (1984), *African Flower* (1985), and *If Love* (1989). A Guggenheim recipient, Newton is professor of music at the University of California, Irvine.

REFERENCES

BIRNBAUM, LARRY. "The Soul of the Church." *Down Beat* (November 1991): 24–25.

KERNFELD, BARRY. "James Newton." In the *New Grove Dictionary of Jazz.* London, 1988, p. 172.

ANTHONY BROWN

New York African Society for Mutual Relief. The first African-American society founded in New York City, the New York African Society for Mutual Relief was formed in 1808 by Peter WILLIAMS, Sr., a carpenter and eloquent orator, and a group of businessmen, tradesmen, and clergy from throughout the city. On March 23, 1810, it received its charter of incorporation from the state legislature, and until about 1830 this achievement was celebrated with an annual parade that assembled many leaders of the African-American religious and political communities. The society sought to provide insurance and financial aid to its members, their families, and others who would otherwise have been unable to obtain satisfactory insurance and assistance.

Among the early members of the society were many of the most unsuccessful African Americans in the city during the period, including a number of artisans, bootmakers, mechanics, soap chandlers, real estate salesmen, and a pickle manufacturer, as well as such notable editors and clergymen as James VARICK, Peter WILLIAMS, Jr., and Samuel E. CORNISH. In 1812 the defalcation by an officer of the society depleted the treasury, but funds were quickly reestablished, and investments were soon made in rental property. In 1820 a building was constructed, and later property was purchased at 27 Greenwich Avenue and rented to provide funds for the society's relief fund.

From its beginning the principles and organization of the society provided a model for other associations started by African Americans in New York City, such as the Dorcas Association, the Phoenix Society, the Clarkson Society, and the Wilberforce Benevolent Society. With the proliferation of associations formed by African Americans in the decades prior to the Civil War, the importance of the Society for Mutual Relief diminished.

Starting in the 1850s the society appears to have been relatively self-perpetuating because of its strong financial base, and membership seems to have been restricted to about sixty-five financially secure members who made relatively few demands upon the society's resources. During this period the annual rent collected from property was ten times greater than that collected through membership dues. After the NEW YORK CITY DRAFT RIOTS OF 1863, abolitionist Charles B. RAY became a leader of the society and dispensed funds to victims of violence and property loss. In 1892 the society had about fifty members, and it appears that it remained in existence into the early twentieth century. Its function during its later phase is unclear, however, and it has since passed out of existence.

REFERENCES

OTTLEY, ROI, and WILLIAM J. WEATHERSBY, eds. *The Negro in New York*. New York, 1967.

RIPLEY, C. PETER, ed. *The Black Abolitionist Papers*. Chapel Hill, N.C., 1985–1992.

WILLIAM J. MOSES

New York City. The founding by the Dutch of the colony of New Netherland in 1624 and its principal city, New Amsterdam, was soon followed by the importation of African slaves in 1626 (*see* SLAVE TRADE). Africans were an integral part of the economic development of the colony as the Dutch West India Company enslaved Africans for use on public works. Unlike other colonies in the New World, those in bondage to the company had certain basic rights such as baptism, marriage, and some legal standing afforded by the courts in a colony that operated without a formal slave code (*see* BLACK CODES; SLAVERY). Indeed, some Africans occupied a status termed "half-freedom," which released them from bondage for an annual payment to the company and the use of their labor at unspecified times. The precise extent of African slavery is unclear during this period, but it was increasing in the late 1650s.

A more restrictive form of bondage was introduced with the English conquest of New Netherland in 1664. Under the English, the colony became New York and the main city was renamed New York City. By 1741, blacks numbered 20 percent of the city's 11,000 population. English fears of a slave uprising became quite pronounced after the April 6, 1712 insurrection of approximately two dozen slaves. The hysteria following the insurrection resulted in the temporary closing of Elias Neau's Catechism School for Negroes, the first school for blacks in British North America, opened in 1704. In March of 1741 a rash of ten fires occurred (eight in six days) which many residents construed to be the beginning of a slave rebellion. Whether a form of protest against slavery or a revolt to overthrow slavery, some thirteen blacks were burned at the stake, sixteen hung along with four whites, and seventy-one deported.

Since the area's early settlement by the Dutch in the seventeenth century, blacks resided not only on Manhattan Island, or the city itself, but also lived in Brooklyn. A 1698 census of the province revealed no free blacks in Kings County (then a collection of independent villages that included Brooklyn), but indicated that there were 296 slaves, which constituted 15 percent of the county's population of 2,017. By 1738, Kings County was the leading slave holding county in New York, and by 1790 blacks accounted for more than one-third of the population. The agricultural economy of King's County accounts for the small number of free blacks—only 46—and the large number of slaves, 1,482. In comparison, 33 percent, or 1,036, of New York City's black population was free. By 1820, only seven years before mandatory emancipation in the state, half of Kings County's black population remained enslaved. In 1820, more than 60 percent of white families in Kings County owned slaves, compared to 18 percent in New York City.

Slavery in New York City was not overthrown by overt rebellion, but by those in the state who recognized the contradiction between a slave society and the democratic rhetoric of the REVOLUTIONARY WAR; this recognition culminated in the passage of the gradual abolition law of 1799. In the final years of the institution in New York City most slave holding units were of small size. In 1790, 75 percent of slave holders in the city owned only one or two slaves.

The gradual emergence of a free black population led to the formation of a separate black institutional life in the 1790s and early nineteenth century. Black members dissatisfied with the discriminatory treatment they received within white churches left to form their own churches. African Americans attended segregated schools since they were excluded from most white schools. The best known school in early New York City was the African Free School, founded by the largely white NEW YORK MANUMISSION SOCIETY in 1787. Blacks also started their own schools and formed mutual aid societies like the NEW YORK AFRICAN SOCIETY FOR MUTUAL RELIEF in 1810, which was designed to aid the poor, widows, orphans, and disabled. The creation in 1827 of the nation's first black newspaper, FREEDOM'S JOURNAL, by John RUSSWURM and Samuel CORNISH, provided a means of communication and discussion relevant to free blacks and the antislavery movement. In 1800 black Methodists in New York City, led by Peter WILLIAMS, consecrated the Zion Church, which in time became the founding congregation of the AFRI-

CAN METHODIST EPISCOPAL ZION CHURCH. His son, Peter WILLIAMS, Jr., founded the first black Episcopal church in New York City, St. Phillips African Church in 1819. Other leading antebellum figures raised in New York City included abolitionists Henry Highland GARNET and Alexander CRUMMELL. New York City also had some immigration of persons of African descent from the Caribbean in the late eighteenth century. Haiti was the largest source of emigrants, of whom the best known was the prominent lay Roman Catholic Pierre TOUSSAINT.

Some free blacks prospered in this period of transition from slavery to freedom which occurred simultaneously with the movement of New York City's economy toward "metropolitan industrialization." In 1800 more than one in three free male blacks worked as artisans, and by 1810, despite the economic hardships wrought by the Embargo Act of 1807, which prohibited exports from the United States to any foreign country, nearly three in ten male blacks were still classified as artisan. The embargo, which had been instituted to avoid war with British and French warships seizing American neutral vessels, did not reverse black economic opportunities in New York. These opportunities, however, decreased over the next decades as prejudice and discrimination from employers, the consuming public, native workers, and a poor competitive immigrant working class combined to drive blacks out of recently acquired skilled jobs and exclude them from newly developing industrial jobs. The economic position of blacks was fragile in the early nineteenth century. Attacks on individual black property owners by poor whites had begun during the first two decades of the nineteenth century and foreshadowed the antiabolitionist and antiblack riots of 1834 and 1835.

The position of African Americans was threatened by restrictions on their right to vote and an erosion of their economic status in the antebellum era. New York City blacks were affected after 1821 by the revised state constitution which retained a prohibitive $250 property qualification for voting for black males while eliminating property qualifications for white male voters. Occupational opportunities for free blacks also declined as they were forced out of many unskilled jobs due to competition from the increasing immigrant Irish population.

The perception of blacks as a racially inferior and degraded people coupled with the animosities fueled by economic competition resulted in numerous attacks on blacks, perhaps the most notable being the infamous CIVIL WAR draft riot of 1863 in which the Colored Orphan Asylum was burned down, almost one hundred persons were killed, and many blacks fled the city. Lincoln's Emancipation Proclamation of 1862 (see EMANCIPATION) had turned the war from one to preserve the Union to one to end slavery. Immigrant workers unable to pay the $300 "commutation fee" to avoid the draft and fearful of the job competition from emancipated blacks much prophesied by Democratic party propaganda ventilated their racial prejudices and economic fears upon the city's small black population.

Blacks fleeing the draft riots in 1863 were driven from downtown Brooklyn and New York City. Some found refuge in the Weeksville-Carrsville area of Kings County, named after local blacks. This area is located in present-day Bedford-Stuyvesant. The Weeksville-Carrsville area dates from the 1830s and was an acknowledged neighborhood by the 1840s. A sense of racial solidarity and assertiveness existed in the neighborhood; Weeksville blacks petitioned, albeit unsuccessfully, in 1869 to have a black appointed to the Brooklyn Board of Education so that they could have a say in the governance of the five "colored" schools. (In 1882 Phillip A. White became the first black on the Brooklyn Board of Education.) The distinctive black character of Weeksville and other parts of the Ninth Ward (which included part of present-day Bedford-Stuyvesant) was lost by 1870 as whites purchased property and moved into the area touted as excellent for "genteel suburban residences." However, more was lost than the character of the neighborhood, for as immigrants came to Brooklyn and New York City they and their offspring forced blacks out of skilled and semiskilled jobs.

Despite the contributions of black New Yorkers to the Union victory, including the formation of the Twentieth United States Colored Infantry, the referendum in New York State advocating equal suffrage was defeated. Equal suffrage for black New Yorkers would not come until the passage of the FIFTEENTH AMENDMENT to the U.S. Constitution in 1870. Between 1870 and the turn of the century African Americans continued to contribute to the establishment of new institutions and organizations in their community. The *New York Age,* founded in 1887 under the editorship of T. Thomas FORTUNE, became one of the leading black newspapers in the nation. In the early years of the twentieth century Charles ANDERSON, a close ally of Booker T. WASHINGTON, was a leading black Republican politician. During the same years Tammany Hall organized the UNITED COLORED DEMOCRACY, its black auxiliary. During these years, the city's black population rose significantly from 17,580 in 1860 to 33,888 by 1890. Nevertheless, blacks remained less than 2 percent of the total population as southern and eastern European immigrants swelled the city's population.

In 1900, after the 1898 consolidation of the five boroughs (Manhattan, Brooklyn, Queens, the Bronx, and Staten Island), New York City had

60,000 black residents. By 1920, it had the largest black population of any city in the country, though less than 3 percent of the population was black. The city's ethnic diversification was accompanied by considerable social upheaval as groups contended for jobs and living space. African Americans, who had lived in the Greenwich Village area of Manhattan, were slowly moving northward and by the 1890s were residing in substantial numbers in the infamous San Juan Hill area (centered on the West Side of Manhattan between Sixtieth and Sixty-sixth Streets on Tenth and Eleventh avenues), so named because of the frequent interracial battles there. The worst disturbance during these years was the August 1900 antiblack riot when policemen joined the white mobs in attacking blacks all along Eighth Avenue between Twenty-seventh and Forty-second streets.

Seeking the security of new neighborhoods, better housing stock, and the concomitant status, blacks took the opportunity to move into the middle-class community of HARLEM, created by vacant apartments in an overbuilt housing market, and the entrepreneurial skills of a black realtor, Philip A. PAYTON, and his Afro-American Realty Company organized in 1904. Many of the major African-American social, fraternal, and religious institutions relocated from their downtown quarters to Harlem by the early 1920s. The African Methodist Episcopal Zion ("Mother Zion"), St. Philip's Protestant Episcopal Church, and Abyssinian Baptist Church were some of the prominent churches that reestablished themselves in Harlem. The "Great Migration" of blacks from the South and the Caribbean was intensified by the demand for labor in the North during the WORLD WAR I years. The black population of New York City increased from 60,666 in 1900 to 152,407 in 1920. Of Manhattan's black population of 109,133 in 1920, two-thirds lived in Harlem.

New York City also became the center of increased Caribbean immigration. Approximately 25 percent of Harlem's black population were foreign-born by the mid-1920s, with the vast majority of the foreign-born composed of Caribbean immigrants. Although the foreign-born percentage decreased 16.7 percent by 1930 due to restrictive immigration laws, West Indian immigrants continued to play an important role in the economic, intellectual, and political life of New York City. By 1930, an estimated one-third of New York City's black professionals were from the Caribbean. Harlem was home to many prominent Caribbean intellectuals such as journalist and African Blood Brotherhood leader Cyril BRIGGS, socialist organizers Frank CROSSWAITH and H. H. HARRISON, and nationalist leaders W. A. DOMINGO and Ethelred Brown. In 1919 Caribbean immigrants founded New York City's leading black newspaper, the *Amsterdam News*.

By this time, Harlem had become the center of New York's black life, containing not only the working class, but also the small but influential black middle class. In 1919, the Equitable Life Assurance Society placed on the market the beautiful brownstones on W. 139th Street designed by Stanford White which had been off limits to black buyers. Within eight months, members of the black bourgeoisie had purchased them and they became known as "Striver's Row." Other streets, such as Edgecomb Avenue and St. Nicholas Place, became middle- and upper-income black enclaves. The diverse black nationalities and artistic communities of Harlem contributed to its heterogeneous class composition and cosmopolitan reputation in the 1920s.

Throughout the first half of the twentieth century Harlem was the cultural and ideological capital of black America. In the 1920s, it became the center of both a literary renaissance (*see* HARLEM RENAISSANCE) and the black nationalistic movement of Marcus GARVEY—another Caribbean immigrant—and his UNIVERSAL NEGRO IMPROVEMENT ASSOCIATION (UNIA). From his Harlem headquarters, Garvey instilled a new racial pride while advocating the decolonization of Africa from European rule. The UNIA established several businesses, including the ill-fated Black Star Line of ships, which was intended to facilitate commerce between Africa and African-Americans. Its promoters hoped the UNIA would play a role in the repatriation of blacks from the racially repressive climate of the United States to freedom in an independent Africa. Garveyism was the nationalistic manifestation of the NEW NEGRO movement's search for racial pride and assertiveness in the struggle for freedom.

The literary ferment of the Harlem Renaissance produced numerous authors and poets who celebrated their African and African-American heritage. In such works as Langston HUGHES's *Weary Blues* (1926), Jean TOOMER's *Cane* (1923), and Countee CULLEN's poem "Heritage" (1925), black writers extolled the culture and character of Africa. The cosmopolitan nature of the Renaissance is seen in the number of West Indian artists who played an instrumental role in the literature, such as Claude MCKAY and Eric WALROND. Artists and their literary promoters, such as the black sociologist and editor of the NATIONAL URBAN LEAGUE magazine OPPORTUNITY, (1923–1944), Charles S. JOHNSON, sought to create a new and more positive image for African Americans through the arts which might be absorbed by the larger society. The NATIONAL ASSOCIATION FOR THE ADVANCEMENT OF COLORED PEOPLE, the leading civil rights organiza-

Demonstration march in New York City, early twentieth century. (Prints and Photographs Division, Library of Congress)

tion in the United States, had its offices in Harlem, as did its journal, the CRISIS (1910–).

Harlem had a vibrant nightlife which was soon discovered by white theatergoers, critics, publishers, and intellectuals. The dominant form of black popular music was JAZZ. One of the roots of jazz was locally-based ragtime and Harlem stride piano, as performed by musicians such as Eubie BLAKE, Fats WALLER, and James P. JOHNSON. Another root of jazz was found in New Orleans and other southern cities. Southern jazz followed black migrants north and became the popular dance music of the 1920s through the 1940s. New York City soon became a music center for jazz. White New Yorkers found black music and entertainers readily available in Harlem nightclubs. Connie's Inn and the COTTON CLUB were two of the most famous clubs in Harlem in the twenties. Owned by white underworld figures, they featured black bands, singers, and chorus-line dancers. Duke ELLINGTON and his

band, and singer Lena HORNE were among the major attractions at the Harlem clubs. The appreciation of black music did not carry over into the human sphere, however, and many of the white-owned clubs excluded black patrons.

The period of the twenties and thirties was one in which the city's black population demanded greater participation or control of the institutions in their communities. In Harlem, blacks demanded positions at Harlem Hospital from which they had been excluded, as well as control of Harlem's district leaderships, clubhouses, and representation. In 1929, Charles Fillmore, a REPUBLICAN, became the city's first black district leader. In 1935, Herbert Bruce, a West Indian immigrant, became the DEMOCRATIC PARTY's first black district leader. In the first five years of the GREAT DEPRESSION, West Indian politicians made significant gains in the Democratic party. By 1952, four of the five Democratic district leaders in

Harlem were West Indians. Four of the five founding members of the Harlem branch of the COMMUNIST PARTY were West Indians. In part these trends were the result of African-American domination of the black posts within the Republican party and the greater accessibility of the Democratic party, which had far less black involvement until the New Deal. West Indians cooperated with African-American Democrats in attempts to gain black control over the Harlem Nineteenth and Twenty-first Assembly Districts. Despite some degree of tension between African Americans and West Indians, race far more than nationality determined the condition of blacks in the city and nation. By the 1930s, the first wave of West Indian immigrants that entered the country at the beginning of the twentieth century lived in neighborhoods segregated by race but not divided by black ethnic or class differences.

By the latter half of the 1920s the Garvey movement had collapsed with his imprisonment and deportation. The stock market crash of 1929 and accompanying depression eroded interest in the Renaissance. Still, Harlem remained dynamic, as the struggle for equality intensified as the black unemployment rate in the city grew to nearly double that of whites and threw nearly half of Harlem's families onto relief. The injustice of employment discrimination in Harlem retail and chain stores in the midst of the depression added insult to injury. Blacks initiated successful boycotts in Harlem in the 1930s, forcing department stores, utilities, and transportation companies to reverse their policies and hire blacks. Boycotts and protest marches were important weapons in breaking down the prejudice-induced barriers that existed during the Great Depression. The 1935 riot in Harlem (see HARLEM RIOT OF 1935) and the accompanying violence directed at white businesses helped sensitize political and civic leaders to the need for change. With the onset of the preparedness drive for WORLD WAR II, New York City became the headquarters for A. Philip RANDOLPH's movement for the March on Washington in 1941 to protest discrimination in the armed forces and among federal contractors. This led to the creation of a Federal FAIR EMPLOYMENT PRACTICES COMMITTEE in 1941 to insure blacks their fair share of jobs in defense industries.

World War II ended the depression and illustrated the contradiction of a country fighting against racist Nazi ideology with two armies, one white and one black. The shooting of a black soldier by a white policeman in the Hotel Braddock in Harlem touched off another riot on August 1, 1943 (see HARLEM RIOT OF 1943). A critical factor contributing to the outbreak of the riot was the erroneous rumor that the soldier had been killed by the policeman. As the evening progressed crowds gathered at the local precinct, the Braddock Hotel, and at Sydenham Hospital, where he supposedly died. Rioting broke out around 10:30 P.M. with the breaking of store windows centering on 125th Street and continued for two days. The human cost of the riot was significant, with 6 people killed, all black, and 185 people injured, mostly black. Arrests of blacks numbered more than 550, with most in custody for burglary and reception of stolen goods. Estimates were that some 1,450 stores were damaged.

In comparison to the Detroit riot of June 21 of the same year (see DETROIT RIOT OF 1943), the loss of life and physical injury were considerably less, but the events of August 1st and 2nd came as a surprise in America's most cosmopolitan city in which the mayor, Fiorello La Guardia, was popular in the black community. Frustration with the continuation of racism was the underlying cause of the riot. Pictures of the earlier Detroit riot showing black victims of white mobs and police were carried by New York newspapers along with numerous articles on white violence and discrimination against black servicemen. On the local level the riot was in part sparked by black discontent with employment discrimination, with police brutality, and La Guardia's apparent retreat from liberal policies (such as his approval of the Navy's use of Hunter College as a segregated training facility for its WAVES [Women's Reserves]). La Guardia's subsequent approval of the Metropolitan Life Insurance Company's plan to build a tax-exempt quasi-public housing project (Stuyvesant Town) also incurred the wrath of blacks familiar with Metropolitan Life's policy of black exclusion and residential segregation.

Following the riot, La Guardia moved to implement policies that the black community had advocated. Within one week of the riot, the Office of Price Administration announced the opening of an office to investigate food price-gouging in Harlem. Within two weeks, La Guardia inaugurated a series of radio broadcasts to promote racial harmony. The New York City Board of Education created a course on Intercultural Relations for teachers which emphasized African-American contributions. The mayor also announced that any discrimination in tenant selection for Stuyvesant Town was illegal. The riot stimulated greater efforts at improving race relations.

WORLD WAR II had a salutary effect upon the black condition, stimulating African-American migration to the North and the acquisition of industrial jobs. In 1944, the election of Adam Clayton POWELL, JR. to the United States Congress, and the election of Powell's successor to the New York City Council, Communist party member Benjamin J. DAVIS, contributed to the growth of militant black political leadership in Harlem.

Malcolm X addresses a rally in Harlem, June 29, 1963. (AP/Wide World Photos)

In the post–World War II era, the black population grew, heavily augmented by migration from the South and the Caribbean. The passage of state and federal discrimination legislation in housing and employment aided the expansion of the black middle class and black outmigration to other boroughs and suburbs. Between 1940 and 1950, Bedford-Stuyvesant emerged as an overwhelmingly black ghetto and by 1960 black residents had expanded into the contiguous parts of Crown Heights and Brownsville. The Greater Bedford-Stuyvesant area developed into the largest black community in New York City. Nearly 40 percent of the city's blacks made their home in Brooklyn by 1970. The South Jamaica–St. Albans–Cambria Heights area of Queens also blossomed as a large area of black settlement after World War II. The black populations in other boroughs were significantly augmented by the increase in black immigration from the Caribbean following

the reform of immigration laws in 1965. The 1980 census indicated that 300,000 New Yorkers were born in the non-Hispanic Caribbean, 80 percent of whom had arrived since 1965. The center of the Caribbean black community shifted in the 1970s from the Harlem and Bedford-Stuyvesant neighborhoods to Crown Heights, East Flatbush, and the Flatbush sections of central Brooklyn. In 1980, 54.8 percent of the city's West Indian population lived in Brooklyn, with only 7.4 percent living in Manhattan. Large West Indian settlements have developed in southeastern Queens and the northeast Bronx. By the mid-1980s, many of the more prosperous West Indians had moved to the Springfield Gardens, Cambria Heights, and Laurelton sections of Queens. The rise of West Indians to national prominence was evidenced in the careers of former congresswoman, presidential candidate, and daughter of Barbadian immigrants, Shirley CHISHOLM, and Colin POWELL, the first black chairman of the Joint Chiefs of Staff and son of Jamaican immigrants.

Postwar New York City continued to serve as a beacon for black immigrants from the South and Caribbean immigrants alike, but many did not find northern cities to be the urban promised land. Employment discrimination, housing segregation, periodic instances of police brutality, and inadequate education served to disillusion some with life in New York. In the 1950s, the NATION OF ISLAM had sent its most talented organizer, minister, and spokesman, MALCOLM X, to New York City. Malcolm X not only built the Harlem Mosque into a major force in the city, but he also significantly increased the national following of the Nation of Islam through his vehement condemnations of America's history of virulent racism. His assassination in upper Manhattan in 1965 was a major setback to the advocates of black nationalism and black empowerment.

Despite their disillusionment, blacks continued their quest for empowerment in the city. The expanding black population helped elect black politicians to many new offices. Hulan JACK, an immigrant from Guyana, became the first black Manhattan borough president in 1953. Anna Arnold HEDGEMAN became a high-ranking aide to Mayor Robert Wagner in the 1950s. J. Raymond JONES, a native of St. Thomas in the Virgin Islands, was selected to the leadership of Tammany Hall (the regular Democratic organization of Manhattan) in 1964. Other prominent politicians include Charles RANGEL, who replaced Adam Clayton Powell, Jr., as Harlem's congressman in 1970, and Percy SUTTON, who was Manhattan borough president from 1966 to 1977.

In 1989, the greatest triumph of black political power in New York City was the election of David DINKINS, a product of Harlem's vital political scene, to the mayor's office. The administration of Dinkins, however, was plagued with the problems troubling all major cities. Some of these problems included the continuation of crime at unacceptable levels, an overburdened educational system, a growing underclass, a deteriorating physical infrastructure, poor minority-community relations with the police, and stagnating black impoverishment.

Despite its many problems, New York City continues to be the center of African-American cultural life in the United States. In almost every area of the arts, New York City remains one of the centers for innovations, and black New Yorkers, both native and transplanted, continue to make enduring contributions. The city has a long history of black classical and theatrical music, dating back to the early decades of the century, when Will Marion COOK, Harry T. BURLEIGH, J. Rosamund JOHNSON, Scott JOPLIN, and Eubie BLAKE composed for the theater and con-

cert hall. In the second half of the century, musicians such as William Grant STILL, Paul ROBESON, Leontyne PRICE, Martina ARROYO, and André WATTS have had significant associations with New York.

New York City has both been a home of numerous JAZZ movements and the place of residence for musicians such as Bud POWELL, Charlie PARKER, Sonny ROLLINS, Max ROACH, Miles DAVIS, Ornette COLEMAN, and Cecil TAYLOR. Popular RHYTHM AND BLUES groups such as Frankie Lymon and the Teenagers and Little Anthony, starting as street corner harmonists, were formed in New York City. Folk musicians associated with New York City include LEADBELLY, Josh WHITE, Sonny TERRY, Brownie MCGHEE, and calypso and popular singer Harry BELAFONTE. There have also been a number of important dancers in New York City, including Florence MILLS, Pearl PRIMUS, and Asadata DAFORA, along with more recent performers such as Arthur MITCHELL and the DANCE THEATER OF HARLEM, Alvin AILEY, and his successor Judith JAMISON, and modern dancer Bill T. JONES. New York City has also been home to tap dancers such as Bill "Bojangles" ROBINSON and Charles "Honi" COLES (see also TAP DANCE).

Beginning in the late 1970s, the most significant contribution of black New Yorkers to popular music was the creation and development of RAP music, which originated in the housing projects of the Bronx, Manhattan, and Queens. Among the first important rap artists were Afrika Bambaata, Grand Master Flash and the Furious Five, the Sugar Hill Gang, and Run-DMC. Other important New York City rappers include LL Cool J, Kool Moe Dee, Krs-One, and Public Enemy.

There have also been a number of important black writers and artists associated with New York City since the Harlem Renaissance. James BALDWIN, a native of Harlem, used the city for the setting of several of his novels, including *Go Tell It on the Mountain* (1953). Ralph ELLISON lived in New York for most of his adult life, and much of his novel *Invisible Man* (1952) is set in the city. Other writers associated with New York City for significant portions of their careers include Zora Neale HURSTON, Nella LARSEN, John O. KILLENS, Lorraine HANSBERRY, Samuel R. DELANY, Paule MARSHALL, Audre LORDE, Albert MURRAY, Gloria NAYLOR, Melvin TOLSON, and Ann PETRY.

African-American painters and sculptors from New York City include Romare BEARDEN, Jacob LAWRENCE, Richmond BARTHE, Augusta SAVAGE, and Jean-Michel BASQUIAT.

The racial divide prevalent in New York City was perhaps highlighted by the electoral defeat of Mayor Dinkins by former U.S. District Attorney Rudolph

Giuliani in 1993. An important factor in the election was the criticism directed at Dinkins by those who believed he excessively restrained the police when rioting broke out in Crown Heights in August 1991 between blacks and Jews after the accidental death of a black youth hit by a Hasidic driver and the subsequent murder of a Jewish rabbinical student. The event polarized the city, and brought militant community-based black protest, largely led by Brooklyn minister Rev. Al SHARPTON, to public attention. In the 1993 election, 76 percent of the white vote went for Republican candidate Giuliani in a city with a five-to-one Democratic majority in registered voters, while 95 percent of the black vote went to Dinkins. In 1989, when the city was less intensely divided than four years later, Giuliani had received 71 percent of the white vote and Dinkins had received 91 percent of the black vote. Given these figures, it is difficult not to sense the increasing racial polarization in the city and to feel uneasy about New York City's future.

See also NEW YORK STATE.

REFERENCES

BERNSTEIN, IVER. The New York City Draft Riots: Their Significance for American Politics in the Age of the Civil War. New York, 1990.

CONNOLLY, HAROLD X. A Ghetto Grows in Brooklyn. New York, 1977.

JOHNSON, JAMES WELDON. Black Manhattan. New York, 1930.

CAPECI, DOMINIC J., JR. The Harlem Riot of 1943. Philadelphia, 1977.

CRUSE, HAROLD. The Crisis of the Negro Intellectual. New York, 1967.

DAVIS, THOMAS G. A Rumor of Revolt: "The Great Negro Plot" in Colonial New York. Amherst, Mass., 1985.

FREEMAN, RHONDA G. The Free Negro in New York City in the Era Before the Civil War. New York, 1994.

GRAY, BRENDA. Black Female Domestics during the Depression in New York City, 1930-1940. New York, 1993.

KASINITZ, PHILIP. Caribbean New York: Black Immigrants and the Politics of Race. Ithaca, N.Y., 1992.

LEWIS, DAVID LEVERING. When Harlem Was in Vogue. New York, 1979.

MOSS, RICHARD. Slavery on Long Island: A Study in Local Institutional and Early African American Communal Life. New York, 1993.

OSOFSKY, GILBERT. Harlem: The Making of a Ghetto, 1870–1930. New York, 1966.

OTTLEY, ROI, and WILLIAM J. WEATHERBY, eds. The Negro in New York: An Informal Social History 1626–1940. New York, 1967.

SCHATZBERG, RUFUS. Black Organized Crime in Harlem, 1920–1930. New York, 1993.

SCHEINER, SETH M. Negro Mecca: A History of the Negro in New York City, 1865–1920. New York, 1965.

SORIN, GERALD. The New York Abolitionists: A Case Study of Political Radicalism. Westport, Conn., 1971.

WALKER, GEORGE E. The Afro-American in New York City, 1827–1860. New York, 1993.

WHITE, SHANE. Somewhat More Independent: The End of Slavery in New York City, 1770–1810. Athens, Ga., 1991.

LARRY GREENE

New York City Draft Riot of 1863. The New York City Draft Riot of 1863 was the most violent of several urban insurrections that occurred during the Civil War. In Detroit, Toledo, Harrisburg, and Cincinnati the economic and social disruption caused by the war provoked violent protests and intensified the racism directed against northern free blacks. The violence in New York City was a direct response to federal implementation of the military-conscription act, but other conditions contributed to the magnitude of the insurrection. Longstanding economic competition between working-class whites and African Americans, particularly between Irish immigrants and blacks on the city's wharves, had strained race relations. A strong local Democratic party organization nurtured anti-Republican sentiment, and an inflammatory pro-Confederate and racist press fueled racial hatred and popular resentment against federal government policies.

Beginning on July 13, white mobs paralyzed the city. Numbering in the thousands and scattered throughout the city, the rioters overwhelmed the city's meager police force. They besieged the New York Tribune offices in search of the paper's Unionist editor, Horace Greeley. They ravaged the home of the city's provost marshal, and threatened the lives of other prominent Union sympathizers. But the mobs directed much of their wrath on the city's black community. Black New Yorkers were harassed, brutally beaten in the streets, and driven from their homes. The mobs singled out black institutions, symbols of racial progress, for destruction. They burned the Colored Orphan Asylum and looted the Colored Seamen's Home. Black residents fled their homes in terror and took refuge outside the city. Some, in desperation, sought protection under police custody in the municipal jails. The rioters murdered at least eleven blacks and injured hundreds of others. Union army regiments, some recent arrivals from the Gettysburg battlefield, were brought in to restore order.

The rioting and the government's forceful response resulted in at least 105 deaths and hundreds of other casualties. Most of the dead and wounded were rioters. Property damage was extensive; in some cases the mobs razed entire city blocks. Losses exceeded $1.5 million, or about $16 million by present standards. Black residents and businesses suffered several thousand dollars in property losses. A special committee of New York City merchants raised over $50,000 to compensate many of the black victims and to rebuild the Colored Orphan Asylum. But no monetary reparations could relieve the psychological devastation or remove the specter of the mob's lynch law. Broken and dispirited by the five days of terror, many blacks left the city. By 1865, New York City had lost 20 percent of its black population.

REFERENCE

BERNSTEIN, IVER. *The New York City Draft Riots.* New York, 1990.

MICHAEL F. HEMBREE

New York Manumission Society. This association, intended to promote the emancipation and improvement of African Americans, first met on January 25, 1785, in lower Manhattan; it was officially organized ten days later as "The New York Society for promoting the manumission of slaves and protecting such of them as have been or may be liberated." Charter members included John Jay (who was the society's first president 1785–90), Alexander Hamilton (its second president, 1790–91), John Murray, Jr. (its treasurer until 1819), James Duane (a judge), Robert Troup (a lawyer), and William Shotwell (a Quaker businessman). Noah Webster was another early member of the society. All the original members were white. Although these men were committed to the gradual emancipation of African Americans, they shared a commitment to property that necessitated a conservative course of action—many of the members were themselves slave owners. The main functions of the society were to push for manumission legislation; litigate on behalf of slaves who were mistreated, unfairly enslaved, or seeking freedom; and promote the education of African Americans, primarily through the administration of the AFRICAN FREE SCHOOL. One of its original goals was realized in 1799 when New York State adopted a gradual manumission statute.

In November 1787 the African Free School launched its endeavors when it admitted its first twelve students. In 1814 the original school was destroyed by fire, but in January 1815 the African Free School Number One was opened at 245 William Street, educating forty pupils of both sexes. The Af-rican Free School Number Two was opened on Mulberry Street near Grand Street in 1820 with accommodations for five hundred students. By 1833 there were seven branch schools of the Free School in lower Manhattan with a total enrollment of over fourteen hundred students, but in the following year the society relinquished administration of this system to the city, and shortly thereafter the aims of the school were altered as white students were admitted.

Cadwallader D. Colden joined the society in 1792 and from 1812 to 1831 served as its president; during part of his tenure he was also the mayor of the city and the lieutenant governor of the state. In 1821 the membership of the society stood at about one hundred active members. Much of the society comprised members of the Society of Friends (Quakers), who from the society's earliest days had disproportionately filled positions of responsibility.

After dispensing its funds to various organizations committed to the betterment of African Americans, the society officially closed in 1849. While it existed, it had been the most significant African-American antislavery educational organization in the city, though it always remained patrician in its structure and somewhat paternalistic in its relations with New York City blacks.

REFERENCE

MOSELEY, THOMAS ROBERT. A History of the New York Manumission Society. Ph.D. diss., University of Michigan, 1963.

WILLIAM J. MOSES

New York Slave Conspiracy of 1741. The actual existence of a widespread insurrectionary conspiracy in the so-called "Great Negro Plot" or "New York Conspiracy" of 1741 is a subject of considerable scholarly debate. Most historians, notably Charles and Mary Beard and Herbert Aptheker, have maintained that the conspiracy was a product of paranoid fantasies by white New Yorkers. However, some scholars, including Gary Nash and Thomas Davis, have used the account published in 1744 by Daniel Horsmanden, the judge who presided over the trial, to argue that there was a core truth to the accusations. These scholars find convincing evidence in Horsmanden's account that slaves in New York City during 1741 were openly expressing their hostility to their masters and committing sporadic, violent acts against white-owned property. These disagreements notwithstanding, what is beyond question is that for their alleged involvement in the conspiracy, thirty-four people, twenty-six of them black, were hanged or burned at the stake in New York City in the summer of 1741.

For good reasons there was wide discontent among the laboring classes of New York, both free and slave. The winter of 1740–1741, remembered for years as "the hard winter," was especially difficult for the city's poorest inhabitants. In the spring the price of wheat was extremely high and in response a group of the city's bakers refused to bake until the price fell, leading to widespread hunger.

In 1740 the city's slaves were accused of poisoning the water supply, causing much of the white population to rely on bottled water for months. These suspicions turned to hysteria in March and April of 1741, when fires struck an unusually high number of buildings in the city, including the governor's house, the secretary's office, the King's Chapel, and soldiers' barracks. Most theories on the fires involved collusion between poor whites and slaves. Some speculated that Catholic priests were also involved.

One hundred and fifty slaves and twenty-five white suspects, including seventeen soldiers, were arrested. Among those indicted was Mary Burton, an indentured servant girl who worked as a prostitute at a tavern. While being interrogated, Burton confessed that the tavern keeper was the leader of a ring of poor whites and slaves that planned to burn down the entire city and kill its white inhabitants. Besides the twenty-six slaves executed, seventy were banished to the West Indies. Burton, the tavern keeper, his wife, and a man accused of being a Spanish priest, were also executed.

REFERENCES

APTHEKER, HERBERT. *American Negro Slave Revolts.* New York, 1943.
DAVIS, THOMAS J. *A Rumor of Revolt: "The Great Negro Plot" in Colonial New York.* New York, 1985.
HORSMANDEN, DANIEL. *The New York Conspiracy.* 1744. Reprint. Boston, 1971.
NASH, GARY B. *Red, White, and Black: The Peoples of Early America.* Englewood Cliffs, N.J., 1974.
SZASZ, FERENC M. "The New York Slave Revolt of 1741: A Re-Examination." *New York History* 48 (1967).

THADDEUS RUSSELL

New York Slave Revolt of 1712.

In the spring of 1712, about two dozen slaves in colonial New York City plotted to rebel against the harsh treatment by their owners. On April 6, two of the plotters put a torch to their master's outhouse, planning to kill anyone who came to put out the fire. As peo-

ple rushed to douse the flames, the rebels shot or stabbed them, killing nine men and wounding seven.

News of the revolt spread quickly and the plotters dispersed to avoid capture. New York's governor called out the militia and posted sentries all around the town. Within two days, the slaves were captured; however, six killed themselves rather than be taken into custody.

Thirty-nine slaves were charged with murder or as accessories to murder, and four were indicted for assault. Several were unjustly accused due to the panic and hysteria the revolt created; in addition, the prosecutor, Attorney General May Bickley, relied on the suspect testimony of two plotters who cooperated in return for immunity. Nevertheless, eighteen of those indicted were later acquitted for lack of evidence. Twenty-five slaves were executed: Twenty, including a woman, were hanged; one was suspended in chains until he died; three were burned to death, one of them by a slow fire that burned for eight or ten hours; another was broken on the wheel.

As a result of the revolt, New York's lawmakers toughened their slave code (*see* BLACK CODES). Among the provisions: Slaves who met in groups of three or more could be given forty lashes, and crimes punishable by death included burning barns, outhouses, stables, and stacks of corn or hay.

REFERENCE

SCOTT, KENNETH. "The Slave Insurrection in New York in 1712." *New-York Historical Society Quarterly* 45 (January 1961): 43–74.

JANE LUSAKA

New York State. The state of New York has had a black presence almost from the beginning of its existence as the Dutch colony of New Netherland in the seventeenth century. From colonial times to the present, blacks have been a continuous and important factor in New York. A black population first developed in 1626 in the southern part of New Netherland in the city of New Amsterdam, called New York City after the English conquest of 1664. The Dutch imported and enslaved Africans to work on farms, estates, and public works. The institution of SLAVERY continued, expanded, and became harsher. By the late seventeenth century, New York had a manorial system along the Hudson Valley, employing white tenant farmers to work the lands. However, the limited number of white immigrants led to the purchase of blacks from the lower South, West Indies, and eventually Africa. By the eighteenth century the African presence, either as slaves or free persons, was established in central New York. Blacks soon began to make distinctive contributions to New York's culture. The Anglo-Dutch and African holiday of "Pinkster," celebrated in the early summer at the time of Pentecost, generated distinctive African-derived songs and dances (*see* FESTIVALS) and was widely celebrated in Albany and elsewhere along the Hudson Valley from the middle of the eighteenth to the early nineteenth century. Slavery was also well established on Long Island. The first published poet in North America was a Long Island slave, Jupiter HAMMON, whose poetry was published as early as 1760.

By 1790, the enslaved African population as counted in the census amounted to 21,324, giving New York the largest black population and the most well-developed institution of slavery north of the Mason-Dixon Line. With slavery came not acquiescence, but conspiracy and revolt. Blacks seeking freedom were unsuccessful in the NEW YORK CITY SLAVE REVOLT OF 1712 and failed again in the NEW YORK CITY SLAVE CONSPIRACY OF 1741. The participants and many innocent bystanders were brutally executed, but the thirst for freedom remained unquenched. In February 1775 there was a slave conspiracy in the Kingston area of New York, and slaves were restive elsewhere. That year, armed conflict erupted against Great Britain in the battles of Lexington and Concord (*see* AMERICAN REVOLUTION). Blacks contributed to the patriot cause in New York, fighting with Gen. "Mad" Anthony Wayne in his capture of Stony Point; blacks were at Valley Forge and with Revolutionary forces at the Battle of Saratoga. Some blacks who received promises of EMANCIPATION fought with the British and were evacuated with them at the war's end from ports in New York City and Staten Island for the West Indies and Nova Scotia.

The incompatibility of slavery with the natural rights philosophy of the American Revolution led to the formation of the NEW YORK MANUMISSION SOCIETY in 1785 and the passage of a state gradual emancipation law in 1799. The law freed all children born to slave women after the 4th of July 1799. Males became free at twenty-eight years of age, and females at the age of twenty-five. New York completed the abolition of slavery with the passage of the Emancipation Act of 1827. These abolition laws, coupled with an earlier act passed by the New York Assembly in 1781 manumitting all blacks serving with the state's military forces in the Revolutionary War, contributed to the growth of New York state's free black population. At the New York State Constitutional Convention meeting in 1821, Democratic-Republicans succeeded in eliminating property qualifications for white male voters, but retained a $250

qualification for black males. Even before this act of blatant discrimination, African Americans, free of bondage but not of discrimination, had set about the formation of an institutional network comprised of their own churches, benevolent societies, newspapers, and literary societies. They organized conventions to combat discrimination, poverty, and illiteracy among free blacks and to oppose slavery. In 1821, the AFRICAN METHODIST EPISCOPAL ZION denomination was formed in New York City and established congregations across the state and eventually in other states. The AFRICAN METHODIST EPISCOPAL denomination, based in Philadelphia, also established churches in New York. The earliest black Baptist church in the state, the ABYSSINIAN BAPTIST CHURCH, was founded in New York City in 1808. These churches provided the leadership and coordinating centers for black participation in the antebellum antislavery effort and the UNDERGROUND RAILROAD.

Sojourner TRUTH, born Isabella Baumfree, a Dutch-speaking slave in the Hudson Valley in 1797, became one of the leading antislavery speakers of the antebellum era. She obtained her freedom in 1827 when the state finally abolished the last vestige of slavery through a process of gradual emancipation. In 1843 she experienced a call to testify the word of God and to the evils wrought against her people and gender, and she assumed the stirring name of Sojourner Truth. She became a part of the women's movement in the late 1840s and eloquently spoke out against the double exploitation of black women in bondage due to both their race and gender.

Numerous fugitives from southern slavery fled to New York or passed through New York on their way to Canada. It has been estimated that more than 1,000 fugitives passed through Elmira between 1840 and 1850. Central New York contained many routes and stations on the underground railroad, like St. James A.M.E. Church in Ithaca, which hid many fugitives in the church basement. Auburn was an important underground railroad site in central New York, centered on Harriet TUBMAN's house on the outskirts of town. She escaped from bondage herself in 1849 and made between eleven and nineteen trips into the South, leading some estimated 300 people from bondage. Sympathies for those seeking refuge were strong in a number of centers, such as Syracuse. Harriet Powell, a slave to a visiting Mississippi family, was assisted by Syracuse abolitionists such as the Rev. Jermain W. LOGUEN in her escape to Canada, as was William Henry "Jerry" McReynolds, a fugitive slave dramatically rescued from police headquarters. Stephen Myers, a black antebellum leader from Albany, helped many FUGITIVE SLAVES in their flight to Canada. At Albany, the Underground Railroad veered east into New England and west toward Utica and beyond. One of the central figures for the Underground Railroad was Henry Highland GARNET, the militant black abolitionist, minister, and community leader. The activity on the Underground Railroad greatly intensified after 1850 with the passage of a strong federal FUGITIVE SLAVE LAW.

The development of the underground railroad in upstate New York was made possible by the extensive evangelical ferment and abolitionism of the Great Awakening in a region of upper New York state known as the "burned-over district," including such cities as Syracuse and Rochester, and became perhaps the most fervently abolitionist region of the nation. Beriah Green, president of the Oneida Institute in Whitesboro, made the school into a center of immediatist abolitionism and a pioneer in integrated higher education with the enrollment of black students. A number of black antislavery leaders graduated from the Oneida Institute, such as Henry Highland Garnet, Alexander CRUMMELL, and Jermain W. Loguen. Garnet, a Presbyterian minister from Troy, addressed the 1843 National Convention of Colored Citizens meeting in Buffalo with the call for a mass insurrection of those enslaved. Abolitionists given to more moderate tactics like moral persuasion rejected this call for violent action against slavery. The call was a reflection of black frustration about the continuation of slavery and the failure of moral persuasion tactics of Garrisonian abolitionism (see ABOLITION). Among those who differed with Garnet's approach was Frederick DOUGLASS, the nation's most famous black abolitionist, a Rochester resident, and publisher of North Star newspaper, who advocated electoral support for the Liberty party and collaboration with white abolitionists.

Abolitionist activity throughout upstate New York, while contributing significantly to the growing opposition to slavery and its expansion into the West, was by no means representative of all New Yorkers. Beriah Green and the abolitionist members of the First Presbyterian Church of Whitesboro were forced out by a conservative faction under the leadership of the pastor. In other areas of central New York—such as Syracuse, Elmira, and Peterboro—churches split over the slavery question. The abolitionists organized "come-outer churches," so named because they had come out of organizations corrupted by silence or indifference to the sin of slavery.

New York state's most famous white abolitionist was John Brown, who set out to seize the arms at the federal arsenal at Harpers Ferry in Virginia (now part of West Virginia) in 1859, which was to have been the first blow sparking a massive insurrection among slaves (see JOHN BROWN'S RAID). Brown had been known in central New York as a religious man and

fervent hater of slavery. He had purchased a farm in North Elba from Liberty party leader Gerrit Smith where he lived from 1843 to 1851. New Yorker Gerrit Smith became one of the "secret six" of prominent white abolitionists who gave John Brown financial aid.

Brown had been in contact with Frederick Douglass, Jermain Loguen, and Harriet Tubman concerning his liberation plans. Many black New Yorkers, including Douglass and Garnet, thought the plan was foolhardy, but gave Brown equivocal support. Shields Green, an escaped slave from Charleston living in Rochester, was the only black from New York state actually participating in the raid. Green was a well-built man of about twenty-five years of age when he was introduced to John Brown by Frederick Douglas in 1859. A few months later, on October 16, 1859, the ill-fated raid commenced and in so doing furthered the process of disunion that would end African-American slavery.

Slavery was ultimately ended by the secession of the South (see CIVIL WAR) and the subsequent efforts of the federal government to restore the Union. Following the Emancipation Proclamation of January 1, 1863, the war to preserve the Union also became a war of emancipation, one in which blacks would finally be allowed to become soldiers for the Union. A black company was sent from Syracuse, and New York City formed the 20th, 26th, and 31st regiments. The contributions of black soldiers to the Union war effort did not deter critics of the Emancipation Proclamation who believed that a war to preserve the Union had been perverted into a war to free blacks. The Union establishment of the draft led to the worst urban rioting in American history in New York City in the summer of 1863. Immigrant workers unable to pay the commutation fee to avoid the draft and hostile to blacks from years of job competition in the antebellum era focused their anger upon blacks.

New York City had been a center of "Copperhead" or Peace Democratic party sentiment during the Civil War. Party leaders like Gov. Horatio Seymour and New York City Mayor and later U.S. Rep. Fernando Wood were constantly critical of Lincoln's conduct of the war, the Emancipation Proclamation, the use of black troops, and finally the draft. For five days in July the city was under siege, white abolitionists were in danger, and black residents were subject to physical attack and even death. While New York City was the center of antiblack violence and Copperheadism in the state, the 1863 draft riots in the city (see NEW YORK CITY DRAFT RIOTS OF 1863) stimulated attacks upon blacks in the Hudson Valley–Mohawk region of the state. In Poughkeepsie, the Catherine Street African Methodist Episcopal Zion Church was attacked by a mob of drunken white soldiers. The governor had to ask assistance from the Vermont Volunteers to restore order. Many blacks in Tarrytown were forced to abandon their homes and seek refuge in places like Buttermilk Hill until federal gunboats appeared on the Hudson to restore order.

African Americans in New York had to wait five years before the ratified FIFTEENTH AMENDMENT granted them the right to vote on an equal basis with whites. The inundation of the North with freedmen following emancipation and the Civil War, predicted by Democratic party politicians seeking to exploit the fears of the immigrants and working class, never materialized. While the years between the Civil War and WORLD WAR I were ones of economic expansion and industrial growth, New York's black population did not participate in this fully or equally—in part because of segregated unions that kept blacks out of most skilled industrial jobs. It was with the onset of World War I and the interruption of the flow of European immigrants (*see* IMMIGRATION) that the northern demand for labor stimulated southern black migration to northern cities like New York City, Rochester, and Buffalo and the subsequent entrance of blacks into the state's industrial labor force. The Great Migration increased the black population of not only the major metropolitan area, New York City, but also in smaller cities like Buffalo, which experienced an increase in its African-American population from 1,698 in 1900 to 13,563 in 1930.

New York City's expanding African-American urban population became the cultural center of black America and the capital of the NEW NEGRO movement, which emphasized race pride, a concern for the decolonization of Africa, and the assertion of a unique black contribution to the cultural fabric of the United States. These trends were manifest everywhere in New York from the passage of the 1918 Civil Rights Act of New York State, which prohibited discrimination in areas of public accommodation, resort, or amusement, to Marcus GARVEY's New York City–based nationalistic organization the UNIVERSAL NEGRO IMPROVEMENT ASSOCIATION (UNIA). HARLEM became the center of an artistic and literary "renaissance" in the 1920s. Cities other than New York, while not possessing the magnetism of the HARLEM RENAISSANCE or the dynamism accompanying the Garvey movement, experienced a rapid increase in their black population and black institutions. In Buffalo, the migration led to the emergence of new community leaders and the creation and expansion of community organizations. From the 1920s through the GREAT DEPRESSION and WORLD WAR II years, Buffalo's black churches grew in number and such new organizations as the NATIONAL URBAN LEAGUE, the primarily black Michigan Avenue YMCA, the NATIONAL ASSOCIATION FOR THE ADVANCEMENT OF COLORED PEOPLE (NAACP), and the UNIA also appeared in the city. During the World War I era, white strikes and the hiring of replacement workers provided a means of entrance for blacks into Buffalo's heavy industry, such as railroad companies and steel mills. However, at Buffalo's Bethlehem Steel and Wickwire Steel mills, African Americans were usually given the most arduous jobs, such as in the blast furnace room. But the wages from these jobs were far superior to those available in the South. By 1940 the attraction of industrial jobs had increased Buffalo's black population to 19,000.

Progress was limited in the decade of the 1920s. The central region of upstate New York did not offer the economic opportunities that major industrial centers had afforded black migrants during the WORLD WAR I years. Returning black soldiers after the war found the racism of the KU KLUX KLAN had spread from the South and was successfully recruiting converts in this region by targeting Catholics and Jews as well as blacks. Emmet D. Smith, a native Mississippian, began recruiting members in 1923 from his base in Binghamton, N.Y. In response to the Klan and to less blatant and aggressive forms of racism, civil rights organizations were formed over the next two decades. The Interracial Committee of Binghamton was organized in 1932 and eventually became the Broome County Urban League. The NAACP opened belatedly a local branch in Syracuse to deal with persistent racial problems. The Ku Klux Klan's post–World War I search for new members north of the Mason-Dixon Line proved fruitful in upstate New York. The ebullience that opened the decade waned especially after the stock market crash of October 1929, and the nation descended into the GREAT DEPRESSION.

The cultural energy of the 1920s Harlem Renaissance diminished, but a new community-based activism arose in urban cities like New York, directing its energies toward discriminatory municipal agencies and Harlem department stores refusing to hire blacks in the midst of the Great Depression. Sufi Abdul Hamid began the initial boycott of Harlem merchants in 1934 and was later joined by prominent members of the black clergy, John B. Johnson and Adam Clayton POWELL, Jr. In March 1935, Harlem erupted into a riot protesting the discriminatory employment practices of 125th Street merchants and the past use of excessive force by the police. Powell and other leaders led a successful protest effort to secure employment for blacks as drivers and conductors on the city bus lines and subways. Black civic groups and civil rights organizations addressed similar issues in other cities of upstate New York.

The World War II years increased the flow of black migrants from the South to northern cities looking

Inmates lie on the ground outside Attica State Prison as others are stripped and searched following a rebellion in which the prisoners gained control of the prison, September 1970. (AP/Wide World Photos)

for work in a labor market revived from the throes of the Great Depression. The economic picture for African Americans in the state brightened significantly during the war years, but race relations still required much improvement, as was evidenced by the outbreak of a major riot in Harlem in 1943 (*see* HARLEM RIOT OF 1943). Black New Yorkers made progress in the post–World War II years, but many remained mired in poverty while others were assimilated into the economic mainstream. Defense industries provided jobs for the state's black population, though not in numbers corresponding to the black component of the population. Perhaps more important than the largely temporary defense jobs was the spirit of racial democracy that emerged from the ashes of World War II, which made officially sanctioned racism unacceptable. African Americans, having made their contribution on both war and home fronts, were unwilling to accept the continuation of racial discrimination without challenge.

The post–World War II era has been both one of progress as well as stagnation. After the war, many states passed antidiscrimination legislation covering the fields of employment and housing. New York was part of this movement. The state legislature passed the Ives-Quinn Bill in 1945, which prohibited employment discrimination based on race, color, religion, and national origin. These categories were ex-

panded to include age and gender discrimination in 1956 and 1964. The law was also amended in 1952 to cover discrimination in the area of public accommodations. The state further amended the law in 1955 to prohibit discrimination in public housing and later in 1961 to outlaw discrimination in private housing. In New York City in 1953, Hulan JACK became the first black borough president of Manhattan, at the time the highest ranking black elected-official in the county. J. Raymond JONES ascended the DEMOCRATIC PARTY ladder in 1964 to become the first black leader of the Manhattan Democratic party. Western New York joined the movement towards black elected officials as Buffalo elected Arthur O. Eve to the New York State Assembly in 1966. By 1966, the assembly contained eight blacks or 5.3 percent of the total number of assemblymen, while the New York State Senate held three black senators or 5.1 percent of the total number of senators. This represented an improvement, although blacks were 8.4 percent of the state's population.

By 1990 there were almost 3 million African Americans in New York state. Rochester (231,636 in 1990) was 34.5 percent black, Buffalo (328,123) was 30.7 percent black, while Syracuse (163,860 in 1990) was 20.3 percent African American. The increasing black percentage of New York cities, together with redistricting, has resulted in an increase in black political power. In 1989, David DINKINS was elected as the first black mayor of New York City. The expanding number of minority legislators has resulted in the establishment of a black and Puerto Rican legislative caucus. In 1993 there were twenty-one African-American members of the state legislature and five state senators. The influence of the black vote was manifested in the spring of 1993, when Carl H. McCall was chosen state comptroller by a special election of the state legislature. The growth and the passage of state and federal antidiscrimination employment legislation coupled with fair housing laws has also led to an expanded and increasingly suburbanized black middle class, with blacks elected to office in some of the more integrated suburbs.

The growth of the African-American population in New York towns outside of New York City has not been without racial tension and turmoil. Some municipalities sought to limit the size of the black population and segregate it residentially by restricting the housing opportunities available to minorities. Federal District Judge Leonard B. Sand ruled in 1985 that officials of the city of Yonkers intentionally segregated housing and schools by race. The city was locked in a bitter twelve-year battle with the NAACP and the Justice Department. Through 1993, Yonkers paid $1.6 million in fines and an estimated $15 million in legal fees in opposing the court's order to implement an integration plan. Yonkers provided several hundred units of co-ops and condominiums for minorities, with 565 (80 percent) units located in predominantly white eastern and northwestern Yonkers. This compromise plan was not approved by Judge Sand because many low-income people could not afford the housing, nor did the number of units satisfy the original order. The Yonkers situation demonstrates the limitations of racial integration in New York's suburbs.

A garish incident that focused attention on race relations in upstate New York started in late 1987, when fifteen-year-old Tawana Brawley of Wappingers Falls, N.Y. (a town in the Hudson River Valley), claimed that on November 28 of that year she had been kidnapped, sexually assaulted, physically defiled, and verbally abused by four white men: two off-duty policemen, a New York assistant prosecutor, and a utility worker. Her supporters, who included Alton Maddox, Jr., and C. Vernon Mason, her lawyers, and the Rev. Al SHARPTON, claimed that the case explored the true nature of American racism. Ten months after the original incident, a 170-page report from a grand jury convened by New York State Attorney General Robert Abrams concluded that the entire incident was a hoax. The publicity Al Sharpton received from the case catapulted

him to regional, and later national, prominence as a black spokesperson.

The incident, which revealed the depths of black anger and rage at the state, was one indication that New York state's inner city areas (along with suburban pockets of decay) continue to deteriorate, with crime more vicious, real income lower, and an educational system inferior to that existing in 1964 when riots erupted in Harlem and Rochester's black neighborhoods. The 1993 defeat of Mayor Dinkins by a white candidate, former federal prosecutor Rudolph Giuliani, in a city where registered Democrats outnumber Republicans five to one, reflected an election in which race is more of a determinant of voting patterns than ever before. For a portion of the state's African-American population, the American dream still awaits fulfillment.

See also NEW YORK CITY.

REFERENCES

BLOCH, HERMAN. *The Circle of Discrimination: An Economic and Social Study of the Black Man in New York.* New York, 1969.

COLES, HOWARD. *The Cradle of Freedom: A History of the Negro in Rochester, Western New York, and Canada.* Rochester, N.Y., 1941.

FARLEY, ENA. *The Underside of Reconstruction in New York: The Struggle over the Issue of Black Equality.* New York, 1993.

FIELD, PHYLLIS FRANCES. *The Politics of Race in New York: The Struggle for Black Suffrage in the Civil War Era.* Ithaca, N.Y., 1982.

FORDHAM, MONROE, ed. *The African-American Presence in New York State History: Four Regional History Surveys.* Albany, N.Y., 1989.

FREEMAN, RHONDA G. *The African American Presence in New York State History.* Albany, N.Y., 1989.

KOBRIN, DAVID. *The Black Minority in Early New York.* Albany, N.Y., 1971.

MABEE, CARLETON. *Black Education in New York State.* Syracuse, N.Y., 1979.

MCMANUS, EDGAR J. *A History of Negro Slavery in New York.* Syracuse, N.Y., 1966.

LARRY GREENE

Niagara Movement. The Niagara Movement, which was organized in 1905, was the first significant organized black protest movement in the twentieth century, and represented the attempt of a small but articulate group of radicals to challenge the then-dominant accommodationist ideas (*see* ACCOMMODATIONISM) of Booker T. WASHINGTON.

The Niagara Movement developed after failed attempts at reconciling the two factions in African-

American political life: the accommodationists, led by Booker T. Washington, and the more militant faction, led by W. E. B. DU BOIS and William Monroe TROTTER. A closed-door meeting of representatives of the two groups at Carnegie Hall in New York City in 1904 led to an organization, the Committee of Twelve for the Advancement of the Interests of the Negro Race, but the committee fell apart due to the belief of Du Bois and Trotter that Washington was controlling the organization.

In February 1905, Du Bois and Trotter devised a plan for a "strategy board" which would fight for civil rights and serve as a counterpoint to Washington's ideas. Since they knew Washington was most popular among whites, they resolved to form an all-black organization. Along with two allies, F. L. McGhee and C. E. Bentley, they set a meeting for that summer in western New York, to which they invited fifty-nine businessmen and professionals who were known to be anti-Washingtonites.

In mid-July 1905, Du Bois went to Buffalo. He had difficulty arranging hotel reservations, and crossed to the Canadian side of Niagara Falls. Fearing reprisals by Washington, who had sent spies to Buffalo, the radicals kept their conference secret. On July 11–14, 1905, twenty-nine men met and formed a group they called the Niagara Movement, both for the conference location and for the "mighty current" of protest they wished to unleash. Du Bois was named general secretary, and the group split into various committees, of which the most important was Trotter's Press and Public Opinion Committee. The founders agreed to divide the work among state chapters, which would "cooperate with congressmen and legislators to secure just legislation for the colored people," and pursue educational and informational programs. Movement members would meet annually.

The Niagara Movement's "Declaration of Principles," drafted by Du Bois and Trotter and adopted at the close of the conference, was a powerful and clear statement of the rights of African Americans: "We believe that this class of American citizens should protest emphatically and continually against the curtailment of their political rights." The declaration went on to urge African Americans to protest the curtailment of civil rights, the denial of equal economic opportunity, and denial of education; and the authors decried unhealthy living conditions, discrimination in the military, discrimination in the justice system, JIM CROW railroad cars, and other injustices. "Of the above grievances we do not hesitate to complain, and to complain loudly and insistently," they

Group portrait of members of the Niagara Movement. (Special Collections and Archives, University of Massachusetts, Amherst Library)

stated. "Persistent manly agitation is the way to liberty, and toward this goal the Niagara Movement has started. . . ."

At the end of its first year, the organization had only 170 members and was poorly funded. Nevertheless, the Niagarites pursued their activities, distributing pamphlets, lobbying against Jim Crow, and sending a circular protest letter to President Theodore Roosevelt after the BROWNSVILLE INCIDENT in 1906. That summer the movement had its second annual conference, at Harpers Ferry, W.Va. This was an open meeting, and the conference speeches, and the tribute to John Brown (*see* JOHN BROWN'S RAID), aroused much publicity.

The Niagara Movement, despite its impressive start, did not enjoy a long life. There was, from the start, determined opposition by Booker T. Washington—he prevented sympathetic white newspapers, and even many black ones, from printing the declaration—which dissuaded many blacks from joining or contributing funds. The loose organization, with only token communication between state chapters, and the radical nature, for the time, of such forthright protest, also contributed to the movement's decline. Not long after the Harpers Ferry Conference, factional struggles broke out between Du Bois and Trotter, as well as disagreements over the role of women in the movement. By the end of the summer of 1907, Trotter had been replaced as head of the Press Committee, and his supporters grew disenchanted with the movement. Du Bois tried to keep it going, guiding the movement through annual conferences in 1908 and 1909, after which it largely ceased to exist.

However, even in its decline, the movement left a lasting legacy. In 1908, Du Bois had invited Mary White Ovington, a settlement worker and socialist, to be the movement's first white member; by 1910 he had turned to the search for white allies by joining the newly organized NAACP. Despite its predominantly white leadership and centralized structure, the NAACP was really the successor to the Niagara Movement, whose remaining members Du Bois urged to join the NAACP. (However, William Monroe Trotter and his faction of the Niagara Movement never affiliated with the new organization.) The NAACP inherited many of the goals and tactics of the Niagara Movement, including the cultivation of a black elite which would defend the rights of African Americans through protest and lobbying against oppression and the publicizing of injustice.

REFERENCES

APTHEKER, HERBERT. *A Documentary History of the Negro People in the United States.* Vol. 2. Secaucus, N.J., 1951.

FOX, STEPHEN R. *The Guardian of Boston: William Monroe Trotter.* New York, 1970.

HARLAN, LOUIS R. *Booker T. Washington: The Wizard of Tuskegee, 1901–1915.* New York, 1983.

GREG ROBINSON

Nicholas Brothers, dancers. Fayard (1914–) and Harold (c. 1921–) Nicholas were born and reared in Philadelphia, where their parents played in a pit band called the Nicholas Collegians, which performed regularly at the Standard Theater. Fayard gravitated toward show business at a young age, claiming that the live performances and shows he saw as a child (such as Leonard Reed and his partner, Willie Bryant), were his first great influences. The children began their own professional career as the Nicholas Kids and for a short time danced with their sister Dorothy in different East Coast venues.

In 1930, the brothers danced on a popular Philadelphia radio show called the "Horn and Hardart Kiddie Hour." However, it was during an appearance at the Pearl Theater in Philadelphia that Frank Schiffman, the manager of the Lafayette Theater in Harlem, recruited the brothers to dance in New York. When they opened in New York, their name was changed to the Nicholas Brothers, and they joined the ranks of the famous "brothers" tap acts of the twentieth century.

On April 10, 1932, they moved to the COTTON CLUB, where they performed with the top bands of the period such as Jimmie Lunceford, Lucky Millinder, Duke ELLINGTON, and Cab CALLOWAY. Harold, who had a good soprano voice, did an impression of Cab Calloway that the club broadcast each night on a coast-to-coast radio show. Throughout the 1930s the Cotton Club was their "home." The Nicholas Brothers were known as "the Show Stoppers" because they literally stopped the show each night as the closing act. Perhaps because Fayard and Harold were children, they were the only African-American performers permitted to mingle with the exclusively white patrons of the club. The elegant rhythms of the young stars quickly propelled them to fame.

Fayard and Harold frequently left their regular act at the Cotton Club to tour with international shows such as Lew Leslie's *Blackbirds of 1936,* which had a successful run in London, or to perform in films. Their first film, *Pie, Pie Blackbirds* (1932), featured them in an appearance with Eubie BLAKE and his orchestra. During their career they appeared in more than fifty films including *Kid Millions* (1934), *Big*

The Nicholas Brothers: Fayard (left) and Harold. (Photographs and Prints Division, Schomburg Center for Research in Black Culture, The New York Public Library, Astor, Lenox and Tilden Foundations)

reographer incorporated the brothers' own moves into their routine. In the show, Harold executed a sliding split through the legs of eight lined-up chorus girls while Fayard did a flying leap over them. In 1940 they worked with choreographer Nick Castle to develop a stunt that involved climbing up a wall, doing a back flip, landing in a split and returning to their feet—all on the beat.

During their nearly five decades in show business, Fayard and Harold toured the world from Africa to Europe. In the 1960s they appeared as guests on numerous TV shows and in 1965 performed as part of Bob Hope's Christmas special for the troops in Vietnam. In the 1970s, Fayard won a Tony Award for his choreography in the Broadway hit *Black and Blue*, and in 1980 both he and Harold received an award as part of a celebration honoring fifty years of men in dance. Their Lifetime Achievement Award, presented at the Kennedy Center in 1991, crowned the brothers' career as one of the best and most popular tap acts of the twentieth century.

REFERENCES

FRANK, RUSTY. *Tap: The Greatest Tap Dance Stars and Their Stories*. New York, 1990.

STEARNS, MARSHALL, and JEAN STEARNS. *Jazz Dance: The Story of American Vernacular Dance*. New York, 1964.

JENNIFER DEVERE BRODY

Broadcast of 1936, Calling All Stars (1937), *Down Argentine Way* (1940), *Tin Pan Alley* (1940), *Great American Broadcast* (1941), *Sun Valley Serenade* (1941), and *The Pirate* (1948). The brothers were among the select few who dubbed their own taps for film.

From the time they were small both Fayard and Harold danced with agility, grace, and sophistication. Even when they displayed their astonishing acrobatic ability, they managed to do so with elegance. They choreographed many of their own dance routines and improvised on stage with assurance and flair. The full use of their limber bodies and the exceptional use of their hands distinguished their dancing. The Nicholas Brothers perfected the innovative technique of doing *full* splits (as opposed to jazz or half splits), and they popularized acrobatic moves such as alternately jumping over each other's heads in splits while descending a staircase, as they did in the finale of *Stormy Weather* (1943). Their "classic" tap style flawlessly blended ballet, eccentric dancing, flash, and acrobatics.

When they worked with George Balanchine on the Broadway show *Babes in Arms* (1937), the great cho-

Nickerson, Camille Lucie (1888–April 27, 1982), musician. Born in New Orleans in 1888, Camille Nickerson was a pianist, singer, and educator best known for her collection and performance of creole folk songs. She received her bachelor's degree from Oberlin Conservatory of Music (1916), then taught in her father's music school, the Nickerson School of Music in New Orleans (1916–1926). In 1926 she accepted a position at Howard University, where she established the Junior Preparatory Music Department. A Rosenwald Fellowship in 1931 enabled her to attend Oberlin's graduate school and pursue her folk music research. She received a master's degree in 1932. Nickerson also studied in New York at the Juilliard School and Columbia University.

Beginning in the 1930s, Nickerson dressed in creole costume and sang folk songs as "the Louisiana Lady" on tour in America and (in 1954), in France, where her concerts were sponsored by the United States Information Agency. She retired in 1962, having received numerous honors and awards. Her publications include articles about and arrangements of

2020   NIX, ROBERT NELSON CORNELIUS

many creole songs. The best known include "Chère, Mo Lemmé Toi," "Lizette, To Quitté la Plaine," "Fais Do Do," and "Michieu Banjo." Nickerson served on the boards of several professional and civic organizations and was president of the national association of Negro musicians from 1935 to 1937.

REFERENCE

MCGINTY, DORIS. "Conversation with Camille Nickerson." *Black Perspective in Music* 7, no. 1 (1979): 81–94.

MILDRED DENBY GREEN

Nix, Robert Nelson Cornelius (August 9, 1905–June 22, 1987), congressman. Robert Nix was born in Orangeburg, S.C., where his father, Nelson, was dean of State Agricultural and Mechanical College (now South Carolina State College). While living with family members, Nix attended Townsend Harris High School in New York City. He attended Lincoln University in Pennsylvania, from which he graduated in 1921. Nix earned a degree from the University of Pennsylvania law school in 1924. The following year he opened his own law office in Philadelphia.

Nix became active in DEMOCRATIC politics during the late 1920s and was elected committeeman from Philadelphia's Forty-Fourth Ward in 1932; he retained his post until his death. From 1934 to 1938, he was a special deputy attorney general in the revenue department and went on to serve for many years as special assistant deputy attorney general.

In 1958, Nix defeated two opponents in a special election to fill a vacancy left by Earl Chudoff in the House of Representatives. By winning the election, Nix became Pennsylvania's first black congressman. Nix was not a particularly colorful or attention-seeking legislator, and throughout his twenty-year career, he endured opponents' accusations of absenteeism and of his close identification with the regular Democratic party. Nix's tenure was not without accomplishments, however. During his years in the House, he served on the Veterans' Affairs Committee and the Foreign Affairs Committee. In 1977, he became chairman of the Committee on the Post Office and Civil Service. On the Foreign Affairs Committee, Nix held hearings on political prisoners in such allied countries as South Korea, which were the recipients of foreign aid.

In 1978, Nix lost his seat in the House to William Gray III. He returned to Pennsylvania and continued to work as a committeeman for the Forty-Fourth Ward. In addition, he worked in the law firm he created with his son Robert Nix, a state Supreme Court judge in Pennsylvania. At age eighty-eight, Nix died of a heart attack at the Medical College of Pennsylvania.

REFERENCES

CLAY, WILLIAM L. *Just Permanent Interests: Black Americans in Congress, 1870–1991.* New York, 1992.
"Lawmaker at Work." *Baltimore Afro-American,* February 2, 1963, p. 3.
"Philadelphia's Robert Nix is the 4th Negro Solon." *Jet* (June 5, 1958): 10–11.

KAREN E. REARDON
DURAHN TAYLOR

Nixon, Edgar Daniel (July 12, 1899–February 25, 1987), civil rights leader. E. D. Nixon was born in Robinson Springs, near Montgomery, Ala., the son of Wesley and Susan (Chappell) Nixon. Wesley Nixon was a tenant farmer and, in later years, a Primitive Baptist preacher (*see* PRIMITIVE BAPTISTS). Susan Nixon died when her son was nine, and the boy was reared in Montgomery by his paternal aunt, Winnie Bates, a laundress. He received only the most rudimentary education and at thirteen began full-time work, initially in a meat-packing plant, then on construction crews, and in 1918 as a baggage handler at Montgomery's railway station. Thanks to friendships that he made in this job, he managed in 1923 to obtain employment as a Pullman car porter, a position that he held until his retirement in 1964.

Exposed by his work to the world beyond Montgomery, Nixon grew increasingly hostile to racial segregation. He became an enthusiastic proponent of A. Philip RANDOLPH's efforts in the late 1920s and early 1930s to unionize the Pullman porters, and in 1938 he accepted the presidency of the new union's Montgomery local (*see* BROTHERHOOD OF SLEEPING CAR PORTERS). In 1943 he organized the Alabama Voters League to press for the registration of Montgomery's blacks as voters, and though the campaign provoked a vigorous white counterattack, Nixon himself achieved registration in 1945.

Montgomery's black community was sharply divided between the middle-class professionals who resided near the campus of Alabama State College for Negroes, and the working-class blacks who lived in the city's western neighborhoods. When the Montgomery branch of the NATIONAL ASSOCIATION FOR THE ADVANCEMENT OF COLORED PEOPLE (NAACP), dominated by the Alabama State College professionals, failed to support Nixon's voter registration drive actively, Nixon began organizing the poorer blacks of west Montgomery in an effort to take over the branch. He was defeated for branch president in 1944 but was elected in 1945 and reelected in 1946, in a series of acrimonious campaigns.

In 1947 Nixon was elected the NAACP's state president, defeating the incumbent, Birmingham newspaper editor Emory O. Jackson. But national NAACP officials, hostile to his lack of education, arranged in 1949 for his defeat for reelection to the state post, and in 1950 he also was ousted from the leadership of the Montgomery branch. In 1952, however, he won election as president of the Montgomery chapter of the Progressive Democratic Association, the voice of Alabama's black Democrats. And in 1954 he created a great stir in the city by becoming a candidate to represent his precinct on the county Democratic Executive Committee; though unsuccessful, he was the first black to seek public office in Montgomery in the twentieth century.

During his years with the NAACP, Nixon had become a close friend of Rosa L. PARKS, the branch secretary. When Parks was arrested on December 1, 1955, for a violation of the city's bus segregation ordinance, she called Nixon for assistance. After he bailed her out of jail, Nixon began calling other black leaders to suggest a boycott of the buses on the day of Parks's trial, December 5, to show support for her. The idea, which black leaders had frequently discussed in the past, was greeted enthusiastically by many. The black Women's Political Council began circulating leaflets urging the action, and black ministers supported it from their pulpits. The boycott on December 5 proved so successful that black leaders decided to extend it until the city and the bus company agreed to adopt a pattern of bus segregation that would not require the unseating of passengers who were already seated. The MONTGOMERY IMPROVEMENT ASSOCIATION was formed to run the boycott, and Nixon was chosen the organization's treasurer (*see* MONTGOMERY BUS BOYCOTT).

Nixon, however, became increasingly unhappy with the association's president, the Rev. Dr. Martin Luther KING, Jr. Nixon associated King with the Alabama State College professionals, and he felt that King's growing fame was depriving Nixon and the mass of poorer blacks whom Nixon represented of the credit for the boycott's success. After King moved to Atlanta in 1960, and the Rev. Ralph D. ABERNATHY followed him there in 1961, Nixon engaged in a lengthy struggle with Rufus A. Lewis, the most prominent figure among his rivals in the middle-class Alabama State College community, for leadership of Montgomery's blacks. The struggle culminated in the 1968 presidential election, when Nixon and Lewis served on alternative slates of presidential electors, both of which were pledged to Hubert H. Humphrey. The Lewis slate of electors defeated Nixon's slate handily in Montgomery. Nixon

thereafter slipped into an embittered obscurity. He accepted a job organizing recreational activities for youth in one of the city's poorest public-housing projects, a position that he held until just before his death in 1987.

REFERENCES

GARROW, DAVID J. *Bearing the Cross: Martin Luther King, Jr., and the Southern Christian Leadership Conference*. New York, 1986.

THORNTON, J. MILLS III. "Challenge and Response in the Montgomery Bus Boycott of 1955–1956." *Alabama Review* 33 (1980): 163–235.

J. MILLS THORNTON III

Noble Drew Ali (January 8, 1886–1929), religious leader. Timothy Drew, more commonly known as the Noble Drew Ali, was born in Simpsonbuck County, N.C. It is not clear either when Ali migrated north or when he came into contact with Eastern philosophy. Although he received no formal education, Ali developed an appreciation for Oriental religions. Deeply moved by their racial inclusivity, particularly that of ISLAM, he saw an opportunity for African Americans to be influenced by its thinking. In 1913, at the age of twenty-seven, he established the first Moorish Science Temple of America in Newark, N.J.

Central to Ali's philosophy was the importance of racial identity. In his opinion, the lot of the blacks in America was due to their inaccurate knowledge of themselves. Moreover, once blacks gained a proper understanding of who they were, he believed both salvation and victory over their oppressors would be obtainable. He thus urged his followers no longer to recognize the racial designations given them by Europeans, and to call themselves Moors, Moorish-Americans, or Asiatics. Ali also published and distributed the *Holy Koran* of the Moorish Holy Temple of Science, which served as a catechism for temple members.

By the mid-1920s, the movement had spread throughout the United States and temples had been established in Detroit, Pittsburgh, Philadelphia, New York, and Chicago. In fact, headquarters for the temple were eventually relocated to Chicago, which proved to be both Ali's crowning achievement and his dethroning miscalculation. Since the Moorish Science phenomenon had grown beyond one person's control, he decided to appoint several educated black men to leadership positions within the organization. Shortly after the appointments, however, it became clear to Ali that his understudies were situating themselves to seize control of the movement.

After learning that some of the leaders had become rich by exploiting the rank-and-file membership, Ali rebuked them and called for an end to the corruption. Nevertheless, tension within the group continued to rise until one of Ali's opponents was killed. Even though he was not in Chicago at the time of the murder, Ali was arrested for the crime upon his arrival in the city. In 1929, while waiting to be tried, he was mysteriously killed, apparently beaten to death either by members loyal to his opposition or by the police.

REFERENCES

FAUSET, ARTHUR HUFF. *Black Gods of the Metropolis: Negro Religious Cults in the Urban North.* Philadelphia, 1944.

PAYNE, WARDELL J., ed. *Directory of African American Religious Bodies.* Washington, D.C., 1991.

QUINTON H. DIXIE

Noone, Jimmie (April 23, 1894–April 19, 1944), jazz clarinetist. Jimmie Noone is one of the most admired of the first generation of New Orleans jazz musicians (*see* JAZZ). His style was absorbed by, among others, Jimmy Dorsey and Benny Goodman and thus was a crucial component of the swing clarinet idiom of the 1930s. Noone was born on Stanton Plantation a few miles downriver from New Orleans, moved to the city, and began playing the clarinet around 1910 under the tutelage of Sidney BECHET. He began his full-fledged professional career with Buddy Petit in the Young Olympia Band c. 1915. In 1917 and 1918, Noone spent a season touring in vaudeville with the creole Band, then moved to Chicago definitively at the end of 1918 to play with Joe "King" OLIVER. Between 1920 and 1926, Noone worked in Doc Cook's big band and, unusual for a musician of his background, studied with one of Chicago's foremost classical clarinetists. From 1926 to 1931 Noone led quintets of unusual instrumentation, most notably at the Apex Club; their recordings are judged to be landmarks of jazz clarinet virtuosity. Noone led a number of larger bands in Chicago during the 1930s with several brief forays to New York City. Shortly before his death he moved to southern California, where he was heard on some notable radio broadcasts (available on recordings) with one of the first "revival" bands of New Orleans veterans led by "Kid" ORY.

REFERENCES

KENNEY, WILLIAM HOWLAND III. "Jimmie Noone, Chicago's Classical Jazz Clarinetist." *American Music* 4 (1986): 145–158.

WANG, RICHARD. "Jimmie Noone," In *The New Grove Dictionary of Jazz.* New York, 1988.

LAWRENCE GUSHEE

Normal Institute. *See* Avery Normal Institute.

Norman, Jessye (September 15, 1945–), opera singer. Born in Augusta, Ga., Jessye Norman was a soprano of promise from an early age. At sixteen she entered the Marian ANDERSON competitions, and although she did not win, she auditioned at Howard University with Carolyn Grant. Her acceptance was delayed until she completed high school. She followed her undergraduate training at Howard (B. Music., 1967) with summer study at the Peabody Conservatory under Alice Duschak before enrolling at the University of Michigan for study with Elizabeth Mannion and Pierre Bernac.

A travel grant allowed Norman to enter the International Music Competition in Munich in 1968, where she won first place with performances of Dido's Lament (Henry Purcell) and "Voi lo sapete" from Pietro Mascagni's *Cavalleria rusticana.* She was immediately engaged for her operatic debut as Elisabeth in Richard Wagner's *Tannhäuser* by the Deutsche Oper (1969), with which she later appeared in Giuseppe Verdi's *Aida* and *Don Carlo,* Meyerbeer's *L'africaine,* and as the Countess in Mozart's *Le nozze di Figaro.* In 1972 she sang Aida at La Scala and Cassandre in Covent Garden's production of Berlioz' *Les troyens,* making her recital debuts in London and New York the next year.

Norman's American stage debut came on November 22, 1982, when she appeared as both Jocasta in *Oedipus Rex* (Stravinsky) and Dido in Purcell's *Dido and Aeneas* with the Opera Company of Philadelphia. The following year, she made her debut with the Metropolitan Opera as Cassandre in Berlioz' *Les troyens,* subsequently offering a performance as Didon in the same opera, as well as the Prima Donna and Ariadne in *Ariadne auf Naxos* (Richard Strauss).

As recitalist, guest orchestral soloist, presenter of master classes, and recording artist, Norman was acknowledged as a musician of the highest rank. She was heard in nearly every major American city by 1990 and appeared frequently in telecasts starting in 1979 when she gave a concert version of the first act of Wagner's *Die Walküre* with the Boston Symphony Orchestra conducted by Seiji Ozawa.

Norman has excelled in French and German repertories, stylistically and linguistically, while remain-

"Jessye Norman." In Charles Moritz, ed. *Current Biography*. New York, 1976, pp. 292–295.

DOMINIQUE-RENÉ DE LERMA

Soprano Jessye Norman singing in Carnegie Hall in New York City, at a benefit for AIDS research and services, 1993. (AP/Wide World Photos)

ing faithful to her roots in the spiritual. With a voice ranging from a dark mezzo-soprano to a dramatic soprano, she has not hesitated to reintroduce works outside of the mainstream repertory (e.g., Gluck and Haydn operas), or to perform songs of the musical theater. She has appeared on numerous recordings, including Beethoven's *Fidelio;* Berlioz' *Mort de Cléopatre;* Bizet's *Carmen;* Gluck's *Alceste;* Mahler's *Das Lied von der Erde;* Offenbach's *Tales of Hoffmann;* Purcell's *Dido and Aeneas;* Schoenberg's *Gurre-Lieder;* Strauss's *Four Last Songs* and *Ariadne auf Naxos;* Verdi's *Aida,* Wagner's *Lohengrin* and *Die Walküre;* and Weber's *Euryanthe.* Other notable recordings include *Spirituals, Spirituals in Concert* (with Kathleen Battle), and *Jessye Norman at Notre-Dame.*

REFERENCES

BERNHEIMER, MARTIN. "Jessye Norman." In *The New Grove Dictionary of Music and Musicians.* Vol. 13, p. 283. London, 1980.

EWEN, DAVID. "Jessye Norman." In *Musicians Since 1900: Performers in Concert and Opera.* New York, 1978, pp. 586–587.

North Carolina. The black presence in North Carolina dates from 1526, when a large Spanish expedition from the West Indies tried to plant a colony near Cape Fear. English settlement of North Carolina in the 1650s assured the adoption of a slave system similar to that taking root in VIRGINIA, and the Fundamental Constitutions of 1669 fixed the status of Africans as slaves.

SLAVERY, however, grew slowly in North Carolina. A treacherous coastline and poor harbors compelled slave holders to purchase slaves from other colonies and to bring them overland. Relatively few slaves arrived by sea, and most of those came from other colonies or the West Indies. Even fewer were imported directly from Africa. In 1712 the entire black population of North Carolina did not exceed 800, probably less than one-tenth of the colony's total population.

The rapid expansion of slavery after the mid-eighteenth century raised the number of slaves to 100,572 by the 1790 census. Between 1820 and 1860 the slave population, reaching 331,059 in the latter year, stabilized at between 32 and 33 percent of the aggregate population. In 1860 sixteen counties in the coastal plain and piedmont counted black majorities. Most of those counties produced cotton or tobacco. Rice and naval stores also depended heavily on slave labor.

The legislature enacted basic slave codes in 1715 and 1741. By the 1850s the slave code prohibited slaves from learning to read or write; intermarrying or cohabiting with free blacks; hiring their own time; and preaching at a prayer meeting where slaves of different masters were gathered. Despite such oppressive measures, manifestations of African culture persisted. Documented instances of the RING SHOUT and JOHNKONNU celebration occurred in North Carolina (see FESTIVALS). Moreover, examples of conical fishing huts, based on African architectural methods, dotted the Outer Banks as late as the 1880s.

North Carolina produced a number of exceptional blacks during the antebellum period. In 1829 David WALKER, a free black from Wilmington, published his *Appeal,* which demanded the immediate abolition of slavery. John Carruthers Stanly of New Bern was the largest black slave holder in the South, at one time owning 163 slaves. George Moses HORTON of Chatham County, a slave poet, published three volumes of his verse.

One of the largest black-owned businesses in the country in the early twentieth century was the Durham-based North Carolina Mutual and Provident Association, a life insurance company. Its success was an inspiration to many other black businesses in the early part of the century and helped make Durham "the capital of the Negro middle class." The leaders of the company in 1908 (from left to right) were Dr. A. M. More, J. M. Avery, President John Merrick, and (far right) General Manager C. C. Spaulding. (North Carolina Division of Archives and History)

During the CIVIL WAR thousands of slaves defected to Union troops in eastern North Carolina. As many as 5,000 black North Carolinians bore arms for the Union army. After the war the first freedmen's convention in the South assembled in Raleigh in September 1865. A total of 117 black delegates represented forty-two counties. They sought ownership of land, education, normalization of marriage, equal protection of the law and an end to discrimination, and the regulation of hours of labor.

Between 1868 and 1900 more than 100 blacks served in the North Carolina General Assembly. In addition, the Second Congressional District sent four black representatives to Congress between 1872 and 1901. George Henry White, who served from 1897 to 1901, was the last black to sit in Congress until 1929.

After EMANCIPATION Democrats resorted to violence to weaken blacks' political power. During RECONSTRUCTION, the KU KLUX KLAN launched a reign of terror across the piedmont to destroy the biracial coalition of blacks and whites in the Republican party. The Democrats succeeded in regaining office, but they were unable to extirpate black political strength. The white supremacy campaigns of 1898 and 1900 accomplished that purpose. Democratic violence and intimidation crushed a political coalition of Populists and Republicans that swept elections in 1894 and 1896. The Democratic counterrevolution resulted in the WILMINGTON RIOT (November 10, 1898), disfranchisement, and segregation.

Headquarters of the North Carolina Mutual and Provident Association, Durham, N.C., 1906. (North Carolina Division of Archives and History)

Despite political setbacks, efforts at black community building advanced during those years of repression. Black clubs, lodges, societies, and churches offered members an opportunity to promote racial uplift and community causes without intrusion from whites. In the decades after Reconstruction between one-third and one-half of all black North Carolinians belonged to churches. The BAPTISTS and AME Zion churches accounted for more than 80 percent of all black church members (see AFRICAN METHODIST EPISCOPAL ZION CHURCH).

During segregation blacks struggled to progress economically and materially while challenging discriminatory laws and policies. Durham emerged as the capital of the black middle class, and its NORTH CAROLINA MUTUAL LIFE became the largest black-owned company in the nation. Durham also became the center of a vibrant musical tradition in both gospel and blues (see DURHAM, NORTH CAROLINA).

Most blacks, however, remained mired in agricultural or domestic work. Fully two-thirds of black farmers were tenants in 1910. Whereas blacks composed three-fourths of the labor force (primarily female) in the tobacco industry, the textile and furniture industries barred them from all but menial positions. The NEW DEAL did little to improve blacks' economic status. Indeed, in some respects it worsened conditions as sharecroppers were evicted from homes and farms and whites supplanted blacks in industrial jobs. Even so, the black middle class became increasingly active in politics during the 1930s as it deserted the party of Lincoln for the party of Franklin D. Roosevelt.

WORLD WAR II was a watershed for black North Carolinians. The Great Migration that had begun during World War I accelerated as North Carolina lost an astonishing 14.8 percent of its black population during the 1940s. Moreover, the Durham manifesto, enunciated by fifty-nine prominent southern blacks in 1942, demanded an end to segregation and a commitment to equal economic opportunities and complete political rights.

During the CIVIL RIGHTS MOVEMENT of the 1950s and 1960s North Carolina played a crucial role. The Greensboro sit-ins that began February 1, 1960, spread across the South (*see* SIT-INS). That same year the STUDENT NONVIOLENT COORDINATING COMMITTEE (SNCC) was organized at Shaw University in Raleigh. Reflecting the strength of its economically powerful black middle class, North Carolina contributed a number of key national figures to the civil rights movement, including Floyd McKissick, national director of the CONGRESS OF RACIAL EQUALITY (CORE); Ella J. BAKER, executive director of the SOUTHERN CHRISTIAN LEADERSHIP CONFERENCE (SCLC) and founder of SNCC; Jesse JACKSON, president of the student body at North Carolina A&T College in Greensboro in the early 1960s; and Julius L. Chambers, the Charlotte attorney who successfully brought before the Supreme Court the *Swann* v. *Charlotte-Mecklenburg Board of Education* case (1970), which established court-ordered busing to break the pattern of segregated schools.

Since 1968 blacks have returned to the North Carolina General Assembly as representatives and senators; won election as mayors of such major cities as Raleigh, Durham, and Chapel Hill; served in cabinet and judicial posts, including the state supreme court; and in 1992 elected two representatives to Congress after almost a century's absence. In 1990 blacks constituted 22 percent (1,456,323) of the state's population. Significantly, the 1980 census revealed that black in-migration (92,991) surpassed black outmigration (72,475). Yet economic disparities remained wide. Black per capita income in 1990 ($7,926) was only 55 percent of white per capita income ($14,450).

REFERENCES

ANDERSON, ERIC. *Race and Politics in North Carolina: The Black Second.* Baton Rouge, La., 1981.
CROW, JEFFREY J., PAUL D. ESCOTT, and FLORA J. HATLEY. *A History of African Americans in North Carolina.* Raleigh, N.C., 1992.

JEFFREY J. CROW

North Carolina Mutual Life Insurance Company. Founded by seven black men who each pledged fifty dollars, the North Carolina Mutual and Provident Association (renamed the North Carolina Mutual Life Insurance Company in 1919) opened in Durham, N.C. on April 1, 1899 in order to provide insurance for black families. The Mutual sold primarily industrial insurance, which was obtained for as little as three cents a week by industrial laborers, and which paid out correspondingly small amounts for sickness and death claims. In the summer of 1900, the Mutual went into debt, the income from its policies unable to pay for the claims on them, and all its founding members except the president, John Merrick, a successful businessman, and Aaron Moore, a physician who became secretary, withdrew. Merrick and Moore loaned personal funds to the Mutual to prevent it from going defunct, and promoted Charles Clinton SPAULDING to general manager.

By the end of 1902, after Merrick and Moore had loaned the Mutual an additional $600, its profits were finally greater than its losses, and by 1906 it had quadrupled its number of policyholders, its growth corresponding first to expansion within North Carolina, then expansion to South Carolina and the reinsurance of smaller black insurers who could not meet state regulations, which at that time were being strengthened. In 1913 the Mutual demonstrated its strength by raising $100,000 in order to meet a higher state deposit requirement. During World War I, the Mutual's life insurance in force grew from $5,000,000 to $26,000,000, because a dramatic increase in cotton prices brought greater prosperity to southern blacks.

Embodying Booker T. WASHINGTON's popular philosophy that blacks would overcome prejudice with economic development, the Mutual drew attention to itself and to Durham because the growth of its assets enabled it to launch numerous subordinate institutions, such as the Merrick-Moore-Spaulding Land Company (1907), a real estate company; Mechanics and Farmers Bank (1908, with a branch in Raleigh, 1922); Banker's Fire, a fire insurance company (1920); Mutual Building & Loan Association (1921); the National Negro Finance Corporation (1924); and the Mortgage Company of Durham (1929)—in effect bringing economic development to the black community of Durham by itself.

In 1926, after territorial expansion that followed the black migration north and that also included Southwestern states, Spaulding, now president, a position he would retain until his death in 1952, realized that the income from expansion did not compensate for the operating costs and had the Mutual retrench, not to expand again until 1938. This retrenchment, along with its conservative investments in real estate, government bonds, and especially mortgage loans protected the Mutual during the GREAT DEPRESSION. At $39,000,000 just before the stock market crash of 1929, the Mutual's life insurance in force never fell below $33,000,000 during the Depression.

The prosperity the Mutual experienced during World War II, during which time its insurance

John Merrick, founder of the North Carolina Mutual Life Insurance Company. (Photographs and Prints Division, Schomburg Center for Research in Black Culture, The New York Public Library, Astor, Lenox and Tilden Foundations)

in force increased from $51,000,000 to over $100,000,000, enabled it to offer its policyholders dividends for the first time and to compete with the mainstream companies that now insured blacks at standard rates.

The promotion of racial solidarity during the 1960s brought blacks back to the Mutual from white insurers. The urban riots of the late '60s put pressure on white corporations to invest in black communities, and corporations such as General Motors, IBM, Chrysler, Procter and Gamble, Sun Oil, and Atlantic Richfield did so by buying more than $400,000,000 in insurance contracts between 1969 and 1971 from the Mutual, making it the first black company to pass the billion-dollar mark.

The Mutual's tenfold growth in insurance in force from the early 1970s to the early 1990s enabled it to maintain its status as the nation's largest black insurance company. To stimulate growth, the Mutual gradually began to phase out its industrial insurance and replace it with ordinary life insurance, and, through its subsidiary, NCM Capital, to enter the pension and corporate-fund management business.

REFERENCE

WEARE, WALTER B. *Black Business in the New South: A Social History of the North Carolina Mutual Life Insurance Company.* Chicago, 1973.

SIRAJ AHMED

North Dakota. African Americans in early North Dakota lived in a region in which SLAVERY and the CIVIL WAR had a minimal effect. Located in the far northern edge of the nation's central plains, its residents at the time of the Emancipation Proclamation consisted of Native American peoples, some soldiers, and Missouri River steamboat workers. Then as well as now, the state had a frontier character, remote and often harsh. Serious settlement in the late 1800s and early 1900s involved a business and professional gentry of New England background and massive waves of land-seeking European immigrants. The experience of black men and women in North Dakota differed, therefore, from that of their counterparts elsewhere in America.

The black proportion of the state's population was never large. The 1990 census total, 3,524, represented only one-half of 1 percent, and that figure—the highest in history—consisted primarily of personnel and families at the Minot and Grand Forks air bases. Yet population figures can be misleading. Black individuals have been part of North Dakota's life at every moment of recorded history. Pierre Bonga, a black employee of the North West Fur Company, had a son born at Pembina on the Red River in 1802, and a man named York was part of the Lewis and Clark party as it wintered at the Mandan villages in 1804 on its way to the Pacific Coast.

The Missouri River brought the first handfuls of black Americans from New Orleans and St. Louis to the Dakotas. In the 1820s fur trade there were such famous frontiersmen as James BECKWOURTH and Edward Rose. The heyday of the river freight and passenger trade was from 1832 to 1885. Early photos show black crew members on almost every steamer moored along Bismarck's waterfront. On U.S. Army garrison duty between 1892 and 1894 at Fort Buford, at the confluence of the Missouri and Yellowstone rivers, were three companies of the black 25th Infantry and two companies of the 10th Cavalry. Black maids and servants lived at almost every northern Dakota military post. The cattle industry, with roots in Texas and Colorado, first entered the northern rangelands in 1880. Accordingly, a number of black trail riders and cooks could be found in the badlands and river breaks of western Dakota. One black cowboy, James Williams, working near Me-

(Top) African-American threshing crew, around 1915; (bottom) Second Baptist Church of Bismark, N.Dak., around 1916. (State Historical Society of North Dakota)

dora, is still remembered: "He lassoed a goose in mid-air."

The railroads that crisscrossed the Dakota plains starting in the 1870s brought black employees to the state for over a half century. They came occasionally as construction crews but more often as individuals. Many North Dakota children saw their first black person in the role of cook or porter on trains at the village station. Black railroad employees eventually took up residence at major terminal centers. A "colored section" of town—actually one or two blocks —could be found in Grand Forks, Devils Lake, Bismarck, and particularly in Minot. Wives and children arrived, and soon there were black churches, taverns, lodges, and cafés. Though short-lived, these institutions flourished, especially in the first decades of the twentieth century.

It was free land that enticed most black Americans to settle in North Dakota in a permanent fashion. At least ninety-five African Americans are known to have taken land under some sort of homestead arrangement between 1870 and 1915. Most were men, but some were single women, and many had families. In addition, twenty black individuals purchased already developed farm lands. Seldom living in groups, they lived at ease among the tens of thousands of newly arrived white settlers. One owner, William Thornton Montgomery, farmed a thousand acres of Dakota's best Red River Valley land from 1884 until 1897. This former slave, son of the well-known Benjamin Montgomery (of Davis Bend, Miss.) lived in Fargo and employed white families on his "plantation" in the north.

Business-minded townsmen arrived in the early decades of settlement. At least forty barbers set up small shops that flourished for a dozen or so years. In Bismarck, William H. W. Comer was an exception. A barber in Fort Lincoln, he moved to the newly founded city and erected several blocks of commercial buildings. Operating a four-chair establishment, he was a promoter of note; he gave $1,000 to the fund that would entice the territorial government to choose Bismarck as the state's capital city. Another barber of significance was Julius F. Taylor, who had a multichaired shop in Fargo for over a decade starting in 1880. Leaving the Dakotas, he entered the newspaper business in Salt Lake City, Utah, and later in Chicago. At least two dozen other black men and women were part of the early twentieth-century business world. They operated small cafés, hotels, livery barns, junk yards, and saloons, usually as solitary entrepreneurs in all-white towns and villages.

After 1900, a seasonal type of worker began arriving during early planting and at harvest time. Wheat grew on millions of acres, and thousands of "extra hands" of all races came by railroad from eastern cities. Though the census took place in the spring, the totals show a considerable black presence: 1900, 286; 1910, 617; 1920, 467. Specialized farm machinery slowed the influx, and by 1950 summer-time laborers came only in a trickle. The North Dakota population was also affected by two other forces: the dry years of the 1930s and WORLD WAR II employment demands. Residents, white and black, left by the thousands. Indeed, by mid-century there were only a half dozen small-town African Americans and even fewer black farmers. Small-town baseball teams, however, had black players through the 1930s; Satchel PAIGE spent a summer in Bismarck.

U.S. Air Force bases starting in 1957 at Minot and Grand Forks brought a new surge of black personnel and their families to North Dakota. Black population figures rose from 257 in 1950 to 777 in 1960, and to 2,494 in 1970. These same years saw a modest rise in the numbers of college-oriented black students and professors. Some Air Force and university people subsequently established local roots, working in the trade and professional job categories. An estimated 400 African Americans listed in the 1990 census fell into this permanent category. African Americans who resided through the decades in North Dakota's farm or small-town settings were fortunate; they suffered only minimal discrimination. But all was not rosy. The flood of seasonal workers changed the picture. Local residents disliked outsiders, white or black. It was then that No Negroes Allowed signs appeared in restaurants and hotels. The state, in fact, passed an antimiscegenation law in 1909 that remained in effect until 1955 (see MISCEGENATION).

It is also clear that many African Americans were successful farm and business managers. They were usually involved in the social life of the communities; some were active in politics. Their children attended school more persistently than the offspring of many other ethnic groups. A disproportionately large number in the 1930s, for example, attended schools of medicine, law, and engineering. The recipient of the 1976 Roughrider Award, North Dakota's most prestigious official honor, was Era Bell Thompson, a farm girl from Driscoll, who achieved fame as an author and as international editor of *Ebony* magazine.

REFERENCES

SHERMAN, WILLIAM C., and PLAYFORD V. THORSON, eds. *Plain Folk*. Fargo, N.Dak., 1988.
THOMPSON, ERA BELL. *American Daughter*. St. Paul, Minn., 1986.

WILLIAM C. SHERMAN

Northrup, Solomon (c. 1808–1863), author of slave narratives. Solomon Northrup was born free on a farm in Minerva, N.Y. His father was a former Rhode Island slave who had been freed in his owner's will. Northrup spent the first half of his life on the family farm, farming and working as a violinist and laborer in the Minerva area. At the age of thirty-three or so, a series of bizarre events pulled Northrup into slavery.

In 1841 Northrup was approached by two strangers, who asked him to play in the band with their traveling circus. After catching up with the circus, Northrup was drugged, beaten, and sold to slave traders. He was then shipped to New Orleans, where he was purchased by a planter in the Red River region of Louisiana. Northrup spent the next twelve years as a slave under several owners in the region.

In 1852 Northrup met Samuel Bass, an itinerant Canadian carpenter, and the two plotted to arrange Northrup's freedom. Bass sent a letter to two white businessmen in Saratoga who had been acquaintances of Northrup. The letter eventually reached Henry Northrup, the former owner of Northrup's father, who traveled to Louisiana and made legal arrangements to free Northrup. Northrup finally returned to his family in Glens Falls, N.Y., in January 1853.

Spurred on by the success of Harriet Beecher Stowe's UNCLE TOM'S CABIN, Northrup immediately set out to write the narrative of his enslavement. He enlisted the help of David Wilson, a local writer, and the two finished the book within three months. *Twelve Years a Slave: Narrative of Solomon Northrup* was published in the summer of 1853 and became an immediate success. It sold more than 30,000 copies over the next ten years and was reprinted several times in the nineteenth century after Northrup's death.

Since its publication Northrup's narrative has served as an important resource for scholars of slavery. Like many other SLAVE NARRATIVES, *Twelve Years a Slave* discusses in detail the ways in which slaves presented a servile facade to their owners while practicing subtle acts of subversion and resistance. In recent years, Northrup's recollections have been cited as refutation of the slave's image as a passive, ingratiating figure.

The publication of *Twelve Years a Slave* resulted in yet another set of bizarre circumstances that led to the capture of Northrup's kidnappers. In 1854 the book caused one of its readers to recall meeting the two men and Northrup shortly after the abduction. Northrup met with the reader and confirmed the recollection, and shortly thereafter the two suspected kidnappers were arrested and charged by New York authorities. Though they were widely assumed to be guilty, the two suspects were released on legal technicalities.

Northrup was paid $3,000 by the original publisher of his narrative. He used that money to purchase a house in Glens Falls, where he lived in relative obscurity and practiced carpentry for the last ten years of his life. The circumstances of his death are uncertain, but the name on the deed to his house was changed to his wife's name in 1863.

See also Henry Walton BIBB; William Wells BROWN.

REFERENCES

BLASSINGAME, JOHN. *The Slave Community: Plantation Life in the Antebellum South.* New York, 1972.
NORTHRUP, SOLOMON. *Twelve Years a Slave: Narrative of Solomon Northrup.* 1853. Reprint. Baton Rouge, La., 1965.
OSOFSKY, GILBERT, ed. *Puttin' on Ole Massa: The Slave Narratives of Henry Bibb, William Wells Brown, and Solomon Northrup.* New York, 1969.

THADDEUS RUSSELL

Norton, Eleanor Holmes (June 13, 1937–), civil rights leader. Born in Washington, D.C., Eleanor Holmes graduated from Antioch College in 1960, received an M.A. in American history from Yale University in 1963, and a law degree from Yale in 1965. Norton was a leader of the STUDENT NON-VIOLENT COORDINATING COMMITTEE (SNCC), and was a participant in the MISSISSIPPI FREEDOM DEMOCRATIC PARTY. In 1965, Holmes joined the American Civil Liberties Union (ACLU), where she served as a civil rights lawyer for five years. In 1967, she married Edward Norton, also a lawyer. The couple, who were separated in 1992, had two children. In 1968, Eleanor Holmes Norton gained attention for her active defense of freedom of speech when she represented segregationist presidential candidate George Wallace in his struggle to obtain permission from the City of New York for a rally at Shea Stadium. Keenly interested in fighting both race and gender discrimination, Norton published an article on black women in the well-known anthology *Sisterhood Is Powerful* (1970). "If women were suddenly to achieve equality with men tomorrow," she wrote, "black women would continue to carry the entire array of utterly oppressive handicaps associated with race. . . . Yet black women cannot—must not—avoid the truth about their special subservience. They are women with all that that implies."

In 1970, Norton was appointed chair of the New York City Commission on Human Rights by Mayor John Lindsay. Her achievement in detailing and correcting discriminatory practices led to a position as cohost of a weekly local television program on civil rights. In 1973, Norton helped organize a National Conference of Black Feminists, and in 1975 she cowrote *Sex Discrimination and the Law: Cases and Remedies,* a law textbook dealing with legal remedies to gender inequality.

In 1977, President Jimmy Carter appointed Norton as chair of the Equal Employment Opportunity Commission, a post she held until 1981. Charged with investigating complaints of discrimination, Norton was a visible and respected force within the Administration. In 1982, she accepted a post as professor of labor law at Georgetown University. Throughout the 1980s, she was also a regular media commentator on civil rights and affirmative action issues.

In 1990, Norton announced her candidacy for the position of District of Columbia delegate to the U.S. House of Representatives. Despite the revelation during the campaign that she owed back taxes, she was elected to Congress. She soon won praise even from her opponents for her involvement in community affairs as well as for her work in assuring Washington's fiscal viability and cutting the District's budget. She also lobbied in Congress for District statehood. In 1992, the same year Norton won reelection, she won attention for her offer to escort women seeking abortion information at clinics past antiabortion picketers, and later for her denunciation of the verdict in the Rodney King trial, which she contended was as shameful as the actual beating of King. Since the House vote in 1993 to give delegates limited voting privileges on the floor, Norton has become the first District representative to vote in Congress. In recognition of her prestige, President Bill Clinton agreed that as chair of the District of Columbia Subcommittee on Judiciary and Education, Norton would be responsible for the nomination of candidates for local U.S. Attorney and federal judgeships, the first elected District of Columbia official to be privileged.

REFERENCES

HARDY, GAYLE S. *American Women Civil Rights Activists: Biographies of 68 Leaders, 1825–1992.* Jefferson, N.C., 1993.

HAYWOOD, RICHETTE, "Eleanor Holmes Norton takes D.C. Seat." *Ebony* 46 (January 1991): 105–106.

EVAN A. SHORE
GREG ROBINSON

Norton, Kenneth Howard "Ken" (August 9, 1943–), professional boxer. Born in Jacksonville, Ill., Ken Norton spent two years playing fullback for Northeast Missouri State before joining the Marine Corps in 1963. Norton entered the ring for the first time while stationed at Camp Pendleton near San Diego; he began his professional career in November 1967 with a knockout against Grady Brazell. In 1973, he fought Muhammad ALI twice, first winning and then, in a rematch, losing the North American Boxing Federation (NABF) heavyweight title. Norton fought George FOREMAN for the world heavyweight title in 1973, but lost by a knockout in two rounds. He fought for the title again in 1976 and lost to Ali in fifteen rounds. When the World Boxing Council (WBC) heavyweight titleholder, Leon SPINKS, refused to meet Norton, the number-one contender, WBC proclaimed Norton its champion on March 29, 1978. Norton held the championship until his first title defense, which he lost to Larry Holmes on June 9, 1978. After his loss to Holmes, Norton entered the ring only five more times: in his last fight, on May 11, 1981, he was knocked out in the first round by Gerry Cooney. At his retirement, Norton had boxed a total of fifty matches, of which he had won all but seven.

In 1975, Norton starred in *Mandingo,* a movie set on a Louisiana slave-breeding plantation; he also appeared in a sequel, *Drum,* in 1976. Following his retirement as a fighter, Norton played a small role in television's *The A-Team,* appeared as a print-ad model, provided color commentary on boxing for ABC's coverage of the 1984 Olympics, and managed the career of his son, the professional linebacker Ken Norton, Jr. In 1986, Norton, Sr., suffered a near-fatal automobile accident, from which he recovered slowly and with great difficulty. Norton has been married twice and has four children.

REFERENCES

ASHE, ARTHUR R., JR. *A Hard Road to Glory: A History of the African-American Athlete Since 1946.* New York, 1988.

The Ring Record Book and Boxing Encyclopedia. New York, 1987.

WHITE, PAULA S. "Winning Hook-ups." *Essence* 14 (February 1984): 60.

WILEY, RALPH. "Like Father, Like Son." *Sports Illustrated* 67 (October 12, 1987): 74–76ff.

ALEXIS WALKER

Nubin, Rosetta. *See* Tharpe, "Sister" Rosetta.

Nugent, Pete (c. 1910–), tap dancer. Pete Nugent was the leader of the sophisticated trio Pete, Peaches, and Duke with Irving "Peaches" Beaman and Duke Miller. This small, elegant, tightly coordinated team flourished in the 1920s and '30s, and its members were greatly admired for the precision of their tap work. Having left his middle-class home in Washington, D.C., at the age of sixteen, Nugent worked his way up from a $25-a-week job in vaudeville on the Theater Owners Booking Association circuit to the 1923 Broadway production of *Runnin' Wild* and on to *Honeymoon Lane* with Kate Smith in 1926. Nugent formed his original tap team with Beaman in Chicago in 1928; Miller was added in 1931. The trio's act opened with a precise ensemble routine, moving on to solos danced at a steadily increasing tempo. The trio was best known for its "one man exit," in which, facing the audience in single file and moving sideways with small, quick, perfectly synchronized steps, the dancers disappeared into the wings. The collaboration ended in 1937 when Duke Miller died of pneumonia.

Nugent was a dancer in the tradition of soft-shoe exponents Eddie RECTOR and Jack Wiggins. Nugent perfected Wiggins's "tango twist." The name evokes a maneuver of hips quickly twisting from side to side, but Nugent turned it into a floating half turn using heel and taps. Nugent was also a generous teacher who staged many of the team's acts. He appeared in the Los Angeles production of Duke EL-LINGTON's musical *Jump for Joy* (1941) and danced with Billy ECKSTINE's bebop-influenced big band in 1944.

With the decline of vaudeville, Nugent's career declined in the 1940s, and he left dancing in 1952. He was working as a business manager for a Motown group in the mid-1960s, after which there is no further indication of his whereabouts.

REFERENCE

STEARNS, MARSHALL, and JEAN STEARNS. *Jazz Dance: The Story of American Vernacular Dance.* New York, 1968.

CONSTANCE VALIS HILL

Numbers Games. Numbers games were a pervasive form of gambling in African-American urban communities from around the turn of the century until the late 1970s, when state lotteries and other forms of legalized gambling were instituted. Until that time, the local numbers runner was a familiar figure in black neighborhoods throughout the United States, especially in Harlem, and daily street life was often organized around placing bets and collecting winnings.

There are accounts of policy gambling in New York's white and black communities well before the Civil War, but it was not until decades later that numbers games gained real popularity among African Americans. Extremely high rates of participation made policy gambling a central economic feature of African-American urban life, with small businesses such as bars, hairdressers, and candy stores serving as collection points, or "drops."

In the nineteenth century, winning numbers were chosen from a lottery or roulette wheel. By the 1920s, rather than using lotteries, the results of which could be easily manipulated, bankers drew the winning result from the last three digits of the total volume of the daily New York Stock Exchange trades. Although odds varied from place to place, even within New York City, players attempting to match the winning numbers faced odds of one thousand to one. Those odds could be enhanced by "combinating," or betting on several groupings of the same numbers. Winners stood to gain returns of five hundred to one or even greater on a bet of as little as five or ten cents, but that return represented only a small percentage of the total bettings. Winners traditionally paid 10 percent of their winnings to the runner, who was responsible for taking bets and making payments. The runner was often a charismatic fixture in the neighborhood, and a prodigious mathematician. The most famous runner in the heyday of Harlem's 1920s numbers racket was "Walking Jack," the nickname of Alec Jackson, who was capable of retaining hundreds of numerical combinations in his memory daily. A similar figure, but from a later period, was evoked by MALCOLM X in his autobiography's presentation of West Indian Archie.

For approximately every one hundred runners there was one collector, who organized the day-to-day workings of the operation, and together with the runner took up to 25 percent of total bets as a salary. The collector was also responsible for bribing police and vice squads. At the top of the organization was the "wheel" or banker, of whom there were dozens in Harlem in the 1920s. The bankers were millionaires who controlled huge sums of money and lived legendarily lavish lifestyles financed by a percentage of total winnings as high as 36 percent. The most famous policy banker of the 1920s was Casper Holstein (1877–1944), a West Indian–born former porter who ruled his gambling empire from Harlem's Turf Club, and had a reputation as a powerful tycoon during the HARLEM RENAISSANCE. Considered one of the most important black philanthropists of the 1920s, Holstein sponsored writing prizes for *Opportunity Magazine* (see OPPORTUNITY) and donated money to build Harlem's first Elks Lodge. He later became increasingly involved in West Indian nationalist movements, and had all but left numbers by the time of his death in 1944. Another important banker was Madame Stephanie St. Clair, who in the 1920s and 1930s openly boasted of her status as "Harlem's Policy Queen."

New York's numbers games were traditionally the biggest such enterprise in the country—Brooklyn had its own set of winning numbers—but African-American communities in many cities, including Buffalo, Milwaukee, and Paterson, N.J., supported policy gambling. Chicago's numbers industry was started by "Policy Sam" Young before the turn of the century, and by 1930 there were 350,000 bets per day being given to "policy kings" like John "Mushmouth" Johnson and Dan Johnson. The $12 million-per-year industry controlled black votes in Chicago, and contributed hundreds of thousands of dollars per year to the campaigns of William Hale "Big Bill" Thompson, who in return only minimally enforced gambling laws.

There were many ways for bettors to choose numbers, but one of the most common demonstrates how closely numbers gambling was intertwined with African-American urban culture. Numbers were often chosen with the aid of "dream books," which assigned numerical figures to powerful words, or to the appearance of certain themes in a dream. When the beloved comedienne Moms MABLEY died in 1975, many gamblers bet and won with 769, the dream book number for death. In addition to dream books, many gamblers used birthdays, anniversaries, or other significant dates to select numbers. In 1969, when Willie MAYS hit his 599th home run, huge numbers of gamblers bet the next day on the number 600—unsuccessfully, as it turned out.

In the late 1920s and early '30s, two forces combined to create changes in the policy gambling industry in New York. First, the Manhattan District Attorney's office made a concerted effort to shut down the numbers racket in Harlem, a move that was only partially successful due to the police cooperation that had made widespread policy gambling possible in the first place. Second, white gangsters—Dutch Schultz in particular—who had previously concentrated on prohibition liquor activity, saw the huge profits of numbers games and started to enter the business. Although Schultz's career in numbers was brief, control of the industry did change hands. From the 1940s until well into the 1960s, numbers games were dominated by white organized crime figures.

Despite the fact that policy gambling was no longer a locally controlled business, numbers thrived in Harlem. Reliable statistics are difficult to find, but by the 1960s it was estimated that the New York numbers games employed thousands of people in a $600-million annual industry, representing as much as 60 percent of Harlem's total economic life. The importance of policy gambling in African-American urban life up to the present is validated by the portrayal of numbers runners and policy bankers in the works of writers such as Ralph ELLISON, James BALDWIN, and Malcolm X.

Although groups like The Forty Thieves, and figures such as Ellsworth Raymond "Bumpy" Johnson, the inspiration for the movie *Shaft* (1971), had remained active in policy gambling under the domination of Jewish and Italian organized crime figures, it was only during the 1960s that blacks began to reassert their presence in the industry. This sometimes meant demonstrating their power by becoming involved in politics. In the 1964 presidential election, for example, some runners were instructed to offer a one-dollar free play to Harlemites who promised to register and vote against Barry Goldwater. By this time there had been many changes in the way numbers games ran. Average bets had increased to fifty cents or one dollar, and the corresponding payoffs were much higher. Also, the winning number was now determined not by the New York Stock Exchange volume, but by the last three digits of the total amount of money betted—the pari-mutuel "handle"—at the local harness racing track.

In 1980, attempts by New York and many other states to preempt numbers games with institutionalized legalized lotteries led to public demonstrations in Harlem. The state prevailed, and these lotteries, combined with the opening of Off-Track Betting offices, as well as the enforcement of laws that made the taking of more than five hundred numbers bets a felony, weakened the popularity of "Harlem's favorite indoor sport." Nonetheless, policy gambling continued to be a prominent feature of urban life, though increasingly run by Latinos.

Numbers games have been attacked as a means of exploiting poor blacks. Indeed, policy gambling has undoubtedly had an adverse net financial affect on African Americans and their communities, with masses of working-class or chronically unemployed people regularly wasting a significant portion of their income. However, arguments have also been made, particularly when policy gambling was being threatened by lotteries starting in the 1970s, that numbers games at least kept money in African-American neighborhoods, financed small black businesses, or even occasionally saved them from bankruptcy. Those factors, as well as the traditional thrill of gambling, have kept numbers gambling alive, with law enforcement officials in New York, Atlanta, St. Louis, Detroit, and Baltimore regularly closing down operations.

REFERENCES

COOK, FRED J. "The Black Mafia Moves into the Numbers Racket." *New York Times Magazine*, April 4, 1971, pp. 26–27, 107–108, 110, 112.

DRAKE, ST. CLAIR. *Black Metropolis: A Study of Negro Life in a Northern City.* New York, 1945.

IANNI, FRANCIS A. J. *Black Mafia: Ethnic Succession in Organized Crime.* New York, 1975.

McCALL, GEORGE J. "Symbiosis: The Case of Hoodoo and the Numbers Racket." In Alan Dundes, ed. *Mother Wit from the Laughing Barrel: Readings in the Interpretation of Afro-American Folk Culture.* Jackson, Miss., 1990, pp. 419–427.

McKAY, CLAUDE. *Negro Metropolis.* New York, 1968.

JONATHAN GILL

Nursing.   The first three American nurse-training schools were established in 1873: Massachusetts General Hospital in Boston, Bellevue Hospital in New York, and the New Haven Hospital in Connecticut. These early schools operated within hospitals, but in keeping with the "Nightingale Tradition" they enjoyed a degree of faculty autonomy and a separate funding apparatus, and they employed women as nurse supervisors. Within a very short period, however, this relatively autonomous structure was eclipsed, as hospitals came to dominate nursing education. Two factors—insufficient capital and endowment, and the demand for more science-based instruction—enabled hospital administrators quickly to gain hegemony in nursing education. Out of a desire to raise the status of the "trained nurse" and to gain control over instruction, white nurse leaders organized what would be renamed, in 1911, the American Nurses Association (ANA). Its official organ, the *American Journal of Nursing,* commenced publication in 1901.

In August 1879, Mary Eliza MAHONEY became the first black graduate nurse when she received her diploma from the New England Hospital for Women and Children, in Boston. She was an exception to the rule of racial exclusion practiced by the vast majority of hospital nurse-training schools in the North and by all such institutions in the South. The pattern of widespread denial of admission to black women left African-American communities with few alternative means of training. Blacks and white philanthropists accordingly created a separate parallel network of nurse-training schools and hospitals. In 1886, John D. Rockefeller contributed the funds for the establishment of a school of nursing at the Atlanta Baptist Seminary (now Spelman College), a school for black women. This institution bears the distinction of being the country's first school of nursing established within an academic framework.

During the 1890s, the establishment of a nationwide network of black hospitals and nursing schools gained momentum as black physicians, educators, community leaders, and women's clubs grew alarmed at the high rates of black morbidity and mortality. In 1891, Daniel Hale WILLIAMS, the first surgeon to perform an open-heart suture, founded PROVIDENT HOSPITAL and Nurse Training School in Chicago. Three years later, he was also instrumental in creating the FREEDMEN'S HOSPITAL and Nurse Training School in Washington, D.C. Under the aegis of Booker T. WASHINGTON, the Tuskegee Institute School of Nurse Training in Tuskegee, Ala., came into existence in 1892. In the same year, the Hampton Nurse Training School and Dixie Hospital in Hampton, Va., began accepting students. In October 1896, the black women of the Phillis Wheatley Club founded the only black hospital and nurse-training school in New Orleans. The Phillis Wheatley Sanitarium and Training School for Nurses, like its sister institutions, began rather inauspiciously, in a private residence consisting of seven beds and five patients. This institution was later renamed the Flint Goodridge Hospital and Nurse Training School and eventually incorporated into Dillard University. On October 4, 1897, Alonzo Clifton McClennan, an 1880 graduate of the Howard University Medical School, founded the Hospital and Nursing Training School in Charleston, S.C. Anna Decosta Banks, one of the first graduates of the Dixie Hospital School of Nursing, became the first head nurse of that black institution. By 1920, there were approximately two hundred black hospitals and thirty-six black nurse-training schools.

African Americans established these institutions in order to provide black patients with access to health care and to provide black women with opportunities to enter the nursing profession. Daniel Hale Williams declared in a 1900 address before the Phillis Wheatley Club of Nashville, "In view of this cruel ostracism, affecting so vitally the race, our duty seems plain. Institute hospitals and training schools. Let us no longer sit idly and inanely deploring existing conditions."

These early black nursing schools were, for the most part, as deficient in quality and standards as were many of their white counterparts. In keeping with prevailing practices, student nurses were exploited as an unpaid labor force. In every institution they performed all the domestic and maintenance drudgery, attended the patients, and dispensed medicine. It was not inconsequential that one of the early Tuskegee catalogs noted that the major admission requirement for the nursing program consisted of a

The first graduating class of Freedmen's Hospital Nursing Training School in Washington, D.C., in 1896. Sara Iredell Fleetwood (top left) became the first black superintendent of the nursing school in 1901. (Prints and Photographs Division, Library of Congress)

strong physique and stamina to endure hardship. In spite of the attendant difficulties and the mediocre instruction, hundreds of black women graduated from these segregated hospital nursing programs and went on to render invaluable service to black patients.

The process of becoming a nursing professional involved more than earning a diploma; as important for advancement was the acquisition of specialized training or graduate education. Black women nurses in this period encountered virtually insurmountable obstacles in their quest for more training. Indeed, for black graduate nurses, challenging career opportunities and employment in hospitals, visiting-nurses' associations, and municipal departments of health proved to be as difficult to obtain as sympathetic work environments that held out possibilities for promotion to supervisory and administrative positions. The vast majority of black graduate nurses, like their untrained predecessors, worked in private duty, usually for white families, for whom they frequently were expected to perform domestic household chores in addition to providing nursing care—all for lower wages than were paid to white nurses. Professional opportunities for black graduate nurses were often bleaker in the South than in the North. For many black women graduate nurses, however, the most galling assault to professional esteem was the denial of membership in the ANA. Only the members of

the alumnae association of the Freedmen's Hospital in Washington, D.C., who had obtained ANA membership prior to 1911 escaped this most visible manifestation of professional ostracism.

Determined to repudiate the ANA's exclusionary practices, Martha Franklin, a black graduate of the Women's Hospital in Philadelphia, launched a separate black nursing organization. Franklin joined forces with Adah Belle THOMS, president of the Lincoln Hospital Nursing Alumnae Association, in August 1908, to convene a meeting of fifty-two nurses at St. Mark's Episcopal Church in New York City. Out of this meeting emerged the National Association of Colored Graduate Nurses (NACGN). In 1912, the NACGN's members numbered 125; by 1920, it boasted a membership of 500. In 1928, in order to facilitate communication and to foster a greater sense of professional involvement among black nurses, NACGN president Carrie E. Bullock founded and edited the organization's official organ, the *National News Bulletin*. She encouraged black nurses to pursue postgraduate education by persuading the Julius Rosenwald Fund to establish for them a special Rosenwald fellowship program.

From the outset, the NACGN leadership made the integration of their profession a top priority. However, it would take twenty years, the emergence of a cadre of strong and resourceful leaders, and the crisis of World War II for black nurses to gain entrée into the ANA and to win full acceptance into the profession. In the mid-1930s, the NACGN received a much-needed boost from the general education board of the Rockefeller Foundation and from the Rosenwald Fund. These timely grants enabled the NACGN to employ Mabel K. STAUPERS and to move into permanent headquarters at Rockefeller Center, where all the major national nursing organizations had offices. Eventually, Staupers and then–NACGN president Estelle Massey Riddle succeeded in winning recognition and acceptance for black nurses. Central to this victory was Staupers's successfully orchestrated campaign to eliminate quotas established by the Armed Forces Nurse Corps during World War II.

Initially, the War Department had established a quota for African Americans of 56 nurses, 120 doctors, and 44 dentists to tend the wards designated for black troops. In 1943, after considerable agitation, Staupers received notice that the navy, heretofore the most hostile branch of the services, had decided to place the induction of black nurses under consideration. The army took more affirmative action and raised its quota of black nurses from 56 to 160. In an effort to attract public attention to the unfairness of quotas, Staupers met with First Lady Eleanor Roosevelt in November 1944, at which time she described in detail the discrimination and humiliation black nurses suffered in the armed forces.

When in January 1945 Surgeon General Norman T. Kirk announced the possibility of a draft to remedy a nursing shortage within the armed forces, Staupers immediately challenged him, "If nurses are needed so desperately, why isn't the army using colored nurses?" Her question exposed the hypocrisy of the draft call. Afterward she encouraged nursing groups, black and white, to write letters and send telegrams protesting the discrimination against black nurses in the army and navy nurse corps. This ground swell of public support for the removal of quotas that so severely restricted the enrollment of capable and willing black women proved effective.

Buried beneath an avalanche of telegrams and seared by the heat of an inflamed public, Kirk, Navy Rear Adm. W. J. C. Agnew, and the War Department declared an end to quotas and exclusion. On January 20, 1945, Kirk stated that nurses would be accepted into the Army Nurse Corps without regard to race; five days later, Agnew announced that the Navy Nurse Corps was now open to black women. Within a few weeks, Phillis Daley became the first black woman to break the color barrier and receive induction into the navy corps. The end of discriminatory practices by a key American institution helped to erode entrenched beliefs about the alleged inferiority of black health-care professionals and paved the way for the integration of the American Nurses' Association.

In 1948, the ANA's House of Delegates opened the gates to black membership, appointed a black nurse as assistant executive secretary in its national headquarters, and witnessed the election of Estelle Riddle to the board of directors. The decision to grant individual membership to black nurses barred from state associations in Georgia, Louisiana, South Carolina, Texas, Virginia, Arkansas, Alabama, and the District of Columbia was followed by the adoption of a resolution to establish biracial committees in district and state associations to implement educational programs and promote development of harmonious race relations.

The removal of the exclusionary barriers convinced Staupers and the leadership of the NACGN that their organization was now obsolete. Thus, during the NACGN's 1949 convention the members voted to dissolve. In the following year, Staupers, now president of the NACGN, presided over its formal dissolution.

In December 1971, a new generation of black nurses wrote another chapter in black nursing history. Dissatisfied with the integration meted out to them, black nurses launched a new organization, the National Black Nurses Association (NBNA). Of the ten published objectives of the NBNA, four concerned the obligation of black nurses to act as advocates for improving the health care of black people. The remaining six focused on efforts to promote the professional development of black nurses. The existence of this new organization suggests that the earlier dissolution of the NACGN had been premature.

REFERENCES

GAMBLE, VANESSA. *Black Community Hospitals: A Historical Perspective.* New York, 1987.

HINE, DARLENE CLARK. *Black Women in White: Racial Conflict and Cooperation in the Nursing Profession, 1890–1950.* Bloomington, Ind., 1989.

STAUPERS, MABEL KEATON. *No Time for Prejudice: The Story of the Integration of Negroes in Nursing in the United States.* New York, 1961.

DARLENE CLARK HINE

Oakland, California. *See* San Francisco and Oakland, California.

OBAC Writers' Workshop. The Organization of Black American Culture (OBAC) was founded in Chicago in 1967, and its writers' workshop has survived longer than any other literary group of the BLACK ARTS MOVEMENT. Originally conceived by a small group of intellectuals that included Hoyt Fuller, the editor of *Negro Digest,* the poet Conrad Kent Rivers, and Gerald McWorter (Abdul Alkalimat), its purpose has been to nurture artists and, in keeping with the general agenda of the Black Arts movement, to develop close ties between artists and the black community in a collective endeavor to revolutionize black culture and black consciousness. The acronym OBAC, pronounced "oh-bah-see," echoes the Yoruba word *oba,* which refers to royalty and leadership.

Like many other Black Arts organizations, OBAC was predicated on a conception that artists have a special role to play as leaders of a cultural revolution. Accordingly, the original vision of OBAC was broad, comprising three separate "'workshops"—writers, visual artists, and community relations—but not overlapping the work of groups such as the AS-SOCIATION FOR THE ADVANCEMENT OF CREATIVE MUSICIANS (AACM), founded in 1965, and nascent theater groups such as the KUUMBA Workshop,

which formed shortly after OBAC. The visual arts workshop, led by Jeff Donaldson, soon evolved into an independent group, AFRICOBRA (1968), and the community workshop disbanded. Within a couple of years OBAC became exclusively a writers' workshop, and it has continued to thrive in that form.

Several of the position papers issued by OBAC during its early days have been collected in *Nommo: A Literary Legacy of Black Chicago* (1983), an anthology celebrating the first two decades of the workshop. While these manifestos state OBAC's objectives clearly, the group's structure and activities equally reveal its fundamental values. Foremost among the tenets in OBAC's statement of purpose were (1) the establishment of a black aesthetic; (2) the encouragement of the highest quality of literary expression; (3) the identification of critical standards for black writing; and (4) the development of black critics. Other objectives included fostering a spirit of cooperation among writers, issuing publications, and conducting readings and forums for the public. To achieve these goals, OBAC has always remained an independent, community-based organization, free of institutional affiliations. OBAC publishes a newsletter, *Cumbaya,* and a magazine, *Nommo.* In addition to sponsoring traditional readings and forums, OBAC has conducted readings in public places such as bus stops and taverns. At weekly meetings members and visitors read their works and receive criticism from members of the group.

Among its alumni OBAC boasts many well-known writers. The poets include Hakai MAD-

HUBUTI (Don L. Lee), Johari Amini, Carolyn ROD-
GERS, Sterling Plumpp, and D. L. Crockett-Smith.
The fiction writers include Cecil BROWN and Sam
Greenlee. Some, such as Angela JACKSON and Sandra
Jackson-Opoku, have published fine work in several
genres. Regardless of individual differences, OBAC
writes hold in common a commitment to produce
work that in some sense derives from and speaks to
the black community. OBAC's emphasis on public
readings reflects this commitment, and it has produced a group of writers who are skilled and charismatic readers of their own work. The workshop itself embodies the vision of literary activity that at
once expresses and enlivens the culture of the black
community.

REFERENCES

PARKS, CAROLE A., ed. Nommo: A Literary Legacy of
    Black Chicago (1967–1987). Chicago, 1987.
SMITH, DAVID LIONEL. "Chicago Poets, OBAC, and
    the Black Arts Movement." In Werner Sollors and
    Maria Diedrich, eds. The Black Columbiad. Cam-
    bridge, Mass., 1994.

DAVID LIONEL SMITH

Oblate Sisters of Providence.

Oblate Sisters of Providence.   The Oblate Sisters of Providence, an order of black nuns, pioneered
in the area of black Catholic education in America.
The order was founded in Baltimore in 1828 by a
group of free women of color who had fled the turmoil of slave insurrections on the French island colony of San Domingo. Elizabeth Lange, one of the
order's founding members, had already been involved in educating black children in Baltimore when
she was approached by a local priest with the idea of
founding a "religious society of virgins and widows
of color." Three other Haitian women joined Lange
in the formation of the community, and the four
took their vows as sisters on July 2, 1829. Lange
served as the order's first Mother Superior. The Oblates' chapel, built in 1836, became an important center for worship among black Catholics in Baltimore.
There, members of the black Catholic community
could be baptized, married, confirmed, and buried
(see ROMAN CATHOLICISM).

While tuition and boarding fees were charged at St.
Frances Academy, the Oblates' school, the sisters
made a regular practice of caring for and educating
homeless and orphaned children. Non-Catholic children were also accepted as students. The Oblates
taught both academic and trade subjects. Despite frequent difficulties, the Oblates were ever expanding.
Their own numbers grew and the order drew

African-American women in addition to women
from San Domingo. The order of the Oblate Sisters
of Providence is still in existence, and members of the
order are at the forefront of leadership of black nuns
in America. St. Frances Academy, the original
school, continues to operate as well.

REFERENCES

GERDES, SISTER M. REGINALD, O.S.P. "To Educate
    and Evangelize: Black Catholic Schools of the Ob-
    late Sisters of Providence (1828–1880)." U.S.
    Catholic Historian 7 (Spring/Summer 1988): 183–
    199.
SHERWOOD, GRACE H. Oblates' Hundred and One
    Years. New York, 1930.

JUDITH WEISENFELD

Odell Waller Case.

Odell Waller Case.   Between 1940 and 1942 the
Odell Waller case became a matter of deep concern to
many Americans, black and white, because of what it
demonstrated between economic status, political
power, and race to the quality of justice in the United
States. On September 27, 1940, Odell Waller, a
twenty-three-year-old black sharecropper from Pitt-
sylvania County in southside Virginia was sentenced
to death for killing his landlord, a white man named
Oscar W. Davis, after a hasty trial before an all-white
jury. There was no doubt that Waller had shot Davis,
arguably in self-defense, during a dispute arising over
Davis's refusal to give the Waller family its share of
the wheat crop, but otherwise the case was full of
ambiguities.

Waller's plight attracted the attention of the Workers Defense League, an organization founded by the
Socialist Party in 1936, and other groups. After
Waller's conviction the WDL led a campaign to save
him that attracted national attention and won the support of numerous prominent Americans. For many
people Waller became a symbol of the country's racial and economic problems. The case had a profound and lasting impact on those most closely
involved in his defense, especially Pauli MURRAY and
Morris Milgram, deepening their commitment to
work on behalf of poor blacks.

The WDL's principal argument was that Waller
had not been tried by a jury of his peers. Not only
were all the jurors white, six were landlords who
hired sharecroppers; and unlike Waller and others in
similar economic straits, all had paid Virginia's poll
tax. The WDL's efforts succeeded in winning five
reprieves and led to an extraordinary commutation
hearing conducted by Gov. Colgate W. Darden, Jr.
But the defense lawyers failed to convince either the

Virginia or the federal courts or Gov. Darden that Waller's constitutional rights had been violated, and on July 2, 1942, Waller was put to death in Virginia's electric chair in Richmond.

REFERENCE

SHERMAN, RICHARD B. *The Case of Odell Waller and Virginia Justice, 1940–1942*. Knoxville, Tenn., 1992.

RICHARD B. SHERMAN

Odetta (Gordon, Odetta Holmes Felious)

(December 31, 1930–), folk singer. Born in Birmingham, Ala., Odetta—as she is invariably known—grew up in Los Angeles, where her family moved when she was six. By the age of thirteen she was studying piano and singing. She also taught herself to play the guitar. She studied classical music and musical theater at Los Angeles City College, and performed in a 1949 production of *Finian's Rainbow* in San Francisco. In the early 1950s, Odetta, with her rich contralto voice, emerged as an important figure on the San Francisco and New York FOLK MUSIC scenes. With the encouragement of Harry BELAFONTE and Pete Seeger, she began performing and recording more widely, presenting an eclectic repertory of spirituals, slave songs, prison and work songs, folk ballads, Caribbean songs, and BLUES (*My Eyes Have Seen*, 1959; *Sometimes I Feel Like Cryin'*, 1962). She also appeared in the film *Sanctuary* (1961).

In the early 1960s Odetta began to address political and social issues. She became an important advocate for civil rights, and took part in the historic 1963 civil rights march in Washington, D.C. Throughout the 1960s and '70s Odetta continued to perform internationally and record (*Odetta Sings the Blues*, 1967). In 1974 she appeared in the television film *The Autobiography of Miss Jane Pittman*. In 1986 she presented a concert marking forty years of her life as a performer. This was released as a live recording (*Movin' It On*, 1987). She has received acclaim throughout the world as one of the central figures of modern folk music.

REFERENCES

ARMSTRONG, DON. "Odetta: A Citizen of the World." *Crisis* 90, no. 6 (June–July 1983): 51–52.

GREENBERG, MARK. "Power and Beauty: The Legend of Odetta." *Sing Out* 36, no. 2 (August–October 1991): 2–8.

ROSITA M. SANDS

Ogawa, Florence Ai. *See* Ai.

O'Hara, James Edward (February 26, 1844–
September 15, 1905), politician and lawyer. James O'Hara was born a free black in New York City, the son of an Irish merchant and a West Indian woman. The family moved to the West Indies (probably St. Croix in the Danish West Indies) in 1850, where O'Hara spent much of his youth and probably acquired much of his education. At some point he returned to the United States and in 1862 was a missionary schoolteacher in North Carolina territory that had been captured from the Confederacy. After the war, O'Hara acquired political expertise as a clerk for the North Carolina constitutional convention of 1868, where he drafted proposed new laws. Through 1869 he performed similar work for the state legislature. O'Hara moved to Washington, D.C., and studied law at HOWARD UNIVERSITY for about two years. Although he did not finish his degree, he completed his studies in North Carolina and was admitted to the bar in 1873. He moved to Enfield and began a law practice.

In 1872, O'Hara was elected chair of the county board of commissioners in Halifax County, N.C., and served until 1878. Halifax, a cotton-growing region, was prosperous and populous; African Americans comprised half of its population. Holding positions that afforded them considerable control over both taxes and fiscal disbursements, O'Hara and his fellow commissioners (four blacks and a CARPETBAGGER) found themselves charged with numerous counts of graft and fraud by white Democrats, almost from the beginning of their terms. O'Hara and the other commissioners were indicted (and acquitted) fifteen times, a reaction indicating the extent to which whites were willing to go in their ultimately successful attempts to eliminate black political power. African Americans nonetheless continued to exercise a measure of power even after North Carolina was "redeemed" in 1876, particularly in the Second Congressional District, which sent four blacks to the U.S. Congress between 1872 and 1900. James O'Hara was one of six black delegates to the state constitutional convention in 1875. After two unsuccessful bids for the congressional nomination 1874 and 1876, a losing effort for the House seat in 1878, O'Hara was finally elected to the House in 1882. When he took office in 1883, he was the only African American in the House of Representatives.

In Congress, James O'Hara was a lonely champion of civil rights. Most of the measures he introduced died in committee. After the U.S. Supreme Court declared the Civil Rights Act of 1875 unconstitutional, O'Hara introduced an unsuccessful constitutional amendment in 1883 that would have restored the rights in that bill. Another thwarted effort was O'Hara's amendment to an interstate commerce bill of 1884, which would have provided equal accommodations on trains. Although the amendment passed, its effects were nullified by another amendment, sponsored by white southerners, which held separate accommodations to be equal. O'Hara tried in 1883 to provide financial remuneration to depositors of the failed Freedmen's Savings Bank and Trust Company, but this bill also found scant support. O'Hara did manage to garner greater funding for North Carolina waterfront projects.

Although reelected in 1884, O'Hara was defeated in the 1886 election by a white Democrat. O'Hara retired from national politics but remained active in local Republican politics. He practiced law in New Bern, N.C., until his death in 1905.

REFERENCES

ANDERSON, ERIC. "James O'Hara of North Carolina: Black Leadership and Local Government." In Howard N. Rabinowitz, ed., *Southern Black Leaders of the Reconstruction Era.* Urbana, Ill. 1982.
CHRISTOPHER, MAURINE. *America's Black Congressmen.* New York, 1971.

ALLISON X. MILLER

Ohio. Ohio occupies a special place in the history of African Americans. Located on slavery's fringe, abutting western Virginia and across the Ohio River from Kentucky, Ohio played a crucial role in both the UNDERGROUND RAILROAD and the abolitionist movement. Although the Northwest Ordinance of 1787 outlawed slavery in the area, proslavery forces still tried to make Ohio a slave state. They failed to overturn the antislavery provisions of the Ordinance at the 1802 Ohio Constitutional Convention. The state constitution, which took effect when Ohio entered the Union in 1803, denied blacks suffrage, but left no other restrictions on civil rights. Antiblack delegates introduced a series of black codes at the 1804 Ohio legislative session. Blacks were denied the right to hold political office, to serve in the state militia, to serve on juries, to testify against whites in court, to receive public charity, or to send children to public schools. Beginning in 1807, the law required blacks to register and post a $500 bond when they entered the state.

Black codes did not keep African Americans from coming to Ohio, however. While sizable communities were established in Cincinnati, Chillicothe, Steubenville, Columbus, Cleveland, and other places, most settled in rural areas, especially in the southwestern part of the state, where they worked in agriculture or on the Ohio River trade. Blacks settled in clusters of a few families, and built close-knit communities. The church was the institutional core around which everyday life and culture was organized. During the 1820s and 1830s, the Reverend Wallace Shelton of Cincinnati and other black missionaries spread the independent church movement to Ohio. They inspired blacks to break off from white denominations and organized dozens of AFRICAN METHODIST EPISCOPAL (AME) and BAPTIST congregations, including the nation's first Black Baptist Association. By 1860, almost every community had one of each denomination. Associated with churches were missionary associations, temperance societies, Sunday schools, and mutual-aid societies such as Xenia's Colored United Association. Community residents also formed Masonic lodges and other fraternities and schools. Except in Cincinnati, which had the state's largest black community and was renowned for the quality of its black schools, Ohio blacks attended one-room schools supported by meager black community funds.

Ohio was notable during the antebellum years as a hotbed of abolitionism, where liberal whites joined with blacks in the struggle against slavery and worked to help "fugitives" escape from slavery to freedom. Ohio served as one of the main routes of the Underground Railroad, and slaves from Virginia and Kentucky escaped via Ohio to Canada. Black abolitionists such as Cleveland's William Howard Day and Columbus political activist David Jenkins organized antislavery conventions to petition against slavery and appoint lobbyists who would press white legislators to grant blacks civil rights and suffrage. Poet James Madison BELL, born in Gallipolis, was active in antislavery activities with John Brown, a white Ohio settler who later gained fame at Harpers Ferry (*see* JOHN BROWN'S RAID). During the 1840s, Ohio Rep. Joshua Giddings helped lead the challenge to the "gag rule" on antislavery petitions.

Cincinnati was a citadel of the abolitionist movement. James G. Birney edited *The Philanthropist,* an influential antislavery newspaper, and Levi Coffin, a Quaker who came to Cincinnati from Indiana, was nicknamed "President of the Underground Railroad," for his efforts in developing escape routes in Michigan and elsewhere and organizing escape missions.

The Western Reserve, a nine-county region in the state's northeast corner (including Cleveland), which was primarily settled by New Englanders and Quakers, was especially notable for racial liberalism. Cleveland's public schools remained integrated and hired black teachers. Oberlin College in Lorain County, dominated by abolitionists almost from its inception in the 1830s, was the first American college to admit large numbers of black students, and the town of Oberlin remained an open and interracial community throughout the century. In 1855, John Mercer LANGSTON, a former slave and attorney and future U.S. congressman, was elected to the office of township clerk in Brownhelm, thus becoming one of the first black elected officials in the nation. Mount Union College in Alliance also began accepting black students during the 1850s. During this period, the Western Reserve was heavily settled by free black refugees from North Carolina, including the parents of African-American novelist Charles CHESNUTT.

Elsewhere in the state, blacks also found educational opportunity. In the 1850s, President Horace Mann of Antioch College in Yellow Springs opened the college's door to blacks, and in 1856 the Cincinnati Conference of the Methodist Episcopal Church opened Wilberforce University in nearby Tawawa Springs. Designed as a black college, it was in reality closer to a prep school. After the Civil War, it was augmented by the founding of a sister institution, Central State University.

Although slavery was prohibited in Ohio, the institution left its mark everywhere. It was common for Kentucky slaves to be hired for work in Ohio tobacco plantations and factories and ferried across the river for daily labor. Slave owners were protected by law when vacationing or traveling in the state with their slaves or transporting them through the state en route to another jurisdiction that recognized slavery. In 1841 abolitionists convinced the Ohio Supreme Court to declare the state a safe haven for runaway slaves, though the Federal Fugitive Slave statutes remained in effect.

Nevertheless, the state was far from ideal in its race relations. Conflict was severest in southern Ohio, where most of the state's blacks lived and whose residents were largely Southern-born migrants who retained proslavery and/or antiblack attitudes and feared masses of blacks escaping or migrating across the Ohio River. Cincinnati, despite its abolitionist movement, periodically exploded in waves of violence instigated by fearful whites wishing to drive away black residents. The worst racial violence broke out in 1829 and temporarily cut the city's black population in half (with financial aid from Ohio Quakers, the refugees founded the Wilberforce colony in Canada). Despite further violence in 1839 and 1841, black migration to Cincinnati continued. The American Colonization Society, which advocated sending blacks back to Africa, was popular throughout Ohio.

The CIVIL WAR ushered in a new era in the history of black Ohioans. After the war broke out, several volunteer black companies formed, but were refused military service. Instead, blacks were organized into labor gangs. A "Black Brigade" built fortifications to protect Cincinnati from rebel attacks. Determined to

participate in the struggle, some blacks, such as Wilson Bruce Evans, "passed" for white so that they could fight. During the war years, the state's black population increased as escaping or emancipated slaves migrated north, mostly to rural areas. Antiwar "Copperhead" Democrats lead by Clement Vallandigham played on urban white fears of black competition, and white (mainly Irish) workers in Toledo and Cincinnati rioted in 1862. When Massachusetts organized a black regiment in 1863, John Mercer LANGSTON and O. S. B. Wall, a shoe store proprietor, recruited about 900 blacks for the Massachusetts 54th Volunteers. Soon after, Gov. David Todd, desperate to fill enlistment quotas, organized blacks into the 127th Ohio Volunteers. Ultimately 5,000 Ohio blacks served in the Union Army.

By the end of the war, a narrow Unionist majority controlled the state. The Christian Commission and other organizations were established by elite whites to aid the freedpeople. Whites set up hospitals, schools, job-placement services (mostly in domestic labor), and relief efforts. However, most white Ohioans were unwilling to grant blacks equal rights—let alone suffrage. In January 1865, Ohio blacks, meeting at Xenia, established a state branch of the National Equal Rights League and during the succeeding years lobbied for enfranchisement. Ratification of the FIFTEENTH AMENDMENT—rejected by Ohio in 1869 and barely passed in 1870—brought blacks voting rights and the right to sit on juries.

However, blacks continued to face problems and sometimes violent opposition. Segregation was widespread on streetcars and railroad trains and in hotels, restaurants, theaters, and schools. Most significant, they were locked into low-paying, dead-end domestic and personal-service jobs. Few were able to secure high-paying jobs in Ohio's factories and mines. However, blacks fought back. Through lawsuits based on federal civil-rights legislation, they desegregated streetcars and railroads. Using the political power of the ballot, blacks forced state authorities to admit them to state orphanages and institutions and obtained equal funding for black schools.

Blacks also united to elect black lawmakers. Cincinnati's George Washington WILLIAMS was elected to the state's House of Representatives in 1879—the first black to serve. Williams, a lawyer and preacher, wrote *The History of the Negro Race in America,* the first important history of African Americans. In 1881, Cleveland attorney and Justice of the Peace John P. Green, one of the most prominent politicians in the United States, was also elected to the House.

Benjamin W. ARNETT was probably the most important black Ohio legislator. A distinguished clergyman, Arnett was elected to the Ohio House of Representatives in 1885, and he served a brief by significant term. In 1887, largely as a result of Arnett's lobbying, legislators passed a law desegregating state schools and repealed the law forbidding interracial marriage. In 1888, Arnett left the legislature and became a bishop of the AME Church.

Laws prohibiting discrimination in public accommodations were passed in 1884 and 1894. However, these political gains did not eradicate discrimination and segregation in Ohio. Lawsuits to enforce equal access were expensive and damage awards often failed to ensure compliance. Blacks remained wary of the commitment of white parties to black rights, and a few formed their own political parties. In 1897, S. J. Lewis ran for governor as the candidate of the Negro Protective Party, a small third-party movement. Most blacks remained trapped in low-status jobs, with no way to advance out of poverty. A few black Ohioans, however, did achieve prominence in the second half of the nineteenth century. Cincinnati's Peter Clark, America's first black Socialist, was an important educator and labor leader in the 1870s and 1880s. Col. Charles YOUNG, a native of Ripley, was the highest-ranking African American soldier of the pre–WORLD WAR I era. Poet Paul Laurence DUNBAR of Dayton, author of such works as *Majors and Minors* (1896), was the first widely regarded black American writer. AME Bishop Daniel PAYNE came to WILBERFORCE UNIVERSITY in 1863, turned it into a thriving black community and intellectual center and remained as its president until his death thirty years later.

By 1900 more than 70 percent of black Ohioans lived in cities, primarily Cleveland, Cincinnati, Columbus, Dayton, Youngstown, Toledo, Akron, and Springfield. The population shift from country to city, matching a decline in the state's agricultural economy, took place within the context of a precipitous decline in black-white relations in the state, following a national pattern. While blacks were not disenfranchised, informal segregation in restaurants, theaters, and public places became universal, even in the liberal Western Reserve, and racial conflict increased. School integration was sometimes slow, and black teachers were fired from interracial positions. In 1892 a black man accused of murdering a white woman and raping her daughter was lynched at Oxford, triggering a wave of a dozen LYNCHINGS and lynching attempts during the next fifteen years. Race riots broke out in Akron in 1900 (following the lynching of a black man accused of raping a white child) and at Springfield in 1904 and 1906. The Springfield riots were prompted by underlying tensions over desegregated schools, black population growth, strikebreaking and labor competition, and the scapegoating of blacks for the town's crime and vice. In both incidents, white mobs invaded the town's African-American community, made indiscriminate attacks on residents, and destroyed homes and property. City authorities refused to intervene. The riots, which resembled Southern models, attracted nationwide attention.

World War I spawned the migration of thousands of blacks to Ohio, most to urban areas, whose black communities ballooned. Between 1910 and 1920, the black population of Cleveland quadrupled, while those of Toledo and Youngstown tripled, and that of Dayton doubled. While some black workers found industrial jobs, most were shunted into low-paying service jobs at the bottom of the industrial ladder. The institution of a strict color bar continued to promote racial solidarity across class lines, but many established black residents scorned the uneducated working-class newcomers. However, elite blacks made self-conscious efforts at racial uplift and improvement of conditions, and they formed chapters of the NAACP and/or YMCA and YWCA branches in such cities as Dayton, Cleveland, Columbus, and Cincinnati. Hallie Quinn BROWN, president of the Ohio Federation of Colored Women's Clubs from 1905–1912, became a national leader of the Women's Club movement.

Black urban population growth continued through the 1920s and 1930s and coincided with the building of a new residential environment. Building codes, zoning laws, city plans, restrictive covenants and discrimination by realtors assured the creation of neighborhoods segregated on the basis of housing type and cost. Blacks were confined by poverty and racism in the most dilapidated neighborhoods in the city. Blacks who tried to move into white neighborhoods, like Cleveland's Dr. Charles Garvin in 1926, were greeted with violence. The growth of the black industrial proletariat promoted the organization of ghetto communities, and their wages supported a small black professional class. Many black communities contained music and entertainment districts as well as baseball clubs such as the Columbus Blue Birds and the Cleveland Buckeyes. Despite the success of "Don't-Buy-Where-You-Can't Work" campaigns in Cleveland and elsewhere at forcing shopkeepers to hire black workers, the Great Depression in Ohio brought widespread misery. Overtaxed community institutions were unable to respond effectively to poverty and poor health care.

World War II brought renewed migration to the cities of Ohio. Between 1940 and 1960, Cincinnati's black population increased by 72,000, while 172,354 new blacks settled in Cleveland, and Dayton and Toledo again doubled their black populations. The Civil Rights Movement was active throughout the state during these decades and succeeded in laying the foundations for later actions. Cleveland and Cincinnati had major efforts throughout the era, but a few groups in smaller areas were notable. The Vanguard League of Columbus founded in 1940 was a black-led, interracial mass movement that filed lawsuits to obtain equal access to public accommodations and boycotted and picketed stores that refused to hire blacks. It declined, however, after World War II. Columbus blacks eventually helped to build a successful chapter of the CONGRESS OF RACIAL EQUALITY (CORE) in the 1960s. By 1964 it had 100 members and was a powerful protest and lobbying group to assure just distribution of federal government aid to poor blacks.

During the 1960s, Ohio's economy began to shift from a primary focus on heavy industry to service and technology. The postindustrial economy required fewer workers and produced a proliferation of low-paying jobs. Blacks who had finally achieved long-sought admission to industrial employment and unions were the first to be laid off. Ultimately, deindustrialization led to a restructuring of the social geography of the metropolis, with whites concentrated in suburbs and poor blacks in center city areas. In 1966, anger over chronic discrimination and police harassment led to a racial uprising in Dayton.

Over time, blacks were able to transform city-population growth into political power. On November 7, 1967, Carl B. STOKES of Cleveland ushered in a new stage in American history when he became the first African American elected mayor of a large city. In the ensuing years, the black quest for political power met with success in most parts of the state. Some cities, however, thwarted black political aspirations. Cincinnati's at-large city council voting assured the defeat of many minority group candidates. Columbus annexed adjacent white suburbs to maintain a white electorate.

By 1990, African Americans were an essential political force in Ohio politics. Cincinnati had a black mayor, Dwight Tillery, as well as a black city council member; Columbus boasted three city council members, two state representatives, and a state senator; Dayton had a black mayor, Richard Clay Dixon, four municipal judges, and six city council members. Cleveland blacks wielded the most political power, having not only elected a black mayor, Michael R. White, and black city and state officials, but an African-American U.S. Congressman, Louis STOKES. In 1992 Eric Fingerhut was also elected to Congress from the Cleveland area. However, a 1993 legislative redistricting plan upheld by the U.S. Supreme Court threatened to erode some of these gains.

Black political power, however, was not accompanied by widespread economic empowerment. Some African Americans did succeed and entered careers in sports and entertainment or in business, medicine, law, and other professions. Notable black Ohioans include athlete Archie Griffin, athlete and executive Oscar ROBERTSON, jazz artist Art TATUM, opera singer Kathleen BATTLE, Nobel Prize-winning novelist Toni MORRISON, actress Ruby DEE, writer Russel Atkins, and poet/critic Mari EVANS. Government employment and teaching positions in secondary and higher education promoted the birth of a large, new black middle class. However, the economic shift from industry to service and high technology hit black Ohio with great force. By 1980, the state's African Americans had double-digit unemployment levels, and many were living in poverty. The economic picture remained bleak through the early 1990s.

REFERENCES

CACCOMO, JAMES F. *Hudson, Ohio and the Underground Railroad.* Hudson, Ohio, 1992.

GERBER, DAVID A. *Black Ohio and the Color Line, 1860–1915.* Urbana, Ill., 1976.

HEMMONS, WILLA MAE, ed. *The State of Black Cleveland.* Cleveland, 1989.

KUSMER, KENNETH. *A Ghetto Takes Shape: Black Cleveland, 1870–1930.* Urbana, Ill., 1976.

MCCLUSKEY, JOHN A. *Blacks in Ohio: 7 Portraits.* Cleveland, 1976.

QUILLIN, FRANK URIAH. *The Color Line in Ohio: A History of Race Prejudice in a Typical Northern State.* 1913. Reprint. New York, 1969.

TAYLOR, HENRY LOUIS, JR. "The Northwest Ordinance and the Place of Ohio in African-American History." *The Old Northwest* 14 (1988): 131–144.

———. "On Slavery's Fringe: City-Building and Black Community Development in Cincinnati, 1800–1850." *Ohio History* 95 (1986): 5–33.

———. "Spatial Organization and the Residential Experience: Black Cincinnati in 1850." *Social Science History* 10 (1986): 45–69.

TAYLOR, HENRY LOUIS, JR., ed. *Race and the City: Work, Community, and Protest in Cincinnati, 1820–1970.* Urbana, Ill., 1993.

WATSON, WILBUR H. *The Village: An Oral Historical and Ethnographic Study of a Black Community.* Atlanta, Ga., 1989.

WESLEY, CHARLES H. *Negro Americans in Ohio: A Sesquicentennial View.* Wilberforce, Ohio, 1953.

HENRY LOUIS TAYLOR, JR.

Oklahoma. Oklahoma has occupied a varied role in African-American history. Created as an Indian homeland, the area became a center of black slavery, then was a locus of complex interaction between African Americans and Native Americans. After the Oklahoma territory was opened to non-Indian settlement in 1889, Oklahoma was briefly a land of promise for blacks fleeing the oppression of white America. Once whites began to dominate the territory, African Americans fought a rearguard action in support of their civil rights and economic independence. There followed a long period of rigid control by whites, occasionally broken by black civil rights victories. Eventually, the state's African Americans pushed successfully for entry into the economic and social mainstream.

The history of blacks in Oklahoma begins in the 1830s with the notorious Trail of Tears, by which Native Americans from the so-called Five Civilized Tribes—the Creeks, Cherokees, Choctaws, Chickasaws, and Seminoles—were expelled from their lands in Georgia, Alabama, and other areas of the Southeast. With them went thousands of their African-American slaves, as well as some free blacks. Native American groups had widely differing slave systems. The Choctaw and Chickasaw had most of the slaves, and were perhaps the harshest masters. The Creeks and Cherokees were divided between pro-slavery (often part-white or white-educated) and antislavery factions, which—like the Seminoles—had influential black and *métis* (mixed race) community members. Slaveholding Indians transferred their agricultural system to the new land. Some planted cotton, but most slaves were employed growing foodstuffs and serving as domestics. There were two failed antislavery rebellions in the area. In 1841 some 200 slaves revolted near Webber's Falls but were overtaken and defeated near the Texas border by armed federal troops, then brought back to their masters. In 1853 a rebellion by free blacks was crushed by soldiers from Fort Washita. As in white slaveholding areas, the social and legal status of blacks in Indian territories declined through the antebellum period. Even free blacks were denied suffrage, and often education.

The CIVIL WAR disrupted the Indian slave economy, and caused internal warfare. In 1861 federal troops left the Indian territories, which were taken by the South. Pro-Union Cherokees, Creeks, and Seminoles, as well as the small free black population, were forced to flee to Kansas. When Union troops retook the area one year later, pro-slavery Indians gathered in the lands of the pro-Confederate Choctaws and Chickasaws. In 1863 the pro-Union faction of the Cherokees voted to emancipate Cherokee slaves.

In 1866, after the THIRTEENTH AMENDMENT abolished slavery in the United States, federal representatives met with Native American leaders, who were not covered by the amendment, at Forth Smith, Arkansas, to force emancipation by treaty. The "Northern" (pro-Union) faction of the Creeks was represented by chief Cow Tom, an African-American Creek chieftain. The Native Americans officially signed treaties to grant African Americans citizenship and farms. The Chickasaw, a group of some 5,000, refused to admit their 2,000 freedmen to citizenship or to furnish them any tribal land, claiming the federal government had given them the option of expelling their black slaves. As a result, the Chickasaw freedmen remained without legal status anywhere for forty years. The Cherokees, some 22,000 strong, gave their 2,500 slaves six months to claim residence within the area they controlled. Many blacks who had been resettled in distant regions and were unable to meet the deadline were excluded. After protests from the Convention of the Negroes of Indian Territory, which assembled at Scullyville in January 1870, Freedmen's Bureau and other federal agents applied pressure to assure them land and citizenship rights. In the twenty-five years after the Civil War, the ex-slaves and their families were absorbed into the Native American groups. Unlike in the rest of the United States, most blacks secured title to land. Among the federal troops who patrolled the region and defended against encroachment by white squatters were the African American "buffalo soldiers" of the 9th and 10th Cavalry. Meanwhile, blacks organized unsuccessful petition and lobbying movements for the granting of federal-owned or leased land in the Indian territory to be granted to black settlers.

In 1889 the Oklahoma territory was created and opened to non-Indian settlement. No racial barriers were created to land ownership, and Oklahoma already had a thriving black farming class. Hundreds of blacks were among the settlers who rushed into the territory to stake a claim. By 1890 there were 3,000 black homesteaders in Oklahoma, who grew cotton or food crops. As further lands were opened to settlement, black boosters began to promote Oklahoma as a promised land for African Americans, and urged Southerners to migrate. The leading propagandist for Oklahoma was E. P. McCabe. McCabe, a black political leader from Kansas who had twice been State Auditor, the highest black elected official in the West, had settled in the territory in 1890. McCabe believed that if enough African Americans came to Oklahoma, the territory could become a separate black state, where blacks could develop political and economic autonomy. He also hoped to be named territorial governor. McCabe called for blacks to found their own towns as centers of economic and political power. He bought land near Guthrie and built up a short-lived model all-black community, which he named Langston after Virginia Congressman John Mercer LANGSTON. He set up a newspaper, *The Langston Herald,* to attract immigrants.

Some twenty-five black towns were founded. As Langston University sociologist Mozell C. Hill noted in his study of black towns in the 1940s, they were set up amid strong white and Indian resistance, and their residents tended towards separatism. The most famous town was Boley, founded in 1903 and noted for its annual Black Rodeo. A showplace of the independent black economy, the thriving town and its surrounding area had some 3,000 black residents by 1906, with all-black churches, stores, restaurants, and community organizations. However, white gerrymandering and fraud ultimately robbed it of its potential status as county seat and center of political power, and the town never became economically important.

Though Oklahoma's black population climbed to 55,000 by 1900 and 113,000 by 1910, too few blacks and too many whites migrated to the territory for McCabe's plan for black control to be realized. Still, many blacks were elected to office. Green Currin and David J. Wallace sat in the territorial legislature, and various blacks served on school boards, and as tax collectors, aldermen, and in other positions. McCabe was appointed territorial assistant auditor. Bass

One of those who hoped in vain that Oklahoma could become a racially egalitarian enclave in the South was Edward Prescott McCabe, a former state auditor for Kansas who moved to Oklahoma in the 1890s to further this goal. (Archives and Manuscripts Division of the Oklahoma Historical Society)

Reeves became a famous U.S. marshal, and many blacks were made deputy sheriffs or appointed to other posts.

Most of the black migrants were farmers, who settled in rural areas, as did railroad workers, cowboys, and other laborers. There were few skilled white laborers in the area, and African Americans were quickly integrated into the territorial economy. Meanwhile, artisans and merchants migrated to the growing cities of Oklahoma City, Tulsa, Guthrie, and Muskogee, and formed prosperous black business districts.

The surrounding communities developed fraternal and community institutions. Newspapers such as the *Muskogee Cimiter* were founded. Several churches sprang up and were united into the Oklahoma State Baptist Convention in 1895. Schools were opened, the first one in Oklahoma City in 1892. In 1897 a land grant college, the Colored Agricultural and Normal University (also known as Langston University) was established at Langston under the leadership of the distinguished educator Inman PAGE, a graduate of Brown University.

As Oklahoma's white population grew in the 1900s, race relations worsened. Blacks were excluded from juries and public office, and found increasingly less economic opportunity. Lynching and segregation grew more common in the territory, especially in "Little Dixie," the southeastern portion of the state that was largely settled by white Southerners. In 1906 Oklahoma applied for statehood. Oklahoma's black population formed numerous groups, such as the Afro-American Independent Suffragist League and the Suffrage League of Oklahoma Territory, to press for guarantees of voting rights. Nevertheless, the state constitution, drafted by conservative Democrats, included provisions for separate schools, and limits on the franchise. Despite the pleas of the Negro Protective League and the Afro-American League, the federal government admitted Oklahoma to the union in 1906. The first state legislature, over the objections of the lone African-American representative, Albert C. Hamlin, segregated public transportation and waiting rooms, and made interracial marriage a felony.

Some African Americans responded to the new restrictions by leaving the state. From 1910 through 1912, a group of some 1,300 blacks, consisting largely of skilled farmers, moved to the Canadian provinces of Alberta and Saskatchewan, most settling together near Edmonton. Though they were legal immigrants, white Canadians feared an influx of African Americans, and applied pressure to halt the flow of immigrants. A small group of Oklahoma blacks immigrated to Liberia. In 1913 Chief Alfred Sam came to Oklahoma from the Gold Coast to sell stock and

This family was part of the burgeoning increase in Oklahoma's African-American population in the twenty years after it was opened to general settlement in 1889. The migration to Oklahoma Territory and the establishment there of more than twenty all-black towns was motivated in part by the vain hope that the territory would not adopt the prevailing southern system of racial discrimination. (Prints and Photographs Division, Library of Congress)

arouse interest in his Akim Trading Company, promising free transportation to Africa for stockholders. His movement sparked widespread interest, and about sixty black Oklahomans traveled to the Gold Coast before the company failed and they were forced to return.

Most blacks remained in the state. Oklahoma soon became a civil rights battleground. Church leaders such as E. W. Perry, pastor of Oklahoma City's Tabernacle Church and president of the Oklahoma Baptist Convention, lectured to white and interracial groups about racial problems. The activist Oklahoma City chapter of the NATIONAL ASSOCIATION FOR THE ADVANCEMENT OF COLORED PEOPLE, the state's first NAACP chapter, was founded in 1913. In 1915, the Oklahoma City *Black Dispatch* was founded by crusading editor Roscoe Dungee. Dungee became a leading spokesperson for Oklahoma blacks during his fifty-year editorial career, and in 1930 helped combine local NAACP branches into a powerful state chapter.

In 1910 the Oklahoma legislature, spurred on by radicals anxious to assure white domination over the state's large and relatively affluent black population, struck a powerful final blow at black political power in the form of laws which required literacy and property qualifications for voters, but included a "grandfather clause" exempting most whites. The NAACP joined with white Oklahoma Republicans to oppose the measure, and the U.S. Supreme Court ruled in *Guinn* v. *United States* (1915) that "grandfather clauses" were unconstitutional. However, the state responded by requiring those affected to register within a short period or be permanently disenfranchised. As a result of such discrimination, few blacks were able to vote in the state during the following decades. The same year, whites passed a law segregating telephone booths, the nation's first such law.

On the local level, Tulsa and Oklahoma City passed stringent residential segregation ordinances in 1916. The U.S. Supreme Court ruled most such laws unconstitutional the following year, and the two cities passed milder ordinances in accordance with the ruling. City officials did not enforce the laws strictly, but residential covenants kept most African Americans trapped in dilapidated housing in neighborhoods with poor city services. In 1933 "Alfalfa Bill" Murray, an outspoken white supremacist, segregated city housing by executive order, after proclaiming martial law to prevent "bloodshed" arising from blacks in white areas. The state Supreme Court voided the order in *Allen* v. *Oklahoma City* (1935).

During the first half of the twentieth century, Oklahoma African Americans were victimized by poverty, isolation, and white violence. After 1910 chronic agricultural depression and soil erosion, combined with taxation and white harassment, cut deeply into the size and value of black-owned land in the state. Many farmers were forced to sell their land to white planters or to lease it to oil companies for a pittance. Many blacks moved to the rapidly growing cities, and found work as low-paid manual laborers or domestic servants. Others were forced into tenant labor, and lived the same penurious existence that tenant farmers in the South did. The GREAT DEPRESSION further impoverished tenant farmers, despite the efforts of the interracial Southern Tenant Farmers Union to organize cooperatives and win higher prices. The state's black population declined during the 1930s, as black "Okies" left in search of opportunity in California or Texas.

As the state's culture was progressively Southernized, lynchings and racial violence in the state became so common that during World War I a contingent of Oklahoma black soldiers being shipped to military camps carried banners warning whites, "Do Not Lynch Our Relatives While We Are Gone." Tulsa became a KU KLUX KLAN center noted for weekly whippings of blacks. In 1921 a black Tulsa bootblack was falsely accused of the rape of a white woman. The local white population erupted into a riot. Despite resistance by armed blacks, a white mob invaded the black neighborhood, randomly shooting unarmed blacks and ultimately setting off bombs that leveled most of the district. Overt racial violence tapered off after 1930, though the threat of it remained. In 1935 the NAACP won an important victory in the U.S. Supreme Court decision *Hollins* v. *Oklahoma*, which overturned a death-penalty rape conviction because of systematic racial prejudice in jury selection.

Oklahoma's best-known black natives, writer Ralph W. ELLISON and historian John Hope FRANKLIN, writing of their childhoods in the Oklahoma of the 1920s and '30s, asserted that although discrimination was widespread, many remaining independent black towns and institutions nurtured a powerful sense of pride and assertiveness in Oklahoma's blacks. During the period, Oklahoma black communities boasted a thriving culture. Churches occupied a central place in black life, and around them grew social groups such as the Oklahoma grand lodge of the Prince Hall Masons, which had 150 lodges in the state by the 1940s. Theaters such as Tulsa's Dreamland and Oklahoma City's Aldridge featured plays, vaudeville shows, and later, movies. Meanwhile, JAZZ developed in the state. Southwestern jazz bands, of which the Blue Devils were the most famous, were created in Oklahoma, and nurtured musicians such as Walter Page, Lester YOUNG, Count BASIE, and Oklahoma natives Jimmy RUSHING, Jay McShann, and Don BYAS. Charlie CHRISTIAN, one of the fathers of the electric guitar, grew up in Oklahoma City, before joining the Benny Goodman band in 1939. Ralph Ellison noted that what was known as "Kansas City" jazz was in large part an Oklahoma product. Oklahoma has also been the home of distinguished blacks in other fields. Some of the more notable natives are rodeo star "Bill" PICKETT, poet Melvin TOLSON, and singer Leona MITCHELL.

The first cracks in the wall of Oklahoma racial discrimination came in the years after World War II. Blacks, long plagued by inadequate, underfunded schools, had been pushing unsuccessfully for teacher salary equalization and an end to school discrimination since the 1939 Oklahoma Supreme Court case *Simmons* v. *Board of Education* (brought by wealthy oil magnate and civil rights leader Jake SIMMONS). The first concrete victory against unequal education came in January 1948, when NAACP attorney Thurgood MARSHALL took the case of Ada Lois Sipuel, who had applied to the University of Oklahoma Law School and was rejected on racial grounds, to the U.S. Supreme Court, which ordered her admitted. Oklahoma quickly created a law school at (unaccredited) Langston University. The NAACP responded by bringing suit on behalf of George McLaurin, charging that education at Langston was unequal. In September 1948, a federal court ordered McLaurin admitted to the University of Oklahoma. The University's regents admitted him and other blacks, but they required black students to attend class in a separate, adjoining room, and set up special segregated sections of campus buildings. The NAACP again brought suit, and in *McLaurin* v. *Oklahoma* (1950), the U.S. Supreme Court struck down such segregated facilities.

The decision opened the doors of Oklahoma's university system on an equal basis to African Americans, and served as an important precedent for the Court's BROWN V. BOARD OF EDUCATION OF TOPEKA, KANSAS public school desegregation four years later. In 1955, following *Brown*, voters passed a constitutional amendment assuring equal funding for Oklahoma black schools, and began a multiyear process of peaceful integration, in the face of heavy and occasionally violent white opposition. In the early 1960s the legislature passed a law mandating the teaching of black history in public schools.

The CIVIL RIGHTS MOVEMENT broke down Oklahoma's established system of segregation. Oklahoma City and Tulsa, home of many of the state's blacks, were the first areas affected by demonstrations. In 1958 members of Oklahoma City's NAACP Youth Council, led by teacher Clara Luper, sat in at department stores and lunch counters and forced desegregation of thirty-nine downtown stores. The demonstrations soon expanded, but the process was distressingly slow. Still, by 1964 almost all state public accommodations had been forced to desegregate. In 1965, following legislative reapportionment, black voters assured the election of John White, Archibald Hill, and Curtis Lawson, the first African Americans elected to the state legislature in almost sixty years. That year, E. Melvin Porter became the first black state senator. In 1968 Hannah Atkins was elected to the legislature, the first black woman to serve. In 1988 she was named Oklahoma Secretary of State, and then was appointed by President George Bush to take charge of the U.S. Consumer Product Safety Commission.

In the years since the 1960s, Oklahoma African Americans have had their share of both problems and triumphs. Black legislators have continued to play an important role in the running of state affairs, and hundreds of blacks now occupy elected or appointed offices in Oklahoma. Economic empowerment, however, has lagged behind political gains. A few businesses, such as the Simmons Development Co., American Beauty Products Co., and the Oklahoma City *Post-Dispatch* have continued to thrive. However, despite Oklahoma's "Black Gold" program, aimed at encouraging minority business growth, in the 1990s African Americans continue to represent a disproportionate share of the state's poor and unemployed.

By the 1990s the University of Oklahoma Law School had become a symbol of the success of the black struggle for equality. Once the focus of the state's resistance to desegregation, the school now listed among its faculty Anita F. Hill, who gained fame as U.S. Supreme Court nominee Clarence THOMAS's accuser (see also HILL-THOMAS HEARINGS.) In 1992 it named Ada Lois Sipuel Fisher, whom it had sought to exclude in the 1940s, to its board of trustees. Yet, despite such official integration, obtaining quality education was a particular problem. Langston University remained underfunded and inadequate. Residential segregation within the sprawling urban areas of Oklahoma City and Tulsa continued to restrict the number of students attending biracial schools. In 1972 the Oklahoma City school board adopted the controversial "Finger Plan," which involved busing of black students to all-white schools. By 1990 local black parents were urging an expanded busing plan, this time including adjacent suburbs, to avoid the effective resegregation of city schools.

REFERENCES

ALDRICH, GENE. *Black Heritage of Oklahoma.* Edmond, Okla., 1973.

ELLSWORTH, SCOTT. *Death in a Promised Land: The Tulsa Race Riot of 1921.* Baton Rouge, La., 1982.

FRANKLIN, JIMMIE LEWIS. *Journey Towards Freedom: A History of Blacks in Oklahoma.* Norman, Okla., 1982.

GREENBERG, JONATHAN D. *Staking a Claim: Jake Simmons and the Making of an African-American Oil Dynasty.* New York, 1990.

HAMILTON, KENNETH MARVIN. *Black Towns and Profit: Promotion and Development in the Trans-Appalachian West, 1877–1915.* Urbana, Ill., 1991.

HILL, MOZELL C. "Basic Racial Attitudes Towards Whites in the Oklahoma All-Negro Community." *American Journal of Sociology* 49 (May 1944): 519–522.

KNIGHT, THOMAS. *Black Towns in Oklahoma: Their Development and Survival.* Washington, D.C., 1975.

LITTLEFIELD, DANIEL. *The Chickasaw Freedmen: A People Without a Country.* Westport, Conn., 1980.

RADER, BRIAN P. *The Political Outsiders: Blacks and Indians in a Rural Oklahoma County.* San Francisco, 1978.

TOLSON, ARTHUR L. *The Black Oklahomans, A History: 1541–1972.* New Orleans, 1974.

WASHINGTON, NATHANIEL JASON. *Historical Development of the Negro in Oklahoma.* Tulsa, Okla., 1948.

GREG ROBINSON

O'Leary, Hazel Rollins (May 17, 1937–   ), corporate executive. Hazel Rollins was born and raised in the seaport city of Newport News, Va. She graduated from Fisk University in Nashville, Tenn., in 1959 and earned a law degree from Rutgers in 1966. In New Jersey she began a career in law enforcement, serving as an assistant state attorney general and later as an Essex County prosecutor. In the early 1970s O'Leary moved to Washington and became a partner at the accounting firm of Coopers and Lybrand. She later joined the Federal Energy Administration during the Ford presidency. She served in Jimmy Carter's Energy Department as head of the Economic Regulatory Administration. While there, Rollins befriended John F. O'Leary, the deputy energy secretary. The couple married in 1980 and formed an en-

President Clinton looks on as Energy Secretary Hazel O'Leary speaks before the Federal Fleet Conversion Task Force, December 9, 1993. Though one of the least well-known members of Clinton's cabinet, she has distinguished herself by her vigorous investigation of the history of radiation experimentation on human subjects. (AP/Wide World Photos)

ergy consulting firm, O'Leary Associates. John O'Leary died in 1987, and Hazel O'Leary closed the consulting firm.

In 1989 O'Leary was named executive vice president for corporate affairs at the Minneapolis-based Northern States Power Company, one of the largest gas and electric utilities in the Midwest. She was in charge of environmental affairs, public relations, and lobbying. As an energy policymaker O'Leary advocated decreased dependence on oil and coal, promoted fuel conservation, and helped develop a program at Northern States Power to generate electricity with windmills. She has also been a proponent of nuclear power, and her goals include the creation of safe storage methods for nuclear waste.

The policy of Northern States Power regarding the storage of nuclear waste earned her some criticism from environmental groups. In 1990 Northern States sought to build nuclear storage facilities at Prairie Island, Minnesota, next to the Mdewakanton Sioux Indian Reservation. After the Sioux protested, a judge prohibited an expansion of the nuclear waste site. O'Leary then drafted a compromise with regulators that permitted Northern States to open the storage facility on a reduced scale. Her background in energy regulation and her commitment to conserva-

tion attracted the attention of President Bill Clinton, who in 1993 offered O'Leary the post of secretary of energy. When confirmed, O'Leary became the first woman ever to hold that post.

REFERENCES

New York Times, January 19, 1992.
NIXON, WILL. "Bill and Al's Green Adventure." *Environmental Magazine* (May 1993).
Washington Post, January 19, 1993.

JAMES BRADLEY

Oliver, Joseph "King" (May 11, 1885–April 8, 1938), cornetist and bandleader. Joseph Oliver was born in Donaldsville, La., and raised in New Orleans. He began his music studies on trombone, and eventually switched to cornet and trumpet. While still a teen he began performing at dances, at parades, and in brass bands, although he made his living at times as a butler. Oliver's first important work (1916–1919) came with bandleader Edward "Kid" ORY, who gave him his nickname. Oliver moved to Chicago in 1919 to play in bassist Bill Johnson's band. He also co-led a band with clarinetist Lawrence Duhé. In 1921 Oliver performed in San Francisco.

The next year found him back in Chicago, where he led the enormously influential "hot" style Creole Jazz Band, including clarinetist Jimmie NOONE, at the Royal Gardens Cafe, later known as the Lincoln Gardens. In 1922 Oliver called on trumpeter Louis ARMSTRONG, who had substituted for him in Ory's group, to join the band. Oliver's classic 1923–1924 ensemble, which also included clarinetist Johnny DODDS, his brother drummer Baby DODDS, pianist Lil Hardin (*see* Lil Hardin ARMSTRONG), trombonist Honore Dutrey, and Bill Johnson on banjo and double bass, is among the first great jazz ensembles, and is certainly the greatest authentic New Orleans-style ensemble to record. The group's 1923–1924 recordings, with their spontaneous polyphony and surging, four-to-the-beat rhythmic attack on "Riverside Blues," "Tears," "Weatherbird Rag," "Dipper Mouth Blues," "Chimes Blues," and "Canal Street Blues," rank with recordings by Jelly Roll MORTON the same year as among the earliest African-American New Orleans–style jazz recordings.

Armstrong left the Oliver band after a tour of the Midwest in 1924, and in that year Oliver disbanded the Creole Jazz Band and recorded duos with Jelly Roll Morton. From 1924–1927 Oliver led a larger group called the Dixie Syncopators, including tenor saxophonist and clarinetist Barney BIGARD, and also played again with Ory. In the late 1920s and early

1930s he led his own groups, with a somewhat sweeter, more bluesy sound ("Someday Sweetheart," 1927, "Too Late," 1929, "Sweet Like This," 1929). During these years Oliver also served as a sensitive accompanist for blues singers such as Sippi WALLACE and Victoria Spivey.

Oliver was a pioneering jazz trumpeter, with an unadorned but highly expressive style. The recorded solo breaks he traded with Louis Armstrong in 1923–1924 show that his talent and influence also lay in straight and plunger-muted voicelike passages. In his final years Oliver was plagued by financial setbacks and failing health, including the gum disease that would make performing on cornet difficult. In the early and mid-1930s he toured with his own ensembles in the South and Southwest. In 1937 he quit music, and thereafter worked at a fruit stand and as a pool hall attendant. He died in Savannah, Ga., in 1938.

REFERENCES

ALLEN, WALTER C., and BRIAN RUST. *King Joe Oliver.* London, 1955.
ARMSTRONG, LOUIS. *Satchmo, My Life in New Orleans.* New York, 1955.
SCHULLER, GUNTHER. *Early Jazz: Its Roots and Musical Development.* New York, 1968.

LAWRENCE GUSHEE

Olympic Movement, The. The first modern Olympic Games were held in 1896, in Athens, Greece, the homeland of the ancient Olympic competitions, traditionally dated as beginning in 776 B.C. Since 1896 the Olympic Games have been held every four years, except for interruptions caused by the two world wars. The first Winter Olympiad was held at Chamonix, France, in 1924, and, like the summer games, the winter games have been held quadrennially. Starting with the Winter Olympics in Lillehammer, Norway, in 1994, the Winter Olympics will be held in even-numbered years in between the years of the Summer Olympics. Relatively few persons of African descent have participated in the Winter Olympics. The only African-American medalist has been figure skater Debi THOMAS, holder of the 1986 U.S. and world titles, who won a bronze medal in figure skating at the 1988 Calgary games. The professional football player Herschel WALKER was a member of the American bobsledding team at the 1992 Albertville Winter Games.

Despite the scarcity of African Americans in the Winter Olympics, black Americans have been involved in the Olympic movement almost from the beginning. It has been the scene of some of the greatest triumphs and most controversial moments in the history of African-American athletic competition. Though there has never been a "color line" barring African Americans from participating on American Olympics teams, there were subtle forms of racism present in the early years of the Olympic movement. The International Olympic Committee (IOC) and the founder of the Olympic movement, the French baron Pierre de Coubertin (1863–1937), were sympathetic to European colonialism and comfortable with invidious distinctions between European civilization and the peoples and cultures of the colonized world. An example of the sort of racism the Olympic movement endorsed were the so-called Anthropology Days, held at the 1904 St. Louis games, the first Olympic competition held in the United States. This was little more than a racial sideshow in which Africans, Asians, and American Indians engaged in mock athletic competition to the amusement of the spectators.

Nonetheless, Coubertin believed that Olympic competition could produce an "aristocracy of sport," which could serve as a basis for enhanced cooperation between nations and races. Coubertin attempted to stage "African games" in 1925 and 1929; he blamed the failure of these abortive competitions to take place on the efforts of colonialists. But Coubertin and the IOC had little interest in the participation of black Africans in the regular Olympics. No black sub-Saharan team competed in the Olympics until Nigeria and the Gold Coast (later Ghana) sent small contingents to the 1952 Helsinki games. Since the 1960s black Africans have excelled in many summer Olympic sports, especially distance events. Abebe Bikila of Ethiopia won the Olympic Marathons in 1960 and 1964, and several Kenyans won other distance events at Mexico City in 1968. At the 1988 Seoul games, Kenyan men won the events at 800 meters, 1,500 meters, 3,000-meter steeplechase, and at the 5,000 meters.

African-American runners began to make their mark early in the Olympic movement and have since become the dominant performers among American track-and-field Olympians. The first African-American Olympian medalist was George C. Poage, who won a bronze medal in the 400-meter hurdles race at the 1904 St. Louis games, representing the Milwaukee Athletic Club. The first African-American gold medalist was John Baxter Taylor, who ran on the winning 1600-meter relay team at the 1908 London games. Between 1924 (Paris) and 1936 (Berlin) fifteen African-American men won Olympic medals in track-and-field events (track-and-field events for women were initiated at the 1928 Amsterdam Games).

The first African-American athlete to attain worldwide fame through Olympic competition was Jesse OWENS (1913–1980), a remarkable track-and-field performer who had already set a number of world records before his four-gold-medal performances at the 1936 Berlin games. The 1936 games are remembered both as a victory for Nazi propaganda and as Jesse Owens's personal triumph in the face of Nazi racism. Nazis, who treated blacks as subhumans not fit to compete with Aryans, were disdainful of black athletes. Owens won gold medals in the 100- and 200-meter races, the 4 × 100-meter relay, and the long jump. One of the most enduring stories of the Olympics is the refusal of Nazi dictator Adolf Hitler to shake Owens's hand after his victory in the 100 meters. Although there are different explanations for Hitler's snub, the most likely account holds that Nazi racial ideology was a large factor in Hitler's act. In his victory in the face of Nazi contempt, Owens served as a surrogate for all Americans opposed to Hitler and Nazism. But when Owens returned to the United States, racism of another kind denied Owens certain honors he surely deserved. President Franklin Delano Roosevelt neither invited him to the White House nor conveyed his congratulations, while the Amateur Athletic Union suspended him for an imagined act of insubordination and denied him the Sullivan award that was given annually to the outstanding amateur athlete. These acts of racial discrimination, however, should not obscure the fact that Olympic competition was among the most integrated venues for African-American athletes in the 1920s and 1930s.

African-American athletes continued to distinguish themselves in TRACK-AND-FIELD competition at postwar Olympiads. Among the most important figures of the quarter-century following World War II were Harrison Dillard (gold medals in the 100-meter dash and 110-meter high hurdles in 1948 and 1952, respectively), Wilma RUDOLPH (gold medals in the 100- and 200-meter dash and the 4 × 100 relay in 1960); Rafer Johnson (gold medal in the decathlon in 1960 and lighter of the Olympic torch in the opening ceremonies of the 1984 Los Angeles Olympics); Bob Hayes (gold medal in the 100-meter dash in 1964); and Bob Beamon, whose long jump of 29′ 2½″—almost two feet longer than the existing record—was the single most spectacular achievement of the 1968 Mexico City games.

African-American participation in the Summer Olympic Games has long extended beyond the track-and-field events. The first sport other than track and field which included black athletes was weightlifting. John Terry was a member of the 1936 team, John Davis was the Olympic champion in the heavyweight division at both the London (1948) and Helsinki

(1952) games, and James Bradford won silver medals in that division at both the Helsinki and Rome (1960) games. In the sport of judo (see MARTIAL ARTS) George Harris was the first African American to make an American Olympic team, competing at the 1964 Tokyo games. Allen Coage won a bronze medal as a heavyweight at Montreal (1976), and Edward Liddie won a bronze in the extra-lightweght class at the 1984 Los Angeles games.

African Americans have won medals in almost every Olympic sport. Anita DEFRANTZ won a bronze medal at the 1976 Montreal games as a member of the rowing team. In 1980 she was awarded the Olympic Order medal for opposing President Jimmy Carter's ordered boycott of the 1980 Moscow games (because of the Russian invasion of Afghanistan), and in 1986 she was elected a member of the IOC. In WRESTLING, Lloyd Keaser won a silver medal in the lightweight division in 1976, and Greg Gibson won a silver medal as a heavyweight in 1984. In the sport of cycling, Oliver "Butch" Martin, Jr., was a member of the 1964 American Olympic team, and Nelson VAILS won a silver medal in the 1984 Olympic sprint competition. The first African-American member of an American Olympic FENCING committee was Uriah Jones, who participated in the 1968 Mexico City games. Black fencers earned positions on American Olympic teams in 1972, 1976, 1980, and 1984, and Peter Westbrook won a bronze medal in the saber competition at the Los Angeles Games. The silver-medal winning women's VOLLEYBALL team at the Los Angeles games included three African-American players, including the team's star player, Flo HYMAN. Americans have dominated BASKETBALL competition since it was first held in 1936. African Americans who have won gold medals include Don Barksdale (1948), Bill RUSSELL (1950), K. C. JONES (1956), Oscar ROBERTSON (1960), Walt Hazzard (1964), Spencer Haywood (1968), JoJo White (1968), Phil Ford (1976), Quinn Buckner (1976), Michael JORDAN (1984), and Patrick Ewing (1992). Jordan and Ewing, along with Charles Barkley and Earvin "Magic" JOHNSON, were among the professional National Basketball Association all-stars who overwhelmingly defeated their opposition in the largely African-American "dream team" at the 1992 Barcelona Olympics.

Olympic gold medals have launched several African-American boxers into successful careers as professional champions. Floyd PATTERSON, who won the Olympic middleweight championship at the 1952 games, eventually became heavyweight champion of the world. Joe FRAZIER and George FOREMAN won gold medals in the heavyweight (now super heavyweight) division in 1964 and 1968 respectively, and both went on to become professional heavy-

George Foreman, the victor in the heavyweight boxing division at the Summer Olympics in Mexico City in 1968, congratulated at the medal ceremonies. An astonishing twenty-six years later, in 1994, he won the professional heavyweight title. (AP/Wide World Photos)

weight champions. Sugar Ray LEONARD, who won a gold medal as a light welterweight in 1976, later won several world championships as a professional. The most famous African-American boxing champion was probably Muhammad ALI, who as Cassius Clay won an Olympic gold medal in the light heavyweight division in 1960 and went on to an extraordinary career as both a pugilist and black nationalist activist.

The politics of race and South Africa's policy of apartheid were central issues in the Olympic movement in the 1960s and 1970s. The IOC was reluctant to ban South Africa from the Olympic movement, and South Africa was allowed to participate in the 1960 Olympics because Avery Brundage, the president of the IOC, believed the claims of the South African representative that racial discrimination played no role in the selection of athletes. This was a

transparent fiction, and by 1964, in part through pressure from the Organization of African Unity (OAU), South Africa was suspended from participation. In 1968 the IOC voted to admit a racially mixed South African team. This led to a proposed boycott, and the IOC bowed to massive pressure and excluded the South African team just as the competition was about to begin. Under pressure from black African nations, the IOC also banned a Rhodesian team from the 1972 Olympics. A team from Zimbabwe was admitted in 1980. Following significant changes in the apartheid laws, South Africa was readmitted to the 1992 Olympic games at Barcelona.

The proposed return of South Africa to the Olympics for 1968 led Harry Edwards, a young sociology professor at San Jose State University, to call for a boycott of the games by African Americans, in protest against South African apartheid and racial conditions in the United States. Among those who chose not to participate in the Olympics were basketball players Elvin Hayes, Bob Lanier, Wes Unseld, and Lew Alcindor (later known as Kareem ABDUL-JABBAR). Some of those athletes who chose to take part in the games found themselves embroiled in even bigger controversy. The African-American sprinters Tommie Smith and John Carlos, gold and bronze medal winners respectively in the 200-meter dash, raised black-gloved fists above their heads during the medals ceremony. This Black Power demonstration resulted in their expulsion from the Olympic village, since the IOC saw their symbolic protest as an unacceptable form of political interference in the games. George Foreman's flag-waving demonstration after his gold-medal victory was seized upon by critics as evidence that Smith and Carlos were misguided rebels.

There have been a number of outstanding African-American performers in recent Olympics. In 1984

Carl LEWIS became the first Olympic performer since Jesse Owens in 1936 to win four track and field medals in one Olympiad (gold medals in the 100- and 200-meter dash, the long jump, and the 4 × 100 meter relay). Lewis won the 100-meter dash at the 1988 Seoul games after the apparent winner, Ben Johnson of Canada, was stripped of his medal for steroid use. Lewis was awarded the gold medal, as well as also winning a gold in the long jump and a silver in the 200-meters. At the 1992 Barcelona games, Lewis won gold medals in the long jump and in the 4 × 400-meters. Lewis's eight gold medals are the most earned by any track and field athlete since the early years of the century.

At the 1988 Seoul games Florence GRIFFITH-JOYNER, or "Flo Jo" as she was popularly known, tied Wilma Rudolph's 1960 record of three gold medals by winning gold medals in the 100- and 200-meter races and the 4 × 100-meter relay. Her striking appearance and dazzling track outfits were as much dis-

Carl Lewis (left) in the long jump at the Summer Olympics in Barcelona, Spain, in 1992. Lewis won the event, one of eight gold medals he has captured in Olympic competition. (AP/Wide World Photos) Florence Griffith-Joyner (right) running in the 200-meter dash at the U.S. Olympic Track and Field Trials in Indianapolis in 1988. (AP/Wide World Photos)

In the photograph to the left, in a gesture that for many epitomized a year of black protest and rage, sprinters Tommie Smith (center) and John Carlos (right) offered the Black Power salute—a black glove on a clenched and upraised fist—during the playing of the U.S. national anthem at the 1968 Summer Olympics in Mexico City. Smith and Carlos, respectively gold and bronze medal winners in the 200-meter dash, were promptly dismissed from the national team. A number of other black medal winners at the games engaged in similar, if more muted, protests. (Photographs and Prints Division, Schomburg Center for Research in Black Culture, The New York Public Library, Astor, Lenox and Tilden Foundations) Cheryl Miller, in the photograph to the right, after leading the U.S. women's basketball team to an 85–55 gold medal victory over South Korea at the 1984 Olympics in Los Angeles. (AP/Wide World Photos)

cussed as her track accomplishments. Jackie JOYNER-KERSEE (whose brother, Al Joyner, also an Olympic gold medal champion, married Florence Griffith in 1987) was acknowledged as "America's best all-around female athlete" after the 1988 Seoul games, where she won the heptathlon, the most demanding event in women's track and field. Joyner-Kersee went on to become the first woman to win two Olympic gold medals in the heptathlon after a repeat victory in the 1992 Barcelona games. In 1992 Dr. Leroy WALKER became the first African American to be elected president of the United States Olympic Committee. The visibility of Olympic competition will continue to attract the most talented athletes from around the world, including African Americans, and in all likelihood the games will draw various forms of symbolic political protests as well.

REFERENCES

GUTTMANN, ALLEN. *The Games Must Go On: Avery Brundage and the Olympic Movement.* New York, 1984.

HART-DAVIS, DUFF. *Hitler's Games: The 1936 Olympics.* New York, 1986.

HOBERMAN, JOHN. *The Olympic Crisis; Sport, Politics, and the Mortal Order.* New Rochelle, N.Y., 1986.

———. "Olympic Universalism and the Apartheid Issue." In F. Landry, M. Landry, and M. Yerle, eds. *Sport: The Third Millennium.* Saint-Foy, Quebec, 1991.

LAPCHICK, RICHARD E. *The Politics of Race and International Sport.* Westport, Conn. 1975.

MANDELL, RICHARD. *The Nazi Olympics.* New York, 1971.

JOHN M. HOBERMAN

Opera. Since its inception in early seventeenth-century Florence, Italy, opera has been the dominant form of staged musical storytelling in the European musical tradition. During the last two centuries of its evolution, African Americans and persons of African descent have played an important role in its development as an art form.

African settings and characters were often included in the plots of early opera. Indeed, the first important opera, Claudio Monteverdi's *Orfeo* (1607), included a female moor in the finale. Cleopatra was a common role in early opera, most notably in George Frideric Handel's *Giulio Cesare* (1724), as was the Carthaginian princess Dido, in Henry Purcell's *Dido and Aeneas* (1689), numerous settings of *Didone Abbandonata* (as in Tommaso Albinoni's of 1725), and in later opera such as Hector Berlioz's *Les Troyens* (1858). Other operas from the standard repertory with an African setting or characters include Mozart's *Die Zauberflöte* (1791), Gioacchino Rossini's *L'Italiana in Algeri*

With an extraordinary range of more than three octaves, Elizabeth Taylor Greenfield, the "Black Swan," had a successful international concert career, which included a command performance before Queen Victoria. (Photographs and Prints Division, Schomburg Center for Research in Black Culture, The New York Public Library, Astor, Lenox and Tilden Foundations)

(1813), Giacomo Meyerbeer's *L'Africaine* (1865), and Giuseppe Verdi's *Aida* (1865) and *Otello* (1889).

African Americans have been active in opera as performers and singers since the early nineteenth century. In nineteenth-century America the boundaries between high and low musical cultures were not as rigid as they would later become. Like many of their contemporaries, black and white, trained singers often performed in minstrel and vaudeville shows (*see* MINSTRELS/MINSTRELSY), as well as in the concert hall or opera house. One of the first prominent African-American operatic singers was Elizabeth Taylor GREENFIELD. Born a slave in Mississippi, but raised free in Philadelphia, Greenfield was known as "the Black Swan" and performed with a troupe of African-American opera singers in the United States, Canada, and England throughout the 1850s and '60s. In 1854, Greenfield sang with tenor Thomas J. Bowes (1836–c. 1885), whom critics called "the American Mario" or "the colored Mario," after Italian opera star Conte di Candia Mario. Bowers, possibly the greatest American male singer of the period, chose "Mario" as his preferred stage name and refused to sing to segregated audiences or in concert halls from which African Americans were barred. Opera selections were also included in the program of the multitalented LUCA FAMILY, a father and four sons who performed as vocalists, pianists, and violinists. After the deaths of the father, Alexander C. Luca, and one brother, tenor Simeon G. Luca, the three remaining brothers joined with the Hutchinsons, a famous abolitionist singing family, for a concert tour of the Midwest that advertised a program of "Humor, Sentiment, and Opera!" In the late 1860s and '70s, the two HYERS SISTERS, Anna Madah and Emma Louise Hyers, achieved renown for concerts featuring scenes from such operas a Verdi's *Il Trovatore* and *La Traviata,* and Gaetano Donizetti's *Lucia di Lammermoor.* Another prominent singer, soprano Marie Selika Smith (c. 1849–1937), who named herself Selika after the African princess in *L'Africaine,* performed in the United States and Germany during the 1870s and '80s. One of the most important performers of this period was Sissieretta Joyner JONES, known as "the Black Patti"—after the great soprano Adelina Patti—whose celebrity was established in 1892, when she was asked to give a recital at the White House for President Benjamin Harrison. In 1896, Jones formed her own troupe, the Black Patti Troubadors, which featured her in operatic excerpts.

African Americans were barred from performing in major opera houses in the United States. As a result, many well-qualified singers either pursued careers in Europe or confined their performances to recitals and the concert stage. Newspapers and magazines from the late nineteenth century stated that black artists were frequently exploited by their white managers, who garnered their financial support from both the white and black communities. Generally, African-American singers could count on two or three years of concertizing before white audiences ceased to find them novel or exotic, which forced them to turn to studio teaching as a means of making a living. There were two notable exceptions to this rule: Jones, "the Black Patti," who, in founding her own troupe, extended her singing career by fifteen years; and Nellie Brown Mitchell (1845–1924), who debuted in New York and Boston in the 1870s and, after becoming the leading soprano for James Bergen's Star Concert Company, created the Nellie Brown Mitchell Concert Company in Boston in 1886. One of Mitchell's unusual achievements was her staging of a juvenile operetta called *Laila, the Fairy Queen,* with an ensemble of fifty African-American girls ages five to fifteen, at a Boston musical festival in 1876. Mitchell's concert company lasted approximately ten years, after which Mitchell turned to private teaching in the mid-1890s.

The first known African-American opera company was the Colored American Opera Company of Philadelphia and Washington, D.C., which staged Julius Eichberg's *Doctor of Alcantara* for enthusiastic audiences in both cities in 1873 and returned in 1879 with performances of Gilbert and Sullivan's *H.M.S. Pinafore.* Twelve years later, Theodore Drury (1867–c. 1943), a highly trained tenor and impresario, founded his own company. Drury began by presenting operatic selections and expanded the company's repertory to include full operas at the turn of the century. Between 1900 and 1910, as well as sporadically into the 1930s, the Theodore Drury Opera Company appeared in New York, Boston, Providence, and Philadelphia. Works performed included Georges Bizet's *Carmen,* Charles Gounod's *Faust,* Verdi's *Aida,* Pietro Mascagni's *Cavalleria Rusticana,* the Ruggiero Leoncavallo's *I Pagliacci.* The productions were advertised as social affairs attended by prominent social figures and concluded with supper and dancing to Walter F. Craig's orchestra.

One unique contribution that African-American singers made to vocal literature was the development of the concert SPIRITUAL, a fusion of melodies derived from African-American religious chanting with the harmonies of the European art song. For many African-American vocalists, the first exposure to classical singing occurred in church or while listening to a recital of sacred music and spirituals. Because they were not allowed on the opera stage, many classically trained African-American singers became primarily known as recitalists and their repertories frequently included spirituals as well as European art songs and arias. One of the first recitalists to come to

prominence in the twentieth century was the tenor Roland HAYES. Among those who followed in his path was contralto Marian ANDERSON. Initially barred from the operatic stage in the United States, Anderson became a peerless recitalist with a wide repertory of arias, songs, and spirituals. The most dramatic moment in her career occurred in 1939, when, after being barred from performing in a Washington, D.C., concert hall, Anderson gave an outdoor recital—introduced by Secretary of the Interior Harold Ickes—on the steps of the Lincoln Memorial. Nevertheless, major opera houses remained inaccessible to African Americans for another fifteen years. Other prominent African-American recitalists of the middle decades of this century included sopranos Inez Matthews (1917–1950), Ellabelle Davis (1907–1960), and Dorothy MAYNOR. Catherine Yarborough (1903–1986) appeared in the United States only in musical comedy, but sang the role of Aida in Europe, where she was known as Caterina Jarboro. In the next generation, leading singers included Muriel Rahn (1911–1961), Carol Brice (1918–1985), and contralto Louise Parker (1926–1986), a favorite of both Leopold Stokowski and Paul Hindemith.

Outside the concert hall, African-American singers were often confined to operatic roles in works that had all-black casts such as Virgil Thomson's *Four Saints in Three Acts* (1933) and George Gershwin's *Porgy and Bess* (1935) or "ebony" versions of *Carmen* and other opera classics. Bass Paul ROBESON and baritones Jules BLEDSOE and William Warfield (1920–), each used the character of Joe in Jerome Kern's *Showboat* (1927) to launch their careers. Todd DUNCAN and Donnie Ray Albert (1950–) also began by singing the role of Porgy in the Gershwin opera. Other singers, such as Lawrence Winters (1915–1965) and Charles Holland (1910–1987), the first black principal to sing at the Paris Opera (he debuted there in *Aida* in 1954), performed extensively in Europe.

Although some major companies, such as the New York City Opera, cast African Americans as early as the 1940s, the Metropolitan Opera in New York City did not drop its color line until 1955, when Marian Anderson sang Ulrica (traditionally a dark-skinned role) in Verdi's *Un Ballo in Maschera.* Louis Gruenberg's *Emperor Jones,* which calls for a character of African descent in the title role, had premiered at the Met in 1933; at the time, white baritone Lawrence Tibbett was cast over Paul Robeson, who was an obvious candidate for the part. Anderson's debut at the Met was soon followed by the appearances of baritone Robert MCFERRIN, SR., and coloratura soprano Mattiwilda DOBBS. In 1954, Dobbs, who had been signed two years earlier by La Scala in Milan, Italy, performed in Richard Strauss's *Ariadne auf Naxos* at New York's Town Hall before making her debut at the San Francisco Opera in 1955 and at the Met in 1956, where she sang Gilda in Verdi's *Rigoletto*. In 1958, soprano Gloria Davy (1936–) became the first African American to sing the role of Aida at the Met.

The engagement of African-American operatic singers without any limitation to a select number of traditionally dark-skinned roles did not fully occur with major opera companies before the 1960s. The career of Mississippi-born Leontyne PRICE marks the acceptance of the African-American diva by the operatic establishment in the United States. In 1955, Price's televised performance of the title role in Giacomo Puccini's *Tosca* caused a sensation; she debuted at the Met six years later, after having established a successful career in Europe. In 1966, Price opened the new Metropolitan Opera House at New York's Lincoln Center in a role especially written for her in the world premiere of Samuel Barber's *Antony and Cleopatra*. (The production was choreographed by Alvin AILEY.) Between 1955 and 1965, ten African-American singers debuted at the Met: Price, Anderson, McFerrin, Davy, Dobbs, Grace Bumbry (1937–), George Shirley (1934–), Martina Arroyo (1939–), Felicia Weathers, and Reri Grist (1932–), who had appeared in the original cast of Leonard Bernstein's *West Side Story* in 1957. Other black singers who came to prominence in the 1950s and 1960s were Margaret Tynes (1929–), Betty Allen (1930–), Hilda Harris (1936–), Gwendolyn Killebrew (1942–), Esther Hinds (1943–), Faye Robinson (1943–), and Shirley VERRETT.

The 1970s and '80s witnessed the recognition of numerous African-American divas, among them Carmen Balthrop (1948–), Barbara Hendricks (1938–), Leona Mitchell (1949–), Roberta Alexander (1949–), and Harolyn Blackwell. The two most prominent African-American women singing in opera in the 1980s and early '90s were soprano Kathleen BATTLE and dramatic soprano Jessye NORMAN. Battle, who rose to fame after starring in a 1975 production of Scott Joplin's *Treemonisha* on Broadway, debuted at the Met as the Shepherd in Richard Wagner's *Tannhäuser* in 1978; Norman sang in the major opera houses of Europe throughout the 1970s before her first appearance at the Met in Berlioz' *Les Troyens* in 1983. In 1991, the two singers performed together in a well-received concert of spirituals at New York City's Carnegie Hall.

Throughout the history of opera in the United States, male African-American singers have not enjoyed the same success as their female counterparts. Many believe that this can be attributed to a reluctance to have black male singers in mixed-race casting. Among those who have been active in opera since the 1970s are Seth McCoy (1928–), Andrew

Frierson (1927–), and McHenry Boatwright (1928–1994). Musical theater has been the dominant genre for Rawn Spearman (1924–), while Thomas Carey (1931–) and Eugene Holmes (1934–) were primarily active in Europe. Bass-baritone Simon ESTES, the first black male singer to star in the Wagner Festival at Bayreuth, Germany, also made his name in Europe in the 1970s before debuting at the Met in 1981. Two singers whose promising careers were cut short, respectively by cancer and AIDS, were baritones Ben Holt (1955–1989) and Bruce Hubbard (1952–1991). Among the leading singers of the current generation are Kevin Short (1960–), Antonio Green (1966–), and Vinson Cole (1950–).

By the beginning of the twentieth century, African Americans had also begun to compose opera, although the lack of financial support frequently made it impossible for their works to be staged. The first significant African-American composer was Harry Lawrence FREEMAN, who wrote fourteen grand-style operas including *The Octoroon* (1904), *Voodoo* (1911), and the early jazz opera *The Flapper* (1929). In addition to being one of the first African Americans to conduct a symphony orchestra in a rendering of his own work—*O Sing a New Song*, presented in Minnesota in 1907—Freeman founded the Freeman School of Music in 1911; the Freeman School of Grand Opera in 1923, and the Negro Opera Company in 1920. Among Freeman's contemporaries was Clarence Cameron WHITE, whose opera *Ouanga*, set in Haiti in the early 1800s, was first presented in a concert version in New York City at the New School for Social Research in 1941. The opera was not staged until 1959, when it was performed at the Central High School Auditorium in South Bend, Ind. Subsequently, it received a successful run with the Dra-Mu Opera Company in Philadelphia. RAGTIME composer Scott JOPLIN never saw a performance of his three-act opera *Treemonisha* (1911) in his lifetime, although his first opera, *A Guest of Honor*, was staged in St. Louis in 1903 (its score is now lost). One of the most respected and prolific composers of the mid twentieth century was William Grant STILL who collaborated with his wife, librettist Verna Arvey, and whose works include *Troubled Island* (1938)—which takes as its subject the Haitian revolt at the turn of the nineteenth century—*Blue Steel* (1935), *A Bayou Legend* (1941), *A Southern Interlude* (1942), and *Highway No. 1, USA* (1963). Ulysses Simpson Kay (1917–) came to prominence in the late 1950s with *The Juggler of Our Lady* (1956), which was followed by such works as *The Capitoline Venus* (1971), *Jubilee* (1976), and *Frederick Douglass* (1986). In recent years, two major operas have been composed by Anthony DAVIS, the founder of the instrumental group Episteme. Davis's *X (The Life and Times of Malcolm*

Anthony Davis at the piano in New York University's Loeb Student Center, 1983. (Allford/Trotman Associates)

X) (libretto by Thulani Davis), premiered at the New York City Opera in 1986; *Under the Double Moon,* with a libretto by Deborah Atherton, premiered at the Opera Theatre in St. Louis in 1989. In 1992 Davis's *Tania,* about the kidnapping and subsequent exploits of newspaper heiress Patricia Hearst, was premiered in Philadelphia by the American Music Theater Festival.

The development of African-American operatic talent has been furthered by the establishment of educational programs and opera companies for aspiring singers. Fisk University, Hampton University, Morgan State University, Virginia State University, and Wilberforce College, all traditionally black schools, have produced major operatic talent. By the mid-twentieth century, several African-American opera companies emerged, including the Imperial Opera Company (1930), the National Negro Opera Company (1941), the Dra-Mu Opera Company (1945), and the Harlem Opera Company (c. 1950). The 1970s witnessed a flourishing of African-American productions with the establishment of two major companies, Opera/South (1970) and the National Ebony Opera (1974), founded specifically to create professional opportunities for African-American performers, writers, conductors, and technicians. In addition to European grand opera, Opera/South has produced such works as William Grant Still's *Highway No. 1, USA* and *A Bayou Legend* (which, though written in 1941, received its world premiere in 1974), and Ulysses Kay's *Jubilee* and *The Juggler of Our Lady.*

As opera has become more accessible to African-American artists, major opera houses have produced new works and also revived lost or neglected works by African-American composers. Leroy Jenkins's *The Mother of Three Sons* premiered at the New York City Opera in 1991. In 1993, Duke ELLINGTON's (1899–1974) unfinished opera, *Queenie Pie,* was performed for the first time at the Brooklyn Academy of Music. The Lyric Opera of Chicago and the American Music Theater Festival in Philadelphia have jointly commissioned a new opera by Anthony Davis, *Amistad,* telling the story of the 1839 capture of the eponymous slave ship and the liberation of its captors. *Amistad* will be premiered in 1997. African-American singers are widely recognized both for their artistic excellence and popular appeal. However, male performers continue to claim that they are not cast as readily as women in European opera. African-American composers continue to encounter resistance to works about African-American subjects. "The opera world is looking for fresh blood," observed librettist Thulani Davis. "Does a black composer have the same shot? I hope the answer is yes."

REFERENCES

DUNCAN, JOHN. "Negro Composers of Opera." *The Negro History Bulletin* (January 1966): 79–80, 93.

HEYMONT, GEORGE. "Blacks in Opera." *Ebony* (November 1981): 32–36.

KORNICK, REBECCA HODELL. *Recent American Opera: A Production Guide.* New York, 1991.

PLOSKI, HARRY A., and JAMES WILLIAMS, eds. *The Negro Almanac.* Detroit, 1989.

ROSEN, CAROLE. *Opera.* Poole, U.K., 1983.

SOUTHERN, EILEEN. *The Music of Black Americans: A History.* New York, 1983.

TROTTER, JAMES M. *Music and Some Highly Musical People.* Boston, 1881.

DOMINIQUE-RENÉ DE LERMA

Operation Breadbasket. Operation Breadbasket was established as an economic arm of the SOUTHERN CHRISTIAN LEADERSHIP CONFERENCE (SCLC) in September 1962 to put "bread, money and income into the baskets of black and poor people." In the early 1960s civil rights activists were increasingly concerned about poverty and unemployment in urban areas. SCLC started Operation Breadbasket to improve the economic situation of African Americans by demanding jobs for black workers and fostering the growth of black businesses. The Rev. Fred C. Bennett, SCLC field secretary, was the first National Director of Operation Breadbasket.

Operation Breadbasket sought to organize black consumers to win economic concessions from major corporations, a tactic modeled on the work of the Rev. Leon SULLIVAN in Philadelphia in the early 1960s. The group encouraged ministers to organize boycotts and pickets to pressure companies to increase African-American employment and strengthen the relationship of large corporations to black-owned businesses. The first Operation Breadbasket campaign was launched in Atlanta, where activists won a commitment for 5,000 jobs over a five-year period. After this victory, affiliates were established in eight southern states and targeted a variety of institutions, including government agencies and laundry firms.

By the mid-1960s, as civil rights activists gradually began to shift their focus to the North, SCLC sought to establish a northern base for Operation Breadbasket. Although chapters were formed in several northern cities, Operation Breadbasket had its biggest influence in Chicago, where it was established in 1966. Jesse JACKSON, a student at Chicago Theological Seminary and later associate pastor at Fellowship Baptist Church, and the Rev. Clay Evans, pastor at Fellowship Baptist Church, met with local ministers and laid the groundwork for a Chicago chapter of Operation Breadbasket.

The first Chicago campaign was directed at Country Delight Dairy Products. In 1966 Operation Breadbasket picketed stores that carried Country Delight until the dairy company agreed to hire forty-four additional black workers. The group moved onto other dairy companies until eventually the entire industry had conceded to the demands. Operation Breadbasket also targeted the supermarket industries, including the A&P, High-Low, and Red Rooster chains, and demanded that they improve their quality and service, hire black workers, and make greater use of black businesses. Jackson came to play the central role in Chicago Operation Breadbasket and in August 1967 the Rev. Dr. Martin Luther KING, Jr., appointed him as national director, hoping to develop Operation Breadbasket into a national organization.

Operation Breadbasket was successful at winning agreements from major corporations, but had few mechanisms in place to ensure compliance. Once a formal agreement was reached, it was difficult to monitor progress. For instance, in May 1967, A&P agreed to hire 770 permanent African-American workers and 1,200 teenagers over the summer. The company did not comply, however, until Operation Breadbasket renewed protests in 1970.

After the initial successes of winning job commitments from large corporations, Operation Breadbasket began to focus on black business development. Activists believed that support for black-owned businesses would improve the economic health of the black community as a whole. In 1967 Operation Breadbasket held a "Trade Exposition and Seminar on Negro Businesses" in Chicago. In 1969 and 1970 this was expanded into the "Black Minorities Business and Cultural Exposition" to advertise black products. They also sponsored a Black Christmas to encourage spiritual affirmation as well as promote black merchandise. At the end of 1969 business leaders formed the Breadbasket Commercial Association, Inc. to institutionalize business interests with Operation Breadbasket.

By 1971 Operation Breadbasket had begun to decline. The group had assumed too many projects. In addition to initiating their own campaigns, they organized free breakfast programs, helped plan the POOR PEOPLE'S WASHINGTON CAMPAIGN in 1968, opposed cuts in welfare, and supported electoral candidates. Operation Breadbasket was also unable to expand into a national organization. This was partly because of a lack of resources and coordination, but some SCLC members felt that Jackson maintained firm control over the organization and that his aim was not to expand Operation Breadbasket but to build his own base in Chicago. This tension constrained Jackson and frustrated the national SCLC leadership. In addition, charges of patronage and financial improprieties were made against Operation Breadbasket which tarnished its image. As a result, Operation Breadbasket was increasingly unable to implement its programs or organize sustained protests.

In December 1971, Jackson left SCLC, dissolved Operation Breadbasket in Chicago, and formed an independent organization, OPERATION PUSH (People United to Serve Humanity) which adopted many of the tactics and goals of Operation Breadbasket. Without Jackson, Operation Breadbasket lost much of its momentum, but in the 1990s it continues to exist as a part of SCLC, although it has no independent program or staff.

REFERENCES

MASSONI, GARY. "Perspectives on Operation Breadbasket." In David J. Garrow, ed. *Chicago 1966: Open Housing Marches, Summit Negotiations, and Operation Breadbasket*. Brooklyn, N.Y., 1989.

REYNOLD, BARBARA. *Jesse Jackson: The Man, the Movement, the Myth*. Chicago, 1975.

PAM NADASEN

Operation PUSH (People United to Serve Humanity). Founded in late 1971 by the Reverend Jesse JACKSON, Chicago-based Operation PUSH has always advocated a program demanding greater support of black-owned or -operated businesses and strongly encouraging corporations to hire more minority employees. With Jackson as its charismatic leader, Operation PUSH organized boycotts of companies unwilling to make agreements requiring increased minority hiring; combining his oratorical skills and national influence, Jackson was capable of effectively threatening the business of recalcitrant corporations. Originally called People United to Save Humanity, Operation PUSH grew out of, and originally had an agenda very similar to, the SOUTHERN CHRISTIAN LEADERSHIP CONFERENCE's Operation Breadbasket, which Jackson headed until 1971.

One of its initiatives, PUSH for Excellence, or PUSH/EXCEL, was another plan inspired by Jackson to empower African Americans, this time through education. In the later 1970s PUSH/EXCEL received much national attention and substantial amounts of federal and private aid to establish programs to help minority schoolchildren. Several years later, auditors' reports concluded that the organization lacked concrete goals and an effective administrative structure. While it was scaled down considerably, PUSH/EXCEL continued to attempt to make schooling for black children a more enriching experience.

When Jackson left Operation PUSH in 1983 to lead his presidential campaign, the organization foundered. By the end of the 1980s it was financially insecure after a poorly supported boycott of the sporting goods company Nike left it deeply in debt. In early 1991 PUSH was forced to lay off temporarily all twelve of its salaried workers. After a plea from Jackson, prominent African Americans, black businesses, and community groups cooperated to raise the funds necessary to return Operation PUSH to a more sound financial footing.

Although he no longer held an official leadership position, Jesse Jackson remained a spokesman and adviser for Operation PUSH. In 1991 he announced a political agenda for Operation PUSH that was similar to the campaigns of the early 1980s, but that incorporated pressing new concerns, such as the AIDS crisis and the problem of Haitian refugees. Operation PUSH continued to be a vocal advocate of black enterprise and entrepreneurs and continued to urge African-American youths to stay in school and not to use drugs or alcohol. In 1993 Jackson announced an Operation PUSH campaign to "save the children" of Chicago. This was part of a larger effort on the part of progressive black organizations to curb urban violence and increase opportunities for African-American children. Other initiatives forwarded by PUSH in the 1990s included cultural sensitivity training for police officers and proposals that youthful first-time criminal offenders be counseled by local ministers. In 1993, led by national executive director Janette Wilson and chief executive officer Rev. Willie T. Barrow, Operation PUSH continued its crusade for an empowered black community.

REFERENCES

HOUSE, ERNEST R. *Jesse Jackson and the Politics of Charisma: The Rise and Fall of the PUSH/Excel Program.* Boulder, Colo., 1988.

REYNOLDS, BARBARA. *Jesse Jackson: The Man, the Movement, the Myth.* Chicago, 1975.

JOHN C. STONER

Opportunity: Journal of Negro Life. *Opportunity* was the official organ of the NATIONAL URBAN LEAGUE; the first issue appeared in January 1923. Under the editorship of sociologist Charles Spurgeon JOHNSON, the journal tried to approach African-American life though a self-consciously "scientific" point of view, in contrast to the supposedly subjective emphasis of the NATIONAL ASSOCIATION FOR THE ADVANCEMENT OF COLORED PEOPLE journal CRISIS and its editor, W. E. B. DU BOIS.

Opportunity's circulation grew from 4,000 in 1923 to 11,000 in 1927. Despite its supposed concentration on sociology, during the 1920s the magazine played an important role in encouraging young writers and artists of the HARLEM RENAISSANCE. It sponsored yearly literary contests and award dinners at which writers such as Langston HUGHES and Countee CULLEN met contacts who would eventually publish their work. Among early contributors to *Opportunity* were James Weldon JOHNSON, Claude MCKAY, Angelina Weld GRIMKE, Gwendolyn BENNETT, and Sterling BROWN.

The era of optimism and creative ferment at *Opportunity* subsided somewhat with the departure of Johnson in 1929. He was succeeded by Elmer A. Carter, who published much poetry and fiction but emphasized the original vision of *Opportunity* as a sociological journal. The 1930s saw dissent on the editorial board concerning the role of the magazine. The declining circulation worried some, who argued that *Opportunity* should be a popular magazine. Others thought that it should serve mainly as the house organ of the National Urban League. The board never decided on a single policy, so *Opportunity* served a variety of purposes throughout the 1930s, printing news, economic and social criticism, poetry, short stories, and articles about the Urban League. Literary criticism flourished in regular contributions by Alain LOCKE and Sterling Brown. Carter even attempted in 1931 to revive the literary contests, which had ended in 1928. But the GREAT DEPRESSION strained *Opportunity*'s ability to publish, as private donations shriveled up and as individual subscriptions were harder to sell.

The 1940s were no easier, as wartime rationing limited paper and printing supplies. In an April 1942 editorial, Carter described the journal's dire financial straits and appealed for additional funds from its readers. Carter resigned later that year and was replaced by Madeline Aldridge. *Opportunity* began publishing on a quarterly basis in January 1943. Its content and style did not change significantly but did focus on African Americans' perceptions of the war. Despite the financial difficulties the journal faced, it remained an important forum for wartime discussions of racial equality and freedom and emerged as a champion of integration. After WORLD WAR II, *Opportunity* published fewer literary pieces, as the rise of periodicals dedicated to black artistic advancement provided another "proving ground" for young talent. Dutton Ferguson assumed editorship in 1947. *Opportunity,* however, had seen its best days. Its last issue appeared in 1949.

REFERENCES

DANIEL, WALTER C. *Black Journals of the United States.* Westport, Conn., 1982.

JOHNSON, ABBY ARTHUR, and RONALD MAYBERRY JOHNSON. *Propaganda and Aesthetics: The Literary Politics of Afro-American Magazines in the Twentieth Century.* Amherst, Mass., 1979.

ELIZABETH MUTHER

Oratory. Oratory as it is generally understood refers to the practice of eloquent public speaking. In Aristotle's classic formulation oratory, or rhetoric, is that branch of discourse which involves the persuasive use of the spoken word.

Aristotle defined three primary types of persuasive oratory: (1) *forensic,* the judicial oratory of the classroom, the purpose of which is to prove the justice or injustice of some past action; (2) *epideictic,* the oratory of ceremony, the purpose of which is to display sentiments appropriate to such formal occasions as dedications, commemorations, inaugurations, and funerals; and (3) *deliberative,* the oratory of the public forum, the purpose of which is to persuade an audience to act or to accept a particular point of view as to the future. While the Aristotelian categorization of

oratory provides a useful system through which to understand African-American oratory, it is important to note that the African-American oratorical tradition's links both to Anglo-American Protestant evangelism and to traditional African oratorical practice provide it with a character quite distinct from the classical forms of oratory formulated by Aristotle.

From Anglo-American Protestantism black oratory adopted the rhetorical form of the jeremiad, a sermon form that combines several of the Aristotelian types of oratory into a single discourse. The jeremiad typically has three structural elements: an opening reference to the promise of the past, a central criticism of the present failure to realize that promise, and a closing declaration of the future redemption of that promise. For the African-American oratorical tradition, the thematic promise of the jeremiad has remained constant: It is the attainment of freedom from slavery, of equal rights, and of collective empowerment. While most of the great African-American orators have envisaged the fulfillment of this promise to secure equality for African Americans as coming in the United States, others have argued that its fulfillment is to be realized through a return to Africa and the establishment of a free African homeland. In both cases, figurative imagery of Africa as a lost physical, cultural, and spiritual paradise plays a central role in the imagination of future freedom and equality.

As the religious origins of the jeremiad indicate, the African-American oratorical tradition has strong links to American religious thought. Many of the greatest African-American political orators have been preachers, and black political oratory generally employs Biblical language and imagery with great effect. African-American oratory also has strong roots in the sermonizing of black folk preachers, and the jeremiad as a rhetorical form is very well suited to the characteristic calm-to-storm structure of the folk sermon. With its movement from a slow, deliberate opening to an increasingly cadenced and assertive middle section to a rapturous, climactic conclusion, the calm-to-storm sermon mirrors in oratorical style the argumentative structure of the jeremiad.

While the Bible has provided the central written text for African-American oratory, early black folk preachers and orators, many of whom were illiterate, were also influenced by the primarily oral nature of traditional West African oratory. In traditional West African society storytellers (known as griots) and learned expositors of customary lore and law employed oratory as a powerful means of ensuring the unity and stability of the community. The use of such rhetorical devices as call-and-response exchanges with listeners and rhythmic repetition of words and phrases is characteristic of such oral traditions, and in the African-American oratorical tradition it has become an effective means of endowing oratory with the power of communal ritual.

Because slavery deprived African Americans of significant access to print, folk oratory became a powerful resource in early African-American efforts to establish and maintain a unified sense of community and shared purpose. Despite the celebratory and unifying nature of some of the traditions that contributed to the development of African-American oratory, the conditions of slavery and of subsequent discrimination and segregation faced by the black community created an African-American oratorical tradition that is characteristically denunciatory and exhortatory, concerned not only with fashioning community and consensus but also with depicting injustice and demanding redress. The most powerful use of black oratory has been as a means of protesting against the institutions of slavery, segregation, and discrimination.

Although oratory is a verbal art, recorded examples of early black oratory are extremely rare. But it is possible to gain some sense of eighteenth- and nineteenth-century oratory through the printed work of prominent early African-American writers, some of whom were also noted orators. The earliest work preserved includes that of prerevolutionary figures such as Jupiter HAMMON, Phillis WHEATLEY, Olaudah EQUIANO, George Moses HORTON, John MARRANT, and Benjamin BANNEKER. Although most were remarkable for their forthright condemnation of slavery, Jupiter Hammon, the first African-American author to publish exhortatory work, gained prominence as a religious author and apologist for slavery. In his "Address to the Negroes in the State of New York," the central role of the Bible as an authoritative oratorical text is already quite apparent. However, as Hammon's speech makes clear, the Bible was sometimes employed to justify slavery rather than condemn it:

> Now whether it is right, and lawful, in the sight of God, for them to make slaves of us or not, I am certain that while we are slaves, it is our duty to obey our masters. . . . The apostle Paul says, "Servants, be obedient to them that are your masters. . . . Not with eye service, as men pleasers, but as the servants of Christ doing the will of God. . . ."

With the flood of ideas and liberation rhetoric that accompanied the American and French revolutions and especially the Haitian revolution of 1801, black orators began to construct their own liberation rhetoric. Arguments against slavery were strengthened and extended by appeals to African-related themes found in the Bible and in history, providing African Americans with a greater sense of cultural history, unity, and purpose. A particularly good example of this new development is Prince HALL's "Charge Delivered to the Brethren of the African Lodge, Charlestown, Massachusetts" of June 25, 1792. Hall, the founder of African-American Masonry, began by citing "some of our forefathers, for our imitation," and providing brief portraits of Tertullian, Cyprian, St. Augustine, and Fulgentius, all North African fathers of the Roman Catholic church. After giving his audience this sense of a distinguished African historical community, Hall encouraged them to follow the example of those forefathers despite "being deprived of the means of education in your younger days, as you see it is at this day with our children." Although such deprivation was unjust and discouraging, Hall concluded by urging his audience to "have patience, and look forward to a better day; Hear what the great Architect of the universal world saith, *Aethiopia shall stretch forth her hands unto me.*"

Hall makes use here of the oldest and one of the most frequently employed metaphors for the fulfillment of the promise of freedom and equality for African Americans—the Biblical verse concerning Egypt and Ethiopia: "Princes shall come out of Egypt; Ethiopia shall soon stretch forth her hands unto God" (Ps. 68:31). By interpreting Ethiopia as a reference to all African, black preachers and political orators from the time of Hall to the present have been able to present the promise of the future as a destiny ordained for all Africans by God.

Another example of oratory inspired by Africa is William Hamilton's 1815 "Oration on the Abolition of the Slave Trade" in New York, an address heavily weighted toward the promise and history of Africa and the violation of that continent by Europeans. Hamilton's Africa is first presented rationally and scientifically as the probable site of the origin of man and of a great and peaceable kingdom. That kingdom, however, has been violated, and Hamilton shifts to an emotional portrayal of the loss of Africa as the loss of Eden:

> O! Africa, thou first fair garden of God's planting, thou once delightful field and original nursery for all those delicious fruits, tasteful herbage, and fragrant plants, that man highly prises, thou track of earth over which the blest luminary, the sun, delights to make his daily splendid pass, thou spot of earth, where fair science first descended and the arts first began to bud and grow; how art thou chang'd and fallen.

By 1830 black orators and writers had gained the confidence to attack slavery with vehemence in all public forums, not only in front of black audiences. The most noteworthy of these attacks was made by the free black David Walker (1785–1830) of Boston, one of the first black orators to employ the jeremiad as an aggressive and militant argument for abolition. In his *Appeal to the Coloured Citizens of the World* (1830), Walker called for universal emancipation. Although the *Appeal* is a written document, it provides a good indication of the characteristics of Walker's militant abolitionist oratory. Taking his inspiration from the success of the black Haitian liberator Toussaint L'Ouverture, Walker argued that all blacks were linked by chains of blood and destiny and that there could be no emancipation of American blacks without simultaneous emancipation of blacks in Africa and in the West Indies. Walker was not only a pioneer in liberation oratory but also one of the first African Americans to employ Protestant evangelical oratory both to condemn slavery and to critique white culture as a whole.

Uncompromising oratory such as Walker's and that of the white abolitionist William Lloyd Garrison, an equally vehement orator, helped set the stage for more intense antislavery oratory by both blacks and whites in the abolition movement. The general approach of these orators was to carry the rhetoric of liberation directly to the masses through open-air platform oratory that focused on the horrors and atrocities of slavery as an American institution. Among the primary sources of audience attraction during antislavery rallies were the many fugitive slaves who narrated in graphic and poignant language their personal experiences in bondage.

Narrative oratory developed into a powerful rhetorical form as orators combined personal experience with vigorous antislavery arguments. One of its pioneers was the ex-slave Henry Highland Garnet, who often opened his verbal assault on slavery with the words "I was born in slavery and have escaped to tell you and others what the monster has done and is still doing." At a time when most antislavery orators adopted a rhetoric of argumentation and moral persuasion, Garnet openly called for violent insurrection as the only means to lasting liberation. In *An Address to the Slaves of the United States of America* (1843), Garnet, as a militant advocate bent on insurrection, passionately called his listeners to arms:

> Brethen, arise, arise! Strike for your lives and liberties, now is the day and the hour. Let every slave throughout the land do this, and the days of slavery are numbered. You cannot be more oppressed than you have been—you cannot suffer greater cruelties than you suffer already. Rather die free men than live to be slaves. Remember that you are four millions!

Part of the reason that fugitive slave narratives were such powerful reinforcements to oratorical attacks on slavery as an institution was that they functioned as a form of testimony—a direct relation of the facts of experience—which carried a naturally greater ring of truth and persuasiveness that could be obtained by even the most closely reasoned abstract arguments. Because of this direct, unadorned force the fugitive slave narrative also served as a very effective vehicle for oratory directed against the unequal treatment of women. Sojourner TRUTH, an emancipated slave who became a noted orator against slavery, also gained prominence as an advocate of women's rights. The direct and colloquial bearing of her 1851 speech "Woman's Rights" provides some indication of the power of testimonial argument.

> Look at my arm! I have ploughed, and planted and gathered into barns, and no man could head me! And a'n't I a woman? I could work as much and eat as much as a man—when I could get it—and bear de lash as well! And a'n't I a woman? I have borne thirteen chilern, and seen 'em mos' all sold off to slavery, and when I cried out with my mother's grief, none but Jesus heard me! And a'n't I a woman?

In addition to Sojourner Truth, other celebrated African-American abolitionist orators of the pre–Civil War period include Charles Lenox REMOND, Samuel Ringgold WARD, Martin R. DELANEY, William Wells BROWN, Harriet TUBMAN, J. W. C. PENNINGTON, Alexander Crummell, James McCune SMITH, and Frederick Augustus Washington Bailey, better known as Frederick DOUGLASS. It was Douglass who best exemplified the abolitionist oratorical style.

While still a young boy in slavery, Douglass had read avidly and recited endlessly the various gems of British and American political speech making contained in *The Columbian Orator,* a popular instructional anthology of oratory first published in 1797. After his escape to freedom, Douglass honed his talent by giving numerous antislavery speeches under the auspices of William Lloyd Garrison's American Anti-Slavery Society. But it was only after his break with Garrison in the late 1840s (Garrison did not permit his protégés, white or black, much room for independent thought) that Douglass entered his full maturity as an orator. Douglass combined lacerating indignation at the institution of slavery with a sense of the profound failure of the ideals of American liberty in confronting the challenge of slavery. In his 1852 Rochester, N.Y., address, "The Meaning of July Fourth for the Negro," he challenged the deepest beliefs of his audience.

> What, to the American slave, is your Fourth of July? I answer; a day that reveals to him, more than all other days in the years, the gross injustice

and cruelty to which he is the constant victim. To him, your celebration is a sham; your boasted liberty, an unholy license; your national greatness, swelling vanity; your sounds of rejoicing are empty and heartless; your denunciations of tyrants, brass-fronted impudence; your shouts of liberty and equality, hollow mockery; your prayers and hymns, your sermons and thanksgivings, with all your religious parade, and solemnity, are, to him, mere bombast, fraud, deception, impiety, and hypocrisy—a thin veil to cover up crimes which would disgrace a nation of savages.

Douglass remained an eloquent spokesman for African Americans through the Civil War and Reconstruction and until his death in 1895. Despite the abolition of slavery and the attempts during Reconstruction to secure fundamental rights for African Americans, it became apparent during the last quarter of the nineteenth century that resistance to African-American equality was not only strong but apparently increasing. After a brief period of optimistic celebration, black oratory once more became primarily concerned with the problems of racial discrimination, now manifested in a more subtle way by institutionalized segregation.

Among the gifted orators of the postbellum years are Alexander CRUMMELL, Henry McNeal TURNER, and George Washington MURRAY, but the most influential orator of the late nineteenth century was undoubtedly Booker T. WASHINGTON. Washington's oratory is in many ways a radical departure from the tradition of black political oratory. Reacting to the environment of growing institutionalized racism, Washington advocated a policy of political accommodation paired with economic advancement as the only feasible path for the advancement of African Americans. Washington's most famous speech, the cornerstone of his national fame, was his address to an audience of prominent white Southerners at the Cotton States' Exposition in Atlanta on September 18, 1895. It remains the single most controversial oration in African-American history. In the speech, which advocated accommodation to southern segregation, Washington characteristically avoids all of the confrontational elements of the antislavery jeremiad. His tone is restrained, conciliatory, and respectful, the structure of the address is deliberative, as Washington merely lays out his theme and then discusses it in detail; rather than taking the position of the oppressed so as to confront the establishment, Washington adopts the position of the establishment so as to criticize and challenge the black worker:

To those of my race who depend on bettering their condition in a foreign land or who underestimate the importance of cultivating friendly relations with the Southern white man, who is their next-door neighbour, I would say: "Cast down your bucket where you are"—cast it down in making friends in every manly way of the people of all races by whom we are surrounded.

Washington's policies were accepted at first my most African Americans as the most advisable, pragmatic position in view of the difficult situation. However, within a few years such a conciliatory position seemed to many African Americans to be wholly insufficient as a means of improving their situation. The decisive challenge to accommodation was soon put forward by Washington's rival for leadership of the African-American community, W. E. B. DU BOIS. Though Du Bois was better known as a writer than as an orator, he was a master of committed political rhetoric as well as being one of the greatest writers of his generation. Du Bois proposed an aggressive program that would challenge the legal boundaries of American social and political life, demanding immediate social and political integration so that African Americans would exercise "the right of freemen to walk, talk, and be with them that wish to be with us." In his "Niagara Address to the Nation," delivered at the second annual conference of the NIAGARA MOVEMENT at Harpers Ferry, W. Va., in 1906, Du Bois invoked the spirit of John Brown and revived the aggressive jeremiad oratory of Frederick Douglass. After lamenting the regression of the political and economic situation of African Americans since the Civil War, he declared the Niagara movement's unceasing devotion to the struggle for equality. Playing on the lyrics of the "Star-Spangled Banner," he represented the battle for equality as one that concerned the ideals of the entire nation. "It is a fight for ideals, lest this, our common fatherland, false to its founding, become in truth the land of the thief and the home of the slave—a byword and a hissing among the nations for its sounding pretensions and pitiful accomplishment." True to the jeremiad tradition, Du Bois concluded on an optimistic, prophetic note: "And we shall win. The past promised it, the present fortells it. . . . All across the skies sit signs of promise. . . . The morning breaks over the blood-stained hills."

Du Bois's leadership and outspoken oratory marked the beginning of the twentieth century's tradition of aggressive advocacy for civil rights. There were a variety of rhetorical and oratorical strategies employed by civil rights advocates, ranging from the almost impassioned rhetorical denunciations of accommodationism and segregation of William Monroe TROTTER and A. Philip RANDOLPH to the more measured, though equally antisegregationist, oratory of leaders such as Walter WHITE, Mary McLeod BETHUNE, Roy WILKINS, and Whitney YOUNG, Jr.

The opening decades of the twentieth century were also marked by a significant increase in African nationalism. The central biblical metaphor of "Ethiopia stretching out her hands" was effectively recycled into the philosophy of a new nationalist movement, the UNIVERSAL NEGRO IMPROVEMENT ASSOCIATION, led by Marcus GARVEY. In a speech delivered at Liberty Hall in New York City during the Second International Convention of Negroes in August 1921, Garvey combined the language of antislavery oratory with that of an emergent black nationalism:

> It falls to our lot to tear off the shackles that bind Mother Africa. Can you do it? You did it in the Revolutionary War. You did it in the Civil War; you did it at the battles of the Marne and Verdun; you did it in Mesopotamia. You can do it now marching up the battle heights of Africa. Let the world know that 400,000,000 Negroes are prepared to die or live as free men.

Despite the strength of Garvey's nationalist movement, the main course of African-American political oratory remained with efforts to gain equality for African Americans within American society. Many of the prominent national leaders of this struggle in the 1930s and '40s viewed the law as the central battleground for black rights and the courtroom rather than the auditorium as the critical venue. It took decades for this slow, patient strategy to yield significant results, culminating in the 1954 *Brown* v. *Board of Education* decision.

The succeeding two decades witnessed a remarkable flowering of black oratory as black Americans employed diverse oratorical strategies in a determined effort to win the fight against segregation and discrimination. The two major oratorical figures of this era were the Rev. Dr. Martin Luther KING, Jr., and MALCOLM X, contrasting in their approach and their goals but united in their commitment to challenge American racism. Both men recognized the need to move the struggle from the courtrooms to the streets, from the law libraries to the churches and mosques, from the mind to the soul.

Martin Luther King, Jr., came to national attention through his role in the 1955 Montgomery, Ala., bus boycott. Through King's leadership the boycott grew into a movement and spread across the South. In his assault on white resistance, King was a shrewd tactician of the direct-action nonviolent movement. In his capacity as a black preacher, he was able to harness to the movement the one element that had sustained and buttressed black America since slavery—the black church. The ideological theme that King adopted for his national resistance movement was "love your enemies, for they know not what they do." Through the use of biblical allusion and the eloquent cadences of pulpit address, King's oratory picked up the traditional stylistic devices of black political oratory and allied them to the moral and political force of nonviolent protest.

While King's appeals to love and to nonviolence enabled him to gain considerable support from the northern white liberal establishment, these same fundamental tenets proved increasingly frustrating during the 1960s as the pace of social change slowed and the problems King confronted became more complex and intractable. In fact, there had always been a tension in King's oratory between the patience that many associated with nonviolence and the urgent need for action that was felt within the civil rights movement. As King declared in his *Letter from a Birmingham Jail* in 1962, "justice too long delayed is justice denied." Nonetheless King's oratory is generally known for a determined optimism that is not at odds with urgency but is in fact grounded on an unshakable conviction as to the moral and ethical rightness of the civil rights movement.

During the March on Washington of August 28, 1963, more than 250,000 Americans—about sixty thousand of them white—gathered in Washington, D.C., and marched to the Lincoln Memorial. Late in the afternoon King came to the lectern and delivered his "I Have a Dream" speech. After reading for several minutes from a prepared text, he began to improvise, sharing with the crowd his vision of a new society in a slowly building conclusion that exemplifies the power of the jeremiad form. In this passage, perhaps the most famous in all his oratory, King skillfully makes use of the repetitive cadences of the phrase "I have a dream" to magnify the unifying effect of the culminating biblical passage:

> I have a dream that one day this nation will rise up. . . .
> I have a dream that my four little children will one day . . . not be judged by the color of their skin but by the content of their character.
> I have a dream today!
> I have a dream that one day every valley shall be exalted and every hill and mountain shall be made low, the rough places will be made plain, and the crooked places will be made straight, and the glory of the Lord shall be revealed, and all flesh shall see it together.

King's speech concluded with an elevated and memorable coda on the capacity of the American political system to be inclusive and to overcome old barriers and animosities:

> When we let freedom ring, when we let it ring from every village and hamlet, from every state and every city, we will be able to speed up that day when all of God's children, black men and

The Rev. Dr. Martin Luther King, Jr., addressing a crowd on May 12, 1965. King frequently went on brief northern tours to publicize and finance his efforts with the SCLC. (Prints and Photographs Division, Library of Congress)

white men, Jews and Gentiles, Protestants and Catholics, will be able to join hands and sing in the words of that old Negro spiritual: "Free at last! Free at last! Thank God Almighty, we are free at last!"

In sharp contrast to the church-based oratory of King is the militant and retaliatory rhetoric of Malcolm X, who called for total separation from white America and the establishment of a black nationalist state in America. Despite the lack of support given to Malcolm X by the national civil rights organizations, he was so successful as a public orator that he quickly gained adherents to his militant position on race relations. As a Muslim, Malcolm X had little recourse

in his oratory to biblical metaphors, nor did he often adopt the sort of revelatory, ecstatic closing exemplified in King's "I Have a Dream" speech. Instead Malcolm X employed carefully constructed repetitive sentence structures that would clarify the course of his reasoning, simplifying and organizing the logic of a usually incisive attack on accepted ideas about race relations. In the following selection from his speech in Detroit to the Northern Negro Grass Roots Leadership Conference (November 10, 1963), he employs these strategies to dismiss conciliatory attitudes in relation to the civil rights struggle and to address a jeremiad against those of his audience who held such views:

As long as the white man sent you to Korea, you bled. He sent you to Germany, you bled. He sent you to the South Pacific to fight the Japanese, you bled. You bleed for white people, but when it comes to seeing your own church being bombed and little black girls murdered, you haven't got any blood. You bleed when the white man says bleed; you bite when the white man says bite; and you bark when the white man says bark.

Following the deaths of both Malcolm X and Martin Luther King, Jr., the focus of the civil rights struggle shifted from the streets and community centers to the halls of Congress and from there to the campaign trail leading to the White House itself. The two outstanding orators who best represent this shift are Barbara JORDAN and the Rev. Jesse JACKSON. Elected as a member of the House of Representatives from the state of Texas in 1972, Jordan quickly distinguished herself as an unrelenting advocate of equal rights for blacks and for women and as an outstanding orator willing to confront difficult issues. In 1975 she became widely known for her participation in the impeachment debates following the Watergate cover-up, and in 1976 she became the first African-American woman invited to deliver the keynote address at a Democratic national convention. Through her oratorical brilliance Jordan paved the way for fuller participation by blacks and women in national political life.

Jesse Jackson, a devoted follower of Martin Luther King, Jr., in the SOUTHERN CHRISTIAN LEADERSHIP CONFERENCE (SCLC), gained national prominence as a spokesperson for black issues following his mentor's death in 1968. A preacher by background, like King, Jackson worked initially in communities across the United States, attempting both to instill hope in his audiences and to inspire them for the political struggles that lay ahead.

Since the 1970s Jackson has become a direct and frank critic of the internal problems that plague the African-American community—drugs, family instability, inadequate education, unemployment, self-destructive values, and a host of others. Because of the severity of these internal problems, one of Jackson's aims has been simply to provide the black community with the strength to confront and survive them. His oratory is structured around messages of hope and survival that are often formulated as ritualistic chants and slogans: "Repeat after me, 'I may be poor, but I am Somebody!'"; "Down with dope, up with hope"; "Red, Yellow, Black, White, all are precious in God's sight." Although dissenters accused Jackson of being gimmicky and manipulative, such affective appeals serve an important psychological function, one rooted in the experience and suffering of people in need of hope, healing, and a sense of community.

In the early 1990s no voice spoke as eloquently or as poignantly about the needs of African Americans as that of Marian Wright EDELMAN, who started her career as a lawyer working with the poor in Mississippi and in 1973 founded the Children's Defense Fund, an advocacy organization for children, particularly poor, minority, and handicapped children. Edelman's oratory, like Jackson's, is intended to sustain an audience that often feels discouraged, ignored, or willfully misunderstood: "One has to remember the seasons. . . . That in the barest points of winter, one really does have to remember that leaves and buds are beginning to blossom now in a new recognition by the country that it is in deep trouble."

By embodying the experiences, the aspirations, the struggles, and the demands of the African-American community, oratory operates at a suprapersonal level and functions to unite a discontented but determined people. As such, oratory remains a sustaining legacy in the life, culture, and history of African Americans.

REFERENCES

BARKSDALE, RICHARD, and KENNETH KINNAMON, eds. *Black Writers of America.* New York, 1972.

BREITMAN, GEORGE, ed. *Malcolm X Speaks: Selected Speeches and Statements.* 2nd ed. New York, 1989.

FONER, PHILIP S., ed. *The Voice of Black America: Major Speeches by Negroes in the United States, 1797–1971.* New York, 1972.

GLENN, ROBERT W. *Black Rhetoric: A Guide to Afro-American Communication.* Metuchen, N.J., 1976.

HOWARD-PITNEY, DAVID. *The Afro-American Jeremiad: Appeals for Justice in America.* Philadelphia, 1990.

JACQUES-GARVEY, AMY, ed. *The Philosophy and Opinions of Marcus Garvey.* 1922, 1925. Reprint. New York, 1992.

MEIER, AUGUST, ELLIOT RUDWICK, and FRANCIS L. BRODERICK, eds. *Black Protest Thought in the Twentieth Century.* 2nd ed. Indianapolis, 1971.

MILLER, KEITH D. *Voice of Deliverance: The Language of Martin Luther King, Jr., and Its Sources.* New York, 1992.

PORTER, DOROTHY, ed. *Early Negro Writing: 1760–1837.* Boston, 1971.

WALKER, ROBBIE JEAN, ed. *The Rhetoric of Struggle: Public Address by African American Women.* New York, 1992.

RICHARD L. WRIGHT

Oregon. African Americans visited Oregon as early as 1579, when the mixed-race crew of Francis Drake stopped there during his global circumnavigation. The first documented African American in Oregon was Markus Lopeus, who arrived in August 1788 as a member of the crew of the *Lady Washington,* a vessel owned by Boston businessmen wanting to enter the fur trade with the natives of the northwest coast. The *Lady Washington,* captained by explorer Robert Gray, stopped first at the Cape Verde islands to take on supplies. There, Gray hired Lopeus, a native, as cabin boy. Lopeus was killed in an encounter with native inhabitants at Tillamook, Ore. The best-known early African-American explorer was York, the slave of William Clark of the Lewis and Clark expedition.

African Americans were also present in the frontier activities of the British, French, and Spanish in Oregon. During the fur-trading era (1820–1840), the western frontier appeared to provide an appealing alternative for African Americans to the rigid slave system of the South and the harsh discrimination of the North and East. Upon their arrival, however, many African Americans discovered that their status in what would become Oregon was problematic.

The wagon trains of the antebellum era (1843–1859) brought pioneers who carried with them the seeds of violent race-based controversy. The persistent antiblack traditions of the pioneer period assured that, at least until World War II, Oregon would attract little African-American migration. For example, in 1850, a black woman, Rose Allen, rode to Oregon hidden in a large box. The white family with whom she traveled feared the uncertainty of her status in the western territories and allowed her to emerge only at night.

On the other hand, some African Americans prospered. Moses "Black" Harris, a former mountain man, was a well-known guide. George Washington Bush was already a prosperous man when he arrived in the Northwest at the age of fifty-two. He settled with his family in the area of present-day Washington state. A former employee of the Hudson's Bay Company, he turned to farming and was so successful that in one year when wheat was in short supply he turned down high prices for his crop, and gave grain and seed to his neighbors so that they would not have to go without. He played a principal role in retaining Washington for the United States when the division of the old Oregon territory was negotiated with the British in 1846.

The Organic Code of the Oregon territory's provisional government banned slavery in 1843, but a year later passed a black exclusion law. When Oregon became an official U.S. territory in 1849, a new black exclusion law was adopted. This provision was temporarily repealed in 1853, but when Oregon became a state in 1859, the state constitution included an article forbidding black residence, employment, property holding, and voting. Oregon supported the Union in the CIVIL WAR, but supplemented earlier antiblack legislation with new laws banning African Americans from juries, establishing a black poll tax, and forbidding interracial marriages. Although the exclusion law was rarely enforced (in fact, records suggest that only one black man, Jacob Vanderpool in 1851, was expelled from Oregon because of his race), it was not repealed until 1926. The ban against interracial marriage remained law until 1955.

The establishment of JIM CROW laws proceeded in the late nineteenth century, and in 1906 the State Supreme Court pronounced them legal. It is a testament to the effectiveness of the antiblack laws of Oregon's pioneer and early statehood periods that the African-American presence there continued to be small through the eve of WORLD WAR II. The census of 1850 listed 207 African Americans in Oregon, although this figure may overrepresent the black population at the time. The number of black residents did not exceed 1,000 until the 1890 census (the actual count was 1,186); by 1920 it reached 2,144 (0.3 percent of the total population); it increased only to 2,565, or 0.2 percent of the population, by 1940. Perhaps because of this legacy of hostility, Oregon was not a destination of African Americans during the Great Migration of the interwar years.

Nonetheless, an "accommodation" emerged in this era around racial matters, which was understood and tolerated uneasily on each side of the color line. For African Americans, it meant relative freedom from the overt forms of racial hatred and violence found in other regions as long as they kept within their assigned "place." Within certain limits, African Americans were able to resist oppression and plan a better future. One unintended result of segregation, for example, was the emergence of an active black business community. The black-owned Golden West Hotel of Portland, catering to African-American railroad workers, was the largest such enterprise west of the Mississippi River.

The "accommodation," however, did not mean an absence of racial tension. In the 1920s, Oregon had the largest KU KLUX KLAN movement in the western United States. The Klan held full-regalia parades, practiced terrorism, and exercised significant political power, electing a member governor in 1923. Because the African-American population was so small, the Klan's primary targets were Jews, Catholics, and other non-Protestants.

By the 1930s, the organized influence of the Klan declined due to internal conflicts and financial fraud. The economic hardships of the GREAT DEPRESSION, however, hardened the lines of the racial status quo. Many of the black-owned businesses that had previously thrived collapsed.

World War II was the turning point in the modern African-American experience in Oregon. Portland became the center of a large shipbuilding industry, and thousands of African Americans were recruited and imported to work in the Kaiser Shipyards there. From 1940 to 1943 the area's black population increased tenfold, to over twenty thousand.

During and following the war, the new resources of population size and economic power produced political activism that transformed Oregon African-American life. But the state's attitudes toward blacks continued to exhibit two conflicting tendencies. The passage of laws concerning fair employment (1949), public accommodations (1953), and fair housing (1957) characterized a new era of black civil rights, and some African Americans, through skill, circumstances, and hard work, rose to impressive heights of influence. Still, Oregon continued to have a reputation among African Americans as a place where considerable private prejudice survived, and many blacks continued to suffer the legacies of earlier discrimination. The last third of the twentieth century has seen a continuation of some of these tendencies, as witnessed in part by a new wave of radical racialism in the form of neo-Nazi and skinhead activity.

By the 1990 census, Oregon's African-American population had reached 46,178, representing 1.6 percent of the total population. Most of the black population is centered in Portland, the state's largest city, and its two suburban counties, Washington and Multnomah (with a combined total of 37,191 black residents). The only other Oregon counties with African-American populations exceeding 2,000 were Marion County (site of the state capitol and location of the state prison), with 2,132, and Lane County (site of Eugene, the state's second-largest city and location of a major state university), with 2,107. The black presence in rural central and eastern Oregon is very sparse. Six such counties have single-digit black population figures and two counties, Sherman and Gilliam, have no African-American residents at all.

REFERENCES

DOUGLASS, JESSIE. "Origins of the Population in Oregon in 1950." *Pacific Northwest Quarterly* 41 (April 1950): 100–101.
HOROWITZ, DAVID A. "The Klansman as Outsider." *Pacific Northwest Quarterly* (January 1989): 12–20.
McLAGAN, ELIZABETH. *A Peculiar Paradise: A History of Blacks in Oregon, 1788–1940.* Portland, Oreg., 1980.
MILLNER, DARRELL. "The Death of Markus Lopeus: Fact or Fantasy? First Documented Presence of a Black Man in Oregon, August 16, 1788." *Trotter Institute Review* (Summer 1991): 19–22.

DARRELL MILO MILLNER

Organ, Claude H., Jr. (October 16,1928–), surgeon. Born in Marshall, Tex., Organ earned a B.S. in 1948 from Xavier University in New Orleans, and an M.D. in 1952 from Creighton University School of Medicine in Omaha, Neb. He earned an M.S. in surgery from Creighton in 1957. From 1957 to 1959, Organ served as a lieutenant commander in the Medical Corps of the United States Navy. He returned to Creighton University in 1960 as an instructor in surgery. He was subsequently named Assistant Professor of Surgery from 1963 to 1968, Associate Professor of Surgery from 1966 to 1971, and Professor and Chairman of the Department of Surgery from 1971 to 1982. Organ was the first African American to chair a department of surgery at a predominantly white medical school. In 1982, he became Professor of Surgery at the University of Oklahoma Science Center.

The father of seven children, three of whom also became physicians, Organ was President of the Nebraska Urban League (1964–1968), Director of Father Flanagan's Boys Town (1969 to 1983), Chairman of the Board of Trustees of Xavier University (1976 to 1978), President of the Southwestern Board of Surgery (1984), and Chairman of the American Board of Surgery (1984–1986). He received the Sinkler Award in 1970, and the Distinguished Service Award from the Minority Medical Educators of America in 1986. Organ published many scholarly articles in medical journals, and, along with Vernon J. Henderson, M.D., he edited *A Century of Black Surgeons: The USA Experience* (1987).

REFERENCES

CLOYD, IRIS, ed. *Who's Who Among Black Americans, 1990/91.* Detroit, 1990.
"Super Surgeon." *Ebony* (January 1978): 88.

LYDIA MCNEILL

Organization of Black American Culture. *See* OBAC Writers' Workshop.

Origins of African Americans. *See* African-American Origins.

Ory, Edward "Kid" (c. 1889–January 23, 1973), jazz trombonist and band leader. Although Kid Ory prided himself on his ability to play many instruments, it is by his rough-hewn but highly expressive and idiosyncratic style that he is known. Born on a farm in St. John Baptist Parish, near New Orleans, Ory moved to the city around 1910 and by 1917 had formed a highly successful musical partnership with cornetist Joe "King" OLIVER (with the young Louis ARMSTRONG an occasional substitute and eventual replacement in 1919) and clarinetist Johnny DODDS. Ory moved to California in the fall of 1919 and led New Orleans-style bands in Los Angeles and the San Francisco Bay area. In 1922, a small group under his leadership made the first, albeit only locally distributed New Orleans-style recordings by African Americans.

Moving to Chicago in 1925, Ory played in many of the most important jazz recordings made by bands led by Armstrong (Hot 5 and Hot 7), Joe Oliver, Lil ARMSTRONG, and "Jelly Roll" MORTON. Not long after his return to California in 1930, Ory retired from music for a decade. A "second career" began in 1941 and lasted until about 1965 with long-term California engagements as well as extensive tours. His bands of this period comprised a wide variety of musicians, from New Orleans contemporaries to younger swing players, and they made a great many widely distributed recordings, many of them of considerable musical merit. Plagued by illness, Ory retired and moved to Hawaii in 1966. He is noted as the composer of two traditional jazz standards, "Ory's Creole Trombone" and "Muskrat Ramble."

REFERENCE

HOSIASSON, JOSÉ. "Kid Ory." In *The New Grove Dictionary of Jazz*. New York, 1988.

LAWRENCE GUSHEE

Osborne, Estelle (1901–1981), nurse. Born Geneva Estelle Massey in 1901 in Palestine, Tex., the eighth of eleven children of Hall and Bettye Massey, Estelle Osborne completed Prairie View Teachers College at age sixteen. She taught for two years in rural schools before starting nursing education in October 1920 at St. Louis Hospital no. 2, which later became Homer G. Phillips Hospital. She began a discussion group, which, at her graduation in 1923, became the alumni association. She served as its first president. After achieving the highest score on the Missouri state nurses' examination, she pursued an active career that both enriched her profession and contributed to the health of many people in the South.

As an African-American nurse Osborne accomplished several notable firsts. She earned both bachelor's (1930) and master's (1931) degrees at Teachers College, Columbia University; she was appointed to a committee of the National Organization for Public Health Nursing (1934); she conducted Rosenwald-funded research on poverty and health in the South; she served as superintendent and director of nursing at the Homer G. Phillips School of Nursing in St. Louis (1940); she was a consultant with the National Nursing Council for War Service (1943); she taught at the schools of nursing at Harlem Hospital and New York University (1945); and she represented the American Nurses' Association (ANA) at the International Council of Nurses in Stockholm (1949). Her marriage to Akron physician Bedford N. Riddle ended in divorce, and she later married Herman Osborne in New York. There were no children from either marriage.

Osborne filled leadership positions as president of the National Association of Colored Graduate Nurses (1934–1939) and as Educational Director of the Freedman's Hospital School of Nursing in Washington, D.C. She was a member of the ANA board of directors (1948–1952) and the board of directors of the American Journal of Nursing Company (1951); she was also assistant director for general administration of the National League for Nursing (1954).

In recognition of her achievements, Osborne was honored with the Mary Mahoney Award (1946), membership in the ANA Hall of Fame (1954), and honorary membership in Chi Eta Phi and the American Academy of Nursing (1975). After retirement in 1966, Osborne moved to Oakland, Calif., where she died on December 12, 1981. The Nurses Educational Fund, Inc., annually offers the Estelle Massey Osborne Memorial Scholarship for an outstanding African-American nurse seeking a master's degree.

REFERENCES

CARNEGIE, M. ELIZABETH. *The Path We Tread: Blacks in Nursing, 1854–1990,* 2nd ed. New York, 1991.
Obituary. *Newsletter of the National Black Nurse's Association 9* (January 1982): 1, 2.
SAFIER, GWENDOLYN. "Estelle Osborne." In *Contemporary American Leaders in Nursing.* New York, 1978.

PATRICIA E. SLOAN

Osteopathic Medicine. See Health and Health Care Providers.

Overton, Anthony (March 21, 1865–July 3, 1946), businessman. Although it is known that he was born in Monroe, La., in 1865, little is known of the early life of Anthony Overton. While university records are incomplete, Overton claimed that he attended Washburn College and graduated from the University of Kansas with an LL.B. in 1888. In the same year he married Clara Gregg. For several years, Overton was a judge of the Municipal Court in Topeka, Kans. In 1898 he established the Overton Hygienic Manufacturing Company in Kansas City, Kans. Overton moved the company to Chicago, Ill., in 1911, where it quickly expanded, becoming popular for a "High Brown Face Powder" and other toiletry products.

Overton's business interests flourished in Chicago; in the early 1920s, he established a bank, a life insurance company, and the *Chicago Bee*, a newspaper. Eschewing luxuries himself, Overton reinvested most of his profits back into his own enterprises. The Douglass National Bank was reportedly the first national bank owned and run by African Americans in the state of Illinois.

In 1924 Overton also organized the Victory Life Insurance Company, the first black-owned insurance company to be permitted to conduct business in the state of New York, where strict regulations and legal reserve requirements made entry into the insurance market extremely difficult. As a result of the success of this company, Overton received the NAACP's SPINGARN MEDAL in 1927. Overton's empire collapsed during the GREAT DEPRESSION, however, when both the bank and the insurance company failed. The insurance company later reorganized under different management.

But the depression did not claim either the Overton Hygienic Manufacturing Company or the *Chicago Bee*, and Overton led these companies until his death. He was an active member of the board of directors of the Chicago Urban League, as well as a number of fraternal organizations. He died in Chicago in 1946.

REFERENCE

Obituary. *Journal of Negro History* 32, no. 3 (July 1947): 394–396.

JOHN C. STONER

Owen, Chandler (April 5, 1889–1967), political journalist. Chandler Owen was born in Warrenton, N.C., and graduated from Virginia Union University in Richmond, Va., in 1913. He pursued graduate work at the New York School of Philanthropy and at Columbia University as a NATIONAL URBAN LEAGUE fellow. Owen severed ties with the league

after he met A. Philip RANDOLPH and in 1916 joined the Socialist party. In November 1917, Owen and Randolph began publishing the MESSENGER, an independent monthly with a Socialist party orientation; in early issues, they framed pacifist objections to WORLD WAR I, supported armed defense against mob violence directed at African Americans, promoted radical industrial unionism, and voiced support for the social goals of the Russian Revolution. Owen and Randolph served brief jail sentences for their radicalism, and the *Messenger*'s offices were ransacked several times in the early 1920s by the authorities.

In the early 1920s Owen had become disillusioned with radical politics, and was especially embittered when socialist garment workers' unions denied membership to his brother. In 1923 he left the *Messenger* to become managing editor of Anthony OVERTON's *Chicago Bee,* a liberal African-American newspaper, but maintained ties with Randolph and used the *Bee* to muster support for Randolph's campaign to unionize the Pullman car porters (*see* BROTHERHOOD OF SLEEPING CAR PORTERS).

During the 1930s and WORLD WAR II Owen continued to move to the right, and was active in the REPUBLICAN PARTY. He served as a speechwriter and publicity chairman of the Negro division for Wendell Willkie's 1940 presidential campaign. During this period Owen also wrote about black anti-Semitism for the Anti-Defamation League of B'nai B'rith. Despite his private reservations about the Roosevelt administration, he served as a consultant on race relations for the Office of War Information (he wrote the office's pamphlet *Negroes and the War* (1942), a tabloid-size publication that praised the New Deal), and projected worse treatment for blacks if Hitler were to win.

In his later life Owen continued to serve as a speechwriter and political consultant for major Republican presidential candidates, including Thomas Dewey in 1948 and Dwight Eisenhower in 1952.

REFERENCE

KORWEIBEL, THEODORE, JR. *No Crystal Stair: Black Life and the "Messenger," 1917–1928.* Westport, Conn., 1975.

ELIZABETH MUTHER

Owens, James Cleveland "Jesse" (September 12, 1913–March 31, 1980), athlete. Born in 1913, the tenth surviving child of sharecroppers Henry and Emma Owens, in Oakville, Ala., Jesse Owens moved with his family to Cleveland, Ohio, for better economic and educational opportunities in the early

1920s. His athletic ability was first noticed by a junior high school teacher of physical education, Charles Riley, who coached him to break several interscholastic records and even to make a bold but futile attempt to win a place on the U.S. Olympic team. In 1933 Owens matriculated at Ohio State University on a work-study arrangement and immediately began setting Big Ten records. In Ann Arbor, Mich., on May 25, 1935, he set new world records in the 220-yard sprint, the 220-yard hurdles, and the long jump and tied the world record in the 100-yard dash.

In the racially segregated sports world of 1936, Owens and Joe LOUIS were the most visible African-American athletes. In late June, however, Louis lost to German boxer Max Schmeling, making Owens's Olympic feats all the more dramatic. At Berlin in early August 1936, he stole the Olympic show with gold-medal, record-making performances in the 100 meters, 200 meters, long jump, and relays. All this occurred against a backdrop of Nazi pageantry and Adolf Hitler's daily presence and in an international scene of tension and fear. Out of that dramatic moment came one of the most enduring of all sports myths: Hitler's supposed "snub" in refusing to shake Owens's hand after the victories. (Morally satisfying but untrue, the yarn was largely created by American sportswriters.)

Business and entertainment offers flooded Owens's way in the wake of the Berlin games, but he quickly found most of them were bogus. Republican presidential candidate Alf Landon paid him to stump for black votes in the autumn of 1936. After that futile effort, Owens bounced from one demeaning and low-paying job to another, including races against horses. He went bankrupt in a dry-cleaning business. By 1940, with a wife and three daughters to support (he had married Ruth Solomon in 1935), Owens returned to Ohio State to complete the degree he had abandoned in 1936. However, his grades were too low and his educational background too thin for him

Jesse Owens was a one-man refutation of the athletic inferiority of blacks. His four gold medals in the 1936 Berlin Olympics discomfited the Nazi hosts of the games as well as racists on both sides of the Atlantic. Here Owens runs in a heat of the 200-meter dash. (AP/Wide World Photos)

to graduate. For most of World War II, Owens supervised the black labor force at Ford Motor Company in Detroit.

In the era of the cold war, Owens became a fervent American patriot, hailing the United States as the land of opportunity. Working out of Chicago, he frequently addressed interracial school and civic groups, linking patriotism and athletics. In 1955 the U.S. State Department sent him to conduct athletic clinics, make speeches, and grant interviews as means of winning friends for America in India, Malaya, and the Philippines.

In 1956 President Dwight D. Eisenhower sent him to the Melbourne Olympics as one of the president's personal goodwill ambassadors. Refusing to join the CIVIL RIGHTS MOVEMENT, Owens became so politically conservative that angry young blacks denounced him as an "Uncle Tom" on the occasion of the famous black-power salutes by Olympic athletes Tommie Smith and John Carlos at Mexico City in 1968. Before he died of lung cancer in 1980, however, Owens received two of the nation's highest awards: the Medal of Freedom Award in 1976, for his "inspirational" life, and the Living Legends Award in 1979, for his "dedicated but modest" example of greatness.

REFERENCES

BAKER, WILLIAM J. *Jesse Owens: An American Life.* New York, 1986.

MANDELL, RICHARD D. *The Nazi Olympics.* New York, 1971.

WILLIAM J. BAKER

P

Pace, Harry Herbert (January 6, 1884–July 26, 1943), insurance executive and music publisher. Born in Covington, Ga., Harry H. Pace studied at Atlanta University, where he edited the school newspaper and became a student and protégé of W. E. B. DU BOIS. After receiving his bachelor's degree in 1903, Pace went into the printing business with Du Bois in Memphis, Tenn. In 1905 the partners put out the short-lived magazine *The Moon Illustrated Weekly,* the first illustrated African-American journal. After the failure of the printing business in 1906, Pace taught Greek and Latin for two years at Lincoln Institute in Jefferson City, Mo., then returned to Memphis, becoming a cashier at the city's Solvent Savings Bank.

During his time in Memphis, Pace published short stories and articles. His work eventually appeared in such publications as the CRISIS, *Forbes Magazine, Colored American Magazine,* and the *New York Sun.* He also sang in church choirs and in community concerts, and began writing song lyrics. In 1908 he met composer W. C. HANDY, with whom he began a collaboration. The pair's first song, "In the Cotton Fields of Dixie," was published in Memphis that year. In 1909, they formed the Pace & Handy Music Company, a sheet-music business. The company published many songs, including Handy's "Memphis Blues" (1909) and "St. Louis Blues" (1914), and Pace's own "The Girl You Never Have Met" (1909).

In 1913, Pace left Memphis and took the post of secretary-treasurer of the Standard Life Insurance Company of Atlanta. (One of his office boys was Walter Francis WHITE, whom he sponsored and recommended to the NAACP.) During the following years, Pace traveled the country as a life insurance and music agent, securing contracts for Handy's band and music. In 1920 Pace left Atlanta to become president of the Pace & Handy Publishing Company, by then based in New York. Composer William Grant STILL was hired as chief arranger, and future bandleader Fletcher HENDERSON was a song plugger.

Although Pace improved the financial stability of the company, he disliked Handy's business methods. In 1921 Pace resigned from the publishing company and formed the Pace Phonograph Company, the first black-owned record company. The company issued records under the Black Swan label. While it recorded many types of music, it was primarily noted for its BLUES records. Although Black Swan was enormously successful in its first year of business, overexpansion and white competition bankrupted the company in 1923. After Black Swan's failure, Pace left the music business and in 1930 he sold his publishing interests.

In 1925 Pace founded the Northeastern Life Insurance Company in Newark, N.J. After it was incorporated into the Supreme Liberty Life Insurance Company in Chicago four years later, Pace became the new company's president and built it into the largest black-owned business in the North during the 1930s. He wrote a self-help book, *Beginning Again* (1934), and served as editor of the company's monthly newspaper, *The Guardian.* (His assistant was future publisher John H. JOHNSON, who began his career by assembling a news digest from black periodicals for Pace.) Besides his insurance business, Pace attended the Chicago Law School, receiving his law degree in 1933, and was active in DEMOCRATIC PARTY politics.

In the late 1930s, Pace cut back on his black community activities. In 1942, he opened a law office in downtown Chicago and bought a house in a white suburb. According to John Johnson, disgruntled employees accused Pace, who was extremely light-skinned, of trying to "pass" for white, and threatened to demonstrate outside his house. The criticism hurt him deeply. He withdrew further from the black community and died the following year.

REFERENCES

JOHNSON, JOHN H., and LERONE BENNETT, JR. *Succeeding Against the Odds.* New York, 1989.

SOUTHERN, EILEEN. *The Music of Black Americans: A History.* New York, 1983.

GREG ROBINSON

Page, Alan Cedric (August 7, 1945–), football player and lawyer. Born in Canton, Ohio, Alan Page grew up with aspirations of pursuing law and developing his talent in FOOTBALL. He received his B.A. from the University of Notre Dame in 1967, where he became an All-American defensive end. Page went on to play professionally for the Minnesota Vikings from 1967 to 1978. In 1971, he became the first defensive player in the history of the National Football League to receive the Most Valuable Player Award. From 1978 to 1981, Page played for the Chicago Bears. He was named an All-Pro defensive tackle ten times and in 1988 was inducted into the NFL Hall of Fame.

After his rookie season with Minnesota, Page enrolled in the law school at the University of Minnesota. Unable to devote the necessary time to his studies, he put off law school until 1975. He reenrolled at the University of Minnesota, where he was able to complete his degree in 1978. From 1978 to 1981, during off-seasons with the Bears, Page practiced at the corporate law firm of Lindquist & Vennum in Minneapolis, where he continued to work full-time after his retirement from football in 1981. In 1985, Page moved to the office of the Minnesota attorney general, specializing in employment litigation. In 1993, he was elected to the Minnesota Supreme Court, the first African American to be on that court.

REFERENCE

MARGOLICK, DAVID. "At the Bar." *New York Times,* January 1, 1993, pp. A1, A19.

LISA MARIE MOORE

Page, Inman Edward (December 29, 1853–December 23, 1935), educator. Born a slave in Warrenton, Va., Inman Page moved with his parents, Horace and Elizabeth Page, to Washington, D.C., in 1858. He attended private school, and then worked his way through newly created HOWARD UNIVERSITY as a groundskeeper and janitor. In 1871, while still a student, he was appointed a clerk to Freedman's Bureau President O. O. Howard. In 1873 he left Howard and moved to Brown University in Providence, R.I., becoming one of the first two African Americans to attend. A brilliant student, Page shined as an orator, winning contests and being selected as class orator in his last year. In his junior year Page was selected to write a history of his class.

Page received his bachelor's degree from Brown in 1877. He was hired immediately after by the Natchez Seminary in Natchez, Miss. The following year, he was hired as the first African-American teacher at the new Lincoln Institute in Jefferson City, Mo. In 1880, the same year Page received an A.M. degree from Brown University, he was named president of Lincoln by the trustees, and gave up teaching to devote his time to administrative duties. Page served as president for eighteen years. During his tenure, he doubled the institute's enrollment and endowment. He organized a state teacher's convention for blacks in 1883 and was also elected its president.

In 1898 Page left Lincoln Institute (he would return temporarily as interim president in 1922–1923), and was hired as the first president of the Colored Agricultural and Normal University (known after 1941 as Langston University) in Langston, Oklahoma Territory. The small, underfunded university, which had just 187 students in 1900, was little more than a grammar school with a few college-level classes. Page pushed unsuccessfully for a strong, well-rounded academic curriculum. The university had 1,000 students by the time he resigned in 1915, following disputes with trustees, who may have desired a more conservative president.

In 1916 Page was named president of Western Baptist College, then in Macon, Mo. Two years later, he became president of another Baptist institution, Roger Williams College in Nashville, Tenn. In 1921 Page returned to Oklahoma, and was named principal of Oklahoma City's Douglass High School (one of his students there was writer Ralph ELLISON). He remained at Douglass until his death in 1935. He was buried on the campus of Langston University, and memorialized by the Inman Page Library at Lincoln University, Page Hall at Langston University, and public schools in Guthrie and Oklahoma City.

REFERENCES

BREAUX, ELWYN E., and THELMA D. PERRY. "Inman Page, Outstanding Educator." *Negro History Bulletin* (May 1969): 8–12.

ELLISON, RALPH. "A Tribute to Inman Page" and "Going to the Territory." In *Going to the Territory.* New York, 1986, pp. 113–119, 120–145.

GREG ROBINSON

Paige, Leroy Robert "Satchel" (July 7, 1906– June 8, 1982). By far the best known of those who played baseball in the relative obscurity of the Negro Leagues (*see* BASEBALL), pitcher and coach Satchel Paige became a legendary figure from Canada to the Caribbean basin. Born in a shotgun house (a railroad flat) in Mobile, Ala., to John Paige, a gardener, and Lulu Paige, a washerwoman, he combined athletic prowess and exceptional durability with a flair for showmanship. In 1971, the Baseball Hall of Fame made Paige—Negro League ball incarnate—its first-ever selection from the (by then defunct) institution.

Paige gained his nickname as a boy by carrying satchels from the Mobile train station. Sent to the Mount Meigs, Ala., reform school at age twelve for stealing a few toy rings from a store, he developed as a pitcher during his five years there. After joining the semipro Mobile Tigers in 1924, he pitched for a number of Negro League, white independent, and Caribbean teams until he joined the Cleveland Indians as a forty-two-year-old rookie in 1948. The first African-American pitcher in the American League, Paige achieved a 6–1 record that helped the Indians to the league pennant. His first three starts drew over 200,000 fans.

But it was in the Negro Leagues and Caribbean winter ball that Paige attained his status as independent baseball's premier attraction. During the 1920s and 1930s, he starred for the Birmingham Black Barons and the Pittsburgh Crawfords, where he teamed up with catcher Josh GIBSON to form what was possibly baseball's greatest all-time battery. Between 1939 and 1947, Paige anchored the strong Kansas Monarchs staff, winning three of the Monarchs' four victories over the Homestead Grays in the 1942 Negro League World Series. Developing a reputation as

Leroy "Satchel" Paige. (Photographs and Prints Division, Schomburg Center for Research in Black Culture, The New York Public Library, Astor, Lenox and Tilden Foundations)

a contract jumper, he led Ciudad Trujillo to the 1937 summer championship of the Dominican Republic and later pitched in Mexico, Cuba, and Venezuela.

Playing before an estimated 10 million fans in the United States, Canada, and the Caribbean, the "have arm—will pitch" Paige, according to his own estimates, threw 55 no-hitters and won over 2,000 of the 2,500 games in which he pitched.

The 6'3½", 180-pound Paige dazzled fans with his overpowering fastball (called the "bee ball"—you could hear it buzz, but you couldn't see it), his hesitation pitch, and unerring control. Stories of him intentionally walking the bases full of barnstorming white all-stars, telling his fielders to sit down, and then striking out the side became part of a shared black mythology. "I just could pitch!" he said in 1981. "The Master just gave me an arm. . . . You couldn't hardly beat me. . . . I wouldn't get tired 'cause I practiced every day. I had the suit on every day, pretty near 365 days out of the year."

Probably the most widely seen player ever (in person), Paige was a regular at the East-West Classic (the Negro League all-star game), and also appeared on the 1952 American League all-star squad. His 28 wins and 31 losses, 476 innings pitched, 3.29 earned run average in the majors represented only the penultimate chapter of a professional pitching career that spanned five decades.

Paige ended his working life as he began it, on the bus of a barnstorming black club, appearing for the Indianapolis Clowns in 1967. In 1971, after the Hall of Fame belatedly began to induct Negro Leaguers, he led the way. As his Pittsburgh Crawfords teammate Jimmie Crutchfield put it, when Paige appeared on the field "it was like the sun coming out from behind a cloud."

REFERENCES

HOLWAY, JOHN B. *Josh and Satch: A Dual Biography of Josh Gibson and Satchel Paige.* Westport, Conn., 1991.

RUCK, ROB. *Sandlot Seasons: Sport in Black Pittsburgh.* Champaign-Urbana, Ill., 1987.

ROB RUCK

Painting and Sculpture.   From the time of their first arrival in the New World, Africans were involved in a wide range of artistic endeavors. Much of the early art of African Americans was folk art and was a part of the routines of life and work. Africans were involved in a wide range of craft activities, including the construction of houses, the casting of iron fences, the fashioning of baskets and pottery, and the making of quilts. This art often displayed a distinctive African sensibility, and partook of traditional African practices such as the decoration of the gravesites.

African-American participation in European styles of fine artwork was slower to develop. This was both because of the unfamiliarity of Africans with the conventions of European art, and the deliberate exclusion of blacks from access to the training and clients needed for successful careers as artists. Despite these handicaps, the achievements of African Americans in painting and sculpture are rich and distinguished. Their history comprises determined individuals who, in addition to the usual struggles of artists to make a livelihood, had to overcome the additional burdens of discrimination (with black women having gender bias to contend with as well), as well as racist assumptions about the artistic abilities of persons of African descent.

It is likely that persons of African descent first created European artworks at the behest of their masters and white patrons, who wished them to make copies of works in fashionable styles. This process began surprisingly early. By 1724 the Boston print shop of Thomas Fleet had two slave artisans, Pompey and Cesar Fleet, who made woodcuts to accompany broadside ballads and small books. Most of the black artisans in eighteenth-century America were anonymous. Primarily located in cities, both free blacks and slaves worked as silversmiths, goldsmiths, watchmakers, and makers of powderhorns, among other crafts. References to them are scarce and primarily glimpsed in newspaper advertisements for their services or in notices for runaway slaves.

Those painters whose names were recorded include Neptune Thurston, an eighteenth-century Rhode Island slave whose artistic prowess, according to a nineteenth-century tradition, was an early inspiration for the renowned artist Gilbert Stuart. Scipio MOORHEAD, a Boston slave, almost certainly painted a portrait of Phillis WHEATLEY which served as the basis for the frontispiece to the 1773 London edition of her works. Wheatley returned the favor in her poem "To S. M. a Young African Painter, on Seeing his Works," the first recorded critical evaluation of an African-American artist:

> To show the lab'ring bosom's deep intent,
> And thought in living characters to paint,
> When first thy pencil did those beauties give,
> And breathing figures learnt from thee to live,
> How did those prospects give my soul delight,
> A new creation rushing on my sight?

Nineteenth-Century Art

Most of the work of nineteenth-century African-American artists is imitative of European and American conventions of technique and appropriate subject matter. The lack of a self-conscious "black aesthetic" in nineteenth-century African-American art has bothered some later critics such as Alain LOCKE, who view this period as one of relatively little importance. But this perspective slights the achievements of these artists and overlooks the efforts they made and the indignities they withstood to be accepted by their peers.

Many of these early black artists were limners—humble, often informally trained, and itinerant portrait painters. One of the first was Joshua JOHNSON or Johnston of Baltimore. His origins, parentage, and almost all other pertinent information about his life are unknown; indeed, there is considerable debate on whether Joshua Johnson was of African descent. While there were black painters in Baltimore in the early nineteenth century, the racial identity of the considerable body of work identified as that of Joshua Johnson is uncertain.

In a December 19, 1798, advertisement in the *Baltimore Intelligencer,* Joshua Johnson posted an announcement wherein he described himself as a "self-taught genius" who had overcome "many insuperable obstacles" in his efforts to become an artist. This perhaps is a reference to his African-American background; but unfortunately for historians, the advertisement is silent on the race of the artist.

Johnson's style and some documentary evidence indicate that he came under the influence of the prominent painters Charles Wilson Peale and his nephew Charles Polk Peale. Johnson's paintings of Maryland's elite were distinguished by an individual sense of character and fine attention to detail. Critics have described Johnson as the "brass tack artist" because of his repetitive use of the same sofa, studded with brass upholstery tacks, in many of the depictions of his subjects. Johnson painted few black subjects, though he has been tentatively identified as the painter of the matched portraits of Daniel COKER and Abner Coker, two early ministers of the AFRICAN METHODIST EPISCOPAL (AME) CHURCH.

Painter, lithographer, and daguerreotypist Jules LION was born in France and later settled in New Orleans. He was listed as a painter and lithographer in the 1838 city directory. An advertisement lists Lion as a daguerreotypist in 1840 and credits him with the introduction of this medium to New Orleans. Although there are no extant examples of his painting, he is known to have exhibited successfully at the Exposition of Paris in 1833, cofounded an art school in New Orleans in 1841, and taught drawing at the College of Louisiana. Lion typifies many early African-American artists who worked in diverse genres and media. He remained active in the New Orleans area, traveling back to France periodically until his death in 1866.

Robert Scott DUNCANSON was hailed at the height of his career as the "best landscape painter in the West" by eastern critics. Born in Seneca County in upstate New York, Duncanson was raised in Monroe, Mich., located at the western tip of Lake Erie, and by the early 1840s had moved to Cincinnati. His landscapes such as *Blue Hole, Little Moon River* (1851) and *The Land of the Lotus Eaters* (c. 1861) are excellent examples of the luminous Hudson River School landscape style.

His commissions included photographs, portraits, still lifes, and landscapes, and in the Belmont House in Cincinnati (now the Taft Museum) he executed the first murals by a black artist. In the early 1850s he probably collaborated with the African-American daguerreotypist James Presley BALL in an enormous rolling panorama (over half a mile of canvas) that depicted in its unfolding the history of African Americans in the United States.

Duncanson was fairly light-skinned and this perhaps eased his access to white artistic circles, though the snubs he did receive, such as his failure to be elected to the National Academy of Design in New York, left him greatly disturbed. His physical and mental health deteriorated toward the end of his life. He made a distinctive contribution to the tradition of American landscape painting by becoming the first African-American artist to appropriate the landscape as a vehicle to express his own cultural heritage and identity.

Boston, a major center for black cultural life in the nineteenth century, was the home of four painters of significance: William SIMPSON, Nelson PRIMUS, Edward BANNISTER, and Edmonia LEWIS. William Simpson was listed in the Boston directories of 1860 and 1866. Critics of the period recall his strong talents as a portrait-painter and his skill as a draftsman of exceptional ability. William Wells BROWN recalled that Simpson began as a youth "drawing instead of following his class work," later studying with Matthew Wilson in 1854. Very little is known about Simpson's career, and few works are extant. Nelson Primus, born in Hartford, Conn., moved to Boston in 1864. He started out as a carriage painter in about 1858, and then professionally began a career as a portrait painter. In 1859 he won a medal for drawing at the State Agricultural Society Fair. While he received high praise in Boston, his career was only partially successful in the East, and he later moved to San Francisco, where he continued to paint.

Edward Mitchell Bannister was a first-rate landscape painter and portraitist in late nineteenth-century New England. Born in New Brunswick, Canada, to a father from Barbados and a local woman, he grew up with an early appreciation of the arts, encouraged by his mother. In 1850 he moved to Boston, where he worked as a hairdresser. As an artist he was largely self-taught, and by 1860 he had acquired a considerable local reputation. During the CIVIL WAR Bannister was a leader in the effort to obtain equal pay for black soldiers, and he painted a portrait, not extant, of Colonel Robert Gould Shaw, commander of the 54th Massachusetts Regiment.

Bannister's painting *Under the Oaks* (now lost) won a first place at the Centennial Exposition in Philadelphia in 1876. African-American newspapers and periodicals such as the *A.M.E. Church Review* proudly took note of Bannister's accomplishment. His work, influenced by the English landscape artist John Constable and the French Barbizon School, often featured seascapes and carefully textured studies of clouds and trees. In 1870 Bannister moved to Providence, R.I., where, unusually for a black professional of his era, he was fully accepted by his white peers, and was a cofounder of the socially prestigious Providence Art Club. At his death in 1901 the Providence Art Club hosted a memorial exhibition of more than one hundred of his works, a testament to his contribution to the American landscape tradition and to the high admiration of his fellow artists, patrons, and admirers.

The most prominent black sculptor of the nineteenth century was the remarkable Edmonia Lewis. Many of the specifics of her biography remain unclear. Lewis was born in upstate New York to an African-American father and a mother of mixed Chippewa and African-American descent. Orphaned at an early age, "Wildfire" (her Indian name) was raised in Canada West (now Ontario) among the Chippewa. She attended Oberlin College, but found herself embroiled in unseemly and unfounded accusations of poisoning two of her classmates, and was obliged to leave in 1863, and moved to Boston. The traumatic impact of the charges, which almost certainly had a racial basis, left Lewis distrustful of outsiders, and fostered an already strong sense of somewhat stubborn independence and self-sufficiency.

The city directory of Boston lists Lewis as a sculptor for the years of 1864 and 1865. Boston's vital black and abolitionist community provided Lewis with numerous opportunities, and she created portrait busts of many of the leading abolitionist figures. In 1866, with the money earned from sales of a plaster bust of Colonel Robert Gould Shaw, she moved to Rome. She befriended the large community of American artists in Rome and started carving in marble. *Forever Free* (1867–1868), probably her best-known work, is a commemoration of the Emancipation Proclamation. Although her work was deeply shaped by neoclassicism, she was influenced as well in both subject matter and style by her African-American and Indian backgrounds. After the 1880s she became less active and gradually cut off contacts with Americans. Lewis became a fervent Roman Catholic, and she executed some religious sculpture. Little is known about the last thirty years of her life, but it is believed that she was living in Rome as late as 1909.

Henry Ossawa TANNER was the leading African-American painter of the late nineteenth and early twentieth centuries. Born in Pittsburgh, Pa., he was encouraged in his artistic ambitions at an early age by a supportive and relatively comfortable family—his father was an AME bishop—and the intellectual community of Philadelphia. He was one of the first black artists to study at the Pennsylvania Academy of Fine Arts, studying with Thomas Eakins in 1880 and 1881, but withdrew after a racial incident. In 1891 he sailed for Europe, traveling to Italy and settling in Paris, where he experienced a freedom unknown in the

United States. He would remain in Paris for the rest of his life, making brief trips home. While in France he executed two realistic genre paintings, *The Banjo Lesson* (1898) and *The Thankful Poor* (1893–1894), displaying the influence of Eakins; these painting represent Tanner's most realistic depictions of contemporary African-American life. For the remainder of his career he concentrated on visionary religious paintings in muted hues, such as *Daniel in the Lion's Den* (1895) and *The Raising of Lazarus* (1896), a prize-winner at the Paris Salon of 1897. Tanner's example and personal encouragement would be an inspiration for several generations of African-American artists. Two painters who became pupils of Tanner were William HARPER and William Edouard SCOTT. Harper was a landscapist in the tradition of the Barbizon painters, and had admirable technical skill. Scott's landscapes displayed the influence of Turner's use of light. Scott later became known for his paintings of Haitian peasants.

The two leading black sculptors at the end of the century were Meta Vaux Warrick FULLER and May Howard JACKSON. Meta Vaux Warwick, who married the pioneer African-American neurologist Solomon Carter FULLER, was born in Philadelphia and at an early age became curious about art through her older sister, an art student. Throughout her early education, her interest in art grew and her talent blossomed. She won a scholarship to the Pennsylvania School of Industrial Art and won a prize for *Process of the Arts and Crafts* (1897), a massive bas-relief composition of thirty-seven figures. After graduation she continued her studies in 1899, attending lectures at the Colarossi Academy in Paris and later working with Auguste Rodin. She was among the earliest American artists to be influenced by African sculpture and folklore in such works as *Spirit of Emancipation* (c. 1918), *Ethiopia Awakening* (1914/1921), and *The Talking Skull* (1937). Her early works had a power and fierceness that many critics found frightening. After her marriage and a devastating fire in 1910 that destroyed much of her early work, she stopped sculpting for a period of years and created stage designs for theater groups in the community. When she resumed her career her work was more technically and emotionally mature, largely consisting of themes centered on African-American culture, history, and leadership.

May Howard Jackson was educated at J. Liberty Todd's Art School in Philadelphia and won a scholarship to the Pennsylvania Academy of Fine Arts in that city. Jackson was primarily a sculptor of portrait busts and portrait groups such as *Mother and Child* (1929) and *Head of a Negro Child* (1929). In many of her works she went beyond her classical training to depict the wide range and uniqueness of African-

American physiognomy. Jackson had a studio in Washington, D.C., and exhibited professionally at the National Academy of Design and the Cocoran Gallery of Art. She won a prize from the HARMON FOUNDATION in 1928. However, the general indifference of the public, despite many critical plaudits from writers including Alain Locke and W. E. B. DU BOIS, filled her life with frustration and anger.

Charles Ethan PORTER was a painter of still lifes and landscapes. Born in Connecticut, he attended the National Academy of Design and later traveled to Paris to study, evidently through the generosity of Mark Twain. Porter established a studio in Rockville, Conn., in 1884. He specialized in still lifes with elaborate floral arrangements and fruit displays, painting primarily for local white patrons. He exhibited intermittently at the National Academy of Design of New York and the American Society of Painters in Watercolor. In 1910 he became a charter member of the Connecticut Academy of Fine Arts, his only known professional association.

Laura Wheeling WARING, like Charles Ethan Porter, was a native of Connecticut. Born in Hartford, she studied at the Pennsylvania Academy of Fine Arts and at the Académie de la Grande Chaumière in Paris. In 1914 she won a Cresson Foreign Traveling Scholarship, which enabled her to travel to Europe and North Africa. Her interest in portraiture of African Americans of both humble and distinguished origins won a high prize, and her painting *Anna Derry Washington* (c. 1930s) received the Harmon Foundation gold medal in 1927. Her studies rendered women powerful and dignified, through intense images of poised strength. After she settled in Philadelphia, her portraits of leading African-American figures, including Marian ANDERSON, George Washington CARVER, and James Weldon JOHNSON were exhibited widely. Many of her busts were commissioned by the Harmon Foundation. A memorial exhibition of these works was displayed at Howard University in 1949.

Harlem Renaissance and the New Negro Movement

The celebrated March 1925 issue of *Survey Graphic*, reprinted under the title THE NEW NEGRO (1925), heralded the arrival of the movement known as the HARLEM RENAISSANCE. It established Alain Locke, a Philadelphia-born critic and educator and Howard University professor, as the movement's mentor and chief booster. Locke, in addition to his many other activities during the Harlem Renaissance, became the first important critic and historian of African-American art, and was the author of pathbreaking books, including *Negro Art: Past and Present* (1936) and *The Negro in Art* (1940). Locke urged African-

American artists to follow the example of Parisian modernists—notably Picasso and Matisse—and incorporate the stylistic innovations of African art and sculpture into their work, and to fashion a "racially expressive art." Locke initiated the call for African-American art and painting to be not merely imitative of dominant European and American styles but to develop its own self-conscious aesthetic.

The burgeoning of publications during the Harlem Renaissance provided a crucial forum for young black artists to showcase and experiment with images reflective of a cultural identity specific to African Americans. Among those active in the production of illustrations, caricatures, graphic design for book and magazine covers, and genre drawings were Aaron DOUGLAS, Gwendolyn BENNETT, Bruce Nugent, Charles ALSTON, E. Sims CAMPBELL, Laura Wheeling Waring, and Lois Mailou JONES. These artists were well respected among their peers, even if at times the "new" imagery of the New Negro provoked resistance and disdain from the older generation of black intellectuals.

Another crucial figure who encouraged visual arts during the Harlem Renaissance was a white real-estate developer and philanthropist, William E. Harmon (1862–1928), who founded the Harmon Foundation in 1922. The foundation, which sponsored the Harmon Awards for Distinguished Achievements Among Negroes in Fine Arts, created exhibitions that toured the United States through the mid-1930s. This activity, much of it supervised by his longtime assistant Mary Beattie Brady (1897–), provided an opportunity and showcase for black artists to gain national and even international recognition that otherwise would not have been available to them.

Aaron Douglas was probably the best-known artist to emerge from the Harlem Renaissance, noted for his murals and paintings as well as his book and periodical illustrations. Douglas was born and educated in Kansas. After teaching in Kansas high schools, he came to New York in 1924, where he began studies with Winold Reiss, a German painter with a keen interest in American Indians and African Americans.

Douglas soon became a popular and prolific illustrator for periodicals such as *The Crisis, Opportunity, Theatre Arts Monthly, Sun, Boston Transcript, American Mercury, Vanity Fair, Fire!!*, and the special March 1925 issue of *Survey Graphic*. Douglas created images based on traditional African forms and stylized cubist elements. The striking mural series "Aspects of Negro Life" (1933–1934) at the Countee Cullen Branch of the New York Public Library (now the Schomburg Center for Research in Black Culture) are among his most compelling creations.

Palmer HAYDEN was born in Widewater, Va., where he was educated in country schools. He began to draw at age four, inspired by his brother. Palmer Hayden was primarily a self-taught painter who intermittently took courses and studied with various artists. In 1927 he entered the Harmon Foundation competition, won first prize and $400, and left to study and exhibit in Paris.

Hayden's early works were figurative and landscape compositions. Early narrative paintings such as *Midsummer Night in Harlem* (1936) and *The Janitor Who Paints* (1936) are realistic reflections of the stark realities faced by African Americans in general and African-American artists in particular. His most famous work is probably the JOHN HENRY series (1944–1947), twelve paintings depicting events from the folk legend.

The aesthetics and creativity of the Harlem Renaissance were not limited to New York City, and flourished in places such as Cleveland, San Francisco, Atlanta, Philadelphia, Boston, Washington, D.C., and Chicago. Many of the artists who did migrate to New York came from small towns in the South. These communities provided environments that gave artists a continuously rich supply of cultural material. William Henry JOHNSON came from such a town—Florence, S.C. Johnson arrived in New York in 1918 and worked at odd jobs, sending money home to his family and saving the rest to enroll in art school. In 1921 he enrolled in the National Academy of Design. He left for Paris in 1926 and won the Harmon Foundation prize in 1929. He lived for most of the 1930s in Denmark, returning to the United States shortly before the outbreak of World War II. In 1939 he changed his style from one heavily influenced by the postimpressionism of Cézanne and Matisse to flat, bright, expressively colored, essential forms that appeared "naive." Johnson felt that these works were a pictorial equivalent of the heart of African-American experience. Compositions such as *Jesus and Three Marys* (1939), *Going to Church* (1940–1941), and his *Folk Family* series recall his cultural roots and his quest to understand African aesthetics and symbolism. He suffered severe mental deterioration in 1947 and was institutionalized for the remainder of his life.

Archibald J. MOTLEY, born in New Orleans and raised in Chicago, painted numerous portraits of family, friends, and models. In 1928 he entered the Harmon Foundation competition and won the gold medal for *Octoroon Girl* (1925); many of Motley's works display an interest in the varieties and textures of African-American skin color. Though his best-known work is probably *Mending Socks* (1924), a sensitive depiction of his grandmother, much of his work focuses on the BLUES and JAZZ scene in Chicago, in canvases such as *Blues* (1929) and *The Liar* (1934). Unlike many Harlem Renaissance-generation artists who tried to depict African Americans in dig-

William H. Johnson painting outside, probably in Chartres, France, 1927. (William H. Johnson papers, Archives of American Art, Smithsonian Institution)

nified settings, many of Motley's paintings portray blacks dancing, drinking, and carousing, but in such a way as to evoke liveliness and vitality rather than stereotypes.

Sargent JOHNSON was born in Boston. His father was of Swedish ancestry; his mother was Cherokee and African American. Early in his youth Johnson was orphaned and sent to live for a while with his maternal aunt, the sculptor May Howard Jackson. In 1915 he moved to San Francisco and set up a studio in his backyard, after studying at the A. W. Best School of Art and the California School of Fine Art. Johnson was talented in many media and worked in wood, terra-cotta, plaster, copper, cast stone, mosaic, ceramic clay, and polychrome porcelain on steel. He was also adept at lithographs, etching, and drawing. Remaining in the Bay Area for the duration of his life, he exhibited regularly with the Harmon Foundation and won awards in 1927 and 1928.

Even though Johnson lived far from Harlem, he was greatly influenced by the call of the New Negro movement to employ the aesthetics of traditional African arts as well as Mexican and Native American art forms. His sculpture captured elegant linearism and a

Elizabeth Prophet. (National Archives)

simple and direct approach to form, derived from the study of African masks and Mexican folk art. During the 1930s he became active in the Works Progress Administration—later the WORKS PROJECT ADMINISTRATION (WPA)—as an artist, later becoming unit supervisor in the Bay Area, the highest post in the WPA held by a black artist. Some of his most important pieces were *Sammy* (1927), his copper mask series (c. 1930–1935), and *Forever Free* (1933).

Richmond BARTHE was the Harmon Foundation's most celebrated and widely exhibited sculptor. His figurative style was most popular from the 1920s through the 1940s. Early in his career his work was bought by the Whitney Museum of American Art and the Metropolitan Museum of Art. Born in Bay St. Louis, Miss., he arrived in Chicago in 1924, entered the School of the Art Institute of Chicago to study painting, and produced his first sculpture three years later. These works helped him win a Julius Rosenwald Fellowship to study in New York.

Barthe worked in clay, plaster, and bronze, and his technical and conceptual skill in the execution of the figure and portrait bust was highly regarded. During the 1930s he worked for the WPA, creating bas-relief murals. Much of his inspiration, especially in his later years, came from the world of theater and dance. The power of movement and the effort to capture kinetic motion in a sculptural form greatly fascinated him. He is known for such compositions as *Feral Benga* (1935), *The Negro Looks Ahead* (1937), and *Mother and Son* (1938).

The life of sculptor Nancy Elizabeth PROPHET was marked by abject poverty, remarkable skill, and a tenacious will to establish herself as an artist. Prophet was born in Providence, R.I.; little else is known about her early life. She had little encouragement to become an artist, but despite this she enrolled in the Rhode Island School of Design in 1918. In 1922 she studied at the École des Beaux Arts in Paris, and she continued to live, work, and exhibit in France until 1932. She had the support and admiration of W. E. B. Du Bois and Henry Tanner, who helped her exhibit with the Harmon Foundation in 1930. In 1930 her recently completed *Congalaise* was purchased by the Whitney Museum of American Art. Prophet worked in marble, alabaster, granite, plaster, clay, bronze, and wood. Her portrait busts were intense, powerful technical executions that abstracted the human character to reveal the qualities of inner strength.

In 1932 she returned to America to teach at Spelman College with Hale WOODRUFF. The position gave her little time to sculpt, and she left after 1945. Thereafter, she lived in poverty and obscurity in Providence, and much of her later work is either incomplete, lost, or was destroyed by her own hand.

Lois Mailou Jones had an exceptional career of success, achievement, productivity. She was born in Boston, educated in local schools, and supported by her parents in her decision to become an artist. She attended classes at the Boston Museum School of Fine Arts, and in 1930 she was invited to teach design and watercolor at Howard University. In 1931 she won an honorable mention at the annual Harmon Foundation exhibition for her drawing *Negro Youth*

(1929). After 1937 Jones studied in Paris and Africa, living for a while in Haiti. Jones's work includes portraits, landscapes, and abstractions, all highlighting her facility with color, texture, and design, and in such diverse media as painting, drawing, watercolor, and stage and costume design.

James Lesesne WELLS was the acknowledged "dean of Negro printmakers." Born in Atlanta and educated in Jacksonville, Fla., he later studied at the National Academy of Design, and Teachers College at Columbia University. In 1930 he won the gold medal from the Harmon Foundation for the painting *The Flight into Egypt* (1929). However, he later largely abandoned painting for printmaking, and won a Harmon Foundation award for a woodcut, *Escape of Spies from Canaan* (1932). He was proficient in a wide range of techniques, including intaglio, wood, and linoleum blocks, as well as painting and drawing. His

Lois Mailou Jones in her studio. (Photographs and Prints Division, Schomburg Center for Research in Black Culture, The New York Public Library, Astor, Lenox and Tilden Foundations)

works concentrated on biblical and religious subjects and were greatly influenced by African sculptural forms, as well as the Renaissance master woodcuts of Albrecht Dürer and those of twentieth-century German expressionists. In 1926 he joined the faculty of Howard University, and he continued to produce prints of great quality and complexity for the remainder of his career.

James PORTER, born in Baltimore, was educated at Howard University and later became head of its Art Department. He was a painter of traditional portraits, and won prizes in the Harmon Foundation exhibitions of 1929 and 1933. He authored the first seminal history of African-American art, *Modern Negro Art* (1943). He traveled widely studying, painting, lecturing, writing, exhibiting his work, and providing a critical foundation as the first major African-American art historian.

Hale Woodruff was the founder of the Atlanta School of Art. He was educated at the John Herron Art Institute in Indianapolis, the Académie Scandinave, and the Académie Moderne in Paris, where he lived for several years. He won a bronze medal in the Harmon Foundation competition of 1926. After his return from Europe in 1931 he started to teach at ATLANTA UNIVERSITY, where he established a successful art program. His first paintings were landscapes and figure studies. In 1934 he studied mural painting with Diego Rivera and became increasingly interested in social realism. From 1938 to 1939, under the auspices of the WPA, he created the famed AMISTAD MUTINY mural series at Talladega College, Alabama, detailing the events surrounding an 1841 shipboard slave mutiny and its aftermath. He helped establish a major competition and collection of art at Atlanta University to encourage young artists, and in 1963 was a cofounder of the artists' group Spiral. In 1946 he joined the faculty of New York University, where he remained until his retirement. In the later years of his career his canvases were greatly influenced by abstract expressionism and traditional African art.

Edwin HARLESTON was a portrait painter who had an uncanny ability to capture the character and personality of his subjects, imbuing them with great humanity. He studied for eight years at the Boston Museum of Fine Art and later assisted Aaron Douglas with the murals at Fish University. Shortly before his death he won a Harmon Foundation award for portrait painting.

John Wesley HARDRICK was a landscape and portrait painter who received minimal attention during his lifetime. Born in Indianapolis, he was educated at the John Herron Art Institute in his hometown and remained in the Indianapolis area throughout his life. He exhibited at the Harmon exhibitions and won a bronze medal in 1927. Hardrick created several murals for churches and high schools during his career.

Malvin Gray JOHNSON, born in Greensboro, N.C., did not live long enough to realize the full potential of the psychological distinctiveness of his early portraits. Johnson was educated at the National Academy of Design, and his work shows a great interest in African-American subject matter, along with efforts akin to Cézanne and later postimpressionists in the radical simplification of form. In 1929 Johnson won a first prize in the Harmon Foundation exhibition.

Black Art and the New Deal

By 1934 the GREAT DEPRESSION had put eleven million to fifteen million people out of work. Ten thousand of these jobless citizens were artists. Many artists, black and white, were in desperate need of support. In 1935 President Franklin D. Roosevelt created the Works Progress Administration (WPA). Its purpose was to create all kinds of jobs at every level of the skill ladder, preserving professional and technical skills while helping individuals retain their self-respect. Artists in the program were paid $15 to $90 a month for a variety of assignments. The program was essentially terminated by 1939. In some areas, bowing to local custom, the WPA programs were segregated, though in other places programs were integrated; in many places, most notably in Harlem, there were separate programs for African-American artists. The WPA gave many artists a sense of collective purpose and provided them with the resources to develop their talent for the first time.

One of the leading figures in Harlem's artistic circles in the 1930s was the sculptor Augusta SAVAGE. One of thirteen children, she came to New York from Cove Springs, Fla., in 1921 to study in the free art program at Cooper Union. She overcame numerous obstacles in her life, and was an artist dedicated to the recognition of black artists. Her best work displays extraordinary power, energy, and technical prowess.

In 1929, after sculpting *Gamin,* a head of a Harlem youth, she won the first of two Rosenwald fellowships that allowed her to study in Paris, to work at the studio of Elizabeth Prophet, and to study at the Académie de la Grande Chaumière for three years. She won citations at the Salon d'Automme and the Salon Printemps and a medallion at the Colonial Exposition of the French government. In 1932, upon her return from Europe, she opened the Savage Studio of Arts and Crafts in Harlem on 143rd Street. Many young artists, such as Norman LEWIS, William ARTIS, Ernest CRICHLOW, Elba Lightfoot, Morgan and Marvin SMITH, and Gwendolyn KNIGHT, came to study with her. Among her contributions to the arts was her role in establishing the Harlem Community Art Center in 1937. She created a large plaster sculpture, *Lift Every Voice and Sing* (also known as *The Harp*), for the 1939 New York World's Fair, although there were no funds to preserve the 16-foot-tall piece, and it was destroyed after the exhibition. After World War II she moved to upstate New York, her active artistic involvement greatly diminished, and she drifted into obscurity.

As the WPA projects began to expand, the Harlem Artist Guild was formed in 1935 to address issues of equality and representation of black artists on WPA projects. Aaron Douglas was the first director of the guild, and Augusta Savage followed as director the next year. By 1936 Savage was an assistant supervisor for the WPA FEDERAL ARTS PROJECT. At about this time, Charles ALSTON, who created important works as a muralist, realist painter, and illustrator, established a studio at 306 West 141st Street; "306" soon became the social center of the Harlem arts community. Without the assistance of the guild, Charles Alston and Vertis Hayes may have never completed their murals for Harlem Hospital. Georgette Seabrooke POWELL, a young New York artist trained at Cooper Union, contributed less controversial murals to that site, as did Elba Lightfoot. Powell also painted murals for Queens General Hospital.

The largest and most influential school to play a critical role in this area was the Harlem Community Art Center. It began as an outgrowth of the Uptown Art Laboratory, another project of Augusta Savage. In 1937 Gwendolyn Bennett replaced Savage as its director. The center served up to four thousand students a month, and became a model for other WPA art centers. It is the longest-active art center still in operation from this period.

Selma Hortense BURKE, a young sculptor who migrated from North Carolina, studied in New York, Paris, and London, and later taught at the Harlem Community Art Center. Burke created works in stone, wood, and metal that were imbued with clarity of line, mass, and strength of spiritual character. Toward the end of World War II she won a competition to execute a bronze plaque of President Franklin D. Roosevelt, and he sat for her several times. Most experts believe that, uncredited, Burke's design was used for the relief of Roosevelt on the face of the dime.

A number of African-American artists came to prominence during the 1930s. Ernest Crichlow, a resident of Brooklyn, became a teacher at the Harlem Community Art Center. Like Charles Alston, Crichlow created compositions influenced by social realism, often commenting on the conditions and culture of the African-American community. Gwen-

dolyn Knight was a quiet young painter who moved to New York from Barbados. She was active at "306" and the Harlem Community Art Center, and later married the artist Jacob LAWRENCE. Richard LINDSEY was a native of North Carolina and came to New York to study at the National Academy of Design. He was active in the exhibitions of the Harmon Foundation and at the Harlem Community Art Center, where he also worked. Lindsey was a painter and printmaker, but very little of his work has survived.

Chicago also produced a number of prominent artists during the 1930s. Rex GORLEIGH, born in Wynne, Pa., was another painter who taught at the Harlem Community Art Center. Educated at the Art Students League and the University of Chicago, he later studied in France, worked at the WPA in Greensboro, N.C., and later became director of Chicago's South Side Community Art Center (SSCAC), which had opened in 1940. Despite its relatively short existence, the SSCAC had a number of distinguished artists, including Gorleigh, Charles WHITE, Margaret BURROUGHS, Eldzier CORTER, Gordon PARKS, Archibald Motley, and Charles SEBREE.

White established the medium of drawing in charcoal, ink, pencil, and collage as a means to depict semiabstract figures with intense drama. These idealized portraits and studies often had historical subject as their focus. White continued using this style throughout his life, though he became less iconographic and more individualized in his later years. He was active in the WPA as well as the SSCAC.

Burroughs was educated at the Art Institute of Chicago, was a versatile artist in painting, printmaking, and sculpture, and was a significant figure in Chicago area arts education. Cortor was primarily drawn to depictions of African-American women, reflecting their alienation from society and their introspection in positional studies using bedrooms and mirrors as stages. Sebree was a sensitive portraitist.

Another Chicago artist was Ellis WILSON. A Kentucky native, Wilson came to study at the Art Institute of Chicago. He was active in the Harmon Foundation exhibitions, the Savage Studio, and the Federal Arts Project. His mature style is based on strong color, flat figures in outline that document the black working class community.

Allan Rohan CRITE was born in Plainfield, N.J., and moved to Boston to study art. He was one of the few African-American artists to be hired for the WPA Federal Arts Project in Boston. Many of Crite's early subjects were paintings of street scenes and portraits. The balance of his career was spent developing complex studies of religious and spiritual themes.

One of the most active centers for African-American art in the 1930s and 1940s was KARAMU

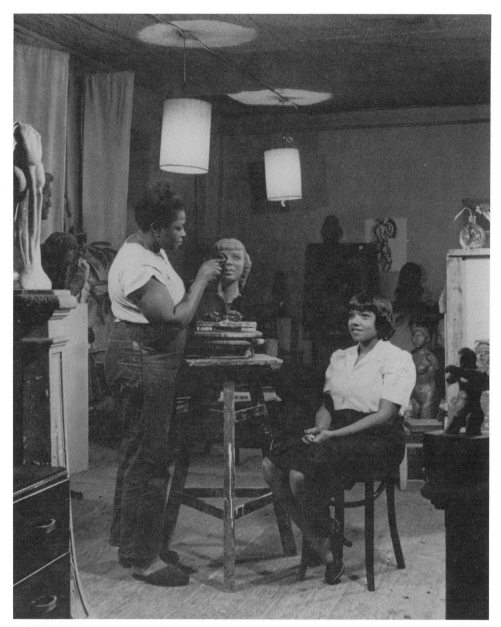

Selma Burke working in her studio with a model. (Photographs and Prints Division, Schomburg Center for Research in Black Culture, The New York Public Library, Astor, Lenox and Tilden Foundations)

PLAYHOUSE, founded in Cleveland in 1915. Karamu Playhouse was an interracial settlement house designed to address the cultural needs of the urban poor. By the time of the Great Depression it was recognized for its theater group. It was not until funding came from the WPA that it established a strong visual arts program. Hughie LEE-SMITH studied at the Cleveland Institute of Arts and became part of the Ohio Federal Arts Project. His painted imagery is figurative and realistic, with metaphysical references to surreal or romanticized landscapes. Lee-Smith was active in numerous portrait commissions and was

greatly respected for his technical skill in watercolor, prints, and drawing. A significant part of his career was spent teaching at the Arts Students League in New York in addition to painting and exhibiting widely.

Elton FAX, born in Baltimore, moved to New York and worked with Augusta Savage and the Harlem Community Art Center. Later he became active in the Maryland Federal Arts Project. He was a versatile painter, printmaker, illustrator, and educator, and was the author of several books on the lives of black artists. Fax played an important role in the development of regional art programs from Baltimore to New York.

Folk Artists

One of the most important forms of African-American artistic expression in the twentieth century has been by "folk" artists. This is a difficult term to define, but generally refers to artists who have not had the benefit of formal academic training and whose work often appears "naive" in its artistic conventions, as in the handling of perspective and shadowing. Many folk artists took up art as an avocation later in their lives, after their retirement, a religious call, or a critical change in lifestyle or career.

Clementine HUNTER was born on Hidden Hill Plantation in Louisiana and worked as a sharecropper. Late in life, Hunter began to paint at the encouragement of one of her guests. She had a prolific career in exhibiting and painting canvases that recalled, with humble reverence, her memories of life in Louisiana.

Horace PIPPIN, born in West Chester, Pa., began to paint later in life, despite an injury to his painting arm during World War I. He started painting by using a hot iron poker to burn the image on a piece of wood. Pippin then slowly painted in the details with numerous layers of oil paint. Many of his intensely detailed paintings relived his haunted memories of the war. His work also includes visions of childhood experiences (including his version of southern black rural life, a reality he never experienced), landscapes, interiors, and his visions of a utopian and peaceful world. During his last years, Pippin's subtle and profoundly moving art achieved great acclaim. He was an ordinary man with an extraordinary sensibility for observing the world around him.

Minnie EVANS, born in Pender County, N.C., created compositions inspired by visions and dreams after a voice on Good Friday in 1935 directed her to "draw or die." Her imagery consisted of a fusion of bright colors with figurative and abstract human and plant forms. She worked in watercolor, crayon, graphite, oil, acrylic ink, collage, enamel, and tempera. Sister Gertrude MORGAN, who lived most of her life in New Orleans, was adept at a wide range of other forms of expression. She was not only a gifted painted but a singer and preacher as well. After she was "called" to a missionary vocation, she used her artistic abilities to spread the word of God. Believing herself to be the bride of Jesus Christ, her paintings had large areas of white—a color of holiness—which were filled with painted images of redemption and revelation.

There have also been a number of important African-American folk sculptors. William EDMONDSON, born in Davidson County, Tenn., near Nashville, spent his working career as a farmhand. Upon retirement he began to carve, in part because of a command from God. He collected old limestone curbstone, and made grave-markers for people in the community who had minimal funds to lay a headstone. As his skill increased, he produced images with great spirituality, humanity, and power. Religious figures, birds, ordinary and heroic individuals, and what he called "critters and varmits (sic)" were his favorite subjects. In 1937 he became the first African-American artist to be given a one-person show by the Museum of Modern Art. Elijah PIERCE was a barber, preacher, and wood carver. He was born in Baldwyn, Miss., and lived most of his life in Columbus, Ohio. Morality, ethics, and the stories of the Bible inspired many of the wooden panels he carved and painted. He painted his carvings in bright colors, energizing the message of his medium and visualizing the message of his pictorial sermons.

Perhaps the most remarkable of African-American folk sculptors was James HAMPTON, who migrated from Elloree, S.C., to Washington, D.C., where he worked as a janitor. A loner, he created *The Throne of the Third Heaven of the Nations' Millennium General Assembly* (c. 1950–1964), which was not known until it was found in a garage long after his death. It consists of more than 185 objects, mostly old furniture, lightbulbs, and other household objects, covered with aluminum, silver, and gold foil and ornately decorated. The heavy use of metallic paper is a symbolic reference to heavenly or celestial light. The work evokes a heavenly and spiritual place, and though Hampton drew on biblical sources, notably the book of Revelations in creating his masterpiece, the precise program is unclear.

Postwar Modernism

Although one cannot define a single African-American aesthetic during the 1930s, the dominant perspective was social realism. One reason for this was the desire of most African-American artists to convey political themes in a realistic form that was programmatically consistent with the aesthetic that was typical for most WPA projects. Although figurative painting continued to predominate in the postwar period, African-American artistic expression became more diverse, and responded to the proliferation of modernist styles.

The African-American artist to be affected most directly by abstract expressionism was Norman Lewis. A native New Yorker, Lewis trained with a variety of artists, including Augusta Savage. In the 1930s he painted a number of powerful paintings in the social realist mode, demonstrating his strong sympathies for the unemployed and homeless. In the later 1930s and 1940s he experimented with the cubist simplification of form, and visually tried to convey the innovations of bebop jazz, which led to an abstract style by the late 1940s. Some critics complained that he was turning his back on depictions of African Americans, though his work often continued to comment on the CIVIL RIGHTS MOVEMENT and other important social issues. Although Lewis was among the earliest American artists to take up the cause of pure abstraction, until recently his name had been conspicuously left out of the canon of abstract expressionist innovators.

Jacob Lawrence was a painter and printmaker who began his career in the mid-1930s, quickly established himself as an important modernist, and developed a style based on expressive flat forms and direct color. He was greatly influenced by Augusta Savage, Charles Alston, and Henry Bouveran when he worked at the Harlem Community Art Center. His primary subject matter was African-American life and history told in a narrative format, in such works as the sixty panels of the . . . The Migration Series (1940–1941), a visual history of the Great Migration. Other important works include the Toussaint Loverture (1938) series, consisting of forty paintings; the thirty works in the Harlem series (1942–1943); and other connected thematic treatments of John Brown, Frederick DOUGLASS, African-American craftsmen, and a general treatment of the theme of freedom in American history. Jacob Lawrence was the first modernist painter of critical significance to emerge from the New Negro movement.

Beauford DELANEY came to New York in the 1920s from Knoxville, Tenn. A sensitive portraitist, in the 1930s he experimented with brightly colored abstractions, and his subsequent portraits are highly expressionistic in their presentation. After World War II he lived in Paris. His brother Joseph DELANEY was a figurative painter who was greatly influenced by the social realist painters and sought to create expressive, atmospheric compositions that reflected urban stresses in the life of large urban areas such as New York. Thomas Sills was a laborer turned painter who moved to New York City from North Carolina. He painted "brushless" canvases with abstracted forms and colors, and was active artistically from the 1950s through the early 1970s.

One of the most important African-American abstractionists was Alma THOMAS, who studied at Howard University in the 1920s before beginning a long career of teaching in the Washington, D.C., public school system. In 1943 she cofounded the first integrated gallery in Washington, D.C., the Barnett-Aden gallery. Her own work was fairly conventional until the early 1950s, when she began to produce the colorful and lyrical abstract canvases she is best known for.

Elizabeth CATLETT, a native of Washington, D.C., studied at Howard University and later with Grant Wood at the University of Iowa. She is a sculptor of immense power, vision, and technical skill. Her media include printmaking, wood, stone, plaster, clay, and bronze. Motherhood, women, and the struggle of oppressed people have been the central themes of her compositions throughout her life. Mexican themes were important in her art after her marriage to Mexican artist Francisco Mora and her expatriation to his country.

Like Catlett and Beauford Delaney, a number of important African-American artists expatriated themselves after World War II. Ronald JOSEPH moved to Europe in the 1940's, primarily living in Brussels. An abstractionist from the late 1930s, his restrained compositions received little recognition in the United States and for many decades he had little contact with American artists, though he was making a comeback at the time of his sudden death in 1992. Herbert GENTRY moved to Paris after World War II and studied at the Grande Chaumière. Linear movement and biomorphic form have been among his major concerns. Though primarily abstractions, a number of his canvases have featured the representation of masks. In 1960 he settled in Stockholm, Sweden. Ed Clark moved to Paris in 1952; his paintings were often abstractions of the human figure. Other expatriates include Lawrence Potter (1924–1966), primarily a color field abstractionist, and Walter Williams (1920–), whose work often imaginatively evokes African-American childhood.

The Civil Rights Movement and the Visual Arts

The civil rights movement of the 1960s was a turning point for black art and culture. A number of important artworks were directly inspired by the movement, such as Norman Lewis's Processional (1964), Jacob Lawrence's The Ordeal of Mary (1963), and Elizabeth Catlett's Homage to My Young Black Sisters (1968) and Malcolm X Speaks for Us (1969). In 1963 Romare BEARDEN contacted Norman Lewis and Hale Woodruff and formed Spiral, a group of twelve African-American artists committed to supporting the civil rights movement and furthering its connection to African-American art. They held their first group show in 1964. The group had largely disbanded by 1965, though their impact as a politically conscious African-American artist collective outlived the short duration of the movement.

One of the central figures in Spiral, Romare Bearden was in his own right one of the most significant African-American artists of the postwar period. Born in Charlotte, N.C., he was raised in Harlem and was a lifelong New Yorker. He was primarily a portrait-

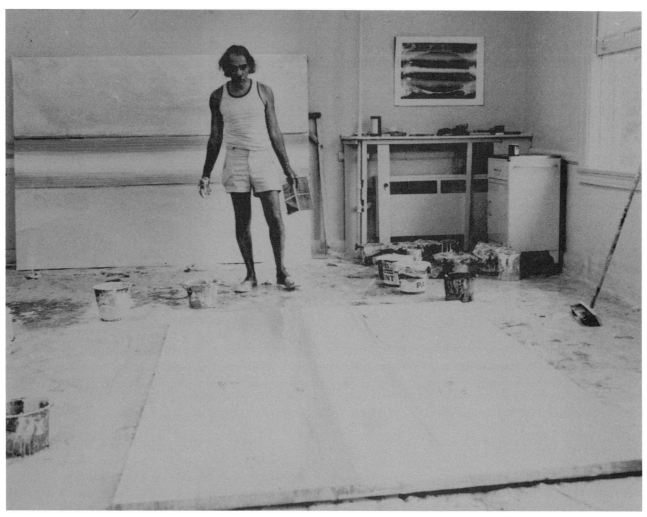

Ed Clark in his New York studio. (Photographs and Prints Division, Schomburg Center for Research in Black Culture, The New York Public Library, Astor, Lenox and Tilden Foundations)

ist, and Spiral had a major impact on his art, which subsequently concentrated on painted, mixed media collages that depicted the African-American experience with a strong emphasis on spirituality. Bearden was also an important writer on African-American art. His works include the posthumous *History of African-American Artists* (1993), cowritten with Harry Henderson.

Benny ANDREWS, like Bearden, was an activist and an expressive figurative painter who also worked in collage, with modeling paste and acrylic. Andrews was concerned that black artists express themselves on a wide range of issues. He was active in teaching in prisons in Queens, New York, and he cofounded the BLACK EMERGENCY CULTURAL COALITION (BECC) in 1969. John BIGGERS, who was raised in North Carolina and who taught for many decades at Texas Southern University, was a figurative artist in the tradition of Charles White, and was profoundly influenced by numerous visits to Africa. His draw-

ings and murals were some of his most distinguished contributions to the field.

By the late 1960s the BLACK ARTS MOVEMENT was giving rising to a new type of African-American art: community based, militant, and African-centered in its politics. In 1968 the Chicago-based AFRICOBRA (African Commune of Bad Relevant Artists) painted the *Wall of Respect* in a black Chicago neighborhood, and started a vogue of the painting of community murals in the late 1960s and 1970s. This aesthetic had other venues besides murals. Nelson Stevens, one of the founders of Africobra, painted in "Kool-Aid" colors and produced prints that contained nationalistic positive images of black males, females, and heroic icons such as MALCOLM X.

Vincent SMITH was influenced by the Black Arts movement, avant-garde jazz and blues of the 1960s, and African art. Many of his oil paintings are mixed media explorations of the black experience, and his etchings and monoprints are eloquent narratives on the distinctive nuances of African-American life. Faith RINGGOLD, in contrast, executed huge reconfigured paintings of the American flag. She was an outspoken feminist and activist who used her art to redefine the role of women. Her paintings evolved into painted story quilts, telling complex narratives in a geometric format.

Other strategies for confronting viewers with unsettling observations on the nature of the relation between blacks and American society include those explored by Barkley HENDRICKS, who has painted large, portrait images of African-Americans against stark and vaguely ominous white canvases. Betye SAAR uses mixed media, including found objects and advertising images, as in her *The Liberation of Aunt Jemina* (1972). Mel EDWARDS uses found or discarded metal objects such as parts of machines and tools to create metaphors of the exploited classes within American society, as in his *Lynch Fragment Series,* a lifelong, continuous series of explorations in form and structure.

Bob THOMPSON worked in flat, brightly colored figures and compositions that resembled the work of European masters, including Nicolas Poussin and the Fauves. His work had a strong symbolic component. His development was cut short by his untimely death. Emilio CRUZ, once a studiomate of Thompson's, shared similar artistic concerns. Cruz has been occupied throughout his career with symbolism, spirituality, and the holistic sense of humanity and personal artistic development. The mood, tempo, and improvisational structure of jazz have been integral to his creative process.

Contemporary African-American Art

The diversity in medium, style, and philosophy within African-American art has burgeoned since the 1970s. In part this reflects the increasing heterogeneity of contemporary art, as well as the new prominence and confidence of black artists as they see themselves as part of the world at large.

Among the most important of recent African-American abstractionists has been William T. WILLIAMS. He works in large-scale abstractions characterized by the use of geometry, illusion, and complex surface textures, creating subtle moods and atmospheres as he attempts to realize his inner visions. Al LOVING also works in an abstract idiom. Spatial relationships, color, and illusion dominate his large acrylic canvases and small watercolor collages. His forms appear suspended in space, amplifying the sense of illusion. Other abstract artists include Jack WHITTEN, who explores surface textures and organic structures that resemble intensely magnified sections of human skin or the tile mosaics of ancient floor patterns. Whitten is also interested in human efforts

to decorate and ornament skin, as in the African practice of scarification. Oliver JACKSON, a California painter, explores the power and energy of nature. In his paintings humanity is often reduced to a subordinate element within the grand scale of his oversized acrylics. Jackson is also a sculptor and woodcarver of power, skill, and vision. Raymond SAUNDERS has developed a very personal style in which the environment around him is reflected in large studies, illuminated by iconographic messages embedded in the surface of the picture plane. Saunders uses the popular language of the community to create a visual text of ideas, images, and symbolic metaphors.

Sam GILLIAM exhibited unorthodox canvases in the 1972 Venice Biennale, which broke his connection to "easel" art. The huge canvases were painted on the studio floor by pouring buckets of paint on the surface and moving the pigment across the canvas with brooms. Later he extended this process by cutting and repasting sections of these canvases, configuring them into large shaped paintings, juxtaposing bright color, texture, and form. In other commission projects he would wrap entire buildings or drape interior spaces with his creations. Gilliam has been fascinated with the processes of paint, light, color, and texture.

Another contemporary style was exemplified in the work of the highly publicized and controversial work of Jean-Michel BASQUIAT. Although often dismissed as a mere graffiti artist, he expanded and redefined the nature of abstract expressionist painting, through the use of energetic figures and text in his works. Basquiat reorganized the nature of the picture plane by using popular imagery and mixed media on grand-scale surfaces to make biting commentaries on society. He was especially concerned with the politics of African-American art within the larger society. His early stardom and the media attention he garnered, as well as his early death, have to some extent obscured his true worth, which will become clearer in passing decades.

Robert COLESCOTT's signature style of figurative paintings is intended to place African Americans within the canons of Western art traditions. In the *Knowledge is the Key to the Past* series (1970s), Colescott re-creates famous historical compositions by European artists and replaces the subjects with black characters. The results are satirical indictments of Western society which disturb white and black viewers. Bold color and complex compositions combined with the gesturally painted figures amplify the importance of the issues involved. His sociopolitical commentaries with their deft skewering of stereotypes have often provoked controversy, negative reactions, and great debate about the relevance of his themes.

A number of recent artists have combined Afrocentric themes with a proactive stance on conceptual art. Howardena PINDELL is a multitalented artist and writer who works in a wide range of media, including painting, prints, video, performance art, and installations. Her works are provocative and have often been compared to those of Colescott for their political stance. David HAMMONS, like Pindell, has invited controversy through his creations from hair balls, wine bottles, greasy paper bags, bottle caps, snowballs, coal, chicken wings, and barbecued ribs. Hammons treats even the most despised and hidden aspects of the black experience with a sense of reverence. Houston CONWILL's inventiveness creates sculpture, installations, and performance art that recall the time, place, and memory of African and African-American cultural rituals of the past. He has been preoccupied with defining the nature of sacred space in the African-American community.

Richard HUNT and Martin PURYEAR are two of the most distinguished African-American sculptors. Both work in distinct styles. Hunt works in metal, usually steel, creating works that are derived from plant and animal forms. The metal is shaped to convey the illusion of a series of plants growing in space. Puryear creates objects and forms inspired by architectural structures and everyday objects essential to the lives of African, Asian, and American Indian peoples. His materials include wood, metal, fiber, stone, and wax. The expanded scale of the objects often sets up a psychological juxtaposition that challenges the notion of the function and role of the objects as art.

The current bounty of contemporary African-American art in some ways represents the culmination of the work of many generations of creative black painters and sculptors. African-American artists first had to struggle simply to gain access to the world of fine art. Once the barriers were beginning to be breached, they were faced with the equally important task of finding their own distinctive voice, and demanding that it be heard and given respect. Amid the turbulence of the contemporary artistic scene, few groups have been as important as African-American artists in directing the attention of artists to issues such as race, gender, identity, culture, politics, and a critical self-examination of the operations of the art world itself. At the same time, one cannot pigeonhole African-American art to one type of expression; black artists have created and are creating works in styles and forms ranging from quiet intellectual contemplation to works of militant engagement. The accomplishments of African-American art are testament to the creative expectations of black artists as they meld the complexities of their African and multiethnic American heritages with their personal artistic visions. Its achievements will endure and invent ever new forms of visual expressiveness.

REFERENCES

BEARDEN, ROMARE and HARRY HENDERSON. *A History of African-American Artists: From 1792 to the Present.* New York, 1993.
BENEZRA, NEAL. *Martin Puryear.* Chicago, 1992.
CANNON, STEVE, KELLIE JONES, and TOM FINKELPEARL. *David Hammons: Rousing the Rubble.* Cambridge, Mass.; 1991.
Columbus Museum of Art. *Elijah Pierce: Woodcarver.* Seattle, Wash., 1992.
Connecticut Gallery, Inc. *Charles Ethan Porter.* Marlborough, Conn., 1987.
Dallas Museum of Art. *Black Art: Ancestral Legacy.* Dallas, 1989.
DRISKELL, DAVID. *Two Centuries of Black American Art.* Los Angeles, 1976.
FULLER, EDMUND R. *Visions in Stone: The Sculpture of William Edmundson.* Pittsburgh, 1973.
GOOD-BRYAND, LINDA, and MARCY S. PHILIPS. *Contextures.* New York, 1978.
———. *Hidden Heritage: Afro-American Art, 1800–1950.* Bellevue, Wash., 1985.
HARTIGAN, LYNDA ROSCOE. *Sharing Traditions: Five Black Artists in Nineteenth-Century America.* Washington, D.C., 1985.
Howard University Gallery of Art. *James A. Porter: Artist and Art Historian—The Memory of the Legacy.* Washington, D.C., 1992.
KING-HAMMOND, LESLIE. *Masks and Mirrors: African-American Art, 1700–Now.* New York, 1995.
LEWIS, SAMELLA. *Art: African-American.* Los Angeles, 1993.
———. *The Art of Elizabeth Catlett.* Claremont, Calif., 1984.
LIVINGSTON, JANE, and JOHN BEARDSLEY. *Black Folk Art in America, 1930–1980.* Washington, D.C., 1982.
LOCKE, ALAIN. *The Negro in Art.* New York, 1940.
NEWBERGER MUSEUM OF ART. *Melvin Edwards Sculpture: A Thirty-Year Retrospective, 1963–1993.* Seattle, Wash., 1993.
PERRY, REGENIA. *Free Within Our Selves: African American Artists in the Collection of the National Museum of American Art.* Washington, D.C., 1992.
Philadelphia Museum of Art. *Henry Ossawa Tanner.* Philadelphia, 1991.
PORTER, JAMES A. *Modern Negro Art.* 1943. Reprint. Washington, D.C., 1993.
POWELL, RICHARD. *Homecoming: The Life and Art of William Henry Johnson.* Washington, D.C., 1992.
REYNOLDS, GARY A., and BERYL J. WRIGHT, eds. *Against the Odds: African-American Artists and the Harmon Foundation.* Newark, N.J., 1989.
ROBINSON, JONTLYLE TERESA and WENDY GREENHOUSE. *The Art of Archibald J. Motley, Jr.* Chicago, 1991.
STEIN, JUDITH E. *I Tell My Heart: The Art of Horace Pippen.* Philadelphia, 1994.

Studio Museum in Harlem. *Beauford Delaney: A Retrospective*. New York, 1978.

————. *Harlem Renaissance: Art of Black America*. New York, 1987.

————. *Memory and Metaphor: The Art of Romare Bearden, 1940–1987*. New York, 1991.

————. *Tradition and Conflict: Images of a Turbulent Decade, 1963–1973*. New York, 1985.

TURNER, ELIZABETH HUTTON, ed. *Jacob Lawrence: The Migration Series*. Washington, D.C., 1993.

WEEKLEY, CAROLYN J., and STILES TUTTLE COLWILL with Leroy Graham and Mat Ellen Hayward. *Joshua Johnson: Freeman and Early American Portrait Painter*. Williamsburg, Va., 1988.

WHEAT, ELLEN HARKINS. *Jacob Lawrence: American Painter*. Seattle, Wash., 1986.

WILLIS-THOMAS, DEBORAH. *Black Photographers, 1840–1880: An Illustrated Bio-Bibliography*. New York, 1985.

WILSON, JAMES L. *Clementine Hunter: American Folk Artist*. Gretna, La., 1988.

LESLIE KING HAMMOND

Pan-Africanism. The term *Pan-Africanism*, in its most general sense, refers to a movement that seeks to unite and promote the welfare of all people identified with, or claiming membership in, the African or black race. Pan-Africanism is based on the idea of overcoming vast differences in language, ethnicity, religion, and geographical origin. A degree of cultural unity despite these divisions has to some extent already been achieved among the African population of the United States, due to forced interethnic mingling without regard to cultural or regional background during the SLAVERY experience. Slavery forged African Americans into a truly Pan-African people, who came to share a belief in a common destiny, deriving from the historic humiliations of slavery, colonialism, and racism. On a more positive note, Pan-Africanists also insist on recognizing the historic importance of contributions that Africa and the black race have made to civilization and human progress since the dawn of history.

Pan-Africanism assumes that the political unification of Africa will contribute to the welfare of all black people of African descent, whether or not they actually live in Africa. The African-American scholar, W. E. B. DU BOIS, defined Pan-Africanism as "the idea of one Africa uniting the thought and ideals of all peoples of the dark continent," but observed that the idea had stemmed "naturally from the West Indies and the United States." Pan-African and black nationalist sentiments in the United States and in the Caribbean have provided much of the ideology for nationalist and decolonization movements on the African continent.

During the period 1957–1974, most of the colonial powers withdrew, at least formally, from their African colonies. Since then, political Pan-Africanism has focused on removing the vestiges of colonialism, particularly in South Africa, and on promoting economic and political unity among African nations. The institution that presently seeks to accomplish geopolitical unification of the continent is the Organization of African Unity (OAU), founded in 1963. In the United States, the best-known African-American support organization is TRANSAFRICA, founded in 1977.

Documents illustrating the history of Pan-Africanism began to appear during the late eighteenth century. Of signal importance was *The Interesting Narrative of the Life of Olaudah Equiano or Gustavus Vassa, the African, Written by Himself* (1787) (*see also* Olaudah EQUIANO). Equiano's tract, published in England, has been identified by historian Imanuel Geiss as "proto-Pan-Africanism," but it lacked the militant self-assertiveness that is associated with the modern movement. Equiano, who had been enslaved as a child and traveled as a cabin boy to the New World, believed for a time that the African condition could be improved by resettling Christianized Africans from Europe and the Americas in Africa. Although he came to abandon that plan, he remained committed to the destruction of African slavery through the agencies of Christian missionary activity, free trade, and the establishment of an African nationality.

In 1787, British reformers began a campaign to resettle England's so-called "black poor" in the West African colony of Sierra Leone. Abolitionists (*see* ABOLITION) saw themselves as creating a center for missionary activity and African redemption from the SLAVE TRADE. Their efforts were supported by a small cadre of proto–Pan-Africanists, but Equiano eventually came to oppose African resettlement.

The diversity of the peoples who settled Sierra Leone illustrated the complexities of Pan-African identity. The first settlers were a mixed group, including African-American loyalists who had been evacuated with the British after the AMERICAN REVOLUTION and runaway slaves from the West Indies. A second group of immigrants came from Canada—ex-slaves who had fought on the British side in the American War for Independence and then temporarily settled in Nova Scotia (*see* LOYALISTS IN THE AMERICAN REVOLUTION). A third element also came from Nova Scotia, but ultimately derived from a group known as maroons, escaped slaves who had formed independent colonies in the mountains of Jamaica (*see* MAROONAGE). These maroons, after staging an unsuccessful revolt in 1795, were deported first to Nova

Scotia and then to Sierra Leone. A fourth group were the so-called "recaptives," persons of various African ethnicities deposited in Sierra Leone over the years after being recaptured from slave traders by the British fleet.

Black Americans showed an immediate interest in Sierra Leone. A group of settlers arrived from the United States in 1816, transported by Capt. Paul CUFFE, a man of mixed African and American Indian ancestry. Along with James FORTEN, a black sailmaker of Philadelphia, Cuffe hoped to develop Christianity, commerce, and civilization in Africa, and to further thwart the slave trade, while providing a homeland for African Americans. This emigrationist variety of American Pan-Africanism was undermined in 1817, however, with the formation of the American Society for Colonizing the Free People of Color in the United States, usually called the AMERICAN COLONIZATION SOCIETY (ACS). Because the ACS included a number of prominent slave holders in its leadership, and expressly denied any sympathy for abolition, the black American population was generally hostile to it. With the death of Cuffe, Forten became silent on the subjects of black nationalism and Pan-Africanism.

African Americans who supported the movement, as did Peter WILLIAMS, SR., and John RUSSWURM, were subjected to considerable public scorn. In the early nineteenth century, black Americans went through one of their periodic frenzies of name changing, in an attempt to affirm their American loyalties. At this point even some of the more millitant nationalist and Pan-Africanist organizations began to prefer the designation "Colored" over "African." Notable exceptions were the AFRICAN METHODIST EPISCOPAL CHURCH (AME) and the AFRICAN METHODIST EPISCOPAL ZION CHURCH (AMEZ).

The ideologies of black nationalism and Pan-Africanism evolved in the climate of the American and French revolutions, which gave currency to ideas of republican government, and inspired certain classes of Africans to think of creating an African nation-state. One should not, however, assume that Pan-Africanism was simply an imitation of European or United States' ideology. It arose simultaneously with the European nationalisms and was a cognate rather than a derivative. C. L. R. James viewed the Haitian slave revolt (1791–1803) as the decisive event in the history of Pan-Africanism (see HAITIAN SLAVE REVOLT). Du Bois observed that the Haitian revolt led to the Louisiana Purchase and thus had a direct effect on white Americans' conceptions of nationalism and Manifest Destiny. It can be argued that Pan-Africanism and black nationalism in the Haitian republic were historically intertwined with the growth of the American nation and its conception of Manifest Destiny.

The Haitian revolt provided the impetus for the abortive revolution of the Jamaican Maroons in 1795. It also inspired early Pan-Africanism in the United States. Prince HALL, the Masonic lodge master from Massachusetts, and sometime advocate of emigration, expressed his admiration of "our African brethren . . . in the French West Indies." There is no way of determining the extent to which Pan-Africanism touched the imaginations of the slave population of the United States, but there is some evidence that they were influenced by it. Herbert Aptheker has speculatively linked the slave conspiracy of Gabriel Prosser (see GABRIEL PROSSER CONSPIRACY) to the revolution in Haiti. The conspiracy of Denmark Vesey (see DENMARK VESEY CONSPIRACY) was said to have been inspired by the Haitian revolt, and Vesey was reputed to have dreamed of a black supernation uniting the southern states to the Caribbean.

Pan-African sentiments were strong among the African-American population of the early republic. The so-called Free African Societies of New York, Boston, and Rhode Island often expressed their identity with other Africans on both sides of the Atlantic. Early black newspapers revealed an interest in the history of Africa and the destiny of the African race. Overt identification with African affairs became unfashionable, however, when in 1816 the American Colonization Society was founded for the purpose of resettling the so-called "free people of color" in the colony of Liberia. David WALKER published an incendiary *Appeal Together with a Preamble, to the Colored Citizens of the World* in 1829, in which he denounced Liberian colonization. Another early pamphleteer was Maria STEWART, who, although she referred to herself as an African, was equally hostile to the colonization movement. So too was Richard ALLEN, an organizer of the AME church, who believed in the unity of African peoples and a special God-given mission for them, but steadfastly opposed any talk of Liberian colonization.

Peter Williams, Sr., an Episcopal priest in New York, took a more tolerant view of African colonization. He eulogized Paul Cuffe, memorializing his voyages to Africa, and he remained friendly with John Russwurm, even after the latter was burned in effigy by anti-emigration activists. Classical black nationalism became practically indistinguishable from Pan-Africanism in the mid-nineteenth century. Between 1850 and 1862 the quest for a national homeland represented a desire to create, in Henry Highland GARNET's words, "a grand center of Negro Nationality." Although Martin DELANY and a number of other black nationalists focused on Cuba and South America as possible sites for this "grand center," most black nationalists were inevitably drawn to Africa as the logical focus for a scheme of universal Negro improvement. Alexander CRUMMELL, a protégé of Peter Williams, made his peace with the American Colonization Society, and settled his hopes on Liberia. The entire generation of classical black nationalists, like the hero of Martin Delany's novel *Blake* (1859), believed in a commonality of interests among all African people, whether in Africa, the Caribbean, Europe, or North America.

At the time of the American CIVIL WAR, the Constitution of the African Civilization Society (1861) represented the Pan-African agenda in terms of "the civilization and Christianization of Africa, and of the descendants of African ancestors in any portion of the earth, wherever dispersed. Also the introduction of lawful commerce and trade into Africa." It also stated a commitment to "Self-Reliance and Self-Government, on the principle of an African Nationality, the African race being the ruling element of the nation, controlling and directing their own affairs."

The heavy emphasis on Christianity and civilization among nineteenth-century Pan-Africanists was among its more notable features. The cultural nationalism in the 1850s was universalist in its concepts and did not seek to promote an alternative to European or American definitions of culture. Even when celebrating the history of Africa's past attainments, nineteenth-century Pan-Africanists ironically betrayed an attachment to European definitions of progress and civilization. The early Pan-Africanists' appreciation for the African past was usually limited to a fascination with Egyptian grandeur and its Ethiopian roots.

Nonetheless, Pan-Africanism, in its attraction to Egyptian origins of civilization, initiated the movement known in the late twentieth century as Afrocentrism (*see* AFROCENTRICITY). William Wells BROWN and other nineteenth-century African Americans celebrated the accomplishments of the ancient Egyptians and made high claims for the potential of native Africans untouched by European decadence. This fascination with Egypt appeared even in the writings of Frederick DOUGLASS, who normally disparaged the idea of racial pride. Edward Wilmot BLYDEN, a West Indian migrant to Liberia, who is often called the father of modern Pan-Africanism, claimed ancient Egypt as his ancestral heritage. In recent years, the "Egyptocentric" approach to African history, championed by the Senegalese scholar Cheikh Anta Diop, has been immensely popular among some factions of American Pan-Africanists.

Blyden, like many later Pan-Africanists, was increasingly interested in contemporary African cultures and folklore. He was well known in the United States, where he traveled and lectured extensively. Blyden advocated the study of West African languages and cultures in the African schools and universities, and insisted that pristine African societies were culturally and morally superior to those of primeval Europe. The Sierra Leone physician, Africanus Horton, likewise defended traditional African cultures. Toward the end of the century, younger scholars, like J. E. Casely Hayford of the Gold Coast and the American W. E. B. Du Bois, also celebrated Egypt, Ethiopia, and Meroë (in the Sudan) as black sources of world civilization. At the same time, they followed in the tradition of Blyden by encouraging a respect for traditional African village life as manifested in the cultures of sub-Saharan Africa.

In 1885 Otto von Bismarck convened the so-called Berlin Conference at which the European powers partitioned the continent of Africa, and the Congo was consigned to the "protectorship" of Leopold II, King of the Belgians. While the partition awakened mixed emotions among many black Americans, Blyden, Crummell and the African-American historian George Washington WILLIAMS hoped, at first, that the Belgian model would provide a workable plan for attacking the slave trade and promoting "the three Cs." By 1890, however, Williams had denounced Leopold for his brutal exploitation of the Congo. Byden, the Pan-Africanist par excellence, continued to praise Leopold as late as 1895. Crummell supported European colonialism until his death in 1898, because of his belief that the British would hinder the spread of ISLAM and suppress the Arab slave trade in the Sudan. Nonetheless, Africans and black Americans were becoming increasingly disillusioned with European colonialism. Booker T. WASHINGTON, for example, spoke out against British imperialism, and became active in the Congo Reform Association. Washington also encouraged African missionary activities, industrial education, and colonial reform, while his political machine contributed to a series of conferences on Africa. Washington worked behind the scenes to organize a missionary conference at the Atlanta Exhibition in 1895, where participants included Alexander Crummell and the AME Bishop, Henry McNeal TURNER.

Black missionary activity in Africa gave rise to a religious manifestation of Pan-Africanism called "Ethiopianism." The movement derived its name from its adherents' obsession with the cryptic biblical prophecy, "Ethiopia shall soon stretch forth her hands unto God (Psalms 68:31)." Crummell, Blyden, and other Christian preachers had long employed the allusion in their sermons, but the Ethiopian movement was an independent movement of the African masses and a departure from traditional Christianity. It was what some scholars have referred to as a revitalization movement, in that it revived Christian teaching by adapting it to the indigenous cultures. It often preserved elements of ancestral religions and carried with it a strong antiwhite feeling. The new militancy is often attributed to the inspiration of Bishop Turner, who visited South Africa in 1898, preaching religious independence and establishing the AME church there. In short order, however, the zeal of South African Christians exceeded Turner's expectations, as Africans declared their independence not only from the white churches, but also from the African-American–dominated AMEs. Thereafter, a much larger independent church movement came into being, revealing attitudes that were both nationalistic and Pan-Africanistic.

St. Clair DRAKE and George Shepperson have described the political aspect of Ethiopianism as an element of Pan-African consciousness, spreading rapidly northward and eastward, and becoming more strident in its attacks on colonialism. In Nyasaland, now known as Malawi, John Chilembwe led a premature revolt in 1914, which has been attributed to the influences of Chilembwe's studies in the United States and his exposure to Ethiopianism after his return to Africa. Later in the century, in Kenya in the 1950s, the Mau Mau movement had ties to the Ethiopian millenialism that Jomo Kenyatta called "The New Religion in East Africa." It was from the Ethiopian movement that the slogan "Africa for the Africans" began to take on radical political implications. Ethiopianism is important as at least one of the sources of the RASTAFARIAN movement in Jamaica.

Edwin S. Redkey has detected grassroots Pan-Africanism in the movement that established all-black towns in Oklahoma during the 1890s. The Rev. Orishatukeh Faduma, a Yoruba man from Barbados, became a missionary in Oklahoma, where he recruited for Chief Alfred C. Sam's back-to-Africa movement. J. Ayodele Langley has shown that Sam, a Twi speaker from the Gold Coast, eventually received the moral support of Casely Hayford, despite the latter's original skepticism. William H. Ferris, John E. BRUCE and Du Bois, all protégés of Alexander Crummell, had been connected with Faduma, through their association with the AMERICAN NEGRO ACADEMY. The academy also included among its honorary members Duse Muhammad Ali, the London-based Sudanese nationalist who was editor of the *African Times and Orient Review*.

Ferris and Bruce, although well acquainted with the failure of Chief Sam's back-to-Africa movement, nevertheless became supporters of Marcus Garvey's similar repatriation effort after World War I. Marcus Garvey's UNIVERSAL NEGRO IMPROVEMENT ASSOCIATION revealed in its very name the traditional concern of Pan-Africanism. Garvey was less successful as a repatriationist than some of his predecessors, but he did a great deal to generate mass enthusiasm for African nationalism and the Pan-African movement. Garvey was an inspiration to a generation of African political leaders, and his name became a household word in small towns throughout the black world.

After Garvey's death, his second wife, Amy Jacques Garvey, remained an important figure in the movement.

Garvey did much to popularize the idea of African independence, and he was unexcelled in his celebration of Africa's ancient glories. William H. Ferris, John E. BRUCE, Carter G. WOODSON, Arthur Schomburg, and J. A. ROGERS contributed to Marcus Garvey's newspaper, *Negro World,* and did much to popularize the notion that black peoples of the upper Nile were the unrivalled progenitors of world civilization. Pan-Africanist cultural expressions in the tradition of Blyden were certainly more obvious among Garveyites than among those intellectuals who disassociated themselves from the Garvey movement.

In 1900 Henry Sylvester Williams, a Trinidad barrister, and Bishop Alexander WALTERS of the AME Zion church, convened the London Conference, widely regarded as the first international meeting to apply the term *Pan-African* to its program. W. E. B. Du Bois, although he played an important role in the London Conference, never referred to it as the first Pan-African Congress, reserving that distinction for the meeting that he called in Paris in 1919 at the time of the Paris Peace Conference, following World War I. The convention brought together fifty-seven delegates from Africa, the West Indies, and United States, but American participation was limited because of the refusal of the United States government to grant passports. Ida B. WELLS, who was accredited as a representative of Garvey's UNIA was thus unable to attend, and William Monroe TROTTER was forced to pose as a ship's cook in order to get to Paris. Du Bois was assisted in setting up the Congress by his connections to the NATIONAL ASSOCIATION FOR THE ADVANCEMENT OF COLORED PEOPLE (NAACP), and the influence of the Senegalese Deputy, Blaise Diagne. Du Bois insisted that the Congress had influenced the Peace Conference to establish a Mandates Commission for administration of the former German colonies. Du Bois worked with the Pan-African Congress at its subsequent meetings of 1921, 1923, and 1927.

During the 1920s, a cultural development known as the NEW NEGRO movement, centered in such urban centers as Harlem, Washington, D.C., and Chicago, contributed to the development of cultural Pan-Africanism. The movement found expression in the literary Garveyism of Ferris, Bruce, and Rogers, but the term came to be associated with the publication of Alain LOCKE's *The New Negro* (1925). The so-called HARLEM RENAISSANCE, an offshoot of this New Negro movement, was much indebted to cultural developments in Europe and the United States after World War I, including "primitivism," cultural relativism, and the Freudian revolution in sexual values. In the view of Sterling BROWN and Arthur P.

Davis, this fostered a "phony exotic primitive" stereotype and "grafted primitivism on decadence." Sentimental Pan-Africanism, as expressed in the sensual imagery of Countee CULLEN's poem "Heritage," appealed to wealthy whites and influential white intellectuals, but avoided Pan-Africanism as a political ideology. Although Locke included an article on Pan-Africanism by Du Bois in *The New Negro,* he dismissed Garveyism. The works of Charles T. Davis, Tony Martin, and David Levering Lewis are essential correctives to the view of the Harlem Renaissance that emphasizes bohemian aestheticism to the neglect of political Pan-Africanism and the Garvey movement.

During the 1930s, Pan-African cultural nationalism came to be identified with the NÉGRITUDE movement, defined by francophone black intellectuals, René Maran, Leopold Sédar Senghor, and Aimé Césaire. *Négritude* emphasized such mythic traits of the African personality as sensuality, emotional sensitivity, and the purported softness of the black man. Cheikh Anta Diop has lamented the relationship of Négritude to the primitive stereotype and has opined that "the Negritude movement accepted this so-called inferiority and boldly assumed it in full view of the world." Indeed, many African and African-American intellectuals did celebrate African "primitivism." Nineteenth-century black intellectuals had shown little interest in the culture of the masses, aside from the occasional militant Christianity expressed in the Negro spirituals. Twentieth-century intellectuals celebrated black American folk culture for its "pagan," pre-Christian elements and its Pan-African cultural connections.

Data collected by Leo Frobenius, the German scholar, interpreted in the light of social science, heightened the interest of Du Bois, Aimé Césaire, and Leopold Senghor in the cultures of pre-colonial, sub-Saharan Africa. This led black American intellectuals to a reappraisal of their folk heritage and its African roots. The development of ANTHROPOLOGY (*see also* ANTHROPOLOGISTS), with its doctrine of cultural relativism and its ties to scientific relativism, made possible an increased respect for "primitive" cultures. The concepts of Franz Boas and Melville Herskovits contributed to the metaphysical foundations of a new African cultural nationalism that merged modernism with primitivism. Fashionable modern artists, such as Picasso and Modigliani, demonstrated their discontent with the conventional norms of European cultural expression by borrowing from African graphic modes. The increasing respectability of JAZZ, after its celebration by European and American audiences, was another factor in the transformation of Pan-African cultural nationalism.

In 1939 the Council on African Affairs was organized by Paul ROBESON and Max YERGAN, with Ralph BUNCHE and the novelist René Maran on the board of management. The council was promoted by numerous prominent black individuals and organizations throughout the 1940s, but came under attack during the Red Scare of the 1950s. Meanwhile the Fifth Pan-African Congress was held in Manchester, U.K., in 1945. Du Bois was accorded a place of honor in Manchester, although Pan-African leadership by this time had passed from African-American to African leadership, represented by Kwame Nkrumah, Nnamdi Azikewe, and Jomo Kenyatta. Older West Africans, such as Ras T. Makonnen and George Padmore, continued to play significant roles. Padmore, a Trinidadian who had participated in the Manchester Conference, gained considerable influence with Nkrumah, who as president of Ghana (the former Gold Coast), hosted a conference in the Ghanaian capital of Accra in 1958. Shirley Graham, the only American officially in attendance, read an address by her husband, W. E. B. Du Bois, who was hospitalized in Moscow.

Since formation of the Organization of African Unity, black Americans have supported the Pan-African movement from a distance. The major emphasis in recent years has been on the struggle against apartheid in the Republic of South Africa. The efforts of African Americans in support of the South African struggle have been moderately successful. Black Americans have been unable to exert much influence over American foreign policy regarding Western and Central Africa, regions of the continent that have experienced much economic hardship and domestic unrest. The hopes of Garvey and Du Bois for an economically prosperous Africa have not yet been realized despite the attainment of political independence.

REFERENCES

AJALA, ADEKUNLE. *Pan-Africanism: Evolution, Progress and Prospects.* London, 1974.

CARLISLE, RODNEY. *The Roots of Black Nationalism.* Port Washington, N.Y., 1975.

CROMWELL, ADELAIDE. *An African Victorian Feminist: The Life and Times of Adelaide Smith Casely Hayford.* London, 1992.

DIOP, CHEIKH ANTA. *Black Africa: The Economic and Cultural Basis for a Federated State.* Westport, Conn., 1978.

DRAKE, ST. CLAIR. *The Redemption of Africa and Black Religion.* Chicago, 1970.

GEISS, IMMANUEL. *The Pan-African Movement.* New York, 1974.

JAMES, C. L. R. *A History of Pan-African Revolt.* Washington, D.C., 1969.

LANGLEY, J. AYODELE. *Pan-Africanism and Nationalism in West Africa, 1900–1945.* Oxford, U.K., 1973.

LEMELLE, SID. *Pan-African Connection.* Dover, Mass., 1983.

MARTIN, TONY. *The Pan-African Connection.* Dover, Mass., 1983.

MILLER, FLOYD. *The Search for a Black Nationality: Black Colonization and Emigration, 1787–1863.* Urbana, Ill., 1975.

MOSES, WILSON J. *The Golden Age of Black Nationalism 1850–1925.* Hamden, Conn., 1978.

REDKEY, EDWIN S. *Black Exodus.* New Haven, 1969.

WILSON J. MOSES

Pan-African Orthodox Church (The Shrine of the Black Madonna).

The Pan-African Orthodox Church, which is more commonly known as the Shrine of the Black Madonna, was established in Detroit, Mich., on March 26, 1967, by the Rev. Albert B. Cleage, Jr., an ordained minister in the UNITED CHURCH OF CHRIST. While this is the recognized date for its inception, the church actually began with a remnant of several earlier congregations. It has now grown from one congregation into a denomination.

A longtime resident of Detroit, Cleage returned home in 1951 after a rocky but productive pastorate in Springfield, Mass., in order to assume ministerial duties at St. Mark's Presbyterian Mission. St. Mark's was a middle-class black congregation, and although the Cleage family had long been a part of the city's black elite, Cleage was greatly disturbed by the privilege and complacency of his parishioners. Finally, in March 1953 Cleage led "a group of dissidents" out of St. Mark's, charging that the overly pious Sunday morning Christianity at the church had become intolerable.

A week later Cleage and his followers established the Central Congregational Church. For most of the next decade he and his church enjoyed a respectful honeymoon. However, problems at Central began to surface in 1964, when Cleage was informed that several members of his parish were pleased with neither his preaching nor his politics. Over the years following the exodus from St. Mark's, Cleage became increasingly involved with radical political organizations, and, shortly after his appearance in November 1963 at the National Negro Grassroots Leadership Conference, tension between black nationalist and moderate members of Central came to a head (*see* BLACK NATIONALISM).

Although the conference was held at King Solomon Baptist Church in Detroit, many of Central's parishioners did not agree with the choice of MALCOM X (a man they saw as advocating violence as a means of change) as a keynote speaker. Moreover, they felt the integral role Cleage played in organizing the meeting would somehow taint the reputation of Central. And following a May 1964 *Illustrated News*

reprint of Cleage's black nationalist platform, unhappy members of Central appealed to the Detroit Metropolitan Association of the United Church of Christ for intervention.

In a special hearing of the association's church and ministry committee, a request on behalf of the dissidents (who remained anonymous, supposedly for their protection) was made that association funds for Central Church be withdrawn until Cleage's ministry was brought in line with the mission of the United Church of Christ. Indirectly, the committee was interested in finding out two things: first, whether or not Cleage was indeed a black nationalist; and second, if so, whether or not his black nationalism was Christian. Cleage refused to cooperate on the grounds that no one in his congregation had ever approached him with a complaint, and since the names of the petitioners were withheld, it was possible the association itself was behind the inquisition. In any event, he believed the association had no right to interfere in the internal affairs of an autonomous congregation.

In the end Cleage and those parishioners loyal to him won both the battle and the war when those opposed to the church's black nationalist leanings withdrew their membership from Central. Three years later, on March 26, 1967, Easter Sunday, a large painting of a black Virgin Mary was unveiled at the church. Subsequently, the name of the congregation was changed to the Shrine of the Black Madonna, and in 1971 the Black Christian Nationalist Movement was officially inaugurated.

Initially, Cleage envisioned the movement as an ecumenical endeavor, with each participating congregation maintaining membership in its respective denomination. To some extent, this is the case. The "Mother Shrine" in Detroit has maintained its affiliation with the United Church of Christ. The Pan-African Orthodox Church, whose name is intentionally related to the AFRICAN ORTHODOX CHURCH of Bishop George Alexander MCGUIRE, has three congregations, a farm in upper Michigan, and a publishing house.

REFERENCES

CLEAGE, ALBERT B., JR. *Black Christian Nationalism: New Directions for the Black Church.* New York, 1972.

———. *Black Messiah.* New York, 1968.

QUINTON H. DIXIE

Parker, Charles Christopher "Charlie"

(August 29, 1920–March 23, 1955), jazz alto saxophonist. Charlie Parker, often known as "Bird" or "Yardbird," was the primary architect of the style of jazz called bebop, which revolutionized jazz, taking it from dance music to a black musical aesthetic and art form (*see* JAZZ). He accomplished this as performer, composer, and theorist.

Parker was born in Kansas City, Mo. When he was eleven his mother bought him an alto saxophone. By the time he was fifteen he had become a professional musician, leaving school at the same time. At first his playing was ridiculed, but after he spent some time at a retreat in the Ozark Mountains of Missouri his technique grew immensely, and during the next couple of years he played in and around the Kansas City area. During this period he learned his craft mainly by sitting in and playing in bands, where he absorbed all he could about music.

In 1939 Parker made his first visit to New York. He stayed about a year, playing mostly in jam sessions. After that he began playing in the band of Jay McShann, touring in the Southwest, Midwest, and East. It was with this band that Parker made his first recording, in Dallas in 1941. At the end of 1942 he joined the Earl HINES orchestra, which featured trum-

As the prime creator of bebop, Charlie Parker was an improviser of incandescent genius on the alto saxophone and a model and inspiration for several generations of jazz musicians. This photograph is from 1946, during Parker's run at Billy Berg's club in Los Angeles. (Frank Driggs Collection)

peter "Dizzy" GILLESPIE. Bird and Dizzy began an informal partnership that launched the beginning of bebop. A strike by the American Federation of Musicians made it impossible to make records for several years, and the early period of bebop's development is largely undocumented. In 1944 Parker, along with Gillespie and other modern players, joined the Billy ECKSTINE band. This band was one of the first to introduce the innovations being developed in the music, and it provided a platform for Parker's new improvisations.

In 1945 Parker began to record extensively with small groups that included Gillespie. His playing became more familiar to a larger audience and to other musicians, even though the new music was criticized harshly by critics. At the end of 1945 he took a quintet to California for what turned out to be an ill-fated trip. Audiences and musicians in the West were not familiar with bebop innovations, and Parker's addiction to heroin and alcohol finally forced him into the Camarillo State Hospital. He stayed there during the second half of 1946 and was released in January 1947. He did make several important recordings for the Dial record company before and after his stay at the hospital.

Parker returned to New York in April 1947 and formed a quintet featuring his protégé Miles DAVIS on trumpet, Duke Jordan on piano, Tommy Potter on bass, and Max ROACH on drums. Between 1947 and 1951 Parker left a permanent imprint on jazz. With the quintet he recorded some of his most innovative compositions: "Now's the Time," "Koko," "Anthropology," "Ornithology," "Scrapple from the Apple," "Yardbird Suite," "Moose the Mooche," "Billie's Bounce," "Confirmation," and others. In addition to playing in his own quintet, Parker worked in a variety of other musical groups, including Afro-Cuban bands and a string chorus, which he led during 1950. He was featured soloist in the Jazz at the Philharmonic series, produced by Norman Granz. Parker's main venue continued to be his quintet, which changed members several times but still was vital. Within his quintet he worked in nightclubs, recording studios, and radio broadcasts, and made his first trip to Europe in 1949, returning there the next year for an extensive stay in Sweden, where he worked with Swedish musicians.

Parker's lifestyle continued to create problems for himself and his family. In 1951 he lost his cabaret card in New York because of his constant confrontations with narcotics police. This kept him from playing in New York clubs for over two years. His alcohol and drug use precipitated a downward financial spiral from which he never recovered. In 1953 he presented a landmark concert in Toronto with Gillespie, Bud POWELL on piano, Charles MINGUS on bass, and Max Roach on drums. The concert was at Massey Hall and featured many of the pieces Bird and Dizzy had created during the 1940s: "Night in Tunisia," "Hot House," "Wee," and others. This was Parker's last great musical statement. After the Toronto concert his physical and mental health deteriorated to the point where he attempted suicide several times, finally committing himself to Bellevue Hospital in New York. His last public performance was early in March 1955 at Birdland, the New York City club named after him. On March 23 he died of heart seizure in the New York apartment of his friend Baroness Pannonica de Koenigswarter.

Parker's contributions to jazz are extensive. He took saxophone playing to a level never reached before and in so doing led the way for others, not only saxophonists but all instrumentalists. He was able to weld prodigious skill with poetic content, and he left hours and hours of recordings of wondrous improvisations. Parker's playing struck fear in the hearts of many musicians and made some put down their instruments. John COLTRANE, the gifted performer of the 1950s and 1960s, moved from alto to tenor saxophone because he felt that Parker had played all that was going to be played on the alto. Parker frequently composed using the harmonic structures of established melodies as the basis of his works. He did not invent this technique but used it more than anyone else before or since. In his improvisations he used all the intervals of the scales. In his harmonic structures he consistently used chords made up of eleventh and thirteenth intervals in order to take harmony out of the diatonic system and into chromaticism. Parker was clearly one of America's most innovative and prolific artists.

REFERENCES

GIDDINS, GARY. Celebrating Bird: The Triumph of Charlie Parker. New York, 1987.
MORGENSTERN, DAN, ET AL. Bird and Diz: A Bibliography. New York, 1973.
REISER, ROBERT G. Bird. New York, 1962.
RUSSELL, ROSS. Bird Lives. New York, 1973.

WILLIAM S. COLE

Parker, Charles Stewart (March 31, 1882–January 10, 1950), botanist. Charles Stewart Parker was a botanist and mycologist (specializing in fungi). He was born in Corinne, Utah, and received his bachelor's degree in botany from Trinity College in 1905. After earning a master's degree from Washington State College in 1923, his Ph.D. dissertation, "A Taxonomic Study of the Genus *Hypholoma* in North America," followed in 1932 at Pennsylvania State College.

Parker continued his botanical studies as director of a field expedition to Mexico and as a member of a survey party in Washington State during 1921–1922. The body of his research included descriptions of a new subgenus and a section of the genus *Carex*. He also wrote detailed definitions of thirty-nine species of plants. Several plants were named for him (e.g., a new species of sweet pea, *Lathyrus Parkeri,* and a new variety of *Rosa Spaldingii* called *Var. Parkeri.*).

Parker served as professor of botany at Howard University from 1924 until he retired as department chair and professor emeritus in 1947. He was affiliated with many academic organizations, among them the Mycology Society, the Botanical Society, the Phytopathological Society, the British Mycology Society, and the Torrey Botanical Club. Parker died in Seattle, Wash.

REFERENCES

CATTELL, JACQUES, ed. American Men of Science. 8th edition. Lancaster, Pa., 1949.
Obituary. Science 3 (February 3, 1950): 122.

VIVIAN OVELTON SAMMONS

Parks, Gordon, Jr. (December 7, 1934–April 3, 1979), filmmaker. Gordon Parks, Jr., was born in Minneapolis, Minn., the child of Sally Alvis and author, photographer, and director Gordon PARKS, Sr. He attended the American School in Paris and graduated from White Plains (N.Y.) High School in 1952. He served two years in the United States Army (1956–1957), and in the early 1960s performed folk music in Greenwich Village coffeehouses.

Using the name Gordon Rogers to avoid trading on his father's fame, Parks shot still photographs for two major Hollywood films, *Burn* (1969) and *The Godfather* (1972). He also worked as a cameraman on his father's first film, *The Learning Tree,* released in 1969.

In the 1970s, Parks, Jr., directed four feature films. The first, *Superfly* (1972), remains one of the best-known BLAXPLOITATION films, although it was criticized for its unapologetic portrayal of a black drug dealer triumphing over the white mob. The film and the score by Curtis MAYFIELD were extremely successful. Made for less than $500,000, the film eventually grossed $24.8 million. Parks next directed *Thomasine and Bushrod* (1974), and then *Three the Hard*

Way (1974). In 1975, he directed his last feature film, *Aaron Loves Angela.*

Parks moved to Kenya in 1979 and started his own film company, Africa International Productions/Panther Film Company. He died in Nairobi that same year when his plane exploded on the runway after an aborted takeoff.

REFERENCES

BOGLE, DONALD. *Blacks in American Film and Television: An Encyclopedia.* Westport, Conn., 1988.

MAPP, EDWARD. *Directory of Blacks in the Performing Arts.* Metuchen, N.J., 1990.

ELIZABETH V. FOLEY

Parks, Gordon, Sr. (November 30, 1912–), photographer. A true Renaissance man, *Life* magazine photographer Gordon Parks has achieved international recognition in a wide variety of other fields including filmmaking, letters, and music. He has also pioneered as the first mainstream African-American photojournalist and as the first African American to direct a major Hollywood film.

Gordon Parks was born in Fort Scott, Kans., the youngest in a farming family of fifteen children. His mother's death when Parks was sixteen, along with his aged father's rapidly failing ability to manage a household, led to the family's break-up, and Parks moved north to live with a married sister in Minneapolis. Unwelcome in his brother-in-law's home, the teenager was soon on his own, struggling to attend high school and support himself.

The Great Depression ended his formal education, but Parks seized every opportunity to learn by reading and attending closely to the talented individuals he encountered in his various jobs. As a teenager and later as a young husband and father, he worked as a bellhop, musician, semipro basketball player, and member of the Civilian Conservation Corps, primarily in the Midwest but also for a brief time in Harlem, New York. Relative security came with a position as a railroad dining car waiter. All the while Parks wrote, composed, and read, absorbing on his own what he had been unable to study in school.

The picture magazines of the day—*Vogue, Harper's Bazaar,* and especially the brand new *Life* magazine (first issued in November 1936)—caught Parks's imagination. A newsreel cameraman's in-person presentation of his latest battle-action footage in a Chicago movie theater inspired Parks to take up photography himself, and in 1937 he acquired his first camera. Largely self-taught, he took his earliest photographs with only a few pointers from the camera

Gordon Parks, Sr. (Photographs and Prints Division, Schomburg Center for Research in Black Culture, The New York Public Library, Astor, Lenox and Tilden Foundations)

salesman. Quickly mastering technique, he intuitively found the subjects most meaningful to him. The same local Minneapolis camera store soon gave him his first exhibition.

A successful fashion assignment for a stylish Minneapolis department store caught the attention of Marva (Mrs. Joe) Louis, who encouraged Parks to establish himself in Chicago. His fashion background served him well there (as it would later throughout his years at *Life*) photographing Gold Coast socialites. In his spare time, he documented the grim poverty of the city's South Side, the fast-growing Chicago enclave of African Americans displaced from the rural South who came north for jobs in the heavy industries surrounding the Great Lakes.

This socially conscious camera work won for the young photographer, now responsible for a growing family of his own, the very first Julius Rosenwald Fellowship in photography. The 1942–1943 stipend enabled Parks to work with photographic mentor Roy Stryker in Washington, D.C., at the Farm Security Administration. This was the closing years of the influential NEW DEAL agency that had undertaken a pioneering photo documentation of depression conditions in urban and rural America.

Parks continued with Stryker until 1947, first as a correspondent for the Office of War Information, and later at the Standard Oil Company of New Jersey, photographing the face of America for the company's public relations campaign. In the brief months before he began to work for *Life* magazine in 1948, Parks photographed for *Vogue* and *Glamour* and also authored two books on photographic technique: *Flash Photography* (1947) and *Camera Portraits: The Techniques and Principles of Documentary Portraiture* (1948).

Early in his more than two decades at *Life,* Parks spent two influential years assigned to the magazine's Paris office, where he covered fashion, the arts, celebrities, and political figures. The experience was seminal, providing a rich window on the diversity of contemporary creative expression as well as an opportunity for international recognition. Moreover, like other African Americans, he found the European experience, with its relative lack of racial barriers, especially liberating.

Back in the United States during the 1950s and early '60s, Parks executed hundreds of photographic assignments for *Life* that reflect the magazine's far-ranging coverage: popular culture, high fashion, arts, entertainment, sports, national events, and the personalities of business, labor and politics. Parks's direct, realistic style of photographing life in America and abroad won him international renown as the first African-American photojournalist.

Parks's longest assignment began in 1961, when he traveled to Brazil to photograph the slums of Rio de Janeiro. His story of Flavio da Silvia, a poverty-stricken Brazilian boy whom Parks found dying of asthma, attracted international attention that resulted in Flavio and his family receiving gifts, medical treatment, and, finally, a new home. At the same time, with the emerging CIVIL RIGHTS MOVEMENT, Parks undertook a new role at *Life:* interpreting the activities and personalities of the movement, in words as well as pictures, from a personal perspective. His 1971 anthology *Born Black* is a collection of these essays and images.

A gifted storyteller, Parks began his chronological autobiographical book cycle in 1963 with *The Learning Tree,* a well-received novel that drew on the author's own childhood experiences and memories. This was followed in 1966 by *A Choice of Weapons,* a powerful first-person narrative that recounted the events and influences that enabled Parks to overcome societal prejudice and personal hardship. It is the most insightful of the series, illuminating the development of a sensitive and self-confident young man as he grows into what he will become, an artist of universal conscience and compassion.

Parks also gained distinction as a poet, composer, and filmmaker, becoming in 1969 the first African American to direct a major Hollywood film. He also produced and wrote the script for *The Learning Tree* and directed a number of other films, including the highly popular *Shaft* (1971), *Leadbelly* (1976), and *The Odyssey of Solomon Northup* (1984), about a free black sold into slavery. In addition, Parks has completed the music for a ballet about the Rev. Dr. Martin Luther KING, Jr., and has worked on a novel based on the life of J. M. W. Turner, the English nineteenth-century landscape painter.

Parks is the recipient of numerous professional awards, organization citations, and honorary degrees, among them Photographer of the Year from the American Society of Magazine Photographers (1960) and the Spingarn Medal from the NAACP (1972).

His greatest satisfaction and motivation is expressed in his prologue to *Moments Without Proper Names,* one of his three books of poems accompanied by his photographs:

> I hope always to feel the responsibility to communicate the plight of others less fortunate than myself, to show the abused and those who administer the abuses, to point up the pain of the underprivileged as well as the pleasures of the privileged—somehow to evoke the same response from a housewife in Harlem as I would from a seamstress in Paris or a butcher in Vladivostok.
>
> In helping one another we can ultimately save ourselves. We must give up silent watching and put our commitments into practice.

REFERENCES

BUSH, MARTIN H. *The Photographs of Gordon Parks.* Wichita, Kans., 1983.
HANNAN, TERRY. *Gordon Parks, Black Photographer.* Champaign, Ill., 1972.
TURK, MIDGE. *Gordon Parks.* New York, 1971.

JULIA VAN HAAFTEN

Parks, Rosa Louise McCauley (February 4, 1913–), civil rights leader. Rosa McCauley was born in Tuskegee, Ala. She lived with relatives in Montgomery, where she finished high school in 1933 and attended Alabama State College. She met her husband, Raymond Parks, a barber, and they married in 1932. Rosa Parks worked as a clerk, an insurance salesperson, and a tailor's assistant at a department store. She was also employed at the time as a part-time seamstress by Virginia and Clifford Durr, two white residents of Montgomery who were staunch supporters of the black freedom struggle.

Rosa Parks. (© Flip Schulke/Black Star)

Parks had been active in civil rights work since the 1930s. She and her husband supported the Scottsboro defendants, a notorious case in which nine young black men were convicted in 1931 on questionable evidence for raping two white women. In 1943, Parks became one of the first women to join the Montgomery NAACP. She worked as a youth adviser, served as secretary for the local group from 1943 to 1956, and helped operate the joint office of the NAACP and the BROTHERHOOD OF SLEEPING CAR PORTERS. In addition, she worked with the Montgomery Voters League to increase black voter registration. During the summer of 1955, with the encouragement of the Durrs, Parks accepted a scholarship for a workshop for community leaders on school integration at the Highlander Folk School in Tennessee. It was an important experience for Parks, not only for the practical skills of organizing and mobilizing she learned, but because the racial harmony she experienced there nurtured and sustained her activism.

Popularly known as the Mother of the Civil Rights Movement, Parks is best known for her refusal to give up her seat for a white man on a segregated bus in Montgomery on December 1, 1955, an incident which sparked the MONTGOMERY BUS BOYCOTT.

Contrary to popular belief, Parks was not simply a tired woman who wanted to rest her feet, unaware of the chain of events she was about to trigger. As she wrote in *Rosa Parks: My Story,* "the only tired I was, was tired of giving in." Parks was a veteran of civil rights activity and was aware of efforts by the Women's Political Council and the local NAACP to find an incident with which they could address segregation in Montgomery.

Parks was actively involved in sustaining the boycott and for a time served on the executive committee of the MONTGOMERY IMPROVEMENT ASSOCIATION, an organization created to direct the boycott. The intransigence of the city council was met by conviction and fortitude on the part of African Americans. For over a year, black people in Montgomery car-pooled, took taxis, and walked to work. The result was a ruling by the United States Supreme Court that segregation on city buses was unconstitutional.

As a result of her involvement in the bus boycott, Parks lost her job at the department store in Montgomery. In 1957, she and her husband moved to Detroit, where she worked as a seamstress for eight years before becoming administrative assistant for Congressman John CONYERS, a position she held until 1988. After she moved to Detroit, Parks continued to be active in the CIVIL RIGHTS MOVEMENT and joined the SOUTHERN CHRISTIAN LEADERSHIP CONFERENCE (SCLC). She participated in numerous marches and rallies, including the 1965 march from Selma to Montgomery.

In the mid-1980s she was a supporter of the free South Africa movement and walked the picket lines in Washington, D.C., with other antiapartheid activists. She has made countless public appearances, speaking out on political issues as well as giving oral history lessons about the civil rights movement. In 1987, ten years after the death of her husband, she founded the Rosa and Raymond Parks Institute for Self-Development in Detroit, a center committed to career training for black youth. The institute, a dream of hers, was created to address the dropout rate of black youth.

Parks, an international symbol of African-American strength, has been given numerous awards and distinctions, including ten honorary degrees. In 1979, she was awarded the NAACP's prestigious Spingarn Medal. In 1980, she was chosen by *Ebony* readers as the living black woman who had done the most to advance the cause of black America. In the same year she was awarded the Martin Luther King, Jr., Nonviolent Peace Prize by the Martin Luther King, Jr., Center for Nonviolent Social Change. In addition, the SCLC has honored her by sponsoring the annual Rosa Parks Freedom award.

REFERENCES

BROWN, ROXANNE. "Mother of the Movement." *Ebony* (February 1988): 68–72.

GARROW, DAVID, ed. *The Montgomery Bus Boycott and the Women Who Started It: The Memoir of Jo Ann Gibson Robinson.* Knoxville, Tenn., 1987.

PARKS, ROSA. *Rosa Parks: My Story.* New York, 1992.

PAM NADASEN

Parks, Suzan-Lori (May 10, 1963–), playwright. Suzan-Lori was born in Fort Knox, Ky., the daughter of a U.S. Army officer. She moved around the United States with her family and completed high school in Germany. She then attended Mt. Holyoke College, graduating in 1985, and continued her education at the Drama Studio in London. There she studied acting in preparation for a career as a playwright.

Several of her plays have been produced, most notably at BACA Downtown, an offshoot of the Brooklyn Arts Council. In 1989, her *Imperceptible Mutabilities in the Third Kingdom* was produced there to favorable reviews. In 1989, BACA produced *The Death of the Last Black Man in the Whole Entire World,* which was also performed as part of the Yale Winterfest in 1992. In 1991 Parks completed a thirty-minute film, *Anemone Me,* with collaborator Bruce Hainley. The same year, her play *Devotees in the Garden of Love* was produced by the Actors Theater of Louisville, Ky. In 1992 she was commissioned to write two plays, *Venus,* for the Women's Project of New York, and *The America Play,* for the Theatre for a New Audience, also in New York.

In 1991 and 1992 Parks was a writer-in-residence at The New School in New York. She has been a guest lecturer in dramatic writing at New York University, Yale University, the University of Michigan, and the Pratt Institute. She has received numerous grants and awards, including an Obie Award in 1990 for *Imperceptible Mutabilities,* National Endowment for the Arts grants in 1990 and 1991, and a Rockefeller Foundation grant in 1990.

In her plays and scripts Parks is concerned with poetic voice as well as with the representation of the African-American experience. Her evocative, dreamlike style has its roots in Gertrude Stein's investigations into language as well as poet Adrienne KENNEDY'S poetic, nonnarrative dramas.

REFERENCE

SOLOMON, ALISA. "To Be Young, Gifted, and African American." *Village Voice,* September 11, 1989, pp. 99–102.

ELIZABETH V. FOLEY

Parsons, Lucy (1853–March 7, 1942), anarchist labor organizer. Little is known about the early life of Lucy Parsons. She claimed to have been born the daughter of a Mexican woman, Marie del Gather, and a Creek Indian, John Waller. Orphaned at age three, she said, she was then raised on a ranch in Johnson County, Tex., by her maternal uncle. However, later research has pointed to the likelihood that she was of at least partial African-American descent and born a slave in Texas. In about 1870 she met Albert Parsons, a former Confederate soldier turned radical Republican, and married him in 1871 or 1872.

Forced to flee Texas because of their mixed marriage, the couple settled in Chicago in 1873 and became heavily involved in the revolutionary elements of the labor movement. In 1877, Lucy Parsons took on the financial responsibility of her household by opening up a dress shop after her husband was blacklisted from the printing trade. In 1878, she began writing articles about the homeless and unemployed, Civil War veterans, and working women for *The Socialist.* She also gave birth to two children within the next few years. Known for being a powerful writer and speaker, Lucy Parsons played a crucial role in the workers' movement in Chicago. In 1883, she helped found the International Working People's Association (IWPA), an anarchist-influenced labor organization that promoted revolutionary direct action toward a stateless and cooperative society and insisted on equality for people of color and women. Parsons became a frequent contributor of the IWPA weekly newspaper the *Alarm,* in 1884. Her most famous article was "To Tramps," which encouraged workers and the unemployed to rise up in direct acts of violence against the rich.

Although primarily a labor activist, Parsons was also a staunch advocate of the rights of African Americans. She wrote numerous articles and pamphlets condemning racist attacks and killings; one of her most significant pieces being "The Negro: Let Him Leave Politics to the Politician and Prayer to the Preacher." Published in the *Alarm* on April 3, 1886, the article was a response to the lynching of thirteen African Americans in Carrollton, Miss. In it, she wrote that blacks were victimized only because they were poor and that racism would inevitably disappear with the destruction of capitalism.

In 1886, Parsons and the IWPA worked with the other industrial trade unions for a general strike in support of the eight-hour work day that began on the first of May and involved almost 80,000 workers. Five days later, at a rally at Haymarket Square in support of the strike, a bomb was hurled at police officers after they attacked the demonstration. Police blamed the IWPA and began rounding up anarchist leaders, including Albert Parsons. Lucy Parsons took the lead in organizing their defense, and after they had all been convicted of murder, she traveled the country speaking on behalf of their innocence and raising money for their appeals, facing repeated arrests herself. In November of that year, her husband was hanged along with three other Haymarket defendants.

After her husband's death, Parsons continued revolutionary activism on behalf of workers, political prisoners, people of color, the homeless, and women. In 1892, she published the short-lived FREEDOM'S JOURNAL, which attacked lynchings and black peonage. In 1905, she participated in the founding of the Industrial Workers of the World, an anarcho-syndicalist trade union. Also in that year, she published a paper called the LIBERATOR. In 1927, she was made a member of the National Committee of the International Labor Defense, a Communist-led organization that defended labor activists and unjustly accused African Americans such as the "Scottsboro Nine" and Angelo HERNDON. After working with the COMMUNIST PARTY for a number of years, she finally joined the party in 1939, despairing of the advances of both capitalism and fascism on the world stage and unconvinced of the anarchists' ability to effectively confront them. After almost fifty years of continual activism, Parsons died in a fire in her Chicago home in 1942. Viewed as a threat to the political order even in death, her personal papers and books were seized by the police from the gutted house.

REFERENCES

ASHBAUGH, CAROLYN. *Lucy Parsons, American Revolutionary*. Chicago, 1976.

ROEDIGER, DAVE. *Haymarket Scrapbook*. Chicago, 1986.

JOSEPH W. LOWNDES

Passing. The word "passing," an Americanism not listed in the first edition of the *Oxford English Dictionary,* refers to a crossing of a line that divides social groups. Everett Stonequist cites a great variety of cases, including Jews passing as Gentiles, Polish immigrants preferring to be German, Italians pretending to be Jews, the Japanese *Eta* concealing their group identity to avoid discrimination, the Anglo-Indians passing as British, and the Cape Coloured as well as mixed bloods in the West Indies and Latin America moving into the white groups. One could add many other cases, such as whites and blacks passing as Mexicans, or Chinese-Americans passing as Japanese. There was some passing from white to black in the United States, for example, by musicians.

Passing is used most frequently, however, as if it were short for "passing for white," in the sense of crossing over the color line in the United States from the black to the white side. Louis Wirth and Herbert Goldhamer see in passing "an attempt on the parts of Negroes to enter into the white community in a fashion which would otherwise be forbidden because of racial barriers." Ratna Roy defines passing as "assimilating into white society by concealing one's antecedents."

Racial passing is a phenomenon of the nineteenth and the first half of the twentieth centuries. It thrived in a modern social system in which, as a primary condition, social and geographic mobility prevailed, especially in environments such as large cities that provided anonymity to individuals. A second constitutive feature for passing was a widely shared social-belief system, according to which certain descent characteristics, even invisible ones, were viewed as more deeply defining than physical appearance, individual volition, and self-description, or than social acceptance and economic success.

A child whose ancestors come from groups X and Y could theoretically live as an X, a Y, or an XY. In the United States, for example, the child of Irish and Italian parents may be Irish, Italian, Irish-Italian, "simply American," or become, as by marriage, a member of another ethnic group. Yet some types of ancestry (often those associated in the United States with the term "race" rather than "ethnicity") deny a descendant the legitimate possibility of choosing certain forms of identification (including even X-ness, the identity of one parent, of three grandparents, or of fifteen out of sixteen ancestors), because the identity of the remaining other part of the ancestry (Y-ness) is considered so dominant that the individual is believed to be "really" a Y. The description of Roxy in Mark Twain's *Pudd'nhead Wilson* (1894) gives full expression to this paradoxical racial identification: "To all intents and purposes Roxy was as white as anybody, but the one-sixteenth of her which was black out-voted the other fifteen parts and made her a negro. She was a slave, and salable as such." William Javier Nelson called the United States a "hypodescent" society in which children of a higher-caste and a lower-caste parent are assigned the lower-parent status, a procedure deriving from slavery. It is quite possible that the first printed instances of the expression "passing for white" appeared in runaway slave bills. In hypodescent societies, X-ness is seen not as an "ethnic option" (Mary Waters's useful term) for $XY,$ nor as a legitimate parental legacy but only as a "disguise." Hence XY is considered a Y who is "passing for" but "not really" an X.

This "fiction of law and custom" (Mark Twain) may seem odd in a social system that cherishes social mobility and espouses the right of individuals to make themselves anew by changing name, place, and fortune, and which has produced famous parvenus and confidence men. In Gustave de Beaumont's novel *Marie* (1835), one of the first works of fiction to thematize racial passing, the narrator Ludovic makes this point explicity:

> A Massachusetts bankrupt can find honor and fortune in Louisiana, where there is no inquiry into the ruin he experienced elsewhere. A New Yorker, bored by the ties of a first marriage, can desert his wife on the left bank of the Hudson and go take another on the right bank, in New Jersey, where he lives in undisturbed bigamy. . . . There is but one crime from which the guilty can nowhere escape punishment and infamy: it is that of belonging to a family reputed to be *colored*. The color may be blotted out; the stain remains. It seems that people find it out even when it is invisible; there is no refuge secret enough, no retreat obscure enough, to hide it.

The coexistence of the cult of the social upstart and the condemnation of the racial passer constitutes the parameters in which the phenomenon of passing took place. In the era of passing, the notion also found support that no one could "always tell" Y's by certain ineffaceable characteristics and visible signs such as their eyes or fingernails or the babies they might generate even generations later. Because this is, however, not really true, passing highlights an area of social ambiguity and insecurity. Stories of passing may appeal to modern readers' fascination with the undecidable or offer the assurance of some firmness in at least one individual identity (that based on racial ancestry) in a world of fluidity.

This makes tales of passing allegories of modernization that may appeal to people as they move toward more general identifications and experience anxieties about giving up old homes and families. In a generally mobile society, the world of passing suggests, despite its first appearance, an unchangeable hold of origin and community. One may thus say that "passing" is a misnomer since it is used only to apply to cases of people who are *not* presumed to be able to pass legitimately from one class to another, but who are believed to remain identified by a part of their ancestry throughout their lives. Ironically, the language speaks only of those persons as passing who, it is believed, cannot really pass.

The experience of passing can be differentiated in various ways. The person who passes *voluntarily* may be doing it for a variety of motives that push him out of one group and pull him into another one: possibility of economic advancement and benefits (opportunism); interracial courtship and marriage (love); escape from slavery, proscriptions, and discrimination

(political reasons); and for many other motives such as for curiosity, for kicks (an "occasional thrill"), for the love of deception, for revenge, and for investigative purposes (most famously by Walter Francis WHITE). A person may also pass *inadvertently* when being mistaken for white and failing to protest; and *involuntarily,* be it because the individual may be too young to decide for himself (*The Garies and Their Friends*) or because it is arranged for him by others without his knowledge ("Tristan," *A Romance of the Republic*).

Passing may be undertaken *full-time,* twenty-four hours a day, or it may be *"part-time"* (Joel Williamson) or *"segmental"* (Louis Wirth), for job purposes on a certain time segment on a daily basis or for avoiding segregation in transportation, entertainment, restaurants, and hotels. It may be *permanent,* at least by intention, for the duration of an individual's life; or it may be full-time, but temporary or *sporadic* (for a shorter or longer period of a person's life, for one purpose or scheme, such as escaping from slavery, finding a job, completing a program of education, or simply while waiting for an advantageous moment to "come out"). This sporadic form of passing is sometimes associated with sexual cross-dressing and transvestism: in William Wells BROWN's *Clotel; or, The President's Daughter* (1853) or William and Ellen CRAFT's *Running a Thousand Miles for Freedom* (1860), for example, runaway slave women dress up as white men (Marjorie Garber).

Passing may be arranged by a secretive individual alone; revealed to some confidants, friends, siblings, or family members; or it may be done in the open, forcing others to pretend that they do not know: According to Edward Byron Reuter, "much 'Passing' is more a matter of acceptance or indifference than of actual and successful concealment." It may be planned by others; it may even "be unknown to the person who is passing" (for example, in stories of orphans, foundlings, or switched babies). It may be done collectively by several family members (*A Romance of the Republic*), siblings (*The House Behind the Cedars*), or friends, a couple, a whole family (*Colcorton*), a town, or other large groups (*Black No More*).

Passing may be experienced as a source of conflict or not. Fear and "constant anxiety" (*Century*) of discovery may so much intensify the stress, which the person who passes experiences, that giving up the subterfuge may come as a relief. "It is a great risk, and they live in almost daily fear of exposure." ("The Adventures of a Near-White," *Independent* [1913].) Louis Wirth writes:

> For even though a person could not be identified by means of any physical marks as having Negro ancestry, there is always the possibility that

someone who knew him as a Negro may discover his present mode of existence, or the possibility that he may have to account for his family and his early life. Even where the chance of such discovery is slight, there may be such constant anxiety and daily fear that the individual prefers to remain within the Negro community.

And Mary Helen Washington makes similar observations about Nella Larsen's treatment of the theme of passing:

> The woman who passes is required to deny everything about her past: her girlhood, her family, places with memories, folk customs, folk rhymes, her language, the entire long line of people who have gone before her. She lives in terror of discovery—what if she has a child with a dark complexion, what if she runs into an old school friend, how does she listen placidly to racial slurs? And more, where does the woman who passes find the equanimity to live by the privileged status that is based on the oppression of her own people?

Washington also stresses that the word *passing* may "connote death—in the black community dying is often referred to as 'passing.'"

Some who pass may feel like cowards, traitors, or losers: For example, at the end of *The Autobiography of an Ex-Colored Man* the narrator feels that he has sold his birthright for a mess of pottage. Some may also simply miss the familiar world of their pasts, their friends, and families. They may feel obliged to deny their closest relatives and friends: Thus, in the presence of her white male companion, Angela has to pretend not to recognize her own sister Virginia in Jessie FAUSET's *Plum Bun* (1929); and the subject of Langston HUGHES's "Passing" (1934) cannot speak to his mother in the street. An elaborate passing scenario is developed by the writer Garvin Wales in Hamilton Basso's novel *The View From Pompey's Head* (1954): To keep his racial background a secret, Wales has to hide his own mother, and his agent sends her checks for her whole life. Because of this family-disrupting aspect of passing—fully exploited by melodramatic films like *Imitation of Life*—family loyalty and race solidarity may be jointly invoked in an argument against passing.

Yet passing does not always have to be as conflictual as is often assumed. Wirth stresses that the people who tell their stories are more likely to be the ones who suffered from the experience: "The successful and well-adjusted person who passes is not likely to be heard from." Passing may even lead the individual who succeeds in it to a feeling of elation and exultation, an experience of succeeding as a trickster-hero who crosses a significant boundary and sees the world anew. Passing may thus lead to the higher insights of rising above and looking through the "veil" of the color line, to an experience of revelation, to seeing while not being seen—learning about the freemasonry of whiteness; surreptitiously joining an enemy camp—like a spy, a Trojan horse, a living reminder of the absurdity of racial divisions. People who cross the line in this sense, "by reason of their fair skins, are able to gain information about what white people are doing and thinking that would surprise many of them. Often have I gone into the South in my capacity of newspaper correspondent, and as a white man secured vast quantities of information on the race and other questions." Thus writes the anonymous author of "White, but Black" in the 1924–1925 *Century Magazine*. In William Henry's novel *Out of Wedlock* (1931), Mary Tanner devises a scheme for her children to pass and marry leading whites in order to undermine racial prejudice.

For reasons such as these, passing was often perceived as a threat by whites. Elmer A. Carter describes the 1924 Virginia Act to Preserve Racial Integrity as an effort "to stem the tide of pseudo Caucasians who are storming the Anglo-Saxton ramparts." The act included a provision that made it a "felony to make a willfully false statement as to color," and Walter White reports that in 1926 he was threatened by the sheriff of a Southern town with an indictment for passing for white. Blacks may react protectively toward the person who passes (Shiny in *The Autobiography of an Ex-Colored Man*), may be indifferent, or may be "ever the quickest to reveal the identity of those who seek to 'pass'" (*Century*).

The presence of people who are "neither black nor white and yet both" undermines the seeming certainty of the most important American racial boundary, and characters who threaten such boundaries may, like Joe Christmas in William Faulkner's *Light in August* (1932), be turned into sacrificial scapegoats. African-American writers like Langston Hughes, George SCHUYLER, and Walter Francis White have explored the comic potential in passing and have used it to criticize white and black hypocrisy.

How widespread a phenomenon was passing? Since quantitative data do not exist, writers have offered dramatically heterogeneous estimates. Many African Americans have reported that they personally knew friends or relatives who were passing. In 1931 Caleb Johnson reported the HARLEM assumption that more than 10,000 "have 'passed,' and are now accepted as white in their new relations, many of them married to white folks, all unsuspected." Jessie Fauset stated in an interview with the PITTS-BURGH COURIER that about 20,000 blacks were passing in New York alone. An unsigned editorial by the sociologist Charles S. JOHNSON in OPPORTUNITY (1925), entitled "The Vanishing Mulatto," alerted readers to a possible interpretation of the U.S. Census statistics of 1900, 1910, and 1920. According to those figures 2,050,686 Negroes were classified as mulattoes in 1910, but only 1,660,554 in 1920. Some mulattoes, the editorial concedes, were undoubtedly recounted as blacks, but others must also have faded "into the great white multitude." Drawing on Hornell Hart, Johnson further notes a possible increase of 162,500 native whites from 1900 to 1910 and a corresponding disappearance from the black group of 355,000! E. W. Eckard assumed more modestly that there were nationally 2,600 cases per year from 1920 to 1940, but T. T. McKinney believed in 1937 that the figure was 10,000 per year; Walter Francis White claimed that every year "approximately twelve thousand white-skinned Negroes disappear." According to Harold Asbury (1946), approximately 30,000 African Americans were passing each year so that "more than 2,000,000 persons with colored blood have crossed the line since the end of the Civil War." Factoring in possible descendants of people who passed, he goes on to report the "conservative" estimate "that there are at least between 5,000,000 and 8,000,000 persons in the United States, supposed to be white, who actually possess Negro blood." About 10 percent of the 346 families Caroline Bond Day studied had members who passed, but Gunnar Myrdal did not consider her group a representative sample. Edward Reuter concluded that the "actual number of persons who have left the race and are accepted as white is impossible to determine. There is a tendency to grossly exaggerate the number." Passing was undoubtedly significant locally. The Seventh Ward in NEW ORLEANS, for example, was known as the "Can't Tell Ward" (Burton Peretti), and in the 1920s, a theater in Washington hired "a black doorman to spot and bounce intruders whose racial origins were undetectable to whites" (Constance Green).

Uncertainty has not kept writers from advancing speculations not only about the general figures but also about age and sex distribution among the population of people who pass. For example, Earnest Hooton expressed his belief that it is the younger rather than the older ones who pass; and according to Charles S. Johnson's "Vanishing Mulatto," while there were 1,018 black males per 1,000 females, there were only 886 mulatto males per 1,000 females—permitting the conclusion that men "travel more and are not so dependent as women on family connections." This sex-ratio approach suggested that men were more likely to pass than women, an assumption shared explicitly by Edward Byron Reuter. Although fictional literature often presented men as more successful at passing than women (e.g., John as opposed to Rena in Charles Chestnutt's *House Behind the Ce-*

dars; or Johnson's ex-colored man as opposed to the heroines of Larsen's and Fauset's novels), we have no evidence to support the belief that men have passed at a greater rate than women. Louis Wirth writes that "the sex ratio can give no indication of what the total amount of passing is unless one were to assume that females do not pass." Caleb Johnson assumed the opposite, with little evidence: "While there are no statistics to support the conclusion, there is strong reason for the belief that many more women than men cross the color line from Negro to white. This is partly due to the fact that sexual attraction is stronger between the light male and the darker female than in the opposite direction. It is a matter commented on by numerous scientific observers, who agree that the male Negro almost universally prefers a woman of his own color or darker, while the primitive sex-appeal of the octoroon girl is highly potent with the average young white male. Moreover, the social act of 'passing' is easier for the girl than for the man." Joseph Washington rightly reminds us that "the knowledge of the sex distribution of blacks who *passed* was even less adequate than the knowledge of the color distribution."

Though now relegated to a footnote in cultural history, the phenomenon of passing "unleashed tremendous anxiety and fascination among whites" (Joseph Washington) and, from the 1850s to the 1930s, was "the favorite theme in Negro fiction" (Edward Byron Reuter). Passing was swept aside in social history by the CIVIL RIGHTS MOVEMENT and in literature by the Richard Wright school. As Nathan Huggins put it, "Passing is passé." A generation later, the time may be ripe for case studies of known individuals who passed (for example, the Trinity College-trained Theophilius John Minton Syphax, who, for 45 years, was the white Wall Street lawyer T. John McKee until he revealed his true identity shortly before his death in 1948; or the Columbia graduate William E. Jackson, who disclosed his racial background when he married the white woman Helen Burns in New York in 1925). At the same time, a full-fledged cultural investigation could be conducted of the period in which passing created much fascination for both black and white Americans.

REFERENCES

ADAMS, BRUCE PAYTON. The White Negro: The Image of the Passable Mulatto Character in Black Novels, 1853–1954. Ph.D. diss., University of Kansas, 1975.

ARBERY, GLENN CANNON. "Victims of Likeness: Quadroons and Octoroons in Southern Fiction." *Southern Review* 25, no. 1 (Winter 1989): 52–71.

BAKER, RAY STANNARD. *Following the Color Line: American Negro Citizenship in the Progressive Era.* 1908. Reprint. New York, 1964.

BERZON, JUDITH R. *Neither White Nor Black: The Mulatto Character in American Fiction.* New York, 1978.

BROWN, STERLING. *Negro Poetry and Drama* and *The Negro in American Fiction.* 1937. Reprint. New York, 1969.

BULLOCK, PENELOPE. "The Mulatto in American Fiction." *Phylon* 6 (1945): 78–82.

DAVIS, F. JAMES. *Who Is Black? One Nation's Definition.* University Park, Pa., 1991.

DEVEREUX, GEORGE. "Ethnic Identity: Its Logical Foundation and Its Dysfunctions." In George DeVos and Lola Romanucci-Ross, eds. *Ethnic Identity: Cultural Continuities and Change.* Palo Alto, Calif., 1975.

HOLMES, THOMAS ALAN. Race as Metaphor: "Passing" in Twentieth-Century African-American Fiction. Ph.D. diss. University of Alabama, 1990.

JACKSON, BLYDEN. "A Golden Mean for the Negro Novel." *College Language Association Journal* 3, no. 2. (December 1959): 81–87.

KINNEY, JAMES. *Amalgamation! Race, Sex, and Rhetoric in the Nineteenth-Century American Novel.* Westport, Conn., 1985.

KLINEBERG, OTTO, ed. *Characteristics of the American Negro.* New York, 1944.

MENCKE, JOHN G. *Mulattoes and Race Mixture: American Attitudes and Images.* Studies in American History and Culture, No. 4. Ann Arbor, Mich., 1979.

REUTER, EDWARD BYRON. *The Mulatto in the United States: Including a Study of the Rôle of Mixed-Blood Races Throughout the World.* 1918. Reprint. New York, 1969.

———. *Sex and Race.* 3 vols. 1941, 1942, and 1944. Reprint. St. Petersburg, Fla., 1967, 1972, and 1984.

ROGERS, J. A. *Nature Knows No Color-Line.* 1952. Reprint. St. Petersburg, Fla., 1980.

ROY, RATNA. The Marginal Man: A Study of the Mulatto Character in American Fiction. Ph.D. diss. University of Oregon, 1973.

SOLLORS, WERNER. *Neither Black Nor White and Yet Both: Thematic Explorations of Interracial Literature.* New York, 1989.

STONEQUIST, EVERETT V. *The Marginal Man: A Study in Personality and Culture Conflict.* 1937. Reprint. New York, 1961.

———. "Race Mixture and Mulatto." In Edgar T. Thompson, ed. *Race Relations and the Race Problem: A Definition and an Analysis.* Durham, N.C., 1939.

WASHINGTON, JOSEPH R., JR. *Marriage in Black and White.* Boston, 1970.

WILLIAMSON, JOEL. *New People: Miscegenation and Mulattoes in the United States.* New York, 1980.

YARBOROUGH, RICHARD. The Depiction of Blacks in the Early Afro-American Novel. Ph.D. diss., Stanford, 1980.

ZACK, NAOMI. *Race and Mixed Race.* Philadelphia, 1993.

ZANGER, JULES. "The 'Tragic Octoroon' in Pre–Civil War Fiction." *American Quarterly* 18 (1966): 63–70.

WERNER SOLLORS

Patents and Inventions. The U.S. Constitution (Article 1, Section 8) empowered Congress "to promote the progress of science . . . by securing to authors and inventors the exclusive right to their respective writings and discoveries." The first U.S. Patent Act, passed in 1790, had two basic purposes: to protect inventors from unauthorized use of their work, and to provide the public with increased access to information about useful inventions.

While free blacks were legally entitled to hold patents prior to the Civil War, few actually received them. The first African American known to have received a patent was Thomas L. Jennings, for a dry-cleaning process (March 3, 1821). Following him was Henry Blair, who patented a corn-seed planter in 1834 and a cottonseed planter in 1836. In 1843, Norbert RILLIEUX patented a refining process that revolutionized the sugar industry.

Blacks were hindered, however, from participating fully in the system. They did not have routine access to apprenticeships in the white-dominated crafts and trades, and, therefore, to the kind of training and experience that would have helped nurture their inventive skills. As a result, black inventors had to rely almost entirely on their own initiative. Furthermore, their products tended to evolve out of occupations that had been predetermined as acceptable for blacks—e.g., domestic service, carpentry, and agriculture. Within these constraints, a few African Americans developed successful, important inventions. Some, like Jennings, achieved wealth and social visibility, which they subsequently used as leverage in campaigns aimed at improving the lot of black Americans.

Slaves were not entitled to hold patents, yet some developed creative implements and techniques that enhanced the efficiency of their masters' businesses. Slave craftsmen emerged as a small, elite group distinct from field laborers and domestic servants. Because of their legal standing, the question arose as to who (if anyone) was entitled to ownership of their inventions. In 1857, one Mississippi slave owner claimed the rights to his slave's invention, a cotton scraper regarded as an innovative laborsaving device. The federal government denied this claim, reinforcing the prohibition on ownership by slaves but also declining to grant slave owners the privilege of "owning" the fruits of a slave's inventive genius. In response, the Confederate Patent Act asserted the ownership rights to slave owners in such cases. It was no mere coincidence that Joseph Davis, the brother of Confederate President Jefferson Davis, had earlier been denied a patent on a steamboat propeller invented by his slave, Benjamin Montgomery.

After the Civil War, no one was excluded from taking out a patent on grounds of race or legal status.

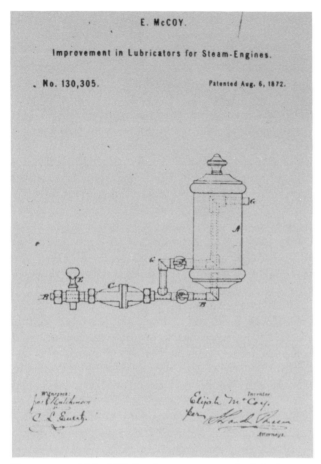

E. McCOY.

Improvement in Lubricators for Steam-Engines.

No. 130,305.   Patented Aug. 6, 1872.

Patent no. 130, 305 for improvement in lubricators for steam engines by Elijah McCoy, August 6, 1872. (Photographs and Prints Division, Schomburg Center for Research in Black Culture, The New York Public Library, Astor, Lenox and Tilden Foundations)

The result was a dramatic increase in the number of patents awarded to blacks. On August 10, 1894, the names and inventions of ninety-two blacks were read into the *Congressional Record*. By 1900, blacks had been awarded over 400 patents. Among them was A. P. Ashbourne, for the processes relating to food preparation. In 1872, Elijah MCCOY received the first of many patents on automatic engine lubrication, processes critical to the railroad and shipping industries. Jan MATZELIGER received a patent (March 20, 1883) for his invention of a shoe-lasting machine, followed by four others also relating to the technology of shoemaking. In the mid-1920s, after decades of innovative work in botany and agriculture at Tuskegee Institute, George Washington CARVER took out patents for a cosmetic and for pigment-producing processes. Such inventions reflected the ongoing concentration of blacks in service and manual-labor occupations—a pattern influenced not just by social tradition but also by the emphasis that black leaders such as Booker T. WASHINGTON placed on industrial and technical education as the most promising path of opportunity for African Americans.

This path was consistent with the pressures of American urbanization. By the turn of the twentieth century, as blacks migrated to the cities, many had entered technical occupations in government and industry. Andrew F. HILYER, an attorney in Washington, D.C., patented a room humidifier in 1890; Robert Pelham, a newspaper publisher in Detroit, patented a tabulating machine in 1905 and an adding machine in 1913; Garrett MORGAN of Cleveland, a gas mask in 1914 and an automatic traffic signal in 1923. Granville WOODS and Lewis LATIMER contributed to the emergence of electricity as an energy replacement for gas. Woods, known as the "black Edison," patented a telegraph transmitter in 1884 and, subsequently, devices to facilitate railway electrification. In 1881, Latimer patented a method for producing carbon filaments and became part of the research team of the Edison Electric Light Company.

Access to a career as an inventor became more difficult as the growing complexity of technology changed the character of innovation and discovery. In the twentieth century, the solitary, self-motivated inventor was replaced by teams of salaried researchers, often with advanced degrees, working in large companies or government-sponsored laboratories. Few blacks qualified for such positions, and those who did often faced discrimination by prospective employers. This sheds light on why the participation of blacks in patenting and invention is proportionately lower today than it was a hundred years ago.

REFERENCES

BAKER, HENRY E. *The Colored Inventor: A Record of Fifty Years.* 1915. Reprint. New York, 1968.

JAMES, PORTIA P. *The Real McCoy: African-American Invention and Innovation, 1619–1930.* Washington, D.C., 1989.

KLEIN, AARON. *Hidden Contributors: Black Scientists and Inventors in America.* New York, 1971.

PHILIP N. ALEXANDER

Patterson, Charles R. (?–1910), carriage manufacturer. Originally from Virginia, Charles R. Patterson settled in Greenfield, Ohio, where he worked as a blacksmith before opening a buggy repair shop in 1865. His mechanical skills helped him prosper, and eventually his firm, C. R. Patterson & Sons, began manufacturing carriages and wagons. It grew to employ forty skilled mechanics and eventually produced twenty-eight buggy models, including phaetons, school wagons, funeral hearses, and surreys. One particularly popular model, a doctor's buggy, was used throughout the Southwest and Midwest.

After Patterson's death, his son Frederick Douglass Patterson (1871–1932), became general manager of the company. Frederick had been the first black student to graduate from the local high school. After receiving a bachelor of arts degree from Ohio State University in Columbus, he taught history at Louisville High School. In 1901 he married Estelline Postell of Hopkinsville, Ky. That same year he resigned his teaching position and returned to Ohio to work in his father's firm. Under Frederick's leadership the firm became the largest African-American–owned manufacturing company in the United States, producing 500 new vehicles and earning $75,000 annually.

In 1916 with the introduction of the Patterson-Greenfield, Frederick Patterson became the country's first and only black manufacturer of automobiles. By 1919 he had built thirty cars, but lacking the capital for production-line techniques, he was not able to compete with other manufacturers. Nevertheless, C. R. Patterson & Sons continued to be successful, building truck bodies as well as the bodies for school buses used all over Ohio, and bus bodies for the Cincinnati transit system. Frederick Patterson was a member of the Executive Committee of the National Negro Business League and the Greenfield Business League. The firm dissolved six years after his death.

REFERENCES

HARTSHORN, WILLIAM NEWTON. *An Era of Progress and Promise, 1863–1910.* Boston, 1910.

REASONS, GEORGE, and SAM PATRICK. *They Had a Dream.* Vol. 3. Los Angeles, Calif., 1971.

LYDIA MCNEILL

Patterson, Floyd (January 4, 1935–), boxer. The second youngest heavyweight champion in BOXING history, Floyd Patterson was born in 1935 in Waco, N.C., one of eleven children of Thomas and Anabelle Patterson, and grew up in the slums of Brooklyn. A wayward youth, he attended Wiltwyck School, a correctional institute (1945–1947), where he learned to read and box. He was taken up by Cus D'Amato, who observed his quick hands and punching power. He twice won the Golden Gloves and took the gold medal in the middleweight division at the 1952 Olympics. He then turned pro, and quickly became a contender for the heavyweight crown vacated by Rocky Marciano. On November 30, 1956,

he KO'd forty-three-year-old light-heavyweight champion Archie MOORE for the title.

Patterson seemed too gentle a person for his chosen career; once he helped retrieve an opponent's mouthpiece. After attaining the title, he defeated four nondescript challengers until matched with Ingemar Johansson on June 26, 1959. Patterson was knocked down seven times in the third round and lost in an upset. He went into seclusion, returning to the ring one year later to knock out Johansson in the fifth, becoming the first heavyweight titlist to regain the crown. On September 25, 1962, he fought the awesome Sonny LISTON, who knocked out Patterson in the first round, a defeat that caused him to sneak out of Chicago in disguise. Their rematch in 1963 ended with the same result. Patterson retired in 1972, finishing with a record of 55–8–1.

Patterson has served as head of the New York State Athletic Commission, and in 1985 was appointed director of Off-Track Betting. He was elected to the Boxing Hall of Fame in 1977 and the Olympic Hall of Fame in 1987.

REFERENCE

PATTERSON, FLOYD, with MILTON GROSS. *Victory Over Myself.* New York, 1962.

STEVEN A. RIESS

Patterson, Frederick Douglass (October 10, 1901–April 26, 1988), educator. Born in Washington, D.C., the son of Willam Ross and Mamie Lucille Patterson, Frederick Douglass Patterson attended Prairie View State College in Prairie View, Tex., from 1915 to 1919. He then studied veterinary medicine at Iowa State College in Ames, Iowa, and in 1923, after receiving his degree, he accepted a position as professor of veterinary science and chemistry at Virginia State College in Petersburg, Va. Meanwhile, he continued his studies during summer terms, receiving an M.S. degree from Iowa State University in 1927, whereupon Virginia State College promoted him to director of agriculture. In 1928, Patterson became professor of bacteriology and head of the veterinary division at TUSKEGEE INSTITUTE. In 1933, the year after he received a Ph.D. in agriculture from Cornell University, he was named director of the School of Agriculture.

In 1935, the same year he married Catherine Moton, daughter of Robert Russa MOTON, the president of Tuskegee Institute, Patterson replaced his father-in-law as president. Given Patterson's relative youth and administrative inexperience, the choice was widely viewed as nepotism, though he proved to be an effective and forceful administrator. Patterson remained as president until 1953, presiding over several changes. In 1937, for example, Tuskegee inaugurated a new division of domestic service, with a four-year college program in nutrition and personal service. In 1940 the George Washington Carver Foundation was established at Tuskegee to fund scientific research by African Americans. Two years later, after America's entry into World War II, Patterson lobbied sucessfully for the creation of a black Army Air Corps base at the Institute, where the now-famous Tuskegee Airmen were trained. Patterson acquiesced in military segregation, infuriating many black leaders, but supported civil rights efforts by Charles Gomillion and others at Tuskegee. In an essay in the widely publicized collection, *What the Negro Wants* (1944), edited by Rayford LOGAN, Patterson presented a moderate integration platform, and strongly pushed for voting rights and equal opportunity for southern blacks.

Patterson's greatest achievement was founding the UNITED NEGRO COLLEGE FUND. In 1943 he wrote an article in the *Pittsburgh Courier* about the financial problems of black colleges, and called a meeting of college presidents to discuss finances. After Patterson pointed out the need for a streamlined charitable organization and the power of an organized appeal, twenty-seven college presidents agreed to establish a united fund. The organization, named the United Negro College Fund (UNCF), chartered in 1944, raised $765,000 for black colleges in its first year. Since then it has remained the largest outside source of funds for historically black colleges. Later, from 1964 to 1966, Patterson served as the UNCF's President.

Patterson remained involved in educational funding efforts throughout his career. In 1947 he was named to the landmark President's Commission on Higher Education, where he argued for federal aid to higher education. In 1953, after leaving Tuskegee, he was named president of the Phelps-Stokes Fund, where he organized the Cooperative College Development Program to assign federal money to improvement of and maintenance of the physical plant of black colleges. After leaving the Phelps-Stokes Fund in 1970, Patterson headed the Robert R. Moton Memorial Institute for ten years, during which time he established the College Endowment Funding Plan, developed to boost black college endowments and make them less dependent on federal funding for ongoing expenses.

Patterson retired in 1981. In 1987, he was awarded the Presidential Medal of Freedom for his educational efforts, and the following year received the NAACP's SPINGARN MEDAL for his educational and humanitarian work. Patterson died in New Rochelle, N.Y. on April 26 of that year.

REFERENCE

PATTERSON, FREDERICK DOUGLASS. *Chronicles of Faith: The Autobiography of Frederick Douglass Patterson.* Tuscaloosa, Ala., 1991.

GREG ROBINSON

Patterson, William (August 27, 1891–March 5, 1980), lawyer, activist. William Patterson was born in San Francisco, Calif. When he was young, his father left the family to become a missionary, while his mother worked as a domestic to raise their children. Patterson took jobs as a sea porter, a dishwasher, and an elevator operator, among other things, to help support his family and put himself through school. In 1911 he graduated from Tamalpais High School and entered the University of California at Berkeley to study engineering. He attended on and off for several years before deciding to go to the Hastings College of Law in San Francisco, where he earned his J.D. in 1919.

While in college, Patterson became politically active, combatting racism and urging African Americans not to fight in WORLD WAR I, which he felt was a "white man's war." After considering going to Liberia, he instead chose to move to New York City where he opened a law firm with two friends in 1923. In New York in the midst of the HARLEM RENAISSANCE he was exposed to left-wing ideas and met such influential black activists as Paul ROBESON and W. E. B. DU BOIS. During this period he actively supported the International Labor Defense protests on behalf of Nicola Sacco and Bartolomeo Vanzetti, two Italian anarchists whose radical political views and status as immigrants contributed heavily to their conviction and subsequent execution in 1927 for the murder of a paymaster.

As a result of his political activity, Patterson came to the conclusion that economic exploitation and the capitalist system lay at the root of black oppression. In 1927 he joined the COMMUNIST PARTY, U.S.A., and went to the Soviet Union for three years to study at the University of the Toiling People of the Far East in Moscow. There he found a society he thought was free of racial, class, and religious prejudice. Patterson returned to the United States in 1930 and two years later was elected to the Central Committee of the Communist party and ran for mayor of New York on the Communist party ticket. From 1932 until 1946 he served as executive director of the International Labor Defense (ILD), a radical legal-action group strongly influenced by the Communist party. As head of the ILD in the 1930s, Patterson helped coordinate the legal strategy and political protests on behalf of the SCOTTSBORO CASE defendants, nine young African-American men falsely accused of raping two white women. (All but the youngest were sentenced to death.)

In 1938 Patterson moved to Chicago and two years later married Louise Thompson, with whom he had three children. While there, Patterson organized Chicago's South Side and wrote for and edited various communist newspapers, including the *Daily Record* and the *Daily Worker*. From 1946 to 1956 he served as executive director of the Civil Rights Congress, an organization often aligned with the Communist party that defended the civil rights and liberties of African Americans and radical political activists. In 1951 he and Paul ROBESON presented a petition to the U.N. charging the United States with genocide by "deliberately inflicting on [African Americans] conditions of life calculated to bring about [their] physical destruction" through executions, lynchings, and systematic terrorism. In the same year he edited a book, *We Charge Genocide: The Crime of Government Against the Negro People*. Because of his involvement in the Civil Rights Congress and the Communist party, Patterson was called before the House Committee on Un-American Activities in 1950 and found in contempt four years later for refusing to answer questions. He spent three months in prison before the decision was reversed upon appeal.

Patterson's political activity declined in the later years of his life, but he still firmly believed in a society free of racism and poverty. In 1971 he published his autobiography, *The Man Who Cried Genocide,* and in 1978 he was awarded the Paul Robeson Memorial Medal by the Academy of Arts in East Germany. Although he died in 1980 after a prolonged illness, a foundation which bears his name carries on his commitment to social justice by awarding grants to supporters of the "people's struggle."

REFERENCES

HORNE, GERALD. *Communist Front? The Civil Rights Congress, 1946–56.* Rutherford, N.J., 1987.
PATTERSON, WILLIAM. *The Man Who Cried Genocide: An Autobiography.* New York, 1971.

PAM NADASEN

Patton, Charley (1887?–April 28, 1934), blues guitarist and singer. Charlie Patton was born in the heart of the Mississippi Delta, near Edwards, Miss. His date of birth is in dispute, with 1881, 1885, and 1887 often given. As a child Patton worked on farms, and began to play guitar. By most accounts, in his early teens he was already performing at parties, work camps, juke joints, and picnics in the area around Jackson and Yazoo City. By around 1912 Patton's family had moved to Will Dockery's Plantation, near Drew, Miss., where he performed with Willie Brown, Dick Bankston, and Tommy Johnson. Patton lived there until he was thirty-four years old, working as a field hand and wagon driver. He also performed as an itinerant musician, helping to create the distinctive and haunting solo guitar-and-voice style known as the Delta blues. Patton at first became well known locally for his dazzling, percussive virtuosity and churning rhythms on bottleneck slide guitar. His singing voice was deep and rough, and he often added falsetto or spoken effects. His repertory was diverse, including not only BLUES and FOLK, but also RAGTIME, popular, and religious songs. As a composer he shaped material from his own experience and from his own point of view. In "High Water Everywhere," for example, he chronicled the 1927 flood that devastated the Mississippi Delta region.

Even during his own lifetime, a legend grew up around Patton. As a publicity stunt he was billed as "The Masked Marvel" on some of his recordings. If there is little truth to the claim that he alone founded the Delta blues, he was nonetheless among the first musicians to record in that idiom, and he had a decisive impact on blues musicians who followed him. His recordings were made between 1929 and 1934, when he was living in the Lula and Holly Ridge areas, and established him as a pioneer of the country blues. These songs, some of which had accompaniment by Willie Brown on guitar and Henry Sims on violin, failed to achieve popularity outside the Delta, perhaps because they did not convey the comic talent Patton displayed in live performance. His most significant recordings, which were made in Richmond, Ind., and in New York, include "Pony Blues" (1929), "Down the Dirt Road" (1929), "Frankie and Albert" (1929), "Moon Going Down" (1930), "High Sheriff Blues" (1934), and "Oh Death" (1934). Patton died in Indianola, Miss., of a heart attack.

REFERENCES

FAHEY, JOHN. *Charley Patton.* London, 1970.
SACRE, ROBERT, ed. *The Voice of the Delta: Charley Patton and the Mississippi Blues Tradition, Influences and Comparisons.* Liège, Belgium, 1987.

JONATHAN GILL

Paul, Nathaniel (c. 1793–1839), minister and abolitionist. Nathaniel Paul was born free in Exeter, N.H., the son of a veteran of the American Revolution. He was one of five brothers of Thomas PAUL, the well-known Boston minister and community leader. Nathaniel Paul likely attended the Free Will Academy, an interracial minister's training school in Hollis, N.H., run by the Free Will Baptists. In 1820 he founded the Albany African Church Association, a black congregation in Albany, N.Y. Two years later, he became pastor of Albany's First African Baptist Church, and taught a Sunday school for African-American adults. A strong advocate of black education and self-improvement, Paul was also the founder and first president of the Union Society of Albany for the Improvement of the Colored People in Morals, Education, and the Mechanic Arts.

In addition to his clerical duties, Paul was an active abolitionist. In 1827 his address commemorating the termination of slavery in New York State was printed in the newspaper *Freedom's Journal,* and subsequently appeared in pamphlet form. Paul also called for an end to the international SLAVE TRADE. A moderate anticolonizationist, Paul contributed articles to FREEDOM'S JOURNAL and *The Rights of All* attacking the AMERICAN COLONIZATION SOCIETY. Despite his opposition to African settlement, Paul supported emigration to Canada, and in 1830 he and his brother Benjamin joined the Wilberforce Settlement in Upper Canada (now Ontario). In 1831, Paul was sent to England by community leaders to collect funds for a manual labor training college at Wilberforce.

Paul arrived in England in 1832. The next year he married an English woman and began traveling on speaking tours with well-known British Abolitionists such as John Scobie, George Thompson, and Thomas Clarkson, as well as the American antislavery leader William Lloyd Garrison (*see* ABOLITION). On July 13, 1833, Paul attended a notable meeting at Exeter Hall in London, during which he, Garrison, and Irish patriot Daniel O'Connell spoke against the American Colonization Society.

Paul remained in England until 1836, when he returned to Wilberforce. There, he became involved in a dispute over the funds, some $8,000, that he had raised for the Wilberforce project. Paul maintained that his expenses had amounted to over $7,000, and that this, combined with his $50 monthly salary, left him in debt for his efforts. He therefore refused to surrender the money he had raised. When the colony's leaders protested, Paul left the settlement. The Wilberforce settlement disbanded soon after. Meanwhile, Paul returned to Albany, and was named pastor of the city's Hamilton Street Baptist Church. He remained at that position until his death three years later.

REFERENCE

RIPLEY, C. PETER, ET AL., eds. *The Black Abolitionist Papers.* Vol 2, *Canada.* Chapel Hill, N.C., 1987.

SABRINA FUCHS

Paul, Thomas (September 3, 1773–April 13, 1831), minister and missionary. Born free in Exeter, N.H., Thomas Paul was the son of a laborer who fought in the American Revolution. Educated at a Baptist school in Hollis, N.H., Paul was ordained a Baptist minister at West Nottingham, N.H., on May 1, 1805.

Paul moved to Boston, where he became a leader of the town's growing African-American community. Angered by the segregation of blacks, who were confined to Negro pews at Baptist churches, Paul organized a black congregation on August 8, 1805, and helped raise funds for the construction of the African Meeting House on Beacon Hill, designed for all faiths. The Meeting House was finished late in 1806. As the sole black-owned public building in the city, it rapidly became a community center. Paul was Chaplain of Prince Hall's black Masonic lodge, and when Hall died in 1807, Paul became recognized as leader of Boston's African-American community. As one of the few ordained African-American Baptist ministers, such was Paul's fame that, in 1808, he was asked to come to New York and create a black Baptist congregation. Paul remained in New York a few months, where, on July 15, 1809, he founded the ABYSSINIAN BAPTIST CHURCH. Shortly thereafter, he returned to Boston.

In 1815, Paul traveled to England under the aegis of the Baptist Missionary Society of Massachusetts. Hailed by English abolitionists, he returned committed to the antislavery cause. In 1823, Paul petitioned the Missionary society to send him to Haiti. He arrived in Port-au-Prince in July. The Haitian government was friendly, and Paul at first termed the country "the best and most suitable place offered to emancipated people of color, for the enjoyment of liberty and equality." However, he brought on strong opposition by preaching Protestantism to the devoutly Catholic Haitians, and he was hindered by his poor command of French. He returned shortly after arriving, having decided conditions were not yet ripe for a mass emigration of North American blacks.

Once back in Boston, Paul threw himself anew into the antislavery struggle. He became a close associate of David Walker, with whom he worked on FREEDOM'S JOURNAL (1827–1829), the first African-American newspaper. Paul also befriended abolitionist William Lloyd Garrison. In 1829, Paul retired from his pulpit. He died in Boston two years later. His three children became teachers and abolitionists.

REFERENCES

DOWLING, JOHN. "Rev. Thos. Paul and the Colored Baptist Churches." In *Baptist Memorial and Monthly Record* 8 (1849): 295–301.

SOBEL, MECHAL. *Trabelin' On: The Slave Journey to an Afro-Baptist Faith*. Westport, Conn., 1979.

GREG ROBINSON

Payne, Daniel Alexander (February 24, 1811–November 2, 1893), minister. Daniel Alexander Payne was the principal figure in the AFRICAN METHODIST EPISCOPAL CHURCH (AME) during the second half of the nineteenth century—a period one historian even termed "the era of Bishop Daniel Payne." Payne was born in Charleston, S.C., to free black parents who provided for his early education. He established his own school in 1828 but was forced to close it when the South Carolina legislature prohibited the teaching of blacks. Leaving Charleston in 1835, he studied for two years at the Evangelical Lutheran Seminary in Gettysburg, Pa., but left because of failing eyesight. He obtained a license to preach and in 1839 became the first African-American clergyman ordained by the Franckean Evangelical Lutheran Synod (*see* LUTHERANISM). He opened a coeducational school in Philadelphia in 1840 and soon became involved in the antislavery movement.

Although Payne briefly served a white Presbyterian congregation in Troy, New York, he was never given charge of a Lutheran parish, so in 1841 he associated with the AME church. He hesitated to join the denomination because many members opposed an educated clergy. Payne's preference for formal, liturgical worship and learned ministers contrasted with the emotional, spontaneous style of many of the denomination's pastors and congregations. But his untiring efforts to standardize AME worship, improve religious education, and preserve a record of the denomination's history eventually earned the respect of church leaders. Elected a bishop in 1852, he shaped the character and policies of the denomination over the next four decades. Under his leadership, the AME church expanded its home and foreign missions, reorganized its publication program, and established hundreds of congregations among the recently emancipated slaves, a major factor in the denomination's rapid growth after the Civil War.

A noted educator, author, and theologian, Payne was named president in 1863 of WILBERFORCE UNIVERSITY, the first black-controlled college in the United States. He made the institution solvent, attracted capable students and faculty, and enhanced its reputation. Although he left the presidency of Wilberforce in 1876, he remained active in its administration until his death.

Payne wrote numerous poems, essays, speeches, and sermons for the African-American press. His autobiographical *Recollections of Seventy Years* (1888)

Forced at a young age from his native Charleston, S.C., for teaching blacks to read, Daniel Alexander Payne later became senior bishop of the African Methodist Episcopal Church and a preeminent intellectual and spiritual leader of late nineteenth-century black America. (Prints and Photographs Division, Library of Congress)

and *History of the African Methodist Episcopal Church* (1891) are important contributions to African-American literature and valuable sources for nineteenth-century African-American history. He was a conspicuous figure in the World Parliament of Religions at the World's Columbian Exposition in Chicago (1893).

REFERENCE

COAN, JOSEPHUS R. *Daniel Alexander Payne: Christian Educator*. Philadelphia, 1935.

ROY E. FINKENBINE

Payton, Philip A., Jr. (February 27, 1876–August 29, 1917), Harlem realtor. Philip Payton was born and raised in Westfield, Mass. In 1898 he received a bachelor's degree from Livingston College in Salisbury, N.C. The following year he moved to

New York City, where he worked at various jobs, including one as a janitor in a real estate office.

In 1900 Payton opened his own real estate business in Harlem, which advertised: "Management of Colored Tenements a Specialty." After nearly a year of little success, he benefited from a squabble between two white landlords, one of whom turned over a building to Payton to get even with his competitor. More generally, Payton benefited from a depressed market in Harlem real estate, and was soon renting extensively to African Americans in the previously almost all-white neighborhood of HARLEM. Other white landlords began to let him manage their "black" buildings. By 1904 he had become the most prominent African-American realtor in New York City. In that year Payton founded the Afro-American Realty Company, which specialized in acquiring five-year leases on Harlem property owned by whites and subsequently renting them to black tenants. In several cases, Payton evicted white tenants and replaced them with African Americans. In its four years of existence, Payton's company played a pivotal role in opening Harlem to African Americans. The black press dubbed Payton the "Father of Harlem."

The realty company ran into severe difficulties in 1906, when forty-three stockholders in the company sued Payton for fraud and embezzlement. The suit was dismissed on the grounds that Payton was only one of several officers in the company. But the company itself was found guilty of misrepresentation, and several stockholders were awarded compensation for lost investments. Payton was also criticized outside the company for charging higher rents to black tenants than to whites. Payton and the company continued to do business, but the lawsuit, along with several unsuccessful speculations, weakened the company, which closed its doors in 1908.

After the demise of his company, Payton continued to operate in Harlem as a real estate agent. He died in Harlem in 1917.

REFERENCE

OSOFSKY, GILBERT. *Harlem: The Making of a Ghetto: Negro New York, 1890–1930.* New York, 1966.

THADDEUS RUSSELL

Payton, Walter Jerry (July 25, 1954–), football player. Walter Payton was born and raised in Columbia, Miss. He began playing football as a junior at Columbia High School. After graduation Payton attended Jackson State University in Mississippi where he established himself as a star running back, earning the nickname "Sweetness." In 1974, after three and

one-half years of coursework, Payton graduated from Jackson State as the all-time leading scorer in NCAA history with 464 points scored rushing and kicking.

Payton was selected by the Chicago Bears in the first round of the 1975 National Football League (NFL) draft and went on to become one of the greatest running backs in football history. On November 20, 1977 he set the NFL single-game rushing record with 275 yards against the Minnesota Vikings. In 1977 and 1978 Payton was named the NFL Most Valuable Player. Over his twelve-year professional career, all with Chicago, he rushed for more than 1,000 yards in ten seasons and was selected for the Pro Bowl ten times. Payton retired in 1987 as the NFL's career rushing record-holder with 16,726 yards gained.

After his retirement Payton took up race car driving, managed his own company, 34 Enterprises, and purchased several restaurants and nightclubs. In 1993 he joined an unsuccessful St. Louis effort to bring an expansion NFL team to that city. Payton was inducted into the Football Hall of Fame in 1993.

REFERENCES

PORTER, DAVID L. *Biographical Dictionary of American Sports: Football.* New York, 1987.
WILBON, MICHAEL. "Payton Spirited in St. Louis." *Washington Post,* September 28, 1993, p. D1.

THADDEUS RUSSELL

Peace Mission Movement.   *See* Father Divine.

Peake, Mary S. (1823–February 22, 1862), teacher. Born in Norfolk, Va., the daughter of a free woman of color and a white Englishman, Peake was educated at a school for free African Americans in Alexandria, Va. She returned to Norfolk at the age of sixteen, and in 1847, with her mother and stepfather, moved to Hampton, Va. As a young woman, she had secretly educated slaves, and sometime around 1850 she founded the Daughters of Zion, a benevolent society for impoverished and indigent African Americans. She married Thomas Peake, a former slave, in 1851.

When the Civil War began, Peake had been teaching African-American children in Hampton, Va.; after Hampton was occupied by the Union Army early in the war, schoolchildren recommended Peake to an agent from the AMERICAN MISSIONARY ASSOCIATION (AMA) who had come South to start a school for

African Americans who had seized their freedom behind Union lines. In September 1861, Peake became the first teacher to be hired in the first AMA school. Her daytime classes of fifty or sixty children at Fortress Monroe included her own daughter; at night, Peake conducted classes for adults. She also conducted a Sabbath school, and infused all her teaching endeavors with a highly religious sensibility.

Peake died from tuberculosis soon after she began her work in African-American education; the school at Fortress Monroe formed the nucleus of what became the renowned African-American college, HAMPTON INSTITUTE.

REFERENCE

LOCKWOOD, LEWIS C. *Mary S. Peake: The Colored Teacher at Fortress Monroe.* 1863. Reprint. New York, 1969.

MARTHA E. HODES

Peck, David John (19th century), physician. David Peck was probably the first African American to graduate from an American medical school. A native of Pennsylvania, he was the son of John Peck, who settled in Carlisle. Records at the University of Chicago indicate that in 1847 he graduated from Rush Medical School with the notation "colored" beside his name. Later in 1847 he joined William Lloyd Garrison, Martin Robison DELANY, and other abolitionists in making speeches in Ohio. The 1850 Philadelphia City Directory listed him as being at 223 Lombard Street, where he practiced medicine. In the early 1850s Delany advised him to rescind his plans to settle in California and unite in an effort to found a Negro republic in Central America. Delany told Peck he would not succeed in California among white doctors, whereas in Central America his color would be an advantage.

Shortly thereafter, Peck moved to Nicaragua, where he became a prominent practitioner and was nominated as port physician over an Englishman of eleven years' standing. Although Delany's proposal for a republic did not succeed and he returned to the United States, Peck remained in Nicaragua and became chairman of a local committee charged with drafting resolutions for a municipal council. The date of his death, like his birthdate, is unknown.

REFERENCES

MORAIS, HERBERT M. *History of the Negro in Medicine.* New York, 1967.
ROLLIN, FRANK A. *Life and Public Services of Martin R. Delany.* New York, 1969.

VIVIAN OVELTON SAMMONS

Peete, Calvin (July 18, 1943–), golfer. Peete is the most accomplished African American to compete on the Professional Golfers' Association (PGA) tour through the 1990s. He achieved this distinction despite an unlikely personal background for professional GOLF. Born in Detroit, one of nineteen children, Peete moved with his family to Pahokee, Florida, where he grew up. After dropping out of high school, he made his living selling trinkets and wares to migrating farm workers who followed the seasonal crops of fruits and vegetables from northern Florida. On one of his trips north to Rochester, N.Y., Peete was lured out by a group of friends who told him they were going to a party. Instead they took him to a golf course where he agreed to follow them around, and eventually took some shots. After playing that day, he subsequently devoted all his spare time to golf. His game quickly improved, even though he was hampered with a deformed left arm—he could not fully straighten it—as a result of a childhood accident. Most golf experts consider a straight left arm essential for a good swing.

Within two years Peete was playing scratch golf (zero handicap), but he had no aspirations to become a professional, since he did not think that a black man could earn a living playing golf. He remembers the Sunday afternoon when he was watching a televised tournament (it was the 1968 American Golf Classic), and Lee ELDER—at the time the most promising black professional on the PGA Tour—was in a playoff with Jack Nicklaus, the most renowned golfer of all time. Elder didn't win the playoff, but the fact that he was in it, competing for thousands of dollars, prompted Peete to renew his commitment to golf.

Peete didn't earn his PGA playing card until 1971, and in the next three years he struggled to maintain his eligibility to compete on the PGA Tour, finishing 96th, 105th, and 108th, respectively, on the PGA Tour earnings list. It was in 1978 that the thirty-five-year-old Peete won his first tournament, the Greater Milwaukee Open. In 1982 he became the second black multiple winner on the PGA tour when he won the Greater Milwaukee Open, the Anheuser-Busch Classic, the BC Open, and the Pensacola Open. His third-place finish in the 1982 PGA Championship, one of the tour's major events (the others are the Masters, the U.S. Open, and the British Open), demonstrated his ability to compete at the highest level of the sport. He won the Georgia-Pacific Atlanta Classic and the Anheuser-Busch Classic again in 1983, and the Texas Open in 1984.

By 1984, Peete had earned almost $1.25 million, by far the most money earned playing golf in such a short period by an African American. He was honored by *Golf Digest* magazine as the Most Improved Player of 1983, and named to its All-American Team.

The Golf Writers' Association awarded him the prestigious Ben Hogan Award.

Despite his unorthodox swing, Peete distinguished himself as the most consistent striker of the golf ball in the sport, regularly leading all other professionals in the category of driving accuracy (the ability to land the first shot on the fairway) and greens in regulation (landing the ball on the green on the first shot for par 3s, the second shot for par 4s, and the third shot for par 5s).

The PGA requires its members to have graduated from high school in order to compete in the Ryder Cup match (the prestigious biennial competition pitting the best American professionals against the best European professionals). Peete passed the test for his high school equivalency in 1982, and was selected as a member of the 1983 U.S. Ryder Cup team. Peete and Lee Elder remain the only African Americans to have competed on the team.

Despite his accomplishments on the professional golf tour, Peete did not convert his success into significant commercial gain. Unlike white golf professionals with similar tour statistics, he received no major national commercial endorsement offers or advertising contracts. Thus, despite the significant liberalization in other areas of opportunity for African-American golfers, a subtle form of discrimination continues to exist.

REFERENCES

ASHE, ARTHUR. *Hard Road to Glory: 1946–Present.* New York, 1988.

BARKOW, AL. *The History of the PGA Tour.* New York, 1989.

DIAZ, JAMIE. "Big Role Model, Barren Stage." *New York Times,* May 4, 1990, p. B1.

"Something Had to Be Done." *Golf Illustrated* (September 1991).

WHITE, CAROLYN. "Peete: 'There May Be No Blacks' in Tour in 3 to 5 Years." *USA Today,* April 5, 1990, p. 6E.

LAWRENCE LONDINO

Penniman, Richard Wayne. *See* Little Richard.

Pennington, James William Charles (January 1807–October 22, 1870), minister, abolitionist. Born James Pembroke, a slave in Queen Anne's County, Md., James Pennngton early became an expert blacksmith and carpenter, and taught himself to read, write, and do figures. In 1827, he escaped via the Underground Railroad, and was hidden by a Quaker couple in Petersburg, Pa., for whom he briefly worked. Around 1830, he traveled to the Brooklyn area (Kings County, N.Y.), taking the name James W. C. Pennington. While there, Pennington worked as a coachman and gained fame in the black community for his forthright opposition to the American Colonization Society. In the year 1831–1832, he was elected a delegate to the Negro Convention in Philadelphia. In the meantime, he began teaching, and decided to become a minister. He taught himself Greek and Latin. Yale College Divinity School, which barred blacks, allowed Pennington to listen to lectures. In 1840, he was hired as pastor of the Talcott Colored Congregational Church in Hartford, Conn. In 1848, he was hired by the First Colored (later Shiloh) Presbyterian Church in New York City. He returned to Hartford in 1856.

Pennington did not confine himself to ministerial duties. He took on the position of teacher at Hartford's Free African School. In 1841, he wrote for school use *A Textbook of the Origin and History of Colored People,* one of the earliest African-American history books. Pennington glorified blacks' African heritage and denounced negative racial stereotypes. He was also the first black member of the previously all-white Hartford Central Association of Congregational Ministers. In 1841, he formed and became leader of the Union Missionary Society, a forerunner of the American Missionary Association.

Pennington's chief fame, however, was as an abolitionist. In 1843, he attended the World's Antislavery Convention in London, and subsequently toured Paris and Brussels, giving antislavery speeches and sermons. In 1849, he wrote his autobiography, *The Fugitive Blacksmith,* which achieved a major success. Having revealed his identity, Pennington feared recapture, and in 1849, he accepted an invitation to England, where he attended the World Peace Conference, and gave antislavery lectures under the auspices of the British and Foreign Antislavery Society. He was lionized in England and Europe, and raised a great deal of money for African missions and abolitionism. In 1849, "in trust" for other black Americans, Pennington was awarded an honorary Doctor of Divinity degree from the University of Heidelberg in the German States. After the Fugitive Slave Act was passed in 1850, he visited the island of Jamaica. Despite his continuing opposition to African colonization, he recommended black settlement in Jamaica. British friends eventually bought his freedom, and he returned to America in 1853.

Pennington's later years were plagued by troubles. He was accused by opponents (mainly anticlerical Garrisonians) of misusing the funds he had raised for his freedom. In 1853, he was criticized for joining a Presbyterian association which included slaveholders. Like most black ministers, he was poorly paid and faced financial problems. His reputation was finally destroyed when his alcoholism was revealed. In 1858, Pennington left Hartford, and served six different congregations in the North and postbellum South over the next twelve years. A trip abroad in 1861 was financially unsuccessful, and while in England, he was briefly imprisoned for stealing a book. Shortly after taking a teaching post in Jacksonville, Fla., in 1870, he took sick and died.

REFERENCE

BLACKETT, R. J. M. *Beating Against the Barriers: Biographical Essays in Nineteenth-Century Afro-American History*. Baton Rouge, La., 1986.

GREG ROBINSON

Pennsylvania. The history of African Americans in Pennsylvania covers more than three centuries. Located in the northeast section of the United States, the Commonwealth of Pennsylvania was one of the original thirteen American colonies. While Pennsylvania's African-American residents have tended to live in the major metropolitan areas of Philadelphia and Pittsburgh, there is a long and rich history even outside these areas.

As early as 1639, African people are recorded as being in servitude to Swedish settlers in the Delaware Valley region of southeast Pennsylvania. William Penn (1644–1718), an English Quaker (*see* SOCIETY OF FRIENDS), came to the region in 1681, to found a colony originally called "Penn's Woods," but which later was renamed Pennsylvania. In 1684, the ship *Isabella* arrived in the new city of Philadelphia carrying the first documented slaves in Pennsylvania. Penn was a slave owner; at his Bucks County estate, Pennbury, he owned as many as twelve slaves at one time.

For several reasons, SLAVERY in Pennsylvania was neither as widespread nor as enduring an institution as it was in the South. First, the early settlers of British Quaker and German Pietist backgrounds preferred to labor and perform chores themselves, and their religious beliefs convinced many of them that slavery was immoral. Second, Pennsylvania did not have a plantation economy based upon tobacco or cotton. Most Pennsylvania slaves worked as laborers, domestics, or craftspeople. A few slaves, as well as some free blacks, worked at charcoal iron forges. Charcoal iron was used in the manufacture of tools, utensils, and firearms, and this industry ultimately

played a decisive role in helping the American colonies win their independence.

Soon after Pennsylvania was settled, an abolitionist movement arose in the colony, beginning with the Germantown protest of 1688, an antislavery petition drafted by a group of Mennonites. By 1701, slave manumission had begun, and in 1711, the colony banned the SLAVE TRADE. The law was vetoed by the English Parliament, and slave importation was not definitively halted until 1767. The revolutionary spirit led several well-known Pennsylvanians, including Benjamin Franklin and Thomas Paine, to become involved in antislavery activities. In 1775, the Pennsylvania Abolition Society, the first abolitionist organization in American history (*see* ABOLITION), was formed in Philadelphia.

By the early eighteenth century, Pennsylvania was home to a significant free black community. In 1707, the Pennsylvania assembly received a petition from some free hired white workers, who resented labor competition from black craftsmen, to restrict black skilled laborers. In 1725–1726, the assembly enacted a "Black Code," which sought to control all Pennsylvania blacks (*see* BLACK CODES). Under the Pennsylvania code, free blacks were fined for socializing with slaves; if suspected of vagrancy, a free black could be enslaved. Meanwhile, if a slave was convicted of a crime and executed, the slave owner was compensated for his loss. The effect of the Black Code was to coerce blacks and prevent them from forming a unified community.

During the AMERICAN REVOLUTION, African Americans fought at several places in Pennsylvania, including Brandywine, and were present at Valley Forge. Several blacks crossed the Delaware River with George Washington at the Battle of Trenton in December 1776, but blacks also fought on the side of the British (*see* LOYALISTS IN THE AMERICAN REVOLUTION). When the British evacuated Philadelphia for Nova Scotia in 1778, many blacks left with them. By the end of the war, the African Americans who remained in Philadelphia formed a close-knit community under the leadership of Richard ALLEN and Absalom JONES. In 1787, Allen and Jones organized the FREE AFRICAN SOCIETY, which led to the founding of the AFRICAN METHODIST EPISCOPAL CHURCH in 1794.

Pennsylvania's African Americans entered the nineteenth century with hopes of being full-fledged American citizens. The 1790 Pennsylvania state constitution conferred on all freemen the right to vote, and free blacks therefore enjoyed a measure of political freedom. In 1780, Pennsylvania passed a gradual abolition act stipulating that no African-American slave born in the state would be enslaved past the age of twenty-eight. However, slavery was not finally extinguished in the state until the 1840s. During this period, black communities began to grow up throughout the state. From 1800 to 1820, African Methodist Episcopal (AME) churches were started in southeast and central Pennsylvania towns such as West Chester, Carlisle, Shippensburg, and Lewiston. There were blacks as far west as Erie at least as early as 1787, but the first real settlement of blacks in the northwest of the state came with the Battle of Lake Erie during the WAR OF 1812. Commodore Oliver Perry had a number of blacks serving in his fleet, and several black sailors, including Isaac Hardy aboard the *Niagara,* were killed in the battle. Following the battle's end, a few black veterans settled in Erie. Starting with this core group, Erie's black population eventually grew large enough to warrant the creation of a local chapter of the AMERICAN COLONIZATION SOCIETY by whites anxious to send them to Africa. Meanwhile, a small black community grew up in Pittsburgh, growing to some 200 people by 1810.

During the early nineteenth century, black Pennsylvanians united against slavery, whose existence, in the form of slavecatchers, threatened their lives in Pennsylvania. The Keystone State had numerous "stations" on the UNDERGROUND RAILROAD, the most active being those near the state's southern border such as York, Philadelphia, Chester, Lancaster, Chambersburg, Pittsburgh, and Uniontown. In 1821, white residents of the town of Kennett Square successfully resisted the kidnapping of a fugitive slave. The same year, the legislature forbade justices of the peace to aid in slavecatching and mandated trials for FUGITIVE SLAVES. In 1826, Pennsylvania passed a "personal liberty" antikidnapping law requiring warrants. The Pennsylvania Anti-Slavery Society was formed in 1837 in Harrisburg to promote abolitionism. In 1838, William Whipper started the first black journal in Pennsylvania, the *National Reformer.* By 1846, several antislavery newspapers, including the *Mystery* of Pittsburgh, the *Mercer Luminary* of Mercer, the *Clarion of Freedom* of Clarion, and the *Pennsylvania Freeman* of Philadelphia, had been founded.

Slavecatching remained a serious threat. In 1842, Maryland slavecatcher Edward Prigg seized Margaret Morgan, a black woman fugitive, in York and took her back to Maryland. Pennsylvania indicted Prigg under the personal liberty law, but Maryland claimed the law was unconstitutional. The case went to the U.S. Supreme Court later that year, which in *Prigg* v. *Pennsylvania* struck down the Pennsylvania law, ruling that states could neither hinder nor be forced to help federal officials under Fugitive Slave acts. Pennsylvania passed a stronger antikidnapping act in 1847, banning the use of state officials and prisons in fugitive slave cases. This act aided the founding of communities by fugitive slaves, including "Freedom Road" in Mercer County, "Africa" in Franklin County, Wilmore in Cambria County, "Hayti" in Chester County, and "Guinea Run" in Bucks County.

With the passage of the federal FUGITIVE SLAVE ACT of 1850, however, these communities dispersed and forays into Pennsylvania by slavecatchers became common and often disrupted community life. In 1850, for instance, slavecatchers attempted to abduct two freeborn black women in Harrisburg. The same year, white and black Harrisburgers raised money to buy freedom for the fugitive slave James Phillips, who was kidnapped in the city and taken south.

The most sensational attempted kidnapping of fugitive slaves in Pennsylvania touched off the CHRISTIANA REVOLT OF 1851 in Lancaster County. On September 11, 1851, a Maryland slave owner and three federal marshals surrounded the house of William Parker, a local free black, demanding the return of fugitives hiding in the house. Parker and the fugitives opened fire and killed the slave owner. Parker later fled to Canada via the Underground Railroad, while others arrested in the "riot," defended by lawyer Thaddeus Stevens, were acquitted.

However, Pennsylvania also had a strong proslavery and antiblack element. Pennsylvania had a reputation as "the most southern Northern state," and JIM CROW facilities became increasingly common over time. The Philadelphia area was the site of at least four major race riots during the antebellum era. Meanwhile, the black community in Columbia, led by businessman/activist Stephen Smith (c. 1797–1873), was threatened by whites. In 1834, white mobs carried out two riots during which they destroyed considerable property in the black area of town. The following year, antiblack leaders organized boycotts and threats in an unsuccessful attempt to drive away Smith and others in the town's black population. Abolitionist speakers such as Frederick DOUGLASS were not always welcome in the state. During a speech in Harrisburg in 1847, Douglass was pelted with eggs by a mob. Perhaps the burning of Pennsylvania Hall, an abolitionist meeting hall, in Philadelphia in 1837 was the event that best symbolized how deeply divided Pennsylvania was on the slavery question.

The progressive spirit of antebellum Pennsylvania's African Americans is reflected in their community life, especially in the form of black newspapers, schools, and churches. The black church, which often signified the presence of a tiny black community within largely white counties, continued to grow. By the late 1850s, AME churches had been founded in Meadville in the northwest and Wilkes-Barre in the northeast, and in 1857 Philadelphia alone had at least eighteen black churches. Pennsylvania also became a leader in nurturing educational institutions for blacks. As early as 1818, Philadelphia offered public support for black schools, and segregated education for black children expanded throughout the period. In 1854, the state passed a law requiring segregated schools in districts with twenty or more black students. Meanwhile, the Institute for Colored Youth (later Cheyney State College) was founded by Quakers in Philadelphia in 1837. In 1853, Ashmun Institute was founded as a liberal-arts school in Chester County and was renamed Lincoln University in 1866. These two leading educational institutions are among the oldest historically black colleges in the United States, as well as—with Wilberforce University—the only ones in the North.

Black Pennsylvanians remained politically active throughout the antebellum period. Both the national convention movement, begun in 1830 and based in Philadelphia, and its Pennsylvania chapter were centers of organization. The fight for the ballot was a major unifying issue. In 1835, a Luzerne County black man sued to exercise his right to vote, but a county court ruled him ineligible. In 1837, the Pennsylvania Supreme Court ruled that blacks had no right to vote. The same year, fearing the potential voting power of blacks, the state legislature inserted the word "white" before "freeman" in the new state constitution's voting rights cause. Philadelphia's Robert PURVIS drafted a petition to the legislature: "The Appeal of Forty Thousand Citizens Threatened with Disenfranchisement"—but it was ignored. Pennsylvania's convention movement led the struggle for voting rights. In 1841, a State Convention of Colored Freemen was held in Pittsburgh, while Harrisburg was the site of the 1848 State Convention of Colored Citizens and the 1865 State Rights Convention. However, the ballot was not restored to Pennsylvania blacks until passage of the FIFTEENTH AMENDMENT in 1870.

When Pennsylvania joined the Union cause following the outbreak of the CIVIL WAR in 1861, African Americans in Pennsylvania were anxious to volunteer for military service. That year, a contingent of Pittsburgh blacks called the Hannibal Guards came forward, and Philadelphia blacks readied themselves for combat. Neither group, however, was allowed to fight until 1863, when blacks were admitted to the Union Army. Some Pennsylvania blacks enlisted in the 54th and 55th Massachusetts Volunteer Colored Infantry. In June 1863, on the eve of the Battle of Gettysburg, Camp William Penn was established not far from Philadelphia to train black Union soldiers in the Commonwealth. White officers organized ten regiments of the U.S. Colored Regiments (the 3rd, 6th, 8th, 22nd, 24th, 25th, 41st, 43rd, 45th, and 127th

Regiments). They fought on southern battlefields and served duty during the RECONSTRUCTION era.

Following the end of the Civil War, Pennsylvania's black population increased as a result of migration from the South. In Johnstown, for example, the Bethlehem Steel Company began recruiting southern black laborers in 1873, and other businesses followed. The new migrants created social and religious institutions such as the Cambria African Methodist Episcopal Zion Church, founded by ex-Maryland blacks recruited by the Rosensteel Tannery in 1873 and the Mount Olive Baptist Church, set up by railroad workers in 1876. In the early twentieth century, migrants from Clayton, Ala., established Johnstown's Shiloh Baptist Church. The migration, especially to Philadelphia, swelled into a significant movement in the 1880s.

Civil rights efforts intensified in the late nineteenth century. In 1881, after a black man in Meadville successfully sued in county court to have his children admitted to an all-white school, the Pennsylvania legislature officially integrated the state's schools. The same year, following a decade of voter organization and lobbying by black state conventions and the National Equal Rights League, the Pennsylvania Equal Rights Bill was passed. It banned racial discrimination in public accommodations. However, equal-rights laws proved ineffective; judges and juries refused to punish offenders or award damages to black plaintiffs. Meanwhile, Jim Crow facilities, common in the state before 1865, became increasingly universal. Semiofficial educational discrimination continued well into the twentieth century. Violence was a constant threat. In August 1911, Zachariah Walker, a drunken black worker in the the growing steel town of Coatesville, shot a policeman. The next day, Walker was lynched, in an incident that shocked the nation and sparked the expansion of the newly founded NATIONAL ASSOCIATION FOR THE ADVANCEMENT OF COLORED PEOPLE (NAACP).

During the late nineteenth and early twentieth centuries, the burgeoning black communities concentrated on developing educational facilities. Booker T. WASHINGTON's philosophy of industrial education influenced the creation of several schools, such as the Berean Industrial School, founded in Philadelphia in 1899; the Downington Industrial School, founded in 1905; and the Chester Industrial School, founded in 1899. (In 1913, the more academically oriented Cheyney Training School for Teachers—later Cheyney State Teacher's College, which grew out of the old Institute for Colored Youth—was founded.) Access to education created a vital audience for black newspapers, and by 1909, fourteen black newspapers had been created in the state in such towns as Steelton, Wilkes-Barre, and Harrisburg.

The most prominent organs were the *Philadelphia Tribune* and the nationally circulated *Pittsburgh Courier,* which remain in publication. Political organizations also flourished. In 1911, Harry Bass became the first African American in the Pennsylvania Assembly.

Beginning in 1915–1916, the Great Migration triggered by the start of World War I and the cutoff of European immigration transformed Pennsylvania's black communities. Pennsylvania companies such as Midvale Steel, Atlantic Refining, Franklin Sugar, and Hog Island Shipyards recruited thousands of southern African Americans. As steel plants such as Carnegie Steel and Jones & Laughlin hired black workers, black communities sprang up in industrial suburbs such as Homestead near Pittsburgh. Though most of the migrants went to Philadelphia and Pittsburgh, other communities, such as Johnstown, also welcomed large numbers of southern migrants. Competition for scarce housing and leisure facilities led to large-scale racial tension. In 1917–1918, racial rioting broke out in Chester and Philadelphia. In 1923, a shootout between blacks and white police in Johnstown resulted in KU KLUX KLAN cross-burnings and an order from the mayor, partially enforced, expelling Johnstown's black population.

Despite the discrimination, black culture in Pennsylvania thrived, with lodges, music clubs, settlement houses, and chapters of the YOUNG MEN'S CHRISTIAN ASSOCIATION (YMCA) and sports teams being common cultural centers. By 1925, colored chapters of the YMCA had been established in Philadelphia, Pittsburgh, Sewickley, Harrisburg, and Wilkes-Barre, and FRATERNAL ORDERS such as the Masons, Elks, Odd Fellows, and others had chapters throughout the state. Meanwhile, Pittsburgh's Hill District became famous for its jazz clubs, and many local residents, including Earl "Fatha" HINES, Roy ELDRIDGE, and Billy STRAYHORN went on to jazz celebrity. Philadelphia's music scene was distinguished by notable classical musicians such as contralto Marian ANDERSON and the all-black Philadelphia Concert Orchestra. In 1934 Leopold Stokowski conducted the premiere of William Levi DAWSON's *Negro Folk Symphony* with the "mainstream" Philadelphia Orchestra. Baseball teams such as Ed Bolden's Darby-based Hilldale Club, the Pittsburgh Crawfords, the Harrisburg Giants, the Homestead Grays, the Philadelphia Stars, and Erie's Pontiac club were favorites of Pennsylvania fans.

The Great Depression brought serious unemployment and poverty to much of Pennsylvania's black population. In response, blacks organized community relief efforts and organized politically. Black leaders such as NAACP field secretary Daisy LAMPKIN campaigned for civil rights, while activists such as Crystal Bird FAUSET, assistant personnel director of the Philadelphia office of the WORKS PROJECT ADMINISTRATION (WPA), campaigned to obtain federal jobs and relief for blacks. In 1938, Fauset was elected to the Pennsylvania legislature from a largely white district, becoming the first African-American woman ever elected to a statehouse.

The coming of WORLD WAR II brought renewed black migration to Pennsylvania and led to increased social and economic opportunity. In 1942, under pressure from Washington, state industries began to hire African Americans for government defense contract jobs. Meanwhile, the Pennsylvania legislature passed a law banning racial discrimination in unions, which had long been a major obstacle to black advancement in industry. However, progress remained slow and uncertain. In 1946, whites instigated a race riot in a black neighborhood of Philadelphia.

Beginning in the 1950s, civil rights efforts increased in Pennsylvania. Elected officials such as state Reps. Homer S. Brown and K. Leroy Irvis (who was named speaker of the Pennsylvania House in 1977) played a prominent role in securing such equal-rights action as the 1961 open-housing law. In 1958, the same year that Robert N. C. NIX of Philadelphia was elected Pennsylvania's first black U.S. congressman, the NAACP led demonstrations that succeeded in desegregating a housing project in Erie. Perhaps the most notable action of the civil rights era concerned Philadelphia's Girard College. In 1966, blacks capped a centurylong protest against their exclusion from the school with demonstrations. In 1968, after a legal campaign supervised by civil rights lawyer William T. COLEMAN, the U.S. Supreme Court ordered the college to admit African Americans. In other cities, the push for social justice focused on community group efforts. In Reading, for example, blacks and whites formed the Reading-Berks Human Relations Council in 1966 to seek solutions to racial problems. However, discrimination persisted, and the resulting frustration helped spark racial uprisings such as those in Philadelphia in 1964 and Pittsburgh in 1968. Beginning in 1967, efforts by blacks, supported by the U.S. Labor Department, to obtain equal hiring and union membership in the heavily white housing and construction industry through the "Philadelphia Plan" and "Pittsburgh Plan" failed to dismantle black exclusion and led to bitter labor strikes.

In the later decades of the twentieth century, the position of blacks in Pennsylvania remained uncertain. Although 80 percent of the state's African-American community was concentrated in Allegheny, Delaware, Dauphin, and Philadelphia counties, black communities continued to grow. Growth was particularly impressive in the north of the state, in cities such as Williamsport and Erie.

Meanwhile, African Americans developed considerable political clout. On the local level, Philadelphia elected W. Wilson Goode as its first African-American mayor in 1983. On the state level, by 1993, there were fifteen black state representatives and three senators, and in 1994, state Rep. Dwight Evans finished a strong second in the Democratic gubernatorial primary. On the national level, U.S. Rep. William Grey III attained the position of House Majority Whip before his resignation from office in 1990. The fight for economic empowerment has been more difficult. Beginning in the 1970s and increasing in the 1980s, industrial downsizing in factory communities such as Chester and Johnstown led to high levels of black unemployment and poverty.

African-American Pennsylvanians have made significant contributions in diverse fields. Some notable figures are writer David BRADLEY, born in Altoona; composer/musicologist Harry T. BURLEIGH, born in Erie; Hall of Fame catcher Roy CAMPANELLA, born in Philadelphia; basketball legend Wilt CHAMBERLAIN, born in Overbrook (Philadelphia); performer/educator Bill COSBY, born in Philadelphia; jazz musician John COLTRANE raised in Philadelphia; educator-critic Alain LOCKE, born in Philadelphia; civil rights and gay activist Bayard RUSTIN, born in West Chester; painter Henry Ossawa TANNER, born in Pittsburgh; singer/actress Ethel WATERS, born in Chester; open-heart-surgery pioneer Dr. Daniel Hale WILLIAMS, born in Hollidayburg; and playwright August WILSON, born in Pittsburgh.

REFERENCES

BLOCKSON, CHARLES L. African Americans in Pennsylvania: A History and Guide. Baltimore, 1994.

CARTER, ALICE ROSTON. Can I Get a Witness? Growing Up in the Black Middle Class in Erie, Pennsylvania. Erie, Pa., 1991.

DICKERSON, DENNIS C. Out of the Crucible: Black Steelworkers in Western Pennsylvania, 1875–1980. Albany, N.Y., 1986.

DOWNEY, DENNIS, and RAYMOND M. HYSTER. No Crooked Death: Coatesville, Pennsylvania and the Lynching of Zachariah Walker. Urbana, Ill., 1991.

GOTTLIEB, PETER. Making Their Own Way: Southern Blacks' Migration to Pittsburgh, 1916–1930. Urbana, Ill., 1987.

GREGG, ROBERT S. Sparks From the Anvil of Oppression: Philadelphia's African Methodists and Southern Migrants, 1890–1940. Philadelphia, 1993.

HARRIS, RICHARD E. Politics and Prejudice: A History of Chester, Pennsylvania Negroes. Apache Junction, Ariz., 1991.

HOPKINS, LEROY, and ERIC LEDELL SMITH. The African Americans in Pennsylvania. Harrisburg, Pa., 1994.

MCBRIDE, DAVID, ed. Blacks in Pennsylvania History: Research and Educational Perspectives. Harrisburg, Pa., 1983.

MOSS, EMERSON I. African Americans in the Wyoming Valley, 1778–1990. Wilkes-Barre, Pa., 1992.

NASH, GARRY B. Forging Freedom: The Formation of Philadelphia's Black Community, 1720–1840. Cambridge, Mass., 1991.

SLAUGHTER, THOMAS P. Bloody Dawn: The Christiana Riot and Racial Violence in the Antebellum North. New York, 1991.

ERIC LEDELL SMITH

Pentecostalism. Among scholars of Pentecostalism there are two schools of thought as to the emergence of this religious phenomenon. The first school, identified with Vinson Synan, William Menzies, and James Goff, argues that Charles Parham (1873–1929) was the founder of the Pentecostal movement and that it began in Kansas in 1901. The competing school, which includes Walter Hollenweger, James Tinney, J. Douglas Nelson, Cecil R. Robeck, and Edith Blumhofer, argues that the Azusa Street Revival in Los Angeles from 1906 to 1913 was the true beginning and William J. SEYMOUR the pivotal person.

The second school focuses on Azusa Street and Seymour because they were the originating center of Pentecostalism throughout the United States and in Scandinavia, Great Britain, Brazil, Egypt, and India, where it spread. The revival defined Pentecostalism, shaped its interracial relations, and gave it its multicultural character. The first school designates Parham because he was the first proponent to link glossolalia with the biblical Pentecost event recounted in several chapters in the Book of Acts and to define this experience as the baptism of the Holy Spirit.

In 1901 Charles Parham operated the Bethel Bible School in Topeka, Kans. A major religious experience for him was the baptism of the Holy Spirit as described in the Bible, the Book of Acts, chapter 2. The HOLINESS MOVEMENT during the 1800s identified this experience as sanctification. The Wesleyan wing of the Holiness Movement defined the experience in terms of cleansing, while the Calvinist or Reformed wing saw it as empowerment for Christian living. Both positions understood the experience as subsequent to justification. The Reformed advocates described sanctification as a progressive process, while the Wesleyan advocates described it as an instantaneous event.

In the late 1890s Parham joined those who sought to categorize discrete experience beyond justification and sanctification. In January 1901 Parham identified glossolalia with the third experience and linked this experience instead of sanctification with Acts 2. He began preaching this new doctrine within Holiness circles in the Midwest.

In 1905 William J. Seymour, who was black, enrolled in Parham's school in Houston despite the white man Parham's enforcement of segregation laws that prevented Seymour from sitting with the white students. While Seymour adopted the new doctrine, he failed at the time to have the actual experience himself. In 1906 he carried the new doctrine to California in response to an invitation to become pastor of a small black Holiness congregation in Los Angeles headed by Julia Hutchins. Hutchins and the other members established a congregation of Evening Light Saints after withdrawing from the Second Baptist Church, which had refused to embrace their Holiness message. Hutchins, however, rejected Seymour's addition to Holiness teaching and barred him from the pulpit. Edward Lee and, later, Richard Asberry invited Seymour to resume preaching at their homes.

After Seymour and others began speaking in tongues, they outgrew the "house church," and Seymour secured larger facilities at 312 Azusa Street, the former sanctuary of First AFRICAN METHODIST EPISCOPAL CHURCH (AME). Seymour's revival on Azusa Street attracted the attention first of local whites and blacks, especially those involved in the Holiness community. But soon participants from the Holiness Movement across the United States converged by the thousands on Azusa Street to observe events, examine the new doctrine, and experience glossolalia. Within twelve months the Azusa Street Mission spawned an international movement and began a journal, *Apostolic Faith*. From 1906 to 1908, *Apostolic Faith,* the Azusa Street Mission, and Seymour held the loosely bound movement together and provided it with a center and leadership.

Like its Holiness counterpart, Pentecostalism was basically local and regional and headed by both blacks and whites, as well as both women and men. In many places local and regional movements took over entire Holiness congregations and institutions. African-American Holiness leaders who embraced Pentecostalism along with all or some of their associated congregations included W. H. Fulford (d. 1916), William Fuller (1875–1958), Charles Harrison MASON (1866–1961), and Magdalena Tate (1871–1930).

Early Pentecostalism emerged as a strongly interracial movement and struggled with its interracial identity at a time when American society was segregated. Frank Bartleman, a white Azusa Street participant and reporter, stated that at the revival "the color line was washed away in the blood [of Jesus Christ]." While Baptist, Methodist, Presbyterian, and Holi-

ness people lived in racially segregated congregations, associations, and denominational structures, the black and white Pentecostals pastored and preached to and fellowshipped and worshipped with each other between 1906 and 1914, and many joined the predominantly black Pentecostal-Holiness group, the CHURCH OF GOD IN CHRIST. The Pentecostal leadership was strongly anti–KU KLUX KLAN and was often the targets of Klan terrorism because of their interracial sympathies.

But racism came to counter the interracial nature of early Pentecostalism. Parham exhibited racist behavior and a patronizing attitude toward his black counterparts, especially Seymour; in 1908 blacks withdrew from the Fire-Baptized Holiness Church (later called Pentecostal Holiness Church); in 1913 another black group withdrew from the Pentecostal Holiness Church; in 1914 a white group withdrew from the Church of God in Christ; and in 1924 a white group withdrew from the half-black Pentecostal Assemblies of the World, which was led by a black minister, Garfield Thomas Haywood.

While segregation among Pentecostals came to follow the pattern of American Christianity after the Civil War, there were exceptions. Blacks and whites continued to struggle together to structure their interracial relationships during the height of segregation in the United States. In 1924 the Church of God in Christ adopted the Methodist model of establishing a minority transgeographical conference, specifically a white conference to unite the white congregations across the United States that belonged to the predominantly black denomination. In 1907 and 1931 several different groups of blacks and whites entered and withdrew from the Pentecostal Assemblies of the World.

Theologically, Pentecostalism split early into two camps over the doctrine of God: Trinitarian and Oneness. The Oneness doctrine, as opposed to the classic Christian doctrine of the Trinity, claimed that Jesus was the name of God and that God expressed Godself in the form of the Father, Son, and Holy Spirit but was not three persons in one. The Trinitarians confessed the traditional Christian doctrine of the Trinity and rejected the Oneness interpretation. While the existing black Pentecostal denominations, such as the Church of God in Christ, United Holy Church, and Church of the Living God, remained Trinitarian, many independent black Pentecostal congregations in the Midwest, especially those associated with Haywood, rejected Trinitarianism. Oneness denominations identified themselves as Apostolic churches (*see* APOSTOLIC MOVEMENT).

Haywood and the Pentecostal Assemblies of the World are the parents of most black Apostolic denominations in the United States. Significant leaders of the movement included Robert C. Lawson (1881–1961), who organized the Church of Our Lord Jesus Christ of the Apostolic Faith in 1919, Sherrod C. Johnson (1897–1961), who organized the Church of the Lord Jesus Christ of the Apostolic Faith in 1930, and Smallwood Williams, who organized Bible Way Churches of Our Lord Jesus Christ Worldwide in 1957.

While Pentecostal denominations opened more forms of ministry to women than other Protestant denominations, only a few granted women equality with men. Among black Pentecostals, full male–female equality existed only in denominations founded by black women. Magdalena Tate's denomination, the oldest Pentecostal denomination founded by a black woman, was among the Holiness groups that joined Pentecostalism after their establishment. During 1903 she founded in Tennessee the Church of Living God, Pillar and Ground of the Truth. The other major grouping of Pentecostal denominations founded by black women withdrew from the United Holy Church of America, which ordained women to the ministry but denied them the bishopric. In 1924 Ida ROBINSON founded the Mt. Sinai Holy Church to rectify this inequality. In 1944 Beulah Counts (d. 1968), an associate of Robinson, organized the Greater Mt. Zion Pentecostal Church of America.

Crossing Trinitarian and Apostolic divisions is a stream within Pentecostalism called the deliverance movement. The deliverance movement grew out of the white healing movement of the 1940s associated with William Branham that produced Oral Roberts, Gordon Lindsay, and A. A. Allen. The deliverance movement among black Pentecostals is related to Arturo Skinner (1924–1975), who expanded the traditional black Pentecostal emphasis on healing to include exorcisms and heightened the accent on the miraculous. In 1956 he established the Deliverance Evangelistic Centers, with headquarters in Newark, N.J. Deliverance ministries emerged in traditional Pentecostal congregations such as Faith Temple Church of God in Christ under Harry Willis Goldsberry (1895–1986) in Chicago. In urban centers there emerged new independent congregations that competed with traditional black Pentecostals; Benjamin Smith (b. 1926), who founded the Deliverance Evangelistic Center in Philadelphia in 1960, and Richard Hinton, who founded Monument of Faith Evangelistic Center in Chicago in 1963, were two of the best-known leaders of these congregations.

Although Pentecostals are stereotyped as other-worldly, studies have shown a social activist stream within black Pentecostalism. A number of black Pentecostal denominations and leaders joined the Fraternal Council of Negro Churches and participated in the marches for black employment during the 1930s.

Robert C. Lawson cooperated with Adam Clayton POWELL, JR., and other leading Harlem ministers in campaigns for black employment. J. O. Patterson (1912–1990) of the Church of God in Christ and other ministers participated in local civil rights campaigns in Memphis, Tenn., and other southern cities and towns in the late 1950s. Smallwood Williams led the legal battle against segregated public schools during the 1950s in Washington, D.C. Arthur Brazier (b. 1921), Louis Henry Ford (b. 1914) and other Pentecostal clergy were active in the CIVIL RIGHTS MOVEMENT in Chicago and other northern cities in the 1960s.

Studies of the black Pentecostal leadership note the occurrence of a cadre of black Pentecostals who identify with twentieth-century theological liberalism. Relations between liberal Protestantism and black Pentecostalism occur on a number of levels. A significant number of Pentecostals are graduates of liberal seminaries, some as early as the 1940s. They are graduates of schools such as Temple University, Oberlin, Union Theological Seminary (New York City), Duke, Emory, and McCormick. And the first accredited Pentecostal, and only African-American, seminary, Charles Harrison Mason Theological Seminary, is a member of Interdenominational Theological Center (ITC), a consortium of African-American seminaries affiliated with mainline denominations. The Church of God in Christ, the sponsor of Mason Seminary at ITC, embraces theological liberalism from a black perspective in the preparation of an educated clergy. A number of black Pentecostal leaders are also involved in the ecumenical movement that liberal Protestantism embraces: Herbert Daughtry (b. 1931) participates in some World Council of Churches programs, and Ithiel Clemmons (b. 1921) participates in regional and local ecumenical councils.

Black Pentecostalism also includes leaders who identify with evangelicalism. Black Pentecostals associated with the evangelical movement are often graduates of evangelical seminaries such as Fuller, Gordon-Conwell, and Trinity Evangelical Divinity School. Leaders such as William Bentley (b. 1926 and George McKinney (b. 1932) are active members of the National Association of Evangelicals along with the National Black Association of Evangelicals.

During the 1970s black Pentecostalism intersected with the "Word of Faith" movement spurred by Kenneth Hagin and his message of healing, prosperity, and positive confession. Fredrick Price (b. 1932) emerged as the Word of Faith leader among black Christians after establishing Crenshaw Christian Center of Los Angeles in 1973.

During the 1970s Pentecostalism influenced the historic black denominations, especially the AME Church. Neo-Pentecostal ministers occupy some ma-

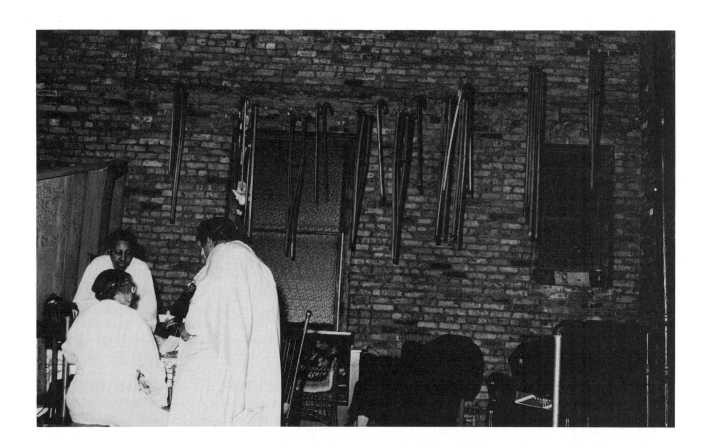

(Top) A Pentecostal church in Chicago in 1941. The crutches and canes of those previously healed hang on the wall. (Bottom) Easter Sunday, April 1941, at a Pentecostal service. (Prints and Photographs Division, Library of Congress)

jor AME pulpits. The focal point for the movement during the early 1970s was St. Paul AME Church in Cambridge, Mass., under the pastorate of John Bryant (b. 1948). During the period, college campuses became centers for the growth of Pentecostalism among black students, particularly through the college gospel choir movement.

Black Pentecostals have been leaders within the black religious music movement since the early 1900s. Black Pentecostalism became the carrier of black religious folk music, noted for its call-and-response, improvisation, polyrhythms, and diatonic harmonies. By the 1920s Arizona Juanita Dranes (b. 1905) and Sallie Sanders were popular gospel singers. Dranes and Sanders began the tradition of the Baptist and Pentecostal leadership of the GOSPEL MUSIC movement. By the 1980s black Pentecostals such as Andrae CROUCH, Edwin HAWKINS, Walter Hawkins, Shirley CAESAR, the Clark Sisters, and the Wynans dominated the gospel music movement.

From its beginning at the Azusa Street Revival in 1906, black Pentecostalism has grown to become the second-largest religious movement among African Americans and one of the fastest-growing religious movements in the United States and around the globe, especially in the Third World.

REFERENCES

BURGESS, STANLEY M., and GARY B. McGEE. *Dictionary of Pentecostal and Charismatic Movements.* Grand Rapids, Mich., 1988.

DUPREE, SHERRY S., ed. *Biographical Dictionary of African-American Holiness-Pentecostals, 1880–1990.* Washington, D.C., 1989.

JONES, CHARLES EDWIN. *A Guide to the Study of Black Participation in Wesleyan Perfectionist and Glossolalic Pentecostal Movements.* Metuchen, N.J., 1987.

DAVID D. DANIELS III

People United to Save Humanity. *See* Operation PUSH.

Perry, John Edward (April 2, 1870–May 15, 1962), physician. John Edward Perry was born in Clarksville, Tex., the son of Anderson Perry, a former slave who became a farmer, and his wife Louisa (White). He attended Bishop College, Marshall, Tex., graduating with a B.A. in 1891. After earning an M.D. at Meharry Medical College (1895), he opened a general practice in rural Mexico, Mo., but soon moved to Columbia, Mo., where he practiced

until 1903. He settled in Kansas City, Mo., in 1903.

Perry's experience with hostile racial attitudes while a student at the Post-Graduate Medical School, Chicago (1897–1898), galvanized his commitment to increase the number and quality of health-care facilities open to both African-American patients and African-American physicians. In 1903 he became affiliated with the Douglass Hospital, in Kansas City, Kans., a hospital for blacks founded by Dr. S. H. THOMPSON in 1898. Perry spearheaded an effort to persuade the city government and medical establishment that a public facility for blacks was essential to the health and well-being of the community at large. As a result, the all-black Kansas City General Hospital No. 2 came into existence in 1910. Perry served as its chief of surgical service (1910–1941). Also, in 1910 he founded a private facility known as the Perry Sanitarium and Nurse Training School (later, the Wheatley-Provident Hospital), serving as superintendent until 1930. In 1945, at the age of seventy-five, he came briefly out of retirement to manage the Houston (Tex.) Hospital for Negroes.

Perry served on the boards of Lincoln University (Missouri) and Meharry Medical College and was active in the Negro YMCA program in Kansas City. He became the twenty-fourth president of the National Medical Association in 1923.

REFERENCES

COBB, W. MONTAGUE. "John Edward Perry, M.D., 1870–." *Journal of the National Medical Association* 48 (1956): 292–296.

PERRY, J. EDWARD. *Forty Cords of Wood: Memoirs of a Medical Doctor.* Jefferson City, Mo., 1947.

PHILIP N. ALEXANDER

Perry, Rufus Lewis (1834–1895), minister and writer. Rufus Lewis Perry was born a slave to the Rev. and Mrs. Lewis and Maria Perry. Both his parents were slaves in Smith County, Tenn. His father also was a Baptist minister and carpenter. Using his skills in carpentry, his father was able to secure work and save enough money to move the family to Nashville. Here young Rufus was classified as a free person, and learned to read and write while attending a school for free Negroes.

This good fortune was short-lived, for in 1841 when Perry was seven years of age his father escaped slavery by fleeing into Canada. The remaining family was sent back to the plantation, and back to a life of slavery. Plantation life was not easy upon his return. His education proved to be a handicap. Not only did his master consider Perry's ability to read and write "dangerous," but his fellow slaves resented his learning. So in August 1852, his master decided it would be best to sell Perry to a trader who was to take him to Mississippi. However, before the trader had an opportunity to sell Perry, he escaped and eventually settled in Canada.

Following a conversion experience in 1854, Perry felt called to the Christian ministry and later enrolled in the class of 1861 at Kalamazoo Seminary in Kalamazoo, Mich. He was ordained October 9, 1861, and was called as pastor of the Second Baptist Church in Ann Arbor, Mich., that same year. Perry would go on to pastor churches in St. Catharine's, Ontario, and Buffalo, N.Y. He is best known for his work with Baptist publications and missionary societies. He either edited or coedited five journals in his lifetime, including the *Baptist Weekly,* the *People's Journal,* and the *National Monitor.* Perry also served as corresponding secretary of the Consolidated American Baptist Missionary Convention, the American Educational Association, and the American Baptist Free Mission Society.

REFERENCES

SIMMONS, WILLIAM J. *Men of Mark: Eminent, Progressive and Rising.* 1887. Reprint. New York, 1988.
WASHINGTON, JAMES M. *Frustrated Fellowship: The Black Baptist Quest for Social Power.* Macon, Ga., 1986.

QUINTON H. DIXIE

Petersen, Franklin E. (March 2, 1932–), military officer. Born in Topeka, Kans., Franklin E. Petersen graduated from Topeka High School in 1949. Following one year at Topeka's Washburn University, he joined the United States Marine Corps in June 1950. In October 1952, Petersen became the first African-American Marine Corps officer commissioned in the Naval Aviation Cadet Program. In April of the following year, he reported to Marine Attack Squadron 212 stationed in Korea, where he completed sixty-four combat missions, earning six Air Medals and the Distinguished Flying Cross.

Following his return to the United States, Petersen continued his education at George Washington University in Washington, D.C. (B.A. degree, 1967; M.A., 1973) and served as operations officer for the Marine Reserve Training Department at Willow Grove, Pa. In 1968, Petersen became the first African American to command a tactical air squadron in the Navy or Marine Corps, when he took command of Marine Fighter Attack Squadron UMFA 314 at Chu Lai Air Base, in South Vietnam. That same year, his squadron received the Hanson Award for Aviation, given to the best fighter squadron in the Marine Corps. Flying more than 280 combat missions, Petersen was awarded the Legion of Merit, a Combat Action Ribbon, and a Purple Heart.

From 1969 to 1972, Petersen served as special assistant to the Commandant for Minority Affairs. In 1979, while serving as chief of staff for the 9th Marine Amphibious Brigade, he was promoted to brigadier general, the first African American to earn that rank in the history of the Marine Corps. Prior to his retirement in 1988, Petersen, in command of Marine Corps Development and Education in Quantico, Va., had achieved the rank of lieutenant general and was the senior ranking aviator in the Navy and the Marine Corps.

REFERENCES

DABS, HENRY E. *Black Brass: Black Generals and Admirals in the Armed Forces of the United States.* Freehold, N.J., 1985, p. 144.
HAWKINS, WALTER L. *African American Generals and Flag Officers.* Jefferson, N.C., 1993, pp. 172–174.
SHAW, HENRY I., JR., and RALPH W. DONNELLY. *Blacks in the Marine Corps.* Washington, D.C., 1976, pp. 62–63, 75–80.

BENJAMIN K. SCOTT

Peterson, Oscar Emmanuel (August 15, 1925–), pianist and composer. Born in Montreal, Oscar Peterson first studied music at the insistence of his father, a railroad porter who made all his children study an instrument in order to escape the poverty of Montreal's small black community. Peterson began piano lessons at age six, and first recorded in a boogie-woogie style while still in high school. As a teenager, he played on a weekly radio show in Montreal, and from 1944 to 1949 he worked with Johnny Holmes, who led one of Canada's most prominent dance bands.

Peterson, one of the few Canadians to reach a position of prominence in American JAZZ, began his international career in 1949, when producer Norman Granz heard him on a radio broadcast from a Montreal club; it was the beginning of a musical relationship that lasted more than four decades. Granz arranged for Peterson to perform that same year at New York City's Carnegie Hall with a touring group of jazz stars known as Jazz at the Philharmonic. Peterson toured regularly with the group until 1953, when he formed a trio with Barney Kessel, and then Herb Ellis, on guitar and Ray Brown on bass. Although Peterson toured Great Britain in 1955 with Ella

The Oscar Peterson Trio (from left to right: Ray Brown, Oscar Peterson, and Herb Ellis) on their return to the United States after a four-week tour of Europe with the Jazz at the Philharmonic band, March 14, 1956. (UPI/Bettmann)

FITZGERALD, and was in great demand as a sideman with Louis ARMSTRONG, Lester YOUNG, Fred Astaire, Billie HOLIDAY, and Coleman HAWKINS, it was as leader of this trio, and a later trio with drummer Ed Thigpen, that he gained his reputation as a genteel but virtuosic improviser, combining the light touch of Nat "King" COLE and Teddy Wilson with the drive and invention of Art TATUM.

Peterson settled in Toronto in 1958, helping to found and manage the Advanced School of Contemporary Music, and continued touring with his trio until 1967, when Ray Brown left. He subsequently recorded and toured prolifically, often as the house pianist for Granz's Pablo Records, with Ella Fitzgerald, Clark TERRY, Dizzy GILLESPIE, Stan Getz, and Niels-Henning Orsted Pederson. In addition to compositions such as "Hallelujah Time," "Children's Tune," "The Smudge," and "Lover's Promenade," Peterson has composed longer works such as *Canadian Suite* (1965) and *Easter Suite* (1984). Although he is one of the most-traveled musicians in jazz, Peterson has always maintained a home in Canada. In 1991 he was named to a three-year term as chancellor of York University in Toronto, and in 1993 he was invested as a Companion of the Order of Canada.

REFERENCES

LEES, GENE. *Oscar Peterson: The Will to Swing*. Toronto, 1988.

LYONS, LEN. *The Great Jazz Pianists*. New York, 1983.

PALMER, RICHARD. *Oscar Peterson*. Tunbridge Wells, England, 1984.

DOUGLAS J. CORBIN

Petry, Ann Lane (October 12, 1908–), writer. Anne Lane was born to middle-class parents in Saybrook, Conn. The daughter of a pharmacist, she graduated from the University of Connecticut School of Pharmacy (formerly the Connecticut College of Pharmacy) in 1931 and worked for a while in her father's drugstore. Yet from the time she created a slogan for a perfume advertisement while still in high school, she was convinced she could be a writer. In 1938 she married George D. Petry and moved to New York City.

Ann Petry in 1946, at the time of the publication of her first novel, *The Street*. (AP/Wide World Photos)

In New York, Petry began serving a kind of writer's apprenticeship as a journalist for two Harlem newspapers, the AMSTERDAM NEWS and *The People's Voice*. (From 1944 to 1946, she would also study creative writing at Columbia University.) This experience exposed her to the gritty world of Harlem's poverty, violence, crime, and economic exploitation that gave her early fiction its absorbing cast and distinctive signature. Her first published story, "On Saturday the Siren Sounds at Noon," appeared in the CRISIS in 1943. Finding the story "Like a Winding Sheet" similarly engaging, *Crisis* published it in 1945. Collected in Martha Foley's *Best American Stories of 1946*, "Like a Winding Sheet" brought Petry national attention and a Houghton Mifflin Literary Fellowship Award to complete what became her best known and most celebrated novel, *The Street* (1946), the first by a black woman to sell more than one million copies.

In *The Street,* Petry focuses on the thwarted and naive efforts of a young black woman to secure a decent living for herself and her son. Petry closely documents the defeating conditions of the ghetto on a woman. She shows an especially critical sensitivity to the notion of the woman as a spectacle, as a body to be looked at and made the object of male sexual desire and exploitation. In her second novel, *Country Place* (1947), Petry shifts her focus from Harlem to Monmouth, Conn. Here she uses the effect that a violent storm has on the people who live in a small town to intricately weave strands of class conflict, bloodlines, and social responsibility. Many of these themes are reworked in Petry's next work, *The Narrows* (1953), a novel about the taboo and ultimately tragic relationship between a black man and a white woman. Petry does not skirt the history of sexual and racial politics that weighs on their relationship, a history that makes the white woman's cry of rape and the black man's subsequent lynching inevitable.

Petry joins urban and rural scenes in her only collection of short stories, *Miss Muriel and Other Stories* (1971). Of the stories in this diverse collection, standing out are those in which Petry experiments with the point of view of precocious, introspective child narrators. Set variously in Harlem, small-town upstate New York, and Connecticut, these stories show geography to be the dominant factor in Petry's writing. Other works include four children's books: *The Drugstore Cat* (1949), *Harriet Tubman, Conductor of the Underground Railroad* (1955), *Tituba of Salem Village* (1964), and *Legends of the Saints* (1970).

REFERENCE

MCKAY, NELLIE. "Ann Petry's *The Street* and *The Narrows:* A Study of Influence of Class, Race, and Gender on Afro-American Women's Lives." In

The Changing Status of American Women from the 1930s to the 1950s. New York, 1985.

DEBORAH MCDOWELL

Pettiford, Oscar (1922–1960), bass player. Oscar Pettiford's mother, a Choctaw, taught music theory; his father, of Cherokee and black ancestry, was a veterinarian who led the family's musical troupe throughout the South and the Midwest. Pettiford was born in Okmulgee, Okla. (Creek Nation), and was three when his family relocated to the Minnesota vaudeville circuit. He danced and sang on stage and at fourteen started playing bass, rapidly developing a prowess for it without much training. African-American bassists like Adolphus Alsbrook and Milt HINTON inspired Pettiford; the latter talked him out of quitting music. He began playing with guitar innovator Charlie CHRISTIAN and multireed player Jerome Richardson as they passed through Minneapolis, and made an acetate recording with them in 1939. In 1942, Pettiford joined Charlie Barnet's orchestra and went to New York. He played the famous jam sessions at Minton's Playhouse, with Thelonious MONK and others, which laid the foundation for bebop, and by 1944 co-led with trumpeter Dizzy GILLESPIE the first working bebop combo, at the Onyx Club on Fifty-second Street.

With expanded personnel and under saxophonist Coleman HAWKINS's leadership, this band recorded bebop's first records on February 16, 1944. Pettiford's solo on "The Man I Love" drew favorable comparisons with the stylistic elasticity of the recently deceased Jimmy BLANTON; however, the guitarlike expressiveness of both musicians developed independently. Later that year, Pettiford performed with Gillespie's first orchestra, then Boyd Raeburn's orchestra. From 1945 to 1948 he toured with the idol of his youth, Duke ELLINGTON, then joined the big band of Woody Herman, with whom he premiered his remarkable though untutored cello playing. A hand broken during a Herman-band softball game kept him inactive for eighteen months, but by 1951 he co-led with trombonist J. J. JOHNSON a band playing at the American Officers' Club in Tokyo.

Pettiford was dismissed from this important tour for his heavy drinking. He returned to New York and led the house band at the Cafe Bohemia until 1958. He was probably the last significant combo leader to attempt thwarting inexperienced musicians with abrupt key changes and rapid tempos. Pettiford's most enduring composition, "Bohemia After Dark," stems from this period and is derived from two Native American melodic strains. After a European tour in the late 1950s he settled in Copenhagen, where he died in 1960 from what was described as a "polio-like virus." Despite being temperamental, Pettiford was well loved by musicians. Gillespie called him a "driving force" in creating modern jazz, and his Bohemia-period pianist Dick Katz remembered his "unself-conscious quality" and "genuine urge to play," with or without an audience.

REFERENCES

GITLER, IRA. *Jazz Masters of the Forties*. New York, 1966.

HUNT, D. C. "Oscar Pettiford: Absolute Artistic Clarity." *Jazz Journal* 26, no. 8 (1973): 6.

RON WELBURN

Pharmacy. The science of preparing and dispensing medicines evolved in tandem with the medical profession, although in the early days pharmacists were a more eclectic and diverse group than physicians. Advances in pharmaceutical knowledge and practice often came not from "recognized" physicians (who generally did their own dispensing) but from self-taught, itinerant healers. A tradition of lay healing flourished because of the inadequacies of organized medicine.

In America, blacks were part of this tradition since colonial times. Some slaves, known for their wisdom in folk cures, developed effective salves and potions that were used in plantation practice. In 1729, a slave in Virginia perfected a root-and-bark mixture said to have been useful in the treatment of syphilis. Cesar, a slave in South Carolina, discovered a remedy for rattlesnake bite that was published in the *South Carolina Gazette* in 1751. Wilcie J. Elfe, a slave assistant to a pharmacist in Charleston, S.C., essentially managed his master's drugstore during the 1850s. While carrying out the routine work of mixing drugs and filling prescriptions, he also formulated original recipes that were widely distributed.

With the growing professionalization of pharmacy as a distinct branch of health care in the nineteenth and early twentieth centuries, African Americans sought the requisite training to establish themselves in practice. The first college of pharmacy in the United States was the Philadelphia College of Pharmacy, founded in 1821, but few blacks attended until the mid-twentieth century (a total of sixty-two from 1900 to 1950; earlier numbers are unknown). Other white schools admitted blacks, although the numbers fluctuated widely; the Temple School of Pharmacy, for example, graduated fifteen blacks in 1926 and none in 1934.

Most aspiring black pharmacists received their training at black (or predominantly black) schools. The earliest school, begun in 1868, was attached to HOWARD UNIVERSITY. Howard's first pharmacy graduate was James Thompson Wormley, who earned his degree in 1870. Black pharmacy schools—now defunct—were also attached to Meharry Medical College (1889–1937); Shaw University (1891–1918); and New Orleans University (1900–1914). Meharry graduated 569 pharmacists, Shaw graduated 125, and New Orleans graduated 59. The Washington (D.C.) College of Pharmacy, a short-lived proprietary school (ca. 1922–1926), graduated approximately seventy-five pharmacists before closing due to lack of funds, accreditation problems, and competition with Howard.

In 1980, four out of seventy-one pharmacy schools were attached to predominantly black universities: Howard, Xavier (in New Orleans), Florida A&M, and Texas Southern. Though pharmacy requires a shorter and less costly training program than either medicine or dentistry, the representation of black pharmacists among the total number of practitioners in 1980 (2.3 percent) was lower than that of black dentists and black physicians (2.9 percent and 2.6 percent, respectively). This shortfall of pharmacists has exacerbated the problem of health care in traditionally underserved urban and rural areas, where pharmacists often act in place of physicians as primary-care providers.

As a professional group, black pharmacists operated for many years within the National Medical Association (which also included black dentists). They established their first autonomous body, the National Pharmaceutical Association (NPA), on August 18, 1933. A new NPA, founded by Chauncey Ira Cooper, dean of the Howard University College of Pharmacy from 1941 to 1972, came into existence in 1947. The first number of the new NPA's official periodical, *Journal of the National Pharmaceutical Association*, appeared in 1954. The National Pharmaceutical Foundation was established in 1972 by Ira C. Robinson, Cooper's successor as dean at Howard, to promote the interests of minority pharmacists and the pharmaceutical needs of minority communities.

REFERENCES

CULP, ROBERT W. "The Genesis of Black Pharmacists in America to 1900." *Transactions and Studies of the College of Physicians of Philadelphia* 42 (April 1975): 401–411.

ROBINSON, IRA C., comp. and ed. *First National Symposium on Progress and Problems of Black Pharmacists in America, Feb. 21–22, 1976, Houston, Texas: Proceedings*. Silver Springs, Md., 1976.

PHILIP N. ALEXANDER

Phelps-Stokes Fund. Founded in 1911 to administer a bequest from Caroline Phelps Stokes (1854–1909), the Phelps-Stokes Fund (PSF) is a nonprofit foundation governed by a volunteer board of trustees and headquartered in New York City. Stokes, one of America's first women philanthropists, provided in her will that income from an $800,000 estate be used to increase educational opportunities for African Americans, Africans, North American Indians, and needy whites, and to create housing for the poor in the city of New York.

Stokes was inspired by the example of her two charitable grandfathers, one of whom, Anson Green Phelps, had been prominent in the New York Colonization Society, an organization that repatriated freed slaves to Liberia. PSF's continuing commitment to that country derives from this historic connection. The first two board presidents, Isaac Newton Phelps Stokes and Anson Phelps Stokes, agreed that PSF should focus particularly, but not exclusively, on "Negro education," dispense its own income to support programs, and undertake surveys and reports to delineate the needs of target groups.

During their tenures, spanning the years 1911–1944, and that of Thomas Jesse Jones, director of education from 1917 to 1946, PSF made numerous small grants and produced landmark reports: *Negro Education in the United States* (1916), *Education in Africa* (1922), *Education in East Africa* (1924), and *The Problem of Indian Administration* (1928). These men's extensive contacts with officers of major foundations helped PSF increase its influence and gain access to

financial support. Jones was succeeded by Channing TOBIAS, who marshaled the resources of the fund by decreasing the number of grants awarded from PSF income and concentrating his efforts on attracting revenue from other agencies to address his primary concerns of domestic education and race relations.

The organization's proficiency in administering grants and delivering services was greatly enhanced during the 1950s and 1960s, under Frederick Douglass PATTERSON. Deeply committed to the historically black colleges, Patterson organized the Cooperative College Development Program, dispensing more than six million dollars in federal aid to improve facilities and upgrade funding capabilities. His initiative ultimately resulted in the formation of the United Negro College Fund.

Succeeding Patterson in 1970, Franklin H. WILLIAMS expanded the funding base, established a Washington office, and substantially increased staff. While he revitalized all areas of the fund's charter commitments—institutionalizing a Native American program, initiating support for poor white colleges in Appalachia, and sponsoring research and its dissemination through publications, conferences, lectures, and special events—his major achievements resulted from the fund's increased ability to support African students. He secured nearly eighteen million dollars from the U.S. Agency for International Development to administer two southern African scholarship programs, and he solicited private donations that supported the Bishop Desmond Tutu Southern African Refugee Scholarship Fund.

Board of Trustees of the Phelp-Stokes Fund, 1984. (Photographs and Prints Division, Schomburg Center for Research in Black Culture, The New York Public Library, Astor, Lenox and Tilden Foundations)

Wilbert J. LeMelle succeeded to the presidency after Williams's death in 1990. His attention has been focused on enhancing PSF's advocacy role in the area of domestic education, sponsoring research that investigates the effects of educational reform policies on minority youth.

REFERENCE

Phelps-Stokes Fund Papers. Schomburg Center for Research in Black Culture, New York.

ENID GORT

Philadelphia, Pennsylvania. When William Penn arrived on the shores of the Delaware River in 1682 to establish the Pennsylvania Colony, the area was inhabited by Delaware Indians, Dutch, Swedes, British settlers, and free and enslaved Africans. Penn selected and named Philadelphia to be the capital of the colony. The early city was small: 1,200 acres, two miles in length from east to west between the Delaware and Schuylkill rivers, and one mile in width from north to south. The boundaries remained unchanged until the consolidation of 1854, which made the county of Philadelphia coterminous with the city, incorporating many districts and townships, including Northern Liberties, Spring Garden, Southwark, Moyamensing, Passyunk, and Blockley into the city of Philadelphia.

Scant references exist to the early presence of blacks in the colony; however, by 1720 they numbered at least 2,500 in PENNSYLVANIA. Many were slaves. There is evidence of their collective activities by various acts of proposed and enacted legislation. The first restriction imposed in 1693 required that Africans carry passes. Later, other acts prohibited their assembly and determined where and when they could meet. The 1790 Census recorded 210 slaves in the city and 384 in the county, but Pennsylvania's Gradual Abolition of Slavery Act of 1780 applied only to children born after the act, freeing them after service to their enslaved mothers' owners for twenty-eight years. Therefore, in addition to apprenticeship, a number of black children were indentured servants, adding an additional element of separation and rendering them still not free.

Despite these limitations, Philadelphia blacks developed a community in the eighteenth century. In 1786 a petition for a burial ground was presented. A year later, the Free African Society was formed. This was the first beneficial society, established by Richard ALLEN and Absalom JONES in Philadelphia and comprised blacks and a few white Quakers. Some members of the Society were part of the group that had petitioned for a burial ground.

Richard Allen recorded that the beginning of the African Church in Philadelphia occurred in 1787. Though there is considerable scholarly disagreement on the precise sequence of events, and the date of the famous incident when Allen, Jones, and their fellow black congregants were ejected from St. George's Church, by the late 1780s a number of blacks who had previously worshipped with whites began leaving those churches to establish their own places of worship. At first they worshipped in private dwellings. Later they were able to formally dedicate their own buildings.

The African Church, later the First African Church of St. Thomas (Protestant Episcopal), was dedicated in 1794. Jones was its first pastor. Bethel Methodist Church, the oldest real estate continuously owned by blacks in the United States, was dedicated in 1796. Allen was its first pastor. In 1816 Allen and others organized the African Methodist Episcopal Church, the first black denomination. African Zoar Methodist Church was formed in 1794 by another group of blacks who left St. George's and worshipped for some time in their homes in Campingtown, an area in Northern Liberties. Later, in 1796, on ground adjacent to property owned by Lunar Brown, a member and trustee, they formally dedicated their church. METHODISTS and EPISCOPALIANS were not the only groups to lose black parishioners. In 1809 nine black men and women received a letter of dismission from the First Baptist Church of Philadelphia. They established the First African Baptist Church in that year in the Spring Garden district, near Northern Liberties. The First African Presbyterian Church was established in 1811 by men and women led by John GLOUCESTER. These and many more black churches came into existence providing for the growing black population, schools, burial grounds, and meeting places. Not only do census figures indicate an increase in the black population, but the proliferation of institutions also attests to the population's increase and potential influence. Perhaps the most notable event in the early history of black Philadelphia was the yellow fever epidemic of the summer of 1793, which claimed about one-tenth of the city's 50,000 residents. Under the mistaken belief that African Americans had natural immunity to the disease, city leaders appealed to blacks to help treat and bury the dead. Some whites criticized blacks for trying to profit from the crisis. Jones and Allen rebutted the accusations in their jointly written *Narrative of the Proceedings of the Black People During the Late Awful Calamity in Philadelphia* (1794).

There were nineteen black churches in the city and county of Philadelphia by 1847. Eighty-four percent

Huey P. Newton, national defense minister of the Black Panthers, raises a clenched fist as he speaks to a convention sponsored by the Black Panthers in Philadelphia, September 5, 1970. He is surrounded by Black Panther security guards as he spoke to an estimated 5,000 people in Temple University's McGonigle Hall with another 1,000 people outside the auditorium unable to gain entrance. (AP/Wide World Photos)

of black persons living in the city who were surveyed that year by the Pennsylvania Abolition Society indicated church membership. In addition to the denominations mentioned, a large percentage of blacks were members of various other denominations: Roman Catholic, African Methodist Episcopal Zion, and Society of Friends. Later, some black Philadelphians were members of the Shaker community established in Philadelphia by Rebecca Cox Jackson. Few blacks, however, attended interracial churches.

Literary and secret societies also came into existence in the 1800s. Beneficial society membership increased in every area in the city and county from 1837 to 1847. Their purpose was the relief of members who were unable to work, the interments of deceased members, and the relief of widows and orphans. Occupational organizations such as Humane Mechanics,

Coachman's Benevolent Society, Union Sons of Industry, and African Porter's Benevolent Society also were formed. These institutions and real property owned by blacks were seen by whites as symbols of upward mobility and power and were targeted for violence and destruction.

Prominent black Philadelphians such as sail maker James FORTEN, the aforementioned ministers Richard Allen and Absalom Jones, educator Sarah DOUGLASS, dentist Jacob White, and members of the Bowser and the Bustill families were well known. Indeed, they were influential in the formation, growth, and development of Philadelphia's black community. Many also raised their voices against slavery and became prominent early abolitionists. In 1830, with Allen as president, the first National Negro Convention was held in Philadelphia. Other Philadelphia abolitionists included the three granddaughters of James Forten: Margaretta, Sarah, and Harriet Forten, and leader of the Underground Railroad, William STILL.

Individual and collective economic enterprises began as early as 1810 with the founding of the African Insurance Company. Joseph Randolph was president, and Cyrus Porter and William COLEMAN, were treasurer and secretary, respectively. The company had capital in the amount of $5,000 in $50 shares. A financial panic in 1814 and a subsequent depression caused its failure. Two young black men, Derrick Johnson and Joseph Allen, initiated the African Fire Association (AFA) in 1818. There were more than 7,000 blacks in the city at that time, and its formation caused a "great excitement among the members of the [white] fire and hose companies." Whites successfully argued that black fire companies were unnecessary and would be unproductive. Thereafter the founders of the AFA, a potentially powerful political organization, were persuaded and encouraged to desist by some members of the black community.

Pennsylvania's Constitution in 1790 declared that a "freeman" 21 years of age who had resided in Pennsylvania for two years and paid a state or county tax "shall enjoy the rights of an elector." Though there was some African-American suffrage in the late eighteenth century and early nineteenth century in Pennsylvania, it was on a very small scale. The increasing black population in the city and county, along with their ownership of property valued at more than $300,000, caused the Pennsylvania Supreme Court in 1837 to declare that the Negro was not a "freeman" within the context of the Constitution. Revised a year later, Pennsylvania's Constitution prohibited black property owners from voting, stipulating that the vote belonged to every "white freeman," regardless of realty holdings. In 1848, blacks again petitioned for the right to vote, and in 1849, there was an election–day riot. Blacks regained the vote in 1871, and another riot ensued after that election, resulting in the murder of political leader Octavious V. Catto. The years 1829, 1835, 1838, and 1849 were tumultuous and in 1838 there were major riots against the black community which destroyed their churches, meeting halls, residences, the African Grand Lodge of Masons Hall (Pennsylvania Hall), and the Shelter for Colored Orphans.

Despite these setbacks, black Philadelphia's institutional life grew in the second half of the nineteenth century. Businessmen and philanthropists such as Stephen Smith (1797?–1873) helped found the Institute for Colored Youth, the Home for Destitute Colored Children, the House for the Aged and Infirm Colored Persons, Mercy Hospital, and the House of Refuge. Many prominent black Philadelphians such as Robert Bogle, James LeCount, James Prosser, Jer-

emia Bowser, and Peter Augustine made their fortunes in the catering industry. The black community supported a number of newspapers—five by the end of the nineteenth century—including the *Philadelphia Tribune,* founded in 1884, the oldest continually published black newspaper in the United States. The artistic and intellectual attainments of Philadelphia's black middle class were considerable. Benjamin T. TANNER, a bishop in the A.M.E. Church, edited the *Christian Recorder* and *AME Church Review* and made them into important forums for black intellectual and religious thought. His son, Henry Ossawa TANNER, became the leading black artist of his generation. In the middle decades of the twentieth century, the granddaughter of Bishop Tanner, Sadie Tanner Mossell ALEXANDER and her husband, Raymond Pace ALEXANDER, became lawyers and leaders in the civil rights struggle for Philadelphians. Arthur Huff FAUSET, a distinguished folklorist and urban sociologist, also was an advocate for improving housing conditions for black Philadelphians. His sister, Jessie Redmon FAUSET, was a leading novelist of the HARLEM RENAISSANCE, and in novels such as *The Chinaberry Tree* (1931) provided a sensitive portrait of Philadelphia's black elite. Though originally from a poor background, Marian ANDERSON became active at an early age in the middle-class musical culture of her local church, and the Philadelphia community financially supported her training and early career. By the 1930s, she was one of the leading concert performers of her generation.

In 1899 W. E. B. DU BOIS's work, *The Philadelphia Negro,* was published. The monumental sociological study examined the history and present condition of blacks in Philadelphia.

After 1900 there were considerable changes in Philadelphia's black community. Between 1900 and 1960, Philadelphia's black population increased more than 800 percent. Conditions were often difficult for the new migrants. There were jobs, but new migrants met much hostility. In 1918 there was a riot that resulted in the deaths of four blacks and many injuries. Philadelphia was not prepared to house the multitude of people who came seeking refuge. Overcrowded slums quickly developed in North and South Philadelphia, and residential segregation began. Although public housing had been available to whites, it was not until 1943 that public housing became available for blacks in North Philadelphia. In response to the increase in population, neighborhoods changed, the number of public and parochial schools increased and became more segregated, and more black churches came into existence. East Calvary Methodist Church, pastored by the charismatic Charles A. TINDLEY, attracted a large number of migrants from the South. Purchasing property on affluent Broad Street (circa 1924), East Calvary continued to grow and later became Tindley Temple (1925).

Although many black Philadelphians registered Republican, the New Deal attracted the loyalty of many who were less affluent, and the majority of black voters soon became Democrats. Philadelphia has long been a city of machine politics. Blacks benefited from political patronage, were elected ward leaders, and eventually won seats on city council and the courts. In 1938 Crystal Bird FAUSET, running as a Democrat from a Philadelphia district, became the first black woman in the United States elected to a state legislature. The population continued to increase because of wartime employment opportunities. The many government installations, including the Philadelphia Navy Shipyard, provided jobs for migrants.

The 1960s and '70s were turbulent times for black Philadelphians. The emergence of a new militancy among them was evidenced by community protest meetings, race riots, and BLACK PANTHER PARTY rallies. Many of the rallies occurred, with the encouragement of Father Paul Washington, at the Church of the Advocate, an Episcopal church in the heart of North Philadelphia. Again, churches were influential in community improvement as evidenced by Opportunities Industrialization Center (OIC), a self-help organization founded by the Rev. Leon SULLIVAN.

Girard College, a segregated school in North Philadelphia, was established by the will of Stephen Girard for white male orphans and administered by the Board of City Trusts. Initial litigation to invalidate the will was begun in 1954 by attorney Raymond Pace Alexander. Later, another black attorney, Cecil B. Moore, not only renewed legal action, but rallied blacks to march around the wall of the college until it figuratively "came down." Moore was a criminal attorney known for representing indigent defendants *pro bono*. Moore increased the membership of the NAACP and eventually won election to city council. The combination of litigation and continued community pressure and moral outrage succeeded in the school's integration in 1968. (Even after the end of legal segregation, however, residential segregation patterns left the de facto segregation of Philadelphia's schools largely intact.)

With more blacks in influential positions and a large, black voting population, W. Wilson Goode was elected Philadelphia's first black mayor in 1983, with 91 percent of the black vote. Although reelected four years later, his political career was marred by the bombing of the MOVE compound in May 1985. After years of sparring with a black nationalist organization, MOVE, that rejected most contact with outsiders, Philadelphia police dropped bombs into its com-

pound, killing six, and started a fire that burned down fifty adjoining homes and left 200 people homeless. All of black Philadelphia—and, indeed, most of the city's residents—were devastated at the loss of innocent lives and the destruction of a stable, black neighborhood in West Philadelphia.

Despite these difficulties, Philadelphia's black community is proud of its history as one of the centers of African-American institutional life for more than three centuries. Some of the leading monuments to black Philadelphia are the Afro-American Historical and Cultural Museum, opened in 1976, the All-Wars Memorial to Black Soldiers, unveiled in 1934, and the homes of the writer Frances Ellen Watkins HARPER and the painter Henry O. TANNER. Philadelphia has been home to a number of prominent jazz musicians, including Dizzy GILLESPIE, John COLTRANE, and the three Heath brothers: Percy, Al, and Jimmy. It also has been a center for black popular music. Other black Philadelphians who have achieved renown in recent decades include comedian Bill COSBY , and William Gray III, former congressman, ambassador to Haiti, and president of the UNITED NEGRO COLLEGE FUND.

REFERENCES

ALLEN, RICHARD. *The Life Experience and Gospel Labors of the Rt. Rev. Richard Allen.* Introduction by George A. Singleton. Nashville, Tenn., 1983.

DU BOIS, W. E. B. *The Philadelphia Negro.* New York, 1971.

FRANKLIN, VINCENT P. "Voice of the Black Community: *The Philadelphia Tribune,* 1912–1941." *Pennsylvania History* (1984): 261–284.

LANE, ROGER. *William Dorsey's Philadelphia and Ours: On the Past and Future of the Black City in America.* New York, 1991.

LAPSANSKY, EMMA JONES. "Since They Got Those Separate Churches: Afro-Americans and Racism in Jacksonian Philadelphia." *American Quarterly 32,* (Spring 1980): 54–78.

NASH, GARY B. *Forging Freedom.* Cambridge, Mass., 1989.

SERNETT, MILTON C. *Black Religion and American Evangelicalism.* Metuchen, New Jersey, 1975.

SHANNON, JANET HARRISON. Community Formation: Blacks in Northern Liberties, 1790 to 1850. Ph.D. diss., Temple University, 1991.

ULLE, ROBERT F. A History of St. Thomas' African Episcopal Church, 1794–1865. Ph.D. diss., University of Pennsylvania, 1986.

WEIGLEY, RUSSELL W., ed. *Philadelphia: A 300-Year History.* New York, 1982.

WINCH, JULIE. *Philadelphia's Black Elite.* Philadelphia, 1988.

JANET HARRISON SHANNON

Philanthropy and Foundations. The beginnings of organized African-American philanthropy can be traced to the early black churches, mutual aid societies, and fraternal organizations among free blacks in the late eighteenth century. The introduction of black self-help organizations resulted from the economic insecurity of free blacks in northern cities when the state provided little or no social welfare assistance. This spontaneous social organization also helped to form a distinctive African-American culture. Robert Harris, a scholar of early black self-help organizations, stated, "The benevolent societies combined African heritage with American conditions to transform an amorphous free black population into a distinct free black community. . . . In the final analysis, the early black benevolent society functioned as the wellspring for Afro-American institutional life."

The first black American mutual aid organization we know of was the African Union Society of Newport, R.I., founded in 1780. The society was primarily concerned with the moral rectitude of free blacks and provided material assistance by recording births, deaths, and marriages and by seeking to apprentice black youths in useful trades. Another of the earliest mutual aid organizations, African Lodge No. 459 (later renamed the Prince Hall Grand Masons), was founded in Boston in 1787 in Prince HALL and was the first black freemasonic society. The lodge provided members with protection against reenslavement due to delinquent debts and provided the poor with food and other provisions. The FREE AFRICAN SOCIETY OF PHILADELPHIA was founded in 1787 to provide material aid to free blacks and support to religious institutions.

In the first half of the nineteenth century black churches and mutual aid organizations were active in the abolitionist movement, including the UNDERGROUND RAILROAD, by raising money, donating goods and services, and volunteering their time on behalf of escaping slaves. Through collective action, groups such as the International Order of Twelve Knights, the Daughters of Tabor, and the Knights of Liberty, all founded in the 1850s, were responsible for liberating and sheltering thousands of slaves through the Underground Railroad. Collectively these organizations used the financial and volunteer contributions of black Americans to provide other black Americans with social services that they could not obtain through government or from most white charitable organizations, though some white philanthropies, such as the various state abolition societies, were important sources of material support for African Americans. Further, since the leaders of these organizations, in particular black ministers, received financial support directly from the black community,

they could speak freely about the community's aspirations for equal rights without fear of financial repercussions from those who disagreed with their positions.

In most of the South before emancipation there existed a de facto ban on black mutual aid societies, and Virginia, Maryland, and North Carolina legally prohibited such organizations. Despite the hostility, southern free blacks successfully maintained benevolent societies. Among such groups were the Resolute Beneficial Society of Washington, D.C., established in 1818; the Burying Ground Society and the Beneficial Society of Richmond, Virginia, both formed in 1815; and the Brown Fellowship Society (1790), Christian Benevolent Society (1839), Humane Brotherhood (1843), and Unity and Friendship Society (1844), all of Charleston, S.C.

Before the Civil War most black philanthropy was concentrated at the local level. In 1835 there were forty black mutual aid organizations in Baltimore and eighty in Philadelphia. In the latter city in 1848 almost half of the adult free black population was affiliated with African-American philanthropic societies.

Some of the early black benevolent societies included both men and women in the same organization. The African Benevolent Society of Newport, R.I., founded in 1808, accepted free blacks without regard to gender, as did the African Marine Fund of New York City. In general, women only belonged to organizations that stressed education, but were not ordinarily members of other types of benevolent societies. There were, however, female auxiliaries for most of the groups, and black women played a key role in literary associations.

Notwithstanding the separate and unequal living conditions that characterized the lives of black and white Americans during the eighteenth and nineteenth centuries, it is important to note that many black organizations also provided the larger white society with services and other assistance during times of emergency. For example, during the great plague that struck Philadelphia in 1793, the Free African Society provided the entire city with extensive nursing and burial services.

Following the end of the Civil War, there was a national concern to establish programs that would enable the freed slaves, many of whom could not read or write, to become self-sufficient. The Freedmen's Bureau, officially known as the BUREAU OF FREEDMEN, REFUGEES, AND ABANDONED LANDS, was formed by Congress in 1865, and along with nearly a hundred independent volunteer freedmen's aid societies, sought to provide assistance to both ex-slaves and impoverished whites. During the bureau's seven-year tenure, it established more than four thousand schools and forty hospitals, as well as distributing free food.

In the late nineteenth and early twentieth centuries, philanthropists from the North played a crucial role in disbursing aid to African Americans in the South. Notwithstanding the combined efforts of the bureau and the freedmen societies, when Julius Rosenwald started his eponymous fund in 1917, there was not a single standard public eighth grade or high school in the South for black children. Between 1913 and 1932, Rosenwald helped establish 5,357 public schools in fifteen southern states. A key feature of this effort was that in each case, the local black community contributed to the building of the schools by donating both money and labor. In later years, the Rosenwald Fund would support fellowships for black schoolteachers, black hospitals, and efforts to improve black-white relations.

By far, the most influential foundation in shaping black educational opportunities was the General Education Board (GEB), which was founded by John D. Rockefeller in 1902. The GEB was involved in all aspects of black education during the early to mid-1900s, including encouraging consolidation of one-room schools, training teachers, and providing transportation for students in rural areas. Between 1902 and 1960 the GEB distributed $62.5 million in support of black education. In addition to the Rosenwald Fund and the General Education Board, other, smaller philanthropic institutions that were active in promoting educational opportunities for black Americans include the Peabody Fund, the SLATER FUND, and the PHELPS-STOKES FUND.

The Peabody Fund, established in 1867, was intended to popularize the idea of universal education as a means of integrating ex-slaves and poor whites into the emerging bourgeois southern order. The organizers of the fund were concerned about the dangers of an unruly, uneducated class of paupers in a society lacking a significant public welfare structure. The Peabody Fund gave considerable material aid to southern schools until 1910, when it was merged into the Slater Fund, which had pursued a similar program of educational promotion since its founding in 1882.

The Slater Fund particularly applauded and assisted the work of black educators such as Booker T. WASHINGTON, who accepted the racial status quo in the South and insisted that the primary means of black advancement was through the acquisition of industrial skills. Between 1891 and 1911 the Slater Fund supported a few model industrial schools such as HAMPTON INSTITUTE (Va.) and Washington's Tuskegee Institute (now TUSKEGEE UNIVERSITY) (Ala.), eventually giving these two schools one-half

of its annual appropriations. After 1911 the fund pursued its interest in manual training by preparing black teachers in county training schools; it helped build 384 such schools in the South over the next two decades. In 1937 the Slater Fund merged with the Jeanes Fund and the Virginia Randolph Fund to form the Atlanta-based Southern Education Fund, which still exists.

Another important source of philanthropy for black education, the Phelps-Stokes Fund, was founded in 1911 to administer a bequest from Caroline Phelps Stokes to increase educational opportunities for black Americans, Native Americans, and poor whites. The fund made several small grants to black educational institutions from its founding until the 1940s, when its emphasis shifted to supporting historically black colleges through the Cooperative College Development Program. Through this program the fund dispensed more than six million dollars to black colleges and helped establish the UNITED NEGRO COLLEGE FUND in 1943, a joint fund-raising effort by over thirty historically black colleges and universities.

As the role of foundations in African-American education grew, at least two issues arose. First, what was the appropriate type of education for black Americans? Most foundations began their efforts by supporting industrial education to provide training for specific, often rural, trade skills rather than a liberal arts education in the humanities or sciences. With these interests in mind, foundations provided support for Tuskegee Institute and Hampton Institute, among others. (The Rosenwald Fund was largely an exception to this.) Second, throughout the Jim Crow era, foundations generally accepted the idea of separate schools for black Americans. To be sure, funding for integrated education in the early twentieth-century South was a near impossibility. As a result, foundations sought to develop and strengthen separate black educational institutions rather than encourage integrated institutions. An additional problem was the attempt of the foundations to placate the white South, and the conviction of many foundation leaders that academic education for African Americans was pointless. For example, in 1899, a trustee of the GEB was quoted as stating, "The Negro should not be educated out of his environment. Industrial work is his salvation. . . . Except in the rarest of instances, I am bitterly opposed to the so-called higher education of Negroes." Many foundations relied on their experiences in helping to shape black education in the United States as a guide for developing similar educational programs in Africa.

By the 1930s many of the remaining foundations were paying greater attention to academic education. In addition, several foundations supported comprehensive studies of the adverse socioeconomic conditions and legal barriers confronting African Americans. For example, the Laura Spelman Rockefeller Memorial Fund financed *The Negro in American Civilization* (1930), the Phelps-Stokes Fund supported a never-completed encyclopedia project on black Americans (1930s and 1940s), and the Julius Rosenwald Fund Provided support for *Alien Americans: A Study of Race Relations* (1936). The most influential study of black America in the middle decades of the century, *An American Dilemma* (1944), by the Swedish-born scholar Gunnar Myrdal, was supported by the Carnegie Corporation of New York. The report concluded that the American dilemma was the inconsistency between the stated belief in equality and social justice for all and the documented legal barriers that prevented black Americans from fully participating in American society.

The strategies employed by foundations to promote black-white relations have changed markedly over time. Concerned that black Americans be sufficiently moral and upstanding, foundations in the early twentieth century supported the Negro Boy Scouts, the National Negro Business League, and, later, the NATIONAL URBAN LEAGUE. However, beginning at the end of World War I, as foundations began to recognize black Americans' long-standing desire for equality and began to fear that continued denial of their aspirations might encourage them to become communists, foundations became more interested in supporting black and white cooperation. In 1919, the Rosenwald Fund helped to create the Commission on Interracial Cooperation (CIC) to bring together black and white community leaders throughout the South. The fund also provided support for the American Council on Race Relations and the SOUTHERN REGIONAL COUNCIL, the successor to the CIC.

Despite the role of white institutions in philanthropy for African Americans, black self-help has been a significant force in the field throughout the twentieth century. Black fraternal orders that emerged close to the turn of the century have over time adapted to modern needs. One such organization, the Ancient Egyptian Arabic Order Nobles Mystic Shrine, Inc., was founded in 1893. With 47,000 members in the 1990s, this organization runs programs to address delinquency and drug abuse, and supports medical research on health problems of special concern to blacks. Another, the Improved Benevolent Protective Order of Elks of the World, was founded in 1898, and claims 450,000 members. It supports a variety of causes, including scholarships, for which it raises one million dollars annually. Despite such activities, however, many fraternal orders have experienced dramatic declines in membership. Since

the end of World War II, one alternative source of black philanthropy has been the growing ranks of collegiate associations. The eight largest black fraternities and sororities have a combined membership of well over 650,000. In terms of direct material aid, the black church has been the most enduring source of black self-help. Perhaps the best-known example of church welfare was the "Peace Mission" in New York's Harlem, operated during the GREAT DEPRESSION, by FATHER DIVINE. Father Divine operated grocery stores nationwide, fed the hungry full meals for ten cents apiece at his own restaurants, and published and distributed newspapers and magazines for which his followers often volunteered to work. He was also known for the free meals he provided the hungry on Sundays.

As the CIVIL RIGHTS MOVEMENT came of age in the 1950s and 1960s, black Americans mobilized their collective financial and volunteer resources, along with those of their supporters, to challenge and eventually overturn laws that sanctioned keeping black and white Americans separate but equal. The black church, with its independent leaders, as exemplified by the Rev. Dr. Martin Luther KING, Jr., and T. J. Jemison, harnessed and directed a national effort involving several hundred thousand children, women, and men to volunteer in marches, sit-ins, and demonstrations. Moreover, the nonprofit civil rights organizations that gained new prominence during this time for example, the NATIONAL ASSOCIATION FOR THE ADVANCEMENT OF COLORED PEOPLE (NAACP), the NAACP LEGAL DEFENSE AND EDUCATIONAL FUND, the CONGRESS OF RACIAL EQUALITY (CORE), and the SOUTHERN CHRISTIAN LEADERSHIP CONFERENCE (SCLC), have been replicated by other groups concerned with ensuring equality for women and Asians, Latinos, and Native Americans, as well as gays and lesbians.

White foundations not only provided some support for many of the civil rights organizations but also began to fund projects aimed at directly promoting black socioeconomic advancement through education and redistributive social programs. In particular, the Rockefeller and Ford foundations were at the forefront of these efforts. The Rockefeller Foundation launched its equal opportunity program, which primarily focused on supporting integrated higher education. Between the mid-1960s and the mid-1970s, grants were awarded to predominantly white colleges located throughout the United States to recruit minority students.

Stating that full equality for black Americans was the most urgent concern challenging the country, the Ford Foundation launched an unprecedented effort to improve the socioeconomic and political conditions of the urban poor, among whom black Americans were disproportionately represented. Between 1960 and 1970 the Ford Foundation awarded more than $25 million for its Great Cities School Improvement project, which focused on assisting major urban school districts to become more responsive to the needs of black children with rural backgrounds, and the Gray Areas project, which focused on the health, housing, welfare, and employment needs of residents in urban cities. The Gray Areas project served as the model for several of the education and training provisions that were later authorized in the Economic Opportunity Act of 1964. Ford also established major programs to support civil rights organizations, voter education, black colleges, and community economic development.

The Ford Foundation's activism was not without repercussions. For example, in 1967 a Ford-supported demonstration project in New York to encourage local community control of public school districts led to school strikes as the local councils, teachers' unions, and school board struggled for control of the public school system. Similarly, when Carl STOKES was elected as the first black mayor of Cleveland, many charged that the election outcome had been influenced by Ford-sponsored voter education programs. The concern that foundations had undue influence in public matters led in part to the Tax Reform Act of 1969, which placed new restrictions on foundation activities in several areas, including voter registration.

Before the 1970s there were few black Americans on the boards or professional staffs of foundations. However, as a consequence of the civil rights movement, black Americans are now represented at every level within foundations and are key decision makers in determining how limited philanthropic resources will be allocated to address unlimited needs. For example, Franklin A. THOMAS, a black American, was named president of the Ford Foundation, the largest foundation in the United States, in 1979. As a result of these developments, the black community has both a continuing tradition of philanthropy and self-help within its own community and has started a new chapter as individual black Americans begin to help shape the funding priorities of older philanthropic institutions in helping everyone.

In the 1970s black Americans began to develop new types of charitable organizations to confront both old and new problems. Despite significant socioeconomic progress among black Americans, a significant proportion continued to require a broad range of social services. In addition, the increased support of black charitable organizations by government agencies and foundations led some to question whether these organizations could be as independent to advocate on behalf of black Americans' interests as the black church had in the past.

Recognizing the need to develop new ways to provide an independent, black-controlled funding source to support black-run social protest and social service organizations, a number of black fund-raising organizations emerged in various cities across the United States to raise money from African Americans to support black organizations. In 1972 a number of these groups formed the National Black United Fund (NBUF). NBUF's mission was to develop a fund-raising mechanism that would allow them to raise money primarily from African Americans throughout a particular city and distribute that money to black organizations.

For many years, one national charitable organization, the United Way, had sole access to the federal government's work-site charitable payroll deduction campaigns. Through these campaigns, federal workers agreed to contribute a given amount of money from each paycheck to charity. In the early 1980s, NBUF won a series of court cases that challenged United Way's monopoly to access the federal government's work-site charitable payroll deduction campaigns and was allowed to participate in these campaigns. Later, NBUF began to gain access to the campaigns of private employers.

NBUF's success has enabled a wide range of women, minorities, and special interest groups to develop identical organizations to raise money for their causes. Further, the development of black charitable organizations has resulted in greater responsiveness to the black community from all charitable organizations seeking contributions from black Americans.

Perhaps the most interesting new development is the establishment of foundations by African Americans. For example, the Jackie Robinson Foundation, named after the man who broke the color barrier of organized baseball in 1947, focuses on supporting educational programs for youth. More than two hundred years after blacks had to rely on pooling their modest contributions to develop a different form of philanthropy, a growing number of black Americans have amassed enough wealth to create their own foundations and to underwrite major charitable activities. For example, businessman Reginald Lewis made a contribution of two million dollars to HOWARD UNIVERSITY and three million dollars to Harvard University, among many other contributions. Entertainer Bill COSBY made a historic gift of twenty million dollars to SPELMAN COLLEGE as one of his many charitable contributions. The diverse mix of approaches that African Americans have developed indicates that black philanthropy will remain an important vehicle through which the community will continue to help themselves and others.

While black Americans have a long history of providing financial and volunteer resources to help themselves, these efforts often have been advanced or hindered by the funding priorities of wealthy white philanthropists and foundations. Of the thousands of foundations that have been created in the United States, only a handful have had a sustained interest in issues of social justice and equality of black Americans. This interest has resulted in support of African-American causes in the overlapping areas of education, policy research studies, and civil rights. Like the evolution of black philanthropy, foundations have awarded or declined support for projects based, in part, on the social norms and values that were accepted at a given time.

REFERENCES

CARSON, EMMETT D. "The Evolution of Black Philanthropy: Patterns of Giving and Voluntarism." In *Philanthropic Giving: Studies in Varieties and Goals.* New York, 1989, pp. 92–102.

———. *A Hand Up: Black Philanthropy and Self-Help in America.* Washington, D.C., 1993.

———. "Patterns of Giving in Black Churches." In *Faith and Philanthropy in America.* San Francisco, 1990, pp. 232–252.

DILLARD, JEMS HARDY, et al., *Twenty Year Report of the Phelps-Stokes Fund, 1911–1931.* New York, 1932.

EMBREE, EDWIN R., and JULIE WAXMAN. *Investment in People: The Story of the Julius Rosenwald Fund.* New York, 1949.

HARRIS, ROBERT L., JR. "Early Black Benevolent Societies, 1780–1830." *Massachusetts Review* (Autumn 1979): 603–625.

JONES, THOMAS JESSE. *Educational Adaptations: Report of Ten Years' Work of the Phelps-Stokes Fund, 1910–1920.* New York, 1920.

MAGAT, RICHARD. *The Ford Foundation at Work: Philanthropic Choices, Methods, and Styles.* New York, 1979.

NIELSEN, WALDEMAR A. *The Big Foundations.* New York, 1972.

RHIND, FLORA M., and BARRY BINGHAM. "Philanthropic Foundations and the Problem of Race." In *U.S. Philanthropic Foundations: Their History, Structure, Management, and Record.* New York, 1967.

STANFIELD, JOHN H. *Philanthropy and Jim Crow in American Social Science.* Westport, Conn., 1985.

WILLIE, CHARLES V. "Philanthropic and Foundation Support for Blacks: A Case Study from the 1960s." *Journal of Negro Education* 50 (1981): 270–284.

EMMETT D. CARSON

Philippine-American War. After the Philippines became an American colony at the conclusion of the SPANISH-AMERICAN WAR, a local rebellion against American rule was led by Emilio Aguinaldo, the Filipino leader. African-American soldiers and officers took an active part in the effort to crush the rebellion.

Though in 1898 the Filipinos initially welcomed the American help against the Spanish, once it became clear that the Americans would not be leaving, the Filipinos began to fight for their independence. All four of the African-American regular army regiments (Ninth and Tenth Cavalry and Twenty-fourth and Twenty-fifth Infantry) and two volunteer regiments raised in 1899 (Forty-eighth and Forty-ninth Volunteer Infantry) participated in the fighting in the islands, mainly in Luzon. All of the action was related to the pacification campaign and consisted of either patrols through the jungle, brief encounters with small groups of partisans, or tasks involved with civil government. The dense terrain, American unfamiliarity with the local inhabitants, and the irregular nature of the combat made it difficult for the U.S. force.

The Army made no differentiation in its assignment and utilization of the African-American soldiers. For example, two companies of the Twenty-fourth Infantry, under the command of Capt. Joseph Batchelor, spent several weeks marching several hundred miles through the mountains of central Luzon. Most of the time they did not face any opposition; on a few occasions the two companies encountered a few Filipino combatants. On much more typical assignments, companies of the regiments garrisoned small towns to exert American authority. They served as local police, collected taxes, and helped restore communication lines.

There were a number of African-American officers serving in the war, the vast majority with the volunteer regiments. Many of them had been enlisted men in the regular Army, though others had been officers in the volunteers in the recently concluded Spanish-American War. They led their units on patrols, captured insurgent leaders, and conducted pacification campaigns. They also encountered racial prejudice from some American officers and enlisted men who refused to treat them as equals. In 1901, newly appointed 2d Lt. Benjamin O. DAVIS, Sr., began his forty-eight-year career as an officer with service in the Philippines, mainly involved with civil government duties on the island of Samar.

Both at home and in the Philippines, some individuals raised the question of why African Americans should fight against other people of color. Though the insurgents made an effort to appeal to them along the color line, the effort was largely unsuccessful. One of the few exceptions was David Fagen, a member of the Twenty-fourth Infantry. In November 1899 he deserted, joined the insurgents, and quickly rose to the rank of captain. Several years later he was reported killed. The Army also executed two other African-American deserters.

REFERENCES

NALTY, BERNARD C. *Strength for the Fight: A History of Black Americans in the Military*. New York, 1986.

ROBINSON, MICHAEL C., and FRANK N. SCHUBERT. "David Fagen: An Afro-American Rebel in the Philippines, 1899–1901." *Pacific Historical Review* 44 (1975): 68–73.

MARVIN E. FLETCHER

Photography. African Americans shaped the practice of photography from its origin in 1840 and have participated in its history as practitioners and subjects. The larger American public was fascinated with the daguerreotype as soon as Louis Jacques Mandé Daguerre (1787–1851) publicized the process in France in 1839. The French inventor Nicéphore Niepce (1765–1833) produced the earliest extant photographic image made by a camera obscura in 1827. After the death of Niepce, Daguerre successfully fixed an image and in January 1839 announced to the Paris press his discovery, which he named the Daguerreotype. Six months after the public announcement of the process in Paris, Jules LION, a free man of color, a lithographer, and portrait painter, exhibited the first successful daguerreotypes in New Orleans.

The African-American public was enthusiastic about Daguerre's process of making likenesses (which we now call photographs). These were numerous free black men and women who established themselves as daguerreans, photographers, inventors, artists, and artisans who had gained local and national recognition in their respective cities. Portraits of prominent and lesser-known African Americans were produced regularly in galleries and studios throughout the country. The portraits of well-known African Americans soon became popular, and the practice of private photography—the photographing of individuals for personal collections and albums—became more and more the artistic method for creating a likeness. Most of the photographs taken at this time were not intended for publication or public presentation, but noted citizens and other families from all walks of life thought it important to have their likenesses preserved for posterity.

During most of photography's early history, images produced by African-American photographers presented idealized glimpses of family members in romanticized or dramatic settings. Photographers such as C.M. BATTEY and James VANDERZEE sought to integrate elements of romanticism and classicism, as did the painters of the previous centuries. Most photographs taken in the early years were made to commemorate a special occasion in the sitter's life—such as marriage, birth, graduation, confirmation, and anniversaries—or the achievement of a particular social or political success.

One of the earliest known photographical studies in America of African-American physiognomy was conducted in 1850 by Harvard scientist Louis Agassiz and J. T. Zealy, a white daguerreotypist in Columbia, S.C. The latter was hired to take a series of portraits of African-born slaves on nearby plantations. The daguerreotypes were anatomical studies of the faces and the nude upper bodies of African men and women. The photographs were to give visual evidence of the "natural difference in size of limbs, heads, and configurations of muscles," thereby establishing a theory that blacks were different and inferior. Much of the work of the nineteenth-century black photographers was in sharp contrast to these scientific and stereotypical images.

"Joe" by J. P. Ball, 1893. Joe was a cook for the Ming family, who were among Helena, Mont.'s wealthier pioneers. (Montana Historical Society, Helena)

The first publicized exhibition of a work by a black photographer was held on March 15, 1840, in the Hall of the St. Charles Museum in the city of New Orleans. The exhibition, reported to have drawn a large crowd, was organized and sponsored by the artist, Jules Lion. In 1854, Glenalvin Goodridge, a black photographer from York, Pa., won the prize for "best ambrotypes" (a process using a wet plate) at the York County fair. Other black photographers who won distinction in the nineteenth century at exhibitions and expositions include James Presley BALL, who exhibited his daguerreotypes in 1855 at the Ohio Mechanics Annual Exhibition, and Harry Shepherd, who won the first prize at the 1891 Minnesota State fair and later exhibited photographs of the TUSKEGEE INSTITUTE (now University) at the Paris Exposition in 1900. In 1895, Daniel Freeman, known as the first black photographer in Washington, D.C., exhibited his works in the Negro Building at the 1895 Atlanta Exposition.

Between the end of the Civil War and the turn of the nineteenth century, numerous itinerant photographers flourished in the North. But even earlier, several African-American photographers were able to open their own studios. In the 1840s and '50s, James BALL and Augustus Washington (1820–?) operated galleries in Cincinnati, Ohio, and Hartford, Conn.; Jules Lion had his own studio in New Orleans. (Ball and Washington were active abolitionists who often used their photographic skills to expose the inhumane institution of slavery and promote the abolitionist movement.) Harry Shepherd opened his first portrait gallery in St. Paul, Minn., in 1887, where he employed eight attendants. He advertised that "his patrons are among all classes—from the millionaires to day wage workers." Shepherd was one of the few African-American members of the National Photographers Association of America.

Fanny J. Thompson, a musician and composer living in Memphis, Tenn., in the 1880s, studied

"Domestic Science Class" by C. M. Battey, taken at Tuskegee Institute. (Tuskegee University, Library Archives)

photography and was one of the first to record African-American women working in the field. The Goodridge brothers—Glenalvin, Wallace, and William—began their careers in York, Pa., in the 1850s, before settling in East Saginaw, Mich., in 1866. They opened their first studio the following year. In 1884 they were commissioned by the U.S. Department of Forestry to photograph views of the Saginaw Valley woodlands.

At the turn of the century, photography expanded in a variety of ways. Newspapers, journals, and books published photographic images. Courses in photography were offered in schools and colleges, and correspondence courses were also available. C. M. Battey, an accomplished portraitist and fine-art photographer, was a noted educator in photography. Battey founded the Photography Division at Tuskegee Institute in Alabama in 1916. In 1917, CRISIS magazine highlighted Battey in the "Men of the Month" column as "one of the few colored photographers who has gained real artistic success." The most extensive portrait series of African-American leaders produced in the nineteenth century and early twentieth century was done by Battey. His photographic portraits of John Mercer LANGSTON, Frederick DOUGLASS, W. E. B. DU BOIS, Booker T. WASHINGTON, and Paul Laurence DUNBAR were sold nationally and were reproduced on postcards and posters.

Between 1900 and 1919, African-American photographers flourished in larger cities, producing images of both rural and urban experiences. They included Arthur Bedou (1882–1966) of New Orleans; King Daniel Ganaway (1883–?) of Chicago, who in 1918 received first prize in the John Wanamaker Annual Exhibition of photographers; and Arthur Laidler Macbeth (1864–?) of Charlestown, S.C., Baltimore, and Norfolk. Macbeth won many awards and citations for his photographs and was among the pioneers in motion pictures. He invented "Macbeth's Daylight Projecting Screen" for showing stereopticon and moving pictures in the daytime.

In 1911, Addison SCURLOCK, who was HOWARD UNIVERSITY's official photographer, opened a studio in Washington, D.C., which he operated with his wife and sons, Robert and George, until 1964; after that time, his sons continued to operate the studio. In New York City, James VanDerZee, undoubtedly the best known of black studio photographers, began capturing the spirit and life of New York's Harlem in the 1920s and continued to do so for more than fifty years.

During the period of the HARLEM RENAISSANCE through the GREAT DEPRESSION and the New Deal, photographers began to exhibit their work widely in their communities. In the 1920s, young black pho-

tographers who viewed themselves as artists moved to the larger cities in search of education, patronage, and support for their art. Harlem was a cultural mecca for many of these photographers. In 1921 the New York Public Library's 135th Street branch in Manhattan (now known as the Schomburg Center for Research in Black Culture) organized its first exhibition of work by black artists, entitled "The Negro Artists." Two photographers, C. M. Battey and Lucy Calloway of New York, displayed six photographs in this exhibition of over sixty-five works of art. The HARMON FOUNDATION was one of the first philanthropic organizations to give attention, cash awards, and exhibition opportunities to black photographers. These awards came to be known as the William E. Harmon Awards for Distinguished Achievement Among Negroes. In 1930, a special prize of $50 for photographic work was added in the name of the Commission on Race Relations.

A year earlier, James Latimer Allen (1907–1977) exhibited his portraits of African-American men, women, and children in a Harmon Foundation exhibition. Allen also photographed such writers of the

"Portrait of Family" by Richard S. Roberts. (Photographs and Prints Division, Schomburg Center for Research in Black Culture, The New York Public Library, Astor, Lenox and Tilden Foundations)

period as Alain LOCKE, Langston HUGHES, Countee CULLEN, and Claude MCKAY. Other photographers active between 1920 and '40 included several students of C. M. Battey, among them Elise Forrest Harleston (1891–1970) of Charleston, S.C., and P. H. Polk (1898–1985) of Tuskegee, Ala. Harleston opened a photography studio with her painter husband, Edwin HARLESTON, after studying with Battey in 1922. Polk opened his first studio at Tuskegee in 1927. The following year he was appointed to the faculty of Tuskegee Institute's photography department, photographed prominent visitors such as Mary McLeod BETHUNE and Paul ROBESON, and made extensive portraits of scientist-inventor George Washington CARVER. Richard S. ROBERTS (1881–1936) of Columbia, S.C., began studying photography through correspondence courses and specialist journals, and opened his studio in the early 1920s. According to Roberts's advertisements, his studio took superior photographs by day or night. Twin brothers

Morgan (1910–1993) and Marvin SMITH (1910–) were prolific photographers in Harlem in the 1930s and early '40s. They photographed members of the community, as well as political rallies, breadlines during the Great Depression, families, and "Lindy Hoppers" in the SAVOY BALLROOM.

During the Depression, numerous images were taken of the lives of African-Americans. The Resettlement Administration, later known as the Farm Security Administration (FSA), was created in 1935 as an independent coordinating agency; it inherited rural relief activities and land-use administration from the Department of the Interior, the Federal Emergency Relief Administration, and the Agricultural Adjustment Administration. Between 1935 and '43, the FSA photography project generated 270,000 images of rural, urban, and industrial America. Many of the heavily documented activities of the FSA were of black migrant workers in the South. In 1937, Gordon PARKS, SR. decided that he wanted to be a photog-

Street mass meeting, 125th Street, Harlem, N.Y., by Morgan and Marvin Smith, c. 1938. (Photographs and Prints Division, Schomburg Center for Research in Black Culture, The New York Public Library, Astor, Lenox and Tilden Foundations)

rapher after viewing the work of the Farm Security Administration photographers. He was hired by the FSA in 1941, and during WORLD WAR II he worked as an Office of War Information correspondent. After the war, he was a photographer for Standard Oil Company. In 1949 he became the first African-American photographer to work on the staff of *Life* magazine.

Roy DECARAVA is the forerunner of contemporary urban photography. He studied art at Cooper Union in New York City, the Works Progress Administration's Harlem Art Center, and the George Washington Carver Art School. In 1955, DeCarava collaborated with Langston HUGHES in producing a book entitled *The Sweet Flypaper of Life,* which depicted the life of a black family in Harlem. In 1952, DeCarava received a Guggenheim Fellowship; he was one of the first black photographers to win the award. In 1954, he founded a photography gallery that became one of the first galleries in the United States devoted to the exhibition and sale of photography as a fine art. DeCarava founded the Kamoinge Workshop for black photographers in 1963.

From the 1930s through the '60s, photographers began working as photojournalists for local newspapers and national magazines marketed to African-American audiences, including *Our World,* EBONY, JET, *Sepia,* and *Flash,* among others. Only a few African-American photojournalists, most notably Gordon Parks, Sr., Richard SAUNDERS, Bert Miles, and Roy DeCarava, were employed for the larger picture magazines such as *Life, Look, Time, Newsweek,* and *Sports Illustrated.* Most of them learned photography while in the military and studied photography in schools of journalism.

This period also encompassed the beginning of reportage and the documentation of public pageantry and events. In the 1930s smaller hand–held cameras and faster films aided photographers in expressing their frustration and discontent with social and polit-

Mr. Dean, sheet metal foreman, and Mr. Reese, operational officer, at the National Youth Administration School of Bethune-Cookman College, Daytona Beach, Fla., January 1943, by Gordon Parks. (Prints and Photographs Division, Library of Congress)

ical conditions within their communities. The CIVIL RIGHTS MOVEMENT was well documented by photographers such as Moneta SLEET, Jr. (New York and Chicago); Jack T. Franklin (Philadelphia); Charles "Teenie" Harris (Pittsburgh); Howard Morehead (Los Angeles); Bertrand Miles (New York); Austin HANSEN (New York); and U.S. Information Service Agency photographers Richard Saunders and Griffith Davis.

Between 1935 and the early 1990s, musical pioneers were the frequent subjects of Chuck Stewart (1927–), Milt HINTON, Roy DeCarava, and Bert Andrews (1931–1993), who photographed performing artists in the studio, on stage, and in nightclubs. Milt Hinton received his first camera in 1935 while he was playing in Cab CALLOWAY's band. As a jazz bassist and photographer, Hinton photographed his musician friends and colleagues. In 1950, Chuck Stewart, who studied photography at Ohio University, began photographing jazz musicians and vocalists on stage and in his studio in New York City. His photographs were used for album covers, publicity stills, and illustrations for books and articles of jazz. Stewart photographed virtually every well-known musician and vocalist between 1950 and '90; his coverage includes blues, bebop, fusion, salsa, and popular music. Bert Andrews photographed black theatrical productions on and off-Broadway from the early 1960s through the early 1990s. Among the production companies whose plays he photographed are the NEGRO ENSEMBLE COMPANY, the New Federal Theatre, and the Frank Silvera Writers' Workshop.

During the active years of the civil rights and Black Power movements—the early 1960s through the 1970s—a significant number of socially committed men and women became photographers, documenting the struggles, achievements, and tragedies of the freedom movement. STUDENT NON-VIOLENT COORDINATING COMMITTEE (SNCC) photographers Doug Harris, Elaine Tomlin, and Bob Fletcher were in the forefront in documenting the voter registration drives in the South; Robert SENGSTACKE, Howard Bingham, Jeffrey SCALES, and Brent Jones photographed the North and West Coast activities of the BLACK PANTHER party and desegregation rallies. Between 1969 and 1986, six African-American photographers received the coveted Pulitzer Prize in photography. The first to win the award was Moneta Sleet, Jr., in 1969 for his photograph of Coretta Scott KING and her daughter at the funeral of the Rev. Dr. Martin Luther KING, Jr. Following in subsequent years were Ovie Carter (1975) for international reporting for his photographs of famine in Africa and India; Matthew Lewis (1975) for his portrait studies of Washingtonians; John White (1982) for work published in the *Chicago Sun Times;* Michel Du Cille (1985) for the photographs of the Colombian earth-

The Kamoinge Workshop, founded in 1963 by New York-based African-American photographers, supports and publicizes the work of black photographers. The name of the workshop comes from a Kikuyu word for "people working together." Members of the workshop in this 1974 photograph are (from left to right, back row) Adger Cowans, Ray Frances, Herbert Randall, Daniel Dawson, Beauford Smith, Herbert Robinson, Al Fennar, and Shawn Walker. (Front row, left to right) Herman Howard, Ming Smith, Jimmy Mannas, Lou Draper, Calvin Wilson, and Tony Barboza. (© Shawn Walker)

quake; and Ozier Muhammad (1985) for international reporting for the photographic essay "Africa: The Desperate Continent."

In the 1970s, universities and art colleges began to offer undergraduate and graduate degrees in photography, and African-American photographers began studying photography and creating works for exhibition purposes. Others studied in community centers and workshops. The symbolic and expressive images of the works produced in the 1980s and '90s offer sociological and psychological insights into the past, as well as examinations of contemporary social themes, such as racism, unemployment, child and sexual abuse, death and dying. Most of these works are informed by personal experienced. Significant contributors to the development of this genre are Albert CHONG, Sulaiman Ellison, Roland Freeman, Todd Gray, Chester HIGGINS, Lynn Marshall-Linnemeier, Willie Middlebrook, Jeffrey SCALES, Coreen SIMPSON, Lorna SIMPSON, Elisabeth Sunday, Christian Walker, Carrie Mae WEEMS, Carla Williams, and Pat Ward WILLIAMS.

REFERENCES

COAR, VALENCIA HOLLINS. *A Century of Black Photographers: 1840–1960.* Providence, R.I., 1983.
CRAWFORD, JOE. *The Black Photographers Annual,* Vol. 1. Brooklyn, N.Y., 1972.

————. *The Black Photographers Annual.* Vol. 2. Brooklyn, N.Y., 1974.

————. *The Black Photographers Annual.* Vol. 3. Brooklyn, N.Y., 1976.

————. *The Black Photographers Annual.* Vol. 4. Brooklyn, N.Y., 1980.

DeCarava, Roy, and Langston Hughes. *The Sweet Flypaper of Life.* 1955. Reprint. Washington, D.C., 1984.

Parks, Gordon. *Born Black.* Philadelphia, 1971.

————. *A Choice of Weapons.* New York, 1966.

————. *Moments Without Proper Names.* New York, 1975.

Willis-Thomas, Deborah. *Black Photographers, 1840–1940: An Illustrated Bio-Bibliography.* New York, 1985.

————. *Black Photographers, 1940–1988: An Illustrated Bio-Bibliography.* New York, 1989.

Deborah Willis-Thomas

Physics, the study of matter and energy and their various interactions. The results of physics lead to a fundamental understanding of the physical processes that occur in the universe. This knowledge allows the prediction of the future behaviors for given systems of matter and energy, and the possibility to construct devices that can serve a multitude of useful purposes.

The first publicly known African-American scientist was Benjamin BANNEKER. His contributions to invention, astronomy, and publishing are well documented (Bedini 1972). However, it took more than a century after the work of Banneker to produce the first black with a doctorate degree in any field in the United States. This was Edward A. BOUCHET, who earned his Ph.D. in physics from Yale University (1876). His experimental dissertation was titled "Measuring Refractive Indices." Bouchet spent most of his adult life (twenty-six years) as a high school teacher of physics and chemistry at the Institute for Colored Youth in Philadelphia. His excellent teaching and personal concern for students inspired many of them to pursue advanced degrees in a variety of subject areas and professions (Mickens 1989).

Elmer Samuel IMES was the second African American to earn a doctorate in physics (University of Michigan, 1918). His research activities were pioneering efforts in the then-new area of infrared spectroscopy. Imes's work, in addition to revealing the detailed spectra of certain diatomic molecules, also helped in the experimental verification of quantum theory and, for the first time, allowed the accurate determination of atomic distances. After a career in industry, Imes returned to Fisk University, where he continued his research in infrared spectroscopy.

There are no records to indicate that any African American received the doctorate in physics during the 1920s (Greene 1946); however, for the period 1934–1942, at least eleven were awarded the doctorate. Several of these persons had distinguished careers in research, education, and/or administration. James Raymond Lawson (Ph.D. 1939, University of Michigan) taught at Fisk University and directed its Molecular Spectroscopy Research Laboratory; he served as the school's president from 1967 to 1976. After leaving Fisk, Lawson became director of the Office of University Affairs at NASA (1976–1982). Warren Elliot Henry (Ph.D. 1941, University of Chicago) has always been identified as a physicist, although his doctorate is in physical chemistry. During World War II, he was a staff member of the Radiation Laboratory of the Massachusetts Institute of Technology. His academic experiences include teaching and research at Morehouse College, the University of Chicago, Tuskegee Institute, and Howard University. Henry also held senior staff positions at the Naval Research Laboratories (1948–1960) and Lockheed Missiles and Space Company 1960–1969). He has published many research articles and is known internationally for his work on magnetic interactions.

Legal decisions by the U.S. Supreme Court in the 1950s and '60s allowed African Americans greater access to the nation's universities. Thus, the number who pursued and obtained the doctorate in physics increased. A conservative estimate is that in 1990, approximately 250 had the degree. Out of this small group come individuals who have provided leadership for major research and education organizations. Among them are Walter Eugene Massey, director of the Argonne National Laboratory (1979–1984), president of the American Association for the Advancement of Science (1988), and director of the National Science Foundation (1991–); James Stith, president of the American Association of Physics Teachers (1992); and Robert Ellis, Jr., head of experimental projects at the Princeton Plasma Physics Laboratory (1988–1989). Many individuals have obtained international recognition for their research: Shirley Ann Jackson, in theoretical solid-state physics; Anthony Johnson, nonlinear optics; Harry Morrison, quasiparticle and pseudo-particle spectra in many-body systems; Carl Albert Rouse, theory of the sun's interior structure; James Edward Young, theoretical and mathematical physics.

The undergraduate origins of African-American recipients of the doctorate in physics continue to be largely the historically black colleges and universities. The leading institutions have been FISK UNIVERSITY, HOWARD UNIVERSITY, and Virginia State College (now University). The physics doctorate program at Howard University began in 1960, and by 1991 had granted more than thirty Ph.D.'s to African Americans. Other doctoral programs exist at Alabama A & M University (begun in 1986) and Hampton University (1992).

REFERENCES

BEDINI, SILVIO A. *The Life of Benjamin Banneker.* New York, 1972.
GREENE, HARRY W. *Holders of Doctorates among American Negroes.* New York, 1946.
MICKENS, RONALD E. "Bouchet and Imes: First Black Physicists." In *Proceedings of the 12th Annual Meeting and 16th Annual Day of Scientific Lectures of the National Society of Black Physicists.* Holmdel, N.J., 1989, pp. 1–14.

RONALD E. MICKENS

Pickett, Bill (December 5, 1871–April 2, 1932), cowboy and rodeo star. Bill Pickett, whose parents were of mixed African-American and Cherokee ancestry, was born and raised in a ranch community near Austin, Tex. He apparently attended a private school but quit after the fifth grade to work on neighboring ranches. Pickett was the first to use and perfect a special type of "bulldogging," a method of long-horned steer wrestling that involved throwing a bull by biting the upper lip of the animal, which was popular in wild west shows. By the late 1880s, Pickett was performing bulldogging and other rodeo stunts on a semiprofessional basis, appearing in carnivals and county fairs in Texas and surrounding states.

In the 1890s, while still a "working cowboy," Pickett and his brothers organized a small company called the Pickett Brothers Bronco Busters and Rough Rider Association. It was a family business offering services for taming wild horses and cattle. During this time, Pickett also performed his bulldogging publicly under the direction of a series of white managers.

Between 1907 and the late 1920s, Pickett, popularly known as the "Dusky Demon," was a star attraction with the Miller brothers' renowned Oklahoma-based 101 Ranch Wild West Show, which toured the western and midwestern United States and also appeared at Madison Square Garden in New York City in 1907. The show toured England, Canada, Argentina, and Mexico, where in 1908 Pickett allegedly rode a fighting bull for a remarkable seven and a half minutes. That same year, Pickett moved his family to the 101 Ranch in Marland, Okla.

Pickett was well liked and highly praised in the rodeo world for his character and talents, though in the beginning of his rodeo performance days pro-

moters and managers tended to deemphasize his black ancestry, promoting him as a "colored" man and requiring him to dress as a Mexican bullfighter. Among Pickett's admirers was celebrated humorist and stage personality Will Rogers, also of part Cherokee ancestry, who worked with Pickett and knew him throughout his career.

Although he temporarily retired from the 101 Wild West Show in 1919, Pickett remained a vigorous rancher and cowboy well into his fifties and sporadically entered local bulldogging contests. Pickett left the 101 Ranch briefly in the early twenties, moving his family to Oklahoma City, where he worked in the stockyards and as a millhand. In 1924 he returned to professional bulldogging and to the Millers' Wild West Show.

In the late 1920s, Pickett performed little bulldogging but continued to work as a ranch hand. In 1932 he was kicked in the head by a horse he was trying to tame and died of the head wounds he received. In 1971 Pickett became the first black cowboy to be inducted into the National Rodeo Cowboy Hall of Fame, part of the National Rodeo Cowboy Hall of Fame and Western Heritage Center in Oklahoma City. In 1987 a statue of Pickett was erected in Fort Worth, Tex., and in 1994 the U.S. postal service issued a commemorative postage stamp in his honor.

REFERENCE

HANES, BAILEY C. *Bill Pickett, Bulldogger: The Biography of a Black Cowboy.* 1977. Reprint. Norman, Okla., 1984.

LOUISE P. MAXWELL

Pickett, Wilson (March 18, 1941–), singer and songwriter. Born in Prattville, Ala., Wilson Pickett began singing in church as a child and was in a number of small-town GOSPEL MUSIC groups in his youth before moving to Detroit, Mich., to live with his father in 1955. There he continued to sing gospel until 1959 when a neighbor, Willie Schofield, asked him to join the popular RHYTHM AND BLUES group, the Falcons, of which Schofield was a member. This group also included Eddie Floyd, Sir Mack Rice, and Joe Stubbs. Pickett wrote numerous songs for the group, including "I Found a Love," which became a chart hit for the group in 1962 on the Lupine label.

In 1963 Pickett, who by that time was well known in the burgeoning Detroit music scene, went solo and released two songs on Lloyd Price's Double LL label which became hits on the national rhythm and blues charts that year—"If You Need Me" and "It's Too Late." The following year Pickett signed with Atlan-

Detroit soul singer Wilson Pickett made his reputation on songs of sexual bravado, such as "In the Midnight Hour" and "Funky Broadway." (AP/Wide World Photos)

tic Records and began a fruitful relationship with musicians from the Stax label in Memphis, Tenn. His 1965 hit, "In the Midnight Hour," was cowritten with Steve Cropper and performed with the Stax house band, Booker T. and the MGs. Known for his ferocious, sexual vocal style, a strong, raspy delivery punctuated by melodic screams, Pickett, who often went by the sobriquet "Wicked" Wilson Pickett, went on to make rhythm and blues hits for the rest of the decade, including "Don't Fight It" in 1965, "Mustang Sally," "634–5789," and "Land of a Thousand Dances" in 1966, and "Funky Broadway" in 1967.

In the early 1970s, Pickett began producing more rock-influenced soul, with hits that included a remake of the Archies' "Sugar, Sugar," and "Engine Number Nine" in 1970, and a successful version of the Beatles "Hey Jude" in 1971. In the same year he recorded the highly successful "Don't Let the Green Grass Fool You" and "Don't Knock My Love Pt. 1."

Pickett's popularity declined, however, throughout the 1970s. In the 1980s he continued to be active in the concert circuit but played mostly smaller venues in the United States and abroad. In the early 1990s, there was a revival of interest in Pickett's music with the release of a two-disc retrospective, *Man and a Half* (1991), his induction into the Rock and Roll Hall of Fame (1991), and the popularity of *The Commitments* (1991), a film about an Irish soul group who idolized Pickett. By this time, however, Pickett said he was ready to retire and move aside for younger artists to come up in the business.

REFERENCES

HIRSHEY, GERRI. *Nowhere to Run: The Story of Soul Music.* New York, 1984.
LIGHT, ALAN. "Rock & Roll Hall of Fame." *Rolling Stone* (February 7, 1991): 56.

JOSEPH W. LOWNDES

Pierce, Elijah (March 5, 1892–May 9, 1984), artist, barber, lay preacher. Known for his "sermons in wood," Pierce carved hundreds of reliefs, figures, and tableaus with themes from religious and secular life. Born on a plantation in Baldwyn, Miss., he was the son of a freed slave. Pierce began carving small animals early in his childhood. As a young man, he managed several jobs, finally settling on barbering. Combined with the lay preaching he began in the 1930s with his second wife, Cornelia West Houeston, Pierce worked at the nexuses of black society—the church and the barbershop. His subjects included autobiography, popular sayings, animals, moral lessons, biblical stories, and current events. His visual sources included magazines, newspapers, radio and television, religious publications, and popular books.

Well known in Columbus, Ohio, where he settled in 1923, by the early 1970s Pierce was discovered by folk art enthusiasts and was exhibited nationally. He did not transform his work to accommodate the interests of this new audience. He was initially cast as an idiosyncratic "outsider" artist, and it was only in the late 1980s that the art community came to appreciate him as the gifted artist, master storyteller, and genial moral authority he was. Pierce received numerous awards, including first prize at the International Meeting of Naive Art in Zagreb, Yugoslavia (1973) and the National Heritage Fellowship, National Endowment for the Arts (1982). The Elijah Pierce Art Gallery and his home are designated as a national historic site (1983). The largest public collection of his work is held at the Columbus Museum of Art (Ohio).

REFERENCE

Elijah Pierce, Woodcarver. Columbus Museum of Art. Columbus, Ohio, 1992.

HELEN M. SHANNON

Pierce, Samuel Riley (September 8, 1922–), politician and lawyer. Born and raised in a middle-class family in the New York City suburb of Glen Cove on Long Island, N.Y., Samuel Pierce was a football star at Cornell University. After graduating in 1945 and acquiring a law degree from Cornell in 1949, he entered REPUBLICAN PARTY politics, and soon held a number of important political and legal positions. He served as an assistant undersecretary of labor (1954–1956) and counsel of the House Anti-Trust Subcommittee (1956–1957). Pierce was also appointed by New York Gov. Nelson Rockefeller to fill vacancies in Manhattan's Court of the General Sessions in 1959 and 1960, though he failed to be elected by the voters both times.

A political conservative, Pierce was touted in the mid-1960s by FEDERAL BUREAU OF INVESTIGATION director J. Edgar Hoover as a preferable "moderate"

The only African-American member of President Ronald Reagan's cabinet was Housing and Urban Development Secretary Samuel Pierce. In this 1982 address, Pierce discussed possible federal budget cuts to cities before the Conference of Mayors. (AP/Wide World Photos)

alternative to more "radical" black leaders such as Roy WILKINS and the Rev. Dr. Martin Luther KING, Jr. From 1970 to 1973 Pierce served as the general counsel to the Justice Department in the Nixon administration.

From 1961 to 1970, and again from 1973 to 1981, Pierce was an associate and later partner in the New York law firm of Battle, Fowler, Jaffin & Kheel. In the 1960s and '70s, he also served as director for a number of companies, including Prudential Insurance, General Electric, and International Paper.

Pierce had a reputation as a loyal Republican who would not make waves, and in 1981 he was selected as President Ronald Reagan's secretary of Housing and Urban Development (HUD). The appointment was viewed by many as pure tokenism; Reagan clearly had little interest in urban issues, and Pierce was his lone African-American cabinet member. Under Reagan, HUD's budget was slashed dramatically with no protest from Pierce, who subsequently earned the nickname "Silent Sam" for his low public profile.

In 1989, after he left public office, it was revealed that kickbacks and favoritism were rampant in Pierce's department; several close associates of his were subsequently indicted for fraud, bribery, and lying to Congress. In 1993 and '94 Lance Wilson and Deborah Gore Dean, both chief assistants to Pierce at HUD, were sentenced to prison terms of six and twenty-one months, respectively. Though Pierce was not charged with any wrongdoing as of 1994, his administration of HUD was lax, at best.

REFERENCE

ELLIOT, JEFFREY M. *Black Voices in American Politics.* New York, 1986.

JAMES BRADLEY

Pinchback, Pinckney Benton Stewart (May 10, 1837–1921), politician. Born free in Macon, Ga., P. B. S. Pinchback was the son of William Pinchback, a white planter, and Eliza Steward, his emancipated slave, who was of mixed blood. Along with his brothers and sisters, Pinchback was taken to Cincinnati to escape enslavement by his white relatives at his father's death. Denied any share of his father's estate, Pinchback went to work as a steward on a Mississippi riverboat. In 1862, during the early stages of the Civil War, he volunteered for the Union Army in New Orleans and was assigned to recruit for the Corps d'Afrique and a cavalry company where he protested the unequal treatment of African-American troops.

Pinckney B. S. Pinchback. (Prints and Photographs Division, Library of Congress)

Pinchback played an important role in establishing the REPUBLICAN PARTY in Louisiana following the war, and was elected to the state's 1867 Constitutional Convention. He was president of the state senate in 1871, and served as lieutenant governor at the death of Oscar J. Dunn. He became acting governor during the impeachment of Gov. Henry Clay Warmoth. Pinchback was an advocate of universal suffrage, civil rights, the legal suppression of discrimination, and tax-supported education. He moved away from the Radical Republicans in 1871 and supported the reelection of Ulysses S. Grant.

There was backing for Pinchback's own nomination for governor in 1872, but he withdrew in favor of W. P. Kellogg. Elected congressman-at-large, he also served as governor again and was then elected to the U.S. Senate. He was unseated when the election was contested, however. Under Gov. F. T. Nicholls, Pinchback was appointed to the State Board of Education, where he was instrumental in founding Southern University. He became surveyor of customs at the port of New Orleans. Pinchback was a keen businessman, dealing in cotton, and a founder of the Mississippi River Packet Co. He was admitted to the bar in 1886.

Pinchback moved to New York City, then to Washington, D.C., in 1897, where he resumed his political career, supporting Booker T. WASHINGTON, and became a leader of the city's light-skinned social elite. He married Nina Hawthorne; they were the parents of six children. One grandson was Jean TOOMER, the HARLEM RENAISSANCE novelist. Pinchback died in 1921 and was buried in New Orleans.

REFERENCE

HASKINS, JAMES. *Pinckney Benton Stewart Pinchback.* New York, 1973.

MICHEL FABRE

Pindell, Howardena (April 14, 1943–), artist. Howardena Pindell grew up in Philadelphia and studied art at Philadelphia Art College and Flasher Memorial Art Program from 1948 to 1960. In 1965 she received her B.F.A. from Boston University and in 1967 completed her M.F.A. at Yale University. She was hired as an exhibition assistant at the Museum of Modern Art in New York City in 1967 and remained at the museum for over ten years, attaining the post of associate curator in the Department of Prints and Illustrated Books. (She was, at the time, one of the very few African Americans to hold a position of authority at a major American art museum.) Pindell left the museum in 1979 and became Professor of Art at the State University of New York, Stony Brook.

In the late 1960s and early 1970s, Pindell worked full time at the Museum of Modern Art and pursued her own art at night in a small New York City apartment. From 1970 to 1976 she made images from sequins, glitter, paper hole punchings, and the stencils they left behind, and placed them on sewn grid formations sprayed with powder, pigment, or hair. She occasionally numbered the hole punchings to represent the odometer records kept by her father on family road trips when she was a child. In 1977 Pindell began creating "video drawings" which were photographs taken from the television screen and covered with numbered locations randomly chosen on the surface of the image.

In 1979 Pindell's style changed significantly after she was injured in an automobile accident and suffered memory lapses which motivated her to make memory the central subject in her images. Pindell's best known memory pieces are from the early 1980s when she traveled to Japan and India and created collages from postcards (*The Japanese Memory Series, The India Memory Series,* 1982–1985). Each collage presents several locations comprised of postcards sliced in long strips and pieced together to create an obviously reconstructed scene (*Durga I, Durga II,*

1984). Her piece *Hiroshima Disguised* (1982) used a sandlike surface resembling Japanese dry gardens and nuclear ash interrupted by small photos of Japan that tried to show the effects of nuclear war.

Pindell's involvement in political issues facing African-American artists also influenced her work after 1979. For most of the 1970s Pindell allied herself with feminist artists who could not get their work exhibited at major institutions and she helped found the Artists-in-Residence Gallery (A.I.R. Gallery, 1971) as an alternative exhibition space for women artists of all races. In 1979 she joined the Committee Against Racism in the Arts and in 1980 she made the video *Free, White, and Twenty-One,* depicting the hypocritical politics of the feminist movement toward black women (also the painting *Free, White, and Plastic* [#114]). Pindell's 1989 series of works, *Autobiography,* focused on issues of identity and self-definition facing women of color, as well as the relationship between the public and private realms of women's lives (*Separate but Equal,* 1986–1989). In some of her recent work she has traced her body onto the canvas and painted her face and other body parts as integral components of the composition.

Pindell's work has been exhibited at the A.I.R. Gallery (1972, 1973), the New Museum in New York City (1980, 1981), Los Angeles Municipal Arts Gallery (1982), Museum of Modern Art (1985), the Studio Museum in Harlem (1986), the Cyrus Gallery in New York City (1989), and the College Art Gallery at SUNY, New Paltz (1993). A retrospective of her painting and drawing from 1972–1992 was held at the Davison Art Center, Wesleyan University, in 1994. That year she also was the recipient of the Studio Museum in Harlem's Artist Award.

REFERENCES

Hine, Darlene Clark, ed. *Black Women in America: An Historical Encyclopedia.* New York, 1993.
Howardena Pindell: Autobiography. Gallery brochure. New York, 1989.
Howardena Pindell: Odyssey. Gallery brochure. New York, 1986.

Lowery Stokes Sims

Pippin, Horace (February 22, 1888–July 6, 1946), painter. One of the foremost self-taught painters of the twentieth century, Horace Pippin was born in West Chester, Pa. A disabled WORLD WAR I veteran, he initially took up art in the 1920s to strengthen his wounded right arm. By the late 1930s Pippin's distinctive and diverse images of his childhood memories and war experiences, scenes of everyday life,

landscapes, portraits, biblical subjects, and American historical events had found enthusiastic local supporters such as critic Christian Brinton, artists N. C. Wyeth and John McCoy, collector Albert C. Barnes, and dealer Robert Carlen.

In the eight years between his national debut in a 1938 group exhibition at New York's Museum of Modern Art and his death at the age of fifty-eight, Pippin's productivity increased and his paintings entered major private and museum collections on the East and West Coasts. In 1947 Alain LOCKE described Pippin as "a real and rare genius, combining folk quality with artistic maturity so uniquely as almost to defy classification."

A descendant of former slaves, the artist was raised by Harriet Pippin (1834–1908). It is unknown today if Harriet was his mother or grandmother. Her eyewitness account of the 1859 hanging of the abolitionist John Brown provided the basis for Pippin's 1942 painting on that subject, which depicted her as the sole African-American woman in the crowd of onlookers.

In 1891, the family relocated to the resort town of Goshen, N.Y., where they worked as domestic servants. As a boy, Pippin showed a strong interest in drawing, winning his first set of crayons and a box of watercolors for his response to an advertising contest for an art supply company. Pippin rendered the warm family circle of his boyhood in the memory picture *Domino Players* (1943; Phillips Collection).

He attended a segregated one-room school until 1902. After working as a porter at the St. Elmo Hotel for seven years he relocated to Paterson, N.J., finding employment crating oil paintings with a moving and storage company. Prior to his service in World War I, Pippin variously toiled in a coal yard, in an iron foundry, and as a used-clothing peddler.

In 1917, the twenty-nine-year-old Pippin enlisted in the New York National Guard, serving as a corporal in what would subsequently become the 369th Colored Infantry Regiment of the 93rd Division of the United States Army. Landing in Brest in December 1917, Pippin and his regiment first worked laying railroad track for two months prior to serving at the front lines in the Argonne Forest under French command.

While in the trenches, Pippin kept illustrated journals of his military service, but only six drawings from this period survive. He later wrote that World War I "brought out all the art in me." In October 1918 Pippin was shot through the right shoulder by a German sniper and was honorably discharged the following year. Awarded the French Croix de Guerre in 1919, he received a retroactive Purple Heart in 1945.

In 1920 Pippin married the twice-widowed Ora Fetherstone Wade, who had a six-year-old son. Sup-

Woman Taken in Adultery by Horace Pippin. (National Archives)

porting themselves on his disability check and her work as a laundress, they settled in West Chester, where she owned a home. A community-spirited man, Pippin helped organize a black Boy Scouts troop and served as commander of the local American Legion for black veterans. As therapy for his injured arm, he began making pictures in 1925 by burning images on wood panels using a hot iron poker. At the age of forty he expanded to oil paints, completing his first painting, *End of the War: Starting Home,* in 1930 (Philadelphia Museum of Art).

Pippin first received public attention when he exhibited two paintings in the Chester County Art Association annual of 1937. Immediately following this debut, John McCoy and Christian Brinton facilitated an exhibition for Pippin at the West Chester Community Center, a hub of local black activities. Within a year Pippin was included in Holger Cahill's "Masters of Popular Painting" at New York's Museum of Modern Art.

Art dealer Robert Carlen of Philadelphia mounted Pippin's first gallery show in 1940, comprising twenty-seven works including *Abraham Lincoln and His Father Building Their Cabin on Pigeon Creek* (Barnes Foundation), *Buffalo Hunt* (Whitney Museum of American Art), and *Cabin in the Cotton* (Art Institute of Chicago). Introduced to Pippin's work by Carlen, the renowned art collector Albert Barnes wrote two catalog essays on the artist. At his invitation, Pippin visited Barnes's Foundation to see his world-famous painting collection and to attend art appreciation lectures. This exposure did not alter his characteristic approach to his art, although from then on Pippin added still-life compositions to his repertory, of which there are many examples in Barnes's collection.

In the years between his first Philadelphia show in 1940 and his death in 1946, Pippin had solo exhibitions at New York's Bignou Gallery (1940), the Arts Club of Chicago (1941), the San Francisco Museum of Art (1942), and New York's Downtown Gallery (1944). Among the museums that purchased his work during his lifetime were the Pennsylvania Academy of Fine Arts (*John Brown Going to His Hanging*); Buffalo's Albright Knox Gallery (*Self-Portrait*); and Washington's Phillips Collection (*Domino Players*). Early collectors included Philadelphia's Main Line society and such well-known actors and writers as Edward G. Robinson, Charles Laughton, Claude Rains, John Garfield, Ruth Gordon, S. J. Perelman, and Clifford Odets.

Pippin's commissioned works were varied. For the Capehart Collection in 1943 he executed a painting inspired by Stephen Foster's "Old Black Joe" (private collection); in 1944 *Vogue* magazine requested him to paint an image on the theme of cotton (Brady Museum, Cuernavaca); his painting *The Temptation of Saint Anthony* (1945; private collection) was created for an invited competition sponsored by the film producers David L. Loew and Albert Lewin, who also asked Salvador Dali, Marc Chagall, and Giorgio de Chirico, among others, to respond to a Guy de Maupassant short story.

Mrs. Pippin was hospitalized with mental problems in March 1946. She died four months later, two weeks after the artist himself had succumbed to a stroke on July 6, 1946. Of the 137 works on paper, fabric, and wood that Pippin was known to have created, approximately ten percent are today unlocated. He once summed up his approach to paintings: "Pictures just come to my mind. I think my pictures out with my brain, and then I tell my heart to go ahead."

REFERENCES

BARNES, ALBERT. "Horace Pippin." In *Horace Pippin Exhibition*, Carlen Gallery. Philadelphia, 1940.

BEARDEN, ROMARE. "Horace Pippin." In *Horace Pippin*, The Phillips Collection. Washington, D.C., 1976.

LOCKE, ALAIN. "Horace Pippin." In *Horace Pippin Memorial Exhibition*, The Art Alliance, April 8–May 4, 1947. Philadelphia, 1947.

RODMAN, SELDEN. *Horace Pippin: A Negro Painter in America*. New York, 1947.

STEIN, JUDITH E., et al. *I Tell My Heart: The Art of Horace Pippin*. New York, 1993.

JUDITH E. STEIN

Pittman, Portia Marshall Washington (June 6, 1883–February 26, 1978), pianist and teacher. Portia Marshall Washington was born to Booker T. WASHINGTON and Fanny Norton Smith Washington in Tuskegee, Ala. Although Washington was famous

for his advocacy of vocational training for African Americans, he nonetheless sent his daughter to elite white private schools in New England. In 1895, she was enrolled at the Framingham State Normal School (now Framingham College) in Massachusetts. At the all-white girls' school, Washington began to study the piano seriously, but her father brought her back to Tuskegee in 1899 in response to criticisms of his daughter's elite education. In 1901, after a year at Tuskegee, Portia Washington entered Wellesley College in Massachusetts, but left after encountering racial discrimination and political controversy. Her withdrawal from Wellesley attracted the attention of the national and black press. William Monroe Trotter, a fierce opponent of Washington, wrote that Washington's children were "not taking to higher education like a duck to water," while the *New York Times* criticized the double standard that a Wellesley education for his daughter represented for Booker T. Washington.

In 1902, Washington enrolled at the all-white Bradford Academy in Massachusetts, where she continued her musical education. After graduating from Bradford in 1905 (its first black graduate), she spent a summer traveling in England and France, then moved to Berlin to study piano under Martin Krause, a former pupil of Franz Liszt. There Washington encountered an old friend, architect William Sidney Pittman, a former Tuskegee teacher and alumnus. She broke off her musical studies and sailed home with Pittman, in 1907, marrying him at Tuskegee in October 1907.

The Pittmans moved to Washington, D.C., where Portia bore three children between 1908 and 1912. She gave her first American piano recital at the Metropolitan African Methodist Episcopal Church, playing, among other pieces, the spiritual "Sometimes I Feel Like a Motherless Child," as arranged by her friend, the Anglo-African composer Samuel Coleridge-Taylor. For a while, William Pittman ran a successful architectural practice, but when business worsened, Portia began teaching private piano lessons to help support the family. In 1913, Pittman moved the family to Dallas, Tex., in hopes of finding more work. Portia thrived in the Dallas musical world. She led several school and church choirs, gave piano lessons, presided as chairman over the Texas Association of Negro Musicians, and taught music at Booker T. Washington High School. In 1927, she directed a 600-voice, high-school choir in a highly acclaimed performance of black spirituals for the National Education Association's convention at Dallas's Park Auditorium. Pittman's architectural practice continued to suffer, and he became increasingly depressed and even violent. When he struck their daughter Fanny, Portia finally left him and moved with her daughter to Tuskegee in 1928, where she taught music for sixteen years.

After retiring from Tuskegee in 1944, Portia Pittman dedicated herself to honoring her father's memory. She helped preserve the rural Virginia cabin in which he was born, and she founded the Booker T. Washington Foundation to provide scholarships for needy black students. Permanently estranged from her husband, Portia Pittman moved back to Washington, D.C., in 1949, living in poverty until the local branch of the Tuskegee Institute Alumni Association provided her with an apartment. Pittman died at eighty-seven in Washington, D.C.

REFERENCES

HARLAN, LOUIS R. *Booker T. Washington: The Wizard of Tuskegee, 1901–1915.* New York, 1983.

STEWART, RUTH ANN. *Portia: The Life of Portia Washington Pittman, the Daughter of Booker T. Washington.* Garden City, N.Y., 1977.

FRANCES A. ROSENFELD

Pittman, William Sidney (April 21, 1875–April 3, 1958), architect. William Sidney (sometimes spelled "Sydney") Pittman was born and raised in Montgomery, Ala. He was raised by his mother and never knew his white father. His mother sent him to Tuskegee Institute in 1892, where he was soon assigned to make alterations in the home of Tuskegee's president, Booker T. WASHINGTON. Pittman graduated from Tuskegee's department of mechanical and architectural drawing in 1897, entered Drexel Institute in Philadelphia on an architectural scholarship and, after graduating in 1900, spent five years teaching architecture at Tuskegee.

In 1905, Pittman moved to Washington, D.C., where he established an architectural office. Two years later, after returning from a trip to Europe, he married Portia Washington (*see* Portia PITTMAN), Booker T. Washington's daughter; shortly afterward Pittman designed and built a home for his family in Fairmont Heights, Md. He subsequently designed the headquarters for the 12th Street Branch of the YMCA in Washington, D.C., (whose membership was African American) and the National Training School in Durham, N.C. His C. P. Huntington Memorial Building in Alabama was a combination of architectural styles, featuring a Greek temple–style entrance facade with the tripartite elevation of a Renaissance palace. Perhaps the high point of Pittman's career was the "Negro Building" at the 1907 Jamestown Tricentennial Exposition, which was designed and constructed entirely by African Americans; it made Pittman the first African American to be given a federal government architectural contract. This two-story structure was a major engineering feat for its time, because despite the decorative colonial-revival colonnade and classical Greek portico of its exterior, the interior auditorium was column-free.

The next fifteen years saw a decline in both Pittman's professional career and personal life. Although he was proud of his accomplishment and was a strong believer in advancing black businesses, he proved to be an irascible and difficult colleague. He began to receive fewer architectural contracts from whites and also found that black contractors were approaching white architects instead of him. His plans for the Lincoln Memorial Building, which he hoped would become the first theater and office building owned and operated by African Americans, collapsed when the company he had founded to construct it lost financial support. In 1913, he moved his family and practice away from the Washington, D.C., area, to Dallas, Tex., to escape the shadow of his father-in-law. Shortly after his arrival in Texas, Pittman succeeded in constructing the Dallas Pythian Temple (later the headquarters of the Dallas Union Bankers Life Insurance Company), but only after bitter arguments with employees. His resentment of his wife's musical success, which often brought more income into his household than his own work did, caused his marriage to deteriorate. Following a household altercation in 1928, Portia separated from her husband and moved back to Tuskegee with their daughter Fanny.

In 1931, Pittman began a weekly newspaper called *Brotherhood Eyes,* in which he attacked members of the black community whom he considered hypocritical. Among these members were self-indulgent ministers and business owners who hired white workers over outspoken black workers. He was sued for libel for one such attack in 1936, but was acquitted.

According to accounts by his wife, William Pittman was sent to the Leavenworth, Kans., federal penitentiary for a later statement made in the paper, but Portia was able to secure her husband's release through her friendship with one of President Franklin D. Roosevelt's assistants. Pittman's final twenty years have not been clearly documented; he was absent from the *Dallas City Directory* from 1937 through 1946. After 1928, he was not listed as a practicing architect. He died in Dallas after a long illness.

REFERENCES

DOZIER, RICHARD K. "Black Architects and Craftsmen." *Black World* (May 1974): 10–12.

STEWART, RUTH ANN. *Portia: The Life of Portia Washington Pittman, the Daughter of Booker T. Washington.* Garden City, N.Y., 1977.

DURAHN TAYLOR

Pittsburgh, Pennsylvania. Prior to the Civil War, Pittsburgh's blacks were typical of those in most northern cities—they were few in number, impoverished, and victimized by racial discrimination. Blacks arrived with the very earliest colonial settlers—as trappers, pioneers, soldiers, and slaves—once the area became a British possession in 1763, at the conclusion of the Seven Years' War. A few of these early settlers prospered. By 1800, for example, Ben Richards, a butcher, had accumulated a fortune by provisioning nearby military posts. Nonetheless, opportunities for most were quite limited, and the black population grew slowly. In 1850, blacks comprised only two thousand people—less than 5 percent of the city's population—and were centered in "Little Hayti," an area in the Lower Hill district where housing was cheap and close to downtown.

This community, although small, was active and assertive. One of its leading citizens, John Vashon, operated a fashionable bath house and barbershop. Another, John Peck, was a wigmaker and barber. Vashon, Peck, and Lewis Woodson, a barber and schoolteacher, were active in the antislavery movement. The best-known leader was Martin R. DELANY, who lived in Pittsburgh from the early 1830s until 1856. He edited one of Pittsburgh's early black newspapers, *The Mystery,* from 1843 until 1847.

Despite its small size and its poverty, Pittsburgh's pre–Civil War African-American community supported a remarkable number of institutions. These included an AME (African Methodist Episcopal) church, an AME Zion church, four benevolent societies, a private school, a cemetery, a militia company, a newspaper, and a temperance society.

In the years between the Civil War and World War I, black Pittsburghers made impressive gains. From 1870 to 1900, Virginia migrants helped swell their numbers from 1,162 to 20,355, making theirs the sixth-largest black community in the nation. In 1875, following years of protests and boycotts, they forced the desegregation of the city's public schools. And, although they remained largely excluded from the city's booming iron and glass industries, by the early 1900s they boasted eighty-five businesses and supported numerous clubs dedicated to social and cultural uplift. The community erected its own Home for Aged and Infirm Colored Women, a Working Girls' Home, and a Colored Orphans' Home.

Churches which catered to the district's elite—Ebenezer Baptist, Grace Memorial Presbyterian, Bethel AME, Warren ME, and St. Benedict the Moor Roman Catholic—were also active in community affairs. A number of groups—including the Aurora Reading Club, the Frances Harper League, the Wylie Avenue Literary Society, the Homewood Social and Literary Club, the Emma J. Moore Literary and Art Circle, and the Booker T. Washington Literary Society—promoted the cultural life of the community through reading and discussing literature. In addition, the prestigious Loendi Club, established in 1897, invited outstanding speakers to address its members and the black community.

African Americans in Pittsburgh also enjoyed an active musical life in the late nineteenth century. Community interest in classical music was reflected in the creation of three black concert and symphony orchestras at this time. One was founded by William A. Kelly, a coal miner and graduate of Oberlin; a second by Dr. C. A. Taylor, who had played in the Toronto Civic Orchestra; and a third by David Peeler, a local contractor and builder.

Between World War I and 1930, the city's black community grew rapidly. The cutoff of European immigration occasioned by World War I forced employers in Pittsburgh to seek out black workers to fill their depleted labor force. The iron and glass industries hired large numbers of African Americans for the first time. This touched off a migratory wave of Southerners that enlarged the region's black population. In Pittsburgh, the number of blacks rose from 25,000 to 55,000, while in the nearby mill towns of Aliquippa, Homestead, Rankin, Braddock, Duquesne, McKeesport, and Clairton, their numbers increased from 5,000 to 23,000.

Migrants brought energy and creativity to the local community. One of the most notable examples of this was Robert VANN, under whose leadership the PITTSBURGH COURIER, founded in 1910, became by the 1930s the black newspaper with the largest circulation in the country. Born in North Carolina in 1879, Vann earned his undergraduate degree at Virginia Union University in Richmond, Va. He then attended law school at the University of Pittsburgh, attracted by the availability of an Avery Scholarship for black students.

The *Courier*'s masthead—"Work, Integrity, Tact, Temperance, Prudence, Courage, Faith"—reflected Vann's faith in the American Dream. The paper endorsed the philosophy of Booker T. WASHINGTON: "Concentrate your earnings, and make capital. Hire yourselves, produce for yourselves, and sell something for yourselves." As a conservative journal, it supported World War I, opposed socialism, had no sympathy for unions, and applauded restrictive quotas on immigrants. An associate of Vann's, Daisy LAMPKIN (c. 1884–1965), was an active black Republican suffragist and national field secretary for the NAACP from 1935 to 1947.

The cultural life of black Pittsburgh flourished in the interwar years. By the 1930s it had two of the best teams—the Homestead Grays and the Pittsburgh Crawfords—ever to play baseball. In 1936, the Crawfords fielded five eventual Hall of Famers—Satchel PAIGE, Josh GIBSON, James "Cool Papa" BELL, Oscar CHARLESTON, and Judy JOHNSON. Pittsburgh was also an active jazz center, and prominent jazz musicians who grew up there include Lena HORNE, Billy STRAYHORN, Kenny CLARKE, Billy ECKSTINE, Roy ELDRIDGE, Mary Lou WILLIAMS, and Art BLAKEY. The local nightlife was centered on the intersection of Wylie and Fullerton Avenues, an area of nightclubs and cabarets.

Economically and politically, however, the community suffered. Few blacks enjoyed occupational mobility in the mills, partly because of white prejudice and partly because they had entered the city just as its steel industry had stopped growing. Black migrants entered the industrial work force at the bottom and had almost no success in moving up. Abraham Epstein's 1918 study "The Negro Migrant in Pittsburgh" found that 95 percent of black industrial workers were in unskilled positions. Investigations five years later by two black graduate students, Abram Harris and Ira Reid, in "The Negro in Major Industries and Building Trades of Pittsburgh" (later incorporated into Reid's study *Social Conditions of the Negro in the Hill District of Pittsburgh of 1930*) found blacks still mired at the bottom of the job ladder, and experiencing difficulty holding on to even those lowly jobs. A situation that was bleak during the 1920s turned disastrous during the Great Depression, when 33 to 40 percent of black adults were unemployed. A study of 2,700 black families found 41 percent destitute and another 33 percent living in poverty.

Moreover, blacks were unable to exercise political influence commensurate with their numbers. Pittsburgh's hills dispersed blacks among several "minighettos," so that the Hill district—the city's major black neighborhood—housed only 41 percent of the area's black residents. This fragmentation caused political weakness and apathy that have been denounced by generations of community leaders. The distinguished career of Homer Brown as a community activist, state legislator, and local judge in the 1930s, 1940s, and early 1950s was a striking exception to this condition.

In the 1950s, the economic and political problems of African Americans were compounded by the destruction of the Lower Hill—home to thousands of residents—for the sake of "urban renewal." Because no provision was made for their resettlement, those who were uprooted crowded into other neighborhoods, notably East Liberty and Homewood-Brushton, precipitating the abandonment of those areas by whites and more established middle-class blacks.

Nonetheless, blacks took tentative steps toward political power. In 1954 they helped elect their first city council member, Paul Jones; in 1958, they elected K. Leroy Irvis to the Pennsylvania legislature, and over the next three decades of a distinguished career Irvis served as minority whip, majority whip, and (twice by acclamation) speaker of the Pennsylvania House. Black political power was fragile, however. This was demonstrated in 1985, when blacks wound up with no representation on the city council. By 1989, following widespread protests and the abolition of an at-large electoral system, two blacks were elected to council from districts with large black majorities.

Political leadership was sorely needed, for Pittsburgh blacks suffered from many of the same social ills as their counterparts elsewhere. Indeed, in 1980, Pittsburgh blacks had a somewhat higher proportion of female-headed families and a higher infant mortality rate than blacks nationally. They also lived on an income that was only 57 percent that of local whites, and suffered an unemployment rate 2.3 times the local rate for whites.

Despite these travails, the condition of Pittsburgh's blacks was not altogether bleak. The riots following the assassination of the Rev. Dr. Martin Luther King, Jr., were less violent in Pittsburgh than in many other cities, and, at least through the 1980s, Pittsburgh was not overrun by drugs, which made its crime rate substantially lower than that of cities like Cleveland, Detroit, and Chicago, and even lower than supposedly "safe" cities like Minneapolis and Syracuse. If older black institutions, such as the great Negro League teams or the *Pittsburgh Courier*, became defunct or were greatly diminished in stature in the postwar years, black Pittsburgh has continued its cultural vitality. In jazz, Erroll Garner, Ahmad Jamal, Stanley Turrentine, Dakota Staton, and George BENSON show that Pittsburgh continues to produce outstanding talent. In letters, John WIDEMAN (winner of the PEN/Faulkner Award) and August WILSON (winner of the Pulitzer Prize) have added luster through their novels and plays set in Pittsburgh. Nonetheless, black Pittsburghers still must cope with the legacy of their economic and political burdens.

REFERENCES

BLACKETT, RICHARD J. M. "Freedom, or the Martyr's Grave: Black Pittsburgh's Aid to the Fugitive Slave." *Western Pennsylvania Historical Magazine* 61 (January 1978): 117–134.

BODNAR, JOHN, WILLIAM SIMON, and MICHAEL P. WEBER. *Lives of Their Own: Blacks, Italians, and Poles in Pittsburgh, 1900–1960.* Urbana, Ill., 1982, pp. 117, 186.

———. "Migration, Kinship, and Urban Adjustment: Blacks and Poles in Pittsburgh, 1900–1930." *Journal of American History* 66 (December 1979): 548–565.

BUNI, ANDREW. *Robert L. Vann of the Pittsburgh Courier: Politics and Black Journalism.* Pittsburgh, 1974.

DARDEN, JOE. *Afro-Americans in Pittsburgh: The Residential Segregation of a People.* Lexington, Mass., 1973.

DICKERSON, DENNIS C. "The Black Church in Industrializing Western Pennsylvania, 1870–1950." *Western Pennsylvania Historical Magazine* 64 (October 1981).

———. "Black Ecumenism: Efforts to Establish a United Methodist Episcopal Church, 1918–1932." *Church History* 52 (December 1983): 470–491.

———. *Out of the Crucible: Black Steelworkers in Western Pennsylvania, 1875–1980.* Albany, N.Y., 1986.

EDMUNDS, ARTHUR J. *Daybreakers: The Story of the Urban League of Pittsburgh: The First Sixty-Five Years.* Pittsburgh, 1983.

EPSTEIN, ABRAHAM. *The Negro Migrant in Pittsburgh.* Pittsburgh, 1918.

GLASCO, LAWRENCE. "Double Burden: The Black Experience in Pittsburgh." In S. P. Hays, ed., *City at the Point.* Pittsburgh, 1989, pp. 69–109.

GOTTLIEB, PETER. *Making Their Own Way: Southern Blacks' Migration to Pittsburgh, 1916–1930.* Urbana, Ill., 1987.

HARRIS, ABRAM. *The New Negro Worker in Pittsburgh.* M.A. thesis, University of Pittsburgh, 1924.

LUBOVE, ROY. *Twentieth Century Pittsburgh: Government, Business, and Environmental Change.* New York, 1969.

REID, IRA DEA. *The Negro in Major Industries and Building Trades of Pittsburgh.* M.A. thesis, University of Pittsburgh, 1925.

———. *Social Conditions of the Negro in the Hill District of Pittsburgh.* Pittsburgh, 1930.

RUCK, ROB. *Sandlot Seasons: Sport in Black Pittsburgh.* Urbana, Ill., 1987.

SAPOLSKY, STEVEN, and BARTHOLOMEW ROSELLI. *Homewood-Brushton: A Century of Community-Making.* Pittsburgh, 1987.

SIZEMORE, BARBARA. *An Abashing Anomaly: The High-Achieving Predominantly Black Elementary School.* Pittsburgh, 1983.

TUCKER, HELEN A. "The Negroes of Pittsburgh." In *Charities and the Commons,* 1909. Reprinted in Paul U. Kellog, *Wage-Earning Pittsburgh* (no. 6 of *The Pittsburgh Survey*). New York, 1974, pp. 424–436.

WILLIAMS, MELVIN D. *Community in a Black Pentecostal Church: An Anthropological Study.* Pittsburgh, 1974.

WILMOTH, ANN G. *Pittsburgh and the Blacks: A Short History, 1780–1875.* Ph.D. diss., Pennsylvania State University, 1975.

LAWRENCE A. GLASCO

Pittsburgh Courier. The *Pittsburgh Courier* was for several decades among the most influential African-American newspapers in the United States. Founded in January 1910 by Edwin Nathaniel Harleston, a security guard with an interest in literary endeavors, the weekly publication was nurtured into prominence under the guidance of Robert L. VANN. An attorney and acquaintance of Harleston's, Vann was asked to handle the fledgling newspaper's incorporation procedures and to solicit financial investors. By the autumn of 1910, however, Harleston had resigned from the ownership group and Vann was named editor. Vann accepted $100 a year in *Courier* stock shares as compensation, and by 1926 he was the majority stockholder.

When the *Courier's* first issue was published, the black population in Pittsburgh was approximately 25,000, but only one of the city's six newspapers carried any news concerning the African-American community. That paper, the *Pittsburgh Press,* carried black-oriented items in a segregated section titled "Afro-American News," but its content was generally of sensational crime and other lurid aspects of

The Chicago offices of the *Pittsburgh Courier* in 1941. In the early 1940s, the newspaper had a national circulation and a wide readership throughout black America. (Prints and Photographs Division, Library of Congress)

black life. Under Vann's leadership the *Courier* flourished, reaching a circulation of 55,000 in the early 1920s. This was accomplished by a number of adept strategies which included hiring well-known journalist George SCHUYLER in 1925 to write his "View and Reviews" column.

That same year Vann sponsored Schuyler on a nine-month tour of the South to write a series of on-the-road observations. This strategy allowed the *Courier* to build a national circulation among African-American readers, particularly in southern cities with large black populations. At the same time, Vann was increasing the paper's national advertising, hiring additional professional staff, and focusing on national stories.

As the *Courier* broadened its national coverage, its attention to local events weakened. Still, by the end of the 1920s, H. L. Mencken observed that the *Courier* was the "best colored newspaper published." A significant operational decision was the construction of the *Courier*'s own printing and production plant in 1929. During the Great Depression the *Courier* was able to keep and conserve its revenues because it maintained its own production facility.

It was also during the 1930s that the *Courier* undertook one of its first major campaigns as a national opinion leader for African Americans. At issue was the enormously popular radio program "Amos 'n' Andy." The *Courier* attacked the racial stereotypes presented in the program and in 1930 and 1931 launched a drive to obtain one million signatures on a petition to remove it from the air. Although the effort fell some 400,000 signatures short of its goal, the *Courier* firmly established its place as a national forum for African-American expression.

During the 1930s, *Courier* readers could faithfully follow the exploits of heavyweight champion Joe Louis, and the paper's increase in circulation coincided with Louis's reign. Journalists such as P. L. Prattis, William G. Nunn, and sportswriter Chester Washington joined the staff and the paper launched various crusades against Jim Crow discrimination and for civil rights.

Vann died in 1940 and his wife Jessie Ellen (Matthews) Vann succeeded him as publisher. By May 1947, the *Courier* attained a circulation high of 357,212 readers nationally. It championed the causes of racial equality in the U.S. armed forces and covered black military achievements in World War II. Although it also covered the black baseball circuit, emphasizing the Homestead Grays over the major league locals, the Pittsburgh Pirates, the *Courier* fought vigorously for the integration of major league baseball.

During the 1950s and 1960s the *Courier* experienced steady declines in circulation, and in 1966 it was purchased by the Sengstacke Group, which continued the weekly as the *New Pittsburgh Courier*.

REFERENCES

BUNI, ANDREW. *Robert L. Vann of the Pittsburgh Courier*. Pittsburgh, 1974.

WOLSELEY, ROLAND E. *The Black Press, USA*. Ames, Iowa. 1990.

CLINT C. WILSON II

Plato, Ann (c. 1820–?), poet. All that is known about Ann Plato is that she was the author of *Essays; Including Biographies and Miscellaneous Pieces in Prose and Poetry* (1841) and that she was a member of the Colored Congregational Church, Hartford, Conn., of which James W. C. PENNINGTON was pastor. Her birthdate is speculative, her date of death unknown. All other biographical data about Plato rests upon the content of her poems, and inferences based on such work are risky.

Using the evidence of the poems, scholars speculate that she may have had an American Indian father and a brother named Henry, that she joined the church when she was thirteen, that she was a teacher of very young children, and that she was in her early teens when she began to teach.

Essays, the second book published by a black American woman in the United States, is a slight but significant work containing sixteen essays, four biographical eulogies, and twenty poems. It is unique as the work of an African American during the mid-nineteenth century, neither slave narrative nor autobiography, decidedly apolitical in concerns and "ladylike" in tone. The content is historically informative, revealing through the brief biographies aspects of the lives of ordinary northern black women at the time and giving expression through the essays of the values espoused by many New England blacks at the time. The poems, of limited metrical variety and clearly the work of a young person, concern themselves largely with morality and mortality and show a lyric gift.

REFERENCE

WARREN, NAGUEYALTI. "Ann Plato." In Jessie Carney Smith, ed. *Notable Black American Women*. Detroit, 1992, pp. 853–854.

QUANDRA PRETTYMAN

Platters, The, rock-and-roll vocal group. Formed by Herbert Reed in Los Angeles in 1953, the Platters became one of the most successful vocal groups in popular music in the 1950s. In addition to Reed, the original members of the Platters were Tony

WILLIAMS, David Lynch and Alex Hodge. The group had little success until 1954, when Samuel "Buck" Ram, a songwriter and big band arranger, took over, adding the female vocalist Zora Taylor to the group and replacing Hodge with Paul Robi. The group's 1955 recording of Ram's "Only You" reached number one on the rhythm-and-blues charts, and number five overall. That song, with Williams's soaring falsetto, smooth backing vocals, and a light rhythmic accompaniment, became an important stylistic bridge between older, more established vocal groups and the then-emerging sounds of rock and roll. "Only You" also made the Platters the first black group to "cross over" to a white rock-and-roll audience. "Only You" was followed the next year by Ram's "The Great Pretender," which became the number-one-selling record in the United States and England. In 1956, the group also appeared in the films *Rock Around the Clock* and *The Girl Can't Help It*. From the mid-1950s through the late 1960s, the Platters sang on almost forty hit records, including "My Prayer" (1956), "It Isn't Right" (1956), "The Magic Touch" (1956), "Twilight Time" (1958), "Smoke Gets in Your Eyes" (1958), and "Enchanted" (1959).

During this time, the Platters also made numerous appearances on television, and became a successful concert and nightclub act in the United States and abroad, but their popularity was damaged by an incident in 1959 in which they were arrested in a Cincinnati hotel on drug and prostitution charges. Personnel changes, including Williams's replacement in 1961 by Sonny Tyner, and Robi and Taylor's replacement in 1966 by Nate Nelson and Sandra Dawn, also had a negative effect. In the 1970s Tony Williams, who had pursued an unsuccessful solo career, waged and eventually lost a long legal battle with Ram for the exclusive right to use the group's name. As a result, two separate groups began to call themselves "The Platters." Both groups, each with many personnel changes, continued to tour in the 1980s and '90s.

REFERENCES

GILLETT, CHARLIE. *The Sound of the City: The Rise of Rock and Roll*. London, 1983.

The Story of Rock: The Late Fifties. Milwaukee, Wis., 1991.

WHITCOMB, IAN. *After the Ball: Pop Music From Rag to Rock*. New York, 1973.

ROBERT W. STEPHENS

Pleasant, Mary Ellen "Mammy" (August 19, 1814–January 11, 1904), abolitionist, entrepreneur. By her own account, Mary Ellen Pleasant was born in Philadelphia in 1814 to a father who was a rich merchant from the Sandwich Islands and a mother who was a free black woman. The more common report, however, is that she was born a slave in either Virginia or Georgia, and there are conflicting accounts of how she made her way to the Northeast. (One account contends that a planter named Price bought her freedom and sent her to Boston to be educated.)

Pleasant lived in Boston in the 1830s and became friends with William Lloyd Garrison and other abolitionists (*see* ABOLITION). She married Alexander Smith, reputedly a Cuban painter, who left her a legacy of $45,000 when he died, urging her to use it to aid the abolitionists. Her second husband, John Pleasant, was apparently an overseer, but little else is known about him, and his role in her later life is slight.

In 1849, Mary Pleasant came to San Francisco where she opened a restaurant and boarding house which prospered in the midst of the Gold Rush. She ran the boarding house until 1858, and her boarders included many who became important in California history, including David Broderick, William Sharon, and David S. Terry. Throughout the 1840s and '50s, she often went to rural areas to rescue slaves who had been illegally brought to California by their masters. She also campaigned for the civil rights of free blacks in California.

In 1858, Pleasant returned east. According to some versions of her story, she spent time in Canada where she befriended John Brown. However, Pleasant's connection to John Brown has never been clearly documented. As the story goes, she gave Brown $30,000 to finance the attack of Harper's Ferry (*see* JOHN BROWN'S RAID). But available records do not indicate that Brown ever received such a large sum of money, and while it is certain that Pleasant did aid in the undertaking, her exact role is unclear.

Pleasant returned to San Francisco after the Civil War and became the housekeeper of a banker named Thomas Bell. She apparently was able to extract large sums of money from Bell, enough to open the House of Mystery, which soon became a notoriously successful house of ill repute. W. Sherman Savage has argued that Pleasant's reputation as a keeper of such houses in late nineteenth-century San Francisco came to obscure her earlier contribution to civil rights and the abolitionist cause.

Thomas Bell died in 1892, and Pleasant remained at the House of Mystery until 1899, when she was ordered out by a Federal judge, who called her a "scheming, trafficking, crafty old woman." She died in 1904, alone and apparently impoverished. On her tombstone is the inscription "She was a Friend of John Brown."

REFERENCE

LOGAN, RAYFORD W., and MICHAEL R. WINSTON, eds. *Dictionary of American Negro Biography*. New York, 1982.

ANDREW BIENEN

Plessy v. Ferguson.

Plessy v. Ferguson. In *Plessy* v. *Ferguson,* 163 U.S. 537 (1896), the Supreme Court upheld an 1890 Louisiana statute that required railroads to provide separate but equal accommodations for blacks and whites, and forbade persons from riding in cars not assigned to their race. It gave constitutional sanction to virtually all forms of racial SEGREGATION in the United States until after World War II.

Plessy arose as part of a careful strategy to test the legality of the new Louisiana law. In September 1891, elite "persons of color" in New Orleans formed the "Citizens Committee to Test the Constitutionality of the Separate Car Law." They raised three thousand dollars for the costs of a test case. Albion Tourgee, the nation's leading white advocate of black rights, agreed to take the case without fee. Tourgee, a former judge, was a nationally prominent writer most noted for his novel about Reconstruction, *A Fool's Errand.*

In June 1892, Homer A. Plessy purchased a first-class ticket on the East Louisiana Railroad, sat in the "white" car, and was promptly arrested and arraigned before Judge John H. Ferguson. Plessy then sued to prevent Ferguson from conducting any further proceedings against him. Eventually his challenge reached the United States Supreme Court.

Before the Court, Tourgee argued that segregation violated the THIRTEENTH AMENDMENT's prohibition of involuntary servitude and denied blacks equal protection of the laws, which was guaranteed by the FOURTEENTH AMENDMENT. These amendments, along with the Declaration of Independence, Tourgee asserted, gave Americans affirmative rights against invidious discrimination. He asserted that the Fourteenth Amendment gave constitutional life to the Declaration of Independence, "which is not a fable as some of our modern theorists would have us believe, but [is] the all-embracing formula of personal rights on which our government is based." Joining Tourgee in these arguments was Samuel F. Phillips, a former solicitor general of the United States, who in 1883 had unsuccessfully argued the *Civil Rights Cases.*

The Court rejected Tourgee's arguments by a vote of 7 to 1. In his majority opinion, Justice Henry Billings Brown conceded that the Fourteenth Amendment was adopted "to enforce the absolute equality of the two races before the law," but asserted that the amendment "could not have been intended to abolish distinctions based upon color, or to enforce social, as distinguished from political equality, or a commingling of the two races." Ignoring the reality of the emerging JIM CROW South, the Court denied that "the enforced separation of the two races stamps the colored race with a badge of inferiority." Brown believed that segregation was not discriminatory because whites were also segregated from blacks. Thus, if segregation created a perception of inferiority "it is not by reason of anything found in the act, but solely because the colored race chooses to put that construction upon it." Reflecting the accepted social science and popular prejudices of his age, Brown argued:

> Legislation is powerless to eradicate racial instincts or to abolish distinctions based upon physical differences, and the attempt to do so can only result in accentuating the difficulties of the present situation. If the civil and political rights of both races be equal, one cannot be inferior to the other civilly or politically. If one race be inferior to the other socially, the Constitution of the United States cannot put them upon the same plane.

Thus, as long as segregated facilities were "equal" they were permissible. Segregation had now received the sanction and blessing of the Supreme Court.

In a bitter, lone dissent, Justice John Marshall Harlan, a former slave owner, acknowledged that the "white race" was "the dominant race in this country." But, as Harlan read the Constitution,

> in the eye of the law, there is in this country no superior, dominant, ruling class of citizens. There is no caste here. Our Constitution is color-blind, and neither knows nor tolerates classes among citizens. In respect of civil rights, all citizens are equal before the law. The humblest is the peer of the most powerful. The law regards man as man, and takes no account of his surroundings or his color when his civil rights as guaranteed by the supreme law of the land are involved.

Harlan protested that the Court's decision would "stimulate aggressions, more or less brutal and irritating, upon the admitted rights of colored citizens" and "encourage the belief that it is possible, by means of state enactments, to defeat the beneficent purposes which the people of the United States had in view when they adopted the recent amendments to the Constitution." In prophetic language, Harlan asserted, "The thin disguise of 'equal' accommodations for passengers in railroad coaches will not mislead any one, nor atone for the wrong this day done." Harlan argued that the Louisiana law was "inconsistent with the personal liberty of citizens, white and black" and "hostile to both the spirit and letter of the Constitution of the United States."

Harlan's voice was that of a prophet ignored by his own age. More than five decades would pass before the Supreme Court recognized the fundamental truth of his dissent. Meanwhile, the South built a social and legal system rooted in racial segregation. In January 1897, Homer Plessy pled guilty to attempting to board a "white" railroad car and paid a twenty-five-dollar fine.

REFERENCES

FINKELMAN, PAUL, ed. *Race, Law, and American History*. Vol. 4, *The Age of Jim Crow: Segregation from the End of Reconstruction to the Great Depression*. New York, 1992.

KULL, ANDREW. *The Color Blind Constitution*. Cambridge, Mass., 1992.

LOFGREN, CHARLES A. *The Plessy Case: A Legal-Historical Interpretation*. New York, 1987.

LOGAN, RAYFORD W. *The Betrayal of the Negro*. Reprint of *The Negro in American Life and Thought: The Nadir, 1877–1901*. New York, 1965.

WOODWARD, C. VANN. *The Origins of the New South, 1877–1913*. Baton Rouge, La., 1951.

———. *The Strange Career of Jim Crow*. New York, 1955.

PAUL FINKELMAN

Podiatry.   The health specialty dealing with the human foot, also called chiropody, saw its beginnings in the United States around the mid–nineteenth century. The first podiatry offices or clinics opened in Boston and Philadelphia in the 1840s. African Americans became active in the profession almost from the start, earning a level of recognition that was more elusive in other health fields.

Compared to medicine, for example, podiatry was an accessible career. The training required little financial outlay and involved a relatively flexible combination of apprenticeship, classroom instruction, and on-the-job experience. The great demand for podiatric treatment among blacks, concentrated as they were in service occupations that required them to be on their feet much of the time, ensured a steady clientele for black podiatrists. Some black podiatrists also managed to generate a substantial white clientele because whites were less apt to be concerned about a black coming into contact with their feet than, say, with their abdomen (as a physician or surgeon might have to).

Census records for 1870 and 1880 list one Hannah Prosser (later Bosley) living in Lancaster County, Pa., with substantial wealth accrued in part from her activities as a "corn doctoress." Alexander Clark prospered as a manicurist and podiatrist in Philadelphia, and published a forty-six-page pamphlet entitled *The Feet and Hands: How to Take Care of Them* (1896) at a time when few podiatric texts existed.

Several blacks became charter members of the National Association of Chiropodists (NAC). Robert H. Hardin, Virgil D. Pumphrey, Leroy R. Dago, and Thomas W. Tives, all of Chicago, attended the NAC's inaugural convention in 1912. Also in attendance were members of the Emanuel family. Jonah Emanuel, born a slave in 1858, began practicing podiatry in 1884. He was the only black charter member of the Pedic Society of New York (1896), and served as the first vice president of the New York County Pedic Society, an all-black group incorporated in 1916. Jonah's brother, William Emanuel, a resident of Chicago, established a practice in which he was later joined by his wife, Fannie, and their three sons, William H., Floyd S., and McKinley.

The attendance of so many blacks at the NAC's inaugural convention sparked a discussion about their admission to membership; it was decided that excluding them would represent "undue discrimination." In educational opportunity, as in professional affiliation, the color line was less rigidly enforced than in other fields. A small but steady stream of black graduates emerged from the Illinois College of Chiropody, First Institute of Podiatry (New York), Ohio College of Chiropody, Temple School of Chiropody, and other institutions.

Still, African Americans had little or no voice in the NAC, which in 1958 changed its name to the American Podiatry Association (APA). In 1972, more than twenty black APA members met to discuss questions of visibility and recruitment. This caucus led a year later to blacks establishing their own organization, the National Podiatry Association (NPA). In 1978, Theodore H. Clarke became the first black president of the APA, which had never had a black officeholder of any rank. Clarke worked with the NPA and APA to recruit more blacks into the field. Partly as a result of these efforts, the proportion of black enrollment at podiatry schools nearly doubled between 1976 and 1985, from 3.3 percent to 6.5 percent.

REFERENCES

HOLLOWAY, LISABETH M. "Women and Minorities in the Profession." In Lisabeth M. Holloway, ed. *A Fast Pace Forward: Chronicles of American Podiatry*. Philadelphia, 1987, pp. 132–138.

JERRIDO, MARGARET. "Early Blacks in Chiropody." In Lisabeth M. Holloway, ed. *A Fast Pace Forward: Chronicles of American Podiatry*. Philadelphia, 1987, pp. 78–81.

PHILIP N. ALEXANDER

Poetry, Black.   *See* Literature.

Poetry, Dialect.   *See* Dialect Poetry.

Poindexter, Hildrus A. (May 10, 1901–1987), physician. Hildrus A. Poindexter was born in Memphis, Tenn. He graduated from Lincoln University, Pa., in 1924 and earned an M.D. from Harvard University in 1929 and an M.S. and Ph.D. (bacteriology) from Columbia University in 1929 and 1930, respectively. Poindexter was a Rockefeller Foundation Traveling Fellow in 1932 and joined the faculty of Howard University College of Medicine in 1931 as an assistant professor of bacteriology, preventive medicine, and public health. He rose to the rank of full professor in 1937. Poindexter was a first major (lieutenant colonel) in the U.S. Army Medical Corps from 1934 to 1947. In 1947 he became surgical and medical director of the U.S. Public Health Service Medical Mission to Liberia.

Poindexter was the recipient of numerous awards, including the Bronze Star (1944). In 1963 he became the first African American to receive the National Civil Service League Career Service Award, the same year in which he was given the Distinguished Public Health Service Award of the Agency of International Development. Two years later he received both the National Medical Association's Distinguished Service Award and the U.S. Public Health Service Meritorious Award.

He was a fellow in the American Medical Association, the American Association for the Advancement of Science, and the American Public Health Association. He also held membership in the National Medical Association, American Society for Tropical Medicine, American Society of Protozoology (commissional officer), Association of the U.S. Public Health Service Masons, Omega Psi Phi, and Beta Kappa Chi.

Poindexter wrote more than one hundred publications dealing with tropical medicine, microbiology, and public health. He received honorary degrees from Lincoln University (1946), Dartmouth College (1956), and Howard University (1961). He was the only African-American tropical-disease specialist with the U.S. Armed Forces during World War II.

REFERENCES

POINDEXTER, H. A. *My World of Reality.* Detroit, 1973.

SAMMONS, V. *Blacks in Sciences and Medicine.* New York, 1990, pp. 192–193.

WILLIAM D. WALLACE

Poindexter, James Preston (1819–February 7, 1907), minister and abolitionist. James Poindexter was freeborn in Richmond, Va., the son of a woman of black and Cherokee descent and a white journalist. He attended schools there until he was ten years old, when he was apprenticed to a barber. In 1837, he moved to Columbus, Ohio. In his successful career as a barber, Poindexter counted many prominent townspeople among his clients, contacts which were useful for Poindexter in his political career.

In Columbus, Poindexter joined and occasionally preached at the Second Baptist Church. However, in 1847, after a black family that had once owned slaves was admitted to the congregation, he and many others left Second Baptist Church and formed the Anti-Slavery Baptist Church. In 1858, Poindexter returned to Second Baptist Church and served as pastor for forty years. A great orator, his sermons on abolition and other subjects were often published in the local newspapers. Poindexter was also an active agent for the UNDERGROUND RAILROAD and, during the CIVIL WAR, formed the Colored Soldiers Relief Society. By the end of the Civil War, Poindexter had become recognized as a leader of the African-American population of Columbus.

In 1873, Poindexter became the first black to be nominated by the REPUBLICAN PARTY for a seat in the Ohio House of Representatives, though he lost the election. Three years later, he was a delegate-at-large to the Republican national convention, where he met and developed close ties with Rutherford B. Hayes. The next year, after Hayes was elected president, Poindexter supported Hayes's controversial policy of removing federal troops from the South, arguing that racism would end only if blacks and southern conservatives worked together. He lobbied hard for the post of consul to Haiti, but Hayes awarded it to John Langston Mercer.

In 1880, Poindexter became the first black elected to the Columbus City Council, and he was also named to the board of trustees for the Ohio School for the Blind. In 1884, he was appointed to fill a vacancy on the Columbus Board of Education and was subsequently reelected four times. At the school board, Poindexter fought for integrated schools and the improvement of the conditions of schools in black neighborhoods.

In 1887, he was made a director of the State Forestry Bureau, and Louisville State University awarded him a doctor of divinity degree. After leaving the pastorate of the Second Baptist Church in the last years of the nineteenth century, Poindexter remained in retirement in Columbus until his death from pneumonia.

REFERENCES

MINOR, RICHARD C. "James Poindexter: Elder Statesman of Ohio." *Ohio History* (1947).
SIMMONS, WILLIAM J. *Men of Mark*. Cleveland, Ohio, 1887.

LYDIA MCNEILL

Pointer Sisters, The, pop singing group. The Pointer Sisters, Ruth (March 19, 1946–), Anita (January 23, 1948–), Bonnie (July 11, 1950–), and June (November 20, 1954–), were born and raised in Oakland, Calif., the daughters of Elton and Sarah Elizabeth Pointer, both ministers in the West Oakland Church of God. The sisters grew up in a highly religious household, and their exposure to music came through their church choir. As they matured, they began to perform secular music, and were exposed to a wide variety of musical styles, from JAZZ to country. In 1969 their friendship with producer David Robinson led to work as backup singers with local San Francisco musicians such as Taj Mahal, Tower of Power, and Boz Scaggs.

After a brief, unsuccessful relationship with Atlantic Records, the Pointer Sisters signed a contract with ABC/Blue Thumb Records in 1973. Their debut album, *The Pointer Sisters,* mixed BLUES and soul styles with vocal harmonies and costumes that evoked the female singing groups of the 1940s. The single "Yes We Can Can" reached number eleven on the Billboard pop charts, and they soon became popular guests on television variety shows. Their second album, *That's A Plenty* (1974), produced the Grammy Award–winning single "Fairytale." In 1974 the Pointer Sisters also became the first African-American female group to appear at Nashville's Grand Ole Opry, and the first to reach the top of Billboard's country and western charts.

Despite their stylistic eclecticism, the Pointer Sisters were rarely given the opportunity by their producers to record and perform in anything other than a 1940s-style nostalgic imitation of the Andrews Sisters. In 1977, after Bonnie left to pursue a solo career with Motown Records, the Pointer Sisters, now a trio, recorded *Energy,* which yielded two pop singles, "Fire," and "Happiness." In the early and mid-1980s, the trio produced a succession of highly successful pop-oriented rhythm and blues singles, including "Slow Hand" (1981), "What a Surprise" (1981), "So

Excited" (1982), "I Need You" (1983). Their recordings of "Jump" (1983) and "Automatic" (1984) won Grammy Awards. In 1985 the trio again switched record labels, this time to RCA, where they recorded *Slammin'* (1988). By the early 1990s they had moved to Motown, where they recorded *Right Rhythm* (1991). The Pointer Sisters continue to record regularly and perform to large audiences.

REFERENCES

COLLIER, ALDORE. "Pointer Sisters Shed Old Look, Old Clothes to Reach New Heights." *Jet* (April 15, 1985): 58.
HOERBURGER, ROB. "Hot Together." *Rolling Stone* (February 12, 1987): 90.

SUSAN MCINTOSH

Poitier, Sidney (February 20, 1927–), actor, director, and filmmaker. The youngest of eight children, Sidney Poitier was born in Miami and reared on Cat Island in the Bahamas. He was forced to leave school at fifteen in order to work on his parents' tomato farm, and then moved to Miami to live with his married brother Cyril. Shortly thereafter, Poitier left for New York City, enlisted in the U.S. Army, and served as a physiotherapist until World War II ended in 1945. Upon his return to New York, he supported himself with a series of menial jobs, while studying to become an actor. After an unsuccessful audition, he spent six months trying to rid himself of his West Indian accent and eventually became a member of the AMERICAN NEGRO THEATRE, for which he often played leading roles. He also won minor parts in the Broadway productions of *Lysistrata* (1946) and *Anna Lucasta* (1948), before trying his hand at film. In 1950 he married Juanita Hardy, a dancer, with whom he had three children; Poitier and Hardy were eventually divorced.

Poitier's big break came when he was cast as a young doctor in Twentieth Century Fox's "racial problem" film *No Way Out* (1950). Leading roles followed in such films as *Cry, the Beloved Country* (1951), *Go Man Go* (1954), *Blackboard Jungle* (1955), *Band of Angels, Edge of the City,* and *Something of Value* (the last three all released in 1957). With his performance as an escaped convict in *The Defiant Ones* (1958), Poitier became the first African American to be nominated for an Oscar in the best actor category; he also won the New York Film Critics and Berlin Film Festival awards for best actor. The next year, Poitier took on the title role in Otto Preminger's motion picture version of *Porgy and Bess* (1959), for which he was also critically acclaimed.

Sidney Poitier in his Academy Award–winning performance in *Lilies of the Field* (1963). (AP/Wide World Photos)

As an actor, Poitier was known for sensitive, versatile, and eloquent interpretations and powerful on-camera presence as well as his good looks. He was one of the first African Americans to become a major Hollywood star, and during the 1960s played leads in many influential and controversial films. After originating the role of Walter Lee Younger on Broadway in Lorraine HANSBERRY's *A Raisin in the Sun* (1959), Poitier was featured in such diverse films as *Paris Blue* (1960), *Pressure Point* (1961), *A Patch of Blue* (1965), *The Bedford Incident* (1965), *Duel at Diablo* (1966), *Guess Who's Coming to Dinner?*, *In the Heat of the Night* and *To Sir, with Love* (all 1967). In 1963, he became the first African American to win an Academy Award for best actor for his performance in *Lilies of the Field*.

The late 1960s proved a transitional period for Poitier, who was accused of portraying unrealistic "noble Negro" or "ebony saint" characters by the militant black community. He confessed to feeling himself caught between the demands of white and black audiences, and attempted to diversify his roles by taking on such films as *They Call Me Mr. Tibbs!* (1970), *A Warm December* (1973), and *The Wilby Conspiracy* (1975), and applying his talents to directing. In 1968, Poitier joined with Paul Newman, Steve

McQueen, Dustin Hoffman, and Barbra Streisand to form First Artists, an independent production company. The popular western *Buck and the Preacher* (1972) marked his debut as both director and star; *A Warm December* and the hit comedy *Uptown Saturday Night* (both 1974), *Let's Do It Again* (1975), and *A Piece of the Action* (1977) all featured him in this dual role. In 1975 he was elected to the Black Filmmakers Hall of Fame; his film *Let's Do It Again* earned him the NAACP Image Award in 1976. That year, Poitier married the actress Joanna Shimkus, with whom he had two children. His autobiography, *This Life,* was published in 1980.

Over the next decade, Poitier concentrated on directing such works as *Stir Crazy* (1980), *Hanky Panky* (1982), *Fast Forward* (1985), and *Ghost Dad* (1990). In 1982 he became the recipient of the Cecil B. DeMille Golden Globe Award and the Los Angeles Urban League Whitney M. Young Award. Poitier returned to acting briefly in 1988 for starring roles in *Shoot to Kill* and *Little Nikita,* both of which were released that year.

In addition to creative filmmaking, Poitier has produced a record album called *Sidney Poitier Reads the Poetry of the Black Man* and narrated two documentaries on Paul ROBESON: *A Tribute to the Artist* (1979) and *Man of Conscience* (1986). In recognition of his artistic and humanitarian accomplishments, he was knighted by Queen Elizabeth II, and the NAACP honored him with its first Thurgood Marshall Lifetime Achievement Award in 1993.

REFERENCES

EWERS, CAROLYN H. *The Long Journey: A Biography of Sidney Poitier.* New York, 1969.
MARILL, ALVIN H. *The Films of Sidney Poitier.* Secaucus, N.J., 1978.
POITIER, SIDNEY. *This Life.* New York, 1980.

ED GUERRERO

Polite, Carlene Hatcher (August 28, 1932–), novelist. Born in Detroit, Mich., Carlene Hatcher Polite attended Sarah Lawrence College and the Martha Graham School of Contemporary Dance. A recipient of a National Foundation on the Arts and Humanity fellowship (1967) and a Rockefeller Foundation fellowship (1968), Polite had a career that fused art and social activism, and encompassed literature, dance, and politics. After having been a dancer with the Concert Dance Theatre of New York from 1955 to 1959, she returned to Detroit, where she danced with the Vanguard Playhouse, taught dance, and became involved with the local and state Democratic Party. She was elected to the party's State Central Committee in 1962. The following year she served as an organizer of the Northern Negro Leadership Conference and coordinator of the Detroit Council for Human Rights. Shortly after the Council closed in 1964, she moved to Paris. There, she continued to dance, but writing became her primary interest. Her first novel, *The Flagellants*, was published in France in 1966, and in the United States in 1967. The book concerns a young black couple thwarted in their search for love and self-identity by an oppressive society. They lacerate each other in a series of verbal attacks, and in the end are driven apart.

Polite returned to the United States in 1971, but her Paris experiences informed her second novel, *Sister X and the Victims of Foul Play* (1975), which recounts the life and death of a female black dancer in Paris, and again delineates in direct, almost brutal fashion the cancerous effects of racism. Polite's fiction is experimental, relying more on unconventional techniques such as the extended monologue than on more traditional means such as plot. Polite has been a member of the English Department at the State University of New York at Buffalo since 1971.

REFERENCE

METZGER, LINDA, ed. *Black Writers: A Selection of Sketches from Contemporary Authors.* Detroit, 1989.

MICHAEL PALLER

Politics and Politicians. African-American Politics has been divided into three sections: a brief Overview, Antebellum Politics, and Reconstruction to the Present. See also the articles on individual states and cities, as well as the following related articles: ABOLITION; AFFIRMATIVE ACTION; CIVIL RIGHTS MOVEMENT; CIVIL WAR; COMMUNIST PARTY OF THE UNITED STATES; CONGRESSIONAL BLACK CAUCUS; DEMOCRATIC PARTY; FIFTEENTH AMENDMENT; MAYORS; PRESIDENTS OF THE UNITED STATES; RECONSTRUCTION; REPUBLICAN PARTY; SOCIALISM; SUFFRAGE, NINETEENTH-CENTURY; SUFFRAGE, TWENTIETH-CENTURY.

Overview

African-American politics has a long, complex, and frequently painful history. By definition slaves were noncitizens, outside of the political process. Yet in various ways slaves contrived to fashion a political role for themselves, such as through NEGRO ELECTIONS DAY festivals in New England. During the Colonial period, free blacks tried to enter the political process whenever possible, but were unable to exercise significant influence on the political system. In the half century following the end of the AMERICAN REVOLUTION, free black voting was largely restricted, but through petitions, community organizations, emigrationist activities, newspapers, and eventually the ANTEBELLUM CONVENTION MOVEMENT, free blacks expressed themselves politically.

Beginning in the 1830s, at the same time that the ABOLITION movement offered blacks a voice within a national reform movement, blacks themselves set up numerous committees and organizations to struggle for suffrage, civil rights, and education. Nevertheless, the political status of African Americans remained uncertain, and it eroded during the late 1840s and 1850s as a result of growing white racism, immigrant labor competition, FUGITIVE SLAVE LAWS, and other factors. Many African Americans became convinced that freedom in the United States was unattainable, and turned their attention to colonization schemes in Africa, Canada, Haiti, and other places.

The outbreak of the CIVIL WAR galvanized blacks, who saw the war as a struggle for their liberation. Throughout the first two years of the war, African-American leaders such as Frederick DOUGLASS campaigned for blacks to be armed and devoted their attention to securing aid for freemen who escaped behind Union lines, as well as civil rights and suffrage for the free black community. By 1862 blacks were permitted to enlist in the Union Army. Thousands joined, recognizing the importance of the struggle, and black leaders served as recruiting agents.

For a brief period during RECONSTRUCTION, fortified by constitutional amendments guaranteeing equal citizenship and suffrage and white northern efforts to ensure southern compliance, black males for the first time participated fully in the electoral system. Black elected officials, sponsored by southern Republican parties in exchange for black voting support, appeared on the national scene, and black state legislators and convention delegates made decisive contributions to the political culture of their states. Meanwhile, there was widespread black involvement in municipal politics in the South's few cities of importance. Richmond, Va., had thirty-three black city council members between 1871 and 1896, while in the deep South, leaders such as William Finch of Atlanta and Holland THOMPSON of Montgomery, Ala., were elected to positions on city councils. In 1873 Mifflin GIBBS was elected a municipal judge in Little Rock, Ark. Many smaller towns elected black mayors. Between 1870 and 1900 twenty African Americans were elected to the House of Representatives, and two served in the Senate.

However, white Southerners never really accepted blacks as equal members of the body politic, and following the withdrawal of northern pressure—both military and political—from the South during the mid-1870s, the scope of black public participation narrowed. Black officeholding all but disappeared, and black voting power was vitiated by voting fraud, intimidation of voters, and electoral devices such as redistricting. As early as 1878 the city of Atlanta changed from ward elections to at-large voting to dilute the black vote. Other cities soon followed suit. Even where black suffrage was unfettered, the dissolution of southern Republicanism left blacks no effective weapon against one-party Democratic regimes other than through alliance with third parties such as the Populists, who were ambivalent about black support.

In the upper South, black Republicans continued to be elected in small numbers. George WHITE, an African American, represented North Carolina in Congress into the new century, while blacks such as Richmond's John MITCHELL served on city councils in Virginia into the 1890s. Violence and legislative action against black voting during the 1890s cut off even these avenues of influence.

Meanwhile, the political influence of blacks in the urban North also diminished. In the immediate post-bellum period, some blacks were elected to office. In 1866, with the aid of white voters, state representatives Charles Mitchell and Edwin Walker of Boston became the first blacks elected to office from a large urban area. In 1876 George L. Ruffin was elected to Boston's Common Council. However, in most cities, the percentage of African Americans in the population remained too small for blacks to play a significant role, and as immigrant-backed machines hostile to blacks took control of city governments, black voting power diminished. Moreover, city governments were often dependent on state legislatures, which controlled budgets and selected police chiefs and other officials. These outside bodies could act to curtail or eliminate black voting strength. (Similarly, in 1871 the U.S. Congress stripped Washington, D.C., whose population was one-third black, of its elected government.) Even after many cities obtained "home rule" at the end of the century, Progressive elites instituted at-large voting and granted power to unelected city commissions and civil service workers to curb the power of blacks and white ethnics.

Through most of the late nineteenth century, the Republican party maintained its alliance with both southern and northern black populations through government appointments and support for education. Many black voters and party leaders measured party support not through its defense of civil rights but by the amount of political patronage granted the black community. Still, as early as the 1870s many blacks grew dissatisfied with shrinking party patron-

age and the party's inaction over violations of black rights, and distanced themselves from the Republicans. Beginning in the 1880s some blacks flirted with joining the Democrats. However, neither party was willing to risk alienating white voters or grant more than token assistance in exchange for the black vote. Others joined third parties or attempted to build up separate black institutions but were unable to mount effective challenges to prevailing political trends.

By 1900 virtually all southern blacks were disfranchised, while their counterparts in the North were unable to exert significant influence. A few political clubs, such as New York's UNITED COLORED DEMOCRACY, were formed, but they were merely satellite party groups, given minor patronage positions in exchange for promoting white candidates. Black political power remained largely dormant for a generation, except for the influence black strongmen such as Charles ANDERSON in New York City, Robert CHURCH, Jr., in Memphis, and, above all, Booker T. WASHINGTON wielded over Republican party patronage. The ratification in 1920 of the Nineteenth Amendment, which enfranchised black women as well as white women, had little discernible impact on black political strength. In the first years after the turn of the century, the border states were the only places with significant African-American influence on municipal government. For example, in 1890 Harry Smythe Cummings became the first of several blacks over the following years to sit on the Baltimore City Council.

The Great Migration of southern blacks to northern and midwestern cities during the late 1910s and '20s (see MIGRATION/POPULATION) brought in its wake large numbers of new voters. The voting power of the increased population was strengthened by the increasing ghettoization and residential concentration of African Americans. Their votes were organized in exchange for patronage by ward leaders selected by urban machines, such as New York's J. Raymond JONES and Chicago's William DAWSON. In many places, city council and other municipal elected offices remained largely powerless, and ward committeemen positions were the most powerful city jobs most blacks held. In a few areas, blacks became a large enough segment of the population to elect black officials. In 1915, after the creation of a largely black district in Chicago, Republican Oscar DEPRIEST won election to the city's Board of Alderman. In 1919 Charles ROBERTS was elected to New York City's Aldermanic Board. Similarly, Frank Hall was elected to the Cincinnati City Council in 1931. The growing strength of black organizations was evidenced by DePriest's election in 1928 as the first northern black congressman. As importantly, the migration and the GREAT DEPRESSION helped foster increasing black community militancy, and civil rights joined patronage as a primary concern of African-American voters.

During the 1930s, as a result of aid from New Deal federal social programs, urban machine involvement, and labor union activism, the majority of black voters were drawn into the Democratic Party coalition. Meanwhile, black Democratic elected officials, beginning with Arthur MITCHELL in 1934, entered Congress as well as state legislatures and municipal bodies. While the Democrats did not commit to civil rights action or provide aid proportionate to the level of black support, they made symbolic gestures toward the black community and instituted several relatively race-neutral government programs. While blacks backed Democratic candidates, many remained registered Republicans. A small number of blacks supported minor parties, notably the Communist Party, whose advocacy of civil rights and interracialism won it the support or approbation of many African Americans.

In the years after WORLD WAR II, black political activity increased. The war brought renewed migration to the North of southern blacks, who swelled urban voting blocs. The migration made possible the election of larger numbers of black officials such as Harlem, N.Y., minister Adam Clayton POWELL, JR., who in 1941 became the first African-American member of the New York City Council, and who three years later was elected to Congress.

At the same time, civil rights became a national issue. In 1948, the adoption of a strong civil rights platform plank at the Democratic National Convention prompted a walkout by some white Southerners. Democratic presidential candidate Harry Truman was elected nevertheless, and his victory helped demonstrate the electoral clout of urban African Americans. Gradually, over the following years, northern Democrats championed that party's transition to a strongly problack position.

Postwar black population growth in the urban North continued to be heavy, and its effects were heightened by declining white populations, as whites migrated to nearby suburbs. In 1953 New York State assemblyman Hulan JACK was elected to the powerful position of Manhattan borough president. Soon after, Newark and Detroit, two cities with heavy concentrations of black residents, gained their first black city councilmen.

In 1944 the U.S. Supreme Court struck down the "white primary," a leading method by which southern blacks were deprived of the ballot. The decision increased both southern black voter registration and pressure for suffrage rights. Beginning with the South Carolina Progressive Democratic party in 1944, blacks formed satellite political organizations

to encourage voter registration and unity. The secular migration of rural blacks to southern industrial centers also accelerated during the 1950s, and all the deep South states had majority urban populations by 1960. The large potential vote the migrants made up was partially unleashed by registration efforts and the reduction of barriers to registration. A few blacks even won election to office. In 1948 Oliver Hill became Richmond's first black city councilman in a half century, and in 1957 Hattie Mae White was elected to Houston's school board.

To neutralize the power of the black vote, both white Southerners and their northern counterparts adopted various electoral stratagems: At-large elections were instituted for political offices; runoff elections assured a solid white bloc vote against black candidates; cities annexed adjacent white suburbs to dilute the percentage of blacks in the city; black areas were divided or merged with nearby white areas to prevent the formation of black majority districts (Tuskegee, Ala., gerrymandered its black voters out of the city, a move struck down by the U.S. Supreme Court in 1960 in *Gomillion* v. *Lightfoot*).

The CIVIL RIGHTS MOVEMENT of the 1960s made possible the return of blacks as full-fledged actors on the national political scene. Not only did the movement's demonstrations bring black concerns temporarily to the top of the American political agenda, but also grassroots lobbying and voter registration efforts, through such organizations as the MISSISSIPPI FREEDOM DEMOCRATIC PARTY, and the *National Democratic Party of Alabama* gave masses of previously disfranchised southern blacks a channel for political self-expression. The culmination of the nonviolent movement's triumphs was the VOTING RIGHTS ACT OF 1965, which banned most of the measures used to curb black voting. The black vote unleashed by the act, and its subsequent extensions and amendments, completely transformed the southern political landscape and made possible the election of large numbers of black officials. By 1970 black city councilmen and state representatives had been elected in several southern states, and in 1972 Andrew YOUNG of Georgia and Barbara JORDAN of Texas became the first southern blacks elected to Congress in the twentieth century. Meanwhile, throughout the country, the conjunction of white urban depopulation and the growing power of black political organizations brought about an explosion of black mayors of large cities (beginning with Carl STOKES of Cleveland and Richard HATCHER of Gary, Ind. in 1967), members of Congress (including Edward BROOKE, who in 1966 became the first African-American member of the U.S. Senate in the twentieth century). However, legal challenges to existing electoral districts and systems were unavailing, and many states, both in and outside of the South, continued to practice both "massive resistance and more subtle forms of subterfuge to thwart black electoral progress. As a result, change was continually retarded.

Despite the unprecedented political and electroal strides made by African Americans, the future of black politics remains uncertain. An African-American political class, made up of elected officials and black political leaders such as Jesse JACKSON, has grown up during the years since 1965. Through such forums and networks as the CONGRESSIONAL BLACK CAUCUS, formed in 1971, its members have succeeded in articulating black concerns within mainstream political channels and in obtaining a certain share of national political influence (in part a result of the disproportionately high seniority rate of blacks in Congress). However, entrenched racism and the poor socioeconomic status of African Americans remain obstacles to full integration of the community into the nation's body politic. Even as blacks such as Virginia governor C. Douglas WILDER demonstrate crossover electoral appeal, black frustration with mainstream party policies that appear to downplay their needs has resulted in chronic low voter turnout and has led some frustrated activists to turn from mainstream political parties toward independent black institutions.

Antebellum Politics

African-American involvement in American politics began in the period from 1619 through 1865. During much of that time, the historical record of African-American political involvement is thin. Nevertheless, there is much to indicate that African-American political activity, both as part of the larger American body politic and as African Americans' organizing institutions that mirrored and challenged their white counterparts, often was an offshoot of African values and customs.

COLONIAL ERA

African-American politics began in the seventeenth century, and political participation grew during the eighteenth. The most direct actors were free African Americans. Two categories of political participation were available to them during this era: pressure and electoral politics. As an example of the former category, we find that in New Netherlands (later New York) in 1661, free blacks petitioned the director-general and lords councillors of the colony to mandate that their adopted children be recognized as free. The petition was granted. In 1726 a free black petitioned the chief justice of the General Court in North Carolina, asking the colonial judiciary to uphold his free status and voluntary choice of association. The court denied this request. In 1769, a group of free

blacks in Virginia successfully petitioned the House of Burgesses to have their families exempted from taxation.

As for electoral participation, the small free black population was allowed to participate in certain places. In the thirteen colonies, prior to the Revolution, there was sporadic voting by free blacks. Only four southern colonies explicitly denied free blacks the vote, and even in these colonies it is not improbable that here and there people willingly acquiesced in the casting of an occasional ballot by a black man or a mulatto. The earliest record of such black voting came from South Carolina, where the 1701 and 1703 gubernatorial elections were marked by widespread complaints over free black votes.

The legal flexibility that made free black voting possible resulted from the fact that there were free blacks at that time, and their existence went all but unnoticed. The vast majority of African Americans during the colonial era were slaves, who could not legally vote or engage in formal political activities. Some slaves may have been allowed to vote in close elections by their plantation masters. Historical research has uncovered such practices in Rapide Parish—dubbed "the ten-mile district"—in Louisiana, and these practices continued from the early nineteenth century until the eve of the Civil War. However, manipulated as this voting was, it did develop a group of individuals who were at least socialized into the evolving political process.

The slaves' exclusion from electoral participation did not mean that they were entirely cut off from political expression. Such expression can, of course, be found—indirectly—in the acts of slaves who resisted punishments, escaped, purchased their freedom, or revolted, or who destroyed the property of the masters. This behavior, motivated by ingrained concepts of freedom and liberty fueled by memories of one's own or one's forebears' liberty in an African past, as well as responding to an immediate situation of oppression, contained a clear political message.

Moreover, slaves played an active role in the political culture in some areas of Colonial and early national New England through the celebration of NEGRO ELECTIONS DAY as part of the Colonial election day festivities. The ceremonial election of black "governors" and "kings" began in the mideighteenth century in ports and administrative centers with large slave populations. The earliest evidence of the ceremony is from Salem, Mass., in 1741; Newport, R.I., in 1756, and Hartford Conn., from sometime before 1766. It quickly spread throughout New England and adjacent areas such as Albany, N.Y., with black leaders' "jurisdictions" shrinking to the county or town level as more towns participated. Although this was only ceremonial voting, it was an exercise that probably helped to develop black political leadership and promoted the organization of the slave community. At least it represented the demand by African Americans to participate in the public life of the larger society, as filtered through their own appreciation of African political traditions. In some areas, such as New Hampshire, black community members even formed "slave courts" that regulated the conduct of slaves and punished offenses.

The Colonial political system did shape the fledgling efforts of African Americans to participate in the political process. For example, whether the election was for "governor" or "king" seems to have depended on the type of colony in which the election was held: Blacks in charter colonies, which elected their own governors, had black "governors," while those in royal colonies, whose governors were appointed by the king of England, selected "kings." Similarly, there were rude party divisions of blacks into "Tories" and "Whigs" (based on masters' political leanings). The institutions African Americans built covertly expressed their struggle against political powerlessness and satirized the white institutions that surrounded and excluded them.

However, the immediate context of the white election day ritual was not the only operative variable in the establishment of Negro Elections Day. There was also the influence of the African background and heritage. The religious-political Adae ceremony of the Ashanti provides an illustration of a similar custom. Other customs—the coronation ritual of the Maradi, and the harvest festival of the Jukun-speaking peoples—similarly illustrate those ceremonial traditions. Indeed, peoples of African heritage in Brazil, Martinique, Cuba, and other areas of the New World engaged in similar election proceedings. Descriptions of the ritual in Newport clearly indicate African features such as songs, dances, drums, and games. Also, the ritual took place, as in Africa, in a large open space under a tree. After the 1820s, with the emancipation of most northern blacks, Negro Elections Day ceremonies declined, and were largely replaced with carefully staged parades that commemorated the end of local slavery. Unlike the election day ceremonies, the emancipation parades often had an explicitly oppositional political component.

REVOLUTIONARY AMERICA

When the First Continental Congress met in September 1774, African Americans' political participation, save for events such as slave revolts, had not really arrived at the stage of coherent collective action. The rare political actions of blacks were still individual, and they lacked a strong sense of community and racial consciousness. However, by the time that revolutionary America had transformed itself into an independent nation and developed a federal system, African-American politics had begun to evolve beyond the strictly individual stage, to achieve some collective bases of action.

The revolutionary struggle that led to the creation of the United States of America had a profound effect on African-American ideology and political activities. Blacks, conscious of the irony of white colonists campaigning for "liberty" while denying it to their slaves, made use of revolutionary rhetoric and the wartime needs of the country to carve out a political space for themselves. Between 1773 and 1774 African Americans in Massachusetts presented five collective antislavery petitions to the General Court, Massachusetts's governing body. One of the early petitioners, from 1773, challenged the legislators, "We expect great things from men who have made such a noble stand against the designs of their fellow-men to enslave them." Scores of other petitions protesting slavery and discrimination were presented to the legislatures of the newly independent states in the following years.

When war broke out, many free African Americans joined the fledgling American army, recognizing that military service was a traditional mark of citizenship. Partly for the same reason, white authorities soon attempted to bar blacks from military service. Once white opposition to arming slaves, at least in the northern states, melted away under pressure of military necessity, blacks enlisted in disproportionate numbers in the Continental Army. Meanwhile, slaves in Virginia, promised freedom by royal governor Lord Dunmore if they fought on the side of England, rushed in large numbers to his offshore base.

Revolution in America did little to improve the political participation of African Americans. Four of the new state constitutions denied free blacks the right to vote; five more states would eventually deny it, and only four would never deny it. (*See* Appendix 11.9). Thus only four of the thirteen original colonies—plus Vermont, admitted to the Union in 1791—permitted African Americans to vote. In all of these four states—Massachusetts, New Hampshire, Rhode Island, and New York—the Negro Elections Day celebrations continued to be observed regularly, though New York imposed a discriminatory property requirement for black voters in 1821. In Connecticut, which denied African-American suffrage in 1818, the blacks' last "governor" held office shortly before the Civil War.

Nevertheless, the petitions and military service did exert an influence on the new governments in the years after the war's end. State legislatures in the North passed gradual abolition statutes, and even southern states passed laws simplifying manumission. Many veterans were freed, and some were franchised. Wentworth CHESWILL of New Hampshire, probably the first person of African descent elected to office in North America, served as a justice of the peace as early as 1768, and was town selectman for New Market, N.H., several times after 1780. In 1806 he was an unsuccessful candidate for the state senate. In 1831 Alexander TWILIGHT of Vermont became the first African American elected to a state legislature.

Most of the states abolished the slave trade within their borders, although the U.S. Constitution delayed federal action until 1808. Meanwhile, African Americans and white antislavery allies appealed to the judiciary, bringing a handful of test cases challenging slavery in state courts. In 1783 Quock Walker brought a freedom suit in Massachusetts. Judge Richard Cushing ruled slavery incompatible with the state's constitution, resulting in the effective end of slavery in Massachusetts. By 1800 a number of northern states had passed emancipation statutes.

The development of two opposing national political parties, the Federalists and the Democratic-Republicans (later the Democratic party), increased black political involvement. To the extent that blacks participated in campaign and electoral politics, they overwhelmingly supported the Federalists, led in part by such antislavery figures as Alexander Hamilton and John Jay, over Thomas Jefferson and the Democrats, who were identified with slavery and southern interests. The Federalist Party sought the support of black leaders such as New York City's Joseph Sidney and Philadelphia's Absalom JONES, and in 1809 established a black political club, the Washington Benevolent Society, which maintained active branches in Boston and New York City. Black voting played a notable role in the Federalists' narrow victory in New York in 1813.

With the changing structure of government and electoral context came a change in political protest behavior. Not only did African Americans send their petitions and memorials to various state executives and legislatures, but by 1797 they were also sending petitions to the Congress of the United States. On January 23, 1797, four African Americans living in Philadelphia petitioned Congress though Representative John Swanwick of Pennsylvania for a redress of their grievances, which were related to a North Carolina law of 1788 that provided for the capture and reselling of illegally manumitted slaves. Seven days after the petition arrived, Congress debated whether to accept or reject "a petition from fugitive slaves." By a vote of 50–33, Congress rejected the petition. This initial petition was soon followed by another, which arrived in "the second day of the new century," in 1800. Absalom Jones had his representative, Robert Waln of Pennsylvania, present a petition to Congress to demand the banning of the SLAVE TRADE and the 1793 Fugitive Slave Act. However, Congress voted 85–1 not to consider the petition.

Thus, in this early national period, when African-American political participation was still closely circumscribed by denials of the right to vote, to serve on juries, to hold office, and to bring a legal suit against a white person, black political participation showed signs of expanding and extending itself into new directions. Not only did African Americans show increasing inclination to exert pressure and redirect their focus, they now began to take on a collective impulse. The influence of the African heritage and background was a strong spur to organization, in the form of mutual aid and fraternal organizations, educational societies, and black religious organizations, which grew up in African-American communities and served as the centers of collective effort and activism. For example, in Rhode Island, on November 10, 1780, free blacks established the African Union Society; in Massachusetts they formed The Sons of Africans Society in 1808. New York saw an African Society in 1809; Pittsburgh, an African Education Society in 1832; Boston, an African Lodge in 1787; and New York City, an African Marine Foundation in 1810. That these groups bore African names was no mere accident of simple naming. In the extant constitutions, preambles, laws, minutes, proceedings, resolutions, and reports of these African organizations, a budding "race consciousness" and sense of racial solidarity is openly expressed. Out of this sense of race-based community came the collective action that marked antebellum black pressure politics.

"Africa" did not simply provide the internal cohesion for these interest/pressure groups; it would also become a symbol of freedom and liberty. With the beginning of the emigration and colonization efforts, the influence of Africa directly reentered the contextual political realities of African Americans. The initial pioneering effort of Paul CUFFE, who personally returned thirty-eight free Negroes to Sierra Leone in 1815, was institutionalized (though substantially changed) in December 1816, when the AMERICAN COLONIZATION SOCIETY (ACS) was formed. Five years later, the society established the colony of Liberia. Although the two efforts had outwardly similar objectives, Cuffe sought Africa as a place of freedom and liberty. On the other hand, the motives of the society were at best mixed and questionable, since the society wished to send free blacks to Africa in part to eliminate what they saw as the anomalous position of the free black in the North. The implication that free blacks have no role to play in American society soon came under attack by African Americans, who saw the ACS as racist, and this served to catalyze their subsequent organizing efforts.

Finally, the late 1820s saw the beginning of African-American newspapers, which provided a forum for spokespersons who would take up the struggle on behalf of their "colored fellow citizens." (FREEDOM'S JOURNAL, founded in New York City in 1827, was the earliest.) The numerous efforts of such individuals and papers heralded not only a rising sense of solidarity and community but also vindicated the acts of pressure and protest in the revolutionary and the early national period that seemed, at first blush, so futile.

Thus elements of the African background provided the underpinning for fledgling African-American pressure group activity in the new nation by 1830. The first Negro convention was held on September 20, 1830, in Philadelphia, with delegates from seven states. Another convention met the next year, and black conventions subsequently were organized four times during the 1830s, three times in the 1840s, and twice in the 1850s. At the 1864 Syracuse, N.Y., national convention, the movement reorganized itself into the National Equal Rights League. The national convention movement directed, albeit in a rather unstable way, a mass self-help movement of the churches, mutual aid societies, and fraternal organizations, and took these efforts into the political area. With the emergence of such mass political action in both the electoral and protest areas, African-American politics had come of age.

The national organization, where possible, set up state and local affiliates. Some state and local auxiliaries pursued policies and directions independent of those of the national organization. When they were meeting and functioning properly, the national, state, and local bodies issued resolutions, petitions, prayers, and memorials addressed to state legislatures and to Congress. While their chief interest was the antislavery struggle, the conventions acted on other issues as well. Political rights such as suffrage, jury service, and repeal of discriminatory legislation were major concerns. Despite their support of abolitionist groups, the convention members also chided the AMERICAN ANTI-SLAVERY SOCIETY, founded in 1833, for its unwillingness to champion "social equality."

Temperance, education, and moral reform stood high on the agenda of many Negro conventions and allied groups throughout the era. Equally important was the fight for women's equality and voting rights. As early as Maria STEWART in the 1830s, African-American women played prominent roles in black politics. Just as many white feminists became politically committed through abolitionist activities, so black leaders from Sojourner TRUTH to Frederick Douglass attended feminist conferences and pressed for the end of gender discrimination.

The convention movement was supplemented by countless local political committees and pressure groups that campaigned for civil rights and educational opportunity. Black groups formed in the early 1830s, such as the Phoenix Society in New York City and the AMERICAN MORAL REFORM SOCIETY, based in Philadelphia, added civil rights petitioning to their temperance and educational efforts. Meanwhile, African Americans in New York City and Philadelphia organized committees to protest denials of equal suffrage and to stimulate black political involvement. African Americans in Boston successfully lobbied to overturn a state law fobidding racial intermarriage, and organized protests that desegregated most of the state's railroads. In 1855, the Legal Rights Association sued in a New York City court protesting segregated streetcars and won a judgment. In 1849 Benjamin Roberts pursued a test case challenging segregated schools in Boston to the Massachusetts Supreme Court. Although he lost, the state legislature integrated the schools in 1855.

ABOLITIONIST AMERICA

In December 1833 the American Anti-Slavery Society, the first national abolitionist organization, was founded in Philadelphia. This marked the awakening of abolition as a full-fledged sociopolitical movement, and it catapulted blacks into the center of the political system. The electoral efforts of most free blacks in this era were focused on their work for and participation in a host of antislavery third parties. They attended their conventions and served as low-level officers at the conventions, especially as secretaries. They succeeded in having resolutions and platforms adopted that called for equality. They campaigned for the standard-bearers of these parties. Where they could, they voted for these candidates. And in several states in the expanding new nation, these antislavery parties sought to have the state extend suffrage to free blacks, but to no avail.

When the first antislavery party, the Liberty party, was formed on April 1, 1840, at Albany, N.Y., it announced that its goal was "the absolute and unqualified divorce of the General Government from Slavery, and also the restoration of equality of rights, among men, in every state where the party exists or may exist." The Liberty party's leaders reached out to free blacks, and shortly after the founding of the party, influential black leaders began to associate with it, attending party conventions and providing what limited electoral support they could muster. In return, the Liberty Party welcomed black supporters into party councils and leadership positions. The brightest spot in the party's history was the election of John M. LANGSTON on the party's ticket to a township clerk position in Ohio in 1855. Langston's nomination for office was the first ever given an African American by a political party. Despite this achievement, the Liberty Party was unable to compete with subsequent abolitionist parties. Its numbers declined through the 1850s, and it dissolved in 1860.

African Americans also became involved in the Free Soil party. At its founding convention in Buffalo, N.Y., on August 9, 1848, the party adopted a platform calling for the exclusion of slavery from the District of Columbia and the territories of the United States, though it conceded the legality of slavery in existing states. While the party called for jury trials for captured fugitive slaves, it made no commitment to expanding black equality, and many of its leaders opposed black suffrage. Free blacks participated in the convention, and later in the campaign, despite the party's limited positions on equality and the liberation of slaves. Although unsuccessful in its initial presidential bid, the party tried again in 1852. This time the national nominating convention adopted a resolution favoring black suffrage, and elected Frederick Douglass secretary of the convention. Despite the work of Douglass and other free blacks, the party polled fewer votes than it had in 1848, and dissolved after the election.

There were other antislavery parties in which African Americans participated. Frederick Douglass attended the convention of the new National Liberty party in Buffalo, N.Y., on June 14–15, 1848. The party's poor performance in the 1848 presidential election—which may have been the consequence of its stiff competition from the Liberty party and the Free Soil party—led to its collapse soon afterward. Another party, the Political Abolition party, took up the struggle in 1856. It had an even more dismal showing than expected; it collected only 484 votes for its presidential candidate. It did not again contest a presidential election.

The antislavery parties were never large organizations, although they helped swing the balance in several elections. Their failure during the 1850s was largely the result of the entry of the Republican Party into the political fray. The Republicans captured the political imagination of many free blacks, and a significant degree of their support. In 1860 the Republican party candidate, Abraham Lincoln, won the presidency, with the overwhelming support of free blacks and attentive slaves.

EMIGRATIONIST POLITICS

Beginning in the 1840s, the African heritage began to influence African-American political participation and action in a new and more direct way, through the doctrine of African-American political nationalism. The historians John Bracey, Jr., August Meier, and Elliott Rudwick describe the dynamics of this era:

> In the 1840s a number of converging developments turned Negro ideologies in more nationalist directions: the essential failure of the antislavery movement to liberate the slaves; the evidences of racism among many white abolitionists . . . increasing trends toward disfranchisement and segregation in public accommodations in many of the northeastern states, combined with the continuing pattern of discrimination in the Old Northwest that made the black man's condition there similar to that in the South; and the growing hopelessness of the economic situation. . . .

One result of the growing estrangement of African Americans from the mainstream of American politics was the national convention movement's increasing withdrawal from interracial groups and endorsement of independent black political organizations. Of course, this trend did not contradict its members' goal of equality in the United States. While blacks were nationalistic about their color, and were determined to build separate black institutions, their nationalism did not preempt their demands for inclusion as Americans. Black institutions were created as a halfway measure, as a means to the end of integration.

The events of the 1850s aggravated the obstacles confronting African Americans. The Fugitive Slave Act of 1850 made life unsafe and dangerous for large numbers of free blacks, and the Kansas-Nebraska Act threatened to extend slavery into new territories. Finally, the U.S. Supreme Court's decision in the 1857 DRED SCOTT DECISION, that blacks had no rights as United States citizens and that a state could not forbid slavery, was responsible for convincing large numbers of black activists of the necessity for radical action. A few supported the idea of a violent overturning of the slave system, and threw their support to the white abolitionist John Brown, who planned a slave insurrection. At the same time, a number of African Americans mounted emigration and colonization efforts. Some emigrationists favored mass emigration to Africa. For them, Africa would be the place to create a great nation, a place where freedom and liberty would prevail and a place where an African nation might arise that would eventually rival that of America. Larger numbers moved to the relatively safe haven of Canada. Others favored Haiti, Central America, or other places. National emigration conventions were held in 1854, 1856, and 1858.

CONCLUSION

On the eve of the Civil War, the essential features of African-American political culture had taken form and had started to mature. The dual influences of America and Africa had converged in the era of abolitionism and black nationalism to shape a political culture that had one message: In a society where racism is a permanent feature, equality and liberty for

African Americans could not be left solely to the efforts of whites; instead, in a time of political and democratic restriction, a special role had to be played by African Americans themselves.

Reconstruction to the Present

During the Reconstruction era, stretching from 1865 through 1877, the nature of African-American politics was radically transformed. The Fifteenth Amendment, ratified in 1870, gave African-American men the right to vote. Before the Civil War only a segment of the African-American community in the North was allowed to participate in politics; during the Reconstruction era, the entire community was permitted to participate. The results were striking, electing twenty African-American congressmen, two senators, a governor, six lieutenant governors, numerous local officials, state legislators, and delegates to state constitutional conventions. In addition to the figures who served in official positions, Reconstruction also energized large elements of the African-American community in political struggles. How-

ever, the gains achieved during Reconstruction were largely overturned in the years after the political compromise of 1877, when federal troops were withdrawn from the southern states, where most African Americans lived.

By the turn of the century, most southern states had adopted poll taxes, literacy tests, and other measures that disfranchised the vast majority of their black populations. Segregation was rigidly imposed on African Americans, whose hard-won citizenship rights were largely ignored. Even in the northern states, where African Americans retained voting rights, de facto housing and employment discrimination eroded the dream of equality. From the 57th until the 70th congresses there were no African-Americans in the House or the Senate, and few local or state officials. In the face of such burdens, blacks organized what political protests they could.

The political struggle of African Americans from the end of Reconstruction to at least the 1960s, and in many ways to the present, has been focused on one goal: to reshape the political landscape so that the

Black Reconstruction members of Congress in 1872: (from left) Sen. Hiram Revels (R.-Miss.), Reps. Benjamin Turner (R.-Ala.), Robert C. DeLarge (R.-S.C.), Josiah T. Walls (R.-Fla.), Jefferson Long (R.-Ga.), Joseph H. Rainey (R.-S.C.), and Robert B. Elliot (R.-S.C.). (Photographs and Prints Division, Schomburg Center for Research in Black Culture, The New York Public Library, Astor, Lenox and Tilden Foundations)

political and economic liberties of African Americans would be restored. When this goal was unworkable through major party politics, some blacks turned in independent, and sometimes separatist, directions. As early as the 1880s, many blacks, particularly in the North, grew dissatisfied with the Republican party, which refused to act effectively against deteriorating race relations or to offer the black electorate patrongae commensurate with its voting support. Black activists such as T. Thomas FORTUNE and Peter H. CLARK urged African Americans to be politically independent and either explore the possibility of supporting the Democratic party or establish an independent political party. Neither party was generally prepared to offer significant rewards. The resulting frustration led some African Americans to eschew major party politics altogether.

THIRD PARTY POLITICS
Beginning in the 1870s, many black voters supported factions and splinter groups of the Republicans such as the National Republicans and the Greenback party, as well as statewide organizations such as Virginia's Readjusters. These groups generally opposed the tight-money, probusiness slant of the mainstream Republicans. While they supported racially liberal platforms and welcomed black electoral support, most of these groups were not interested in campaigning for black interests or soliciting black participation in party activities.

The first national third party that blacks supported was the Prohibition party, whose presidential campaigns attracted a solid core of black voters through the midtwentieth century. The Prohibition Party did not target civil rights issues, but their radical reform message encompassed black interests. Temperance had long been a concern of black leaders in an attempt to raise the moral image and economic standing of African Americans. The elite nature of the party, particularly in the South, offered blacks with middle-class aspirations a measure of status, and the movement's strong Christian ideology contributed to general ideals of racial harmony and fairness. During the 1884 and 1888 campaigns, Prohibitionists realized that blacks represented swing votes on temperance measures, so the party reached out to them, sponsoring interracial rallies with black speakers and inviting African Americans to join organizing committees and convention delegations. For example, the African Methodist Episcopal bishop Henry McNeal TURNER spoke for Prohibition Party candidates and was a delegate to the party's 1888 national convention. Philadelphia had a strong black Prohibitionist party in the late nineteenth century, at times supported by such stalwarts of black Philadelphia life as AME bishop Benjamin TANNER and physician

John Roy Lynch was a three-term Republican congressman from Mississippi in the 1870s and '80s. In pamphlets and memoirs, Lynch was a stalwart defender of the accomplishments of black Reconstruction-era politicians. (Photographs and Prints Division, Schomburg Center for Research in Black Culture, The New York Public Library, Astor, Lenox and Tilden Foundations)

Nathan MOSSELL. Also, the Prohibition Party generally opposed urban Democratic machines dominated by white ethnics, who were traditional antagonists of the black community. During the twentieth century, as the party grew more racially restrictive and black elites found other political channels, support for the Prohibitionists waned.

The Populist Party, the political arm of an agrarian movement of the 1890s, revolved around a platform of democratic reform, debt relief, and monetary expansion that appealed to southern and midwestern black farmers who supported party candidates for president and for state offices. Prominent southern blacks such as former Georgia state legislator Anthony Wilson supported the party. Many Populists, such as Tom Watson of Georgia, called for interracial economic unity and took radical positions in support of the legal rights of African Americans. Populists helped elect black officials, such as North Carolina congressman George White in 1896. Populist representatives often voted funds for black education. However many white Populists were ambivalent about black participation and voting support, fearing white racist backlash, and were cautious about challenging discrimination. With the help of voting fraud and manipulation in Black Belt areas, southern Democrats beat back Populist challenges during the 1890s. Some Populist leaders, such as the South Carolina senator "Pitchfork" Ben Tillman, had rarely disguised their racial demagoguery. Others, such as Georgia's Tom Walton, underwent a notorious transformation, from supporting interracial cooperation during the heyday of the Populist era to becoming a virulent racist and defender of lynching. Black populists also despaired of joint black-white efforts. John B. Payner, a Texas Populist who was one of the party's leading orators, became an embittered supporter of separate black institutions, acknowledging that the price for their survival was a subservient relation to white authorities.

As a result of their own entrenched racism, many Populists responded by supporting black disfranchisement campaigns. Despite the reversal of southern Populist leaders on black issues, small numbers of blacks continued to support the declining party during its presidential campaigns of 1900, 1904, and 1908.

During most of the twentieth century, when the vast majority of blacks in the South were unable to vote, the center of black voting strength and political influence shifted to the urban North. The record of black activity in third parties during the first half of the twentieth century reveals a strong tie between black political participation and the politics of eco-

nomic protest. A few blacks offered support for candidates running on economic reform platforms, including the Progressive (Bull Moose) party in 1912 and the Progressive party in 1924, despite the refusal of party leaders to seat black delegates or to reach out to black voters. However, in 1948 Henry Wallace, running for president on the Progressive party ticket, campaigned strongly for black votes. Wallace made civil rights a centerpiece of his platform and organized integrated tours of the South. However, while he was supported by such black leaders as Paul ROBESON and W. E. B. DU BOIS, a strong Democratic party platform on civil rights sharply reduced Wallace's appeal.

Throughout this period, the Communist, Socialist, and other workers' parties repeatedly sought and gained black support for their ideologies and platforms. In the late nineteenth century a number of African-American leaders, such as Peter H. Clark of Cincinnati and T. Thomas Fortune, expressed sympathy with socialist ideas. The Socialist party, founded in 1901, gained few black converts in its first two decades, though W. E. B. Du Bois expressed strong sympathy with socialism as early as 1907 and briefly joined the party in 1912. It vigorously denounced the exploitation of workers, but subordinated race to class in its policies, refusing to recognize the special problems facing African Americans. Many of its leaders held racist views, and while the party platform opposed disfranchisement and leaders such as Eugene V. Debs publicly opposed racial discrimination, the Socialists offered no special support for black interests. After World War I, the party's platform became more inclusive. Larger numbers of blacks, inspired by African-American Socialist orators such as A. Philip RANDOLPH, H. H. HARRISON, Cyril V. BRIGGS, Richard MOORE, Chandler OWEN, and Frank CROSSWAITH, moved to support party candidates.

The Communist party of the U.S.A., formed in 1921, shared the class-based approach of the Socialists. By the end of the 1920s, in accordance with Moscow's ideological support of non-Western nationalism, the party developed a platform calling for worker unity in the North and African-American "self-determination" in the southern Black Belt. While black party membership was always low, the Communists attempted to exert a disproportionate influence on black life. Unlike the Socialists, the Communists'—especially in the South—actively shifting position on the Nazi-Soviet alliance destroyed its southern base. The decline of the Communist and Socialist parties after 1950 was accompanied by the formation of several minor Marxist political parties, notably the Trotskyist-influenced Socialist Workers' party, beginning in the 1950s.

John Conyers has served his Detroit district in the U.S. House of Representatives since 1965. His thirty-year tenure is the longest for any African-American member of Congress. (AP/Wide World Photos)

Probably the most influential African-American Trotskyist was the West Indian historian and theorist C. L. R. JAMES, who lived in the United States from 1938 until his expulsion in 1953. Tiny parties such as the Workers' World party drew black support during the 1980s. These parties have actively sought a black constituency through powerful denunciations of racism and integrated leadership but have been unable, due in part to lack of money for broad-based campaigns, to draw more than a tiny percentage of the black vote.

Beginning in the 1960s, various New Left and other radical parties without large black constituencies have sponsored black candidates for political office. For example, in 1968 during the height of the antiwar movement, Dick GREGORY, an African American, ran for president on the Freedom and Peace party's ticket. In 1992 Leonora B. Fulani, running as the presidential candidate of the New Alliance party, became the first black minor party presidential

Charles Evers leaves his car to vote in Fayette, Miss.'s municipal elections. Evers was a candidate for mayor of the city. (AP/Wide World Photos)

candidate to qualify for federal matching campaign funds.

SEPARATIST PARTIES

The antimainstream impulse is largely the consequence of the political discrimination that the white majority in various states has used to block the entrance of blacks into mainstream political parties. An equally significant development, however, is the appearance and growth of independent black political parties and factions throughout the twentieth century. The southern states, particularly Mississippi, have provided the most promising conditions for these independent parties. Yet the appearance of national black separatist parties in 1904, 1960, and 1992 indicates that the impulse is not limited to the South.

The first black party was the Negro Protective party, formed in Ohio in 1897, but this was not a truly independent organization. Taking advantage of black discontent over Republican inattention to black needs, the Ohio Democratic party financed a small group of black Democrats and independents, who formed a party and ran a slate of candidates for governor and lesser state offices on a platform of civil rights and control of white mobs. Many "party" candidates were paid off by Republicans to withdraw their candidacies so as not to cut into the black Republican vote. The party's gubernatorial candidate, Sam J. Lewis, received only 477 votes. The few remaining candidates for other posts did even worse.

The first nationally based black political party was the National Liberty party, which grew out of local Civil and Personal Liberty leagues. On July 5, 1904, a convention of the leagues was organized at St. Louis and was attended by delegations from thirty-six states. Iowa editor George Edwin Taylor was chosen as the party's presidential candidate. The party gained only a few votes, and it disappeared after the election.

Although two independent black presidential candidates ran in Alabama in 1960, on the ticket of the Afro-American Party, and received 1,485 votes, the next serious attempt to build a nationwide black party came with the formation of the Freedom Now Party. Organized by African-American lawyer Conrad Lynn as a national party in 1963 at a convention in Washington, D.C., during the famous March for Jobs and Freedom, it ran candidates in elections in New York, California, and Connecticut. When these candidates did poorly in November elections, it switched strategy to concentrate its efforts exclusively on Michigan. In 1964 the party ran a slate of thirty-nine candidates for statewide office in that state, hoping to demonstrate its electoral strength and to educate black voters. All the candidates were badly beaten, however, and the party dissolved soon after the election.

The Rev. Jesse Jackson addresses the annual convention of People United to Save Humanity (PUSH), of which he is the director, Chicago, July 9, 1981. Jackson compared Ronald Reagan's budget policies to cyanide-laced drinks that he said would kill America's economy in the future if the country continued to swallow them. (AP/Wide World Photos)

In the years after 1964, black activists tried on numerous occasions to establish national black parties, but without success. In 1968 the Peace and Freedom Party (not to be confused with the aforementioned Freedom and Peace party, which appeared in 7 states and got nearly 48,000 votes for Dick Gregory) was created. Run by an alliance of white leftists and members of the BLACK PANTHER PARTY, the party selected Eldridge CLEAVER as its presidential candidate. It was on the ballot in some 5 states, and Cleaver received almost 37,000 votes. However, the alliance disintegrated soon after the election, although some candidates ran on the Peace and Freedom ticket in California statewide elections in 1970. In 1976 the National Black Political Assembly, an outgrowth of the 1972 National Black Convention, formed the National Black Independent Political Party. However, handicapped by poor funding and bad management, it succeeded neither in persuading well-known black elected officials to run for president, nor in gaining sufficient signatures to place the party slate on the ballot in any state. In 1980 the National Black Independent Political party held a founding convention to form a nucleus of support for a 1984 campaign but was unable to overcome internal debate, and its platform was overshadowed by Jesse Jackson's independent black candidacy for the presidential nomination of the Democratic party. In 1992, after Jackson declined to seek the Democratic party nomination, Ron Daniels, former chair of the National Black Political Assembly, ran for president on the Campaign for a New Tomorrow ticket, but had difficulty getting his name on the ballot in many states and finished poorly.

More notably successful have been satellite black political organizations. While black-supported and -run, these have oriented themselves within existing party structures and groups. During the end of the nineteenth century and the first part of the twentieth century, this independent spirit expressed itself in the form of numerous "Black and Tan" factions in Republican parties of southern states such as Texas, Louisiana, and Tennessee. Black delegates to state conventions, opposed by "lily-white" delegations, would try to gain their groups a fair share of patronage and political influence. If defeated at the state level, they would form their own slate of delegates and candidates for local office, and appeal to the national conventions for recognition. Often, deals would be struck. Occasionally, as in Louisiana and Mississippi in the 1920s, the Black and Tan faction would win clear-cut control of patronage.

Most factions petered out by the turn of the century, however, as increasing numbers of blacks were disfranchised or left the Republicans and as the party courted white southern support. Sometimes party presidential candidates such as Theodore Roosevelt would recognize the black delegates, but once nominated refuse to award them their share of the spoils. In 1920 the Texas Black and Tans, tired of this strategy, went so far as to run their own candidates for the position of Republican presidential electors, receiving some 27,000 votes. In Virginia in the early 1920s a "lily-black" party ran newspaper editor John R. MITCHELL for governor. The Tennessee and Texas Black and Tans disappeared in the early 1930s, as patronage and national party support dried up.

During the 1930s, southern blacks turned to the Democratic Party. However, excluded by white-dominated state parties, they began building shadow parties. The first example of this was the South Carolina Progressive Democratic party. Formed at a convention in Columbia in May 1944, the party was designed to build support for Franklin D. Roosevelt's Democratic candidacy while evading the state's white primary. Its representatives attended the national convention in an unsuccessful attempt to unseat the regular state delegation, and sponsored a black candidate for U.S. senator, who won some 4,500 votes in the election. While the party continued after the

Carol Moseley-Braun, the first black woman elected to the U.S. Senate, at her victory celebration in Chicago in 1992. With her is her son Matthew, fifteen. (AP/Wide World Photos)

election, it reformed as a political caucus group, working in voter registration and unsuccessfully challenging the regular state delegation at the 1948 and 1956 conventions before being absorbed completely into the state party. (In 1970 South Carolina blacks, dissatisfied with the fused party, formed a short-lived new political party, the United Citizens' party.)

Two notable examples of satellite parties are the Mississippi Freedom Democratic party (MFDP)) and the National Democratic party of Alabama (NDPA). The MFDP, created in 1964, was formed as part of an effort by the Student Nonviolent Coordinating Committee (SNCC) and other civil rights groups to dramatize the state's denial of voting rights to blacks and involve long-disfranchised Mississippi African Americans in the political process. The MFDP sponsored candidates for office in the Mississippi Democratic party primary, and sent a delegation to the 1964 Democratic national convention, urging without success that their delegation be seated in place of the white-only regular state delegation. In 1968, however, the MFDP [reorganized as the Loyal Dem-

ocratic Party of Mississippi (LDPM)] succeeded in unseating the Mississippi delegation. While the party continued to operate into the 1970s, it was unable to elect large numbers of candidates to state or local office and eventually became part of the state Democratic Party, without a distinct status. The NDPA, one of a number of black political organizations in Alabama during the 1960s, was organized in 1968 to remedy the failure of the Alabama Democratic Party to open its organization to African Americans. In that year, the NDPA, inspired by the success of the MFDP, successfully fought to obtain recognition as the official state delegation at the Democratic national convention. While its platform and activity pushed the regular party into a more progressive racial posture, the NDPA was also unable to survive the 1970s as an independent black political organization.

Despite the overwhelming lack of political success of third parties and independent movements, their value has been in displaying the fitness of black candidates and sponsoring their inclusion in American political culture in periods when and in areas where, if dependent on mainstream political parties and institutions alone, African Americans would clearly have been underrepresented in this sphere of the American political process.

The independent black political movements in particular have provided the community with its best opportunity to compete in the general election for seats in the U.S. Senate. The mainstream parties have not yet provided adequate support or opportunity. Of the twenty African-American senatorial candidates in general elections from 1920 to 1990, seventeen ran on third-party or African-American party tickets. Similarly, of all the African-American gubernatorial candidates in general elections, the vast majority were sponsored on either third-party or African-American party tickets, mostly the latter. The first such African-American gubernatorial candidate in this country was Sam J. Lewis in Ohio in the 1897 state election; he ran as the candidate of the Negro Protective Party. Through 1990, L. Douglas Wilder, Mervyn Dymally, and George Brown are the *only* African Americans to have received a major party nomination for governor or lieutenant governor and survive until the general election. At the city level, African-American mayors prior to the Voting Rights Act of 1965 had to run on small African-American or third-party tickets to play a political role. As the black percentage of the population of major cities has increased, it has become easier to elect black mayors.

Similarly, in majority black districts, for the state legislature it has been relatively easy to elect black candidates. Also, seventy-one African Americans were elected to the U.S. House of Representatives, all on major party tickets, between 1865 and 1992.

Separatist and independent parties reveal that African Americans have never completely forgotten or abandoned their African heritage. Although African Americans have more often and more strongly supported the major and minor parties, they shared the frustration and search for channels of political power that drove others to form separatist groups. Even if it remained a minor channel of blacks' political activity, the independent impulse shows a stubborn ability to survive.

THE DUAL IMPULSES IN AFRICAN-AMERICAN POLITICS IN THE FUTURE

Just why the impulses motivating African-American politics assume these patterns may be illuminated by the remarks of Samuel Du Bois Cook, who writes, "Black political parties are, after all, expressions of radically abnormal conditions and consequences—basic defects in the political system. They have had a special mission—correction of those fundamental dif-

(Left to right) Former New York mayor David Dinkins; Earl Graves, publisher of *Black Enterprise Magazine;* Ron Brown, President Clinton's secretary of commerce. (Allford/Trotman Associates)

ferences. . . ." (Cook 1972). He continues, "Black political parties fostered the notion and ideal of self-help, self-propulsion, group consciousness and solidarity, and political sensitivity, awareness and appreciation."

Harold CRUSE offers these thoughts on African-American political parties as a means to achieve liberation:

> The politics of ethnicity is more exactly the "politics of plurality." The demise of the civil rights era, beginning with 1980, points to political organization as the only alternative. Political organization also permits a renewed opportunity to make up for longstanding organizational deficiencies that have hampered black progress in economic, cultural, educational, and other social fields.

Cruse asserts that the "only option left" is to "organize an independent black party." Moreover, he argues, the ultimate aim of this black party would not be solely for the "expedient purposes of electoral politics." As he sees it, the African-American political party should not simply be an electoral political entity, but among other things a cultural political entity—that is, concerned with preserving those crucial values emanating from what we have here called the background impulses, such as self-help, self-propulsion, group consciousness, self-determination, and self-liberation.

Which of the two motors driving African-American politics—the mainstream or the separatist independent—will come to dominate the political lives of America's black men and black women remains to be seen. Clearly, the second impulse will continue as long as there is political discrimination and racism in the American political system. The separatist impulse, moreover, gives African-American politics much of its unique flavor and may prove to be the most enduring cultural legacy of African-American political activism.

REFERENCES

AMER, MILDRED L. Black Members of the United States Congress. Washington, D.C., 1991.

APTHEKER, HERBERT, ed. A Documentary History of the Negro People in the United States. New York, 1951.

———. "Slave Guerrilla Warfare" and "Buying Freedom." In Herbert Aptheker, ed. To Be Free: Studies in American Negro History. New York, 1948, pp. 11–30.

BELL, HOWARD H. A Survey of the Negro Convention Movement, 1830–1861. New York, 1969.

BERLIN, IRA. Slaves Without Masters: The Free Negro in the Antebellum South. New York, 1974.

BRACEY, JOHN, JR., AUGUST MEIER, and ELLIOTT RUDWICK, eds. Black Nationalism in America. New York, 1970.

BROOKE, EDWARD. The Challenge of Change: Crisis in Our Two-Party System. Boston, 1966.

COOK, SAMUEL DU BOIS, Black Political Parties: An Historical and Political Analysis. New York, 1972.

CRUSE, HAROLD. Plural but Equal: Study of Blacks and Minorities and the American Plural Society. New York, 1987.

DRAPER, THEODORE. The Rediscovery of Black Nationalism. New York, 1970.

FIELD, PHYLLIS F. The Politics of Race in New York: The Struggle for Black Suffrage in the Civil War Era. Ithaca, N.Y., 1982.

FLEMING, G. JAMES. An All Negro Ticket in Baltimore. New York, 1960.

HAMILTON, CHARLES V., ed. The Black Experience in American Politics. New York, 1968.

HENRY, CHARLES. Culture and African American Politics. Bloomington, Ind., 1990.

LINK, ARTHUR S. "The Negro as a Factor in the Campaign of 1912." Journal of Negro History 32 (1947): 81–89.

LOGAN, RAYFORD, and IRVING COHEN. The American Negro. Boston, 1920.

MERRITT, R. L. Symbols of American Community, 1735–1775. New Haven, Conn., 1966.

OLBRICH, EMIL. The Development of Sentiment on Negro Suffrage to 1860. Madison, Wis., 1912.

PORTER, DOROTHY, ed. Early Negro Writing, 1760–1837. Boston, 1971.

———. Negro Protest Pamphlets: A Compendium. New York, 1969.

PORTER, KIRK, and DONALD JOHNSON, eds. National Party Platforms, 1840–1964. Urbana, Ill., 1966.

REIDY, JOSEPH. "Negro Election Day and Black Community Life in New England, 1750–1860." In Kenneth L. Kusmer, ed. Black Communities and Urban Development in America 1720–1990: The Colonial and Early National Period. New York, 1991, p. 234.

SCOTT, JAMES C. Domination and the Acts of Resistance: Hidden Transcripts. New Haven, Conn., 1990.

SMITH, ROBERT S. "The Black Congressional Delegation." Western Political Quarterly 34 (1981): 203–221.

SWEET, LEONARD I. Black Images of America, 1784–1870. New York, 1976.

THOMAS, LAMONT. Rise to Be a People: A Biography of Paul Cuffe. Urbana, Ill., 1986.

WALTON, HANES, JR. Black Politics: A Theoretical and Structural Analysis. Philadelphia, 1972.

———. "Black Presidential Participation and the Critical Election Theory." In Lorenzo Morris, ed. The Social and Political Implications of the 1984 Jesse Jackson Presidential Campaign. New York, 1990, pp. 49–64.

———. The Negro in Third Party Politics. Philadelphia, 1969.

WESLEY, CHARLES. Neglected History. Washington, D.C., 1969.

WHITE, JOHN. *Black Leadership in America, 1895–1968.* New York, 1985.

WHITE, SHANE. " 'It Was a Proud Day': African Americans, Festivals, and Parades in the North, 1741–1831." *Journal of American History* 81 (1994): 13–50.

HANES WALTON, JR.
MERVYN DYMALLY

Polk, Prentice Herman (November 25, 1898–December 29, 1984), photographer. Prentice Herman Polk was born in Bessemer, Ala., and began drawing as a child. He started his study of photography through a correspondence course that he paid for with ten dollars change he mistakenly received after buying a candy bar at a local store. From 1916 to 1920 he attended Tuskegee Institute in Tuskegee, Ala., and studied photography under C. M. BATTEY, the Institute's official photographer. Polk relocated to Chicago in 1924 and worked as an apprentice to African-American photographer Fred Jensen. For three years Polk sold his photographs door to door throughout Chicago; in 1927 he returned to Tuskegee and opened a photography studio.

In 1928, following the death of Battey, Polk was appointed to the faculty of the Tuskegee photography department. From 1933 to 1938, he served as head of the department and was the school's official photographer. Polk relocated to Atlanta in 1938 and opened a photography studio, but his family remained in Tuskegee, and within a year he rejoined them at their home. In 1939, he opened a studio in Tuskegee and again began serving as Tuskegee Institute's official photographer, a post he held into the 1980s.

Polk's opus comprised formal studio portraits, genre scenes, images of sharecroppers, and official school pictures for Tuskegee. He created photographs of African Americans in the Tuskegee community, as well as such notable visitors as Mary McLeod BETHUNE, Roland HAYES, Paul ROBESON, Henry Ford, W. C. HANDY, and Eleanor Roosevelt. His photographic studies of George Washington CARVER chronicled the success of Carver's experiments. Polk was especially interested in representing the familiar and the commonplace through his photographs of the everyday life of Alabama's former slaves and sharecropper families.

In 1981, an exhibition of Polk's photographs was held at Washington, D.C.'s Corcoran Gallery, and his work was also shown in museums in New York City, Los Angeles, Washington, and Birmingham, Alabama. Polk retired in 1982 and died in Tuskegee three years later.

REFERENCES

DUVALL, LYNN. "P. H. Polk: Carry Me Home." *Southern Exposure* 13 (July/August 1985): 38–45.

SUPER, GEORGE LEE, MICHAEL GARDEN, and NANCY MARSHALL, eds. *P.H. Polk: Photographs.* Atlanta, 1980.

WILLIS-THOMAS, DEBORAH. *Black Photographers, 1840–1940: An Illustrated Bio-Bibliography.* New York, 1985.

DEBORAH WILLIS-THOMAS

Pollard, Frederick Douglass "Fritz" (January 27, 1894–May 11, 1986), football player and coach. Fritz Pollard was born in Chicago to a family of accomplished athletes; his father was an outstanding boxer and his older brothers were prominent FOOTBALL players. He followed in their footsteps and became a star football and track athlete in high school and college. He was a standout professional football player and the first African-American coach in the National Football League (NFL). When he died in 1986, no other African American had been named head coach of an NFL team.

Pollard was an exceptional running back at the Albert G. Lane Technical High School in Chicago. He also excelled at track—he was the top hurdler and

Fritz Pollard, a College All-Star at Brown University during the 1910s and in the 1920s the first African-American coach in the NFL, at his alma mater in 1954 as he is inducted into the National Football Hall of Fame. (AP/Wide World Photos)

quarter-miler in Cook County, Ill., for three straight years—and played baseball (Porter 1987).

After he completed high school, the wealthy Rockefeller family was instrumental in getting Pollard to attend Brown University—John D. Rockefeller's alma mater—where Pollard played football and ran track. At 5 feet 8 inches and 150 pounds, Pollard was a sterling running back and defensive player on the 1915 Bruins team that met Washington State in the Rose Bowl (then known as the Tournament of Roses) game. On January 1, 1916, Pollard became the first of many African Americans to participate in the Rose Bowl.

The next season, his elusive running propelled Brown to victory in its first eight games and to its first-ever victory over Harvard. Following the 1916 season, Pollard was the second African American to be named All-American in football. (He was preceded by Harvard's William LEWIS, who was selected in 1892).

Although he was a remarkable athlete, perhaps Pollard's greatest accomplishment was in a nonplayer position. In 1920, he coached the Akron Pros to an undefeated season and the championship of the American Professional Football Association (APFA). When the APFA became the NFL, Pollard again led the Pros to a winning season.

Throughout his athletic career—from high school through the professional ranks—Pollard faced discrimination from hostile fans who often yelled "kill the nigger," opposing players who sought to injure him because of their antipathy toward African Americans, and restaurant and hotel owners who refused him service and lodging. He would later lament, "Jackie Robinson had an easy time next to me." Still, he excelled at every level in football and became a role model for many African Americans involved in sport.

REFERENCES

PORTER, DAVID L. *Biographical Dictionary of American Sports: Football.* Westport, Conn., 1987.

RIFFENBURGH, BEAU. *The Official NFL Encyclopedia.* New York, 1986.

RUST, ART, and EDNA RUST. *Art Rust's Illustrated History of the Black Athlete.* Garden City, N.Y., 1985.

OTHELLO HARRIS

Pomare, Eleo (1937–), choreographer, dancer, teacher. Before moving to Harlem at the age of ten, Eleo Pomare spent his childhood in Cartagena, Colombia, San Andres, and Panama. After receiving a diploma from the High School of Performing Arts in

New York City, he continued his dance training with Louis Horst, José Limón, and Curtis James, and by 1958 was directing his first company. Through a John Hay Whitney Fellowship, Pomare spent two years (1962–1964) studying initially with Kurt Jones in West Germany and later with Expressionists in Holland. There he organized a second company that was well received in Holland, Sweden, Germany, and Norway.

By 1965, Pomare returned to the United States seeking an artistic connection to American culture. His company performed throughout the United States and later toured successfully in Asia, Africa, Canada, Spain, Australia, and the West Indies.

Pomare's distinctive style is characterized by unexpected shapes that twist, bend, fall, and lean in continuous organic movement. With a keen musical sense, he creates sculptures-in-motion that extend, expand, and slice through space. They can be lush and lyrical, or bold, driving, and direct. Some of his characteristic works include *Missa Luba* (1965), *Blues for the Jungle* (1966) and *Las Desenamoradas* (1967).

Pomare often creates dances based on visual and literary works or socio-political issues. In 1988, he

Eleo Pomare portrays a drug addict in a performance of *Blues for the Jungle* (1966), as choreographed by Pomare. (Photographs and Prints Division, Schomburg Center for Research in Black Culture, The New York Public Library, Astor, Lenox and Tilden Foundations)

was selected by the American Dance Festival to participate in a three-year project entitled "The Black Tradition in American Modern Dance" set up to showcase and preserve modern dance classics by African-American choreographers. He has produced dances for the Alvin AILEY American Dance Theater, the Dayton Contemporary Dance Company, The National Ballet of Holland, Balletinstituttet (Oslo, Norway), the Cleo Parker-Robinson Dance Company, the Australian Contemporary Dance Company, and the Ballet Palacio das Artes (Belo, Horizonte, Brazil).

As a founder and the first artistic director of Dancemobile (1967), Pomare helped bring free professional dance concerts to the streets of New York City. For his outstanding contributions to modern dance, January 7, 1987 was declared Eleo Pomare Day by the Borough President of Manhattan. Pomare is the recipient of a Guggenheim Fellowship and several awards from the National Endowment of the Arts.

REFERENCES

EMERY, LYNNE FAULEY. *Black Dance in the United States From 1619–1970.* California, 1972.
ESTRADA, RIC. "3 Leading Negro Artists and How They Feel About Dance in the Community." *Dancemagazine* (November 1968): 45–60.
GOLDEN, BERNETTE. "Eleo Pomare Dance Company." *Black Creation* 4, 2 (Winter 1973): 16–18.
LONG, RICHARD A. *The Black Tradition in American Dance.* New York, 1989.

JACKIE MALONE

Poole, Elijah.   *See* Muhammad, Elijah.

Poor, Salem (c. 1758–?), Revolutionary War soldier. Salem Poor was born free in Massachusetts, probably in 1758. We know little about his early life, except that he married young. In 1775, he left his wife to enlist in the Massachusetts Militia. Following the outbreak of war at Lexington and Concord, he joined the Patriot forces in Boston. On June 17, 1775, Poor served at the Battle of Bunker Hill (actually fought on Breed's Hill), helping to repulse several British charges. Some later accounts have credited him with the killing of British Lt. Col. James Abercrombie.

So exceptional was Poor's bravery that on December 5, 1775, fourteen Massachusetts officers signed a petition to the General Court, the colony's legislature, which stated, "A Negro Man Called Salem Poor . . . in the late Battle of Charleston, behaved like an Experienced Officer, as Well as an Excellent Soldier, to Set Forth Particulars of his Conduct Would Be tedious, Wee Would Only begg leave to say in the person of this Sd. Negro Centers a Brave & gallant Soldier . . ." The petition suggested the Continental Congress offer Poor "The Reward due to so great and Distinguisht a Caracter." There is no record of any reward actually given to Poor.

In June 1775, Gen. George Washington barred black soldiers from military service, but permitted those already serving, such as Poor, to finish their tours of duty. At the end of 1775, Washington reversed his order. Poor reenlisted and served at least through 1776, seeing action at the Battle of White Plains and retreating to the winter camp at Valley Forge. Nothing is known of his later life. African-American historians have often pointed to Poor's heroism as an example of the African-American contribution to the nation's founding. Poor appeared on a U.S. commemorative postal stamp in 1975.

REFERENCE

QUARLES, BENJAMIN. *The Negro in the American Revolution.* Williamsburg, Va., 1961.

GREG ROBINSON

Poor People's Campaign.   The Poor People's Washington Campaign was conceived in 1967 by the Rev. Dr. Martin Luther KING, Jr., and other SOUTHERN CHRISTIAN LEADERSHIP CONFERENCE activists as a means of extending the civil rights agenda to include broad-based demands for economic justice. In the context of massive unrest in urban black communities, King and his colleagues felt that constitutional rights were inadequate to alleviate the crushing poverty and exploitation still faced by the majority of African Americans. At the same time, with the strategy of peaceful protest fast losing ground among the urban poor, they were eager to conduct a campaign that would reassert the legitimacy of a nonviolent approach to social change. In a mood of deep pessimism, the Poor People's Campaign was born.

Initially, the campaign's primary goal was to achieve federal legislation that would ensure full employment, establish a guaranteed income, and promote construction of low-income housing. To that end, organizers intended to bring thousands of poor people from a variety of racial and ethnic backgrounds to Washington, D.C., where they would conduct massive civil disobedience demonstrations and disrupt the city until the government acceded to their demands. The campaign would dramatize the urgency of the poor's plight through mass demonstrations and the erection of a tent city within plain sight of the federal government. The campaign, declared King, would highlight the need for a "new turn toward greater economic justice" in a society more concerned with property and profits than with people.

The campaign was set to begin on April 22, 1968. While the planning stage had been marked by sharp dissension within SCLC's ranks about the wisdom and feasibility of such an effort, King had insisted on pushing ahead with the project. He interrupted final preparations in order to travel to Memphis, Tenn., where he supported striking sanitation workers. After his assassination there on April 4, the SCLC, now under the untested leadership of the Rev. Ralph ABERNATHY, decided to press forward with the campaign as a fitting tribute to King's memory.

The first group of travelers to Washington arrived on April 28; they were later joined by caravans from Tennessee, New Mexico, Chicago, the Mississippi Delta, and elsewhere. With a permit to house 3,000 people on a fifteen-acre strip of land in West Potomac Park, the construction of Resurrection City began on May 13; its population peaked at 2,500 in late May.

From there, organizers led daily sojourns to federal agencies, presenting demands that outlined a predominantly economic agenda.

The highlight of the campaign was Solidarity Day, which drew a crowd of 50,000–100,000 (according to press and police estimates) to the Lincoln Memorial on June 19 for music and speakers, including Coretta Scott King. Rev. Abernathy, in his speech, underscored the need for economic justice and an end to racism. Though he acknowledged that his effort did not match King's, Abernathy believed he had solidified his own position at SCLC's helm and that the campaign had successfully brought together the nation's poor and galvanized grassroots efforts to eradicate poverty.

From the start, however, the campaign was plagued by crises—timing problems, lack of coordination, inadequate resources, poor leadership, the absence of a clearly focused program, and interethnic frictions. Demonstrations at government agencies were spottily attended, and they failed to produce the mass arrests organizers had hoped would mobilize the community and lead to nationwide boycotts. Resurrection City was marred by heavy rains that lasted throughout most of the campaign, and it was not the model of nonviolence and interracial harmony that

Sign-carrying participants in the southern leg of the Poor People's Campaign march through Atlanta, Ga., on the way to Washington, D.C., May 10, 1968. (AP/Wide World Photos)

King had envisioned; by June 6, only three hundred residents remained. In addition, internal disputes over direction and goals divided action-oriented militants from more cautious figures such as Bayard RUSTIN, who opposed the use of civil disobedience.

At the same time, campaigners faced growing hostility from local and national government leaders. Before the Poor People's Campaign had even begun, it had been roundly criticized by President Lyndon B. Johnson and by moderate civil rights leaders such as NATIONAL ASSOCIATION FOR THE ADVANCEMENT OF COLORED PEOPLE Executive Secretary Roy WILKINS. Southern congressional leaders had sought to prevent the mass mobilization from taking place, and local media had stirred fears of insurrection if large numbers of poor descended on the city *en masse*. Black Mayor Walter WASHINGTON arranged for police training in riot control before the marchers arrived. As the campaign continued through June, the patience of those in power wore increasingly thin; the Justice Department refused a second extension of Resurrection City's permit, and police not only began to respond violently to demonstrators, they launched an unprovoked tear-gas attack on the encampment itself.

On June 19, Rev. Abernathy declared, "Today, Solidarity Day, is not the end of the Poor People's Campaign. In fact, today is really only our beginning." But just five days later, as hundreds of protestors were being arrested at the Capitol grounds, the tent city was surrounded by more than 1,500 police, who evacuated and sealed off the camp. Organizers and participants straggled home to continue the struggle. The campaign had not achieved its goals, and its failure helped bring to a close the civil rights era in which Martin Luther King had been so instrumental.

REFERENCES

FAGER, CHARLES. *Uncertain Resurrection: The Poor People's Washington Campaign.* Grand Rapids, Mich., 1969.

GARROW, DAVID. *Bearing the Cross: Martin Luther King, Jr. and the Southern Christian Leadership Conference.* New York, 1986.

GILBERT, BEN W., et al. *Ten Blocks from the White House: Anatomy of the Washington Riots of 1968.* New York, 1968.

KING, MARTIN LUTHER, JR. *Where Do We Go from Here? Chaos or Community.* Boston, 1967.

MARSHALL HYATT

Population.   *See* Migration/Population.

Port Chicago Mutiny.   On July 17, 1944, a massive explosion destroyed the Port Chicago naval ammunition base on the Sacramento River near San Francisco Bay, killing 320 naval personnel and civilians. Of the 320 dead, 202 were black ammunition loaders. Because of the Navy's official policy of segregation, black enlistees at Port Chicago were restricted to ammunition loading, the most dangerous and physically demanding work at the base. None of the surviving ammunition loaders were given leave after the explosion; three weeks later 328 of them were ordered to return to their jobs at the rebuilt pier. The men refused, and 258 of them were arrested and held under guard on a prison barge. Within a few months, fifty of the men were court-martialed, convicted of mutiny, and given sentences from eight to fifteen years' imprisonment.

Soon after the mutiny trial, the NAACP Legal Defense Fund took up the case, waged a publicity campaign on behalf of the convicted men, and directed their appeal before the Judge Advocate General of the Navy in 1945. At the appeal, NAACP Legal Defense Fund director Thurgood MARSHALL introduced evidence that black enlistees at Port Chicago were restricted to the most dangerous work, given no special training in ammunition loading, subjected to forced competition by the officers, and systematically barred from receiving promotion. Despite Marshall's efforts, the convictions were upheld.

The fifty Port Chicago mutineers were released from prison in 1946, but were held on Navy ships for several months as a "probationary period" before receiving dishonorable discharges from the service. The status of the discharges was later changed to honorable, but the convictions were never overturned.

REFERENCE

ALLEN, ROBERT L. *The Port Chicago Mutiny.* New York, 1989.

THADDEUS RUSSELL

Porter, Charles Ethan C. (c. 1847–March 6, 1923), painter, educator. Born in either 1847 or 1848 around Rockville or Hartford, Conn., Charles Porter was typical of late nineteenth-century African-American professional artists in being the child of free northern parents. From 1869 to 1873, he studied at the National Academy of Design, possibly the first black student at the country's premier art school. In the 1870s he began to exhibit still lifes.

Three years after returning to Hartford in 1878, Porter traveled to Europe, with a letter of introduction from Mark Twain. He lived in Paris for three years, but neither enrolled in the École des Beaux Arts nor exhibited in the annual salons, government-sponsored institutions that offered official sanction to artists. However, he clearly studied such contemporary artists as the French painter of flowers Henri Fantin-Latour. Porter spent the rest of his life in Hartford and New York, where the conservative tastes of his patrons eventually stultified his style. In his later years, he was forced to barter his paintings for food. Porter fell from critical view after his death in 1923, and his reputation did not recover until the mid-1980s. The extant works reveal the art of a deft handler of paint who thrived on the transient nuances of flowers and fruit. His critical reception has suffered as much from his having been an African-American artist of the seemingly minor genre of still-life painting as from his relative isolation in Hartford, away from artistic centers that could have maintained his name.

REFERENCE

Charles Ethan Porter, 1847?–1923. Connecticut Gallery. Marlborough, Conn., 1987.

HELEN M. SHANNON

Porter, James Amos (December 22, 1905–February 28, 1970), artist and art historian. Through his writing, painting, and teaching, Porter helped establish African-American art history as a scholarly field. Born in Baltimore, Md., Porter received a B.S. in art from Howard University in 1927, and later that year he joined the faculty as instructor of drawing and painting in the Department of Art and Architecture. Howard was Porter's base for the remainder of his career. There he became the most influential African-American art teacher of his generation.

In 1933 Porter took a sabbatical, moved to New York, and attended classes at the Art Students League of New York and at Teachers College of Columbia University. From 1935 to 1937 he pursued an M.A. in art history at New York University.

Porter had begun exhibiting paintings by 1928, when he received honorable mention for a portrait, *Sarah*, at the annual show of the Harmon Foundation. He exhibited six paintings with the organization, and in 1933 he won the Arthur Schomburg Portrait Prize in figure painting for *Woman Holding a Jug* (1933). Porter was best known for his portraits, but all his work was influenced by the decorative

techniques of the Fauves, with a realist style drawn from direct observation.

In 1935, Porter spent the summer visiting museums in Europe and studying art at the Sorbonne in Paris as part of a Rockefeller Foundation grant. His paintings received recognition in 1940, when he was included in the American Negro Exposition in Chicago; in 1945, when he was awarded a second Rockefeller Foundation grant; and in 1948, when the Barnett-Aden Gallery in Washington, D.C., presented a solo exhibition of his work.

While teaching at Howard, Porter wrote *Modern Negro Art* (1943), which became the basic source on African-American art history; it was one of the first works to treat the iconography of African art in relationship to African-American visual arts. Porter also wrote a catalog on Laura Wheeler WARING for Howard University Gallery (1949); a monographic study, *Robert S.* DUNCANSON: *Midwestern Romantic-Realist* (1951); and numerous reviews for the JOURNAL OF NEGRO HISTORY.

From 1945 to 1946 Porter traveled to Cuba and Haiti, where he studied painting and collected teaching materials for use at Howard University. Some of his most widely exhibited paintings, such as *On a Cuban Bus* (1946), were inspired by this trip. In 1953,

African Nude by James A. Porter. (National Archives)

Porter was appointed head of the Art Department and Director of the Art Gallery at HOWARD UNIVERSITY, a position he held until his death in Washington, D.C., in 1970. He received a *Washington Evening Star* research grant in 1963 to travel to West Africa and was awarded the National Gallery of Art Medal in 1966.

Porter studied an African-American tradition in the visual arts, and while he acknowledged the influence of African art on black American artists, he also insisted that a "black art" would not develop out of imitations of African works. In Porter's view, social analysis and criticism were central to the African-American artistic tradition, and he stressed the black artist's commitment to realist depictions of everyday life rather than abstract compositions.

REFERENCES

DRISKELL, DAVID. *Hidden Heritage: Afro-American Art, 1800–1950.* San Francisco, 1987.

"Internationally Known Artist and Author: Head of Art Department at Howard University, James A. Porter." *Negro History Bulletin* (April 1970): 99.

MILTON, NARISSA LONG. "James A. Porter." *Negro History Bulletin* (October 1954): 5–6.

SAMELLA, LEWIS. *Art: African-American.* New York, 1978.

NANCY YOUSEF

RENEE NEWMAN

Port Royal Experiment.   The Port Royal Experiment has often been termed a "rehearsal" for RE-CONSTRUCTION. The experiment was designed to discover whether African Americans liberated from their slavemasters could work as free laborers. On November 7, 1861, planters on the South Carolina Sea Islands fled the United States Navy, leaving their enslaved laborers on the land. Military forces led by Lieut. Gen. William W. Reynolds occupied and looted the islands. William W. Pierce, a civilian attorney from Boston, was assigned to scout the land and direct efforts on behalf of the "contrabands" of war now under their control. He went north, and in Boston and New York joined with abolitionists and reformers such as Edward Philbrick to form an educational association named Gideon's Band. Shortly thereafter, missionary teachers arrived to assist the newly independent blacks.

Missionaries from Gideon's Band, later assisted by the American Missionary Association, opened schools in the face of military hostility and racism. Within a short time, conflict emerged over the use of the land. Northern officials wanted to grow cotton to ease the wartime shortage. Freedmen, however, were used to laboring for others and interpreted "free labor" to mean independence. Like many whites, they preferred subsistence farming to wage labor on cash crops as part of large work groups. Eventually, many blacks were coerced by the military into growing cotton on abandoned plantations. Pierce, a free labor advocate, ordered blacks to plant cotton on the abandoned plantations. The federal government provided supplies and meager salaries for the freedmen. At the same time, cotton agents and soldiers lined their pockets with commissions and profits on the cotton.

On July 7, 1862, Congress passed a bill that effectively displaced the absentee white landowners, and in March 1863, their abandoned properties were divided into lots and sold. Although 2,000 acres were bought by groups of blacks, who pooled their wages, most of the lands were bought by military officers and speculators. A consortium of abolitionists headed by Philbrick and Edward Atkinson, a Boston textile manufacturer, bought eleven plantations. They wished not only to profit, but to prove the superiority of black wage work. Philbrick opened plantation stores and stocked fine goods, hoping to create a desire for cash among African-American farmers.

In January 1865, Gen. William T. Sherman awarded all unclaimed land to the freedmen. Several months later, however, President Andrew Johnson

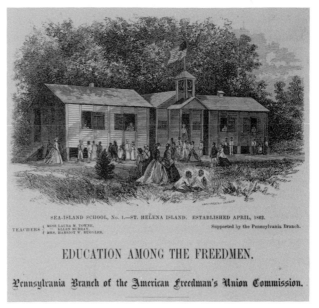

EDUCATION AMONG THE FREEDMEN.

Pennsylvania Branch of the American Freedman's Union Commission.

One of the top priorities in the South Carolina Sea Islands after they were secured by Union forces in 1862 was education of the freedmen. Many northern female abolitionists, black and white, went to South Carolina as schoolteachers. (Prints and Photographs Division, Library of Congress)

allowed planters to reclaim land not already sold to investors. In early 1866, freedmen who refused to sign lease agreements with white owners were forced off the land by the military. Some left; others contracted to work for planters. A few did manage to retain title to lands.

Despite the small and isolated nature of Port Royal, the experiment aroused great attention in antislavery circles. The failure of the experiment, as far as black uplift was concerned, presaged the later collapse of Reconstruction. Differences between northern free labor ideology and black desire for autonomy would again appear, and the fragility of black independence in the face of white opposition would once again be demonstrated.

REFERENCES

FONER, ERIC. *Reconstruction: America's Unfinished Revolution, 1863–1877*. New York, 1988.

ROSE, WILLIE LEE. *Rehearsal for Reconstruction: The Port Royal Experiment*. New York, 1964.

ELIZABETH FORTSON ARROYO

Postal Service. The first organized mail delivery system in what is now the United States was a private messenger service instituted in the seventeenth century by Southern plantation owners using mostly African-American slaves as carriers. More than fifty years later, in 1691, the British crown awarded a grant to Thomas Neale, who appointed New Jersey Governor Andrew Hamilton as his deputy postmaster general while Neale remained in England. The earliest mention of African Americans in the British Royal Post is a reference to "black riders as mail carriers" in an entry in the journal of Hugh Finlay, surveyor of post roads and post offices, made May 17, 1774.

The Post Office Department (POD), successor to the Royal Post, was established by the Second Continental Congress in 1775. Its records contain no evidence of black employees until 1800, when the first of several letters dealing with African-American employment appeared in official postal correspondence. Gideon Granger was appointed Postmaster General under Thomas Jefferson in 1801 and within six months of taking office wrote three letters concerning blacks as carriers of the country's mail. His March 23 letter to the chairman of the Senate Post Office Committee detailed his position. "An objection exists," he wrote, "against employing negroes or people of color in transporting the public mails of a nature too delicate to ingraft into a report which may become public, yet too important to be passed over

without full consideration. . . . After the scenes which St. Domingo [then a part of Haiti where a successful slave uprising had taken place] has exhibited in the world we cannot be too cautious in attempting to prevent similar evils in the four Southern states . . . where there is so great a proportion of blacks as to hazard the tranquility and happiness of the free citizens." He continued, "By travelling from day to day . . . they . . . will learn that a man's rights do not depend on his Color. They will in time become teachers to their brethren . . . an organized corp circulating our intelligence openly." And he concluded, "It is easier to prevent the evil. . . ."

Congress acted immediately and in 1802 passed a statute providing "that from and after the first day of November next no other than a free white person shall be employed in carrying the mail of the United States." The penalty for disobeying the law was "the sum of fifty dollars, one moiety [half] thereof to the use of the United States, and the other moiety thereof to the person who shall sue for, and prosecute the same. . . ." The law was reenacted in 1810 and again in 1825, when the penalty was reduced to twenty dollars. Except for an 1828 ruling that permitted blacks to haul mailbags from stagecoach to the post office "under white supervision," the regulation remained on the books until 1865, when Congress approved an act removing "all disqualifications of color in carrying the mail."

In 1867 John W. Curry was employed in the Washington, D.C. post office; he is thought to be the first black mail carrier in the POD. The period of Reconstruction (1865–1877) also saw the appointment of blacks as postal clerks, watchmen, laborers, and messengers. It was during this time that the first black postmaster, Benjamin Boseman, a physician, was installed at Charleston, S.C. in 1873.

Minnie Cox, believed to be the first black woman postmaster, was appointed at Indianola, Miss., in 1891 and, in what the Post Office described as "a crusade against the few negro postmasters in this state," became the target of a citizens' campaign to have her removed from office. In a series of letters to President Theodore Roosevelt and the Post Office Department, A. B. Weeks gave his reasons for Cox's proposed ouster from the $1,100 per annum post. "We have here a colored woman as postmistress . . . the wife of the railroad postal messenger. . . . I think it unfair that one family should have both offices, especially as they have no children to support and are very wealthy. . . . I want to be appointed . . . I am entitled to the office . . . I need the office to support my family . . . [I] was raised a Democrat, but . . . I have seen . . . prosperity under yourself . . . for this reason I come to the ranks of the Republican party."

When Postmaster General Henry C. Payne refused to bow to demands that a white postmaster be named, Cox was subjected to death threats and her husband was ordered to leave town. Finally, after more than a year of intimidation, she resigned. On January 3, 1903, postal officials wired: "Postmaster's resignation is not accepted. Office is to remain closed until Postmaster-General orders it reopened." A congressional inquiry followed.

When William Howard Taft was elected president in 1909, the naming of blacks as postmasters ended. Woodrow Wilson's postmaster general, Albert S. Burleson, instituted rules of segregation in 1913, and many blacks were removed from office. Those who remained were mostly railroad clerks, who sought to protect their interests by founding the National Alliance of Letter Carriers.

The First World War (1917–1921) prompted renewed concerns about African-American acts of espionage, and mailing bans were instituted against black publications. After the war, however, blacks increased in the postal population and by 1928 were 15 to 30 percent of the workforce in some large city offices. For the next fifty years the POD was a source of part-time employment for African Americans working toward professional careers, including Dr. Charles DREW, actor Sherman Hemsley, and Adm. Samuel Gravely.

Under President Franklin D. Roosevelt blacks were 10 percent of the federal workforce in 1938, and they were mostly in the postal service. Segregation was endemic, and in 1941 and 1943 the president issued executive orders designed to end discrimination against black employment during World War II.

The decade of the 1940s saw several relevant events. One was the issuance of the first stamp honoring an African American, Booker T. Washington. In 1941 Ralph E. Mizelle, a black attorney, was appointed to the POD Solicitor's office. The postal war effort again included an effort to deny mailing privileges to black publishers who criticized the United States. After World War II the Senate heard allegations of "many cases of discrimination because of race . . . that neither the Department nor its field officials have taken steps to remedy. . . ." Several years later Joseph A. Clarke became the first black special assistant to an assistant postmaster general.

It was only after the CIVIL RIGHTS MOVEMENT began and new executive orders banning discrimination were issued in the 1960s that the POD appointed larger numbers of blacks to supervisory positions. The black firsts of the decade were Charles A. Preston, postal inspector, 1962; Leslie M. Shaw, postmaster of a major city (Los Angeles), 1963; Ena M. St. Louis, postal attorney (female), 1964; and Ronald B. Lee, assistant postmaster general, 1969.

Promotion into middle management remained elusive, however, as examination announcements were often unposted and advancement opportunities were extended by written invitation or by word of mouth to selected individuals. A 1969 executive order sought to end that practice by mandating that "recruitment activities reach all sources of job candidates."

Political patronage was removed from the postal arena just as blacks began to achieve significant political power, and in 1970 Congress created the United States Postal Service (USPS) as an independent government agency. The position of postmaster general was removed from the president's cabinet, and a board of governors was given oversight of the corporation. A commission was installed to rule on postage fees and a citizens' advisory committee was charged with deciding on subjects and designs for postage stamps. George E. Johnson, an African American, was one of the original governors, and the USPS was made subject to all previously enacted civil rights acts.

In January 1971 only fifty-four of almost thirty thousand postmasters were black, the fewest of any minority, including American Indians and Aleutians. The Equal Opportunity Act was passed, and AFFIRMATIVE ACTION became a stated goal of the USPS. In 1977 Emmett E. Cooper was appointed the first black regional postmaster general. Bonnie F. Guiton was the first black to serve on the Postal Rate Commission when she was appointed in 1985.

At the end of 1991, blacks were 21.1 percent of the USPS workforce of 728,121. In contrast, 2.9 percent of all postmasters were African Americans. Two of forty-two Level II executives and 121 (10.6 percent) of the 1,137 Level I executives were black, representing a 0.5 percent decrease from 1990.

In 1992 the USPS issued a volume featuring illustrated biographical sketches of twenty-eight African Americans depicted on U.S. postage stamps, some of which were designed by black artists. The book is called *I Have a Dream*. (For a list of African Americans depicted on postage stamps, *see* Appendix 15.3.)

REFERENCES

GLENN, AL, ed. *History of the National Alliance of Postal Employees*. Washington, D.C., n.d.

MORONEY, RITA L., ed. *History of the U.S. Postal Service 1775–1984*. Washington, D.C., n.d.

SPERO, STERLING, and ABRAM HARRIS. *The Black Worker*. New York, 1931.

JOHNNIE LOCKETT THOMAS

Postlewaite, Joseph William (1827–1889), bandleader and composer. Born a slave in St. Louis,

Mo., J. W. Postlewaite published his first composition, "Concert Hall Grand Waltz," in 1845. His most popular works were "St. Louis Greys Quick Step" (1852), "Annie Polka Mazurka" (1854), and "Recreation Schottisch" (1854). Between 1845 and 1880 Postlewaite led several bands, including Postlewaite's Quadrille Band (1857), Postlewaite's Cotillion Band (n.d.), Postlewaite's Orchestra (1873), the St. Louis Great Western Band (1874), and the Great Western Reed and String Band (1875). His known published compositions include 15 waltzes, 7 schottisches, 6 marches and quicksteps, 4 mazurkas, 1 lancer, 1 polka, 1 polka redowa, and 1 schottische quadrille. At the end of his career, Postlewaite lived and worked in the Chestnut Valley district of St. Louis, where in 1885 Scott JOPLIN set up his base of operations and launched the RAGTIME era.

REFERENCES

FLOYD, SAMUEL A. "A Black Composer in Nineteenth-Century St. Louis." *19th Century Music* 4, no. 2 (1980): 121–133.
———. "J. W. Postlewaite of St. Louis: A Search for His Identity." *Black Perspective in Music* 6, no. 2 (1978): 151–167.

SAMUEL A. FLOYD, JR.

Poussaint, Alvin Francis (May 15, 1934–), psychiatrist, educator, and author. Born in East Harlem in New York City, Alvin Poussaint attended Stuyvesant High School and graduated from Columbia College (B.A., 1956) and Cornell University Medical College (M.D., 1960). He took postgraduate training at the University of California's Neuropsychiatric Institute in Los Angeles, where he served as chief resident in psychiatry from 1964 to 1965. From 1965 to 1967, he was southern field director of the Medical Committee for Human Rights in Jackson, Miss., providing medical care to civil rights workers and aiding in the desegregation of health facilities throughout the South. In 1967, Poussaint became an assistant professor at Tufts University Medical School. He remained there for four years (1965–1969) before joining the faculty of the Harvard Medical School. At Boston's Judge Baker Guidance Center, he counseled families traumatized by the murder of a relative or friend.

Poussaint's research included the psychological and social adaptation of children of interracial marriages, the nature of grief, and the pharmacological treatment of smoking and bed wetting. He was a founding member and treasurer of the BLACK ACADEMY OF ARTS AND LETTERS in 1969. Two years later

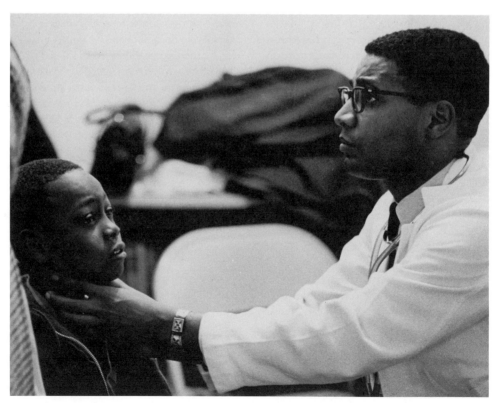

Dr. Alvin Poussaint examines a young patient at a clinic set up for residents without access to medical care in Miles, Holmes County, Miss., by the Medical Committee for Human Rights, 1965. Dr. Poussaint served as resident physician. (© Charmian Reading)

Poussaint became an initial member of the Rev. Jesse JACKSON's organization OPERATION PUSH (People United to Save Humanity). He also served as an advisor to Jackson during the 1984 presidential campaign.

One of the nation's leading psychiatrists, Poussaint has researched and written widely on such social issues of concern to African Americans as poverty, unemployment, self-esteem, parenting, and violence. He has written several books, including *Why Blacks Kill Blacks* (1972), an examination of the effects of white racism on black psychological development. He was coauthor with James P. Comer of *Black Child Care* (1975; reissued as *Raising Black Children,* 1992), a study of the cultural biases faced by African-American youths. Poussaint also served as a consultant to *The Cosby Show* from 1984 to 1992 and *A Different World* from 1986 to 1993. He reviewed script dialogue to ensure that the two television series presented positive images of blacks and were free of stereotypes and discriminatory content. In 1993, Poussaint became professor of psychiatry and associate dean of student affairs at Harvard Medical School. A year later, he became the director of the Media Center for Children at the Judge Baker Children's Center. Poussaint has been a fellow at a number of organizations, including the American Psychiatric Association, the American Association for the Advancement of Science, and the Orthopsychiatric Association.

REFERENCES

HENDRIX, KATHLEEN. "Alvin Poussaint: Upbeat About the Black Psyche." *Los Angeles Times,* June 24, 1988, Sec. 5, p. 1.

TROUTT, DAVID D. "Alvin F. Poussaint—Psychiatrist Goes Prime Time to Shape Persona of Blacks." *Los Angeles Times,* June 10, 1990, Sec. M, p. 3.

ROBERT C. HAYDEN

Powell, Adam Clayton, Jr. (November 29, 1908–April 4, 1972), congressman, civil rights activist, and clergyman. Adam Clayton Powell, Jr., was born in 1908 in New Haven, Conn. Shortly thereafter his father, Adam Clayton POWELL, SR., left New Haven for New York City to assume the pastorship of the ABYSSINIAN BAPTIST CHURCH in Harlem. The elder Powell, a prominent minister, sought the best for his only son, educating him at the elite Townsend Harris High School, then sending him to Colgate University, a largely white school in Hamilton, N.Y. In 1932 Powell received an M.A. in religious educa-

tion from Columbia University Teachers College. By the time Powell had graduated from Colgate in 1930 and returned home, the United States was mired in the GREAT DEPRESSION. Young Powell was named an assistant pastor at the Abyssinian Church. Powell was not content, however, to concern himself exclusively with pastoral matters. With the depression as backdrop, young Powell rallied for help for Harlemites from City Hall, and goaded the residents of Harlem to protest second-class treatment of African Americans. He declaimed from both pulpit and streetcorner, leading marchers not only to City Hall, but to the doorsteps of the ill-staffed and racially discriminatory Harlem Hospital. Older Abyssinian deacons considered him unpredictable, even impatient. But the younger members of the church adored him, and were eager to follow his lead. In the winter of 1937 Powell was named minister of the Abyssinian Baptist Church to succeed his father. He was twenty-nine years old. The congregation boasted more than 10,000 members and was probably the largest Protestant Church in the United States. During the next few years, Powell, in his forceful and flamboyant manner, became the most visible leader of the boycott campaign to break the bottleneck of discrimination that existed in stores. Melding together the often factious groups that comprised the "Don't Buy Where You Can't Work" campaign, Powell's tactics were hugely successful and emulated in other cities. He pressured New York utilities, including Consolidated Edison, to hire blacks. His boycotting tactics forced the New York City private bus companies for the first time to hire black drivers. Liberals and progressives from the world of politics were invited to appear in the Abyssinian pulpit. The mix was eclectic. They were animated by the spirit of progressive reform in the manner of Robert LaFollette and Franklin D. Roosevelt, as well as black nationalist sentiments inspired by Marcus GARVEY. Powell turned the church stage into a personal bully pulpit.

Powell was a natural for the political arena, and in 1941, running as an Independent, he became the first black to win election to the New York City Council. Although he would thereafter usually run as a Democrat, he always maintained his independence from the Democratic machine. Before his first term was over, he decided to run for Congress from a newly created district that would, for the first time, enable a black to be elected from Harlem. With help from the left-wing East Harlem Congressman Vito Marcantonio, the powerful Abyssinian church, and the vibrant artistic community of Harlem, Powell launched a two-year campaign that saw him elected the first black in 1944 to Congress from the Northeast. His Washington debut was typically controversial. In fall 1945, when the Daughters of the American Revolution (DAR) refused to allow jazz pianist Hazel Scott, the second of his three wives, to perform on the stage of Constitution Hall, Powell assailed First Lady Bess Truman in the press because of her continued connections with the DAR. President Truman was livid, and Powell was never invited to the White House while Truman was President.

Powell's talent for attracting attention and making enemies soon made him the congressional leader in the fight for civil rights legislation. Working closely with Clarence MITCHELL, Jr. and the NAACP in 1950 he offered an amendment to current legislation, which came to be known as the Powell Amendment, forbidding any federal support for segregated facilities. Powell would repeatedly introduce this amendment over the next several years. Politically he was liberal, but he was also a shrewd opportunist. In 1956 Powell backed President Eisenhower's reelection bid, a move that angered Democrats. Four years later, however, Powell heartily campaigned for the Kennedy-Johnson ticket. Coinciding with Kennedy's victory, Powell had gained sufficient seniority to become chairman of the powerful House Education and Labor Committee. The influence of his powerful po-

Adam Clayton Powell, Jr., January 10, 1967. (Prints and Photographs Division, Library of Congress)

sition, however, would not be felt until 1964, when President Johnson's heightened domestic agenda went into full action. Powell was instrumental in passage of the war on poverty legislation, on which he and Johnson collaborated. These included increased federal aid to school programs, increasing the minimum wage, and the Head Start Program for preschool children. Billions of dollars flowed through the Powell committee. In 1964 the Civil Rights Act finally saw the core of the Powell Amendment enacted into law. From 1961 to 1967 Powell was one of the most powerful politicians in the United States, and certainly the most powerful African American. He was both an American insider and outsider, working inside the halls of Congress, and identifying with the masses who remained on the outside as one of the most riveting stump speakers in the country. He often engaged in one-upmanship with Martin Luther KING, Jr. By the time his congressional career ended there would be more than sixty pieces of major legislation with his imprimatur.

Powell's political downfall began when, in 1960, he accused Esther James, a Harlem woman, of corruption. James successfully sued for libel. Powell refused to pay, and before he finally agreed to settle in 1966 Powell had accumulated enormous amounts of bad publicity because of his sometimes mercurial and sybaritic behavior. In January 1967 House members, led by southern Democrats and Republicans, refused to seat Powell until a committee could investigate his conduct, citing his indiscretions and personal lifestyle. The House committee set up to investigate Powell's conduct, the Celler Committee, chaired by New York Republican Emanuel Celler, decided to fine Powell, strip away his seniority, and have him repay money that had gone to his third wife, Yvette Diago Powell, while she had been on his payroll. The full House, however, ignored the recommendations of the Celler Committee and voted to expel Powell from Congress in March 1967. It was the first time since 1919 that the House had expelled one of its members. Powell vowed to fight the case all the way to the Supreme Court. He won a special election in March 1967 to fill his own vacant seat, and was re-elected in 1968, though he remained outside of Congress. In 1968 he barnstormed the United States, rallying black and white students on college campuses to fight for equality and end American involvement in Vietnam, peppering his defense with his catchphrase, "Keep the faith, baby." He was mentioned in 1968 as a favorite-son presidential candidate from New York. In 1969, in his last decision from the Supreme Court, Chief Justice Earl Warren ruled that Adam Clayton Powell had been unconstitutionally expelled from Congress. Back in Congress, however, Powell was without the power he had once yielded, returning as a freshman, because the Court had not ruled on the matter of his seniority and lost back pay. In 1970 he lost his last reelection bid to Charles RANGEL by 150 votes. He spent the last two years of his life on the island of Bimini, in the Bahamas, where he said he was working on his memoirs, which never were published. He died of cancer in a Miami hospital on April 4, 1972, four years to the day from Martin Luther King's death.

REFERENCES

HAYGOOD, WIL. *King of the Cats: The Life and Times of Adam Clayton Powell, Jr.* Boston, 1993.
JACOBS, ANDY. *The Powell Affair: Freedom Minus One.* New York, 1973.
POWELL, ADAM CLAYTON, JR. *Adam by Adam: The Autobiography of Adam Clayton Powell, Jr.* New York, 1971.

WIL HAYGOOD

congressman. Following his retirement, the elder Powell became increasingly involved in political efforts to end job discrimination and expand employment opportunities for African Americans. He also published three books: an autobiography, *Against the Tide* (1938); *Picketing Hell* (1942); and *Riots and Ruins* (1945). Powell died in New York City in 1953.

REFERENCES

HAMILTON, CHARLES V. *Adam Clayton Powell, Jr.: The Political Biography of an American Dilemma.* New York, 1991.
HICKEY, NEIL, and ED EDWIN. *Adam Clayton Powell and the Politics of Race.* New York, 1955.
POWELL, ADAM CLAYTON, SR. *Against the Tide.* New York, 1938.
WASHINGTON, JOSEPH R. *Rulers of Reality and the Ruled Races: The Struggle of Black Ministers to Bring Afro-Americans to Full Citizenship in America.* Lewiston, N.Y., 1990.

THADDEUS RUSSELL

Powell, Adam Clayton, Sr. (May 5, 1865–June 12, 1953), clergyman. Adam Clayton Powell, Sr., was born to a sharecropping family in Soak Creek, Franklin County, Va. In 1875 his family moved to West Virginia, where he lived through adolescence. In 1884 Powell left home for Rendville, Ohio, where he worked as a coal miner, attended the Rendville Academy, and became an ardent Baptist. In 1887 he moved to Washington, D.C., where he enrolled in Wayland Seminary and College (which later became part of Virginia Union University) and received a B.A. in 1892.

In 1893 Powell was hired as pastor of Immanuel Baptist Church in New Haven, Conn., a position he held for fifteen years. In 1908 he was hired by the ABYSSINIAN BAPTIST CHURCH, the oldest black Baptist church in New York City, then located at West 40th Street in Manhattan. Under Powell's leadership the church acquired land uptown, and, in 1923, moved to West 138th Street in Harlem. Powell worked to expand the role of the church beyond Sunday services, opening a community center at the new location, managing a home for the aged, and operating soup kitchens for the needy during the GREAT DEPRESSION. By the mid-1930s the church under Powell's leadership had become the largest Protestant congregation in the United States, with fourteen thousand members.

Powell retired in 1937 and was succeeded as pastor by his son, Adam Clayton POWELL, JR., the future

Powell, Colin Luther (April 5, 1937–), Army officer, chair of the Joint Chiefs of Staff. Born and raised in New York City, Colin Powell grew up in a close-knit family of Jamaican immigrants in the Hunts Point section of the Bronx. After attending public schools, Powell graduated from the City College of New York (CCNY) in 1958. Although his grades were mediocre, he discovered an affinity for the military. Participating in CCNY's Reserve Officer Training Corps (ROTC) program, he finished as a cadet colonel, the highest rank attainable. Like all ROTC graduates, Powell was commissioned as a second lieutenant after completing college.

Powell served for two years in West Germany and two years in Massachusetts, where he met his wife, Alma. In 1962, already a captain, Powell received orders to report to Vietnam. He was one of the second wave of more than 15,000 military advisers sent by the United States to Vietnam and was posted with a South Vietnamese Army unit for most of his tenure. During his first tour of duty, from 1962 to 1963, he was decorated with the Purple Heart after being wounded by a Viet Cong booby trap near the Laotian border.

After returning to the United States, Powell spent almost four years at Fort Benning in Georgia, serving as, among other things, an instructor at Fort Benning's Army Infantry School. In 1967, now a major, he attended an officers' training course at the United States Army Command and General Staff College at

Gen. Colin Powell, the first African American to serve as chairman of the Joint Chiefs of Staff, became a national hero after the successful conclusion of the war in the Persian Gulf in 1991. Here he addresses the Chicago Council of Foreign Relations in November 1992. (AP/Wide World Photos)

Fort Leavenworth, Kans., finishing second in a class of more than twelve hundred. In the summer of 1968, Powell was ordered back to Vietnam. On his second tour, Powell primarily served as a liaison to Gen. Charles Gettys of the American Division and received the Soldier's Medal for his role in rescuing injured soldiers, including Gen. Gettys, from a downed helicopter.

Powell returned to the United States in mid-1969 and began moving between military field postings and political appointments, a process that would become characteristic of his career. In 1971, after working in the Pentagon for the assistant vice chief of the Army, he earned an M.B.A. from George Washington University in Washington, D.C. Shortly thereafter, Powell was accepted as a White House Fellow during the Nixon administration and was attached to the Office of Management and Budget (OMB), headed by Caspar Weinberger. In 1973, after a year at OMB, Powell received command of an infantry battalion in South Korea; his mission was to raise morale and restore order in a unit plagued by drug abuse and racial problems. He then attended a nine-month course at the National War College and was promoted to full colonel in February 1976, taking command of the 2nd Brigade, 101st Airborne Division, located at Fort Campbell, Ky.

In 1979 Powell was an aide to Secretary of Energy Charles Duncan during the crisis of the nuclear accident at Three Mile Island in Pennsylvania and the oil shortage caused by the overthrow of the shah of Iran. In June of that year, while working at the Department of Energy (DOE), he became a brigadier general. Powell returned to the field from 1981 until 1983, serving as assistant division commander of the Fourth Infantry (mechanized) in Colorado and then as the deputy commanding general of an Army research facility at Fort Leavenworth. In mid-1983, he became military assistant to Secretary of Defense Caspar Weinberger. In 1986, Powell, by then a lieutenant general, returned to the field as the commander of V Corps, a unit of 75,000 troops in West Germany. The following year, in the wake of the Iran-Contra scandal, he returned to serve as President Ronald Reagan's national security adviser. During the Intermediate Nuclear Forces (INF) arms-control negotiations with the Soviet Union, Powell was heralded as being a major factor in their success.

In July 1989, Powell, a newly promoted four-star general, was nominated by President George Bush to become the first black chairman of the Joint Chiefs of Staff, the highest military position in the armed forces. As chairman, Powell was responsible for overseeing Operation Desert Storm, the 1991 international response to the 1990 Iraqi invasion of Kuwait. Through his commanding and reassuring television presence during the successful Persian Gulf War, Powell became one of the most popular figures in the Bush administration. Reappointed chairman in 1991, he was the recipient of various military decorations as well as a Presidential Medal of Freedom from Bush. In the same year, the NAACP gave Powell the SPINGARN MEDAL, its highest award for African-American achievement.

When Bill Clinton was elected president in 1992, he and Powell had differences over Clinton's plan to substantially reduce the defense budget. Powell also disagreed with Clinton's proposal to end the ban on homosexuals in the military and was instrumental in limiting the scope of the change. Powell retired from the Army in September 1993 at the end of his second term as chairman of the Joint Chiefs. Upon his departure, President Clinton awarded him his second Presidential Medal of Freedom.

REFERENCES

MEANS, HOWARD. *Colin Powell: Soldier/Statesman—Statesman/Soldier*. New York, 1992.

POWELL, COLIN, with Joseph E. Persico. *My American Journey*. New York, 1995.

ROBERTS, STEVEN V., with Bruce Auster and Gary Cohen. "What's Next, General Powell?" *U.S. News and World Report* (March 18, 1991): 50–53.

ROWAN, CARL. "Called to Service: The Colin Powell Story." *Reader's Digest* (December 1989): 121–126.

JOHN C. STONER

Powell, Earl "Bud" (September 27, 1924–August 1, 1966), jazz pianist. Born in New York's Harlem, Bud Powell was raised in a musical family and began to study piano at age six. After leaving school at the age of fifteen, he played regularly in New York night clubs, and by the mid-1940s he emerged as the most important pianist in the new jazz style, known as bebop. He first rose to prominence in the big band of Cootie WILLIAMS, an association that provided his first professional recordings in 1944. Thereafter, he played in numerous bebop combos, with Charlie PARKER, Dizzy GILLESPIE, and Fats NAVARRO, among others. Powell was particularly noted for his performances on up-tempo pieces, soloing with immense creativity and an exhilarating technical execution. Among his best known compositions are "Un Poco Loco," "Hallucinations," and "Glass Enclosure."

Powell was hospitalized several times during the late 1940s and early '50s. Thereafter, his deteriorating mental and physical condition hampered his ability to consistently capture the energy that made his earlier performances so memorable. He lived in Paris from 1959 to 1964, performing and recording frequently there until his return to New York, where he died in 1966.

REFERENCE

GITLER, IRA. *Jazz Masters of the Forties,* 1966. Reprint. New York, 1983, pp. 110–130.

GUTHRIE P. RAMSEY, JR.

Powell, Georgette Seabrooke (August 2, 1916–), artist, and art therapist. Georgette Seabrooke Powell was born in Charleston, S.C. Her father, George W. Seabrooke, was a restaurant and hotel owner; her mother, Anna C. Seabrooke, was a homemaker. Powell attended the Harlem Art Workshop and then the Cooper Union Art School (1933–1937). In 1935, she won first prize for painting at the Cooper Union for a work called "Church Scene."

Powell was one of six African-American artists commissioned by the Federal Arts Project of the WORKS PROJECT ADMINISTRATION (WPA) in 1936 to create a series of murals for Harlem Hospital. Powell's work, "Recreation in Harlem," was designed for the nurse's recreation room. But it and three other murals were rejected by both the Harlem Hospital Superintendent and the New York City Commissioner of Hospitals, who objected to displaying the work of black artists featuring black subjects on hospital walls (one reason they offered for their objections was that Harlem might not be a predominantly black neighborhood in the future). However, pressure from federal and local officials led to a reversal of the rejections and the murals were painted. In 1937, Powell painted a mural for a children's play room in Queens General Hospital.

Powell was also interested in other applications of art and in the late 1950s entered the emerging field of art therapy (the use of art in a therapeutic treatment setting). She returned to school and studied art therapy at the Turtle Bay Music School in New York City (1959–1960), obtained a B.F.A. from Howard University (1973), and did additional work at the Washington (D.C.) School of Psychiatry. She worked as an art therapist until 1978. In 1975, she founded Tomorrow's World Art Center, in Washington, D.C., a community organization offering instruction and a range of other programs in the visual arts. Powell's work was included in the 1992–1993 traveling exhibition *Alone in a Crowd,* featuring the work of black artists of the 1930s and 1940s.

REFERENCE

HARLEY, RALPH L., ed. *Afro-American Art and Artists.* Kent, Ohio, 1970.

MICHAEL PALLER
KIM ROBBINS

Powell, William Frank (June 26, 1845–c. January 23, 1920), educator and diplomat. William Powell was born in Troy, N.Y., of mixed American Indian and black descent. He attended public schools in New York City and studied for a time at the School of Pharmacy there and at Ashman Institute (later Lincoln University) in Pennsylvania, before graduating from the New Jersey Collegiate Institute in 1865. In 1869, Powell began teaching at a school for free blacks in Leesburg, Va. He opened a similar school in Alexandria, Va., the following year and taught there for five years.

In 1875, Powell became principal of a school in Bordentown, N.J., and soon was active in New Jersey REPUBLICAN PARTY politics. From 1881 to 1882, he worked as a bookkeeper for the U.S. Treasury in Washington, D.C. Two years later, in 1884, Powell was elected district superintendent of schools in Camden, N.J., where he introduced many innovations, including manual training in the school system. Because of Powell's high educational standards, enrollment in black schools increased, and the Camden school system became a model for black education in New Jersey. After 1886, Powell resumed his career as a high school teacher.

In 1881 and again in 1891, Powell refused diplomatic assignments, but in 1897 he accepted President William McKinley's appointment as minister to Haiti. Relations between the United States and Haiti, which were strained at the time, improved during Powell's tenure. He successfully negotiated the cancellation of special taxes against U.S. merchants and clerks in Haiti, and obtained the release of the U.S. vice-consul general. In 1897, a crisis developed between Haiti and Germany over whether Haitian courts had jurisdiction over foreign citizens, and Germany threatened to shell the Haitian capital. With the support of some Haitian politicians, Powell suggested that the United States make Haiti a U.S. protectorate. The U.S. State Department rejected the suggestion, but Powell was instrumental in defusing the crisis.

Powell resigned in 1905—there is some suggestion that the State Department thought he had become too close to the Haitians—and returned to his home in Camden. In 1907, Powell was awarded an LL.D. by Lincoln University. In 1909, he became active as an editorial writer for the black newspaper *Philadelphia Tribune*. Relatively little is known about Powell's later years or the circumstances of his death, though he probably died on January 23, 1920.

REFERENCES

CREW, SPENCER R. *Black Life in Secondary Cities*. New York, 1993.

HEINL, ROBERT, and NANCY GORDON HEINL. *Written in Blood: The Story of the Haitian People*. Boston, 1978.

LOGAN, RAYFORD W. *Haiti and the Dominican Republic*. New York, 1968.

WRIGHT, MARION M. *The Education of Negroes in New Jersey*. New York, 1941.

LYDIA MCNEILL

Powers, Georgia (October 19, 1933–), politician. Born in Springfield, Ky., Powers attended Louisville Municipal College from 1940 to 1942. She worked at odd jobs until 1962, when her political career began. Initially, she worked for Wilson Wyatt, who ran for the U.S. Senate in 1962. She then worked as campaign chairperson for various senate, mayoral, and gubernatorial candidates. In 1964, she was elected to the Jefferson County, Ky., Democratic Executive Committee, the first African American to serve on that body. In 1968, she spoke at the Democratic National Convention on behalf of Hubert Humphrey.

After activity on both the political and civil rights fronts, Powers ran successfully for a seat in the Kentucky State Senate. She was the first black and the first woman ever elected to it. She introduced many innovative bills, including the first open housing law in the South, low-cost housing bills, a proposal to eliminate "race" from Kentucky motor vehicle operators' licenses, and an amendment of the Kentucky Civil Rights Act (1966) to eliminate discrimination based on race, sex, and age. After retiring in 1988 at the age of sixty-five, Powers wrote her autobiography, *Pride, Passion, and Politics*. Among her many awards are the King/Kennedy Award: Kentucky Young Democrats (1968), the University of Louisville Board of Trustees Appreciation Award (1978), the Woman of the Year Award from the Women's Coalition (1978), and the Clarence Mitchell Award, given by the Kentucky NAACP for her leadership in promoting human rights legislation (1980).

REFERENCES

MATNEY, WILLIAM C., ed. *Who's Who Among Black Americans*. New York, 1991.

SMITH, JESSIE CARNEY, ed. *Notable Black American Women*. Detroit, Mich. 1992.

NEIL GOLDSTEIN

Pozo, Chano (Pozo y Gonzales, Luciano) (January 7, 1915–February 2, 1948), drummer and composer. Chano Pozo was born in Havana, Cuba. As a young man growing up in Solar el Africá, a tough neighborhood of former slave quarters in Havana, Pozo drummed for African-derived Lucumi ceremonies. His mastery of Afro-Cuban religious music led to success in popular music. In the 1930s his songs won prizes at Carnival, and he developed a reputation that preceded his arrival in New York City in 1937.

In 1947 Dizzy GILLESPIE hired Pozo. As the first conga player to perform with a jazz band, Pozo broadened the appeal of Afro-Cuban music. His best-known composition is "Manteca." A virtuoso improviser and showman, Pozo delivered the unexpected. During one solo he might bend over backward, picking up a handkerchief with his teeth while drumming; during the next he might do something completely different. Pozo helped make Gillespie's band *Metronome*'s Band of the Year in 1947.

From 1947 to 1948 Pozo toured with Gillespie, teaching him the Afro-Cuban chants and rhythms that transformed Gillespie's music. The Gillespie/Pozo collaboration was cut short by Pozo's death in a bar fight in New York City.

A conga drummer of legendary brilliance, Pozo played a key role in the fusion of African-derived Latino music and bebop that became known as Afro-Cuban jazz, and his influence on later Latin jazz and salsa musicians has been profound.

REFERENCES

GILLESPIE, DIZZY, and AL FRASER. *To Be or Not to Bop: Memoirs.* New York, 1979.
ROBERTS, JOHN STORM. *The Latin Tinge: The Impact of Latin American Music on the United States.* New York, 1979.

ERNEST BROWN

Prater, Dave. *See* Sam and Dave.

Presbyterians. The African-American constituency of the Presbyterian church dates from the 1730s, when the Rev. Samuel Davies began to evangelize slaves of Scotch-Irish Presbyterian immigrants in the Valley of Virginia. Davies reported instructing and baptizing 150 slaves in 1757. Unlike the BAPTISTS and Methodists (*see* METHODIST CHURCH), American Presbyterians failed to attract large numbers of blacks in either the South or the North. At the end of the nineteenth century there were fewer than 30,000 African Americans in the northern and southern Presbyterian churches combined. These two major branches of Presbyterianism had split in 1861 over the Civil War but closed ranks in 1983. The black minority has grown slowly. By 1990 it was reported that only 2.47 percent, or 64,841 of the almost three-million-member reunited Presbyterian Church in the U.S.A. (PCUSA) were African Americans.

Reputedly, Presbyterian slaves were well instructed in the rudiments of Christianity. Many were taught to read and recite the creed and passages of the Bible by their owners. The emphasis of Puritan Presbyterians on a trained clergy and a literate laity had the effect of exposing black Presbyterians to pious learning as indispensable for Christian discipleship. The Presbyterians, however, were slow to oppose slavery. The issue was first raised in 1774 at a meeting of the Synod of New York and Philadelphia, but no action was taken. In 1787 the synod approved the ultimate goal of abolition; however, successive deliverances of the General Assembly induced the practice of Presbyterians to condemn slavery in principle while warning local judicatories not to interfere with the civil order.

The first black Presbyterian preacher was John CHAVIS, born in Granville County, N.C., in 1763. From 1801 to 1808 he served as a missionary to slaves in Virginia and opened a school that was patronized by many leading white families. The first African-American pastor was John GLOUCESTER, manumitted by Gideon Blackburn, a Tennessee missionary, to preach the gospel. In 1807 Gloucester was permitted by the Presbytery of Philadelphia to organize the First African Presbyterian Church, which competed with Richard ALLEN's Bethel AFRICAN METHODIST EPISCOPAL CHURCH for members from the burgeoning black community of South Philadelphia. Gloucester's three sons entered the Presbyterian ministry. Jeremiah organized Second African of Philadelphia in 1824, James organized Siloam in Brooklyn in 1847, and Stephen served the Lombard Central church of Philadelphia. Among the earliest black congregations in the North were Shiloh in New York City (organized 1822) and Washington Street in Reading, Pa. (1823). The first black Presbyterian congregation in the South was Beaufort-Salem, organized in Sheldon, N.C. in 1828. The Ladson Presbyterian Church of Columbia, S.C. (1828), was first governed by white elders and named after the white minister who was its first pastor. The slaves of the members of the First Presbyterian Church of Macon, Georgia, organized the Washington Avenue Church of that city in 1838.

After the Civil War, blacks spurned the southern branch of the church, the Presbyterian Church in the United States (PCUS), and rallied to the northern PCUSA missionaries following the Union armies. Many became members of the northern church. Fewer than 4,000 blacks remained in the southern church, which tried to organize them into an independent Afro-American Presbyterian Church in 1874. That effort was abandoned in 1916 because of poor support from whites. During RECONSTRUCTION the northern church launched a mission to attract and minister to the recently freed people. By 1882 its Board of Missions for Freedmen sponsored two universities, LINCOLN UNIVERSITY, near Oxford, Pa., and Biddle University (later Johnson C. Smith) in Charlotte, N.C., two colleges, five boarding schools, and 138 parochial schools. Following the Presbyterian tradition of educational excellence, these institutions made a signal contribution far beyond the ranks of the black constituency. Until the church's Board of National Missions phased it out in the twentieth century, this remarkable educational system enrolled 19,166 students and 494 teachers. At its peak the board supervised 438 churches and missions, 388 schools, 272 ministers, and 27,916 communicants.

Black Presbyterians caucused for greater recognition and freedom as early as 1859, when their ministers began meeting with black Congregational clergy in Philadelphia. Prior to the Civil War Samuel CORNISH, Theodore WRIGHT, Henry Highland GARNET, and J. W. C. PENNINGTON, all Presbyterian clergy, were leading black abolitionists (*see* ABOLITION). Lucy Craft LANEY, daughter of a Presbyterian minister and born a slave, founded the Haines Normal Institute in Augusta, Ga., in 1867. In 1891 Daniel J. Sanders became the first black president of J. C. Smith University. Blacks in the northern church became more assertive with the establishment in 1894 of the Afro-American Presbyterian Council. Its purpose was to create more fellowship among themselves in an overwhelming white church and greater influence in the boards and agencies of the denomination. At the turn of the century outspoken black pastors like Francis J. GRIMKÉ of the Fifteenth Street Presbyterian Church in Washington, D.C., and Matthew ANDERSON of Berean in Philadelphia consistently fought racism in the church and the proposed mergers of the northern church with the PCUS and the Cumberland Presbyterian Church, both with lingering Confederate allegiances.

Pressure from the African-American constituency moved the northern church to begin elevating blacks to key positions. In 1938 Albert B. McCoy became the first black executive of the Unit of Work for Colored People. Charles W. Talley was appointed field representative of the Atlantic Synod in 1945. During this period George Lake Imes became field representative for Negro Work in the North and West. He was followed by Robert Pierre Johnson, who served as associate stated clerk of the General Assembly in 1972. Jesse Belmont Barber, Frank T. Wilson, Emily V. Gibbes, Elo Henderson, Mildred Atris, Rachel Adams, and Bryant George were among the black men and women who served in prominent executive positions after World War II.

Lawrence W. Bottoms was an executive of the PCUS prior to his election in 1974 as its first black moderator. The PCUS began to respond to civil rights agitation after 1969. Under Bottoms's leadership in new church development in black communities and with the rising militancy of a newly formed Black Leadership Caucus, African-American membership in the southern church doubled to about 8,000 before the 1983 merger with the United Presbyterian Church (formed by the union of PCUSA and the United Presbyterian Church of North America in 1958).

Northern black Presbyterians figured prominently in the civil rights program of the National Council of Churches during the 1960s. The Afro-American Presbyterian Council of 1894 went through several reincarnations and finally developed into the Concerned Presbyterians in 1963 and Black Presbyterians United in 1968. The former caucus, with white allies, enabled the election of the controversial pastor of St. Augustine Presbyterian Church in the Bronx, Edler G. HAWKINS, as the first black moderator of the United Presbyterian Church in 1964. This group was also a major factor in the creation of the Commission on Religion and Race, which steered the church through the 1960s and played a leading role in the BLACK MANIFESTO call for slavery reparations in 1969 and the Angela DAVIS crisis of 1971. Gayraud S. Wilmore, a professor at the Pittsburgh Theological Seminary, J. Metz Rollins, a pastor and civil rights activist in Tallahassee, and Robert Stone, a New York City pastor, were chosen to head this unprecedented commitment of the church to the struggle led by the SOUTHERN CHRISTIAN LEADERSHIP CONFERENCE. Since the union, Asian, Hispanic, and Native-American minorities have played a larger role in the church's program in racial and intercultural affairs. African Americans, however, came together across regional lines in 1983 to form a National Black Presbyterian Caucus, which continues to monitor church policy and practice in the field of racial and ethnic relations.

REFERENCES

MURRAY, ANDREW W. *Presbyterians and the Negro: A History*. Philadelphia, 1966.

SWIFT, DAVID E. *Black Prophets of Justice: Activist Clergy Before the Civil War*. Baton Rouge, La., 1989.

WILMORE, GAYRAUD S. *Black and Presbyterian: The Heritage and the Hope*. Philadelphia, 1983.

GAYRAUD S. WILMORE

Presidents of the United States. Through their ability to veto legislation, appoint judges, command the armed forces, and influence public opinion (from the so-called bully pulpit), presidents of the United States have made decisions that have affected the lives of African Americans, as they have affected the lives of all Americans. At the same time, the actions of African Americans, in their struggle against slavery and their quest for civil rights, have determined the issues that presidents must confront and, in so doing, have shaped the office of the presidency.

The issue of the presidency as it relates to African-American history may be divided into three parts: the first, from the beginning of the executive office to the assassination of Abraham Lincoln; the second, from the succession of Andrew Johnson to the administration of Harry Truman; and the third, from the election of Dwight D. Eisenhower to the presidency of Bill Clinton. These periods are demarcated by two pivotal events in the history of African Americans—the Emancipation Proclamation of 1863 (*see* EMANCIPATION) and the BROWN V. BOARD OF EDUCATION OF TOPEKA, KANSAS decision in 1954. Like SLAVERY and the CIVIL RIGHTS MOVEMENT, these events serve as markers in the shifting scope of the influence, power, and purpose of the presidency.

From George Washington to Abraham Lincoln
When the presidency began, there were approximately 700,000 African Americans in the country—the vast majority of whom were slaves. Four of the first five presidents were slaveholders from Virginia, a state in which slavery had once flourished, but where the deterioration of the soil and the declining price of tobacco had made the institution less profitable. Reflecting on this, *George Washington* (1789–1797), a Virginia planter and the nation's first president, remarked in 1794 that slaves were "a very troublesome species of property." Like other presidents of the "Virginia Dynasty," Washington testified to the complexities of slave owning in his state—one that had paradoxically engendered both slavery itself and the republican notions of freedom found in the Constitution. On the one hand, Washington held a paternalistic view toward his slaves which was supported by a belief in their inferiority. "[T]he Blacks are so bad in their nature that they have not the least gratitude for the kindness that may be showed to them," he remarked. Yet unlike many of his contemporaries, Washington seemed able to recognize the accomplishments of individual African Americans, such as the Boston poet Phillis WHEATLEY who had written a poem in his honor. As president, Washington refused to interfere with the course of slavery. Twice he declined to lend his name in support of gradual emancipation: once to a group of Quakers (*see* SOCIETY OF FRIENDS) and a second time to a band of Maryland legislators who sought the demise of slavery in their own state. Similarly, he refused to support the Marquis de Lafayette, who planned to begin a colony of free blacks in French Guiana on the northern coast of South America.

Once he left office, however, Washington indicated on several instances that he wished to see an end to the "peculiar institution." "[T]here is not a man living, who wishes more sincerely than I do, to see a plan adopted for . . . abolition," he wrote. His will offered freedom to his personal slave, Billy Lee, and to the remainder of his slaves (with the exception of orphaned children and the elderly) upon the death of his wife, Martha. An inventory of Washington's plantation in 1799, the year of his death, revealed 317 slaves. Many were field hands, but there were also 11 house servants, 38 skilled artisans, 18 elderly, and 143 children.

Washington was followed in office by one of the few early presidents who did not own slaves, *John Adams* (Federalist, 1797–1801) of Massachusetts. While Adams's administration witnessed the sharp increase in southern slavery that followed Eli Whitney's production of the cotton gin, he made few public pronouncements on slavery. Most of his time as president was spent conducting foreign policy—trying to avoid war with France. In his later years, when the sectional crisis deepened, Adams spoke openly against the expansion of slavery, hoping to preserve western lands for white settlers. "If the gangrene is not stopped, I can see nothing but insurrection of the blacks against the whites . . . till at last the whites will be exasperated to madness," he wrote in 1819.

Thomas Jefferson (Democratic-Republican, 1801–1809) was a Virginia slave owner who, like Washington, personally struggled with the morality of slavery. Jefferson wrote on the subject often. In 1776, he included in a draft of the Declaration of Independence a section (deleted in the final document) condemning George III for foisting slavery upon the American people and for perpetuating a "cruel war against human nature [by] violating the most sacred right to life and liberty in the persons of a distant people who never offended him, capturing and carrying them into slavery in another hemisphere." This would remain Jefferson's strongest indictment of slavery and the SLAVE TRADE. He backed away from such rhetoric as he grew older. His guiding national principle that "all men are created equal" has been variously interpreted, though it is clear at the time that "all men" included only white males. In his *Notes on the State of Virginia* (1785), which contained sections attacking slavery, Jefferson also put forth his belief in the mental inferiority of blacks. African-American scientist Benjamin BANNEKER wrote in protest to Jefferson in 1791, sending along an almanac he had prepared as proof of the capabilities of members of his race. Banneker also criticized the president on the hypocrisy of writing about freedom and equality while "detaining by fraud and violence so numerous a part of my brethren under groaning captivity and cruel oppression." Jefferson responded only that he had yet to witness proof that nature had given blacks "talents equal to other colors of men," and largely ignored Banneker's insights.

Jefferson's actions as president had great impact on the course of slavery and the lives of African Americans. He believed his purchase of the Louisiana Territory in 1803 would provide enough land for a thousand years of westward migration and secure for small, independent farmers a future with limited federal government. Much of this land became the property of slave owners, however, and its purchase set the stage for later controversies over whether the expansion across the continent would be one of freedom or slavery. Jefferson's administration also saw the cessation of the slave trade in 1808. This fundamentally changed the nature of slavery and slave culture in the United States, as henceforth almost all slaves would be born on American soil. It also transformed certain states where slavery had become less profitable (including Jefferson's Virginia) into exporters of slaves to other regions of the country.

The issue of slavery pressed upon Jefferson greatly, though there remained a paradoxical gap between his writings and actions. In 1809, after leaving the White House, he wrote, "nobody wishes more ardently to see a revolution . . . of the condition of slavery, and certainly nobody will be more willing to encounter every sacrifice for that object." Yet the "revolution" he proposed fell along the lines of colonization rather than MANUMISSION. Unlike Washington, Jefferson continued buying and selling slaves during his presidency. He also did not free his slaves in his will. Even the mulatto Sally HEMINGS, with whom it is often alleged he had a long affair, lived and died in slavery—though Jefferson did make provisions in his will to free her sons.

James Madison (Democratic-Republican, 1809–1817), who had served as Jefferson's Secretary of State, largely hoped to continue his predecessor's vision of an agrarian republic. During his two-term administration, Madison spent much of his time trying to mitigate the effects of Jefferson's 1807 embargo on American trade with foreign nations and waging the subsequent WAR OF 1812. Like other members of the "Virginia Dynasty," Madison acknowledged the evils of slavery, but did not act against it. "The whole Bible is against Negro slavery, but the clergy do not preach this, and the people do not see it," he wrote. Along with Jefferson, he believed that colonization offered a feasible method of eradicating slavery. After leaving office in 1819, he proposed a gradual emancipation that would resettle manumitted slaves in the vacant western territories, though nothing came of it. Madison did not free his slaves in his will.

Virginian *James Monroe* (Democratic-Republican, 1817–1825) had served as Madison's secretary of state and secretary of war. As president, he faced the first true test of the unity of a nation half-slave and half-free. This was the question of whether slavery would be allowed in the newly organized state of Missouri. On this great and pressing issue, Monroe made little comment. He did not discuss it with his cabinet until March 1820 when a compromise was about to be approved by Congress (the MISSOURI COMPROMISE allowed slavery in Missouri, but forbade it in any other land acquired in the Louisiana Purchase above 36 degrees 30 minutes, the southern boundary of Missouri). Monroe then opposed the measure, arguing against imposing any restrictions on new states that had not been placed on existing states—in effect, that slavery should not be expressly forbidden from new states. The aged Thomas Jefferson was more outspoken on the issue. He ardently supported the southern position in 1820. To the end, Jefferson re-

mained a troubled, but firm, supporter of slavery. Recognizing the dangers the institution posed for the harmony of the nation, he remarked, "We have the wolf by the ears; and we can neither hold him, nor safely let him go. Justice is in one scale, and self-preservation in the other."

Like the Virginian presidents before him, Monroe was a proponent of colonization. He served as president of the AMERICAN COLONIZATION SOCIETY—an organization which proposed to gradually manumit slaves and resettle them in Africa with compensation for their former owners. In 1822, the society named its first settlement on the west coast of Africa (in what later became Liberia) Monrovia in his honor.

John Quincy Adams (Democratic-Republican, 1825–1829), son of former president John Adams and a native of Massachusetts, pursued a different vision of the nation's future than the Virginian presidents. He hoped to strengthen the role of the national government in domestic affairs—advocating federal funding of canals, turnpikes, and a national university. Few of these plans were realized. Adams's power as president was undercut by the popular perception that he had made a "corrupt bargain" with Henry Clay to win the 1824 election. Nevertheless, on several occasions Adams proposed measures which suggested his willingness to act on behalf of minority and disfranchised peoples, such as African and Native Americans. In 1826, for instance, he attempted to send U.S. delegates to a conference of Latin American countries in Panama, but was blocked in this effort by southern senators who opposed the presence of black delegates from Haiti. Adams's greatest efforts in this regard came upon the resumption of his congressional career in 1831, following his term as president. Remaining a member of the House of Representatives until his death in 1848, Adams became a tireless supporter of free speech. Although not an abolitionist, he defended the rights of antislavery groups to present petitions to Congress over an imposed "gag rule" which prohibited congressmen from reading, printing, or commenting in any way on the subject of slavery.

Adams's efforts on behalf of abolitionists greatly annoyed his successor, *Andrew Jackson* (Democrat, 1829–1837). Jackson, quite unlike Adams, had risen to national fame as a military hero and Indian fighter, winning the Battle of New Orleans and defeating the Creeks in Mississippi and the Seminoles in Spanish Florida. He also owned slaves. Before assuming the presidency, he had served as a congressman from Tennessee and purchased an estate, the Hermitage, which in 1809 was worked by about twenty slaves (Jackson would later develop it into a major cotton plantation). After losing the 1824 presidential election to Adams, Jackson began building a new political coalition of western expansionists, opponents of financial concentration, and others who helped usher in the so-called era of the common man. Some historians have characterized Jacksonian democracy in different terms, however, seeing it as a celebration of white supremacy. There are several reasons for this. In office, Jackson continued his war against Indians, relocating tribes west of the Mississippi. He also was vehement in his condemnation of the rising abolitionist and antislavery sentiment—such troublemakers, he believed, would split the DEMOCRATIC PARTY's national alliance into sectional camps. Jackson and his followers not only imposed the above-mentioned gag rule on congressional petitions, but also outlawed abolitionist mailings. In 1835 Jackson reported to Congress that these "inflammatory appeals to the passions of the slaves [would] produce all the horrors of a servile war."

If Jackson's policies were anathema to abolitionists, they could also arouse the ire of southern aristocrats who feared "too much democracy." Slave owners particularly objected to Jackson's attempts to enforce a high national tariff (a prospect always unpopular among a group dependent on trade). Sen. John C. Calhoun of South Carolina—the most heavily enslaved state in the nation—led a state convention in 1832 which argued that states had the right to nullify such federal legislation. Nullification was seen by Calhoun and others as necessary, not only to keep plantation slavery profitable, but to stop future federal assaults on slavery itself. Jackson pressed Congress for a "Force Bill" to coerce South Carolina to comply.

Jackson was followed in office by his vice president, *Martin Van Buren* (Democrat, 1837–1841), a former governor of New York. The Panic of 1837 and the depression that followed cast a pall over his administration. Van Buren tried to continue Jackson's policies and pledged not to interfere with slavery. For instance, he opposed abolishing slavery in the District of Columbia without the consent of the slaveholding states. In 1840, the Democrats renominated Van Buren on a platform, that, among other things, declared its opposition to ABOLITION.

After his defeat in the 1840 presidential election, however, Van Buren began to work for forces opposed to the expansion of slavery. In 1848, he headed the presidential ticket for the Free-Soil party, which aimed at banning slavery from western lands for the benefit of free white labor.

The 1840 Whig convention nominated *William Henry Harrison* (Whig, 1841), who like Jackson, had been a war hero. Harrison was descended from Virginia aristocracy, but had spent his adult life in the Old Northwest—in particular Indiana Territory, where he had served as governor. Because of this,

there was uneasiness in the Whig party (formed in opposition to Jackson) about how Harrison would fare in the South on election day. This was one of several reasons for balancing the ticket with John Tyler as vice presidential candidate. Tyler, a true Virginia aristocrat, was a staunch states-rights supporter and slave owner. His views were not considered particularly important before the election, as vice presidents were yet to play an important role in national politics. When Harrison died after less than a month in office, however, *John Tyler* (Whig, 1841–1845) assumed the presidency. Tyler's views alienated him among the Whig nationalists who had helped to elect Harrison. When he vetoed two bills proposing to establish a national bank, the Whigs deserted him—his entire cabinet, save Daniel Webster, resigned. Tyler's inclination to support the "rights" of southern states expressed itself in his efforts to annex Texas and bring it into the Union as a slave state—an act which was against the wishes of many leaders of both parties. After his term as president, Tyler retired to his Virginia plantation, Sherwood Forrest. At the outbreak of the CIVIL WAR, he was elected to the Confederate Congress, but he died before that assembly met.

Taking up Tyler's call for westward expansion, and ultimately the expansion of slavery, the southern Jacksonian Democrats rallied behind *James K. Polk* (Democrat, 1845–1849) of Tennessee, who defeated the Whig candidate Henry Clay in 1844. (Polk also triumphed over the antislavery Liberty party candidate James G. Birney.) Like his predecessors in office, Polk wished to keep the subject of slavery out of national politics, yet the course he pursued made this impossible. After the annexation of Texas in 1845, Polk pressed for the acquisition of California and New Mexico—initiating a war with Mexico to secure this land (*see* MEXICAN WAR). The acquisition of such vast territory thrust the issue of slavery, and more specifically the expansion of slavery, into the national political debate once again. It became the central issue of the brief administration of Polk's successor, *Zachary Taylor* (Whig, 1849–1850). Taylor had grown up in a prosperous planter family in Kentucky, and after serving as an officer in the Mexican War, purchased cotton plantations in Louisiana and Mississippi. Whig leaders seized upon his popularity after his victory in the Battle of Buena Vista and drafted him as their candidate. He was thrust into a national crisis with little political experience—particularly inflammatory was the question of whether to admit California as a free or slave state. While Sen. Henry Clay of Kentucky was working out a compromise over what to do with the land acquired from Mexico, Taylor died of a sudden attack of cholera on July 9, 1850.

After Taylor, the presidency passed to three northern Democrats. Because of their tolerance and, at times, support of slavery, these last three presidents before the Civil War—Fillmore, Pierce, and Buchanan—have been referred to as "Doughfaces." Polk's immediate successor, *Millard Fillmore* (Whig, 1850–1853), of New York State, was full of praise for Clay's COMPROMISE OF 1850, which, among other things, admitted California as a free state and outlawed the slave trade in Washington, D.C. Another feature of the compromise, which Fillmore signed, however, was the FUGITIVE SLAVE LAW. This greatly enhanced the powers of federal authorities to seize African Americans who were accused of being runaway slaves. It denied them trial by jury and the right to testify in court. It also served to increase the awareness among northerners of the brutality of slavery—as blacks were seized, chained, and dragged back to the South.

Franklin Pierce (Democrat, 1853–1857), who followed Fillmore, had largely built and operated the Democratic party in New Hampshire. Like other Democrats, he wished to limit the size of the national government and viewed reformers (like abolitionists) with suspicion and intolerance. Though he vowed to lessen the rising sectional conflict in his campaign speeches, this proved impossible. The most pressing problem was the right of southerners to bring slaves into the territory of Kansas. Pierce endorsed a proposal by Illinois Sen. Stephen A. Douglas to allow the people of the territory to settle the question themselves. This solution of "popular sovereignty," however democratic-sounding it seemed, was anathema to those who opposed slavery in the North, as it effectively overturned the 1820 Missouri Compromise which had banned slavery from these areas. The result was a bloody civil war in Kansas. Pierce was attacked by Free Soilers such as Salmon P. Chase and Charles Sumner, and by the Independent Democrats in his own party.

Because of this divisiveness created within his own party, Pierce did not secure the Democratic nomination in 1856. The man who did, *James Buchanan* (Democrat, 1857–1861) of Pennsylvania, was even more strongly in support of the South on the issue of slavery. Fortunately for his own political career, he had been out of the country (serving as minister to Russia) during the controversy over Kansas. Buchanan was elected with strong support from Southerners, who correctly judged he would not interfere with slavery's expansion. Believing that territorial legislatures could not prohibit slavery in territories, Buchanan pushed northern Supreme Court justices to formally invalidate the Missouri Compromise in the DRED SCOTT DECISION (1857). He further worsened the sectional crisis by endorsing the admission of Kansas as a slave state against its antislavery majority.

The presidential election of 1860 brought the sectional crisis to a breaking point, as evidenced by the scramble within factions of the Democratic party to find suitable nominees. Northern Democrats nominated Stephen A. Douglas of Illinois. Southern Democrats nominated John Breckenridge of Kentucky. Former Whigs and members of the newly formed (largely anti-Catholic and anti-immigrant) Know-Nothing party chose Senator John Bell of Tennessee. Against these three, the REPUBLICAN PARTY, founded in 1854, ran *Abraham Lincoln* (Republican, 1861–1865) of Illinois. The platform of the Republican party called for, among other things unacceptable in the South, an end to the expansion of slavery. Lincoln's election, brought about by nearly unanimous support of northern states, showed southern leaders that henceforth they could be consistently defeated in national elections by the more heavily populated North. Seven southern states seceded—South Carolina, Georgia, Florida, Alabama, Mississippi, Louisiana, and Texas. Buchanan, as a lame duck, refused to surrender federal property and denied the legality of secession. He left the matter of responding to the seizure of Forts Sumter and Pickens to his successor.

Upon taking office, Lincoln tried to be considerate of the several slaveholding border states that were yet to cast their lot with the Confederacy. In this climate, Lincoln vowed in his inaugural address (March 4, 1861) not to interfere with slavery where it legally existed, and to enforce the Fugitive Slave Law. Arkansas, Tennessee, North Carolina, and Virginia eventually chose to secede in April and May of 1861; Missouri, Kentucky, Maryland, and Delaware chose to remain within the Union.

Despite the bold reaction of the secessionists, Lincoln was generally viewed as a moderate on the issue of slavery. During his well-known senatorial debates with Stephen A. Douglas in 1858, Lincoln had explained his view that slavery was a moral wrong, one that contradicted the promise of equality in the Declaration of Independence. He had also warned of the divisiveness of the issue, remarking that "A house divided against itself cannot stand." At the same time, however, Lincoln had stated that, like Douglas, he believed in the superiority of the white race and opposed racial intermarriage and black suffrage. His support of the American Colonization Society and his suggestion that African Americans consider emigration to Haiti and Liberia had alienated radical abolitionists. At the start of the Civil War, Lincoln pledged only to fight to preserve the Union—whether that meant freeing all or none of the slaves. By 1862, however, as parts of the Confederacy began to fall and slaves began to take their own freedom,

Sojourner Truth with President Abraham Lincoln after their meeting on October 29, 1864. (Prints and Photographs Division, Library of Congress)

Lincoln recognized that the salvation of the Union rested with the abolition of slavery. His Emancipation Proclamation of January 1, 1863, applied only to areas under Confederate control. Yet it changed the meaning of the Civil War, making it a struggle to secure the rights of *all* Americans to freedom. His decision to enroll slaves as soldiers helped to secure a Union victory. By April 1865, nearly 200,000 men and women of African descent had joined the United States military as soldiers and laborers.

Grateful African Americans appreciated Lincoln's efforts to recognize their contributions to the war effort. In 1864, 519 African Americans contributed $580.75 to purchase a handsome gold-clasped Bible for Lincoln. A spokesman for the group called him "blessed." Lincoln responded to the group from Baltimore: "It has always been a sentiment with me that all mankind should be free." Lincoln's death in 1865 was a great tragedy to African Americans, some of whom bestowed upon him the status of a deity. In South Carolina, freedmen referred to him as "Uncle Sam," and cried that the "government was dead." One man declared, "Lincoln died for we, Christ died for we, and me believe him de same mans." The

AFRICAN METHODIST EPISCOPAL CHURCH, holding its forty-eighth annual session in Baltimore, resolved that "the death of the great President will be made the occasion of continuing the work [for complete freedom]."

From Andrew Johnson to Harry Truman

There were twenty administrations between 1865 and 1954, and with few exceptions they were either indifferent to the conditions of black Americans or sought to placate white Americans at the expense of blacks. It made little difference which party was in power in the White House or on Capitol Hill. The plight of African Americans in a JIM CROW South and hostile North went largely ignored.

Abraham Lincoln had given some thought to the intertwined issues of race and sectional politics in his plan to rebuild the nation after the end of the Civil War. In his lenient proposal, southern states would be readmitted into the Union upon compliance with a few simple procedures. Lincoln's plan required the southern states to recognize the end of slavery, but it did not specify that blacks be given full political rights. As historian Kenneth Stampp wrote, "For Lincoln Reconstruction was to be essentially a work of restoration, not innovation: it was the old Union— the Union as it was—that he hoped to rebuild."

Lincoln's assassination brought the antisecessionist, but prosouthern *Andrew Johnson* (Republican, 1865–1869) to the presidency. Johnson was born in North Carolina, but spent most of his life in Tennessee. A Jacksonian Democrat, he was the only southern senator to remain loyal to the Union after secession. He had been a slaveholder himself, yet had disdain for the plantation aristocracy that dominated the political, economic, and social life of the antebellum South. In part this can be attributed to his humble beginnings. Johnson held deep convictions about black inferiority, and the Reconstruction policies he pursued as president offered little civil rights protection. He came into conflict with Radical Republicans in Congress who wished to ensure not only black citizenship and voting rights, but also protection of civil liberties. Johnson's veto of the Freedmen's Bureau (*see* BUREAU OF FREEDMEN, REFUGEES, AND ABANDONED LANDS) and the Civil Rights Act of 1866 and his effort to remove Edwin Stanton from his post as secretary of war led to his impeachment (though not his conviction) by the House of Representatives. He remained a fairly weak executive afterward.

Ulysses S. Grant (Republican, 1869–1877), a native of Ohio and former supreme commander of the Union Army, did not pursue a clear or consistent Reconstruction policy. His administration was riddled with corruption, and the greatest efforts on behalf of African Americans during his tenure came from Congress. There were some bright spots in Grant's administration, however. His support of the Enforcement Act of 1874 helped to reduce the violence of the KU KLUX KLAN and his endorsement of the Civil Rights Act of 1875 helped to lessen discrimination in hotels and public accommodations (though this act was declared unconstitutional in 1883). Grant also appointed the first two African Americans to serve in the diplomatic corps. In 1869, he named Ebenezer Don Carlos BASSETT minister resident and consul general to Haiti; in 1871, he chose James Milton Turner to fill the same position in Liberia.

While the Grant administration had seen some small achievements for African Americans, the election of *Rutherford B. Hayes* (Republican, 1877–1881) proved a disaster. The popular vote resulted in an apparent victory for Hayes's Democratic opponent, Samuel Tilden, yet the returns of several southern states were disputed. In order to secure these votes for Hayes, Republican officials secretly conceded to southern Democrats their willingness to withdraw federal troops from the South and relinquish control of federal patronage there as well. The COMPROMISE OF 1877 suspended federal concern with such issues as black suffrage, civil rights, and integration, and brought the return of local white Democratic rule in the South. In the years that followed, state-supported segregation (so-called Jim Crow legislation) became widespread in the South. Hayes devoted much of his term to strengthening his party and the office of the presidency, which had been very badly damaged by his predecessors, and to pursuing civil service reform. In his retirement, Hayes worked for charitable causes, among them improving the education of poor white and black children.

Hayes's successor, *James A. Garfield* (Republican, 1881), of Ohio, served as president for only 200 days before being shot by religious extremist Charles K. Guiteau. The election campaign had not been concerned with the worsening plight of African Americans, but had been dominated by issues concerning currency reform, civil service, and the restriction of Chinese immigration. For the nation's ills, including the racial troubles in the South where LYNCHING was becoming increasingly common, Garfield's policy was: "Time is the only cure."

Chester A. Arthur (Republican, 1881–1885), a former New York State lawyer, succeeded Garfield as president. Arthur was an antislavery Whig before joining the Republican party. He served his presidential post more as an administrator than a reformer. He did, however, sign the Pendleton Civil Service Reform Act of 1883 which began the gradual process of opening federal jobs to competitive examination. Though it was not until the 1940s that the majority of

federal jobs were filled in this manner, the Civil Service provided a major source of employment for African Americans.

The Democratic administrations of *Grover Cleveland* (Democrat, 1885–1889; 1893–1897), who was from Buffalo, N.Y., did not greatly differ from those of his Republican predecessors. Cleveland pursued a modest and inactive course on racial matters. He was conservative on the currency issue, an anti-imperialist, and a supporter of big business. Like other presidents of this period, he neglected to address the continuing assaults on African-American rights. He did, however, maintain a cordial relationship with Frederick DOUGLASS, inviting him on several occasions to dine at the White House. Cleveland's successor, *Benjamin Harrison* (Republican, 1889-1893) from Indiana, the grandson of William Henry Harrison, continued the federal neglect of issues involving African Americans. His concerns lay primarily with expanding the boundaries of the Union, securing naval bases in the Caribbean and the Pacific, and attempting to annex Hawaii.

The spirit of imperialism continued with *William McKinley* (Republican, 1897–1901). McKinley led the nation into war against Spain after public outcry over the brutality of Spanish rule in Cuba. Over one-quarter of the U.S. invasion force entering Cuba was African American (*see* SPANISH–AMERICAN WAR). These soldiers served in their own regiments and lived in segregated quarters. They played a crucial role in winning the battle of San Juan Hill. It is a testament to the complexity of the relationship between imperialism and racism that white Americans were enraged over Spanish misrule in Cuba, while most did not bridle at injustices to blacks at home. Both may be linked to what Rudyard Kipling called "the White Man's Burden," the patronizing belief that it was the duty of white civilization to protect "lesser" races.

After McKinley's assassination by anarchist Leon Czolgosz, New Yorker *Theodore Roosevelt* (Republican, 1901–1909) became president. Roosevelt, who also held patronizing views of other civilizations, nonetheless won African-American approval by closing the Indianola, Miss., post office rather than acceding to white demands that he dismiss the black postmistress there and by insisting on appointing an African American as collector of the port of Charleston, S.C.—despite powerful southern senatorial opposition. Blacks were also encouraged by Roosevelt's invitation to Booker T. WASHINGTON to lunch at the White House, which, in the worsening racial climate of the early twentieth century, evoked a storm of protest from southern whites. In fact, Roosevelt and Washington, founder of Tuskegee Institute, maintained a close relationship throughout his administration. It was through Roosevelt's support of federal patronage that Washington was able to build his powerful "Tuskegee machine."

Roosevelt, however, sometimes acted in ways which angered his black supporters. For instance, he spoke favorably of southern traditions and falsely asserted that most lynchings were caused by black sexual assaults on white women. His worst action in this regard came in 1906 after a riot broke out in Brownsville, Texas (*see* BROWNSVILLE, TEXAS, INCIDENT). He summarily discharged three companies of the black Twenty-fifth Regiment for their involvement in a shootout with white citizens with little proof of their guilt. No action by Roosevelt hurt and angered African Americans more.

William Howard Taft (Republican, 1909–1913), Roosevelt's hand-picked successor, had earned a poor reputation among black voters even before his election in 1908. While secretary of war, Taft endorsed black ballot restrictions and criticized as "useless"

higher education for African Americans. He also was responsible for the Brownsville incident when serving as secretary. His inaugural address declared that "the best friend of the southern Negro is the southern white man," thereby indicating his approval of a conservative approach to federal involvement in southern racial issues. Taft appointed far fewer blacks to office than Roosevelt and even removed many of those who had positions in government—thus lessening the effectiveness of the Tuskegee machine. He also permitted segregation to be introduced in some federal buildings where it had not previously existed. His actions caused many blacks to shift their allegiance to the Democratic party, a process that had begun after Roosevelt's Brownsville decision.

Woodrow Wilson (Democrat, 1913–1921), a Virginian who had served as governor of New Jersey, was helped into office by this small but important movement of black voters to the Democratic party. Wilson, however, did not return the favor for this

When Booker T. Washington dined at the White House with Theodore Roosevelt on October 17, 1901, it provoked an enormous protest by white Southerners who complained that it was a dangerous step toward social equality. Despite the innocuous nature of Roosevelt's gesture, African Americans were also aware of the symbolic significance of the luncheon, as this commemorative card indicates. (Prints and Photographs Division, Library of Congress)

election support. In fact, the most conspicuous defect in his first administration was its attitude toward black Americans. Many of his closest advisers were white Southerners with few ties to the black community. Once in office, they terminated the remaining patronage that Republicans had conferred on black supporters. Wilson further demonstrated his loyalties to the South by rigidly segregating the few remaining black workers from white officeholders in government. Wilson told a leader of the NATIONAL ASSOCIATION FOR THE ADVANCEMENT OF COLORED PEOPLE (NAACP), "I have thought about this racial thing for twenty years and I see no way out. It will take a very big man to solve this thing." In November 1914, William Monroe TROTTER led a black delegation to the White House to protest Wilson's actions. Wilson met with the delegation only briefly and then dismissed them. Most of Wilson's attention focused on foreign policy, directing the United States' involvement in WORLD WAR I and trying to secure a lasting peace settlement with the creation of a League of Nations.

In the first presidential election after World War I, the Republican candidate, *Warren G. Harding* (Republican, 1921–1923), of Ohio, campaigned on a platform calling for a return to normalcy. Harding solidly won the black vote (it was the first election in which women, black or white, were allowed to vote). A few months after taking office, however, Harding made a speech on race relations in Birmingham, Ala., in which he asserted his belief in the social separation of blacks and whites. "Racial amalgamation there cannot be," he said. After Harding's death in August 1923, *Calvin Coolidge* (Republican, 1923–1929) of Vermont succeeded him as president. Coolidge maintained a conservative administration, cutting taxes and keeping the tariff high, and acting little on behalf of African Americans.

Meanwhile, leaders of the Democratic party—particularly those in northern cities—had continued their efforts to bring blacks into their fold. These politicians had taken careful note of the large black migrations from the South and tried to wean the newcomers from their Republican allegiances. They urged blacks to register to vote and gave local black leaders modest amounts of patronage. By 1928 this strategy began to show results, as the losing Democratic presidential candidate, Alfred Smith, did well among black voters.

The newly elected president, *Herbert Hoover* (Republican, 1929–1933) of Iowa, faced the worst depression in the history of the nation after the stock market crash of October 1929 (*see* GREAT DEPRESSION AND THE NEW DEAL). This proved disastrous for the worsening relation between African Americans and the Republican party. Hoover's policies did not help in this regard, for he gave few federal appointments to blacks and remained silent on the more than fifty lynchings of blacks that took place during his administration. Another slight came when Hoover's administration arranged to send Gold Star Mothers to France to visit the graves of their sons. African-American mothers were segregated and given inferior accommodations. Furthermore, in 1930 Hoover nominated to the Supreme Court the conservative Judge John J. Parker of North Carolina, who ten years earlier had said that the participation of blacks in politics was a "source of danger to both races." The NAACP fought the nomination, and the Senate withheld Parker's confirmation.

In the presidential election of 1932, blacks strongly supported the Democratic candidate, *Franklin D. Roosevelt* (Democrat, 1933–1945) of New York. African American support of Roosevelt increased during his first administration. In the election of 1936, he gained between 70 and 80 percent of the black vote. Their hopes rested on Roosevelt's plan for a New Deal in which the government would assume greater responsibility for the national welfare. At the time of his election, roughly one-quarter of the labor force was unemployed. No president had recognized African Americans as Roosevelt did. Roosevelt appointed many African Americans to government positions and solicited their political opinions—though his "black brain trust" was derided by critics as little more than window dressing.

Despite this, some New Deal programs ignored the plight of African Americans, and others were openly discriminatory. The Civilian Conservation Corps (CCC) maintained a policy of strict segregation, and the Agricultural Adjustment Act hurt both black sharecroppers and tenant farmers. The Social Security Act, by excluding agricultural and domestic workers from its provisions, excluded huge numbers of African Americans from benefit. Nevertheless, none could deny that the New Deal was immensely important to black people. One-third of all low-cost federal housing went to black families; two-fifths of the young men working in CCC camps were black; one-sixth of those participating in student-work programs of the National Youth Administration were black.

Many gains made by black Americans in this period also came through their own collective action. A. Philip RANDOLPH, head of the BROTHERHOOD OF SLEEPING CAR PORTERS, pressured Roosevelt (with a threatened march on Washington in 1941) to issue Executive Order 8802 banning discrimination in defense industries. Eleanor Roosevelt was a more consistent supporter of African-American rights than her husband. She invited black groups to the White House, visited black schools and federal projects, and

In 1947 Harry S. Truman became the first U.S. president to address a national convention of the NAACP, delivering his speech from the steps of the Lincoln Memorial. (Prints and Photographs Division, Library of Congress)

spoke to numerous groups. When she was photographed while being escorted by two Reserve Officers' Training Corps cadets from Howard University, blacks circulated the picture widely as an example of the broad egalitarianism of the occupants of the White House.

In many ways the CIVIL RIGHTS MOVEMENT (the so-called Second Reconstruction) began in the post–WORLD WAR II years during the administration of Missourian Harry S. Truman (Democrat, 1945–1953). By 1946 Democrats and Republicans alike knew they would have to compete for the growing black vote in urban-industrial states like California, Illinois, Michigan, Ohio, Pennsylvania, and New York. Truman, therefore, had political reasons for supporting black rights. However, he was also a man of strong moral convictions and worked to lessen racial division. He began the desegregation of the armed forces, and, on December 5, 1946, signed an executive order establishing the President's Committee on Civil Rights. A year later, when the committee delivered its report, *To Secure These Rights*, it recommended the enactment of federal legislation against lynching, segregation, and poll taxes. The committee's report further called for laws guaranteeing voting rights and equal employment opportunity. Truman sent a special message to Congress in

February 1948 embracing the committee's recommendations. Truman's support for a civil rights bill and a civil rights plank in the party platform brought a rift in the Democratic convention of 1948. Conservative southern Democrats walked out and formed the States' Rights (or "Dixiecrat") party. Despite this, Truman won a narrow but decisive victory over New York Gov. Thomas E. Dewey for a second term. Although some of his reform plans were approved by Congress—an increase in minimum wage, an expansion of Social Security benefits, the construction of low-income housing—Truman's efforts at civil rights protection were blocked. Truman hoped, among other things, to make lynching a federal crime, to provide federal protection for black voters, and to abolish poll taxes. Despite his only limited success in these areas, his recommendations helped to shape the civil rights agenda of liberal Democrats for the next twenty years.

From Dwight Eisenhower to Bill Clinton

Prior to the 1952 presidential election, African Americans had, through intense lobbying, gained a modest commitment by Presidents Franklin D. Roosevelt and Harry Truman to racial equality. Yet while Truman's civil rights efforts were stronger than Roosevelt's, a continuity in presidential behavior at

Gloria Richardson (left), a leader in the integration movement; Dr. Rosa L. Gragg (center) of the National Association of Colored Women's Clubs; and Diane Nash Bevel (right), representing the Southern Christian Leadership Committee, are interviewed on leaving the White House where President John Kennedy asked three hundred representatives of women's organizations to back his civil rights programs, July 9, 1963. (AP/Wide World Photos)

least on a personal level had been established. Many in the civil rights and African-American community held high hopes that such a commitment would continue under the new Republican president, *Dwight D. Eisenhower* (Republican, 1953–1961). But Eisenhower, born in Texas and raised in Kansas, spent much of his campaign courting southern white voters. To make matters worse, he chose a place that could hardly have been noticed—Wheeling, W. Va.—to give his major civil rights address. Events, however, forced Eisenhower to play a more active role in the advancement of civil rights. The BROWN V. THE BOARD OF EDUCATION OF TOPEKA, KANSAS (1954) decision against segregation came shortly after his election. It was the most crucial legislative turning point in the history of African Americans since the Emancipation Proclamation. It shifted the weight of the Constitution to be on the side of integration. In the wake of the *Brown* decision, Eisenhower, albeit with great reluctance, sent federal troops to Little Rock, Ark., in 1957 to ensure school desegregation and quell the violence that had erupted at Central High School. More than the personal commitment that had inspired Roosevelt and Truman, the *Brown* decision gave the president an institutional

commitment to enforce the law of the land that now included "equality."

In the wake of the 1954 decision, Eisenhower made substantive efforts on behalf of African Americans. In 1955 he appointed E. Frederick MORROW as administrative assistant to the president. Morrow was the first African American to hold a position on the White House staff. Also during the Eisenhower administration, Congress passed the Civil Rights Act of 1957, which established the Commission on Civil Rights and provided an additional assistant attorney general for the civil rights division in the justice department. Congress supplemented this act with passage of the 1960 Civil Rights Act, which gave additional power to the attorney general for protection of voting rights.

During the 1960 presidential campaign, *John F. Kennedy* (Democrat, 1961–1963) of Massachusetts seemed a promising alternative to the conservative Eisenhower. He openly objected to the arrest in Atlanta of the Rev. Dr. Martin Luther KING, Jr., telephoning Coretta King to express his sympathy. His brother Robert contacted the judge in the case and got King out on bail. As president, Kennedy brought more African Americans into federal offices than any

Civil rights leaders gather with President John Kennedy at the White House. (Prints and Photographs Division, Library of Congress)

before him. He appointed black Americans to serve in several important positions: commissioner for the U.S. Commission on Civil Rights; assistant to the secretary of labor; Housing and Home finance administrator; and ambassadors to Norway and Niger. Kennedy also appointed Thurgood MARSHALL as a justice to the U.S. Court of Appeals for the Second Circuit. He established the President's Committee on Equal Employment Opportunity and supported a policy of the Department of Health, Education, and Welfare to bar funds to segregated schools. Kennedy also issued three executive orders that aided African Americans, dealing with fair employment opportunities, nondiscrimination in grant-in-aid programs, and nondiscrimination in federally assisted housing.

However, his administration was a disappointment to many African-American leaders. Although Kennedy continued the use of federal marshals in both Mississippi and Alabama to enforce school desegregation, he did so only as a last resort. Like Eisenhower, he was reluctant to antagonize white Southerners and attempted to negotiate the entrance of black students with state governors until this proved impossible. More importantly, Kennedy failed to follow through on his campaign promise to draft civil rights legislation. It was not until the last year of his presidency—pressed by civil rights leaders

and his brother Robert, the attorney general—that John Kennedy submitted a full and comprehensive civil rights bill to Congress. Supported by Kennedy's successor after the president's assassination in November, 1963, the Civil Rights Act of 1964 empowered federal officials to combat discrimination in a number of areas: voting rights, public accommodations, and public school systems.

The administration of *Lyndon B. Johnson* (Democrat, 1963–1969), from Texas, was the high-water mark for the new institutional role of the president in regard to civil rights. It also further committed the office of the president to the civil rights cause. Johnson sent three landmark civil rights bills to Congress: the 1964 Civil Rights Act (mentioned above), the VOTING RIGHTS ACT OF 1965, and the Open Housing Law of 1968. He also backed the controversial Philadelphia Plan, which, it was hoped, would promote fair employment in industries, like construction, in which racial discrimination was widespread. The Johnson presidency expanded the responsibilities of the federal government to care for social welfare. For the first time since the 1930s, the government created a host of new social programs to combat poverty. Kennedy had begun to move along this path when he increased minimum wage (from $1.00 to $1.25) and Social Security benefits. Johnson brought

President Lyndon Johnson with civil rights leaders. (© Flip Schulke/Black Star)

to fruition some programs Kennedy had suggested, including Medicare (1965) and Medicaid (1966). He also initiated new programs to fight what he called a "war on poverty." The centerpiece of this effort was the Economic Opportunity Act (and the Office of Economic Opportunity) which sponsored vocational training, remedial education, college work-study loans, and other such programs. It also created programs for youths, such as the Jobs Corps, the Neighborhood Youth Corps, and VISTA (Volunteers in Service to America), which sent volunteers into troubled communities to teach and provide social services. These programs provided aid to a disproportionate share of African Americans.

Johnson also made several significant appointments. He promoted Thurgood Marshall to the Supreme Court—the first African American to hold that position. Johnson also chose Robert WEAVER to serve as secretary of Health, Education, and Welfare, making him the first African American to hold a cabinet position. Unfortunately, the disastrous and escalating war in Vietnam became Johnson's first priority (*see* VIETNAM WAR) diverting not only his attention from domestic issues, but government funds as well. The KERNER REPORT issued by the National Advisory Commission on Civil Disorders in 1968,

concluded that American society was becoming increasingly segregated and unequal.

Richard M. Nixon (Republican, 1969–1974), a former congressman from California, came to the presidency in the midst of a white backlash against expanded social and political opportunities for African Americans. Nixon understood his constituency to be "the silent majority"—described by Richard Scammon and Ben Wattenberg as "unyoung, unblack, and unpoor." His mandate, as he understood it, was for the federal government to retreat from local communities. Nixon withdrew both institutional and personal support from the issue of racial equality. He seldom spoke on the subject of civil rights and continued the Republican policy of appointing a few token African Americans to subcabinet posts and, like Eisenhower, one to the White House office staff. Legislatively, Nixon pressured the Department of Health, Education, and Welfare to continue funding school districts that had failed to integrate and reduced the amount of federal grants to many social welfare programs. In 1973, he abolished the Office of Economic Opportunity. It was only with great reluctance that Nixon signed the 1972 Equal Employment Opportunity Commission Act, as well as the 1970 renewal of the 1965 Voting Rights

President Jimmy Carter signing the Humphrey-Hawkins bill. Coretta Scott King stands at far right. (Photographs and Prints Division, Schomburg Center for Research in Black Culture, The New York Public Library, Astor, Lenox and Tilden Foundations)

Act. The Justice Department, however, continued to pursue AFFIRMATIVE ACTION cases during Nixon's tenure, somewhat against the president's wishes. The moderate and liberal justices of the Supreme Court, however, extended the reach of federal civil rights protection in many areas, ruling in favor of forced busing (1971), which Nixon opposed, and the right to an abortion (1973).

After Nixon was forced from office due to the exposure of the Watergate scandal, his successor was Michigander *Gerald R. Ford* (Republican, 1974–1977). (Nixon's first vice president, Spiro Agnew, had previously resigned in an unrelated criminal case.) In public, Ford continued the policies of his predecessor. He seldom spoke on the problem of racial discrimination and failed to issue a single executive order on behalf of civil rights. The majority of the statements that Ford did make were negative—attacking busing, for instance. During his time in office, he made one appointment of an African American to a cabinet position, William COLEMAN at the Department of Transportation.

Georgian *Jimmy Carter*'s (Democrat, 1977–1981) election to the presidency was aided greatly by African-American support. Carter acknowledged this debt by attending many African-American ceremonies and functions throughout the country. At these gatherings Carter not only restated his commitment to racial equality, but praised civil rights leaders, particularly his fellow Georgian, Martin Luther King, Jr. Once in office, Carter appointed more African Americans to cabinet and subcabinet positions and federal judgeships than all other presidents combined up to that point. These appointments included Patricia HARRIS as secretary of Housing and Urban Development—the first black woman to serve in the cabinet. Carter signed some ten executive orders, most designed to reorganize and consolidate the federal civil rights apparatus. One sought to increase participation of black colleges in federally sponsored programs. Carter's greatest failings in the eyes of his African-American supporters came when he refused to endorse a bill making the birthday of Martin Luther King, Jr. a federal holiday, and when he dismissed U.S. Ambassador Andrew YOUNG.

Ronald Reagan (Republican, 1981–1988) was born in Illinois but lived most of his life in California. He won the presidency voicing a conservative ideology. He supported the views of a coalition of Southerners who wanted not merely a "benign neglect" of African-American rights, but also a reversal of their gains in the area of equality. Reagan advanced the notion, through his highly effective public speeches, that civil rights leaders were the new racists and the enemies of civil rights progress. Reagan's addresses attacked not only busing, but other civil rights programs like affirmative action. He appointed numer-

ous African-American conservatives who agreed with his policies of curtailing civil rights regulation to cabinet and subcabinet positions. They were selected to offer the rhetorical justification for his proposed reduced federal effort in terms of civil rights. Thus at the Equal Employment Opportunity Commission (EEOC) and at the Department of Housing and Urban Development (HUD), Clarence THOMAS and Samuel PIERCE slowed the process of enforcement of existing civil rights laws.

Reagan's executive orders were designed to reduce the federal government's involvement in curbing discrimination. Executive Order 12320 revoked President Carter's order to increase participation of black colleges in federally sponsored programs. Reagan reorganized and recast the U.S. Civil Rights Commission when it came up for renewal by giving it a conservative membership and chairman. He also vetoed the Civil Rights Restoration Act of 1988—though Congress eventually overrode the veto.

The Reagan administration not only failed to enforce civil rights laws, but also cut both the budget and the staff to those agencies dedicated to that

Chairman of the Joint Chiefs of Staff Colin Powell appearing with President George Bush in May 1991 shortly after the conclusion of the Persian Gulf War. (AP/Wide World Photos)

cause—the staff of the Civil Rights Division was reduced from 210 in 1981 to 57 in 1985. The Reagan legacy for the presidency and African Americans—with the exception of his signing of the Martin Luther King, Jr., Holiday Bill and the 1988 Open Housing Law—is one that reversed the direction of civil rights policy taken during the preceding generation.

George Bush (Republican, 1989–1993) had served as Reagan's vice president for eight years. He won the presidency not only by running political advertisements that appealed to racist sentiment, but also by courting the same southern electoral coalition that had achieved victory for his predecessor. Bush's rhetoric echoed his Republican predecessor's in its negative views on affirmative action, quotas, and busing. He voiced support for civil rights and racial equality, but opposed many of the techniques that came into existence in the 1960s and '70s to implement those causes. Bush vetoed the Civil Rights Restoration Act of 1991 but signed a watered-down and weakened version of the bill. Bush's African-American appointees were, like those under Reagan's administration,

conservative and divisive in the African-American community. His most important appointment was the controversial nomination and confirmation of Clarence Thomas to the Supreme Court (*see also* HILL–THOMAS HEARINGS).

African Americans generally supported the election of *Bill Clinton* (Democrat, 1993–) from Arkansas. Their voices helped to secure key states in the general election, including Georgia. Clinton held his inaugural on the day of the celebration of Martin Luther King's birthday. He nominated four blacks to cabinet positions—Ron BROWN (Commerce Department), Mike Espy (Department of Agriculture), Jesse BROWN (secretary of veterans affairs), and Hazel O'LEARY (energy secretary). He also named Joycelyn ELDERS as surgeon-general, though she resigned in late 1994. While African Americans greeted Clinton's administration as a change for the better, there was concern among members of the CONGRESSIONAL BLACK CAUCUS on some specific issues. Not only did Clinton appoint David Gergen, a former aid to Ronald Reagan, to an important White House post, but

After the 1992 elections, which sent a record number of African Americans to Congress, the forty members of the Congressional Black Caucus reached new heights of influence. Meeting in March 1993 are (from left to right), Vice President Al Gore, President Bill Clinton, Rep. Kweisi Mfume of Maryland, and Sen. Carol Moseley-Braun of Illinois. (AP/Wide World Photos)

he also, in 1993, abandoned his support of Lani Guinier, a black legal scholar, for the job of chief civil rights enforcer in the Justice Department.

Overall, then, in the period since 1954, several Democratic presidents sponsored and orchestrated major civil rights bills that have advanced the social, political, and economic position of African Americans. Republican presidents have, in general, either stalled these measures by failing to enforce them or by placing people within the bureaucracy to limit their implementation. While Democratic presidents have fashioned a new institutional role for the presidency in the area of civil rights, the Republicans have reformulated and recast that role in a negative and reverse fashion. Whether partisanship will move toward a bipartisan stance in these matters remains to be seen.

The office of the president has, often through the pressure of African Americans, expanded greatly in scope since its founding in 1789. While the vast majority of presidents in this nation's history have tried to ignore the plight of African Americans, they have often been forced to do otherwise. The freedom that slaves took for themselves during the course of the Civil War no doubt influenced Lincoln's call for emancipation; the threatened march on Washington by A. Philip Randolph caused Franklin D. Roosevelt to increase the number of jobs available to African Americans; the ceaseless efforts of NAACP workers to combat the discrimination in a Jim Crow South or a hostile North brought about legislation (*Brown v. Board of Education*) and forced Eisenhower to act on behalf of integration. Although no African American has yet to attain the executive office, the scope, influence, and purpose of the presidency will no doubt continue to both shape and be shaped by the lives of African Americans.

REFERENCES

BERMAN, WILLIAM. *The Politics of Civil Rights in the Truman Administration*. Athens, Ohio, 1979.

BURK, ROBERT F. *The Eisenhower Administration and Black Civil Rights*. Knoxville, Tenn., 1984.

COX, LAWANDA. *Lincoln and Black Freedom: A Study in Presidential Leadership*. Columbia, S.C., 1981.

FARENBACHER, DON E. "Only His Stepchildren: Lincoln and the Negro." *Civil War History* 20 (1974).

FERLING, JOHN E. *The First of Men: A Life of George Washington*. Knoxville, Tenn., 1988.

FRANKLIN, JOHN HOPE, and ALFRED A. MOSS, JR. *From Slavery to Freedom*. New York, 1988.

GRAHAM, HUGH DAVIS. *The Civil Rights Era: Origins and Development of National Policy*. New York, 1990.

HARVEY, J. C. *Black Civil Rights During the Johnson Administration*. Jackson, Miss., 1973.

———. *Black Civil Rights During the Kennedy Administration*. Jackson, Miss., 1971.

———. "Civil Rights, Blacks, and the Reagan Administration." In Mfanya Donald Truman, ed. *Institutional Racism and Black America*. Needham Heights, Mass., 1985.

MEIER, AUGUST, and ELLIOTT RUDWICK. *From Plantation to Ghetto*. New York, 1964.

MELLON, MILTON T. *Early American Views on Negro Slavery*. With an introduction by Richard B. Morris. New York, 1969.

MORROW, E. FREDERICK. *Black Man in the White House*. New York, 1963.

PANETTA, LEON E., and PETER GALL. *Bring Us Together: The Nixon Team and the Civil Rights Retreat*. Philadelphia, 1971.

SHULL, STEVEN A. *The President and Civil Rights Policy: Leadership and Change*. Westport, Conn., 1989.

SITKOFF, HARVARD. *A New Deal for Blacks*. New York, 1978.

SMITH, ROBERT C. "Black Appointed Officials: A Neglected Area of Research in Black Political Participation." *Journal of Black Studies* 14 (March 1984): 369.

———. "The Political Behavior of Black Presidential Appointees, 1960–1980." *Western Journal of Black Studies* 8 (Fall 1984): 139–147.

WALTERS, RONALD W. *Black Presidential Politics in America: A Strategic Approach*. Albany, N.Y., 1988.

WHALEN, CHARLES, and BARBARA WHALEN. *The Longest Debate: A Legislative History of the 1964 Civil Rights Act*. Calvin John, Md., 1985.

WOLK, ALLAN. *The Presidency and Black Civil Rights: Eisenhower to Nixon*. East Brunswick, N.J., 1975.

MERVYN M. DYMALLY
WILLIAM SERAILE
HANES WALTON, JR.
MELVIN R. WILLIAMS

Price, Florence Beatrice Smith (April 9, 1887–June 3, 1953), composer, concert pianist, and organist. Florence Price, born Florence Smith in Little Rock, Ark., was the first African-American woman composer to achieve national recognition. She was the third child of Dr. James H. Smith, Little Rock's first black dentist, a published author, inventor, and civil rights advocate, and of Florence Irene Gulliver, a school teacher with some musical training who later was a successful businesswoman. Florence Smith attended the New England Conservatory of Music from 1903 to 1906, graduating with an artist's diploma in organ music and a teacher's diploma in piano. There she studied composition with Wallace Goodrich and Frederick Converse and privately with the composer George Whitefield Chadwick, director of the conservatory.

Smith taught for a time at the Cotton-Plant Arkadelphia Academy (1906–1907) and Shorter College

In 1933, when the Chicago Symphony Orchestra premiered her Symphony in E Minor, Florence Price became the first black female composer to have a work performed by a major American symphony orchestra. (Photographs and Prints Division, Schomburg Center for Research in Black Culture, The New York Public Library, Astor, Lenox and Tilden Foundations)

(1907–1910) in Little Rock, and later headed the music department at Clark University (1910–1912) in Atlanta. In 1912 she returned to Little Rock and married Thomas J. Price, an attorney and partner of Scipio Africanus Jones, one of Arkansas' most distinguished black lawyers. When she married, Florence Price abandoned her college teaching career and set up a private studio at her home. Little Rock had become racially intolerable by the mid-1920s, and the Price family settled in Chicago in 1927. It was here that Price established herself as a concert pianist, teacher, and nationally acclaimed composer.

During the 1920s she began to win awards for her compositions and her music was published by Theodore Presser, G. Schirmer, McKinely, Gamble Hinged, and Carl Fischer. In 1932, Price achieved national recognition when she won first prize in the Wanamaker Music Composition Contest for her

Symphony in E. Minor (her first symphony). With its premiere in June 1933 by the Chicago Symphony Orchestra under the baton of Frederick Stock, Price became the first African-American woman to have an orchestral work performed by a major American orchestra. In 1934, her Piano Concerto in One Movement was premiered by the Woman's Symphony Orchestra of Chicago (Ebba Sundstrom, conductor) with the black pianist Margaret BONDS. The Michigan W.P.A. Orchestra under Walter Poole premiered her Symphony No. 3 in 1940.

Price wrote over three hundred compositions, including symphonies, concertos, chamber works, art songs, and settings of SPIRITUALS for voice and piano. Her art songs and arrangements of spirituals were sung by many of the most renowned singers of the day, including Marian ANDERSON, Etta Moten, and Blanche Thebom. Her best-known spiritual arrangement, "My Soul's Been Anchored in De Lord," was recorded by Marian Anderson, Ellabelle Davis, and Leontyne PRICE. She also wrote popular music and orchestrated arrangements for the WGN radio symphony orchestra in Chicago.

Rising to prominence in the 1930s, much of Price's early music, including the Symphony in E Minor and the piano concerto, fall within the context of American musical nationalism. Her instrumental music reflects the influence of her cultural heritage, incorporating spirituals, spirituallike themes, and such characteristic dance music as the "Juba" dance within classical forms. Her music also represents a high point of the NEW NEGRO movement in the arts, which included the works of other composers such as William Grant STILL and William Levi DAWSON. Price died in Chicago in 1953.

REFERENCES

BROWN, RAE LINDA. Selected Orchestral Music of Florence B. Price in the Context of Her Life and Work. Ph.D. diss., Yale University, 1987.
———. "William Grant Still, Florence Price, and William Dawson: Echoes of the Harlem Renaissance." In Samuel Floyd, Jr., ed. Black Music in the Harlem Renaissance. Westport, Conn., 1990.
———. "The Woman's Symphony Orchestra of Chicago and Florence B. Price's Piano Concerto in One Movement." American Music 11, no. 2 (Summer 1993): 185–205.
GREEN, MILDRED. Black Women Composers: A Genesis. Boston, 1983.

RAE LINDA BROWN

Price, Joseph Charles (February 10, 1854–October 25, 1893), clergyman and educator. Born in Elizabeth City, N.C., Joseph Price was the son of a slave father, Charles Dozier, and free mother, Emily Pailin. After his father was sold away, his mother married David Price who gave Joseph his name and raised him as his own son. The family moved to New Bern, N.C. in 1862, where they joined the AFRICAN METHODIST EPISCOPAL (AME) ZION CHURCH. Joseph attended the St. Cyprian Episcopal School, later known as the Lowell Normal School of New Bern, N.C.

Price taught for four years (1871–1875) in Wilson, N.C., and graduated in 1881 from Lincoln University (in Oxford, Penn.), with a degree in theology. He was very active and popular while in college, winning several oratorical prizes. The AME Zion Church licensed him to preach in 1876, and he was ordained a deacon and elected a delegate to the 1880 General Conference. His oratorical skill soon propelled him to considerable fame within the church.

Price was a supporter of the Zion Wesley Institute, which trained American blacks for missionary service in Africa. His fund-raising efforts eventually led to the establishment of the Zion Wesley College in Salisbury, N.C. in 1882. In 1885 he advocated changing the name of the institution to Livingstone College, after the African missionary. Livingstone College was incorporated in 1885, the same year that Price garnered contributions to the college from white philanthropists such as William E. Dodge, Collis P. Huntington, and Leland Stanford. Price struggled to establish Livingstone College as a leading black liberal arts institution. In 1922 W. E. B. DU BOIS wrote that, if Price had lived, Livingstone College might have become a "black Harvard."

Price was a powerful and influential orator whose natural leadership skills were cut short by his untimely death at the age of forty. In 1890 he became chairman of a group of 445 African Americans who established the Citizens' Equal Rights Association of the United States. The association published a pamphlet which advocated the philosophy that education, lawful behavior, and financial security would assist in the acquisition of equal rights. Price was also elected president of National Afro-American Rights League, founded by T. Thomas FORTUNE in 1890. Both groups became inactive in the early 1890s due to internal conflicts and a lack of funding.

There is some speculation that, except for his early death, Price might have proved a natural counterpoint to Booker T. WASHINGTON's leadership of the black community in the South at the turn of the century. While optimistic and willing to work toward an alliance with the white South, Price was unwavering in his commitment to the immediate accordance of full citizenship rights to African Americans.

Price died on October 25, 1893, and was buried at Livingstone College. He was survived by his wife and four young children. In *The Souls of Black Folk* (1903), Du Bois wrote: ". . . for a time Price arose as a new leader, destined, it seemed, not to give up, but to reinstate the old ideals in a form less repugnant to the white South. But he passed away in his prime."

REFERENCES

LOGAN, RAYFORD W., and MICHAEL R. WINSTON, eds. *Dictionary of American Negro Biography*. New York, 1982.

THORNBROUGH, EMMA LOU. *T. Thomas Fortune: Militant Journalist*. Chicago, 1972.

WALLS, WILLIAM JACOB. *Joseph Charles Price: Educator and Race Leader*. Boston, 1943.

DEBI BROOME

Price, Mary Violet Leontyne (February 10, 1927–), opera singer. Born in Laurel, Miss., the soprano Leontyne Price came to be regarded as a *prima donna assoluta* during her exceptionally long operatic career (1952–1985).

Her parents had been involved in the musical life of Laurel, and provided her with piano lessons from the age of four. Soon thereafter, she joined her mother in the church choir and, after attending a recital by Marian ANDERSON in Jackson, Miss., in 1936, she resolved on a career in music. At that time, African-American women could aspire in music only for roles in education, and it was with that major in mind that Price enrolled at Central State College in Ohio. Before she graduated in 1949, however, her vocal talent was manifest and she was encouraged to enter the Juilliard School of Music, where she studied with Florence Kimball. As Mistress Ford in a school production of Verdi's *Falstaff*, she attracted the attention of American composer Virgil Thomson, who enlisted her for the role of Cecilia in a 1952 revival of his *Four Saints in Three Acts* (1934), a work calling for an all-black cast, thus initiating her professional career and terminating her formal study.

Following this production in New York and performances at the Paris International Arts Festival, she was engaged for the role of Bess in George Gershwin's *Porgy and Bess,* with which she toured in Berlin, Paris, and Vienna into 1954. In November of that year, she made her New York debut at Town Hall. The following February she appeared in the title role of Puccini's *Tosca* on television, later adding Mozart's *Die Zauberflöte* and *Don Giovanni,* and Poulenc's *Dialogues des Carmélites* to her NBC telecasts. In 1956, she sang the role of Cleopatra in Handel's *Giulio Cesare.*

Leontyne Price as Leonora in Giuseppe Verdi's *Il Trovatore* in 1963. (AP/Wide World Photos)

It was in the Poulenc opera as Madame Lidoine that she made her debut with the San Francisco Opera in 1957, following this with the leading soprano roles with that company in Verdi's *Il Trovatore* and Puccini's *Madama Butterfly* and debuts that year at the Arena di Verona, Covent Garden, and the Vienna Staatsoper (*Aida*). Her debut with the Lyric Opera of Chicago was as Liù in Puccini's *Turandot* (1959).

The Metropolitan Opera had only begun adding black singers to its roster in 1955 with Marian Anderson and Robert MCFERRIN, followed by the debuts of African-American artists Mattiwilda DOBBS (1956), Gloria Davy (1958), and Martina ARROYO (1959). Actually, Price had already appeared in the Metropolitan Opera Jamboree, a fund-raising broadcast from the Manhattan Ritz Theater, April 6, 1953, when she performed "Summertime" from *Porgy and Bess,* but her formal debut was as Leonora in Verdi's *Il Trovatore* on January 27, 1961, when she won an unprecedented forty-two-minute ovation, fully justifying her selection as the leading lady to open the next Met season (as Puccini's Minnie in *La Fanciulla del West*) and that of the next year (repeating her 1957 Vienna role of Aida, in which she was heard each season for the following five years). During the last six years of the "old Met," she particularly excelled in the Italian repertory (as Liù in Puccini's *Turandot,*

Cio-Cio-San in Puccini's *Madama Butterfly,* and Elvira in Verdi's *Ernani,* which she had sung for Herbert von Karajan at the 1962 Salzburg Festival).

The new home of the Metropolitan Opera at Lincoln Center was inaugurated in 1966 with a new opera by Samuel Barber, *Antony and Cleopatra,* written specifically for her. When she concluded her career in opera performances on January 3, 1985, with *Aida* at the Metropolitan Opera, she had proved her interpretive leadership in the Italian repertories of Verdi and Puccini, but she has expanded the previously practiced limits to move far past any stereotypes, excelling in German, Spanish, French, and Slavic works, as well as in spirituals and other American literature. Her principal opera roles, in addition to those mentioned, were the Prima Donna and Ariadne (*Ariadne auf Naxos*), Amelia (*Un Ballo in Maschera*), Fiordiligi (*Così fan tutte*), Donna Anna (*Don Giovanni*), Tatiana (*Eugene Onegin*), Minnie (*La Fanciulla del West*), Leonora (*La Forza del Destino*), Manon (*Manon Lescaut*), and the title role in *Tosca.*

Her recorded legacy is extensive. In addition to many of the operatic roles in which she appeared on stage—Bizet's *Carmen,* Mozart's *Don Giovanni* and *Così fan tutte,* Puccini's *Madama Butterfly* and *Tosca,* Verdi's *Aida, Un Ballo in Maschera, Ernani, La Forza del Destino,* and *Il Trovatore*—she has recorded Samuel Barber's *Hermit Songs* and music of Fauré, Poulenc, Wolf, and R. Strauss, as well as Verdi's *Requiem* and Beethoven's *Ninth Symphony.* She has also recorded excerpts from *Porgy and Bess* (with her then-husband William Warfield), an album of popular songs with André Previn (*Right as Rain*), and *Swing Low, Sweet Chariot,* a collection of fourteen spirituals. In 1992 RCA reissued on compact disc forty-seven arias by Price under the title *Leontyne Price: The Prima Donna Collection,* arias which had been recorded between 1965 and 1979.

REFERENCES

BLYTH, ALAN. "Mary Violet Leontyne Price." In *The New Grove Dictionary of Music and Musicians,* vol. 15. London, 1980, pp. 225–226.

"Leontyne Price." In Nicholas Slonimsky, ed. *Baker's Biographical Dictionary of Musicians,* 7th ed. New York, 1992, p. 1363.

LYON, HUGH LEE. *Leontyne Price: Highlights of a Prima Donna.* New York, 1973.

SARGEANT, WINTHROP. *Divas.* New York, 1973, pp. 134–167.

DOMINIQUE-RENÉ DE LERMA

Price, Samuel Blythe "Sammy" (October 6, 1908–April 14, 1992), jazz pianist. Sammy Price was born in Honey Grove, Tex., and grew up in Waco, where he learned to play alto saxophone, and in Dallas, where he studied piano with Portia Pittman, the daughter of Booker T. WASHINGTON. In 1925 Price joined the Alphonse Trent Orchestra as a Charleston dancer. Later that year he got his first job as a pianist, and soon he was leading his own big band in Dallas. In 1927 he toured with the *Let's Go Show,* and in the late 1920s he performed with Benny Long, Lem Johnson, and Leonard Chadwick. Price lived in Kansas City, Chicago, and Detroit before settling in New York City in 1937. There he began a lengthy association with Decca Records. He supervised and selected personnel for record dates and was a staff pianist, recording with many of the top blues and gospel musicians of the area, including Sister Rosetta THARPE, Peetie Wheatstraw, and Blue Lu Barker. Price also led his own group, the Texas Blusicians, which at times included Lester YOUNG, Ike Quebec, J. C. Heard, and Big Sid CATLETT. In the 1940s Price recorded for Mezz Mezzrow's King label as both solo boogie-woogie pianist and accompanist for Mezzrow and Sidney BECHET. During this time Price also organized the first black-run jazz festival in Philadelphia.

By the late 1940s Price was much in demand for his charming and muscular boogie-woogie style, and he toured Europe in 1948. Price returned to Dallas in the early 1950s as the owner of two nightclubs, but by 1955 he had embarked on another tour of Europe, an engagement he repeated in 1956 and 1957. In 1957 he moved back to New York to play with Henry "Red" Allen at New York's Metropole club, a gig that he interrupted in 1960 to tour with *Tambourines to Glory,* the gospel song-play by Langston HUGHES. During this time he also recorded several albums, including *Blues and Boogie* (1955) and *The Price Is Right* (1956).

Except for the late 1960s, when he briefly left the music business to work in community affairs and run Down Home Meat Products, Price's musical career flourished. He performed frequently at concerts and festivals in the United States and Europe, occasionally with a group known as Two-Tenor Boogie, and recorded *Midnight Boogie* (1969), *Fire* (1975), *Black Beauty* (1979), and *Play It Again, Sam* (1983). His last major appearance was at the Weill Recital Hall at Carnegie Hall as part of the 1991 JVC Jazz Festival. Price died of a heart attack in New York at the age of eighty-three.

REFERENCE

PRICE, SAMMY. *What Do They Want?* New York, 1990.

IRA BERGER

Pride, Charley Frank (March 18, 1938–), country singer and guitarist. Born in Sledge, Miss., Charley Pride grew up steeped in the African-American Mississippi Delta BLUES culture he encountered on his parents' sharecropper farm, but as a child gravitated toward the country music that was largely favored by whites. He taught himself guitar by the age of fourteen, but by his late teens he was concentrating on becoming a professional baseball player. Aside from a two-year stint in the Army, Pride played for Negro American League teams in Detroit, Memphis, and Birmingham from 1955 to 1959. Starting in 1960 he worked off-season as a tin smelter in Great Falls, Mont., and during the season played for the Class C Pioneer League team there, occasionally singing for the fans between innings. He also sang occasionally in nightclubs, where country music producers from Nashville heard him. After a brief time in the major leagues with the Los Angeles Angels in 1961, he returned to Montana. A final, unsuccessful tryout for the New York Mets in 1963 convinced Pride to give up baseball. On the trip back to Montana, he stopped off in Nashville, where his velvety baritone quickly earned him a reputation in the local country music scene.

From the mid-1960s on, Pride's love songs, starting with "Atlantic Coastal Line" (1965) and "Snakes Crawl at Night" (1965), were among the most popular recordings in country music, and Pride quickly became the first African-American star in country music since DeFord BAILEY more than three decades earlier. However, the all-white country music industry at first proved wary of an African-American star and took advantage of Pride's "white" sound, hiding the fact of his race. His first recordings were released without the usual publicity photos, and indeed, some country disc jockeys who knew Pride's race boycotted his music. Nonetheless, country music fans embraced Pride from the start and gave him numerous hit singles, including the Grammy Award–nominated "Just Between You and Me" (1966), "All I Have to Offer You Is Me" (1969), "Is Anybody Going to San Antone?" (1970), "Kiss an Angel Good Morning" (1973), "My Eyes Can Only See as Far as You" (1976), and "You're My Jamaica" (1979). Pride won the Country Music Association's Entertainer of the Year award in 1971, and that year he also won two Grammy Awards, for best sacred album (*Did You Think to Pray?*) and best gospel performance ("Let Me Live"). During this time he also toured extensively and became one of the few African Americans to perform at Nashville's Grand Ole Opry.

Since the 1970s Pride's success has continued unabated, with hit recordings including "Honky Tonk Blues" (1980), "I'm Missin' Mississippi" (1984), and "Amy's Eyes" (1989). In recent years Pride, who

Country singer Charley Pride performing in Los Angeles, Calif., April 4, 1987. (AP/Wide World Photos)

married in 1956 and has three children, has also pursued a career in business. He owns three radio stations and a cattle ranch in Dallas and is a majority shareholder of First Texas Bank in Dallas, where he lives.

REFERENCES

BURTON, CHARLIE. "Charley Pride." *Rolling Stone* (May 27, 1971): 52–53.

MILLARD, B. "Alone in the Spotlight." *Journal of Country Music* 14, no. 2 (1992): 18–22.

JONATHAN GILL

Primitive Baptists. The "Primitive" or "Antimission" Baptists (also known as "Old School," "Old Line," "Hardshell," "Square Toed," or "Old" Baptists) separated from mainstream Baptists in the early nineteenth century, in opposition to Baptist participation in the emerging evangelical Protestant culture. Primitive Baptists, who considered themselves descended from the original "primitive" Church, objected to missionary activities they believed were inconsistent with a Calvinist belief in predestination. They also opposed national organizations that threatened local church autonomy, and a centralized, paid "hireling" clergy. They denounced ministerial education, Bible and tract societies, and Sunday schools as innovations, and as "human institutions" contrary to the Bible and historic Baptist principles. Their opponents charged them with retreat from Christian responsibility in the world, and with a morbid inward-turning faith.

The split among Baptists involved African Americans as well, although few joined the Primitive party. For example, the Huntsville (Ala.) African Baptist Church (today the St. Bartley Primitive Baptist Church), the historic center of Black Primitive Baptists, was established with seventy-six members in 1820. Following its pastor, the Rev. William Harris, a free black, it entered the white Flint River Baptist Association the following year. When division came in the late 1820s, the church joined the Primitive faction. Forced out of the white association after the Civil War, the Huntsville church joined with other black Primitive Baptists to form the Indian Creek Primitive Baptist Association in northern Alabama. In 1895, the association had some 2,000 members.

Around 1906 there was a movement among Black Primitive Baptists for a national convention. This led to an organizational meeting in Huntsville, Ala., the following year called by Elders Clarence Francis Sams of Florida, James H. Carey of North Carolina, and George S. Crawford of Florida. Eighty-eight elders from seven southern states attended and organized the National Primitive Baptist Convention of the United States of America, headquartered in Tallahassee, Fla. The Convention, still the major Primitive Baptist body, had some 600 churches and 250,000 members in the early 1990s. Evident by the existence of a national organization—albeit a loose organization without centralized authority—National Primitive Baptists tend to be less theologically rigid than their white counterparts. They remain committed to sixteen articles of faith, including the doctrine of divine election and visible sainthood, baptism by immersion, and foot washing as a form of religious observance.

However, the National Primitive Baptists do not impose a common confession on associations and individual congregations, resulting in some variation in belief, especially concerning social action. Despite their ideological opposition to political action and other "worldly activities," the churches do serve as community centers and churches do supply funds to needy members. In 1967 the convention even considered a proposal to establish foreign missions, though it ultimately rejected the idea.

REFERENCES

Discipline of the Primitive Baptist Church. Tallahassee, Fla., 1966.

PIEPKORN, ARTHUR CARL. "The Primitive Baptists of North America." *Concordia Theological Monthly* 42, no. 5 (May 1971): 297–313.

SUTTON, JOEL BRETT. Spirit and Polity in a Black Primitive Baptist Church. Ph.D. diss., University of North Carolina, 1983.

TIMOTHY E. FULOP

Primus, Nelson A. (1842/43–May 29, 1916), painter. Born in Hartford, Conn., in either 1842 or 1843, Primus began an apprenticeship in 1858 with George Francis, the owner of a Hartford carriage works, to learn the carriage painting trade. Francis supported Primus's ambition to become an artist and gave him basic lessons in portraiture and landscape. Primus's early artistic efforts won him local recognition, and in 1859 he received a medal for drawing from the Connecticut State Agricultural Society. Although primarily self-taught, Primus studied painting informally in Hartford with Elizabeth Gilbert Jerome from 1860 to 1862.

In 1864 he moved to Boston to establish himself as a portrait painter. There he married and enjoyed some success as "Primus of Boston." He painted well-recieved portraits of local white Bostonians such as F. J. Allen, the proprietor of Astor House (n.d.) and Lizzie May Ulmer, a minor Boston actress (1876). He also depicted religious scenes and biblical subjects in such paintings as *Christ Before Pilate* and *Madonna,* both of which are now lost. He could not support himself by his commissions and had to work as a carriage painter and bookseller. Primus tried unsuccessfully to persuade his colleague, the prominent black landscapist Edward Mitchell BANNISTER, to introduce him to the wealthy, white abolitionist patrons who might have provided him with valuable commissions. In letters to his mother, Primus specualted that Bannister was jealous of his work; he also lamented that his poverty prevented him from traveling and studying art in Europe.

In 1895, Primus left Boston (his wife had died in 1876) and moved to San Francisco in hopes of finding more work. By 1897 he had settled in the city's Chinatown section where, except for a brief stay in Seattle, he lived for the remainder of his life. Financial success still proved elusive for Primus in San Francisco, and he drew almost all of his commissions from the Chinese community. Dogged by continual obscurity and poverty, Primus had to work occasionally as model for life-drawing classes at the Mark Hopkins Institute of Art.

Primus painted in a realistic, almost photographic, style, infusing many of his portraits with a sense of emotional drama. He copied several of his Chinatown portraits from the photographs of Arnold Genthe and Oscar Maurer, who shared a studio in San Francisco in the early 1900s. (Although Primus may have known the white photographers, no direct documentation of their relationship exists.) *The Crying Boy* or *Oriental Child* (1900) is a direct copy of an 1898 Maurer photograph. The painting depicts a despondent, young Chinese boy standing alone in a dark and shadowy street with a group of adults in the background. *The Fortune Teller* (1898), probably a copy of Genthe's photograph of the same name (n.d.), presents a sage in traditional Chinese costume seated at a sidewalk table with the tools of his trade spread around him; a sign announcing his profession in Chinese calligraphy hangs above.

Few other of Primus's paintings from his San Francisco years survive. *Portrait of a Lady* (a.k.a. *Lady with Golden Hair*, 1907) is a detailed study of a white woman with brilliantly colored red hair. As in many of his portraits, Primus presents here a side view of the subject's face dramatically spotlighted against a dark background. His last extant work, *Christ Being Lowered from the Cross* (1914), is a colorful deposition scene of huge proportions (twelve by fifteen feet). Primus died of tuberculosis at San Francisco Hospital in 1916. The Oakland Museum in California has acquired some of his work.

REFERENCES

LEWIS, SAMELLA S. *Art: African American.* New York, 1978.

McElroy, Guy C., Richard J. Powell, and Sharon F. Patton. *African-American Artists 1880–1987: Selections from the Evans-Tibbs Collection.* Seattle, Wash., 1989.

FRANCES A. ROSENFELD

Primus, Pearl (November 29, 1919–October 29, 1994), dancer and choreographer. Primus was born in Trinidad and raised in New York City, where she attended Hunter College. After graduating in 1940 with a degree in biology, she received a scholarship to study at the New School for Social Research in New York. Primus made her professional debut in New York in 1943, performing her own *African Ceremonial.* She then began performing at the Cafe Society Downtown, an integrated nightclub, and in 1944 she gave her first solo recital, performing to poetry and the music of folksinger Josh WHITE. That show met with such success that it moved to Broadway. In 1946, Primus appeared in a New York revival of *Showboat,* as well as in Louis Gruenberg's opera *The Emperor Jones* at the Chicago Civic Opera.

From the 1940s until her death in 1994, choreographer and dancer Pearl Primus was in the forefront of the black dance movement. In 1991 she was awarded the National Medal of Arts. (© Leandre Jackson)

Primus, who founded her own dance company in 1946, was best known for her "primitive" dances. She was famed for her energy and her physical daring, which were characterized by leaps up to five feet in the air. Dance critics praised her movements as forceful and dramatic, yet graceful and deliberately controlled. During this time Primus often based her dances on the work of black writers and on racial issues. In 1944, she interpreted Langston HUGHES's *The Negro Speaks of Rivers* (1944), and in 1945 she created *Strange Fruit,* based on the poem by Lewis Allen about a lynching. *Hard Time Blues* (1945) is based on a song about sharecroppers by folksinger Josh White. In 1949, Primus received a grant from the Julius Rosenwald Foundation to study dance in Central and West Africa. In the years that followed, she also studied and danced throughout the Caribbean and the southern United States. She drew her subjects from a variety of black cultures and figures, ranging from African stonecutters to Caribbean religious practices to rural life in the American South.

Primus married the dancer and choreographer Percival BORDE in 1954, and began a collaboration that ended only with his death in 1979. In 1959, the year Primus received an M.A. in education from New York University, she traveled to Liberia, where she worked with the National Dance Company there to create *Fanga,* an interpretation of a traditional Liberian invocation to the earth and sky. In 1978, Primus received a Ph.D. in Dance Education from New York University. The following year she created *Michael, Row Your Boat Ashore,* about the 1963 Birmingham, Ala., church bombing. From 1984 to 1990 Primus served as a professor of ethnic studies, and artist in residence at the Five Colleges consortium in Massachusetts. In 1990, she became the first chair of the Five Colleges Dance Consortium. Her original dance company eventually grew into the Pearl Primus Dance Language Institute, where her method of blending African-American, Caribbean, and African influences with modern dance and ballet techniques is taught. In 1991, President George Bush honored Primus with the National Medal of Arts.

REFERENCES

Emery, Lynne Fauley. *Black Dance: From 1619 to Today.* Salem, Mass., 1988.
Thorpe, Edward. *Black Dance.* London, 1989.
Wright, Patricia. "The Prime of Miss Pearl Primus." *Contact* 10, no. 3 (February 1985): 13–16.

ELIZABETH V. FOLEY

Prince (Nelson, Prince Rogers) (c. June 7, 1958–), singer and composer. Prince Rogers Nelson, who goes by the name Prince, is reluctant to divulge information about his early years. He was born to two JAZZ musicians in an interrracial marriage and raised in Minneapolis, Minn. He began playing music at a very young age, alternating among piano, keyboards, guitar, and drums. He formed his own band, Grand Central, while still in junior high school. Prince made his first demonstration record in 1976, playing all the parts of the music himself. In 1978, after his manager subtracted several years from Prince's age and heralded him as "a new Stevie WONDER," Prince signed a contract with Warner Brothers and made *For You*. That album combined several African-American musical styles, taking the heavy bass of funk and mixing it with the dance beat of disco, while providing an overall feeling of rock in both arrangement and content. His second album, *Prince* (1979), was a great commercial success, producing the hit single, "I Wanna Be Your Lover."

Prince, who adopted a visually androgynous persona in photos, public appearances, and performances, first received notoriety for sexually explicit lyrics on his third album, *Dirty Mind* (1980), which included songs about incest, oral sex, and a ménage-à-trois. His breakthrough album, *1999* (1982), included the hit songs "1999" and "Little Red Cor-

vette," both of which featured a vocal style ranging from a reedy falsetto to a muscular baritone.

In 1984 Prince produced, wrote, scored, and starred in the film *Purple Rain*, whose soundtrack sold more than seventeen million copies and won an Oscar for best original music score, in addition to three Grammy Awards and three American Music Awards. After this, Prince continued to pursue film projects. His film *Under the Cherry Moon* (1987) failed to achieve wide popularity, but his soundtrack for *Batman* reached the top of the popular album charts in 1989. His film *Graffiti Bridge* (1992) achieved only moderate success.

Since 1987 Prince has recorded his own albums and produced music by others in Paisley Park Studios, a Minneapolis production facility built with the assistance of Warner Brothers. In 1987 he also released *Sign o' the Times*, which combined the rhythms of funk with GOSPEL and pop styles, but it failed to muster significant appeal. In 1992 he released an album whose title was a symbolic representation that he thereafter officially adopted as his name.

In recent years Prince has worked with many prominent figures in popular music, including Chaka Khan, Sheena Easton, Stephanie Mills, the Bangles, Stevie Nicks, Sheila E, Patti LaBelle, and M. C. Hammer. He has also collaborated with the gospel singer Mavis Staples, and in the late 1980s he worked several times with the jazz trumpeter Miles DAVIS. Although Prince has a huge international following, he has remained committed to his home state. He owns two nightclubs in Minneapolis and lives on a thirty-acre estate in Chaussen, a small town thirty miles from Minneapolis.

REFERENCES

KALOGERAKIS, GEORGE. "Prince and the Revelation." *Vanity Fair* 56 (November 1993): 128.

KARLEN, NEAL. "Prince Talks." *Rolling Stone* (October 18, 1990): 56.

DAVID HENDERSON

Pop musician Prince in an appearance at New York City's Apollo Theater in 1993. (AP/Wide World Photos)

Prince, Lucy Terry (c. 1730–August 21, 1821), poet. The history of African-American poetry begins in 1746 with Lucy Terry Prince, who at the age of sixteen wrote a vivid verse of rhyming couplets describing a victorious Native-American raid in Deerfield, Mass. Prince's poem is the most complete contemporary account of the murder of two white families who resided in a section of town called the Bars. "Bars Fight, August 28, 1746" became part of Deerfield's oral tradition, remaining unpublished until 1855, when it appeared in a volume of local history. The poem may also have been sung as a ballad.

Prince was known in her community as a story-teller, and her home became a meeting place to hear her orations. Prince's New England community also remembered her for two outstanding uses of orator-ical skills. In one, she spoke for three hours before the Board of Trustees of Williams College in an ulti-mately unsuccessful plea for one of her sons to gain admission to the school. In the other, she defended herself before the United States Supreme Court in a land-claims case against a neighbor. Prince won the case and earned high praise from Supreme Court Jus-tice Samuel Chase.

Lucy Terry was born in Africa and brought to New England as an infant slave. In 1756 she married Abijah Prince, a manumitted slave who then pur-chased his wife's freedom. The couple moved to Ver-mont, where Abijah had been given land, and their son, Cesar (one of six children), served in the Amer-ican Revolution.

REFERENCE

KAPLAN, SIDNEY, and EMMA NOGRADY KAPLAN. *The Black Presence in the Era of the American Revolution.* Amherst, Mass., 1989.

MARTHA E. HODES

Prince, Nancy Gardner (September 15, 1799–?), traveler and memoirist. Nancy Prince was born of free parents in Newburyport, Mass. Little is known of her remarkable life beyond her account in *Narra-tive of the Life and Travels of Mrs. Prince* (1850). Prince's narrative offers a unique glimpse at working-class African-American life in the nineteenth century in its depiction of a free black family in a seafaring New England town. Her ancestors included a Native-American grandmother who was captured and enslaved by the English and an enslaved African grandfather who fought at Bunker Hill. Her stepfa-ther, an African seaman who escaped slavery by jumping ship, was pressed into service during the War of 1812 by a British privateer and died in 1813. Prince's account of the economic hardships faced by free blacks at this period, though brief, is particularly valuable.

At the age of fourteen, Nancy Gardner was work-ing as a domestic servant for a family of seven. In February 1824, she married Nero Prince, who was employed as a servant in the court of Alexander I. That April, the only female on board, she sailed to Russia, where she remained for nearly ten years. She operated a boardinghouse for schoolchildren and set up a business making baby linen and children's gar-ments, employing a journeywoman and apprentices. Prince's narrative of her years in Russia is a unique travel account, both in its black authorship and in its perspective on Russia, with eyewitness accounts of historical events and social occasions.

Ill health forced Prince to return to the United States in 1833; her husband remained in Russia, where he died soon after. In the United States, Prince struggled to support herself and was involved in sev-eral abolitionist and charitable enterprises. She helped found, but was unable to maintain, a home for black orphans in Boston.

In 1840, she sailed for Jamaica to teach and evan-gelize the emancipated slaves. Although in 1842 she was briefly successful in setting up a Free Labor School for destitute young women, the personal dif-ficulties of a single woman supporting herself, com-bined with internal conflicts of her various sponsors, doomed most of her efforts. Out of a desire to "sup-port [herself] by [her] own endeavors," rather than avail herself of the "benevolent societies for the sup-port of Widows," she published her narrative, fol-lowed by a second edition in 1853 and a third in 1856. Neither the time nor place of her death is known.

REFERENCE

WALTERS, RONALD G. Introduction to *A Black Wom-an's Odyssey through Russia and Jamaica: The Narra-tive of Nancy Prince*, by Nancy Prince. New York, 1990.

QUANDRA PRETTYMAN

Prison Labor. One of the most enduring images of the postbellum South is the chain gang, consisting of convicts in striped prison uniforms, chained together and laboring alongside the roadway. The chain gang was only one of the forms of prison labor developed in the late nineteenth century. Although prison labor was found in all areas of the country, it was in the South that it was most important and was practiced in its most distinctive and most brutal forms. The southern prison system made use of black labor as early as the late 1850s. As white Southerners became increasingly concerned about the region's expanding free black population, they increasingly turned to the state prison as a means of control. As the black prison population expanded, so too did the existing prison leasing system. For many years, southern states had allowed lessors to use prison labor within the prison itself, but in 1858, Virginia was the first state to allow railroad and canal companies to take free black con-victs out of the prison to labor.

This system of leasing out black convicts expanded in the aftermath of the CIVIL WAR as southern states tried to control millions of blacks previously contained in slavery on individual plantations. In most cases, state finances were insufficient to meet the growing demands of the state penitentiary, and the South's growing industrial economy was short of capital, thus providing an ideal setting for the growth of convict leasing. Leasing convicts to private contractors and corporations relieved the government from responsibility for maintenance of the prison population and provided employers with a cheap, manageable, and readily available labor supply.

During the 1860s and early '70s, states began to experiment with convict labor, offering short lease periods for mainly agricultural and railroad labor. By 1880, every ex-Confederate state had implemented a convict leasing system. Although convicts were used for virtually every conceivable type of labor, they were used primarily on railroads in the 1870s and in mines in the '80s and '90s.

The growth of the convict lease system was associated with a radical shift in the racial composition of the prison population. Prior to the Civil War, the majority of the prison population had been white; but by 1880, nine-tenths of the South's prison population was black. Taking almost all blacks, save the sick or infirmed, out of the prisons themselves enabled prison officials to maintain a racially segregated prison system. By 1890 there were an estimated 27,000 convict laborers in the South.

Men were the primary source of convict labor, working in turpentine and phosphate camps in Florida and on railroads and in mines in other states, but black women, who comprised the majority of the female prison population, were also used in the convict leasing system. Women were kept apart from the male prison population and were employed as cooks, washerwomen, and in other domestic chores. (Less than 10 percent of the total prison population was female.)

Prisoners used in the convict lease system, some as young as nine years old, endured horrific work conditions. They worked under armed guard; frequently they wore leg irons and were chained together at their ankles. Convicts labored from ten to fourteen hours a day and were allowed no breaks other than a short time to eat lunch and dinner. Sanitary conditions in the camps were life-threatening, and many prisoners died from disease and malnutrition. Overwork and beatings claimed the lives of others. Of the convicts who suffered these intolerable conditions, approximately half had been sentenced for minor theft or burglary.

While the convict lease system satisfied employers' demands for cheap labor and provided tremendous profits for the state, not all whites united behind the system. Foremost among the opponents of convict leasing were white workers whose jobs were threatened by convict labor. Other opponents included residents where convict camps were established, opposition political parties, and moral reformers. Under mounting pressure from reformers, southern politicians began organizing investigative committees in the 1880s to study conditions in the convict camps. Their reports, revealing the terrible abuses of the system, galvanized the media behind the opponents' cause, and public opinion began to turn against the convict lease system.

The Tennessee legislature succumbed to the protestations of miners in 1895, becoming the first state to abolish the convict lease system. Prison reform associations were organized in several southern states to work with ministers, labor unions, and newspapers, toward abolishing the system. By 1913, six states—Louisiana (1901), Mississippi (1906), Oklahoma (1907), Georgia (1907), Texas (1910), and Arkansas (1912)—had outlawed the system. Only Alabama continued to lease convicts to private corporations until it abolished the system in 1919, becoming the last state to do so.

Although the use of convict labor by private employers was prohibited throughout the South, the use of convict labor did not cease. Instead, southern states turned to state-owned prison farms and public chain gangs to employ prisoners. Defenders of this new system argued that the worst abuses of the old convict leasing had been removed by placing the state in control. Although reformist activity and exposes continued to attack the abuses of the system and managed to curb its use in the 1920s and 1930s, southern states continued to use state-controlled convict labor as late as 1960.

Vivid images of the system exist in literature, film, and song. In the 1930s the musicologist John A. Lomax visited numerous prison work camps to capture the frequently haunting music of prison laborers. The best known of the singers Lomax met was Huddie LEDBETTER, whose music was shaped by the experience of working twelve to fourteen hours a day on prison farms. Convict work songs serve as powerful reminders of the horrors of the chain gang, while also demonstrating that black convicts managed to fuse their own culture with their work experiences to create a distinctive folk art that survives even to the present. Even after the decline of prison labor, it continued to be acknowledged in African-American culture through ersatz testaments such as Sam COOKE's "Chain Gang" (1960).

REFERENCES

AYERS, EDWARD L. Vengeance and Justice: Crime and Punishment in the Nineteenth-Century South. New York, 1984.

NOVAK, DANIEL A. *The Wheel of Servitude: Black Forced Labor After Slavery.* Lexington, Ky., 1978.
WOODWARD, C. VANN. *Origins of the New South, 1877–1913.* Baton Rouge, La., 1951.

LOUISE P. MAXWELL

Proctor, Henry Hugh (December 8, 1868–May 12, 1933), clergyman and civil rights activist. Henry Hugh Proctor was born near Fayetteville, Tenn., to former slaves Richard and Hannah (Murray) Proctor. After attending public school in Fayetteville, he became a teacher in Pea Ridge, Tenn., and then teacher and principal of the Fayetteville public school. He attended Central Tennessee College in Nashville from 1884 to 1885 and then studied at Fisk University, became friendly with W. E. B. DU BOIS, a fellow student, and finally received his B.A. in 1891. In 1894 Proctor graduated from Yale Divinity School and was ordained a Congregational minister. He became pastor of the elite First Congregational Church in Atlanta, Ga., a black church built and funded by the AMERICAN MISSIONARY ASSOCIATION (AMA), whose congregation formed, in one commentator's words, the "black Atlantan social register." He served there until 1920.

In 1903 Proctor cofounded and became first president of the National Convention of Congregational Workers Among Colored People, which was designed to make Southern black Congregational churches self-sufficient, as well as to improve theology departments and promote black hiring in AMA colleges. In 1904, the National Council of Churches named him to the largely symbolic post of assistant moderator. The same year, he obtained his Doctor of Divinity Degree from Atlanta's Clark University.

In 1906, in the aftermath of the notorious riot in Atlanta (*see* ATLANTA RIOT OF 1906), Proctor joined with white attorney Charles T. Hopkins to form the Interracial Committee of Atlanta, which was mildly successful in reducing racial tension. The two men recruited forty blacks and whites to draw up plans for reducing racial tensions. Proctor decried the lack of recreational facilities for black youth, and so he made the First Congregational Church into an institutional church, providing sports, schools, and employment counseling, as well as a kindergarten, library, girl's home, and model kitchen. Proctor designed an auditorium that seated one thousand, and in 1910 he organized the Atlanta Colored Music Festival. He regarded the SPIRITUAL as a powerful weapon of black pride. His pastoral service and musical work were so popular that the membership of the First Congregational rose from one hundred in 1900 to one thousand when he left in 1920.

Proctor was an expert orator, best known for his speech "The Burden of the Negro," which he delivered hundreds of times. In it, Proctor preached self-help and discipline. He counseled elite blacks to devote themselves to aiding the black masses, while retaining their "social reserve" against interclass mixing. Proctor was influenced by Du Bois and Booker T. WASHINGTON, both of whom were his personal friends. Although conservative on many political issues, he fought black disenfranchisement and supported civil rights efforts. He also wrote religious articles and two books, *Sermons in Melody* (1916) and *Between Black and White* (1925).

In 1919, Proctor spoke to African-American troops in Europe. When he returned to the United States the following year, he assumed the pastorate of the Nazarene Congregational Church in Brooklyn, and in 1926 he became moderator of the New York City Congregational Church Association, an organization of black clergymen. Proctor died in New York.

REFERENCES

LEWIS, DAVID LEVERING. *W. E. B. Du Bois: Biography of a Race, 1868–1919.* New York, 1993.
PROCTOR, HENRY HUGH. *Between Black and White: Autobiographical Sketches.* Boston, 1925.

SABRINA FUCHS

Professional Organizations. Professional associations regulate entry into their respective professions, set standards for their practice, provide training and forums for the exchange of information among members, and serve as formal and informal networks through which members advance their careers. Until the middle of the twentieth century, most major American professional associations excluded African Americans from membership. Blacks responded by organizing their own societies. Even after they achieved equality in the general associations, African-American professionals maintained separate organizations to address their special needs in the often overwhelmingly white professions.

The first African-American professional associations were established on a local level in the late-nineteenth century. Excluded from the Medical Society of the District of Columbia, black doctors founded the National Medical Society in 1870. Physicians in other cities and states organized similar societies in the next two decades. In 1895, African-American physicians formed the National Medical Association (NMA), the first national black professional society. (The American Medical Association [AMA], the country's largest and most prestigious medical society, officially adopted a color bar in 1872.) At first, the NMA included related medical professions in addition to physicians, but these soon began to establish their own organizations. The National Dental Association arose in 1897, the National Association of Colored Graduate Nurses in 1908, and the National Pharmaceutical Association in 1933.

The National Negro Business League (NNBL) was founded in 1900 by Booker T. WASHINGTON. While primarily an organization of businesspeople, it also included special sections for lawyers, pharmacists, morticians, real-estate brokers, and bankers. In 1909, the lawyers' section became the National Negro Bar Association and remained affiliated with the NNBL until 1925. Reconstituted as an independent organization in that year, the National Bar Association (NBA) also forged links among the many local black legal societies, the first of which, the Colored Bar Association of Mississippi, was founded in 1891. The NBA regularly took a strong stand on civil rights issues and emphasized the need for African-American lawyers especially in light of the important role they could play in the struggle for equal rights.

By the late 1940s, color barriers in the larger American professional associations were beginning to fall. In 1943, the American Bar Association adopted a resolution stating that membership was "not dependent upon race, creed, or color." Others followed suit. When blacks were admitted to the American Nurses Association in 1948, the National Association of Colored Graduate Nurses dissolved. In 1948, E. Franklin FRAZIER became the first African American to head a predominantly white professional association when he was elected president of the American Sociological Association. Only in the 1970s did several others achieve similar positions. A major milestone was reached in 1994, when Lonnie Bristow was elected to the presidency of the venerable, powerful AMA.

Nevertheless, progress in integrating the mainstream professional associations was slow. Many local societies remained segregated through the 1960s, and because some of the national organizations required members to belong to the local groups, this remained an effective bar to participation by blacks, especially in the South. Moreover, many black professionals in the late 1960s and early 1970s believed that the general organizations did not serve them adequately. Members of some professions formed caucuses within the general professional associations to press them to take stronger stands against discrimination and white cultural biases, recruit more minority practitioners, and find ways to better serve the African-American community as a whole. In many cases, these caucuses evolved into independent national organizations, joining the older associations such as the NBA and the NMA in serving the grow-ing number of African-American professionals in the 1980s and 1990s.

See the Appendix for a listing of black professional organizations.

DANIEL SOYER

Professor Longhair (Byrd, Henry Roeland "Roy") (December 19, 1918–January 30, 1980), rhythm and blues pianist and singer. Born in Bogalusa, La., Henry Byrd was raised in extreme poverty in New Orleans by his mother. He learned about music as a child by listening to the BLUES and boogie-woogie styles played in the nightclubs of New Orleans. He earned spare change by street dancing, and played percussion in the informal children's bands which often followed and supplemented legitimate marching bands. In 1926 Byrd also performed as a stuntman in the CJK Medicine Show in New Orleans. He began playing blues guitar, and in his late teens taught himself piano after finding an abandoned upright instrument in an alley.

In the early 1930s Byrd worked as a dancer with Champion Jack Dupree, but later in the decade he was supporting himself largely by boxing and gambling, and worked in the Civilian Conservation Corps in 1937. Byrd married briefly in 1940 and served in the Army from 1942 to 1944. After the war he worked as a cook, but his time was mainly spent roaming barrelhouses and nightclubs, playing piano. Byrd led his first ensembles in the late 1940s, and became known as "Professor Longhair" because of his collar-length, processed hair. He had his first regionally popular record in 1949, and shaved his hair off to commemorate its title, "Bald Head." In that year he also recorded "Byrd's Blues" and "Her Mind Is Gone."

Although Professor Longhair eventually came to personify post–World War II New Orleans music, in the 1950s his quirky vocal style and diffident personality kept his music from attaining national recognition on the scale of Fats DOMINO. Nonetheless, Professor Longhair was, along with Domino and Dave Bartholemew, a dominating presence in the eclectic and lively Gulf Coast RHYTHM AND BLUES scene. He was a brilliant, flamboyant pianist, who assimilated elements of rhythm and blues, Tex-Mex, rhumba, calypso, and dixieland into his basic strutting and riffing barrelhouse piano style. His boogie-woogie left-hand rhythms, complemented by right-hand triplet figures, constituted a style that became virtually synonymous with New Orleans piano. Always an eccentric, he often kept time by kicking a drum, or even the piano itself, a practice that proved helpful to dancers, but destructive to his instruments. His singing perfectly matched the humorous lyrics he wrote, and he often accompanied himself with infectious whistling. During this time Professor Longhair, who was also known as "Fess," recorded and performed as the leader of ensembles with such typically whimsical names as the Shuffling Hungarians or the Blues Scholars.

In 1954 a stroke put Professor Longhair in the hospital for almost a year, and from then on he was plagued by health problems. Nonetheless, his "Tipitina" (1954), "No Buts No Maybes" (1957), and "Baby, Let Me Hold Your Head" (1957) were regional hits, and his 1959 "Go to the Mardi Gras," which he had recorded almost a decade earlier, eventually grew to become the city's unofficial anthem. However, during this time his music never transcended local popularity, and later in the 1950s, when his career slumped, he became destitute. He had remarried, and his new wife ran a laundry in their home in order to support them. In 1960 he was arrested onstage during a Mardi Gras performance and charged with possession of marijuana. Professor Longhair gave up music in 1964 and began to make his living by gambling and janitorial work.

Professor Longhair was rediscovered in 1969 and came to greater prominence than ever, with a busy schedule of performing and recording (*Houseparty New Orleans Style,* 1971–1972), both in the United States and in Europe. In the 1970s he gained a large following among whites, and performed annually at the New Orleans Jazz and Heritage Festival. His last recording was *Crawfish Fiesta* in 1979, and that year he appeared in the documentary *Piano Players Rarely Play Together.* Despite his health problems, his playing remained as vigorous as ever, and he gave his last performance three days before he died in his sleep in New Orleans. Although Professor Longhair achieved wealth and fame in the decade before his death, it was only in the 1980s that he attained legendary status as one of the most vital of all American musicians.

REFERENCES

BERRY, JASON. *Up from the Cradle of Jazz: New Orleans Music Since World War II.* Athens, Ga., 1986.

JONES, TAD. "Professor Longhair." *Living Blues* 26 (March–April 1976):16–29.

LICHTENSTEIN, GRACE, and LAURA DANKNER. *Musical Gumbo: The Music of New Orleans.* New York, 1993.

JONATHAN GILL

Prophet, Nancy Elizabeth (1890–1960), sculptor. Born in Providence R.I., in 1890, Nancy Elizabeth Prophet attended the Rhode Island School of Design, where she studied drawing and painting with an emphasis on portraiture while supporting herself by working as a domestic. She graduated from the school in 1918 and in 1922 left the United States to study at the École des Beaux Arts in Paris. It is not known when she began sculpting, but soon after her arrival in France, she produced *Silence,* an early portrait in marble. In the 1920s and 1930s she exhibited her work in several notable galleries in Paris, gaining the attention of Countee CULLEN, W. E. B. DU BOIS, and Henry TANNER, all of whom became strong supporters of her work.

Prophet's sculpture in both wood and marble tends toward austerity, yet her portraits can be remarkably sensitive. Contemporary critics noted both her outstanding technical mastery and the power of her expression. Tanner's recommendation led Prophet to submit two sculptures to the 1930 Harmon Foundation exhibition, where she won the Otto Kahn Prize for *Head of a Negro.* Shortly after returning permanently to the United States in 1932, Prophet won first prize at the twenty-first annual Newport Art Association exhibition for *Discontent.*

Head of a Negro by Elizabeth Prophet. (National Archives)

In the following year, W. E. B. Du Bois persuaded Prophet to accept a teaching position at SPELMAN COLLEGE. She remained on the faculty at Spelman until 1944, initiating a sculpture program, teaching classes in clay modeling and in the history of art and architecture and, with painter Hale WOODRUFF, expanding the arts department. Unfortunately, Atlanta offered few opportunities for the black artist to exhibit her work; perhaps for this reason, she returned to Rhode Island in 1945.

After a showing of her work at the municipal library in Providence, Prophet's career ebbed. Having lost many of her previous contacts and without a steady source of income, she returned to work as a domestic. Many of her works were lost in this period, some deliberately destroyed by the artist, others irreparably damaged through neglect. When Prophet died in Providence in 1960, it was necessary to raise a special burial fund to keep her from a pauper's grave.

REFERENCE

REYNOLDS, GARY A., and BERYL J. WRIGHT. *Against the Odds: African-American Artists and the Harmon Foundation.* Newark, N.J., 1989.

DOROTHY DESIR-DAVIS

Propositions 48 and 42: NCAA Bylaw 14.3.

Whether freshmen should compete in American intercollegiate athletics has been debated for a century. The issue, however, acquired distinct racial overtones only in 1983, when the National Collegiate Athletic Association (NCAA), the country's governing body for major intercollegiate athletics, adopted Proposition 48. Effective in 1986, the NCAA required that in order to be eligible to compete as a freshman, a student-athlete must have a 2.0 grade point average on a scale of 4.0 in eleven "core" courses (four English, three mathematics, and two each in social sciences and natural sciences), as well as either a 700 total score on the Scholastic Aptitude Test (SAT) or a 15 total score on the American College Test (ACT).

Historically black colleges in particular opposed Proposition 48, contending that the test scores were arbitrary and the tests themselves discriminated against lower-income minorities, often in neglected inner-city schools. Athletic grants-in-aid could still be received by "partial qualifiers"—those who had the requisite grades but not the test scores—but they could not play or practice their sport during the freshman year and lost one of their four years of eligibility.

Proposition 48, lobbied by the American Council on Education, was a reaction to the low academic standards of the previous decade, when only a 2.0 high school grade point average was required for athletic aid, without regard for the nature of the courses taken. Many athletes, often African Americans, were recruited for their athletic ability, were maintained in college while playing and then discarded upon completing their eligibility, without receiving meaningful higher education. Tony Rice, a Notre Dame quarterback among the first made ineligible under Proposition 48, expressed its rationale: "It was tough, not being able to play. . . . But . . . I was able to get a foot down on my classes."

The NCAA commenced research on the effects of Proposition 48, but before meaningful data were available, its 1989 convention passed Proposition 42, barring athletic aid to partial qualifiers. While 85 percent of the African-American athletes entering Division I schools between 1987 and 1990 qualified, African Americans constituted two-thirds of the partial qualifiers. Half of all partial qualifiers play football or men's basketball, sports in which America's colleges serve as professional development teams.

The emotional protest of Georgetown basketball coach John Thompson, who walked off the court before his team's next two games, brought massive publicity to the issue, and led to a change by the 1990 convention, prior to the effective date. While Proposition 42's bar to athletic aid was retained, need-based aid was approved. Two years later, after a prestigious commission created by the Knight Foundation refocused public attention on the commercialization of college revenue sports, additional changes were made, sponsored by a newly powerful President's Commission within the NCAA. Effective August 1995, a 2.5 average in thirteen core courses will be required, though indexing could bring it as low as 2.0 if an SAT combined score of 900 or an ACT score of 21 is achieved. More significant in terms of minimizing exploitation of major college athletes, 25 percent of whom are African-American, is requiring that athletes meet the minimum grade point average requirements throughout their college careers and complete a steadily increasing portion of their degree requirements in order to remain eligible.

REFERENCES

ASHER, MARK. "Presidents Play the Numbers; Debate over SAT, Grades." *Washington Post,* June 30, 1991, p. B1.

DAVIS, TIMOTHY. "An Absence of Good Faith: Defining a University's Educational Obligation to Student-Athletes." *Houston Law Review* 28 (1991): 743–790.

GREENE, LINDA S. "The New Rules of the Game: Academic Integrity or Racism?" *St. Louis University Law Journal* 28 (1984): 101–151.

LEDERMAN, DOUGLAS. "Arthur Ashe, Defender of Black Athletes, Urges Colleges to Help Them Meet More Stringent Standards." *Chronicle of Higher Education,* February 12, 1992, pp. A37, A40.

GORDON A. MARTIN, JR.

Prosser, Nancy

Prosser, Nancy (fl. 1800), activist. The presence of African-American women in slave revolts and other forms of resistance under slavery does not figure prominently in the remaining records of such events. Women were often active participants in insurrections, however, and Nancy Prosser exemplifies such women. Nancy's husband, Gabriel, was the leader of a rebellion that was to involve some one thousand enslaved African Americans near Richmond, Va., in 1800 (*see* GABRIEL PROSSER CONSPIRACY). Nancy was active in making the swords and other weapons that the group planned to use in their attack on the city. The plan was exposed, and key members of Gabriel and Nancy's group were rounded up by the state militia. Gabriel and approximately thirty-five other participants were hanged. Although Nancy's fate is not known, she also may have been hanged, as other black women were who participated in such revolts.

REFERENCES

APTHEKER, HERBERT. *American Negro Slave Revolts.* New York, 1943.

JUDITH WEISENFELD

Provident Hospital

Provident Hospital. On May 4, 1891, Provident Hospital and Training School, the first black-controlled hospital in the United States, opened on the south side of Chicago. The racially exclusionary policies of Chicago nursing schools had prompted Daniel Hale WILLIAMS, a prominent African-American surgeon, to found the institution. The establishment of Provident Hospital would also benefit African-American patients and physicians. Its doors would be open to them at a time when those of most other hospitals in Chicago were not.

Williams did not conceive of the hospital as an exclusively black enterprise but as an interracial one. During its early years Provident reflected its founder's vision. However, by 1915 the hospital had evolved into a predominantly black institution. This evolution resulted primarily from a rise in institutional racism and residential segregation in Chicago. A change in leadership at Provident Hospital also contributed to its development as a black institution. When Williams resigned as medical director in 1894 to become surgeon-in-chief at Freedman's Hospital, a professional and personal rival, Dr. George Cleveland HALL, assumed the position. Hall strengthened the hospital's ties with the African-American community.

Provident won renown as a medical center. Two years after its founding, Daniel Hale Williams performed one of the first successful open-heart operations there. By 1914 its nurse-training school, the first established by a hospital to train black students, had graduated 118 black women from twenty-four states. In 1928 it was one of the seventeen black hospitals approved by the American College of Surgeons and one of the fourteen approved by the American Medical Association for internship training. In 1940 Provident was one of the seven black hospitals that offered specialty training, and it also had more approved residency programs than any other black hospital. That same year, most of the nation's African-American physicians who had become board certified in specialties had trained there.

In 1929 Provident became the site of a pioneering experiment in black medical education and black hospital reform when it affiliated with the University of Chicago. However, the union ended in 1944. Several factors contributed to its demise, including the growing indifference of the university, financial problems and mismanagement at Provident, and the fact that Chicago's black community came to view the project as Jim Crowism.

Because it predominantly served poor residents on Chicago's south side, Provident Hospital, almost from its inception, suffered from financial problems. As was true at other black hospitals, these problems escalated after the desegregation of medical facilities in the 1960s. Desegregation resulted in an exodus of physicians and patients from Provident. Such losses increased the hospital's financial vulnerability, and it was unable to provide up-to-date medical facilities. In 1965 it was forced to close its nurse-training school.

Still, Provident Hospital struggled to survive. In August 1982 it moved into a new, modern facility. The move did not reverse Provident's fortunes; debts continued to increase and the patient census continued to decline. In September 1987 Provident closed. Since then, several attempts have been made to reopen it. However, it remains unclear whether a resurrected Provident Hospital would be run by a government agency as an extension of Cook County Hospital or by a private group from the African-American community.

REFERENCES

BUCKLER, HELEN. *Daniel Hale Williams: Negro Surgeon.* 2nd ed. New York, 1968.

MATTHEWS, HENRY B. "Provident Hospital—Then and Now." *Journal of the National Medical Association* 53 (1961): 209–224.

VANESSA NORTHINGTON GAMBLE

Pryor, Richard Franklin Lenox Thomas

(December 1, 1940–), comedian. Born in Peoria, Ill., Richard Pryor overcame a troubled life in an extended family headed by his grandmother, Marie Carter, to become a preeminent comedian, film star, screenwriter, producer, and director, beginning in the early 1960s.

During Pryor's boyhood, Peoria was like the Deep South. Segregation and discrimination in housing, employment, and places of public accommodation were deeply embedded in southern Illinois. Forty percent of the black population of Peoria was unemployed, while 32 percent worked for the WORKS PROJECT ADMINISTRATION (WPA). Odd jobs supported the rest, including the Pryor family, which ran small carting firms, pool halls, and, Pryor claimed, houses of prostitution. Peoria remained segregated for a time even after the 1954 Supreme Court decision that forbade it.

At eleven, Pryor, the son of Gertrude Thomas and Leroy "Buck" Carter Pryor, and, he once said, the seventh of twelve "Pryor kids," began acting at the Carver Community Center under the guidance of the drama teacher, Juliette Whittaker. Over the years she became the recipient of some of Pryor's performing awards; he also contributed to the private school she later founded, the Learning Tree.

After dropping out of school, Pryor joined the army in 1958, where his life was no less troublesome. After military service, he worked for his father's carting firm and the Caterpillar factory in Peoria. He also haunted the local clubs and watched television for the appearances of African-American entertainers such as Sammy DAVIS, Jr., and Bill COSBY, personalities he wanted to emulate and eventually replace.

Within a few years Pryor was playing small clubs in East St. Louis, Chicago, Windsor (Canada), Buffalo, Youngstown, and Cleveland. Much of his comic material was drawn from his army service and the early Cosby comedy routines. By 1964 he had attracted enough attention to be booked for his first national television appearance, on Rudy Vallee's *Broadway Tonight* show. Three years later, after stops on the Ed Sullivan, Merv Griffin, and Johnny Carson shows, Pryor appeared in the film *The Busy Body*

with Sid Caesar and other comedians—the first of more than forty films he acted in, wrote, produced, and/or directed into the early 1990s. His first major role was in *Lady Sings the Blues* (1972), with Diana ROSS, in which Pryor played a character called Piano Man.

The Richard Pryor Show ran briefly on NBC-TV for part of 1977. It was innovative and conveyed a wide range of both comedy and tenderness, but it was too daring for the executives of NBC. Amid legal wrangling, the show went off the air and, typically, Pryor laid the blame on NBC. In 1984, he played himself as a boy in *Pryor's Place,* a children's show that aired on Saturday mornings. It too was short-lived, this time without recrimination.

From 1970 through 1979, Pryor starred or costarred in twenty-one films. He contributed to the script of *Blazing Saddles* (1973), and in the same year wrote for and appeared on *The Flip Wilson Show* and was a cowriter for Lily Tomlin's television specials, for which he won Emmy Awards in 1973 and 1974. He continued to perform in clubs and theaters around the country; these performances provided material for his two *Richard Pryor Live in Concert* films (both in 1979). The recordings of his performances earned him three Grammy Awards: *That Nigger's Crazy,* 1974; *Is It Something I Said,* 1975; and *Bicentennial Nigger,* 1976. *That Nigger's Crazy* also became a certified gold and platinum album.

In 1980 he produced his first film, *Bustin' Loose,* starring himself and Cicely TYSON. Two years later he produced and wrote *Richard Pryor: Live on the Sunset Strip. Jo Jo Dancer, Your Life Is Calling,* which Pryor produced, directed, and helped write, was based upon his near-fatal self-immolation that occurred when he was freebasing cocaine in 1980. In 1986, Pryor, who had also survived two heart attacks, discovered that he had multiple sclerosis, but he continued to perform onstage.

Pryor was known as a "crossover" star: one who appealed to both black and white moviegoers. This label resulted from the "buddy" films he made with Gene Wilder—*Silver Streak* (1976), *Stir Crazy* (1980), and *See No Evil, Hear No Evil* (1989)—although he had starred with white actors in sixteen other movies. Few of Pryor's films during the 1980s were memorable, not even the concert film *Richard Pryor: Here and Now* (1983). But *Richard Pryor: Live on the Sunset Strip,* released only the year before, most typified his pungent, raunchy comedy that echoed the African-American man in the street, which was precisely what made Pryor the great comedian he was.

When he was at his peak, few comedians could match Pryor's popularity. Most contemporary comedy is said to be "post-Pryor," because of the standards he set. His life was his act, but he shaped his personal experiences into rollicking comedy. His major themes were racism in its several forms and the battle of the sexes. Usually, the women bested the men. His topics were current and to the point, and his favorite character was an old, foul-mouthed, wise black man named Mudbone from Mississippi.

REFERENCES

HASKINS, JIM. *Richard Pryor, a Man and His Madness: A Biography.* New York, 1984.

WILLIAMS, JOHN A., and DENNIS A. WILLIAMS. *If I Stop I'll Die: The Comedy and Tragedy of Richard Pryor.* New York, 1991.

JOHN A. WILLIAMS

Psychology and Psychiatry. Today's psychiatrists and psychologists acknowledge that psychological principles are inevitably culturally biased. In the United States, mental health approaches often have favored the white middle and upper classes. The CIVIL RIGHTS and black consciousness movements made whites more aware of both overt and covert manifestations of racial prejudice; nonetheless, a great deal remains to be accomplished. All psychiatrists are very much a product of their society, and many of them have been influenced in varying degrees by the white supremacist attitudes that permeate the culture. Unfortunately, merely receiving psychiatric or psychoanalytical training does not purge practitioners of racist beliefs. As a consequence, blacks have suffered discrimination from one of the most humanitarian branches of medicine—psychiatry.

During the antebellum period, many white professionals argued that mental illness was greater among free blacks in the North than among southern slaves because black people were not thought to be capable of adult independence. These professionals concluded that SLAVERY was a benign institution protecting blacks from psychological development. Blacks were believed to be fragile misfits who could not cope with the rigors of a competitive society.

Perhaps the most dramatic example of psychological theory being used in a politically repressive way against blacks comes from the work of Dr. Samuel Cartwright. This example underscores the invidious nature of cultural bias often inherent in the theory and practice of psychology and psychiatry. Dr. Cartwright was a surgeon and psychologist summoned to a Louisiana plantation in 1851 to investigate the causes for the high percentage of slave runaways. After many weeks of study, he concluded that the slaves who ran away to freedom were suffering from a mental disease he dubbed *drapetomania*—literally, the "flight-from-home madness." This illustration is germane to blacks' current predicament because Dr. Cartwright accepted slavery as normal, as did many whites at the time, and considered it an appropriate social arrangement for African Americans. Black rejection of this norm was viewed as pathological. Cartwright's tactic (perhaps unknowingly) was to use psychology, with the trappings of objective scientific research, not only to justify slavery, but to indoctrinate the slaves into believing that their mental health meant being happy on the plantation. Any slave, of course, who accepted Cartwright's "scientific" theories was an accomplice in his or her own oppression.

At the turn of the century, psychologist G. Stanley Hall stated that medical treatment of the races was as different as applying the same veterinary medicine practices to different animal species. Racists asserted that the black brain was smaller and less developed than the white's (*see* RACE, SCIENTIFIC THEORIES OF); thus, blacks were not capable of managing a high degree of civilization. Many early psychiatrists believed that the black person's psychological development was more childlike and less complex than that of the white person. In a leading textbook in 1908, psychologist William McDougall stated that blacks had an "instinct of submission." Psychiatrists often committed rebellious African Americans (and nonconformist whites, as well) to mental institutions. During the height of the civil rights movement, workers complained that police often brought them to state mental institutions, where they were held involuntarily. Southern white psychiatrists did not generally condemn such practices, nor did many lend their voices to the struggle for black equality.

Psychoanalytic theory is profoundly culture-bound because it was primarily developed in a Western European, Judeo-Christian society. In the United States, it has largely been addressed to affluent, white clients who share cultural values of individual success and personal happiness. Psychologists or psychiatrists, in fact, have often unwittingly supported the mental health of white racists, thereby becoming agents for the status quo. There were psychiatrists practicing in Mississippi in the 1960s, for example, who would not see black patients and who were open to segregationists. They did not see white racism in any way as a mental health issue. Some psychiatrists, furthermore, have tended to serve as purveyors of the values of the white middle class as models for sound mental health.

By catering to a well-to-do clientele, psychiatrists and psychologists express a greater commitment to meeting the mental health needs of the affluent than to satisfying those of minority groups and the poor.

As a result, blacks and others have been confined to overcrowded state mental institutions and public clinics. Often the service provided for minorities is minimal or custodial. Because of a combination of racial and socioeconomic factors, emotionally disturbed blacks seldom receive mental health treatment during the early stages of their distress. Frequently, their illnesses progress to a stage of incapacitation before services are provided—often by commitment to public psychiatric facilities. This commitment is usually involuntary; thus, it is no wonder that in some black communities the psychiatrist is viewed with the same fear as the police officer. Often a black patient's first contact with a psychiatrist is when the doctor signs a paper ordering the involuntary incarceration of the patient in a prisonlike hospital far away from the community.

Psychiatrists and psychologists are not the only ones to blame for this state of affairs. However, they must bear part of the burden of guilt for maintaining a perspective that frequently ignores the plights of blacks. Too often, they prefer patients, who, like themselves, are verbally skillful and well educated. Racial and economic discrimination, as well as de facto segregation, has allowed countless numbers of professional social workers, psychologists, and psychiatrists to go through years of training while seeing few, if any, black patients. As a result, most have not had an opportunity to confront their own prejudices or deficits in cross-cultural contacts. Charles Pinderhughes, a black psychiatrist, suggests that many psychotherapists have unconscious needs to be in helping and controlling roles. They want their patients to accommodate to them or imitate their style or approach. For a black patient, this kind of relationship with a white therapist can easily imitate a masterslave dynamic, which can produce barriers to successful therapy, although admittedly similar issues may be sometimes present in same-race interactions.

Many professional prejudices are manifested subtly, camouflaged in psychiatric jargon, which stereotypes minority patients as "hostile," "not motivated for treatment," "not psychologically oriented," "passively uncooperative," and so forth. These categorizations are often code words indicating that someone is not suitable for psychotherapeutic treatment. Such people may be subtly discouraged from returning to the clinic or relegated to "lesser" therapies such as drug treatment and crisis intervention.

At other times, a few psychiatrists have aligned themselves with racist policies and used "objective" psychiatric concepts to support their positions. I was witness to a group of white psychiatrists in Mississippi in 1965 who opposed the integration of their hospital unit because "it would be bad for the mental health of both whites and blacks." Another example

of bias in psychiatry is the frequency with which angry black people who have suffered severe discrimination are inappropriately labeled "paranoid" or "schizophrenic."

Historically, black patients treated in mental health facilities have been twice as likely as whites to be diagnosed initially with schizophrenia (Bel and Mehta, 1981). Using more objective testing, or more thorough evaluation, many of these "schizophrenics" are found to be suffering from other diagnoses—notably, depression. Depression is generally regarded as a more episodic than chronic illness with a better prognosis than schizophrenia. Blacks tend to seek treatment much later in the illness, and therefore have developed more severe symptoms. However, there is a consistent pattern of misdiagnosis of depression among African-American clients. Part of this reflects psychiatric training, which often considers depression an upper-class disease. In the 1950s and '60s, psychiatrists in training were taught that clinical depression was rare among blacks.

Other stereotypes about the black family have been reported by white investigators as a result of cultural biases and inadequate research. Negative labels and simplistic generalizations abound. In *The Mark of Oppression* by Abram Kardiner and Lionel Ovesey, 1951, two white psychiatrists used psychoanalytic techniques to study some blacks and describe the scars inflicted on the black personality by racism. However, in doing so, they highlighted the so-called pathological symptoms to suggest that all blacks are emotionally sick. In their view, African Americans are filled with a pervasive self-hatred. This kind of research has led to blacks being evaluated from the perspective of a deficit model, or perspectives of cultural deprivation. During the 1960s, "culturally deprived" became a code phrase for poor blacks. Implicit in the concept of "cultural deprivation" has been the assumption that the standards of the dominant white middle-class culture represent norms by which all other cultures may properly be measured. Therefore, inner-city blacks are seen as culturally deprived, rather than more appropriately as culturally different.

In many circumstances psychiatry acts as a bridge between social science and cultural and political values. This fact has created problems for the black community in its relationship to mental health concepts. The uneven training of many psychiatric workers has made it difficult for them to distinguish deviant, unhealthy behavior from what is merely culturally different behavior. For example, a black man who believes that a white police officer might shoot him for the slightest wrong move is probably not paranoid; such a feeling could be a likely sign of mental imbalance in a middle-class white man. It has taken a long time for many mental health practitioners to realize that the life experiences of blacks differ from those of whites and, as a result, so do their social and psychological adaptations.

Techniques in psychology have been slow to change to adequately serve different cultural and socioeconomic groups. Some training programs today are beginning to offer more exposure to minority issues. Fortunately, recent forms of therapy such as cognitive, behavioral, and psychopharmacological treatments have made mental health care more suitable to a wider variety of patients. In the past few decades, psychiatric institutions have begun to be concerned about meeting the mental health needs of blacks and other minorities.

Nonetheless, there are still some mental health workers inclined to help blacks adapt and adjust to their "situation," while remaining unconcerned with eliminating racism in society—or even in their own practices. Many blacks avoid treatment with white psychiatrists who they feel will not understand them. Therefore, there is a critical need for mental health professionals to be taught an antiracist and culturally sensitive approach to their clients.

For instance, psychological testing is usually based on biased standardizations that in many instances do not apply to blacks. The Minnesota Multiphasic Personality Inventory, a widely used measure of personality functioning, originally (1943) had a femininity-masculinity scale that often depicted black men as feminine because of cultural biases in the coded questions. Intelligence (IQ) tests abound with biases that discriminate against blacks and other ethnic groups in the testing and scoring. It is not surprising that blacks score lower than whites on average since the tests were standardized to measure achievement on the basis of a white middle-class model. Nevertheless, racist theorists have incorrectly used the IQ differences shown by such tests to postulate the genetic inferiority of blacks—even after researchers have rescinded their earlier claims, now stating that there is no such thing as a culture-free test. This "scientific racism," restating in new terms that whites are superior, has been used by government policymakers and others to justify the continued oppression and segregation of blacks. Fortunately, many prominent social scientists, both black and white, have successfully attacked the doctrine of scientific racism, creating a consensus that IQ tests measure specific skills, not intelligence per se.

Until World War II there were few black psychiatrists to refute the "scientific racists." They worked in isolated, predominantly white settings without significant contact with their black colleagues. Since that time, the number of black psychiatrists has steadily grown, albeit slowly. Currently, there are approximately fourteen thousand black psychiatrists and twelve hundred black psychologists practicing in America.

Solomon Carter FULLER was the first black psychiatrist in the United States. The son of a coffee planter and governmental official, Dr. Fuller was born in Liberia in 1872 and came to the United States at age seventeen. After attending black colleges in the South, he received his M.D. degree from Boston University in 1897. Despite his rapid rise professionally in a white setting, he gave considerable time and effort to the recruitment and training of black physicians.

Perhaps the greatest inspiration to black psychiatrists came from Franz Fanon, the black revolutionary psychiatrist from Martinique. He gained a worldwide reputation and a place in history through his monumental works, originally published in French, *Black Skin, White Masks* (1952; translation 1967) and *The Wretched of the Earth* (1961; translation 1966), which explored the psychological condition of oppressed blacks and advocated violent struggle to obtain liberation. Fanon was not just a theoretician but an activist who participated in the Algerian revolution and developed psychiatric programs that emphasized reeducation through milieu therapy. Fanon's insights about black-white relations penetrated the civil rights movement in the United States and helped to provide the psychological underpinnings of the BLACK POWER MOVEMENT.

Similarly, Kenneth CLARK, a black American psychologist, has been a pioneer in the effort to bring social science to bear on the liberation of blacks in the United States. He documented the psychologically damaging effects on children of both races of a segregated school system. His studies were cited in the United States Supreme Court decision of 1954 outlawing legal school segregation (*see* BROWN V. BOARD OF EDUCATION). This ruling paved the way for the civil rights struggles of the ensuing years, in which Clark played a leading role. Young black psychologists and psychiatrists have been inspired by his example and have seen that they, too, can intervene directly in the institutional processes that affect the well-being of blacks.

In 1968, the Association of Black Psychologists (ABP) was founded in the midst of criticism of the American Psychological Association for its limited vision and its support of the racist character of American society. The following year, in 1969, the Black Psychiatrists of America (BPA) was formed. The group was autonomous but closely tied to the American Psychiatric Association in order to eliminate institutional racism in the practice and programs in psychiatry throughout the country. Many white clinicians deplored the formation of these groups and attacked them as separatist. Nevertheless, it was clear that black clinicians needed to form action groups for an assault on racism in psychiatric practices.

The formation of these groups forced the breakdown of previously all-white committees and councils in the national organizations and brought about the formation of subcommittees to specifically examine issues of minority clients, bias in testing, and the racism in traditional psychology and psychiatry. Now, both the American Psychiatric Association and the American Psychological Association have permanent committees on minorities. In addition, the BPA publishes a quarterly journal, *BPA Quarterly,* and the ABP publishes the *Journal of Black Psychology.*

One result of the formation of the BPA was the appointment of African-American psychiatrist Jeanne SPURLOCK to the joint position of Deputy Medical Director of Minority and National Affairs and Director of the American Psychiatric Association/National Institutes of Mental Health Minority Fellowship Program by the American Psychiatric Association in 1974. Many alumni from this program serve minority communities and are involved in all levels of academic and clinical psychiatry.

Since the formation of the ABP and BPA, many black psychiatrists and psychologists have joined the faculty of major universities and assumed new administrative and policy-making roles. This has led to the increase in available black clinicians, and increased research on minority mental health. Black clinicians have made their presence felt by publishing articles and books about the plights of blacks and the effects of white oppression. Many of these works have been read by white therapists as well as by a large segment of the lay population. As a result, white attitudes within the mental health field are slowly changing.

In the spirit of Afrocentrism, a group of theorists, Na'im Akbar, Wade Nobles, Joseph White, and others, have proposed an African psychology, separate from European-based psychology. Prominent among the cultural values advocated by these black psychologists are group-centered behavior, strong kinship bonds, inherent feelings of cooperation over competition, a "feeling" or affective orientation, and an overarching religious orientation that provides structure, direction, and a philosophy of the interrelatedness of all things.

This psychology builds on strengths that have enabled African Americans to cope adaptively with the racism experienced during and after slavery. Nobles argues that black psychology derives from positive features of basic African philosophy which dictate the values, customs, attitudes, and behavior of Africans in Africa and the New World.

Many black clinicians are working toward the incorporation of some of these new perspectives into American psychiatry. Some of them have rejected traditional psychiatry, perceiving Western psychiatry as another form of cultural genocide against African Americans. However, the concept of a unique black psychology has been rejected by leading African and African-American psychiatrists who insist that, although there are cultural differences in the clinical manifestations of emotional disorders, the underlying psychological mechanisms are similar across cultural lines. Just as a purely European psychology is too narrow a model for all humanity, an African psychology is also too narrow, even for African Americans, because Africans have merged, whether by choice or force, with so many cultures around the world.

Because traditional psychiatry has not been responsive to the needs of blacks, many have turned to other helping institutions and individuals in the community. Most important has been the church and the black minister. Nonetheless, in recent years, black Americans' interest in psychiatry has grown. Both middle-class and poor blacks have increased their utilization of psychological services. It is now the responsibility of decent citizens to remove the last vestiges of racist practices within the mental health field to ensure a greater acceptance of psychiatry and psychology on the part of minorities and the poor.

REFERENCES

AKBAR, NA'IM. "African Roots of Black Personality." In W. D. Smith, K. H. Burlew, M. H. Mosley, and W. M. Whitney, eds. *Reflections on Black Psychology.* Washington, D.C., 1979.

BELL, CARL, and HARSHAD MEHTA. "Misdiagnosis of Black Patients with Manic-Depressive Illness." *Journal of the National Medical Association* 73, no. 2 (1981): 101–107.

BURLEW, A., KATHLEEN HOARD, W. CURTIS BANKS, HARRIETTE PIPES MCADOO, and DAUDI AJANI YA AZIBO, eds. *African American Psychology: Theory, Research, and Practice.* Newbury Park, 1992.

CLARK, KENNETH. *Dark Ghetto.* New York, 1965.

JONES, REGINALD L., ed. *Black Psychology.* New York, 1972.

KOVEL, JOEL. *White Racism: A Psychohistory.* New York, 1970.

NOBLES, WADE. *African Psychology: Toward Its Reclamation, Reascension, and Revitalization.* Oakland, Calif., 1986.

RUIZ, DOROTHY S., ed. *Handbook of Mental Health and Mental Disorder Among Black Americans.* New York, 1990.

THOMAS, ALEXANDER, and SAMUEL SILLEN. *Racism and Psychiatry.* New York, 1972.

WHITE, JOSEPH L. *The Psychology of Blacks: An Afro-American Perspective.* Englewood Cliffs, N.J., 1984.

ALVIN F. POUSSAINT

Public Health.   Concerned with the study, organization, development, and maintenance of standards of health for a population, public health is a field that takes into account the needs of individuals, but focuses on communities—cities and towns, regions, countries, and even entire continents. Concepts and approaches in the field have undergone several changes during the past two centuries. Through the first half of the nineteenth century, the emphasis was on "containment," or reliance on methods of quarantine to curb the spread of disease by isolating infected from non-infected people. With the acceptance of the so-called germ theory in the latter half of the nineteenth century, quarantine methods were supplemented—and in some instances supplanted—by efforts to control communicable disease through immunization programs and the application of sanitary principles on a population-wide basis. The twentieth century saw both an expansion of the role of government in public health and a widening of perspectives in the field to include factors other than disease, such as economic status, race, and lifestyle, in an attempt to maintain health standards.

In the United States, an agency with major responsibility for public health is the U.S. Public Health Service (USPHS). Founded in 1798 as the Marine Hospital Service, primarily to treat illnesses of merchant seamen, the USPHS assumed its current designation through an act of Congress in 1912 and gradually expanded its role in public health oversight and control. The agency's interest in matters affecting the health of all segments of the population, including African Americans, was a factor in the appointment of blacks to the service at a time when few held positions of authority or responsibility within the federal government.

Algernon Brashear Jackson (1878–1942) and Roscoe Conkling BROWN (1884–1962) were among the early African-American professionals to hold positions in public health work. A physician by training, Jackson was appointed during WORLD WAR I to work in a program aimed at reducing venereal infections among black Army troops. In 1922, he established a public health curriculum at HOWARD UNIVERSITY, "to train young colored men and women in this most important field of service to humanity." Brown served during World War I as a member of the Army's Commission on Training Camp Activities. A dentist, he had relinquished his practice in 1915 to devote himself to public health work. He joined the USPHS in 1919 and served successively as a lecturer and director of "colored work," as a health education specialist and health consultant, as chief of the Office of Negro Health Work, as a public health adviser, and as chief of the Special Programs Branch. Brown is perhaps best remembered for his promotion and

supervision of the National Negro Health Movement. This movement, initiated in 1915 by Booker T. WASHINGTON, was placed on a permanent year-round basis in 1930 with support from the USPHS and other organizations. It was headquartered at the USPHS under Brown's direction from 1932 until 1950, at which time it was closed as part of an effort to generate a more racially integrationist outlook within the federal health service. Among his colleagues, Brown was known affectionately as "Mr. Public Health."

Opportunities for service in the field of public health expanded during the 1930s and '40s. For African Americans, this trend was facilitated by the USPHS leadership of Surgeon General Thomas Parran, who was noted for his progressive thinking on health policy; by support from agencies such as the Julius Rosenwald Fund (JRF); and by aggressive lobbying on the part of black professional groups such as the National Medical Association (NMA). The NMA established a Commission on Public Health in 1938. By 1940, a campaign to convey the urgency of African-American health interests to Congress and federal agencies was under way. The JRF provided grants for public health training through fellowships offered by the USPHS under the auspices of state health boards.

As a result, the 1940s saw a marked increase in the number of African Americans active in public health work. Over 800 public health nurses were employed in official and unofficial agencies; many physicians were involved with health clinics, especially in programs relating to venereal disease and tuberculosis; several health centers were administered by African Americans; and the USPHS and the U.S. Children's Bureau assigned a number of blacks to responsible staff positions. The USPHS, for example, included on its roster Drs. Virginia M. Alexander and William B. Perry, who managed the Slossfield Health Center, in Birmingham, Ala. The center became a pioneer experiment in community-based health care for low-income African Americans. USPHS senior surgeons (later, medical directors) Drs. John B. West and Hildrus A. POINDEXTER received commissioned assignments to, among other posts, the United States Mission in Liberia. Dr. Walter H. Maddux, a professor of pediatrics at Meharry Medical College, served for a period with the U.S. Children's Bureau. In 1944, no less than eight state and five city health departments employed black health officers, as did nongovernmental agencies such as the National Tuberculosis Association and the Planned Parenthood Federation. A decade earlier, one commentator noted, "the number of Negroes holding important positions in public health could be numbered on the fingers of one hand."

The trend continued after the war. Charles C. Johnson, Jr., and Edward B. Cross became, in 1969, the first African Americans to attain the rank of assistant surgeon general. That year, Cross also served as acting surgeon general. Dr. Audrey F. Manley received her USPHS commission in 1976. In 1988, she became the first African-American woman to be appointed assistant surgeon general and, a year later, the first woman to serve as deputy assistant secretary for health (U.S. Department of Health and Human Services). In 1993, Joycelyn ELDERS became the first African American to hold the post of surgeon general, the chief executive officer of the USPHS.

The integration of African Americans into the public health services has been a contributing factor in the improvement of health indicators for all segments of the population during the last fifty years. A marked disparity, however, persists between the white and black populations. In 1989, the infant mortality rate among American blacks was more than double that for whites, while adult whites could expect to live an average of five years longer than their black counterparts. The most alarming statistics relate to pockets of urban poverty, where lack of access to health services is endemic. One report published in 1990 demonstrated that the life expectancy rate among residents of New York's central Harlem health district, for example, was lower than in Bangladesh, one of the world's poorest nations.

REFERENCES

CORNELY, PAUL B. "Public Health as a Professional Career." *Journal of the National Medical Association* 36 (May 1944): 71–78.

JAYNES, GERALD DAVID, and ROBIN M. WILLIAMS, JR., eds. *A Common Destiny: Blacks and American Society.* Washington, D.C., 1989.

PRICE, DAVID E. "Programs of the Public Health Service." *Journal of the National Medical Association* 57 (March 1965): 104–108.

U.S. Public Health Service. *Commissioned Corps Centennial, January 4, 1889–January 4, 1989: "A Century of Service with Distinction."* Washington, D.C., 1989.

KENNETH R. MANNING

Public Relations.   Under the free enterprise system, public relations is the management function that identifies, establishes, and maintains mutually beneficial relationships between an organization and the various publics on whom its success depends. Historically, very few African Americans have had national influence in the mass media or in the businesses that support them, like public relations. The first Af-

rican Americans who worked in mainstream white businesses were tapped to assist a few of the major progressive national corporations as they reached out to the black community to increase awareness of their concern and interest.

Joseph Vardrey Baker, editor of the *Philadelphia Tribune,* for example, left the paper in 1934 to become a public relations consultant for the Pennsylvania Railroad Company. From this experience, where he assisted in the company's efforts to reach the African-American community, Baker became one of the first blacks to open his own public relations agency. He received nationwide recognition in the profession, and had major corporations as clients, including RCA, Proctor and Gamble, NBC, the Dumont Network, and Scott Paper. Baker became the first black to serve as a chapter president of the Public Relations Society of America, and he was also the first accredited by the association.

Also connected with the Joseph Baker Agency was Barbara Morris, who joined the concern in the 1950s and later served as president of the company. The first black woman to handle major corporate accounts, she worked for NBC, handling Roxie Roker, later of television's *The Jeffersons,* and for RCA the popular singer Harry BELAFONTE and opera singer Marian ANDERSON. In 1973, Morris left the Baker Agency to become manager of community relations and urban affairs for a major mainstream firm, Sun Oil Company. Morris served as a role model and mentor for others in public relations, particularly the women she befriended.

Pepsi-Cola took an active role in hiring blacks in the 1960s to bolster their sagging sales to the African-American community. When Harvey C. Russell was hired as a vice-president for special markets in 1962, he was the highest ranking black executive for an international American business. Russell had a long and successful career with Pepsico, and was joined in 1965 by H. Naylor FITZHUGH. For Fitzhugh, who in 1933 became the first African American to receive an MBA from the Harvard Business School, this was the culmination of a long career at HOWARD UNIVERSITY, where he was called the "dean of black business."

Others who entered corporate public relations at this time include Frank Seymour and Gerald Lundy, who launched a Detroit-based advertising and public relations firm in the 1950s; Joe Block, who took a position with the Greyhound Corporation in 1962; and Eddie Attkinson, who worked for the Carnation Company in the 1970s. Perhaps the best known black public relations official of this era was D. Parke Gibson, who served as the president of the National Association of Market Developers (NAMD), a black professional organization, and was the author of two books, *The $130 Billion Negro* (1969), and *$70 Billion in the Black* (1978).

Gibson's clients included the government of Bermuda, Columbia Pictures, the Miller Brewing Company, P. Lorillard, and the Brown and Williamson Tobacco Company. Gibson and other black public relations officials worked on developing black-owned campaigns and programming, and fostering community goodwill through having companies sponsor awards for Mother and Father of the Year, give minority scholarships, and sponsor minority art.

Only a handful of African Americans worked in the mainstream entertainment arena at a level of national influence, "handling publicity," as it was termed in the 1950s. Vincent Tubbs worked as a reporter in Atlanta, Norfolk, and Baltimore, and served as a newspaper reporter for the *Baltimore Afro-American* during World War II. After the war, at the request of President Franklin D. Roosevelt, who met him during Tubbs's tour of duty, Tubbs studied and reported on colonialism in Africa. His report became the basis for development of provisions concerning the Trusteeship Council of the United Nations. Tubbs subsequently became editor of the *Baltimore Afro-American* newspaper, *Ebony,* and then *Jet* magazine.

Through his contacts and persistence, Tubbs was hired on the staff of the publicity director at Warner Brothers, and became the first African-American press agent for a major motion picture company. He handled publicity for such Warner Brothers' TV series as 77 *Sunset Strip, Cheyenne, Maverick, Sugarfoot, Surfside Six,* and *Roaring Twenties.* Later he moved to American International Pictures, where he managed publicity for such stars as Vincent Price and Boris Karloff.

Bob Jones, born in Fort Worth, Tex., in 1936 moved to Los Angeles, where he worked as an entertainment editor for several newspapers. Though Rogers & Cowan, the leading entertainment public relations firm of the time, was at first reluctant to hire Jones, he secured a position there in 1968, where he represented James BROWN, the Jackson Five (*see* JACKSON, MICHAEL AND FAMILY), the SUPREMES, and Buffy Saint-Marie. In 1970 he took a position as publicity manager for MOTOWN's International Management Company, where he stayed until 1987. Other pioneers in the area of entertainment public relations included Victoria Lucas at Rogers and Cowan and Sandra Livingston at Paramount Pictures.

During the years of the civil rights movement, African Americans began to target politics as an area for expansion. The effects of voter registration persistence paid off, as more and more blacks became political leaders and elected officials. In the arena of political public relations, very few African Americans had international influence, but Ofield Dukes was

one who did. Dukes grew up on the lower east side of Detroit, called "Black Bottom." While in high school, he covered sports for the Detroit edition of the *Pittsburgh Courier.* After he graduated from Wayne State University, he served as assistant editor of the *Michigan Chronicle,* where he won three national awards for his news, editorials, and feature writing in the 1960s.

In 1965, Dukes was encouraged by Hobart Taylor, Jr., a prominent white attorney in Detroit who had become an adviser to President Lyndon B. Johnson, to accept a position in Washington as deputy director of public affairs for the President's Committee on Equal Employment Opportunity. In addition to involvement with the Johnson White House, Dukes served on the Democratic Party's inaugural committee, helping arrange Johnson's 1964 presidential inauguration, and then became a member of the public relations staff of Vice President Hubert H. Humphrey in 1966.

In 1969, Dukes opened his own firm, Ofield Dukes & Associates. Working in the political arena of public relations at the international and national levels, he obtained the first major public relations contract held by an African-American company with an African country—Liberia. Among other national activities, Dukes worked with Democratic presidential election campaigns after 1968.

Others involved in political public relations included John C. Calhoun, a community relations chief in the federal government from 1969 through 1977; Bill Cherry, a public relations expert for numerous politicians in the same period; Paul Brock, deputy director of communications for the Democratic National Committee from 1974 to 1978; and Alexis Herman, President Bill Clinton's publicist in the 1980s and 1990s.

In the 1980s, public relations saw a new wave of African Americans who were not content to work exclusively developing relations to the black community, or working with African-American clients. Attempts to enter the highest tier of management have been mixed, though there have been some success stories. Caroline Jones Advertising, Inc., a full-service agency, is one of the few agencies that has received general marketing accounts. Donna Brooks, who worked for fourteen years at Burson-Marsteller, the world's largest public relations firm, where she served as the first African-American vice president, left in 1990 to establish Brooks, Robinson & Rashid (later BR&R Communications, Inc.), where the clients included the Sara Lee Corporation and Johnson's Wax.

During the 1990s, BR&R handled a highly successful project for the Sara Lee Corporation, "The Frontrunners Program," which annually saluted women in government, the arts, business, and the humanities at a dinner and awards ceremony held in New York. In addition to the awards presentations, which included videotaped stories about the honorees, the multiracial, multicultural program featured a corporate-style video presentation about the Sara Lee Corporation that was a part of their public relations image-enhancement campaign.

Many recently organized public relations firms have had difficulty getting beyond being viewed as minority vendors. As a result, some firms such as the Philadelphia-based Crawley, Haskins and Rogers (organized 1989) refuse to take positions as minority subcontractors in larger public relations contracts. Other African-American firms deal with the problem by assuming ongoing relations with larger firms. Focus Communications, a public relations firm established in Dallas in 1980, in 1991 assumed the position of an independent, in-house firm within Hill & Knowlton, one of the largest public relations firms in the country.

In the area of entertainment public relations, by the 1990s more African-American stars began to place their work in the hands of African-American publicists. Among this group were Eddie MURPHY, Spike LEE, Michael JACKSON, and Bill COSBY. These stars demanded that African-American publicists have access to the same wide array of resources as others.

Many of the most prominent African-American publicists have been women. Terrie Williams worked as a publicist for Eddie MURPHY, Miles DAVIS, Bobby BROWN, Charnett Moffett, New Line Cinema, The Samuel Goldwyn Company, Kid 'N' Play, Martin Lawrence, Sinbad, Anita Baker, and Dawnn Lewis. In 1991, Williams was awarded the Matrix Award for Women in Communications, for career excellence in public relations. Pat Tobin has handled publicity for Spike Lee, as well as for a number of political campaigns, including work for the Mondale/Ferraro presidential bid in 1984, and work on the 1984 and 1988 presidential campaigns of Jesse JACKSON.

Claudette Roper worked for seven years on the *Donahue Show*, in a working relationship that ended in some bitterness, before she obtained a position at Carsey-Warner, Bill Cosby's production company. Paul Brock served as communications counselor for Tony Brown Productions, and in 1987 coordinated its Buy Freedom Campaign, an effort to get African Americans to patronize community-based enterprises.

In politics, Bob Brown worked with the communications staff of the Nixon and Ford administrations, while Amelia Partier served as communications director of the Carter administration in the late 1970s. A number of first ladies have hired African-American press secretaries. Annette Samuels, Barbara Taylor,

and Anna Perez worked respectively for Rosalyn Carter, Nancy Reagan, and Barbara Bush.

Recent innovations include the burgeoning of market research. Ken Smikle founded Target Market News in 1987, and in 1991, Business Wire, a mainstream data service began offering services about black consumers. In 1989, a number of African-American executives formed an association of black-owned marketing and media firms, the African American Marketing and Media Association.

Despite improvements, many public relations officials still think black consumers are being slighted. In the early 1990s, advertisers spent only two percent of their marketing dollars in direct advertisements for an African-American population that spent $270 billion yearly. In fact, the industry spent only about $700 million in direct advertising to African-American consumers, compared with the $34 billion that the nation's top 100 advertisers spent to reach all consumers.

By the year 2010, it is estimated that African Americans will have $900 billion in spending power. Some have argued African-American consumers need to renew their focus on products and campaigns that are sensitive to their needs. In the 1960s and 1970s, the selective patronage campaign led by Leon Sullivan in Philadelphia and Jesse Jackson's nationwide Operation Push demonstrated the power of economic selectivity in purchasing by members of the black community, as well as a renewed and more sophisticated selectivity that would aid black consumers in rewarding, through their purchases, only those who cared about them.

By the 1990s, major corporations developed a strategy that allowed them to bypass black-owned media organizations almost entirely, while aiming their marketing overtures at black consumers (and the general market) as they positioned African-American superstars from various fields as pitchers for mass volume sales or as spokespersons endorsing products. Thus, unlike campaigns targeting the general market, and unlike the 1970s and 1980s, without using public relations overtures to establish a presence in the black community, companies just sold products, often making disproportionately high profits from the black community (on cornmeal products, hair care products, soft drinks, shoes, and moving pictures, for example), while they ignored other aspects of the community's needs and wishes.

Many argued that major American corporations were effectively threatening all but the strongest African-American–owned public relations, advertising, and marketing firms. This was true as well for other black businesses that depended upon public relations, advertising, and marketing, such as radio, newspapers, and magazines. Without contracts for overtures to the black community, public relations agencies and advertising agencies failed in larger numbers.

African-American owners of media-related businesses had just begun to see some opportunities open to them in the 1980s as the nation became conscious that its citizenry was more racially and culturally diverse. In the 1990s, with corporations shutting them out of the system that used and created black images, they had few options to keep their businesses on solid economic ground. Although some black-owned firms struggled to be viewed as general market businesses, and fought to obtain some contracts, even when they had proved their expertise they seldom won contracts for general market accounts. Thus there were nearly restricted to the segmented markets that included African-American, Latino, and Asian communities.

REFERENCES

DATES, JANNETTE L., and WILLIAM BARLOW. *Split Image: African Americans in the Mass Media*. Washington, D.C., 1990.

GIBSON, D. PARKE. *The $30 Billion Negro*. New York, 1969.

———. *$70 Billion in the Black: America's Black Consumers*. New York, 1978.

HACKER, ANDREW, *Two Nations: Black and White, Separate, Hostile, Unequal*. New York, 1992.

JANNETTE L. DATES

Purvis, Charles Burleigh (c. April 14, 1842–1929), physician and educator. Charles Purvis, the son of prominent abolitionist Robert Purvis, was born in Philadelphia, most likely in 1842 (though sources differ). He was educated at Oberlin College and the Medical College of Western Reserve University (M.D., 1865), and served as an acting assistant surgeon (with the rank of first lieutenant) for the U.S. Army. In 1869 he joined the staff at FREEDMEN'S HOSPITAL in Washington, D.C., as well as the faculty of the Howard University Medical School. This was the beginning of Purvis's fifty-seven-year association with the Howard University Medical School as a faculty member and administrator.

Purvis's reform activities paralleled his rising professional career. In 1869 he served as a Pennsylvania delegate to the national Convention of Colored Men of America. He also joined forces with Washington-area black physicians, supported by Massachusetts senator Charles Sumner, seeking to gain admission to the all-white Medical Society of the District of Columbia.

In 1881 Purvis gained national attention when President James A. Garfield was shot by an assassin; Purvis was one of the doctors brought in to treat the president. The following year, President Chester A. Arthur appointed Purvis surgeon-in-charge of Freedmen's Hospital in Washington. Under Purvis's leadership the hospital experienced significant growth.

Purvis's social philosophy reflected the civic ideals held by many among the African-American social elite of the Progressive era. He defended social welfare assistance for impoverished blacks on the grounds that class and color handicaps were at the root of their poverty. However, Purvis also stressed temperance, education, and self-reliance as the most effective means for people to end their poverty.

Though a prominent civic leader, Purvis was not without his critics. He exercised tight control over the administration of Freedmen's Hospital. Purvis impeded the famed surgeon Dr. Daniel Hale Williams when Freedmen's political controllers employed Williams to succeed Purvis as the hospital's chief surgeon from 1894 to 1898. The conflict that ensued between Purvis and Williams led to the latter's resignation in 1898.

When Purvis himself resigned from Howard in 1907, the university hailed his career at the school and Freedmen's Hospital. In 1908 the Howard trustees appointed him professor emeritus and made him a member of the university's board of trustees—a post Purvis held until 1926 when he was in his eighties. He died in Los Angeles in 1929.

REFERENCES

HARLAN, L. R. et al. *The Booker T. Washington Papers*. Urbana, Ill., 1975.

MORIAS, H. M. *The History of the Negro in Medicine*. New York, 1968.

DAVID MCBRIDE

Purvis, Harriet Forten (1810–1875), abolitionist. Harriet Forten Purvis was born in Philadelphia, Pa., in 1810, the daughter of James E. and Charlotte Forten. As the daughter of a wealthy black businessman, Harriet Forten enjoyed a life of privilege. She received a formal education from private tutors and became acquainted with the social reformers, black leaders, and other distinguished guests who visited the Forten home. Her marriage to Robert Purvis in 1832 united two of the most prominent black Philadelphia families.

Harriet Purvis dedicated her public life to abolitionism (*see* ABOLITION). She accompanied her husband to England in 1834 and assisted him in his anti-slavery work with British reformers. She maintained the Purvis country home in Byberry, Pa., as a major station on the UNDERGROUND RAILROAD. She helped establish the Philadelphia Female Anti-Slavery Society and organize the society's annual antislavery fairs. In 1838 and 1839 she represented her society at the Anti-Slavery Convention of American Women. Later she joined the Pennsylvania Anti-Slavery Society and served as the society's last secretary.

Purvis also demonstrated a lifelong commitment to women's rights. She spoke publicly on women's issues, advocated universal suffrage, and after the Civil War became an active member of the American Equal Rights Association (*see* SUFFRAGE, NINETEENTH-CENTURY).

REFERENCES

RIPLEY, C. PETER, et al., eds. *The Black Abolitionist Papers,* Vol. 3, *The United States, 1830–1846.* Chapel Hill, N.C., 1991.

STERLING, DOROTHY, ed. *We Are Your Sisters.* New York, 1984.

MICHAEL F. HEMBREE

Purvis, Robert (August 4, 1810–April 19, 1898), abolitionist and political leader. Robert Purvis was born in Charleston, S.C., the second of three sons of William Purvis, a British cotton merchant, and Harriet Judah, a free woman of color. A staunch opponent of SLAVERY, William Purvis instilled his hatred of the "peculiar institution" in his sons. Robert Purvis gave his first antislavery speech when he was seventeen.

In 1819 William Purvis sent his family to Philadelphia, intending eventually to settle with them in England. The children were enrolled in the Pennsylvania Abolition Society's Clarkson School, and Robert later attended Amherst College in Massachusetts. In 1826 William Purvis died, leaving the bulk of his fortune—some $200,000—to his sons. When the eldest son died without issue, his brothers received his share. A shrewd businessman, Robert Purvis put his legacy to good use, investing in bank stock and real estate.

Light-skinned and wealthy, Purvis rejected suggestions that he relocate and "pass." in 1831 he married Harriet Forten (*see also* Harriet Porter PURVIS), the daughter of African-American businessman and abolitionist James FORTEN. With his Forten in-laws he threw himself into the antislavery struggle. A tireless member of the Philadelphia Vigilance Committee, he sheltered runaways and conveyed them to the next "safe house" in his carriage. With William Lloyd

Robert Purvis, the son of a wealthy South Carolina cotton broker, was a notable abolitionist, philanthropist, and leader of Philadelphia's black residents for many decades. The inheritor of a considerable fortune from his father and owner of a large estate outside of Philadelphia, Purvis was likely the wealthiest African American of his day. (Prints and Photographs Division, Library of Congress)

Garrison, he was a founding member of the AMERICAN ANTI-SLAVERY SOCIETY in 1833, and in 1834 he crossed the Atlantic to meet leaders of the British antislavery movement. With his father-in-law, he helped steer white abolitionists, among them Garrison and Arthur Tappan (*see* ABOLITION), away from African colonization and toward a sweeping program designed to achieve racial equality. Purvis also had a profound influence on his young niece, educator and social reformer Charlotte Forten, who spent much of her early life in the Purvis household.

For two decades the Purvises lived in an elegant home in Philadelphia, where they entertained abolitionists from the United States and Europe. In 1842, with racial violence escalating, they moved to an estate in Byberry, some twelve miles outside Philadelphia.

Purvis welcomed the outbreak of the Civil War, demanding that President Abraham Lincoln make EMANCIPATION his goal. With the end of the war came an invitation to head the Freedmen's Bureau (*see* BUREAU OF FREEDMEN, REFUGEES, AND ABANDONED LANDS). However, Purvis declined the offer, fearing that this was a ploy by President Andrew Johnson to keep the support of African-American voters even as he set about destroying the bureau.

Initially a staunch REPUBLICAN, Purvis became disheartened as the party retreated from the principles it espoused during RECONSTRUCTION. In the Philadelphia mayoral race of 1874, his endorsement of the Democratic candidate was denounced by other African-American leaders. He was also criticized for his stance on the FIFTEENTH AMENDMENT, which was ratified in 1870. A lifelong champion of women's rights, Purvis contended that African-American men should not be enfranchised unless women received the vote.

In the last two decades of his life Purvis assumed the role of an elder statesman, tending his garden, orchard, and livestock. He died in Philadelphia at the age of eighty-seven, survived by his second wife and four of his eight children.

REFERENCES

BOROMÉ, JOSEPH A. "Robert Purvis and His Early Challenge to American Racism." *Negro History Bulletin* 30 (1967): 8–10.

WINCH, JULIE. *Philadelphia's Black Elite: Activism, Accommodation, and the Struggle for Autonomy, 1787–1848.* Philadelphia, 1988.

JULIE WINCH

Puryear, Martin (1937–), sculptor. The oldest of seven children, sculptor Martin Puryear attended both elementary and secondary school in Washington, D.C. His father, Reginald, worked as a postal service employee, and his mother, Martina, taught elementary school. He developed strong interests in biology and art, and aspired to be a wildlife illustrator. Always interested in working with his hands, Puryear as a young man made numerous objects, including guitars, chairs, and canoes.

Puryear entered Catholic University in Washington in 1959. Although initially a biology major, he shifted in his junior year to the study of painting and sculpture. Following graduation in 1963, Puryear entered the Peace Corps and served for two years in Sierra Leone, where he taught English, French, art, and biology. In addition to his teaching, he studied the craftsmen of West Africa, particularly the carpenters, from whom he learned a wide variety of traditional techniques. In 1966 he moved to Stockholm, where he enrolled at the Swedish Royal Academy. In addition to his formal studies in printmaking, Puryear pursued an interest in Scandinavian woodworking and began to work independently, making wood sculptures in the studios of the academy. He traveled widely during his two years in Stockholm, visiting the Soviet Union and western Europe, as well as the region of Lapland in northern Scandinavia.

In 1968 Puryear returned to the United States, and the following year he entered Yale University to study sculpture at the graduate level. In addition to his exposure to the part- and full-time faculty (including James Rosati, Robert Morris, Richard Serra, and Salvatore Scarpitta) at Yale, Puryear visited New York often, familiarizing himself with recent developments in contemporary art. Following receipt of his master of fine arts degree in 1971, he taught at Fisk University in Nashville for two years. His first important sculptures were made in the early 1970s, and these were shown in a solo exhibition held in 1973 at the Henri Gallery in Washington and at Fisk.

In 1973 Puryear left Fisk and established a studio in Brooklyn. The following year he accepted a teaching position at the University of Maryland, and he commuted between New York and College Park, Md., from 1974 to 1978. It was during this period that his work became known to a larger audience. In 1977 the Corcoran Gallery of Art in Washington, D.C., organized the first museum exhibition of his work; this show included *Cedar Lodge* (1977), a large, quasi-architectural sculpture, as well as *Some Tales* (1977), a wall-mounted sculpture consisting of six linear wooden elements. In the same year, Puryear created *Box and Pole* for Art Park in Lewiston, N.Y. For this first outdoor commission, the sculptor constructed a wooden box made of milled wood with dovetailed corners, and a hundred-foot-tall pole, thereby contrasting the concentrated strength of the former with the upward, seemingly infinite reach of the latter.

If 1977 found Puryear being accorded increasing attention in the art world, it was also a time of great loss. On February 1, 1977, his apartment and studio—including virtually all of the sculptor's work to date—were lost in a fire. The following year he left the East Coast to accept a teaching position at the University of Illinois, Chicago; he lived in Chicago until 1991. During this period, Puryear achieved ever-increasing recognition and was included in numerous important group exhibitions (including the Whitney Biennial in 1979, 1981, and 1989; the Museum of Modern Art's International Survey of Recent Painting and Sculpture, in 1984; and the Walker Art Center's Sculpture Inside Outside, in 1988). In 1989 he was selected as the sole American representative to exhibit in the twentieth São Paulo Bienal in Brazil, and he received the grand prize for his installation of eight works. The same year, he received a John D. and Catherine T. MacArthur Foundation Fellowship. In the fall of 1991, a large retrospective of Puryear's work opened at the Art Institute of Chicago. This exhibition of some forty sculptures toured to the Hirshhorn Museum and Sculpture Garden, Washington, D.C.; the Museum of Contemporary Art, Los Angeles; and the Philadelphia Museum of Art.

During the 1980s, Puryear's work grew to full maturity. He has pursued a number of different sculptural directions simultaneously, including approximately forty wall-mounted sculptures, many in the form of nearly circular "rings"; increasingly large-scale, three-dimensional sculptures, most made principally of wood but often incorporating new materials such as wire mesh and tar; and, finally, several outdoor commissions, some of which were sited permanently.

Puryear concentrated on the "ring" sculptures between 1978 and 1985. Constructed primarily of thin wood strips laminated in place and often painted, the "rings" are the sculptor's most refined work to date. Around 1984 they evolved into larger, more imposing wall-mounted works that grew increasingly independent of the supporting wall. A sculpture such as *Greed's Trophy* (1984), in the collection of New York's Museum of Modern Art, suggests an enormous hunting trap, its wire-mesh shape projecting nearly five feet from the wall. At this time Puryear also began to apply tar to his wire-mesh surfaces—in

a work such as *Sanctum* (1985), in the collection of the Whitney Museum of American Art—and this new element grants the undulating surface of the sculpture a sense of spatial enclosure as well as a tremendous physical presence. Since the mid-1980s, Puryear's sculpture has grown in new directions, as the artist has pressed the boundaries of abstraction to include allusions to living forms as well as objects. Finally, throughout the 1980s Puryear worked with distinction and great range in public, completing *Bodark Arc* (1982), commissioned for the Nathan Manilow Sculpture Park, south of Chicago, and *Ampersand* (1987–1988), commissioned for the Minneapolis Sculpture Garden. Throughout his work, Puryear has demonstrated a remarkable ability to create sculpture with multiple references, in which viewers discover images, memories, and allusions through their experience of the works.

REFERENCES

BENEZRA, NEAL. *Martin Puryear*. Chicago, 1991.
DAVIES, HUGH M., and HELAINE POSNER. *Martin Puryear*. Amherst, Mass., 1984.
JONES, KELLIE. *Martin Puryear*. Jamaica, N.Y., 1989.

NEAL BENEZRA

PUSH.   *See* Operation PUSH.

Quakers. *See* Society of Friends (Quakers).

Quarles, Benjamin (January 28, 1904–), historian. Born in Boston, Mass., in 1904, the son of a subway porter, Benjamin Quarles entered college at the age of twenty-three and received degrees from Shaw University (B.A., 1931) and the University of Wisconsin (M.A., 1933; Ph.D., 1940). He taught at Shaw, served as dean at Dillard University, and has chaired the history department at Morgan State University.

Quarles began his scholarly career at a time when racist assumptions hampered research and writing on African-American history (*see* HISTORIANS/HISTORIOGRAPHY). White historians questioned whether blacks could write objective history; and they believed that African-American history lacked sufficient primary sources for serious research and writing. Quarles proved both notions were false. Building on the pioneering research of Carter G. WOODSON and other black historians of the previous generation, Quarles confirmed the existence of a rich documentary record of African-American life and culture. His early writings demonstrated both his careful research and his ability to present a balanced historical narrative. His essays in *Mississippi Valley Historical Review* in 1945 and 1959 were the first from a black historian to appear in a major historical journal.

Benjamin Quarles. (Photographs and Prints Division, Schomburg Center for Research in Black Culture, The New York Public Library, Astor, Lenox and Tilden Foundations)

Stuyvesant quilters. (© Martha Cooper/City Lore)

Quarles's first scholarly article, "The Breach Between Douglass and Garrison," appeared in the *Journal of Negro History* in 1938 and revealed his interest in race relations. Many of his subsequent studies have explored the way in which blacks and whites have helped shape each other's identity on individual and collective levels. In *Lincoln and the Negro* (1962) and *Allies for Freedom: Blacks and John Brown* (1974), Quarles investigated the relationship between blacks and two notable whites in American history. Quarles focused on the eighteenth and nineteenth centuries, particularly the collective contribution of African Americans in two dramatic events in *The Negro in the Civil War* (1953) and *The Negro in the American Revolution* (1961). In *Black Abolitionists* (1969), he highlighted their participation in the nation's most important social reform movement.

Quarles has shared with his contemporary John Hope FRANKLIN an optimistic appraisal of racial progress in American history. He has brought his scholarship to the classroom through two textbooks, *The Negro in the Making of America* and *The Negro American: A Documentary History,* and he has advanced African-American history as a contributing editor of *Phylon* and as associate editor of the *Journal of Negro History.*

REFERENCES

McFEELY, WILLIAM F. "Introduction." In Benjamin Quarles. *The Negro in the Civil War.* 1953. Reprint. New York, 1989, pp. 3–6.

MEIER, AUGUST. "Introduction: Benjamin Quarles and the Historiography of Black America." In Benjamin Quarles. *Black Mosaic: Essays in Afro-American History and Historiography.* Amherst, Mass., 1989, pp. 3–21.

MICHAEL F. HEMBREE

Queen Ida.   *See* Guillory, Ida Lewis "Queen Ida."

Quilt Making.   For many generations African-American women in the South engaged in the art of making patchwork quilts. Motivated by a need to provide insulation against the cold winters spent in drafty slave cabins, early African-American female slaves transformed brightly colored scraps of calico from the "Big House" and plantation sewing rooms into beautiful geometric designs. Patterns for the quilts were cut and sewn together into coverlets during the few leisure hours of slave existence. The coverlets were combined with a cotton interlining and muslin backing, all of which were later quilted or joined together. Southern African-American women still host "quilting bees" where groups assemble around a wooden frame and the three parts of the quilt (design top, cotton interlining, and muslin backing) are quilted into a single cover.

Quilt making, per se, is not a West African tradition, as the warm climate of the continent does not necessitate heavy bed covering. Documentation does not support, however, a Euro-American origin of that craft. The tradition of certain categories of patchwork quilt making, which are still preserved in the South, probably originated with African slaves and derived from woven and appliquéd textiles found in West and Central Africa. Decorative quilt art is not exclusively an African-American phenomenon. Examples are also made by the Amish, Pennsylvania Germans, and other ethnic groups in America. Euro-American examples, however, are usually more formal and complex in design than those made by African-American women in the South. African-American quilt patterns were handed down from generation to generation, and it is not uncommon for women to possess samplers that illustrate some of the most frequently depicted designs. The patterns are generally geometric, and some of the most popular are "Sawtooth," "Single Irish Chain," "Double Irish Chain," "Pineapple," "Wedding Ring," "Rising Sun," "Triangles," and "Lone Star." One of the most common patterns made by African-American women in the Deep South is the "Crazy Quilt," which combines scraps of materials of many sizes and shapes in an informal arrangement with an absence of the geometric designs that characterize most examples. This type of random color and patterning, which appears primarily in African-American quilts made in the Deep South, is apparently indigenous.

Two of the most unusual examples of nineteenth-century African-American quilt art, which differ from the typical geometric or random patterning, are the "Harriet Quilts" in the collections of the Smithsonian Institution, the National Museum of American History, and the Museum of Fine Arts in Boston. These quilts were made by Harriet Powers (1837–1911), an African-American woman who lived in Georgia. Born a slave in 1837 near Athens, Ga., Powers was the wife of a farmer who, after her emancipation, engaged in the art of quilt making as a hobby. The quilt in the Smithsonian's collection was completed c. 1885 and is a vivid depiction of eleven scenes from the Old and New Testaments. The Boston quilt was made in 1898 and included fifteen scenes combining religious and astronomical symbolism. Unlike other surviving quilts made by African Americans during the nineteenth century, Powers's only two known surviving quilts were created by appliquéing or stitching neatly compartmentalized patterns against a solid background. That technique has been compared with the centuries-old tradition of royal appliquéd tapestries made in the Republic of Benin (formerly Dahomey) in West Africa. That tradition might have been introduced to Powers through the influx of hundreds of Dahomean slaves who were brought to central Georgia well into the nineteenth century.

REFERENCES

FRY, GLADYS-MARIE. "Harriet Powers: Portrait of a Black Quilter." *Missing Pieces: Georgia Folk Art 1770–1976* (1977): 72–77.

PERRY, REGENIA A. *Selections of Nineteenth-Century Afro-American Art.* Museum exhibit brochure. New York, 1976.

REGENIA A. PERRY

Quinland, William Samuel (October 12, 1885–April 6, 1953), pathologist. Born in 1885 in Antigua, British West Indies, William Samuel Quinland studied to become a teacher before moving to the United States. In 1918 he received a B.S. from Oskaloosa College in Iowa, and, in 1919, an M.D. from Meharry Medical College in Nashville, Tenn.

In 1919 Quinland became the first recipient of a Rosenwald Fellowship for postgraduate study in pathology and bacteriology at Harvard Medical College in Cambridge, Mass. He studied at Harvard until 1922, during which time he worked as an assistant in pathology at Peter Bent Brigham Hospital in Boston. In 1922 he returned to Meharry, where he served as professor and head of the pathology department until 1947. From 1922 to 1947 Quinland also worked as a pathologist at George W. Hubbard Hospital, and was the associate medical director there from 1931 to 1937. From 1947 until his death in 1953, he was chief of laboratory service at the Veterans Administration Hospital in Tuskegee, Ala.

Quinland published numerous articles in such periodicals as the *Journal of the National Medical Association* and the *Boston Medical and Surgical Journal.* He was the first black named to the American Association of Pathologists and Bacteriologists (1920), the first black diplomate of the American Board of Pathology (1937), and the first black fellow of the College of American Pathologists (1947).

REFERENCE

SAMMONS, VIVIAN OVELTON. *Blacks in Science and Medicine.* New York, 1990.

LYDIA MCNEILL

Quinn, William Paul (c. 1788–February 21, 1873), bishop, African Methodist Episcopal (AME) Church. Little is known of the early life of Paul Quinn other than that he was born in a British colony about 1788. Bishop Daniel Alexander PAYNE, historian of the AFRICAN METHODIST EPISCOPAL CHURCH (AME), states that Quinn was born in British Honduras (now Belize) to Catholic parents. (Other accounts suggest he was born in Calcutta, India, to Hindu parents.) He migrated to the United States when very young, lived in Pennsylvania, and worked briefly as a lumberjack. According to Payne, Quinn was introduced to organized religion at an early age by Samuel Collins, an itinerant Methodist preacher, in West Chester, Pa.

By 1808, Quinn was a member of the Methodist Episcopal Church in Bucks County, Pa. He was licensed to preach in Bucks County in 1812 and attended the first AME general convention in Philadelphia in 1816. The AME ordained him a deacon two years later, and he held several pastorates in New Jersey and Bucks County. Following a disagreement with Bishop Richard ALLEN, the church's principal founder, Quinn left the denomination about 1827 and ministered to an independent congregation of about 150 in New York.

Quinn petitioned to return to the church in June 1828, but was not readmitted until its 1833 conference—two years after Allen's death. Quinn was then sent by the AME to the Western Pennsylvania and Ohio region as an itinerant preacher. In 1838, he became an elder in the AME and an assistant bishop under Morris BROWN the following year.

By 1844 Quinn had organized an astounding 120 congregations and 50 Sunday schools in the Midwest, some under arduous circumstances in the slave states of Kentucky and Missouri. A big man, he often intervened personally when fights arose that disrupted his religious meetings. He was assaulted twice during such intrusions. In 1834, Quinn published *The Origins, Horrors and Results of Slavery,* an impassioned pamphlet denouncing slavery, especially targeting the South Carolina legislature, which had passed laws that year preventing Negro education and employment in trading establishments.

On May 19, 1844, Quinn was consecrated bishop, the fourth in the history of the AME Church. At Bishop Morris Brown's death, in 1849, Quinn became the denomination's senior bishop and he settled in Richmond, Ind. He was a notable figure in the AME leadership until he became ill and was relieved of active duties in 1872. Paul Quinn died in Richmond. Many AME churches and a college in Waco, Tex., are named after him.

REFERENCES

BERRY, L. L. *A Century of Missions of the African Methodist Episcopal Church.* New York, 1942.

PAYNE, DANIEL A. *A History of the AME Church.* Vol. 1. Nashville, 1891. Reprint. New York, 1968.

PORTER, DOROTHY, ed. *Early Negro Writing: 1760–1837.* New York, 1971.

SMITH, CHARLES SPENSER. *A History of the AME Church.* Vol. 2. Philadelphia, 1922. Reprint. New York, 1968.

QADRI ISMAIL

Ra, Sun. *See* Sun Ra.

Race, Caste, and Class. In his influential 1944 study, *An American Dilemma,* Gunnar Myrdal characterized the peculiar nature of race relations in the United States as the most important problem facing the country. Social scientists have offered several theoretical frameworks to understand and conceptualize the complexities of this dilemma. Gordon Allport, for example, wrote of "prejudice" as being at the heart of American race relations (*The Nature of Prejudice,* 1958). Later theorists have written of "institutional racism" (Louis L. Knowles and Kenneth Prewitt eds., *Institutional Racism in America,* 1969), or "internal colonialism" (Robert Blauner, *Racial Oppression in America,* 1972) as frameworks for the interpretation of race relations.

Although none of these approaches has won universal acceptance, the so-called caste-class model presented by Lloyd Warner and popularized by Gunnar Myrdal has been the most influential and enduring. Beginning with a 1936 essay, "American Caste and Class," and continuing with the study of a small southern city in *Deep South* (1941), Warner and his colleagues argued that race relations in the United States could be best understood as analogous to the traditional caste system of India.

Having earlier studied a small community in New England (given the pseudonym "Yankee City"), Warner was struck by differences in intergroup relations in the two cities. Unlike Yankee City, where members of white ethnic groups experienced some mobility within the "social class" structure (even though they rarely reached the highest level), in the town they called "Deep South," all blacks seemed to be ranked below all whites, without any hope of upward mobility. This characteristic of southern race relations along with the taboo against interracial marriage suggested to Warner and his associates that a fundamentally different social structure existed in the South.

The concepts of "prejudice" and "race" were considered and rejected as explanations of this organized social system, which systematically separated the races and subordinated all blacks to whites. Warner and his associates observed that even the most liberal members of white southern society shared dominant cultural ideas about the social incompatibility of the two groups and carefully avoided social contact with blacks. They noted that race relations in the South had all the earmarks of a caste system such as existed in India. Yet southern society was not static. While blacks and whites were separated by impermeable barriers, social hierarchies existed within each community which allowed for some social mobility within each group. To express these two aspects of the town's social structure, the researchers settled on "caste and class," a nomenclature combining both aspects of community dynamics. A substantial number of community studies and essays by Warner and his colleagues provided additional plausibility to their approach to race relations in the United States and led to its widespread acceptance among social scientists. To the general public this analogy with the Indian caste system was persuasive, especially after the more popular work by Gunnar Myrdal, *An American Dilemma,* appeared a few years later.

Within this study, which became enormously popular because of its focus on the disjuncture between the American creed of equality for all and the systematic subordination of blacks, Myrdal defended the caste and class thesis. Myrdal put his greatest emphasis on the closed nature of black and white groups. He saw the ban against interracial marriage as "one expression of the still broader principle . . . that *a man born a Negro or a white is not allowed to pass from the one status to the other as he can pass from one class to another."*

Myrdal focused on the "permanent disabilities" African Americans faced "solely because they are 'Negroes' in the rigid American definition and not because they are poor and ill-educated." His observation cut through rationalizations of white dominance based on alleged black inferiority, lack of wealth, or education. Unlike recent immigrants, he argued, African Americans were locked in their "caste" by their artificial racial definition. These arguments seemed cogent given the institutionalized system of racial separation that had developed in the South.

For all its commonsense persuasiveness, however, the caste and class model of American race relations was from the beginning seriously flawed. As a model of a system of stratification or inequality, the caste-class approach ignored fundamental distinctions already developed by both Karl Marx and Max Weber, the two authors who contributed most to this area. According to Weber, the three fundamental forms of stratification were "classes," "status groups," and "castes." Classes (as Marx also agreed) were groups based exclusively in the market or economy, while status groups rose out of a system which ranked individuals within a hierarchy of prestige or honor. Membership in classes was a factor of personal achievement in the marketplace through ownership of wealth or occupations held. Membership in status groups was dependent upon acceptance by their members and conformity to the groups' style of life, which frequently included in-group marriage. Castes, unlike status groups, included the added dimension of being religiously sanctioned.

Based on these distinctions, the groups about which Warner and Myrdal wrote were in reality status groups rather than classes. Warner defined a "social class" as "the largest group of people whose members have intimate access to one another," a definition that coincides exactly with Weber's definition of status groups. In practice Warner often used the

terms class and status interchangeably, another indication that the difference was not one that was well grasped by him.

Neither Warner nor Myrdal appeared to comprehend the true nature of India's caste system from which they derived their analogy. Warner, a social anthropologist who spent many years studying preliterate societies in Australia, never studied up close a caste system such as that of Hindu India. He based his conclusions on secondhand observations and conversations. As the African-American sociologist Oliver Cromwell COX pointed out in his book *Race, Caste and Class* (1948), this misunderstanding of the Indian caste system led to a fuzziness and inconsistency in the school's discussion of the hypothesized American caste system. Contradictory evidence seemed to be ignored. For example, Cox noted that though Warner adopted the definition of caste proposed by the well-known anthropologist A. L. Kroeber, he ignored Kroeber's conclusion that a caste system was not possible in Western societies. Furthermore, neither Warner nor Myrdal seemed to be aware of the essentially religious foundation of the Indian caste system. As Max Weber pointed out in *Economy and Society,* "status distinctions [in caste systems] are . . . guaranteed not merely by conventions and laws, but also by religious sanction." The complete absence of religious sanctions in maintaining racial separation in the United States was a matter not even commented on by the members of the caste-class school.

Nor was the analogy of American race relations with the Indian caste system original to either Warner or Myrdal. Cox traced the use of the analogy at least as far back as the middle of the nineteenth century. A number of prominent scholars, including William I. Thomas in 1904 and Ray Stannard Baker in 1908, made use of the analogy in their discussions of race relations in the South, sometimes applying the term "color line" and frequently the concept of "caste." So popular was the concept that it appeared in sociological textbooks early in the twentieth century. For his part, Myrdal acknowledged his own indebtedness for the concept to earlier usages in the 1930s by the Chicago University sociologist Robert E. Park.

Another area of ambiguity revolved around the perceived "form" of the caste-class social structure. While agreeing upon the existence of a "color line" or "caste line" separating all blacks from all whites, the location and even the shape of the line were disputed by members of this school. Hypotheses varied depending upon perceptions of the individual class structures of blacks and whites. Long before the writings of Warner and Myrdal, Robert E. Park argued in 1928 that the caste line had moved from an earlier horizontal to a vertical position. As the occupational structure of blacks became more differentiated, Park held, blacks and whites more and more "looked across" a vertical line rather than "up and down" along a horizontal line.

In *Deep South,* the caste line is portrayed as neither horizontal nor vertical but as *diagonal,* a position the authors argued best represented the disproportionate concentration of blacks at the bottom of their class structure. The horizontal line, Warner argued, was shifting toward a vertical position as the black class structure became similar to that of the whites and closer to "equivalency." Myrdal, on the other hand, argued that black and white class structures were shifting but would remain fundamentally asymmetrical, with blacks overrepresented in the lower classes, while whites would remain concentrated in the middle class. This situation Myrdal represented by a "diagonal curve" underscoring his conviction that a fundamental inequality would remain between blacks and whites. He further held that even in the event of a similar distribution across classes, whites of the same class would still look "down" on blacks rather than "across" as suggested by Warner's use of the term "equivalent."

Closely connected to disagreements over the position and shape of the caste line were the varying views on the essence of a "caste" system among members of the school. Cox pointed to this serious problem when he wrote that "to John Dollard, the essence of caste is 'a barrier to legitimate descent'; to W. Lloyd Warner, it is endogamy; to Guy B. Johnson, it is the achievement of 'accommodation'; to Robert E. Park, 'etiquette is the very essence of caste.' " Even the southern taboo against interracial marriage, Cox argued, was not sufficient reason for the use of the caste analogy. Classes, tribes, sects, and "any other social groups which think they have something to protect," he pointed out, have disapproved of intermarriage.

Given the many flaws in the caste-class model, why did it enjoy such longstanding popularity? While the many conceptual problems discussed above demonstrate the inadequacies of the model there is no denying its intuitive appeal at a time when 90 percent of African Americans resided in a solidly segregated JIM CROW South. It is just this intuitive appeal that may have been its undoing. As more and more African Americans moved to northern cities between the two world wars and into the 1950s, the caste-class model began losing its attractiveness. Though segregation and discrimination were widely practiced in the North, these practices lacked the legal backing of southern Jim Crow laws. Interracial marriage, for instance, though discouraged in the North by racial custom, was not proscribed by law. As St. Claire DRAKE and Horace R. CAYTON observed in *Black Metropolis,* their exhaustive two-volume study of Chicago's African-American community in the mid-1940s, though a color line existed in Chicago as in the Deep South, in Chicago and other northern cities it was "not static; and sometimes the job ceiling was pierced and broken." In the North, some whites offered at least "lip service" to the democratic creed of equality. Though in a "Methodological Note" to *Black Metropolis,* Warner held that despite differences in the two cities, there was a "status system of the caste type" in *Black Metropolis,* the caste-class model nevertheless lacked persuasiveness when applied to northern cities like Chicago.

During the 1940s and '50s millions of blacks migrated to the industrial cities of the North and West in a massive population shift that eventually led almost half of the African-American population out of the South. As the CIVIL RIGHTS MOVEMENT got under way, it was the call for long denied rights, an end to segregation at lunch counters, restaurants, and other public accommodations, not an end to the legal ban on interracial marriage that dominated the movement's agenda. With rising educational levels among blacks, and increased occupational diversity and geographical dispersion, the caste-class model had lost its intuitive appeal. Lacking a firmer grounding in social facts, it could not serve as the basis of the Movement's rallying cries. Civil rights, black power, and desegregation of public accommodations proved to be more powerful images to rouse opponents of racial inequality. The term "caste" seemed absent from the vocabulary of protestors. Within the academic community, scholars tested new conceptual models of American race relations such as "institutional racism" and "internal colonialism." In the rough and tumble of the civil rights movement it was increasingly the call for "black power" that brought crowds to their feet or protestors into the streets. Observations of racial inequality in housing, the job market, income and wealth continue to be made by scholars, journalists, and activists alike. And while there is still no consensus on the most accurate model of American race relations, the caste-class approach has all but disappeared from the discourse on racial inequality.

REFERENCES

Cox, Oliver C. *Caste, Class, and Race.* Garden City, N.Y., 1948.

Davis, Allison, Burleigh Gardner, and Mary R. Gardner. *Deep South: A Sociological Anthropological Study of Caste and Class.* Chicago, 1941.

Drake, St. Clair, and Horace R. Cayton. *Black Metropolis: A Study of Negro Life in a Northern City.* New York, 1945.

Glenn, Norvall. "White Gain from Negro Subordination." In Gary Mars, ed. *Racial Conflict.* Boston, 1971, pp. 106–16.

LANDRY, BART. "The Enduring Dilemma of Race in America." In Alan Wolfe, ed. *America at Century's End*. Berkeley, Calif. 1991, pp. 185–207.

MYRDAL, GUNNAR. *An American Dilemma: The Negro Problem and American Democracy*. New York, 1944.

BART LANDRY

Race, Scientific Theories of. It was not until the early nineteenth century that race received systematic attention in a scientific manner, although ideas about racial difference had existed for centuries. Scientific racism and the marshaling of empirical data to support theories of racial inferiority/superiority intensified during the early 1800s after the expansion of knowledge within the biological sciences enhanced the professional status of science in Europe and America. By the late eighteenth century, however, Enlightenment philosophers had already laid a foundation for later typologists with a series of natural history treatises that classified races according to environmental and geographic conditions.

David Hume's *Of National Characters* (1748) and Baron Montesquieu's *Spirit of Laws* (1748) both explained how local climatic factors had produced the human "varieties" that Europeans encountered during imperialist voyages. The influential classification system of Johann Friedrich Blumenbach, with its five types—Caucasian, Mongolian, Ethiopian, African, and Malayan—would, at century's end, provide an important typological framework for empiricists who increasingly assigned race significance as a static, biological entity during the next half century.

Scientific theories of race in Europe and America during the first half of the nineteenth century were directly linked to speculations on the role of evolution in the development of plant and animal diversity. Monogenists, one of the two more popular kinds of racial theorists during the period, asserted that all human races could be traced to the traditional biblical story of Adam and Eve, but that a process of "degeneration" left each distinct type at various stages of mental, moral, and physical development. Polygenists, on the other hand, maintained that God created an Adam and Eve for each racial group and that immutable biological differences among races belonging to individual species resulted from these separate acts of creation.

Both monogenism and polygenism buttressed social and political support for slavery in the United States and imperialist expansionism abroad, but the latter theory did generate some degree of skepticism among American adherents because of its inherent challenge to biblical doctrine. Lauded quite frequently by Louis Agassiz, a Harvard naturalist, in many lectures during the 1840s, the biologic argument for "separate species" reinforced societal fears about the alleged deleterious evolutionary effects of miscegenation, or race mixing, between blacks and white Americans.

Samuel George Morton, in *Crania Americana* (1839), analyzed hundreds of craniometric measurements and assembled a scale of development which asserted the inferiority of Native Americans, blacks, and women, a feat that was surpassed only by the work of Josiah C. Nott and George R. Gliddon, two indefatigable champions of polygenism. Their most famous publication, *Types of Mankind* (1854), declared that zoological investigations proved that races constituted "permanent" types.

Charles Darwin's *Origin of Species* (1859) challenged static representations of race types with its materialist theory of evolutionary change and its pronouncement that human evolutionary "progress" extended beyond the six thousand years that the classic biblical interpretation offered. Despite the fact that Darwin had undermined monogenism and polygenism by pointing to the importance of change in the development of biological diversity and a common origin for human evolutionary experience, polygenists—physical anthropologists, in particular—persisted in their claims for static racial types.

Among racial typologists, the "cephalic index," a facial angle measurement developed by Anders Retzius (1796–1860), supplied an important statistical dimension for anthropometric and craniometric studies into the early twentieth century. Many physical anthropologists inferred from Darwin's work and these measurements, for instance, that high mortality rates among late nineteenth-century black Americans forecast imminent "extinction," and that mental and physical distinctions rather than the economic and political disfranchisement that characterized the experience of blacks in post-Reconstruction America explained the high disease rates.

Darwin's work also became a catalyst of hereditary and genetic explanations of racial distinctions in the late nineteenth and early twentieth centuries, when eugenists launched aggressive campaigns for human action to transform the evolutionary process with social policies designed to promote good "breeding" among the better "stocks." Charles B. Davenport, an influential biologist, initiated a series of studies to determine the influence of sterilization and immigration restriction on "defectives" in 1910 at the Eugenics Records Office in Cold Spring Harbor, Long Island, just ten years after Mendel's laws on heredity were rediscovered and almost thirty years after Francis Galton, a cousin of Darwin, first coined the term "eugenics" in 1883.

During the first half of the twentieth century, significant challenges to biologic and genetic characterizations of race stressed the importance of environmental and cultural factors in human behavior. Franz Boas and other reform-minded physical anthropologists criticized earlier anthropometricians and pointed to overlapping physical variation, while social scientists, such as W. E. B. DU BOIS, and reformers, such as Anna Julia COOPER, provided stark analyses of the persistent socioeconomic conditions that maintained racial disparities in health, education, and general economic status. By the mid-twentieth century, a coalition of cultural and physical anthropologists, empirical sociologists, and geneticists would also advance the biological data from populational genetics that affirmed overlapping genetic variation to undermine static portraits of race and intelligence depicted in many IQ studies.

The most powerful statement rejecting the biological model of race came by a group of scientists who signed the UNESCO Statement on Race in 1950 and 1951, largely acknowledging the view that studies of human variation should be "population-based" in order to trace the prevalence of particular patterns of human variation to selective environmental factors. It would also become apparent through the revelation of Nazi experiments during World War II and the Tuskegee Study on the Effects of Untreated Syphilis in the Negro Male (1932–1972) that static genetic and biologic representations of race did not disappear with the emergence of the cultural/environmental model during the early twentieth century (*see* TUSKEGEE SYPHILIS EXPERIMENT). Although most anthropologists and biologists have abandoned older theories of race based on static and permanent morphological distinctions, ongoing debates about the genetic basis of intelligence and other social phenomena continue to fuel discussions about the scientific importance of race.

REFERENCES

APTHEKER, HERBERT, ed. *Against Racism: Unpublished Essays, Papers, Addresses, 1887–1961*. Amherst, Mass., 1985.

BANTON, MICHAEL. *Racial Theories*. Cambridge, U.K., 1987.

GOULD, STEPHEN JAY. *The Mismeasure of Man*. New York, 1981.

KEVLES, DANIEL. *In the Name of Eugenics*. Berkeley, Calif., 1985.

MAYR, ERNST. *The Growth of Biological Thought*. Cambridge, Mass., 1982.

MONTAGU, ASHLEY. *Statement on Race*. New York, 1951.

NOTT, JOSIAH C., and G. R. GLIDDON. *Types of Mankind*. Philadelphia, 1854.

OMI, MICHAEL, and HOWARD WINANT. *Racial Formation in the United States: From the 1960s to the 1980s*. New York and London, 1986.

GERARD FERGERSON

Radio.

Radio. African-American radio can be divided into three general periods of historical development: blackface radio (1920–1941), black-appeal radio (1942–1969), and black-controlled radio (1970 to the present). Blackface radio was characterized by the appropriation of African-American music and humor by white entertainers, who performed their secondhand imitations for a predominantly white listening audience. During this period, black people were essentially outside of the commercial broadcasting loop; they were marginal as both radio entertainers and consumers. In the era of black-appeal radio, African Americans entered into the industry as entertainers and consumers, but the ownership and management of the stations targeting the black radio market remained mostly in the hands of white businessmen. This situation constrained the development of independent black radio operations, while the radio industry in general prospered from it. During the most recent period, African Americans have striven to own and operate their own radio stations, both commercial and public. In addition, they have established black-controlled radio networks and trade organizations. However, the percentage of African American–owned stations still lags far behind the percentage of black listeners.

The appropriation of black song, dance, and humor by white entertainers who blackened their faces with charcoal goes back to the early days of slavery. The resulting radical stereotypes were embedded in the blackface minstrel tradition (*see* MINSTRELS/MINSTRELSY), which dominated American popular entertainment in the antebellum period, and remained resilient enough in the postbellum years to reappear in film and radio in the early decades of the twentieth century. Popular black music styles like blues and jazz were first performed on the radio by white performers like Sophie Tucker, the first singer to popularize W. C. HANDY's "Saint Louis Blues," and Paul Whiteman, the so-called king of jazz in the 1920s. A parallel trend developed with respect to black humor with the emergence of AMOS 'N' ANDY (starring Freeman Gosden and Charles Correll) as radio's most popular comedy series.

Indeed, *Amos 'n' Andy* was radio's first mass phenomenon: a supershow that attracted 53 percent of the national audience, or 40 million listeners, during its peak years on the NBC network in the early 1930s. In addition, the series provoked the black community's first national radio controversy. Robert Abbot, editor of the CHICAGO DEFENDER, defended Gosden and Correll's caricatures of black urban life as inoffensive and even humane. Robert Vann, editor of the PITTSBURGH COURIER, countered by criticizing the series as racist in its portrayal of African Americans. He also launched a petition campaign to have the program taken off the air that amassed 740,000 signatures—but to no avail. The petition was ignored by the Federal Radio Commission. Meanwhile, *Amos 'n' Andy* dominated black comedy on radio throughout its heyday as the "national pastime" in the 1930s. In addition to Gosden and Correll, the other major blackface radio entertainers of the era included George Mack and Charles Moran, known as the Two Black Crows on the CBS network, as well as Marlin Hunt, who created and portrayed the radio maid Beulah on the series of the same name.

During the period when blackface comedy performed by whites dominated the portrayal of African Americans over the airways, its audience was mostly white; fewer than one in ten black households owned a radio receiver. There were black entertainers and actors who managed to get hired by the radio industry in the pre–World War II era, and for the most part they were restricted to playing stereotyped roles. The renowned black comedian Bert WILLIAMS was the first important black performer to be linked to commercial broadcasting, in the 1920s; he was featured on a New York station doing the same routines he popularized while performing in blackface on the Broadway stage. During the Great Depression, as if to add insult to injury, a number of black actors and actresses who auditioned for radio parts were told that they needed to be coached in the art of black dialect by white coaches if they wanted the jobs. This perverse chain of events happened to at least three African-American performers: Lillian Randolph (*Lulu and Leander Show*), Johnny Lee (*Slick and Slim Show*), and Wonderful Smith (*Red Skelton Show*). The most famous black comic to appear regularly on network radio in the 1930s was Eddie ANDERSON, who played the role of the butler and chauffeur Rochester on the *Jack Benny Show*. Anderson was often criticized in the black press for playing a stereotypical "faithful servant" role, even as he was being praised for his economic success and celebrity.

After blackface comedy, the African-American dance music called JAZZ was the next most popular expression of black culture broadcast over the airways in the 1920s and 1930s. As was the case with humor, the major radio jazz bands were made up of white musicians, and were directed by white bandleaders like Paul Whiteman, B. A. Rolfe, and Ben Bernie. The first black musicians to be broadcast with some regularity on network radio were New York bandleaders Duke ELLINGTON and Noble SISSLE. A number of influential white radio producers like Frank and Ann Hummert, the king and queen of network soap operas, began to routinely include black doctors, teachers, and soldiers in their scripts. In addition, the federal government produced its own radio series, entitled *Freedom's People,* to dramatize the participation of African Americans in past wars, and it recruited Paul ROBESON as a national and then international radio spokesman for the U.S. war effort. But at the end of the war, the government withdrew from the domestic broadcasting sphere, allowing the logic of the marketplace to reassert itself. Then with the advent of the new television networks, and their subsequent domination of the national broadcasting market, radio was forced to turn to local markets in order to survive as a commercial enterprise. Inadvertently, this led to the discovery of a "new Negro market" in regions where African Americans' numbers could no longer be ignored by broadcasters. This was especially the case in large urban centers, where nine out of ten black families owned radios by the late 1940s. The result of this convergence of economic necessity and a mushrooming listening audience was the emergence of black-appeal radio stations and the rise of the African-American disc jockey—two interrelated developments that transformed the landscape of commercial radio in the postwar era.

A few black DJs were playing records over the airways in the 1930s; they worked through a brokerage system that charged them an hourly fee for airtime. The disc jockeys, in turn, solicited advertising aimed at the local black community and broadcast it in conjunction with recorded "race" music. Jack L. Cooper pioneered this approach in Chicago on his radio show *The All Negro Hour,* which first aired on WSBC in 1929. At first, he developed a live variety show with local black talent, but within two years he had switched to recorded music in order to cut costs. He played jazz discs, hosted a popular "missing persons" show, pitched ads, made community-service announcements, and also developed a series of weekend religious programs. This format was successful enough to make him into a millionaire; by the end of the 1930s, he had a stable of African-American DJs working for him on a series of black-appeal programs broadcast on two stations. In the 1940s, Cooper was challenged as Chicago's premier black disc jockey by Al Benson, who also built up a small radio empire on local outlets with his own style of black-appeal programming. Cooper targeted the middle-class African-American audience; he played the popular big-band jazz recordings of the day and prided himself in speaking proper English over the air. Benson played the down-home blues of the era and spoke in the vernacular of the new ghetto populace, most of whom were working-class southern migrants. A new era of black radio was at hand.

By the end of the 1940s, there was a growing number of aspiring DJs in urban black communities ready to take advantage of the new "Negro-appeal" formats springing up on stations throughout the country. In Memphis, Nat D. Williams was responsible for broadcasting the first African-American radio show there, on WDIA in 1948; he also created the station's new black-appeal format and launched the careers of numerous first-generation African-American DJs over WDIA's airways. Two of the most important were Maurice "Hot Rod" Hulbert, who moved on to become the dean of black disc jockeys in Baltimore, on WBEE; and Martha Jean "the Queen" Stienburg, who later became the most popular black DJ in Detroit, on WCHB. In 1950, WERD, in Atlanta, became the first African-American–owned radio station in the country when it was purchased by J. B. Blayton, Jr. He appointed his son as station manager and then hired Jack "the Rapper" Gibson as program director. Other black-appeal stations that came into prominence during the early 1950s included WEDR in Birmingham, Ala.; WOOK in Washington, D.C.; WCIN in Cincinnati; WABQ in Cleveland; KXLW in St. Louis; and KCKA in Kansas City, which became the second African American–owned radio outlet in the nation in 1952. By 1956 there were over four hundred radio stations in the United States broadcasting black-appeal programming. Each of these operations showcased its own homegrown African-American disc jockeys, who were the centerpiece of the on-air sound.

The powerful presence and influence of the African-American DJs on the airways in urban America in the 1950s stemmed from two sources. On the one hand, they were the supreme arbiters of black musical tastes; they could make or break a new record release, depending on how much they played and promoted it. On the other hand, the black disc jockeys were also the new electronic griots of the black oral tradition, posturing as social rappers and cultural rebels. As such, they collectively constituted a social grapevine that was integral not just to the promotion of rhythm and blues, but also to the empowerment of the growing civil rights movement in the South. Black-appeal radio stations like WERD in Atlanta and WDIA in Memphis, as well as Al Benson's shows in Chicago, played a vital role in informing people

about the early civil rights struggles. In a speech to black broadcasters late in his life, civil rights leader the Rev. Dr. Martin Luther KING, Jr., paid special tribute to disc jockeys Tall Paul White (WEDR, Birmingham), Purvis Spann (WVON, Chicago), and Georgie Woods (WHAT, Philadelphia) for their important contributions to the civil rights efforts in their respective cities.

During the 1950s, African-American radio DJs also had a profound effect on commercial radio in general. Some stations—such as WLAC in Nashville, a high-powered AM outlet heard at night throughout the South—devoted a hefty amount of their evening schedules to rhythm and blues records. In addition, the white disc jockeys at WLAC (John R., Gene Noble, Hoss Allen, and Wolfman Jack) adopted the on-air styles, and even dialect, of the black DJs. Many of their listeners, both black and white, thought that WLAC's disc jockeys were African Americans. This was also the case on WJMR in New Orleans, where the white DJs who hosted the popular *Poppa Stoppa Show* were actually trained to speak in black dialect by the creator of the show, an African-American college professor named Vernon Winslow. Other white DJs who became popular by emulating the broadcast styles of their black counterparts included Dewey Phillips in Memphis; Zenas "Daddy" Sears in Atlanta; Phil Mckernan in Oakland, Calif.; George "Hound Dog" Lorenz in Buffalo, N.Y.; and Allen Freed in Cleveland. Freed moved on to become New York City's most famous rock and roll disc jockey, before his fall from grace as the result of payola scandals in the early 1960s.

Payola, the exchange of money for record airplay, was a common practice throughout the radio industry. It was an easy way for disc jockeys to supplement the low wages they were paid by their employers. Hence, many well-known black DJs were adversely affected by the payola exposés. Some lost their jobs when their names were linked to the ongoing investigations, and an unfortunate few were even the targets of income-tax-evasion indictments. The industry's solution to the payola problem was the creation of the "top forty" radio format, which in effect gave management complete control over the playlists of records to be aired on their stations. Formerly, the playlists had been determined by the individual DJs. This change led to the demise of both the white rock-and-roll disc jockeys and the black "personality" DJs associated with rhythm and blues, and then "soul" music. Black-appeal stations were centralized even further by the emergence of five soul radio chains in the 1960s, all of which were white-owned and -managed. By the end of the decade, these corporations controlled a total of twenty stations in key urban markets with large African-American populations like New York, Chicago, Memphis, and Washington, D.C. The chain operations not only established standardized top forty soul formats at their respective outlets, thus limiting the independence of the black DJs they employed, but they also eliminated most of the local African-American news and public-affairs offerings on the stations.

In spite of the trend toward top forty soul formats, a number of black personality DJs managed to survive and even prosper in the 1960s. The most important were Sid McCoy (WGES, WCFL), Purvis Spann (WVON), and Herb Kent (WVON) in Chicago; LeBaron Taylor and Georgie Woods (both WDAS) in Philadelphia; Eddie O'Jay in Cleveland (WABQ) and Buffalo (WUFO); Skipper Lee Frazier (KCOH) in Houston; the Magnificent Montegue (KGFJ) in Los Angeles; and Sly Stone (KSOL) in San Francisco. LeBaron Taylor and Sly Stone went on to successful careers in the music industry—Taylor as a CBS record executive and Stone as a pioneering pop musician. The Magnificent Montegue's familiar invocation, "Burn, baby, burn," used to introduce the "hot" records he featured on his show, inadvertently became the unofficial battle cry of the 1967 Watts rebellion. The new mood of black militancy sweeping the nation also found its way into the ranks of the African-American DJs, especially among the younger generation just entering the radio industry. Two of the more influential members of this "new breed," as they came to be known, were Del Shields (WLIB) in New York and Roland Young (KSAN, KMPX) in San Francisco. Both men independently pioneered innovative black music formats, mixing together jazz, soul, and salsa recordings.

The 1970s ushered in the current era of black-owned and -controlled radio operations, both stations and networks. In 1970, of the more than three hundred black-formatted stations, only sixteen were owned by African-Americans. During the next decade, the number of black-owned stations rose to 88, while the number of formatted stations surpassed 450. Some of the more prominent African Americans who became radio station owners during this era included entertainers James BROWN and Stevie WONDER, Chicago publisher John JOHNSON, and New York City politician Percy SUTTON. In particular, Sutton's Harlem-based Inner City Broadcasting (WLIB-AM, WBLS-FM) has been the national trendsetter in a black-owned-and-operated radio from the early 1970s to the present. In 1977, African-American broadcasters organized their own trade organization, the National Association of Black-Owned Broadcasters. By 1990 there were 206 black-owned radio stations—138 AM and 68 FM—in the country.

It was also during the 1970s that two successful black radio networks were launched: the Mutual Black Network, founded in 1972, which became the Sheridan Broadcasting Network in 1979; and the National Black Network, started in 1973. Both of these operations provide news, talk shows, public affairs, and cultural features to their affiliate stations throughout the nation. In the 1980s, the Sheridan network had over one hundred affiliates and 6.2 million weekly listeners; in addition to news and public affairs, it offered a wide range of sports programming, including live broadcasts of black college football and basketball games. The National network averaged close to one hundred affiliates and four million weekly listeners in the 1980s; its most popular programs, in addition to its news reports, were journalist Roy Woods's *One Man's Opinion* and Bob Law's *Night Talk.*

Two major formats have dominated black-owned commercial radio in the 1970s and 1980s—"talk" and "urban contemporary." Talk radio formats emerged on African-American AM stations in the early 1970s; in essence, they featured news, public affairs, and live listener call-in shows. By this time, the FM stations dominated the broadcasting of recorded music due to their superior reproduction of high fidelity and stereo signals. The AM stations were left with talk by default. Inner City Broadcasting initiated the move toward talk radio formats among African-American stations when it turned WLIG-AM, which it purchased in New York City in 1972, into "your total news and information station" that same year. The logic of the commercial radio market encouraged many of the other black AM operations, such as WOL-AM in Washington, D.C., to follow suit. Likewise, Inner City Broadcasting also pioneered the urban contemporary format on WBLS-FM during this same period. Much of the credit for the new format is given to Frankie Crocker, who was the station's program director at the time. In order to build up WBLS's ratings in the most competitive radio market in the country, Crocker scuttled the station's established jazz programming in favor of a crossover format featuring black music currently on the pop charts along with popular white artists with a black sound. The idea was to appeal to an upscale black and white audience. The formula worked to perfection; WBLS became the top station in the New York market, and scores of other stations around the country switched to the new urban contemporary format. One example was WHUR-FM, owned by Howard University in Washington, D.C. The station's original jazz and black-community-affairs format was sacked in favor of the urban contemporary approach in the mid-1970s. The new format allowed WHUR to become one of the top-rated stations in the Washington market. In the process, it gave birth to an innovative new nighttime urban contemporary style called "quiet storm," after the Smokey Robinson song of the same name. The architect of this novel format was Melvin Lindsey, a former Howard student and WHUR intern.

The 1970s and 1980s also marked the entrance of African Americans into the public broadcasting sphere. By 1990, there were thirty-two public FM stations owned and operated by black colleges around the country, and another twelve controlled by black community boards of directors. These stations are not subject to the pervasive ratings pressures of commercial radio, giving them more leeway in programming news, public affairs, talk, and unusual cultural features. Many of these stations—such as WCLK-FM, owned by Clarke College in Atlanta; WSHA-FM, owned by Shaw College in Raleigh, N.C., and WVAS-FM, from Alabama State University in Montgomery—have adopted the jazz formats abandoned by African-American–owned commercial FM stations. Others, like WPFW-FM in Washington, D.C. (the number one black public radio outlet in the country), have developed a more ambitious "world rhythms" format embracing the many musics of the African diaspora. In general, the growth of black public radio has expanded the variety and diversity of African-American programming found on the airways, while also increasing the numbers of African Americans working in radio.

REFERENCES

DATES, JANNETTE, and WILLIAM BARLOW, eds. *Split Image: African Americans in the Mass Media*. Washington, D.C., 1989

DOWNING, JOHN. "Ethnic Minority Radio in the USA." *Howard Journal of Communication* 1, no. 4 (1989); 135–148.

EDMERSON, ESTELLE, "A Descriptive Study of the American Negro in U.S. Professional Radio, 1922–1953." M.A. thesis, University of California at Los Angeles, 1954.

FERRETTI, FRANK, "The White Captivity of Black Radio." *Columbia Journalism Review* (Summer 1970); 35–39.

WILLIAM BARLOW

Ragtime. Ragtime was the first music of African-American origin to play a significant role in American popular culture. It had both vocal and instrumental forms, flourished from the late 1890s until the late 1910s, and had important exponents among both black and white composers.

A major element of antebellum black music in the public mind was syncopated rhythm. This and similar rhythms were used to caricature black music and were widely heard in minstrel shows that toured the nation, bringing an incipient ragtime to public consciousness (*see* MINSTRELS/MINSTRELSY). Ragtime as a distinct genre came to public notice at the 1893 World's Fair in Chicago, one piece that was played there reportedly being Jesse Pickett's "Dream Rag." The term "ragtime" first appeared in print on song publications of 1896, possibly the earliest being Ernest Hogan's "All Coons Look Alike to Me," which included a syncopated "Choice Chorus, with Negro 'Rag,' Accompaniment." As this quotation indicates, the black roots of ragtime were acknowledged from the very beginning.

Vocal Ragtime

Most early ragtime songs were known as "coon songs," "coon" being a then-widely used contemptuous term for blacks. These songs typically had lyrics in stereotypical black dialect and played upon such negative themes as black men being shiftless, lazy, thieving, gambling, and violent; of black women being mercenary and sexually promiscuous. A typical song lyric would be "I don't like no cheap man / Dat spends his money on de 'stallment plan." (Bert Williams and George Walker, 1897). Adding to the songs' negative impressions were sheet music covers that usually portrayed African Americans in grotesquely exaggerated caricatures. With the relatively insensitive ethnic climate of the time, there was little protest from the black community; black artists—including such sophisticated individuals as composer Will Marion COOK and poet-lyricist Paul Laurence DUNBAR—contributed to the genre.

Not all early ragtime songs were abusive, even though they retained racial stereotypes. Among those whose popularity outlived the ragtime years was Howard and Emerson's "Hello! Ma Baby" (1899), which celebrates courtship over the telephone. "Bob" COLE and J. Rosamond JOHNSON, black artists who were sensitive to the stigma of demeaning lyrics, wrote their enormously successful "Under the Bamboo Tree" (1902) to demonstrate that a racial song could express tasteful and universally appreciated sentiments.

Around 1905, the ragtime song began to lose its overtly racial quality and came to include any popular song of a strongly rhythmic character. Typical examples were "Some of These Days" (1910) and "Waiting for the Robert E. Lee" (1913). Irving Berlin's hit song "Alexander's Ragtime Band" (1911) which was regarded by many as the high point of ragtime, retains only slight racial suggestions in its lyrics and these are nonderogatory.

Instrumental Ragtime

Ragtime developed both as a solo-piano vehicle and as an ensemble style for virtually all instruments. Ensemble ragtime was played by marching and concert bands, by dance orchestras, and in such diverse combinations as xylophone-marimba duos and trios, piano-violin duos, and mandolin-banjo groupings. Solo-piano ragtime was heard on the vaudeville stage, in salons and brothels, in the home parlor, and on the mechanical player piano.

Ragtime was closely associated with dance. In the early days, the two-step was most common, along with such variants as the slow-drag. The cakewalk remained popular throughout the ragtime years but was a specialty dance reserved mostly for exhibitions and contests. In the 1910s many new dances joined the ragtime category, including the one-step, foxtrot, turkey trot, grizzly bear, and such waltz variants as the Boston, hesitation, and half-and-half. The tango and maxixe, though Latin-American rather than ragtime dances, were performed to syncopated music and became part of the ragtime scene in the mid-1910s.

Piano Ragtime

Ragtime was published primarily for the piano and contributed significantly to the development of American popular music and jazz piano. Piano ragtime, like the ragtime song, flourished as published sheet music, but it also existed as an improvised art, giving it a direct link to early jazz (*see* JAZZ). However, since improvised ragtime was not preserved on sound recordings, we have little detailed knowledge of it.

The defining elements of ragtime were established by 1897, when the earliest piano rag sheet music appeared. Of primary importance was the syncopation, for it was from this uneven, ragged rhythmic effect that the term "ragtime" was derived. As applied to piano music, syncopation typically appeared as a right-hand pattern played against an even, metric bass. Around 1906 a new pattern, known as secondary ragtime, gained acceptance. This is not true syncopation, but the shifting accents within a three-note pattern create a polyrhythmic effect that was successfully integrated with the other ragtime gestures. After 1911, dotted rhythms made inroads into ragtime, further diluting the distinctiveness of the early ragtime syncopations.

The form into which ragtime was cast, though not a defining element, was consistent. The form followed that of the march and consisted of a succession of sixteen-measure thematic sections, each section being evenly divided into four phrases. Typically the two opening thematic sections were in the tonic key and were followed by one or two sections (known as the "trio") in the subdominant key. (As an example of the key relationships, if the tonic key were C, the subdominant key would be F.) Diagrammatically,

with each section depicted with an upper-case letter, the form with repeats might appear as AA BB A CC or AA BB CC DD. To these patterns might be added four-measure introductions to A and to C and interludes between repeats of C or between C and D. Though these patterns were typical, they were not invariable; many rags used different numbers of sections and different key relationships.

Blues, another style that emerged from the African-American community, had some influence on the rags of a few composers, particularly in the use of so-called blue notes (*see* BLUES). What in later years was to become known as the classic twelve-bar blues form made its earliest appearances in piano rags. The first known example was in "One O' Them Things?" (James Chapman and Leroy Smith, 1904), in which a twelve-bar blues replaces the usual A section. Both the form and the term appear in a New Orleans ragtime publication of 1908, A. Maggio's "I Got the Blues." The first blues to achieve popularity was W. C. HANDY's "Memphis Blues" (1912), which combines twelve-bar blues and sixteen-bar ragtime sections and was subtitled "A Southern Rag." Through the rest of the ragtime era, the term "blues" was applied indiscriminately to many rags.

Though instrumental ragtime lacked the direct verbal communication possible with the lyrics of ragtime songs, early published rags conveyed a racial connotation with cover pictures that caricatured blacks, frequently in an offensive manner. As with the songs, piano ragtime's gradual acceptance as American music rather than as an exclusively racial expression was matched with the discontinuance of racial depictions.

The Composers and Performers

The first ragtime performer to acquire fame was vaudeville pianist, singer, and composer Ben Harney, who appeared in New York in 1896 with "plantation negro imitations." Though he was known as "the first white man to play ragtime," his racial origins remain uncertain.

The publication of piano ragtime began in 1897 with "Mississippi Rag," by white bandmaster William Krell. Several months later, Tom Turpin, with his "Harlem Rag," became the first black composer to have a piano rag published. Turpin, a St. Louis saloon keeper, was an important figure in the development of ragtime in that city and reportedly had composed this piece as early as 1892. The most prominent ragtime success of 1897 was Kerry Mills's "At a Georgia Campmeeting," known in both song and instrumental versions and recorded by the Sousa Band, among others.

Piano ragtime quickly caught on, and in the years 1897–1899 more than 150 piano rags were published, the most important and influential being Scott JOP-LIN's "Maple Leaf Rag" (1899). Joplin was a composer with serious aspirations, and his frequent publisher John Stark adopted the term "classic ragtime" to describe the music of Joplin and others he published. These included black Missourians James Scott, Arthur Marshall, Louis Chauvin, Artie Matthews, and such white composers as J. Russel Robinson, Paul Pratt, and Joseph Lamb. Though virtually all classic rags are superior examples of the genre, the term did not embrace any single style. Nor were classic rags the best known. More popular were the easier and more accessible rags of such composers as Ted Snyder, Charles Johnson, Percy Wenrich, and George Botsford.

New York City, with its flourishing entertainment centers and music publishing industry (Tin Pan Alley), naturally attracted many ragtimers. Because of the competition and high musical standards in the city, some of the more adept ragtime pianists developed a virtuosic style known as "stride." Among the leaders of this style were Eubie BLAKE, James P. JOHNSON, and Luckey ROBERTS. These musicians—along with such figures as Joe Jordan, Will Marion Cook, Bob Cole, and J. Rosamond Johnson—also became involved in black musical theater, which made extensive use of ragtime.

Bandleader James Reese EUROPE disliked the term "ragtime" but became one of the most influential musicians on the late ragtime scene in New York. In 1910 he formed the Clef Club, an organization that functioned both as a union and booking agency for New York's black musicians. As music director for the popular white dance team of Irene and Vernon Castle, beginning in 1914, Europe created a demand both for black music and for black dance-band musicians.

Many who were admired during the ragtime years left little or no record of their music. Among these were "One-Leg" Willie Joseph, Abba Labba (Richard McLean), and "Jack the Bear" (John Wilson). "Jelly Roll" MORTON was active from the early ragtime years but did most of his publishing and recording in the 1920s and 1930s. Tony Jackson was widely praised as a performer and composer but is remembered today primarily for his song "Pretty Baby." There were many black women active as performers, but they are now forgotten because they did not publish or record. Thus, the history of ragtime is slanted in favor of those who can be documented.

Reaction to Ragtime

Within the context of the genteel parlor music of the 1890s, ragtime was shockingly new. Nothing like it had ever been heard. For some, ragtime became America's statement of musical independence from Europe; it was hailed as a new expression, reflecting this nation's exuberance and restlessness. American youth, regardless of race, embraced the music as its own.

Inevitably, opposition to ragtime emerged. One sector of opposition was generational—the ever-present syndrome of the older generations rejecting the music of the younger. There was also opposition from musical elitists, those who objected to a music that lacked a proper pedigree and feared it would drive out "good music." Some denied that ragtime was at all innovative; they argued that the ragtime rhythms had been used by the European "old masters" and in various European folk musics. Then there were the blatant racists, who rejected the idea that an American music could have black origins and denied that African Americans were capable of creating anything original. Most of all, they feared that white youth was being "infected" by this developing black music.

Certain parts of African-American society also objected to ragtime. Church groups, noting that ragtime was played in saloons and brothels and used for dancing, concluded that the music contributed to sinfulness. Blacks striving for middle-class respectability were also wary of ragtime because of its lower-class associations. The *Negro Music Journal* (1902–1903), which encouraged blacks to cultivate tastes for classical music, denounced ragtime and denied that it was an African-American expression.

Despite such opposition, ragtime thrived and evolved. During the mid- to late 1910s jazz emerged as an offshoot of ragtime. At first there was little distinctiveness between the two, but by the end of WORLD WAR I jazz had replaced ragtime as the most important vernacular music in America.

REFERENCES

BERLIN, EDWARD A. *Ragtime: A Musical and Cultural History*. Berkeley, Calif., 1980.
———. *Reflections and Research on Ragtime*. Brooklyn, N.Y., 1987.
BLESH, RUDI, and HARRIET JANIS. *They All Played Ragtime*. 4th ed. New York, 1971.
HASSE, JOHN EDWARD, ed. *Ragtime: Its History, Composers, and Music*. New York, 1985.
JASEN, DAVID A. *Recorded Ragtime, 1897–1958*. Hamden, Conn., 1973.
JASEN, DAVID A., and TREBOR TICHENOR. *Rags and Ragtime*. New York, 1978.
RIIS, THOMAS L. *Just Before Jazz: Black Musical Theater in New York, 1890–1915*. Washington, D.C., 1989.
SCHAFER, WILLIAM J., and JOHANNES RIEDEL. *The Art of Ragtime*. Baton Rouge, La., 1973.
WALDO, TERRY. *This Is Ragtime*. New York, 1976.

EDWARD A. BERLIN

Rainey, Gertrude Pridgett "Ma" (April 26, 1886–December 22, 1939), singer. One of the most beloved blues and vaudeville singers of the first three decades in the twentieth century, Ma Rainey— "Mother of the Blues"—was born Gertrude Pridgett in Columbus, Ga. Rainey was the second of five children born to Thomas and Ella Pridgett. She performed in a local show, "A Bunch of Blackberries," at fourteen and married a tent showman, Will Rainey, when she was eighteen. They performed together for several years as a comedy song and dance act, billed as the "Assassinators of the Blues," with the Rabbit Foot Minstrels.

Supposedly, Rainey coined the term "blues" after she began singing the mournful songs that she had heard sung by a young woman along the tent show's route (*see* BLUES). Rainey left her husband after twelve years but continued to follow the TOBA (Theater Owner's Booking Association) circuit as a solo act because she was so popular with country folk, white and black. She sang with jug bands as well as small jazz bands, which included at times Tommy Ladnier, Joe Smith, and Coleman HAWKINS. She was a seasoned performer who sang about the worries and tribulations of country folk in the traditional style of the rural South. Her subject matter was earthy, her renditions were often comedic, yet she did not resort to trivia.

Rainey's first recording, "Moonshine Blues," was produced by Paramount Records in 1923. She recorded a total of ninety-three songs, which included traditional country/folk blues, vaudeville songs, and popular songs. Rainey wrote many of her songs, addressing topics as diverse as the impact of the boll weevil on cotton crops to homosexuality, prostitution, and jail. Although she was overshadowed by her younger counterpart, Bessie SMITH, Rainey had a loyal following until her last days on the tent show circuit in the 1930s. She handled her business affairs well and retired to her native city of Columbus, Ga., where she opened her own theater. She died there on December 22, 1939.

REFERENCE

LIEF, SANDRA. *Ma Rainey: Mother of the Blues*. Amherst, Mass., 1981.

DAPHNE DUVAL HARRISON

Rainey, Joseph Hayne (June 21, 1832–August 1, 1887), congressman. Joseph Rainey was born in Georgetown, S.C., to slave parents Edward and Gracey Rainey. In the 1840s the Raineys bought their freedom, and the family opened a barbershop in Georgetown. Rainey worked in his father's shop until the outbreak of the Civil War, when he was drafted by the Confederacy to military service.

After the war, Rainey became a Republican chairman in South Carolina and served as a member of the Republican state executive committee from 1868 until 1876. In 1868 he served as a delegate to the constitutional convention from Georgetown. He was elected to the state senate, where he acted as chairman of the finance committee. In 1870, he became the first African-American member of the House of Representatives, replacing Republican Benjamin F. Whittemore, who was forced to resign. Rainey was defeated in 1878 by the Democrat John S. Richardson. While in Congress, Rainey supported civil rights legislation, including the Civil Rights Bill of 1875, enforcement of the Fourteenth Amendment, and the Ku Klux Klan Act. He also advocated integration of public schools.

After leaving congressional office in 1878, Rainey served as a special agent of the treasury department until 1881. He then tried unsuccessfully to open a note brokerage and banking business in Washington, D.C. In 1886, he helped operate a coal and wood yard with William H. Chew. Rainey died in Georgetown, Md.

Joseph H. Rainey, a barber before the Civil War, became a four-term congressman from South Carolina and the first African American to preside over the House of Representatives. (Prints and Photographs Division, Library of Congress)

REFERENCE

LOGAN, RAYFORD W., and MICHAEL R. WINSTON, eds. *Dictionary of American Negro Biography*. New York, 1982.

SABRINA FUCHS

RAM.   *See* Revolutionary Action Movement.

Ram's Horn.   The *Ram's Horn,* a New York City weekly newspaper, was founded by Willis A. HODGES and Thomas Van Rensellaer in January 1847. Hodges, a free black from Virginia, started the paper in response to racist editorials in the city's white press. Like the ram's horns in the biblical account of the battle of Jericho, Hodges's paper sought to bring down the "walls of slavery and racial prejudice." The *Ram's Horn* reflected a growing desire among northern black leaders in the 1840s for a more assertive, independent response to slavery and racism. The one extant issue and articles reprinted in other newspapers suggest that the *Ram's Horn* may have been the most militant black newspaper of the antebellum period. Breaking with pacifists in the anti-slavery movement, Hodges openly called for slave insurrection. Frederick DOUGLASS wrote for the paper; John Brown contributed financially and wrote several essays, including "Sambo's Mistakes"—a biting commentary on the lack of militancy among northern free blacks. Van Rensellaer, a local restaurateur, bought Hodges's interest in the *Ram's Horn* in the spring of 1848 but failed to keep the paper in business. Regular publication of the *Ram's Horn* ended in July, although a few issues appeared during the following months.

REFERENCE

GATEWOOD, WILLARD B., JR., ed. *Free Man of Color: The Autobiography of Willis Augustus Hodges*. Knoxville, Tenn., 1982.

MICHAEL F. HEMBREE

Randall, Dudley Felker (January 14, 1914–), poet and publisher. Dudley Felker Randall was born in Washington, D.C. His mother, Ada Viola Bradley, was a teacher; his father, Arthur George Clyde Randall, was a Congregational minister. When Randall was nine, his family moved to Detroit. He became a published poet at thirteen, when the *Detroit Free Press* printed a sonnet he had written (and for which he was paid one dollar).

Randall attended Wayne University (now Wayne State University) and obtained a B.A. in 1948. In 1951, he earned a master's in library science from the University of Michigan. Throughout the 1950s and '60s Randall was a librarian, and he eventually became the head reference librarian at the University of Detroit (1963–1969). But he also continued to write poetry, and from 1969 until 1975, Randall was the university's poet-in-residence.

Perhaps Randall's most important contribution to American culture was the BROADSIDE PRESS, which he founded in 1965. Through the publication of broadsides (individual poems printed on a single sheet of paper) and books sold at affordable prices, Broadside Press gave voice to an entire generation of African-American poets. Among the poets Broadside published are Gwendolyn BROOKS, Nikki GIOVANNI, Robert HAYDEN, Etheridge KNIGHT, Audre LORD, Haki R. MADHUBUTI (a.k.a. Don L. Lee), Sonia SANCHEZ, and Margaret WALKER. In 1977, deeply in debt (due largely to Randall's commitment to selling books at low prices), Broadside was purchased by the Alexander Crummell Memorial Center. Randall was retained as a consultant.

Collections of Randall's poetry include *Poem Counterpoem* (with Margaret G. Burroughs, 1966), *Cities Burning* (1968), *Love You* (1970), *After the Killing* (1973), *A Litany of Friends: New and Selected Poems* (1983), and *Homage to Hoyt* (1984). In 1981, Mayor Coleman YOUNG named Randall as Detroit's first Poet Laureate.

REFERENCES

Contemporary Literary Criticism, Vol. 1. Detroit, 1973.
WELLBORN, RON. "Cities Burning." *Negro Digest* (December 1969): 94–95.

MICHAEL PALLER

Randolph, Asa Philip (1889–1979), labor and civil rights leader. The younger son of James William Randolph (a minister in the African Methodist Episcopal Church), A. Philip Randolph was born in Crescent City, Fla., and raised in Jacksonville. In 1911, after graduating from the Cookman Institute in Jacksonville, the twenty-two-year-old Randolph migrated to New York City and settled in Harlem, then in an early stage of its development as the "Negro capital of the world." While working at odd jobs to support himself, he attended the City College of New York (adjoining Harlem), where he took courses in history, philosophy, economics, and political science.

During his enrollment at CCNY, he also became active in the Socialist party, whose leader, Eugene Debs, was one of his political heroes.

Between 1914 and the early 1920s, Randolph belonged to a group of young African-American militants in New York, the "Harlem radicals," who regarded themselves as the New Negro political avant-garde in American life. Some of them, including Randolph, combined race radicalism with socialism. Others, such as Marcus GARVEY, who arrived in Harlem in 1916, emphasized an Africa-oriented black nationalism—they were averse to movements that advocated social reform or racial integration within the mainstream of American society. But all Harlem radicals defied the old establishment of African-American leadership, though it included so distinguished a member as W. E. B. DU BOIS.

To race radicalism and socialism Randolph soon added an interest in trade unionism, (*see* LABOR AND LABOR UNIONS), which was to form a basic part of

A. Philip Randolph, the chief organizer of the March on Washington movement in the early 1940s, addressing the 1963 March on Washington from the Lincoln Memorial. Though the 1941 March on Washington was called off by Randolph when the federal government agreed to end discrimination by defense contractors, it demonstrated the potential power of mass demonstrations to civil rights activists. (AP/Wide World Photos)

his approach to the struggle for black progress. In 1917, he and his closest socialist comrade in Harlem, Chandler OWEN, founded and began coediting the MESSENGER, a monthly journal that subtitled itself "The Only Radical Magazine Published by Negroes." The *Messenger* campaigned against lynchings in the South; opposed America's participation in World War I; counseled African Americans to resist the military draft; proposed an economic solution to the "Negro problem"; and urged blacks to ally themselves with the socialist and trade-union movements. For its irreverent editorial stands, the *Messenger* came under the close surveillance of the federal government. In 1918, Postmaster General Albert Burleson revoked the magazine's second-class mailing privileges; and in 1919, a Justice Department report ordered by Attorney General A. Mitchell Palmer described the *Messenger* as being "by long odds the most able and most dangerous of the Negro publications."

In 1917, Randolph also helped to organize the Socialist party's first black political club in New York, located in Harlem's Twenty-first Assembly District. And in 1920, the party recognized his growing importance as a spokesman by naming him its candidate for New York State comptroller, one of the highest positions to which a black socialist had been named. He lost in the November elections but polled an impressive 202,361 votes, about a thousand fewer than Eugene Debs polled in New York that year as the Socialist party's candidate for president.

In the early 1920s, Randolph began dissolving his formal ties to the party when it became clear to him that the black masses were not as responsive to the socialist message as he had hoped. This was partly because of their traditional distrust for ideologies they deemed to be un-American; partly because black nationalism was, emotionally and psychologically, more appealing to them; and partly because the Socialist party failed to address the special problems of black exclusion from the trade-union movement. But despite his retirement from formal party activities, Randolph was always to consider himself a democratic socialist.

In 1925, a delegation of Pullman porters approached him with a request that he organize their work force into a legitimate labor union, independent of employer participation and influence. Randolph undertook the task—a decision that launched his career as a national leader in the fields of labor and civil rights. But establishing the BROTHERHOOD OF SLEEPING CAR PORTERS was a far more difficult task than he had anticipated. The Pullman Company had crushed a number of earlier efforts at organizing its porters, and for the next twelve years it remained contemptuous of Randolph's. Not until 1937, after Congress had passed enabling labor legislation, did the Pullman executives recognize the Brotherhood of Sleeping Car Porters as a certified bargaining agent.

This victory gained the brotherhood full membership in the American Federation of Labor (AFL). It also gave Randolph—as the brotherhood's chief delegate to annual AFL conventions—an opportunity to answer intellectuals in Harlem who had criticized him for urging blacks to ally themselves with the trade-union movement. The black intelligentsia then regarded the AFL as a racist institution, most of whose craft unions barred nonwhite membership. How then (his critics argued) could Randolph call on blacks to invest their economic aspirations in organized labor? Randolph maintained, however, that trade unionism was the main engine of economic advancement for the working class, the class to which a majority of the black population belonged. He believed, moreover, that the achievement of political rights, for which all blacks were struggling, would be meaningless without comparable economic gains.

Throughout his tenure as a delegate to the annual conventions of organized labor (in 1955 he became a vice-president of the merged AFL-CIO), Randolph campaigned relentlessly against unions that excluded black workers. When he retired as a vice-president in 1968, the AFL-CIO had become the most integrated public institution in American life, though pockets of resistance remained. Randolph was not the sole instrument of that revolution, but he was its opening wedge, and much of it was owed to his unyielding agitation.

The brotherhood's victory in 1937 also inaugurated Randolph's career as a national civil rights leader; he emerged from the struggle with Pullman as one of the more respected figures in black America. In 1937, the recently formed NATIONAL NEGRO CONGRESS (NNC), recognizing Randolph's potential as a mass leader, invited him to be its president. In accepting, he himself saw the NNC as a potential mass movement. But he was obliged to resign the NNC's presidency in 1940, when he discovered that much of the organization had fallen under communist control. He was to be a resolute anti-communist for the rest of his life. He wrote to a colleague in 1959:

> They [communists] are not only undemocratic but anti-democratic. They are opposed to our concept of the dignity of the human personality, the heritage of the Judeo-Christian philosophy, and hence they represent a totalitarian system in which civil liberties cannot live.

Randolph's withdrawal from the NNC freed him to organize, early in 1941, the March on Washington Movement based on the Gandhian method of nonviolent direct action. It achieved its first major victory in June of that year. Faced with Randolph's

threat to lead a massive invasion of the nation's capital, President Franklin D. Roosevelt issued an executive order banning the exclusion of blacks from employment in defense plants—the federal government's earliest commitment to the policy of fair employment. That breakthrough brought Randolph to the forefront of black mass leadership, making him "the towering civil rights figure of the period," according to James FARMER, one of his younger admirers. The March on Washington Movement disintegrated by the end of the 1940s. But by then Randolph had secured another historic executive order—this one from President Harry S. Truman, in 1948, outlawing segregation in the armed services. Scholars were to see his movement as one of the most remarkable in American history. Aspects of its influence went into the formation of Farmer's CONGRESS OF RACIAL EQUALITY (1942) and Rev. Dr. Martin Luther KING'S SOUTHERN CHRISTIAN LEADERSHIP CONFERENCE (1957), both of which helped to lead the great nonviolent protest movement of the 1960s.

Randolph was the elder statesman of that movement, a unifying center of the civil rights coalition that composed it. His collaboration with its various leaders culminated in the 1963 March on Washington, the largest demonstration for racial redress in the nation's history. Randolph had conceived that event. And it is appropriate that he should have called it a March for Jobs and Freedom; it represented his two-pronged approach, political and economic, to the black struggle.

After 1963, Randolph the architect of black mass pressure on the federal government faded gradually from the scene. In 1964, President Lyndon B. Johnson awarded him the Presidential Medal of Freedom, the nation's highest civilian honor. He spent the remaining years of his active life chiefly as a vice president of the AFL-CIO. He died in 1979, at the age of ninety.

REFERENCES

ANDERSON, JARVIS. *A. Philip Randolph: A Biographical Portrait*. New York, 1973.

BRAZEAL, BRAILSFORD R. *The Brotherhood of Sleeping Car Porters*. New York, 1946.

PFEFFER, PAULA F. *A. Philip Randolph, Pioneer of the Civil Rights Movement*. Baton Rouge, La., 1990.

JERVIS ANDERSON

Rangel, Charles Bernard (June 11, 1930–), politician. Charles Rangel was born and raised in Harlem. His parents separated when he was a small child and he lived with his mother and grandfather.

Rangel dropped out of high school in his junior year and worked at odd jobs until 1948, when he enlisted in the Army. He was deployed to South Korea, where he was stationed for four years and served in the Korean War, earning a Bronze Star Medal of Valor and a Purple Heart.

After the war Rangel returned to high school in New York and received his diploma in 1953. He then entered the New York University School of Commerce, earning a B.S. in 1957. Rangel went on to St. John's University Law School, where he obtained his J.D. in 1960. After law school, Rangel worked as an attorney and provided legal assistance to civil rights activists. In 1961 he was appointed an assistant United States attorney in the Southern District of New York. He resigned from this position after one year and worked as legal counsel to the New York City Housing and Redevelopment Board, as legal assistant to Judge James L. Watson, an associate counsel to the speaker of the New York State Assembly, and as general counsel to the National Advisory Commission on Selective Service. In the winter of 1963–1964 Rangel and his friend Percy SUTTON founded the John F. Kennedy Democratic Club in Harlem, later renamed the Rev. Martin Luther King, Jr., Democratic Club.

Rangel began his career in politics in 1966, when he was elected to represent central HARLEM in the New York state assembly. He served two two-year terms as a leading liberal in the legislature, supporting the legalization of abortion, opposing stiffer penalties on prostitution, and endorsing antiwar protests.

Rangel moved into national politics in 1970, when he narrowly defeated the longtime incumbent congressman Adam Clayton POWELL, Jr., who had represented Harlem since 1945. Once in office, Rangel immediately established as his top priority the elimination of the drug trade. He called for the elimination of foreign aid to Turkey for its cultivation of opium poppies and opposed New York City Mayor John V. Lindsay's plan to issue maintenance doses of heroin to addicts.

In the 1970s Rangel took a leading position as a Congressional dove. He consistently voted to reduce the military budget, opposed the development of the B-1 bomber and nuclear aircraft carriers, and vigorously criticized the war in Southeast Asia. Rangel's liberalism extended to domestic issues as well. He voted for busing to desegregate schools, federal assistance for abortions, the creation of a consumer protection agency, and the implementation of automobile pollution controls.

Rangel gained national exposure in 1974 as a member of the House Judiciary Committee during the impeachment hearings for President Nixon. That year he was also elected chairman of the CONGRES-SIONAL BLACK CAUCUS, a position he held through 1975. In 1975 Rangel became the first African American appointed to the House Ways and Means Committee. Rangel obtained the chairmanship of the influential health subcommittee of the Ways and Means Committee in 1979. In 1980 Rangel became a member of the Democratic Steering and Policy Committee, and in 1983 was made a deputy whip by Speaker of the House Tip O'Neill and appointed chairman of the Select Committee on Narcotics.

Through the 1980s Rangel served as the chief congressional gadfly on drug issues and repeatedly chastised the Reagan and Bush administrations for their "turtlelike speed" in addressing the narcotics crisis. In 1989, as chairman of the House Narcotics Task Force, Rangel led a Congressional delegation to the Caribbean and Mexico to help coordinate the international crackdown on drugs. In recent years Rangel has served as a leading voice against the movement to legalize narcotics.

REFERENCES

CLAY, WILLIAM L. *Just Permanent Interests: Black Americans in Congress, 1870–1991*. New York, 1992.

RAGSDALE, BRUCE, and JOEL D. TREESE. *Black Americans in Congress, 1870–1989*. Washington, D.C., 1990.

THADDEUS RUSSELL

Ransier, Alonzo Jacob (January 3, 1834–August 17, 1882), congressman. Born free in Charleston, S.C., Alonzo Ransier had a very limited education. While he reportedly became a shipping clerk for a merchant in 1850, his whereabouts are uncertain until the end of the CIVIL WAR. In 1865 he was a member of a convention of the Friends of Equal Rights, which drafted and presented a petition to Congress. Ransier quickly became an important figure in South Carolina politics, attending the state constitutional conventions and being nominated for lieutenant governor on the Republican ticket in 1870.

When the Republican slate was elected overwhelmingly in 1870, Ransier became the first African American to hold a high executive post in South Carolina. Further, despite being associated with an administration riddled with corruption and graft, Ransier emerged unscathed. Ransier would remain a Republican loyalist throughout his political career. When Horace Greeley and Charles Sumner attempted to lure African-American support away from President Grant, Ransier staunchly defended Grant and vowed to stay with the mainstream of the party. In 1872 he became the Republican nominee to succeed

Alonzo J. Ransier. (Moorland-Spingarn Research Center, Howard University)

Robert C. DeLarge as one of South Carolina's congressmen. Elected by a comfortable margin, he became a member of the Forty-third Congress in March 1873.

Ransier's tenure in the House was marked by his fervent advocacy of civil rights legislation. Speaking at length in the House, Ransier sharply answered southern white critics of the legislation who claimed that African Americans were against it. Reading from various petitions of conventions and African-American organizations, Ransier sharply criticized his colleagues' attempts to derail the legislation. As the 1875 Civil Rights Bill was increasingly weakened, Ransier and other African-American legislators watched with growing dismay. When the final vote was called in February 1875, Ransier abstained from voting, since the equal education clause that he considered to be vital to the effectiveness of the bill had been removed.

In 1874 Ransier, who had been an outspoken critic of corruption in the South Carolina Republican party, failed to win the Republican nomination. Instead, Charles Buttz, a white man, became the official party nominee. After leaving Washington in 1875, Ransier became the Collector of Internal Revenue for the Second District of South Carolina, a position he held for a year. Afterward, he seems to have had difficulty finding a job, and reportedly worked as a day laborer in Charleston until his death in 1882.

REFERENCES

CHRISTOPHER, MAURINE. *Black Americans in Congress.* New York, 1976.

FONER, ERIC. *Freedom's Lawmakers: A Directory of Black Officeholders During Reconstruction.* New York, 1993.

McFARLIN, ANNJENNETTE SOPHIE. *Black Congressional Reconstruction Orators and Their Orations, 1869–1879.* Metuchen, N.J., 1976.

JOHN C. STONER

Ransom, Reverdy Cassius (1861–1959), bishop. Born in Flushing, Ohio, in 1861, Reverdy C. Ransom was reared by his mother, Harriet Ransom, a domestic and washerwoman. Ransom never knew his father but was given the surname of his stepfather, George Ransom. Harriet Ransom, the major inspiration of Ransom's life, encouraged him to enroll in the AFRICAN METHODIST EPISCOPAL (AME) Church's Wilberforce University in 1881, and he graduated from its Theological Department in 1886. Ransom spent from 1886 to 1912 pastoring AME congregations in cities experiencing the first wave of black migrations north. His efforts to fashion a church program to meet the unique needs of those migrants culminated in the establishment of the Institutional Church and Social Settlement in Chicago, Ill., in 1900–1904.

In the Booker T. Washington–W. E. B. Du Bois struggle for leadership in the African-American community in the early twentieth century, Ransom allied himself with Du Bois and delivered an oration on John Brown (*see* JOHN BROWN'S RAID) at the Second Annual Meeting of the Niagara Movement in 1906. He also was an early supporter of the National Association for the Advancement of Colored People (NAACP), founded in 1909. From 1912 to 1924, Ransom was editor of *A.M.E. Review.* He published numerous articles and authored six books including his autobiography, *The Pilgrimage of Harriet Ransom's Son.* Ecumenical, Ransom attended various World Methodist Conferences, was a member of the Federal Council of Churches, and a founding member of the Fraternal Council of Negro Churches in 1934.

Elevated to the AME episcopacy in 1924, Ransom remained an active bishop until 1952. From 1932 to 1952, he presided over the Third Episcopal District (Ohio, Western Pennsylvania and West Virginia) and was Chairman of the Board of Trustees of his alma mater, Wilberforce University.

REFERENCE

MORRIS, CALVIN S. *Reverdy C. Ransom: Black Advocate of the Social Gospel.* Lanham, Md., 1990.

CALVIN S. MORRIS

Rap. Rap is an African-American term that describes a stylized way of speaking. Salient features of a rap include metaphor, braggadocio, repetition, formulaic expressions, double entendre, mimicry, rhyme, and "signifyin' " (i.e., indirect references and allusions). Folklorists have credited the term to the 1960s black nationalist "H. Rap" Brown, whose praise name "rap" depicted his mastery of a "hip" way of speaking, aptly called rappin'. Although Brown is lauded for the name of this genre, the roots of rap can be traced from southern oral secular traditions such as toasts, folktales, blues, game songs (e.g., "hambone") to northern urban street jive—all of which make use of many of the same features.

While rap's southern antecedents (such as the blues) developed during the antebellum period and the turn of the century, jive emerged in inner city communities as the prototype of rap. Dan Burley, a scholar of jive, discovered that jive initially emerged among black Chicagoans around 1921. The primary context of its development was in secular environs remote from the home and religious centers, such as street corners, taverns, and parks, known among urban habitats as "the streets." Jive can be defined as a metaphorical style of communicating, using words and phrases from American mainstream English but reinterpreted from an African-American perspective. For example, in rap lingo, man becomes "cat," woman becomes "chick," and house becomes "crib." The art of jive resided in its ability to remain witty and original, hence its constant fluctuation in vocabulary over the years (*see* BLACK ENGLISH VERNACULAR).

Between the 1920s and 1950s, jive proliferated on all levels in the urban milieu—from the church to the street corner; but it also was incorporated in the literary works of noted black writers of the time, like Langston Hughes. Alongside its use by writers, jive became the parlance of jazz musicians. "Jam" (having a good time), "bad" (good), and "axe" (instrument) are some jive words commonplace in the jazz vernacular. By the late 1940s and 1950s, this urban style of speaking was introduced over radio airwaves by two Chicago disc jockeys, Holmes "Daddy-O" Daylie and Al Benson, who utilized jive in rhyme over music. Even the boastful poetry of former heavyweight champion boxer Muhammad ALI as well as comedian Rudy Ray Moore, known for popularizing audio recordings of toasts like "Dolemite" and "The Signifying Monkey," moved jive further into the American mainstream.

By the 1960s, jive was redefined and given a newer meaning by black nationalist "H. Rap" Brown, who laced his political speeches with signifyin', rhyme, and metaphor. Although his way of speaking inaugurated the shift from jive to rap, Brown's stylized speech soon gained popular acceptance among young urban admirers as rappin'. It was not, however, until the late 1960s that Brown's speaking style was set to a musical accompaniment by such political poets as the Watts Prophets of Los Angeles, the LAST POETS of Harlem, and singer-pianist poet Gil SCOTT-HERON, who recited rhyming couplets over an African percussion accompaniment.

In the late 1960s and the 1970s, rappin' to music emerged as two distinct song styles: the soul rap and the funk-style rap. The soul rap, a rappin' monologue celebrating the feats and woes of love, was popularized by Isaac Hayes and further developed by Barry White and Millie Jackson. The funk-style rap, introduced by George Clinton and his group Parliament, consisted of rappin' monologues on topics about partying. Unlike the music of the political poets, the love and funk-style raps were not in rhyme but rather loosely chanted over a repetitive instrumental accompaniment. These artists nonetheless laid the foundation for a type of musical poetry begun primarily by African-American youth of the Bronx called rap music: a quasi-song with rhyme and rhythmic speech that draws on black street language and is recited over an instrumental soundtrack.

There are basically two factors that gave rise to rap music. With the overcommercialization of popular dance forms of the 1970s, particularly disco, and the ongoing club gang violence, African-American youth, particularly in New York City, left the indoor scene and returned to neighborhood city parks, where they created outdoor discotheques, featuring a disc jockey and an emcee. These circumstances were an impetus for the development of rap music, which is marked by four distinct phases: the mobile deejay (c. 1972–1978); the rappin' emcee and the emergence of the rap music genre (1976–1978); the early commercial years of rap music (1979–1985); and the explosive sound of rap in the musical mainstream (1986–1990s).

During the first phase, music performed in neighborhood city parks was provided by an itinerant disc jockey, the mobile deejay. Mobile jockeys were evaluated by the type of music they played as well as by the size of their sound systems. Similar to radio jockeys, mobile deejays occasionally spoke to their audiences in raps while simultaneously dovetailing one record after the other, a feat facilitated by two turn-

Jam in the playground at East 102nd Street and FDR Drive, Harlem, New York City. (Henry Chalfant/City Lore)

tables. They were well known in their own boroughs and were supported by local followers. Popular jockeys included Pete "DJ" Jones of the Bronx and Grandmaster Flowers and Maboya of Brooklyn. The most innovative of mobile deejays, whose mixing technique immensely influenced the future sound direction and production of rap music, was Jamaican-born Clive Campbell, known as DJ Kool Herc. He tailored his disc jockeying style after the dub music jockeys of Jamaica, like Duke Reid and U Roy, by mixing collages of musical fragments, referred to as "break beats," from various recordings in order to create an entire new sound track.

Contemporaries of Kool Herc included Grandmaster Flash, Grand Wizard Theodore, and Afrika Bambaataa. Flash extended the Jamaican deejaying style with a mixing technique called backspinning (rotating one record counterclockwise to the desired beat then rotating the second record counterclockwise to the same location, thus creating an echo effect) and "phasing" (repeating a word or phrase in a rhythmic fashion on one turntable during or in between another recording). Grand Wizard Theodore popularized another mixing technique called "scratching" (the rhythmic movement of the tone arm needle of a turntable back and forth on a record). Bambaataa, on the other hand, perfected Herc's style of mixing by extending his break beats to include a variety of musical styles ranging from soul, funk, and disco to commercial jingle and television themes. But, more important, he is credited with starting a nonviolent organization called the Zulu Nation—a youth organization composed of local inner-city breakdancers,

graffiti artists, and rappers—which laid the foundation for a youth mass art movement that came to be known as hip-hop.

Hip-hop not only encompassed street art forms, it also denoted an attitude rendered in the form of dress, gestures, and language associated with street culture.

The second phase of rap music began around the mid-1970s. Since mixing records had become an art in itself, some deejays felt the need for an emcee. For example, with the hiring of Clark Kent and Jay Cee, DJ Kool Herc became the Herculords, a three-man team. At many of his performances, Bambaataa was also accompanied by three emcees, Cowboy (not to be mistaken with Cowboy of the Furious Five), Mr. Biggs, and Queen Kenya. Other noted emcees during this phase were DJ Hollywood, Sweet G, Busy Bee, Kurtis Blow, Grandmaster Caz, and Lovebug Starski (the latter credited with the term "hip-hop"). Emcees talked intermittently, using phrases like "Get up," and "Jam to the beat," and recited rhyming couplets to motivate the audience to dance while the deejay mixed records. However, it was Grandmaster Flash's emcees, the Furious Five (Melle Mel, Cowboy, Raheim, Kid Creole, Mr. Ness), who set the precedent for rappin' in rhythm to music through a concept called "trading phrases"—the exchange of rhyming couplets or phrases between emcees in a percussive, witty fashion, and in synchrony with the deejay's music—as best illustrated by their hit "Freedom" (1980).

During rap's third phase, the early commercial years from 1979 to 1985, rap music was initially recorded by independent record companies like Win-

Sister Souljah addresses drug abuse, black-on-black crime, male rappers, and U.S. politicians through her lyrics and music. (Allford/Trotman Associates)

ley, Enjoy, and Sugar Hill Records. Of the three, Sugar Hill Records, cofounded by Sylvia and Joe Robinson, succeeded in becoming the first international rap record company, producing such artists and groups as Sequence, Spoonie G., Lady B., Grandmaster Flash and the Furious Five, and Sugarhill Gang (best known for recording the first commercial rap song "Rapper's Delight"). Other modes of commercialization included Bambaataa's introduction of "techno-pop"—music created on synthesizers and drum machines—in rap music with "Planet Rock" (1982), recorded by his group, Soul Sonic Force. By the mid-1980s, techno-pop or the electronic influence in rap gave rise to sampling, the digital reproduction of prerecorded sounds—musical or vocal—in whole or fragmentary units anywhere throughout an entire sound track. Among the most popular styles of music sampled by rap deejays is funk, primarily the music of James BROWN.

Bambaataa's musical innovation also provided the transition from the early commercial sound of rap, known as the "old school," to the "new school" rap. The former refers to earlier innovators and performers of rap music—for example, Kool Moe Dee, Melle Mel, Fat Boys, and Whodini, some of whom have continued to perform well into the 1990s. The "new school" performers are basically protégés of the pioneers; they comprise performers in the fourth phase.

In the fourth phase (1986–1990s), rap music gradually moved from the inner city into mainstream popular culture. Although independent record companies continued to dominate (e.g., Tommy Boy, Priority, Def Jam, Next Plateau), major record companies including MCA, Columbia, and Atlantic began recording rap and in some instances distributed for the independent labels. In addition, rap artists from areas outside of New York, Philadelphia, Los Angeles, Oakland, Miami, Atlanta, Houston, and Seattle, emerged as vital forces in the musical mainstream. Another factor that contributed to its growth was the fusion of rap music with hard rock, popularized by the group Run-DMC with their recording of "Rock Box" (1984) and their rendition of Aerosmith's "Walk This Way" (1986). The rap-rock fusion further evolved the new school techno-pop style through its extensive use of electronic instruments such as drum machines and samplers. However, it was the music of Public Enemy, masterminded by producer Hank Shocklee, that became the quintessence of sampling sounds, from James Brown's music and vocal stylings to black nationalists' speech excerpts. Furthermore, the use of sampling, funk-style drum rhythms with heavy bass drum, boisterous-aggressive vocal style of delivery, and/or moderate to excessive application of expletives in the text contributed to what rap artists refer to as a "hardcore" or street-style aesthetic.

Other factors that broadened the appeal of rap in popular culture were the rise of female rap artists (e.g., Roxanne Shante, the Real Roxanne, Salt-N-Pepa, MC Lyte, Queen Latifah, Yo-Yo); and the diversified sound of rap: party rap (e.g., Digital Underground, Kid 'N' Play, Hammer, De La Soul, Biz Markie, Tone Loc, and Young MC); political rap (e.g., KRS-One/BDP, Public Enemy, Sister Souljah, Arrested Development, X-Clan); "gangsta" rap (e.g., Ice-T, Ice Cube, Geto Boys, Schoolly-D, Too Short); and eclectic rap, a cross between party and hardcore (e.g., LL Cool J, Eric B & Rakim, Naughty by Nature, EPMD, Heavy D, Kriss Kross, Das Efx); and rap/jazz fusion (e.g., Digable Planets, Vs3, and Guru).

By the late 1980s, rap music had not only become musically diverse but culturally diverse as well. While a few white rap artists existed in the shadows of their African-American counterparts (e.g., Vanilla Ice), others, like the Beastie Boys, Third Bass, and House of Pain, crossed over into wider acceptance in the 1990s. Also by the late 1980s, the rap scene expanded to include Spanish-speaking performers (whose raps are aptly called Spanglish): Mellow Man Ace, Kid Frost, and Gerardo. Rap music also gained international prominence in places like England, France, Denmark, Germany, and Canada. Much of rap's popularity in these countries was due to the estab-

Ice Cube (foreground) with a member of the group Naughty by Nature. (Allford/Trotman Associates)

lishment of Zulu Nation chapters abroad and the multimedia exposure of rap artists, from recordings to the silver screen.

By the beginning of the 1990s, rap had achieved unprecedented success in the American mainstream as evidenced by its use in advertising, fashion, and other musical genres. But despite its popularity, rap had created much controversy among critics who considered its lyrics to be too hardcore and sexually explicit. Among rap's most controversial artists have been 2 Live Crew and gangsta rappers. Although much of rap's controversy remains unresolved, it continues to appeal to listeners because of its artful use of street jive and funky beats.

REFERENCES

EURE, JOSEPH D., and JAMES G. SPADY, eds. *Nation Conscious Rap*. New York, 1991.

HAGER, STEVEN. *Hip-Hop: The Illustrated History of Breakdancing, Rap Music, and Graffiti*. New York, 1984.

KEYES, CHERYL L. *Rappin to the Beat: Rap Music as Street Culture Among African Americans*. Ann Arbor, Mich., 1992.

NELSON, HAVELOCK, and MICHAEL A. GONZALES. *Bring the Noise: A Guide to Rap Music and Hip-Hop Culture*. New York, 1991.

ROSE, TRICIA. "Orality and Technology: Rap Music and Afro-American Cultural Resistance." *Popular Music and Society*. 13, no. 4 (Winter 1989): 35–44.

TOOP, DAVID. *Rap Attack 2: African Rap to Global Hip-Hop*. Rev. ed. New York, 1991.

CHERYL L. KEYES

Rapier, James Thomas (November 13, 1837–May 31, 1883), congressman, farmer, and teacher. Born the son of a prosperous free barber in Florence, Ala., James Rapier received much of his early formal education in Nashville, Tenn., where his grandmother lived. Deciding that he needed further education, in 1856 Rapier traveled to Buxton, Canada West (now Ontario), a utopian community of African Americans where his father owned property, and began studying again. His proficiency made his tutors encourage him to go on for further study at a teacher's training school in Toronto. He stayed in the city for three years.

As the Civil War raged in the United States, Rapier felt a desire to return and aid in the reconstruction process. After returning to Tennessee in 1863 and participating in several black conventions in Nashville, he became disillusioned when the 1865–1866 Tennessee constitution denied suffrage to African Americans. Borrowing money to purchase some cotton land, he moved to Seven Mile Island in the Tennessee River in Alabama.

Rapier quickly rose in local and state estimation as an intelligent, educated, and reasonable African-American Republican. Despite heated debate about the role of African Americans in the Alabama Republican party, he participated in party conventions and was one of the ninety-six delegates to draft the Alabama constitution. While part of a moderate group that favored less strict disfranchisement provisions and more strict equality statutes, the gains of Rapier and other black delegates were few. They defeated proposals to legalize segregation, but they were also unable to explicitly make discrimination illegal.

As a result of his visible campaigning, Rapier became a target of racist hate across the state. After Rapier and several associates were accused of burning a girl's school, they were hunted by a lynch mob. Rapier escaped, leaving behind his plantation and his belongings; three other men were hanged without legal proceedings. Shortly thereafter, he was completely exonerated by a local magistrate.

Despite the amount of hostile opposition to blacks participating in the electoral process, Rapier, an eloquent orator, won a seat in Congress in 1872 by a plurality of almost 3,200 votes, including significant support from whites. He made several speeches during his first term on the need for RECONSTRUCTION to go further in guaranteeing civil rights, a federally controlled universal education system, and land redistribution to freedmen.

While the 1874 election initially ended with a Democratic victor, Rapier successfully challenged the result and was seated for his second consecutive term. Again, he spoke militantly about civil rights and segregation. In 1876, after gerrymandering by the Alabama legislature, only one predominantly black district remained in Alabama. Both Rapier and congressman Jeremiah HARALSON decided to run for the seat. When Haralson failed to secure the Republican nomination in 1875, he pledged to run as an independent candidate. The two black candidates split the vote and a white Democrat was elected.

Retiring from politics, Rapier settled down to run his farm. Appointed by the lucrative patronage post of Collector of Internal Revenue for the Second Alabama District (1877–1883), Rapier continued to have influence in Republican circles although he was never again a candidate for office. As a result of his lack of faith in Alabama's government, he became an ardent emigrationist, urging African Americans to move to Kansas or to the West to escape racism and discrimination. His health began to decline, and he died of tuberculosis in Alabama in 1883.

REFERENCES

CHRISTOPHER, MAURINE. *Black Americans in Congress.* New York, 1976.

FONER, ERIC. *Freedom's Lawmakers: A Directory of Black Officeholders during Reconstruction.* New York, 1993.

McFARLIN, ANNJENNETTE SOPHIE. *Black Congressional Reconstruction Orators and their Orations, 1869–1879.* Metuchen, N.J., 1976, pp. 257–279.

SCHWENINGER, LOREN. *James T. Rapier and Reconstruction.* Chicago, 1978.

ALANA J. ERICKSON

Rastafarians. The Rastafarian movement originated in the early twentieth century in Jamaica as a black nationalist religious phenomenon. However, its influence in the United States has been less religious and more as a cultural vehicle for a more general Afrocentrism, a political critique of colonialism, and a staple of popular music.

The first Rastafarians came together around Christian preachers in Kingston, Jamaica, who were heavily influenced by the teachings of Marcus Mosiah GARVEY. Garvey was a Jamaican labor organizer, black nationalist, and founder of the UNIVERSAL NEGRO IMPROVEMENT ASSOCIATION who came to the United States in 1916 to develop a repatriation plan for Africans in the DIASPORA. That same year, Garvey predicted the rise of a powerful black king in Africa, citing from the Biblical passage that predicts that "Ethiopia shall soon stretch out her hands unto God" (Psalms 68: 31). When Prince Ras Tafari was

crowned king of Ethiopia on November 2, 1930, these Garveyite Christians welcomed his coronation as a fulfillment of Garvey's prophesy. The movement became popular in some of Kingston's poorest neighborhoods among people who welcomed a promised alternative to Jamaican society.

The new king's family name, Ras Tafari (literally "Lion's Head" in the Ethiopian language of Amharic), and his royal title, Haile Selassie ("Might of the Trinity"), became significant religious symbols for these Jamaicans, who began calling themselves Rastafarians. Selassie, employing the traditional symbols and ideological supports for Ethiopian kingship, referred to himself as "the King of Kings, Lord of Lords, Conquering Lion of the Tribe of Judah"—a reference to the coming of the Messiah in the Book of Revelation—and he claimed to be a direct descendant of King Solomon and the Queen of Sheba. To the Rastafarians, this was proof of the divinity of the man they began referring to as Jah Rastari. Haile Selassie's popularity was furthered by his defiant stance in opposing the invasion of his country by Italy during the Italo-Ethiopian War of 1935–1941.

Central to Rastafarian belief are the notions that the legacy of African slavery is a reincarnation of the Biblical narrative of Exodus and that the political, social, and economic structures of Western society constitute "Babylon," the Biblical society of sin and evil that is to burn in a coming Apocalypse. Freedom and redemption for people of African descent, according to them, can only be achieved through repatriation to Africa, or more specifically Ethiopia or "Zion." For some Rastafarians, this means physical repatriation, while others interpret it as a spiritual destination. The influence of Rastafarianism was enhanced by the state visit of Haile Selassie to Jamaica in April 1966.

Rastafarians generally let their hair grow into "dreadlocks"—long, matted tresses worn both in deference to the Nazarite code in the Book of Numbers forbidding the cutting of hair and in partial imitation of the braids worn by some Ethiopian tribal warriors and priests. They openly endorse the smoking of cannabis (marijuana) as a sacrament, believing that the trancelike state induced by its ritual use creates a communion with God. The colors of the Ethiopian flag—red, gold, and green—are significant to Rastafarians, who don the color in knitted caps or "tams," belts, and badges. Rastafarians are also vegetarian and shun food that is processed or cooked with salt, a process known as "I-tal," and stress the eating of fruits and drinking of homemade juices.

In the late 1960s and early 1970s, Rastafarian culture began gaining popularity among "rude boys," rebellious youth in Kingston's ghettos. However, this was often adopted more as a style by these youths, who grew dreadlocks and danced to the increasingly Rasta-influenced Jamaican popular music, REGGAE. Referred to as "dreads," some of these young Jamaicans came to the United States in the 1970s to take part in gang warfare over the drug trade and over their allegiances to one of the two major political parties in Jamaica, the People's National Party and the Jamaican Labor Party. Throughout the decade there were a number of shootouts, murders, and bank robberies in the United States, especially in Brooklyn and the Bronx, by Jamaican dreads, giving Rastafarians a reputation among the police for extreme violence.

The Rastafarian movement began gaining adherents among African Americans and others in the United States beginning in the 1970s due to the growing popularity of reggae. Jamaican singer Desmond Dekker had a minor hit in the United States in 1972 with the American release of the 1968 song "Israelites," and the next year the film *The Harder They Come* was released, which depicted the ghettos of Kingston, Jamaica, and urban Rastafarian culture there. Reggae musicians such as Bob Marley and the Wailers and Peter Tosh toured the United States repeatedly during that decade, breathing new cultural life into black nationalism while turning dreadlocks into both a political and cultural statement.

In 1990 Rastafarians in the United States received exposure when the U.S. Supreme Court upheld the right of religious expression for Rastafarians, ruling that Rastafarians could not be required to cut their hair in prison. In 1994, Miami, Fla., was host to the International Nyahbinghi Gathering (*nyahbinghi* is Swahili for "Death to white oppressors and their black allies"), a Rastafarian meeting that brought more than 200 delegates from several countries.

Although Rastafarians can be found in almost every African-American community in the United States, actual numbers are difficult to obtain. The reason for this is that, other than a few specific sects such as the Twelve Tribes of Israel, Rastafarians have no church, no organizational structure, and no religious hierarchies. In fact, open discussion and debate about politics, African history, and biblical interpretation are much more highly valued among Rastafarians than strict dogma and structure; consequently, what it means to be a Rastafarian is continually being redefined.

REFERENCES

BARRET, LEONARD E., SR. *The Rastafarians: Sounds of Cultural Dissonance*. Boston, 1988.

MULVANEY, REBEKAH MICHELE. *Rastafari and Reggae: A Dictionary and Sourcebook*. New York, 1990.

OWENS, JOSEPH. *Dread: The Rastafarians of Jamaica*. London, 1982.

WINSTON THOMPSON

Rawls, Louis Allen "Lou" (December 1, 1936–), singer. Born in Chicago and raised on its South Side by his grandmother, Lou Rawls became a member of the Baptist church choir at seven years old. While still in high school, Rawls was performing in a local gospel group, the Teenage Kings of Harmony, with his friend Sam COOKE.

In the early 1950s Rawls moved to Los Angeles where he was recruited by the Chosen Gospel Singers, with whom he made his first recording. In 1955 he joined the Pilgrim Travelers, with Sam Cooke, before entering the army. Three years later he left the service and rejoined the Travelers.

After the Travelers broke up in 1959, Rawls found work as a blues singer in various clubs in Los Angeles. He was performing at the Pandora's Box Coffee Shop for $10 a night when a producer at Capitol Records invited him to make an audition tape, which led to a record contract. In 1962, his debut album, *Stormy Monday (I'd Rather Drink Muddy Water)*, with pianist Les McCann, was released. Rawls followed the album with jazz-and-blues influenced pop songs such as "Tobacco Road" (1964), "Soulin" (1966), and "Love is a Hurting Thing" (1966), which reached number one on the R&B chart and earned him Grammy Award nominations for Best R&B Recording and Best R&B Solo Vocal Performance.

Also in 1966 Rawls released the album, *Lou Rawls Live,* which included his colorful rhyming monologues that were staples of his nightclub act. Rawls continued his success with the song "Dead End Street" (1967), for which he won a Grammy Award for Best Male Rhythm and Blues Vocal Performance. He also began to make occasional television appearances.

In 1975 Rawls began a collaboration with Philadelphia International Records, combining his vocal style with a disco beat and producing such successful works as, "You'll Never Find (Another Love Like Mine)" (1976), "Lady Love" (1978), the LPs *All Things in Time* (1976), and the 1977 Grammy winner *Unmistakably Lou*. In 1993, Rawls released *Portrait of the Blues* on which he sang in a jazz-influenced pop idiom.

Since 1981 Rawls has sponsored the UNITED NEGRO COLLEGE FUND telethon, raising over a $100 million through the early 1990s for the organization.

REFERENCE

"Lou Rawls at Home." *Ebony* (September 1985): 100–102.

BUD KLIMENT

Ray, Charles Bennett (December 25, 1807–August 15, 1886) minister and journalist. Ray was born in Falmouth, Mass., to Joseph Aspinwall and Annie (Harrington) Ray. He studied theology at Wesleyan Seminary in Massachusetts in the 1830s and continued his studies at Wesleyan University in Middletown, Conn. He was ordained a Methodist minister in 1837, and later joined the Crosby Congregational Church. From 1845 until the 1860s, Ray served as pastor of Bethesda Congregation Church.

Ray was an active abolitionist—a member of the AMERICAN ANTI-SLAVERY SOCIETY since 1833—who worked as a "conductor" on the UNDERGROUND RAILROAD. From 1843 until 1858, Ray was a member and then secretary of the New York Vigilance Committee, which aimed at helping runaway slaves. He also served as a member of the American Missionary Association of New York and the Society for the Promotion of Education Among Colored Children. In addition, he was active in the African Society for Mutual Relief, the Congregational Clerical Union, and the Manhattan Congregational Association.

Beginning in 1846, Ray worked as a missionary in New York. In 1837, he was appointed general agent of *The Colored American,* an early African-American weekly, of which he became co-owner in 1839 and editor until its closing in 1842. *The Colored American* supported the Liberty Party in 1839, and Ray served as a secretary at the Liberty Party's Buffalo convention in 1843. He died in New York City in 1886.

REFERENCE

LOGAN, RAYFORD, W., and MICHAEL R. WINSTON, eds. *Dictionary of American Negro Biography.* New York, 1982.

SABRINA FUCHS

Ray, Charlotte E. (January 13, 1850–January 11, 1911), lawyer. Born in New York City, Charlotte Ray was one of seven children of the Rev. Charles Bennett RAY and his second wife, Charlotte Augusta Burroughs. Her father was pastor of the Bethesda Congregational Church and publisher and editor of *Colored American,* an early African-American newspaper. Little is known about Ray's early life, but by 1869 she had secured a position teaching in the Normal and Preparatory Department at Howard University.

In February 1872, Ray graduated from Howard University's Law School, becoming the first African-American woman to receive a law degree from any law school in the nation. On March 2, 1872, she was admitted to the bar of the District of Columbia—just three years after the admission of George Boyer Vashon, the District of Colombia's first African-American lawyer. On April 23, she gained admittance to practice before the Supreme Court of the District of Columbia as well. She was the fifth woman in the United States admitted to the bar of any state.

Ray began a private practice in Washington, D.C., specializing in corporate and real estate law. Despite her abilities, the practice failed to attract sufficient clients. Details of her life after this point are vague. By 1879, she apparently had returned to the New York City area to live and had started teaching in a Brooklyn public school. Sometime before the mid-1880s, she was married to a man with the surname Fraim. By 1897, Ray was living in Woodside, N.Y., where she died at the age of sixty.

REFERENCE

SMITH, J. CLAY, JR. *Emancipation; The Making of the Black Lawyer, 1844–1944.* Philadelphia, 1993.

JO H. KIM

Ray, Henrietta Cordelia (c. 1849–January 15, 1916), poet and teacher. H. Cordelia Ray was born in New York City to Charlotte Augusta (Burrough) and Charles Bennett RAY. She earned a master of pedagogy degree from the University of the City of New York (1891) and taught in the New York City public school system for some thirty years. After her retirement, she tutored pupils in music, mathematics, and languages and taught English literature to classes of teachers. She lived on Long Island with her elder sister Florence; neither of them married, and together they wrote a biography (published in 1887) of their eminent father.

Ray was a prolific and prominent poet. Her ode "Lincoln" was read at the unveiling of the Freedmen's Monument in Washington, D.C. (1876); she published many poems in periodicals, and 146 poems in two collections: *Sonnets* (1893) and *Poems* (1910). Her favorite subjects are a benignly beautiful earth and heaven, Christian idealism and morality, love, literature, and race heroes. Ray's technical skills are unusually rich, including varied stanzaic forms and diverse rhythms and rhyme schemes; however, her language, thought and sentiments often seem stilted and generic. She is fond of archaic diction and syntax, personifications, mythological allusions, and copious adjectives. Her artificial landscapes, abstract musings, and cultured tributes, bereft of the vitalizing heat of personal emotions and concrete realities, remain superior examples of the picturesque, idealistic, and classically sedate verse beloved by readers of her time.

REFERENCE

SHERMAN, JOAN R. *Invisible Poets: Afro-Americans of the Nineteenth Century*, 2nd ed. Urbana, Ill., 1989.

JOAN R. SHERMAN

Rayner, John B. (November 13, 1850–July 14, 1918), Populist leader and educator. John Rayner was born near Raleigh, N.C., to Kenneth Rayner, a prominent politician and planter, and a young slave woman. Though the formally educated Rayner held elective office in Tarboro, N.C., in the waning days of RECONSTRUCTION, his considerable oratorical and organizational abilities would be exercised chiefly in Texas, where he had moved by 1880. First coming to public attention during an 1887 prohibition referendum, Rayner by 1892 was attracted to the People's Party, which promised government intervention to ease farm credit, fair elections, and expanded educational opportunities. By 1894, Rayner was leading the party's efforts to win over predominantly Republican African-American voters, his being among the most notable of southern Populists' sometimes tentative, often clumsy attempts to build biracial coalitions. Named to the state executive committee twice, Rayner traveled the Texas countryside in 1894, 1895, and 1896, speaking, organizing black Populist locals, and converting thousands to the cause. He tried to ensure that county conventions included blacks and nominated congenial candidates, and arranged local alliances with Republicans. By 1896, however, the Populists had begun to succumb to Democratic fraud and intimidation as well as to the reluctance of many white Texans to slough off traditional Democratic allegiances, especially if it meant consorting with erstwhile black Republicans.

Rayner's aspirations dimmed with the collapse of Populism and the subsequent progress of disfranchisement. He accepted a poll tax limitation on suffrage, asking simply that it not spare poor whites. Continuing to campaign among the dwindling African-American electorate, Rayner, at the behest of brewing interests, opposed prohibition and supported an occasional Republican or even a Democrat.

But his hopes for black advancement now focused on vocational education. From 1904 to 1907, he served as financial agent and president of Conroe-Porter Industrial College, an instution initially patterned after Tuskegee. Later (1911–1914), he was associated with a school founded by the Farmers' Improvement Society, a black self-help organization. Preaching deference, he practiced it among the white donors he cultivated. Yet a certain bitterness in his private writings suggest that Rayner, if resigned to defeat, never became entirely reconciled to it.

REFERENCE

CANTRELL, DAVID GREGG. The Limits of Southern Dissent: The Lives of Kenneth and John B. Rayner. Ph.D. diss., Texas A & M University, 1988.

PATRICK G. WILLIAMS

Razaf, Andy (Razafkeriefo, Andreamentania Paul) (December 15, 1895–February 3, 1973), lyricist. The exact spelling of Andy Razaf's real name is often disputed, but the above is generally accepted. Razaf was descended from the royal family of Madagascar. His grandfather, John Louis Waller, a former slave, became consul to that country, where Razaf's mother, Jennie Maria Waller, married Henry Razafkeriefo, the nephew of Queen Ranavalona III, before moving to Washington, D.C., where Razaf was born. His father's political activities took the family to Baltimore, Kansas City, Cuba, and New York around the turn of the century.

Razaf quit school at sixteen to help support the family, working as an elevator operator, butler, and custodian before moving to Cleveland to become a pitcher for a semiprofessional Negro team there. He also wrote newspaper articles, political speeches, and poems, as well as ragtime songs; he wrote his first song at the age of thirteen, and in 1913 sold his song "Baltimo' " to be performed in *The Passing Show*. In 1921 he returned to New York to play briefly for the New York Black Sox, but was soon able to make a living as a songwriter. His first important success was with *Joe Hurtig's Social Maids* show, for which he wrote lyrics in 1922.

In the early 1920s Razaf was a fixture of Harlem's nightclub scene, where he met many of the musicians with whom he would collaborate, including Willie "The Lion" SMITH, Eubie BLAKE (with whom Razaf wrote "Memories of You" in 1930), and James P. JOHNSON. During this time Razaf also met Fats WALLER, who would become his best friend and co-author of some of the most beloved popular songs of the twentieth century (Waller was unrelated to

The lyricist of "Ain't Misbehavin'," "Memories of You," and "Black and Blue," Andy Razaf was a leading figure of the black musical theater of the 1920s. (Photographs and Prints Division, Schomburg Center for Research in Black Culture, The New York Public Library, Astor, Lenox and Tilden Foundations)

Razaf's grandfather). Among their compositions were "Honeysuckle Rose" (1928), "My Fate Is in Your Hands" (1928), "Ain't Misbehavin'" (1929), "Blue Turning Grey over You" (1929), "Keeping Out of Mischief Now" (1932), and "The Joint Is Jumpin'" (1938). One of the duo's most famous songs, "What Did I Do to Be So Black and Blue" (1929), displayed Razaf's longstanding concern with racial injustice. Although Louis ARMSTRONG's influential 1929 version interpreted the song in terms of white racism towards African Americans, Razaf's original lyrics were also directed at intraracial bias against darker-skinned blacks. Many of Razaf's songs first appeared in the Harlem shows that epitomized urban black popular culture in the 1920s. These shows included *Keep Shufflin'* (1928), *Hot Chocolates* (1929), *Blackbirds of 1930* (1930), *Hot Harlem* (1932), and *Rhythm for Sale* (1934).

The greatest vocalists and instrumentalists of jazz and popular music of the 1920s and '30s performed Razaf's music. Among his earliest champions were Louis Armstrong, Mildred BAILEY, and Ethel WA-

ters. Although Razaf was best known for his lyrics, he also made many recordings, including "Yes Sir! That's My Baby" (1925), "Back in Your Own Backyard" (1928), "Go Harlem" (1931) and "Lost Love" (1937).

In the mid-to-late 1930s, Razaf's estrangement from Waller and the diminished popularity of Harlem stage shows sent his career into decline. After *Tan Manhattan* (1940), which he wrote with Blake, Razaf moved to Englewood, N.J., where he failed in an attempt to enter local politics. In 1948 he moved to Los Angeles and lived the remainder of his life in illness and obscurity. Razaf, who married four times, died of kidney failure in North Hollywood at 77.

REFERENCE

SINGER, BARRY. *Black and Blue: The Life and Lyrics of Andy Razaf*. New York, 1992.

BUD KLIMENT

Rebellions.   *See* Urban Riots and Rebellions.

Reconstruction, period that began during the CIVIL WAR and ended in 1877. One of the most controversial and misunderstood eras in American history, it witnessed far-reaching changes in the country's political and social life. For the first time, the national government assumed the basic responsibility for defining and protecting Americans' civil rights. In the South, African-American men were for the first time given the right to vote and hold office, and a politically mobilized black community joined with white allies to bring the REPUBLICAN PARTY—temporarily, as it turned out—to power. Reconstruction was America's first experiment in interracial democracy.

For much of the twentieth century, both scholarly and popular writing presented Reconstruction as an era of unrelieved sordidness in political and social life. According to this view, Abraham Lincoln, before his death, had embarked on a course of sectional reconciliation that was continued by his successor, Andrew Johnson. Their magnanimous efforts were thwarted by vindictive Radical Republicans in Congress, who fastened black supremacy upon the defeated Confederacy. An orgy of corruption and misgovernment soon followed, presided over by unscrupulous CARPETBAGGERS (Northerners who ventured south to reap the spoils of office), SCALA-WAGS (southern whites who cooperated with the Republican party for personal gain), and ignorant and childlike freedpeople, who were incapable of responsibly exercising the political power that had been thrust upon them. After much needless suffering—so the interpretation goes—the South's white community banded together in patriotic organizations such as the KU KLUX KLAN to overthrow these "black" governments and restore "home rule" (their euphemism for white supremacy). Popularized through films such as THE BIRTH OF A NATION, this interpretation rested on the assumption that black suffrage was the gravest error of the Civil War period. It helped to justify the South's system of racial segregation and disfranchisement of black voters.

Although significant criticisms of the traditional interpretation were advanced earlier in the twentieth century, it was not until the 1960s that the older view was finally interred. The "second Reconstruction"—the CIVIL RIGHTS MOVEMENT—inspired a new conception of the first, and in rapid sequence virtually every assumption of the old viewpoint was swept away. In the new scholarship, Andrew Johnson, yesterday's high-minded defender of constitutional principles, was revealed as a racist politician too stubborn to compromise with his critics. Commitment to racial equality, not vindictiveness or mere partisanship, motivated his Radical Republican critics. The period of Radical Reconstruction in the South was shown to be a time of progress for African Americans and the region as a whole. The Ku Klux Klan, whose campaign of violence had been minimized by earlier historians, was revealed as a terrorist organization that beat and killed its opponents in order to deprive blacks of their newly won rights. Most strikingly, African Americans were now shown to be active agents in shaping the era's history, rather than passive recipients of the actions of others, or simply a "problem" confronting white society. Today, scholars differ among themselves on many issues, but all agree that the traditional view of the period is dead, and unlamented, and that blacks must be considered central actors in the drama of Reconstruction.

Reconstruction During the Civil War

Reconstruction began not with the Confederacy's surrender in 1865 but during the Civil War. Long before the conflict ended, Americans were debating the questions that came to form the essence of Reconstruction: On what terms should the southern states be reunited with the Union? Who should establish these terms, Congress or the president? What system of labor should replace plantation slavery? What should be the place of blacks in the political and social life of the South and the nation? One definitive conclusion emerged from the Civil War: The reconstructed South would be a society without SLAVERY.

The destruction of slavery, begun by blacks who fled the plantations in 1861 and 1862, and made into a national war aim by the Emancipation Proclamation of January 1, 1863, powerfully shaped the course of the war and the debate over Reconstruction. No longer could the Lincoln administration speak of allowing the South to return with its prewar institutions and leadership intact.

In December 1863, Lincoln announced a program for Reconstruction. He offered a pardon to all supporters of the Confederacy (except high-ranking officials) who took an oath of loyalty and pledged to accept the end of slavery. When 10 percent of a state's prewar voters took the oath, they could establish a state government and apply for readmission to the Union. New state constitutions would have to prohibit slavery, but otherwise Lincoln gave southern leaders a free hand in legislation. Voting and office-holding were limited to whites. The president, complained abolitionist Wendell Phillips, "frees the slave and ignores the Negro."

Lincoln attempted to implement his Reconstruction plan in Louisiana, portions of which had been occupied by Union troops in 1862. Two years later, elections were held for a constitutional convention, which abolished slavery and sought Louisiana's readmission to the Union. At the same time, the free African Americans of New Orleans—a self-conscious community that included many highly educated, economically successful individuals—pressed for the right to participate in Reconstruction. After meeting with two free black representatives, Lincoln in March 1864 private, and unsuccessfully, urged Louisiana's governor to allow at least some blacks to vote.

As Reconstruction proceeded in Louisiana, it became clear that many northern Republicans were unhappy with Lincoln's program. Foremost among them were the Radicals, a group that had led the opposition to slavery's expansion before the Civil War and had long favored granting equal civil and political rights to free blacks in the North. The most prominent were Rep. Thaddeus Stevens of Pennsylvania and Sen. Charles Sumner of Massachusetts, both longtime proponents of the rights of African Americans. The Radicals now insisted that the federal government had a responsibility to protect the basic rights of the former slaves. By 1864 some went further, announcing that Reconstruction could not be secure without black suffrage (see SUFFRAGE [NINETEENTH CENTURY]). Their stance combined principle and political advantage. The Radicals believed that without the right to vote, blacks would be vulnerable to domination by their former owners; they also understood that unless blacks voted, the Republican party would find it very difficult to win elections in the postwar South.

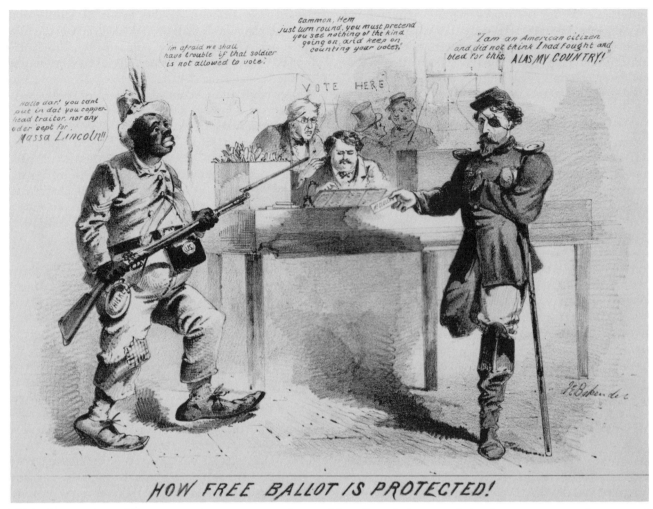

With the coming of Reconstruction, many southern whites feared that any federal attempts to enforce equal protection of the laws would be tantamount to their total disfranchisement, as this cartoon illustrates. (Prints and Photographs Division, Library of Congress)

During 1864, the Radicals became convinced that Lincoln's 10-percent plan was too lenient to "rebels" and did too little to protect African Americans' rights. Enough moderate Republicans agreed that Congress passed the Wade-Davis Bill, which proposed to delay the start of Reconstruction until a majority of a state's white males—not just 10 percent—had taken an oath of loyalty. The new state governments were required to guarantee the equality before the law of black Southerners. Black suffrage, which most Republicans did not at this point support, was not mentioned. Not wishing to abandon his own approach, Lincoln pocket vetoed the bill.

Lincoln and the Radicals differed over Reconstruction, but their breach was not irreparable. Early in 1865, they worked together to secure congressional approval of the THIRTEENTH AMENDMENT, which irrevocably abolished slavery throughout the nation. Shortly thereafter Congress passed, and Lincoln signed, a bill creating the Freedmen's Bureau, an agency empowered to protect the legal rights of the former slaves, provide education and medical care, oversee labor contracts between emancipated blacks and their employers, and lease land to black families.

As the act establishing the Freedmen's Bureau suggested, there was far more to Reconstruction than the problem of forming new state governments and determining who should vote. During the Civil War, the first steps were taken toward addressing the interrelated problems of access to land and control of labor. The most famous of these "rehearsals for Reconstruction" took place on the Sea Islands of South Carolina. When the Union navy occupied the area in 1861, virtually all the white inhabitants fled to the mainland, leaving behind some 10,000 slaves, who sacked the big houses, destroyed cotton gins, and commenced planting corn and potatoes for their own consumption.

Sea Island blacks, however, were not to chart their own course to "free labor." In the navy's wake came whites from the North—military officers, Treasury agents, northern investors eager to resume plantation agriculture, and a group of young teachers and missionaries known as Gideon's Band. Many of the reformers sympathized with African Americans' desire to acquire land. Most government officials and northern investors, however, believed the Sea Island experiment provided a golden opportunity to prove that blacks would work more efficiently and profitably as free laborers than as slaves. Rather than immediately acquiring land, they believed, the former slaves should work for wages and learn the discipline of the free market. The Sea Island experiment produced many improvements in the lives of the area's black population, including access to schools and a rise in their standard of living. However, it also brought disappointment, for when plantations abandoned by their owners were auctioned off by the federal government, only a small amount of land found its way into the hands of the former slaves.

The Sea Island experiment involved a far smaller area and far fewer persons than another rehearsal for Reconstruction, which took place in the Mississippi Valley. Here many slave owners remained on their plantations, declared their loyalty to the Union, and demanded that the army compel their black laborers to remain at work. Military officials, who established "contraband camps" for black refugees, had no desire to care permanently for large numbers of former slaves. They decreed that the former slaves sign labor contracts either with planters who took an oath of loyalty or with investors from the North. They would be paid wages and guaranteed access to schools, and corporal punishment would be prohibited, but they could not leave the plantations without permission of their employers.

Inaugurated in Louisiana, this system of "compulsory free labor" was extended to the entire Mississippi Valley, the home of over half a million slaves, after the Union capture of Vicksburg in 1863. A halfway house between slavery and freedom, the system satisfied no one. Planters disliked not being able to use the whip to enforce discipline, and complained that the former slaves were unruly and refused to obey orders. The freedpeople, for their part, resented being forced to work for white employers, often their former owners, rather than being allowed access to land.

In this optimistic 1868 engraving, a black soldier representing the Freedmen's Bureau restores racial peace in the South by keeping a ragtag mob of ex-Confederates at bay. (Prints and Photographs Division, Library of Congress)

Only occasionally did glimmerings of a different policy appear. In 1863, Gen. Ulysses S. Grant directed that Davis Bend, which contained the plantations of Confederate president Jefferson Davis, be set aside for the settlement of freedpeople. By 1865, Davis Bend had become a remarkable example of self-reliance, with successful cotton farming, a series of schools, and its own system of government.

Early in 1865, a new dimension to the questions of land and labor was added by Gen. William T. Sherman. After capturing Savannah at the conclusion of his famous march to the sea, Sherman met with a group of the city's black leaders. The best guarantee of freedom, they told him, was "to have land, and turn it and till it by our own labor." Four days later, Sherman issued Field Order No. 15, setting aside the Sea Islands and a portion of the South Carolina and Georgia coasts, extending thirty miles inland, for black settlement. Each family would receive forty acres of land, and Sherman later provided that the army could loan them mules. (Thus the phrase FORTY ACRES AND A MULE, which would echo throughout the South.) By June, some 40,000 freedpeople had been settled on 400,000 acres of "Sherman land."

In the spring of 1865, as the Civil War drew to a close, it was apparent that the federal government had not yet worked out its Reconstruction policy. In March, in his second inaugural address, Lincoln called on the nation to bind up its wounds "with malice toward none and charity toward all." But leniency to whites, for Lincoln, did not mean abandoning concern for the rights of blacks. In his last speech, just a few days before his assassination, the president endorsed the idea of limited black suffrage for the Reconstruction South. He singled out former soldiers and those with some education as particularly deserving of the right to vote. This was the first time an American president had called for granting African Americans suffrage, and it illustrated the capacity for growth that had always been the hallmark of Lincoln's leadership.

The Meaning of Freedom

Critical to the debate over Reconstruction were the complex reactions of Southerners, black and white alike, to the end of slavery. That event led inevitably to conflict between blacks seeking to bring substantive meaning to their freedom and planters seeking to retain as much as possible of the old order. Rather than being a predetermined category or static concept, "freedom" itself became a terrain of conflict during Reconstruction, its definition open to different, often contradictory interpretations, its content changing for whites as well as for blacks.

To African Americans, freedom meant independence from white control, autonomy both as individuals and as members of a community that was itself being transformed as a result of emancipation. Blacks relished the opportunity to flaunt their liberation from the innumerable regulations, significant and trivial, associated with slavery. They openly held mass meetings and religious services free of white oversight; they acquired dogs, guns, and liquor (all barred under slavery); they refused to yield the sidewalks to whites. No longer required to obtain a pass from their owners to travel, former slaves throughout the South left the plantations in search of better jobs, family members, or simply a taste of personal freedom. Many moved to southern towns and cities, where, it seemed, "freedom was free-er."

Before the war, free blacks had created a network of churches, schools, and mutual-benefit societies, and slaves had forged a semiautonomous culture centered on the family and church. With freedom, these institutions were consolidated, expanded, and liberated from white supervision.

The family stood as the main pillar of the post-emancipation black community. Under slavery, most blacks had lived in nuclear family units, although they faced the constant threat of separation from loved ones by sale. Reconstruction provided the opportunity to solidify their family ties. Freedpeople made remarkable efforts to locate loved ones from whom they had been separated under slavery. One northern reporter in 1865 encountered a freedman who had actually walked more than six hundred miles from Georgia to North Carolina, searching for the wife and children from whom he had been sold away.

Control over their family life was essential to the former slaves' definition of freedom. Many freedwomen, preferring to devote more time to their families, and wishing to be free from the supervision of white employers (which under slavery often led to sexual exploitation), refused to work any longer in the cotton fields. Black parents strenuously resisted efforts by many planters to force their children into involuntary labor through court-ordered apprenticeships, insisting that they, rather than the employer, would decide when children went to school and when they labored in the fields.

At the same time, African Americans withdrew almost entirely from white-controlled religious institutions, where they had been excluded from a role in church governance and had often been required to sit in the back pews during services. The rise of the independent black church, with METHODISTS and BAPTISTS commanding the largest followings, redrew the religious map of the South. The church played a central role in the black community; a place of worship, it also housed schools, social events, and political gatherings, and sponsored many of the fraternal

Cartoon by Thomas Nast, which appeared in *Harper's Weekly* in 1874. (Prints and Photographs Division, Library of Congress)

and benevolent societies that sprang up during Reconstruction. Inevitably, black ministers came to play a role in politics. Over two hundred held public office during Reconstruction.

Another striking example of the freedpeople's effort to breathe meaning into freedom was their thirst for education. Before the war, virtually every southern state had prohibited the instruction of slaves. Now, adults as well as children thronged the schools established during and after the Civil War. Northern benevolent societies, the Freedmen's Bureau, and, after 1868, state governments provided most of the funding for black education, but the initiative often lay with African Americans, who pooled their meager resources and voluntarily taxed themselves to purchase land, construct buildings, and hire teachers.

The desire for autonomy and self-improvement also shaped African Americans' economic definition of freedom. Blacks wished to take control of the conditions under which they labored and to carve out the greatest degree of economic independence. Most refused to work any longer in gangs under the direction of an overseer, and generally preferred renting land to working for wages. Above all, economic freedom meant owning land of their own. In some parts of the South, blacks in 1865 seized abandoned land, or refused to leave plantations, insisting that the property belonged to them. Many expected the federal government to guarantee them access to land.

If the goal of autonomy inspired African Americans to withdraw from social institutions controlled by whites, and attempt to work out their economic destinies by themselves, in political life "freedom" meant inclusion rather than separation. Recognition of their equal rights as citizens quickly emerged as the animating impulse of black politics. Throughout 1865, blacks organized mass meetings, parades, petitions, and conventions demanding equality before the law and the right to vote. The end of slavery, they insisted, enabled America for the first time to live up to the full implications of its democratic creed by abandoning racial proscription and absorbing blacks fully into the civil and political order.

If former slaves saw Reconstruction as heralding a new era of autonomy and equality, most southern whites reacted to military defeat and emancipation with dismay. Needing to borrow money to resume farming, many small farmers fell into debt and were forced to take up the growing of cotton. By the mid-1870s white farmers, who had cultivated only one-tenth of the South's cotton crop in 1860, were growing 40 percent, and many who had owned their land were tenants.

Planter families also faced profound changes in the aftermath of the war. In a sense, the most arduous task facing former slave owners was adjusting to the world of free labor. Planters understood that the questions of land and labor were intimately interrelated. Many were convinced, a northern visitor reported, that "so long as they retain possession of their lands they can oblige the negroes to work on such terms as they please." Between the planters' need for a disciplined labor force and the freedpeople's quest for autonomy, conflict was inevitable. Blacks, planters complained, insisted on setting their own hours of labor, worked at their own pace, and insisted on the right to conduct their personal lives as they saw fit.

With such polarized forces at work, it fell to the Freedmen's Bureau to attempt to mediate between the contending parties. The bureau's myriad responsibilities included establishing schools for freedmen, adjudicating disputes among blacks and between the races, and attempting to secure for blacks and for white Unionists equal justice from southern courts. Much to the bureau's activity, however, centered on overseeing the transition from slave to free labor.

Some bureau officials believed that the former slaves had to sign labor contracts and go back to work on the plantations. Others—such as Gen. Rufus Saxton, who directed the agency's activities in South Carolina in 1865—sympathized strongly with blacks' aspiration to own land. In the summer of 1865, however, President Andrew Johnson, who had succeeded Lincoln, ordered land in federal hands returned to its former owners. A series of confrontations followed, notably in South Carolina and Georgia, where blacks were forcibly evicted from the land they had been settled on by Sherman. In the end, the vast majority of rural freedpeople remained propertyless and poor, with no alternative but to work as laborers on white-owned plantations. The Freedmen's Bureau attempted to ensure that labor contracts were equitable, and that the former slaves were free to leave their jobs once the contracts had expired. But the ideal of forty acres and a mule was dead. The result was a deep sense of betrayal, which survived among the freedpeople and their descendants long after the end of Reconstruction.

Out of the conflict on the plantations, and with black landownership all but precluded, new systems of labor emerged in the different regions of the South. SHARECROPPING came to dominate the cotton South and much of the tobacco belt of Virginia and North Carolina. In the Louisiana sugar region, an influx of northern capital allowed for the repair of equipment and the resumption of production. Gang labor survived the end of slavery, with blacks working for wages and allowed access to garden plots to grow their own food. In the rice kingdom of coastal South Carolina and Georgia, planters were unable to acquire the large amounts of capital necessary to repair irrigation systems and threshing machinery destroyed by the war, and blacks continued to demand access to land they had occupied in 1865. In the end, the plantations in this region fell to pieces, and blacks were able to acquire land and take up self-sufficient farming.

The Politics of Presidential Reconstruction

To Andrew Johnson fell the task of overseeing the restoration of the Union. Johnson was ill suited for the responsibilities he now shouldered. A lonely, stubborn man, he was intolerant of criticism and unable to compromise. He lacked Lincoln's political skills and keen sense of northern public opinion. Moreover, while Johnson had supported emancipation during the war, he held deeply racist views. A self-proclaimed spokesman for the poor white farmers of the South, he condemned the old planter aristocracy, but believed African Americans had no role to play in Reconstruction.

With Congress out of session until December, Johnson in May 1865 outlined his plan for reuniting the nation. He issued a series of proclamations that inaugurated the period of Presidential Reconstruction (1865–1867). Johnson offered a pardon to all southern whites, except Confederate leaders and wealthy planters (and most of these soon received individual pardons) who took an oath of allegiance. He also appointed provisional governors and ordered conventions held, to which delegates were elected by whites alone. Apart from the requirement that they abolish slavery, repudiate secession, and abrogate the Confederate debt, the new governments were granted a free hand in managing their affairs.

The conduct of the southern governments elected under Johnson's program turned most of the Republican North against the president. White voters by and large returned members of the old elite to power. Alarmed by the apparent ascendancy of "rebels," Republicans were further outraged by reports of violence against former slaves and against northern visitors in the South. But what aroused the most opposition were laws of the new southern governments that attempted to regulate the lives of the former slaves. Known as the BLACK CODES, these did grant the freedpeople certain rights, such as owning property and suing in court. African Americans could not, however, testify against whites, serve on juries or in state militias, or vote.

Responding to planters' demands that the freedpeople be forced back to work on the plantations, the Black Codes required blacks to sign yearly labor contracts. The unemployed were declared vagrants, and could be arrested, fined and hired out to white landowners. Some states limited the occupations open to blacks and tried to prevent them from acquiring land. African Americans strongly resisted the implementation of these measures, and the apparent inability of the white South's leaders to accept the reality of emancipation fatally undermined northern support for Johnson's policies.

When Congress assembled in December 1865, Johnson announced that with loyal governments functioning in all the southern states, Reconstruction was over. In response, Radical Republicans, who had grown increasingly estranged from Johnson during the summer and fall, called for the establishment of new governments with "rebels" excluded from power and black men granted the right to vote.

Most Republicans, however, were moderates, not Radicals. They believed Johnson's plan flawed but desired to work with the president in modifying it, and did not believe that either southern or northern whites would accept black suffrage. Radicals and moderates joined together in refusing to seat the Southerners recently elected to Congress. Early in 1866, Sen. Lyman Trumbull of Illinois proposed two bills, reflecting the moderates' belief that Johnson's policy required modification. The first extended the life of the Freedmen's Bureau, which had been established for only one year. The second, the Civil Rights Bill, defined all persons born in the United States as citizens and spelled out rights they were to enjoy without regard to race—making contracts, bringing lawsuits, and enjoying "full and equal benefit of all laws and proceedings for the security of person and property." The bill left the new southern governments in place, but required them to accord blacks the same civil rights as whites. It made no mention of the right to vote.

Passed by overwhelming majorities in both houses of Congress, the Civil Rights Bill represented the first attempt to define in legislative terms the essence of freedom and the rights of American citizenship. In empowering the federal government to guarantee the principle of equality before the law, regardless of race, against violations by the states, it embodied a profound change in federal-state relations.

To the surprise of Congress, Johnson vetoed both bills. Both, he said, threatened to centralize power in the national government and deprive the states of their authority to regulate their own affairs. Moreover, he believed, blacks did not deserve the rights of citizenship. The vetoes made a complete breach between Congress and the president inevitable. In April 1866, the Civil Rights Bill became the first major law in American history to be passed over a presidential veto.

Johnson had united moderate and Radical Republicans against him. Congress now proceeded to adopt its own plan of Reconstruction. In June 1866, it approved the FOURTEENTH AMENDMENT, which broadened the federal government's power to protect the rights of all Americans. It forbade states from abridging the "privileges and immunities" of American citizens or depriving any citizen of the "equal protection of the laws." In a compromise between Radical and moderate positions on black suffrage, it did not expressly give blacks the right to vote, but threatened to reduce the South's representation in Congress if black men continued to be denied the ballot. The amendment also empowered Congress to take further steps to enforce its provisions.

The most important change in the Constitution since the adoption of the Bill of Rights, the Fourteenth Amendment established equality before the law as a fundamental right of American citizens. It shifted the balance of power within the nation by making the federal government, not the states, the ultimate protector of citizens' rights. The Fourteenth Amendment, and the congressional policy of guaranteeing civil rights for blacks, became the central issue of the political campaign of 1866. Riots that broke out in Memphis and New Orleans, in which white policemen and citizens killed scores of blacks further undermined public support for Johnson's policies.

In the northern congressional elections, Republicans opposed to Johnson's policies won a sweeping victory. Nonetheless, every southern state but Tennessee, egged on by Johnson, refused to ratify the Fourteenth Amendment. The intransigence of Johnson and the bulk of the white South pushed moderate Republicans toward the proposals of the Radicals. In March 1867, over Johnson's veto, Congress adopted the Reconstruction Act, which divided the South into five military districts, temporarily barred many Confederates from voting or holding office, and called for the creation of new governments in the South with suffrage no longer restricted because of race.

The conflict between President Johnson and Congress did not end with the passage of the Reconstruction Act. In 1868 the House of Representatives impeached the president for violating the Tenure of Office Act of 1867, and the Senate came within a single vote of removing him from office. Shortly thereafter, the Republicans nominated Ulysses S. Grant as the party's presidential candidate. Reconstruction was the central issue of the 1868 campaign. Democrats (*see* DEMOCRATIC PARTY) denounced it as unconstitutional, and condemned black suffrage as a violation of America's political traditions. Grant's victory was a vindication of Republican Reconstruction, and it inspired Congress to adopt the era's third constitutional amendment. In February 1869, Congress approved the FIFTEENTH AMENDMENT, prohibiting the federal and state governments from depriving any citizen of the right to vote because of race.

Although it left the door open to suffrage restrictions not explicitly based on race—literacy tests, property qualifications, poll taxes—and did nothing to extend voting rights to women, the Fifteenth Amendment marked the culmination of four decades of agitation on behalf of the slave. As late as 1868, only eight northern states had allowed black men to vote. "Nothing in all history," exclaimed veteran abolitionist William Lloyd Garrison, equaled "this wonderful, quiet, sudden transformation of four millions of human beings from . . . the auction-block to the ballot-box."

Radical Reconstruction in the South

Among the former slaves, the coming of black suffrage in 1867 caused an outburst of political organization. Determined to exercise their new rights as citizens, thousands joined the UNION LEAGUE, an organization closely linked to the Republican party, and the vast majority of eligible African Americans registered to vote. "You never saw a people more excited on the subject of politics than are the Negroes of the South," wrote a plantation manager.

By 1870, all the former confederate states had been readmitted to the Union, nearly all under the control of the Republican party. Their new constitutions, drafted in 1868 and 1869 by the first public bodies in American history with substantial black representation (of about 1,000 delegates throughout the South, over one-quarter were black), represented a considerable improvement over those they replaced. They made the structure of southern government more democratic, modernized the tax system, and guaranteed the civil and political rights of black citizens. A few states initially barred former Confederates from voting, but this policy was quickly abandoned by the new state governments.

Throughout Reconstruction, black voters provided the bulk of the Republican party's support. Although Democrats charged that "Negro rule" had come to the South, nowhere did blacks control the workings of state government, or hold office in numbers equal to their proportion of the total population (which ranged from about 60 percent in South Carolina to around one-third in Arkansas, North Carolina, Tennessee, and Texas). In nearly every state, whites (the much-maligned "carpetbaggers" and "scalawags") controlled the machinery of the Republican party and all but monopolized the top offices—governor, U.S. senator, and major patronage positions. Nonetheless, the fact that well over fifteen hundred African Americans occupied positions of political power in the Reconstruction South represented a stunning departure from past American government.

During Reconstruction, African Americans were represented at every level of government. Fourteen sat in the House of Representatives, and two, Hiram REVELS and Blanche K. BRUCE, represented Mississippi in the Senate. P. B. S. PINCHBACK of Louisiana served briefly as American's first black governor. Other blacks held major state executive positions, including lieutenant governor, treasurer, and superintendent of education. Nearly 700 sat in state legislatures during Reconstruction, and there were scores of black local officials, ranging from justice of the peace to sheriff, tax assessor, and policeman. The presence of black officeholders and their white allies made a real difference in southern life, ensuring that those accused of crimes would be tried before juries of their peers, and enforcing fairness in such prosaic aspects of local government as road repair, tax assessment, and poor relief.

Many of these officeholders had been born free, and around fifty had gained their liberty before the Civil War by manumission, purchase, or escape. In South Carolina and Louisiana, homes of the South's wealthiest and best-educated free black communities, most prominent Reconstruction officeholders had never experienced slavery. A number of black officials had come from the North after the Civil War. But the majority were former slaves who had established their leadership in the black community by serving in the Union army, working as ministers, teachers, or skilled craftsmen, or engaging in Union League organizing.

Given the fact that many of the Reconstruction governors and legislators lacked previous experience in government, their record of accomplishment is remarkable. In many ways, Reconstruction at the state level profoundly altered traditions of southern government. The new governments established the region's first state-supported public school systems, as well as numerous hospitals and asylums for orphans and the insane. These institutions were provided for both blacks and whites, although they were generally segregated by race. Only in New Orleans were the public schools integrated during Reconstruction, and only in South Carolina did the state university admit black students (elsewhere, separate colleges were established for blacks). By the 1870s, in a region whose prewar leaders had made it illegal for blacks to learn and had done little to promote education among poorer whites, over half the children were attending public schools.

In assuming public responsibility for education, Reconstruction governments in a sense were following a path blazed by the North. Their efforts to guarantee African Americans equal treatment in transportation and places of public accommodation, however, launched them into an area all but unknown in American law. Racial segregation—or, indeed, the complete exclusion of blacks from both public and private facilities—was widespread throughout the country. Black demands for the outlawing of such discrimination produced deep divisions in the Republican party. But in the Deep South, where blacks made up the vast majority of the Republican voting population, laws were enacted making it illegal for railroads, hotels, and other institutions to discriminate on the basis of race. Enforcement of these laws varied considerably by locality, but Reconstruction established for the first time at the state level a standard of equal citizenship.

Republican governments also took steps to assist the poor of both races, and to promote the South's economic recovery. The BLACK CODES were repealed, the property of small farmers protected against being seized for debt, and the tax system revised to shift the burden from propertyless blacks to planters and other landowners. Little was done, however, to assist the former slaves in acquiring land. Only South Carolina took effective action, establishing a commission to purchase land for resale on longterm credit to poor families. In general, African-American officeholders tended to place more emphasis on issues relating to civil rights than on the land hunger of the black community.

Rather than on land distribution, the Reconstruction governments pinned their hopes for southern economic growth and opportunity for African Americans on a program of regional economic development. Every state affected by Reconstruction helped to finance the building of railroads, and through tax reductions and other incentives tried to attract northern manufacturers to invest in the region. The program had mixed results. A few states witnessed significant new railroad construction between 1868 and 1872, but economic development in general still remained weak.

Thus, to their supporters, the governments of Radical Reconstruction presented a complex pattern of achievement and disappointment. The economic vision of a modernizing, revitalized southern economy failed to materialize, and most African Americans remained locked in poverty. On the other hand, biracial democratic government, a thing unknown in American history, for the first time functioned effectively in many parts of the South. The conservative oligarchy that had run the South from colonial times to 1867 found itself largely excluded from political power, while those who had previously been outsiders—poorer white Southerners, men from the North, and especially former slaves—cast ballots, sat on juries, and enacted and administered laws.

The Overthrow of Reconstruction

The South's traditional leaders—planters, merchants, and Democratic politicians—bitterly opposed the new governments, denouncing them as corrupt, inefficient, and embodiments of wartime defeat and "black supremacy." There was corruption during Reconstruction, but it was confined to no race, region, or party. Frauds that existed in some southern states, associated primarily with the new programs of railroad aid, were dwarfed by those practiced in the same years by the Whiskey Rings, which involved high officials of the Grant administration and by New York's Tweed Ring, whose depredations ran into the tens of millions of dollars.

The rising taxes needed to pay for schools and other new public facilities, and to assist railroad development, were another cause of antagonism to Reconstruction. The most basic reason for opposition, however, was that most white Southerners could not accept the idea of former slaves voting, holding office, and enjoying equality before the law. Reconstruction, they believed, had to be overthrown in order to restore white supremacy in southern government, and to ensure planters a disciplined, reliable labor force.

In 1869 and 1870, Democrats joined with dissident Republicans to win control of Tennessee and Virginia, effectively ending Reconstruction there. Elsewhere in the South, however, with Reconstruction governments securely entrenched, their opponents turned to a campaign of widespread violence in an effort to end Republican rule. In wide areas of the South, Reconstruction's opponents resorted to terror to secure their aim of restoring Democratic rule and white supremacy. Secret societies sprang up, whose purposes were to prevent blacks from voting and to destroy the infrastructure of the Republican party by assassinating local leaders and public officials.

The most notorious such group was the Ku Klux Klan, an organization of terrorist criminals that in effect served as a military arm of the Democratic party. Led by planters, merchants, and Democratic politicians, the Klan committed some of the most brutal acts of violence in American history. During the 1868 presidential election, Klansmen in Georgia and Louisiana established a reign of terror so complete that blacks were unable to go to the polls to vote, and Democrats carried both states.

Grant's election did not end the Klan's activities; indeed, in some parts of the South they accelerated in 1869 and 1870. The Klan singled out for assault Reconstruction's local leadership. White Republicans—local officeholders, teachers, and party organizers—were often victimized, but blacks bore the brunt of the violence. One black leader in Monroe County, Mississippi, had his throat cut because he was "president of a republican club" and was known as a man who "would speak his mind." In York County, S.C., where nearly the entire white male population joined the Klan (and women participated by sewing the robes the Klansmen wore as disguises), the organization committed eleven murders and hundreds of whippings.

Occasionally, violence escalated from attacks on individuals to wholesale assaults on the local African-American community. Institutions such as black churches and schools, symbols of black autonomy, frequently became targets. In Meridian, Miss., in 1871, some thirty blacks were murdered in cold blood, along with a white Republican judge. At Colfax, La., two years later, scores of African-American militiamen were killed after surrendering to armed whites who were intent on seizing control of the local government.

When the new southern governments proved unable to restore order or suppress the Klan, Congress in 1870 and 1871 adopted three Enforcement Acts, outlawing terrorist societies and allowing the president to use the army against them. These laws continued the expansion of national authority during Reconstruction by defining certain crimes—those aimed at depriving citizens of their civil and political rights—as federal offenses. In 1871, President Grant authorized federal marshals, backed up by troops in some areas, to arrest hundreds of accused Klansmen. After a series of well-publicized trials, in which many of the organization's leaders were jailed, the Klan went out of existence.

Despite the Grant administration's effective response to Klan terrorism, the North's commitment to Reconstruction waned during the 1870s. Many Radical leaders, among them Thaddeus Stevens, had passed from the scene. Within the Republican party, their place was taken by politicians less committed to the ideal of equal rights for blacks. The federal government had freed the slaves, made them citizens, given them the right to vote, and crushed the Ku Klux Klan. Now, it was said, blacks should rely on their own resources, not demand further assistance from the North.

In 1872 a group of Republicans, alienated by corruption within the Grant administration, bolted the party. The Liberal Republicans, as they called themselves, believed that unrestrained democracy, in which "ignorant" voters such as the Irish immigrants of New York City could dominate politics in some locales, was responsible for such instances of corruption as the Tweed Ring. Democratic criticisms of Reconstruction found a receptive audience among the Liberals. As in the North, Liberals believed, the "best men" of the South had been excluded from power while "ignorant" voters controlled politics. The result was corruption and misgovernment. Government in the South should be returned to the region's "natural leaders."

The Liberals nominated Horace Greeley, editor of the New York *Tribune,* to run against Grant in 1872. The Democrats endorsed Greeley as well, and the continuation of Reconstruction became a major issue in the campaign. Grant overwhelmingly won reelection, but the Liberal attack on Reconstruction continued, contributing to a resurgence of racism in the North. Journalist James S. Pike, a leading Greeley supporter, in 1874 published *The Prostrate State,* an influential account of a visit to South Carolina. He depicted a state engulfed by corruption and extravagance, under the control of "a mass of black barbarism." "Negro government," he insisted, was the cause of the South's problems; the solution was to see leading whites restored to political power.

Other factors also weakened northern support for Reconstruction. In 1873, the country plunged into a severe economic depression. Distracted by national economic problems, Republicans were in no mood to devote further attention to the South. Congress did enact one final piece of civil rights legislation, the Civil Rights Act of 1875, which outlawed racial discrimination in places of public accommodation. This was a tribute to Charles Sumner, who had devoted his career to promoting the principle of equality before the law, and who died in 1874.

Nonetheless, it was clear that the northern public was retreating from Reconstruction. Meanwhile, the Supreme Court began whittling away at the guarantees of black rights Congress had adopted. In the *Slaughterhouse* cases (1873), the Court decreed that the Fourteenth Amendment had not altered traditional federalism; most of the rights of citizens remained under state control. Three years later, in *U.S. v. Cruikshank,* the Court gutted the Enforcement Acts by throwing out convictions of some of those responsible for the Colfax Massacre.

By the mid-1870s, Reconstruction was on the defensive. The depression dealt the South a severe economic blow, and further weakened the possibility that Republicans could create a revitalized southern economy. Factionalism between blacks and whites and between carpetbaggers and scalawags remained a serious problem among southern Republicans. In those states where Reconstruction survived, violence again reared its head, and this time the Grant administration showed no desire to intervene. In contrast to the Klan's activities—which had been conducted at night by disguised men—the violence of 1875 and 1876 took place in broad daylight, as if to flaunt Democrats' conviction that they had nothing to fear from Washington. In Mississippi in 1875, white rifle clubs drilled in public, and Republicans were openly assaulted and murdered. When Gov. Adelbert Ames frantically appealed to the federal government for assistance, President Grant responded that the northern public was "tired out" by southern problems and would condemn any interference from Washington. On election day in 1875, armed Democrats destroyed ballot boxes and drove former slaves from the polls. The result was a Democratic landslide and the end of Reconstruction in Mississippi. "A revolution has taken place," wrote Ames, "and a race are disfranchised—they are to be returned to . . . an era of second slavery."

Similar events took place in South Carolina in 1876. Here, where blacks made up 60 percent of the population, Democrats nominated for governor Wade Hampton, one of the state's most popular Confederate veterans. Hampton promised to respect the rights of all citizens, but his supporters launched a wave of intimidation, with rifle clubs disrupting Republican meetings, and freedmen assaulted and sometimes murdered.

Events in South Carolina directly affected the outcome of the presidential campaign of 1876. To succeed Grant, the Republicans nominated Governor Rutherford B. Hayes of Ohio. His Democratic opponent was New York's governor, Samuel J. Tilden. By this time, only South Carolina, Florida, and Louisiana remained under Republican control. The election was so close that whoever captured these states (and both candidates claimed to have carried them) would become the next president. In January 1877, unable to resolve the crisis on its own, Congress appointed an electoral commission composed of senators, congressmen, and Supreme Court justices. Republicans enjoyed an 8–7 majority on the commission; the members decided that Hayes had carried the disputed southern states, and he was elected.

Democrats, who controlled the House of Representatives, could still obstruct Hayes's inauguration, but after secret discussions with representatives of the incoming president they decided not to do so. This was the famous "Bargain of 1877": Hayes would recognize Democratic control of the remaining southern states and Democrats would not block the certification of his election. Hayes became president, promised to end federal intervention in the South, and ordered United States troops, who had been guarding the statehouses in South Carolina and Louisiana, to return to their barracks (but not to leave the region entirely, as is widely believed). Reconstruction was at an end.

The collapse of Reconstruction deeply affected the future course of American development. The South long remained a bastion of one-party Democratic rule, under the control of a reactionary elite who used the same violence and fraud that had helped defeat Reconstruction to stifle internal dissent. The federal government stood by indifferently as the southern states effectively nullified the Fourteenth and Fifteenth amendments and, beginning in the 1890s, stripped African Americans of the right to vote. By the turn of the twentieth century, southern blacks found themselves enmeshed in a complex system of oppression, each of whose components—segregation, economic inequality, political disempowerment, and the pervasive threat of violence—reinforced the others. Although the black institutions created or strengthened after the Civil War—the family, church, and schools—survived the end of Reconstruction, southern governments fell far behind the rest of the nation in meeting their public responsibilities. Long into the twentieth century, the South would remain the nation's foremost economic problem, a region of low wages, stunted economic development, and widespread poverty. Not until the 1960s would the nation again attempt to come to terms with the political and social agenda of Reconstruction.

REFERENCES

BELZ, HERMAN. *Reconstructing the Union: Theory and Practice during the Civil War.* Ithaca, N.Y., 1969.

BROCK, WILLIAM R. *An American Crisis.* London, 1963.

DRAGO, EDMUND L. *Black Politicians and Reconstruction in Georgia.* Rev. ed. Athens, Ga., 1992.

DU BOIS, W. E. B. *Black Reconstruction in America.* New York, 1935.

FITZGERALD, MICHAEL W. *The Union League Movement in the Deep South: Politics and Agricultural Change During Reconstruction.* Baton Rouge, La., 1989.

FONER, ERIC. *Reconstruction: American's Unfinished Revolution, 1863–1877.* New York, 1988.

———. *A Short History of Reconstruction.* New York, 1990.

———. *Freedom's Lawmakers: A Directory of Black Officeholders During Reconstruction.* New York, 1993.

FRANKLIN, JOHN HOPE. *Reconstruction After the Civil War.* Chicago, 1961.

GILLETTE, WILLIAM. *Retreat from Reconstruction 1869–1879.* Baton Rouge, La., 1979.

HOLT, THOMAS. *Black over White: Negro Political Leadership in South Carolina During Reconstruction.* Urbana, Ill. 1977.

JAYNES, GERALD D. *Branches Without Roots: Genesis of the Black Working Class in the American South 1862–1882.* New York, 1986.

KACZOROWSKI, ROBERT. *The Politics of Judicial Interpretation: The Federal Courts, Department of Justice, and Civil Rights, 1866–1876.* New York, 1985.

LITWACK, LEON F. *Been in the Storm So Long: The Aftermath of Slavery.* New York, 1979.

MAGDOL, EDWARD. *A Right to the Land: Essays on the Freedmen's Community.* Westport, Conn., 1977.

MCCRARY, PEYTON. *Abraham Lincoln and Reconstruction: The Louisiana Experiment.* Princeton, N.J., 1978.

MORRIS, ROBERT C. *Reading, 'Riting, and Reconstruction: The Education of Freedmen in the South 1861–1870.* Chicago, 1981.

OLSEN, OTTO H., ed. *Reconstruction and Redemption in the South.* Baton Rouge, La., 1980.

PERMAN, MICHAEL. *The Road to Redemption: Southern Politics, 1869–1879.* Chapel Hill, N.C., 1984.

RABINOWITZ, HOWARD N., ed. *Southern Black Leaders of the Reconstruction Era.* Urbana, Ill., 1982.

RABLE, GEORGE C. *But There Was No Peace: The Role of Violence in the Politics of Reconstruction.* Athens, Ga., 1984.

RANSOM, ROGER L., and RICHARD SUTCH. *One Kind of Freedom: The Economic Consequences of Emancipation.* New York, 1977.

ROSE, WILLIE LEE. *Rehearsal for Reconstruction: The Port Royal Experiment.* Indianapolis, 1964.

STERLING, DOROTHY, ed. *The Trouble They Seen.* New York, 1976.

SUMMERS, MARK W. *Railroads, Reconstruction, and the Gospel of Prosperity: Aid Under the Radical Republicans, 1865–1877.* Princeton, N.J., 1984.

TREFOUSSE, HANS L. *The Radical Republicans: Lincoln's Vanguard for Racial Justice.* New York, 1969.

VINCENT, CHARLES. *Black Legislators in Louisiana During Reconstruction.* Baton Rouge, La., 1976.

WALKER, CLARENCE E. *A Rock in a Weary Land: The African Methodist Episcopal Church During the Civil*

War and Reconstruction. Baton Rouge, La., 1982.
WILLIAMSON, JOEL. *After Slavery: The Negro in South Carolina During Reconstruction, 1861–1877.* Chapel Hill, N.C., 1965.

ERIC FONER

Recording Industry. In the development of sound recording, primarily an enterprise of European Americans, African Americans were initially relegated to the margins of cultural input. Even "coon" songs, a staple of early commercial recordings dating from minstrelsy, were almost invariably sung by whites until World War I. Notable exceptions included Bert WILLIAMS, the great black vaudevillian, and George Washington Johnson, perhaps the first black recording artist, whose hits "The Whistling Coon" and "The Laughing Song" brought him fame and fortune.

The "blues" craze, which swept the country in the 1910s, brought to the fore a number of African-American composers such as "the father of the blues" W. C. HANDY ("Memphis Blues") and Arthur Seals ("Baby Seals' Blues"), as well as a number of white blues writers. "Both Handy and Arthur Seals were Negroes, but the music that they titled 'blues' is more or less derived from the standard popular musical styles of the 'coon song' and 'cake walk' type" (Charters 1959, pp. 34–35). Furthermore, as was the case with coon songs, most of these blues compositions were recorded by whites singing in "Negro dialect" (*see* BLUES).

In 1914, the American Society of Composers, Authors, and Publishers (ASCAP) was founded to protect the rights of songwriters. Membership in the society was generally skewed toward writers of pop tunes and semiserious works. Of the society's 170 charter members, six were black: Harry BURLEIGH, Will Marion COOK, J. Rosamond JOHNSON, James Weldon JOHNSON, Cecil Mack, and Will Tyers. While other "literate" black writers and composers—for example, W. C. HANDY and Duke ELLINGTON—were able to gain entrance to ASCAP, the vast majority of "untutored" black artists were excluded from the society and thereby denied the full benefits of copyright protection.

With the advent of recorded jazz in the late 1910s, patterns of racial exclusion skewed public perceptions of African-American music even more. In 1917, when Victor decided to take a chance on "jass," the band they chose to record was the all-white Original Dixieland Jazz Band. Though they were heavily influenced by the King Oliver Band (which included Louis ARMSTRONG), the Oliver ensemble itself didn't record until 1923 (*see* King OLIVER). The first ensemble of color ever to receive a recording contract was James Reese EUROPE's Syncopated Society Orchestra, signed by Victor in 1914 to supervise a series of dance records for the white dance team of Vernon and Irene Castle, a project directed at mainstream consumption.

It wasn't until 1920, and quite by accident, that an African-American market for African-American records was "discovered." The enterprising black producer/songwriter Perry Bradford convinced the OKeh record company to let him record a black contralto named Mamie SMITH. Her recording of Bradford's "Crazy Blues" sold 7,500 copies a week, mostly to black buyers. Ralph Peer, the OKeh recording director who assisted at the sessions, dubbed these records "race records," and it remained the designation for black music, by black artists, for a black audience until 1949. Smith's overwhelming success ushered in an era of classic blues recordings by African-American women: Ida COX, Chippie Hill, Sarah Martin, Clara SMITH, Trixie Smith, Victoria Spivey, Sippi WALLACE, and the most famous of all, Bessie SMITH, "empress of the blues."

The initial success of the "race market" encouraged the formation of a handful of black-owned independent labels. W. C. Handy and his publishing partner, Harry Pace, started Black Swan in 1921. Mayo "Ink" Williams, head of Paramount's race series, founded Black Patti in 1927. Such labels were soon bought up by the major companies or forced out of the industry. With the onset of the Great Depression, the race market was slowly taken over by OKeh, Columbia, and Paramount. Not a single black-owned label survived the 1920s intact.

As the record companies began to test the limits of the race market, they discovered that there was also a considerable demand for country blues, particularly among southern blacks. In 1924, the same year they acquired the Black Swan catalog, Paramount released Papa Charlie Jackson's "Lawdy Lawdy Blues." This record was followed with releases by Arthur "Blind" Blake and, perhaps the most popular country blues singer of the decade, Blind Lemon JEFFERSON. Throughout the 1920s and early 1930s, a number of companies, including OKeh, Columbia, and Victor, engaged in extensive "field" recordings. As a result, dozens of country blues artists—among them, Furry Lewis, Blind Willie McTell, Mississippi John Hurt, Son HOUSE, Charlie Patton, Huddie "Leadbelly" LEDBETTER, and Robert JOHNSON—were brought to wider public attention. The country blues artist who dominated the 1930s was Big Bill BROONZY.

In the mainstream, it was the era of big band jazz. Again, patterns of racial segregation obscured the origins of the music. A number of African-American bands managed to achieve major success, however.

Jermain Dupree, music mogul and producer of such groups as Kriss Kross, Xscape, and Da Brat. (Allford/Trotman Associates)

Among the best known, Duke Ellington's band became famous through their live broadcasts from the COTTON CLUB in Harlem, New York. William James "Count" BASIE, from the Reno Club in Kansas City, injected jazz with a heavy dose of the blues. Both the Ellington and Basie bands recorded for major labels and were among the few African-American ensembles that could be heard on radio (*see* JAZZ).

In the 1940s, tension between radio and music publishers signaled a new era in black popular music. The National Association of Broadcasters (NAB), representing some six hundred radio stations, formed their own performing rights organization, Broadcast Music Incorporated (BMI), in 1939 and proceeded shortly thereafter to boycott all ASCAP music. The Broadway-Hollywood monopoly on popular music, and its considerable influence in shaping public taste, was challenged publicly for the first time, creating a cultural space for rhythm and blues artists like Arthur "Big Boy" Crudup, Roy Brown, Ivory Joe Hunter, Fats DOMINO, and Wynonie Harris.

The success of these artists in the late 1940s speaks to what critic Nelson George has referred to as "an aesthetic schism between high-brow, more assimilated black styles and working-class, grassroots sounds" (George 1988, p. 10). Until this time, the most notable African-American acts were the more

pop-sounding artists like Nat "King" COLE ("For Sentimental Reasons"), Ella FITZGERALD ("My Happiness"), the MILLS BROTHERS ("Across the Valley from the Alamo"), and the INK SPOTS ("The Gypsy"), all of whom recorded for major labels. These companies failed to appreciate the appeal of R&B in working-class black communities.

With a much smaller horn section and more pronounced rhythm, Louis Jordan and the Tympani Five, something of a transitional act, anticipated the decline of the big bands and helped to define the instrumentation for the R&B combos that followed. JORDAN's material was composed and arranged, but selections like "Saturday Night Fishfry," "Honey Chile," and "Ain't Nobody Here but Us Chickens" evoked blues images not found in most black pop of the day. While Jordan was said to have "jumped the blues," other R&B stars screeched, honked, and shouted. "Suddenly it was as if a great deal of the Euro-American humanist facade Afro-American music had taken on had been washed away by the war" (Jones 1963, p. 171). The raucous styles of such artists as Wynonie Harris ("Good Rockin' Tonight"), John Lee HOOKER ("Boogie Chillen"), saxophonist Big Jay McNeely ("Deacon's Hop"), and pianist Amos Milburn ("Chicken Shack Boogie") all deviated significantly from the sound of mainstream black pop.

Since this music did not readily lend itself to the production styles of the major labels, they decided to ignore the relatively smaller R&B market. This situation made it possible for a large number of independent labels to enter the business. It is estimated that by 1949 over four hundred new labels came into existence. Most important among these were Atlantic in New York City; Savoy in Newark; King in Cincinnati; Chess in Chicago; Peacock in Houston; and Modern, Imperial, and Specialty in Los Angeles. White-owned, except for Don Robey's Peacock label, most of these labels specialized in R&B.

This music found a ready home among independent deejays who often experimented with "specialty" music as an antidote to the trivial popular fare of network radio. Early R&B hits that were popular among both black and white audiences included Fats Domino's "The Fat Man," Jackie Brenston's "Rocket 88," Lloyd Price's "Lawdy Miss Clawdy," and Joe TURNER's "Chains of Love," "Sweet Sixteen," and "Honey Hush." All were recorded for independent labels. Pioneer black deejays like "Jockey" Jack Gibson in Atlanta, "Professor Bop" in Shreveport, and "Sugar Daddy" in Birmingham paved the way for white R&B deejays such as Alan Freed, the self-appointed "father of rock 'n' roll."

With its roots in the deep South, the music that became rock 'n' roll issued from just about every region in the country. Most of its formative influences as well as virtually all of its early innovators were African American: B. B. KING ("The Thrill Is Gone") MUDDY WATERS ("Got My Mojo Working"), Bo DIDDLEY ("Bo Diddley"), Fats Domino ("Ain't That a Shame," "I'm in Love Again," and "Blueberry Hill"), Ray CHARLES ("I Got a Woman"), Clyde MCPHATTER ("A Lover's Question"), Sam COOKE ("You Send Me"), Ruth BROWN ("Mama, He Treats Your Daughter Mean"), Laverne Baker ("Tweedle Dee," "Jim Dandy,"), LITTLE RICHARD ("Tutti-Frutti," "Long Tall Sally," "Rip It Up"), Chuck BERRY ("Maybellene," "Sweet Sixteen," "School Days," "Johnny B. Goode"), the Orioles ("Crying in the Chapel"), the Crows ("Gee"), the Chords ("Sh-Boom"), and the Penguins ("Earth Angel"). Even with the new name, there was no mistaking where this music came from. As late as 1956, *Billboard* referred to the music as "a popularized form of rhythm & blues."

Several dozen "rock 'n' roll" songs were successfully "covered" by white artists in the early years of rock 'n' roll, but the vintage rock 'n' roll years were generally good for black musicians. African-American artists made such significant inroads into the pop market that, for a time, *Billboard*'s pop charts and R&B charts were virtually indistinguishable. At the end of the decade the "payola" scandal threatened to halt their progress. Deejays became the main target of government hearings that were largely orchestrated by ASCAP with support from the major record companies. The deejays were considered largely responsible for the crossover of black music into the pop market.

Chubby CHECKER ushered in the 1960s with "The Twist," which remains the only record to reach number 1 on the pop charts twice, first in 1960 and then again in 1962. It was still listed as the best-selling single of all time well into the 1970s. The twist craze was so powerful that major R&B artists and labels felt compelled to jump on the bandwagon. In 1962 alone, Sam Cooke recorded "Twist the Night Away," Gary "U.S." Bonds released "Dear Lady Twist" and "Twist, Twist Senora," and the Isley Brothers followed their classic "Shout" with "Twist and Shout." Atlantic Records reissued an album of old Ray Charles material as *Do the Twist with Ray Charles*. Relative unknowns Little Eva and Dee Sharp had hits with two twist spin-offs, "The Loco-Motion" and "Mashed Potato Time," respectively.

During this period, R&B producers emerged as artists in their own right. "Uptown rhythm & blues," to use Charlie Gillett's term, was established in Lieber and Stoller's pioneering work with the Drifters ("There Goes My Baby," "This Magic Moment," "Save the Last Dance for Me") in 1959–1960

Grammy Award-winning producers James "Jimmy Jam" Harris III (left) and Terry Lewis, 1992. (Perspective Records)

(Gillett 1970, p. 220). Luther Dixon's work with the Shirelles ("Will You Still Love Me Tomorrow?," "Dedicated to the One I Love," "Soldier Boy"), Phil Spector's with the Crystals ("He's a Rebel," "Da Doo Ron Ron," "Then He Kissed Me") and the Ronnettes ("Be My Baby"), and Berry Gordy's with Martha and the Vandellas ("Heat Wave," "Quicksand," "Dancing in the Street"), the Marvelettes ("Please Mr. Postman"), and the Supremes ("Where Did Our Love Go?" "Baby Love," "Stop! In the Name of Love," "You Can't Hurry Love") developed the style further and rekindled the spirit of early rock 'n' roll. In the hands of these producers, black female vocal harmony groups, known collectively as the "girl groups," became a recognized trend in rock 'n' roll for the first time.

During this period Berry Gordy started the most significant black-owned record label ever—MO-TOWN, which, until its recent sale to MCA (which was itself bought by Matsushita), was the centerpiece of the largest black-owned corporation in the United States. As a businessman, Gordy addressed all aspects of career development for African-American artists such as Marvin GAYE, the TEMPTATIONS, the FOUR TOPS, and Stevie WONDER in addition to the women mentioned above. As a producer, he had an uncanny ability to incorporate white audience tastes without abandoning a black sound.

As the early CIVIL RIGHTS MOVEMENT gave way to the more radical demand for black power, Motown's hegemony over black pop was challenged by a resurgence of closer-to-the-roots, hard-driving R&B from the deep South. Chiefly responsible for the popularization of "southern soul" was a short-lived but highly successful collaboration between Atlantic Records and a number of southern studios, most notably Stax in Memphis (Guaralnick 1986). From 1965 on, artists like Otis REDDING ("I've Been Loving You Too Long"), Wilson PICKET ("Land of 1000 Dances"), SAM AND DAVE ("Soul Man"), Arthur Conley ("Sweet Soul Music"), and Percy Sledge ("When a Man Loves a Woman") echoed the spirit of the new militance with raw, basic recordings easily distinguished from the cleaner, brighter Motown sound.

Stax was originally a white-owned company; its "Memphis sound" created by the house band, Booker T. and the MGs, was the product of cross-racial teamwork. Initially the credits on all Stax recordings read simply "produced by the Stax staff." In the late 1960s, leadership was increasingly taken over by black vice president Al Bell, often under controversial circumstances. Motown was not only black-owned, but virtually all of its creative personnel—artists, writers, producers, and session musicians—were black as well. It was clearly a haven for black talent. Paradoxically, Motown is remembered as being "totally committed to reaching white audiences," while Stax recordings, by contrast, were "consistently aimed at r&b fans first, the pop market second" (George 1988, p. 86).

The two artists who best expressed the spirit of the era were James BROWN and Aretha FRANKLIN. In the 1950s, James Brown's music was intended for, and in many ways confined to, the black community. When he "crossed over," he did so on his terms. His string of uncompromising Top Ten hits ("Papa's Got a Brand New Bag," "I Got You," "Cold Sweat") made few concessions to mainstream sensibilities. His 1968 hit single "Say It Loud—I'm Black and I'm Proud" became an anthem in the struggle for black liberation. Signed to Atlantic records in 1967, Aretha Franklin earned her title "Lady Soul" with her recording "Respect." The vocal and emotional range of her Atlantic releases ("Baby, I Love You," "Natural Woman," "Chain of Fools," "Think," and "Young, Gifted and Black," to name a few) uniquely expressed all the passion and forcefulness of the era.

Two black-led mixed bands in the late 1960s incorporated "psychedelic" sounds into their music—Sly and the Family Stone ("Dance to the Music," "Everyday People," "Hot Fun in the Summertime," "Thank You Falletinme Be Mice Elf Agin," "Family Affair") and the Jimi HENDRIX Experience ("Purple Haze," "All Along the Watchtower"). Chemical indulgence guided the careers of both. Sly married the funk and rock cultures in a way that no other artist,

black or white, had been able to do. Hendrix explored the electronic wizardry of his instrument and recording studio to a greater extent than any other African-American musician. At his Electric Ladyland studios he also logged some eight hundred hours of tape with musicians like Miles DAVIS, John McLaughlin, and other avant-garde jazz notables. None of these tapes was released during Hendrix's lifetime, and he never attracted a black audience to the music with which he was identified.

In the early 1970s a breakthrough of sorts for African-American songwriters was provided by so-called BLAXPLOITATION FILMS. Movies like *Shaft, Superfly,* and *Troubleman* were scored by Isaac Hayes, Curtis MAYFIELD, and Marvin Gaye respectively.

Reflecting the "quieter" mood of the early 1970s was the "soft soul" sound pioneered by Kenny Gamble and Leon Huff and producer-arranger Thom Bell, in league with Sigma Sound Studios in Philadelphia. Working with Jerry Butler, the Intruders, and the Delphonics, Gamble and Huff parlayed a $700 bank loan into thirty million-selling singles in a five-year period. The Philadelphia enterprise hit its stride in 1971 with the formation of Philadelphia International Records (PIR) and a distribution deal with CBS. Harold Melvin and the Blue Notes ("If You Don't Know Me By Now") and the O'Jays ("Back Stabbers," "Love Train") on PIR, the Stylistics ("You Make Me Feel Brand New") on Avco, and the Spinners ("Could It Be I'm Falling in Love") on Atlantic set the standard in black pop for the next few years. Southern soul yielded the velvety smooth Al Green ("Let's Stay Together," "I'm Still in Love with You"). Other artists like the Chicago-based Chi-Lites ("Oh Girl") and the ever-changing Isley Brothers ("That Lady") also followed suit. Soft soul was one of the most formative influences of the trend that would dominate the rest of the decade—disco.

Disco began as deejay-created medleys of existing (mostly African-American) dance records in black, Latino, and gay nightclubs. As it evolved into its own musical genre, its sources of inspiration came, to some extent, from self-contained funk bands such as Kool and the Gang ("Funky Stuff," "Jungle Boogie"), the Ohio Players ("Skin Tight," "Fire"), and Earth, Wind, and Fire ("Shining Star"), but more clearly from "soft soul" and the controlled energy of what came to be known as Eurodisco.

Most of the early disco releases in the United States were by black artists. Among those that made the rare crossover from clubs to radio were "Soul Makossa," an obscure French import by Manu Dibango, "Rock the Boat" by the Hues Corporation, and George McRae's "Rock Your Baby." The first disco hit to reach the charts as disco was Gloria Gaynor's "Never Can Say Good-bye" in 1974. Donna Summer's "Love to Love You Baby" moved disco closer to the surface. And by 1975 Van McCoy and the Soul City Orchestra had established the hustle as the most important new dance craze since the twist.

With the exception of deejay Frankie Crocker on WBLS in New York, disco was systematically excluded from radio. The music received its primary exposure in clubs, popularized only by the creative genius of the disco deejays. Initially shunned by the record companies, the club deejays had to make the rounds to each label individually in order to get records. Organizing themselves into "record pools," disco deejays quickly developed an alternative to the airplay marketing structure of the industry.

Disco's fanatical following turned out to be not only an underground party culture but also a significant record-buying public. By the mid-1970s, the pop charts were bursting with disco acts like the Silver Convention ("Fly, Robin, Fly," "Get Up and Boogie"), Hot Chocolate ("You Sexy Thing"), Wild Cherry ("Play That Funky Music"), K.C. and the Sunshine Band ("Shake Your Booty"), Rhythm Heritage ("Theme from S.W.A.T."), Sylvers ("Boogie Fever"), Johnny Taylor ("Disco Lady"), Maxine Nightingale ("Right Back Where We Started From"), the Emotions ("Best of My Love"), Thelma Houston ("Don't Leave Me This Way"), Rose Royce ("Car Wash"), Brick ("Dazz"), Hot ("Angel in Your Arms"), Taste of Honey ("Boogie Oogie Oogie"), Peter Brown ("Dance with Me"), Yvonne Elliman ("If I Can't Have You"), Chic ("Dance, Dance, Dance"), Heatwave ("The Groove Line"), and, of course, Donna Summer. Most of these acts were black.

The full commercial potential of disco was realized when WKTU, an obscure "soft rock" station in New York, converted to an all-disco format in 1978 and, within months, because the most listened-to station in the country. By 1979 there were some two hundred disco stations broadcasting in almost every major market. Disco records captured eight of the fourteen pop Grammy awards in 1979. Syndicated television programs like "Disco Magic" and "Dance Fever" brought the dance craze to the heartland. Some thirty-six million adults thrilled to the musical mixes of eight thousand professional deejays who serviced a portion of the estimated twenty thousand disco clubs. The phenomenon spawned a subindustry whose annual revenues ranged from $4 billion to $8 billion.

Because of disco's roots, the inevitable backlash had racial overtones. Slogans like "death to disco" and "disco sucks" were as much racial epithets as they were statements of musical preference. In the early 1980s, rock radio reasserted its primacy (and its racism) with a vengeance. Black-oriented radio was force to move in the direction of a new format—urban contemporary (UC). UC was multicultural in its original conception: black artists in the soul, funk, and jazz categories such as Stevie Wonder, Donna Summer, Rick JAMES, Third World, Funkadelic, Quincy JONES, and George BENSON remained central to a station's playlist, and white acts who fit the format like David Bowie or Hall and Oates were added. Paradoxically, UC may well have proven to be a net loss for black artists. While UC provided greater access for white musicians on what had been black-oriented stations, black performers did not gain any reciprocal access to rock radio.

More blatant acts of racial exclusion were occurring in video. In 1983 *People* magazine reported that "on MTV's current roster of some 800 acts, 16 are black." MTV's rejection of five Rick James videos at a time when his album *Street Songs* had sold almost four million copies was rivaled only by their initial reluctance to air even Michael JACKSON's "Beat It" and "Billy Jean" videos. New music video outlets formed in reaction to MTV's restrictive programming policies. Black Entertainment Television (BET) and the long-standing Soul Train provided the primary video exposure for black talent in the early 1980s. Ironically, Yo! MTV Raps subsequently became one of MTV's most popular offerings.

This restricted access for African-American artists occurred during the first recession in the music business since the late 1940s. Recovery, beginning in 1983, was signaled by the multiplatinum, worldwide success of Michael Jackson's *Thriller,* with international sales of some forty million units, making it the largest-selling record of all time. *Thriller* began a trend toward blockbuster LPs featuring a limited number of superstar artists as the solution to the industry's economic woes. Interestingly, quite a few of these superstars—Michael Jackson, PRINCE, Lionel Richie, Tina TURNER, and others—were African Americans.

The phenomenal pop successes of these artists immediately catapulted them into an upper-level industry infrastructure fully owned and operated by whites. In this rarified atmosphere, they were confronted with considerable pressure to sever their ties with the attorneys, managers, booking agents, and promoters who may have been responsible for building their careers in the first place. "Aside from Sammy DAVIS, Jr., Nancy WILSON, and Stephanie Mills," said Nelson George, citing a 1984 *Ebony* story, there were "no other black household names with black management. . . . Michael Jackson, Lionel Richie, Prince, Luther Vandross, the Pointer Sisters, Earth, Wind and Fire, Ray Parker, Jr., and Donna Summer all relied on white figures for guidance" (George 1988, p. 177).

Following their pop successes, these artists were further distinguished from less successful black colleagues in that they were now marketed directly to the mainstream audience, a practice that has since proven successful even with the debut releases of artists like Whitney Houston and Mariah Carey.

A number of cross-racial, pop-oriented duets—Stevie Wonder and Paul McCartney ("Ebony and Ivory"), Michael Jackson and Paul McCartney ("The Girl Is Mine," "Say Say Say"), Diana ROSS and Julio Iglesias ("All of You"), James Ingram and Kenny Rogers ("What About Me?"), Dionne WARWICK and Friends ("That's What Friends Are For"), Patti La-Belle and Michael McDonald ("On My Own"), Aretha Franklin and George Michael ("I Knew You Were Waiting for Me"), and James Ingram and Linda Ronstadt ("Somewhere Out There")—brought a new dimension to the term "crossover." Michael Jackson's and Lionel Richie's "We Are The World" (1985)—the ultimate crossover recording—initiated the phenomenon of "charity rock."

It remained for rap to take African-American music back to the streets (*see* RAP). Rap, one cultural element in the larger hip-hop subculture, began in the South Bronx at about the same time as disco, but, given its place of origin, the movement developed in almost complete isolation for more than five years. In the late 1970s, hip hop was "discovered" in turn by the music business, the print media, and the film industry. Through films like the low-budget *Wild Style* and the blockbuster *Flashdance,* followed by *Breakin'* and *Beat Street,* hip hop was brought to the attention of a mass audience.

In the mid-1980s, early hip-hop culture heroes like Afrika Bambaataa, Kool Herc, and Grandmaster Flash passed the baton to a second generation of artists such as Whodini, the Force MDs, the Fat Boys, and Run-D.M.C., who recorded the first gold rap album, *Run-D.M.C.* (1984). This was a new wrinkle for rap, which had always been based on 12-inch singles. In the relative absence of radio play, even on black radio, rap artists such as Run-D.M.C., UTFO, L.L. Cool J, Whodini, Heavy D. & the Boyz, Salt-n-Pepa, and the Fat Boys made significant inroads into the album and cassette market. Eight of *Billboard*'s top thirty black albums for the week of November 28, 1987, were rap albums. Other rappers also found success in television (the Fresh Prince) and films (Ice-T, Ice Cube).

Beginning as a street movement, rap was initially produced by independent labels, some of which (the notorious Sugar Hill, which has since faded from the scene, and Russell Simmons's Def Jam) were black-owned, all of which were independently distributed. In signing Curtis Blow, Mercury was the only major label to take a chance on rap before it was a proven commodity. Mainstream success, however, demanded the kind of national distribution provided by the major labels. In the mid-1980s, Columbia Records concluded a custom label deal with Def Jam, Jive Records entered into distribution arrangements with both RCA and Arista, Cold Chillin' Records signed a distribution deal with Warner (who also bought a piece of Tommy Boy), Delicious Vinyl entered into a national distribution deal with Island, and Priority contracted with Capitol for national distribution (Garofalo 1990, pp. 116–117).

Roundly criticized for violence, sexism, and bigotry, rap has endeavored to clean up its image while becoming the main target in the controversy over censorship. Following the lead of Nelson George, a number of rap groups including Stetsasonic, Boogie Down Productions, and Public Enemy among others initiated the Stop the Violence Movement aimed specifically at black-on-black crime. West Coast rappers followed with "We're All in the Same Gang." Artists such as Queen Latifah and Salt-n-Pepa have offered a female—if not a feminist—corrective to abusive sexual rantings. Still, highly politicized rappers like Public Enemy and NWA remain controversial, even as they sell millions of records to black as well as white teenagers.

Rap is unique in that it is the only form of African-American popular music that has become more Afrocentric as it has gained in mainstream acceptance. A cursory look at rap's audience also points to a generation gap within the black audience. Nowhere is this separation more apparent than in black radio, which has avoided even completely uncontroversial rap that clearly outsells other selections on their playlists. These stations seem to be making aesthetic and, in some cases, moral judgments that may well run counter to their economic self-interest. Such decisions indicate that rap has become the most visible manifestation of the age and, to a great extent, class differences within the African-American community, even as it bridges the gap among the races.

REFERENCES

CHARTERS, SAMUEL. *The Country Blues.* New York, 1959.

GAROFALO, REEBEE. "Crossing Over, 1939–1992." In Jannette L. Dates and William Barlow, eds. *Split Image: African Americans in the Mass Media.* 2nd ed. Washington, D.C., 1990, pp. 57–127.

GEORGE, NELSON. *The Death of Rhythm & Blues.* New York, 1988.

GILLETT, CHARLIE. *The Sound of the City.* New York, 1970.

GUARALNICK, PETER. *Sweet Soul Music.* New York, 1986.

JONES, LEROI (AMIRI BARAKA). *Blues People.* New York, 1963.

SOUTHERN, EILEEN. *The Music of Black Americans: A History*. New York, 1971.

REEBEE GAROFALO

Rector, Eddie (December 25, 1898–1962), tap dancer. In the early 1920s, this genteel tap soloist perfected a new style of stage dancing that dovetailed one step into another in a seamless flow of sound and movement. Graceful, impeccably dressed, Rector traversed the stage, each motion shaped into a beautiful image. Famous for his sand dance (throwing sand on the floor, the dancer uses the sand's abrasive sounds to amplify his rhythms, whispering like wire brushes on snare drums), and the waltz clog (a delicate style of tap set to a ¾ waltz tempo), Rector is credited with inventing the slap step, and a charming traveling time step called the bambalina. Using his entire body, Rector's dancing emphasized clean, precise footwork.

Born in Orange, N.J., Rector, like many others, began dancing in the children's backup chorus in Mayme Remington's vaudeville act when he was fifteen. In 1914 he played the role of Red Cap Sam in *The Darktown Follies,* then worked on the black vaudeville circuit with partner Toots Davis. He developed his own style, dancing the cakewalk at Coney Island and the Charleston at the Roseland Ballroom. He started in the chorus line and worked up to his own specialty dance in *Darktown Follies of 1916,* in which he was featured in a smooth military routine. Billed as "the Boy in Gray," he wore a top hat and tails—everything was pearl gray, even his spats—and performed his waltz clog routine across the stage and back. In *Dixie to Broadway* (1924), he danced the bambalina with an imaginary partner. He worked with a partner, Ralph COOPER, at Connie's Inn club in Harlem during the late 1920s, tapping out a precise military-drill routine; then he worked with Duke ELLINGTON at the COTTON CLUB, tapping on a big drum, and was a featured dancer in *Hot Rhythm* (1930), *Rhapsody in Black* (1931), *Blackberries of '32,* and *Yeah Man* (1932). His meticulous elegance represented the highest quality of tapping, while his debonair personal performance helped to define the mode of the class acts that would develop shortly thereafter.

REFERENCE

STEARNS, MARSHALL and JEAN STEARNS. *Jazz Dance: The Story of American Vernacular Dance*. New York, 1968.

CONSTANCE VALIS HILL

Redding, Jay Saunders (October 13, 1906–March 2, 1988), writer. Born and raised in a middle-class family in Wilmington, Del., J. Saunders Redding attended Lincoln University in Pennsylvania for one year before transferring to Brown University, where he received his Ph.B. (Bachelor of Philosophy) in 1928 and his M.A. in 1932; afterward, he studied at Columbia University for one year on a graduate fellowship. Redding began his career teaching English at a series of colleges and universities: Morehouse College in Atlanta (1928–1931), Louisville Municipal College (1934–1936), and Southern University in Baton Rouge, La., where he was chair of the English department (1936–1938).

After publication of *To Make a Poet Black* (1939), a critical study unique in its time for its examination of African-American literature from the perspective of a black scholar, the Rockefeller Foundation awarded Redding a fellowship to write *No Day of Triumph* (1942), an exploration of the condition of African Americans in the South. The partly autobiographical book was a critical success, and established Redding's reputation as an acute observer of social realities who spoke eloquently both to black and white Americans about the struggles and the achievements of African Americans. In 1943, Redding returned to teaching, this time as a professor at the Hampton Institute in Virginia, where he remained until 1966, and subsequently at George Washington University (1968–1970) and at Cornell University (1970–1975; as professor emeritus, 1975–1988). He also served as an official of the National Endowment for the Humanities (1966–1970), and as a State Department–sponsored lecturer at colleges and universities in India (1952), Africa (1962), and South America (1977).

During his career, Redding wrote ten books, among them a novel, *Stranger and Alone* (1950), and several sociohistorical studies, including *They Came in Chains: Americans from Africa* (1950), *An American in India* (1954), and *The Negro* (1967). He coedited two anthologies, *Reading for Writing* (1952), with Ivan E. Taylor, and *Cavalcade: Negro American Writing from 1760 to the Present* (1971), with Arthur P. Davis. Redding's many articles and book reviews have appeared in anthologies and in such periodicals as *The Atlantic Monthly, The Saturday Review, The Nation, The North American Review,* and *American Heritage.* While denying neither the specificity of his perspective nor his abiding interest in the experience and culture of African Americans, Redding continually stressed in his works the necessity for full integration of African Americans into the larger community.

Redding received many awards and honorary degrees for his work, including two Guggenheim fellowships (1944–1945 and 1959–1960), a citation from the National Urban League (1950), a Ford Foundation fellowship (1964–1965), and honorary degrees from Brown University (1963), Virginia State College (1963), Hobart College (1964), the University of Portland (1970), Wittenberg University (1977), Dickinson College, and the University of Delaware. Redding died in Ithaca, N.Y., at the age of seventy-one.

REFERENCES

DAVIS, ARTHUR P. *From the Dark Tower: Afro-American Writers, 1900–1960.* Washington, D.C., 1974.

METZGER, LINDA, ed. *Black Writers: A Selection of Sketches from Contemporary Authors.* Detroit, Mich., 1989.

THOMPSON, THELMA BARNABY. "J. Saunders Redding." In *Dictionary of Literary Biography. Vol. 76. Afro-American Writers, 1940–1955.* Detroit, Mich., 1988.

WAGNER, JEAN. *Black Poets of the United States: From Paul Lawrence Dunbar to Langston Hughes.* Trans. Kenneth Douglas. Urbana, Ill., 1973.

STEVEN J. LESLIE

ALEXIS WALKER

Redding, Otis (September 9, 1941–December 10, 1967), soul singer and composer. Otis Redding was one of the most powerful and original singer-songwriters of the 1960s and the mainstay of Stax Records, the Memphis label that became internationally successful releasing gritty southern soul. Born in Dawson, Ga., Redding grew up in Macon, 100 miles to the north. He began playing drums in school and was paid six dollars an hour on Sundays to accompany gospel groups appearing on local radio station WIBB. Redding stayed in school until the tenth grade (1957), but quit to help support his family, working variously at a gas station, as a well-digger, and occasionally as a musician. As a singer, he began to win local talent contests with his spontaneous and tough vocal style. He traveled to Los Angeles in mid-1960, where he recorded four songs, and returned to Macon in 1961, where he cut "Shout Bamalama" for the Confederate label, a minor hit that received airplay on area radio stations. His break came in 1963, when he sang his song "These Arms of Mine" at a Stax recording session of Johnny Jenkins and the Pinetoppers, a group for whom he was guest vocalist and chauffeur. When the record made it into the Rhythm-and-Blues Top Twenty in 1964, Redding's career was launched. Over the next five years, his popularity grew steadily through fiery live performances, hit singles such as "I've Been Loving You Too Long,"

"Try a Little Tenderness," and "I Can't Turn You Loose," and critically acclaimed LPs such as *Otis Blue, The Soul Album,* and *The Great Otis Redding Sings Soul Ballads.* Like Aretha FRANKLIN (who immortalized his song "Respect"), Redding was able to capitalize on the liberal climate of the 1960s, crossing over to white listeners on both sides of the Atlantic. His performances in England in early 1967 so enthralled audiences that he was subsequently named Best Male Vocalist in a poll sponsored by the music publication *Melody Maker,* an accolade won by Elvis Presley the previous eight years. Later in 1967, nestled between rock acts, he captivated an audience of 55,000 at the Monterey Pop Festival in California, one of the milestones of the hippie era. His death in a plane crash near Madison, Wis., on December 10, 1967, came at the peak of his career, and left fans wondering what might have been: "(Sittin' on) The Dock of the Bay," recorded three days before his death, revealed a different, introspective musical direction. It became his biggest record, heading the pop charts for four weeks and becoming a posthumous signature song.

REFERENCE

GURALNICK, PETER. "Otis Redding" and "Stax Goes to Europe/The Big O Comes Home: Triumph and Tragedy." In *Sweet Soul Music.* New York, 1986, pp. 133–152, 308–332.

BUD KLIMENT

Red Summer. "Red Summer" was the term coined in 1919 by NAACP investigator James Weldon JOHNSON to describe the summer and early fall of that year, when twenty-five race riots and other racially based incidents erupted across the United States—the largest in Charleston, S.C.; Washington, D.C.; Chicago; Knoxville, Tenn.; Omaha, Nebr.; and Elaine, Ark. Although the riots had different immediate causes, they had many common roots.

Tensions between blacks and whites were high in the aftermath of WORLD WAR I. Overly rapid demobilization and the end of price controls led to inflation and unemployment. Whites in the North were angered and frightened by the presence of blacks who had migrated during the war, and white Southerners were aroused by blacks' new self-confidence and willingness to challenge the racial status quo. Black soldiers came home from Europe, where they had been treated as equals by the French (one black unit was decorated for bravery), expecting gratitude and employment opportunity. They received neither. There were seventy-six lynchings in a month and a half, a dozen of them of black veterans still in uniform. Racial tensions were augmented by the postwar anti-Bolshevik "red scare." Whites feared radicalism and reacted hysterically to rumors of subversion. Attempts at social change, particularly in the racial status quo, were stigmatized as "radical" and "subversive."

The riots themselves were generally white-instigated affairs, generated by real or fictitious black challenges to white authority. However, unlike most earlier racial disturbances, blacks often actively resisted white violence, and shot and beat white attackers. Radical black leaders such as A. Philip RANDOLPH gave speeches and wrote articles proclaiming blacks' right to commit violence in self-defense.

Red Summer, though brief, convinced many African Americans that their participation in a war for democracy did not mean that white domination in America was going to disappear. The events pushed many blacks into militant action. Some blacks responded by redoubling their commitment to civil rights protest. Others supported black nationalist leaders, notably Marcus GARVEY.

REFERENCE

TUTTLE, WILLIAM M., JR. *Race Riot: Chicago in the Red Summer of 1919.* New York, 1970.

ALANA J. ERICKSON

Reed, Ishmael (February 22, 1938–), author. Ishmael Reed was born in Chattanooga, Tenn., but was raised and educated in Buffalo, N.Y. In high school he discovered the writings of Nathanael West, whose black comedy influenced his own distinctive expressionistic style, and later, at the University of Buffalo (1956–1960), he discovered the works of William Butler Yeats and William Blake, who taught him the importance of creating personal mythological systems. In 1962 he moved to New York City to become a writer. While living on the Lower East Side he encountered a group of young black writers, including Calvin Hernton, David Henderson, and Askia Muhammad Toure, from *Umbra* magazine and workshop, who convinced him of the importance of black literature. His first novel, *Free-Lance Pallbearers* (1967), a parody of Ralph Ellison's *Invisible Man,* is a savage satire of the United States during the Vietnam War years, personified by the President, Harry Sam, who literally eats American children.

In 1967, Reed moved to Berkeley Calif., where he cofounded and published *The Yardbird Reader* (1972–1976), which reflected his new multiethnic spirit, engendered by his move to the multicultural West

Ishmael Reed in 1977. Many of Reed's novels of African-American life combine a sardonic critique of black and American institutions with a finely honed sense of both the comic and the surreal. (© Leandre Jackson)

Coast. His second novel, *Yellow Back Radio Broke-Down* (1969), a surreal western, introduces the theme of the repressive forces of western culture embattled against the life-affirming forces of black culture, which have survived the Middle Passage from Africa to the New World. In this novel Reed presents voodoo religion as a source of authentic black folk culture and values. His next novel, *Mumbo Jumbo* (1972), initiates his countermythology. He argues that there is a conspiracy at the core of the western tradition: Its mythology preaches the glory of the West at the expense of all other cultures. Therefore it is imperative, for Reed, to revise this mythology so that he can expose the lies of the western tradition and affirm the virtues of African civilizations, including Egypt. In later creative works his countermythology, which he usually calls Neo-HooDooism, will draw on many non-European cultures, including Haitian, Black-American, and Native-American. In 1976 Reed cofounded the Before Columbus Foundation, devoted to the dissemination of multicultural literature. *Flight to Canada* (1976), his fifth novel, is a modern slave narrative, defining freedom as the ability to tell one's own story instead of allowing it to be appropriated by alien and hostile cultures. With *Reckless Eyeballing* (1986) Reed continues his exploration of freedom in the explosive area of sexual politics, where he argues against white feminist hegemony. In 1993 he published his ninth novel *Japanese by Spring,* which parodies black neoconservatism and multiethnic abuse of power by the powerful whether they are white, black or yellow.

Even though Reed is known primarily as a novelist, he has produced a number of books of poetry and essays. (He also has had several plays produced, including *Mother Hubbard* (1981) and *Savage Wilds* (1989).) Among his poetry collections are *Conjure* (1972), *Chattanooga* (1974), *A Secretary to the Spirits* (1978), and *New and Collected Poems* (1988). Mostly in free verse, these poems are experimental, humorous, and satiric. In his poetry, as in his fiction, he creates a countermythology, drawing on many non-European cultures for its symbolism. Reed's four books of essays are *Shrovetide in Old New Orleans* (1978), *God Made Alaska for the Indians* (1982), *Writin' Is Fightin': Thirty-Seven Years of Boxing on Paper* (1988), and *Airing Dirty Laundry* (1993). In his essays he tries to refute false and pernicious myths about black people. In recent years he has focused more on black men than on African Americans in general, arguing that they are in a particularly precarious position in American society: that indeed, they are everybody's scapegoat for the evils of the civilization. Reed's impassioned polemics in defense of black men have catapulted him into the center of many heated debates with both black and white feminists. Since all of Reed's works spring from the same individual vision, both the poems and essays help the reader clarify the more significant novels.

Reed is a major innovative writer who relentlessly uses comedy and satire to show the myopia, egotism, and brutality of eurocentric culture. Yet he does not let black culture off scot-free; he criticizes individual blacks when they do not live up to the ideals of freedom and creativity that he finds inherent in the African-American tradition. His critique of the West is often more subtle and penetrating than that of many scholars and is always much more amusing.

REFERENCES

BYERMAN, KEITH E. *Fingering the Jagged Grain.* Athens, Ga., 1985.

FOX, ROBERT ELLIOT. *Conscientious Sorcerers.* Westport, Conn., 1987.

MARTIN, REGINALD. *Ishmael Reed and the New Black Aesthetic Critics.* New York, 1988.

WILLIAM J. HARRIS

Reed, Willis (June 25, 1942–), basketball player, coach, and general manager. A native of Bernice, La., Willis Reed attended Grambling State University in Grambling, La., where he starred as the bas-

A jubilant Willis Reed in 1973 leads his New York Knicks teammates into the locker room after winning the NBA championship against the Los Angeles Lakers. Reed was the center on the exciting Knick teams of the late 1960s and early '70s that captured two NBA titles. (AP/Wide World Photos)

ketball team's center. After his senior year in 1964, Reed was drafted in the second round by the New York Knickerbockers. For his stellar first season of 1964–1965, the 6'10" Reed was named an NBA All-Star and Rookie of the Year. The following season Reed was moved to forward, where he played at All-Star level for two seasons before being moved back to center during the 1967–1968 season. In 1967 Reed was named team captain of the Knicks. Reed remained with the Knicks through the end of his career in 1974. He played on two championship teams, in 1970 and 1973, and was named to the NBA All-Star team seven times. He is remembered most for his play and leadership in the decisive seventh game of the 1970 championship series against the Los Angeles Lakers. After leaving the fifth game with a hip injury and torn muscles in his right thigh, Reed returned to the court in Madison Square Garden for the seventh game, and though he scored only four points, inspired his team to a 113–99 victory. Following the playoffs, Reed became the first player in NBA history to be named Most Valuable Player for the regular season, playoffs, and All-Star game in the same season. Reed also won the MVP award for the 1972–1973 playoffs, when he again led the Knicks to a championship. After suffering several injury-plagued seasons, Reed retired as a player in 1974.

Reed was named head coach of the Knicks in 1977, but was fired after one and a half seasons. Following a string of appointments as assistant coach for NBA teams and as head coach at Creighton University from 1983 to 1987, Reed was hired in the middle of the 1987–1988 season as head coach of the New Jersey Nets. In 1989, he was moved to the Nets' front office to serve as club vice president and general manager. Reed was inducted into the Basketball Hall of Fame in 1981.

REFERENCES

REED, WILLIS. *A View from the Rim.* Philadelphia, 1971.

———. *A Will to Win.* New York, 1973.

LINDA SALZMAN

Reformed Church in America, The. Black people first entered New York City in 1628, the same year the first minister of the Dutch Reformed Church, the Rev. Jonas Michaelius, arrived in New York. The Reformed Church was no different from the colonial Anglican Church and the Roman Catholic Church in its acceptance of slavery as an institution. In his important book *Religion and Trade in New Netherlands,* George L. Smith expresses surprise that the Dutch accepted slavery so readily in New York and New Jersey, when slavery was not legalized in the Netherlands in the sixteenth and seventeenth centuries. He asks: "Why, then, did they so quickly resort to slavery as a scheme of social and economic organization within the Colonies?" (Smith 1973, p. 126). His reply was that the Dutch chose slavery because it was the path of least resistance. However, Smith's answer simplifies the problem.

The truth regarding the Dutch Reformed Church's response to slavery is much more complex. In his article "The Dutch Reformed Church and Negro Slavery in Colonial America" (De Jong 1971, pp. 423–436), Professor Gerald Francis De Jong points out that African slaves provided a ready-made labor force for the Dutch farmers who lived in the Hudson, Raritan, and Minisink valleys of New Jersey. According to De Jong, the Dutch Reformed were among the greatest users of African slaves in New York and New Jersey. Smith informs us that while the ministers were under the supervision of the "Classis" of Amsterdam, "they were in the financial employ of the India Company themselves; which meant that their salaries were in part made possible by the profits of the slave trade" (Smith 1973, p. 126).

In 1652, Peter Stuyvesant, the Director General of New Netherlands, was advised to import directly from Africa as many Africans as the colony needed for the cultivation of the soil. There were a few ministers, among them the Rev. Jacobus Hondius, who in 1679 criticized the slave trade; but most took the position of the Rev. Godfried Ademans, who argued in 1640 that slavery was compatible with Christianity and that the task of the Church was to minister to the soul.

There was no appreciable change in the relationship of the Reformed Church in America toward people of African descent in the eighteenth and nineteenth centuries. Although there were occasional black persons like William Johnson, who was accepted for training as a minister at the New Brunswick Theological Seminary, it was not until the twentieth century that the Church hammered out its commitment in terms of supporting missions to black people and administering a school for black youngsters at Brewton, Ala. The attitude of the Church during the seventeenth and eighteenth centuries was that the liturgy and preaching of the Reformed Church in America was too intellectually demanding for black people. Further, the Church was severely divided over the issue of slavery as an institution.

It was not until the 1950s, when black people in large numbers started to migrate North for economic opportunities and began to attend the Reformed Churches in the inner cities, that the Church was forced to respond to the black presence. The migration of black people from the South, coupled with the push for integration, which was heralded by the CIVIL RIGHTS MOVEMENT led by the Rev. Dr. Martin Luther KING, JR., forced the Church to deal with the black presence which had infiltrated the churches in many inner cities. During the fifties and sixties, the Church responded with a mission in East Harlem and the sponsoring of storefront churches throughout New York City.

To deal with the needs of its black constituency, the Synod of 1969 asked the black membership to establish a Black Council to empower the black membership and to see that their needs were met. In 1972 the Reverend William Moses Howard was appointed executive director of the Black Council and has led it into the 1990s. He has spoken of the role of the Council as a reconciling force in the Reformed Church in America. In defining its purpose within the Reformed Church in America the Council stated: "We, the members of the Black Council, as peers of all other members of the Church, shall seek to reconcile the Church to all of God's people by leading the Church in a ministry to the holistic needs of Black people both within the Church family and beyond."

REFERENCES

DE JONG, GERALD FRANCIS. "The Dutch Reformed Church and Negro Slavery in Colonial America." *Church History* 40:1 (March 1971), 423–436.

ERSKINE, NOEL LEO. *Black People and the Reformed Church in America.* Lansing, Mich., 1978.

SMITH, GEORGE L. *Religion and Trade in New Netherland.* Ithaca, N.Y., 1973.

NOEL LEO ERSKINE

Reggae.   A type of popular music that originated in Jamaica and became successful worldwide, reggae is characterized by a loping yet insistent bass rhythm. Performed largely by black musicians, reggae's appeal in America has traditionally been colorblind, finding favor originally with white listeners and then, more recently, with a core black audience.

Origins

Besides such local musical influences as calypso and mento, reggae has roots in American rhythm and blues, particularly those records made in New Orleans in the 1950s, which Jamaicans enjoyed via U. S. radio broadcasts and on "sound systems," mobile discos where records were played for dancing. To satisfy local demand, competitive sound system promoters such as Duke Reid and Clement Dodd began using primitive equipment to cut their own records, featuring island singers and musicians. Regional playing styles worked a kind of musical alchemy: the local musicians' attempts to simulate American R&B repeatedly came out skewed—they accented the second and fourth beats each measure rather than the first and third. The result, however, was no less appealing to island listeners, and the characteristic reggae rhythm was born. On the first records, released in the early 1960s, this rhythm was accelerated and the music was called "ska," after the scratchy guitar sound which propelled the songs. In subsequent years the rhythm grew slower: at medium tempo, it was called "rock steady"; then, finally, at its slowest, "reggae," after the 1968 release "Do the Reggay" by Toots and the Maytals.

Evolution

As in most popular music, the general term "reggae" actually encompasses many different styles. Two of the most distinctive, "dub reggae" and "deejaying" (also called "toasting"), began to flourish in the late 1960s and early '70s and became synonymous with the music, contributing significantly to its subsequent success, particularly in America. "Dub" refers to versions of reggae songs that have been doctored in the recording studio with echo and other sounds, records on which the vocal and instrumental tracks drop in and out suddenly and the booming bass and percussion tracks dominate. Originating on the "B" sides of reggae 45s, dub evolved considerably through the efforts of such innovative producers as Lee Perry and Augustus Pablo, who in primitive recording studios transformed existing songs into unusual aural collages.

"Toasting," on the other hand, originated live with sound systems, when disk jockeys began to chant boastfully and rhythmically over records to encourage dancers, imitating the staccato chatter of American radio DJs. While remarkably similar to rap music, toasting actually emerged and was recorded years earlier, the specialty of such flamboyant reggae stars as U-Roy and Big Youth. It has even been speculated that records of toasting reggae DJs, played, sold, and heard in the 1970s in American cities with large concentrations of West Indian immigrants (such as New York City) directly influenced the birth of domestic RAP.

The Rastafarian Influence

Paralleling its musical development, certain reggae lyrics began reflecting specific aspects of Jamaican life and culture. By the late 1960s, besides the songs of sex and romance common to all pop music, reggae performers sang about "rude boys" (local street toughs), the harsh lives of the local underclass, and, most notably, the RASTAFARIAN religious sect. Followers of the sect, called Rastas, wore their uncut hair in thick, matted dreadlocks, smoked marijuana as a sacrament, and revered Emperor Haile Selassie of Ethiopia as a god, because of a prediction attributed to back-to-Africa advocate Marcus GARVEY—that a black king, crowned in Africa, would be the Redeemer. Elusively complicated, with roots in mysticism as well as the Bible, Rastafarianism had been present in Jamaica since the 1930s, offering impoverished believers spiritual identity and solace by reaffirming that Africa was their true homeland, and that the captor Babylon (the ruling class or material world) must inevitably fall. Since many Jamaican musicians were Rastafarian, its terminology and beliefs were often incorporated into reggae songs. While uniquely characteristic of the music, reggae's use of Rastafarianism corresponds on a basic level to the message of heavenly deliverance found in American SPIRITUALS, and to the earthly transcendence and catharsis provided by the BLUES.

From Jamaica to the United States

Most of the Americans who discovered reggae in the 1970s were introduced to it in one of two forms. The first, *The Harder They Come,* was a 1972 Jamaican feature film directed by Perry Henzell that starred singer Jimmy Cliff as Ivan Martin, a country boy turned pop star and outlaw. Part comic book and part western, with a percolating reggae sound track, the film found a niche at midnight showings in college towns and art cinemas around the country, where it ran for several years, giving domestic viewers a vibrant first glimpse of the gritty, vibrant world of Jamaican pop. At about the same time, Americans also discovered reggae in the person of Bob Marley and the Wailers. In a career that extended from 1964 until his death from cancer in 1981, Marley was the key individual in the popularization of reggae. Through his many brilliant albums of protest and love songs (including *Catch a Fire, Natty Dread,* and *Exodus*) and his highly charged concert tours, the singer-songwriter became the face, voice, and symbol of reggae for most of the world.

The Changing American Audience

Ironically, reggae's core audience in America was at first comprised largely of white rock fans, who responded to its exoticism, its rocklike drive, and its messages of alienation. They had also heard it first: reggae's earliest inroads beyond Jamaica had been via rock-oriented radio, first in the guise of novelties like the ska song "My Boy Lollipop" or the rock-steady classic "Israelites," hits during the 1960s, and later as audible influences in the work of such premier rock artists as Paul Simon and Eric Clapton. Rock's fascination with reggae reached an apex in the late 1970s, with the international emergence of the new wave-punk rock movement. While many punks voiced solidarity with the inflammatory and apocalyptic aspects of Rastafarianism, reggae's influence was most audible in the new-style rock, which adopted many of its rhythms and recording techniques, especially dub.

In the 1980s and '90s, reggae's black audience in the United States began to increase sizably, due in part to the country's escalating West Indian immigrant population and also to a growing interest in the Afrocentric ideals the music often expresses and reflects. But the primary reason for reggae's catching on with African-American listeners is a musical one: the dominance on the charts of "dancehall style," fast-talking toasting that rose concurrently and intersects considerably with rap music, spawning such intercultural stars as Shabba Ranks.

As reggae's audience shifts and grows, developments in the music have paralleled those in other forms of pop—traditional instrumentation, for instance, has been increasingly replaced by electronic keyboards and percussion. Nevertheless, reggae's widespread popularity in America seems secure, buoyed by the growing interest in all international musics (called "World Beat") that it anticipated.

REFERENCES

DAVIS, STEPHEN, and PETER SIMON. *Reggae Bloodlines.* New York, 1979.

———. *Reggae International.* New York, 1982.

THOMAS, MICHAEL. "Reggae: The Wild Side of Paradise." In *What's That Sound?* New York, 1976, pp. 326–350.

WARD, ED. "Reggae." In *The Rolling Stone Illustrated History of Rock & Roll.* New York, 1980, pp. 445–450.

BUD KLIMENT

Religion.   Carter G. WOODSON, founder of the ASSOCIATION FOR THE STUDY OF NEGRO LIFE AND HISTORY, wrote in 1939: "A definitive history of the Negro Church . . . would leave practically no phase of the history of the Negro in America untouched." Understanding African-American religion—or more accurately, the religious history of peoples of African descent in North America—is crucial for any rounded view of the African-American experience. Religion is often inseparable from culture, as was the case in traditional Africa, and encompasses more than institutional expressions. B. B. KING once said that he felt closest to God when he was singing the BLUES, and African-American art, dance, and literature incorporate and reflect symbols, values, and themes. This essay will focus primarily on some of the principal issues in the study of African-American religious history and culture.

Early historical work on African-American religion, such as that of Carter G. Woodson on "the Negro Church," focused almost exclusively on the institutional history of Protestantism. Yet to view African-American religious history as merely another chapter in the expansion of European Christianity would be to ignore the special circumstances of the religious pilgrimage of African Americans and gloss over the impact of other religious traditions.

Slave Religion

Most Africans who were brought into the colonies of British North America originated from the coast and interior of West and West-Central Africa. Approximately 60 percent of the slaves imported into the territory later known as the United States arrived between 1720 and 1780. Legal United States involvement in the international SLAVE TRADE ended in 1808. Unlike what occurred in much of the New World, the growth of the slave population in the American South was largely by natural increase, and the end of the slave trade did little to retard the increase of the African-American population. In 1825 the United

States had approximately 36 percent (1,750,000) of the slave population in the New World, despite the dramatic increase in the arrival of new imports. For many slaves, knowledge of AFRICA was acquired indirectly and was only one of many cultural influences. Therefore, an understanding of the formative influences on the religious experience of African Americans, while recognizing the importance of the African cultural base, must take into account the New World cultural experience. The formation of an African-American culture was a long historical process, an evolution over time.

Close examination reveals that differences within African-American religious culture are as important as similarities. The religious outlook of someone of African descent in the low country of Carolina and Georgia about 1710, before the impact of the Great Awakening, might understandably be different from that of someone subject to the religious instruction of a white Presbyterian clergyman active in organized plantation missions after 1829. The religious profiles of a member of the Mother Bethel African Methodist Church in Philadelphia in 1880, a communicant of St. Cyprian's Roman Catholic Church in Chicago in 1924, of Zion Baptist Church in rural Mississippi in 1954, and of the Pentacostal C.H. Mason Temple in Memphis today will have significant differences. Generalizations about African-American religion must account for changes over time, geographic variables, and differing population demographics.

Regional geography is an important qualifying factor in understanding the uniqueness of the African-American religious experience in the United States. *Vaudou* in Haiti, the Trinidadian cult of *Shango,* the practices of *santeria* in Cuba, and the *candomble* rituals found in Brazil exemplify a high degree of syncretism between West African traditions and Euro-Christian, principally ROMAN CATHOLIC, culture. In contrast, Africans who were brought or born into the predominantly British environment of North America were more likely to adapt or remodel their religious beliefs and practices in terms of the prevailing regional religious culture—low church Protestant Evangelicalism. Except for the Sea Islands of the Georgia coast (*see* GULLAHS), and a few other places where African slaves were isolated from the dominant white society, the children and grandchildren of those who survived the ordeal of the MIDDLE PASSAGE created a new syncretic religious worldview in America.

Traditional African languages had no single word for *religion*—religion was synonymous with the way of life. Importing Africans into the New World marked a transference of African ways of perceiving and responding to the spirit world, but just how strongly Africanisms survived is subject to debate.

Proponents of the retention of African beliefs and practices point to spirit possession, musical forms, dance patterns such as the "ring shout," mounded-grave decorations, conjuring practices, and the identification of African divinities with specific saints in Roman Catholic folk piety as evidence of the survival of African traditional religion in the New World. The slaves' preference for the baptismal ritual of total immersion ("river baptisms") is often cited as an especially strong link with the West African river cults.

Other scholars have taken the view that traditional African beliefs and practices gradually weakened and in some cases died as the result of the complex interplay of forced acculturation, voluntary adaptation, and assimilation. The terrors of the Middle Passage called into question the omnipotence of the African gods and the ability of the ancestors to come to the aid of the distressed. Dealers in slaves intentionally broke up families and kinship groups and sought to create cultural anomie and linguistic confusion among the new arrivals. Slave buyers shunned the purchase of individuals who had operated as religious specialists in Africa and waged a destructive campaign against all religious practices, including the use of ritual drums, that might serve as the focal point for the reconstruction of traditional African social groups on the plantations.

African slaves in the New World did not receive intensive indoctrination in Christianity for several generations. Europeans at first doubted that Africans had souls worth saving, and owners of slaves in the English colonies initially opposed the introduction of Christianity, not only because of lingering doubts about the religious capacity of the African, but also because of fears that offering baptism to Africans implied spiritual equality and might spark resistance. European missionaries, such as those of the Society for the Propagation of the Gospel that sponsored preaching among Africans in the Carolinas, persisted, and over time converts were made. The conflict between proponents of chattel slavery and the church diminished after the mid-1600s, when new laws partially relieved owners' anxieties by stating that baptism did not alter the civil estate of a slave. By 1706 at least six colonies had legislation stipulating that baptism did not make any change in the slave's status "as to his bondage, or freedom."

In the New World environment, Africans adapted and transformed European language and religious beliefs and in the process created a new African-American identity. The southern-born children and grandchildren of the Africans who participated in the transatlantic passage had to find religious meaning and seek religious expression within the predominantly white Protestant evangelical environment. The outburst of religious revivals in the 1740s and again in the early 1800s helped dismantle the colonial establishment of Anglicanism in the South and Congregationalism in New England and proved attractive to many African Americans, slave and free. Black converts and lower-class whites shared in the evangelical emphasis on conviction of sin, individual salvation, ecstatic worship, and the recompense of heaven.

An African-American Christian population of significant size and, in some places, of surprising independence developed during and after the AMERICAN REVOLUTION. Most black Christians belonged to mixed congregations where the egalitarian legacy of the Great Revival lingered on, despite inroads made by white racism among evangelicals. Independent African-American preachers, such as the Rev. Andrew BRYAN of the First African Church of Savannah, established in 1788, planted numerous congregations, mostly BAPTIST, until a frightened white South curbed the religious freedom of blacks in the wake of the Denmark Vesey insurrection of 1822 (see DENMARK VESEY CONSPIRACY) and that led by Nat Turner in 1831 (see NAT TURNER'S REBELLION). No reliable figures exist for the number of African Americans who became Christians during the era of the pioneer black preachers, but it is important to acknowledge that this experience of relative religious independence and a shared evangelical ethos provided a benchmark by which blacks could judge later efforts to use Christianity as a means of social control.

Although growing numbers of blacks, slave and free, had embraced Christianity by the beginning of the nineteenth century, the camp meetings and other mechanisms used by the evangelical preachers were limited in scope. In some places, such as among the Gullah peoples of the Sea Island district of South Carolina, and in Louisiana, where Roman Catholicism and West Indian–derived practices of VOODOO intermixed, religious syncretism was so strong as to violate mainstream Christian sensibilities. Even in parts of the south, where free blacks and whites experienced common fellowship in local churches, little effort was made to reach the plantation slave.

Although many slave owners were made uneasy by some of the radically egalitarian implications of Christianity, many became convinced that Christianity, properly catechized, could make slaves more docile. In 1829, the Rev. William Capers appealed to plantation owners in South Carolina to allow him to go to their slaves. Supporters of the plantation missions were motivated by the biblical mandate to share the Gospel, but they also wanted to rid the slaves of their "heathen" ways, and, as Capers argued, improve plantation efficiency on the premise that a Christian slave would be more obedient.

Nat Turner's insurrection in 1831 cast doubt on Capers's assertion, but gradually many in the white South were won over to the notion that "lessons on salvation and lessons on duty" were compatible and that the South had a divine mandate to convert and civilize the "children of Ham"—as Africans were often called because of the proslavery interpretation of the story told in Genesis 9. When abolitionists chastised southerners for the sin of slavery, the apologists of "the peculiar institution" pointed to plantation missions as evidence of their fulfillment of the Christian duty to civilize and convert and of the legitimacy of their custodial rule over "the darker race."

Just how strongly, if at all, African-American slaves internalized the religious model placed before them by whites is a difficult question. Was the Christian slave successfully indoctrinated with the notion that piety and obedience were inseparable? Or did Christianity, as expressed in the secret or "hush arbor" meetings of slaves, in their prayers and in their songs (SPIRITUALS), offer a basis from which both individual psychological independence and organized resistance could spring forth? Frederick DOUGLASS reported that he observed fellow slaves who scoffed at the religious pretensions of whites; personally he found hypocrisy at the root of slaveholding Christianity, which he termed "bad, corrupt, and wicked." But he thought of the Christianity of Christ as impartial and "good, pure, and holy." If we are to judge by the testimony of ex-slaves, many of whom eagerly sought to read the Bible for themselves once freedom came, they had successfully appropriated Christianity in order to give meaning to their lives and cope with systematic efforts to deny their humanity. Estimates are that one in seven of the adult slaves belonged to an organized church, primarily Baptist or METHODIST, by the time of the CIVIL WAR, and many more had been exposed to the influence of Christianity.

The religious outlook of the African-American slave was a complex and highly creative adaptation of European Christianity and African traditional religion to everyday needs. A few rejected Christianity altogether and retained Islam or their African religion, or became persistent skeptics. Many slaves originally sought the protection and power of the conjurer, but after a period of religious instruction and Christian baptism, many came to the conclusion that conjuration was the work of the devil. Although masters attempted to enforce discipline through the use of Christianity, the slaves heard the sermons preached in the plantation chapels with a critical ear, sorted out the wheat from the chaff, and constructed a religious story in which they were the chosen of God. Although they might have, as the spirituals reflect, trouble and sorrow in this world, they could hope for the joys of heaven where "de' bottom rail become de' top rail."

Labeled as "otherworldly" and "compensatory," this use of Christianity has been judged dysfunctional by those who emphasize the need for radical political and social transformation. Discussed in the manner of Gary Marx and others, the "opiate-versus-inspiration debate," as it is sometimes referred to, forces our view of the religious culture of the African-American slave into opposing and limiting channels. By recognizing the multiple dimensions of the sacred cosmos operative in the slave quarters and "hush-arbors," we come close to understanding what the African-American slaves meant when they spoke of their beliefs in God as helping them to "keep on keeping on." They testified that they had a "home in glory land" and that no earthly master could close them out of God's house. As historian John Boles wrote, "There was a fateful ambiguity at the heart of the slave response to Christianity, and the fervent rebel, and the passive, long-suffering servant were equally authentic expressions of black religion." Once they had been "killed dead" in the Spirit and were reborn, African-American Christian slaves became participants in another community than that which numbered them with cattle and cotton.

Christianity in the Antebellum North

By focusing too exclusively on the South, we run the risk of missing important facets of the antebellum African-American religious experience. There were individual African-American Christians of note in the North, such as Lemuel HAYNES, the first African American officially ordained to the Christian ministry and who served as pastor of white congregations in New England; Phillis WHEATLEY, who wrote religious verse read in both America and Europe; and Jupiter HAMMON, a slave on Long Island, N.Y., who counseled Christian endurance in the hope of heaven. Though few in number until after 1800, independent black churches were organized in the North. Separated from the bulk of the country's black population, African-American Christians in the North kept the plight of their sisters and brothers in chains in their prayers; supported causes such as temperance and education, so as not to provide the apologists for slavery with an argument that freedom would ruin the slave; served as UNDERGROUND RAILROAD stations; and assisted in the cause of ABOLITION. They organized voluntary associations to support educational endeavors and to care for widows and orphans, and they served as the focal points of black life in the northern city, where prejudice and discrimination were prevalent.

The northern religious landscape took on more definition with the formation of the first black de-

nominations. Following the pattern of white Christians in the post-Revolutionary era, black Christians organized into denominations. Sometimes the struggle for denominational independence was a particularly dramatic one, as was the case with black Methodists in the Philadelphia area led by Richard ALLEN. A former slave and convert to Christianity, Allen was convinced that the plain and simple Gospel as preached by the spiritual heirs of John Wesley, the English founder of Methodism, was best suited to the unlettered black. However, white authorities resisted when Allen and other Philadelphia black Methodists in the 1790s sought greater control over their own religious affairs by establishing their own church. Armed with a decision from the Supreme Court of Pennsylvania in 1816, to the effect that Allen and his coadjutors had a legal right to the church property and self-governance, the AFRICAN METHODIST EPISCOPAL (AME) denomination was organized in 1816. About six years later, black Methodists in New York City likewise achieved denominational independence under the banner of the AFRICAN METHODIST EPISCOPAL ZION CHURCH. As suggested by the label "Methodist," both groups replicated much of white Methodist ritual, doctrine, and polity while seeking to liberate themselves from the prejudicial control of white Methodists.

By the Civil War, the AME church had about twenty thousand members and had planted new missions as far west as California. Urged on by the zealous efforts of Daniel Alexander PAYNE, the AME church established its first institution of higher education (Wilberforce College, now WILBERFORCE UNIVERSITY) and theological school (Payne Seminary) at Xenia, Ohio. The AME Zion denomination numbered about five thousand and would not expand significantly beyond the Northeast until after the Civil War, when the denomination's representatives worked aggressively among the freedmen. Eventually the denomination transferred most of its central operations to North Carolina, where it established a church newspaper and publishing house, and at Livingstone College in Salisbury.

The earliest separate black Baptist congregations appeared in northern cities in the early 1800s. Blacks customarily worshiped with white Baptists, but the "Negro Pew" was tolerated and eventually blacks sought to organize their own congregations. In 1805, Thomas PAUL became the first pastor of the First African (or Joy Street) Baptist Church of Boston, and in 1808 he assisted in the organization of ABYSSINIAN BAPTIST CHURCH in New York City. Independent black Baptist congregations eventually emerged in most northern cities, but the traditional Baptist emphasis on local autonomy retarded the development of regional associations until the formation of the Providence Association in 1834 and the Union Association (1836), both in Ohio, and the Wood River Association (1839) in southwestern Illinois.

Sparked by interest in developing missions in Africa, black Baptists gradually moved toward more national organizations. The American Baptist Missionary Convention became the first such cooperative arrangement in 1840. In the decades after the Civil War, black Baptists debated whether or not to continue partnerships with northern white Baptists in foreign missions and the publication of religious literature. The nationalist or independent spirit finally triumphed in the formation of the first truly national black organization, the NATIONAL BAPTIST CONVENTION, U.S.A., INC., in 1895. The cooperationists formed the Lott Carey Foreign Mission Convention in 1897.

Because of Baptist disunity during most of the nineteenth century, the African Methodist story tends to assume center stage in accounts of the institutional history of African-American religion. Better organized than the Baptists—and fortunate to have denominational historians such as Bishop Daniel A. Payne—the northern-based African Methodists dominate the documentary record. But statistics of denominational membership published by the U.S. Census Bureau reveal that black Baptists outnumbered black Methodists as the century drew to a close. This was largely due to expansion in the South after EMANCIPATION when the ex-slaves, though heavily recruited by agents of the northern-based denominations, black and white, elected to form new congregations in which they could hear preachers familiar with the religous style found in the antebellum plantation congregations.

Civil War to World War II

When slaves deserted their masters during the Civil War or became contraband as Union troops advanced on southern soil, a new religious landscape began to emerge. Eager to read the Bible on their own and worship without white oversight, the freed slaves were convinced that their emancipation was tantamount to the deliverance of the Children of Israel from the pharaoh of Egypt. African-American Christians seized the moment and left the denominations of their former masters in large numbers. The Colored Methodist Episcopal Church was organized in 1870 at Jackson, Tenn., and was comprised principally of former members of the Methodist Episcopal Church, South, who did not desire to join the northern-based African Methodists. As if by spontaneous combustion, black Baptist congregations appeared in great numbers throughout the South. These Baptist churches and their Methodist counterparts in the small towns and rural areas represented the core religious culture of African Americans in the South between the Civil War and World War I. Heavily influenced by the folk practices of the "invisible institution" and often criticized for its demonstrative religious style—with emphasis on dramatic conversion experiences, emotional preaching and "testifying"— southern African-American religion developed its own internal dynamic. African-American churches in the North, with their educated ministers and more formal worship styles, developed differently. On the eve of World War I, therefore, two African-American religious cultures existed: one northern and urban, the other mostly southern and rural.

Despite the cultural differences between the northern and southern black religion, most observers agreed that the church was central to African-American life as the twentieth century dawned. "The Negro Church," Booker T. WASHINGTON wrote in 1909, "was the first institution to develop out of the life of the Negro masses and still retains the strongest hold upon them." "The Negro church of today," W. E. B. DUBOIS had written six years earlier, "is the social center of Negro life in the United States, and the most characteristic expression of the African character." An institution so central to African Americans could not escape internal discussion of the prevailing social and political issues raised in the larger society.

One of the most important issues concerned the role that women should play in male-dominated institutions such as the church, where the pulpit had been traditionally defined as "men's space" and the pew as "women's place." The AME Zion church authorized the ordination of women in the 1890s, the AME church in 1948, and the CME church in 1954. Appealing to the principle of congregational autonomy, the major black Baptist conventions have not legislated policy regarding the ordination of women. Conservative attitudes at the congregational level, where gender bias among the male clergy is strong, has proved to be an obstacle to many women who have sought ordination. The CHURCH OF GOD IN CHRIST, the largest black PENTECOSTAL body, prohibits the ordination of women.

Historically, women have been in the majority in the mainline black denominations, yet men have dominated the leadership. Women serve as "mothers of the church;" are active in missionary societies, educational efforts, and a wide variety of charitable causes; and serve local congregations in numerous capacities, such as teachers, stewardesses, and deaconesses. Yet men hold denominational offices and monopolize the clergy rosters to a greater degree than in the more liberal white Protestant churches. Women who wish to exercise the gift of the Spirit have had to operate as independent evangelists, such as Jarena LEE did after an originally futile appeal to Richard Allen and the African Methodists in the early 1800s. Sojourner TRUTH, Harriet TUBMAN, and Rebecca Cox JACKSON, who eventually joined the Shakers, possessed spiritual gifts which the established black denominations did not formally recognize. Amanda Berry SMITH left the AME Church in order to exercise her ministry more freely, joined the HOLINESS movement, and thereby served as a precursor for the many women who found the freedom to develop their own ministries within the orbit of the burgeoning Pentecostal and Holiness movement, which flourished in the "sanctified" storefronts of the urban North. For example, Elder Lucy Smith (1874–1952) founded All Nations Pentecostal Church in Chicago and conducted a multidimensional ministry that dealt with the material as well as the spiritual needs of her members.

Closed out of male-dominated ecclesiastical centers of power, African-American women developed auxiliary organizations. The Women's Parent Mite Missionary Society of the AME Church, founded in 1874, supported new churches in western United States and in South Africa. Baptist women led by Nannie Helen BURROUGHS formed the Women's Convention of the National Baptist Convention in 1900 and operated the National School for Girls in Washington. Many of these church women were also active in the club movement, which stressed self-help and charitable and civic work, and served as a focal point for women's independent identity. Beset by racism in the larger society and confronted by patriarchal attitudes within their denominations, African-American church women had to confront multiple challenges. They played an especially important role in bringing the gap between church work as traditionally defined and secular reform activity. The demands upon them intensified with the outbreak of World War I.

The centrality of women in the local congregation became all the more apparent because of external social forces in the flight from field to factory once the call for labor went out from the North. After 1910, in the early years of the Great Migration, males, particularly young males, went north lured by the promise of better jobs. Women and the young were left to carry on congregational life. Urbanization proved to be no panacea. Indeed, in poor urban areas, church adherence was increasingly the sphere of women and children. This is especially true of the independent churches, known as "storefronts." In an extensive study done in the 1980s, researchers found that in 2,150 black churches, of various denominations, women outnumbered men by a factor of 2.5 to 1. Some observers have spoken of the "feminization of the black church" because of the relative absence of males, especially young males, in urban congregations. Whether or not the disproportionate representation of females in contemporary black churches is principally a result of the urbanization of African Americans is yet to be determined. It is clear, how-

A river baptism in Aiken, S.C., in the early years of the twentieth century. For many African Americans, no life ceremony had so much significance as baptism. (Prints and Photographs Division, Library of Congress)

ever, that the gender question is one that black Christians, regardless of denominational affiliation, have yet to fully and adequately address.

The urbanization of African-American religion precipitated an institutional crisis in the existing black churches. In 1910 nearly 90 percent of the nation's black population lived in the South, mostly in rural regions and small towns. Since the end of the Civil War, the church had assumed a dominant position in the life of southern blacks, whose institutional development in other areas was restricted by racial apartheid. By default, then, the churches served multiple purposes—worship, education, recreation, and socialization. Northern black leaders, as well as some Southern leaders (e.g., Booker T. Washington) pointed to such problems as overchurching, undereducated ministers, pastors with multiple charges, congregations too small to adequately maintain programs and property, too little emphasis on the social and political problems of the day. Carter G. Woodson referred to rural churches as "mystic shrines" while writing approvingly of northern urban churches as progressive centers of "social uplift." This debate over the mission of the black church was heightened by the Great Migration because it placed new demands upon existing denominational and local church resources and programs.

The population shift put severe strains upon existing denominational structures. Home missionary boards lacked adequate resources to cope with the need in the North, and congregations in the South were left depleted and deserted. Competition among the three major black Methodist bodies prevented a cooperative effort in addressing the needs of the migrants. The National Baptist Convention, U.S.A., Inc., underwent a contentious division in 1915, which resulted in the formation of a rival body, the National Baptist Convention of America Unincorporated, later named National Baptist Convention of America in 1916. The internecine war continued for years, draining away critically needed resources. The secretary of the Home Mission Board of the National Baptist Convention, U.S.A., Inc., reported in 1921: "We have quite a number of destitute fields both North and South and in many cases no opportunity for religious worship."

The regional shift in America's black population portended difficulties because as WORLD WAR I began the black denominations were heavily weighted to the South. In 1916 the U.S. Census of Religious Bodies credited the National Baptists with 2,939,579 members, 89 percent of whom were in the South. The AME Church had 548,355 members and was 81.2 percent southern. The AMEZ Church was 84.6 percent southern with a total membership of 257,169. The CME Church, composed principally of the de-

scendants of ex-slaves, was 95.5 percent southern and 245,749 members strong. None of the Pentecostal or Holiness bodies, which became so important in the urban North after the Great Migration, receive recognition in the 1916 religious census.

In addition to placing strains upon ecclesiastical structures inherited from the nineteenth century and oriented primarily toward the small town and rural church, urbanization offered African Americans new religious options. Baptist and Methodist preachers now had to compete with the agents of the Pentecostal and Holiness churches. These churches played against great emphasis on an intense personal experience of the Holy Spirit. The Church of God in Christ, led by Charles Harrison MASON, held its first Pentecostal general assembly in 1907; having started as a rural church in Mississippi, the denomination grew to become a fixture in the northern city. Ill at ease in the more formal worship services of the established northern churches, many migrants organized prayer bands, started house churches, or moved into the storefronts where speaking in tongues (sometimes referred to as the practice of glossolalia) received the blessing of the Pentecostals. The Church of Christ (Holiness), U.S.A., under the leadership of Elder C. P. JONES, likewise expanded as a result of the burgeoning black populations of urban industrial America. Other Holiness and Pentecostal churches were founded by denominationally-independent religious entrepreneurs who recognized that the migrants from the South desired something that the northern black middle-class churches did not offer.

Many of the migrants wanted religious environments that reminded them of their churches back home, where they were known by name and part of an extended family. The ecstatic worship services and musical styles favored by the Pentecostal and Holiness preachers caught the attention of these ex-Southerners. When hard times befell them in the North, migrants sought out spiritual havens in the urban wilderness. Holiness and Pentecostal churches multiplied everywhere, and existing Baptist and Methodist churches split or sponsored daughter congregations as the migrant population swelled. On occasion, northern black Christians criticized their "brothers and sisters" from the South for falling short of northern cultural expectations and the existing class norms. In turn, migrants shunned some northern black churches, where the elaborate and elegant services made them feel out of place. Some fell away from organized religion all together. Others responded to their crisis of faith in the city by transplanting churches from the South led by the pastors who had followed them northward.

The tension between the two cultural streams that came together after the beginning of World War I is illustrated by the reluctance of the older African-American congregations in Chicago to readily accept GOSPEL music. Gospel music was popularized by Thomas DORSEY, the "father of gospel music," who joined Pilgrim Baptist Church in Chicago in 1921. Unlike the purveyors of commercialized gospel today, early gospel music was church centered. Yet as Mahalia JACKSON, the best-known singer of gospel, learned while growing up in New Orleans, the musical distance between the honky-tonk and a Holiness revival with its beating and tambourine shaking is not that great. Dorsey, building on the work of predecessors such as Charles Albert TINDLEY, was the principal force behind the introduction of blues-like gospel songs into the northern black churches. About 1930, observers of the Chicago scene reported that "Negro churches, particularly the storefront congregations, the Sanctified groups and the shouting Baptists, were swaying and jumping as never before. Mighty rhythms rocked the churches. A wave of fresh rapture came over the people." Jackson earned worldwide acclamation for her solo renditions of gospel classics, and the pioneering touring groups such as the Dixie Hummingbirds and the Five Blind Boys of Mississippi helped make gospel so popular that today it is rare to find a black church, of whatever denomination or class composition, that closes its doors to the gospel sound.

Religious diversity, even dissonance, resonated from the large, densely crowded, black urban centers after World War I. After examining data from the 1926 Federal Census of Religious Bodies, Miles Mark Fisher exclaimed: "Almost in every center, particularly urban, is some unorthodox religious group which makes a definite appeal to Negroes." The Jamaican-born black nationalist Marcus GARVEY discouraged talk of founding a new church, but he and his UNIVERSAL NEGRO IMPROVEMENT ASSOCIATION (1918–1927) had many followers who sought collective redemption in the back-to-Africa ideology. There were also some supporters, such as George Alexander MCGUIRE, the founder of the AFRICAN ORTHODOX CHURCH, who did initiate Garveyite-inspired demonstrations. The UNIA collapsed after the deportation of its "Black Moses" in 1927, but other charismatic personalities came forward offering often exotic visions of heaven on earth. FATHER DIVINE set up a series of Peace Missions during the GREAT DEPRESSION, offering his devotees the unusual mix of "God" in the flesh and a refuge from society's problems. Scores of religious entrepreneurs opened shop in the black ghettos, where they competed with the mainline denominations. Frequently referred to as cults and sects, the groups led by these new messiahs often died when their founders did, but some managed to survive under different leadership, as, for

The ecstatic nature of Pentecostal worship is a primary reason for the rapid growth of the Church of God in Christ in twentieth-century black America. Here, a young convert accepts the Holy Spirit in a Washington, D.C., church in 1942. (Prints and Photographs Division, Library of Congress)

example, the one led by Daddy GRACE (the United House of Prayer for All People). Representatives of the mainline churches frequently decried the proliferation of these alternative groups, arguing, as the Baptist Miles Mark Fisher did, that the principle message of the cults and sects was "Let us prey," not "Let us pray."

The appearance on urban street corners of black adherents of Islam and Judaism added to the perception that African-American religion was undergoing a radical reorientation in the interwar period at the expense of the historic black denominations. The first black Jewish group recognized by the federal religious census was founded in 1896 by William S. CROWDY, a Santa Fe Railroad cook, in Lawrence, Kans. African Americans wearing the yarmulke and speaking Yiddish came to the attention of a wider public in the 1920s. Located primarily in the boroughs of New York City, these teachers of black Hebraism appropriated and adapted the rituals and teachings of Orthodox Judaism (see JUDAISM). Though never large in number, the followers of Rabbi Arnold Ford and other proponents of Black Judaism generated a great deal of interest among the curious and the skeptical.

ISLAM was not entirely unheard of among African Americans before the mysterious figure of W. D.

FARD appeared in the "Paradise Valley" of Detroit in 1930 to wake up the sleeping "Lost-Found Nation of Islam." There is increasing evidence that a small but not insignificant number of enslaved Africans brought knowledge of the Koran and Islamic law to North America. But modern Islam among African Americans begins with the career of NOBLE DREW ALI, a native of North Carolina and founder of Moorish Science in Newark, N.J., about 1913. However, the man who most popularized Islam for African Americans, was the one-time disciple of Wallace Fard, Elijah MUHAMMAD, who capitalized on the interest of urbanized blacks in the religiously exotic. Himself a migrant from Georgia, Muhammad (formerly Elijah Poole) assumed leadership of the NATION OF ISLAM after Fard's disappearance in 1934 and moved its headquarters to Chicago. The Nation's version of Islam did not fare well under the scrutiny of orthodox scholars of the Koran, and eventually the sect broke into rival factions. Nevertheless, it has had a significant impact upon many African Americans, chiefly the young and angry like MALCOLM X who believed that traditional black Christianity was a "pie-in-the-sky" religion.

Attention to the new religious options that appeared in black urban America during the period between World War I and World War II should not be at the expense of the story of the mainline black churches. Stimulated by the crisis brought about by the influx of thousands from the South, the established churches struggled with a redefinition of mission during these decades. Richard R. WRIGHT, JR., examined the record of black church involvement within the public sphere in 1907 and concluded that only a few churches had "attacked the problems of real city Negroes." His own work in Chicago's Institutional Church and Social Settlement, founded by Reverdy RANSOM, and later at Chicago's Trinity Mission and Culture Center, which Wright organized in 1905, convinced Wright that black churches needed a more compelling definition of urban mission than presently at hand. Prior to World War I, outreach primarily involved mission and charity work with the intent of recruiting new members. As Wright and Ransom discovered for themselves, pastors who addressed contemporary social problems born of urban and industrial growth were deemed too radical by denominational officials.

Most black preachers, urban and rural, still thought of sin and salvation in individualistic terms. The black denominations lagged behind their white counterparts in adopting the theological message of the SOCIAL GOSPEL movement with its focus upon the problems of urban America. Beginning with the era of the Great Migration, however, many more black churches incorporated programs into their understanding of "church work" that went beyond the traditional emphasis on praying and preaching. They assisted with needs in housing, employment, education, recreation, and health care. The instrumentalist use of the church to better the community is today so widely accepted that black clergy or congregations who show no interest in everyday problems have little appeal or credibility among African Americans.

Although black denominations were spared the bitter internecine battles that erupted in the 1920s between the white fundamentalists and modernists over such issues as the interpretation of the Creation story in Genesis, their efforts to merge have failed. Concerned about institutional inefficiency and lost oppportunities to influence the larger society and motivated by the ideal that Christ's church be one, representatives of the three principal branches of black Methodism began meetings in 1915 to discuss the possibility of merger. But leaders of the CME church (formerly the Colored Methodist Episcopal church and since 1954 the CHRISTIAN METHODIST EPISCOPAL CHURCH), balked at union because of fears of being dominated by the two larger northern black Methodist bodies: the AME and the AMEZ churches. Division among black Methodists was widened by the segregation of 315,000 in the Central Jurisdiction, a nongeographical entity, of the predominantly white United Methodist Church in 1939 after the merger of the northern and southern branches of Methodism (the segregated structure was abolished in the 1960s). Black Baptists likewise have been unable to heal the divisions within their ranks. The National Baptist Convention, U.S.A., Inc., remains the largest of all black church connections, claiming about 7.5 million members and 30,000 local churches in the late-1980s.

The contemporary black Baptist story is still best told in terms of the local congregation. Ministerial alliances at the local level have fostered interdenominational cooperation where there has been sufficient need for common action. In many congregations, the minister is still the dominant personality. Critics have argued that the domineering role played by the pastor in black congregations has retarded the development of lay leadership. The preeminence of the black minister in African-American religious culture has historical roots. Because of the class and caste attitudes of whites in the South, the ministery remained one of the few professions accessible to blacks. Even in the North, where political boundaries were defined by patterns of residential segregation and black political participation was restricted, black ministers were called upon to speak for their community before local authorities. Participation in electoral and protest politics has engaged the energies of many contemporary black clergy, but they have had to divide their time between their civic roles and their pastoral roles.

Civil Rights Era to the Present

The internal life of African-American churches probably escaped the attention of most of white America until the Rev. Dr. Martin Luther KING, Jr., began to catch the eye and ear of the news media. Rooted deep in the black Baptist tradition, King was schooled in the preaching tradition of the black church of the South. While doing advanced theological training in the North, he became proficient in the major currents of thought among liberal, socially aware Protestants. This made it possible for him to appeal to the conscience of white America during the civil rights struggle (*see* CIVIL RIGHTS MOVEMENT) and to enlist the aid of allies from the more liberal white denominations. Yet the grassroots participation of thousands of black churchgoers who marched and sang and prayed transformed King's protest of racial segregation in Montgomery, Ala., into a mass movement. From the vantage point of these people of faith, a civil rights march was as much a religious crusade as a social movement. While the cause of civil rights united black religious leaders across denominational lines and cemented alliances with progressive forces in the predominantly white Protestant, Catholic, and Jewish communities, there were disharmonious chords. The Rev. Joseph L. JACKSON, who served as president of the National Baptist Convention from 1953 to 1982, resisted the attempt of King and others to move the largest Protestant denomination in the world into activist or protest politics. As a result, King, with the Rev. Ralph David ABERNATHY, Gardner C. Taylor, and others, formed the Progressive National Baptist Convention in 1961 under the motto: "Unity, service, fellowship, peace."

The civil rights movement, of course, was not confined to institutional church circles. Nor are its religious dimensions fully measured by focusing, for example, on the SOUTHERN CHRISTIAN LEADERSHIP CONFERENCE (SCLC) led by King. And of course, organizations with a more secular orientation, such as the STUDENT NONVIOLENT COORDINATING COMMITTEE (SNCC) also had crucial roles to play. But even the members of SNCC were animated by a vision of the day when truth and justice would prevail in the United States. Indeed the bulwark of the civil rights movement, especially in the South, was the grassroots black church, which propelled the crusade that eventually broke down the barriers of legalized segregation. While a form of religious sectarianism among many African Americans has led to withdrawal and isolation from the public sphere, or-

Muslim national convention in Chicago's International Amphitheatre, February 27, 1961. A line of Elijah Muhammad's security men form a barrier in front of the platform. (AP/Wide World Photos)

thodox or mainline black churches have for the most part been instrumental in bringing America closer to Dr. King's dream of the "beloved community."

A dramatic scenario for the reenvisioning of America unfolded in the decade of the 1960s, when the call for Black Power was heard. Originating among young radicals, many of whom were estranged from the traditional black church, the largely secular Black Power movement quickly drew a theological response. It came first from individuals such as James CONE, who were situated in academic environments, but it eventually engaged the thinking of denominational representatives. Their statements revealed both agreement with the diagnosis of the wrongs of American society as portrayed by advocates of Black Power but also some uneasiness regarding the means necessary to achieve a just society. King had taught that nonviolence was ethically essential given the witness of the New Testament. During the civil rights crusade, local churches served as training grounds in nonviolent resistance. In contrast, the more strident advocates of Black Power carried weapons and, rhetorically at least, endorsed their use in conflicts with the police and others in authority. Steeped in the traditional Christian doctrine that the use of violence is a betrayal of the ethics of Jesus, most black Christians remained skeptical of the means the militants justified.

Nevertheless, the Black Power advocates made a lasting impact on black churches. By raising cultural awareness, black nationalists—as Garvey had done in the 1920s and earlier back-to-Africa proponents such as Bishop Henry M. TURNER of the AME church did in the 1880s—stimulated interest in and debate over the essential question of "how black is black religion?" African-American clergy in the predominantly white Protestant groups organized caucuses in which they examined their historic and contemporary relationship with their host denominations. This analysis led to demands for representation in the higher echelons of institutional life, for more black clergy, and for the incorporation of distinctively African-American religious styles in worship. Black Roman Catholics also experienced a renaissance of pride in "blackness," variously defined. Representations of a Black Jesus appeared in Roman Catholic sanctuaries, and the refrains of gospel music could be heard during Mass sung in English following the reforms of Vatican II (1963–1965). In other religious traditions such as the Presbyterian, Episcopal, and Lutheran, African Americans also pressed for a greater appreciation of the rich African and African-American religious heritage.

At the core of the complex religious pilgrimage of peoples of African descent in America is the importance of the local congregation of believers who celebrate together the rites of passage of its members from baptism to Christian burial. Most black churches, however, emphasis preaching over the sacraments, in contrast to the liturgical traditions such as Roman Catholicism and Lutheranism. The spoken word, whether in sermon or song, is at the core of black worship. The roster of celebrated black preachers is long. The Rev. C. L. FRANKLIN of Detroit is but one example. Called "the most imitated soul preacher in history" by the Rev. Jesse JACKSON, Franklin shepherded more than 10,000 members of Detroit's New Bethel Baptist Church at the height of his popularity. He carried the sermon to an art form, was heard on the radio by a large audience, and sold millions of records.

Black churches historically have served as the centers of African-American life and identity. Benjamin MAYS, the distinguished educator in Atlanta and mentor of Martin Luther King, Jr., wrote of the church of his youth in rural South Carolina: "Old Mount Zion was an important institution in my community. Negroes had nowhere to go but to church. They went there to worship, to hear the choir sing, to listen to the preacher, and to hear and see the people shout. The young people went to Mount Zion to socialize, or simply to stand around and talk. It was a place of worship and a social center as well. There was no other place to go." As the twentieth century draws to a close, there is concern as to whether or not black churches will be equipped to meet the challenges of the next millennium. Already there are some who argue that the major black denominations have succumbed to the lure of middle-class America and left the poorest of the poor behind. The Nation of Islam is often credited with being able to reach into the ranks of the youthful street gangs and has had success in making converts among African Americans in the country's prisons. Often overlooked in the media attention given to representatives of the Nation of Islam are the various street ministries sponsored by black churches or independent evangelical preachers and the extensive community services such as "meals on wheels" programs, Head Start schools, and recreational facilities, found in most places where black churches are active.

By strict interpretation, there is no "black church," nor is there one uniform expression of "black religion." There has been a rich and varied tapestry of religious expression and religious institutions among African Americans. There are many black congregations within the predominantly white denominations along with the lengthy list of historic black denominations and independent churches. Pentecostal and Holiness churches have increased in number dramatically since first taking

Muslims bow to Mecca during Muslim Family Day in Prospect Park, Brooklyn, N.Y. (© Martha Cooper/City Lore)

root in the urban North during the World War I era and represent the fastest-growing segment of the African-American religious experience. Formerly criticized as too concerned with exclusively "other-worldly" matters and personal moral failings, they are now recognized as effective community partners in the black population centers across America. This may be because they have successfully blended a demonstrative style of worship—once identified most strongly with the folk religion of the black South—with community involvement, the hallmark of proponents of the Social Gospel.

Contemporary black churches are not without their problems. Few have the economic resources to meet the many demands placed upon them, and effective national structures able to efficiently garner funds and distribute them are for the most part lacking. Many local congregations are clergy-dominated and have not effectively tapped the leadership potential of the laity. Black denominations have yet fully to come to terms with enduring gender discrimination within their midst, especially in terms of access to the pulpit and positions of church governance. Given the generally inadequate state of public education in the country's most heavily urbanized areas,

the black churches could do much more if adequately equipped and motivated. Although the major black denominations have been involved in ecumenical agencies such as the National Council of Churches, there exists no national organization made up exclusively of representatives of the black denominations that could work for a reduction in competition and redundancy at the local level, as well as speak more authoritatively on matters of public concern.

There have been several partially successful attempts at African-American ecumenism: the Fraternal Council of Negro Churches was active from 1934 through the early 1950s and the Black Power-oriented National Conference of Black Churchmen had its heyday from 1967 to 1973. Since 1978 the CONGRESS OF NATIONAL BLACK CHURCHES has coordinated efforts among the major African-American denominations. One of the most successful ecumenical efforts by the black church is the INTERDENOMINATIONAL THEOLOGICAL CENTER, a consortium of six primarily black denominations at the ATLANTA UNIVERSITY CENTER.

During the 1950s when the crusade to break down the walls of prejudice and discrimination crested, some observers wondered what the fate of the black churches would be if racial assimilation replaced racial apartheid. Since the historic African-American denominations had originated in protest to the exclusionary policies prevalent among white Christians, so the argument went, the rationale for separate black religious institutions weakened as the predominantly white denominations became more egalitarian. That African-American religious institutions continue to expand some four decades after Martin Luther King, Jr., trumpeted the call for a new day in the relationship between black and white America should signal that African-American religion has been more than a simple reaction to the religious experiences and practices of Americans of European descent. It stands as an enduring witness to the multicultural texture of the entire American experience. *See also* RELIGIOUS EDUCATION.

REFERENCES

AUSTIN, ALLEN D. *African Muslims in Antebellum America: A Sourcebook.* New York, 1984.

BAER, HANS A., and MERRILL SINGER. *African American Religion in the Twentieth Century: Varieties of Protest and Accommodation.* Knoxville, Tenn., 1992.

BOLES, JOHN B., ed. *Masters and Slaves in the House of the Lord: Race and Religion in the American South, 1740–1870.* Lexington, Ky., 1988.

BURKETT, RANDALL. *Black Redemption: Garveyism as a Religious Movement.* Metuchen, N.J., 1978.

BURKETT, RANDALL, and RICHARD NEWMAN, eds. *Black Apostles: Afro-American Clergy Confront the Twentieth Century.* Boston, 1978.

BURNHAM, KENNETH E. *God Comes to America: Father Divine and the Peace Mission Movement.* Boston, 1979.

CONE, JAMES. *For My People: Black Theology and the Black Church.* Maryknoll, N.Y., 1984.

DAVIS, CYPRIAN. *The History of Black Catholics in the United States.* New York, N.Y., 1990.

EPSTEIN, DENA J. *Sinful Tunes and Spirituals: Black Folk Music to the Civil War.* Urbana, Ill., 1977.

FRAZIER, E. FRANKLIN, and C. ERIC LINCOLN. *The Negro Church in America: The Black Church Since Frazier.* New York, 1974.

GEORGE, CAROL V. R. *Segregated Sabbaths: Richard Allen and the Emergence of Independent Black Churches, 1760–1840.* New York, 1973.

HARRIS, MICHAEL W. *The Rise of Gospel Blues: The Music of Thomas Andrew Dorsey in the Urban Church.* New York, 1992.

HIGGINBOTHAM, EVELYN BROOKS. *Righteous Discontent: The Women's Movement in the Black Baptist Church, 1880–1920.* Cambridge, Mass., 1993.

JACKSON, JOSEPH H. *A Story of Christian Activism: The History of the National Baptist Convention, U.S.A., Inc.* Nashville, 1980.

LINCOLN, C. ERIC, and LAWRENCE H. MAMIYA. *The Black Church in the African American Experience.* Durham, N.C., 1990.

MARTIN, SANDY D. *Black Baptists and African Missions: The Origins of a Movement 1880–1915.* Mercer, Ga., 1989.

MURPHY, LARRY G., J. GORDON MELTON, and GARY L. WARD, eds. *Encyclopedia of African American Religions.* New York, 1993.

PARIS, PETER. *The Social Teachings of the Black Churches.* Philadelphia, 1985.

RABOTEAU, ALBERT. *Slave Religion: The "Invisible Institution" in the Antebellum South.* New York, 1978.

RICHARDSON, HARRY V. *Dark Salvation: The Story of Methodism as It Developed Among Blacks in America.* Garden City, N.Y., 1976.

SERNETT, MILTON. *Black Religion and American Evangelicalism: White Protestants, Plantation Missions and the Flowering of Negro Christianity, 1787–1865.* Metuchen, N.J., 1975.

———, ed. *Afro-American Religious History: A Documentary Witness.* Durham, N.C., 1985.

SMITH, EDWARD D. *Climbing Jacob's Ladder: The Rise of the Black Churches in Eastern American Cities, 1740–1877.* Washington, D.C., 1988.

SOBEL, MECHAL. *Trabelin' On: The Slave Journey to an Afro-Baptist Faith.* Westport, Conn., 1979.

SPENCER, JON MICHAEL. *Protest & Praise: Sacred Music of Black Religion.* Minneapolis, 1990.

WASHINGTON, JAMES M. *Frustrated Fellowship: The Black Baptist Quest for Social Power.* Macon, Ga., 1986.

———, ed. *A Testament of Hope: The Essential Writings of Martin Luther King, Jr.* San Francisco, 1986.

WILLIAMS, ETHEL L., and CLIFTON F. BROWN. *Afro-American Religious Studies: A Comprehensive Bibliography with Locations in American Libraries.* 2nd ed. Metuchen, N.J., 1979.

WILLIAMS, MELVIN D. *Community in a Black Pentacostal Church: An Anthropological Study.* Pittsburgh, 1974.

WILMORE, GAYRAUD. *Black Religion and Black Radicalism: An Interpretation of the Religious History of Afro-American People.* Maryknoll, N.Y., 1983.

WOODSON, CARTER G. *The History of the Negro Church.* 3rd ed. Washington, D.C., 1972.

MILTON C. SERNETT

Religious Education. From the early eighteenth century onward exceptional religious teachers have inspired African Americans to reach beyond the constraints of racial discrimination to discover a connection to and awareness of the Divinity and a higher destiny for their lives. This process began as early as 1701, when the Church of England's SOCIETY FOR THE PROPAGATION OF THE GOSPEL IN FOREIGN PARTS attempted to educate black men for membership in the Christian church. In 1702 the Rev. Samuel Thomas was sent to South Carolina to evangelize among Negroes. By 1705 he could document a thousand slaves belonging to the Church of England. Many learned to read the Bible, and he showed the direct influence of religious instruction upon the reduction of "immorality among the slaves."

The second major educational effort of the Society for the Propagation of the Gospel was under the influence of Elias Neau of New York City. A school was opened in his house in 1704 for the purpose of instructing Negroes. The third important school of the society was established in Charleston, S.C., in 1745, at St. Phillips Church. It had as many as sixty scholars at one time. It annually sent out twenty young Negroes, well instructed in the English language and the Christian faith.

The SOCIETY OF FRIENDS, commonly known as Quakers, showed an early interest in the religious instruction of Negroes from 1757 to 1774. The Friends were among the earliest abolitionists, and their emphasis was upon preparing the slaves for the enjoyment of liberty. They advocated the notion that children be taught by masters or let out to persons who would supervise their religious instruction. This included learning to read and the affirmation of human dignity. However, the austere manner of Quaker worship had relatively little appeal to African Americans.

The Presbyterians sent the Rev. Samuel Davies as a representative of the London Society for the Promotion of Religious Knowledge Among the Poor. In 1747 Davies went to the parish at Hanover, Va., where he reported three hundred Negroes attending his ministry. He baptized one hundred of them and taught them to read and spell. He secured Bibles and Watts's *Psalms and Hymns* for them. He demonstrated that religious instruction made the slaves more faithful, honest, and diligent. The Presbyterian Pronouncement in 1787 implied that their aim was to prepare the Negro for the day of freedom. In 1800 the General Assembly of the Presbyterian Church of Philadelphia recommended the instruction of Negroes in various parts of the country.

In 1785, the Methodist Conference recorded a concern for establishing a Sunday school for poor children, white and black. There arose an evangelical zeal for promoting the spiritual welfare of colored people. The educational success of the Methodists was found in the printing and distribution of books, tracts, sermons, and other literature. In the late 1700s, George Daughaday, a Methodist preacher, was drenched in water in public for conducting a Sunday school for the benefit of the African children in Charleston, S.C. Many black Methodists such as Richard ALLEN tried to combine evangelization with basic education.

The Great Awakening and subsequent eighteenth-century stirrings led Baptists to the wholesale winning of a large number of African Americans to the Christian faith, chiefly in North Carolina, South Carolina, Georgia, and Virginia. However, little formal instruction was given to the converts, even though some became preachers and baptized others. In 1789 the Virginia Baptist Association passed a resolution that condemned slavery as being a violent deprivation of human nature. As the Baptist faith expanded rapidly in the late eighteenth and early nineteenth centuries, a backlash of sorts developed against the emphasis on emotional conversion and uneducated preachers.

Negro ministers benefited educationally from this recognized need. Soon the need for Baptist education went beyond ministerial education to concern with lay instruction. The first efforts in this regard began about 1797 in Pawtucket, R.I. In 1834 the American Baptist Home Mission Society was organized, which proved to be vitally important for furthering black religious education.

The most important innovation in religious instruction for youth in the first half of the nineteenth century was the Sunday school. But with a few exceptions Sunday school instruction was uniformly segregated. Only a few integrated Sunday schools existed in the North, in such places as Philadelphia. The South was slow to adopt the Sunday school, partly because it was identified with black education.

Despite state laws, Sunday instruction flourished, sometimes using oral instruction as a subterfuge to evade antiliteracy laws. Sunday schools that employed texts used the speller and reader for young children and the Bible for older Negroes. After NAT TURNER'S REBELLION in 1831—Turner had attended a Sunday school—religious instruction of slaves, and increasingly education of slaves in any form, was proscribed. Many white missionaries were able to preach to blacks by promising to preach obedience to slave masters.

A few white missionaries participated in denominational campaigns to place white Sunday school workers among blacks. Charles C. Jones was one who in 1842 wrote one of the first books on the history of black education in America, *The Religious Instruction of the Negroes*. While some white Sunday school teachers emphasized subservience to authority in their teaching, others were abolitionist in their teaching.

In 1859, when a Sunday school superintendent from Oberlin, Ohio, was held for two months without trial for work in the UNDERGROUND RAILROAD, four hundred children of the Oberlin Sabbath School Association conducted what may have been the first jail "sit-in." In 1855, William Lloyd Garrison proposed to the AMERICAN ANTI-SLAVERY SOCIETY that it pass a resolution condemning many groups in the

Sunday School Union as being in league and fellowship with the slaveholders of the South.

The Sunday school movement continued to flourish after the Civil War and Reconstruction. In the 1890s and 1900s the International Sunday School Convention hired black staff members to develop parallel organizational structures (i.e., state and local conventions) among the "colored people." Carter G. WOODSON stated in 1912, "Many of these Negroes often learned more on a single Sunday than the average student acquired in a day school during a week."

Not all religious education efforts received favorable review. The Christian Endeavor Movement, organized in 1881 by Francis E. Clark in a Portland, Me., Congregational church, became the model for the formal organizations of youth work in black churches and denominations. Youth between ages ten and eighteen pledged their loyalty to themes of commitment, constancy, faithful attendance, serious Bible study, and prayer. In 1902 I. Garlan Penn and J. W. E. BOWEN published the findings of the Negro Young People's Christian and Educational Congress at a conference in Atlanta, Ga.; the congress was called by a distinguished group of black leaders. Social workers and educators came together to advocate a unified approach to help improve the condition of black youth. In books written about the Negro church, critics such as W. E. B. DU BOIS, George HAYNES, and Benjamin MAYS cited the fact that youth groups lacked clear purpose, had low enrollments and poor attendance, were poorly guided, and had little community outreach. Reports such as these led a few black congregations to employ a social worker, often under the direction of the Christian education department.

Dr. William Lofton, one of the first graduates of HOWARD UNIVERSITY's Dental School, spoke as a trustee of St. Augustine's Catholic Parish in Washington, D.C., at the first black Catholic congress, held July 8–10, 1890. Lofton deplored the fact that the Catholic church provided few schools for black children, while teaching that Catholics should send their children to Catholic schools. His comments led to the establishment of a committee to seek congressional appropriation for blacks in Washington, D.C. The following year, at the second black Catholic congress, Charles Butler, a clerk in the Treasury Department of the federal government, reiterated the same point. He stressed that beyond twelve years of age, there was no Catholic school open to black youth— "Hence they are deprived of an education unless they seek it in a public school, possibly at the loss of their religion." Butler was convinced of the great need for industrial education for black boys. A set of resolutions was passed, calling for the establishment of night schools for Catholics to have access to a religious education.

Black colleges in the South, started after the Civil War, sometimes included Sunday schools in which the faculty would teach. These Sunday schools reached youth who could not qualify for higher academic programs. Frequently white missionaries would start new churches among blacks with a Sunday school initiative that would expand into a church. Such was the case with Lincoln Temple Congregational Church in Washington, D.C. It began as a Sunday school in the former Confederate Army's Wisewell Barracks immediately after the Civil War.

The chairman of the Committee for the Advancement of Colored Catholics and professor of biology at Howard University, Thomas Wyatt TURNER, wrote Archbishop Bonzano in November 1919, alerting him to the pressing need for more colored priests. He called attention to the failure of the church to educate more black students for the priesthood, the policy of the Catholic University to reject the application of blacks, and the neglect of Catholic education for black children.

Throughout the 1920s, 1930s, and 1940s, black churches built large and effective Sunday schools and youth departments. One such was the Metropolitan Baptist Church in Washington, D.C., under the leadership of Rev. Dr. Ernest Clarence Smith, who taught at Howard University and shared in citywide, ecumenical, and national Baptist conventions. Dr. Smith wrote sixteen Christian education books to equip Negroes to participate fully as citizens, "to meet the need of elevating, guiding, and inspiring optimum human nature among black men." The matter of "uplift of the race" through social action and getting out the black vote was epitomized in such leaders as Mary McLeod BETHUNE and Nannie Helen BURROUGHS, who led large numbers of black women within the churches to become actively involved in cleaning up alleys as well as improving educational opportunities for blacks.

Throughout the 1940s and 1950s the religious education efforts of African Americans collaborated with the civil rights struggle in America. Educational departments gave rise to improvement societies and equal opportunity committees such as those in Dexter Avenue Baptist Church in Montgomery, Ala., under Rev. Vernon JOHNS. Religious education efforts included voter registration and literacy training throughout the South. Much of the teaching and organizing was done by black college students.

The 1960s saw a new interest in changing the approaches of religious education among African Americans. The National Committee of Black Churchmen (NCBC), founded in 1967, established an educational committee in 1968. In 1969 members from the black denominations and black representatives of educational staff of predominantly white denominations in the National Council of Churches formed the Black Christian Education Project to address the educational needs of black people, especially those victims of overt oppression. This project formulated an educational design that included components of black history, black church history, and Saturday ethnic schools. Three major workshops at the Krisheim Study Center in Philadelphia between 1969 and 1971 trained leaders and workers from across the nation. Since 1971 the movement toward an explicitly African-American form of Christian education has intensified across the black church. In 1971 a group of editors from several black denominations met for the first time to develop black church curriculum resources. As a result, the Black Ecumenical Curriculum Resource Center was established by the Joint Education Development Department of the National Council of Churches under the leadership of Joe Nash.

In the 1980s, black-owned publishing houses, committed to using black writers and artists, began to market religious education materials especially designed for African Americans. Individual churches, persons writing black children's storybooks, and companies such as Urban Ministries and African-American Images in Chicago, gained popularity. Artistic creations and visual images depicting African and African-American people became prominent. The presence of blacks in the Bible was highlighted. Black-owned religious bookstores sprang up in churches and shopping malls, and the "Africanizing" of religious instruction has created a new audience and a new agenda for the black church.

See also RELIGION.

REFERENCES

CARPENTER, DELORES CAUSION. "Black Women in Religious Institutions." *The Journal of Religious Thought* 46, no. 2 (1989–1990).

DAVIS, CYPRIAN. *The History of Black Catholics in the United States.* New York, 1991.

RICE, EDWIN WILBUR. "Historical Perspectives." In Charles R. Foster and Grant S. Shockley, eds. *Working with Black Youth: Opportunities for Christian Ministry.* Nashville, 1989.

———. *The Sunday School Movement 1780–1917 and the American Sunday School Union 1817–1917.* New York, 1971.

SHOCKLEY, GRANT S. "Black Experience and Religious Education." In Iris V. Cully and Kendig Cully, eds. *Harper's Encyclopedia of Religion.* San Francisco, 1990.

TYMS, JAMES D. *The Rise of Religious Education Among Negro Baptists.* Washington, D.C., 1979.

DELORES CARPENTER

Religious Society of Friends (Quakers). *See* Society of Friends.

Remond, Charles Lenox (1810–December 22, 1873), abolitionist. Charles Lenox Remond was born in Salem, Mass., in 1810, the eldest son of John and Nancy Remond. John Remond, a hairdresser and successful merchant originally from Curaçao, was a prominent figure in Salem's black community and led the campaign to desegregate the city's public schools. Charles Remond received his education from a private tutor and attended integrated schools in Salem.

Remond adopted his parents' anti-slavery commitment as his own. He participated in the early life of the AMERICAN ANTI-SLAVERY SOCIETY (AASS). He embraced the Garrisonian principles of nonresistance and moral suasion, and he acquired the reputation as an eloquent and persuasive anti-slavery speaker. In 1838 he became the first full-time black lecturer hired by the Massachusetts Anti-Slavery Society. Over the following two years, he traveled through New England delivering anti-slavery lectures and organizing a network of local anti-slavery societies.

Remond drew on his lecturing and organizational experience during an eighteen-month tour of the British Isles. He represented the AASS at the World's Anti-Slavery Convention in London in 1840. When the convention refused to seat women delegates, he created a sensation by chastising the assembly for their exclusionary policy and by withdrawing from the proceedings.

Remond continued his anti-slavery lecturing when he returned to the United States in December 1841. He worked with Frederick DOUGLASS on the lecture circuit and participated in the widely publicized "One-Hundred Conventions" anti-slavery tour of midwestern states. Although an advocate of moral suasion, Remond revealed an interest in political anti-slavery as president of the Essex County Anti-Slavery Society in the late 1840s.

In the wake of federal laws and legal decisions restricting black citizenship, Remond became increasingly pessimistic about the prospects for racial progress. In the late 1850s, he judged the anti-slavery movement a failure. He abandoned nonresistance, defended slave revolts, and predicted a violent resolution to the question of southern slavery. In the 1850s, Remond advocated more aggressive tactics in the struggle for equal rights, but he remained committed to racial integration. He continued to oppose expressions of black separatism and criticized those who advocated racially exclusive schools, churches, and reform organizations.

Charles Lenox Remond, a member of a notable family of antislavery activists, was appointed in 1838 as the first black lecture agent of the Massachusetts Anti-Slavery Society and was one of the first black abolitionists to give a public-speaking tour. (Prints and Photographs Division, Library of Congress)

During the CIVIL WAR, Remond recruited black soldiers for the Fifty-fourth and Fifty-fifth Massachusetts regiments. He spoke out on RECONSTRUCTION issues and urged AASS to extend its commitment to racial justice beyond slave emancipation. Remond attended the 1867 meeting of the American Equal Rights Association, but he apparently retired from public life shortly thereafter. He suffered from ill health most of his life. The death of his first wife, Amy Williams, in 1856 and his second wife, Elizabeth Magee, in 1872 further aggravated his condition. Remond spent his last years working as a clerk in the Boston Customs House and died in 1873. (*See also* Sarah Parker REMOND.)

REFERENCES

USREY, MIRIAM L. "Charles Lenox Remond, Garrison's Ebony Echo: World Antislavery Convention, 1840." *Essex Institute Historical Collections* 106 (1970): 113–25.

WARD, WILLIAM EDWARD. Charles Lenox Remond: Black Abolitionist, 1838–1873. Ph.D. diss., Clark University, 1977.

MICHAEL F. HEMBREE

Remond, Sarah Parker (June 6, 1826–December 13, 1894), abolitionist. Born in Salem, Mass., one of eight children, Sarah Remond was the daughter of John Remond, a black immigrant from Curaçao, and Nancy Lenox Remond, daughter of African-American Revolutionary War veteran Cornelius Lenox. The family was noted for its abolitionist activities. In 1832, Remond's mother helped found the Salem Anti-Slavery Society, and her sister Caroline became an active member. In 1835 her father became a life member of the Massachusetts Anti-Slavery Society, and three years later, her brother, Charles Lenox REMOND began lecturing for the Society. In 1835, Sarah Remond completed grade school, but she was denied admission to the local high school on racial grounds, whereupon the family moved to Newport, R.I., returning to Salem after her graduation in 1841. In July 1842, Remond joined her brother as an antislavery lecturer, and began protesting segregation in churches, theaters, and other public places. In a well-publicized incident in 1853 at Boston's Howard Athenaeum, she refused to vacate a seat in the "whites-only" gallery during an opera. Arrested and thrown down the stairs, she subsequently won $500 in damages in a civil suit. In 1856, she was appointed a lecturing agent of the AMERICAN ANTI–SLAVERY SOCIETY and she and her brother covered the Northeast and Midwest. Antislavery leaders hailed her dignified bearing and eloquent speech.

In 1859, Sarah Remond and her brother left for England in order to further the cause of abolition. Denied a visa to France by the American legation in London, who claimed that because of her color she was not an American citizen, Remond toured Great Britain and Ireland. Bitter about the lack of educational opportunity in America, she welcomed the chance to study in Europe. She may have attended the Bedford College for Ladies in the years 1859 to 1861.

Remond stayed in England through the CIVIL WAR, urging the British to support the blockade of the Confederacy and raising money for freed slaves. In 1866, she returned to the United States. She attended the New York Constitutional Convention, where she lobbied unsuccessfully for universal suffrage. In 1867, Remond went back to Europe and settled in Italy, where she spent the rest of her life. She is believed to have studied medicine at the Santa

Maria Nuova Hospital in Florence. Remond received her diploma for "Professional Medical Practice" in 1868, married Lorenzo Pintor in 1877, and died in Rome seven years later.

REFERENCE

BOGIN, RUTH. "Sarah Parker Remond: Black Abolitionist from Salem." In Darlene Clark Hine, ed. *Black Women in American History from Colonial Times through the Nineteenth Century*. Vol. 1. Brooklyn, N.Y., 1990.

KIM ROBBINS

Renaissance Big Five (Harlem Rens).

The premier African-American professional basketball team of the 1930s, the Harlem Renaissance (nicknamed the Rens) was founded by Robert L. Douglas (1884–1979) in 1922, and was named for their home court, the Renaissance Casino Ballroom in HARLEM, NEW YORK. The original team consisted of Clarence (Pat) Jenkins, a former Negro League baseball player; Bill Yancey; John Holt; James (Pappy) Ricks; and Eyre Saith. Later Charles "Tarzan" Cooper and "Wee" Willie Smith joined the team. The Rens were noted for their flashy, quick passing attack, and players seldom dribbled. While the 6'4" Cooper and 6'5" Smith were inside shooters, most of the players relied on outside shots.

During the early 1930s, the Renaissance Casino closed, and the Rens were forced to play all their games on the road as the visiting team. The team bought a $10,000 custom-made bus for travel for the long rides. More importantly, the Rens had just seven players, and members of the team were thus forced to play games virtually without breaks. Still, the Rens reached the peak of their strength during these years. In 1931 the Rens beat their arch rivals, the Harlem Globetrotters, in the World Championship Tournament in Chicago. From 1932 to 1934 the team won 473 games out of the 491 it played, including 88 straight in 1934. In 1933 the Rens played a series of games with the Original (Boston) Celtics, a champion white team, in Cleveland and Kansas City. The Rens won seven of eight contests. In 1939 the Rens achieved a record of 112–7 and were one of eleven teams invited to the World Tournament in Chicago. They were unbeatable in the tournament, and defeated the Oshkosh All-Stars, champions of the National Basketball League (ancestor of the National Basketball Association) to take the the world title. The Rens ended their existence in 1944, as professional basketball integrated. Their record was reportedly an estimated 2,300 victories against 500 losses.

In 1963 the Harlem Renaissance was inducted into the Naismith Memorial Basketball Hall of Fame in Springfield, Mass.

REFERENCE

DICKEY, GLENN. *The History of Professional Basketball*. New York, 1982.

GREG ROBINSON

Reparations.

In May 1969, a man interrupted the Sunday service at the Riverside Church in New York City. Reading from a BLACK MANIFESTO, African-American civil rights activist James FORMAN made several demands. Among them was a call for reparations from whites to African Americans for historic and ongoing repression. In the first phase of this program, white churches and synagogues would pay $500 million to be distributed to African Americans and black community groups.

The demand for reparations was hardly a new phenomenon. Even before the Civil War, various groups advocated the redistribution of wealth or property to African Americans. In 1854, black abolitionist Sojourner TRUTH warned whites that they "owed the colored race a big debt, and if they paid it all back, they wouldn't have anything left for seed." Although its motives were racist, the nineteenth-century AMERICAN COLONIZATION SOCIETY called for government support of their program to provide free transportation and land in Liberia for any blacks willing to settle there. The champion of African emigration in the late nineteenth century, African Methodist Episcopal bishop Henry McNeal TURNER, believed that the government should be financially responsible for the "repatriation" effort.

"FORTY ACRES AND A MULE" became the historic rallying cry for reparations after an abortive experiment on the Sea Islands off the Georgia and South Carolina coasts, where Gen. William T. Sherman granted forty acres of land and the loan of a government mule to some African Americans near the end of the war. However, in mid-1865, under a proclamation of amnesty, President Andrew Jackson returned most of the donated property to its antebellum white owners. Another proposal of the same period would have provided African Americans with free transportation to the American West where, under the Homestead Act, they could obtain free land. In 1890, white Congressman William J. Connell (Republican-Nebraska), prompted by a wealthy and influential constituent, introduced a bill that would grant government pensions to blacks in partial recompense for the suffering of slavery. Various bills would propose pensions for African Americans, always unsuccessfully, until World War I.

Demands for compensation came from other areas. In 1892, in the British colony of Natal (part of present-day South Africa), white British missionary Joseph Booth created an "African Christian Union" whose goal was the uplifting of Africans. Booth foresaw the formation of a Christian nation of Africans. In order to fund its activities, the organization requested that the United States government pay £100 for every African American who volunteered to emigrate.

Proposals for reparations on behalf of African Americans have surfaced continuously throughout the twentieth century from a wide range of voices. In a somewhat obscure 1913 book, *Prophetic Liberator of the Coloured Race of the United States of America: Command to His People,* Arthur Anderson proposed the creation of a black state in the South. In 1928, the COMMUNIST PARTY of the United States argued that African Americans, especially in the South, were a distinct people and had a national identity. As such, the party argued, blacks were entitled to a homeland and had the right to carve out an independent African-American polity in the "Black Belt" states of the South.

Frequently, but not exclusively, demands for reparations have combined ideological radicalism with black nationalism. In 1934, the Chicago-based National Movement for the Establishment of a 49th State advanced its own agenda for redistribution, calling for a new state to be created in the American South. Through the creation of a new polity, blacks would "have the opportunity to work out their own destiny, unbridled and unhampered by artificial barriers." This state would be an "opportunity for the nation to reduce its debt to the Negro for past exploitation."

In 1955 black activist "Queen Mother" Audley MOORE, a former Garveyite and Communist, began her campaign to press for reparations, especially in a pamphlet entitled "Why Reparations? Money for Negroes." Moore believed that there was an effective one-hundred-year statute of limitations for an oppressed group to press legal claims against former captors. At one point in 1962, she even met with President John F. Kennedy to air her views. On the one-hundredth anniversary of the Emancipation Proclamation (see EMANCIPATION), Moore formed the Reparations Committee for the Descendants of American Slaves. The primary demand of $500 million was to be only partial compensation for historic wrongs. Her organization did file suit in at least one court in California.

While Moore's calls for reparations seemed to go unheeded, the subject of reparations was a major component of black nationalist rhetoric during the 1950s and 1960s. In the 1950s, the NATION OF ISLAM called for the establishment of a separate black state. In 1962, its leader Elijah MUHAMMAD asserted that "former slave masters are obligated to provide" choice land for the descendants of slaves to create an African-American nation. In addition, under the Nation of Islam's plan, the United States would support and maintain the population of the proposed black state for at least twenty to twenty-five years until it had reached some level of economic and political autonomy.

In a 1966 platform, the BLACK PANTHER PARTY called for economic restitution from the white community. Citing the promises of "forty acres and a mule" and the example of German aid to Jews after the Holocaust, the Panthers desired monetary payments that would be distributed to "our many communities." Other groups also made calls for reparations. One group located in Harlem, the "Provisional Government of the African-American Captive Nation," advocated the creation of a state, supported and aided by the American government, in all areas south of the Mason-Dixon Line where African Americans constituted a majority. A similar program was advocated by the separatist REPUBLIC OF NEW AFRICA, a nationalist organization headed by Imari Obadele (Richard Henry) and his brother Gaidi Obadele (Milton Henry). The Republic of New Africa (RNA) demanded an independent black nation that would encompass the states of Louisiana, Mississippi, Alabama, Georgia, and South Carolina. Although little support remains for the RNA, Imari Obadele continued to advocate reparations as recently as 1993.

The most vocal of all those urging reparations during the 1960s was James FORMAN, best known as the executive secretary of the STUDENT NON-VIOLENT COORDINATING COMMITTEE (SNCC) from 1961 until 1966. His disruption of the service at the Riverside Church was part of a larger effort to collect money from white churches and synagogues. This program, created by the Black Economic Development Conference, of which Forman was a leader, did not request direct payments to African Americans. Instead, the first $500 million installment would go toward forming, among other things, television stations owned and run by blacks, publishing and printing houses, training centers for job and community skills, and a Southern Land Bank that would provide funds for those who wanted land. The bank and an African-American university proposed by the manifesto would receive over $300 million of the total.

While some response came from the white community, it never approached the demands made by the BEDC. The reparations money received by the

BEDC was reputedly used to create Black Star publications, which distributed black militant writings written by Forman and others. One organization that received its start from funds generated in response to the manifesto was the Black Economic Research Center. Originally started by donations from the National Council of Churches, the Research Center began publishing the *Review of Black Political Economy,* a journal now published under the auspices of the National Economic Association, the professional organization of black economists. In the early issues of the *Review,* Robert S. Browne, director of the Research Center, advocated substantial reparations to correct disparities in wealth between blacks and whites. Struck by data from a survey that showed that blacks only held 2 percent of the nation's wealth, Browne felt that reparations would be an appropriate remedy.

Economist David Swinton, formerly a colleague of Browne's at the Research Center, argued in 1991 that the "gap between black and white America never changes because of the impact of slavery and JIM CROW on the accumulation of wealth—both financial, material, and in terms of human capital." Swinton endorsed reparations of between $700 billion and $1 trillion in order to begin to make a transition to a more economically powerful African-American community. Another group in Maryland, the Black Reparations Commission, placed the recommended payment as high as $4 trillion.

The 1980s saw no decrease in the call for reparations; indeed, many black activists argued that at least some discussion of reparations was required. The Detroit City Council passed a resolution in the late 1980s encouraging some compensation for slavery; a Massachusetts state senator introduced a reparations bill into the state senate in 1989. Arguing in 1992 that the nation owes a singular debt to African Americans above and beyond normal affirmative action programs, sociologist Paul Starr called for the establishment of a privately funded National Endowment for Black America, which would foster the economic growth of the black community. A body of activists and organizations known as the National Coalition of Blacks for Reparations in America (NCOBRA) began to agitate for reparations in 1989. Cochaired by Johnita Scott and Kalonji Olusegun, NCOBRA supported congressional legislation to discuss reparations and attempted to increase public awareness about reparations in the early 1990s.

Calls for reparations to Africa have continued as well. In May 1993, at a summit of African and African-American leaders held in Libreville, Gabon, the Rev. Jesse JACKSON proposed that slave reparations be "paid" to African nations in the form of relief for their external debt. Owed primarily to foreign governments and to multilateral organizations such as the International Monetary Fund and the World Bank, the debt was approximately $255 billion at the time.

The method of payment and its sources are crucial. Should, for example, payments be made by transferring existing assets from non-blacks to blacks until some level of preordained parity is achieved? Or, on the other hand, should the government sanction additional borrowing in order to effect such a transfer? The former strategy is unlikely to be politically acceptable when the group to receive the compensation is a minority of the overall population. The political complications of large-scale reparations would be considerable. Furthermore, it is probable that those who would not benefit from reparations would oppose a major redistribution of their assets.

One of the practical issues of concern to advocates of reparations is whether such an enormous one-time transfer of funds would be distributed to blacks as individuals and families, or to community-based organizations. If the former, would genealogical evidence have to be provided in order to establish that prospective recipients were descendants of enslaved Africans? Also, should payments go to all blacks, or only to those who show palpable evidence of current distress? If the latter, how would these organizations or individuals be identified and their need assessed? What uses could be made of funds on behalf of blacks collectively that would justify reparations payments?

There has been historical precedent for both formal apologies and economic reparations by nation-states to various groups. Japanese-Americans subjected to internment in American concentration camps during World War II have received an official national apology and payment of $20,000 per victim. Various Native-American nations have received settlements in court for prior seizure of their lands and discrimination. Since World War II, the German government has paid about $50 billion in reparations to Holocaust survivors. In 1988, Daimler-Benz, the German industrial giant, agreed to pay the equivalent of almost $12 million to victims of Nazi forced-labor policies and to their families. President Bill Clinton formally apologized to Hawaiians in 1993 for American involvement in the overthrow of the Hawaiian sovereign at the turn of the century. In general, although most whites are hostile to the suggestion, advocates of reparations in the 1990s have been increasingly vocal, and are receiving more and more public attention.

REFERENCES

AMERICA, RICHARD F. *Paying the Social Debt: What White America Owes Black America.* Westport, Conn., 1993.

———, ed. *The Wealth of Races: The Present Value of Benefits from Past Injustices.* New York, 1990.

BITTKER, BORIS. *The Case for Black Reparations.* New York, 1973.

BROWNE, ROBERT S. "The Economic Basis for Reparations to Black America." *The Review of Black Political Economy* 21, no. 3 (1993): 99–110.

CARSON, CLAYBORNE. *In Struggle: SNCC and the Black Awakening in the 1960s.* Cambridge, Mass., 1981.

FORMAN, JAMES. *The Making of Black Revolutionaries.* New York, 1972.

MOORE, AUDLEY. *Why Reparations? Money for Negroes.* Los Angeles, 1969.

PAYTON, BRENDA. "Reparations Now?" *The Nation* 253, no. 1 (July 1, 1991): 10.

WILLIAM A. DARITY, JR.

Republican Party.

Born out of political conflict over slavery, the Republican party forged through the Civil War and Reconstruction a close association with black Americans, an identification that continued in important ways long after the party retreated from the substantive commitments that had first nurtured the connection.

The Emancipation Proclamation (*see* EMANCIPATION) and the THIRTEENTH AMENDMENT provided the foundation; the FOURTEENTH AMENDMENT and FIFTEENTH AMENDMENT, together with the active participation of blacks in Republican politics during RECONSTRUCTION, cemented the relationship. No matter that emancipation had been declared as a war measure and that Abraham Lincoln had explicitly stated that he would maintain slavery if he could thereby save the Union; to blacks, his embrace of emancipation enshrined him ever afterward as the special champion of the race. With radical Republicans in Congress in control of Reconstruction, blacks gained important civil and political rights through constitutional amendments and federal and state legislation. As well, they played prominent roles in Republican Reconstruction governments in the southern states, as members of state legislatures, lieutenant governors, speakers of state houses, and secretaries of state. Between 1869 and 1901, twenty southern black Republicans were elected to the United States House of Representatives and two to the United States Senate.

With the end of radical Reconstruction in 1877, the Republican party began to distance itself from support of black rights. As the DEMOCRATIC PARTY regained control of southern state governments, they moved through the 1890s and early 1900s to disfranchise black voters and to erect the legal underpinnings of a segregated society. With these came the establishment of a one-party South.

Blacks looked in vain for support from Republicans in Washington. Committed to promoting sectional reconciliation, President William McKinley declined to confront such pressing racial issues as disfranchisement and lynching. At first, Theodore Roosevelt appeared to offer more hope: Blacks took heart from his willingness to appoint African Americans to federal offices, his reliance on the advice of Booker T. WASHINGTON, and his strongly stated opposition to lynching. In his second term, however, Roosevelt alienated many blacks, especially by his summary discharge of three companies of black infantrymen who refused to inform on their fellow soldiers who had allegedly shot up the town of Brownsville, Tex.

William Howard Taft proved to be even less supportive. Eager to strengthen southern Republicanism, he followed a policy of not appointing to federal offices anyone whom the local community found objectionable. In practice, that meant the exclusion of blacks from federal posts in the South—a record scarcely offset by some showcase appointments in Washington and in diplomatic and consular positions. Equally troubling was Taft's inattention to problems of segregation, discrimination, disfranchisement, and racial violence.

In the 1920s the Republican party again showed more interest in cultivating lily-white Republicanism in the South than in strengthening the party's traditional ties to blacks. Warren G. Harding and Calvin Coolidge appointed few blacks to federal posts and failed to reverse the policy of segregation in the civil service. Nor was there support for the battle of the NATIONAL ASSOCIATION FOR THE ADVANCEMENT OF COLORED PEOPLE (NAACP) to secure federal antilynching legislation.

In the Hoover administration, too, the desire to cultivate white political support in the South shaped the handling of racial issues. Herbert Hoover ignored black concerns such as racial violence and disfranchisement. He had a mediocre record on black appointments, and some of his principal white appointees were known to be antiblack. Worse than Hoover's neglect of blacks were the actions that blacks interpreted as deliberate slaps to the race: the segregation of Gold Star Mothers on a government-sponsored pilgrimage to visit the graves of American servicemen buried in Europe, and the nomination to the United States Supreme Court of John J. Parker, a circuit court judge in North Carolina who was known to be antiblack and who failed to win confirmation in part because of a vigorous campaign by the NAACP.

The Republican party's record on race loosened the historic ties that had bound blacks to the party of Lincoln; with the acute suffering of the GREAT DE-

PRESSION, many blacks were finally ready to turn Lincoln's picture to the wall and declare their political emancipation. The New Deal brought tangible economic assistance that made a critical difference in the struggle for survival. Moreover, blacks took encouragement from the unprecedented attention they enjoyed from the Roosevelt administration, most notably through the appointment of a Black Cabinet of racial advisers in federal agencies and through Eleanor Roosevelt's public support for the interests of blacks (*see* ROOSEVELT'S BLACK CABINET). With the election of 1936, the majority of black voters (an estimated 71 percent) cast their ballots for Franklin D. Roosevelt, breaking decisively with the historic pattern of support for the party of Lincoln.

A majority of blacks continued to identify themselves as Republicans well after they began voting Democratic in presidential elections. In 1948, attracted by Harry Truman's embrace of civil rights, a majority of blacks for the first time identified themselves as Democrats (a fifth to a quarter of those blacks surveyed continued to call themselves Republicans until 1964). In the election of 1956, black Republicanism enjoyed a brief resurgence as 39 percent of black voters supported Dwight D. Eisenhower. Later, however, the explicit commitment of John F. Kennedy and Lyndon B. Johnson to the cause of civil rights converted a healthy black majority into a nearly unanimous black commitment to the Democratic Party. The anti–civil rights stance of Republican nominee Barry Goldwater in 1964 marked the low point for black Republicanism: 6 percent of black voters supported the Republican ticket in the presidential election, while 8 percent of blacks identified themselves as Republicans. Over the next decades there were modest gains in Republican voting strength (Republican presidential candidates drew from 12 to 15 percent of the black vote in the elections of 1968 through 1980, but slipped to 9 to 10 percent in 1984 and 1988). Republican party identification fell to a low of 3 percent in 1968 but recovered to 9 percent in 1988 and 1992.

In 1928 Oscar DE PRIEST, a Republican from Chicago, became the first black to win election to Congress since Reconstruction. In 1966 Republican Edward BROOKE of Massachusetts won election to the United States Senate, the first (and, through 1992, the only) black to serve in that body in the twentieth century. Under Presidents Ronald Reagan and George Bush a vigorous effort to promote black conservative Republicans had little electoral success, though it did lead to the controversial appointment of conservative black Republican Clarence Thomas to the U.S. Supreme Court in 1991. By 1992, 70 of 7,480, or fewer than 1 percent, of black elected officials in the United States identified themselves as Re-

publicans, including one member of Congress, four state legislators, and five mayors.

REFERENCES

BOSITIS, DAVID. *Blacks and the 1992 Republican National Convention.* Washington, D.C., 1992.

BURK, ROBERT FREDRICK. *The Eisenhower Administration and Black Civil Rights.* Knoxville, Tenn., 1984.

KOUSSER, J. MORGAN. *The Shaping of Southern Politics: Suffrage Restriction and the Establishment of the One-Party South, 1880–1910.* New Haven, Conn., 1974.

LEWINSON, PAUL. *Race, Class, and Party: A History of Negro Suffrage and White Politics in the South.* 1932. Rev. ed. New York, 1965.

SHERMAN, RICHARD B. *The Republican Party and Black America: From McKinley to Hoover, 1896–1933.* Charlottesville, Va., 1973.

WEISS, NANCY J. *Farewell to the Party of Lincoln: Black Politics in the Age of FDR.* Princeton, N.J., 1983.

NANCY J. WEISS

Republic of New Africa. In 1967 Milton Henry, an African-American attorney and former acquaintance of MALCOLM X, and his brother, Richard (1931–), founded the Malcolm X Society, an organization based in Detroit whose purpose was to encourage the establishment of an autonomous black nation within the United States. By 1968 the brothers had adopted new names—Milton became Brother Gaidi Obadele and Richard renamed himself Imari Abubakari Obadele—and issued a call to black nationalists for the creation of an independent black republic in the deep South.

In March 1968, the Obadeles, along with black militant activist Robert F. WILLIAMS, convened several hundred nationalists in Detroit, where a declaration of independence was adopted and the Republic of New Africa (RNA) was established. The delegates called for the creation of an independent, communitarian black nation stretching across "the subjugated territory" of Louisiana, Mississippi, Alabama, Georgia, and South Carolina. The republic's economy would be organized according to the guidelines of *Ujamaa*, the Tanzanian model of cooperative economics and community self-sufficiency, but political rights and freedom of the press would be limited, unions discouraged, military service made compulsory, and men allowed multiple wives.

Soon several "consulates" were established across the country, officials were chosen, and members declared their allegiance to the "provisional government." In its manifestoes, largely written by Imari Obadele, the RNA called on the U.S. government to grant $400 billion in reparations for slavery and racist oppression and to cede the five "homeland" states to the Republic. In anticipation of the government's rejection of the proposal, the RNA's leaders developed a contingency plan of armed resistance in the South and guerrilla sabotage in the North.

Detroit police conducted a violent raid on the RNA's one-year anniversary conference, held in 1969 at the New Bethel Baptist Church. One police officer was killed and four RNA members were wounded after hundreds of rounds of ammunition were fired into the church. Three RNA members were tried and acquitted of murder charges, but one of the accused, Chaka Fuller, was stabbed to death several months later by an undiscovered assailant.

In 1971 the RNA purchased twenty acres of land in Hinds County, Miss., to be used as the capital, El Malik, but the original owner of the land, an African-American farmer, reneged on the agreement. Soon thereafter local police conducted a raid on the RNA headquarters in Jackson, Miss., during which a white police officer was killed. Eleven RNA members including Imari Obadele, president of the provisional government, were arrested and convicted on charges of murder, assault, and sedition. Ten of the "RNA-11" served sentences ranging from two to ten years. Hekima Ana was convicted of firing the shot that killed the officer and was sentenced to life in prison.

Three RNA members who were driving through New Mexico on route to Mississippi to assist the besieged headquarters murdered a police officer when he stopped their car. The three, Michael Finney, Charles Hill, and Ralph Goodwin, then hijacked a commercial airplane and ordered it flown to Cuba. Finney and Hill continue to live in Cuba (Goodwin died there in 1973).

Imari Obadele was released from prison in 1973, but shortly thereafter he and six others were convicted on federal conspiracy charges and incarcerated in a federal prison in Illinois. While serving his seven-year sentence, Obadele filed a civil suit against the FEDERAL BUREAU OF INVESTIGATION (FBI) in 1977 which resulted in the release of government documents confirming that the RNA had been targeted for subversion by COINTELPRO, the FBI's anti-radical program.

Formed at the height of the Black Power movement, the RNA attracted a significant number of sympathizers in both radical and liberal political circles. Communist Party leader Angela DAVIS organized support campaigns for the group and prominent Democratic politicians such as Julian BOND, John CONYERS, and George Crockett provided the legal assistance on various occasions. At the grassroots level, the diffusion of RNA offices in cities throughout the United States attested to the group's position as one of the most popular and influential black nationalist organizations.

Imari Obadele was released from prison in 1980 and went on to pursue an academic career. He received a Ph.D. in political science from Temple University in 1985, and through the late 1980s taught at several colleges, including Beaver College in Pennsylvania and College of Wooster in Ohio. Obadele has also published numerous books and articles on the RNA and black separatism in which he continues to advocate reparations, the acquisition of land, and the establishment of an independent, socialist republic where a distinctive and autonomous black culture could flourish. His works include *War in America: The Malcolm X Doctrine* (1968), *Revolution and Nation-Building: Strategy for Building the Black Nation in America* (1970), and *America the Nation-State: The Politics of the United States from a State-Building Perspective* (1988).

After the imprisonment of most of its leaders the RNA declined in prominence but remained committed to its original principles. In the mid-1980s the group moved its headquarters from Detroit to Washington, D.C., and claimed a membership of between 5,000 and 10,000. The RNA, which considers all African Americans to be citizens of the Republic, periodically holds elections on street corners in black neighborhoods to elect officials for the provisional government.

REFERENCES

LUMUMBA, CHOKWE. "Short History of the U.S. War on the Republic of New Africa." *Black Scholar* 12 (January–February 1981): 72–81.

MILLOY, COURTLAND. "State of a Nation." *Washington Post,* March 30, 1986, p. B3.

OBADELE, IMARI. *Free the Land! The True Story of the Trials of the RNA-11 in Mississippi and the Continuing Struggle to Establish an Independent Black Nation in Five States of the Deep South.* Washington, D.C., 1984.

VAN DEBURG, WILLIAM L. *New Day in Babylon: the Black Power Movement and American Culture, 1965–1975.* Chicago, 1992.

THADDEUS RUSSELL

Revels, Hiram Rhoades (September 1, 1822–January 16, 1901), politician. Hiram Rhoades Revels was the first black man to sit in the U.S. Senate, where he completed the unexpired term of Jefferson Davis. Revels was born in Fayetteville, N.C. His parents, who were free blacks, sent him to an elementary school run by a black woman. Moving north, Revels studied at several seminaries in Indiana and Ohio. He then became a minister in the AFRICAN METHODIST EPISCOPAL CHURCH (AME) and pastored congregations in Indiana, Illinois, Ohio, Missouri, and Maryland. In 1854, Revels left the AME Church after the congregation where he was pastor in St. Louis was divided by squabbling. He joined the ministry of the Presbyterian Church (*see* PRESBYTERIANS) and was posted to Baltimore, where he worked until the outbreak of the CIVIL WAR.

Once hostilities commenced, Revels helped organize the first black regiments in Maryland and Missouri. Leaving the Presbyterian Church, he went south; reunited with the AME Church, Revels became active in Republican politics, serving on the city council of Natchez, Miss., briefly as a state senator, and in 1870–1871 replacing Jefferson Davis in the U.S. Senate.

Compared to other AME ministers who entered RECONSTRUCTION politics, Revels was rather lackluster. During his tenure in the Senate, Revels delivered a few speeches, but none of the legislation he introduced was passed. After his term expired, he returned to Mississippi, left the AME Church, and became a minister in the Methodist Episcopal Church (North). Revels served twice after he left the Senate as President of Alcorn University, Mississippi State College for Negroes.

REFERENCES

WALKER, CLARENCE E. *A Rock in a Weary Land: The African Methodist Episcopal Church during the Civil War and Reconstruction.* Baton Rouge, La., 1982.
WHARTON, VERNON LANE. *The Negro in Mississippi, 1865–1890.* New York, 1967.

CLARENCE E. WALKER

Reverend Ike (Eikerenkoetter, Frederick J.) (June 1, 1935–), religious leader. Born in Ridgeland, S.C., Frederick J. Eikerenkoetter II was educated in public schools. At the age of sixteen, he became an assistant pastor in his father's Bible Way Church. After graduating from high school in 1952, Eikerenkoetter went to Chicago to attend the American Bible College; he received a bachelor's degree in theology in 1956.

After serving two years in the U.S. Air Force Chaplain Corps, Eikerenkoetter returned to South Carolina, where he founded the United Church of Jesus Christ for All People. In 1962 Eikerenkoetter established the United Christian Evangelistic Association (UCEA), a corporate structure that he would

Hiram Revels, a free black from North Carolina and an African Methodist church missionary, became the first African-American U.S. senator when elected in 1871 to complete the unfinished term of Jefferson Davis. Revels later became president of Alcorn Agricultural and Mining College in Mississippi, the first black land grant college. (Photographs and Prints Division, Schomburg Center for Research in Black Culture, The New York Public Library, Astor, Lenox and Tilden Foundations)

maintain throughout his career. He set up the Miracle Temple in Boston in 1964 and moved to New York City in 1966. After operating from a defunct movie theater in Harlem for several years, Eikerenkoetter, by then known as Reverend Ike, moved into a large, vacant movie palace in the Washington Heights section of Manhattan in New York City.

The refurbished building served as the headquarters for Reverend Ike's United Church and Science of Living Institute. Reverend Ike espoused a vision of happiness and personal fulfillment that would come through self-confidence and prosperity. By making donations to his church, people would receive copies of Reverend Ike's Blessing Plan and other assistance that provided the self-confidence that would lead to success.

By 1972 Reverend Ike claimed that more than one million people received the newsletter and magazine of his organization. Average attendances of four thousand people were not uncommon in his New York congregation, and a second, large affilitate met in Boston. Not content to restrict his activities to one or two locales, Reverend Ike began to tour the country, making speeches and collecting money for his church. He was one of the first African-American religious leaders to have a regular television show; taped broadcasts for both radio and television were aired regionally in New York, Chicago, and other cities. By 1982 Reverend Ike claimed that more than seven million people around the world received his quarterly magazine, which often included pieces about his many luxury cars and homes in Beverly Hills and New York.

Critics charged that Reverend Ike was essentially defrauding his congregation and that he was more a con artist than a religious leader. He also came under criticism from black community leaders who believed that his emphasis on personal advancement and economic success failed to aid the black community in its struggle for communal empowerment.

After the 1970s Reverend Ike's ministry was less visible. As late as 1990 he was still circulating pleas for money; in return, the donor would receive a "Holy Blessing Package," followed by "Health, Happiness . . . and More Money. . . ." In the early 1990s he had curtailed many of his national activities. However, through his Manhattan church Reverend Ike continued to support some international evangelistic activities through the UCEA and several outreach programs throughout the country.

REFERENCES

MORRIS, JAMES. *The Preachers*. New York, 1973.
RILEY, CLAYTON. "The Golden Gospel of Reverend Ike." *New York Times Magazine* (March 19, 1975).

VIETS, ELAINE. "Offer of Riches Comes with Strings Attached." *St. Louis Post-Dispatch,* August 7, 1990, p. 3D.

JOHN C. STONER

Revolutionary Action Movement. The Revolutionary Action Movement (RAM) was one of the earliest expressions of revolutionary black nationalism. Founded in 1963, RAM was a Marxist–Leninist organization which believed that violence was the only way to fundamentally alter the structure of American society and "free black people from colonial and imperialist bondage." Based in Philadelphia and New York, RAM claimed several hundred members which included teachers, students, clerks, and businesspeople, all of whom were passionately dedicated to the struggle of which they were a part. RAM was founded by Robert Franklin Williams, former head of a local NAACP branch in North Carolina who gained national attention for advocating black self-defense and was in exile in Cuba, then China, while serving as RAM's president.

RAM's goal was to build a liberation army by educating and mobilizing young African Americans. Through grass-roots organizing, it sought to maintain a base in the black community. The organization published a bimonthly magazine, *Black America*, and distributed a free weekly, *RAM speaks*. RAM also sent out field organizers to form local groups, organize street meetings, and hold African and African-American history classes. RAM worked with more traditional civil rights groups, but its members were critical of their piecemeal reform agenda. On one occasion, RAM joined the NAACP in demonstrations over discrimination on a school construction site. However, they were less interested in integrating the job site than in educating the people on the pitfalls of reform struggles and the necessity of revolutionary organization.

Despite the small size and relative obscurity of RAM, its militant posture and commitment to grass-roots organizing made it a target of FEDERAL BUREAU OF INVESTIGATION infiltration. By 1965, as part of a larger program to undermine radical black organizations, undercover FBI agents had penetrated RAM's structure. On June 21, 1967, New York City and Philadelphia police rounded up seventeen RAM members, including Maxwell Sanford, field chairman of RAM, in predawn raids and seized about 130 weapons. Fifteen members were charged with criminal conspiracy, but they were never brought to trial and charges were eventually dropped. The other two, Herman Ferguson, an assistant principal at a New York City school, and Arthur Harris, unemployed at the time, were convicted of conspiracy to assassinate Roy WILKINS of the NAACP and Whitney YOUNG of the National Urban League and sentenced to three and a half to seven years in prison. After failed attempts at appeals, Harris fled to Sweden, where he remains today, and Ferguson went to Guyana, where he lived for nineteen years. Upon returning to the United States in 1989, Ferguson was immediately taken into custody, but he was released on parole in 1993. That year, a judge ordered the FBI to release his files, which Ferguson is certain will vindicate him. However, the FBI has delayed doing so. In another raid, in September 1967, seven RAM members in Philadelphia were charged with conspiring to assassinate local and national leaders, blow up City Hall, and foment a riot, during which time they planned to poison the city's police force. Charges against RAM members consisted of conspiracy and intent based on fiery speeches or militant rhetoric, rather than acts committed. The testimony of informers was the primary evidence used to convict RAM members, who vehemently denied the allegations and claimed that local police and FBI agents had instituted a frame-up to discredit them.

The FBI infiltration and raids on RAM were devastating. With most of the leadership either in prison, under surveillance, or in hiding, there were few left to sustain the organization's activities. In 1968, RAM collapsed. Some ex-RAM members helped form the Republic of New Afrika, which was intended to be a provisional government of a separate black state within the United States. Despite the short-lived existence of RAM, it was an important example of the changing nature of the black political movement of the sixties: the disillusionment with conventional politics and the desire to effect social and political change by more radical means.

REFERENCES

BRACEY, JOHN H., JR., AUGUST MEIER, and ELLIOT RUDWICK, eds. *Black Nationalism in America.* Indianapolis, 1970.
BRISBANE, ROBERT. *Black Activism: Racial Revolution in the U.S., 1954–70.* Valley Forge, Pa., 1974.

NANCY YOUSEF
PAM NADASEN

Revolutionary War.   *See* American Revolution.

Rhode Island.   The exact date when blacks first arrived in Rhode Island is unknown, although by 1637 Indian warriors captured in the Pequot War were being exchanged for black slaves from the Caribbean. In 1652 the Rhode Island General Court was sufficiently alarmed by the growth of SLAVERY to limit indentured servitude for blacks and whites to ten years. This law was enforced for whites, but not for blacks. Rhode Islanders became leaders in the SLAVE TRADE, which not only became a mainstay in the colony's economy, but made Newport one of the leading slave-trading centers in North America. At first the traders sold their cargoes in the West Indies, but as Rhode Island grew, so did the colony's demand for slaves.

There were four patterns of slavery in eighteenth-century Rhode Island. In Newport the slaves were generally employed as house servants, though there were some workers, both skilled and unskilled. In Providence a similar occupational pattern prevailed, but with slaves employed in a wider variety of occupations and with fewer serving as domestics. In the smaller outlying communities, however, slaves were used much like indentured servants and were put to a variety of tasks.

In the southern part of the colony, across Narragansett Bay from Newport, a form of slavery unique to New England appeared. On the basis of their landholdings, their wealth, their aristocratic lifestyle, and their ownership of slaves, the mid-eighteenth century planters of the Narragansett Country—so named for the local Indians—were compared to their counterparts in Virginia and the Carolinas. In 1755 one in every three residents of South Kingstown was black, and in the same year a census found 712 whites and 418 blacks in Charlestown. The large landowners were cattlemen, sheepmen, and dairymen. With slave labor, they raised hogs and marketed livestock, as well as pork, butter, lard, wool, and wood products. Rhode Island cheese was popular, and the Narragansett pacer, a horse known for its smooth gait, was a preferred mount in both North America and the Caribbean. Most of these goods were ferried across the Bay to Newport and then shipped, but some slaveholders shipped directly from their own piers. Slaves were employed as both ferrymen and on ships which traded along the North American coast and in the Caribbean.

The presence of so large a black population, and the tendency of the slave owners to lend their slaves to one another, to bring them together at harvest time and during holidays, created a strong network among blacks, a fact clearly demonstrated in what the slaves called "'Lection Day." On 'Lection Day, the male slaves came together to elect a slate of black officials who were given, some scholars argue, limited power over the black community to adjudge minor infractions and resolve disputes. A governor, a lieutenant governor, a sheriff, and other officials were elected. Elections were traditionally held on the third Saturday in June, and when the slave population was at its apogee—around mid-century—two elections were held each year, one in North and one in South Kingstown. 'Lection Day itself was the subject of much advance political maneuvering and the voting was carried out amidst considerable pageantry; a parade took place, an all-day picnic was held, and there were games, feasting, and drinking. Slaves were usually given the day off, and those elected to office were generally persons of some standing among their fellow slaves. The wealthy slavemasters supported their favorite slaves, providing them with finery, foodstuffs, and occasionally the loan of horses and carriages. Free blacks continued 'Lection Day festivities until 1841, when the frequent attacks on the participants by racist whites ended the tradition.

Two scholarly debates surround 'Lection Day events. The first is over whether the elections represented a continuation of traditions in West Africa, where the election of officials was common, or whether the slaves were merely emulating the colonists. The second debate is over the extent to which the black officials had any meaningful power in the slave community. The first debate is most easily resolved by saying the two forces leading to elections among the slaves were not mutually exclusive and could have reinforced one another. The second debate is more complex, for while it is clear the slaves tended to vote into office those among them who were most respected, it is far from clear that these men had any significant power. Slavemasters generally reserved such power for themselves.

For much of the seventeenth and eighteenth centuries the terms "black" and "slave" were interchangeable. A gradual emancipation law was passed declaring that all children born into slavery after March 1, 1784, were to be free. Freed from the chains of slavery, black Rhode Islanders left the Narragansett country in droves, and while many left the state, others were attracted to a growing, developing, industrializing Providence. For the latter part of the nineteenth century and into the twentieth, Providence, not the Narragansett country, was the center of black life.

Freedom did not mean equality with whites for nineteenth-century black Rhode Islanders. In 1822, a Rhode Island law disenfranchised black males. African Americans were excluded from participation in Rhode Island's industrial revolution. While jobs opened up for whites in textiles, ironmongering, and other manufacturing concerns, Rhode Island blacks remained confined to domestic work, janitorial services, and similar menial jobs. A 1701 law forbidding interracial marriage remained in force until 1881, and was then repealed by a mere eight votes in the Rhode Island Senate. When Rhode Island began support for common schools in the 1830s, the state set aside funds to educate black children up to the age of ten. School districts were given the option of having integrated or racially segregated schools. Rural areas with a small population generally allowed blacks to attend schools with whites, but in Providence, Newport, and Bristol, all towns with a substantial black population, separate schools were created. Not until 1866 did the General Assembly abolish segregated schools. African Americans also were discriminated against in housing and in receiving bank loans.

Blacks were sometimes subjected to brutal physical attacks. In Providence, two riots led to the destruction of black neighborhoods. The Hardscrabble riots took place in 1824 and were sparked by the failure of some blacks to yield the sidewalk to whites. In 1831, riots in Snowtown lasted three days. In both cases blacks fought back, at times driving off the mobs, but at both times numerous black homes were destroyed.

Black Rhode Islanders responded to racism in varied ways. Some left. In 1826, led by Newport Gardiner, one of the most respected black Newporters, thirty-two blacks sailed for Liberia with support from the AMERICAN COLONIZATION SOCIETY. Others left for New York City, for Boston, and for other cities that were perceived as offering more opportunities for African Americans. Ironically, those who wanted to be schoolteachers, librarians, doctors, dentists, and other professionals often moved to the segregated South, where they could both attend college and work. Other Rhode Islanders organized themselves to serve the black community and fight racism. In 1780, under the leadership of Newport Gardiner, blacks in Newport established the African Union Society. The organization committed itself to aiding blacks by keeping community records, finding training and jobs for black youth, and supporting members in time of financial need. The Providence African Union Society was established at about the same time. In Newport the African Union Society merged in 1808 with the African Benevolent Society, a group established to support a school for black children. Black Freemasonry came to Rhode Island in 1799 with the establishment of Hiram Lodge Number Three. The African Greys, a black military drill company, the members of which purchased their own weapons, was established in 1820. Newspapers were a primary means of communication in nineteenth-century America, and black Rhode Islanders made a number of attempts to establish newspapers of their own. William J. Brown and the Reverend George W. Hamblin briefly published *L'Ouverture,* a monthly, in the 1860s. In 1880, *The Eastern Review* was published in Providence, and in 1891 John C. Minkins edited *The New England Torchlight,* a weekly. None of these newspapers was long lived, but Minkins went on to have a long and distinguished career as a journalist, including five years as the editor-in-chief of the *Evening News.*

Churches were not only central in the spiritual life of African-American Rhode Islanders, but were also important in the struggle for justice. For much of the eighteenth century, most black Rhode Islanders were not Christians, and even those who became Christians had no share in church governance. Blacks were segregated in most of the churches, required to sit either at the back of the church or in segregated balconies. In both Newport and Providence, blacks established churches of their own. In Providence the African Union Meeting House was built with the financial support of both blacks and whites, with African Americans in Boston, Hartford, New Haven, and even Baltimore sending monies. The church was open to black Americans of all denominations. However, the growth of the black population and increased black knowledge of and interest in American theology led to union churches in both cities dividing along denominational lines. In Providence, African Americans left Congdon Street Baptist Church to form Ebeneezer Baptist in 1880, and still others left in 1901 to form Olney Street Church. In 1871, an African Methodist Episcopal Zion Church was established in Providence and three years later an African Methodist Episcopal Church was founded. A similar fragmentation of the churches took place in Newport and elsewhere in the state.

In the twentieth century, Rhode Islanders continued to suffer from discrimination in jobs, housing, and education, but a number of black attorneys were admitted to the bar, notable among them Joseph G. LeCount, who was a leader in the state for the better part of the century. In the 1930s, T. E. Lewis operated an enameling business, hiring in the process a number of fellow blacks. In 1932, Andrew Bell opened a funeral parlor to serve blacks, and like LeCount, Bell was for many years a leader in Rhode Island's black community.

In the 1970s African-American Rhode Islanders began to be employed as bus drivers, college professors, bank tellers, schoolteachers, and policemen, but their numbers remain small. Blacks have made great strides in being elected to public office. Paul Gaines was elected mayor of Newport. Charles Walton is the state's first, and through the early 1990s, the only, black state senator, though a number of state representatives and city councilmen have been elected. No

African American has yet been elected to statewide office. A number of blacks have been named to the judiciary, including Alton Wiley, Edward Clifton, and O. Rogieree Thompson, Rhode Island's first African-American female judge. Blacks have also been appointed to positions in the state's institutions of higher education. In the early 1990s William Truehart was President of Bryan College, John McCray was vice president for student development at the University of Rhode Island, and James Wyche was associate provost at Brown University. Published by Frank Graham, *The Providence American,* Rhode Island's black newspaper, began publication in 1985. There are sufficient numbers of bankers of African-American descent in the state to have formed their own organization. On the one hand some black Rhode Islanders have prospered, but on the other, drug-related black-on-black crime has significantly increased, the rate of black teenage pregnancy has increased, and urban renewal cost blacks in Providence a substantial portion of one of their historic neighborhoods. In this sense, Rhode Island's blacks in the 1990s (there was an African-American population of 39,000 in 1990) mirror the nation, with a few blacks who have made it well into the middle class, and a large number existing at or near the poverty line, and comparatively few in between.

REFERENCES

BARTLETT, IRVING H. *From Slave to Citizen: The Story of the Negro in Rhode Island.* Providence, 1954.

COTTROL, ROBERT J. *The Afro-Yankees: Providence's Black Community in the Antebellum Era.* Westport, Conn., 1982.

COUGHTRY, JAY. *Creative Survival: The Providence Black Community in the Nineteenth Century.* Providence, 1984.

JONES, RHETT S. "Plantation Slavery in the Narragansett Country of Rhode Island, 1690–1790." *Plantation Society in the Americas* 2 (1986): 157–170.

PIERSEN, WILLIAM D. *Black Yankees: The Development of an Afro-American Subculture in Eighteenth Century New England.* Amherst, Mass., 1988.

RHETT S. JONES

Rhodes, Theodore, Jr. (1916–July 4, 1969), golfer. Theodore Rhodes was raised in Nashville, Tenn., in a close-knit family. From his father, who was an avid GOLF fan, a caddie, and an average player, he inherited an interest in the sport. The younger Rhodes started caddying in his early teenage years at local country clubs after school and on weekends to help supplement the family income. But because African Americans were not allowed to play on any of Nashville's courses, public or private, he had to learn to play with other African Americans in public fields, occasionally sneaking a round on a standard course. By the time he was twenty-five he was known as one of Nashville's best players.

In the early 1940s, Joe LOUIS, who had become an avid golfer, heard of Rhodes's golfing prowess on a trip through Nashville and hired him to be his personal instructor. With Louis's financial support, Rhodes played in tournaments across the country, mostly on the fledgling UNITED GOLFERS ASSOCIATION (UGA) tour, also known as the "Neckbone Tour," which was predominantly for African-American players, who were banned from all but a handful of the tournaments of the Professional Golfers Association (PGA). Rhodes also played as Louis's partner in big-money gambling games, usually winning. Rhodes won the UGA National Open four times, 1949, 1950, 1951, and 1957, and more than 150 other tournaments, most against African-American professionals. He also played in the United States Open a few times and in the handful of other events open to African Americans, such as the Los Angeles and Phoenix Opens. His fourteenth-place finish in the 1949 Tam O'Shanter All American Open in Chicago was believed to be the highest finish ever by an African American in a predominantly white tournament.

Rhodes was part of the pioneering group of black professionals, also including Bill Spiller and Charlie SIFFORD, that led the movement eventually forcing the PGA to drop its Caucasian-only clause in November 1961. Because he played in so few PGA tournaments and because the UGA offered meager purses, Rhodes's income from victories never equaled his impressive tournament records. His biggest paycheck was $1,500, from the Ballantine Open in the 1950s, and in his best competitive season he earned about $10,000—while white professionals sometimes earned more than $50,000 a season in the 1950s.

As his health deteriorated in the 1960s, Rhodes curtailed competitive playing and focused on mentoring young African-American talents, including Lee ELDER and Charlie Sifford. Rhodes never received much public acclaim for his golfing prowess because he did not have the opportunity to consistently compete against the best players of his era. But the effortless power and smooth rhythm of his swing earned him the nickname "Straight Arrow." The day before dying of a heart attack in Nashville, he shot thirty-three, three under par, over nine holes on a public course that in 1991 was renamed for him.

REFERENCES

BARKOW, AL. *Gettin' to the Dance Floor*. New York, 1986.

LIPSEY, RICK. "Ted Rhodes." *Golf Magazine* (November 1992): 108–109.

RICK LIPSEY

Rhythm and Blues. The term *rhythm and blues* was a product of the post–World War II music industry's effort to find a new word to replace the category that had been known for several decades as "race records." First used by *Billboard* magazine in 1949, rhythm and blues was intended to describe blues and dance music produced by black musicians for black listeners, so that rhythm and blues—often abbreviated to R&B—was more a marketing category than a well-defined musical style. In effect, R&B reflected the confluence of JAZZ, BLUES, GOSPEL, and vocal harmony group music that took place in cities such as New York, Detroit, Chicago, Memphis, Philadelphia, and New Orleans after World War II. In the 1950s successful marketing efforts that targeted white listeners made rhythm and blues, and the related category of rock and roll, the most popular music not only in the United States but in the rest of the world as well. Although much rhythm and blues music was produced by small, white-owned record labels such as Savoy, Atlantic, and Chess—in the 1960s Motown would be an exception—and was aimed at a multiracial market, rhythm and blues has always drawn its core influences from African-American culture.

The Roots of Rhythm and Blues: Jazz

The most obvious ancestor of rhythm and blues was jazz, which in the 1920s and '30s was black America's popular music, produced mostly to accompany dancing. In the 1940s many big bands featured "honking" tenor saxophonists who played in a bluesy, at times histrionic style that drove dancers to ever more frenzied steps and tempos. Lionel HAMPTON's "Flyin' Home" (1943), with its famous solo by Illinois JACQUET (1922–), was the model for such performances. Many tenor saxophonists followed Jacquet's model, including Bill Doggett (1916–), Arnett Cobb (1918–1989), Ike Quebec (1918–1963), Hal "Cornbread" Singer (1919–), and Willis "Gatortail" Jackson (1928–1987). Important recordings in this style include "Juice Head Baby" (1944) and "Deacon's Hop" (1948) by Big Jay McNeely (1929–) and "The Hucklebuck" (1949) by Paul Williams.

Another jazz influence on rhythm and blues was the jump bands that were popular starting in the mid-1940s. These midsized ensembles, named for their buoyant tempos, combined the extroverted solo style of the honking tenors with the relentless momentum

Jimmy SMITH (1925–), Cannonball ADDERLEY, David "Fathead" Newman (1933–), Eddie Harris (1934–), King Curtis (1934–1971), Stanley Turrentine (1934–), and Ramsey Lewis (1935–) all performed in the bluesy, funky style known as soul jazz. Herbie HANCOCK, a groundbreaking avant-garde jazz pianist in the 1960s, went on to experiment with funk music in the 1970s and RAP in the '80s.

Vocal Groups

The vocal harmonizing groups of the 1940s helped develop the heavily rhythmic backing of passionate vocals that characterize rhythm and blues. Some of these groups were called "doo-wop" groups, after the wordless, nonsense-syllable accompaniments they often sang. The Ink Spots, formed in 1934, were among the earliest important rhythm-and-blues vocal groups, although the group's smooth approach on songs such as "If I Didn't Care" (1939), "To Each His Own" (1946), and "The Gypsy" (1946) was less influential in the development of rhythm and blues than the more heavily rhythmic performances of the MILLS BROTHERS, who had hits with "Paper Doll" (1942) and "You Always Hurt the One You Love" (1944).

After World War II, dozens of important vocal groups, starting with the "bird groups," drew heavily from the gospel tradition and dominated black popular music. Groups such as the Ravens ("Ol' Man River," 1946), the Orioles ("Crying in the Chapel," 1953), the PLATTERS ("Only You," 1955, "The Great Pretender," 1956), the Dominoes ("Sixty Minute Man," 1951), and the Clovers ("Fool, Fool, Fool," 1951; "Good Lovin'," 1953; and "Love Potion Number Nine," 1959), and the 5 Satins ("In the Still of the Night," 1956) used simple arrangements and minimal instrumental accompaniment to highlight their passionate, gospel-style vocals. The Penguins ("Earth Angel," 1954) were notable for their juxtaposition of high falsetto with deep bass voices. The COASTERS had a more raucous and humorous style than other doo-wop groups, evidenced on "Riot in Cell Block No. 9" (1954) and "Charlie Brown" (1959). The Drifters were hugely popular throughout the 1950s and early '60s ("Money Honey," 1953; "Save the Last Dance for Me," 1960; "Up on the Roof," 1962; "On Broadway," 1963; and "Under the Boardwalk," 1964).

In the 1950s and '60s impromptu, street-corner doo-wop–style singing was an essential part of African-American urban life. Solo rhythm-and-blues singers who drew on gospel, vocal harmony, and doo-wop traditions were among the most popular recording artists of the era. An early member of the Drifters, Clyde MCPHATTER, topped the R&B and pop charts with "Without Love" (1956), "Long

Dinah Washington was a rhythm-and-blues singer of passionate intensity, as can be seen in this photograph of her in concert performance at the Newport Jazz Festival. (George West)

of shuffle and boogie-woogie rhythms of pianists Albert AMMONS, Meade "Lux" LEWIS, and Pete Johnson (1904–1967), whose "Roll 'Em Pete" (1938) with vocalist Big Joe TURNER was one of the first great rhythm-and-blues performances. Tiny Bradshaw (1905–1958), Slim Gaillard (1916–1991), and Johnny Otis (1921–1984), the latter a white musician whose bands were largely black, all led jump ensembles. The greatest of the jump band leaders was saxophonist and vocalist Louis JORDAN. His biggest hits, including "Is You Is or Is You Ain't My Baby?" (1944), "Let the Good Times Roll" (1945), "Caldonia" (1945), "Choo Choo Ch'Boogie" (1946), and "Saturday Night Fish Fry" (1940), were novelty numbers suffused with earthy humor. Jordan was a masterful saxophonist in the jazz tradition, yet most of his records were carefully composed, and his rejection of jazz improvisation became a major characteristic of rhythm and blues.

In the late 1950s and '60s, the relationship between jazz and rhythm and blues was sometimes reversed, with musicians—especially the pianist Horace SILVER, who recorded "Opus de Funk" in 1953—drawing inspiration from rhythm and blues. In the 1960s,

Lonely Nights" (1957), and "A Lover's Question" (1958). Jackie WILSON, another falsetto tenor and Drifters' alumnus, had a huge following for his "To Be Loved" (1958), "Lonely Teardrops" (1958), and "Higher and Higher" (1959). Ben E. King (1938–) also worked with the Drifters before recording "Spanish Harlem" (1960) and "Stand by Me" (1960). Frankie Lymon (1942–1968) and the Teenagers achieved great popularity with songs such as "Why Do Fools Fall in Love?" (1956), "The ABCs of Love" (1956), and "I'm Not a Juvenile Delinquent" (1956). A doo-wop group that came to prominence relatively late was Little Anthony Gourdine (1940–) and the Imperials, whose "Tears on My Pillow" was a hit record in 1958.

Gospel music was a direct influence on many important R&B singers. Sam COOKE sang gospel with the Soul Stirrers starting in 1950 and eventually recorded such secular songs as "You Send Me" (1957), "Chain Gang" (1960), and "Another Saturday Night" (1963). Solomon Burke (1936–), who recorded "Just Out of Reach" (1960) and "Got to Get You off My Mind" (1965), also sang in a gospel-influenced R&B style. The vocals and even the themes of Curtis MAYFIELD and the Impressions' "I'm So Proud" (1964) and "People Get Ready" (1965) both have strong connections to black sacred

Earth, Wind, and Fire, under the direction of Maurice White (center front), was one of the most popular black musical groups of the 1970s, performing an innovative combination of jazz, soul, Latin music, and funk. (Frank Driggs Collection)

music. Al GREEN, a child gospel sensation later known for soul recordings such as "Let's Stay Together" (1972) and "Take Me to the River" (1973), returned to the church in the late 1970s and has since concentrated solely on gospel music.

Blues

The urban blues styles of the late 1940s and early '50s, with loud, amplified guitars, anguished vocals, and churning rhythms, are also direct descendants of rhythm and blues. Perhaps the best examples of this influence are MUDDY WATERS, HOWLIN' WOLF, and B. B. KING, all of whom were prominent on the rhythm and blues charts in the 1950s. Bo DIDDLEY ("Who Do You Love," 1955; "Bo Diddley," 1955, "I'm a Man," 1955) and Screamin' Jay Hawkins (1929–), who had a 1956 hit with "I Put a Spell on You," represent a less pure blues style that was nonetheless equally influential in creating rhythm and blues. Big Joe Turner, whose "Roll 'Em Pete" with pianist Pete Johnson is considered one of the founding songs of rhythm and blues, was known in the 1950s for his shouting renditions of "Chains of Love" (1951) and "Shake, Rattle and Roll" (1954), both of which are considered classic examples of a time when rock and roll was virtually synonymous with rhythm and blues. Another early rhythm and blues figure was Arthur "Big Boy" Crudup (1905–1974), a guitarist and singer who was popular throughout the 1940s but was best known for writing "That's All Right" (1946), which became a hit for Elvis Presley in 1954.

Along with the Chicago blues style, a different kind of blues, at once more derived from jazz and country music but with the same reliance on electric instruments, exerted a strong influence on early rhythm and blues. T-Bone WALKER, a singer and guitarist who successfully negotiated the boundary between blues and jazz on "Stormy Monday" (1945), had several hit rhythm and blues-influenced records in the early 1950s, including "Strolling with Bones" (1950) and "Street Walkin' Woman" (1951). Wynonie Harris (1915–1969), a blues shouter with a strong Louis Jordan influence, wrote "Good Rocking Tonight" and had several hits in the mid-1940s. A mellower approach was represented by Roy Brown (1925–1981), Amos Milburn (1926–1980), and Lowell Fulson (1921–), whose "Every Day I Have the Blues" (1950) later became B. B. King's signature tune.

An even more restrained, elegant blues vocal style, used by the "Sepia Sinatras," also gained a large following among rhythm and blues audiences in the 1940s and '50s. Nat "King" COLE started out as a jazz pianist but achieved his greatest acclaim as a singer, starting in 1950 with "Mona Lisa." Other singers in this genre included Cecil Gant (1915–1951) and Charles Brown (1922–).

Ray CHARLES is often grouped with blues singers, but his synthesis of many early rhythm and blues influences, in particular the melding of sacred and secular black music traditions, is unique. Starting in the mid-1950s, he combined a smooth, almost country singing style on ballads with infectious gospel inflection and solid jazz rhythms on both slow and up-tempo numbers, including "I Got a Woman" (1955), "Drown in My Tears" (1955), "What'd I Say?" (1959), "Georgia on My Mind" (1960), and "Hit the Road, Jack" (1961).

Female blues singers often landed on the rhythm and blues charts in the 1950s. Ruth Brown (1928–), who worked with Lucky Millinder (1900–1966) and Blanche Calloway (1902–1978) in the late 1940s, sang in a jump blues style on "Teardrops from My Eyes" (1950), "Mama He Treats Your Daughter Mean" (1952), and "Wild Wild Young Men" (1954). La-Vern Baker (1928–), a niece of the blues singer Memphis Minnie, recorded "Jim Dandy" (1956) and "I Cried a Tear" (1958), both of which were hits on the R&B chart. Etta JAMES, who sang blues on Chess Records, recorded "Something's Got a Hold on Me" in 1962, a song that made her reputation in a rhythm and blues vein. Dinah WASHINGTON had considerable success as a jazz singer before entering the rhythm and blues market with records such as "Baby Get Lost" (1949). Washington later crossed over into the pop field with the ballad "What a Difference a Day Makes" (1959).

New Orleans rhythm and blues almost constitutes its own genre, no doubt because of the city's unique confluence of African-American and creole cultures. Fats DOMINO, whose first hit was "The Fat Man" (1949), became an archetypal crossover success, whose gently rocking voice and piano playing on "Ain't That a Shame" (1955), "Blueberry Hill" (1956), "I'm Walkin'" (1957), "I Hear You Knockin'" (1958), and "I'm Ready" (1959) appealed to a large white audience. Other important New Orleans rhythm and blues musicians include Dave Bartholomew (1920–), Huey "Piano" Smith (1934–), Allen Toussaint (1938–), the Meters, Irma Thomas (1941–), and the Neville Brothers.

Rock and Roll

In the early 1950s, rock and roll—originally a euphemism for sex—was virtually synonymous with rhythm and blues. By the mid-1950s, as more and more white teenagers began to listen to rhythm and blues, the scope of the term *rock and roll* expanded and was primarily applied to white musicians such as Elvis Presley, Buddy Holly (1936–1959), Roy Orbison (1936–1988), or Bill Haley (1925–1981), whose

music copied aspects of rhythm and blues styles but was aimed at white audiences. However, black musicians remained crucial to the development of rock and roll even after the term was being applied mostly to white musicians. Chuck BERRY, whose country-influenced, bluesy tunes were extraordinarily successful with white audiences, exemplified the adolescent themes, rebellious sound and look, and aggressive guitar playing of early rock and roll. His "Maybellene" (1955), "Johnny B. Goode" (1958), and "Sweet Little Sixteen" (1958) became rock standards almost immediately. This was also true of LITTLE RICHARD, whose "Tutti Frutti" (1955), "Long Tall Sally" (1956), and "Good Golly Miss Molly" (1958) brought to early rock and roll a frenetic, updated version of New Orleans piano styles. Chuck Berry and Little Richard were enormously influential in England. In fact, the biggest rock groups of the 1960s, including the Beatles and the Rolling Stones, rebelled against the bland, staid sounds of white pop-rockers like Pat Boone and Paul Anka and began their careers by performing mostly cover versions of black rock-and-roll songs. Other rhythm-and-blues musicians who played an important role in the development of rock and roll include Junior Parker (1927–1971), who recorded "Mystery Train" (1953), "Next Time You See Me" (1957), and "Sweet Home Chicago" (1958), as well as Ike Turner (1931–), Jackie Brenston (1930–1979), Big Mama Thornton ("Hound Dog," 1953), the Isley Brothers ("Shout," 1959; "Twist and Shout," 1962), and Chubby CHECKER ("The Twist," 1960). During the late 1960s, relatively few black musicians remained involved in rock and roll, notable exceptions being Richie HAVENS and Jimi HENDRIX, who had performed as an accompanist with Little Richard, the Isley Brothers, and Ike and Tina TURNER before leading a popular rock ensemble.

Soul

By 1964 black popular music had acquired a new name: soul music. There is no clear chronological or stylistic division between rhythm and blues and soul music, but there are some important differences. Soul music displayed a more pronounced gospel influence, whether in up-tempo, unrestrained shouting or in slower, more plaintive styles. Furthermore, soul's general rejection of extended instrumental soloing marked the continuing retreat of jazz as the popular music of the black middle class. Finally, even though most soul music consisted of solo singing with vocal backgrounds, the influence of carefully arranged close harmonies also waned.

It is no coincidence that soul flourished alongside the black pride movement. The music was made almost exclusively by blacks, at first almost exclusively

Little Richard brought a unique sense of hectic abandon and propulsion to the rock and roll of the 1950s. Despite a highly eccentric personal style, in time he was accepted as one of the great figures of American popular entertainment. Here, in 1990, he celebrates after being awarded a star in Hollywood's Walk of Fame. (AP/Wide World Photos)

for blacks, and was part of a rising black middle-class culture that celebrated black values and black styles in hair and clothing. In addition, soul's secular stance allowed the music to directly confront political issues central to African-American culture in the 1960s. James BROWN, who had been a successful recording artist throughout the 1950s and achieved great popularity in the '60s with live performances and recordings of songs such as "I Got You" (1965) and "I Feel Good" (1965), forever linked soul music and the BLACK POWER MOVEMENT with "Say It Loud, I'm Black and Proud" (1968).

Two record companies, Atlantic and Motown, dominated the soul-style rhythm and blues markets starting in the late 1950s and defined two major ap-

proaches. Atlantic and its Stax subsidiary often concentrated on funky instrumentals. Wilson PICKETT sang with a thrilling gospel feeling on songs such as "In the Midnight Hour" (1965) and "Mustang Sally" (1966). Otis REDDING's brief career included "These Arms of Mine" (1962), "I've Been Loving You Too Long" (1965), "Try a Little Tenderness" (1966), and "Sittin' on the Dock of the Bay" (1967). Ballad singer Percy Sledge (1941–) recorded "When a Man Loves a Woman" (1966) for Stax. Sam and Dave specialized in energetic, shouting vocals on hits such as "Hold On, I'm Coming" (1966), "Soul Man" (1967), and "I Thank You" (1968). Booker T. Jones (1944–) and the MG's personified the Memphis rhythm and blues sound on their instrumental hits for the Stax label, including "Green Onions" (1962) and "Hip Hug-Her" (1967). Aretha FRANKLIN reached her prime at Atlantic in the mid-1960s, when her white producer, Jerry Wexler (1917–), encouraged her to return to her gospel roots. She responded by creating perhaps the defining performances of the soul genre. Her majestic, emotional voice made songs such as "I Never Loved a Man the Way I Love You" (1967), "Respect" (1967), "Chain of Fools" (1967), and "Think" (1968) bona fide soul masterpieces.

If Stax and Atlantic musicians cultivated a funky, gritty sound, the founder of Motown, Berry GORDY, encouraged a sweeter sound, one that came to represent the classic soul sound even more than Atlantic or Stax. Those efforts produced dozens of hits during Motown's peak years in the 1960s by figures such as Marvin GAYE, Stevie WONDER, Mary WELLS, and Gladys KNIGHT. Important vocal groups included Smokey ROBINSON and the Miracles, the Jacksons (see Michael JACKSON), the FOUR TOPS, the TEMPTATIONS, and the SUPREMES.

Atlantic and Motown were by no means the only producers of soul music. Aside from James Brown, perhaps the most important, independent soul musicians of the 1960s were Tina TURNER and her husband, Ike Turner, who had led his own groups and backed the blues guitarist Elmore JAMES in the early 1950s. The duo had a string of influential hits in the 1960s, including "A Fool in Love" (1960), "It's Gonna Work Out Fine" (1961), and "River Deep, Mountain High" (1966).

In the 1970s, soul-style vocal groups remained popular, although the high lead vocals of the early vocal-harmony groups were backed with sleek, electrified rhythms. These groups included the Chi-Lites, the Stylistics, Harold Melvin (1941–) and the Blue-notes, the O'Jays, Earth, Wind and Fire, and the Spinners. Solo singers in the soul idiom in the 1970s included Roberta FLACK, Barry White (1944–), Al Green, and Teddy Pendergrass (1950–), all of whom created slow, emotional ballads and love songs. In the 1980s and '90s, Whitney Houston (1963–) and Luther Vandross (1951–) have continued the tradition of the gospel-influenced singing style that characterizes soul.

Funk

In the mid-to-late 1960s a new style known as "funk," derived from the black vernacular term for anything with a coarse, earthy smell, began to dominate the rhythm and blues charts. James Brown, who had been so influential in the 1950s and early '60s in pioneering soul music, once again broke new ground, this time with stripped-down, forceful rhythms and simple, melodic riffs on "Papa's Got a Brand New Bag" (1965). This style was picked up by Sly STONE on "Dance to the Music" (1968), "Everyday People" (1968), "Hot Fun in the Summertime" (1969), and by George CLINTON's work with his groups Parliament and Funkadelic in the 1970s. Other R&B musicians who adopted the funk style included Isaac Hayes (1938–), who recorded the soundtrack for *Shaft* in 1971, and Curtis MAYFIELD, who recorded *Super Fly* in 1972. Disco music by 1970s figures such as Donna Summer (1948–), Gloria Gaynor (1949–), Kool and the Gang, and Rick JAMES drew directly on funk's interpretation of rhythm and blues.

Although the category of rhythm and blues, created by white music-industry executives to describe a range of musical styles, has undergone dramatic transformations, the term continues to express the essential characteristics of African-American popular music. In the 1980s and '90s, musicians such as Prince (c. 1958–), Lenny Kravitz (1964–), and Living Color have taken inspiration from Little Richard, James Brown, and Jimi Hendrix, while younger musicians such as the group Boyz II Men have updated the close-harmony vocal ensemble sound of the 1940s and '50s. Black popular music—including funk, rock, rap, and pop-gospel ballads—continues to freely borrow and mix jazz, blues, and gospel, validating rhythm and blues as the common ground of modern African-American popular music.

REFERENCES

GEORGE, NELSON. *The Death of Rhythm & Blues.* New York, 1988.

GILLET, CHARLIE. *The Sound of the City.* New York, 1984.

GONZALEZ, FERNANDO. *Disco-File: The Discographical Catalog of American Rock and Roll and Rhythm and Blues, Vocal Harmony Groups, 1902–1976: Race, Rhythm and Blues.* New York, 1977.

GUARALNICK, PETER. *Sweet Soul Music: Rhythm and Blues and the Southern Dream of Freedom.* New York, 1986.

HARALAMBOS, MICHAEL. *Right On: From Blues to Soul in Black America.* New York, 1975.

SHAW, ARNOLD. *Honkers and Shouters: The Golden Years of Rhythm and Blues.* New York, 1978.

PETER EISENSTADT
JONATHAN GILL

Ribbs, William Theodore, Jr. (January 3, 1956–), racecar driver. Willy T. Ribbs was born in San Jose, Calif. The son of an amateur road-racer, he began competitive automobile racing at the age of twenty-one. Ribbs entered a driving school in England to avoid the racism prevalent in the sport in the United States. He began his career renting lightweight, inexpensive cars for beginning racers, and in 1977 he won six of his eleven starts, finished second four times, and third once. For this remarkable success, Ribbs was named the Dunlop Star of Tomorrow Champion, the International Driver of the Year, and won the British Sports Writers Award. The following year, after his return to the United States, his track-side bravado and posturing, as well as his traffic tickets and raucous behavior at a hotel, offended officials at a stock car race in Charlotte, N.C. and Ribbs eventually had his entry withdrawn. After this incident, Ribbs did not race again until 1981.

By 1983 Ribbs was racing in the International Motorsports Association's (IMSA) Trans-Am division (in which cars not built explicitly for racing have been modified for competition). That year he was named the Trans-Am Rookie of the Year for winning five races in that series. Two years later Ribbs's reputation was once again damaged when he was fined $1,000 and suspended by the IMSA for punching a driver he claimed had tried to push him off the track during warm-ups. However, despite numerous difficulties, between 1984 and 1987 Ribbs won more Trans-Am victories than any other driver, and in 1987 and 1988 the IMSA named him GTO driver of the year.

After a failed attempt in 1985 to qualify for the Indianapolis 500, in 1989 the actor Bill COSBY agreed to help Ribbs attract sponsors for a second try. On May 19, 1991, driving a year-old Buick Lola and still lacking sufficient corporate sponsorship, Ribbs became the first African American to qualify for the Indy 500. Two days before the race, the McDonald's Corporation signed on as a major sponsor. But Ribbs's inexperience with the specialized Indy cars resulted in mechanical problems that forced him to retire his car after only six laps of the race.

With continued support from Cosby but without major corporate sponsorship, Ribbs entered some races on the Indy car circuit in 1992, though he failed to get backing for the Indianapolis 500. In 1993 Ribbs raced in the Indianapolis 500 for the second time, finishing twenty-first.

REFERENCES

Associated Press. "Black Driver Qualifies for 500." *New York Times,* May 20, 1991, p. C4.

BONDY, FILIP. "Indy Qualifier Finds Corporate Sponsors Are Slow to Line Up." *New York Times,* May 24, 1991, p. D15.

McALEVEY, PETER. "The Hard Ride of Willy T." *New York Times Magazine* (October 9, 1988): 56.

PETER SCHILLING

Richard, Little.   *See* Little Richard.

Lloyd Richards. (© Shawn Walker)

Richards, Lloyd George (June 29, 1919–), theater director. Lloyd Richards was born in Toronto to Albert and Rose Richards, Jamaican immigrants who soon moved to Detroit. Despite having to help support his family, he graduated from Wayne State University in 1943. He served in World War II in the U.S. Air Force, then worked as a social case investigator in Detroit. In New York in the 1950s he studied with Paul Mann, a proponent of the Stanislavsky method of acting, and made his debut as Pee Wee in Ben Bengal's *Plant in the Sun* (1948).

Following Mann's advice, Richards moved toward directing and theater education. He directed Lorraine HANSBERRY's *A Raisin in the Sun,* which won the New York Critics Circle Award for the 1958–1959 season, and he went on to work with several actors and playwrights through the 1960s. He was head of actor training at the New York University School of the Arts from 1966 to 1972, then became a professor in the department of theater and cinema at Hunter College in New York. In 1969 Richards was appointed head of the Eugene O'Neill Theater Center in Waterford, Conn., and in 1979 he replaced Robert Brustein as dean of the Yale School of Drama.

After his work with Hansberry, Richards's most important director-playwright collaborations have been with Athol Fugard, the South African author of *Master Harold . . . and the Boys,* and with August WILSON. Collaboration with Wilson began in 1982, when Wilson submitted the script of his play *Ma Rainey's Black Bottom* to the O'Neill Theater Center summer workshop. The two blended their talents to create a string of critically acclaimed plays. Following *Ma Rainey's Black Bottom* came *Fences, Joe Turner's Come and Gone, The Piano Lesson,* and *Two Trains Running.*

Wilson wrote the plays and Richards directed and polished them in workshops such as those at the Yale Repertory Theatre and regional theaters throughout the country. In 1986, Richards received a Tony Award as director of *Fences.* At his retirement from Yale in 1991, a chair was established in his name, the first endowed chair in the school and the first honor of its kind named for an African American. Richards is active as a member of the National Council for the Arts and other arts committees and commissions. He continues in the Eugene O'Neill Playwright's Workshop and as head of the Theatre Communications Group.

REFERENCES

ERSTEIN, HAP. "Richards, Wilson Team Up on Prize Dramas." *Washington Times,* November 8, 1991, p. E1.

TURNER, BETH. "Lloyd Richards: The Quiet Force in American Theatre." *Black Masks* (Summer 1986): 2–9.

SANDRA G. SHANNON

Richardson, Gloria St. Clair Hayes (May 6, 1922–), civil rights activist. Gloria Richardson played a major role in Cambridge, Md.'s struggle for desegregation in the 1960s. Born Gloria St. Clair Hayes in Baltimore, she and her family relocated to Cambridge when she was six years old. Richardson graduated from Howard University and married Harry Richardson in 1944. She worked as a manager in her father's drugstore, had two children, and became involved in local politics through her fundraising and development plans for the communities' segregated schools. She separated from Harry in 1958, and in 1962 became chair of the Cambridge Nonviolent Action Committee (CNAC).

In 1963, Richardson and CNAC cochair Inez Grubb appeared at a meeting of the City Council, demanding integration. CNAC subsequently began a program of picketing and sit-ins at City Hall, the county courthouse, and the jail. Richardson and eighty protesters were arrested. In May 1963, the well-publicized "Penny Trials" were held—the mass trial of eighty activists which resulted in each activists being fined one penny and given a suspended sentence.

The sentence did little to curtail the protests of Richardson and her colleagues, and the picketing of government offices and discriminatory businesses continued. On May 31, Richardson appealed to U.S. Attorney General Robert F. Kennedy for a federal investigation into constitutional violations in Cambridge. In mid-June, after the police and the courts attempted to crush the demonstrations with harsh tactics, violence broke out in Cambridge. In response, state troopers sealed off the black community; later Maryland Gov. J. Millard Tawes imposed martial law, and ordered in the National Guard. Throughout the period Richardson continued her nonviolent protests. The disturbances attracted considerable attention: on July 17 President John F. Kennedy criticized the demonstrators for the violent outcome of the protests and the Rev. Dr. Martin Luther KING, Jr. also made public his doubts about some of Richardson's tactics.

Nonetheless, on July 22, 1963, at the invitation of the head of the Civil Rights Division, Burke Marshall, a conference in Washington was convened, and the next day a five point "Treaty of Cambridge" was signed, calling for various forms of economic aid as well as an end to segregation.

Two years later Richardson moved to New York City and began working for a series of nonprofit community organizations. She married Frank Dandridge in 1970, separated from him in 1975, and took a position with the J. Walter Thompson Man Power Development office as a program director. In 1985 she began working for the City of New York's Department of Aging, becoming a program officer in 1990.

REFERENCE

SMITH, JESSIE CARNEY, ed. *Notable Black American Women*. Detroit, 1992.

SUSAN MCINTOSH

Richmond, William "Bill" (August 5, 1763–December 28, 1829), boxer. Bill Richmond was the first American to become a well-known professional fighter, as well as the first to earn fame and fortune fighting in England. Richmond was born into slavery in what was then Cuckoldstown, Staten Island, N.Y. He was the son of a Georgia-born slave and the property of the Rev. Dr. George C. Charlton. As a young boy he caught the attention of an English general, the Earl of Percy, whose troops were occupying New York City in the early stages of the AMERICAN REVOLUTION, after pummeling three of Percy's soldiers at a local tavern. General Percy, a patron of the prize ring, took Richmond as his valet and in 1777 brought him to England, where his position helped carve the path for Richmond's professional career.

After arriving in England, General Percy, who became Duke of Northumberland in 1786, sent Richmond to school in Yorkshire. After three years of schooling, Richmond was apprenticed in York to be a cabinetmaker and served as a journeyman there for the next seven years. Richmond first gained public notoriety for his fighting skills in a brawl at the York races on August 25, 1791. Attending the races with the Duke of Northumberland, Richmond was provoked to fight by a known local troublemaker. The 5'9" 175-pound Richmond beat his 210-pound challenger in the presence of several prominent citizens, including Colonel Leigh, the Duke of Bedford, the Duke of Queensberry, and Sir Charles Bunbarry. Richmond was highly praised for his skill and encouraged to take up BOXING professionally.

Richmond, however, refused and continued to fight only when provoked, especially when taunted about his color. Aside from several private encounters, he publicly entered the boxing ring to meet the challenges of Paddy Green and Frank Meyers, both of whom he beat. It wasn't until 1804, however, that Richmond began a career of professional prize fighting.

Richmond fought several prominent boxers in the following years, suffering disheartening losses to George Maddox in 1804 and to the British favorite, Tom Cribb, in 1805. Richmond temporarily retired following this latter defeat and fought only sporadically thereafter. He reentered the ring in 1809 with a string of victories, culminating in a triumphant rematch with George Maddox.

Shortly after this fight, Richmond again temporarily retired from boxing to open the Horse and Dolphin, a sporting tavern in Haymarket, London, where he had a long and successful career as an innkeeper. In 1809 Richmond became the trainer, patron, and second of fellow African-American boxer, Tom MOLINEAUX, until their parting over personal differences in 1812. Still drawn to the ring, Richmond entered the Pugilistic Club tournament in 1814 at the age of fifty-two and fought sporadically until 1818, before permanently retiring to the Horse and

Dolphin. From his arrival in England to his retirement in 1815, he won twelve bouts and lost two. Richmond died in 1829 at his house in Haymarket.

REFERENCES

EGAN, PIERCE. *Boxiana.* 1812. Reprint. London, 1976.
FLEISCHER, NAT. *Black Dynamite.* 5 vols. New York, 1938–1947.

LOUISE P. MAXWELL

Richmond, Virginia. Richmond's significance in American history is clear. The city has been the capital of Virginia since 1779; it was the capital of the Confederacy during the CIVIL WAR, and it has been the heart of the "myth of the Lost Cause" ever since. Its centrality to African-American history is less well known but no less important. Over the course of the nineteenth century, both before and after the Civil War, Richmond African Americans created a rich, cohesive community, grounded in industrial labor, from which they launched a series of social movements challenging the local status quo. This community and its evolving tradition of struggle enabled African Americans to survive the difficult years of the first half of the twentieth century and, in the second half of the century, to renew their quest for equal rights and justice.

In 1607, a fort was set up at the headwaters of the James River in the Virginia colony. By the 1670s, a trading post, where slaves were among the products sold, was established. Still, the outpost remained tiny for almost a century. When the town of Richmond was incorporated in 1742, it had only 250 inhabitants. Despite its small size, Richmond's central location made it a political center, and it was the site of two legislative conventions in 1775. Four years later, it became the capital of the state.

African Americans played a considerable role in Richmond's early history. Enslaved blacks, who represented nearly half the town's population and much of its skilled and unskilled labor force, built many of Richmond's houses. During the Revolutionary War (*see* AMERICAN REVOLUTION), many blacks were put to labor on public projects. In 1781, fifteen slaves employed as ropewalkers fled behind British lines, following the burning of Richmond by British troops. James Lafayette, a plantation slave who had earned his freedom by spying for the Americans, became a respected resident of Richmond.

Following the end of the Revolutionary War Richmond grew steadily in size. Its black population jumped from 468 in 1782 to 2,900 in 1800. SLAVERY flourished in the city, despite the presence of a group of antislavery Quakers (*see* SOCIETY OF FRIENDS). As a result of liberalized MANUMISSION laws, the city's free black community grew from 40 to 607 during the same eighteen years. FREE BLACKS (SOUTH) lived in integrated areas, and many, such as Mary Lucas and Brazil de Romo, acquired property. The most notable free black was Christopher McPherson, a real estate investor and clerk in the Court of Chancery. Blacks and whites worshipped together at the city's First Baptist Church. However, free blacks were denied voting rights and were subject to numerous petty restrictions—for example, blacks were forbidden to drink and banned from ballplaying, cockfights, and horse races. Legal curbs on both slaves and free blacks accelerated after the discovery in 1800 of Gabriel Prosser's plot for a slave revolt and takeover of Richmond (*see also* GABRIEL PROSSER CONSPIRACY). A skilled blacksmith living outside Richmond, Prosser and his accomplices were executed, but whites remained fearful of slave uprisings.

In the early nineteenth century, as Virginia's soil became depleted and tobacco farming declined, Richmond stagnated. As slavery became unprofitable, the city actually lost one-quarter of its slave population in the 1820s. In 1831, a convention met in the city to discuss abolishing slavery in Virginia, although it quickly disbanded after NAT TURNER'S REBELLION (*see also* NAT TURNER CONTROVERSY) discredited EMANCIPATION efforts.

Beginning in the 1830s, as Richmond became a focal point for railroad traffic, the city was transformed into an industrial and transportation center. While some labor was performed by white immigrants, Richmond was the major urban center for industrial slavery in the antebellum South. Beginning in the 1840s, slaves were employed in large numbers, either through direct ownership or hire, in Richmond's tobacco factories, iron and flour mills (the city had the world's largest flour mill), nearby coal mines and stone quarries; in the construction of buildings, canals, and railroads; and in the hauling, unpacking, and repacking of goods along the city streets and waterways, in warehouses, and on the docks. By the 1850s, half of Richmond's slaves hired their labor, and numerous hiring agencies had emerged to handle the trade.

Tobacco manufacturing was the most labor-intensive industry in antebellum Richmond. Its fifty-two processing plants employed 3,400 slaves in the decade before the Civil War—more than half of all the slaves working in nondomestic labor. The organization of work in these factories left slaves with considerable latitude for decision making. In the chewing and plug segment of the industry, slaves often performed the most skilled work. There were no machines to set the pace. Foremen found work processes regulated by the songs of their operatives and wisely left their cat-o'-nine-tails hanging on the wall. "Overwork" bonuses were used to motivate slaves to exceed production quotas.

The iron industry was second only to tobacco in its reliance on slave labor. It more clearly restricted both the employment and the social lives of its bondsmen, who labored in the larger iron mills such as the famous Tredegar Works, founded in 1836. Only a few slaves held skilled positions; most performed the hot, heavy, and repetitive tasks around the furnaces. Still, employers resorted to "overwork" bonuses, which gave slaves some control over both their pace of work and consumption behavior.

Richmond's other "industry" was the SLAVE TRADE. As Virginia's agricultural sector contracted, "excess" slaves were sold south. Manchester, across the James River, had long been a significant slave market. With the growth of railroad traffic, slave trading became one of the city's most profitable businesses, and Richmond's market became larger than any other city except New Orleans. By 1860, there were thirty-three dealers, private slave jails, and daily slave auctions.

Factory slaves exercised considerable freedom. While many iron workers were housed in company-owned and -controlled "tenements" and enjoyed only limited freedom of movement, so many slaves worked in the tobacco factories that it was uneconomical for their employers to house them. Instead, they were provided with "board money" for lodging and food. They made their own decisions about how to spend or save their "overwork" earnings and "board money."

Slaves in other occupations also enjoyed more autonomy than they would have been allowed in plantation society. Teamsters, boatmen, stevedores, carpenters, plasterers, shoemakers, and barbers chose and controlled much of their work, earning money for themselves as well as their owners. They, too, found their own lodgings and participated in the black community. The systems of "hiring out" and "self-hire" often operated in unskilled as well as skilled work. Building trades laborers, ditch diggers, warehouse laborers, and even domestic servants (female and male) had some experience in bargaining over work conditions and selecting their own residences, spouses, food, and clothing.

The earnings of black workers were central to the development of a vital black community in Richmond. Their sense of independence, empowerment, and exploitation brought a particular cutting edge into the community. Their cash helped to support black boardinghouse keepers, grocers, barbers, tailors, seamstresses, shoemakers, churches, beneficial societies, gamblers, prostitutes, and grogshop owners. Not surprisingly, the dividing lines between slaves and free blacks in antebellum Richmond were frequently vague. Indeed, marriage and kinship, church and beneficial-society membership, and workplace and neighborhood relationships often knitted close bonds between the enslaved and the free.

Two critical social institutions were maintained by—and maintained—Richmond African Americans: the family and the church. These social institutions provided a foundation upon which they built a community that carried them from slavery through Emancipation and into RECONSTRUCTION.

All evidence points to the centrality of family in black life: the naming of children after parents, grandparents, aunts, and uncles; the efforts of free men and women to purchase the freedom of their spouses and children; the thousands of former slaves who sought to gain legal sanction for marriages in 1865 and 1866; and the recurrent laments about marriages broken by the city's numerous slave traders and by sale, particularly in the city, which served as the prime northern terminus in the internal slave trade.

No extrafamilial institution received greater attention than the church. By 1860, five thousand slaves and free blacks belonged to the city's African Baptist and African Methodist churches. In 1841, the First Baptist Church's large congregation split, and its white members left. The church became the all-black First African Baptist Church, though Dr. Robert Ryland, a white man, remained as its pastor until after the CIVIL WAR. The First African Baptist Church, which had more than three thousand congregants by the eve of the Civil War, provided a public forum for voicing opinions and a vehicle for taking collective action and aiding the poor and helpless. It also gave blacks an opportunity to create their own rules for conduct and a mechanism to enforce them.

The Civil War transformed Richmond, which became the capital of the Confederacy in 1862. The war brought an influx of slaves and whites, pressures to restrict the freedoms of free blacks, material privations caused by Yankee blockades and troop movements, fears of impressment into service for the Confederate military, as well as the excitement of possible freedom. Thousands of blacks were forced into public works projects such as the reinforcement of the city's fortifications and the laying of railroad track. In 1864, amid debates by southern leaders over the question of arming slaves, a regiment of black hospital workers was formed into a makeshift regiment and paraded. Slaves, free blacks, and a handful of white Unionists maintained an underground during the war, aiding captured Union soldiers, passing information to the Union Army, and facilitating slave escapes. Black Union soldiers participated in many battles in the Richmond campaign of 1864–1865, including the successful assault on Fort Harrison. Thousands of local blacks lined the streets when black troops appropriately led the Union Army into Richmond on April 3, 1865, signaling an end to the war and the institution of slavery itself.

Race relations remained confrontational after Emancipation. In 1866, whites burned the Second African Church after blacks held a ceremony commemorating the Emancipation Proclamation. The same year, blacks engaged in several demonstrations over their exclusion from horse-drawn cars, and in 1867 federal troops were called in to quell a violent incident sparked by the exclusion.

After Emancipation, black Richmonders continued to build on the base of the extended family linked with the church. They erected a broad network of "secret societies" that fulfilled a multiplicity of purposes: funerals and death benefits, labor organization, collective self-education and self-improvement, religious advancement, political expression, socializing, and the like. The leadership of these organizations—and of the African-American community itself—emerged from the ranks of wage-earning industrial workers, especially tobacco factory workers. The most famous of the fraternal orders were the Grand Fountain United Order of True Reformers and the Independent Order of St. Luke (see also FRATERNAL ORDERS AND MUTUAL AID ASSOCIATIONS).

The years after Emancipation witnessed the emergence of a series of popular movements grounded in the social network that honeycombed black Richmond. African Americans formed schools, notably the Richmond Theological Seminary (later Virginia Union University), which held its first classes in the former Lumpkin's slave jail in 1865. Churches expanded, and several black ministers achieved prominence in the community (including the Rev. John JASPER of the Sixth Mt. Zion Church, celebrated for his 1879 sermon "The Sun Do Move," an attack on the Copernican hypothesis of a heliocentric solar system). The movements for mutual aid and self-help were easily transformed to more overt forms of political organization and expression—parades, mass meetings, collective direct action, armed self-defense, political campaigns, labor organization, strikes, and other methods.

These new forces were concentrated in Jackson Ward, which became the geographic heart of black Richmond as housing segregation became nearly absolute. The wages of industrial workers supported black businesses such as barbershops and restaurants, and an adjacent middle-class black neighborhood developed around Marshall and Clay streets (later absorbed into Jackson ward). In 1872, the conservative "Redeemer" government gerrymandered Richmond's wards to limit black voting influence. The results were the concentration of black voting in Jackson Ward and the creation of safe "black" seats. For the rest of the century, Richmond had a full complement of African-American city councilmen and aldermen.

Black political activity heightened in the 1880s—well after the formal "redemption" of Virginia—in two movements, Readjusterism and the Knights of Labor. Both were grounded in the experiences of working-class African Americans, reflected their central leadership roles within the larger community, and were based on coalitions along class lines with disaffected whites. Black aspirations were expressed through the *Richmond Planet* newspaper, founded in 1883 and edited by journalist-politician John MITCHELL, Jr., from 1884 until 1929, nine years before its demise.

Readjusterism expressed widespread frustrations with the consequences of the depression of 1873–1878. These frustrations gave birth to a new party that gained control of state government. Blacks won several concrete gains: abolition of the whipping post, the restructuring of the tax system to lessen the burden on working people, the appointments of African Americans to the board of education and black principals to head black schools, and funding for a new black elementary school. A black regiment, headquartered in Richmond, was admitted to the state militia, although it disbanded after the SPANISH-AMERICAN WAR when its members insisted on serving under black officers.

In the mid-1880s, both white and black workers in Richmond flocked into the Knights of Labor. Organized into racially separate locals, but often supporting each other, they fought employers for higher wages, shorter hours, and better working conditions; organized producers' cooperatives; challenged convict labor through boycotts and protest movements; and promoted self-education through newspapers, reading rooms, lectures, and drama troupes. By early 1886, ten thousand Richmond workers were organized into more than thirty local assemblies, linked into two district assemblies, one white and one black.

In mid-1886, white and black leaders together led this movement into local politics, forming the Workingmen's Reform Party to contest for control over the local government. Their stunning victory at the polls, however, was soon followed by internal conflict, exacerbated by manipulative politicians from the two entrenched parties. In the midst of this turmoil, the Richmond Knights hosted the national convention of the organization, which brought more than one thousand delegates into the city. Charges of "social equality" and "race mixing" swirled, as some

In the black neighborhoods of Richmond, as in all early twentieth-century cities, stores such as this pharmacy on Leigh Street were hubs of community activity. (Prints and Photographs Division, Library of Congress)

out-of-town delegates launched their own challenges to the emergent JIM CROW system at the Richmond Theater and in local hotels. When the dust had settled, the Knights had lost their momentum.

The Knights' demise signaled more than the end of efforts to build class-based coalitions in Richmond. In the wake of not only this defeat, but also the cooptation of the Readjusters by the mainstream Republicans and the increasing sophistication of the conservative, white elite counterattack, the local African-American community faced the loss of many of the gains they had made since Emancipation.

During the final decade of the nineteenth century and the first decade of the twentieth, the new patterns were set. African-American suffrage was restricted, by law and practice, until the last black councilman was eliminated in 1898. When only 228 black registered voters remained on the rolls in 1903, the Jackson Ward district was broken up. Public spend-

ing confirmed that "separate" would be anything but "equal," as funding for black schools, for the extension of city water, sewage, and electricity, and the improvement of streets in black neighborhoods dried up. In 1900, for example, the city granted $7,722 to white charities, and only $550 to black charities—despite their greater need.

The process of segregation, which had become widespread in the nineteenth century, increased. Segregation, combined with population growth and neglect by landlords, caused the deterioration of the quality of black housing. Occupational opportunities for African Americans also declined, particularly for African-American women. Changes in the tobacco industry—the rise of cigarettes and the impact of technological change—had created jobs for white women, but not for African Americans. For the next half century, Richmond's African Americans found themselves locked into low-paying, unskilled jobs and trapped in poor neighborhoods, with little access to education and scant public voice.

Even in this environment, the extended family, the church, the social network, and the influence of industrial workers provided a foundation for the development of a relatively independent black economy in the first part of the twentieth century. Small businesses proliferated in recreation, amusement, personal services, real estate, as well as barbering (despite efforts by whites to pass "licensing" laws and remove black competition). More sizable concerns emerged in banking and insurance, typically linked to the network of "secret societies." The True Reformers Bank of Richmond, opened in 1888, was the first African-American bank. John Mitchell's Mechanics Savings Bank (also known as the Pythian Bank because of its funding by the Virginia Knights of Pythias) was founded in 1902; it was housed in a four-story building in downtown Richmond and became a symbol of pride for the community. St. Luke's Penny Savings Bank, founded by Maggie Lena WALKER (the first African-American woman bank president and quite probably the first woman bank president of any race) in 1903, grew into the Consolidated Bank & Trust Company, still one of the nation's largest black-owned banks. All these grew directly from fraternal organizations, as did seven major Richmond INSURANCE COMPANIES, notably the Southern Aid Life Insurance Company and National Benefit Life Insurance Corporation (reorganized during the Great Depression as the Virginia Mutual Life Insurance Corporation). This financial network supported an increase in African-American home ownership, even in the face of segregation and an overall shortage of quality housing stock.

While such "self-help" activities nurtured a Washingtonian ideology, their prevalence did not mean that the community had withdrawn from social and political struggle. In 1904, when Richmond's streetcar company segregated its cars, John Mitchell organized a yearlong black streetcar boycott that bankrupted the company, although the city passed a segregation ordinance that broke the boycott. In 1911, Richmond passed a residential-segregation ordinance. Local blacks lobbied against the ordinance, and their campaign culminated in 1917 with the founding of the Richmond NAACP and the overturning of the law following a ruling by the U.S. Supreme Court.

In the political arena, struggle continued as well. In the fall of 1920, black women tried to register to vote, claiming their rights were upheld by the new women's suffrage amendment, the Nineteenth Amendment to the Constitution. A year later, to protest the REPUBLICAN PARTY's "lily-white" southern strategy, local African Americans launched a "lily-black" campaign, running John Mitchell for governor. In the wake of a 1927 U.S. Supreme Court decision outlawing the all-white primary in Texas, Richmond African Americans presented themselves to vote in the Democratic primary election. A decade later they organized the Non-Partisan League for Colored Voters to challenge restrictions on African-American suffrage and conduct voter-registration drives.

During the 1930s, when Richmond blacks faced high unemployment and discrimination in distribution of federal relief, tobacco factory workers sustained workplace organization. Denied membership in the Richmond Central Labor Union and accorded little voice within the Tobacco Workers International Union, locals 12 and 40 were known for their independence, which they expressed in a variety of ways, such as demanding—and winning—the right of African-American workers to be examined by a black doctor when applying for sick benefits. Despite employer intransigence, LABOR UNIONS were transformed and revitalized in the mid-1940s, through linkages with the United Cannery, Agricultural, Packing & Allied Workers of America (UCAPAWA) and the Food, Tobacco, Agricultural & Allied Workers (FTA), both of whom were influenced by white labor radicals and affiliated with the Congress of Industrial Organizations (CIO).

After World War II, the wall of discrimination in Richmond began to crack. The first black firemen and police were hired, and in 1947, after protests, the Richmond Public Library opened its doors to blacks. In 1954, following the U.S. Supreme Court's *Brown* v. *Board of Education* school desegregation ruling, the Richmond schools (headed by future Supreme Court Justice Lewis Powell) remained open, in contrast to other cities in Virginia, and were gradually integrated. Richmond made slow progress integrating its public spaces, but it was spared the violent resistance that occurred elsewhere in the South.

Black voter registration was promoted by the Richmond Citizens Association, founded in 1946, and the Richmond Civic Council, which linked more than eighty churches, labor organizations, fraternal societies, and civil and educational groups. From the low point of fewer than three hundred black registered voters in Richmond in the early twentieth century, 12,518 were on the rolls by the late 1940s. Changes in the city charter in 1948 to elect the city council at large provoked a creative strategy from African-American activists. They selected one member of their ranks for the ballot and then encouraged black voters to employ a "single shot"—to vote only for that candidate and throw away their other eight votes. This concentration of efforts brought the desired results: Oliver Hill, the first black city councilor in fifty years, assumed his seat. Another black political organization, the Crusade for Voters, founded in 1956, provided political leadership in the community during the 1960s. In 1969, with the aid of black community votes, Richmond lawyer and businessman L. Douglas WILDER became the first African American in the Virginia state Senate.

Electoral efforts were inseparably linked to the emergent civil rights movement. As early as 1945, African-American candidates entered the Democratic primary to select Richmond's representative in the House of Delegates, campaigning for abolition of the poll tax, creation of a permanent Fair Employment Practices Commission, repeal of segregation on public carriers, and increased funding for black schools and community health programs. Despite the strategy of participation in the Democratic primary, African-American political organizations remained independent, particularly after white Democrats opted for "massive resistance" to federal demands for school integration in the mid-1950s.

African-American community struggle broadened and deepened in the late 1950s and early 1960s, even as it reflected its historical roots. Activists not only confronted—and defeated—the "massive resistance" strategy, but they launched a boycott and picket of department stores to support demands for equal service. On New Year's Day 1959, black demands for civil rights were expressed in a massive march, whose character, makeup, and tenor harkened to the protest rallies and parades of the Reconstruction era. In September 1963, Richmond hosted the SOUTHERN CHRISTIAN LEADERSHIP CONFERENCE's convention, at a critical moment in the evolution of the national civil rights movement, which echoed the Knights of Labor convention of 1886.

By the mid-1960s, postwar black population increases combined with white migration to the suburbs and beyond led to Richmond's transformation into a near-black-majority city, and the African-American community's struggle for equal rights, justice, and empowerment continued despite obstacles. White leaders turned to the annexation of largely white suburbs and rural areas in last-ditch efforts to dilute the power of the African-American vote. The attempted annexation was blocked by the federal government under the VOTING RIGHTS ACT, and blacks obtained a series of injunctions and court orders against the white-dominated electoral process. For seven years no local elections were held, and when the final obstacles were lifted in 1977, a new city council with a black majority was elected. They, in turn, elected Councilman Henry Marsh III as Richmond's first black mayor. (Mayors are not directly elected by the populace in Richmond, which has since 1954 employed a city manager type of government.) Meanwhile, in 1971 the U.S. Supreme Court over-turned a court-ordered school district consolidation with adjacent suburbs aimed at promoting integration, leading to widespread busing and a fifteen-year campaign to achieve a unitary system.

The past two decades have seen Richmond buffeted by the economic forces that have challenged all of America's cities—deindustrialization, suburban expansion, inner-city decay—and the social problems of poverty, crime, violence, drugs, and hopelessness—that have accompanied them. In 1989, the U.S. Supreme Court's *Richmond v. J. A. Croson Co.* decision, which struck down the city's minority set-aside program, was a heavy blow to the black economy. The election of L. Douglas Wilder as Virginia's governor the same year may have provided a source of hope to local African Americans, but Wilder was unable to significantly change the problems of black Richmond. Whether the "Richmond Renaissance" declared jointly by white and African-American community leaders in the 1980s will usher in a new era depends largely on the degree to which they learn from their own history.

Throughout its existence, Richmond has been the home of large numbers of influential African Americans. Some notable figures include tennis star/activist Arthur ASHE, sculptor Leslie Bolling, actor Charles GILPIN, economist Abram HARRIS, and dancer Bill "Bojangles" ROBINSON. The city's extensive black history was commemorated by the creation of the Jackson Ward National Historic District in 1981.

REFERENCES

BROWN, W. H. *The Education and Economic Development of the Negro in Virginia.* Charlottesville, Va., 1923.

BUNI, ANDREW. *The Negro in Virginia Politics, 1902–1965.* Charlottesville, Va., 1967.

CHESSON, MICHAEL B. "Richmond's Black Councilmen, 1871–1896." In Howard Rabinowitz, ed. *Southern Black Leaders of the Reconstruction Era.* Urbana, Ill., 1982.

DABNEY, VIRGINIUS. *Richmond: The Story of a City.* Garden City, N.Y., 1976.

DEW, CHARLES B. *Ironmaker to the Confederacy: Joseph R. Anderson and the Tredegar Iron Works.* New Haven, Conn., 1966.

FINK, LEON. " 'Irrespective of Party, Color, or Social Standing': The Knights of Labor and Opposition Politics in Richmond, Virginia." *Labor History* 19 (Summer 1978).

GATES, ROBBINS L. *The Making of Massive Resistance: Virginia's Politics of Public School Desegregation, 1954–1956.* Chapel Hill, N.C., 1962.

JACKSON, LUTHER PORTER. *Negro Officeholders in Virginia, 1865–1895.* Norfolk, Va., 1945.

KAUFMAN, STUART. *Challenge & Change: The History of the Tobacco Workers International Union.* Urbana, Ill., 1986.

KNIGHT, CHARLES L. *Negro Housing in Certain Virginia Cities*. Richmond, Va., 1923.

MOORE, JAMES T. "Black Militancy in Readjuster Virginia." *Journal of Southern History* 41 (May 1975).

PINCHBECK, RAYMOND B. *The Virginia Negro Artisan and Tradesman*. Richmond, Va., 1926.

RACHLEFF, PETER J. *Black Labor in Richmond, 1865–1890*. 1984. Reprint. Urbana, Ill., 1989.

SILVER, CHRISTOPHER. *Twentieth Century Richmond: Planning, Politics, and Race*. Knoxville, Tenn., 1984.

PETER J. RACHLEFF

Riddick, George (March 24, 1933–July 12, 1994), clergyman and activist. George Riddick was born in Denver, Colo., and attended the University of Denver. After serving in the United States Quartermaster Corps, he began an internship at Denver Christian Center and then enrolled at the divinity school of the University of Chicago. He became the associate director of the Department of Christian Citizenship with the Church Federation of Greater Chicago. Later, during the 1960s, he worked at Chicago's Department of Social Welfare, where he served as a liaison staff member with the SOUTHERN CHRISTIAN LEADERSHIP CONFERENCE (SCLC), worked with the Rev. Dr. Martin Luther KING, Jr., and became active in Operation Breadbasket, the urban poverty program of the SCLC.

In the 1960s, Riddick also became the pastor of Blackwell Memorial African Methodist Episcopal (AME) Church on Chicago's South Side, as well as the director of pastoral services at Doctors' Hospital in Hyde Park, Chicago. In 1971, he was one of the founding members of People United to Serve Humanity (*see* OPERATION PUSH) with the Rev. Jesse JACKSON.

Riddick hosted the *Saturday Forum* radio program of Operation PUSH for twenty-one years. He received the South Chicago branch of the NAACP Award for Human Rights, as well as the Baptist Student Center's Belle Kinney Wright Award for his work in human relations. In 1992, he was involved in Carol MOSELEY-BRAUN's successful campaign for the U.S. Senate. He died in Chicago in 1994.

KAREN E. REARDON

DURAHN TAYLOR

Riggs, Marlon Troy (February 3, 1957–April 5, 1994), filmmaker. Marlon Riggs was born in Fort Worth, Tex. After a childhood spent in Texas, Augusta, Ga., and Germany, where his father was in the U.S. Army, Riggs received his bachelor's degree from Harvard University in 1978. After a short stint as an assistant with a television station in Texas, he entered the Graduate School of Journalism at the University of California at Berkeley, where in 1981 he received a master's degree in journalism with a concentration in documentary filmmaking. The next year, he began work as a filmmaker. In 1986 Riggs wrote, produced, and directed *Ethnic Notions*, a study of different stereotypes of African Americans. The film won an Emmy Award in 1988. In 1987 Riggs was hired as a professor by the University of California at Berkeley, and held the post of professor of arts and sciences until his death.

In 1988 Riggs began work on *Tongues Untied*, a documentary about black gay men, and in 1989 he received a grant from the National Endowment for the Arts (NEA) for the film. Shortly after beginning the project, Riggs learned he was HIV-positive. He claimed the diagnosis helped personalize the film. The finished work, a mélange of documentary film, poetry, and Riggs's personal reminiscences, was released in 1989. In 1991 *Tongues Untied* became the center of a national controversy after it was scheduled to be shown on the public television series *P.O.V.* Its frank discussions of black homosexuality horrified such conservative critics as Senator Jesse Helms, who attacked the NEA for its sponsorship of Riggs's work. In 1992 conservative Republican presidential candidate Pat Buchanan used a section of the work in a campaign commercial. Riggs, in turn, complained that Buchanan and others distorted his work through selective presentation.

Riggs continued to produce works about the black gay male experience, including the short film *Anthem* (1990) and *Non, Je Ne Regrette Rien/No Regret* (1991) a study of black men in the AIDS epidemic. He also produced films with non-gay themes. In 1989 Riggs wrote and produced *Color Adjustment*, a documentary about images of African Americans in television sitcoms. The work won him a Peabody Award the same year. His last project was "Black Is . . . Black Isn't," an unfinished documentary about African-American intellectuals. While Riggs championed black culture and the fight against racism, he remained critical of black homophobia and silence on AIDS. Riggs died of AIDS at his home in Oakland, Calif., in 1994.

REFERENCE

GUTHMANN, EDWARD. "Marlon Riggs—A Voice Stilled." *San Francisco Chronicle,* April 6, 1994, p. E1.

GREG ROBINSON

Riles, Wilson Camanza (June 27, 1917–), educational administrator. Wilson Riles was born in Alexandria, La. He was orphaned at the age of eleven and taken in by friends of his parents in Elizabeth, La. After high school Riles moved to Flagstaff, Ariz., where he received a B.A. degree from Northern Arizona University (NAU) in 1940. Following his college career, Riles worked as a teacher and administrator for Arizona public schools and then joined the U.S. Army Air Force, serving for three years during World War II. He returned to NAU after the war and received an M.A. degree in 1947.

Riles was a teacher and administrator in the Arizona public school system from 1947 to 1958. He then moved to the Sacramento area, and had a career with the California State Department of Education. In 1965 Riles was named associate superintendent to administer a federally sponsored program to improve education for low-income families, and achieved considerable recognition as an expert on urban education, chairing various commissions during the administrations of Presidents Johnson and Nixon.

In 1969 Riles was promoted to deputy superintendent of public instruction. In 1970 he campaigned against and defeated his supervisor, conservative incumbent Max Rafferty, to become California's superintendent of public instruction. Riles was the first African American to be elected to a statewide office in California. In 1973 he was awarded the fifty-eighth NAACP SPINGARN MEDAL. He was reelected as superintendent in 1974 and 1978, but lost to Bill Honig in the 1982 election. Following his retirement from public service in 1982, Riles founded Wilson Riles and Associates Inc., a business consulting firm in Sacramento, Calif.

REFERENCES

ROBINSON, L. "California's New Education Boss." *Ebony* (May 1971): 54–56.

TURNER, WALLACE. "Black School Chief on Coast Faces Challenge." *New York Times,* May 4, 1982, p. B16.

THADDEUS RUSSELL

Rillieux, Norbert (March 17, 1806–October 8, 1894), inventor. Norbert Rillieux was born in New Orleans, La., to a wealthy French engineer and plantation owner and an African-American mother. Rillieux was free, although it is unclear whether it was he or his mother who had been freed from slavery. His father sent him to Catholic schools in New Orleans and to study engineering at L'École Centrale in Paris. At twenty-four, he became the youngest instructor at the school as a professor in the department of applied mechanics. He published numerous papers on steam technology in engineering journals before returning to the United States in 1840 to perfect and test the evaporator.

Rillieux is remembered for patenting, originally in 1843 and in an improved form in 1846, the multiple-effect vacuum pan evaporator. Previous to his invention, sugar refining was slow and inefficient, making sugar a luxury reserved for the rich or for special occasions. His innovation—heating cane juice in a partial vacuum, thereby reducing the required boiling point, and using the steam produced for further heating, thereby achieving even greater fuel efficiency—increased the rate of sugar production, reduced the price, and made sugar a common household item. Thousands of evaporators were put into operation in Louisiana, the West Indies, and Mexico. The evaporator has also been used in the production of soap, gelatin, and glue, and has been hailed as the greatest invention in the history of American chemical engineering.

After the treatment of African Americans in Louisiana became increasingly oppressive, Rillieux returned to France, becoming the headmaster of L'École Centrale. He then studied Egyptology and contributed to the deciphering of hieroglyphics. He died in France.

REFERENCES

DESDUNES, RODOLPHE. *Our People and Our History.* Translated by Sister Dorothea Olga McCants. Baton Rouge, La., 1973.

MEADE, GEORGE P. "A Negro Scientist in Slavery Days." *Negro History Bulletin* 20, no. 7 (April 1957): 159–163.

SIRAJ AHMED

Ringgold, Faith (October 8, 1930–), painter and sculptor. Born in Harlem, Faith Ringgold was one of three children of Andrew Louis Jones, Sr., and Willi Posey Jones, a fashion designer. She was married to Robert Earl Wallace, a pianist, from 1950 to 1956 and had two daughters in 1952: Michele, an author, and Barbara, a linguist. Ringgold graduated from City College, New York, in 1955, and taught art in New York public schools until 1973. In 1959 she received a master's degree, also from City College. She began spending summers in Provincetown, Mass., in 1957, took her first trip to Europe in 1961, and married Burdette Ringgold in 1962.

Ringgold's work and life exemplify her interests in civil rights and feminism. Some of her early paintings, such as *The Flag Is Bleeding* (1967) are large with stylized figures; others are abstract, like *Flag for the Moon, Die Nigger* (1969). Her radical use of potent national symbols, such as the flag and, later, postage stamps and maps, fiercely counterpointed American values with their ingrained racism. To achieve greater recognition for blacks and women in the mainstream art world, Ringgold participated in demonstrations at the Whitney Museum (1968, 1970) and at the Museum of Modern Art (1968). She was a cofounder in 1971 of Where We At, a group of black women artists. The following year she created a mural at the Women's House of Detention in New York that used only images of women.

The women's movement and Ringgold's close relationship with her mother influenced her to begin using fabrics, traditionally a women's medium, to express her art. She began to make masks and dolls—soft sculptures. Her mother made the dolls' clothes. They portray, among others, the Rev. Dr. Martin Luther KING, Jr., the murdered children of Atlanta (the Atlanta child murder cases of 1979–1982), and various people in the community. Some of Ringgold's paintings were bordered in tankas, cloth frames made by her mother. Ringgold and her mother also collaborated on the production of Sew Real doll kits in 1979.

Ringgold then began working in the medium that brought her acclaim, story quilts. The first, *Who's Afraid of Aunt Jemima?* (1983), is a visual narrative of a woman restaurateur in painting, text, and patchwork. The quilts' stories vividly raise the issues of racism and feminism. As the stories became more complex, Ringgold began to create multiple quilts to encompass them. Each consists of a large painted panel bordered by printed patches pieced together, with text at the bottom. The quilt series are *The Bitter Nest* (1988), *Woman on the Bridge* (1988), and *The French Connection* (1991). Ringgold used one of her quilts as the basis for a children's book, *Tar Beach*, which was a Caldecott Honor Book and received the Coretta Scott King award in 1992. The original quilt was acquired by the Guggenheim Museum.

Ringgold's awards include a grant from the National Endowment for the Arts (1989), Warner Communications' Wonder Woman (1983), and the National Coalition of 100 Black Women's Candace (1986). She holds honorary degrees from Moore College of Art and the College of Wooster, Ohio. A twenty-five-year retrospective of her work traveled between 1990 and 1993. Ringgold has taught at the University of California at San Diego since 1984, spending half the year there. Her designs from *Street Story Quilt* were selected by Judith Lieber for a limited edition of jeweled evening bags. Some of Ringgold's works are in the High, Metropolitan, New-

ark, and Modern Art museums, as well as in private collections.

REFERENCES

FLOMENHAFT, ELEANOR. *Faith Ringgold: A 25 Year Survey*. Hempstead, N.Y., 1990.
MOORE, SYLVIA. *Yesterday and Tomorrow: California Women Artists*. New York, 1989.

BETTY KAPLAN GUBERT

Rivers, Clarence Joseph (September 9, 1931–), Roman Catholic priest and composer. Clarence Rivers was born in Selma, Ala., to Clarence Rufus and Lorraine (Echols) Rivers. He received a B.A. in 1952 and an M.A. in 1956 from St. Mary's Seminary in Cincinnati, Ohio. Rivers undertook further graduate studies at Xavier University in Cincinnati and at Yale University. He also studied liturgy at L'Institut Catholique in Paris and drama at the Catholic University of America.

In 1956 Rivers was ordained a Roman Catholic priest under the auspices of the Archdiocese of Cincinnati. From 1956 to 1966, he taught English at a high school in Cincinnati and served as assistant pastor of St. Joseph and Assumption parishes. In 1969 he became president of Stimuli, Inc., a group which promoted the use of performing arts in religious education. Three years later, he established and became the first director of the Department of Culture and Worship in the National Office for Black Catholics in Washington, D.C.

Rivers gained greatest acclaim for his compositions of contemporary church music. He introduced African-American elements into music for Catholic worship, blending Gregorian chant and other religious music with blues, spirituals, gospel, jazz, and other folk music. Rivers made his debut as a composer in August 1964 when he introduced *An American Mass Program* at the National Liturgical Conference in St. Louis, Mo. A second mass, *The Brotherhood of Man*, was performed at the Newport Jazz Festival in 1967 and in 1969 at the Third Annual Ecumenical Concert of the Cincinnati Symphony Orchestra. His works include *Celebrations* (1969), *Reflections* (1970), and *Soulful Worship* (1974). Rivers also wrote a musical play, "Turn Me Loose," based on the life of Frederick DOUGLASS.

Rivers has lectured widely to various denominational groups, has held workshops, produced concerts, and supervised celebrations for interreligious gatherings. His honors include awards from civic and community organizations and the Gold Medal of the Catholic Art Association, which he won in 1966. In

1978 Rivers received a Ph.D. in religious studies from Union Graduate School in Yellow Springs, Ohio (which became the Union Institute of Cincinnati in 1989).

REFERENCES

LOCHER, FRANCES CAROL. *Contemporary Authors,* vols. 77–80. Detroit, 1979.
SOUTHERN, EILEEN. *Biographical Dictionary of African-American and African Musicians.* Westport, Conn., 1982.

JO H. KIM

Roach, Maxwell Lemuel "Max" (January 10, 1924–), jazz drummer and bandleader. Born in Elizabeth City, N.C., and raised in Brooklyn, N.Y., Roach studied music as a child with his mother, a gospel singer, and received piano lessons from his aunt. He also received music lessons in public school, and by age ten was playing drums in church bands. He performed in Coney Island sideshows such as *Darktown Follies* while in high school. During this time he also began frequenting Minton's Playhouse in Harlem, where he met some of the leading jazz musicians of the day. In 1941 Roach graduated with honors from Brooklyn's Boys' High School. Soon after, he started performing regularly with Charlie PARKER at Clark Monroe's Uptown House in Harlem, and by the next year he had a strong enough reputation to fill in for Sonny GREER for several nights with Duke ELLINGTON's orchestra. In 1943–44 he recorded and performed with Coleman HAWKINS at Kelly's Stable as a replacement for Kenny CLARKE ("Woody'n' You," 1944; "Bu-Dee-Daht," 1944). In 1944 he also joined Dizzy GILLESPIE's quintet at the Onyx Club, becoming a member of the first bebop band to open on 52nd Street, which had become the central location for New York jazz nightclubs. The next year Roach began working with Charlie Parker, an association that would last more than five years. On Roach's first important recording with Parker, the uptempo "Ko-Ko" (1945), Roach has already left swing drumming behind for a bebop style that keeps time on the cymbal, reserving the drums themselves for accents.

Together with Kenny Clarke, Roach redefined the rhythmical and structural architecture of jazz drumming, and created a new solo role for modern jazz drum performance. Initially influenced by the imaginative "melodic" solo style of Sid CATLETT, the driving intensity of Chick WEBB, and the fluid swing and finesse of Jo JONES, Roach distilled their stylistic characteristics through Clarke's polyrhythmic inno-

Max Roach performs on drums. (© Sulaiman Ellison—Photographs and Prints Division, Schomburg Center for Research in Black Culture, The New York Public Library, Astor, Lenox and Tilden Foundations)

vations. By the end of the 1940s, Roach was recognized as one of the leading drummers in jazz. He performed on Miles DAVIS's "Birth of the Cool" recordings (1949), and on Bud POWELL's "Un Poco Loco" (1951). In the early 1950s he continued his prolific career while pursuing studies in composition and tympani at the Manhattan School of Music. From 1954 to 1956 he co-led the Clifford Brown-Max Roach Quintet, which pioneered the hard-driving style known as hard hop (*Study in Brown,* 1955; *At Basin Street,* 1956).

In the 1960s Roach began to combine his music with his politics, with a particular emphasis on racial oppression in both the United States and South Africa. His 1960 recording of *We Insist: Freedom Now Suite* used free-form musical structures, including an emotionally charged interplay between the drummer and his then-wife, vocalist Abbey LINCOLN, to explore the theme of racial oppression in America. That work also used West African drumming and Afro-Cuban percussion to draw parallels between slavery in the U.S., segregation, and apartheid in South Africa.

In the 1960s Roach began to move away from appearing solely in strict jazz contexts. He began performing solo drum compositions as independent pieces, an effort dating back to his "Drum Conversation" (1953). He also recorded original works for vocal choruses and pianoless quartets. In the 1960s Roach taught at the Lenox School of Jazz, and in 1972 he assumed a faculty position at the University of Massachusetts, Amherst. Among Roach's most significant work from the 1970s are duet recordings he made with some of the leading figures from the post-bebop avant garde, including Archie SHEPP, Anthony BRAXTON, Abdullah Ibrahim, and Cecil TAYLOR. In the 1980s, Roach's astoundingly protean career included performances and recordings with a jazz quartet, the percussion ensemble M'Boom, the Uptown String Quartet (with his daughter Maxine on viola), rap and hip hop musicians and dancers. In 1980 Roach recorded an interactive drum solo with a tape recording of the Rev. Dr. Martin Luther KING Jr.'s 1963 "I Have A Dream" speech (*Chattahoochee Red*), and in 1989 he recorded duets with Dizzy Gillespie. Roach, who wrote music as early as 1946 ("Coppin' The Bop"), has in recent years dedicated more and more of his time to composition. His *Shepardsets,* a work for the theater, received an Obie award in 1985, and he has also composed for film and television, and symphony orchestra.

Roach, who has lived in New York all of his life, has in recent years been recognized not only as one of the most important drummers in the history of jazz, but as one of the leading African-American cultural figures of the twentieth century, with a decades-long commitment to fighting racial injustice. In addition to the several honorary doctorates he has received throughout his career, in 1988 Roach became the first jazz musician to receive a MacArthur Foundation "genius award."

REFERENCES

BROWN, ANTHONY. "The Development of Modern Jazz Drumset Artistry." *Black Perspective in Music* 18, nos. 1, 2 (1990): 39–58.

ROACH, MAX. "What Jazz Means to Me." *Black Scholar* 3, no. 2 (1972): 3.

WEINSTEIN, NORMAN C. *A Night in Tunisia: Imaginings of Africa in Jazz.* Metuchen, N.J., 1992, pp. 118–126.

WHITEHEAD, KEVIN. "Max Roach: Drum Architect." *Downbeat* 52, no. 10 (1985): 16.

ANTHONY BROWN

Roberts, Charles Luckeyeth "Luckey" (August 7, 1887–February 5, 1968), jazz pianist, composer, and bandleader. Born in Philadelphia, Roberts studied piano in childhood, performed in touring vaudeville troupes, and began playing piano professionally and composing in his teens after moving to New York City in 1910. In 1911 Roberts composed the score for the show *My People,* the first of his fourteen scores for musicals, and he published numerous compositions, including "Junk Man Rag" (1913) and "Spanish Venus" (1915). During this period he also led his own bands in New York, and toured as a pianist on vaudeville circuits. In 1923 he made several piano rolls, most notably "Mo'lasses." In the 1920s and '30s he worked as a bandleader, touring the East Coast. He also composed larger concert works, including *Whistlin' Pete—Miniature Syncopated Rhapsody,* and in 1939 he performed at Carnegie Hall. Roberts formed a touring orchestra in the 1940s, and from 1940 to 1954 he owned the Rendezvous Club in Harlem, where his nightly solo performances became legendary.

As a stride pianist he was held in high esteem by his colleagues (e.g., James P. JOHNSON and Willie the Lion SMITH). Although no early recordings survive, those extant from later in Roberts's career (1946 and 1958) document a flawless technique coupled with whimsical imagination and elegant decoration. That most of these recorded takes are in C-sharp major or related keys—an unusual detail—supports Eubie BLAKE's observation that "he [Roberts] could only play in one key" (although Blake cites F-sharp as the key [Waldo, p. 113]; apparently Roberts continued to prefer such black-note keys (including B-flat minor) throughout his career. Johnson implies that F-sharp was thought to be especially difficult when he says that he "could catch a key that a player was using, and copy it, even Luckey's" [Brown, p. 86]).

The recordings reveal the work of a gifted and fluent player, adept at a variety of decorative figures that would become the standard (but nevertheless challenging) gestures of stride: tremolo ("Shy and Sly," recorded May 22, 1946), the use of a midrange melody played by the left hand to the accompaniment of rapid arpeggios in the right ("Fandango," March 18, 1958), decorative, chromatic runs ("Pork and Beans," 1946), unexpected harmonic shifts ("Inner Space," 1958), and a large orchestral sound ("Complainin'," 1958). Roberts died in New York in 1968.

REFERENCES

BLESH, RUDI, and HARRIET JANIS. *They All Played Ragtime.* 4th ed. New York, 1971.

BROWN, SCOTT E. *James P. Johnson: A Case of Mistaken Identity.* Metuchen, N.J., 1986.

WALDO, TERRY. *This Is Ragtime.* New York, 1976.

PAUL S. MACHLIN

Roberts, Richard Samuel (November 14, 1881–November 30, 1936), photographer. Born in Fernandia, Fla., Roberts worked with his father as a stevedore in his native town and opened his own business, Gem Studios, in Fernandia, after teaching himself photography through books, magazines, and correspondence courses. In 1920, the Roberts family relocated to Columbia, S.C., when Roberts's wife, who grew up in Columbia, developed health problems and needed to leave the Florida climate. Roberts bought a house and built a photography studio on his property. From 4 A.M. to noon weekdays he worked as a janitor in the local post office, and in the afternoons and evenings he took pictures. By 1922, he had opened another studio, Roberts Studios, at 1119 Washington Street. The Roberts Studio promised "a true likeness" and advertisements in the local newspaper, the *Palmetto Leader,* claimed that "if you are beautiful, we guarantee to make your photographs just like you want them. If you are not beautiful, we guarantee to make you beautiful and yet to retain a true and brilliant likeness of you."

Roberts photographed families and individuals from all economic and social backgrounds either in his studio or in spaces of their choosing. He traveled around South Carolina photographing people in their homes, at funerals, baseball games, birthday parties, in their businesses, or at school. He also documented architectural structures and street scenes. Roberts's compositions are crisp and carefully posed, with his subjects rarely smiling and often facing the camera with penetrating, serious, and dignified expressions.

Roberts took over 10,000 images before he died in 1936. Three thousand glass-plate negatives were buried in crates in the Roberts home until 1986, when the South Carolina Library heard about Roberts's work from one of his old neighbors and began restoring the images. In the same year, Columbia Museum curated "A True Likeness," an exhibit of Roberts's work which featured two hundred of his photographs. Aside from the technical challenges of restoring the photographs, curators tried to identify as many of Roberts's subjects as possible and approached survivors of the 1920s and 1930s, hoping they would recognize themselves or their relatives in the photos. The Roberts collection is by far the most comprehensive photographic collection of early twentieth-century southern black folk life taken by an African American.

REFERENCES

ANDERSON, TONNIA L. . . . *and they called us 'Colored.'* Oklahoma City, 1992.
JOHNSON, THOMAS, and PHILLIP DUNN, eds. *A True Likeness: The Black South of Richard Samuel Roberts, 1920–1936.* Chapel Hill, N.C., 1986.
MEYER. "Columbia, S.C. Richard Samuel Roberts," *Art News,* March 1987, pp. 35, 37.
ROBERTS, BEVERLY. Interview. Columbia, S.C., 1990.
ROBERTS, GERALD. Interview. Columbia, S.C., 1990.

TONNIA L. ANDERSON

Robertson, Oscar (November 24, 1938–), basketball player. Born in Charlotte, Tenn., the youngest of three sons, Oscar Robertson grew up in Indianapolis, Ind., where he led Crispus Attucks High School to two state BASKETBALL championships. The heavily recruited six-foot-five-inch guard proceeded to the University of Cincinnati and became the first black person to play on that school's basketball team. During his college years, Robertson was a three-time all-American and captain of the gold-medal–winning 1960 U.S. Olympic basketball team. Robertson graduated from the University of Cincinnati in 1960 with a B.A. in business administration and was drafted by the Cincinnati Royals.

Robertson, often known by his nickname, "the Big O," was named rookie of the year and averaged 30.5 points per game in his first season in the National Basketball Association (NBA). In 1964 he was named the NBA's Most Valuable Player. Robertson played with Cincinnati until 1969 when he was traded to the Milwaukee Bucks. With the aid of the young Lew Alcindor (later known as Kareem ABDUL-JABBAR), Robertson helped lead his team to a 1971 NBA championship. When he retired in 1974, Robertson had scored 26,710 points, hit 7,694 free throws, and garnered 9,887 assists.

From 1965 through 1972, Robertson served as president of the NBA Players Association. During his tenure, he filed a landmark suit against the NBA in 1970, charging that its reserve clause, tying a player to a team until the team chose to trade him, was illegal. Despite a hostile reaction from the NBA, including a public relations campaign against him, Robertson pressed the suit. In 1976, two years after Robertson retired, the NBA finally gave in and agreed to a settlement that gave players free agency, allowing them to bargain for better contracts. This opened the door to today's higher salaries and contributed to the merger of the NBA and the American Basketball Association that same year.

Robertson is considered one of the finest guards in NBA history, and in 1979 he was elected to the Naismith Basketball Hall of Fame. After retiring from basketball Robertson worked as a sports analyst on ABC radio. In 1981 he founded Orchem, a chemical specialty manufacturer and commodity chemical supplier in Cincinnati, where he serves as president and chief executive officer.

REFERENCES

McCullum, Jack. "Pro Basketball." In *The Sports Illustrated 1992 Almanac*. Boston, 1991.
Porter, David L., ed. *Biographical Dictionary of American Sports: Basketball and Other Indoor Sports*. Westport, Conn., 1988.

                                    Kenya Dilday

Robeson, Eslanda Cardozo Goode (December 15, 1895–December 13, 1965), anthropologist and activist. Eslanda Robeson was born on December 15, 1895, in Washington, D.C. Her father, John Goode, was a clerk in the War Department. Her mother, Eslanda Cardozo, was the daughter of Francis Lewis Cardozo, a prominent pastor and Reconstruction-era politician.

When Eslanda Goode was six, her father died from alcoholism. Her mother moved the family to New York City, where her children could attend nonsegregated schools. Eslanda Goode graduated from Columbia University in 1917 with a bachelor of science degree in chemistry and took a job as histological chemist at New York's Presbyterian Hospital—the first African American employed there in a staff position. It was there, in 1920, that she met Paul ROBESON, who was recovering from a football injury. They were married a year later, and from then on Robeson pursued her career as an anthropologist and journalist while managing her husband's singing and acting commitments. She combined both careers in 1930 when she published *Paul Robeson, Negro*.

In the twenties and thirties, Eslanda Robeson accompanied her husband on most of his travels. At the same time she studied anthropology at the University of London and at the London School of Economics (1936–1937). She received a Ph.D. in anthropology from the Hartford Seminary Foundation in 1945. She also traveled and worked on her own. A trip through Africa in 1936 resulted in a book, *African Journey* (1945), and led to her commitment to African anticolonialism. She was active on the Council on African Affairs, and in a 1946 address before the United Nations Trusteeship Council, urged self-determination for all African people.

Her political activities, a visit to China in 1949 and public support of its government, and her vocal enthusiasm for the Soviet Union led her to be called before Sen. Joseph McCarthy's Subcommittee of the Senate Committee on Government Operations in 1953. From 1958 through 1963 she and her husband lived in self-imposed exile in the Soviet Union. Eslanda Robeson died of cancer in New York City on December 13, 1965.

REFERENCES

Duberman, Martin Bauml. *Paul Robeson*. New York, 1988.
Logon, Rayford W., and Michael R. Winston, eds. *Dictionary of American Negro Biography*. New York, 1982.

                                    Siraj Ahmed

Robeson, Paul (April 9, 1898–January 23, 1976), actor, singer, and political activist. Paul Robeson was born in Princeton, N.J., where his father, William Drew Robeson, was the minister of a local Presbyterian church, and his mother, Maria Louisa Bustill, was a schoolteacher. His childhood was happy, but marred by two defining events. His mother died when he was six, after she was accidentally set on fire at home; and his father lost his church following a fierce dispute among his congregation. After working at menial jobs in Princeton, his father moved first to Westfield and then to Somerville, both in New Jersey, where he again led churches affiliated with the AFRICAN METHODIST EPISCOPAL ZION DENOMINATION.

An uncommonly brilliant student and athlete, Paul Robeson entered Rutgers College (later Rutgers University) in New Brunswick in 1916. Although he was the only black student there, he became immensely popular. He was elected to Phi Beta Kappa as a junior and selected twice (1917 and 1918) as an All-American football player by the famed journalist Walter Camp. After graduating in 1919, he moved to Harlem, and in 1920 entered the law school of Columbia University in New York. To support himself he played professional football on weekends, then turned to acting after winning a role in *Simon the Cyrenian* at the Harlem YMCA in 1921.

Graduating from law school in 1923, he was admitted to the bar and served briefly in a law firm. Then, chafing at restrictions on him as a black, and urged on by his wife, Eslanda Cardoza Goode (a fellow student, in chemistry, at Columbia), he left the law for the stage. He enjoyed immediate success, particularly with the Greenwich Village-based Provincetown Players in Eugene O'Neill's *The Emperor Jones* (1923) and *All God's Chillun Got Wings* (1925). In 1925, with his longtime accompanist Lawrence

Paul Robeson in recital at London's St. Paul's Cathedral in 1958, shortly after the U.S. State Department restored his passport and enabled him to travel abroad once again and resume his international concert career. (AP/Wide World Photos)

Brown, he launched his celebrated career as an interpreter of African-American spirituals and of folk songs from around the world with a concert of the former in New York. He then traveled to Europe and Great Britain (where in 1922 he had been well received as an individual and as an actor in the play *Voodoo*). Critics hailed his acting in the 1925 London production of *The Emperor Jones*.

In the 1928 London production of Jerome Kern and Oscar Hammerstein II's musical *Show Boat*, his stirring rendition of "Ol' Man River" took his popularity to new heights. Although he triumphed again when *Show Boat* opened in New York in 1930, Great Britain was the scene of many of his greatest achievements. In the following years he starred there in a number of plays, including *Othello* (1930), *The Hairy Ape* (1931), and *Stevedore* (1933). Robeson also had prominent roles in almost a dozen films, such as *Sanders of the River* (1935), *Show Boat* (1936), *King Solomon's Mines* (1935), and *Proud Valley* (1941). In most of these efforts, his depictions of a black man contrasted starkly with the images of subservience, ignorance, criminality, or low comedy usually seen on the Hollywood screen.

Handsome and blessed with a commanding physique and a voice of unusual resonance and charm, Robeson might have capitalized on his stage and screen success and ignored politics altogether. However, his resentment of racism and his attraction to radical socialism, especially after an outstanding welcome in the Soviet Union in 1934, set him on a leftward course. A frequent visitor to the U.S.S.R. thereafter, Robeson learned to speak Russian (and eventually almost two dozen other languages, in which he recorded many songs). His son, Paul, Jr., attended school there for several years. Robeson became a dependable supporter of progressive causes, including the rights of oppressed Jews and of antifascist forces in Spain. In London, he befriended several students and other intellectuals, such as Kwame Nkrumah, George Padmore, and Jomo Kenyatta, who would later be prominent in the anticolonialist movements in Africa.

Resettling in the United States in 1939, Robeson joined enthusiastically in the war effort and maintained his stellar position as an entertainer—although racism, including that on Broadway and in Hollywood, still disturbed him. In 1943, his critically acclaimed portrayal of Othello, in the first Broadway production of Shakespeare's play with an otherwise white cast, created a sensation. He was awarded the NAACP's SPINGARN MEDAL in 1945. He fared less well after the war, when the Cold War intensified. In 1946, he vowed to a special committee of the California State Legislature that he had never been a member of the Communist party. However, when accusations continued, he resolutely refused to cooperate with the authorities. Despite his protests, he was identified as a communist by the House Committee on Un-American Activities. Such opposition hampered his career as a recording artist and actor.

In 1949, in a major controversy, he told a gathering in Paris that it was "unthinkable" to him that African Americans would to go war against the Soviet Union, whose fair treatment of blacks was a rebuke to racist American laws and conventions. Later that year, the announcement of his participation in a musical festival sponsored by liberals and leftists in Peekskill, N.Y., led to rioting in the town that left scores of attendees injured. The next year, the State Department impounded his passport. With Robeson refusing to sign an oath disavowing communism, his singing and acting career in effect came to an end. He was widely ostracized by whites and blacks, except those among the far left.

In 1958, the Supreme Court declared the oath and other government rules unconstitutional. That year, Robeson published *Here I Stand,* which combined autobiography with a considered statement of his political concerns and other beliefs. He sang at Carnegie Hall in what was billed as a farewell concert, and also performed in California. Leaving the United States, he was welcomed as a hero in the Soviet Union, which had awarded him the Stalin Peace Prize in 1952, but he fell ill there. Complaining of chronic exhaustion and other ailments, he entered a series of hospitals in the Soviet Union, Europe, and Britain.

In 1963, when he and his wife returned to the United States, to a home in Harlem, he announced his formal retirement. In 1965, Eslanda Robeson died. With a further deterioration in health, including a nervous breakdown, Robeson moved to Philadelphia to live with his sister. A seventy-fifth birthday celebration at Carnegie Hall in 1973 found Robeson (whose illness kept him away) saluted, in a more liberal age, by prominent blacks, liberals, and socialists as one of the towering figures of the twentieth century. In a message to the gathering, Robeson described himself as "dedicated as ever to the worldwide cause of humanity for freedom, peace, and brotherhood." He died in Philadelphia in 1976.

REFERENCES

DUBERMAN, MARTIN B. *Paul Robeson.* New York, 1988.

ROBESON, PAUL. *Here I Stand.* New York, 1971.

ARNOLD RAMPERSAD

Robinson, Bill "Bojangles" (Robinson, Luther) (May 25, 1878–November 25, 1949), tap dancer. The most famous of all African-American tap dancers, Bill Robinson demonstrated an exacting yet light footwork that was said to have brought tap "up on its toes" from the flat-footed shuffling style prevalent in the previous era. Born Luther Robinson in Richmond, Va., he was orphaned when both his parents, Maria and Maxwell Robinson, died in 1885; he and his brothers were subsequently reared by his grandmother, Bedilia Robinson.

Robinson gained his nickname, "Bojangles"—possibly from the slang term *jangle,* meaning "to quarrel or fight,"—while still in Richmond. It was also in Richmond that Robinson is said to have coined the phrase "Everything's copasetic," meaning "fine, better than all right." He ran away to Washington, D.C., earning nickels and dimes by dancing and singing, and then got his first professional job in 1892, performing in the "pickaninny" chorus (in vaudeville, a chorus of young African-American children performing as backup for the featured performer) in Mayme Remington's *The South Before the War.* When Robinson arrived in New York City around 1900, he challenged tap dancer Harry Swinton, the star dancer in *Old Kentucky,* to a buck-dancing contest, and won.

From 1902 to 1914, Robinson teamed up with George W. Cooper. Bound by the "two-colored" rule in vaudeville, which restricted blacks to performing in pairs, Cooper and Robinson performed as a duo on the Keith and Orpheum circuits. They did not, however, wear the blackface makeup performers customarily used. Robinson, who carried a gold-plated revolver, was a gambler with a quick temper. He was involved in a series of off-stage scrapes; it was allegedly his arrest for assault in 1914 that finally put an end to the partnership with Cooper.

After the split, Robinson convinced his manager, Marty Forkins, to promote him as a soloist. Forkins managed to book him at the Marigold Gardens Theater in Chicago by promising its star and producer, Gertrude Hoffman, Robinson's services as dance instructor; Robinson therewith launched his solo career and eventually became one of the first black performers to headline at New York's prestigious Palace Theatre.

Hailed as "the Dark Cloud of Joy" on the Orpheum circuit, Robinson performed in vaudeville from 1914 to 1927. Onstage, Robinson's open face, flashing eyes, infectious smile, easygoing patter, and air of surprise at what his feet were doing made him irresistible to audiences. His tapping was delicate, articulate, and intelligible. He usually wore a hat cocked to one side, and often exited with a Chaplinesque waddle, or with another signature step, a kind of syncopated "camel walk" (which would later be called the "moon walk" by Michael JACKSON). Robinson always danced in split-clog shoes, in which the wooden sole was attached from the toe to the ball of the foot and the rest was left loose, allowing for greater flexibility and tonality. Dancing upright and swinging to clean six-bar phrases, followed by a two-bar break, Robinson set new standards of performance, despite the fact that he invented few new steps.

In 1922, Robinson married Fannie Clay, who became his business manager and secretary. (The marriage was his second: in 1907, he had married Lena Chase, from whom he was divorced in 1922.) After twenty-one years he divorced Fannie and married a young dancer, Elaine Plaines.

Broadway fame came with an all-black revue, *Blackbirds of 1928,* in which he sang "Doin' the New Low Down" while dancing up and down a flight of

Bill "Bojangles" Robinson. (Photographs and Prints Division, Schomburg Center for Research in Black Culture, The New York Public Library, Astor, Lenox and Tilden Foundations)

five steps. Success was immediate: Robinson's performance was acclaimed by the major New York newspapers, and he was heralded by several as the greatest of all tap dancers. The dance Robinson performed in *Blackbirds* developed into his signature "stair dance"; notable for the clarity of Robinson's taps and for its unusual tonalities—each step yielded a different pitch—Robinson's appealing showmanship made it seem effortless. *Brown Buddies* (1930) was kept alive by Robinson's performance, as were *Blackbirds of 1933, The Hot Mikado* (1939), *All in Fun* (1940), and *Memphis Bound* (1945). Largely in recognition of his Broadway success, Robinson was named honorary "Mayor of Harlem" by Mayor Fiorello LaGuardia. In 1939, he celebrated his sixty-first birthday by tapping down Broadway, one block for each year.

Robinson turned to Hollywood, a venue largely closed to blacks, in the 1930s. His films included, *Dixiana* (1930), which had a predominantly white cast, and *Harlem Is Heaven* (1933), with an all-black cast. Robinson also appeared in the films *Hooray for Love* (1935), *In Old Kentucky* (1935), *The Big Broadcast of 1937* (1936), *One Mile from Heaven* (1937), *Road Demon* (1938), *Up the River* (1938), *By an Old Southern River* (1941), and *Let's Shuffle* (1941); in a newsreel about the 1939 World's Fair in Chicago, *It's Swing Ho! Come to the Fair;* and in a short, *Broadway Brevities* (1934). But of all his many stage and film performances, those that brought him the most fame were his appearances with child star Shirley Temple, in *The Littlest Colonel* (1935), *The Littlest Rebel* (1935), *Just Around the Corner* (1938), and *Rebecca of Sunnybrook Farm* (1938). In 1943, the all-black film *Stormy Weather,* with Robinson, Cab CALLOWAY, Lena HORNE, and Katherine DUNHAM's dance troupe, met with some success.

A founding member of the Negro Actors Guild of America, Robinson performed in thousands of benefits in the course of his career and made generous contributions to charities and individuals. Substantially, however, Robinson's career had peaked in the late 1930s, and when he died in 1949 he was in debt. According to contemporary accounts, nearly a hundred thousand people turned out to watch his funeral procession; the numbers testify to the esteem in which he was still held by his community and by the audiences who loved him. The founding of the Copasetics Club in the year that Robinson died ensured that his brilliance as a performer would not be forgotten.

REFERENCES

FLETCHER, TOM. *100 Years of the Negro in Show Business.* New York, 1954.

HASKINS, JIM, and N. R. MITGANG. *Mr. Bojangles: The Biography of Bill Robinson*. New York, 1988.
STEARNS, MARSHALL, and JEAN STEARNS. *Jazz Dance: The Story of American Vernacular Dance*. New York, 1968.

CONSTANCE VALIS HILL

Robinson, Edward Gay (February 13, 1919–), football coach. Eddie Robinson, the football coach at Grambling State University, has won more games than any other college or professional football coach in history. As of the end of the 1994 season, his record stood at 396 wins, 143 losses, and 15 ties. Robinson has lived in Louisiana all his life. Born in Jackson to a family of sharecroppers, he moved to Baton Rouge at the age of nine. He attended Leland College in Baker, La., where he majored in English, held several part-time jobs, and starred on the football team. Robinson went on several recruiting trips with Leland's coach, and he occasionally filled in as coach himself.

After graduating from Leland in 1941, Robinson was hired by the Louisiana Negro Normal and Industrial Institute in Grambling, La. (later Grambling State University) as football coach and director of the athletic program. The job also included the teaching of physical education, organization and direction of the school band and cheerleaders, and writing accounts of the game for the school newspaper.

Robinson soon proved an excellent coach. In his second year, 1942, the Tigers went 8–0. The following two football seasons were canceled because of World War II, and Robinson coached the football team at Grambling High School. He returned to the college in 1945, and spent his entire career there, refusing job offers from college and professional teams. He recruited and coached so successfully that the National Football League drafted more players from Grambling—over 200 by 1993—than from any other college. Among the most notable were fullback Paul "Tank" Younger, end Willie Davis, tackle "Buck" Buchanan, wide receiver Charlie Joiner, and quarterback Doug WILLIAMS. In 1968, Robinson's Tigers gained national attention when they played Morgan State University in New York City's Yankee Stadium, and in 1969, the team first appeared in a nationally televised game. In 1981 Robinson was portrayed by actor Harry BELAFONTE in a television movie, *Grambling's White Tiger*. On October 5, 1985, Robinson won his 324th game, becoming the winningest coach in college or professional football history.

An inspiring speaker, Robinson spent much of the off-season in lecture tours. He won many awards and honors, including the Walter Camp Foundation's Distinguished American Award in 1982, and a Special Recognition Award from the NCAA in 1986, and the 1992 Coach of the Year Award. A former president of the American Football Coaches Association (AFCA) and the National Intercollegiate Athletics Association (NAIA), he was also a member of the NAIA Hall of Fame.

REFERENCES

BRONDFIELD, JEROME. "Here's to You, Mr. Robinson." *Sports Illustrated* 63 (October 14, 1985): 32–34.
DAVIS, O. K. *Grambling Gridiron Glory*. Ruston, La., 1983.

GREG ROBINSON

Robinson, Frank (August 31, 1935–), baseball player and manager. Frank Robinson was born in Beaumont, Tex., the youngest of ten children of Frank and Ruth Robinson. He moved to California with his family at age four and attended school in Oakland, where he played on his high school team and with an American Legion team in Oakland. Robinson signed with the Cincinnati Reds in 1952 after high school and played minor league ball for several seasons before joining Cincinnati in 1956. Robinson was elected Rookie of the Year with the Reds and selected as the National League's Most Valuable Player (MVP) in 1961. He played with Cincinnati for ten seasons until he was traded to the Baltimore Orioles in 1966. Robinson's first year with the Orioles was one of his best: He batted .316 with 49 home runs and 122 runs batted in, winning a Triple Crown, and was named the American League and World Series MVP.

Robinson stayed with Baltimore until 1972, when he was traded to the Los Angeles Dodgers. The next season he was traded to the California Angels and in 1974 he went to the Cleveland Indians. After the season, the Indians announced that Robinson would take over as manager in 1975 while continuing to play, making Robinson the first black manager of a major league baseball team. Robinson continued to play for the Indians until 1976 and remained as manager until he was released in 1977. During his career as a player he accumulated 586 career home runs—the fourth highest lifetime record up to that time. Robinson is the only player to be named MVP in both the National League and the American League.

Robinson went on to manage the San Francisco Giants (1981–1984) and the Baltimore Orioles (1988–1991). In 1989 he was named manager of the year. However, in 1991, he was relieved of his managerial

Frank Robinson as manager of the Baltimore Orioles in 1989. The first African-American manager in major league baseball, Robinson had previously managed the Cleveland Indians and the San Francisco Giants. (AP/Wide World Photos)

duties early in the season (his career record as a manager at the time was 680 wins and 751 losses) and became the Orioles' assistant general manager. Robinson was elected to the Baseball Hall of Fame in 1982.

REFERENCES

The Baseball Encyclopedia. 8th ed. New York, 1990.
ROBINSON, FRANK. *My Life Is Baseball.* Garden City, N.Y., 1975.

KENYA DILDAY

Robinson, Ida Bell (August 3, 1891–April 20, 1946), minister. Ida Bell Robinson became pastor of the Mount Olive Holy Church, of the United Holy Church of America, in Philadelphia in 1917. In 1924 she organized the Mount Sinai Holy Church of America, one of the first Pentecostal denominations founded by an African-American woman. She was

soon consecrated bishop, and began founding churches on the eastern seaboard. By the time of her death, her organization consisted of eighty-four churches from New England to Florida, with missions in Cuba and Guyana. She also operated an accredited elementary–high school. The church's farm in New Jersey housed and employed workers and served as a retreat center for black church organizations.

Robinson was a strong advocate of the right of women to preach and serve as pastors, taught strict prohibitions against divorce and remarriage, and raised a pacifist voice during World War II (attracting surveillance from the FBI). An able preacher and singer, she broadcast her services on radio from New York City in the 1930s and 1940s. The denomination has grown to include over 120 churches, as well as a nursing home in Philadelphia, and to perform missionary work in England.

REFERENCES

FAUSET, ARTHUR HUFF. *Black Gods of the Metropolis: Negro Religious Cults in the Urban North.* Philadelphia, 1944.
FISHER, MILES MARK. "Organized Religion and the Cults." *Crisis* (January 1937): 8–10.

HAROLD DEAN TRULEAR

Robinson, Jack Roosevelt "Jackie" (January 31, 1919–October 24, 1972), baseball player, civil rights leader, businessman. Born in Georgia, the youngest of five children of sharecrop farmers Jerry and Mallie Robinson, Jackie Robinson was raised in Pasadena, Calif., where the Robinson family confronted the West Coast variety of American racism. White neighbors tried to drive the family out of their home; segregation reigned in public and private facilities. Robinson became an outstanding athlete at Pasadena Junior College, before transferring to U.C.L.A. in 1940, where he won renown as the "Jim Thorpe of his race," the nation's finest all-around athlete. Robinson was an All-American football player, leading scorer in basketball, and record-setting broad jumper, in addition to his baseball exploits.

Drafted into the Army in the spring of 1942 Robinson embarked on a stormy military career. Denied access to Officers' Candidate School, Robinson protested to heavyweight champion Joe LOUIS, who intervened with officials in Washington on Robinson's behalf. Once commissioned, Robinson fought for improved conditions for blacks at Camp Riley, Kans., leading to his transfer to Fort Hood, Tex. At

Fort Hood, Robinson was court-martialed and acquitted for refusing to move to the back of a bus. Robinson's Army career demonstrated the proud, combative personality that would characterize his postwar life.

After his discharge from the Army in 1944, Robinson signed to play with the Kansas City Monarchs of the Negro American League. After several months of discontent in the Jim Crow league, Robinson was approached by Branch Rickey of the Brooklyn Dodgers, who offered him the opportunity to become the first black player in major league baseball since the 1890s. Robinson gladly accepted the opportunity and responsibility of this pioneering role in "baseball's great experiment."

In 1946 Robinson joined the Montreal Royals of the International League, the top farm club in the Dodger system. Following a spectacular debut in which he stroked four hits including a three-run home run, Robinson proceeded to lead the league with a .349 batting average. An immediate fan favorite, Robinson enabled the Royals to set new attendance records while winning the International League and Little World Series championships. Robinson's imminent promotion to the Dodgers in 1947 triggered an unsuccessful petition drive on the part of southern players to keep him off the team. In the early months of the season, beanballs, death threats, and rumors of a strike by opposing players swirled about Robinson. Through it all, Robinson paraded his excellence. An electrifying fielder and baserunner as well as an outstanding hitter, Robinson's assault on baseball's color line captured the imagination of both black and white Americans. He batted .297 and won the Rookie of the Year Award (since renamed the Jackie Robinson Award in his honor) en route to leading the Dodgers to the pennant.

Over the next decade Robinson emerged as one of the most dominant players and foremost gate attractions in the history of the major leagues. In 1949 he batted .342 and won the National League Most Valuable Player Award. During his ten years with the Dodgers the team won six pennants and one World Championship. Upon his retirement in 1956 Robinson had compiled a .311 lifetime batting average. He was elected to the Baseball Hall of Fame on the first ballot in 1961.

But Robinson's significance transcended his achievements on the baseball diamond. He became a leading symbol and spokesperson of the postwar integration crusade, both within baseball and in broader society. During his early years in Montreal and Brooklyn, Robinson had adhered to his promise to Branch Rickey to "turn the other cheek" and avoid controversies. After establishing himself in the major

Jackie Robinson waiting for his turn at bat in the on-deck circle while playing for the Brooklyn Dodgers. (Photographs and Prints Division, Schomburg Center for Research in Black Culture, The New York Public Library, Astor, Lenox and Tilden Foundations)

leagues, however, Robinson's more combative and outspoken personality reasserted itself. Robinson repeatedly pressed for baseball to desegregate more rapidly and to remove discriminatory barriers in Florida training camps and cities like St. Louis and Cincinnati. He also demanded opportunities for black players to become coaches, managers, and front office personnel. Baseball officials and many sportswriters branded Robinson an ingrate as controversies marked his career.

Upon retirement Robinson remained in the public eye. He continued to voice his opinions as speaker, newspaper columnist, and fundraiser for the NAACP. A believer in "black capitalism" through which blacks could "become producers, manufacturers, developers and creators of businesses, providers of jobs," Robinson engaged in many successful business ventures in the black community. He became an executive in the Chock Full O' Nuts restaurant chain and later helped develop Harlem's Freedom National Bank and the Jackie Robinson Construction Company. Robinson also became active in Republican Party politics, supporting Richard Nixon in 1960, and working closely with New York Gov. Nelson Rockefeller, who appointed him Special Assistant for Community Affairs in 1966. These activities brought criticism from young black militants in the late 1960s. Ironically, at this same time Robinson had also parted ways with the NAACP, criticizing its failure to include "younger, more progressive voices."

By the late 1960s Robinson had become "bitterly disillusioned" with both baseball and American society. He refused to attend baseball events in protest of the failure to hire blacks in nonplaying capacities. In his 1972 autobiography, *I Never Had It Made,* he attacked the nation's waning commitment to racial equality. Later that year the commemoration of his major league debut led him to lift his boycott of baseball games. "I'd like to live to see a black manager," he told a nationwide television audience at the World Series on October 15, 1972. Nine days later he died of a heart attack.

REFERENCES

ROBINSON, JACKIE, with Alfred Duckett. *I Never Had It Made.* New York, 1972.

ROWAN, CARL. *Wait Till Next Year.* New York, 1960.

TYGIEL, JULES. *Baseball's Great Experiment: Jackie Robinson and His Legacy.* New York, 1983.

JULES TYGIEL

Robinson, Jo Ann Gibson (April 17, 1912–), teacher and civil rights leader. Jo Ann Gibson Robinson was at the forefront of the movement to desegregate public transportation and a leader of the 1955 MONTGOMERY BUS BOYCOTT in Alabama, in which over 50,000 African Americans participated. Born in Culloden, Ga., the youngest of twelve children, Gibson attended Macon public schools before entering Fort Valley State College. She taught in Macon schools for five years, then went to Atlanta University, where she received a master's degree in English in 1948. One year later, Robinson accepted a position as a member of the English department at Alabama State College in Montgomery.

Shortly after moving to Montgomery, Robinson joined the Women's Political Council (WPC), an organization of mostly middle-class black women. The WPC was founded in 1946 by Mary Fair Burks, an English professor at Alabama state, to increase the black community's involvement in civic affairs by promoting voter registration and teaching high school students about politics and government. In 1950, Robinson became president of the WPC, and under her leadership the organization grew to over two hundred members and began to challenge the demeaning form of segregation on the city's buses. The WPC lobbied the city in the early 1950s to revise its seating policy so black passengers would not have to give up their seats for whites or stand over an empty seat reserved for a white rider. In May 1954, Robinson wrote a letter to Montgomery's Mayor Gayle threatening a boycott unless reforms were forthcoming.

After Claudette Colvin, a young black teenager, was arrested in March 1955 for violating a segregation law, Robinson and other black leaders negotiated with the city commissioner about changing the city's seating policy. The meetings yielded very little, and Robinson supported launching a boycott, but other black leaders opposed the idea. When Rosa PARKS, secretary of the NATIONAL ASSOCIATION FOR THE ADVANCEMENT OF COLORED PEOPLE (NAACP), was arrested on December 1, 1955, for refusing to give up her seat for a white man on the bus, members of the WPC were prepared for a boycott. After speaking with E. D. Nixon and Parks, they made a flier calling for a boycott the following Monday. Putting her job on the line, Robinson mimeographed fifty thousand copies late one night at Alabama State and, with help from two of her students, distributed them within forty-eight hours of Parks's arrest. The WPC also planned a mass meeting at the Dexter Avenue Baptist Church for the afternoon of the boycott, at which time it was decided to continue the boycott indefinitely. It was primarily because of the prevoius five years of political groundwork laid by women in the WPC, under the direction of Robinson, that the black community in Montgomery was prepared to endure a boycott that lasted over a year.

Although men were the most visible leaders of the MONTGOMERY IMPROVEMENT ASSOCIATION (MIA), the organization created to coordinate the boycott, women played important roles. Robinson, in particular, was an influential political strategist and an indispensable contributor to the movement. She wielded political power on the executive board of the MIA; served as an important negotiator with the city; produced the MIA newsletter, which not only provided support and encouragement for boycotters, but kept people around the country informed about the progress of the protest; and volunteered time in the car pool to help the thousands of ordinary participants get to work on time. In December 1956, a court order desegregating public transportation ended the boycott. Although the importance of the WPC began to diminish, it nevertheless continued to exist for several years.

Robinson left Alabama State College in 1960 after several teachers had been fired for their participation in the boycott. She taught for one year at Grambling State College in Grambling, La., and then moved to Los Angeles, where she taught English in the public schools until 1976, when she retired. In 1987, Robinson published her memoir of the boycott, *The Montgomery Bus Boycott and the Women Who Started It,* which won the publication prize by the Southern Association for Women's Historians. Through her historical work, Robinson has helped restore women to their proper place in the Montgomery boycott, and through her political commitment, she helped launch one of the most important civil rights struggles in the JIM CROW South.

REFERENCES

BURKS, MARY FAIR. "Trailblazers: Women in the Montgomery Bus Boycott." In Vicki L. Crawford, Jacqueline Anne Rouse, and Barbara Woods, eds. *Women in the Civil Rights Movement: Trailblazers and Torchbearers, 1941–65.* New York, 1990.

HINE, DARLENE CLARK, ed. *Black Women in America: An Historical Encyclopedia.* Brooklyn, N.Y., 1993.

KING, MARTIN LUTHER, JR. *Stride Toward Freedom.* New York, 1958.

ROBINSON, JO ANN. *The Montgomery Bus Boycott and the Women Who Started It: The Memoir of Jo Ann Robinson.* New York, 1987.

PAM NADASEN

Robinson, LaVaughn (1927–), tap dancer. Born into a family of fourteen children in Philadelphia, LaVaughn Robinson was introduced early to the world of tap. His mother taught him a time step (a basic step typically used at the start of a routine in order to synchronize with the accompaniment and with other dancers) when he was seven years old. He grew up dancing on the street corners of Philadelphia, honing his skills in fiercely competitive tap challenges and watching the best of the Philadelphia-based tap acts—the NICHOLAS BROTHERS and the Condos Brothers, for example—perform. Robinson first danced with a "tramp band" of washboards and kazoos on the street, then moved indoors to clubs and bars, where, as a busker, he danced and passed the hat.

Robinson was eventually able to bring the rhythms of the street onto the concert stage. He started to work professionally in 1946, performing as a soloist with the big bands of Tommy Dorsey and Cab CALLOWAY, who in those years always traveled with a tap dancer or tap team. Robinson also toured with singers Ella FITZGERALD and Billie HOLIDAY and performed internationally in clubs, theaters, on radio, and on television. Robinson has taught at the Philadelphia College of the Performing Arts and was a featured performer at Boston's Great Tap Reunion in 1990.

REFERENCE

FRANK, RUSTY. *Tap!* New York, 1991.

CONSTANCE VALIS HILL

Robinson, Mamie.   *See* Smith, Mamie.

Robinson, Maxie Cleveland (May 1, 1939– December 20, 1988), television newscaster. Max Robinson was born in Richmond, Va., and graduated from Armstrong High School in 1957. He attended Oberlin College for one year before dropping out to join the Air Force. Unable to become a pilot because of partial color blindness, he was sent to the Air Force Language Institute at Indiana University to study Russian from 1959 to 1960. After leaving the Air Force, he held odd jobs and resided with different relatives for several years.

In 1965 Robinson got a job as a floor director at a television station, WTOP, in Washington, D.C. Impressed by his on-camera style and voice, producers quickly promoted him to reporter. A few months later, in 1966, he joined rival station WRC-TV, where he stayed for three years. He returned to WTOP in 1969 with the promise of an anchor position and was eventually teamed with Gordon Peterson for the evening news. Robinson was a successful reporter and quickly rose to prominence. He won an Emmy Award and Journalist of the Year Award in 1967. While at WTOP, he also taught television production and communicative arts at Federal City College from 1968–1972. In 1978 Robinson was asked by the American Broadcasting Company (ABC) to head the national news desk in Chicago for the World News Tonight, while Frank Reynolds and Peter Jennings headed the Washington and foreign news desks. When he joined ABC Robinson became the first black network anchor. He continued to win awards for journalism, including a Capital Press Club National Media Award in 1979 and another Emmy Award in 1981.

While at ABC, Robinson helped found the Association of Black Journalists and spoke out about racism in the media. The racism he experienced and the pressure of being a role model led to drinking problems, which interfered with his job performance. In 1983 Robinson was relieved of his coanchorship and the next year took a job as coanchor of the WMAQ evening news in Chicago, where he stayed for one year. In 1987 Robinson was diagnosed with AIDS and died the next year of complications related to his illness. He was the brother of TRANSAFRICA founder Randall ROBINSON.

REFERENCE

BOYER, PETER. "The Light Goes Out." *Vanity Fair* (June 1989): 68–84.

PAM NADASEN

Robinson, Randall (July 6, 1941–), lobbyist and political activist. Randall Robinson was born in Richmond, Va., and educated in segregated public schools. He attended Virginia Union University in Richmond, graduated in 1967, and three years later received his Juris Doctor degree from the Harvard University Law School. In 1970 he went to Tanzania for a year on a Ford Fellowship before moving to Boston to work as a civil rights attorney for a legal aid project and then as a director of a multiservice center. Robinson moved to Washington, D.C., in 1975 to work in the office of Rep. William Clay of Missouri. The next year he became an administrative assistant to Michigan Rep. Charles DIGGS and went to South Africa as a staff member of a congressional delegation.

In 1977, in the midst of massive demonstrations in the United States to pressure the white South African government to put an end to their racist policies, Robinson was named executive director of TransAfrica, a political lobbying group for African and Caribbean causes. Under Robinson, TransAfrica began to play a central role in educating the American public about the evils of apartheid.

Robinson received national attention in 1984 when he organized daily protests in front of the South African embassy in Washington, D.C., which lasted fifty-three weeks. The protests spread to twenty-six cities around the country and to London. More than six thousand people, including twenty-three congres-

sional representatives, were arrested. Robinson also led the fight in Congress for sanctions, which resulted in the Comprehensive Anti-Apartheid Act of 1986. When President George Bush lifted the sanctions in 1991 after Nelson Mandela was released from prison, Robinson opposed this move until there was more evidence of fundamental changes in South African society.

In addition to opposing apartheid in South Africa, Robinson has been an advocate for a number of other causes in Africa and the Caribbean. In the 1980s he opposed U.S. support for Contra guerrillas seeking to overthrow the Sandinista government of Nicaragua, supported the government of Angola and its struggle against South African–backed National Union for Total Independence (UNITA) forces, and invited Maurice Bishop, the president of Grenada, to speak in the United States just before Bishop's assassination and the subsequent invasion by United States forces. In 1993 Robinson called for a peace conference to put a permanent end to the devastation in Somalia. The following year he went on a twenty-seven-day hunger strike to protest the United States policy of turning back Haitian refugees after a military coup ousted democratically elected President Jean-Bertrand Aristide, which led to widespread political repression.

REFERENCES

CHEERS, MICHAEL D. "TransAfrica: The Black World's Voice on Capitol Hill." *Ebony* (July, 1987): 198–114.
ROBINSON, RANDALL. "We Lost—and de Klerk Won." *Newsweek* (July 29, 1991): 8.

PAM NADASEN

Robinson, Roscoe, Jr. (October 11, 1928–July 22, 1993), army general. Roscoe Robinson, Jr., was born in St. Louis, Mo. He graduated from the U.S. Military Academy at West Point in 1951 and became a second lieutenant with the 188th Airborne Infantry Regiment. In 1952 he commanded a rifle company in the KOREAN WAR, for which he was awarded the Bronze Star. After the war Robinson served with the U.S. Military Mission on its tour of Liberia in the late 1950s. In 1964 he earned a master's degree in international relations from the University of Pittsburgh.

During the VIETNAM WAR Robinson, as a lieutenant colonel, commanded the Second Battalion, Seventh Air Cavalry Division. For valor in combat he received the Silver Star with two oak-leaf clusters in

1968. After his Vietnam service Robinson was stationed in Hawaii as part of the Army's Pacific command. Upon his promotion to colonel in 1972, he returned to the mainland United States to take command of the Eighty-second Airborne at Fort Bragg, N.C. Promoted to brigadier general in 1973, he was stationed near Tokyo in 1978 to serve as a deputy commander for the U.S. Army garrison. Robinson received his fourth star in 1982, making him the first black four-star general in the U.S. Army. He served from 1982 until 1985 as a representative to the NATO Military Committee, after which service he retired from active duty. He died in Washington, D.C., in 1993.

REFERENCE

HAWKINS, WALTER L. *African American Generals and Flag Officers: Biographies of Over 120 Blacks in the United States Military.* Jefferson, N.C., 1993.

ALLISON X. MILLER

Robinson, Ruby Doris (April 25, 1942–October 7, 1967), civil rights activist. Born in Atlanta, Ga., Ruby Robinson observed the Montgomery bus boycott as a teenager, and developed a commitment to the black liberation movement. In 1959, as a sophomore at Spelman College, she was inspired by the North Carolina lunch counter sit-ins and became actively involved in the CIVIL RIGHTS MOVEMENT. In protest over rules that prevented blacks from eating at the same lunch counters as white people, Robinson participated in the first Atlanta sit-ins. In 1960 she assisted in the founding of the STUDENT NONVIOLENT COORDINATING COMMITTEE (SNCC).

Undeterred by mob violence and the risk of physical harm, in 1961 she joined the SNCC freedom riders in their bus rides through the deep South; she received a two-month jail sentence for "inflammatory traveling." In 1963 she joined SNCC full-time, becoming a day-by-day organizer and assuming responsibilities as a financial coordinator and administrator. In 1966, as the philosophy of nonviolence was replaced by more militant black nationalism within the movement, Robinson was elected SNCC's executive secretary. Early in 1967, expressing doubt about nonviolence as a method of serious social change, Robinson left SNCC. She died from leukemia later that year.

REFERENCES

HARDY, GAYLE J. *American Women Civil Rights Activists: Biobibliographies of 68 Leaders, 1825–1992.* Jefferson, N.C., 1993.

SMITH, JESSIE CARNEY, ed. *Notable Black American Women.* Detroit, 1992.

NEIL GOLDSTEIN

Robinson, Sugar Ray (Smith, Walker, Jr.) (May 3, 1921–April 12, 1989), boxer. Sugar Ray Robinson was born to Marie and Walker Smith in Detroit. He moved with his mother in 1933 to Harlem, where he attended DeWitt Clinton High School. Representing the Salem Athletic Club, he began BOXING, using the identification card of a Ray Robinson. He won the New York Golden Gloves in 1939 and 1940 and turned professional late in 1940. A reporter described his technique as "sweet as sugar." Robinson won his first forty fights (twenty-six knockouts) until Jake LaMotta beat him on a decision in 1943. He served as a private during World War II, mainly boxing exhibitions on tour with his idol, Joe LOUIS. Robinson demanded fair treatment for blacks in the military, refusing to appear at one show until blacks were allowed into the audience, and getting into a fight with a military policeman (MP) who had threatened Louis for using a phone in a whites-only area.

Robinson won the vacant welterweight (147 pounds) championship on December 20, 1946, in a fifteen-round decision over Tommy Bell. In Robinson's first defense, Jimmy Doyle suffered fatal brain injuries in an eighth-round knockout. When questioned if he had intended to get Doyle into trouble, Robinson responded, "Mister, it's my business to get him in trouble." He moved up to the middleweight division (160 pounds), besting champion Jake LaMotta in the 1951 "St. Valentine's Day Massacre," which got its name from the punishment LaMotta took until the fight was stopped in the thirteenth round. Robinson lost the title on a decision five months later to Randy Turpin in London, making his record 128–1–2. Two months later he regained the title from Turpin with a dramatic tenth-round knockout in New York as he bled heavily from a cut above the left eye. In 1952 he fought Joey Maxim for the light heavyweight championship at Yankee Stadium. He was far ahead on points, but he collapsed after the thirteenth round in 100-degree heat.

Robinson retired from the ring and worked two years as a tap dancer. He returned to boxing in 1955 and in his seventh bout regained the middleweight crown with a second-round knockout of Bobo Olson on December 9, 1955. He lost the title on January 2, 1956, to Gene Fullmer, regaining it in a rematch four months later, knocking Fullmer unconscious in the

Sugar Ray Robinson, a matchless combination of boxing finesse and knockout power, was widely regarded as the finest boxer of his era. In 1951 he celebrates after defeating Jake LaMotta in Chicago for the middleweight title. (AP/Wide World Photos)

fifth. Carmen Basilio dethroned Robinson on September 23 but lost the rematch on March 25, 1958, by decision. Robinson held the middleweight title until defeated by Paul Pender on January 22, 1960. Robinson lost the rematch and two other title bouts, and he retired in 1965. He held the middleweight championship a record five times.

Robinson was renowned for his flashy living. He owned a night club, Sugar Ray's, and other Harlem properties and on tours took a large entourage, including a valet and barber. He appeared in television and films. Once he was well established, he acted as his own manager and was regarded as a tough negotiator. An IRS tax dispute led to a ruling that allowed income averaging. However, Robinson went through $4 million so fast he had to continue boxing well past his prime. In 1969 he moved to Los Angeles, where he established the Sugar Ray Robinson Youth Foundation for inner city youth. He lived there with his second wife, Millie Bruce, until he died of Alzheimer's disease and diabetes. Robinson had a record of 174 (with 109 KO's)–19–6–2. Renowned for his superb footwork, hand speed, and leverage, he was so powerful that he could knock out an opponent when moving backwards. He was elected to the Boxing Hall of Fame in 1967.

REFERENCES

Obituary. *New York Times,* April 13, 1989, I, 1–1.
ROBINSON, SUGAR RAY, and DAVE ANDERSON. *Sugar Ray.* New York, 1969.

STEVEN A. RIESS

Robinson, William, Jr., "Smokey" (February 19, 1940–), singer. In 1954, while still in high school in Detroit, Smokey Robinson formed the Miracles (originally known as the Matadors). The Miracles' distinctive sound was led by Robinson's quivering falsetto and tenor, with vocalists Ronnie White, Bobby Rogers, Pete Moore, and Claudette Rogers (whom he later married), and guitarist Marv Tarplin. In 1958, Robinson signed with Berry Gordy, the founder of MOTOWN Records, and soon became important in the early successes of Motown. He was a popular performer, but also became a significant songwriter and collaborator for Motown on such compositions as the label's first million-selling record, "Shop Around" (1960).

Robinson's other hits include "The Tracks of My Tears" (1965), "Ooo Baby Baby" (1965), and "The Tears of a Clown" (1970), written for the Miracles. He also composed the TEMPTATIONS' hit "The Way You Do the Things You Do" (1964), Mary WELLS's "My Guy" (1964), and Marvin GAYE's number one R&B hit "Ain't That Peculiar" (1965). In 1972, he left the Miracles in order to devote more time to his Motown executive position and songwriting, while beginning a successful solo career that produced 17 solo albums. Robinson's popular 1974 album *A Quiet Storm* was noted for his silky voice floating over a subtle, evocative instrumental background.

Robinson's vocal style is defined by his soft, sophisticated falsetto singing. Although this style was popular with numerous R&B groups of the 1940s and 1950s, it was Robinson's highly influential solo style that was widely imitated by white "blue-eyed soul" vocalists of the 1970s to 1990s. He was equally influential as a songwriter; his ballads defined the Motown sound. In 1986, he was inducted into the Songwriters' Hall of Fame, and he received a Grammy Award for "Just to See Her" in 1987.

REFERENCE

GEORGE, NELSON. *Where Did Our Love Go? The Rise and Fall of the Motown Sound.* New York, 1985. "The miraculous Smokey Robinson: Twenty-five years and still smokin'." *Sepia* (May 1981): 22–25.

KYRA D. GAUNT

Rock, John Sweat (October 13, 1825–December 3, 1866), lawyer, abolitionist, and physician. John Sweat Rock (the middle name sometimes appears as Swett) was born to free parents in Salem, N.J. He was educated in Salem common schools until he was nineteen. From 1844 to 1848, he taught school and studied medicine with two white physicians. In 1850, after an apprenticeship with a white dentist, he began his own

practice in Philadelphia. Two years later, he earned an M.D. degree, graduating from the short-lived American Medical College in Philadelphia. Sometime before 1855, Rock moved to Massachusetts, where he became one of the first black members of the Massachusetts Medical Society.

In Boston, Rock became involved with the abolitionist Lewis Hayden. In the turbulent period after the passage of the 1850 Fugitive Slave Act, he made use of his medical training to treat ill fugitives who had escaped from slavery (*see* FUGITIVE SLAVES). In 1855 Rock participated in the successful campaign to legally desegregate Boston public schools. He became a leader of the city's black community and was one of the speakers at the Faneuil Hall meeting that was held on March 5, 1858, to commemorate Crispus Attucks Day (*see* Crispus ATTUCKS). In his talk Rock celebrated racial pride and beauty, praising "the fine, tough muscular system, the beautiful, rich color, the full broad features, and the gracefully frizzled hair of the Negro."

Rock's interest in black civil rights led him to study law. On September 14, 1861, he was admitted to the Massachusetts bar. Like other black leaders, Rock saw

John Sweat Rock, physician and lawyer, became in 1865 the first black admitted to practice before the U.S. Supreme Court. (Prints and Photographs Division, Library of Congress)

tremendous possibilities for black advancement during the turmoil of the Civil War. He was the first speaker at the Tremont Temple meeting in Boston on January 1, 1863, which was being held to celebrate the enactment of the Emancipation Proclamation (*see* EMANCIPATION). After Congress authorized the raising of African-American troops in 1863, Rock sought recruits for the Fifty-fourth and Fifty-fifth Massachusetts Infantry Regiments and helped to secure equal pay for the black soldiers. In October 1864, as a delegate from Massachusetts to the National Convention of Colored Men held at the Wesleyan Methodist Church in Boston, he praised Abraham Lincoln and the Republican party, and he called for equal opportunities and equal rights for blacks. The capstone of his career came in February 1865, when Rock became the first African-American attorney to be admitted to practice before the U.S. Supreme Court, though, as it turned out, he never actually practiced. Rock's health deteriorated rapidly shortly thereafter, and he died of tuberculosis on December 3, 1866, in Washington, D.C., where he lived with his mother and his son.

REFERENCES

QUARLES, BENJAMIN. *Black Abolitionists.* New York, 1969.
SMITH, J. CLAY, JR. *Emancipation: The Making of the Black Lawyer, 1844–1944.* Philadelphia, 1993.

JO H. KIM

Rodeo. By the 1870s informal rodeo contests had become commonplace throughout the ranch lands of the western United States. Rodeo's early participants were working cowboys, and a significant minority of these cowboys were African Americans. Although he is not thought to have entered any organized contests, Isom Dart, who would go on to notoriety as a cattle rustler, worked as a rodeo clown in Texas and New Mexico and was known as a skilled horseman. It was for his victory in several roping and shooting contests in Deadwood, Ariz., that Nat Love earned the nickname "Deadwood Dick." Love worked as a brand reader for the Gallanger Company, claiming stray cattle and overseeing branding operations.

Popular interest in cowboy sports grew in turn-of-the-century America, even as the railroad began to change the nature of the cattle industry. And as rodeo purses increased, more cowboys began to participate in organized competition and in the popular Wild West Shows. Jesse Stahl, who began his riding career in 1913, competed nationally and earned a reputation as one of the best horsemen in the West. Among the most famous Wild-West Show performers was Bill PICKETT, who worked for the Miller family's 101 Ranch in Oklahoma and toured nationally with the Miller Brothers' 101 Ranch Wild West Show. Pickett is credited with popularizing the sport of bulldogging, in which a steer is wrestled to the ground by its horns. Bulldogging (or steer wrestling) remains one of seven standard events in modern rodeo and is the only standard event so closely linked to the influence of one individual.

Although rodeo provided both economic opportunity and a degree of social equality for its most successful African-American participants, black rodeo performers were often victims of discrimination. Many competitions were closed to them. In his early days, Bill Pickett dressed as a Mexican toreador to be allowed to perform. Other top riders, such as the Mosely brothers, adopted American Indian names. When allowed to compete, black cowboys were often unfairly judged. In the face of such discrimination, many African Americans began to organize their own rodeos. In 1905, the predominantly African-American town of Boley, Okla., held its first rodeo. Black rodeos would grow in popularity throughout the twentieth century.

In 1929, the Rodeo Association of America (RAA) introduced a point-awards structure, designed to standardize rodeo competition in the manner of other amateur sports, and by the 1930s organized rodeo had largely replaced the once popular Wild West Show. A national rodeo circuit arose, and several African Americans achieved success in what became an increasingly professionalized sport. Bull rider Myrtis Dightman of Crockett, Tex., was the first contemporary black rodeo competitor to gain national fame. Beginning in 1964, Dightman qualified for the National Finals Rodeo seven times. In 1967 and 1968, he was ranked third in his event by the Professional Rodeo Cowboy Association. Clarence LeBlanc of Okmulgee, Okla., held the southern regional steer-wrestling title and finished first in average points in the 1978 International Finals Rodeo. In 1983, he finished second in the U.S. national steer-wrestling competition. Charlie Sampson of Los Angeles emerged as the best-known black rodeo star. Sampson, a bull rider, won the Winston Rodeo Series in 1982, and that same year became the first African American to win a world title. He qualified for the National Finals Rodeo in five subsequent years (1981–1985) and in 1984, won the Sierra Circuit title. Fred Whitfield of Cypress, Tex., became the second African-American world rodeo champion when he won the world calf-roping title in 1991.

In 1984, George E. Blair founded the Black World Championship Rodeo. Staging its performances in urban areas of the United States, and especially in the urban Northeast, the Black World Championship Rodeo highlights the performances of black riders and ropers and seeks to educate urban America about the role of the African-American cowboy in settling the western United States.

REFERENCES

ASHE, ARTHUR R., JR. *A Hard Road to Glory: A History of the African Athlete*. 3 vols. New York, 1988.

FREDRICKSON, KRISTINE. *American Rodeo: From Buffalo Bill to Big Business*. College Station, Tex., 1985.

HANES, BAILEY C. *Bill Pickett, Bulldogger*. Norman, Okla., 1977.

KATZ, WILLIAM LOREN. *The Black West*. Seattle, Wash. 1987.

SAVAGE, W. SHERMAN. *Blacks in the West*. Westport, Conn., 1976.

BENJAMIN K. SCOTT

Rodgers, Carolyn (December 14, 1945–), writer. Carolyn Rodgers, a founding member of Chicago's Organization of Black American Culture (OBAC) Writers' Workshop, was among the most popular poets of the BLACK ARTS MOVEMENT. Born in 1945 and raised in Chicago, Rodgers attended the University of Illinois and Roosevelt University, where she received her bachelor's degree. As a member of Gwendolyn BROOKS's writers workshop and OBAC, she became acquainted with Chicago's younger black writers as well as with Brooks and Hoyt Fuller, who became her mentors. With two other OBAC members, Haki R. MADHUBUTI (Don L. Lee) and Johari Amini (Jewel Latimore), she helped found Third World Press, which published her first book, *Paper Soul* (1968).

With *Paper Soul* and *Songs of a Blackbird* (1969), Rodgers established herself as a leading poetic voice of her generation. Her work was admired for the refreshing and sometimes shocking frankness of her poetic voice. Reflecting cultural dilemmas posed by the Black Power movement, her poems explored the conflicts between conformity and rebellion, family and peers, and secular politics and traditional religion. Among her finest poems are those expressing women's frustrations in seeking both respect and love from men.

how i got ovah: new and selected poems (1975), published by Doubleday, reflected the beginnings of Rodgers's turn from militancy, and *The Heart As Ever Green* (1978) marked her transformation into a primarily religious poet. For nearly a decade, she withdrew from public activity, but in the late 1980s she began teaching at Columbia College in Chicago and publishing new poems, mostly on religious themes.

REFERENCES

EVANS, MARI, ed. *Black Women Writers, 1950–1980*. Garden City, N.Y., 1984.

PARKS, CAROLE A., ed. *Nommo: A Literary Legacy of Black Chicago (1967–1987)*. Chicago, 1987.

DAVID LIONEL SMITH

Rodgers, Rod Audrian (December 4, 1938–), choreographer and dancer. Rod Rodgers was born into a family of professional dancers; his parents performed across the United States in the circuit of night clubs and resorts which catered exclusively to blacks. In the early 1960s, Rodgers began his career as a dancer by working in similar clubs.

In 1962 Rodgers moved to New York City and began studying dance with Hanya Holm, Mary Anthony, and Erick Hawkins. He was a member of such dance groups as Dancer's Theatre Company, the Erick Hawkins Modern Dance Company, and the National Dance Teachers Guild. A year later, Rodgers founded the Rod Rodgers Dance Company and the ensemble performed repertory created by Rodgers as well as guest choreographers. The company, which featured seven to twenty dancers, focused on modern dance techniques in order to show that black dancers did not have to limit their modes of expression to traditional African, ethnic, or historically African-American styles.

During the mid-1960s Rodgers choreographed and presented concert dance programs to children in poor neighborhoods in New York City through the Head Start Program. He became director of the dance project of New York City's Mobilization for Youth in 1965 and in the same year was awarded a John Hay Whitney Fellowship which gave him the financial security to work as a full-time dancer and choreographer. During this decade he was also one of the founders of the Association of Black Choreographers.

Rodgers's best-known works, most of which were created in the late 1960s and early 1970s, feature a range of choreographic styles, with an emphasis on abstraction and occasional use of narrative elements. Pieces such as *Percussion Suite* (1966) include dancers wearing or carrying percussion instruments, a technique that has become a trademark of Rodgers's choreography. Other works which were created in the late 1960s include *Tangents,"* which drew upon African traditions of ritual dance; *Now! Nigga . . . ,* which depicted a moment of violent resistance in an urban ghetto; and *Dances in Projected Space,* which consisted of movements accompanied by a slide presentation of abstract art. Rodgers's 1968 tribute to the

Rev. Dr. Martin Luther KING, Jr., *King . . . the Dream* premiered the week after King was assassinated.

In the 1980s and early '90s, the Rod Rodgers Dance Company taught classes and workshops in the company's studio on the Lower East Side. The group has been particularly active in bringing dance programs into public schools, colleges, and community organizations. During the 1990s, the company presented works honoring African-American artists and leaders such as Langston HUGHES, Duke ELLINGTON, Harriet TUBMAN, Rosa PARKS, and Mary McCloud BETHUNE, as well as more abstract pieces, such as *Rhythmdances,* which featured dancers playing handheld percussion instruments. Rodgers has expanded the audience for modern dance by showing that abstract movement and African-American dance traditions can be used to express social commentary on the urban black experience.

REFERENCES

CHATMAN, PRISCILLA. "Making Dance—A Man Sized Job—A Black Dance Artist and His Work." *The Black American* (October 28, 1976).

RODGERS, ROD. "For the Celebration of Our Blackness." *Dance Scope* (Spring 1967): 6–10.

"Rod Rodgers Troupe Offers a New Dance." *New York Times,* December 14, 1970, p. 56: 4.

ZITA ALLEN

Rogers, Elymas Payson (February 10, 1815–January 20, 1861), minister and poet. Born free in Madison, Conn., the son of Chloe (Ladue) and Abel Rogers, a farmer, Elymas Rogers was sent at the age of nine to live with strangers and to attend school. Returning at age fifteen, he worked on a farm with his father. In the early 1830s, Rogers moved to Hartford, where he attended school and joined the Talcott St. Presbyterian Church. In 1835, determined to become a minister, he enrolled at Gerrit Smith's school in Peterboro, N.Y., and left eighteen months later to teach in a public school for African Americans in Rochester, N.Y. He also attended the Onedia Institute in Whitesboro, N.Y. (1837–1841) to prepare for the ministry.

Upon graduation, Rogers moved to Trenton, N.J., where he became principal of a public school and continued his theological studies. On February 7, 1844, he was licensed as a Presbyterian minister, and took charge of the all-black Whitherspoon St. Church in Princeton. In 1846, Rogers moved to Newark and became pastor of the Plane St. Church, where he remained until 1860.

An ardent abolitionist, Rogers is best known for satirical poems. "The Repeal of the Missouri Compromise Considered" (1854–56) features a dialogue between "Freedom" and "Slavery," with the latter gloating over the noxious effects of the Kansas-Nebraska Act and the North-South political struggle. "A Poem on the Fugitive Slave Law" (1855) is an attack on slave-hunting. Rogers declares that the law was made in Hell and violates natural law. Rogers also gave antislavery speeches, notably at the Presbyterian and Congregational Convention in 1857, denouncing the DRED SCOTT DECISION.

Rogers, an active member of the African Civilization Society, long dreamed of traveling to Africa and preaching to the natives. In 1860, he sailed to Sierra Leone as a missionary, and also visited Monrovia, Bassia, Sinoe, and Cape Palmas to further the missionary effort. In early 1861, he fell ill and died in Cape Palmas in West Africa.

REFERENCE

SHERMAN, JOAN R. *Invisible Poets.* Urbana, Ill., 1989, pp. 21–26.

SABRINA FUCHS

Rogers, Joel Augustus (c. 1883–September 6, 1966), historian and journalist. Joel Augustus Rogers devoted fifty years of his life to revisionary scholarship, in a pioneering attempt to recover the black presence throughout history that had been excluded by white historians. He is thought to have been born in 1883, although the exact day is not known, in Negril, Jamaica. After serving in the British Royal Army, he migrated to the United States in 1906, although he did not become a citizen until 1917. Despite having no formal postsecondary education, he learned French, German, Portuguese, and Spanish, and researched European and African library and museum archives. But Rogers's lack of proper scholarly credentials increased the difficulty that, as an African American, he already had in getting his work published, forcing him to publish much of it himself. Furthermore, because his research led him to radical conclusions, few of his scholarly contemporaries recognized him, and later historians who confirmed his claims have left him largely unacknowledged.

Rogers's publications include *One Hundred Amazing Facts About the Negro* (1934), which went to a nineteenth edition; *The Real Facts About Ethiopia* (1936), which grew out of his firsthand experience as a foreign correspondent for the PITTSBURGH COURIER during Italy's invasion of Ethiopia (1935–1936); the monumental three-volume *Sex and Race* (1941–

1944), which documents miscegenation throughout world history and which went to a ninth edition; the two-volume *World's Great Men of Color* (1946), which was republished in 1972; and *Africa's Gift to America* (1959), which discusses the role of African Americans in the development of the United States. Rogers also wrote a series of African-American history for the *Pittsburgh Courier*, which reached tens of thousands of readers, and a weekly series that was published in many African-American newspapers. He died in New York.

REFERENCES

SANDOVAL, VALERIE. "The Bran of History: An Historiographic Account of the Work of J. A. Rogers." *Schomburg Center for Research in Black Culture Journal* 1, no. 4 (Spring 1978): 5–7, 16–19.

TURNER, W. B. "J. A. Rogers: Portrait of an Afro-American Historian." *Black Scholar* 6, no. 5 (January–February 1975): 32–39.

SIRAJ AHMED

Rolle, Esther (c. November 8, 1920–), actress. Esther Rolle was born in Pompano Beach, Calif., probably in 1920, the tenth of eighteen children of parents of Bahamian descent. After her family relocated in Florida, she finished Booker T. Washington High School in Miami, and attended Spelman College in Atlanta for one year before moving to New York City. There, Rolle supported herself by working at a pocketbook factory while trying to break into theater. She was taking drama classes at George Washington Carver School in Harlem when she obtained a scholarship to study acting at New York's innovative New School for Social Research.

During this time, Rolle was introduced to African dance master Asadata DAFORA and became a member of his dance troupe, Shogola Oloba. After many years with the troupe, she became its director in 1960. During her dancing career Rolle continued to pursue her interest in theater, and in 1962 she made her professional acting debut as Felicity in Jean Genet's *The Blacks*. Rolle worked in theater throughout the early 1960s, appearing in such productions as *Blues for Mr. Charlie* (1964), *Amen Corner* (1965), and in Douglas Turner Ward's *Day of Absence* (1965). She made her film debut as Sister Sarah in 1964's *Nothing But a Man*, and in 1967 she became an original member of the Negro Ensemble Company.

Rolle continued to work steadily in the theater through the early 1970s. She was performing in Melvin Van Peebles's *Don't Play Us Cheap* (1972) when a casting director asked her to audition for the role of the maid on *Maude*, a Norman Lear television show being spun off from *All in the Family*. Rolle won the role and, that same year, with the understanding that her character, Florida Evans, would not be a typical maid, she proceeded to turn the limited role into a popular character. In 1974, the characters of Florida Evans and her husband were spun off into a new television series *Good Times*.

Good Times depicted a lower-middle-class family living in a tenement on the South Side of Chicago as they struggled to survive economically in the face of layoffs and unemployment. Originally the show was praised for addressing the economic difficulties faced by many inner-city blacks. However, Rolle and co-star John Amos constantly struggled with producers over the role of the oldest son, played by Jimmie Walker, who was portrayed as a fast-talking, womanizing buffoon, and who increasingly became the central figure of the show. Rolle left the show in 1977 over these and other disputes, but returned in 1978. *Good Times* was canceled in 1979.

Rolle continued to act in other roles on television and in the theater through the late 1970s and 1980s. She won an Emmy award for her performance as a housekeeper in the 1978 television movie *Summer of My German Soldier*. During the 1980s she appeared on such television shows as *Flamingo Road* (1982) and *The Love Boat* (1983, 1985). In 1989, she played a housekeeper in *The Member of the Wedding* at the Roundabout Theater, a role she had originated in Philadelphia four years earlier. Rolle played the matriarch in an American Playhouse remake of *A Raisin in the Sun* (1989) with Danny Glover as the errant son. That same year, she also played the maid, Idella, in the Academy Award-winning film *Driving Miss Daisy*.

In 1990, Rolle became the first woman to win the NAACP chairman's Civil Rights Leadership Award. For her achievements in film and television, Rolle was inducted into the Black Filmmakers Hall of Fame in 1991.

REFERENCES

BOGLE, DONALD. *Blacks in American Films and Television*. New York, 1988.

HELBING, TERRY. "Esther Rolle: Invitation to the Wedding." *Theater Week*, April 3–9, 1989, pp. 13–16.

KENYA DILDAY

Rollins, Theodore Walter "Sonny" (September 9, 1930–), tenor saxophonist and composer. Born in New York in 1930, Rollins began playing piano at the age of nine. Influenced by saxophonist Louis Jordan, he took up alto saxophone and later tenor saxophone. In high school he led an ensemble that included Kenny Drew on piano, Jackie McLean on saxophone, and drummer Arthur Taylor. In the late 1940s he began playing professionally in New York, often with the greatest bebop musicians of the era, including saxophonist Charlie PARKER, drummers Art BLAKEY and Max ROACH, trumpeters Miles DAVIS and Fats NAVARRO, and pianist Tadd DAMERON. He made his first recordings with pianist Bud POWELL in 1949. His most significant early recordings came in his second stint with Davis in 1954, when they recorded his "Airegin," "Doxy," and "Oleo," which have since become standards.

In 1955 Rollins, who had recovered from a heroin addiction, joined the Max Roach–Clifford BROWN quintet (*At Basin Street,* 1956), the leading practitioners of the intense, bluesy style known as hard bop. Rollins played with the group until the death of trumpeter Brown in 1956. He then played again with Davis and Monk, and began to lead his own groups.

The three albums Rollins recorded in 1956 mark not only the emergence of one of the most original and exciting tenor saxophonists in the history of jazz, but a remarkable composer. His compositions from this time include "Valse Hot" and "Blue Seven," as well as "St. Thomas," which shows the Caribbean influence of his mother's family. *Sonny Rollins Plus 4, Saxophone Colossus,* and *Tenor Madness,* with saxophonist John COLTRANE, feature Rollins's "thematic improvisation," in which miniature themes or motifs, as opposed to chord changes or melodies, generate solo ideas. The next two years were equally productive for Rollins, who recorded the pianoless *Way Out West,* as well as *Tenor Titan* and *Freedom Suite.* The latter was an early example of the growing concern among jazz musicians with the connection between the "freedom" of modern jazz composition and performance practice and the struggle for the civil rights of African Americans.

Although by the end of the 1950s Rollins had become, along with John Coltrane, one of the leading saxophonists in jazz, he was increasingly dissatisfied with his playing. He retreated from public performing from 1959 to 1961, and took to practicing on the pedestrian walkway on New York City's Williamsburg Bridge. Rollins returned to playing in 1961, recording *The Bridge.* In 1962 he was briefly associated with free jazz musicians, including Don CHERRY and Billy Higgins (*Our Man in Jazz*). Rollins continued to record and perform, including *Sonny Meets Hawk!,* with tenor saxophonist Coleman HAWKINS. He also wrote and recorded the score for the film *Alfie* (1966). During this time Rollins's playing was unashamedly romantic, yet also capable of sharp, ironic, fiercely dissonant statements, especially on ballads and popular tunes. He also took to leaving the bandstand while playing, and strolling around the nightclub, often wearing bells.

Rollins retired again in 1968, immersing himself in the philosophy and religion of India before reemerging in 1972. Since that time his recordings include *The Cutting Edge* (1974), *Don't Stop The Carnival* (1978), and *G-Man* (1987). Some of his live performances have been recorded, including *The Solo Album,* from a 1985 concert at New York's Museum of Modern Art, which retains his wry, brusque tone and bittersweet inventiveness, often drawing upon a West Indian–accented sense of humor. Rollins, who was the subject of the 1986 film *Saxophone Colossus,* has lived in Germantown, N.Y., for many years, and continues to record and perform throughout the United States, Europe, and Japan.

REFERENCES

BLANQ, C. C. *Sonny Rollins: The Journey of a Jazzman.* Boston, 1983.

SCHULLER, GUNTHER. "Sonny Rollins and the Challenges of Thematic Improvisation." *Jazz Journal* 1, no. 1 (1958).

EDDIE S. MEADOWS

Roman Catholicism. Black Catholics have figured in Roman Catholic history in the continental United States since the sixteenth century. The town of St. Augustine, established in northern Florida in 1565, was composed of Spanish-speaking Catholics, both white and black. The parish registers (baptismal, marriage, and death records), which noted persons of color and their status as slave or free, reveal a multicolored society that was Catholic in religion. From 1738 to 1763, the all-black town of Gracia Real de Santa Teresa de Fort Mose served as a refuge for slaves fleeing the English colonies to the north. All who converted to Catholicism became free. In the Southwest, blacks from Mexico were also among the Spanish-speaking settlers. Africans and mulattoes made up half the original settlers of the city of Los Angeles in 1781.

Slavery was accepted by most Catholics. Catholic slaveholders included bishops, priests, religious communities of men and women, and laypersons. In the Spanish territories and in the French possessions of Louisiana, the Alabama Gulf coast, Illinois, and eastern Missouri, slave owners had to have their slaves baptized and instructed in the Catholic religion. The slave codes prohibited the separation of family members. Although these stipulations were not always carried out, they ensured a minimum of rights that did not exist in the United States. Maryland had the largest concentration of English-speaking Catholic slaves. John Carroll, first Catholic bishop in the United States, wrote in 1785 that there were about three thousand Catholic slaves in Maryland, one-fifth of the state's Catholic population. Maryland Catholics, settlers and slaves, moved to western Kentucky at the beginning of the nineteenth century. At the same period, Haitians—black as well as white Catholics—entered the United States as a result of civil unrest in the former French colony.

In the period prior to the Civil War, when many Protestant churches were divided by the issue of slavery, the Catholic bishops maintained a policy of noninvolvement. Many Catholics supported the southern cause inasmuch as they supported the Democratic party in the North or secessionists in the South. A

Father Smith, a Roman Catholic priest, conducting Mass in Chicago in 1942. The number of African-American Roman Catholics doubled during the interwar years. By 1938 there were three large, well-attended Roman Catholic churches in Chicago. (Prints and Photographs Division, Library of Congress)

few bishops wrote in defense of slavery. Few came out publicly for emancipation once the war began. Catholic leaders in Europe, on the other hand, were in the main opposed to slavery; in 1839 Pope Gregory XVI condemned the slave trade and slavery itself. Certain bishops, like John England of Charleston, S.C., interpreted the pope's language as referring only to international trafficking in slaves. Rome was preparing to correct this misinterpretation when the Civil War ended.

Evangelization efforts for freed slaves began immediately after the Civil War. During the Second Plenary Council of Baltimore in 1866, at the instigation of the archbishop of Baltimore, Martin J. Spalding, the Holy See presented a program whereby a bishop with nationwide jurisdiction would have responsibility for ministry to all blacks. The bishops in general opposed the plan and agreed to a less innovative (and less efficient) approach, making each bishop responsible for missions to the blacks within his diocese. Religious communities such as the Josephites, the Spiritans, the Society of the Divine Word, and the Society of African Missions took up apostolic work among American blacks.

Black lay Catholics took the initiative for evangelization even before the Civil War. The oldest known document relating to black Catholic parish life is the weekly account of a prayer meeting held each Sunday from 1843 to 1845 in the parish hall of the Baltimore cathedral. Some two hundred or more black women and men called the Society of the Holy Family prayed, sang, received spiritual instruction, began a lending library, and established a fund for charitable purposes.

As early as 1824, three free black women began to live the religious life near Bardstown, Kentucky, under the guidance of Charles Nerinckx, a frontier priest from Belgium. Unfortunately, the community was not allowed to continue. Five years later in Baltimore, five black women began to live as religious sisters. They began as schoolteachers for the children of the largely Haitian black community that worshiped in the lower chapel of Saint Mary's Seminary, with the guidance of a French Sulpician priest.

Under the direction of Mary Elizabeth Lange, a Haitian, the first African-American community of nuns was established in 1829, today still known as the OBLATE SISTERS OF PROVIDENCE. In 1831 Rome gave final approval. Almost a dozen years later, in 1842, another community of black sisters was established, this one in New Orleans, by two women of color, Henriette Delille and Juliette Gaudin. These black sisters were known as the Sisters of the Holy Family (no connection with the parish group of Baltimore). In 1916 in Savannah, Ga., a third community of black nuns was founded, the Franciscan Handmaids of

Mary, who eventually moved to Harlem. All three groups still work in the black community in education and social service.

The first black priests in United States were three sons of an Irish-born slaveholder in Georgia, Michael Morris Healy, and a slave woman, Mary Eliza (*see* HEALY FAMILY). There were ten children. Four of the sons were sent to Holy Cross College in Worcester, Mass.; three of them became priests. The eldest, James Augustine Healy, in 1875 became bishop of Portland, Me., the first black Catholic bishop in the United States. The third son, Patrick Francis Healy, became a Jesuit priest and president of Georgetown University, his African-American origins largely unknown. The first black priest who was clearly recognized as black was Augustus TOLTON. Born a slave in Missouri, educated for the priesthood in Rome, and ordained for Alton, Ill., in 1886, he eventually moved to Chicago, where he became the pastor of the first black parish.

Laypersons played an important role in the development of black Catholic culture. Daniel RUDD of Bardstown, Ky., began a black Catholic weekly newspaper that for a few years had a nationwide subscription. Rudd was responsible for organizing five lay congresses of black Catholics, which met between the years 1889 and 1894 in Washington, D.C., Cincinnati, Philadelphia, Chicago, and Baltimore, respectively. These meetings were important because they revealed the social concerns and beliefs of the black Catholic community, their attachment to the Catholic church, and their determination to end racist practices within the church.

Another black Catholic lay leader and organizer of a lay Catholic organization was Thomas Wyatt TURNER, who in 1924 founded the Federated Colored Catholics, a group of African-American lay leaders dedicated to the eradication of racism within the church. Turner challenged the American church and its inertia in race relations. At the same time, the Roman Curia began pressuring the American hierarchy regarding discriminatory practices. In 1920, the Society of the Divine Word began a seminary for the training of black priesthood candidates, first in Greenville and later at Bay St. Louis, both in Mississippi.

The civil rights movement brought a new consciousness to black Catholics. In 1968 the National Black Catholic Clergy Caucus and the National Black Sisters' Conference were formed, and shortly thereafter the National Black Seminarians Association. In 1970, the National Office of Black Catholics was created as an umbrella organization. Gradually, the church hierarchy began to come to terms with racial matters. The United States bishops issued a pastoral letter dealing with racism and its sinfulness in 1979.

Harold Perry, the second black bishop in U.S. history, was ordained in 1966 as auxiliary bishop of New Orleans. By 1991 there were thirteen black bishops, two of them heads of dioceses. In 1984 the black bishops issued a pastoral letter on evangelization within the black community. In 1987 the sixth Black Catholic Congress met in Washington, D.C. That same year a Black Secretariat was established as part of the National Conference of Catholic Bishops, with headquarters in Washington, D.C. It functions as an agency for both the bishops and the nearly two million black Catholics in the country. In most dioceses where there is a significant black population, an office of black ministry, under various titles, serves as a voice and a coordinating center for diocesan affairs and the concerns of blacks.

In 1989 a Washington, D.C., priest, George Stallings, formed a schismatic group, the Imani Temple African American Catholic Congregation. Stallings broke with the papacy and was ordained a bishop in his own church, retaining many aspects of Catholicism. Eventually, another group under Bruce Greening, likewise ordained a bishop, separated in turn from the Imani Temple.

Sanctity has been a part of the history of black Catholicism. The process of canonization was introduced for three black Catholics: Pierre TOUSSAINT, a devout Haitian layman of New York; Mary Elizabeth Lange, the founder of the Oblate Sisters of Providence; and Henriette Delille, cofounder of the Sisters of the Holy Family.

REFERENCES

DAVIS, CYPRIAN. *The History of Black Catholics in the United States.* New York, 1990.
NICKELS, MARILYN. *Black Catholic Protest and the Federated Colored Catholics, 1917–1933: Three Perspectives on Racial Justice.* New York, 1988.
OCHS, STEPHEN. *Desegregating the Altar: The Josephites and the Struggle for Black Priests, 1871–1960.* Baton Rouge, La., 1990.
What We Have Seen and Heard: A Pastoral Letter on Evangelization from the Black Bishops of the United States. Cincinnati, 1984.

CYPRIAN DAVIS

Roosevelt's Black Cabinet.   Disaffected by REPUBLICAN PARTY politics in the decades following the Civil War, victimized by racism, and ravaged by the GREAT DEPRESSION, African Americans transferred their allegiance to Franklin D. Roosevelt and the DEMOCRATIC PARTY during the New Deal when they perceived that his efforts to improve conditions for all citizens included them as well. While Roosevelt did not propose specific civil rights legislation during his administrations, he did move to repeal particularly egregious racial restrictions within the federal government bureaucracy, many of which had been initiated by his Democratic predecessor, Woodrow Wilson. Moreover, the First Lady, Eleanor Roosevelt, remained a vocal and active champion of racial equality. As a consequence of Mrs. Roosevelt's lobbying, of the concerns and interest of former Chicago NAACP president Harold Ickes, a key figure in the Roosevelt administration, and, most important, of concentrated efforts to secure political appointments for blacks, Roosevelt was made aware of the plight of black Americans. In response, African Americans came to view the Democratic party as a haven.

Two seminal events in 1933 helped to set the stage for the appointment of a number of blacks to second-level positions within the administration. The first was the Second Amenia Conference (*see* AMENIA CONFERENCE OF 1933), hosted by Joel Spingarn, the chairman of the board of the NAACP. The second was the Julius Rosenwald Fund meeting to discuss the economic status of blacks. Out of both of these meetings grew a determination to seek and secure appointments of racial advisers in the administration in order to ensure that blacks would not be excluded from New Deal programs. An Interracial Interdepartmental Group (IIG), supported by the Rosenwald Fund, was set up to promote black appointees. Working closely with Ickes and Eleanor Roosevelt, the IIG helped to secure the appointment of at least one black adviser in all but five of some two dozen New Deal agencies by 1937. This network of officeholders became known as the "Black Cabinet."

Appointees included people such as Robert WEAVER, later appointed by Lyndon B. Johnson to serve as the secretary of Housing and Urban Development; Mary McLeod BETHUNE, director of Negro affairs, National Youth Organization; Henry HUNT and Charles Hall, who, along with Weaver, were original members of the IIG; Joseph H. B. Evans, Farm Security Administration; Lawrence A. Axley, Department of Labor; Edgar G. Brown, Civilian Conservation Corps; N. Robinson, Agriculture; and Alfred E. Smith, WORKS PROJECT ADMINISTRATION. Bethune convened the members of this unofficial Black Cabinet in 1935. Thereafter, they met regularly (although unofficially), remaining in constant touch with one another, and creating a network whose purpose and goal was to promote the interests of black Americans. With a greater direct access to power than they had ever had before, they lobbied actively throughout the administration. Although their achievements were limited, they did realize some success. The Black Cabinet helped to ensure that, by 1935, approximately 30 percent of all black Americans participated in New Deal relief programs.

REFERENCES

LOUCHHEIM, KATIE, ed. *The Making of the New Deal: The Insiders Speak.* Cambridge, Mass., 1983.
SITKOFF, HARVARD. *A New Deal for Blacks.* New York, 1978.

CHRISTINE A. LUNARDINI

Ross, Diana (March 26, 1944–), pop singer, actress. Born Diane Ross in a low-income housing project in Detroit, Ross's interest in music began at an early age, when she sang with her parents in a church choir. In high school she studied dress design, illustration, and cosmetology, spending her free time singing on Detroit street corners with her friends Mary Wilson and Florence Ballard. Betty McGlowan was soon added to the group, and the quartet became known as the Primettes. They came to the attention of MOTOWN Records founder Berry Gordy, who used them as background singers for Mary WELLS, Marvin GAYE, and the Shirelles. The group was renamed the SUPREMES, and from the mid-1960s until 1970 they were one of the most popular groups in pop music, with a string of influential hits. In 1970, however, Ross, who had always sought to dominate what was nominally a balanced trio, left to pursue a solo career.

After leaving the Supremes, Ross's popularity continued ("Ain't No Mountain High Enough," 1970), and she also began a career as a film actress. Ross was nominated for an Academy Award for her performance as Billie HOLIDAY in *Lady Sings the Blues* (1972), and starred in *Mahagony* (1975), which yielded the hit ballad "Do You Know Where You're Going To?" the next year. By the mid-1970s Ross was also considered a top disco diva, recording "Love Hangover" (1976) and "Upside Down" (1980). During this time she also had a starring role in the musical film *The Wiz* (1978). Ross reached the top of the pop charts again in 1981 with "Endless Love," a duet with Lionel Ritchie. Since then she has recorded less frequently (*Muscles,* 1982; *Eaten Alive,* 1985; and *Workin' Overtime,* 1989). Ross, who was married from 1971 to 1975 to Robert Silberstine, was remarried in 1985 to the Norwegian shipping tycoon and mountaineer Arne Naess. They have two sons and live in Norway and Connecticut. Ross has had nineteen number-one recordings on the pop charts—the most to date for a solo performer—and continues to perform sporadically in concert and on television.

Pop singer Diana Ross at a free concert in New York City's Central Park in 1983. (AP/Wide World Photos)

REFERENCES

BROWN, GEOFF. *Diana Ross*. London, 1981.

GEORGE, NELSON. *Where Did Our Love Go? The Rise and Fall of the Motown Sound*. New York, 1985.

HIRSHEY, GERRY. *Nowhere to Run: The Story of Soul Music*. New York, 1984.

KAREN BENNETT HARMON

Ross-Barnett, Marguerite (May 21, 1942–February 26, 1992), educator. Born in Charlottesville, Va., Marguerite Ross-Barnett grew up in Buffalo, N.Y. She received a bachelor's degree from Antioch College in 1964 and subsequently studied at the University of Chicago, where she received a doctorate in political science in 1972. A specialist in Indian and African-American politics, she taught at Princeton University, Howard University (where she also served as political science department chair), and Columbia University. In 1975 she published *Electoral Politics in the Indian States: Party Systems and Cleavages* and *The Politics of Cultural Nationalism in South India* in 1976. That same year she coedited *Public Policy for the Black Community: Policies and Perspec-*

tives. In 1983 Ross-Barnett was hired by the City University of New York (CUNY) as vice chancellor of academic affairs and served in that post for three years. In 1985 she published *Images of Blacks in Popular Culture: 1865–1955*, a sociological study, and coedited *Race, Sex, and National Origin: Public Attitudes on Desegregation*.

In 1986 Ross-Barnett was named chancellor of the University of Missouri–St. Louis. A talented administrator, she succeeded in raising enrollment, firming up standards (including inaugurating an engineering program for undergraduates), and raising funds. She was active in community-based outreach, notably by periodic reports to the community, as well as the Bridge Program, an educational program for poor public school children that in 1991 won the Anderson medal from the American Council on Education as outstanding public school initiative of the year.

In 1990 Barnett was appointed president of the University of Houston, a 32,000-student institution, becoming the first African-American woman to head a major university that was not a historically black college. There she continued her commitment to educational reform, offering a "Report to the Community" on the school's future and developing the Texas Center for University-School Partnerships in order to devote university resources to improving public education. In January 1992, suffering from hypoglycemia and cancer, she took a leave of absence from the University of Houston and traveled to Hawaii. She died there a month later.

REFERENCE

Obituary. *New York Times*, February 27, 1992, p. B7.

GREG ROBINSON

Rowan, Carl Thomas (August 11, 1925–), journalist, government official. Born in Ravenscroft, Tenn., the son of a lumber worker, Carl Rowan grew up in poverty. After graduating from local schools in 1942, he saved enough money to attend Tennessee State University. While at Tennessee, Rowan was drafted, and was selected for a special program to train African-American officers in the then segregated U.S. Navy. In 1945, after completing his military service, Rowan registered at Oberlin College in Ohio; he graduated in 1947. Determined to become a journalist, he moved to Minneapolis, and he received an M.A. degree from the University of Minnesota in 1948.

That same year, Rowan was hired as a copywriter by the white-owned *Minneapolis Tribune*, and was made a reporter in 1950, becoming one of the first African American reporters for a large urban daily newspaper. The next year, Rowan toured the southern states, reporting on racial discrimination. His articles (which were collected in the book *South of Freedom* in 1952) won him national attention. Rown continued as a reporter for the *Tribune* for ten years, and won several journalism awards for his coverage of such issues as the U.S. Supreme Court's BROWN V. BOARD OF EDUCATION school desegregation case in 1954, the Bandung Conference of Nonaligned Nations in Indonesia in 1955, and the 1960 civil war in the former Belgian Congo. In 1956 Rowan made a second trip to the South, and was one of the first national journalists to cover the Montgomery Bus Boycott. He recounted his journey in *Go South to Sorrow* (1957). During the late 1950s, he wrote two other books: *The Pitiful and the Proud* (1956), a report on society and culture in India, and *Wait Till Next Year* (1960), a biography of baseball star Jackie ROBINSON.

In 1961 Rowan was appointed deputy assistant secretary of state by President John F. Kennedy. He spent two years in the position, directing the drafting of position papers. Rowan also assisted then–Vice President Lyndon B. Johnson, accompanying him on a tour of the Middle East, India, and Vietnam. In 1962 he was assigned to the U.S. delegation to the United Nations. In January 1963, Kennedy appointed Rowan U.S. ambassador to Finland. Rowan was one of the first African Americans ever assigned as ambassador to a largely white country.

In December 1963, President Lyndon B. Johnson named Rowan to head the United States Information Agency (USIA), replacing Edward R. Murrow. As USIA director, Rowan held by far the highest executive branch position occupied by an African American up to that time. He also attended cabinet meetings and served as a political adviser. Rowan remained at the agency for a little more than a year, before resigning due to friction with Johnson over Vietnam and other policies.

In 1965 Rowan was hired as a columnist and lecturer by the Field Newspaper Syndicate, becoming the first African American with a nationally syndicated column. During the next three decades, Rowan remained one of the most visible and respected journalists in the United States. In addition to his newspaper column, Rowan served as a syndicated radio commentator on the daily program *The Rowan Report*, as a regular panelist/commentator on the syndicated television show *Agronsky & Company* (1976–1988), and as a frequent panelist on *Meet the Press*. During the 1970s, he wrote *Just Between Us Blacks* (1974), a book of essays on racial topics, and *Race War in Rhodesia* (1978). In 1987 he was named annual

president of the prestigious journalists' group, the Gridiron Club. In 1991 Rowan published *Breaking Barriers: A Memoir*. The following year, Rowan founded the Project Excellence program, a million-dollar college scholarship fund. In recognition of his educational efforts, in 1993 the Lynch Annex Elementary School in Detroit was renamed the Carl T. Rowan Community School in his honor.

Rowan was a committed integrationist and mainstream liberal who attacked both conservatives and black nationalists. He and his writings remained controversial. In 1988 Rowan, long a champion of gun control legislation, drew national headlines after he shot and wounded a white man who had broken into his Washington, D.C., home. He was threatened with arrest on charges of possessing an illegal handgun, but the charges were later dropped. Rowan claimed he was the victim of a politically motivated prosecution led by Mayor Marion BARRY, whose administration he had attacked in his column.

In 1986 Rowan wrote and produced *Thurgood Marshall: The Man* (1986), two television documentary programs on MARSHALL's career. In 1987 Rowan began collaborating on Marshall's memoirs, but the project was abandoned when Marshall refused to discuss his Supreme Court cases. Rowan then wrote a biography, *Dream Makers, Dream Breakers: The World of Justice Thurgood Marshall*, which was published in 1993.

REFERENCES

BYNUM, LYNN. *Carl T. Rowan: Spokesman for Sanity*. Minneapolis, Minn., 1971.
ROWAN, CARL T. *Breaking Barriers: A Memoir*. Boston, 1991.

GREG ROBINSON

Rudd, Daniel A. (August 7, 1854–1933), Catholic layman. Daniel A. Rudd was born in Bardstown, Ky., to parents who were slaves and members of the Roman Catholic church (*see* ROMAN CATHOLICISM). After the CIVIL WAR Rudd went to Springfield, Ohio, where an older brother lived, in order to attain a secondary-school education. In 1886 Rudd founded the first Catholic newspaper by and about African Americans, the *Ohio State Tribune,* renamed the *American Catholic Tribune* in the same year. Rudd first published the paper in Springfield, then in Cincinnati, Ohio (1887), and finally in Detroit, Mich. (1894). Rudd believed, wrote, editorialized, and lectured that the Catholic church was the best hope for African Americans, since among religious institutions it alone recognized all people as equals.

Rudd, however, was not blind to the racism within the church. Recognizing the need for cohesion and solidarity among African-American Catholics, he organized the first National Conference of African-American Catholics. At the inaugural meeting in Washington, D.C., held in January 1889, the conferees elected Rudd its president and endorsed his newspaper.

Rudd and his associates carefully took positions to avoid threatening white Catholics, but the conference sessions addressed such substantive issues as Catholic schools for blacks, job and housing equality, and equality in the church. At the conclusion of the 1889 meeting, Rudd and his fellow representatives received a cablegram of blessing and endorsement from Pope Leo XIII's secretary of state. They also visited the White House, where President Grover Cleveland encouraged their efforts.

Rudd continued his involvement with the National Conference of African-American Catholics until 1894 (the last year that it met until 1987) and also participated in the first lay Catholic congress in the United States in 1889. In addition, he lectured throughout the Midwest—in fluent German to the German communities near Cincinnati—and in the East and South. He also was an active participant in the Negro Press Association and the Catholic Press Association. Even as he entered business after the *American Catholic Tribune* ceased publication (the last extant issue preserved is from September 1894, though the paper may have continued until as late as 1899), Rudd remained involved as a layperson in church activities and as a representative to various conferences.

After suffering a stroke in 1932, Rudd returned to Bardstown and died the following year at the age of seventy-nine.

REFERENCES

DAVIS, CYPRIAN. *The History of Black Catholics in the United States.* New York, 1990.

OCHS, STEPHEN J. *Desegregating the Altar: The Josephites and the Struggle for Black Priests, 1871–1960.* Baton Rouge, La., 1990.

PETER SCHILLING

Rudolph, Wilma Glodean (June 23, 1940–November 12, 1994), athlete. Wilma Rudolph, the twentieth of twenty-two children, was born in Bethlehem, Tenn., and raised in Clarksville. As a child, she suffered from scarlet fever and pneumonia and was stricken with polio, which left her without the use of her left leg. She wore a leg brace until the age of nine, when she was able to regain the strength in her legs. By age twelve, Rudolph was the fastest runner in her school. She entered Cobb Elementary School in 1947 and then attended Burt High School in Clarksville, Tenn., where she played basketball and ran track.

Rudolph met Edward Temple, track coach at Tennessee State University, while at Burt. After her sophomore year, Temple invited Rudolph to a summer training camp and began to cultivate her running abilities. In 1956, at age 16, she participated in the Olympics in Melbourne, Australia, where her team won the bronze medal in the 4 × 100-meter relay race. Two years later, Rudolph entered Tennessee State to run track and study elementary education and psychology. She was determined to return to the Rome Olympics in 1960. She trained and ran with the Tigerbelles, the Tennessee State University team, which was one of the premier teams in the country. In 1960, Rudolph became the first woman to receive three gold medals, which she won for the 100-meter race, the 200-meter race, and the 4 × 100-meter relay. She instantly became a celebrity, drawing large crowds wherever she went. The French press called her "La Gazelle." Rudolph retired from amateur running at the height of her career, in 1962.

Rudolph graduated from Tennessee State in 1963 and accepted a job as teacher and track coach at Cobb Elementary School. Although she has lived in many places and has held a number of different jobs, she has invariably dedicated herself to youth programs and education. She worked as the director of a community center in Evansville, Ind., with the Job Corps program in Boston and St. Louis, with the Watts Community Action Committee in California, and as a teacher at a high school in Detroit. In 1981, she started the Wilma Rudolph Foundation, a nonprofit organization which nurtures young athletes.

Wilma Rudolph has received many awards and distinctions. She was chosen in 1960 as the United Press Athlete of the Year, and the next year she was designated Woman Athlete of the Year by the Associated Press. She was inducted in 1973 into the Black Sports Hall of Fame, seven years later into the Women's Sports Hall of Fame, and in 1983 into the U.S. Olympic Hall of Fame. In 1993, she became the only woman to be awarded the National Sports Award. In addition, her autobiography, *Wilma: The Story of Wilma Rudolph,* published in 1977, was made into a television movie. Rudolph's achievements as a runner gave a boost to women's track in the United States and heightened awareness about racial and sexual barriers within sports. In addition, Rudolph has served as a role model and inspiration to thousands of African-American and female athletes, as well as people trying to overcome physical disabilities.

Wilma Rudolph crosses the tape to win the 400-meter relay for the United States at the 1960 Summer Olympics held in Rome, Italy. (AP/Wide World Photos)

REFERENCES

BIRACREE, TOM. *Wilma Rudolph*. New York, 1988.
JACOBS, LINDA. *Wilma Rudolph: Run for Glory*. St. Paul, Minn., 1975.
RUDOLPH, WILMA. *Wilma: The Story of Wilma Rudolph*. New York, 1977.

PAM NADASEN

Ruffin, Josephine St. Pierre (1842–1924), journalist and suffragist. Born in Boston, Josephine Ruffin became extensively active in women's organizations, including the Associated Charities of Boston, the New England Women's Press Association, and the NEW ERA CLUB, which she cofounded and whose newspaper, *The Woman's Era,* she edited. A Union Army recruiter, she worked for the U.S. Sanitation Commission.

A product of black women's alliance with white abolitionists and suffragists, as well as the tradition of black women's club work, Ruffin helped found integrated and "colored" organizations. But as the reaction against integration stiffened, she and others turned from trying to join white clubs to forming their own.

A well-publicized incident occurred during this transformation. Eligible to attend the General Federation of Women's Clubs meeting in 1900 through membership in two predominantly white organizations, Ruffin insisted on going as the New Era Club's president. Despite northern and western support, the southern delegations, led by the president, blocked her admission.

In 1895 the Missouri Press Association's president wrote a publicized letter, accusing black women of having "no sense of virtue and of being altogether without character" (Wesley, 1984, p. 28). Ruffin responded by organizing the first national convention of African-American women, "to teach an ignorant and suspicious world that our aims and interests are identical with those of all good aspiring women" (Wesley, 1984, p. 30). Twenty clubs attended and formed the NATIONAL FEDERATION OF AFRO-AMERICAN WOMEN. They merged in 1896 with the Colored Women's League to form the NATIONAL ASSOCIATION OF COLORED WOMEN, of which Ruffin became vice president.

REFERENCES

BROWN, HALLIE Q. *Homespun Heroines and Other Women of Distinction*. New York, 1988.
GIDDINGS, PAULA. *When and Where I Enter: The Impact of Black Women on Race and Sex in America*. New York, 1984.
WESLEY, CHARLES HARRIS. *The History of the National Association of Colored Women's Clubs, Inc.: A Legacy of Service*. Washington, D.C., 1984.

ELIZABETH FORTSON ARROYO

Ruggles, David (1810–1849), abolitionist and journalist. Born of free parents in Connecticut and educated at a Sabbath School for the Poor in Norwich, Ruggles moved to New York City at the age of seventeen; in 1829 he opened a grocery, with goods of "excellent quality," but no "spiritous liquors." Ruggles initiated his antislavery work with a letter to the Marquis de Lafayette in 1830 seeking the Revolutionary hero's endorsement of immediate ABOLITION. In 1833 he sharpened his speaking skills as a traveling agent for the *Emancipator*, the New York antislavery newspaper. In his speeches he attacked colonization and spoke of antislavery experiences in

New York, of the Conventions of Colored Peoples, and of the recently established Phoenix Society.

With Henry Highland GARNET, Ruggles organized the Garrison Literary and Benevolent Association and was an officer in the New York City Temperance Union. He opened the first known African-American bookshop in New York City, which was located at 67 Lispenard Street, in 1834; it served the abolitionist and black communities until destroyed by a mob in 1835.

In 1834 Ruggles published his first pamphlet, the anticolonization satire *Extinguisher, Extinguished . . . or David M. Reese, M.D. "Used Up."* This pamphlet and the later *An Antidote for a Furious Combination . . .* (1838) attacked the procolonizationist arguments of the Methodist cleric David Reese. Ruggles expanded his abolitionist arguments in the 1835 feminist appeal *The Abrogation of the Seventh Commandment by the American Churches.* The pamphlet, published on Ruggles's own press (another African-American first), stood proslavery arguments and fearful fantasies on their heads, and called for northern feminists to shun or ostracize southern wives of slaveholders. In 1835 he penned numerous articles in William L. Garrison's *Emancipator.*

In 1835 Ruggles founded and headed the New York Vigilance Committee, which protected free blacks from kidnapping. He was a daring conductor on the UNDERGROUND RAILROAD, harboring Frederick DOUGLASS and one thousand other blacks before transferring them north to safety.

A fearless activist and fundraiser, Ruggles also went to the homes of whites where he believed black servants were unlawfully held. He served writs against slavecatchers and directly confronted them in the street. In the frequent columns he wrote for the *Colored American,* he exposed racism on railroads. In 1839 he published a *Slaveholders Directory,* which identified the names and addresses of politicians, lawyers, and police in New York who "lend themselves to kidnapping."

Between 1838 and 1841 Ruggles published five issues of the *Mirror of Liberty,* the first African-American magazine. Circulated widely throughout the East, the Midwest, and even the South, the *Mirror of Liberty* chronicled the activities of the Vigilance Committee, gave accounts of kidnappings and related court cases, and printed antislavery speeches and notices of black organizations. Despite its irregular appearances, the magazine was a significant achievement.

Burdened by a fractious and costly dispute with Samuel CORNISH, accused of mishandling funds, having been jailed for his activities, and suffering from near blindness, Ruggles moved to Northampton, Mass., in 1842. There Lydia Maria Child and the Northampton Association of Education and Industry gave him succor in the 1840s, while he continued his activities on the Underground Railroad. In Northampton, Ruggles overcame his poor health and built a prosperous practice as a doctor of hydropathy, using water in the treatment of various diseases. He attended a huge variety of patients, from the wife of a southern slaveowner to William Lloyd Garrison to Sojourner TRUTH. He died in 1849 from a severe bowel inflammation.

REFERENCES

PORTER, DOROTHY B. "David Ruggles, an Apostle of Human Rights." *Journal of Negro History* 28 (1943): 23–50.

———. "David Ruggles." In *Dictionary of American Negro Biography.* New York, 1982.

GRAHAM RUSSELL HODGES

Rushing, James Andrew "Jimmy"

Rushing, James Andrew "Jimmy" (August 26, 1903–June 8, 1972), jazz and blues singer. Rushing, best known as a vocalist with the Count BASIE orchestra from 1935 to 1950, was born in Oklahoma City, into a family that included a trumpet-playing father, a church-singing mother, and a piano-playing, blues-singing uncle. As a child he studied piano, violin, and voice. His classroom training was in local schools and at Wilberforce University.

Rushing toured professionally in the Midwest and in California before joining Walter Page's Blue Devils (1927–1929) and Bennie MOTEN's Kansas City Orchestra (1929–1935). He began his career in the time before microphones, when a singer had to be heard above the band; Rushing's mature tenor style was direct, articulate, sure-pitched, and rhythmic.

He became widely known after he joined the Count Basie band and performed such songs as "Goin' to Chicago," "Good Morning, Blues," "How Long, How Long," and the self-descriptive "Mr. Five by Five." After leaving Basie in 1950, Rushing variously worked as a soloist, briefly led a band of his own, and toured with other established jazz artists, including Buck Clayton and Benny Goodman. He was in demand for music festivals, studio sessions, and other events, and appeared in several motion pictures. He was widely recorded, both with orchestras and as a featured artist.

REFERENCES

BASIE, COUNT, and ALBERT MURRAY. *Good Morning Blues: The Autobiography of Count Basie.* New York, 1985.

ELLISON, RALPH. "Remembering Jimmy." In *Shadow and Act*. New York, 1972, pp. 241–246.

THEODORE R. HUDSON

Russell, Nipsey (October 13, 1923–), comedian. Born in Atlanta, Ga., Nipsey Russell entered show business before the age of six as a member of a dance team, the Ragamuffins of Rhythm. As an adult, he served four years as a captain in the U.S. Army during World War II, and attended the University of Cincinnati, where he earned a B.A. in 1946. In 1948 he moved to New York City to become a stand-up comedian. Russell was one of the first black comedians to perform without using the black vernacular or making racial references in his act. This brought him the national attention that allowed him to move in the late 1950s from the APOLLO THEATER and Club Baby Grand in HARLEM, where he had been regularly showcased, to more mainstream clubs and television appearances.

One of the first African Americans to be invited to appear on talk shows, Russell was a frequent guest on *The Tonight Show*. As cohost of the *Les Crane Show* (1964–65), he was the first African American regularly employed as a master of ceremonies on a national television program. He was also the first black to appear on television game shows, where he became known for his ability to improvise poetry. During the early 1960s Russell performed at civil rights rallies. He has appeared on numerous television series, including a recurring role on the series *Car 54, Where Are You?* (1961–63), as well as on the short-lived *Barefoot in the Park* (1970–71), an all-black version of the Neil Simon play. In 1978 Russell was singled out for praise by film critics for his song and dance performance as the Tin Man in the movie *The Wiz*. He also appeared that year in NBC's *Hallmark Hall of Fame* production of Arthur Miller's *Fame*. Throughout the 1980s Russell appeared on such television programs as *The Love Boat* and *As the World Turns*, in addition to performing his stand-up act in clubs in Atlantic City, Las Vegas, and the Poconos. In 1985 he hosted a television game show, *Your Number's Up*, which ran for four months. In 1986 he appeared in the film *Wildcats*, and in 1992 he had a part in the Eddie MURPHY movie *Boomerang*. That same year he was nominated for an NAACP Theater Award for his performance as Horace Vandergelder in the Long Beach Civic Light Opera's all-black version of *Hello Dolly*. In 1993 he had a small part in *Posse*, a black western film, and in 1994 he reprised his original role in the film version of *Car 54, Where Are You?* Russell also appeared in HBO's historical documentary *Mo' Funny: Black Comedy in America* (1993).

REFERENCES

KING, SUSAN. "Q & A: Nipsey Russell; Comic Laureate." *Los Angeles Times,* February 7, 1993, p. 83.
PLOSKI, HARRY A., and JAMES WILLIAMS, eds. *The Negro Almanac*. Detroit, 1989.

LYDIA MCNEILL

Russell, William Felton "Bill" (February 12, 1934–), basketball player. Born in 1934, the second son of a laborer in a paper bag factory in Monroe, La., at age nine Russell moved with his family to Oakland, Calif. His parents separated and his mother died while he was still in elementary school, leaving Russell to grow up in "the projects" under the tutelage of an athletically gifted brother and a strong-willed, racially proud father. Young Russell failed in early attempts at both BASKETBALL and FOOTBALL, but by his senior year at McClymonds High School his wiry frame, leaping skills, and uncanny sense of timing marked him as a potentially great defensive basketball player and team leader.

Those strengths blossomed at the University of San Francisco (USF), where Russell enrolled in 1952 on an athletic scholarship. He and roommate K. C. JONES led USF to fifty-five consecutive victories and successive National Collegiate Athletic Association (NCAA) championships in 1955 and 1956. They then joined the United States Olympic basketball team at the summer Olympic Games in Melbourne, Australia. Shortly after the Americans defeated the Soviet Union in the finals 89–55 to win the gold medal, Russell rushed back home to marry his college sweetheart, Rose Swisher, and to sign a professional contract with the Boston Celtics.

For the next thirteen years, the six-foot, ten-inch Russell towered over a professional basketball dynasty, with the Celtics winning eleven of thirteen NBA championships, including eight consecutive crowns from 1958 to 1966. He regularly controlled the tempo, intimidated opponents driving for the basket, and triggered the Celtics' fast break; in almost a thousand games, he averaged 22.4 rebounds and 15.1 points per game, and five times won the Most Valuable Player award. Yet all was not athleticism and awards. On southern exhibition tours with the Celtics, Russell in the late 1950s and early 1960s hated having to stay in segregated hotels and eating places. At the height of his athletic prowess in 1966, he teamed with William McSweeny to produce a strong public assertion of black pride and an angry protest against racism in the form of an autobiography, *Go Up for Glory*.

In 1966, coach Harold "Red" Auerbach became the Celtics' general manager and asked Russell to coach as well as play, making him the NBA's first black coach. That season the Celtics had their string of NBA crowns broken by Wilt CHAMBERLAIN and the Philadelphia 76ers, but the Celtics recovered to take the next two championships under player-coach Russell. In 1969 Russell abruptly retired with a year still remaining on his contract. Welcomed on the college lecture and talk show circuits, he worked as a color commentator for televised NBA games. Never one to avoid a challenge, from 1973 to 1977 he enjoyed moderate success (162 games won, 166 lost) as coach and general manager for a young NBA club, the Seattle Supersonics; ten years later he signed a ten-year contract to coach yet another new, struggling NBA franchise, the Sacramento Kings. After a disastrous beginning record of 18–41, however, he relinquished the coaching reins to become the Kings' vice president.

In 1975 Russell was inducted into the Basketball Hall of Fame, and in 1980, the Professional Basketball Writers' Association voted him the outstanding player in the history of the NBA. *Second Wind: The Memoirs of an Opinionated Man* (1979), written with Taylor Branch, is Russell's frankly recounted autobiography.

REFERENCES

CAPOUYA, JOHN. "Bill Russell, Reconsidered." *Sport* 79 (January 1988), 33–38.

RUSSELL, BILL, as told to William McSweeny. *Go Up for Glory*. New York, 1966.

RUSSELL, BILL, with Taylor Branch. *Second Wind: The Memoirs of an Opinionated Man*. New York, 1979.

WILLIAM J. BAKER

Russwurm, John Brown (October 1, 1799–June 9, 1851), abolitionist and Liberian government official. John Brown Russwurm was born in Jamaica of an unknown slave mother and a white American merchant father, John Russwurm. After eight years as a free black in Jamaica, young John Brown, as he was then known, was sent by his father to Quebec for formal schooling. His father brought the child to Portland, Me., in 1812 when he married Susan Blanchard, who insisted that John Russwurm acknowledge his son's paternity by name. After the death of John Russwurm, Sr., in 1815, John Brown Russwurm stayed with Blanchard until he entered Hebron Academy in Hebron, Me. Later he attended and graduated (in 1826) from Bowdoin College, one of the first black university graduates in the United States. In his graduation speech, Russwurm praised the republic of Haiti and encouraged American blacks to consider settlement there.

Russwurm came to New York City in 1827 and helped found FREEDOM'S JOURNAL, the first black newspaper. The paper employed itinerant, abolitionist blacks to publicize the antislavery cause and gain subscribers across the country and in Europe. *Freedom's Journal* vocalized demands to end southern slavery and gain equal rights in the North. After Samuel CORNISH resigned as coeditor on September 14, 1827, to return to the Presbyterian ministry, Russwurm continued to publish the paper until February 1829. He then scandalized black New York by resigning to take a post in Liberia in despair over any hope for an African-American future in the United States. Generally condemned by his contemporaries, Russwurm in fact anticipated the PAN-AFRICANISM of Alexander CRUMMELL, Henry Highland GARNET, and Edward BLYDEN twenty years later.

Arriving in Monrovia, Liberia, in November 1829, Russwurm quickly gained prominence. He edited the *Liberia Herald* from 1830 to 1835, when he resigned in protest over the AMERICAN COLONIZATION SOCIETY's attempts to control the newspaper. At the same time, he was superintendent of education for Monrovia. Despite his differences with the colonization society, Russwurm served as its agent to recruit American blacks to migrate to Africa. He became fluent in several African languages.

In 1836, Russwurm became the first black governor of the Maryland sections of Liberia. He was an able administrator and successfully established relations with nearby African nations, encouraged arriving African Americans, and worked diplomatically with whites. His administration supported agriculture and trade, and in 1843 completed a census of the colony. Throughout the 1840s, Russwurm negotiated for absorption of the Maryland colony into Liberia. He died, a distinguished leader, on June 9, 1851, five years before that union became reality. A monument was erected to his memory near his burial place in Harper, Cape Palmas, Liberia. Russwurm Island off Cape Palmas is named for him. His shift in favor of colonization offended many in 1829, but he is now remembered as a significant and successful actor in Pan-Africanism.

REFERENCES

BREWER, WILLIAM M. "John Brown Russwurm." *Journal of Negro History* (1928): 413–422.

SHICK, TOM W. *Behold the Promised Land: A History of Afro-American Settler Society in Nineteenth Century Liberia*. Baltimore, 1980, pp. 20–23.

SMITH, JAMES WESLEY. *Sojourners in Search of Freedom: The Settlement of Liberia by Black Americans.* Lanham, Md., 1987.

GRAHAM RUSSELL HODGES

Rustin, Bayard (March 17, 1910–August 24, 1987), activist. Bayard Rustin was a civil rights leader, pacifist, political organizer, and controversial public figure. He was born in West Chester, Pa., in 1910, the last of nine children. He accumulated a colorful personal history, beginning with his youthful discovery that the women he had assumed was his older sister was actually his mother. Reared by his mother and grandparents, local caterers, he grew up in the relatively privileged setting of a large mansion in town. Like the rest of his family, Rustin became a Quaker, maintaining an enduring commitment to personal pacifism as a way of life. Tall, thin, usually bushy-haired, and with an acquired West Indian accent, Rustin was noticed wherever he appeared.

He attended college at West Chester State, then moved to Harlem during the 1930s, where he cultivated a bohemian lifestyle, attending classes at City College, singing with JAZZ groups and at night clubs, and gaining a reputation as a chef. His most notable activity, however, was aligning with the COMMUNIST PARTY through the Young Communist League, a decision based on the party's position on race issues. In 1941 when asked by the party to abandon his program to gain young black recruits in favor of a singular emphasis on the European war effort, Rustin quit the party.

His public personality and organizing skills subsequently brought him to the attention of A. Phillip RANDOLPH, who recruited him to help develop his plans for a massive March on Washington to secure equal access to defense jobs. The two men, despite brief skirmishes, remained lifelong friends. When President Franklin D. Roosevelt capitulated to Randolph's threat to hold the march—though Rustin believed that Randolph should not have canceled the march—Randolph arranged for Rustin to meet with A. J. Muste, the head of the radical pacifist Fellowship of Reconciliation (FOR). Muste came to regard the younger man almost as a son, naming him in 1941 as a field staff member for FOR while Rustin also continued as a youth organizer for the March on Washington Movement.

Now possessed of a reputation as an activist in the politics of race, Rustin was able to offer advice to the members of the FOR cell who became the nucleus for a new nonviolent action organization, the CONGRESS OF RACIAL EQUALITY (CORE). Until 1955

Bayard Rustin's central role in planning the 1963 March on Washington was the culmination of his lifetime of planning, organizing, and agitating for the civil rights movement. (Shawn Walker)

Rustin remained a vital figure in the FOR/CORE alliance, holding a variety of offices within both groups, conducting weekend and summer institutes on nonviolent direct action in race relations, and serving as a conduit to the March on Washington movement for ideas and techniques on nonviolence. In 1947 he worked closely with Randolph again in a movement opposing universal military training and a segregated military, and once again believed Randolph wrong in abandoning his strategies when met with a presidential executive order intended to correct the injustice. They argued briefly and publicly, then reconciled. Rustin is sometimes credited with persuading Randolph to accept nonviolence as a strategy.

Rustin's dual commitment to nonviolence and racial equality cost him dearly. In the summer of 1942, refusing to sit in the Jim Crow section of a bus going from Louisville, Ky., to Nashville, Tenn., he was beaten and arrested. The following year, unwilling to accept either the validity of the draft or conscientious objector status—though his Quaker affiliation made that option possible—he was jailed as a draft resister and spent twenty-eight months in prison. Following his release, in 1947 he proposed that a racially integrated group of sixteen CORE/FOR activists undertake a bus trip through the Upper South to test a recent Supreme Court decision on interstate travel.

Termed the Journey of Reconciliation, the trip was essentially peaceful, although participants encountered violence outside Chapel Hill, N.C., where Rustin and three others were charged with violating the segregation laws. In a sham trial, Rustin and the others were convicted and sentenced to thirty days hard labor on a chain gang. His continuing visible role in racial policies brought him additional arrests and beatings.

After his release from the chain gang, Rustin traveled to India, where he was received by Mohandas K. Gandhi's sons. He had earlier blended strands of Gandhian nonviolence into his conception of pacifism. When the bus boycott developed in Montgomery, Ala., Rustin appeared on the scene to offer support, advice, and information on nonviolence. Martin Luther KING, Jr., accepted his help. But when word leaked of Rustin's former ties to the Communist party and his 1953 conviction on a morals charge—allegedly for homosexual activity—he was rushed out of town. The gossip led to Rustin's resignation from both CORE and FOR in 1955, although he continued the pacifist struggle in the War Resisters League.

A 1952 visit to countries in north and west Africa convinced him of the need to assist Africans in their independence struggle. And he continued to be an active though less visible force in the effort to achieve racial justice, invited by King to assist in the creation of the SOUTHERN CHRISTIAN LEADERSHIP CONFERENCE and to serve as a publicist for the group. Conservative members, however, eventually sought his ouster, and from 1960 until 1963 Rustin had little contact with King.

In 1963, as Randolph renewed his plans for a massive March on Washington, he proposed Rustin as the coordinator for the national event. Though initially opposed by some major civil rights leaders and under surveillance by the FBI, Rustin successfully managed the complex planning for the event and avoided violence. He was named executive director of the A. Philip Randolph Institute in 1964, while continuing to lead protests against militarism and segregation.

REFERENCES

RUSTIN, BAYARD. *Down the Line: The Collected Writings of Bayard Rustin.* New York, 1971.
———. "On the Economic Condition of Blacks." *Crisis.* (March 1985): 24–29, 32.

CAROL V. R. GEORGE

Ryder, Noah Francis (April 10, 1914–April 17, 1964), conductor and educator. After his earliest years in Nashville, Tenn., Noah Ryder was reared in Cincinnati by his stepmother and his father, who taught him piano, other instruments, and African-American spirituals. Ryder played in the high school orchestra, organized a jazz ensemble, and in 1931 entered the HAMPTON INSTITUTE of Virginia, where his performance, composition, and conducting were encouraged by R. Nathaniel DETT and Clarence Cameron WHITE. Ryder formed a quartet later known as the Deep River Boys and, in addition, a jazz group.

Following graduation in 1935, Ryder held three successive teaching-conducting positions in North Carolina, ending at Winston-Salem Teachers College. Handy Brothers Publishers began to issue his spiritual arrangements. From 1941 until 1944, Ryder was choir director at Hampton Institute. He then served two years in the United States Navy, completed a master's degree from the University of Michigan, and became head of the music department at the Norfolk Division of Virginia State College in 1947. He conducted the college choirs, a church choir, and community glee club until 1962 when illness brought an end to his active career but not his musical creativity. At the time of his death in 1964, his spiritual arrangements, for which he is best known, were well established in the choral repertory.

REFERENCE

JOHNSON, MARJORIE S. "Noah Francis Ryder: Composer and Educator." *The Black Perspective in Music* 6 (1978): 19–31.

GEORGIA A. RYDER